D1303748

*To our families,
for their love, patience,
and inspiration.*

Managing and Maintaining a Microsoft® Windows® Server 2003 Environment

Exam 70-290

First Edition

Kenneth C. Laudon, Series Designer
Brian Hill, MCSE, MCSA
Robin L. Pickering

The Azimuth Interactive MCSE/MCSA Team

Carol G. Traver, Series Editor
Kenneth Rosenblatt
Russell Polo
David Langley
Richard Watson, MCSE, MCSA
Stacey McBrine, MCSE, MCSA
Brien Posey, MCSE
Russell Jones, MCSE
Tim Oliwiak, MCSE, MCT
Simon Sykes-Wright, MCSE
Nigel Kay, MCSE
David Lundell, MCSE, MCT
L. Ward Ulmer, MCSE, MCT
Wale Soyinka, MCP
David W. Tschanz, MCSE
Mark Maxwell

PEARSON
Prentice Hall

Upper Saddle River, New Jersey, 07458

Senior Vice President/Publisher: Natalie Anderson
Executive Editor Certification: Steven Elliot
Senior Marketing Manager Certification: Steven Rutberg
Marketing Assistant: Barrie Reinhold
Associate Director IT Product Development: Melonie Salvati
Project Manager, Editorial: Laura Burgess
Editorial Assistant: Jasmine Slowick
Editorial Assistant: Jodi Bolognese
Media Project Manager: Joan Waxman
Senior Managing Editor: Gail Steier de Acevedo
Senior Project Manager, Production: Tim Tate
Manufacturing Buyer: Jessica Rivchin
Art Director: Pat Smythe
Design Manager: Maria Lange
Interior Design: Kim Buckley
Cover Designer: Pat Smythe
Cover Photo: Joseph DeSciose/Aurora Photos
Associate Director, Multimedia: Karen Goldsmith
Manager, Multimedia: Christy Mahon
Full Service Composition: Azimuth Interactive, Inc.
Quality Assurance: Digital Content Factory Ltd.
Printer/Binder: Courier Companies, Inc., Kendallville
Cover Printer: Phoenix Color Corporation

Credits and acknowledgments borrowed from other sources and reproduced, with permission, in this textbook appear on appropriate page within text.

Microsoft® and Windows® are registered trademarks of the Microsoft Corporation in the U.S.A. and other countries. Screen shots and icons reprinted with permission from the Microsoft Corporation. This book is not sponsored or endorsed by or affiliated with the Microsoft Corporation.

Copyright © 2004 by Pearson Education, Inc., Upper Saddle River, New Jersey, 07458.
Pearson Prentice Hall. All rights reserved. Printed in the United States of America. This publication is protected by Copyright and permission should be obtained from the publisher prior to any prohibited reproduction, storage in a retrieval system, or transmission in any form or by any means, electronic, mechanical, photocopying, recording, or likewise. For information regarding permission(s), write to: Rights and Permissions Department.

Pearson Prentice Hall™ is a trademark of Pearson Education, Inc.
Pearson® is a registered trademark of Pearson plc.
Prentice Hall® is a registered trademark of Pearson Education, Inc.

10 9 8 7 6 5 4 3 2 1
0-13-144743-2

Brief Contents

Contents

Welcome to the Prentice Hall Certification Series!

You are about to begin an exciting journey of learning and career skills building that will provide you with access to careers such as Network Administrator, Systems Engineer, Technical Support Engineer, Network Analyst, and Technical Consultant. What you learn in the Prentice Hall Certification Series will provide you with a strong set of networking skills and knowledge that you can use throughout your career as the Microsoft Windows operating system continues to evolve, as new information technology devices appear, and as business applications of computers continues to expand. The Prentice Hall Certification Series aims to provide you with the skills and knowledge that will endure, prepare you for your future career, and make the process of learning fun and enjoyable.

Microsoft Windows and the Networked World

We live in a computer-networked world—more so than many of us realize. The Internet, the world's largest network, now has more than 500 million people who connect to it through an estimated 171 million Internet hosts. The number of local area networks associated with these 171 million Internet hosts is not known. Arguably, the population of local area networks is in the millions. About 60% of local area networks in the United States are using a Windows network operating system. The other networks use Novell NetWare or some version of Unix (Internet Software Consortium, 2003). About 95% of the one billion personal computers in the world use some form of Microsoft operating system, typically some version of Windows. A growing number of handheld personal digital assistants (PDAs) also use versions of the Microsoft operating system called Microsoft CE. Most businesses—large and small—use some kind of client/server local area network to connect their employees to one another, and to the Internet. In the United States, the vast majority of these business networks use a Microsoft network operating system—either earlier versions such as Windows NT and Windows 2000, or the current version, Windows Server 2003.

The Prentice Hall Certification Series prepares you to participate in this computer-networked world and, specifically, for the world of Microsoft Windows 2000 and XP Professional client operating systems, as well as Windows 2000 Server and Server 2003 operating systems.

Prentice Hall Certification Series Objectives

The first objective of the Prentice Hall Certification Series is to help you build a set of skills and a knowledge base that will prepare you for a career in the networking field. There is no doubt that in the next five years, Microsoft will issue several new versions of its network operating system, and new versions of Windows client operating system. In the next five years—and thereafter—there will be a steady stream of new digital devices that will require connecting to networks. Most of what you learn in the Prentice Hall Certification Series will provide a strong foundation for understanding future versions of the operating system.

The second objective of the Prentice Hall Certification Series is to prepare you to pass the MCSE/MCSA certification exams and to receive certification. Why get certified? As businesses increasingly rely on Microsoft networks to operate, employers want to make sure their networking staff has the skills needed to plan for, install, and operate these networks. While job experience is an important source of networking knowledge, employers increasingly rely on certification examinations to ensure their staff has the necessary skills. The MCSE/MCSA curriculum provides networking professionals with a well-balanced and comprehensive body of knowledge necessary to operate and administer Microsoft networks in a business setting.

There is clear evidence that having the MCSE/MCSA certification results in higher salaries and faster promotions for individual employees. Therefore, it is definitely in your interest to obtain certification, even if you have considerable job experience. If you are just starting out in the world of networking, certification can be very important for landing that first job.

The Prentice Hall Certification Series teaches you real-world, job-related skills. About 90% of the work performed by MCSE/MCSAs falls into the following categories, according to a survey researcher (McKillip, 1999):

- Analyzing the business requirements for a proposed system architecture.
- Designing system architecture solutions that meet business requirements.

- Deploying, installing, and configuring the components of the system architecture.
- Managing the components of the system architecture on an ongoing basis.
- Monitoring and optimizing the components of the system architecture.
- Diagnosing and troubleshooting problems regarding the components of the system architecture.

These are precisely the skills we had in mind when we wrote this Series. As you work through the hands-on instructions in the text, perform the instructions in the simulated Windows environment on the Interactive Solution CD-ROM, and complete the problem solving cases in the book, you will notice our emphasis on analyzing, designing, diagnosing, and implementing Windows software. By completing the Prentice Hall Certification Series, you will be laying the foundation for a long-term career based on your specialized knowledge of networks and general problem solving skills.

Preparing you for a career involves more than satisfying the official MCSE/MCSA objectives. As you can see from the list of activities performed by MCSE/MCSAs, you will also need a strong set of management skills. The Prentice Hall Certification Series emphasizes management skills along with networking skills. As you advance in your career, you will be expected to participate in and lead teams of networking professionals in their efforts to support the needs of your organization. You will be expected to describe, plan, administer, and maintain computer networks, and to write about networks and give presentations to other business professionals. We make a particular point in this Series of developing managerial skills such as analyzing business requirements, writing reports, and making presentations to other members of your business team.

Who Is the Audience for This Book?

The student body for the Prentice Hall Certification Series is very diverse, and the Series is written with that in mind. For all students, regardless of background, the Series is designed to function as a *learning tool* first, and, second, as a compact reference book that can be readily accessed to refresh skills. Generally, there are two types of software books: books aimed at learning and understanding how a specific software tool works, and comprehensive reference books. This series emphasizes learning and explanation and is student-centered.

The Prentice Hall Certification Series is well suited to beginning students. Many students will just be starting out in the networking field, most in colleges and training institutes. The Series introduces these beginning students to the basic concepts of networking, operating systems, and network operating systems. We take special care in the introductory chapters of each book to provide the background skills and understanding necessary to proceed to more specific MCSE/MCSA skills. We cover many more learning objectives and skills in these introductory lessons than are specifically listed as MCSE/MCSA objectives. Throughout all Lessons, we take care to *explain why things are done*, rather than just list the steps necessary to do them. There is a vast difference between understanding how Windows works and why, versus rote memorization of procedures.

A second group of students will already have some experience working with networking systems and Windows operating systems. This group already has an understanding of the basics, but needs more systematic and in-depth coverage of MCSE/MCSA skills they lack. The Prentice Hall Certification Series is organized so that these more experienced students can quickly discover what they do not know, and can skip through introductory Lessons quickly. Nevertheless, this group will also appreciate our emphasis on explanation and clear illustration throughout the series.

A third group of students will have considerable experience with previous Microsoft operating systems such as Windows NT. These students may be seeking to upgrade their skills and prepare for the Windows 2000/XP/2003 MCSE/MCSA examinations. They may be learning outside of formal training programs as self-paced learners, or in distance learning programs sponsored by their employers. The Prentice Hall Certification Series is designed to help these students quickly identify the new features of new versions of Windows, and to rapidly update their existing skills.

Prentice Hall Series Skills and MCSE/MCSA Objectives

In designing and writing the Prentice Hall Certification Series, we had a choice between organizing the book into lessons composed of MCSE/MCSA domains and objectives, or organizing the book into lessons composed of skills needed to pass the MCSE/MCSA certification examinations (a complete listing of the domains and objectives for the relevant exam will be found inside the front and back covers of the book). We chose to organize the book around skills, beginning with introductory basic skills, and building to more advanced skills. We believe this is a more orderly and effective way to teach students the MCSE/MCSA subject matter and the basic understanding of Windows network operating systems.

Yet we also wanted to make clear exactly how the skills related to the published MCSE/MCSA objectives. In the Prentice Hall Series, skills are organized into Lessons. At the beginning of each Lesson, there is an introduction to the set of skills covered in the Lesson, followed by a table that shows how the skills taught in the Lesson support specific MCSE/MCSA objectives. All MCSE/MCSA objectives for each of the examinations are covered; at the beginning of each skill discussion, the exact MCSE/MCSA objective relating to that skill is identified.

We also recognize that as students approach the certification examinations, they will want learning and preparation materials that are specifically focused on the examinations. Therefore, we have designed the MCSE/MCSA Interactive Solution CD-ROM to follow the MCSE/MCSA domains and objectives more directly. Students can use these tools to practice answering MCSE/MCSA examination questions, and practice implementing these objectives in a realistic simulated Windows environment.

What's Different About the Prentice Hall Series—Main Features and Components

The Prentice Hall Certification Series has three distinguishing features that make it the most effective MCSE/MCSA learning tool available today. These three features are a graphical illustrated 2-page spread approach, a skills-based systematic approach to learning MCSE/MCSA objectives, and an interactive *multi-channel pedagogy*.

Graphical illustrated approach. First, the Prentice Hall Certification Series uses a graphical, illustrated approach in a convenient *two-page spread format* (see illustration below). This makes learning easy, effective and enjoyable.

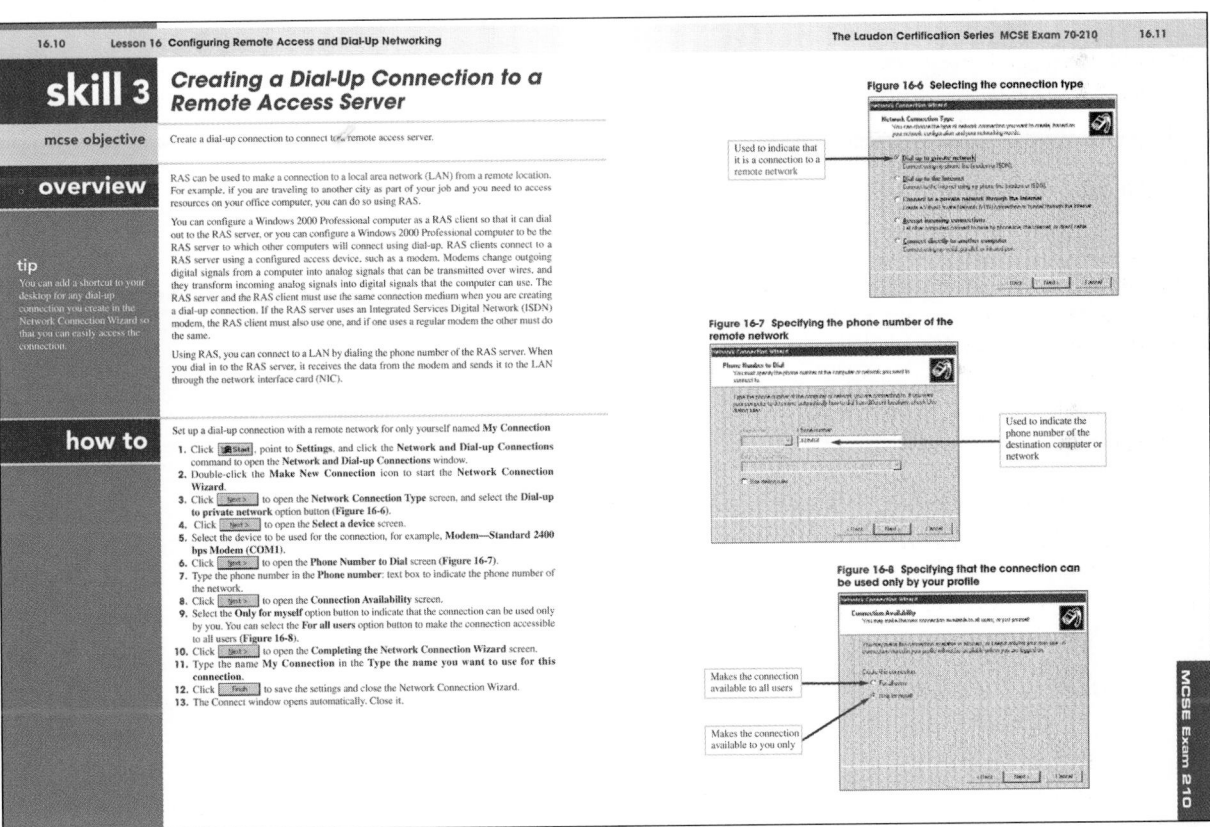

Each two-page spread is devoted to a single skill. On the left-hand side of the two-page spread, you will find a conceptual overview explaining what the skill is, why it is important, and how it is used. Immediately following the conceptual overview is a series of *How To Steps* showing how to perform the skill. On the right hand side of the two-page spread are screen shots that show you exactly how the screen should look as you follow the steps. The pedagogy is easy to follow and understand.

In addition to these main features, each two-page spread contains several *learning aids*:

- *More:* a brief section that provides more information about the skill, alternative ways to perform the skill, and common business applications of the skill.
- *Tips:* hints and suggestions to follow when performing the skill, placed in the left margin opposite the text to which it relates.
- *Caution:* short notes about the pitfalls and problems you may encounter when performing the skill, also placed in the left margin opposite the text to which it relates.

At the end of each Lesson, students can test and practice their skills using three End-of-Lesson features:

- *Test Yourself:* a multiple-choice examination that tests your comprehension and retention of the material in the Lesson.
- *Projects: On Your Own:* short projects that test your ability to perform tasks and skills in Windows without detailed step-by-step instructions.
- *Problem Solving Scenarios:* real-world business scenarios that ask you to analyze or diagnose a networking situation, and then write a report or prepare a presentation that presents your solution to the problem.

Skills-based systematic approach. A second distinguishing feature of the Prentice Hall Certification Series is a *skills-based* systematic approach to MCSE/MCSA certification by using five integrated components:

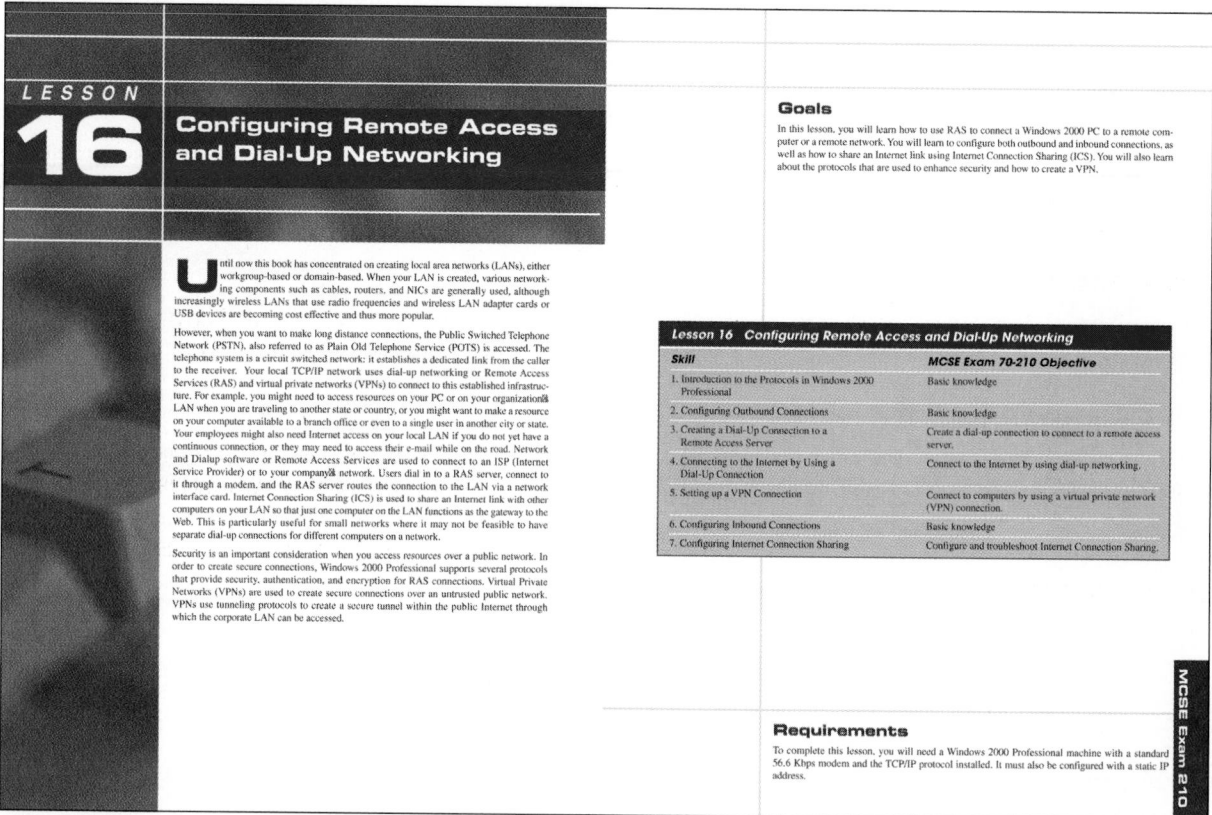

- Main Book—organized by skills.
- Project Lab Manual—for practicing skills in realistic settings.
- Examination Guide—organized by MCSE/MCSA domains and objectives to practice answering questions representative of questions you are likely to encounter in the actual MCSE/MCSA examination.
- Interactive Solution multimedia CD-ROM—organized by MCSE/MCSA domains and objectives—that allows students to practice performing MCSE/MCSA objectives in a simulated Windows environment.
- Powerful Website—provides additional questions, projects, and interactive training.

Within each component, the learning is organized by skills, beginning with the relatively simple skills and progressing rapidly through the more complex skills. Each skill is carefully explained in a series of steps and conceptual overviews describing why the skill is important.

xviii

The Interactive Solution CD-ROM is especially useful to students who do not have access to a Windows network on which they can practice skills. It also is useful to all students who want to practice MCSE/MCSA skills efficiently without disturbing an existing network. Together, these five components make the Prentice Hall Certification Series an effective learning tool for students, increasing the speed of comprehension and the retention of knowledge.

Interactive media multi-channel learning. A third distinguishing feature of the Prentice Hall Certification Series is interactive media *multi-channel* learning. Multi-channel learning recognizes that students learn in different ways, and the more different channels used to teach students, the greater the comprehension and retention. Using the Interactive Solution CD-ROM, students can see, hear, read, and actually perform the skills needed in a simulated Windows environment on the CD-ROM. The CD-ROM is based directly on materials in the books, and therefore shares the same high quality and reliability. The CD-ROM and Website for the book provide high levels of real interactive learning—not just rote exam questions—and offer realistic opportunities to interact with the Windows operating system to practice skills in the software environment without having to install a new version of Windows or build a network.

Supplements Available for This Series:

1. **Test Bank**

The Test Bank is a Word document distributed with the Instructor's Manual (usually on a CD). It is distributed on the Internet to Instructors only. The purpose of the Test Bank is to provide instructors and students with a convenient way for testing comprehension of material presented in the book. The Test Bank contains forty multiple-choice questions and ten true/false questions per Lesson. The questions are based on material presented in the book and are not generic MCSE questions.

2. **Instructor's Manual**

The Instructor's Manual (IM) is a Word document (distributed to Instructors only) that provides instructional tips, answers to the Test Yourself questions and the Problem Solving Scenarios. The IM also includes an introduction to each Lesson, teaching objectives, and teaching suggestions.

3. **PowerPoint Slides**

The PowerPoint slides contain images of all the conceptual figures and screenshots in each book. The purpose of the slides is to provide the instructor with a convenient means of reviewing the content of the book in the classroom setting.

4. **Companion Website**

The Companion Website is a Pearson learning tool that provides students and instructors with online support. On the Prentice Hall Certification Series Companion Website, you will find the Interactive Study Guide, a Web-based interactive quiz composed of fifteen or more questions per Lesson. Written by the authors, there are more than 255 free interactive questions on the Companion Website. The purpose of the Interactive Study Guide is to provide students with a convenient online mechanism for self-testing their comprehension of the book material.

About This Book

Exam 70-290 Managing and Maintaining a Microsoft Windows Server 2003 Environment

This book covers the subject matter of Microsoft's Exam 70-290. The focus in this book is on Windows Server 2003. You will learn about a variety of administrative tools that are used to manage, and maintain the Windows Server 2003 operating system, such as the Control Panel, Active Directory, and Microsoft Management Consoles (MMCs). You will learn about managing hardware, software, user and computer accounts, groups, and network resources. You will also learn how to maintain, manage, and troubleshoot access to network resources. In addition, you will learn how to implement disaster recovery procedures.

The following knowledge domains are discussed in this book:

- Managing and Maintaining Physical and Logical Devices.
- Managing Users, Computers, and Groups.
- Managing and Maintaining Access to Resources.
- Managing and Maintaining a Server Environment.
- Managing and Implementing Disaster Recovery.

How This Book Is Organized

This book is organized into a series of Lessons. Each Lesson focuses on a set of skills you will need to learn in order to master the knowledge domains required by the MCSE/MCSA examinations. The skills are organized in a logical progression from basic knowledge skills to more specific skills. Some skills—usually at the beginning of Lessons—give you the background knowledge you will need in order to understand basic operating system and networking concepts. Most skills, however, give you hands-on experience working with Windows Server 2003 and, in some cases, Windows 2000 Server and Windows XP Professional client computers. You will follow step-by-step instructions to perform tasks using the software.

At the beginning of each Lesson, you will find a table that links the skills covered to specific exam objectives. For each skill presented on a 2-page spread, the MCSE/MCSA objective is listed.

The MCSE/MCSA Certification

The MCSE/MCSA certification is one of the most recognized certifications in the Information Technology world. By following a clear-cut strategy of preparation, you will be able to pass the certification exams. The first thing to remember is that there are no quick and easy routes to certification. No one can guarantee you will receive a certification—no matter what they promise. Real-world MCSE/MCSAs get certified by following a strategy involving self-study, on-the-job experience, and classroom learning, either in colleges or training institutes. Below are answers to frequently asked questions that should help you prepare for the certification exams.

What Is the MCP Program?

The MCP program refers to the Microsoft Certified Professional program that certifies individuals who have passed Microsoft certification examinations. Certification is desirable for both individuals and organizations. For individuals, an MCP certification signifies to employers your expertise and skills in implementing Microsoft software in organizations. For employers, MCP certification makes it easy to identify potential employees with the requisite skills to develop and administer Microsoft tools. In a recent survey reported by Microsoft, 89% of hiring managers said they recommend a Microsoft MCP certification for candidates seeking IT positions.

What Are the MCP Certifications?

Today there are seven different MCP certifications. Some certifications emphasize administrative as well as technical skills, while other certifications focus more on technical skills in developing software applications. Below is a listing of the MCP certifications. The Prentice Hall Certification Series focuses on the first two certifications.

- *MCSA:* Microsoft Certified Systems Administrators (MCSAs) administer network and systems environments based on the Microsoft Windows® platforms.
- *MCSE:* Microsoft Certified Systems Engineers (MCSEs) analyze business requirements to design and implement an infrastructure solution based on the Windows platform and Microsoft Server software.
- *MCDBA:* Microsoft Certified Database Administrators (MCDBAs) design, implement, and administer Microsoft SQL Server™ databases.
- *MCT:* Microsoft Certified Trainers (MCTs) are qualified instructors, certified by Microsoft, who deliver Microsoft training courses to IT professionals and developers.
- *MCAD:* Microsoft Certified Application Developers (MCADs) use Microsoft technologies to develop and maintain department-level applications, components, Web or desktop clients, or back-end data services.
- *MCSD:* Microsoft Certified Solution Developers (MCSDs) design and develop leading-edge enterprise-class applications with Microsoft development tools, technologies, platforms, and the Windows architecture.
- *Microsoft Office Specialist:* Microsoft Office Specialists (Office Specialists) are globally recognized for demonstrating advanced skills with Microsoft desktop software.
- *MCP:* Microsoft Certified Professionals.

What Is the Difference Between MCSA and MCSE Certification?

There are two certifications that focus on the implementation and administration of the Microsoft operating systems and networking tools: MCSA and MCSE. The MCSA credential is designed to train IT professionals who are concerned with the management, support, and troubleshooting of existing systems and networks (see diagram below).

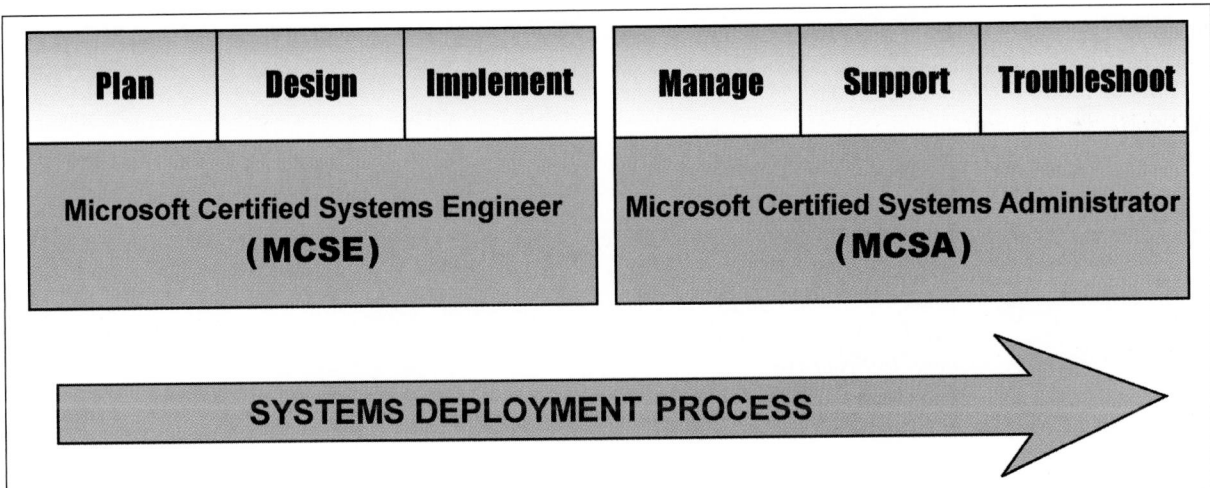

MCSA prepares you for jobs with titles such as Systems Administrator, Network Administrator, Information Systems Administrator, Network Operations Analyst, Network Technician, or Technical Support Specialist. Microsoft recommends that you have six to twelve months experience managing and supporting desktops, servers, and networks in an existing network infrastructure.

The MCSE certification is designed to train IT professionals who are concerned with the planning, designing, and implementation of new systems or major upgrades of existing systems. MCSE prepares you for jobs with titles such as Systems Engineer, Network Engineer, Systems Analyst, Network Analyst, or Technical Consultant. Microsoft recommends that you have at least one year of experience planning, designing, and implementing Microsoft products.

What Does the MCSA on Windows Server 2003 Require?

MCSA candidates are required to pass a total of four exams: three core exams and one elective exam. The list below shows examinations that are included in the MCSA track.

Core Exams (3 Exams Required)

(A) Networking System (2 Exams Required)

- *Exam 70-290:* Managing and Maintaining a Microsoft Windows Server 2003 Environment
  and
- *Exam 70-291:* Implementing, Managing, and Maintaining a Microsoft Windows Server 2003 Network Infrastructure

(B) Client Operating System (1 Exam Required)

- *Exam 70-270:* Installing, Configuring, and Administering Microsoft Windows XP Professional
  or
- *Exam 70-210:* Installing, Configuring, and Administering Microsoft Windows 2000 Professional

Elective Exams (1 Exam Required)

- *Exam 70-086:* Implementing and Supporting Microsoft Systems Management Server 2.0
- *Exam 70-227:* Installing, Configuring, and Administering Microsoft Internet Security and Acceleration (ISA) Server 2000, Enterprise Edition
- *Exam 70-228:* Installing, Configuring, and Administering Microsoft SQL Server 2000 Enterprise Edition
- *Exam 70-284:* Implementing and Managing Microsoft Exchange Server 2003
- *Exam 70-299:* Implementing and Administering Security in a Microsoft Windows Server 2003 Network

As an alternative to the electives listed above, you may substitute the following Microsoft certifications for an MCSA elective:

- MCSA on Microsoft Windows 2000
- MCSE on Microsoft Windows 2000
- MCSE on Microsoft Windows NT 4.0

You may also substitute the following third-party certification combinations for an MCSA elective:

CompTIA Exams:
   CompTIA A+ and *CompTIA Network+*
   CompTIA A+ and *CompTIA Server+*
   CompTIA Security+

What Is the MCSE Curriculum for Windows Server 2003?

MCSE candidates are required to pass a total of seven exams: six core exams and one elective exam. The list below shows the examinations that are included in the MCSE track.

Core Exams (6 Exams Required)

(A) Networking System (4 exams required)

- *Exam 70-290:* Managing and Maintaining a Microsoft Windows Server 2003 Environment
- *Exam 70-291:* Implementing, Managing, and Maintaining a Microsoft Windows Server 2003 Network Infrastructure
- *Exam 70-293:* Planning and Maintaining a Microsoft Windows Server 2003 Network Infrastructure
  and
- *Exam 70-294:* Planning, Implementing, and Maintaining a Microsoft Windows Server 2003 Active Directory Infrastructure

(B) Client Operating System (1 Exam Required)

- *Exam 70-270:* Installing, Configuring, and Administering Microsoft Windows XP Professional
  or
- *Exam 70-210:* Installing, Configuring, and Administering Microsoft Windows 2000 Professional

(C) Design (1 Exam Required)

- *Exam 70-297:* Designing a Microsoft Windows Server 2003 Active Directory and Network Infrastructure
  or
- *Exam 70-298:* Designing Security for a Microsoft Windows Server 2003 Network

Elective Exams (1 Exam Required)

- *Exam 70-086:* Implementing and Supporting Microsoft Systems Management Server 2.0
- *Exam 70-227:* Installing, Configuring, and Administering Microsoft Internet Security and Acceleration (ISA) Server 2000 Enterprise Edition
- *Exam 70-228:* Installing, Configuring, and Administering Microsoft SQL Server™ 2000 Enterprise Edition
- *Exam 70-229:* Designing and Implementing Databases with Microsoft SQL Server™ 2000 Enterprise Edition
- *Exam 70-232:* Implementing and Maintaining Highly Available Web Solutions with Microsoft Windows 2000 Server Technologies and Microsoft Application Center 2000
- *Exam 70-282:* Designing, Deploying, and Managing a Network Solution for a Small- and Medium-Sized Business
- *Exam 70-284:* Implementing and Managing Microsoft Exchange Server 2003
- *Exam 70-297:* Designing a Microsoft Windows Server 2003 Active Directory and Network Infrastructure
- *Exam 70-298:* Designing Security for a Microsoft Windows Server 2003 Network
- *Exam 70-299:* Implementing and Administering Security in a Microsoft Windows Server 2003 Network

As an alternative to the electives listed above, you may substitute the following Microsoft certifications for an MCSE elective:

- MCSA on Microsoft Windows 2000
- MCSE on Microsoft Windows 2000
- MCSE on Microsoft Windows NT 4.0

You may also substitute the following third-party certification combinations for an MCSE elective:

- *CompTIA Security+*
- Unisys UN0-101: Implementing and Supporting Microsoft Windows Server 2003 Solutions in the Data Center

What About Upgrading From a Previous Certification?

Microsoft provides upgrade paths for MCSAs and MCSEs on Windows 2000 so that they can acquire credentials on Windows Server 2003 efficiently and economically. For details on upgrade requirements, visit the following Microsoft Web pages:

http://www.microsoft.com/learning/mcp/mcsa/windows2003/
http://www.microsoft.com/learning/mcp/mcse/windows2003/

Do You Need to Pursue Certification to Benefit from This Book?

No. The Prentice Hall Certification Series is designed to prepare you for the workplace by providing you with networking knowledge and skills regardless of certification programs. While it is desirable to obtain a certification, you can certainly benefit greatly by just reading these books, practicing your skills in the simulated Windows environment found on the MCSE/MCSA Interactive Solution CD-ROM, and using the online interactive study guide.

What Kinds of Questions Are on the Exam?

The MCSE/MCSA exams typically involve a variety of question formats.

(a) Select-and-Place Exam Items (Drag and Drop)

A select-and-place exam item asks candidates to understand a scenario and assemble a solution (graphically on screen) by picking up screen objects and moving them to their appropriate location to assemble the solution. For instance, you might be asked to place routers, clients, and servers on a network and illustrate how they would be connected to the Internet. This type of exam item can measure architectural, design, troubleshooting, and component recognition skills more accurately than traditional exam items can, because the solution—a graphical diagram—is presented in a form that is familiar to the computer professional.

(b) Case Study-Based Multiple-Choice Exam Items

The candidate is presented with a scenario based on typical Windows installations, and then is asked to answer several multiple-choice questions. To make the questions more challenging, several correct answers may be presented, and you will be asked to choose all that are correct. The Prentice Hall Certification Series Test Yourself questions at the end of each Lesson give you experience with these kinds of questions.

(c) Simulations

Simulations test your ability to perform tasks in a simulated Windows environment. A simulation imitates the functionality and interface of Windows operating systems. The simulation usually involves a scenario in which you will be asked to perform several tasks in the simulated environment, including working with dialog boxes and entering information. The Prentice Hall Certification Series Interactive Solution CD-ROM gives you experience working in a simulated Windows environment.

(d) Computer Adaptive Testing

A computer adaptive test (CAT) attempts to adapt the level of question difficulty to the knowledge of each individual examinee. An adaptive exam starts with several easy questions. If you get these right, more difficult questions are pitched. If you fail a question, the next questions will be easier. Eventually the test will discover how much you know and what you can accomplish in a Windows environment.

You can find out more about the exam questions and take sample exams at the Microsoft Website:
http://www.microsoft.com/learning/mcp/default.asp.

How Long is the Exam?

Exams have fifty to seventy questions and last anywhere from 60 minutes to 240 minutes. The variation in exam length is due to variation in the requirements for specific exams (some exams have many more requirements than others), and because the adaptive exams take much less time than traditional exams. When you register for an exam, you will be told how much time you should expect to spend at the testing center. In some cases, the exams include timed sections that can help for apportioning your time.

What Is the Testing Experience Like?

You are required to bring two forms of identification that include your signature and one photo ID (such as a driver's license or company security ID). You will be required to sign a non-disclosure agreement that obligates you not to share the contents of the exam questions with others, and you will be asked to complete a survey. The rules and procedures of the exam will be explained to you by Testing Center administrators. You will be introduced to the testing equipment and you will be offered an exam tutorial intended to familiarize you with the testing equipment. This is a good idea. You will not be allowed to communicate with other examinees or with outsiders during the exam. You should definitely turn off your cell phone when taking the exam.

How Can You Best Prepare for the Exams?

Prepare for each exam by reading this book, and then practicing your skills in a simulated environment on the Interactive Solution CD-ROM that accompanies this series. If you do not have a real network to practice on (and if you do not build a small network), the next best thing is to work with the CD-ROM. Alternatively, it is very helpful to build a small Windows Server 2003 network with a couple of unused computers. You will also require experience with a real-world Windows Server 2003 network. An MCSE/MCSA candidate should, at a minimum, have at least one year of experience implementing and administering a network operating system in environments with the following characteristics: a minimum of 200 users, five supported physical locations, typical network services and applications including file and print, database, messaging, proxy server or firewall, dial-in server, desktop management, and Web hosting, and connectivity needs, including connecting individual offices and users at remote locations to the corporate network and connecting corporate networks to the Internet.

In addition, an MCSE candidate should have at least one year of experience in the following areas: implementing and administering a desktop operating system, and designing a network infrastructure.

Where Can You Take the Exams?

All MCP exams are administered by Pearson VUE and Prometric. There are 3 convenient ways to schedule your exams with Pearson VUE:

- Online: **www.pearsonvue.com/ms/**
- Toll Free in the US and Canada: call (800) TEST-REG (800-837-8734). Or, find a call center in your part of the world at: **http://www.pearsonvue.com/contact/ms/**
- In person: at your local test center. Pearson VUE has over 3,000 test centers in 130 countries. To find a test center near you, visit: **www.pearsonvue.com**

To take exams at a Prometric testing center, call Prometric at (800) 755-EXAM (755-3926). Outside the United States and Canada, contact your local Prometric Registration Center. To register online with Prometric, visit the Prometric web site, **www.prometric.com**.

How Much Does It Cost to Take the Exams?

In the United States, exams cost $125 USD per exam as of January, 2004. Certification exam prices are subject to change. In some countries/regions, additional taxes may apply. Contact your test registration center for exact pricing.

Are There Any Discounts Available to Students?

Yes. In the US and Canada, as well as other select regions around the globe, full-time students can take a subset of the MCP exams for a significantly reduced fee at Authorized Academic Testing Centers (AATCs). For details on which countries and exams are included in the program, or to schedule your discounted exam, visit **www.pearsonvue.com/aatc**.

Can You Take the Exam More Than Once?

Yes. You may retake an exam at any time if you do not pass on the first attempt. But if you do not pass the second time, you must wait fourteen days. A 14-day waiting period will be imposed for all subsequent exam retakes. If you have passed an exam, you cannot take it again.

Where Can I Get More Information about the Exams?

Microsoft Websites are a good place to start:

MCP Program (general): **http://www.microsoft.com/learning/mcp/default.asp**

MCSE Certification: **http://www.microsoft.com/learning/mcp/mcse/**

MCSA Certification: **http://www.microsoft.com/learning/mcp/mcsa/**

There are literally thousands of other Websites with helpful information that you can identify using any Web search engine. Many commercial sites will promise instant success, and some even guarantee you will pass the exams. Be a discriminating consumer. If it was that easy to become an MCP professional, the certification would be meaningless.

Acknowledgments

A great many people have contributed to the Prentice Hall Certification Series. We want to thank Steven Elliot, our editor at Prentice Hall, for his enthusiastic appreciation of the project, his personal support for the Azimuth team, and his deep commitment to the goal of creating a powerful, accurate, and enjoyable learning tool for students. We also want to thank David Alexander of Prentice Hall for his interim leadership and advice as the project developed at Prentice Hall, and Jerome Grant for supporting the development of high-quality certification training books and CDs for colleges and universities worldwide. Finally, we want to thank Susan Hartman Sullivan of Addison Wesley for believing in this project at an early stage and for encouraging us to fulfill our dreams.

The Azimuth Interactive MCSE/MCSA team is a dedicated group of technical experts, computer scientists, networking specialists, and writers with literally decades of experience in computer networking, information technology and systems, and computer technology. We want to thank the members of the team:

Kenneth C. Laudon is the Series Designer. He is Professor of Information Systems at New York University's Stern School of Business. He has written twelve books on information systems and technologies, e-commerce, and management information systems. He has designed, installed, and fixed computer networks since 1982.

Carol G. Traver is the Senior Series Editor. She is General Counsel and Vice President of Business Development at Azimuth Interactive, Inc. A graduate of Yale Law School, she has co-authored several best-selling books on information technology and e-commerce.

Kenneth Rosenblatt is a Senior Author for the Series. He is an experienced technical writer and editor who has co-authored or contributed to over two dozen books on computer and software instruction. In addition, Ken has over five years experience in designing, implementing, and managing Microsoft operating systems and networks. Ken is a co-author of the Prentice Hall Certification Series Exam 70-216, Exam 70-270, and Exam 70-291 textbooks.

Robin L. Pickering is a Senior Author for the Series. She is an experienced technical writer and editor who has co-authored or contributed to over a dozen books on computers and software instruction. Robin has extensive experience as a Network Administrator and consultant for a number of small to medium-sized firms. In addition to this book, Robin is a co-author of the Prentice Hall Certification Series Exam 70-210, Exam 70-215, and Exam 70-270 textbooks.

Russell Polo is the Technical Advisor for the Series. He holds degrees in computer science and electrical engineering. He has designed, implemented, and managed Microsoft, Unix, and Novell networks in a number of business firms since 1995. He currently is the Network Administrator at Azimuth Interactive.

David Langley is an Editor for the Series. David is an experienced technical writer and editor who has co-authored or contributed to over ten books on computers and software instruction. In addition, he has over fifteen years experience as a college professor, five of those in computer software training.

Brian Hill is a Technical Consultant and Editor for the Series. His industry certifications include MCSE 2000 and 2003, MCSA 2000 and 2003, MCSE+I (NT 4.0), CCNP, CCDP, MCT, MCP, Net+, and A+. Brian was formerly Lead Technology Architect and a Bootcamp instructor for Techtrain, Inc. His Windows 2000 experience spans back as far as the first Beta releases. In addition to this book, Brian is also a co-author of the Prentice Hall Certification Series Exam 70-217 and Exam 70-294 textbooks.

L. Ward Ulmer is a former Information Technology Director with eleven years of experience. He began teaching Computer Science in 1996 and has held teaching positions at Patrick Henry Academy and Trident Technical College. He became the Department Chair of Computer Technology Orangeburg-Calhoun Technical College, his current position, in 2000. Ward's certifications include MCSE, MCSA, CCNA, MCP+I, MCT, and CCAI. Ward is a co-author of the Prentice Hall Certification Series Exam 70-217 and Exam 70-294 Project Lab Manuals.

Acknowledgments (cont'd)

Richard Watson has worked in the industry for 10 years, first as a Checkpoint Certified Security Engineer (CCSE), and then as a Lead Engineer for a local Microsoft Certified Solution Provider. Among his many other industry certifications are MCSE on Windows 2000 and NT4, Microsoft Certified Trainer (MCT), Cisco Certified Network Associate (CCNA), and IBM Professional Server Expert (PSE). Richard is currently the President of Client Server Technologies Inc., which provides network installation and support, Web site design, and training in Beaverton, Oregon. Richard is a co-author of the Prentice Hall Certification Series Exam 70-220 and Exam 70-291 textbooks.

Stacey McBrine has spent more than 18 years configuring and supporting DOS and Windows-based personal computers and local area networks, along with several other operating systems. He is certified as an MCSE for Windows NT 4.0, and was one of the first 2000 persons in the world to achieve MCSE certification for Windows 2000. He has brought his real world experience to the classroom for the last 5 years as a Microsoft Certified Trainer. He holds several other certifications for Cisco, Linux, Solaris, and Security. Stacey is a co-author of the Prentice Hall Certification Series Exam 70-293 textbook and Exam 70-270 Lab Manual.

Mark Maxwell is a Technical Consultant and Editor for the Series. He has over fifteen years of industry experience in distributed network environments including TCP/IP, fault-tolerant NFS file service, Kerberos, Wide Area Networks, and Virtual Private Networks. Mark is a co-author of the Prentice Hall Certification Series Exam 70-216 Lab Manual, and has also published articles on network design, upgrades, and security.

Dr. Russell Jones is an Associate Processor and Area Coordinator of Decision Sciences at Arkansas State University and currently holds the Kathy White Endowed Fellowship in MIS. Dr. Jones received his PhD from the University of Texas-Arlington and has been on the ASU faculty for 16 years. He holds certifications from Microsoft, Novell, CompTIA, and Cisco, and is a co-author of the Prentice Hall Certification Series Exam 70-290 Project Lab Manual.

Nigel Kay, MCSE, is a technical writer from London, Ontario, Canada. He has contributed to several published IT certification guides, and is currently the documentation lead for a network security company. Previously, he worked for many years as a Network Administrator. Nigel is a co-author of the Prentice Hall Certification Series Exam 70-293 textbook and Project Lab Manual.

David W. Tschanz, MCSE, MCP+I, A+, iNET+, CIW, is an American who has been living in Saudi Arabia for the past 15 years. There he has worked on a variety of projects related to Web-based information management, training, and applications, as well as computer security issues. He writes extensively on computer topics and is a regular contributor to MCP Magazine. David is a co-author of the Prentice Hall Certification Series Exam 70-220 Lab Manual.

Brien M. Posey, MCSE, has been a freelance technical writer who has written for Microsoft, CNET, ZDNet, Tech Target, MSD2D, Relevant Technologies, and many other technology companies. Brien has also served as the CIO for a nationwide chain of hospitals and was once in charge of IT security for Fort Knox. Most recently, Brien has received Microsoft's MVP award for his work with Windows 2000 Server and IIS. Brien is a co-author of the Prentice Hall Certification Series Exam 70-218 textbook.

Tim Oliwiak, MCSE, MCT, is a network consultant for small- to medium-sized companies. He previously was an instructor at the Institute for Computer Studies, and a Network Engineer for the Success Network. Tim is a resident of Ontario, Canada. Tim is a co-author of the Prentice Hall Certification Series Exam 70-217 Project Lab Manual.

Simon Sykes-Wright, MCSE, has been a technical consultant to a number of leading firms, including NCR Canada Ltd. Simon is a co-author of the Prentice Hall Certification Series Exam 70-293 textbook.

David Lundell is a database administrator and Web developer for The Ryland Group in Scottsdale, Arizona. He holds MCSE, MCDBA, MCSD, MCT, CAN, and CCNA certifications, as well as an MBA from the University of Arizona. David is a co-author of the Prentice Hall Certification Series Exam 70-291 Project Lab Manual.

Wale Soyinka is a systems and network engineering consultant. He holds MCP, CCNA, and CCNP certification. He is the author of a series of lab manuals on Linux, and is a co-author of the Prentice Hall Certification Series Exam 70-218 Lab Manual.

Quality Assurance

The Prentice Hall Certification Series contains literally thousands of software instructions for working with Windows products. We have taken special steps to ensure the accuracy of the statements in this series. The books and CDs are initially written by teams composed of Azimuth Interactive Inc. MCSE/MCSA professionals and writers working directly with the software as they write. Each team then collectively walks through the software instructions and screen shots to ensure accuracy. The resulting manuscripts are then thoroughly tested by an independent quality assurance team of MCSE/MCSA professionals who also perform the software instructions and check to ensure the screen shots and conceptual graphics are correct. The result is a very accurate and comprehensive learning environment for understanding Windows products.

We would like to thank the primary members of the Quality Assurance Team for their critical feedback and unstinting efforts to make sure we got it right. The primary technical editors for this book are Byron Wright and Thomas Lee. Byron Wright (B.Comm., MCT, MCNI) is the Program Director for Information Technology Programs at The University of Manitoba Continuing Education Division. He got his start in the technology industry connecting systems to the Internet in the early 1990s just as the Internet was becoming available to the public. He is also the owner of Applied Innovation, Inc., a consulting company that designs, implements, and maintains both Microsoft and Novell networks. Thomas Lee (MCSA, MCSE, MCT, MVP, Microsoft Regional Director, FBCS) is Chief Technologist at QA, an IT training and consulting company in the UK. He is involved in the development and delivery of a range of leading-edge IT training courses, and in carrying out consulting assignments for QA clients.

Conventions Used in This Book

◆ Bold and/or italicized text enclosed within carets, such as *<Server_name>*, indicates a variable item. The carets and bold/italic formatting are solely to alert you to the variable nature of the enclosed text and will not be present in your file structure. If called on to enter the information referred to within the carets, type only the information itself, not the carets, and do not use bold or italics.

◆ Keys on the keyboard are enclosed within square brackets, such as **[Alt]**. A plus sign (+) between two key names indicates that you must press those keys at the same time, for example, "press **[Ctrl]+[Alt]+[Del]**."

◆ Folder, file, and program names in the text are shown with initial capitals, although their on-screen appearance may differ. For example, in our text, you may see a reference to a Windows folder, but on your screen this folder may be shown as WINDOWS. Similarly, in our text, you may see a reference to the Iishelp folder, although on screen it may appear as iishelp. When typing folder and file names yourself, you may use upper and/or lower case as you choose unless otherwise instructed.

◆ Command line syntax: Commands to be entered at a command prompt are shown in lower case. Square brackets, carets, and/or bold/italic formatting used in command line syntax statements indicate a variable item. As with material shown within carets, if called on to enter such an item, type only the information referred to within the brackets or carets, not the brackets or carets themselves and do not use bold or italics.

◆ The term *%systemroot%* is used to indicate the folder in the boot partition that contains the Windows Server 2003 system files.

Installing, Configuring, and Administering Microsoft® Windows® 2000 Professional Exam 70-210
ISBN 0-13-142209-X

Installing, Configuring, and Administering Microsoft® Windows® 2000 Server Exam 70-215
ISBN 0-13-142211-1

Implementing and Administering Microsoft® Windows® 2000 Network Infrastructure Exam 70-216
ISBN 0-13-142210-3

Implementing and Administering a Microsoft® Windows® 2000 Directory Services
Infrastructure Exam 70-217 ISBN 0-13-142208-1

Managing a Microsoft® Windows® 2000 Network Environment Exam 70-218
ISBN 0-13-144744-0

Designing Security for a Microsoft® Windows® 2000 Network Exam 70-220 ISBN 0-13-144906-0

Implementing, Managing, and Maintaining a Microsoft® Windows® Server 2003 Network
Infrastructure Exam 70-291 ISBN 0-13-145600-8

Planning and Maintaining a Microsoft® Windows® Server 2003 Network Infrastructure Exam 70-293
ISBN 0-13-189306-8

Planning, Implementing, and Maintaining a Microsoft® Windows® Server 2003 Active Directory
Infrastructure Exam 70-294 ISBN 0-13-189312-2

Designing a Microsoft® Windows® Server 2003 Active Directory and Network Infrastructure
Exam 70-297 ISBN 0-13-189316-5

Designing Security for a Microsoft® Windows® Server 2003 Network Exam 70-298
ISBN 0-13-117670-6

Introducing Windows Server 2003

The primary members of the Windows Server 2003 family of operating systems are Windows Server 2003, Standard Edition; Windows Server 2003, Enterprise Edition; Windows Server 2003, Datacenter Edition; and Windows Server 2003, Web Edition. A Windows Server 2003 network offers enhanced features for maintaining your data, network resources, and network services. Windows Server 2003 can be used for file and print servers, application servers, Web servers, domain controllers, DNS (Domain Name System) servers, DHCP (Dynamic Host Configuration Protocol) servers, WINS (Windows Internet Naming Service) servers, terminal servers, remote access servers and VPN (Virtual Private Network) servers.

Windows Server 2003 offers many new security and management-related features and improvements to Active Directory services. Active Directory, introduced in the Windows 2000 environment, provides the directory database and associated services for Window Server 2003. Active Directory stores information about how the network is structured and organized and enables users to identify and locate resources on the network, such as other users and groups, shares, printers, applications, databases, and computers. Active Directory serves as the central repository for network objects and as a central administrative site so that network administrators do not have to individually manage multiple servers. Network resources can be managed from one site because all of the directory information for the network is stored in Active Directory. This data is copied to all of the other domain controllers on the network.

Several new automated management tools are included with Windows Server 2003, such as Microsoft Software Update Services (SUS) and Server Configuration Wizards. Another new tool (available as a separate component) is the Group Policy Management Console (GPMC). GPMC makes managing group policy easier by utilizing Active Directory and its management features. Improvements in the command-line utility provide administrators with the capability of performing most administrative tasks using command console tools. New and enhanced features for storage management have also been introduced in Windows Server 2003, making it easier and more reliable to manage and maintain disks and volumes. Advances in backup and data restoration, such as Volume Shadow Copy and features for connecting to storage area networks (SANs), are also available in the Windows Server 2003 family of products.

Support for the Microsoft .NET framework, XML Web Services, and Internet Information Services (IIS) 6.0 are also important new components of the Windows Server 2003 family of operating systems. The Microsoft .Net framework enhances companies' ability to integrate a variety of software applications, by using XML Web services. XML Web services enable developers to easily create reusable, building-block software applications that can connect to other applications via the Internet. IIS 6.0 is Windows Server 2003's built-in Web server. According to Microsoft, IIS 6.0 has significant architectural improvements and a new process model that improves reliability, scalability, and performance. IIS 6.0 is installed, by default, in a locked down state. An administrator must enable or disable IIS 6.0's system features based on application requirements.

Windows Server 2003 also provides more flexibility, operability, and reliability of network communications. Enterprise Universal Description, Discovery, and Integration (UDDI) services allow organizations to run their own internal UDDI service for intranet or extranet services. This new feature allows developers to find and reuse available organizational Web services. Lastly, a digital streaming media service is also included in the Windows Server 2003 family. This service includes a new Windows Media Player and Windows Media Encoder and other support tools.

Goals

In this lesson, you will learn about the new features of Windows Server 2003 and explore its architecture. You will also learn about the two types of network models used by Windows Server 2003 (workgroups and domains), as well as various network and security services and network protocols supported by Windows Server 2003.

Lesson 1   Introducing Windows Server 2003

Skill	Exam 70-290 Objective
1. Introducing the Windows Server 2003 Family of Operating Systems	Basic knowledge
2. Exploring the Features of Windows Server 2003	Basic knowledge
3. Overview of Windows Server 2003 Operating System Architecture	Basic knowledge
4. Introducing Workgroups and Domains	Basic knowledge
5. Introducing Network Services in Windows Server 2003	Basic knowledge
6. Introducing Network Protocols	Basic knowledge
7. Introducing Network Security Services	Basic knowledge

Requirements

There are no special requirements for this lesson.

Introducing the Windows Server 2003 Family of Operating Systems

exam objective Basic knowledge

overview

The Windows Server 2003 operating system is a flexible, scalable, and user-friendly operating system designed to help you lower your company's overall software maintenance costs. The four main products in the Windows Server 2003 family (as of December 2003) are Windows Server 2003, Standard Edition; Windows Server 2003, Enterprise Edition; Windows Server 2003, Datacenter Edition; and Windows Server 2003, Web Edition **(Figure 1-1)**. There are also 64-bit versions of Windows Server 2003, Enterprise Edition and Datacenter Edition available, which provide enhanced support for memory-intensive applications. However, be advised that some features of Windows Server 2003 are not supported on 64-bit platforms, such as the DOS 16-bit subsystem, Internet Connection Sharing, and support for the .NET framework. For a full list of features not supported in 64-bit Windows Server 2003, see the topic "Features Unavailable on the 64-bit versions of the Windows Server 2003 family" in Windows Server 2003 Help. Finally, there is also a small business edition called Windows Small Business Server 2003.

◆ **Windows Server 2003, Standard Edition** is a network operating system designed to meet the needs of small to medium-sized businesses. This entry-level server platform includes intelligent file and print sharing, secure Internet connectivity and collaboration capabilities, as well as central desktop application and policy management. Windows Server 2003, Standard Edition takes Windows 2000 Server technology, and adds some new and/or improved features, such as Internet Authentication Service (IAS), the Network Bridge feature, and Internet Connection Sharing (ICS), as well as four-way symmetric multiprocessing (SMP) with support for up to 4 gigabytes (GB) of RAM. The result is a secure, reliable, and scalable operating system. Key features of Windows Server 2003, Standard Edition are XML Web Services, file sharing improvements, and the Volume Shadow Copy service. Volume Shadow Copy service allows users to retrieve old copies of files or deleted files without administrative intervention.

◆ **Windows Server 2003, Enterprise Edition** is an operating system built for mission-critical server workloads. Windows Server 2003, Enterprise Edition is designed to meet medium to large companies' applications, Web services, and infrastructure needs. Windows Server 2003, Enterprise Edition supports up to 8 processors and 64 GB of RAM, enterprise-class features such as eight-node clustering and support for up to 32 GB of memory, support for Intel Itanium-based computers, and support for 64-bit computing platforms. In addition to all of the features in Windows Server 2003, Standard Edition, the Enterprise Edition's support for eight-node server clustering provides high availability and disaster tolerance for database management, file sharing, intranet data sharing, messaging, and general business applications. It also increases flexibility in adding and removing hardware in geographically dispersed cluster environments. Microsoft Metadirectory Services (MMS) assists organizations with the integration of identity information from multiple directories, databases, and files with Active Directory providing a unified view for identity information. Hot-Add Memory support allows memory to be added to a computer and made available to the operating system and applications as part of the normal memory pool; no rebooting and no downtime are required. In a server farm running Terminal Services, the Terminal Services session directory feature provides load balancing so that users can easily reconnect to a disconnected session. The Windows System Resource Manager (WSRM)—a feature in both Windows Server 2003, Enterprise Edition and Windows Server 2003, Datacenter Edition—allows an administrator to allocate CPU and memory utilization on a per-application basis. WSRM is a useful tool when consolidating servers.

Figure 1-1 The four main products in the Windows Server 2003 family

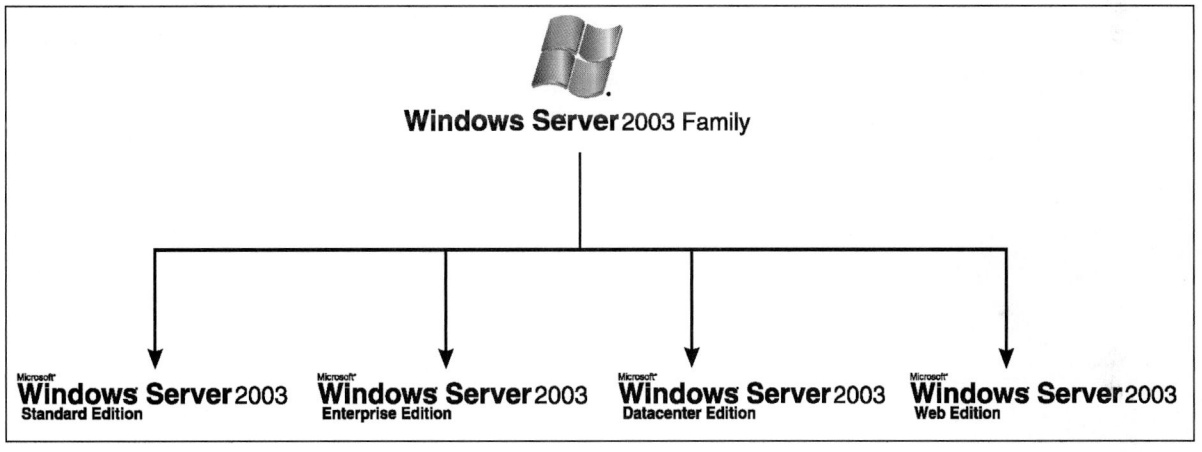

skill 1

Introducing the Windows Server 2003 Family of Operating Systems (cont'd)

exam objective

Basic knowledge

overview

◆ **Windows Server 2003, Datacenter Edition** is built for the highest levels of scalability and reliability required by medium-to-large-sized organizations. Windows Server 2003, Datacenter Edition has all of the features of Windows Server 2003, Enterprise Edition and is the most powerful server operating system Microsoft currently offers. This heavy duty operating system supports up to 32-way SMP, 64 GB of RAM with the 32-bit version, and up to 128-way SMP with individual partitions of up to 64 processors and 512 GB of RAM with the 64-bit version. Standard features include 8-node clustering and load balancing services.

◆ **Windows Server 2003, Web Edition** is a new product within the Windows operating system family. It offers dedicated Web serving and hosting, as well as a platform for building and hosting Web applications, Web pages, and XML Web Services. This edition is intended primarily for use as an IIS 6.0 Web server, a platform for rapidly developing and deploying XML Web services and applications that use ASP.NET technology. Designed specifically for dedicated Web serving needs, Windows Server 2003, Web Edition's functionality has certain limitations. Computers running Windows Server 2003, Web Edition can be members of an Active Directory domain but cannot be a domain controller. It cannot be used alone to apply certain management features such as Group Policy, Software Restriction Policies, Remote Installation Services, Microsoft Metadirectory Services, and Internet Authentication Service (IAS). Windows Server 2003, Web Edition cannot be used to deploy enterprise Universal Description, Discovery, and Integration (UDDI) services, an essential component for enabling discovery and reuse of XML Web services, or Microsoft SQL Server.

more

See **Table 1-1** for a comprehensive list of features included with each version of Windows Server 2003.

Table 1-1 Comprehensive list of features included in each version of the Windows 2003 family of network operating systems

Hardware Support	Web	Standard	Enterprise	Datacenter	Enterprise-64	Datacenter-64
32-bit Intel x86 systems	✓	✓	✓	✓		
64-bit Itanium-based systems					✓	✓
Maximum number of processors	2	4	8	32	8	64
Maximum amount of RAM	2 GB	4 GB	32 GB	64 GB	64 GB	512 GB
Hot add memory support			✓	✓		
Non-Uniform Memory Access (NUMA) support			✓	✓	✓	✓
File Systems and Storage						
Distributed File System (Dfs)	✓	✓	✓	✓	✓	✓
Shadow Copy Restore (requires 2000 or XP client)	✓	✓	✓	✓	✓	✓
Removable and remote storage		Removable storage only	✓	✓	✓	✓
Management Features						
IntelliMirror technologies	Partial	✓	✓	✓	✓	✓
Group Policy Results	Partial	✓	✓	✓	✓	✓
Windows Management Instrumentation (WMI) command line features	✓	✓	✓	✓	✓	✓
Image-based remote installation	✓	✓	✓	✓	✓	✓
Remote Installation Services (RIS)		✓	✓	✓	✓	✓
Windows System Resource Manager (WSRM)			✓	✓	✓	✓
WSRM administrative GUI			✓	✓		
Active Directory						
Active Directory member server	✓	✓	✓	✓	✓	✓
Active Directory domain controller		✓	✓	✓	✓	✓
Metadirectory Services (MMS)			✓	✓	✓	✓
Security						
Encrypting File System (EFS)	✓	✓	✓	✓	✓	✓
Internet Connection Firewall (ICF)		✓	✓		✓	
Public Key Infrastructure (PKI), Certificate Services, and Smart Card	Partial	Partial	✓	✓	✓	✓
Terminal Server						
Terminal Server		✓	✓	✓	✓	✓
Terminal Server Session Directory			✓	✓	✓	✓
Administered through Remote Desktop available	✓	✓	✓	✓	✓	✓
Networking						
Virtual Private Networking (VPN)	Partial	✓	✓	✓	✓	✓
Maximum number of VPN clients	1	1000	Unlimited	Unlimited	Unlimited	Unlimited
Internet Authentication Service (IAS)		✓	✓	✓	✓	✓
Maximum number of RADIUS network access servers for IAS		50	Unlimited	Unlimited	Unlimited	Unlimited
Maximum number of remote RADIUS groups for IAS		2	Unlimited	Unlimited	Unlimited	Unlimited
Network Bridge		✓	✓	✓	✓	✓
Internet Connection Sharing (ICS)		✓	✓		✓	
IPv6 supported	✓	✓	✓	✓	✓	✓
Clustering						
Network Load Balancing (NLB)	✓	✓	✓	✓	✓	✓
Cluster Service			✓	✓	✓	✓
Maximum number of cluster nodes			8	8	8	8
Application Services						
.NET Framework	✓	✓	✓	✓		
Internet Information Services (IIS) 6.0	✓	✓	✓	✓	✓	✓
IIS 6.0 installed by default	✓					
ASP .NET	✓	✓	✓	✓		
Enterprise UDDI Services		✓	✓	✓	✓	✓
Miscellaneous						
Windows Media Services 9 Series		✓	✓	✓		
Fax Service		✓	✓	✓	✓	✓
Services for Macintosh		✓	✓	✓	✓	✓

skill 2

Exploring the Features of Windows Server 2003

exam objective   Basic knowledge

overview

Windows Server 2003 is a network operating system that makes it possible for thousands of computers to share resources and communicate with one another. Windows Server 2003 provides various utilities and services that increase its reliability and scalability, lower the cost of computing and provide a solid foundation for running business applications. Windows Server 2003 has many capabilities, including **(Figure 1-2)**:

◆ **Active Directory:** Windows Server 2003 provides many improvements and new features to Active Directory. These improvements include cross-forest trusts, the ability to rename domains, and the ability to deactivate attributes and classes in the schema so that their definitions can be changed.

◆ **Network security:** Windows Server 2003 supports the Kerberos 5 protocol and Public Key Infrastructure (PKI). Organizations can deploy their own PKI, using Certificate Services and certificate management tools. With PKI, administrators can implement standards-based technologies such as smart card logon capabilities, client authentication (through Secure Sockets Layer and Transport Layer Security), secure e-mail, digital signatures, and secure connectivity, using Internet Protocol Security (IPSec). These features enable Windows Server 2003 to provide secure communication on an open network.

◆ **Automatic installation and configuration:** Using Windows Server 2003, you can automatically install and configure applications, which can save an organization both time and money.

◆ **Familiar appearance and easy server management:** Windows Server 2003 offers an interface similar to other members of the Microsoft Windows operating system family, allowing users to quickly and easily adapt to the Windows Server 2003 environment. Many new tools provided in Windows Server 2003 make it easier to manage your server **(Figure 1-3)**.

◆ **Security from unauthorized logon:** Windows Server 2003 provides security from unauthorized access by prompting users for a logon name and a password when they boot up a Windows Server 2003 computer. In addition, Windows Server 2003's support for Extensible Authentication Protocol (EAP) and smart card login allows an even higher level of security for organizations that require it.

◆ **Network protocols:** Windows Server 2003 supports the most popular network protocols such as TCP/IP, HTTP, PPTP, L2TP, and many others. These protocols make Windows Server 2003 a highly compatible and scalable operating system which allows users, working with different protocols, to interact with one another.

◆ **Connectivity:** In addition to the protocols noted above, Windows Server 2003 operating systems also support NWLink IPX/SPX/NetBIOS Compatible Transport Protocol and AppleTalk, which provide connectivity with Novell NetWare and Apple systems respectively. The Windows Server 2003 operating systems also support dial-up networking and Virtual Private Networks (VPNs).

◆ **Multi-lingual capabilities:** Windows Server 2003 supports a wider range of languages, as compared to its predecessors. Additional languages have been included, increasing the number of users of different languages who can work with the operating system and making it globally functional.

◆ **Web-based Enterprise Management (WBEM):** Web-based Enterprise Management (WBEM) is an industry initiative that establishes management infrastructure standards and provides a way to combine information from various hardware and software management systems. WBEM allows access to data from a variety of underlying technologies and platforms and presents that data in a consistent fashion. Windows Server 2003 makes use of WBEM to track information exchanges between networks and the attached physical components of networks, servers, and workstations. WBEM uses the Common Information Model (CIM) to standardize the utilities used by administrators

Figure 1-2 Windows Server 2003 features

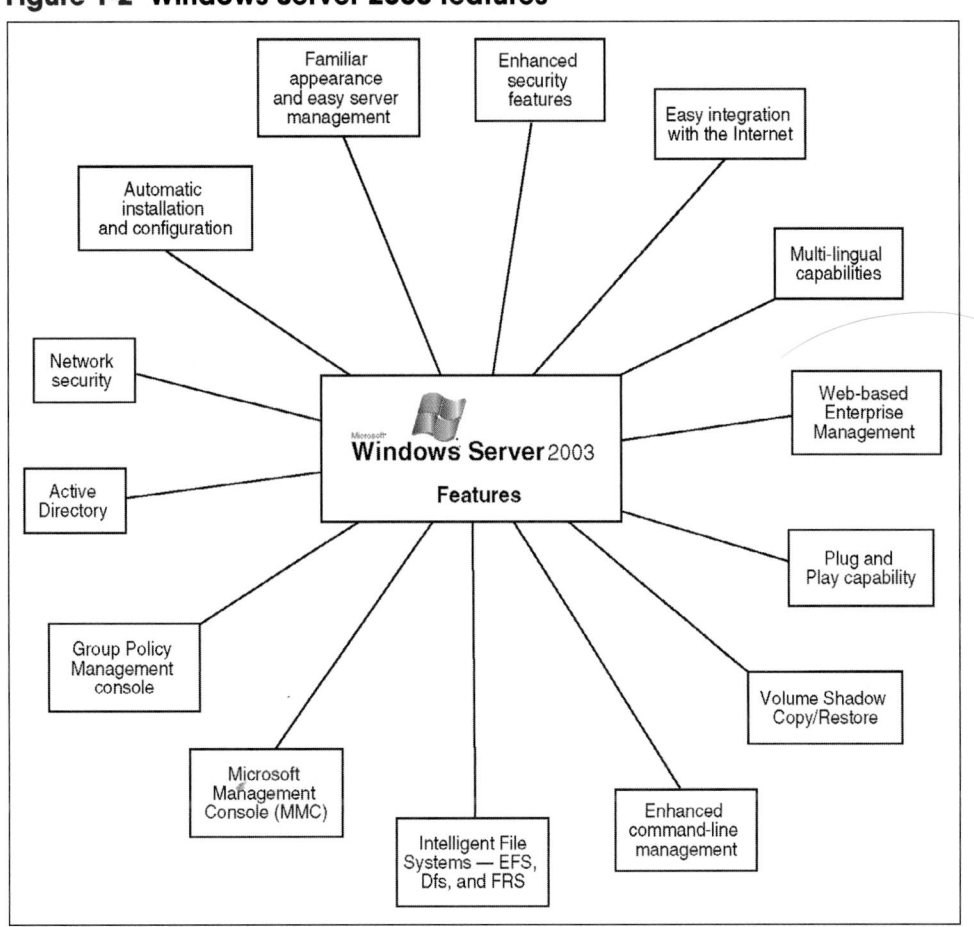

Figure 1-3 File Server Management console

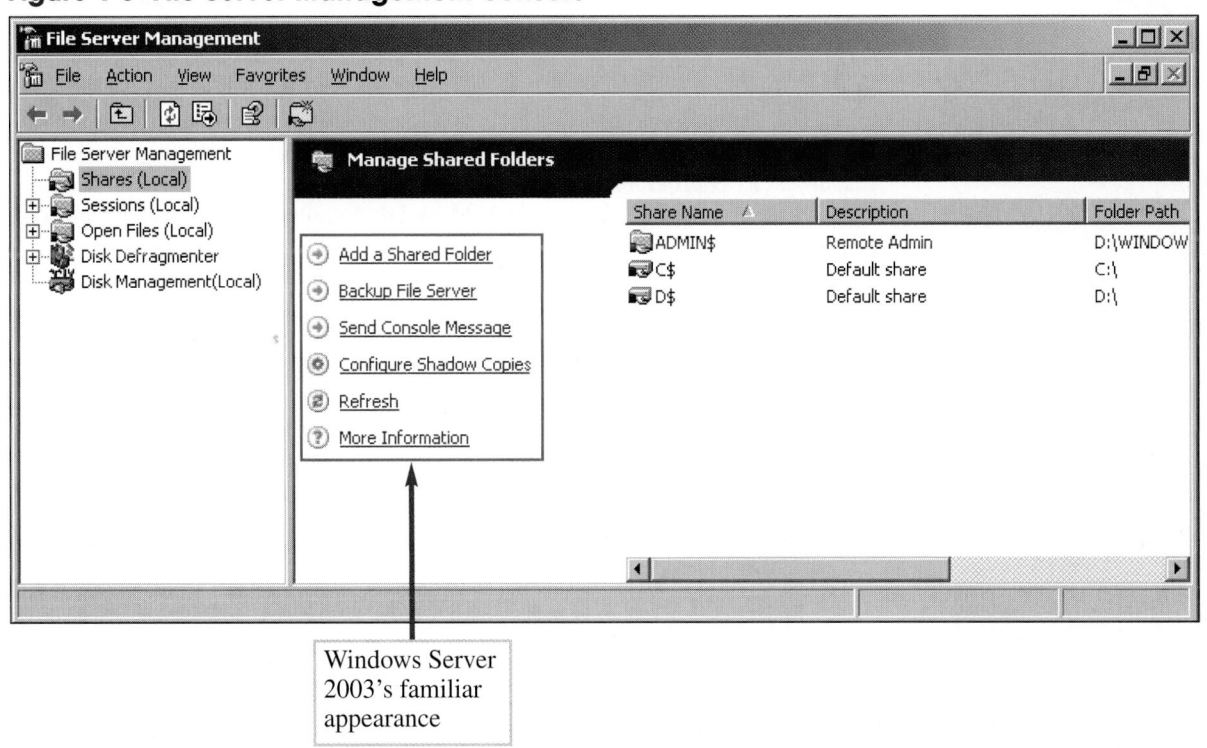

Windows Server 2003's familiar appearance

Exploring the Features of Windows Server 2003 (cont'd)

Basic knowledge

to monitor physical network devices and to get an accurate representation of the relationships between the network and the attached physical devices.

♦ **Automatic detection of Plug and Play hardware devices:** Windows Server 2003 supports automatic detection, installation, and configuration of most Plug and Play hardware devices. When you attach a device to a computer running Windows Server 2003, the operating system automatically detects, installs, and configures it, provided that the necessary drivers are on the server. If the drivers are not available, you will be prompted to install them.

♦ **Volume Shadow Copy/Restore service:** Local Windows file systems include the Recycle Bin on the desktop, from which a user can recover deleted files. The Volume Shadow Service (VSS) enables users to recover deleted files from network shares. Administrators configure VSS to take snapshots (that is, Shadow Copies) of selected NTFS volume shares **(Figure 1-4)**. VSS stores only the changes for the shares, not the entire share content. The service stores as many as 64 versions of a share, depending on disk space. Clients install a software component that adds a Previous Versions tab to the Properties dialog box for the shares on volumes on which Volume Shadow Copy has been enabled. Users select this tab to obtain a point-in-time view of the share and to access its content. If a user deletes a file or a file becomes corrupt, the user can view a prior version of the file and recover it without troubling the administrator.

♦ **Command line management:** A significantly enhanced command-line infrastructure lets administrators perform most management tasks without using a graphical user interface. The ability to perform a wide range of tasks from the command line, by accessing the information made available by Windows Management Instrumentation (WMI), allows the administrator to obtain information relating to various areas of the operating system, as well as control the behavior of services running within the operating system. Through the use of scripting and other administration-oriented utilities, the administrator can automate tasks without the use of a graphical user interface (GUI).

♦ **Intelligent File Systems: Encrypting File System (EFS), Distributed File System (Dfs), and File Replication Service (FRS):** EFS can be used to encrypt and decrypt files to protect sensitive or stored data from intruders. Dfs is an advanced file system that allows users to quickly and easily locate files and folders without having to know their exact location on the network. A single Dfs shared root serves as an access point for other shared folders on the network. This saves users time and effort in locating specific resources. FRS provides multi-master file replication for designated directory trees between designated servers and is used by Dfs to automatically synchronize content between assigned replicas. FRS is also used by Active Directory to automatically synchronize content from the system volume information, across domain controllers.

♦ **Microsoft Management Console (MMC):** The Microsoft Management Console or MMC, introduced with Windows 2000, adds to the manageability of the operating system. MMC is simply a container object for "snap-ins"—utilities that provide an interface and a set of administrative functions. Network administrators can add the snap-ins they use most often to an MMC in order to create a customized managerial tool. These consoles are used to manage the hardware, software, services, and network components of a Windows Server 2003 network.

♦ **Group Policy and Group Policy Management Console:** Group Policy can be used to define settings and allow actions for users and computers. Unlike Local Policy, Group Policy can be used to set policies that apply across a given site, domain, or organizational unit in Active Directory. Management tasks, such as system updates, application installation, user profile management, and desktop-system lockdown, are simplified by using policies. The Group Policy Management Console (GPMC), which is available as a separate download, makes managing Group Policy easier by utilizing Active Directory and its management features **(Figure 1-5)**.

Figure 1-4 Scheduling a Volume Shadow Copy

Schedule options for
creating Volume
Shadow Copies

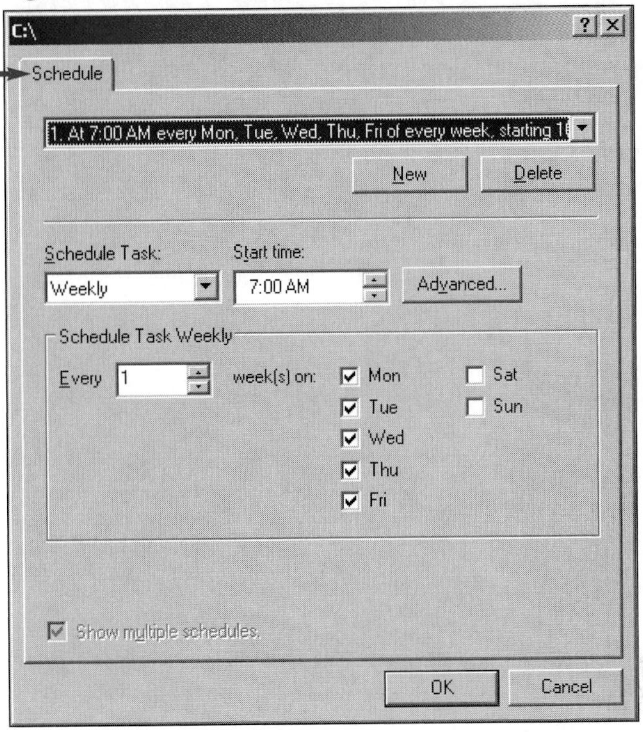

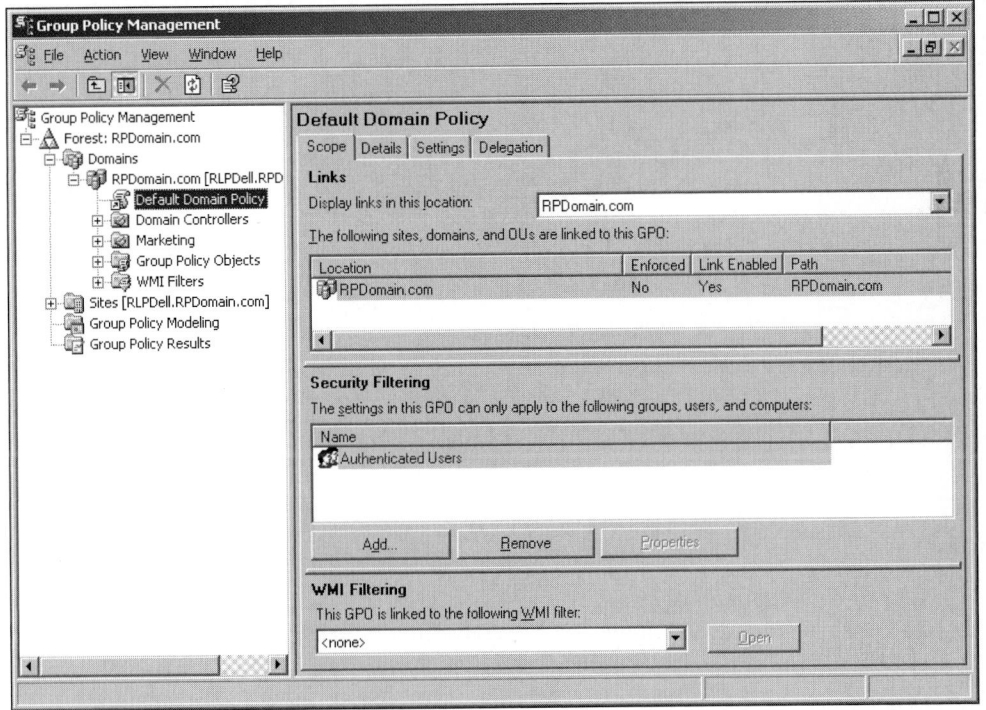

Figure 1-5 The Group Policy Management console

skill 3

Overview of Windows Server 2003 Operating System Architecture

exam objective

Basic knowledge

overview

Understanding Windows Server 2003's operating system architecture will help you to understand the basic functioning of the operating system as it processes the input and output for user requests and operations. Understanding the architecture and being able to differentiate between the various layers of the architecture will make clear the role that they play in the proper functioning of the operating system. As you will see throughout this lesson, Windows Server 2003 is modular, with each module contributing some specific functionality.

Windows Server 2003 architecture has two primary layers: user mode and kernel mode (**Figure 1-6**). Its architecture is basically the same for the Standard, Enterprise, Datacenter, and Web Editions. **User mode** consists of a set of components known as subsystems, responsible for relaying input/output requests to the appropriate kernel mode (defined below) driver through the Input/Output (I/O) system services. There are two types of subsystems: environmental subsystems and integral subsystems.

Environmental subsystems enable Windows Server 2003 to run a variety of applications designed for different operating systems. Environmental subsystems provide **Application Programming Interfaces (APIs)** that an application designed for a foreign operating system needs to interact with Windows Server 2003. An API is a set of definitions of the ways in which one piece of computer software communicates with another. When a foreign application makes an API call, the environmental subsystems accepts it, changes it into a Windows Server 2003 format, and sends it to the kernel mode. The most commonly used API in the environmental subsystems is Win32. The Win32 subsystem includes functionality that enables Win16 and MS-DOS applications to run on Windows Server 2003. Windows Server 2003 also provides many new APIs. However, some APIs that were previously included with Windows 2000, such as built-in POSIX and OS/2 subsystem support, are no longer supported. Environmental subsystems and the programs that they support have no direct access to hardware or device drivers and are limited to the amount of memory assigned to them. When the system needs memory or CPU cycles, environmental subsystems, and the programs that run using the provided API, lose—they are forced to yield CPU and memory if necessary, and are swapped to hard drive space.

Integral subsystems perform various functions that are important for the successful functioning of the operating system such as the creation of security tokens and monitoring user rights and permissions. Integral subsystems run in user mode but perform essential operating system functions. The most important integral subsystems are the Server Service, the Workstation Service, and the Security Subsystem (a collection of services and data structures). The Security Subsystem receives user logon requests and initiates the logon authentication process. The Workstation Service enables client computers to access the network, and the Server Service enables Windows Server 2003 computers to share network resources.

The **kernel mode** layer operates in a protected area of memory and provides services to user mode subsystems, which functionally protects and isolates the hardware from the software. It is also responsible for executing I/O requests and prioritizing hardware and software interrupts based on the precedence of the application or service making the request. An **interrupt** is a request for attention from the processor coming from a hardware device. When an interrupt is generated, the processor suspends its current operations and saves the status of its work. Then, it gives control to a special routine called the interrupt handler, which contains the instructions for dealing with the particular situation that caused the interrupt. Interrupts are generated by various hardware devices to request services or report problems. The processor itself can also issue an interrupt in response to program errors or requests for operating-system services.

Figure 1-6 User mode and kernel mode layers

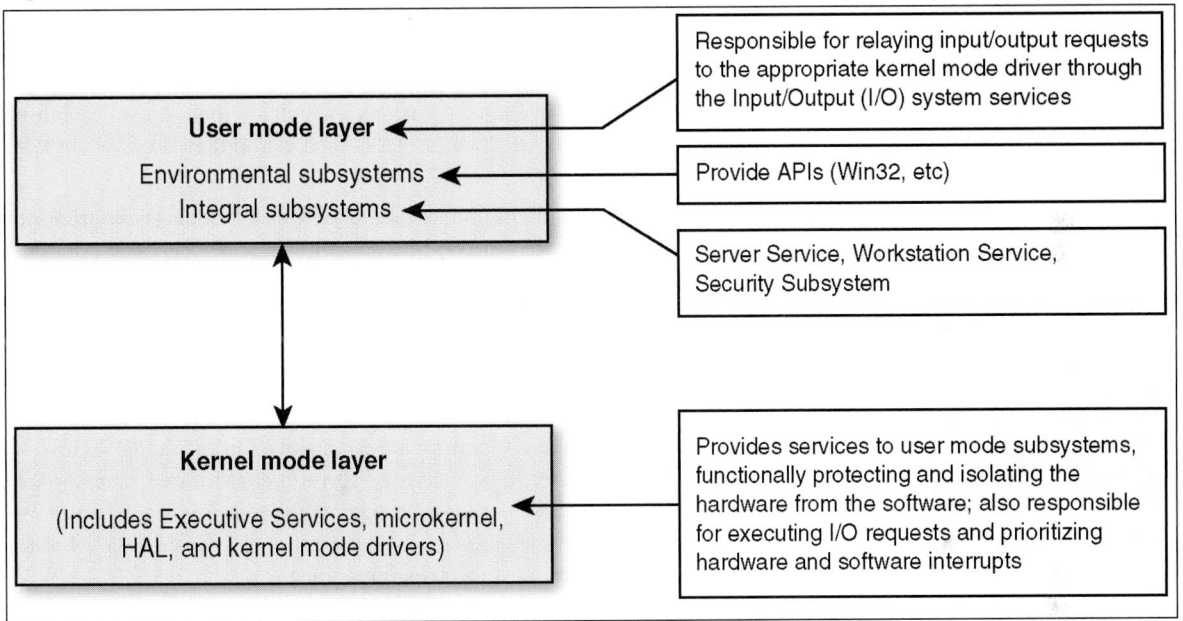

skill 3

Overview of Windows Server 2003 Operating System Architecture (cont'd)

exam objective   Basic knowledge

overview

The kernel mode layer consists of several components including the Executive, the microkernel, the Hardware Abstraction Layer (HAL), and a set of kernel mode drivers. These components make it possible for the kernel mode layer to function properly.

◆ **Executive Services** are responsible for performing I/O requests and object management. It consists of many components. These components provide system services, which can be accessed by user mode processes, as well as internal routines. Key components of the Executive Services are shown in **Figure 1-7**.

  • The **I/O Manager** is responsible for providing input/output services for user and kernel mode processes. The I/O Manager translates all requests for I/O operations into IRPs (Input/Output Request Packets), which are then transmitted through the layered set of drivers in the I/O stack. The components of the I/O Manager include:

    • The file system component that takes the I/O requests and translates them into calls that are designed for specific devices.
    • The device drivers component enables the hardware to accept input or to write output.
    • The Cache Manager augments I/O processes and the write performance of the system by storing disk reads in memory and creating a background cache of the writes to the disk.

  • The **Security Reference Monitor** is responsible for enforcing security policies on the local computer. The Security Reference Monitor is responsible for validating process access permissions against the security descriptor of an object. The Object Manager uses the services of the Security Reference Monitor while validating a process request to access any object.

  • The **Interprocess Communication (IPC) Manager** manages communication between the environmental subsystems and the Executive Services. The environmental subsystems request information (the client role) and the Executive Services responds to the requests (the server role). In this way, the IPC Manager enables the user mode processes to communicate with kernel mode processes. The components of the IPC Manager include:

    • Local Procedure Call (LPC) controls communication between environmental subsystems (client) and the Executive Services (server) on the same computer.
    • Remote Procedure Call (RPC) controls communication between environmental subsystems (client) and the Executive Services (server) on different computers.

  • The **Virtual Memory Manager (VMM)** is responsible for controlling the operation of virtual memory, which provides a private address space for each process and prevents that address space from being used by any other process. The VMM also controls access demands for the hard disk for virtual RAM known as "paging".

  • The **Process Manager** creates and ends processes and threads and manages the process and thread objects. A Windows Server 2003 process is an executable that flows through a logical sequence of events until the appointed action is complete. Technically, an executable program is composed of the base code and related data, a dedicated memory address space, defined system resources, and at least one thread. A thread is the portion of the process being executed.

Figure 1-7 Components of Executive Services

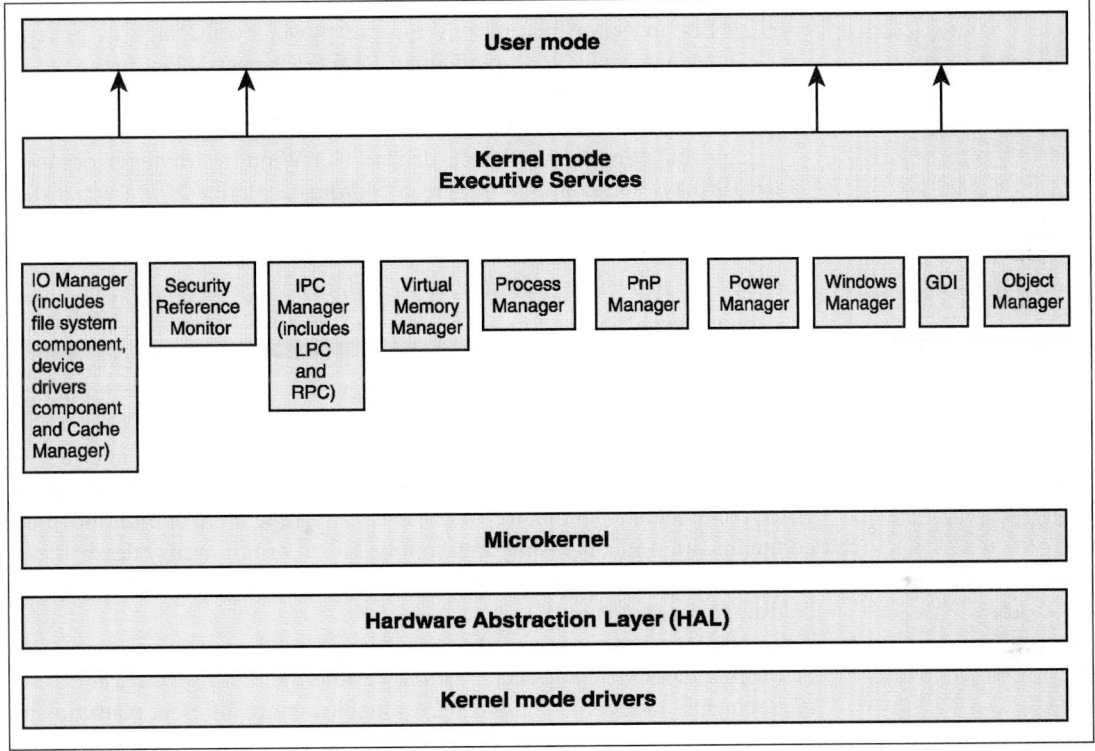

skill 3

Overview of Windows Server 2003 Operating System Architecture *(cont'd)*

exam objective   Basic knowledge

overview

- The **Plug and Play (PnP) Manager** supports boot-time Plug and Play activities that include detection of devices, such as the mouse, keyboard, CD-ROM, etc. The Plug and Play Manager interacts with all of the kernel mode layer components, such as HAL, the Executive Services, and the device drivers, to install and configure Plug and Play devices automatically.
- The **Power Manager** is responsible for controlling all of the power management APIs and coordinating any type of power event, such as generating power management IRPs (Input/Output Request Packets), that helps the CPU go into sleep mode when not in use.
- The **Window Manager** and the **Graphical Device Interface (GDI)** are executed by the Win32k.sys device driver. The Window Manager organizes window displays and controls the screen coordinates defined for a window display. The GDI is used for drawing graphics and controlling graphical displays.
- The **Object Manager** is responsible for creating, managing, and deleting objects associated with system resources such as processes, threads, and data structures.

◆ The **microkernel** is the core of the operating system. The microkernel manages the computer's processors, as well as handles scheduling, interrupts, exception dispatching, and CPU synchronization. Windows Server 2003 is a preemptive operating system, which means that threads can be interrupted or rescheduled.

◆ The **Hardware Abstraction Layer (HAL)** hides the hardware interface details from the end user by acting as an interface between the user and the hardware devices. HAL components handle I/O interfaces, interrupt controllers, and multiprocessor communication mechanisms. Put simply, it is a programming layer that enables the operating system to interact with a hardware device at a general (abstract) level rather than at the detailed hardware level.

◆ **The kernel mode drivers** translate I/O requests into hardware functions. A kernel mode driver is a modular component with a well-defined and specific set of functionality requirements. Kernel mode drivers are portable among different platforms, help provide for easy configuration of hardware and software, are continuously preemptible and interruptible without exception, and are compatible with Symmetric Multiprocessing (SMP). However, because they are allowed access to so many system structures, they are more difficult to debug than user mode drivers and present a greater chance of system corruption. When programming code is executed in kernel mode, the operating system does not perform as many safety checks to ensure the integrity of data and the authentication of user requests. There are three main classifications of kernel mode drivers (**Figure 1-8**):

  - Lowest-level drivers control peripheral devices; for example, a PnP hardware bus driver that controls an I/O bus to which any number of peripheral devices is connected.
  - Intermediate drivers are drivers for device type-specific class drivers. Lowest-level drivers support them. Good examples of intermediate drivers are specific Plug and Play function drivers that manage specific peripheral devices on an I/O controlled by PnP hardware bus drivers.
  - Highest-level drivers are the file system drivers (FSDs) for the FAT (File Allocation Table), NTFS, and CDFS (Compact Disk File System) file systems. Lowest-level drivers always support these drivers and they may also receive support from an intermediate driver.

Figure 1-8 Classifications of kernel mode drivers

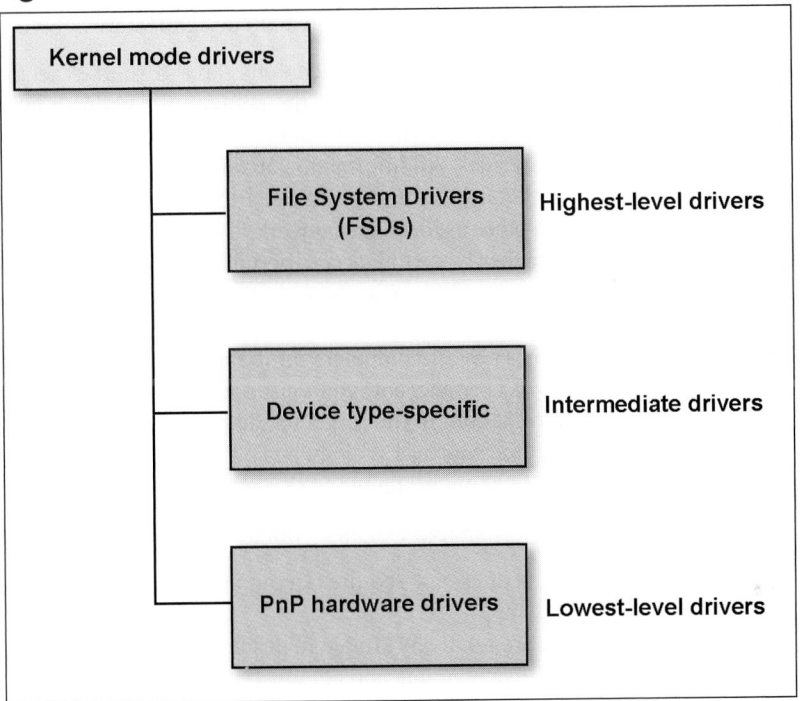

skill 4

Introducing Workgroups and Domains

exam objective   Basic knowledge

overview

The Windows Server 2003 operating system supports workgroups and domains, the two basic network model types that enable users to share common resources.

A **workgroup** or **peer-to-peer network (Figure 1-9)** is a logical group of computers that are interconnected, generally over a local area network (LAN). Workgroups allow users to easily share information and resources. All of the computers in a workgroup share resources as equals, without a dedicated server. The main design features of workgroups are:

◆ The administration of user accounts and resource security in a workgroup is decentralized. Each computer on the network maintains a local security database. This database lists user accounts and resource security information for the computer on which the database resides. All information about users, groups and permissions is stored in the local security database. Each computer user can share resources, such as printers and folders, with other users on the network. Users can also control access to resources stored on their computer by setting access permissions for groups or individual users.

◆ In order for a user to gain access to resources on any computer in the workgroup, he or she must have a user account on that computer. Furthermore, in order to maintain complete access to all computers on the network, if you make changes to the name or password for a user account, you must update each computer in the workgroup with the changed information. If you forget to add a new user account on one of the computers in a workgroup, the new user will not be able to log on to that computer or access resources from it without being prompted for a username and password valid on that system.

There are several advantages to using workgroups to share resources:

◆ A workgroup does not require a computer running Windows Server 2003 to store information.

◆ Workgroups are relatively simple to design and implement. Unlike a domain, it does not require extensive planning and administration.

Workgroups suffer from a number of limitations, including:

◆ A workgroup model is practical only in smaller environments where the computers are located in close proximity.

◆ Microsoft recommends that a workgroup consist of less than 10 computers. If you require a more scalable network that includes computers located in different geographic locations, you must use a domain network model.

Figure 1-9 Workgroup model

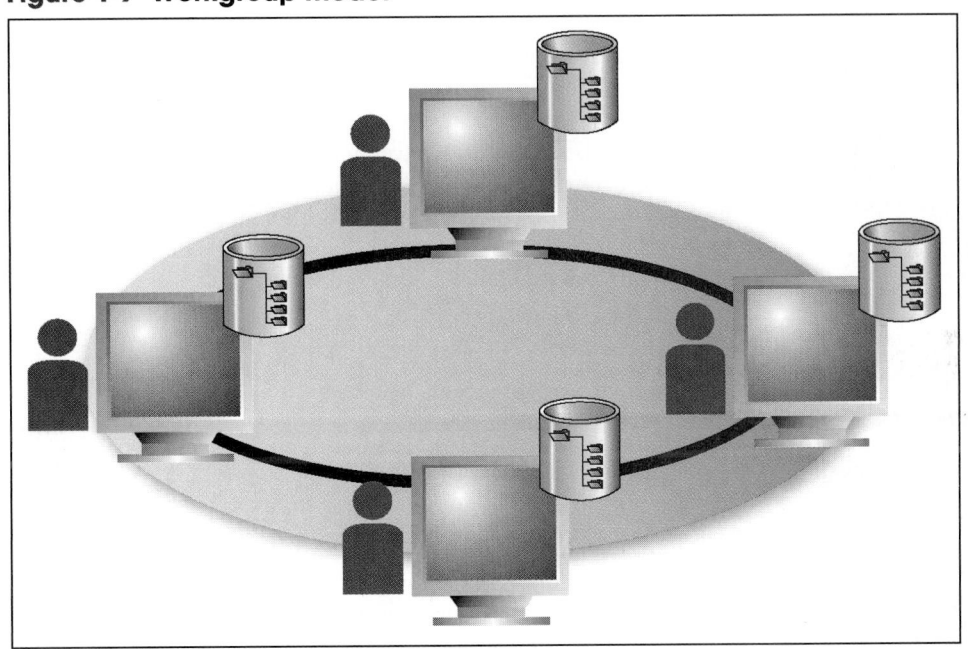

skill 4 | *Introducing Workgroups and Domains (cont'd)*

exam objective

Basic knowledge

overview

A **domain (Figure 1-10)** is a logical grouping of network computers that share a central directory database. The main features of a Windows Server 2003 domain are:

◆ The Active Directory database. As noted in the Introduction to this lesson, Active Directory stores information about how the network is structured and organized and enables users to identify and locate resources on the network, such as other users and groups, shares, printers, applications, databases, and computers. Active Directory serves as the central repository for network objects and as a central administrative site so that network administrators do not have to individually manage multiple servers.

◆ A domain controller, which is a Windows Server 2003 computer on which Active Directory resides. The domain controller manages security-related aspects of user/domain interactions. In a Windows Server 2003 domain, all domain controllers are equals, doing away with the concept of primary and backup domain controllers used in Windows NT. A member server is a domain-based Windows Server 2003 computer that does not have Active Directory installed.

The two main advantages of a domain are:

◆ Security and administration are centralized, meaning that a change to any object within the domain is available to the entire domain.

◆ Domains provide a single logon process for users to gain access to network resources, such as file, print, and application resources for which they have permissions.

The primary limitation of a domain is the added expense incurred from dedicated domain controllers and the staff required to manage them.

Figure 1-10 Domain model

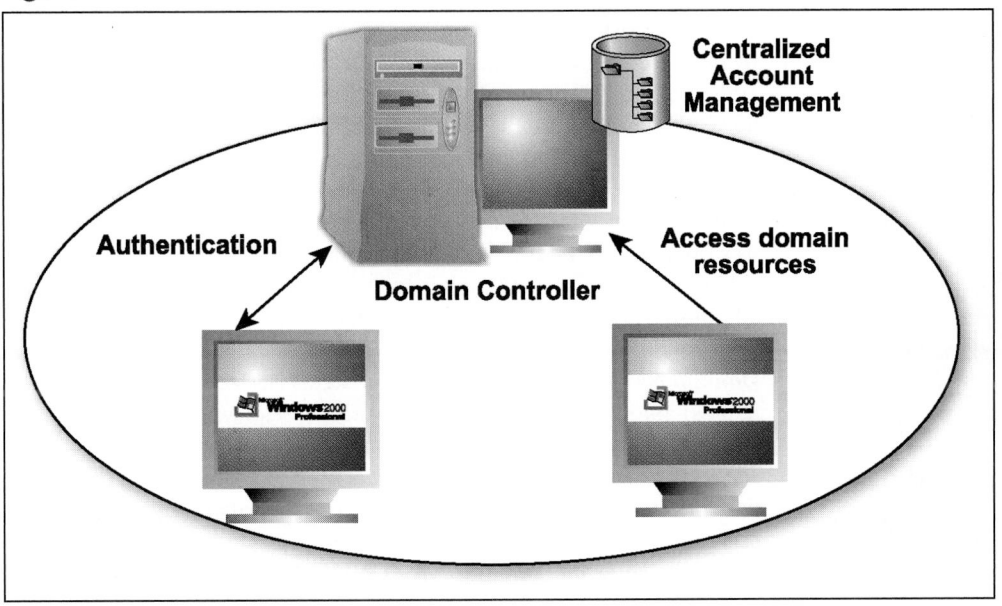

skill 5

Introducing Network Services in Windows Server 2003

exam objective

Basic knowledge

overview

Along with an understanding of the architecture of Windows Server 2003 and the two basic network models used, knowledge of the various network services supported by the operating system is necessary in order to understand the way in which these services help to manage users, workgroups, domains, clients, and servers on a network. The various network services offered by Windows Server 2003 include (**Figure 1-11**):

◆ **Dynamic Host Configuration Protocol (DHCP):** This service is a standard that is used by the DHCP servers on the network. DHCP servers manage the dynamic allocation of IP addresses and the related configuration details for DHCP-enabled clients on your network. The dynamic allocation of IP addresses ensures a unique address for each computer. DHCP provides configuration information to client computers running Windows XP, Windows 2000 Professional, Windows Me, Windows 98, or Windows 95, along with any other computer that supports the DHCP standard. The default setup in most operating systems is for the "client" to retrieve an IP address from the DHCP server. The DHCP server's job is to dynamically assign IP addresses. This simplifies the administration of the TCP/IP configuration because it automates the process of assigning IP addresses to clients.

◆ **Domain Name System (DNS):** The DNS service resolves host names (natural language names) into Internet Protocol (IP) addresses, which are binary digits that enable computers to identify each other, and vice versa. DNS is the main name resolution service for Windows Server 2003 and is used to enable access to computers on a TCP/IP network using the domain name. The Internet also uses DNS to locate various Web servers and hosts on networks around the world.

◆ **Windows Internet Name Service (WINS):** Prior to Windows 2000, the default name resolution service was NetBIOS. Each computer on a network has a computer or NetBIOS name. The NetBIOS name is used to identify the computer on a Microsoft network. When network users want to find your computer on a TCP/IP network, using the NetBIOS name, there must be a method for assigning or mapping an IP address to the computer name. The main method is a WINS server with a database which functions as the lookup directory. As client computers are assigned different IP addresses by the DHCP server as they boot, the WINS database in Windows Server 2003 is dynamically updated resulting in the database staying current. Since NetBIOS was the primary naming scheme in Windows NT, setting up a WINS server is necessary if some of the client computers on your network are running Windows NT, or any other previous version of Windows (such as Windows 9x). In addition, some applications depend on NetBIOS naming. If you do not set up WINS, users can still browse on their subnet using NetBIOS broadcasts, but they cannot make connections to computers on other subnets without the use of other means of computer name resolution, such as an LMHOSTS file.

◆ **Virtual Private Networks (VPN):** VPNs are connections to private networks, such as a LAN, through a non-secure communication channel like the Internet. VPNs use tunneling and encryption protocols to create a virtual tunnel, to exchange information securely. First, a remote client creates a connection with the Internet through a dial-up connection, modem, cable, or any other medium. Then, tunneling and encryption protocols are used to establish a secure channel through the established infrastructure to the LAN. The encryption protocol keeps the data flow private even though it is traveling through the public Internet. The tunneling protocol transports the original, unaltered LAN packet through the Internet by wrapping the packet inside a valid IP packet. This provides a virtual link through the Internet.

Figure 1-11 Networking services offered by Windows Server 2003

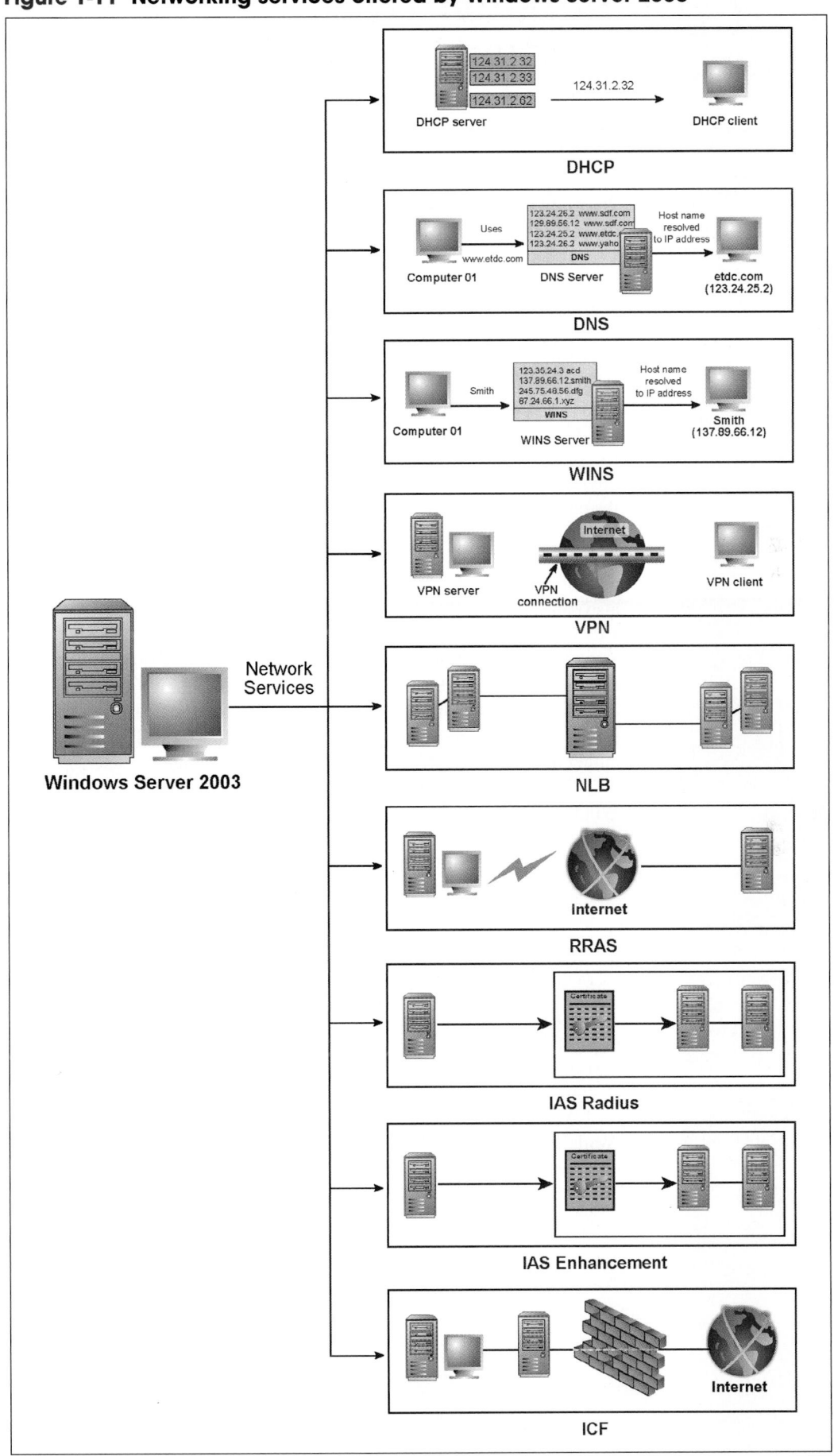

skill 5

Introducing Network Services in Windows Server 2003 (cont'd)

exam objective   Basic knowledge

overview

◆ **Network Load Balancing:** Network Load Balancing (NLB) is provided with Windows Server 2003 to allow certain types of servers (mostly file/print servers and Web servers) to scale to a much larger size than would otherwise be possible. NLB allows you to assign several servers to an NLB cluster, allowing any server in the cluster to respond to any message addressed to the cluster. This provides benefits in increased stability and scalability. This service also provides capacity and scale for Windows VPN gateway deployments. NLB improvements support L2TP VPNs and Point-to-Point Tunneling Protocol (PPTP)-based VPN connections that are protected by IPSec encryption, for increased security for IP traffic.

◆ **Routing and Remote Access Service (RRAS):** RRAS allows remote or mobile workers to connect to a firm's networks so that they can work as if their computers were physically connected to the network. Workers can connect to a LAN by simply dialing the phone number of the RRAS server or through a virtual private network (VPN). RRAS clients connect to an RRAS server using a configured access device. When a client accesses an RRAS server, the RRAS server receives the data from the modem or VPN and routes it to the LAN through a network interface card (NIC). All routing services are also controlled by RRAS **(Figure 1-12)**.

◆ **IAS RADIUS and Load Balancing:** Internet Authentication Service (IAS) is Windows Server 2003's Remote Authentication Dial-In User Service (RADIUS) server component **(Figure 1-13)**. RADIUS is a vendor-independent specification that allows you to central-ize AAA (Authentication, Authorization, and Accounting) duties among several RRAS servers from multiple vendors. RADIUS servers perform all AAA duties, such as logging authentication attempts, and RADIUS clients (which are RRAS servers themselves) establish and terminate connections to and from remote clients. New features of IAS in Windows Server 2003 allow you to configure RADIUS proxies to forward RADIUS requests to groups of IAS servers, instead of relying on a single IAS server. This provides for redundancy, as well as more complete support for the RADIUS specification.

◆ **IAS Enhancements:** New enhancements to RADIUS allow you to centralize AAA ser-vices for wireless users and log information to a Microsoft SQL Server. The benefits of this service include: allowing advanced SQL queries to be performed against network access events across the enterprise, new 802.1X authentication features, cross-forest authentication, and other features. Windows Server 2003's IAS enhancements also provide better tools to diagnose authentication issues and manage network access control.

◆ **Internet Connection Firewall (ICF):** This service is designed for use in a small business. ICF supplies basic protection on computers directly connected to the Internet or on LAN segments. ICF is only available in the Standard and Enterprise editions. Available for LAN, dial-up, VPN, or Point-to-Point Protocol over Ethernet (PPPoE) con-nections, ICF integrates with Internet Connection Sharing (ICS), or with the Routing and Remote Access service.

Figure 1-12 Routing and Remote Access

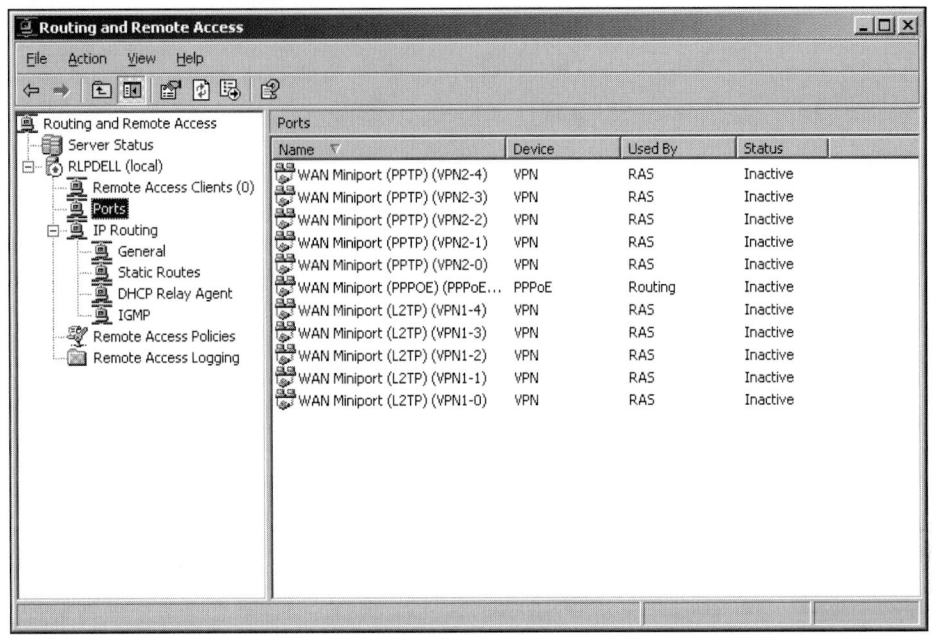

Figure 1-13 Internet Authentication Service

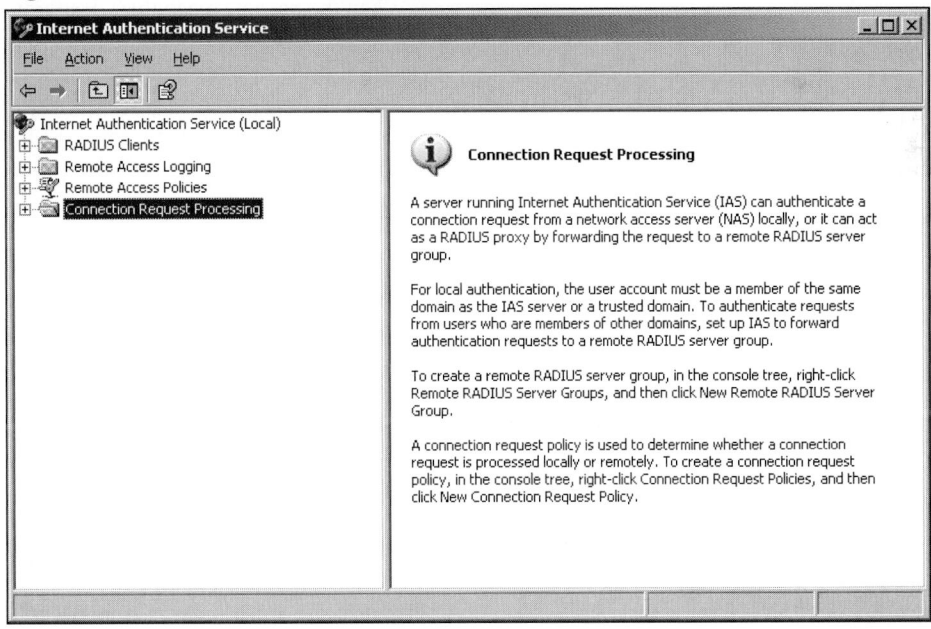

skill 6

Introducing Network Protocols

exam objective   Basic knowledge

overview

Computers on a network must converse in the same language in order for data transfers to be possible. Networking protocols today are typically put into practice as a suite of protocols. A protocol suite is an assemblage of several different networking applications and services that function jointly to make network communications possible. For instance, the term TCP/IP (Transmission Control Protocol/Internet Protocol) actually refers to a whole family of protocols, of which TCP and IP are just two. Rather than make protocols monolithic (which would mean ftp, telnet, and gopher would each have a full network protocol implementation, including separate copies of kernel code for the devices each protocol uses), the designers of TCP/IP broke the job of a full network protocol suite into a number of tasks. Each layer corresponds to a different facet of communication. Network protocols work in conjunction with network services to make Windows Server 2003 a highly scalable and compatible operating system. The main network protocols supported by Windows Server 2003 include **(Figure 1-14):**

◆ **Transmission Control Protocol/Internet Protocol (TCP/IP):** TCP/IP is the core protocol suite used by the Internet and Windows 2003 Server networks. TCP/IP is a scalable and routable transport protocol suite that can be used for both large and small networks. TCP/IP enables you to route messages across networks and between computers using different operating systems and with widely varying structural designs. A router is a special purpose device or computer used to transfer data between networks; a routable protocol ensures that data can cross this network device. A message is broken down into packets before it is transmitted. The packets can follow different routes, but they generally follow one common path. When the packets reach their destination, TCP/IP compiles them again to recreate the original message. TCP/IP defines the rules for connecting networks to each other and for communication between computers on a network. These rules are used to correct errors, manage the routing and delivery of data, and to control all elements of the transmission of data. TCP/IP is suitable for most networks because it is supported by most operating systems and multiple hardware configurations. However, the biggest reason for TCP/IP's use in almost all networks is that it is the protocol used on the Internet. TCP/IP provides an infrastructure that is cross- platform client/server-based, scalable, dependable, and time-tested.

◆ **Point-to-Point Tunneling Protocol (PPTP):** PPTP is a tunneling protocol that is used to create secure connections to corporate networks, over any intermediate network. Secure connections for VPNs are created using either PPTP or Layer Two Tunneling Protocol (L2TP) (see below). Both of these protocols work over dial-up lines, public TCP/IP networks (the Internet), local network links, and WAN links. PPTP uses PPP (Point-to-Point Protocol) to furnish the base packet structure, and MPPE (Microsoft Point-to-Point Encryption) to provide for confidentiality through encryption.

◆ **Layer Two Tunneling Protocol (L2TP):** L2TP is another tunneling protocol used to create VPNs. If you use L2TP, a "tunnel" will be created but data will not be encrypted. L2TP should therefore be used in conjunction with IPSec, which will provide data encryption. When you use L2TP, the message header is compressed while PPTP does not use header compression. In addition, L2TP tunnels all authentication traffic, providing for a much more secure authentication process. Finally, since L2TP is most commonly used in conjunction with IPSec, L2TP typically has a much stronger method of encryption than the more venerable PPTP.

◆ **Hypertext Transmission Protocol (HTTP):** A part of the TCP/IP protocol suite, HTTP is the standard protocol used in the transmission of data across the Internet. HTTP compression is used to compact Web pages to facilitate their rapid transmission between Web servers and clients that have the compression facility. This is particularly useful when only limited bandwidth is available.

Figure 1-14 Network protocols supported by Windows Server 2003

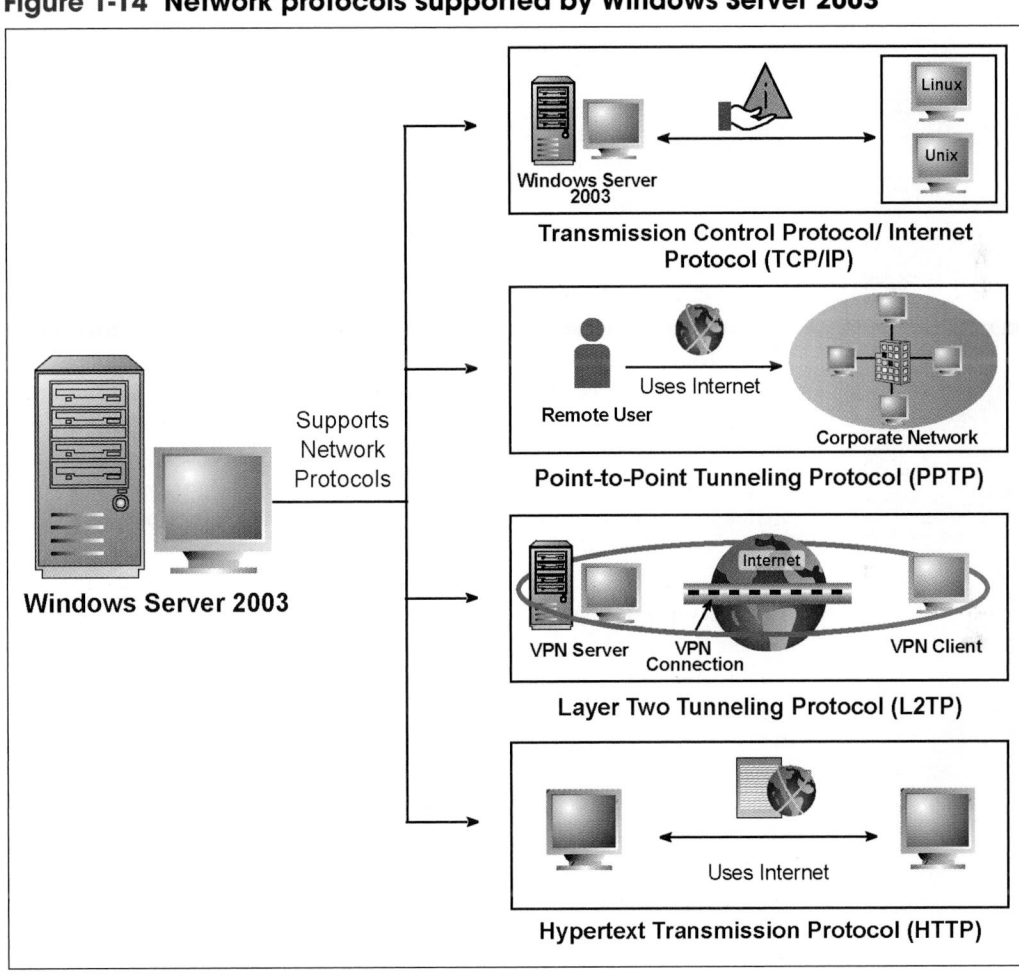

skill 7

Introducing Network Security Services

exam objective

Basic knowledge

overview

In addition to providing support for the various protocols that are used to set the rules for communication, Windows Server 2003 provides special security features to protect your network from unauthorized access. The main security services offered by Windows Server 2003 include **(Figure 1-15)**:

◆ **Kerberos v.5:** Kerberos is a ticket-based authentication protocol that provides high security for authentication traffic by making use of digital signatures and mutual authentication mechanisms. Kerberos is also a vendor-independent industry standard, making pass-through authentication between Windows Server 2003 domains and Unix Kerberos realms possible.

◆ **Public Key Infrastructure (PKI) and Microsoft Certificate Services:** PKI is a system of digital certificates and trusted Certification Authorities (CAs), as well as other registration authorities that issue them, which is used to verify and authenticate the validity of each party in a communication exchange. Digital certificates are documents that can be used to authenticate and secure the exchange of information on any network. A certificate can be used to provide non-repudiation services (through digital signatures) as well as encryption services. Certificates can be used to sign or encrypt e-mail, IPSec communication, authentication information, and many other transmissions, but the most common use of certificates is in encrypting Web-based transactions using SSL. Certificates are digitally signed by the issuing Certification Authority and can be managed for a user, a computer, or a service. The most widely accepted format for certificates is defined by the ITU-T X.509 international standard. Digital certificates help vendors to maintain logs of all of their transactions and to audit and manage certificate requests. In Windows Server 2003, Microsoft Certificate Services are responsible for the issue, renewal, and reissue of digital certificates.

◆ **Encrypting File System (EFS):** EFS is used to encrypt data that is stored in files and folders in order to protect it from unauthorized access. In the EFS encryption technique, important data is secured using an asymmetrical cryptographic key pair: a public key and a private key. Data is encrypted using a random, symmetrical session key (a file encryption key, or FEK). The session key is then encrypted using the user's public key and later decrypted using the user's private key. This technique is the same technique used by many other encryption algorithms (such as PGP and S/MIME), as it provides a high level of security with relatively low overhead.

◆ **Internet Protocol Security (IPSec):** IPSec is a vendor-independent encryption protocol that provides the ability to sign and/or encrypt any IP packet, making it not only vendor independent, but also application independent. IPSec is based on public key encryption, typically using the DES standard, and supports individual packet encryption at up to 3DES levels (168-bit). IPSec also has the ability to dynamically re-key during transmission, meaning that if the data stream is compromised, IPSec can re-key requiring the intruder to begin the process of breaking the encryption anew. IPSec support is provided in Windows Server 2003, Windows XP, and Windows 2000.

◆ **Security configuration tools:** These tools are cost reduction tools provided by Windows Server 2003. They include the Microsoft Management Console (MMC) snap-ins that are used to configure the Windows Server 2003 security settings and to conduct periodic system analyses.

Figure 1-15 Security Services provided by Windows Server 2003

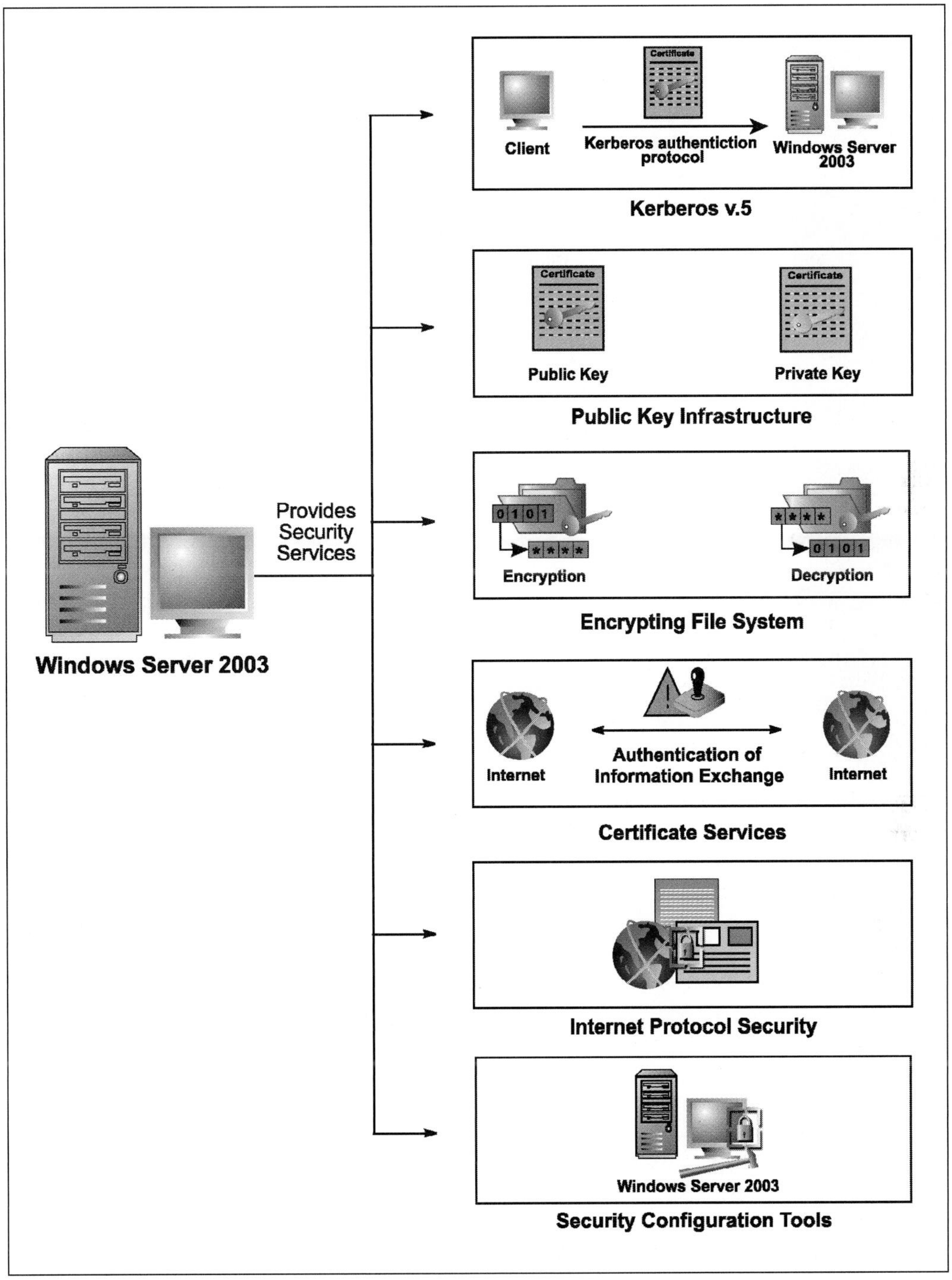

skill 7

Introducing Network Security Services *(cont'd)*

exam objective

Basic knowledge

more

In addition to supporting the various network protocols, such as TCP/IP, PPTP, HTTP, and L2TP, Windows Server 2003 supports Simple Network Management Protocol (SNMP) **(Figure 1-16)**. SNMP is a network management standard widely used to monitor and communicate status information to a network management station (NMS). SNMP is primarily used with TCIP/IP networks and Internetwork Packet Exchange (IPX) networks to efficiently manage network devices, such as servers, routers, bridges, hubs, and workstations, from a centralized network management station. Novell Netware 4.x and below uses the IPX protocol and are often integrated into a Windows environment. All protocols can be configured and managed through the Manage Your Server graphical user interface **(Figure 1-17)**.

Figure 1-16 The SNMP Service Properties dialog box

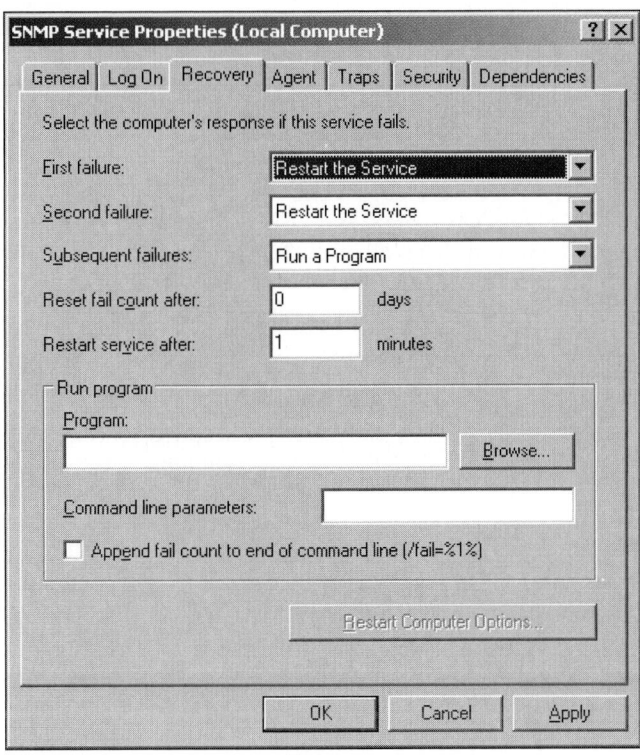

Figure 1-17 The Manage Your Server graphical user interface

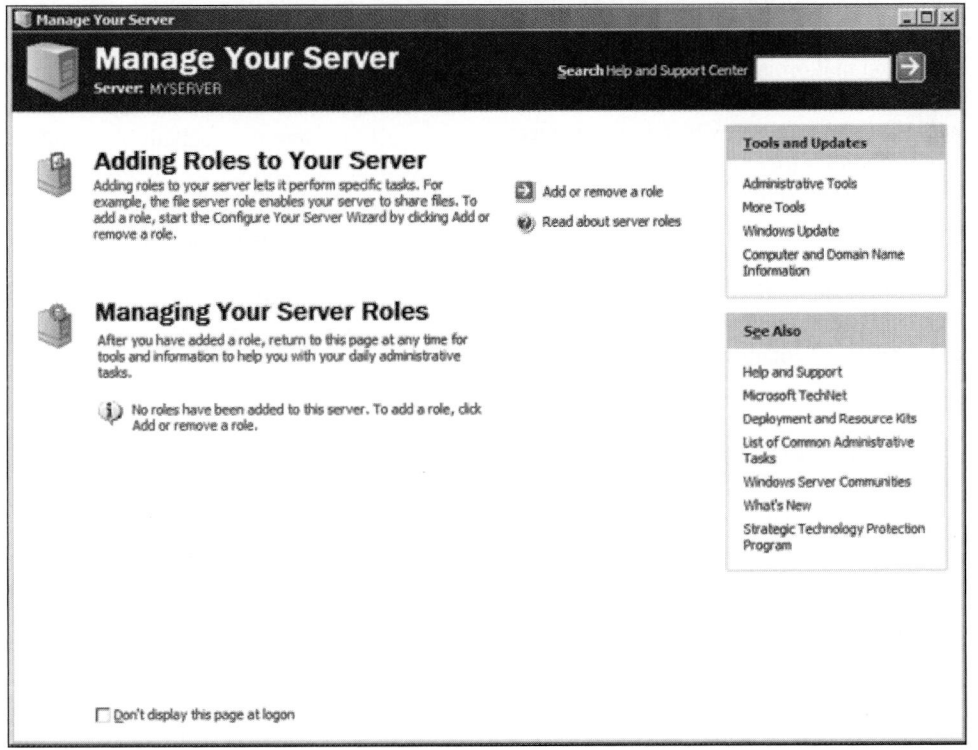

Summary

- The Windows Server 2003 family of operating systems consists of Windows Server 2003, Standard Edition; Windows Server 2003, Enterprise Edition; Windows Server 2003, Datacenter Edition; and Windows Server 2003, Web Edition.

- Windows Server 2003 is an operating system for client/server networks. It can be used for Web servers, as well as for file, print, and application servers. It has all of the features of Windows 2000 Server, along with many new and additional features.

- The features offered by Windows Server 2003 include:

    - Support for improved network, application and XML Web services.
    - Enhanced network security services such as support for the Kerberos protocol and Public Key Infrastructure (PKI).
    - Automatic installation and configuration of applications.
    - Connectivity with Novell Netware and UNIX systems.
    - Automatic detection, installation and configuration most Plug and Play hardware devices.
    - Web-based Enterprise Management (WBEM), which is an industry initiative that establishes management infrastructure standards and provides a way to combine information from various hardware and software management systems. WBEM allows access to data from a variety of underlying technologies and platforms and presents that data in a consistent fashion.
    - Distributed File System (Dfs), which is an advanced file system that allows users to quickly and easily locate files and folders spread across a network. A single Dfs shared root serves as an access point for other shared folders on the network.
    - Better language support than its predecessor versions of Microsoft Windows.
    - Integrated support for client/server and peer-to-peer networks.
    - The Microsoft Management Console (MMC), which provides management functions at a single location for easy accessibility, with the help of administrative tools called consoles.

- Windows Server 2003 Server architecture consists of two primary layers: the user mode and the kernel mode.

- The user mode consists of a set of components known as subsystems that are responsible for relaying input/output requests to the appropriate kernel mode drivers through the I/O system services. There are two types of subsystems:

    - Environmental subsystems, which enable Windows Server 2003 to run a variety of applications designed for different operating systems by providing APIs.
    - Integral subsystems, which perform various functions that are important for the successful functioning of the operating system such as the creation of security tokens, and monitoring user rights and permissions.

- The kernel mode layer consists of

    - Executive Services
    - Hardware Abstraction Layer (HAL)
    - Kernel mode drivers
    - Microkernel

- Executive Services includes many different components, including:

    - The I/O Manager, which is responsible for providing input/output services for device drivers, and translating user mode read and write commands into read or write IRPs.
    - The Security Reference Monitor, which is responsible for implementing security policies on the local computer.
    - The Virtual Memory Manager (VMM), which controls the virtual memory that provides a private address space for each process and protects the address space.

- The Hardware Abstraction Layer hides the hardware interface details from the end user by acting as an interface between the user and the hardware devices.

- The microkernel manages the computer's processors, as well as handles scheduling, interrupts, exception dispatching and CPU synchronization.

- There are three types of kernel mode drivers: Highest-level, Intermediate, and Lowest-level.

- Windows Server 2003 supports both the workgroup and domain network models.

- In a workgroup, the administration of user accounts and resource security is decentralized and each computer on the network maintains a local security database that stores information about users, groups and permissions on the network.

- A domain is a logical grouping of network computers that share a central directory database.

- Windows Server 2003 provides a variety of network services, including DHCP, DNS, and WINS, to enable users to access network data.

- The network protocols supported by Windows Server 2003 include TCP/IP, PPTP, HTTP, L2TP, and IPSec.

- Special security features offered by Windows Server 2003 include EFS, PKI support, and Certificate Services.

Key Terms

Application Programming Interface (API)

Domain

Environmental subsystems

Executive Services

Graphical Device Interface (GDI)

Hardware Abstraction Layer (HAL)

I/O Manager

Integral subsystems

Internet Information Services (IIS) 6.0

Interprocess Communication (IPC) Manager

Interrupt

Kernel mode

Kernel mode drivers

Microkernel

Object Manager

Plug and Play (PnP) Manager

Power Manager

Process Manager

Security Reference Monitor

User mode

Virtual Memory Manager (VMM)

Window Manager

Windows Server 2003, Datacenter Edition

Windows Server 2003, Enterprise Edition

Windows Server 2003, Standard Edition

Windows Server 2003, Web Edition

Workgroup (peer-to-peer network)

Test Yourself

1. Windows Server 2003 uses _____ to manage users, groups, security services, and network resources in an organization by storing the information related to these objects in a centralized database.
   a. Distributed File System (Dfs)
   b. Active Directory
   c. Kerberos protocol
   d. Web-based Enterprise Management (WBEM)

2. Which of the following Windows Server 2003 features is used to track information exchanges between networks and the attached physical components of networks, servers, and workstations?
   a. Web-based Enterprise Management (WBEM)
   b. Microsoft Management Console (MMC)
   c. Public Key Infrastructure (PKI)
   d. Hardware Abstraction Layer

3. The kernel mode layer is made up of:
   a. A set of components known as subsystems.
   b. The Executive Services, the Hardware Abstraction Layer (HAL), the microkernal, and kernel mode drivers.
   c. Two kinds of subsystems: environmental subsystems, and integral subsystems.
   d. A set of system services and internal routine components.

4. The Process Manager is a subcomponent of the:
   a. Environmental Subsystem.
   b. Virtual Memory Manager (VMM).
   c. Executive Services.
   d. User mode.

5. Which of the following operating system architecture components include the Local Procedure Call (LPC) and Remote Procedure Call (RPC), which are responsible for establishing communication between the environmental subsystems and the Executive?
   a. User mode

   b. Interprocess Communication (IPC) Manager
   c. I/O Manager
   d. Hardware Abstraction Layer (HAL)

6. _____ is a tunneling protocol that is used to create virtual private networks (VPNs) through the public Internet. (Choose all that apply.)
   a. PPTP
   b. L2TP
   c. HTTP
   d. TCP/IP

7. Local Procedure Call (LPC) controls:
   a. Communication between environmental subsystems and the Executive Services on different computers.
   b. Security policies on the local computer.
   c. Communication between environmental subsystems and the Executive Services on the same computer.
   d. User logon requests and initiates logon authentication.

8. Which of the following types of drivers are virtual disk, mirror, or device type-specific class driver?
   a. Intermediate drivers
   b. Highest-level drivers
   c. Lowest-level drivers

9. Which of the following operating systems can support ICF with just the software components provided by the network operating system? (Choose all that apply.)
   a. Windows Server 2003, Enterprise Edition
   b. Windows Server 2003, Web Edition
   c. Windows Server 2003, Datacenter Edition
   d. Windows Server 2003, Standard Edition

10. Which of the following most correctly describes the function of Kerberos?
    a. It provides encryption for all data transmissions in the network.
    b. It performs UPN name resolution services.
    c. It provides for secure authentication.
    d. It centralizes AAA for RRAS.

Problem Solving Scenarios

1. You are advising the management of a small fashion design firm in New York City about installing a computer network. Currently, the firm has eight employees working with stand-alone computers in a single office. These computers are currently running Windows 98, but the company is considering upgrading to a network using Windows Server 2003. The company expects to double in size next year and double again the following year. It would like to know if it should set up a simple workgroup network model or a domain network. Prepare a presentation that illustrates the benefits of both models and make a recommendation.

2. You are advising the management of a small consumer products company that makes cooking utensils. The company has a national sales force with which management communicates daily, using telephones and fax machines. Management anticipates moving towards a Windows Server 2003 network environment and would like to use laptop computers in the future as the principal means of communication with the sales force. However, senior management is worried about the security of files and of communications over the Internet. Prepare a report that describes the features of Windows Server 2003 that can address these security concerns.

Installing Windows Server 2003 and Server Hardware Devices

Windows Server 2003 is a user-friendly operating system that you can easily install and configure. Additionally, you can upgrade your old Windows NT Server 4.0 and Windows 2000 Server computers to Windows Server 2003.

The Windows Server 2003 installation process consists of three phases: the pre-copy phase, the text mode phase, and the GUI mode phase. These phases are common to all of the methods of installation. A thorough knowledge of these phases and the functions they perform, at the time of installation, will help you to install Windows Server 2003 in an organized way.

There are two basic ways to install Windows Server 2003: attended and unattended. An attended installation is a sequence of easy-to-follow steps that help you to install and configure Windows Server 2003 on your computer. You can perform an attended installation of Windows Server 2003 using the Windows Server 2003 installation CD-ROM, or by running Winnt32.exe or Winnt.exe (the Setup executable files) over the network from a share. An unattended installation is an automated process that enables you to install Windows Server 2003 on multiple computers over a network. A customized installation script, called an answer file, provides all specifications normally entered by a user during installation.

The upgrade process can be performed either with the Windows Server 2003 installation CD-ROM or an over-the-network execution of the Winnt32.exe or Winnt.exe files. During an upgrade, Windows Server 2003 automatically retains all existing settings for users, groups, permissions, and rights. Therefore, you do not need to reconfigure them after upgrading your system. You can upgrade to Windows Server 2003 from Windows NT Server 4.0, Windows 2000 Server, and Windows 2000 Terminal Server. For earlier versions of Windows NT, you must first upgrade to at least NT 4.0. Windows 2000 Professional, 98, and 95 cannot be upgraded to Windows Server 2003. In most cases, the hardware on which these earlier versions of Windows are installed would not, in any event, have sufficient resources to support an upgrade to Windows Server 2003.

Before installing or upgrading to Windows Server 2003, there are several pre-installation tasks that you should perform that will help you avoid installation problems. If you still encounter problems during installation, there are a number of ways to troubleshoot those problems.

Once you have successfully installed Windows Server 2003, you will also need to install, configure, and monitor server hardware devices. Windows Server 2003 Setup includes a Dynamic Update feature that helps you more easily update drivers and replacement files needed for your system's hardware. Windows Server 2003 also uses driver signing technology to confirm that any drivers being installed have passed the Microsoft certification process. As you install hardware devices, you may also find that you need to use the Add Hardware Wizard if you have any legacy hardware that is not Plug and Play compatible, and the Device Manager to configure and manage various hardware devices.

Goals

In this lesson, you will learn how to install and configure Windows Server 2003. You will also learn how to troubleshoot issues that may arise when you install and configure your server. In addition, you will learn how to install, configure, and monitor server hardware devices.

Lesson 2   Installing Windows Server 2003 and Server Hardware Devices

Skill	Exam 70-290 Objective
1. Identifying Pre-installation Tasks	Basic knowledge
2. Understanding the Different Phases of the Windows Server 2003 Installation Process	Basic knowledge
3. Installing Windows Server 2003 Using the Installation CD-ROM	Basic knowledge
4. Installing Windows Server 2003 Over a Network	Basic knowledge
5. Upgrading Windows NT Server or Windows 2000 Server to Windows Server 2003	Basic knowledge
6. Troubleshooting Failed Installations	Basic knowledge
7. Working with the Add Hardware Wizard	Install and configure server hardware devices. Monitor server hardware. Tools might include Device Manager, the Hardware Troubleshooting Wizard, and appropriate Control Panel items.
8. Working with the Device Manager	Install and configure server hardware devices. Monitor server hardware. Tools might include Device Manager, the Hardware Troubleshooting Wizard, and appropriate Control Panel items. Configure resource settings for a device. Configure device properties and settings.
9. Configuring Driver Signing Options	Install and configure server hardware devices. Configure driver signing options.
10. Working with Hardware Profiles and Event Logs	Install and configure server hardware devices. Monitor server hardware. Tools might include Device Manager, the Hardware Troubleshooting Wizard, and appropriate Control Panel items.

Requirements

To complete this lesson, you will need a computer that meets the minimum hardware requirements for Windows Server 2003, Standard Edition, as set forth in Table 2-1. These minimum requirements include a Pentium 133 MHz processor, a VGA monitor, 128 MB RAM, 3 GB hard disk space (since you will need additional hard disk space beyond the 2.5 GB recommended for installation to complete all of the exercises in this book), a 12X CD-ROM drive, a network interface card (NIC), a mouse, and a keyboard. You will also need a Windows Server 2003 installation CD-ROM.

skill 1   *Identifying Pre-installation Tasks*

exam objective

Basic knowledge

overview

caution

Note that these system requirements are the minimum requirements for a Windows Server 2003 Server installation. If you plan to install any other applications or software, you must have additional resources (hard disk space, RAM, etc).

Before you start the Windows Server 2003 installation process, take some time to plan for the installation. During installation, you will need to provide information about how you want to install and configure Windows Server 2003. Planning will help you to avoid problems during and after the installation. First, you need to make sure that the system on which you plan to install Windows Server 2003, at a minimum, meets the following hardware requirements:

◆ Pentium 133 MHz or faster processor.
◆ VGA monitor.
◆ 128 MB RAM for five or fewer clients and 256 MB for larger networks.
◆ 1.5 GB hard disk space is required for setup; however, at least 2.5 GB hard disk space is recommended.
◆ High-density, 3.5-inch floppy disk drive.
◆ A 12X CD-ROM drive, if installation is performed from a CD.
◆ A network interface card (NIC), if network connectivity is required.
◆ Mouse and keyboard.

Table 2-1 shows the minimum hardware requirements for the different versions of Windows Server 2003.

Other pre-installation tasks are listed below:

◆ Make sure that the hardware components of your system are listed on Microsoft's **Windows Server Catalog**, which is available both on the Windows Server 2003 installation CD-ROM and online, at the Microsoft.com Web site. The Catalog is a list of computers and peripheral devices that Microsoft has confirmed to be compatible with Windows Server 2003.
◆ Determine whether you will be performing a new installation (sometimes called a "clean install") or an upgrade of an existing version of Windows NT Server 4.0 or Windows 2000 Server.
◆ Examine your hard disk partitions. A partition is a part of a hard disk drive that has been sectioned to act as a logically separate unit of storage. Windows Server 2003 may be installed onto an existing partition, if it is large enough, or you may need to create a new partition. Microsoft recommends a partition of at least 2 GB.
◆ Determine the file system format for the partition. Windows Server 2003 supports three different file systems:

  • File Allocation Table (originally known as FAT, now known as FAT16), the 16-bit file system used by DOS and Windows 3.x.
  • FAT32, the 32-bit version of FAT.
  • NTFS, the file system specifically designed to work with Windows NT, Windows 2000, and Windows Server 2003. Microsoft recommends that you select NTFS, as it is the only file system that supports Active Directory, as well as other Windows Server 2003 advanced storage and security features.

Table 2-1 Minimum and Recommended Hardware Requirements

Requirement	Windows Server 2003 System Requirements			
	Standard Edition	Enterprise Edition	Datacenter Edition	Web Edition
Minimum CPU Speed	133 MHz	• 133 MHz for x86-based computers • 733 MHz for 64-bit Itanium-based computers*	• 400 MHz for x86-based computers • 733 MHz for 64-bit Itanium-based computers*	133 MHz
Recommended CPU Speed	550 MHz	733 MHz	733 MHz	550 MHz
Minimum RAM	128 MB	128 MB	512 MB	128 MB
Recommended Minimum RAM	256 MB	256 MB	1 GB	256 MB
Maximum RAM	4 GB	• 32 GB for x86-based computers • 64 GB for 64-bit Itanium-based computers*	• 64 GB for x86-based computers • 512 GB for Itanium-based computers*	2 GB
Multiprocessor Support	Up to 4	• Up to 8	• Minimum 8 • Maximum 64	Up to 2
Minimum Disk Space for Setup	1.5 GB	• 1.5 GB for x86-based computers • 2.0 GB for Itanium-based computers*	• 1.5 GB for x86-based computers • 2.0 GB for Itanium-based computers*	1.5 GB
Recommended Disk Space	2.5 GB	• 2.5 GB	• 2.5 GB	2.5 GB

*The 64-bit versions of Windows Server 2003, Enterprise Edition and Windows Server 2003, Datacenter Edition cannot be successfully installed on 32-bit systems. They are compatible only with 64-bit Itanium-based systems.

skill 1

Identifying Pre-installation Tasks
(cont'd)

exam objective   Basic knowledge

overview

◆ Determine whether the computer on which you are installing Windows Server 2003 will be joining a workgroup or domain. A workgroup, or peer-to-peer network, is a logical group of users that share information and resources on computers that are interconnected, generally over a local area network (LAN). There is no central directory database and network administration is decentralized. Workgroup networks are generally composed of client workstations and have no servers. A domain is a logical group of network computers that share a central directory database. More often than not, you will be joining a domain. If so, you must know the DNS (Domain Name System) name of the domain. If the DNS service is not yet running on the network, it will be installed when you upgrade from Windows NT 4.0 Server to Windows Server 2003 and promote the server to domain controller status, or when you create your first Windows Server 2003 domain controller. Upgrading Windows 2000 Server domain controllers is an easier process because the DNS service and domain database are already compatible with Windows Server 2003. It will just be upgraded to Windows Server 2003.

◆ Decide which optional components available with Windows Server 2003 that you will install. If you decide not to install a particular component at the time of installation, you can always add it at a later date, using the Add or Remove Programs utility.

◆ Any compressed volumes on the computer must be uncompressed before you can upgrade to Windows Server 2003. You can only upgrade to Windows Server 2003 if the drive has been compressed with NTFS compression. Furthermore, if you have disk mirroring configured, you must disable it before you start Setup.

◆ Any anti-virus software installed on the computer should be disabled.

◆ To make sure that any existing applications are compatible with Windows Server 2003, browse the installation CD and open the README.DOC file. This document includes a list of compatible programs. You can also check for software compatibility using the Microsoft Application Compatibility Analyzer tool, which you can find at: **http://www.microsoft.com/windows/appcompatibility/analyzer.mspx (Figure 2-1)**. The Application Compatibility Analyzer consists of a Collector tool, which is used to create a log file of all applications installed on client computers, and an Analyzer tool, which is used to create a database where all of the log files are compiled. Then, you can com pare this database to application compatibility data stored in an online compatibility database at Microsoft. Common applications that will need to be removed are virus-scanning software and third-party network services or client software.

◆ Any UPS (uninterruptible power supply) devices must also be disconnected from the computer on which you are installing Windows Server 2003. These devices are connected via serial cables. They must be detached because Setup will try to detect devices that are attached to serial ports, and a UPS can disrupt the detection procedure.

Be aware that simply because a device or software package is not listed in the Windows Server Catalog or the Microsoft software compatibility database, it does not mean that the device or software will not function. It simply means that the product has not been tested by Windows Quality Labs. In particular, many drivers that are not listed still function properly. The only way to know for sure is to test the device. In general, if the device has a Windows Server 2003 driver, it will typically work properly.

Figure 2-1 Microsoft Application Compatibility Analyzer

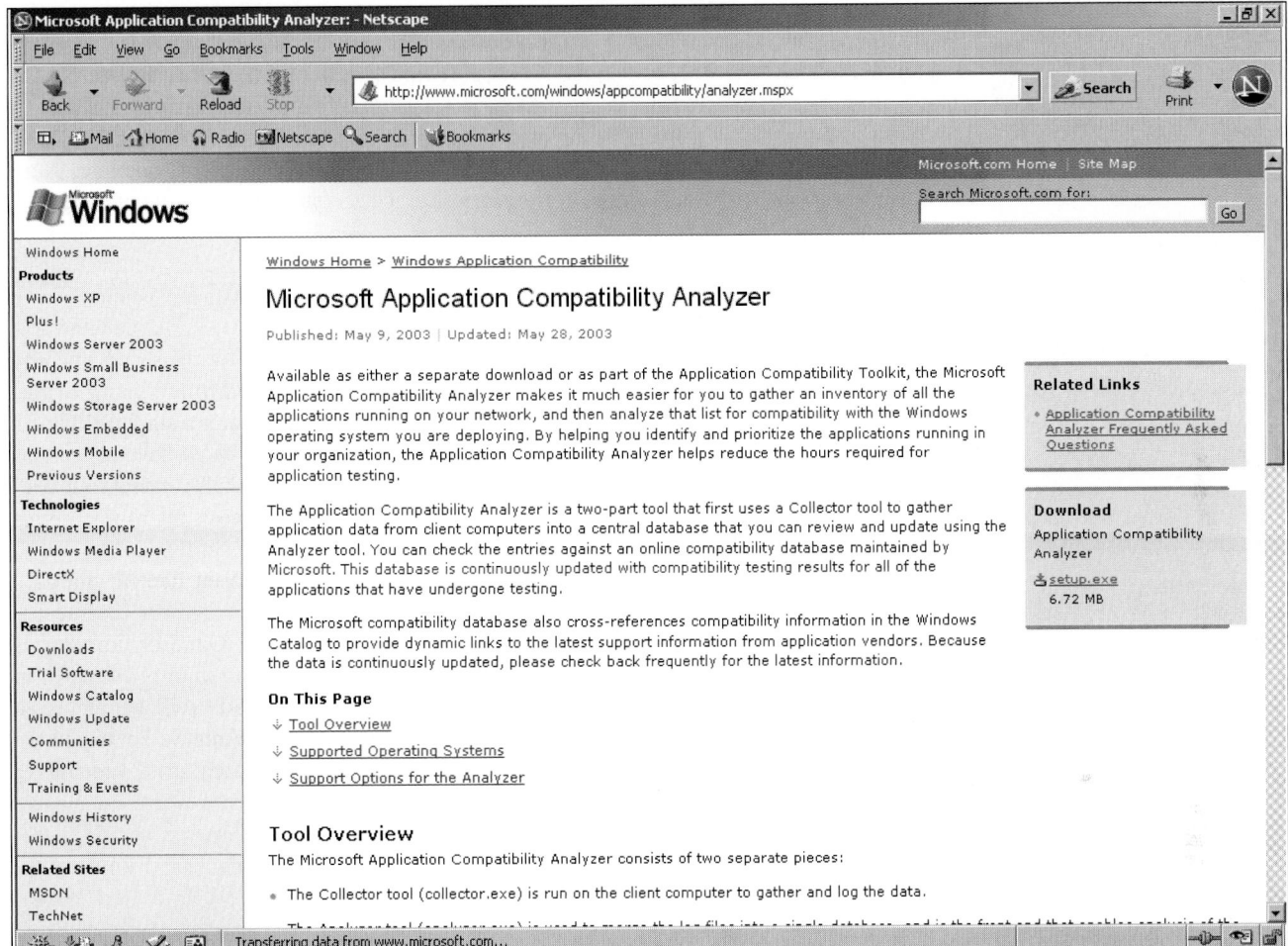

skill 1

Identifying Pre-installation Tasks
(cont'd)

exam objective

Basic knowledge

more

To install Windows Server 2003, you must have both a server software license (i.e, product key) and a license to access or use the server software (a **Client Access License** or **CAL**). There are now two different types of CALs - a User CAL that allows a particular user to access licensed server software from any number of devices, and a Device CAL, which allows any number of users to access licensed server software from a particular device. Note however, that a CAL is not required for anonymous access (such as when connecting to a public Web server).

Microsoft also offers two different licensing modes for Windows Server 2003: **Per Server** and **Per Device or Per User (Figure 2-2)**.

◆ **Per Server licensing mode** provides a specified number of CALs for the server, thereby limiting the number of users and/or devices that can be connected to the server at one time. Per Server licensing is most suitable for small companies using a single Windows Server 2003 computer. If you have multiple servers, each server must have at least as many CALs as the maximum number of users and/or devices that will connect to it concurrently. You must purchase enough CALs for that server to cover all simultaneous users.

◆ **Per Device or Per User licensing mode** (formerly called Per Seat licensing mode) provides a separate CAL for each named user or specified device, which can then access any computer running Windows Server 2003 on the network. This kind of licensing is ideal for large networks where users and/or devices will connect to multiple servers. In fact, in most situations, Per Device or Per User licensing mode will be the most economical choice. However, when you are asked this question during Setup, if you are unsure, select Per Server licensing mode because you can switch from Per Server licensing mode to Per Device or Per User licensing mode, but not the reverse.

Figure 2-2 Types of Windows Server 2003 licenses

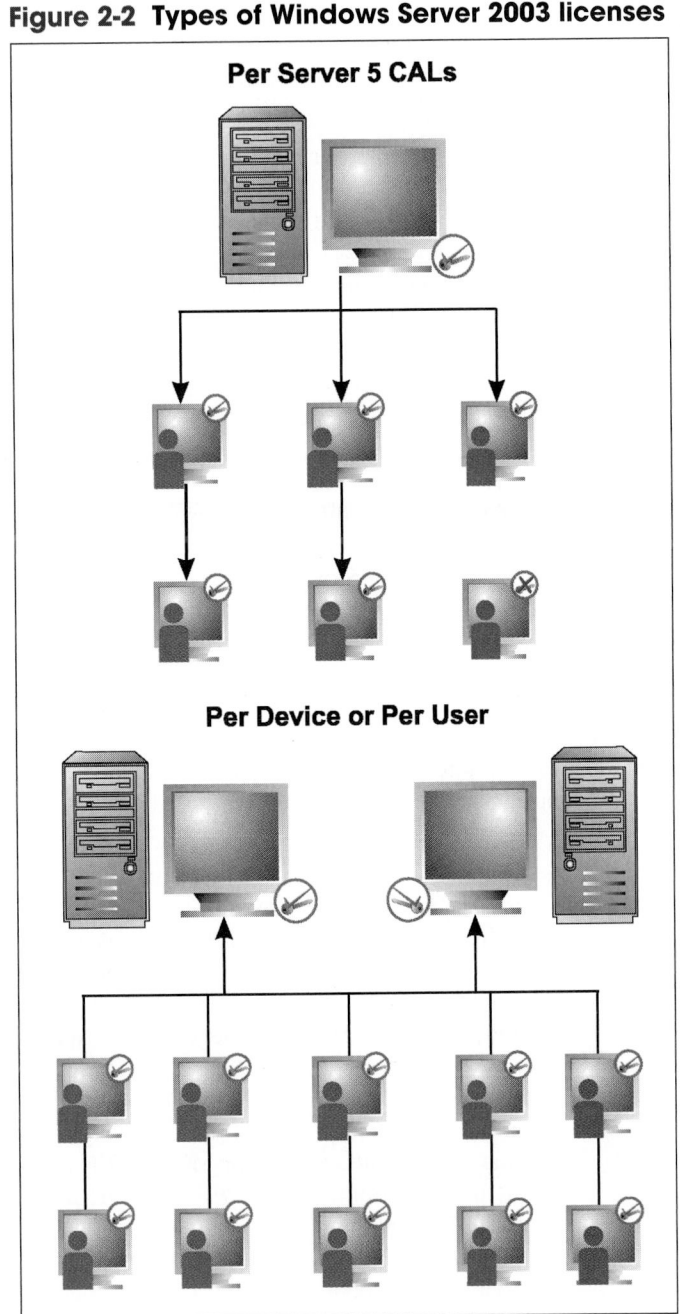

skill 2

Identifying the Different Phases of the Windows Server 2003 Installation Process

exam objective

Basic knowledge

overview

tip

Regardless of which type of installation you choose, the hardware detection process is where problems most frequently occur. If the system becomes unresponsive for more than 1 hour, press the reset button. Setup will continue from where it left off, usually skipping the unresponsive piece of hardware.

Microsoft divides the Windows Server 2003 installation process into three basic phases: the pre-copy phase, the text mode phase, and the GUI mode phase. These phases are common to all methods of installation (**Figure 2-3**).

◆ **The pre-copy phase** starts when you insert the Windows Server 2003 installation CD in the CD-ROM drive of your computer, or double-click the executable file in a shared network folder. The Setup program begins and creates a WIN_NT.~BT temporary directory on the system partition and copies Setup boot files into this directory. Next, a WIN_NT.~LS temporary directory is created and the Windows Server 2003 files are copied from the server into this directory before installation continues.

◆ **The text mode phase** prompts the user for information that is required to complete installation. In this phase:

- You accept the Windows Server 2003 licensing agreement by pressing [F8].
- If the Setup program detects any existing Windows Server 2003 installations, you must select whether to install, repair, or continue with the installation without repairing the existing operating system.
- Information regarding any pre-existing partitions and the free space on your hard disk is displayed by Setup. You need to select the partition on which you wish to install Windows Server 2003.
- You are prompted to select NTFS as the file system for your Windows Server 2003 server.

Then, Setup examines your hard disk and copies the installation files it needs from the temporary directory to the installation directory and then continues the GUI phase.

◆ **The GUI mode phase** consists of three stages: Gathering Information About Your Computer, Installing Windows Server 2003 Networking Components, and Completing Setup (**Figure 2-4**).

tip

At the bottom of the screen, there is a prompt to Press F6 if you need to install SCSI or RAID drivers. After a few minutes the message will go away. However, if you need to install a special device driver you know won't be initialized without the manufacturer's OEM driver, press the **F6** key to install.

- During the **Gathering Information About Your Computer** stage, Setup presents various dialog boxes that collect the information necessary to install and configure Windows Server 2003 security features, as well as various settings, including the date and time, time zone, geographical location, language, computer name, administrative password, and licensing mode.
- In the **Installing Windows Server 2003 Networking Components** stage, you choose between the default Typical settings and Custom settings. When you select Typical settings, you install the networking components that are required to gain access to a network and share network components. Typical settings install three components: Client for Microsoft Networks, File and Print Sharing for Microsoft Networks and TCP/IP using DHCP. This setting configures TCP/IP to obtain IP addresses automatically from a DHCP server on the network. Custom settings are used when you must designate an IP address or add another client, service, or protocol, including Gateway Services for NetWare, NWLink, and AppleTalk.
- In the Completing Setup stage, some final actions necessary for the successful completion of the installation are performed. These include copying remaining files that are important to the installation directory; creating the Start menu and Program Groups, and setting up the print spooler, printers, services, etc.; saving your configuration to the Registry; creating the Repair directory; resetting the Boot.ini file; and removing temporary files and directories that were created during installation (**Figure 2-5**).

Figure 2-3 **The three installation phases**

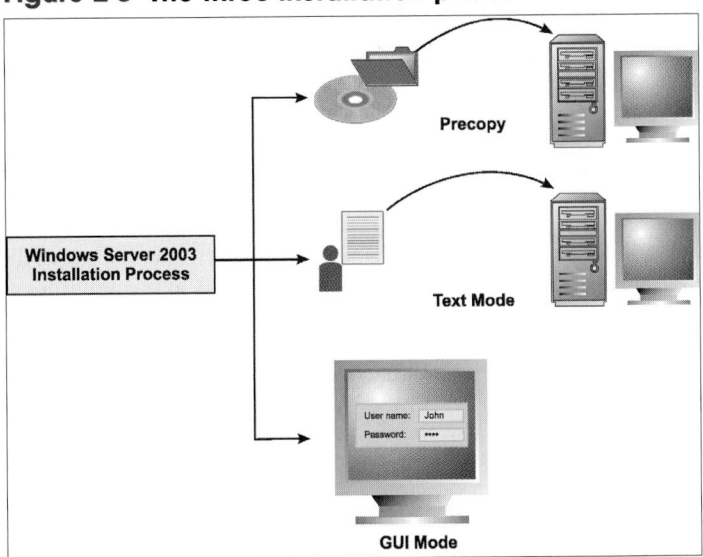

Figure 2-4 **The three stages of the GUI Mode Phase**

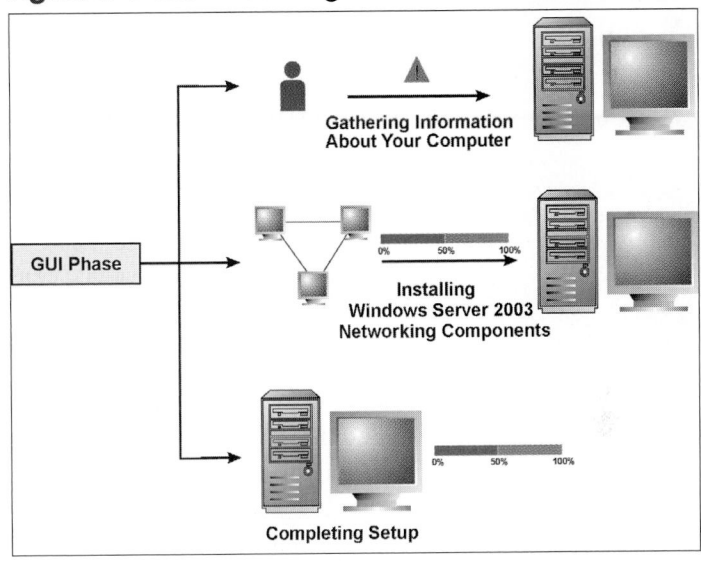

Figure 2-5 **Completing Setup**

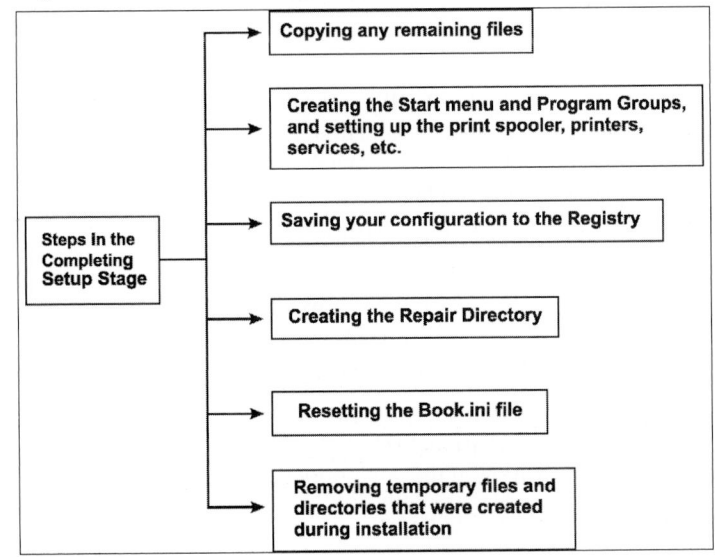

skill 3

Installing Windows Server 2003 Using the Installation CD-ROM

exam objective

Basic knowledge

overview

An attended installation of Windows Server 2003 requires user interaction, in the form of providing information requested by the Windows Server 2003 Setup program. The most common method for an attended installation is using the installation CD-ROM. Full installations are performed on computers that either have no current operating system or that have an operating system that you are going to overwrite.

how to

Install Windows Server 2003, using the installation CD-ROM.

1. Reboot your computer with the **Windows Server 2003 installation CD-ROM** in the CD-ROM or DVD drive of your computer. Note that if you receive the prompt to **Press any key to boot from CD**, press the **[Spacebar]** to boot the computer with the Windows Server 2003 installation CD. If you are not prompted to boot from the CD at all, it is possible that your computer's boot options are not set correctly. In most cases, the boot order should be set to: Floppy, CD, Hard Disk. If this is not the case, you may need to edit your BIOS configuration settings.

2. The **Windows Server 2003 Setup** screen will appear. The edition indicated (Standard, Enterprise, Web, etc.) will depend on the version of the software you installing. Depending on the licensing arrangements with respect to the software you are installing, you may also see a message telling you that you have only a certain period of time in which to activate the installation before it is deactivated (See the More section below for more information on Windows Server 2003's new product activation technology). Press **[Enter]**. The Setup program will then begin loading files to be used during the text-based portion of the installation.

3. The **Welcome to Setup** screen appears (**Figure 2-6**). You are presented with the following choices:
   - To set up Windows now, press ENTER.
   - To repair a Windows installation using Recovery Console, press R.
   - To quit Setup without installing Windows, press F3.
   Press **[Enter]** to continue.

4. The **Windows Licensing Agreement** screen opens (**Figure 2-7**). Press the **[F8]** key to agree to the license and proceed with the installation. Setup will search for previous installations of Windows. If a previous version of Windows is found, the following prompt will appear:
   If one of the following Windows installations is damaged, Setup can try to repair it.
   - To repair the selected Windows installation, press R.
   - To continue installing a fresh copy of Windows without repairing, press ESC.
   Press **[ESC]** to continue with the installation.

5. Windows Setup next displays a list of the existing partitions and unpartitioned space on the computer and offers the following three choices:
   - To set up Windows on the selected item, press ENTER.
   - To create a partition in the unpartitioned space, press C.
   - To delete the selected partition, press D (**Figure 2-8**).

6. You can select an area of free disk space or an existing partition on which to install Windows Server 2003. Use the **[Up]** and **[Down]** arrow keys to select the partition and press **[Enter]**. To create a partition in the unpartitioned space of the first available drive, press the **[C]** key.

tip

If you need to install Windows Server 2003 on a computer connected to a local network using the over the network method, you must open the folder containing the installation files and double-click the appropriate executable file. This will execute Setup over the network.

tip

Delete partitions by first highlighting each partition and then pressing D. Then, to confirm the deletion of the partition or partitions, press L. Note that if there is any data on these partitions, you should make sure that you have a working backup before deleting them.

Figure 2-6 Welcome to Setup

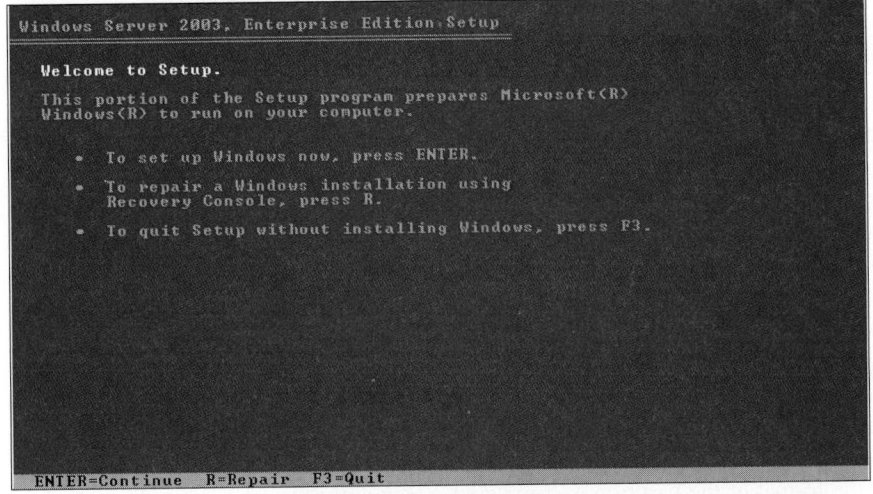

Figure 2-7 Windows Licensing Agreement

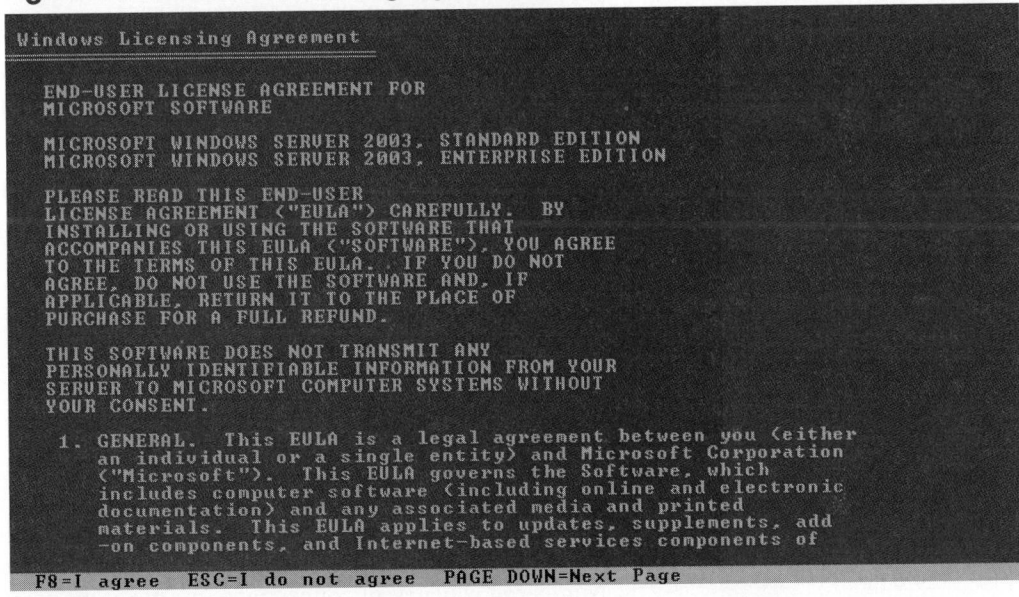

Figure 2-8 List of existing partitions and unpartitioned space

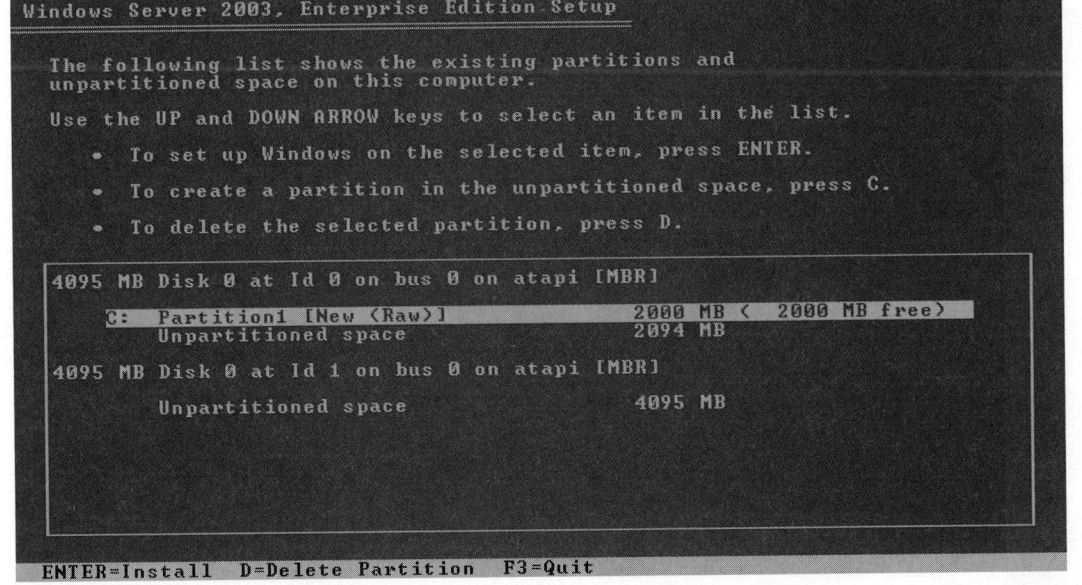

skill 3

Installing Windows Server 2003 Using the Installation CD-ROM *(cont'd)*

exam objective

Basic knowledge

how to

7. The **Create a New Partition** screen appears. Create a partition equal to the maximum (i.e. size of the drive) and press **[Enter]** to create the partition.
8. The **Existing Partitions** screen appears. Verify that the newly created partition is highlighted and press **[Enter]** to continue with the installation.
9. The next screen informs you that the partition that you have just created is not formatted. At this point in the setup, you must choose how the new partition will be formatted (Quick or Normal) and with which file system. Select **Format the partition using the NTFS file system (Quick)** and press **[Enter]** to continue the installation.
10. After the format of the partition is completed, Setup will examine your disks, copy files to the Windows Server 2003 installation folders, and initialize your Windows Server 2003 configuration. This may take several minutes.
11. When completed, the computer will reboot, and the **Windows Server 2003** splash screen appears, followed by the **Windows Server 2003 Setup** screen (**Figure 2-9**). Then, Setup detects and installs the devices on your computer. An Installing Devices progress bar shows you how far the process has progressed. The computer screen may flicker during this process.
12. Next, the **Regional and Language Options** screen opens. Here, you can customize settings for different regions and languages. Accept the default settings, and then click [Next >].

tip

You can modify these settings after installing Windows Server 2003 by opening the Regional Options utility in the Control Panel. Also, in the Regional and Language Options screen, you can click the Customize button to change system or user local settings, and click the Details button to change the keyboard layout.

13. The **Personalize Your Software** screen opens. Type:
    • Your name in the **Name** text box.
    • Your organization's name in the **Organization** text box.
14. Click [Next >]. The **Your Product Key** screen opens. Type the product key in the spaces provided and click [Next >].
15. The **Licensing Modes** screen opens (**Figure 2-10**). Here you must choose either the **Per Server** option, or the **Per Device or Per User** option. If you choose Per Server, enter the number of Per Server concurrent connections based on the actual licenses that you own in the **Number of concurrent connections** spin box if the correct number does not appear by default. Note that in most situations, Per Device or Per User will be the most economical licensing option. However, if you are unsure which licensing mode to use, choose Per Server because you can change to Per User or Per Device at no additional cost, but you cannot convert from Per Device or Per User to Per Server.

caution

The computer name that you enter cannot be the same as any other computer, workgroup, or domain names that exist on your network.

16. Click [Next >]. The **Computer Name and Administrator Password** screen opens. Type:
    • A computer name, such as **Server1**, in the **Computer Name** text box.
    • An **Administrator password** in the Administrator Password text box. Note that if you do not select a password that meets Microsoft's criteria for strong passwords, a message box will appear, recommending that you select a different password that meets those criteria (**Figure 2-11**).
    • The Administrator password again in the **Confirm password** text box.

caution

Keep in mind that passwords are case sensitive.

17. If a modem is detected, the **Modem Dialing Information** screen will appear. Specify the required information about the modem, such as the area code or city code, and click [Next >]. If the computer does not have a modem, you will proceed directly to Step 18.

Figure 2-9 Windows Server 2003 Setup

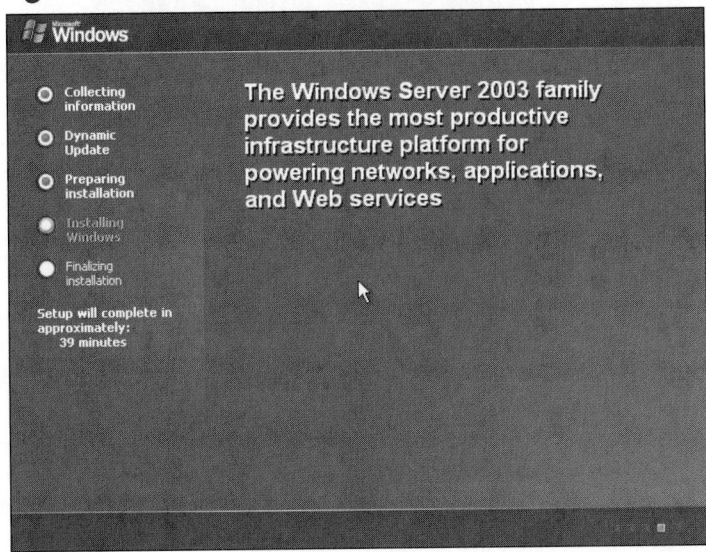

Figure 2-10 Licensing Modes

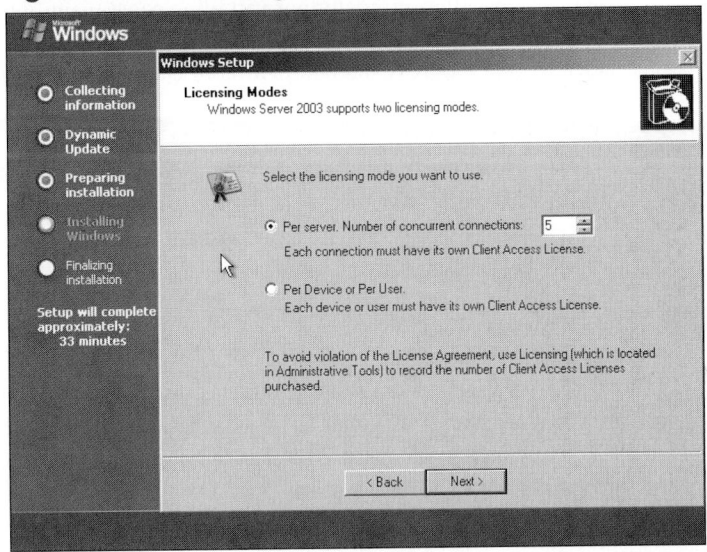

Figure 2-11 Passwords message box

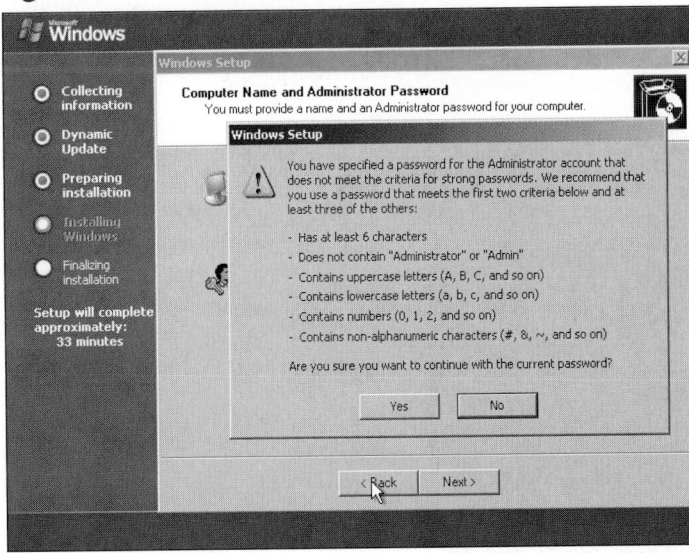

skill 3

Installing Windows Server 2003 Using the Installation CD-ROM (cont'd)

exam objective

Basic knowledge

how to

18. The **Date and Time Settings** screen opens. Set the correct date and time and click [Next >].

19. The Windows Server 2003 Setup screen reappears, and Setup now installs network software that enables you to communicate with other computers, networks, and the Internet. When the **Installing Network** progress bar reaches 100%, the **Networking Settings** screen opens. Select the **Typical Settings** option button and click [Next >].

20. The **Workgroup or Computer Domain** screen opens. Here, you must specify whether you want your computer to join a workgroup or a domain. Accept the default selection **No, this computer is not on a network, or is on a network without a domain. Make this computer a member of the following workgroup** and the default Workgroup name, **WORKGROUP**, by clicking [Next >].

21. The Windows Server 2003 Setup screen reappears once more. Setup now copies files and completes installation, including installing Start menu items, registering components, saving settings, and removing any temporary files used. Progress bars will appear, indicating the progress and completion of each of these tasks, which may take a total of 20–30 minutes.

22. When all tasks have been completed, the computer will reboot to the **Welcome to Windows Microsoft Windows Server 2003** initial logon screen (**Figure 2-12**). Press [Ctrl] + [Alt] + [Delete].

23. The **Log on to Windows** dialog box appears. Enter the password for the Administrator account and click [OK].

more

Windows Server 2003 contains new product activation technology, which means that, in some instances, you must activate your copy of Windows Server 2003 before it can be used (**Figure 2-13**). If your company licenses Windows Server 2003 through one of the Microsoft volume licensing agreement programs, such as Open License, Select License, or Enterprise Agreement, you are not required to activate those licenses.

Product activation works by verifying that a software program's product key has not been used on more computers than intended by the software license. You must use the product key in order to install the software and then it is transformed into an installation ID number. You use an Activation Wizard to provide the installation ID number to Microsoft, either through a secure transfer over the Internet or by telephone.

If you make a substantial number of hardware components changes to your Windows Server 2003 computer, you may have to reactivate Windows Server 2003 within three days in order to continue to log on.

Figure 2-12 Welcome to Windows Microsoft Windows Server 2003

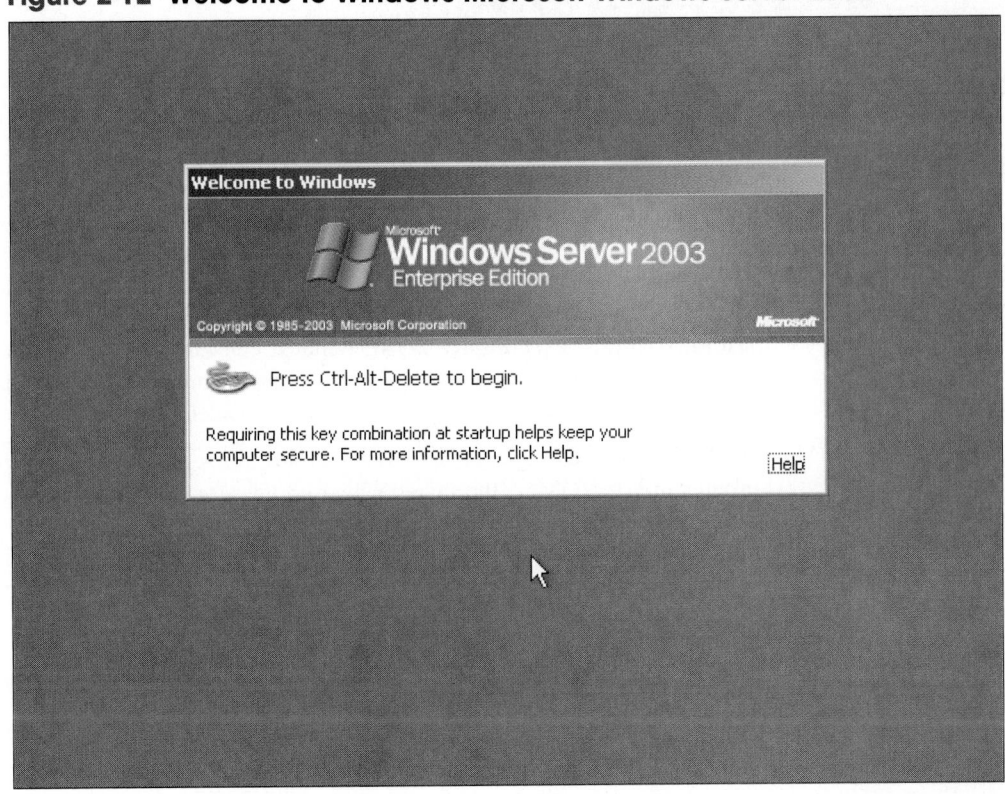

Figure 2-13 Activating the Server License

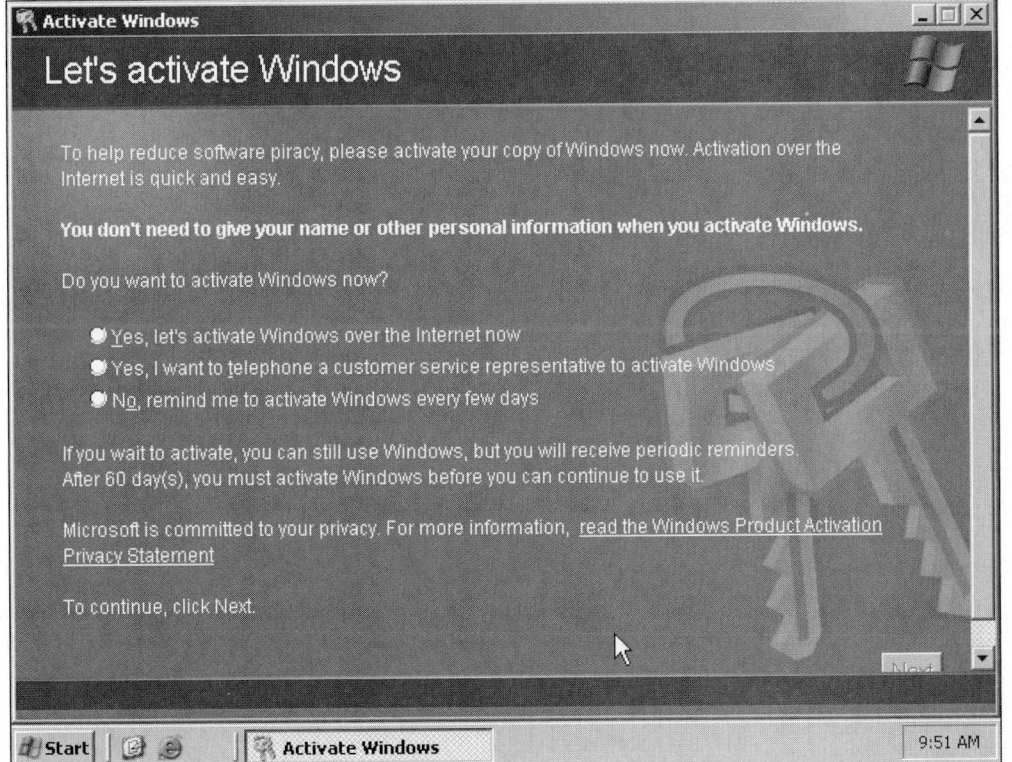

skill 4

Installing Windows Server 2003 Over a Network

exam objective

Basic knowledge

overview

Windows Server 2003 also can be installed over a network. If you are performing a network installation from a shared folder, you must connect to the share, then locate and open the **\I386** folder. If you are connecting to the share from a computer with MS-DOS or Windows 3.x installed, you must run **Winnt.exe**. If you are connecting to the network share from a computer with Windows 9.x, Windows NT 3.51 or higher, or Windows 2000 Server installed, you must run **Winnt32.exe (Figure 2-14)**. Winnt32 can run only on 32-bit computers and makes use of the much more powerful architecture and the multi-threading capabilities of 32-bit machines. Winnt.exe is a 16-bit application used for older computers.

You can run Winnt32.exe (or Winnt.exe) directly by double-clicking it on the Windows Server 2003 installation CD-ROM, in the shared network folder for network installations, or by typing its name at the command prompt. You can also run Winnt32.exe (or Winnt.exe) by clicking Setup.exe, the Windows Server 2003 Setup program. The Winnt32.exe file creates two temporary directories and copies all of the Windows Server 2003 files from the server into these directories for installation purposes.

You can customize the installation of Windows Server 2003 by using switches, such as **C:\Winnt32 /s [sourcepath]**, when you execute Winnt32.exe from the MS-DOS command prompt. Many of the switches for Winnt32 are designed specifically for upgrade situations. **Table 2-2** lists various Winnt32.exe switches.

tip

It is unlikely you will be asked to install Windows Server 2003 on a computer that uses MS-DOS or Windows 3.x because such computers would be quite old, and thus unlikely candidates for Windows Server 2003.

tip

Windows Server 2003 Setup is a graphical user interface program that enables you to modify or perform operations on the Winnt32.exe and Winnt.exe files automatically without executing the switches from the MS-DOS prompt. Use Setup whenever possible to avoid mistakes.

more

An unattended installation is an automated process that enables you to install Windows Server 2003 on multiple computers over a network. A customized installation script, called an **answer file**, provides all specifications normally entered by a user during an installation. The files required to install Windows Server 2003 over a network are stored in a folder called the **distribution folder**. You create the answer files and a distribution folder on a central server or on a host computer by using an application called **Setup Manager** before you start an unattended installation. (Refer to Microsoft Knowledge Base Article—323438 HOW TO: Use Setup Manager to Create an Answer File in Windows Server 2003 at **http://support.microsoft.com/default.aspx?scid=kb;en-us;323438&Product=winsvr2003** for further details on how to install the Setup Manager from the Windows Server 2003 CD). The target computers, on which you are installing Windows Server 2003, access the distribution folder and the answer file on the server during the unattended installation.

Figure 2-14 Winnt.exe and Winnt32.exe

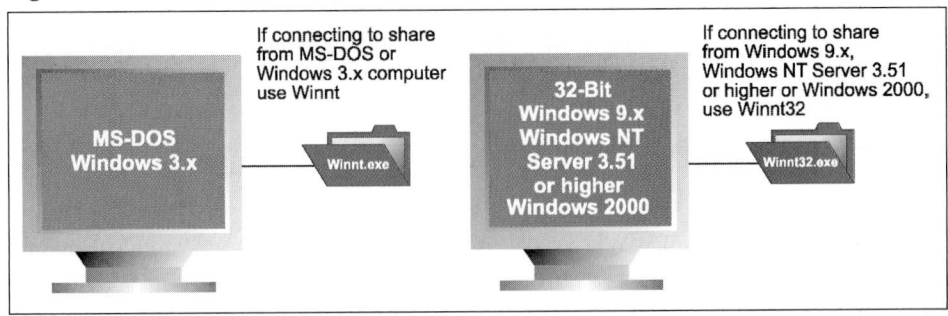

Table 2-2 Switches supported by Winnt32

Switch	Function
/s [sourcepath]	Indicates the location of the Windows Server 2003 files
/tempdrive: drive_letter	Tells Setup to put temporary and final Windows Server 2003 system files on a specified partition
/Unattend or /u	Upgrades your previous version of Windows Server 2003 in unattended Setup mode
/unattend[num][answer_file]	Performs a new installation in unattended Setup mode
/copydir:folder_name	Creates a subfolder within the folder in which the Windows Server 2003 files are installed
/copysource:folder_name	Creates a temporary subfolder within the folder in which the Windows Server 2003 files are installed
/cmd:command_line	Instructs Setup to perform specific commands before the final phase of Setup
/debug[level][filename]	Creates a debug log
/udf:id[.UDF_file]	Includes an identifier that Setup uses to specify how a Uniqueness Database File (UDF) modifies an answer file. An answer file provides the responses needed by the Setup program during an unattended installation. A UDF overrides values in the answer file, and the identifier determines which values in the UDF file are being used.
/syspart:drive_letter	Enables you to copy Setup startup files to a hard disk
/checkupgradeonly	Checks for upgrade suitability with Windows Server 2003
/cmdcons	Adds a Recovery Console option to the operating system selection screen for repairing major problems that cause the GUI boot to fail (usually corrupt or deleted system files). This option cannot be invoked during setup without the use of the /cmd flag (Winnt32.exe) or /e flag (Winnt.exe).
/m:folder_name	Specifies that Setup has copied replacement files from an alternate location
/makelocalsource	Tells Setup to copy all installation source files to the local hard disk
/noreboot	Tells Setup not to restart the computer after the file copy phase of Winnt32.exe is completed so that you can execute another command
/debug[level:filename]	Creates a debug log with a specific level. Default is C:\Windows\Winnt.32.log with a level 2 warning.
/dudisable=yes	Disables Dynamic Update during Setup
/duprepare:[foldername]	Extracts Dynamic Update packages downloaded from Windows Update Web site that reside in the folder specified. Prepares the folder for use as a local Dynamic Updates source for clients
/dushare:[foldername]	Specifies location for Setup to search for Dynamic Update files
/emsport:[comport]	Specifies the serial communication port to use for remote troubleshooting
/emsbaudrate:[baudrate]	Specifies which baud rate to use with EMS's serial port. Valid rates: 9600 (default), 19200, 57600, 115200.

skill 5

Upgrading Windows NT Server or Windows 2000 Server to Windows Server 2003

exam objective

Basic knowledge

overview

Upgrading smoothly to Windows Server 2003 requires careful planning. By following the preliminary steps below, you will save time and improve the likelihood of a smooth and successful upgrade.

◆ Perform a full backup of your computer with a complete recovery procedure.

◆ Run a hardware and software compatibility check from the Windows Server 2003 installation CD. Insert the Windows Server 2003 installation CD in the CD-ROM drive and, when a display appears, follow the prompts for checking system compatibility. If you are connected to the Internet, you can download the latest Setup files (through Dynamic Update) when you run the check. Otherwise, you can insert the installation CD in the CD-ROM drive, open a command prompt, and type:

> **d:\i386\winnt32 /checkupgradeonly** (where **d** represents the CD-ROM drive).

Also, you can check the hardware and software compatibility information in the Windows Server Catalog at:

> **http://www.microsoft.com/windows/catalog/server**

◆ Review the file systems and partitions that exist on the server. You must have at least one NTFS partition on each of your domain controllers. Use NTFS on all server partitions because FAT or FAT32 partitions lack many security features.

◆ If some of your domain controllers run Windows 2000 and some run Windows NT, upgrade the Windows NT domain controllers as soon as possible, to simplify management and troubleshooting, and to strengthen security. Before you upgrade from Windows NT 4.0, you must have installed Service Pack 5 or later. If you have servers or client computers that run Windows NT 3.51, upgrade them to Windows NT 4.0 and Service Pack 5.

◆ If your server has Windows NT 4.0 volume sets, stripe sets, or stripe sets with parity, delete these sets and create new drive configurations with fault tolerance before upgrading. Synchronize your primary and backup controllers before upgrading.

Consider the following three migration paths, relating to domain architecture and Active Directory, when upgrading from Windows NT 4.0:

1. The simplest migration path is an "in-place" upgrade. You would preserve the domain architecture of Windows NT 4.0 in Windows Server 2003's Active Directory structure. You would use the Active Directory Installation Wizard to migrate and upgrade all existing Windows NT 4.0 domain security objects (domain users, groups, and permissions) into Active Directory.

2. As an administrator of a larger organization, you could also choose to migrate Windows NT 4.0 objects from an existing Windows NT 4.0 domain to a brand new Windows Server 2003 forest and Active Directory. In this scenario, you would create trust relationships between the existing Windows NT 4.0 domains (source domains) and the newly created Windows Server 2003 domains (target domains).

3. Taking the third migration path, you would consolidate multiple existing Windows NT 4.0 domains into a single Active Directory domain configuration. You would downsize the existing Windows NT 4.0 domain architecture and increase administrative functionality by migrating Windows NT 4.0 domains into Active Directory organizational units. This is typically the best path from a design standpoint, for future administration, but is also the most difficult.

See **Table 2-3** for a list of the domain and forest functional levels, or modes, that are supported when you upgrade from Windows NT or Windows 2000 to Windows Server 2003.

Table 2-3   Upgrading Domain and Forest Functional Levels in Windows Server 2003 Active Directory

Windows 2000 mixed mode	Permits Windows Server 2003 domains to communicate with Windows NT 4.0 and Windows 2000 domain controllers. This functional level does not support universal groups, group nesting, and enhanced security.
Windows 2000 native mode	In this mode, Windows Server 2003 runs at a Windows 2000 functional level when it is installed into a Windows 2000 Active Directory, running in Windows 2000 native mode. Only Windows 2000 and Windows Server 2003 domain controllers can exist in this environment.
Windows Server 2003 interim mode	Permits the Windows Server 2003 Active Directory to operate with a domain composed only of Windows NT 4.0 domain controllers. Using this mode, environments that upgrade directly from Windows NT 4.0 to Windows Server 2003 can manage large groups more efficiently than by using an existing Windows 2000 Active Directory.
Windows Server 2003 mode*	This mode supports the full Window Server 2003 Active Directory implementation. After all domain controllers are upgraded or replaced with Windows Server 2003, you can raise the domain and then the forest functional levels to Windows Server 2003.

*Caution: The decision to raise the domain or forest functional levels to Windows Server 2003 mode is final. Be certain that you do not need to add Windows 2000 domain controllers anywhere in the forest before performing this procedure. Once the Active Directory forest is upgraded to Windows Server 2003, you cannot add Windows 2000 Active Directory sub-domains.

skill 5

Upgrading Windows NT Server or Windows 2000 Server to Windows Server 2003 (cont'd)

exam objective

Basic knowledge

how to

Upgrade from Windows NT Server or Windows 2000 Server to Windows Server 2003

1. Boot your computer with Windows NT Server or Windows 2000 Server. Insert the Windows Server 2003 installation CD-ROM in the CD-ROM or DVD drive of the computer.
2. In the **Welcome To Windows Server 2003** screen **(Figure 2-15)**, click **Install Windows Server 2003**.
3. Select the **Upgrade** option, then click [Next >].
4. The **License Agreement** screen opens **(Figure 2-16)**. Read the licensing agreement.
5. Select the **I accept this agreement** option button to accept the terms and conditions of the licensing agreement and click [Next >].
6. The **Your Product Key** screen opens.
7. Type the 25-character product key number for Windows Server 2003 in the **Your Product Key** text box and click [Next >].
8. The **Windows Server 2003 Setup** screen opens.
9. In the **Get Updated Setup Files** screen, select **Yes, Download The Updated Setup Files** option **(Figure 2-17)**. Click [Next >].
10. If the Setup finds hardware or software that is not compatible with Windows Server 2003, it will list it in the **Report System Compatibility** screen. Review this report, and click [Next >].
11. If prompted, select the **Yes, Upgrade my drive** option button, and click [Next >].
12. Windows checks the disk space and Setup copies the installation files to your computer and restarts the computer for the text phase of Setup.
13. If a PDC or BDC is being upgraded, the **Active Directory Installation Wizard** starts after Setup is complete, otherwise Setup continues. The rest of the process is the same as for an initial installation.

more

After Windows Server 2003 is installed, you can add Remote Installation Service (RIS) to upload Windows Server images to an RIS server for deployment. Additionally, you can use the Remote Installation Preparation Wizard image format to create and upload Windows Server client computer images on a Windows Server 2003-based RIS Server. After RIS is enabled on the Windows Server 2003 computer, an administrator can use the Remote Installation Preparation Wizard to replicate the installation image of an existing Windows Server client computer (including any locally installed programs and operating system configuration changes) to an available Remote Installation Server on the network. After it is replicated, any supported client computer can remotely install the installation image.

Figure 2-15 The Welcome to Windows Server 2003 screen

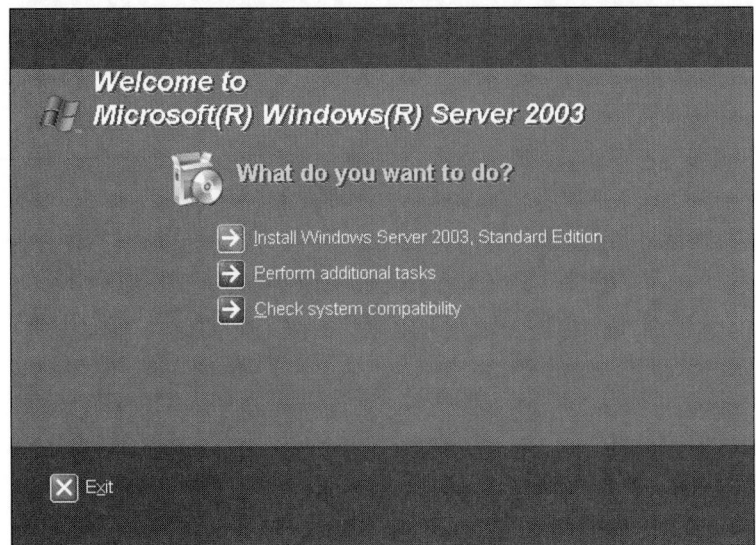

Figure 2-16 The License Agreement screen

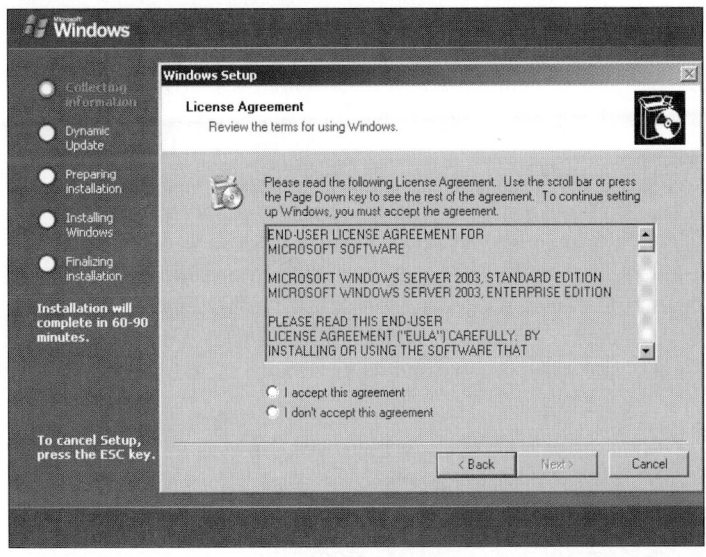

Figure 2-17 The Get Updated Setup Files screen

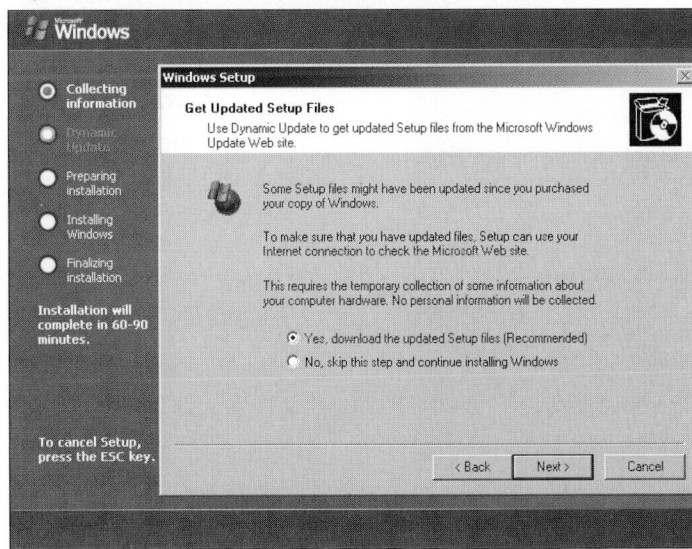

skill 6 | *Troubleshooting Failed Installations*

exam objective

Basic knowledge

overview

tip

If you cannot solve your installation problem, you can call the Microsoft technical support line or visit **www.microsoft.com** for more help.

As you install Windows Server 2003, you may encounter hardware or software-related problems. It is important to be able to troubleshoot these problems in order to achieve a successful installation. Some general problems that may occur during an installation of Windows Server 2003 and their solutions are listed below **(Figure 2-18)**.

◆ **Media errors:** Sometimes the CD you are using may be damaged or the files on the network share you are connecting to may be incomplete. Try a new CD or reinstall the files on the network share. You may have to request a replacement of the installation CD by contacting Microsoft or your vendor.

◆ **Hardware driver errors:** If the drivers for your CD drive are missing or misconfigured, Setup may not run. Bad drivers can also cause difficulty with the network adapter if you are installing from a network boot disk. Replace the CD-ROM drive with one that is supported by your system, install updated drivers, or try another method of installing Windows Server 2003.

◆ **Insufficient disk space:** Microsoft recommends 2.5 GB of available disk space (and 1.5 GB at a minimum) for the installation of Windows Server 2003 on x86-based computers. If you get an insufficient disk space error, use the Setup program to create a partition using existing free space on the hard disk. Delete some outdated data to create more disk space, and create larger partitions that provide sufficient disk space for performing installation, or reformat an existing partition to create more disk space.

◆ **Failure of Windows Server 2003 to install:** This problem may occur if hardware attached to your computer is not in the Windows Server Catalog. Verify that Windows Server 2003 is detecting all of the hardware and that all hardware is in the Windows Server Catalog. You can also use a trial and error approach. Remove all devices that are not indispensable and replace them one at a time until you discover which one is causing the problem.

Some installation malfunctions will generate STOP errors. These messages identify the type of problem that has halted the installation. Some common STOP errors and their solutions are as follows:

◆ **STOP message IRQL_NOT_LESS_OR_EQUAL:** This Stop Message indicates that a kernel-mode process or driver attempted to access a memory location to which it did not have permission, or at a kernel interrupt request level (IRQL) that was too high. A kernel mode process can access only other processes that have an IRQL lower than, or equal to, its own. This Stop message is typically due to faulty or incompatible hardware or software. Start Windows, if you can, and open the System log. You use the Event Viewer to view the System log. To open the Event Viewer, open the Control Panel, double-click Administrative Tools, double-click Event Viewer, and then click System Log. Here, you should be able to find more details about what hardware devices or device drivers are generating the message.

Figure 2-18 Problems that cause failed installations

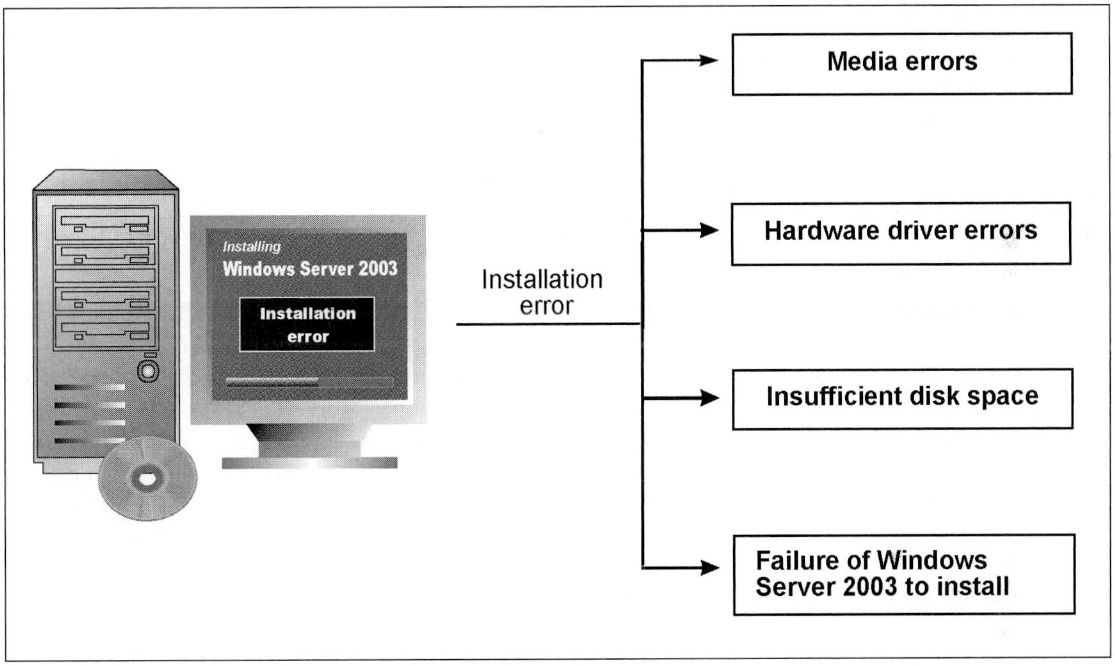

skill 6

Troubleshooting Failed Installations
(cont'd)

exam objective   Basic knowledge

overview

◆ **STOP Message KMODE_EXCEPTION_NOT_HANDLED:** This means that a kernel mode exception has occurred and was not handled. Kernel mode exceptions can happen for a number of reasons. First, you must make sure that you have enough disk space for the installation. Then, you can try removing any new device drivers (or any that you do not need) and, instead, using a standard VGA driver. Make sure that you are running the most up-to-date version of your BIOS, and if you can still boot Windows, use the Last Known Good Configuration. You can choose this option by pressing the F8 key at startup **(Figure 2-19)**.

◆ **STOP Message FAT_FILE_SYSTEM or NTFS_FILE_SYSTEM:** You will see this error message when you have an extremely fragmented drive, you have forgotten to disable disk mirroring, you have a file I/O malfunction, or you did not remove your virus-scanning software and it is causing a conflict. To try to resolve this problem, run **CHKDSK /f**. This utility will check for corruption on the hard drive. Next, reboot the computer. You can also try using the Last Known Good Configuration.

◆ **STOP Message UNKNOWN_HARD_ERROR:** This error message indicates that one of the Registry files may be corrupt. If the computer will not start normally, try starting it with the Last Known Good Configuration. Last Known Good Configuration is a hardware configuration that is available by pressing F8 during startup. If the current hardware settings prevent the computer from starting, Last Known Good Configuration will allow you to start the computer and examine the configuration. When Last Known Good Configuration is used, later configuration changes are lost.

◆ **STOP Message DRIVER_POWER_STATE_FAILURE:** This message indicates that a driver is in an inconsistent or invalid power state. Try disabling the driver identified in the Stop message. You can also update any newly installed drivers or any software that uses filter drivers such as anti-virus or backup programs. Then, rerun the Setup program.

◆ **STOP Message INACCESSIBLE_BOOT_DEVICE:** You will see this message if the I/O system fails to initialize properly. If this happens, your boot sector may be infected with a virus. Run a virus-scanning program to see if this resolves the issue. If not, you likely have a hard disk error.

Figure 2-19 Booting with Last Known Good Configuration

```
Windows 2003 Server Advanced Options Menu
Please select an option:

    Safe Mode
    Safe Mode with Networking
    Safe Mode with Command Prompt

    Enable Boot Logging
    Enable VGA Mode
    Last Known Good Configuration
    Directory Services Restore Mode (Windows 2003 domain controllers only)
    Debugging Mode

    Boot Normally
    Return to OS Choices Menu

Use ↑ and ↓ to move the highlight to your choice.
Press Enter to choose.
```

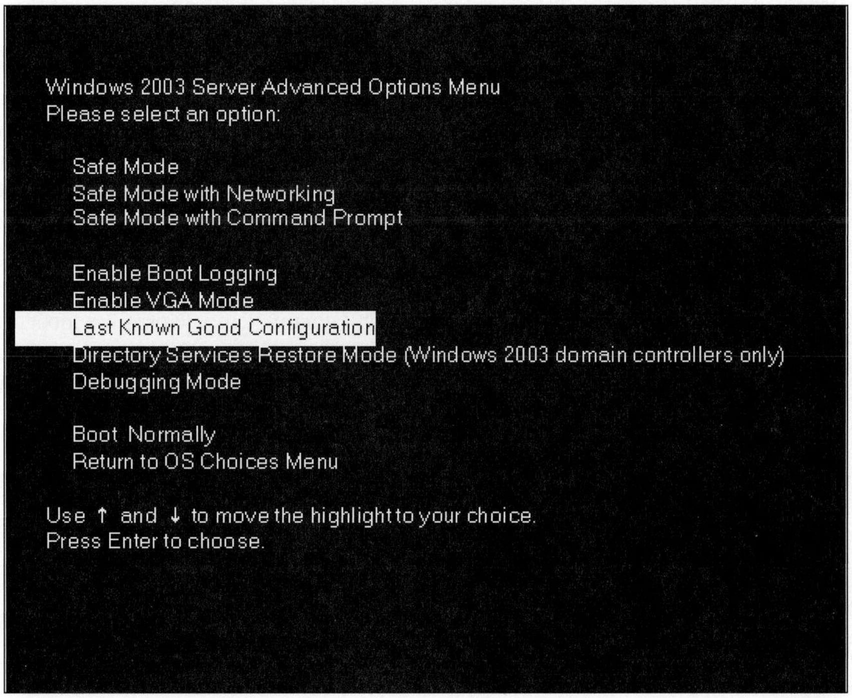

skill 7

Working with the Add Hardware Wizard

exam objective

Install and configure server hardware devices. Monitor server hardware. Tools might include Device Manager, the Hardware Troubleshooting Wizard, and appropriate Control Panel items.

overview

Hardware devices are the physical devices attached to a computer such as the disk drives, CD-ROM drives, monitor, mouse, keyboard, modem, network card, and printer. Installing and configuring hardware devices in the Windows Server 2003 environment is an easy and problem-free procedure because the operating system is **Plug and Play (PnP)** compatible, which means that most common devices will be located and installed automatically.

However, Plug and Play may not work for all devices because some of them may be too old, too new, or too minor to have a device driver included on the installation CD. When Windows Server 2003 does not automatically detect and install a new hardware device (and its associated drivers) that is attached to your system, you may need to use the **Add Hardware Wizard** (**Figure 2-20**) or run a setup program from a manufacturer's supplied CD. Note, however, that only an administrator can install non-Plug and Play devices. Furthermore, if the operating system cannot automatically locate the device driver for a Plug and Play device or if the device driver is not digitally signed, only an administrator will be able to install it.

Windows Server 2003 Setup includes the Dynamic Update feature. **Dynamic Update** downloads critical content to enhance the Setup program. If the computer can connect to the Internet during Setup, you will be prompted to download this new content. You can also skip Dynamic Update during Setup and use Windows Update later. Dynamic Update content includes drivers and replacement files. Drivers are downloaded only for devices that are present in the computer. Replacement files replace the existing files on the installation CD-ROM. No new files are added to the product. Dynamic Update uses the most critical fixes to improve the Setup program and provide a stable operating system.

When you are installing hardware devices, you should make sure that only certified device drivers are installed with the hardware devices. Occasionally, the installation CD includes generic drivers for devices; however, it is always best to use the manufacturer's product CD for the installation of the device driver to ensure that the hardware device functions properly. To avoid installing unsigned device drivers, Windows Server 2003 also provides driver-signing options so that you can check whether the device drivers have been tested and certified by Microsoft. Note that many drivers which are not signed by Microsoft work fine, but those which are signed have been extensively tested and are certified to be compatible. See Skill 9 for a further discussion of driver signing.

When a new hardware device is physically connected to the computer and the computer is booted, Plug and Play will attempt to automatically detect it. However, if this does not happen, an administrator can start the Add Hardware Wizard and it will search for any Plug and Play devices that were not recognized by the operating system at startup. The found devices will be displayed for confirmation, the correct device drivers will be installed, and any necessary resources will be assigned to the device. Next, the installation will be announced, and you will be asked to accept the drivers the Wizard has chosen.

If you start the Add Hardware Wizard and the operating system is not able to locate the device when it performs the search, you can select the **Yes, I have already connected the hardware** option (**Figure 2-21**), click **Next**, and choose from a list of installed devices (**Figure 2-22**). If the device is not on the list, you can select **Add a new hardware device**. Then, you can either have the system attempt to search for and install the hardware automatically again, or you will have to install it manually. This process requires the selection of the hardware category from a list, choosing the manufacturer and model, and the installation of the appropriate driver.

Figure 2-20 The Add Hardware Wizard

Figure 2-21 Is the hardware connected? screen

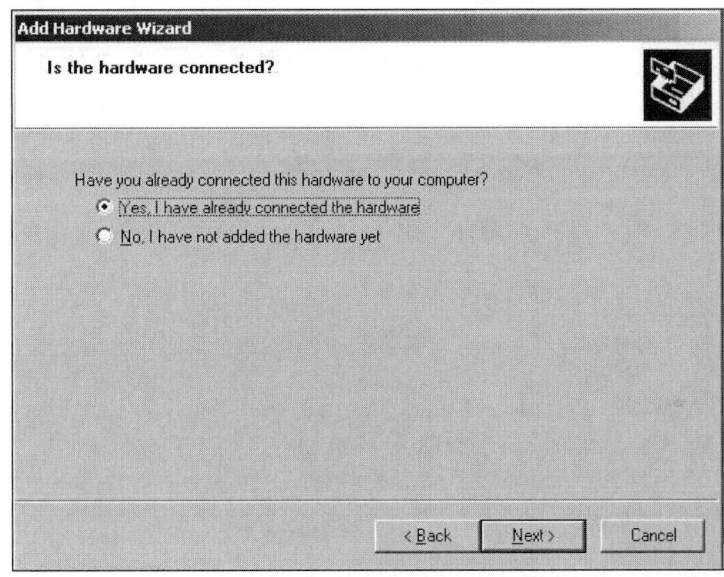

Figure 2-22 The list of installed hardware

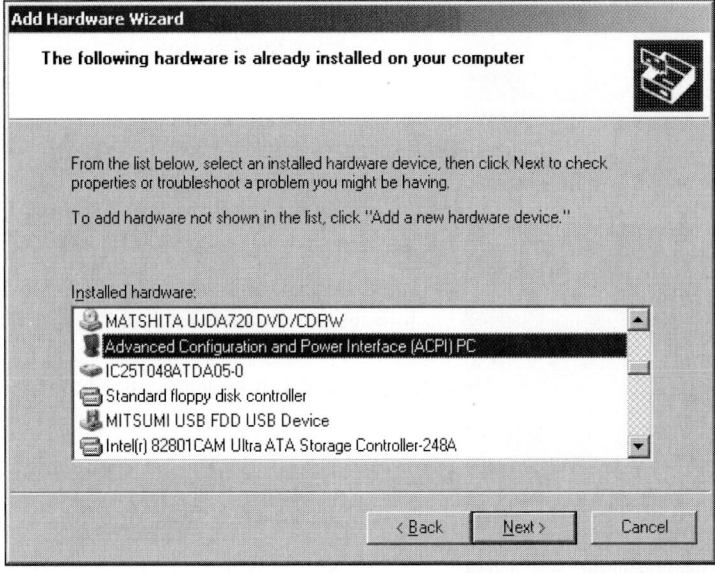

skill 7

Working with the Add Hardware Wizard (cont'd)

exam objective

Install and configure server hardware devices. Monitor server hardware. Tools might include Device Manager, the Hardware Troubleshooting Wizard, and appropriate Control Panel items.

overview

If an installed hardware device is not functioning properly, select an installed device on the screen shown in Figure 2-19 and click **Next**. The **Completing the Add Hardware Wizard** screen includes the **Device status** list box, which will tell you whether the device is functioning correctly or not. The troubleshooter will start when you click **Finish** to close the Wizard. You can also troubleshoot a malfunctioning device on the **General** tab in the **Properties** dialog box for the device. Click `Troubleshoot...` to open the Troubleshooter for the device in the **Help and Support Center**. You will answer a series of questions to attempt to resolve the problem.

how to

Use the Add Hardware Wizard to uninstall and reinstall a device:

1. Log on to the server as an **Administrator**.
2. Click `Start`, click **Run**, and type **devmgmt.msc** in the **Open** text box. Press **[Enter]** or click `OK` to open the Device Manager.
3. Click the plus sign ⊞ next to **DVD/CD-ROM drives**. Right-click the CD-ROM or DVD device and click **Uninstall**.
4. The **Confirm Device Removal** dialog box opens (**Figure 2-23**). Click `OK` to confirm that you want to uninstall the device.
5. If you are prompted to restart the computer, the device will be automatically reinstalled when you reboot. If you are not prompted to restart, proceed to the next step.
6. Close the Device Manager.
7. Click `Start`, and click **My Computer**. The DVD or CD-ROM drive icon has been removed.
8. Click `Start`, point to **Control Panel**, and click **Add Hardware** to initiate the **Add Hardware Wizard**. The **Welcome to the Add Hardware Wizard** screen opens.
9. Click `Next>`. The Add Hardware Wizard will search for, locate, install the device drivers for and configure the DVD or CD-ROM drive automatically (**Figure 2-24**).
10. The **Completing the Add Hardware Wizard** screen opens (**Figure 2-25**). Click `Finish` to close the **Add Hardware Wizard**.
11. If the **System Settings Change** dialog box opens, click **No**. You do not need to restart the computer.
12. Click `Start`, and click **My Computer**. The DVD or CD-ROM drive icon has been restored.
13. Close the My Computer window.

tip

You can also open the Device Manager on the **Hardware** tab in the **System Properties** dialog box or from the **Computer Management** console. To open the **Computer Management** console, right-click **My Computer** on the Start menu and click **Manage**. Then, select **Device Manager** in the console tree.

tip

The Add Hardware Wizard can also be initialized from the **Hardware** tab on the **System Properties** dialog box.

more

Some devices, such as network adapters, must first be installed into a PCI bus slot in the motherboard, while other devices such as printers, mice, keyboards, and scanners connect to the computer through exterior ports. Laptop and notebook computers also support devices called PC Cards which are inserted into PC Card slots.

Some devices are **hot-pluggable**, which means that you can connect and disconnect them while the computer is on and they will be automatically installed and configured with no reboot necessary. Hot plugging and hot swapping are interchangeable terms. Both indicate that a device can be added and removed while the computer is running and the operating system will automatically recognize the change.

tip

Some hardware devices, such as scanners and cameras, the keyboard, mouse, and audio devices have Control Panel applets that you can use to configure their properties.

Figure 2-23 The Confirm Device Removal dialog box

Figure 2-24 Searching for connected hardware

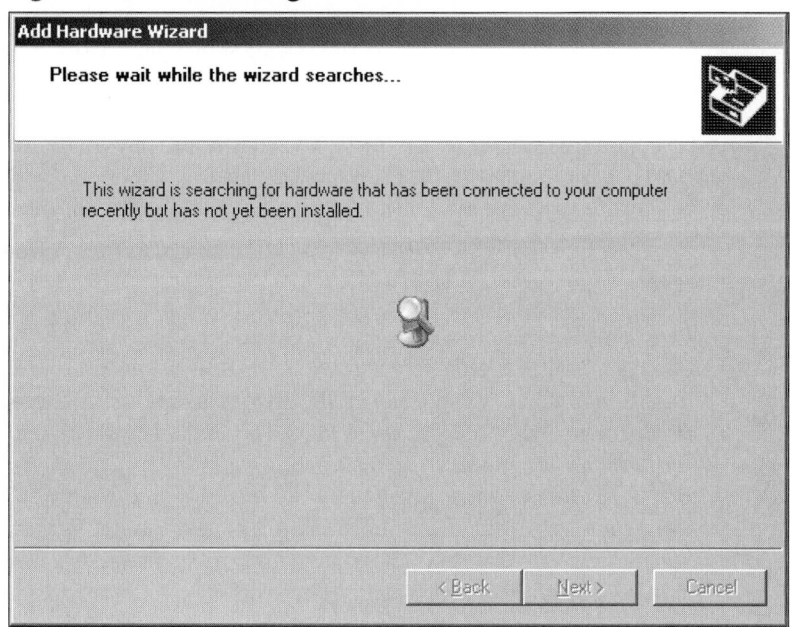

Figure 2-25 Completing the Add Hardware Wizard

skill 8

Working with the Device Manager

exam objective

Install and configure server hardware devices. Monitor server hardware. Tools might include Device Manager, the Hardware Troubleshooting Wizard, and appropriate Control Panel items. Configure resource settings for a device. Configure device properties and settings.

overview

After adding a new hardware device to your system that is not PnP-compatible, you must configure and manage the hardware device. Windows Server 2003 includes the **Device Manager** for this purpose. The Device Manger is a system tool that enables you to:

◆ Verify the status of hardware devices and update the device drivers associated with these hardware devices.

◆ Obtain information about how the hardware is installed and configured (**Figure 2-26**).

◆ Obtain information about how the hardware is interacting with other applications on the computer.

◆ Uninstall hardware devices. As you saw in Skill 7, the Device Manger is used to uninstall a hardware device from the computer. When you uninstall a hardware device, you remove the driver from your computer first (as in the exercise) so that the resources the device used are free. Then, shut the computer down and physically remove the device. When you boot the computer, the Plug and Play feature will no longer detect the device and the hardware configuration will be updated. Note that some devices (such as USB and FireWire devices) are hot-swappable, and can be removed or added to the system without any extra steps.

◆ Disable and enable hardware devices. You do not need to uninstall a device that you want to disable but do not want to physically remove, for example, a modem or a NIC. You can simply disable it, either by using the **Disable** command on the context menu for the device in Device Manager or in the **Device usage** list box on the **General** tab in the **Properties** dialog box for the device. The Registry will be updated so that the device drivers will not be loaded at boot time.

◆ Roll back to a previous version of a driver. This option is useful if you update a device driver for a device that was functioning normally, and the device then malfunctions. You can revert to the driver you were previously using so that the device will work again.

◆ Modify resource settings that are allocated for a device and change advanced settings and properties for devices.

As you have learned, every hardware device you install and configure has associated drivers that enable it to communicate with the operating system. You use the Device Manager to view the driver details, uninstall device drivers (uninstall the device), update to newer versions, or rollback to a previously installed driver. To perform these tasks, right-click the device in Device Manager. The context menu will include some of the commands, depending on the device. You can also click **Properties** to open the Properties dialog box for the device. The **Driver** tab includes buttons for each function (**Figure 2-27**).

Figure 2-26 Devices by connections view provides information about how hardware is installed and configured

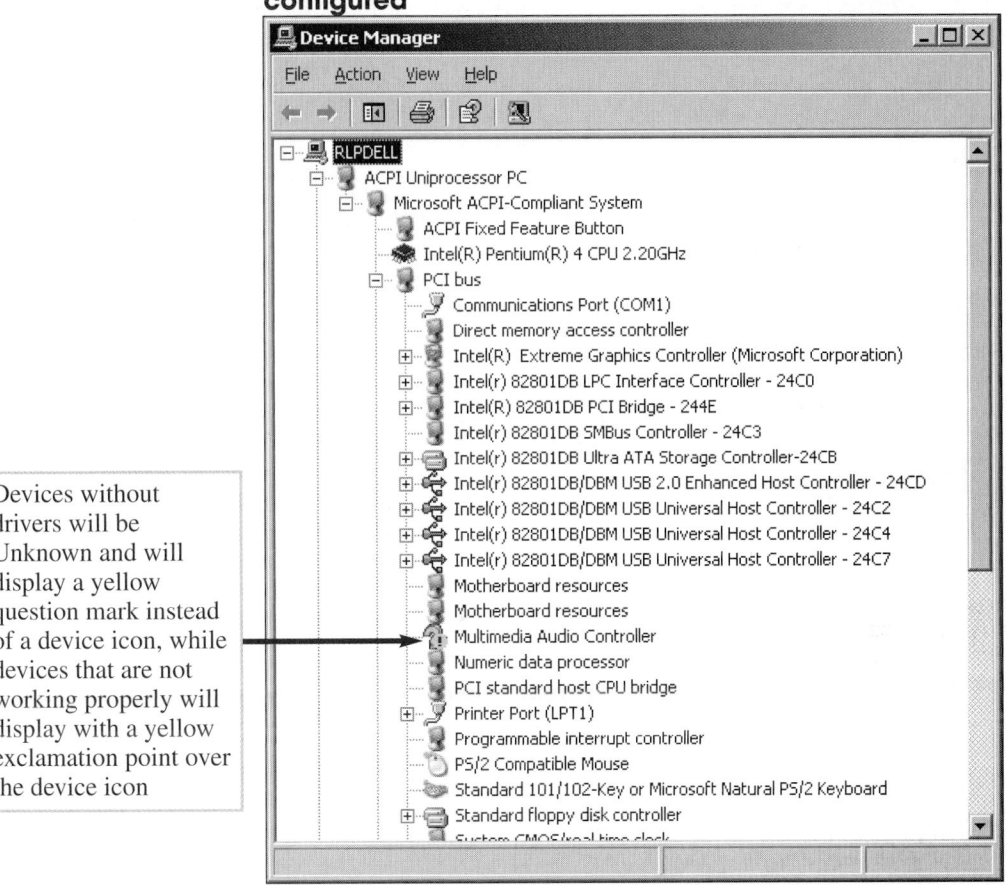

Devices without drivers will be Unknown and will display a yellow question mark instead of a device icon, while devices that are not working properly will display with a yellow exclamation point over the device icon

Figure 2-27 The Driver tab in the Properties dialog box for a device

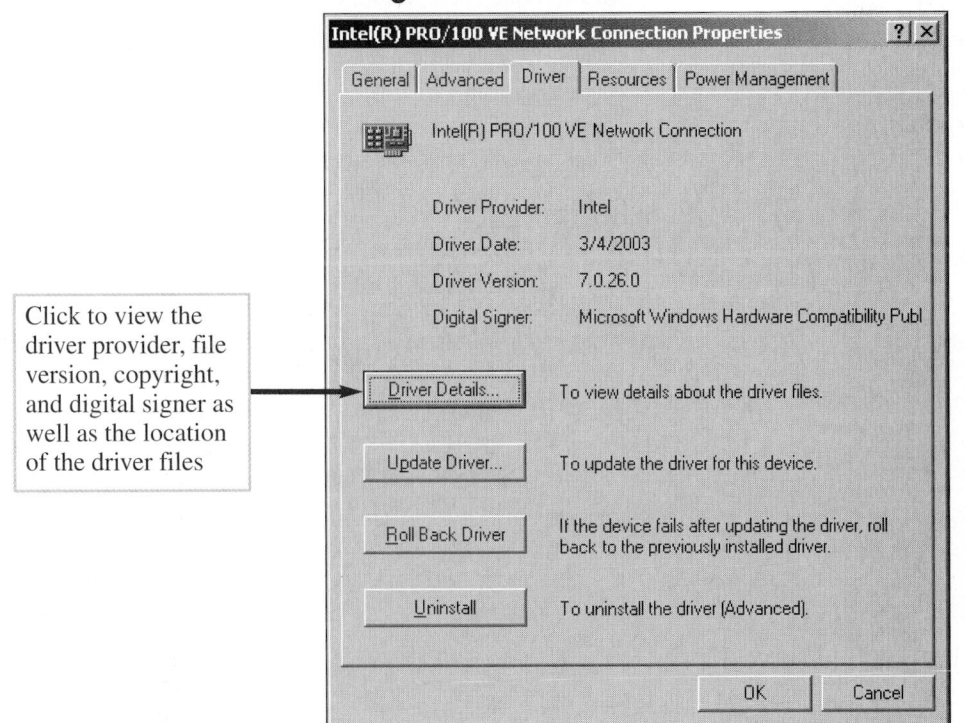

Click to view the driver provider, file version, copyright, and digital signer as well as the location of the driver files

skill 8

Working with the Device Manager
(cont'd)

exam objective

Install and configure server hardware devices. Monitor server hardware. Tools might include Device Manager, the Hardware Troubleshooting Wizard, and appropriate Control Panel items. Configure resource settings for a device. Configure device properties and settings.

overview

Updating the device drivers for hardware devices, in most cases, increases the reliability as well as the functionality, of the drivers. However, when a new version of a device driver is released, you should first test it before upgrading the driver in your production environment. The **Hardware Update Wizard** helps you to install the device driver that is compatible with the hardware device.

The Device Manager displays a graphical list of all the hardware devices installed on your system. The View menu in the Device Manager provides the following views:

◆ The **Devices by type** view is the default view in Device Manager. This view is used to display hardware devices according to their type, such as disk drives, keyboard, monitor, and printer **(Figure 2-28)**.

◆ The **Devices by connection** view is used to display hardware devices according to the connection type such as COM1 or System board.

◆ The **Resources by type** view is used to display the status of the allocated resources such as DMA channels and I/O ports **(Figure 2-29)**.

◆ The **Resources by connection** view displays the status of all allocated resources, DMA channels, I/O ports, IRQ, and memory addresses, by the type of connection used.

◆ The **Show Hidden Devices** view displays devices that are not PnP. This view can also be used to view devices that have been physically removed but whose drivers are still installed by setting an environmental variable. (See Microsoft Knowledge Base Article 241257).

Another benefit of Plug and Play compatibility is that all resources a device must use are automatically configured using system resources that are not currently in use. Moreover, if other devices and their drivers must be reconfigured so that the system can accommodate the new device, this will be done for you too, eliminating most, if not all, resource conflict problems. For example, if you are installing a device that must use several IRQs that are already in use, Plug and Play functionality can almost always find a way to reconfigure the other devices so that an IRQ needed by the new device will be released. For those occasional instances when this cannot be accomplished, you will have to remove or disable the device so that the new device will have access to the system resources it needs.

For older, non-PnP devices, however, you may need to manually configure resource settings on the devices themselves. This is done in various ways, including adjusting the plastic dual-position DIP switches found on some hardware, using jumpers, or by obtaining additional software from the manufacturer. Resources that hardware commonly use are:

◆ **I/O address:** An **I/O address** is a unique hexadecimal number that designates where a memory buffer for a hardware device is located. The memory buffer stores requests generated from a device while the CPU is processing them. I/O address conflicts do not generally occur because there are not enough I/O addresses for all of the devices, but rather because a structured method for address allocation has not been devised. Device conflicts can occur if too many devices try to use the same addresses, or if there are not enough different configuration options so that all devices can find a place to use without hindering another device.

Figure 2-28 Devices by type view

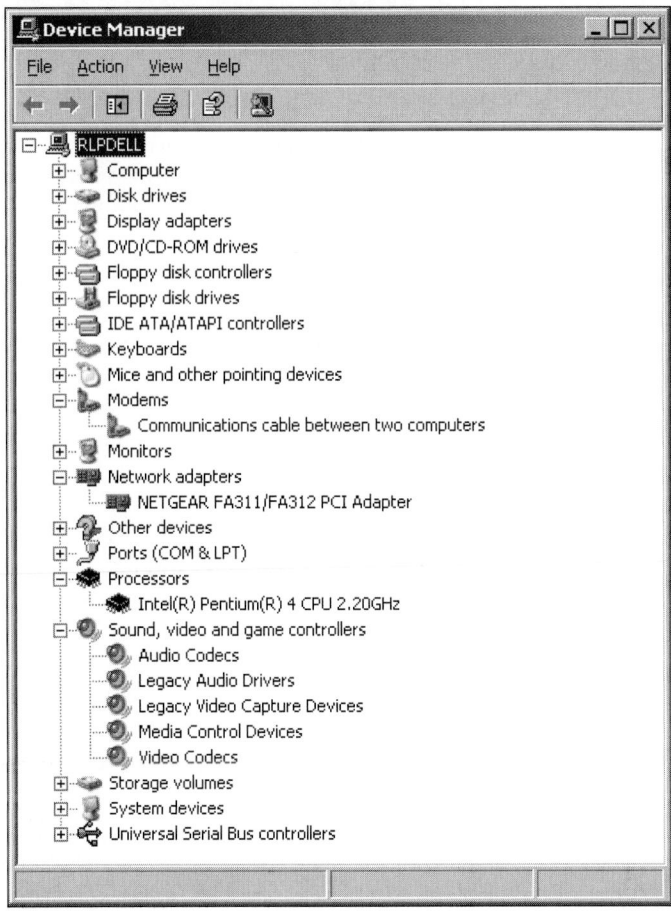

Figure 2-29 Resources by type view

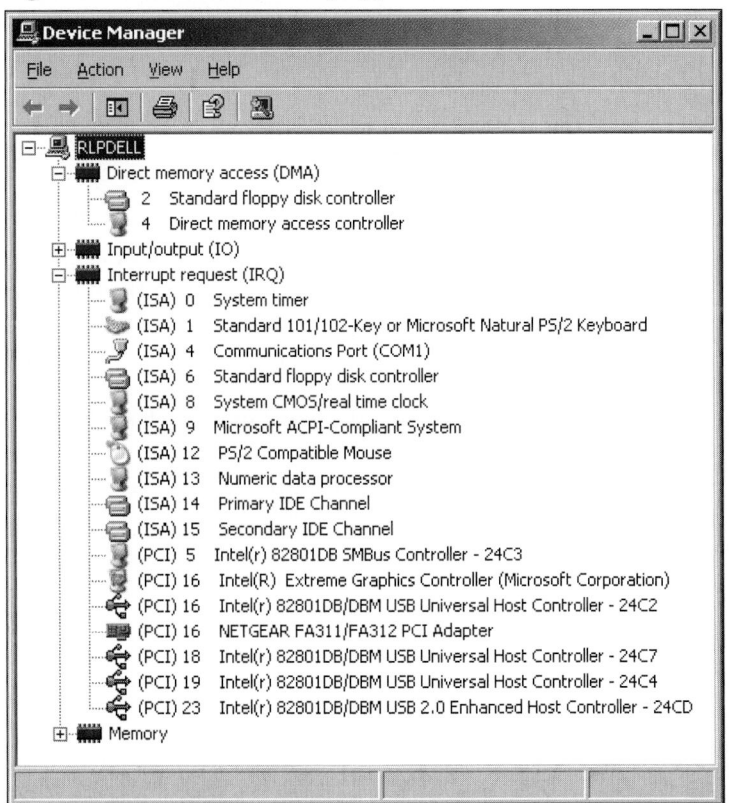

skill 8

Working with the Device Manager
(cont'd)

exam objective

Install and configure server hardware devices. Monitor server hardware. Tools might include Device Manager, the Hardware Troubleshooting Wizard, and appropriate Control Panel items. Configure resource settings for a device. Configure device properties and settings.

overview

- ◆ **DMA (Direct Memory Access) channel:** The function of the DMA channel is to move data directly from the memory of the computer to a device, bypassing the CPU. It is a direct channel from the device to the computer's memory. There are six DMA channels that can be used by a limited number of devices so that the process of transferring data to these devices is accelerated. DMA channel 2 is always used by the floppy drive, but you may have to manually configure the DMA channel for other devices.
- ◆ **Interrupt Request (IRQ):** The function of an IRQ is to "tell" the CPU that a device needs servicing. There are 16 IRQ channels, thus PCs have 16 interrupt settings which run from 0-15. Interrupts can be shared by most Plug and Play devices, but not by most legacy hardware. Windows Server 2003 will automatically configure the IRQs for Plug and Play devices, but for many older devices you will have to set a unique IRQ that will not conflict with any other devices.
- ◆ **Memory addresses:** Memory addresses are particular addresses in the memory of the computer that are used by some hardware devices to transfer data to the CPU. Reserved system memory addresses are not available for use by any other device.

When you must manually install and configure legacy hardware, the manufacturer's documentation will have to be consulted so that you can determine what resources the hardware device must use. Using the **Resources by connection** view in the Device Manager, you can then determine the system resources that are available. In the **Properties** dialog box for the device on the **Resources** tab, select the **Resource setting** you want to change and clear the **Use automatic settings** check box. If the Properties dialog box for the device does not have a Resources tab, you cannot change the resources used by the device. If the Use automatic settings check box is grayed out and inactive, you also will not be able to modify the resources by the device. If you can clear the Use automatic settings check box, select the resource you want to change and click the **Change Setting** button to modify a resource setting **(Figure 2-30 and 2-31)**.

how to

Install and uninstall a network adapter and its device drivers.

1. Click **Start**, point to **Control Panel**, and click **Add Hardware** to initiate the **Add Hardware Wizard**. The **Welcome to the Add Hardware Wizard** screen opens.
2. Click **Next >** and wait for the Add Hardware Wizard to search for new devices.
3. On the **Is the hardware connected** screen, select the **Yes, I have already connected the hardware** option button.
4. Click **Next >** to open the **The following hardware is already installed on your computer** screen.
5. Scroll to the bottom of the **Installed hardware** list and select **Add a new hardware device (Figure 2-32)**.

Figure 2-30 The Resources tab

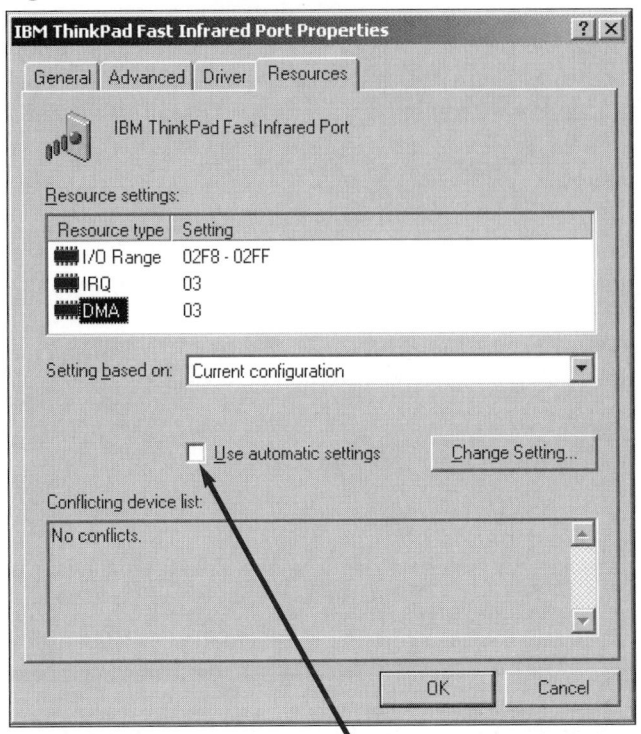

Figure 2-31 The Edit Direct Memory Access dialog box

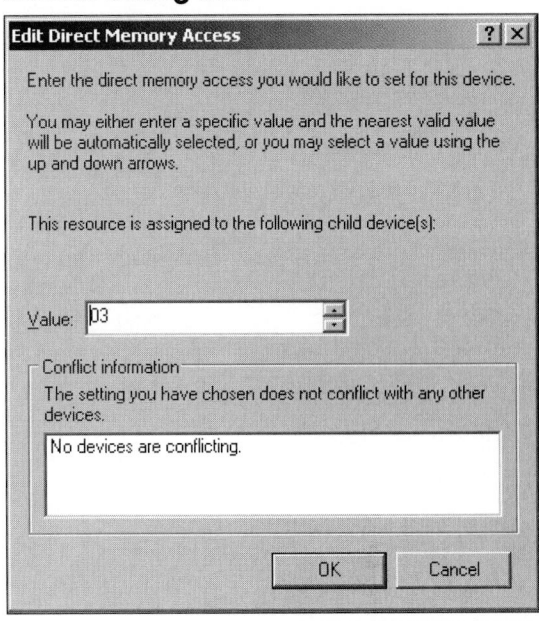

If the Use automatic settings check box is grayed out, you cannot modify the resources used by the device; if you can clear it, click the Change Setting button to modify a resource setting

Figure 2-32 Adding hardware not on the Installed hardware list

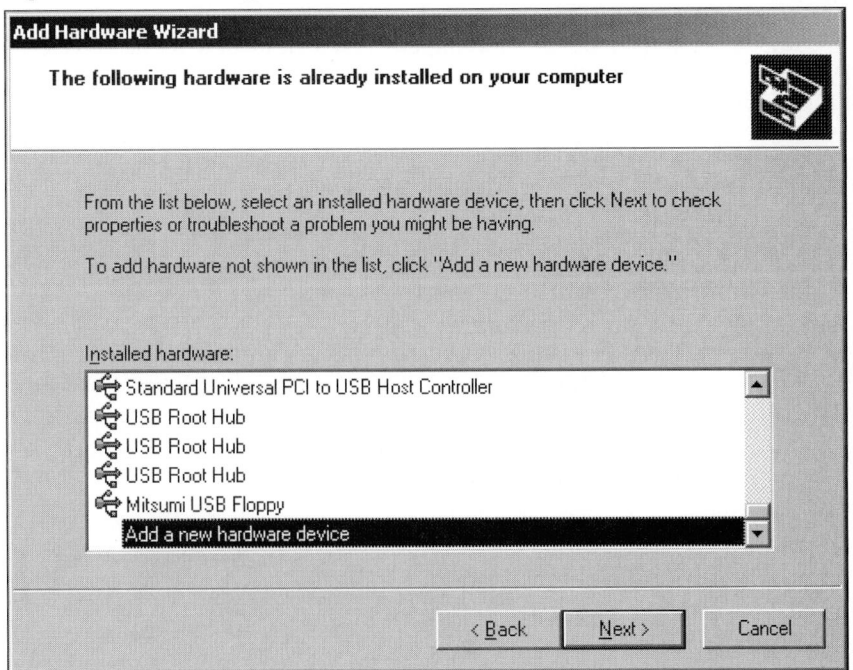

skill 8

Working with the Device Manager
(cont'd)

exam objective

Install and configure server hardware devices. Monitor server hardware. Tools might include Device Manager, the Hardware Troubleshooting Wizard, and appropriate Control Panel items. Configure resource settings for a device. Configure device properties and settings.

how to

6. Click [Next >] to open the **The wizard can help you install other hardware** screen.
7. Select the **Install the hardware that I manually select from a list** option button.
8. Click [Next >] to open the **From the list below, select the type of hardware you are installing** screen. In the **Common hardware types** list, select **Network adapters (Figure 2-33)**.
9. Click [Next >] to open the **Select Network Adapter** screen. Select **Microsoft** in the **Manufacturer** list. Select **Microsoft Loopback Adapter** in the **Network Adapter** list (**Figure 2-34**).
10. Click [Next >] to open the **The wizard is ready to install your hardware** screen.
11. Click [Next >] to start installing the new hardware.
12. Click [Next >] to complete the Add Hardware Wizard.
13. Click [Start], click **Run**, and type **devmgmt.msc** in the **Open** text box. Press **[Enter]** or click [OK] to open the Device Manager.
14. Double-click **Network adapters** to expand the console tree. The Microsoft Loopback Adapter has been installed.
15. Right-click **Microsoft Loopback Adapter** and select **Properties**.
16. Open the **Driver** tab. Click [Uninstall] to open the **Confirm Device Removal** dialog box.
17. Click [OK] to uninstall the drivers for the Microsoft Loopback Adapter.
18. The adapter is removed from the Device Manager.
19. Close the Device Manager.

more

Devices that are not working properly will display in the Device Manager with a yellow exclamation point over the device icon. This is usually due to resource conflicts and you will have to open the Properties dialog box for the device and configure the resources manually depending on what resources are available on the system. Devices that are disabled will display with a red "x" over the device icon. Devices without drivers will be Unknown and will display a yellow question mark instead of a device icon. If you must manually assign resources to a device, when you disable the Use Automatic Settings option, the device will display in the Device Manager with a blue "i" over the device icon.

Double-click a malfunctioning device to open its Properties dialog box. On the **General** tab, you can run the troubleshooter or disable the device for the current hardware profile. On the Driver tab you can view details about the driver files that are loaded for the device, uninstall the driver files for the device, or update the driver files for the device.

Figure 2-33 Selecting the type of hardware to install

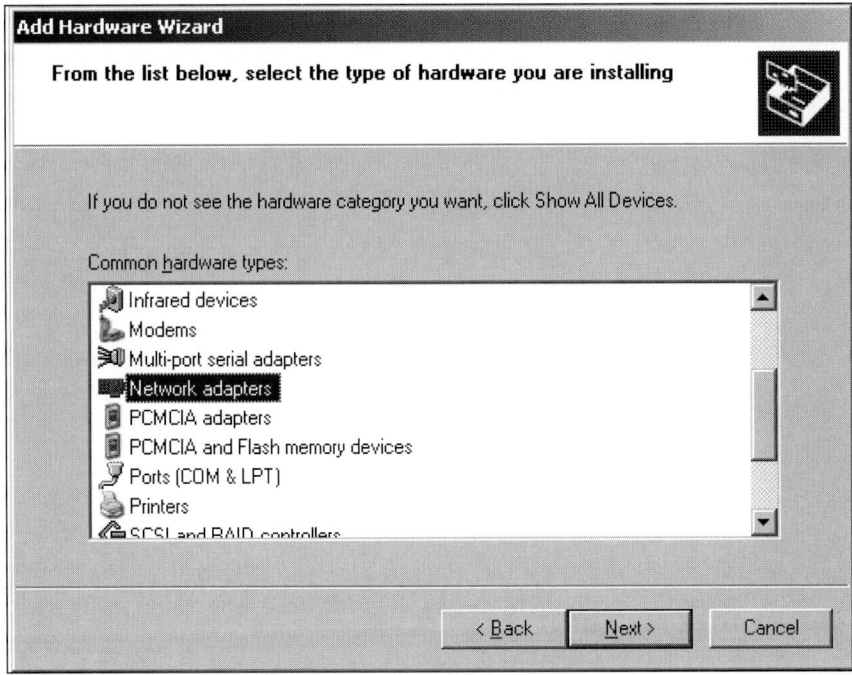

Figure 2-34 The Select Network Adapter screen

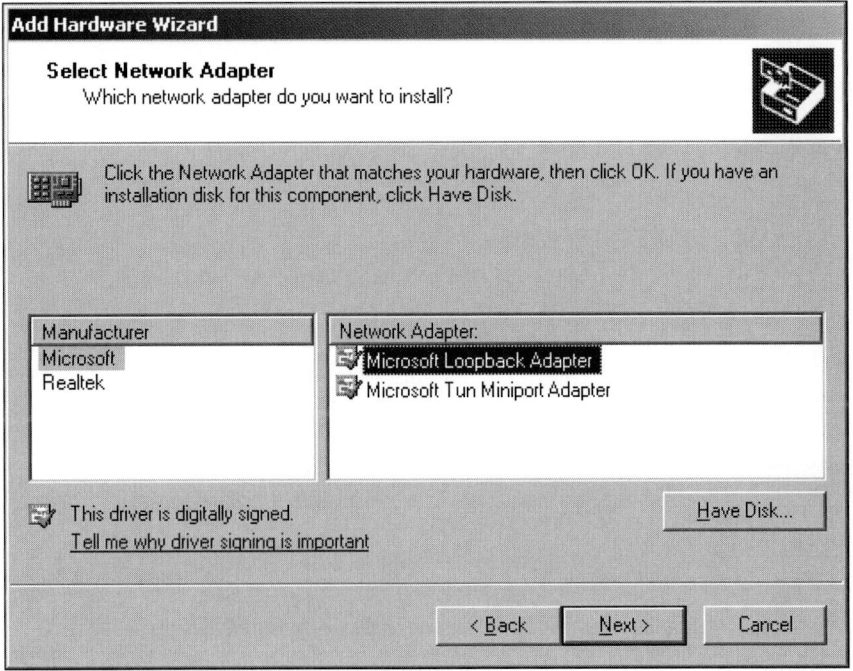

skill 9

Configuring Driver Signing Options

exam objective

Install and configure server hardware devices. Monitor server hardware. Tools might include Device Manager, the Hardware Troubleshooting Wizard, and appropriate Control Panel items. Configure driver signing options.

overview

When you install a new hardware device on your system, it is crucial that reliable driver files for the device are loaded. Defective or bug-ridden drivers can cause considerable problems for your system. Windows Server 2003 uses driver signing options to ensure the use of high quality drivers for any hardware device. **Driver signing** technology is used to confirm for network administrators (and members of the Server Operators group who also have permission to install drivers) that the drivers being installed have passed the Microsoft certification process.

Device drivers developed by a device manufacturer for a hardware device are submitted to the Windows Hardware Quality Lab (WHQL) for testing and certification. If the drivers pass the WHQL tests, they are given a Microsoft digital signature. Microsoft uses digital signatures for device drivers to let users know that drivers are compatible with Microsoft Windows Server 2003. A driver's digital signature indicates that the driver was tested with Windows for compatibility and has not been altered since testing.

Windows uses the presence or absence of a digital signature to evaluate the quality of the drivers it attempts to install. The operating system will warn users if they attempt to install drivers that don't have signatures. System administrators can also choose to set operating system policies that will prevent the installation of drivers that do not have digital signatures. Microsoft encourages the use of digital signatures for drivers to advance system stability, to provide a better user experience, and to reduce total cost of ownership for customers.

There are three levels of driver signing security you can apply:

- ◆ **Ignore:** This level allows any driver to be installed, regardless of whether they have a digital signature or not.
- ◆ **Warn:** The default setting, this level notifies the user if a driver that is being installed does not have the Microsoft digital signature, and prompts the user to either continue or terminate the installation.
- ◆ **Block:** This level prevents the installation of unsigned drivers. The installation program will be unable to install any device drivers that do not have a digital signature.

In the Driver Signing Options dialog box, you can select the **Make this action the system default** check box in the **Administrative option** section. Administrators use this option to ensure that only users with administrative rights can modify driver-signing options.

how to

Configure Windows Server 2003 response to the installation of unsigned drivers.

1. Log on to the server as an **Administrator**.
2. Click [🏁 Start], point to **Control Panel**, and click **System** to open the **System Properties** dialog box **(Figure 2-35)**.
3. Open the **Hardware** tab **(Figure 2-36)**, and click [Driver Signing...] to open the **Driver Signing Options** dialog box.
4. Select the **Block – Never install unsigned driver software** option button to prevent unsigned files from being installed on the server **(Figure 2-37)**.
5. Accept the default **Administrator option** setting, **Make this action the system default**. This setting is used to set the selected driver signing option as the default option for all users that log on to the system.
6. Click [OK] to close the **Driver Signing Options** dialog box.
7. Click [OK] to close the **System Properties** dialog box. The **Block - Never install unsigned software** option has been set on the server to prevent the installation of unsigned driver files.

tip

You can also set driver signing options by setting the Unsigned Driver Installation security setting in the Group Policy snap-in.

Figure 2-35 Opening the System Properties dialog box

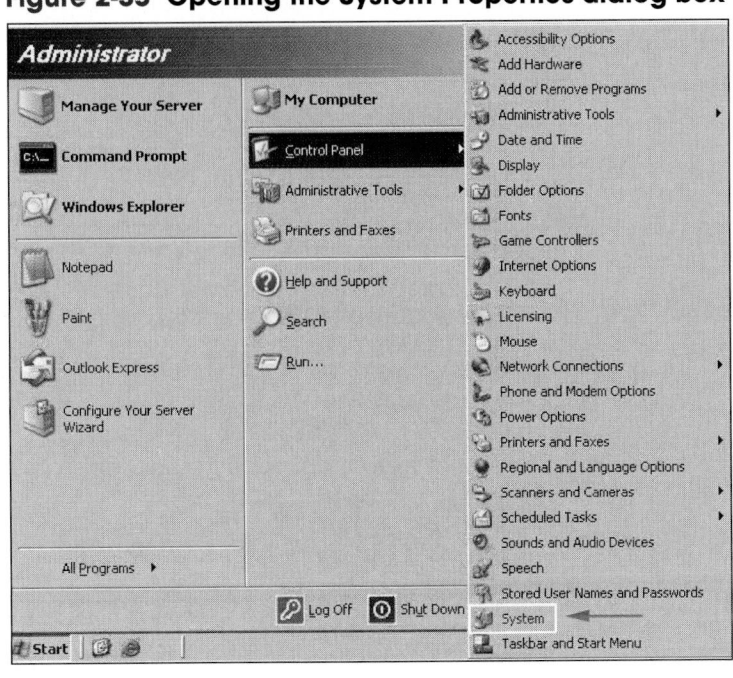

Figure 2-36 The Hardware tab in the System Properties dialog box

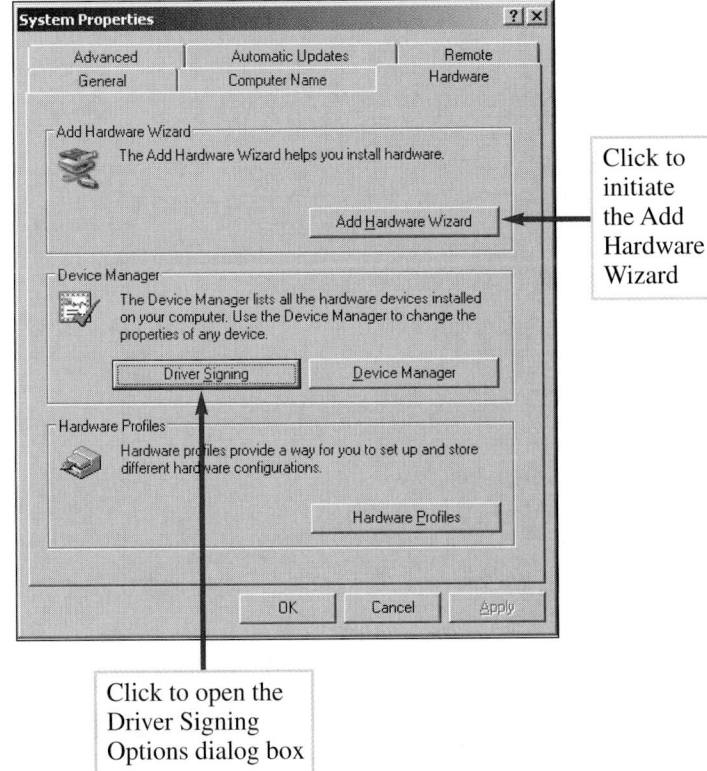

Click to initiate the Add Hardware Wizard

Click to open the Driver Signing Options dialog box

Figure 2-37 The Driver Signing Options dialog box

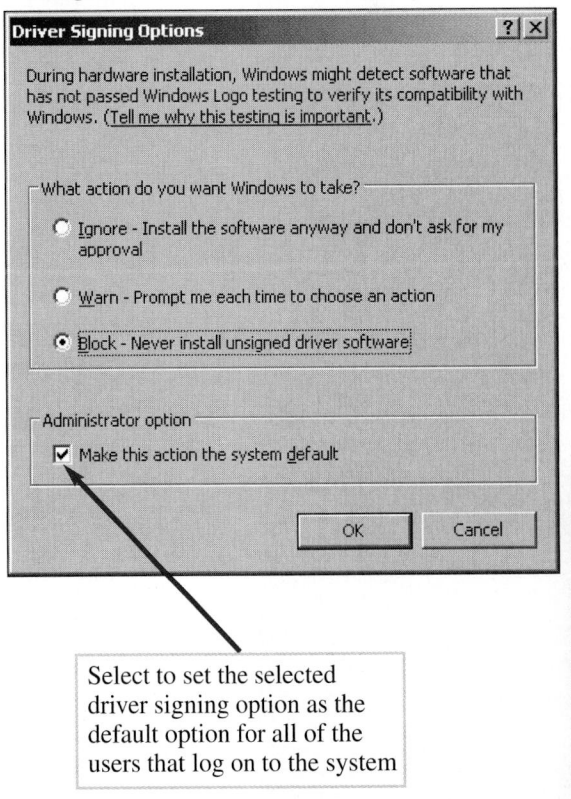

Select to set the selected driver signing option as the default option for all of the users that log on to the system

skill 10

Working with Hardware Profiles and Event Logs

exam objective

Install and configure server hardware devices. Monitor server hardware. Tools might include Device Manager, the Hardware Troubleshooting Wizard, and appropriate Control Panel items.

overview

tip

During the installation of Windows Server 2003, a default hardware profile, Profile 1 (Current), is created. If new hardware profiles are not created, Windows Server 2003 uses the default hardware profile to initialize all hardware devices at system startup.

A **hardware profile** describes the selection of a specific configuration of hardware devices (such as network cards, printers, etc.) at the time the operating system is initialized. Although the configuration of hardware profiles is usually reserved for client operating systems such as Windows 2000 or XP Professional running on portable computers—i.e., laptops—the Microsoft Knowledge Base Article 323338 (HOW TO: Create Hardware Profiles on Windows Server 2003-Based Portable Computers) describes the various ways in which hardware profiles can be configured for Windows Server 2003-based portable computers.

Hardware profiles are most commonly used for situations in which one hardware profile is to be used at one location and another at an alternate location. For example, you might create one hardware profile for when you are using the laptop at a docking station with peripherals such as a printer and network adapter, and another for when you are traveling, when you will need the modem and your portable printer.

Windows Server 2003 displays the hardware profiles that have been created at startup on the **Hardware Profile/Configuration Recovery Menu** screen. You can select the appropriate hardware profile and the system will initialize the associated devices.

A hardware profile, called Profile 1 (Current), is created when you install Windows Server 2003. Every device that is installed at installation will be included in Profile 1. When configuring portable devices running Windows Server 2003 with additional profiles, the profile selections will be either Docked Profile or Undocked Profile.

how to

Create a hardware profile.

1. Log on as an **Administrator**.
2. Click [Start], point to **Control Panel**, and click **System** to open the **System Properties** dialog box.
3. Open the **Hardware** tab, and click [Hardware Profiles...] to open the **Hardware Profiles** dialog box. In the **Available hardware profiles** list, the default profile, **Profile 1 (Current)** will appear (**Figure 2-38**). If the profile is not selected, select it now.
4. Click [Copy...] to open the **Copy Profile** dialog box, which enables you to create a new hardware profile.
5. Type a profile name, **PrinterDisabled (Figure 2-39)**, in the **To** text box, and click [OK]. The new hardware profile appears in the **Available hardware profiles** list.
6. Click [Properties] to open the **Properties** dialog box for the hardware profile.
7. Select the **This is a portable computer** check box, and click the **The computer is undocked** option button (**Figure 2-40**). These options enable the system to recognize that the settings are being configured for a portable computer.
8. Select the **Always include this profile as an option when Windows starts** check box to enable the user to select the hardware profile at startup.
9. Click [OK] to close the **PrinterDisabled Properties** dialog box.
10. Click [OK] to close the **Hardware Profiles** dialog box. Click [OK] to close the System Properties dialog box.
11. Restart the computer. When the **Hardware Profile/Configuration Recovery** menu opens, select the **PrinterDisabled** profile. Log back on as an **Administrator**.
12. Open the **System Properties** dialog box on the **Hardware** tab. Click [Device Manager...] to open the **Device Manager**.

Figure 2-38 The Hardware Profiles dialog box

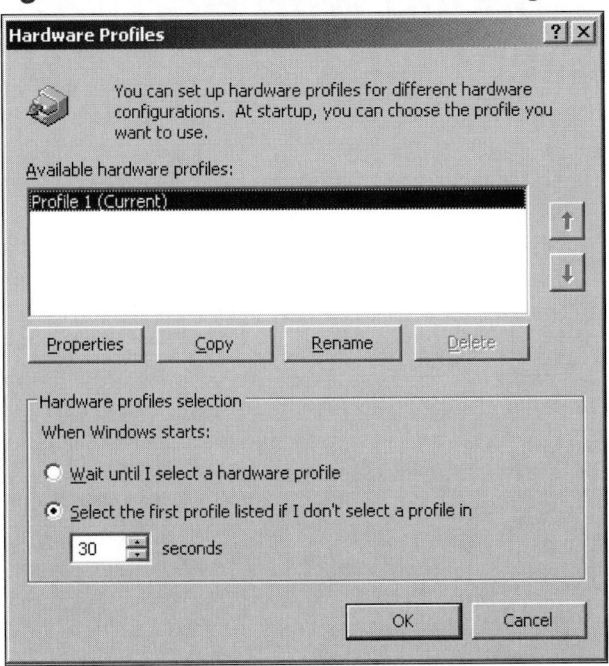

Figure 2-39 Entering a new profile name

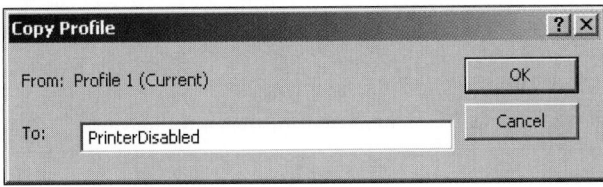

Figure 2-40 Selecting profile property options

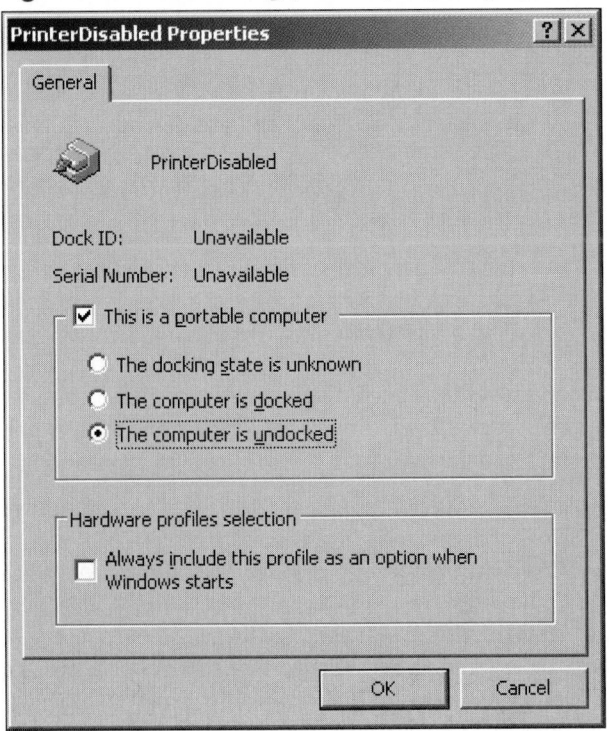

skill 10

Working with Hardware Profiles and Event Logs (cont'd)

exam objective

Install and configure server hardware devices. Monitor server hardware. Tools might include Device Manager, the Hardware Troubleshooting Wizard, and appropriate Control Panel items.

how to

13. Double-click **Ports (COM & LPT)** and then double-click **Printer Port (LPT1)** to open the **Printer Port (LPT1) Properties** dialog box.
14. Select **Do not use this device in the current hardware profile (disable)** on the **Device usage** list. This option disables the device for the current hardware profile (**Figure 2-41**).
15. Click [OK] to close the **Printer Port (LPT1) Properties** dialog box. A red X is inserted over the Printer Port (LPT1) icon in the Device Manager (**Figure 2-42**).
16. Close the **Device Manager**.
17. Click [OK] to close the **System Properties** dialog box. The printer is now disabled for this hardware profile. You may want to log off, log back on with the default profile, and delete the PrinterDisabled profile.

more

tip

When Windows Server 2003 is started, the Event log service starts automatically.

The addition of hardware devices that will be supported by Windows Server 2003 requires network administrators to become familiar with potential system problems related to the configuration and initialization of hardware devices. One reference source administrators can use to identify potential system problems is the System log. The **System log**, which is generated by the Event Log service, records events logged by the operating system or its components, such as the failure of a service or device driver to start at boot-up.

Event logs provide historical information that can help you track down system and security problems. The Event Log service controls whether events are tracked on Windows Server 2003 systems. When this service is running, you can track user actions and system resource usage events. You use the Event Viewer to view Event logs (Start-Administrative Tools-Event Viewer) (**Figure 2-43**). The Event Viewer is used to monitor all activities related to hardware and software on the system. The three logs you will find on all Windows Server 2003 computers are the **Application** log, the **Security** log, and the **System** log. On domain controllers, you will also find the **Directory Service** log and the **File Replication** log (**Figure 2-44**). In the Directory Service log you can view informational events logged by Active Directory, such as when online defragmentation or replication events have occurred, or errors, such as when the domain controller and the global catalog are not communicating. In the File Replication log, events related to changes to file replication or completed replication tasks are recorded. On DNS servers, the **DNS Server** log records events logged by the DNS Server service.

The Application log records events, defined by software developers, such as file errors recorded by applications. The Security log records events that are generated from audited activities on the computer. For example, if you enable logon auditing, you can record successful and/or failed attempts to log on to the system (See Lesson 14). The System log records events logged by Windows system components such as hardware errors, driver problems, and hard drive errors. The three types of events are listed below:

◆ **Error:** An error is logged when an event related to a significant problem, such as data loss or a service failing at startup, occurs.
◆ **Warning:** A warning is logged when an event indicates a possible future problem. For example, when disk space is low, a warning is logged.
◆ **Information:** Information is logged when an event describes the successful execution of an application, driver, or service (for example, when a driver loads successfully).

Figure 2-41 Disabling a device for a hardware profile

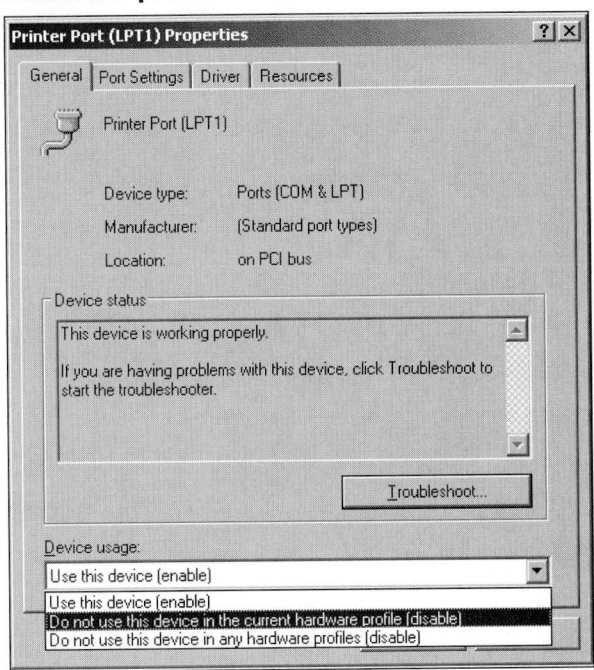

Figure 2-42 A disabled device in Device Manager

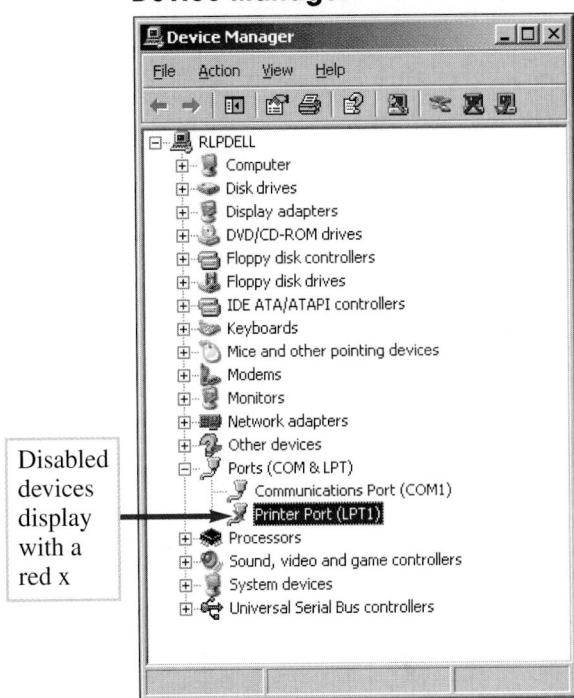

Disabled devices display with a red x

Figure 2-43 Event logs on a member server

The System log records events such as the failure of a service or device driver to start at boot time

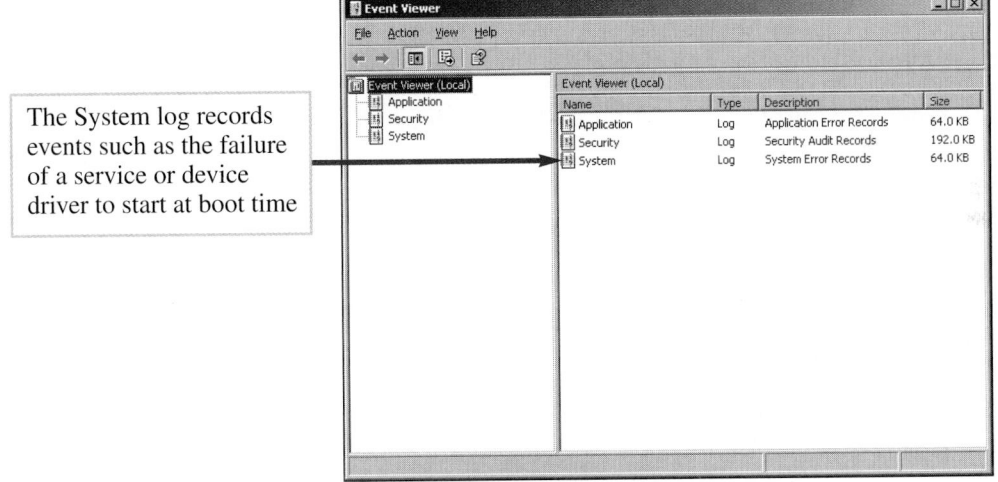

Figure 2-44 Event logs on a domain controller/DNS server

The Directory Service log records events logged by Active Directory

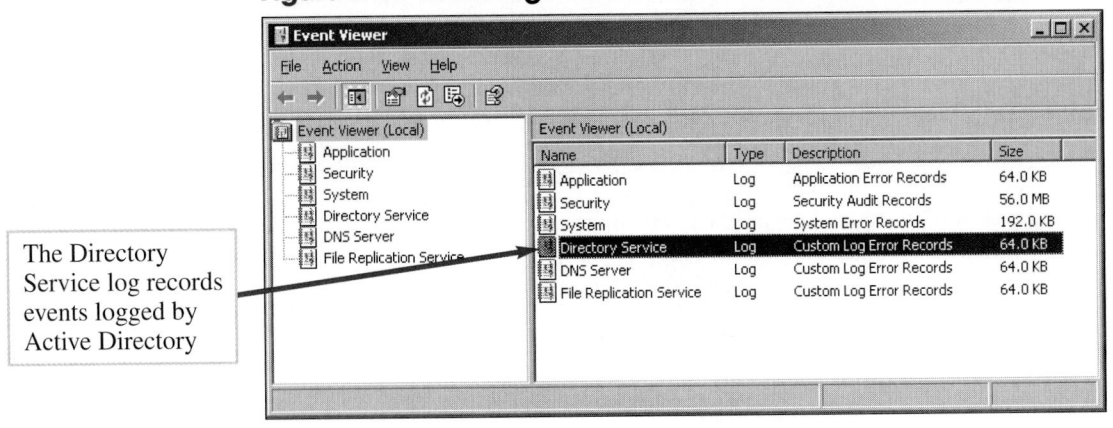

Summary

- Microsoft's minimum installation requirements for Windows Server 2003 are:
  - Pentium 133 MHz or faster processor.
  - VGA monitor.
  - 128 MB RAM for five or fewer clients and 256 MB for larger networks.
  - 1.5 GB hard disk space is required for setup; however, at least 2.5 GB hard disk space is recommended.
  - High-density, 3.5-inch floppy disk drive.
  - A 12X CD-ROM drive, if installation is performed from a CD.
- Pre-installation tasks include making sure that system hardware is listed in the Windows Server Catalog, determining whether you will be performing a clean install or an upgrade, examining existing hard disk partitions, determining the file system format, determining whether the computer will be joining a workgroup or a domain, deciding which optional components you will install, decompressing any compressed volumes, uninstalling any anti-virus software, using the Microsoft Application Compatibility Analyzer to check for software compatibility, and disconnecting any UPS devices.
- To install Windows Server 2003, you must have both a server software license (product key) and a license to access or use the server software (a client access license or CAL).
- There are two different types of CALs—a User CAL that allows a particular user to access licensed server software from any number of devices, and a Device CAL, which allows any number of users to access licensed server software from a particular device.
- There are two different licensing modes for Windows Server 2003: Per Server and Per Device or Per User. Per Server licensing mode provides a specified number of CALs for the server, thereby limiting the number of users and/or devices that can be connected to the server at one time. Per Device or Per User licensing mode (formerly called Per Seat licensing mode) provides a separate CAL for each named user or specified device, which can then access any computer running Windows Server 2003 on the network.
- There are three basic phases in the Windows Server 2003 installation process: the pre-copy phase, the text mode phase, and the GUI mode phase (which itself consists of three phases—Gathering Information About Your Computer, Installing Windows Server 2003 Networking Components, and Completing Setup).
- Windows Server 2003 contains new product activation technology, which means that in some instances, you must activate your copy of Windows Server 2003 before it can be used.
- When you perform a network installation from a shared folder, you must connect to the share and locate and open the \I386 folder. If you are connecting to the share from a computer with MS-DOS or Windows 3.x installed, you must run Winnt.exe. If you are connecting to the network share from a computer with Windows 9.x, Windows NT 3.51 or higher, or Windows 2000 Server installed, you must run Winnt32.exe.
- An unattended installation is an automated process that enables you to install Windows Server 2003 on multiple computers over a network. A customized installation script, called an answer file, provides all specifications normally entered by a user during installation.
- When upgrading Windows NT Server or Windows 2000 Server to Windows Server 2003, first perform a full backup of your computer with a complete recovery procedure; run a hardware and software compatibility check from the Setup CD or from the command prompt (checkupgradeonly); check the hardware and software compatibility information in the Windows Server Catalog; review the file systems and partitions on the server (you must have at least one NTFS partition on each of your domain controllers); if some of your domain controllers run Windows 2000 and some run Windows NT, upgrade the Windows NT domain controllers as soon as possible, to simplify management and troubleshooting, and to strengthen security; upgrade any servers or client computers running Windows NT 3.51 to Windows NT 4.0 Service Pack 5 (in order to upgrade from Windows NT 4.0, Service Pack 5 must be installed); if your server has Windows NT 4.0 volume sets, stripe sets, or stripe sets with parity, delete these sets and create new drive configurations with fault tolerance before upgrading; and synchronize your primary and backup controllers before upgrading.
- There are three upgrade migration paths.
  - An "in-place" upgrade preserves the domain architecture of Windows NT 4.0 in the Windows Server 2003 Active Directory structure. You use the Active Directory Installation Wizard to migrate and to upgrade all existing Windows NT 4.0 domain security objects (domain users, groups, and permissions) into Active Directory.
  - You can also migrate your Windows NT 4.0 objects from an existing Windows NT 4.0 domain to a brand new Windows Server 2003 forest and Active Directory. In this scenario, you would create trust relationships between the existing Windows NT 4.0 domains (source domains) and the newly created Windows Server 2003 domains (target domains).
  - The third migration path involves consolidating multiple existing Windows NT 4.0 domains into a single Active Directory domain configuration. You would downsize the existing Windows NT 4.0 domain architecture and increase administra-

tive functionality by migrating Windows NT 4.0 domains into Active Directory organizational units. This is typically the best path from a design standpoint, for future administration, but is also the most difficult.

◆ Installing and configuring hardware devices in the Windows Server 2003 environment is generally simple because the operating system is Plug and Play compatible. Thus, most common devices will be located and installed automatically.

◆ However, Plug and Play may not work for all devices because some of them may be too old, too new, or too minor to have a device driver included on the installation CD.

◆ Only administrators can install non-Plug and Play devices, devices that do not have a driver included in driver.cab, and device drivers that are not digitally signed.

◆ You will need to use the Add Hardware Wizard, when Windows Server 2003 does not automatically detect and install a new hardware device and its drivers.

◆ The Completing the Add Hardware Wizard screen includes the Device status list box, which will tell you whether the device is functioning correctly or not. A troubleshooter will start when you close the Wizard. You can also troubleshoot a malfunctioning device on the General tab in the Properties dialog box for the device.

◆ Hot-pluggable devices can be connected and disconnected while a computer is running and the operating system will automatically recognize the change. They will be automatically installed and configured with no reboot necessary. Hot plugging and hot swapping are interchangeable terms.

◆ You use the Device Manager to configure and manage the hardware devices. In Device Manager you can view driver details, uninstall device drivers (uninstall the device), update drivers, or rollback to a previously installed driver. You use the Hardware Update Wizard to update device drivers.

◆ Plug and Play compatibility ensures that all resources a device must use are automatically configured using system resources that are not currently in use. The system will reconfigure other devices and their drivers in order to accommodate the new device. This eliminates the majority of resource conflict problems.

◆ For older, non-PnP devices, however, you may need to manually configure resource settings on the devices themselves.

◆ Resources that hardware commonly uses are: I/O address, DMA (Direct Memory Access), channel Interrupt Request (IRQ), and memory addresses.

◆ Driver signing technology is used to confirm that drivers that are being installed have passed the Microsoft certification process. Device drivers are submitted to the Windows Hardware Quality Lab (WHQL) for testing and certification. If the drivers pass the WHQL tests, they are given a Microsoft digital signature.

◆ There are three levels of driver signing security:
  • Ignore: Any driver can be installed whether or not it has a digital signature.
  • Warn: You will be notified if a driver is being installed that does not have a Microsoft digital signature and will have to decide whether or not to install it. This is the default setting.
  • Block: The installation of unsigned drivers is prevented.

◆ A hardware profile describes the selection of a specific configuration of hardware devices when the operating system is started. Hardware profiles are usually used on client operating systems such as Windows 2000 or XP Professional running on portable computers.

◆ The System log, which is generated by the Event Log service, records events logged by the operating system or its components, such as the failure of a service or device driver to start at boot-up.

◆ You use the Event Viewer to view Event logs.

◆ The three logs you will find on all Windows Server 2003 machines are the Application log, the Security log, and the System log.

◆ On domain controllers, you will also find the Directory Service log and the File Replication log.

◆ On DNS servers, the DNS Server log records events logged by the DNS Server service.

◆ The System log records events logged by Windows system components such as hardware errors, driver problems, and hard drive errors. There are three types of events:
  • Error: An error is logged when an event related to a significant problem, such as data loss or a service failing at startup, occurs.
  • Warning: A warning is logged when an event indicates a possible future problem. For example, when disk space is low, a warning is logged.
  • Information: Information is logged when an event describes the successful execution of an application, driver, or service, for example, when a driver loads successfully.

Key Terms

Add Hardware Wizard
Answer file
Client Access License (CAL)
Device Manager
Distribution folder
DMA (Direct Memory Access) channel
Driver signing
Dynamic Update
Event log

GUI mode phase
Hardware device
Hardware profile
Hot-pluggable
Interrupt Request (IRQ)
I/O address
Memory addresses
Per Device or Per User licensing mode
Per Server licensing mode

Plug and Play (PnP)
Pre-copy phase
Product activation
System log
Text mode phase
Windows Server Catalog
Winnt.exe
Winnt32.exe

Test Yourself

1. Information about your computer's configuration that is required to set up your system is prompted for before /during the _____ phase:
   a. Pre-copy
   b. GUI
   c. Text mode

2. Which of the following switches are used to modify the behavior of the Winnt32.exe file? (Choose all that apply.)
   a. /r:[folder]
   b. /copydir:folder_name
   c. /rx:[folder]
   d. /cmd:command_line

3. Which of the following methods allow you to upgrade Windows NT Server 4.0 to Windows Server 2003 on your machine? (Choose all that apply.)
   a. Executing Winnt32.exe over the network.
   b. Using boot disk floppies.
   c. Using a Windows Server 2003 installation CD-ROM.
   d. Executing Winnt.exe over the network.

4. The /udf:id[.UDF_file] switch along with an UDF identifier modifies the _____ file.
   a. startup
   b. source
   c. answer
   d. temporary

5. Which of the following are true for the Per Device or Per User licensing mode?
   a. You can change your licensing mode setting from Per Device or Per User to Per Server licensing at no additional cost.
   b. Enables you to specify a maximum number of concurrent server connections and reject any additional logon attempts.
   c. Requires separate CALs for each device or user.

   d. Is more suitable for companies with small networks using Windows Server 2003 than Per Server.

6. A driver that is not listed in the Windows Server Catalog definitely will not function.
   a. True
   b. False

7. RIS can be used to install which of the following operating systems? (Choose all that apply.)
   a. Windows 2000 Professional
   b. Windows XP
   c. Windows NT 4.0
   d. Windows 2003 Server
   e. Windows Me

8. Which of the following command lines will install the Windows 2003 Recovery Console as part of the operating system installation?
   a. Winnt /cmdcons
   b. Winnt32 /cmdcons
   c. Winnt /cmd: winnt32 /cmdcons
   d. Winnt32 /e: winnt32 /cmdconse
   e. Winnt /e: winnt32 /cmdcons

9. During the installation of Windows Server 2003, you are required to use the manufacturer's drivers for a few different custom hardware devices. These drivers are not signed or listed in the Windows Server Catalog. After installation, you will receive a blue screen occasionally, and you also will receive the error message: IRQL_NOT_LESS_OR_EQUAL. What is the first step you should take in order to resolve this problem with the least amount of administrative effort?
   a. Remove all custom hardware and reboot.
   b. Install generic drivers for each device from the installation CD.
   c. Remove each device one at a time to see which driver is causing the failure.
   d. Contact the manufacturer for updated drivers for each device.

Projects: On Your Own

1. Upgrade a **Windows NT Server 4.0** system to **Windows Server 2003**. Set the licensing mode to Per Device or Per User.
   a. Execute **Winnt32.exe**.
   b. Select the option that initiates the upgrade process.
   c. Accept the License Agreement.
   d. Move to the **Windows Server 2003 Setup** screen.
   e. Specify the size of the partition that you want to create as **2048 MB**.
   f. Select the hard disk partition as **C:New (Unformatted)**.
   g. Move to the **Welcome to the Windows Server 2003 Setup Wizard**.
   h. Move to the **Regional Settings** screen and click **Next**.
   i. Accept the default settings and move to the **Personalize Your Settings** screen.
   j. Specify your name and the organization name.
   k. Move to the **Licensing Mode** screen.
   l. Select the Per Device or Per User licensing mode and move to the **Computer Name And Administrator Password** screen.
   m. Specify the computer name and administrator password.
   n. Move to the **Networking Settings** window.
   o. Accept the default network component and move to the **Workgroup or Computer Domain** screen.
   p. Specify the domain name for your computer, and move to the **Join Computer to Domain** dialog box.
   q. Type your name and password with the permission to join the domain and move to the **Installing Components** screen.
   r. Move to the **Performing Final Tasks** screen that brings you to the **Completing the Windows Server 2003 Setup Wizard** screen. Click **Finish**.

2. Set the driver signing option on a Windows Server 2003 computer to prevent the installation of unsigned driver files.
   a. Log on to the server as an **Administrator**.
   b. Access the **Control Panel** and choose **System** to display the **System Properties** dialog box.
   c. Display the **Driver Signing Options** dialog box.
   d. Specify the option that prevents the installation of unsigned driver files.
   e. Close all dialog boxes.

3. Create a hardware profile and disable the printer for it on a Windows Server 2003.
   a. Log on to the server as an **Administrator**.
   b. Open the **Hardware Profiles** dialog box.
   c. Copy and rename the default hardware profile.
   d. Display the **Properties** dialog box for the selected profile.
   e. Select the **This is a portable computer** check box.
   f. Click the **The computer is docked** option button.
   g. Select the **Always include this profile as an option where Windows starts** check box.
   h. Close all dialog boxes.
   i. Restart the computer. When the Hardware Profile/Configuration Recovery menu opens, select the new profile name. Log back on as an Administrator and open the Device Manager window.
   j. Open the **Printer Port (LPT1) Properties** dialog box.
   k. From the **Device usage** list, select the **Do not use this device in the current hardware profile (disable)** option.
   l. Close all dialog boxes and windows.

Problem Solving Scenarios

1. You are the network administrator for a medium-sized business. Management has recently decided to upgrade the company's network. You have been asked to install Windows Server 2003 on the network. Prepare a detailed report listing the pre-installation tasks you need to carry out before a clean installation of Windows Server 2003 can be performed. Also describe the various phases involved in installing Windows Server 2003.

2. As part of the network upgrade, the network's current member server running Windows NT 4.0 will be upgraded to a Windows Server 2003 domain controller. Draft a report outlining the steps you would take to upgrade the server.

3. You are the network administrator for your company. The Customer Support Manager wants you to set up a computer on which customers can view information about upcoming promotions. For security reasons, the computer should be configured as a stand-alone computer. However, the Customer Support Manager wants the computer to be able to connect to the company network, if necessary. After discussing it with the Customer Support Manager, you decide to set up different hardware profiles on the computer to support these different roles: a stand-alone promotional kiosk and a network client. You now need to create a new hardware profile on the computer. You will also need to disable the network adapter for the profile, make it the default profile, and test if the profile allows access to the company network. Outline the steps you would take to achieve this configuration on the computer.

Introducing Active Directory

Built on the foundation of the Windows 2000 Server operating system, Windows Server 2003 provides a directory service called Active Directory that facilitates the management of resources on multiple servers and multiple clients. Active Directory is a centralized and standardized system that automates network management of user data, security, and distributed resources, and enables interoperation with other directories. Active Directory is designed especially for distributed networking environments.

Active Directory has been enhanced to offer Windows Server 2003 networks lower total cost of ownership (TCO), increased scalability, replication capabilities, and an easy-to-navigate hierarchical organization of network resources. Objects are grouped in a hierarchy of containers that comprise four levels: the forest, the tree, the domain, and the organizational unit (OU).

Active Directory's database is often simply referred to as the directory. The directory contains information about objects—users, groups, computers, domains, organizational units (OUs), and security policies. The directory is stored on servers known as domain controllers, which can be accessed by network applications or services. A domain can have one or more domain controllers. Each domain controller has a writeable copy of the directory and a common set of configuration data which are shared between the domain controllers for the domain in which it is a member.

The Active Directory schema contains formal definitions of every object class that can be created in an Active Directory forest. The schema also contains formal definitions of every attribute that can exist in an Active Directory object. Active Directory uses a global catalog, which stores a partial replica of all objects in all domains in an Active Directory forest. One domain controller in each domain stores a copy of the global catalog and is known as the global catalog server.

Like other directory services, the location of objects and resources within Active Directory is made possible by referencing the Active Directory DNS namespace created at the time Active Directory is first implemented. DNS uses the namespace to resolve a fully qualified domain name to an IP address.

Active Directory architecture consists of three service layers along with interfaces, as well as protocols that facilitate communication between the clients and the directory service. The three layers are the DSA (Directory System Agent), Database, and ESE (Extensible Storage Engine) Layers. The core protocol used to communicate with Active Directory is the Lightweight Directory Access Protocol (LDAP). Active Directory accesses protocols through interfaces such as the Active Directory Services Interface (ADSI), the LDAP API, and Windows Messaging.

Before implementing Active Directory on your Windows Server 2003 computer, you must plan the namespace, OUs, and sites to be created. Then, you can use the Active Directory Installation Wizard to install Active Directory. The Active Directory installation process includes the creation of a new forest, a new domain in an existing forest, a new tree in a forest, or an additional domain controller in an existing domain.

Goals

In this lesson, you will learn the basic concepts of Active Directory and how to install it on Windows Server 2003. You will also learn how to create organizational units (OUs), add objects to an OU, and manage objects in a domain.

Lesson 3 Introducing Active Directory

Skill	Exam 70-290 Objective
1. Identifying the Features of Active Directory	Basic knowledge
2. Introducing Active Directory Architecture	Basic knowledge
3. Examining Underlying Active Directory Concepts	Basic knowledge
4. Introducing the Basic Elements of Active Directory	Basic knowledge
5. Planning the Implementation of Active Directory	Basic knowledge
6. Installing Active Directory	Basic knowledge
7. Working with Microsoft Management Console (MMC) and Snap-Ins	Basic knowledge
8. Creating Organizational Units	Basic knowledge
9. Managing Active Directory Objects	Basic knowledge

Requirements

To complete this lesson, you will need administrative rights on a Windows Server 2003 computer.

skill 1

Identifying the Features of Active Directory

exam objective   Basic knowledge

overview

Active Directory is the directory service for Windows Server 2003. A **directory service** is a database that stores information about network objects. An **object** is any "thing," either tangible or abstract, about which data is stored, such as users, computers, applications, or printers. An object has attributes that hold data describing the concrete identity of the object. As a directory service, Active Directory provides consistent methods to name, describe, locate, manage, and secure information about the objects in a Windows Server 2003 network **(Figure 3-1)**. It is a tool that provides a single point of administration for all resources and connects directories across a network.

Active Directory includes the following features:

◆ **Centralized management:** Active Directory provides a single consistent management interface to centrally manage the users and clients on a Windows Server 2003 network. Centralized management reduces redundancy and lowers the maintenance costs for a network.

◆ **Security:** Active Directory provides enhanced security services using multiple authentication protocols such as Kerberos, X.509 certificates, and smart cards to secure network resources.

◆ **Object-oriented storage:** Active Directory uses objects to represent network resources such as users, groups, and applications. All objects have attributes or characteristics that are associated with them, which define their properties and behaviors. Objects in Active Directory include users, printers, servers, files, folders, shares, and organizational units. The information related to the objects and their attributes is stored in the directory database, which enables faster data retrieval.

◆ **Hierarchical organization:** Active Directory organizes objects hierarchically to simplify access and administration of network resources.

◆ **Multi-master replication:** Active Directory uses **multi-master replication** to create multiple copies, known as replicas, of the directory database and makes them available throughout the network **(Figure 3-2)**. Multi-master replication enhances network performance, ensures the availability of resources, and increases flexibility in distributed environments. Since all domain controllers in a Windows Server 2003 network are equals, all domain controllers replicate Active Directory data rather than having a single master replicator server responsible for updating Active Directory on all of the domain controllers. Therefore, when you make changes to Active Directory on one domain controller, the changes are automatically replicated to all other domain controllers in the domain. All domain controllers are responsible for keeping Active Directory up to date.

◆ **Integration with DNS:** Domain Name System (DNS) is an Internet standard service that translates computer names to Internet Protocol (IP) addresses in order to connect various objects in TCP/IP networks. Active Directory uses the DNS namespace to locate objects within the directory. The DNS contains information used to resolve a fully qualified domain name to an IP address. Because Active Directory names are DNS names, Active Directory references the DNS namespace during the resolution of object queries. For example, a Windows Server 2003 domain name, child.parent.yourdomain.com, identifies a domain named "child" which is a child domain of the domain named "parent". We will explain this process further in Skill 4 of this Lesson.

◆ **Support for Lightweight Directory Access Protocol (LDAP):** Active Directory is integrated with Internet standards through the use of LDAP. **LDAP** is a communication protocol that enables clients to access data in the Active Directory database. It is the protocol used to access Active Directory services, and defines standards for sharing information among computers running Active Directory.

Figure 3-1 Active Directory

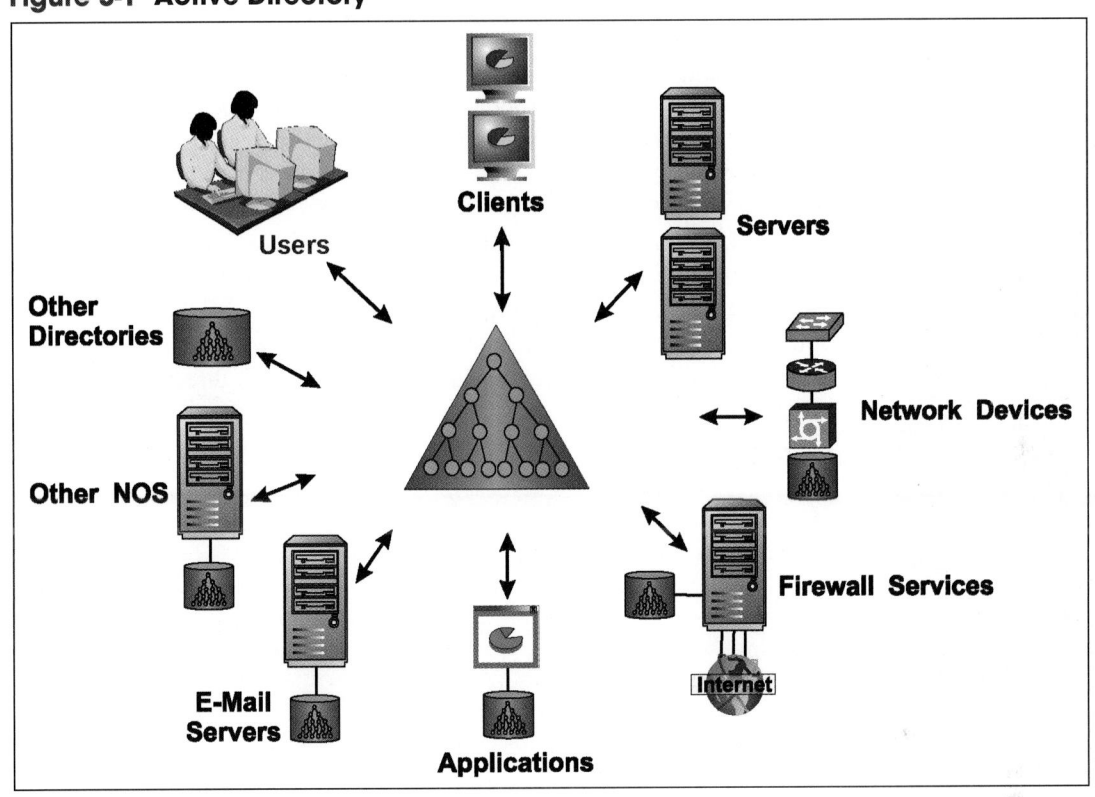

Figure 3-2 Replication

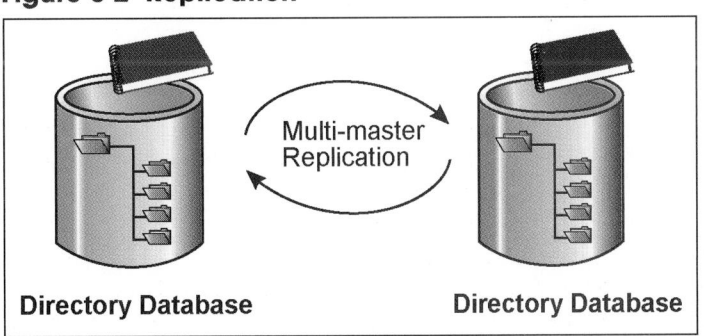

skill 1

Identifying the Features of Active Directory (cont'd)

exam objective

Basic knowledge

overview

◆ **Standard name formats:** Active Directory uses several naming formats, such as Universal Naming Convention (UNC) and LDAP URL, to identify objects on a network. In order to access a network object using the UNC naming convention, you must specify the exact path to it in the following format: **\\servername\sharename**, where **servername** is the name of the server and **sharename** is the name of the shared resource. The LDAP URL format specifies the Active Directory server and the attributed name of the object, which defines the properties associated with it. An example of an LDAP URL is:

LDAP://servername.yourdomain.com/CN=Corp, OU=sys, OU=product,
where CN is the common name of the object and OU is the organizational unit.

◆ **Scalability:** You can expand Active Directory to meet the needs of your organization. Active Directory can include multiple trees and multiple domains per tree, each with one or more domain controllers, enabling you to scale the directory to meet any network requirements.

Table 3-1 summarizes these features.

Table 3-1   Features of Active Directory and their Functions

Feature	Functions
Centralized management	Allows an administrator to manage changes to large numbers of servers (often in remote locations), from a central location through the use of such features as Windows Scripting Host and Terminal Services.
Security	Secures network resources through the use of Access Control Lists (ACLs) for resources stored on NTFS partitions and through the use of multiple authentication protocols.
Object-oriented storage	Information about network elements is stored in the form of objects. These objects can be assigned attributes, which describe specific characteristics about the object. This lets companies store a wide range of information in the directory and tightly control access to it.
Hierarchical organization	Simplifies access and administration of network resources.
Multi-master replication	Provides high performance, availability, and flexibility in distributed environments. Allows an organization to create multiple copies of the directory, known as directory replicas, and place them throughout the network. Changes made anywhere on the network are automatically replicated throughout the network.
Integration with DNS	DNS is used as a locator service, resolving Active Directory domain, site, and service names to an IP address. An Active Directory client queries its configured DNS server for the IP address of the server hosting the directory service, running on a domain controller for a specified domain, to log on to an Active Directory domain.
Support for Lightweight Directory Access Protocol (LDAP)	Integrates Active Directory with Internet standards and enables clients to access Active Directory.
Standard name formats	Used for the identification and access of network objects. Includes naming formats such as Universal Naming Convention (UNC) and LDAP URL.
Scalability	Support for unlimited directory size and unlimited domain controllers, allowing Active Directory to support organizations of any size.

skill 2

Introducing Active Directory Architecture

exam objective

Basic knowledge

overview

Active Directory is built in a layered architecture in which the layers represent the server processes that provide directory services to client applications. Active Directory consists of three service layers, several interfaces, and protocols that work together to provide directory services, and the underlying Data Store **(Figure 3-3)**. The three service layers accommodate the different types of information that are required to locate records in the directory database. Above the service layers in this architecture are the protocols and APIs (APIs are on the clients only) that enable communication between clients and directory services or, in the case of replication, between domain controllers hosting the directory service. The three service layers are listed below:

◆ **Directory System Agent (DSA) Layer:** The DSA is the process that provides access to the data store. The data store is the physical store of directory information located on a hard disk. The DSA is the server-side process that creates an instance of a directory service. Clients use one of the supported interfaces to connect (bind) to the DSA and then search for, read, and write Active Directory objects and their attributes. Applications need to connect to the DSA Layer to access objects in Active Directory through one of the supported interfaces such as LDAP (Lightweight Directory Access Protocol) or ADSI (Active Directory Services Interfaces).

◆ **Database Layer**: The Database Layer provides an object view of database information, thereby isolating the upper layers of the directory service from the underlying database system. The Database Layer is an internal interface. No database access calls are made directly to the Extensible Storage Engine; instead, all database access is routed through the Database Layer.

◆ **Extensible Storage Engine Layer**: This layer has direct contact with the records in the Data Store. It is based on an object's relative distinguished name attribute. This layer can support a database up to a maximum of 16 terabytes (TB) in size.

The **Data Store** (The **Ntds.dit** file) stores the records that make up Active Directory's database. The Ntds.dit file contains the schema information, global catalog, and all of the objects stored on the domain controller. It is stored in the *%systemroot%*\Ntds folder, by default.

Located above the three service layers are APIs and protocols that facilitate communication between the clients and the directory service. The protocols and APIs supported by Active Directory are described in **Table 3-2**.

Figure 3-3 Active Directory Architecture

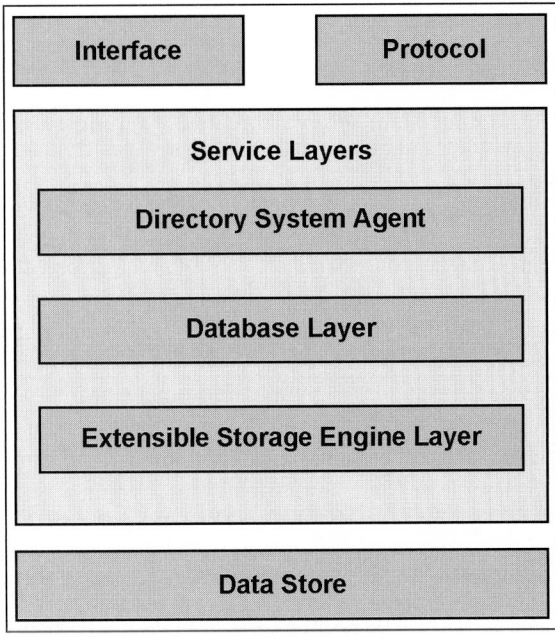

Exam 70-290

Table 3-2 Protocols and APIs supported by Active Directory

Protocol/Interface	Description
LDAP	LDAP is both a protocol and an API. The LDAP protocol is the Active Directory core protocol and is the preferred method of interacting with Active Directory; the LDAP API provides access to the LDAP protocol. The ADSI is the COM interface to Active Directory that uses LDAP as the protocol. LDAP is used by clients to query, create, update, and delete information stored in Active Directory and by domain controllers to communicate with each other.
MAPI-RPC	The MAPI-RPC (Messaging Application Programming Interface-Remote Procedure Call) protocol enables communication with Microsoft Exchange Server components and provides compatibility with existing messaging clients, allowing them to access Active Directory. Active Directory supports the MAPI-RPC address book provider, which allows access to Active Directory (for example, to find the telephone number of a user).
Active Directory Services Interface (ADSI)	The ADSI is an interface that provides a single set of directory service interfaces that are used to manage network objects. This simplifies the development and administration of distributed systems. Administrative tasks, such as adding or deleting an object and managing printers, can be performed using ADSI.
LDAP C API	LDAP API is a C-language API to the LDAP protocol. RFC 1823 specifies the LDAP APIs that are required for a client to gain access to a directory service that supports the LDAP protocol. This API set is relatively simple and supports both synchronous and asynchronous calls to the server. Applications that are written in LDAP are compatible only with LDAP directory services.

skill 3

Examining Underlying Active Directory Concepts

exam objective

Basic knowledge

overview

In order to understand Active Directory, you must first be familiar with the concepts of schema, global catalog, and namespaces.

Schema: The Active Directory **schema** contains formal definitions of every object class that can be created in an Active Directory forest. The schema also contains formal definitions of every attribute that can exist in an Active Directory object. The schema is the database design, which can be extended by adding new object classes or new attributes. Object classes describe the possible directory objects that can be created. Each class is a collection of attributes. When you create an object, the attributes store the information that describes the object. The User class, for example, is composed of many attributes, including Network Address, Home Directory, and so on. Every object in Active Directory is an instance of an object class. Experienced developers and network administrators can dynamically extend the schema by defining new classes and new attributes for existing classes. Active Directory does not support deletion of schema objects; however, objects can be marked as deactivated, providing many of the benefits of deletion. Furthermore, the schema defines the parent object class from which the current object class is derived. In addition, applications can dynamically update a schema by extending the existing classes and defining new classes and new attributes (**Figure 3-4**).

To understand the concept of a schema, think about the characteristics of an automobile. Automobiles belong to different classes such as cars, buses, and trucks. All classes share some common attributes by default, for example, wheels, seats, and engines. On the other hand, objects of each class can also possess other optional attributes. Automobiles, for example, can have accessories, such as CD players, air bags, or power steering, which are their optional attributes.

Global catalog: The **global catalog** stores a full Read-Write replica of all object attributes in the directory for its host domain, and a partial replica of all object attributes contained in the directory for every domain in the forest, along with universal groups and group members (**Figure 3-5**). This gives the global catalog the ability to search the entire forest, but also keeps its database relatively light, allowing for improved replication. The domain controller that maintains the copy of the global catalog is known as the **global catalog server**. In contrast, a standard domain controller (without the global catalog role) normally only stores information about objects located in its domain.

The global catalog also provides universal group membership information. This is necessary since universal groups, by definition, do not exist in any one domain; rather, they exist in all domains in the forest. Universal groups will be covered further in Lesson 7.

As mentioned previously, the global catalog is also used to search for objects in the forest. By default, the partial set of attributes that are stored in the global catalog includes those attributes that are most frequently used in search operations. When information about objects is updated, a global catalog server exchanges this information with other global catalog servers in a forest. This ensures that users have access to the latest information about objects. In most cases, there must be a global catalog server on the network, otherwise users, unless they are a member of the Domain Administrators group, will not be able to log on to the network. This is because a global catalog server must be contacted in order to retrieve universal group memberships and User Principal Name-to-domain mappings.

caution

You cannot delete a schema object; however, you can deactivate an object.

caution

Too many global catalog servers on a network unnecessarily increase replication traffic.

Figure 3-4 Schema

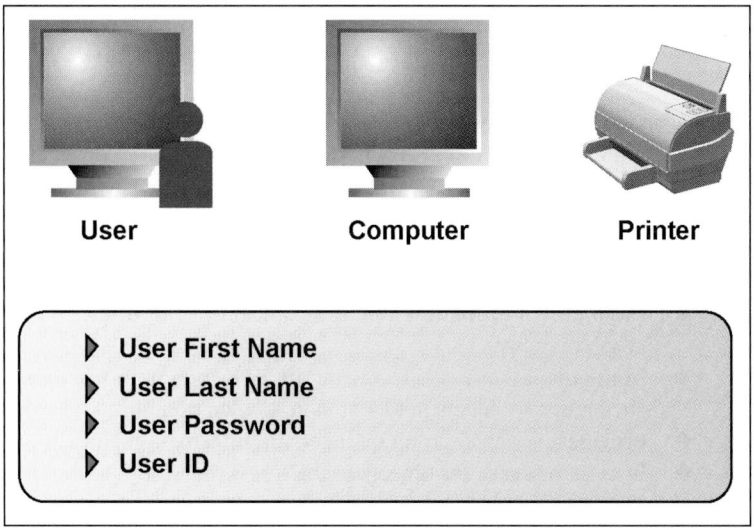

User · Computer · Printer

▷ User First Name
▷ User Last Name
▷ User Password
▷ User ID

Figure 3-5 Global Catalog in Active Directory

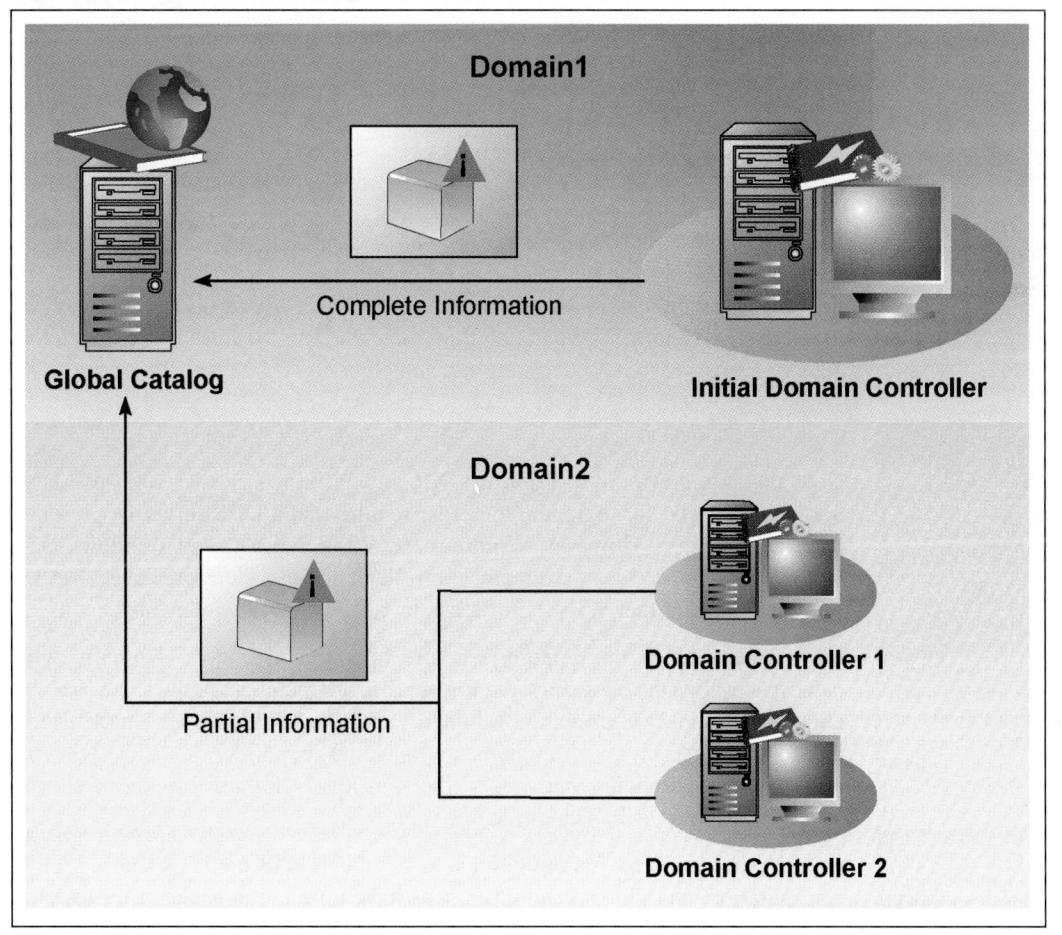

Domain1

Complete Information

Global Catalog · Initial Domain Controller

Domain2

Domain Controller 1

Partial Information

Domain Controller 2

skill 3

Examining Underlying Active Directory Concepts (cont'd)

exam objective

Basic knowledge

overview

A new feature in Windows Server 2003, Universal Group Caching, allows you to configure domain controllers to cache universal group memberships without making those domain controllers global catalog servers. This feature allows you to reduce the total number of global catalog servers on your network considerably, thus reducing overall replication overhead.

To summarize, a global catalog:

◆ Maintains information about all objects in the forest, including universal groups and group members.
◆ Maintains a copy of all objects in all domains in the forest, but only a partial list of attributes for objects not located in its own domain.
◆ Provides universal group membership information and allows users to find resources.
◆ Is used to search for objects in the forest regardless of the location of the data.

Namespace: The resolution of names through the use of Domain Name System (DNS) is central to the operation of Windows networks. Without proper name resolution, users cannot locate resources on the network. It is critical that the design of the DNS namespace be created with Active Directory in mind. All directory services provide a **namespace**, which can be thought of as a bounded area in which the names people use to identify objects are "resolved" or translated in accordance with a naming system or convention. For example, a telephone directory is a namespace where the names of the subscribers are resolved or translated into telephone numbers. Namespaces require a naming system. A **naming system** simply refers to the ways in which a name is specified (see the More section on page 3.14). A naming system supplies a naming service that is available to its users for the purpose of locating directory objects.

Active Directory DNS servers store the information that represents an organization's namespace and work together with the domain controllers to provide correct information to the clients on the location of important Active Directory resources. In the case of a domain logon from a Windows XP computer, for example, it is the DNS server that tells the Windows XP computer where to check the account credentials before the user can be logged on. Without at least one DNS server on a Windows Server 2003 network, a domain controller could not be located.

Note that Windows 2000, Windows XP, and Windows Server 2003 use DNS to locate a domain controller for login and therefore require that a DNS server be present for users in a domain to log on. However, Windows 9x, Windows Me, and Windows NT systems use NetBIOS naming to locate a domain controller, and must therefore have a NetBIOS name resolution method (either WINS, broadcast, or LMHOSTS) in order for users to log on.

Namespaces define the domain structure in Active Directory. Domains with contiguous namespaces, like the ones shown in **Figure 3-6**, are members of the same tree. A tree in Active Directory is simply a grouping of domains with a contiguous namespace. Trees are used for the logical organization of domains, and have no real effect on Active Directory other than naming. The domain that hosts the top-level domain in the tree (in this case, yourdomain.com), is known as the tree root.

On the other hand, forests are defined as a collection of domains sharing the same schema, configuration, and global catalog. Forests have no relation to namespaces, other than being referred to by the forest root domain's name. For instance, you can have a single forest composed of a single tree, as shown in Figure 3-6, or, you can have a single forest composed of multiple trees, as shown in **Figure 3-7**. Domains, trees, and forests are discussed further in Skill 4.

Figure 3-6 Contiguous namespaces (tree)

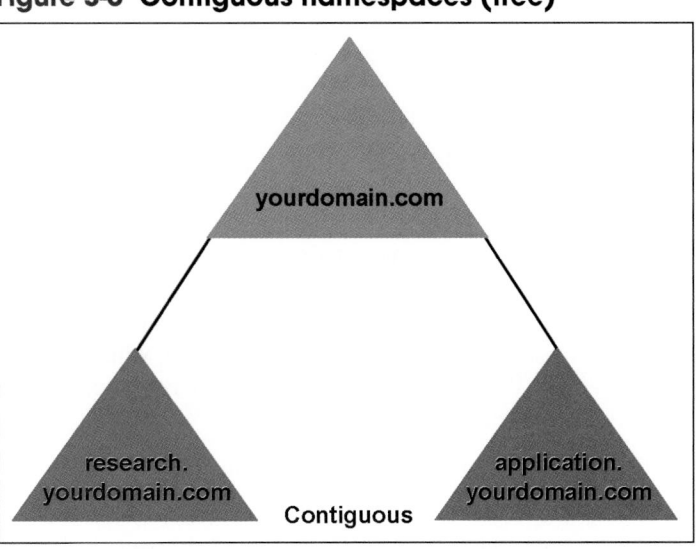

Figure 3-7 Disjointed namespaces (multiple trees)

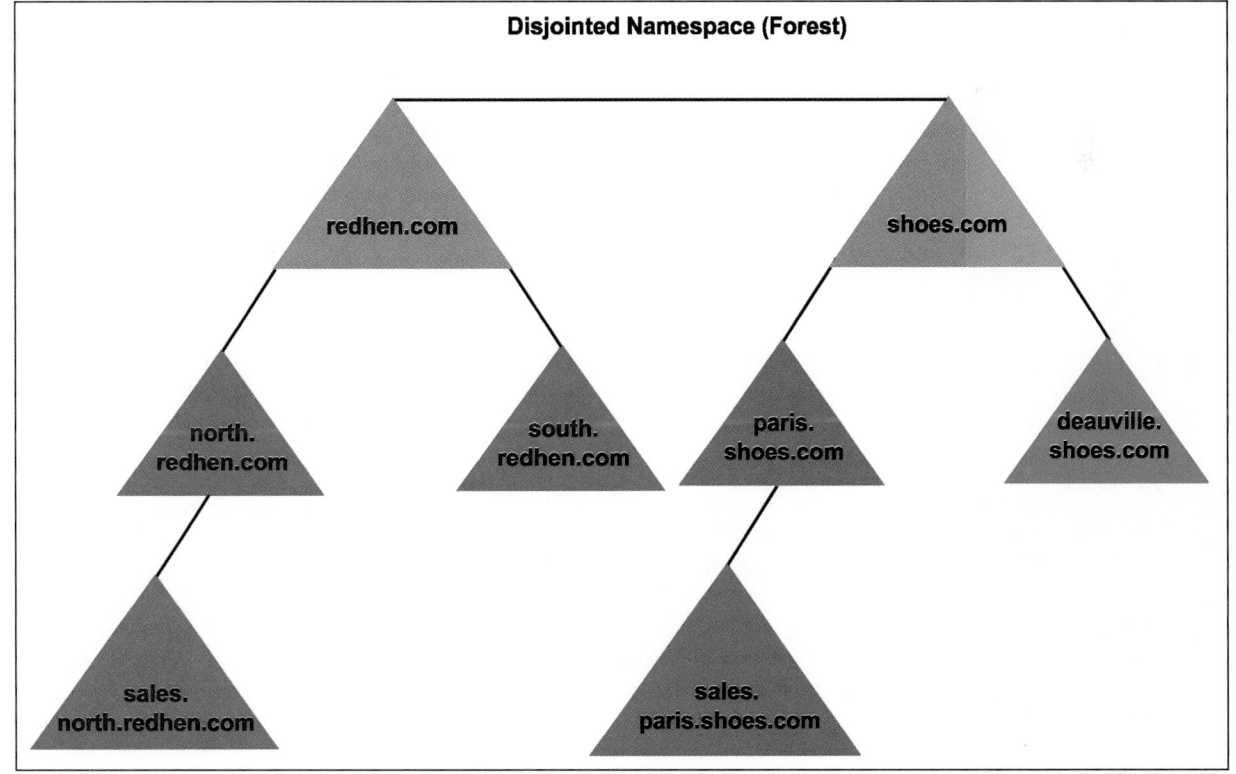

skill 3

Examining Underlying Active Directory Concepts (cont'd)

exam objective

Basic knowledge

more

Active Directory identifies each object in the following ways **(Figure 3-8)**:

Globally Unique Identifier (GUID): A **GUID** defines the identity of an object in Active Directory. When you create an object in Active Directory, the Directory Service Agent (DSA) automatically assigns a 128-bit number as the GUID to the object. Even if you move an object from one domain to another, the GUID remains the same. The Windows operating system identifies each object in the network by a Security Identifier (SID). In Windows Server 2003, in addition to a SID for security principles, an object is also associated with a GUID. However, a GUID never changes, unlike a SID, which is unique only within a domain and changes if an object is moved or renamed. You can track the movement of an object because a GUID is unique across domains.

Distinguished Name (DN): A **Distinguished Name (DN)** is used to uniquely name an Active Directory Object. All objects can be referenced using a Distinguished Name.

For example, the user object **Gregory Johnson**, in the **Accounting** OU, in the **ABC Corp.com** domain can be written as follows:

CN=Gregory Johnson, OU=Accounting, DC=ABC Corp, DC=com,

where CN stands for the common name, OU is the organizational unit, and DC is the domain component name.

Relative Distinguished Name (RDN): A **Relative Distinguished Name** is the portion of the Distinguished Name that uniquely identifies an object within the object's parent container. For example, the RDN for the user object Gregory Johnson is: CN = Gregory Johnson. The DN and RDN for a user object are shown in **Figure 3-9**.

User Principal Name (UPN): A **User Principal Name** is the name of a system user in an e-mail address format. The user name (or "username") is followed by the "at sign" followed by the name of the DNS domain with which the user is associated. An example might look like: **GJohnson@ABCCorp.com**. The UPN is used to identify an Active Directory object and is an acceptable format for user authentication.

tip

The default UPN suffix for a user account is the DNS domain name of the domain that contains the user account.

Figure 3-8 Naming conventions

Distinguished Name	Domain Name/Users/Business Development Group/Team Leaders/Gregory Johnson
Relative Distinguished Name	Gregory Johnson
Globally Unique Identifier	128-bit number → GUID → Retrieves regardless of DN
User Principal Name	Gregory Johnson in yourdomain.com Gregory_J@yourdomain.com

Figure 3-9 The DN and RDN for a user object

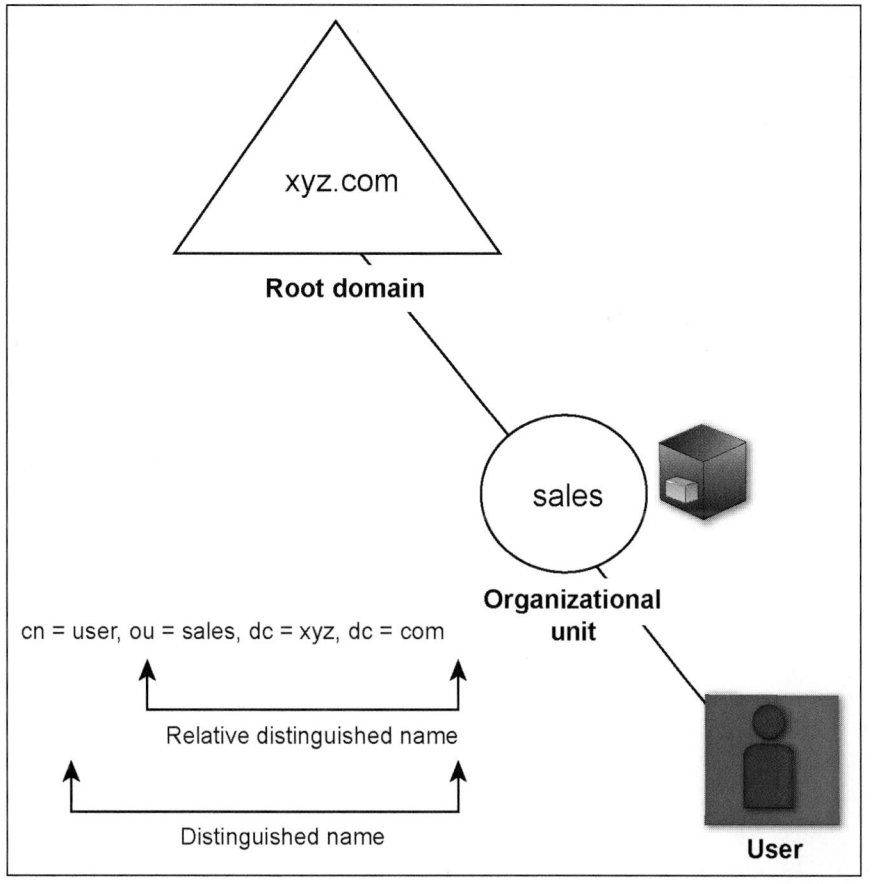

skill 4
Introducing the Basic Elements of Active Directory

exam objective

Basic knowledge

overview

Active Directory organizes resources in a network in a hierarchical structure that is similar to the tree-like structure of folders and subfolders. Active Directory stores information about the network resources and enables administrators and other network users to access this information. Similar to folders and subfolders where a file forms the basic element, objects are the basic elements of Active Directory. These objects are grouped in a hierarchy of containers that comprise four levels: the forest, the tree, the domain, and the organizational units (OU) **(Figure 3-10)**. The physical network structure of Active Directory includes sites, which are used to control replication and authentication when limited bandwidth is an issue. These elements are described further below:

Object: An **object** is any "thing," either tangible or abstract, about which data is stored. It can be a network resource, such as a user, group, printer, or a virtual object such as a forest, tree, domain, or OU.

Each object is defined by a set of attributes related to its properties. When you create an object, the Active Directory is populated with some of the attributes for the object. You can also specify additional attributes for the object. For example, when you create a user account object, Active Directory automatically specifies the Globally Unique Identifier (GUID) for the user account. Other attributes of the user account that you can specify include the user logon name, password, and e-mail address. The common types of objects that can be created in Active Directory **(Table 3-3)** are as follows:

♦ **Computer:** Identifies a computer on the network.
♦ **User:** Consists of information that allows a user to log on to a machine, along with attributes such as first name, last name, and password.
♦ **Group:** Consists of users, computers, and other groups in the forest and simplifies administration of large numbers of objects.
♦ **Shared Folder:** Acts as a pointer to a shared folder on the network.
♦ **Printer:** Acts as a pointer to a printer on the network.

Domain: A **domain** is a group of computers and devices on a network that constitute a single security boundary within Active Directory, but can span more than one physical location. Every domain has its own security policies and security relationships with other domains. Domains co-existing under the same namespace are a single tree. When multiple domains are connected by trust relationships and share a common schema, configuration, and global catalog, they constitute a forest.

A domain consists of the following types of computers in a Windows Server 2003 network:

♦ **Domain controller:** A **domain controller** is a computer that stores a replica of the directory database. When you make any changes to the domain database, Windows Server 2003 automatically updates the information in all of the domain controllers in the domain. A domain controller stores the security policies and security accounts for a domain. A domain controller authenticates a user to log on to the domain and access the shared resources.

♦ **Member server:** A **member server** is a Windows NT 4.0, 2000, or Server 2003 computer that is part of a domain but does not store a replica of the directory database. A Windows Server 2003 member server can perform all Windows Server 2003 services except Active Directory services.

♦ **Client computers:** Client computers are computers running operating systems that can communicate with the Active Directory for user authentication and resource access.

Organizational unit: An **organizational unit** is a container object for organizing objects within a domain. OUs can contain users, groups, resources, and other OUs. For example, you can group objects, such as users, groups, printers, applications, and other network resources

tip

Active Directory can consist of one or more domains, and these domains can be spread across different physical locations.

Figure 3-10 Hierarchical structure of Active Directory

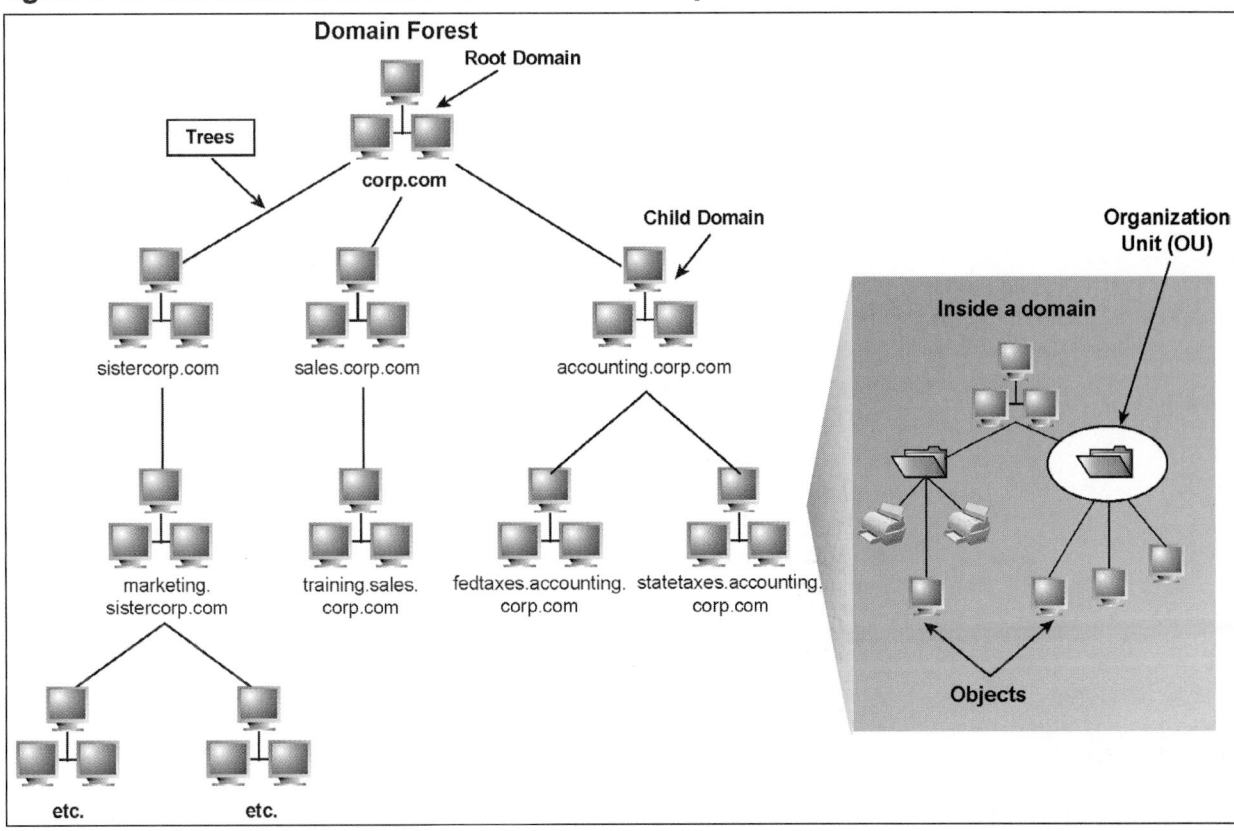

Table 3-3 Types of objects that can be created in Active Directory		
Icon used to represent the object	**Type of object**	**Description**
	Computer	Designates a computer on the network.
	User	Consists of information that allows a user to log on to a computer, along with attributes such as first name, last name, and password.
	Group	Consists of users, computers, and other groups on the network and simplifies administration of large numbers of objects.
	Shared folder	Acts as a pointer to a shared folder on the network.
	Contact	Identifies users who do not have any security permissions and cannot log on to the network. It identifies users for sending e-mails.
	Printer	Acts as a pointer to a printer on the network.

skill 4

Introducing the Basic Elements of Active Directory (cont'd)

exam objective   Basic knowledge

overview

in a domain into one organizational unit. Organizational units enable the delegation of administration to distinct segments of the directory. This provides more flexibility in managing the objects in a business unit, department, or other organizational division. A company with five departments can have one domain for the entire company and five departmental OUs within that domain. The employees in each department will have user accounts, shared files, and shared printers that can be defined as objects in the appropriate OU. Grouping objects into OUs allows for the following object administration:

◆ Creation and organization of child OUs.

◆ Delegation of permissions within specific OUs.

◆ Assignment of Group Policy links.

Tree: A **tree** consists of a set of one or more domains in a hierarchical structure. The first domain created in the forest is called the forest root and this is where the forest name is specified. All domain trees in a forest share the same forest root. If a new tree is created after the forest root, the first domain that is added to this tree is called the **root domain**. The domains under the root domain are called **child domains**, and any domain immediately above another domain is called the **parent domain (Figure 3-11)**. Each tree contains a contiguous namespace, and all domains within that tree follow that contiguous namespace. Within a tree, domains exhibit the following characteristics:

Domains under the root domain possess contiguous names in which the child domain always contains the name of the parent domain. For example, in **Figure 3-11** the parent domain **parent.com** contains two child domains, **childA.parent.com** and **childB.parent.com**. These three domains form a tree.

When multiple domains are created within a tree, a trust relationship is established between the domains such that users in one domain can be authenticated by a domain controller in the other domain. The trust relationship is based on the Kerberos security protocol. According to this protocol, the trust relationship among domains in a tree is transitive and hierarchical. For example, if domain A trusts domain B and domain B trusts domain C, then it is implied that domain A also trusts domain C.

All domains in a tree are members of the same forest.

Forest: A **forest** consists of a group of one or more Active Directory domains that share a common schema, configuration, global catalog, and two-way, transitive trusts **(Figure 3-12).** All trees in a given forest trust each other through transitive two-way trust relationships. Unlike a tree, a forest does not need a distinct name. A forest exists as a set of cross-referenced objects and trust relationships known to the member trees. Trees in a forest form a hierarchy for the purposes of trust.

Sites: A **site** is a location in a network holding Active Directory servers. A site is defined as one or more well connected TCP/IP subnets, meaning that network connectivity is highly reliable and fast **(Figure 3-13)**. A **TCP/IP subnet** is a grouping of devices on a network that share a common IP address range. Dividing a network into subnets is useful for both security and performance reasons.

A site has the following characteristics:

◆ Consists of one or more IP subnets within a physical site which is linked by leased lines or other media to other parts of the organization.

◆ Plays a major role in the Active Directory replication service, which differentiates between replication using a local network connection (intra-site replication) and replication over a slower wide area network (WAN) link (inter-site replication).

Figure 3-11 Multiple domains in a tree

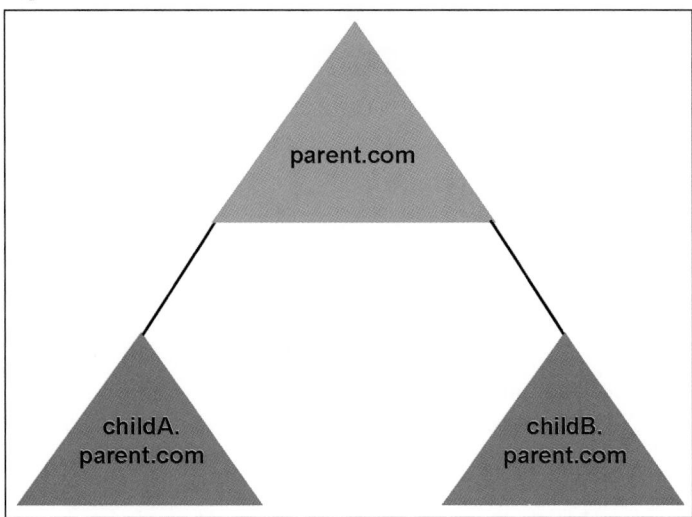

Figure 3-12 Forest

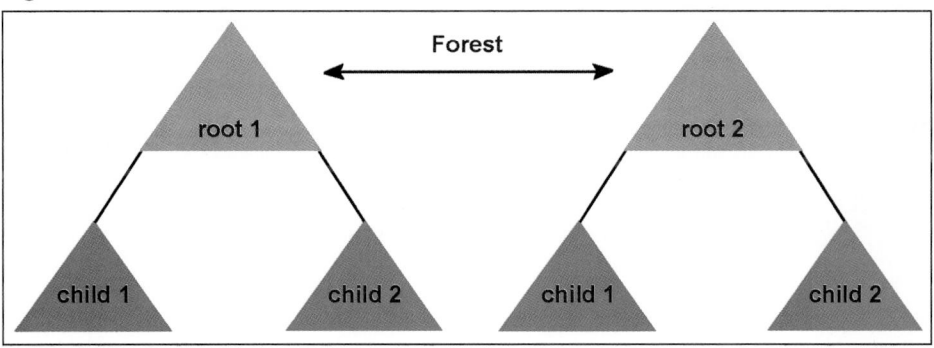

Figure 3-13 Site

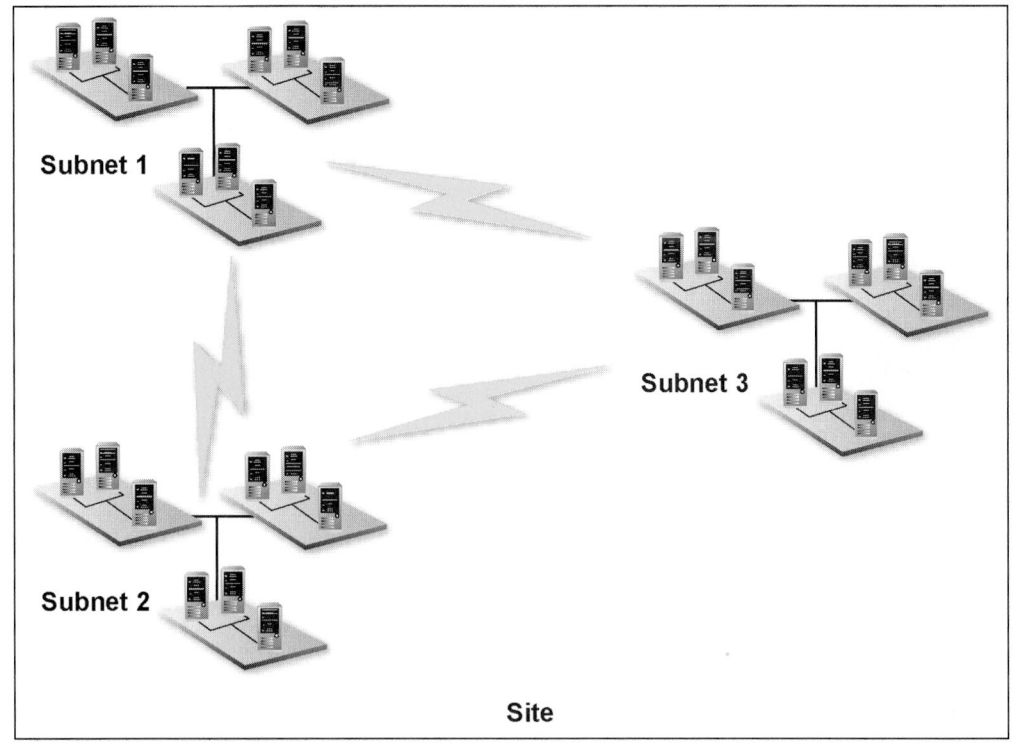

skill 5

Planning the Implementation of Active Directory

exam objective

Basic knowledge

overview

Before implementing Active Directory, you first need to understand the business requirements of your organization and then plan the namespace, sites, domain structure, and organizational units that will be used.

Planning a namespace: Planning the implementation of a new namespace is an important factor before installing Active Directory. In Windows Server 2003, Domain Name System (DNS) servers perform name resolution to resolve computer names to IP addresses, making the access of network resources possible. You need to plan how to integrate Active Directory with the existing DNS and implement Windows Server 2003 DNS. For example, if the external DNS namespace for your organization is yourdomain.com, you can use the same name for the Active Directory namespace or assign a different internal namespace. Assigning the same namespace will enable you to have a single user logon name for the public Internet. For example, username@yourdomain.com would act as both a logon name and an e-mail ID for a user. On the other hand, using different namespaces will simplify administration because the internal and external resources will be easily identified. To decide between having the same or different internal and external DNS names, you must understand their advantages and disadvantages. The advantages and disadvantages of using the same internal and external DNS names as opposed to using separate internal and external DNS names are outlined in **Tables 3-4** and **3-5**.

Designing a site: Planning a site carefully can considerably reduce the possibility that network links will be clogged by replication traffic. In addition, it will allow client computers to access the available resources that are closest to them. When combining IP subnets into sites, you should follow these suggestions:

◆ Combine subnets that run over high bandwidth network connections so they are economical and reliable.
◆ Create one or more sites for domains that spread over two or more far-reaching geographic locations.

Planning a domain structure: After deciding on the namespace philosophy to be used and the site design for Active Directory, you must plan the domain structure. Creating a single domain is recommended, as it reduces the administrative cost to maintain the domain. You can then add organizational units (OUs) that allow you to group objects within the domain. Creating an OU hierarchy for your organization is based on the physical locations of subdivisions, corporate organization, departments, administrative subdivisions, or business functions **(Figure 3-14)**.

Table 3-4 Using the same internal and external DNS names

Advantages	Disadvantages
Only one DNS name needs to be registered.	Results in a complex DNS configuration, due to duplication of effort.

Table 3-5 Using separate internal and external DNS names

Advantages	Disadvantages
The difference between internal and external resources is clear.	Two different naming conventions can be confusing for users.
Easy to manage since separate zones exist for internal and external resources.	Requires registration of multiple DNS names with an Internet DNS (if the internal and external names are not contiguous). When you use separate internal and external namespaces, by default, logon names and e-mail IDs of users are different. You can change this functionality by adding alternative UPN suffixes in the Active Directory Domains and Trusts console.

Figure 3-14 A domain/OU structure for an organization

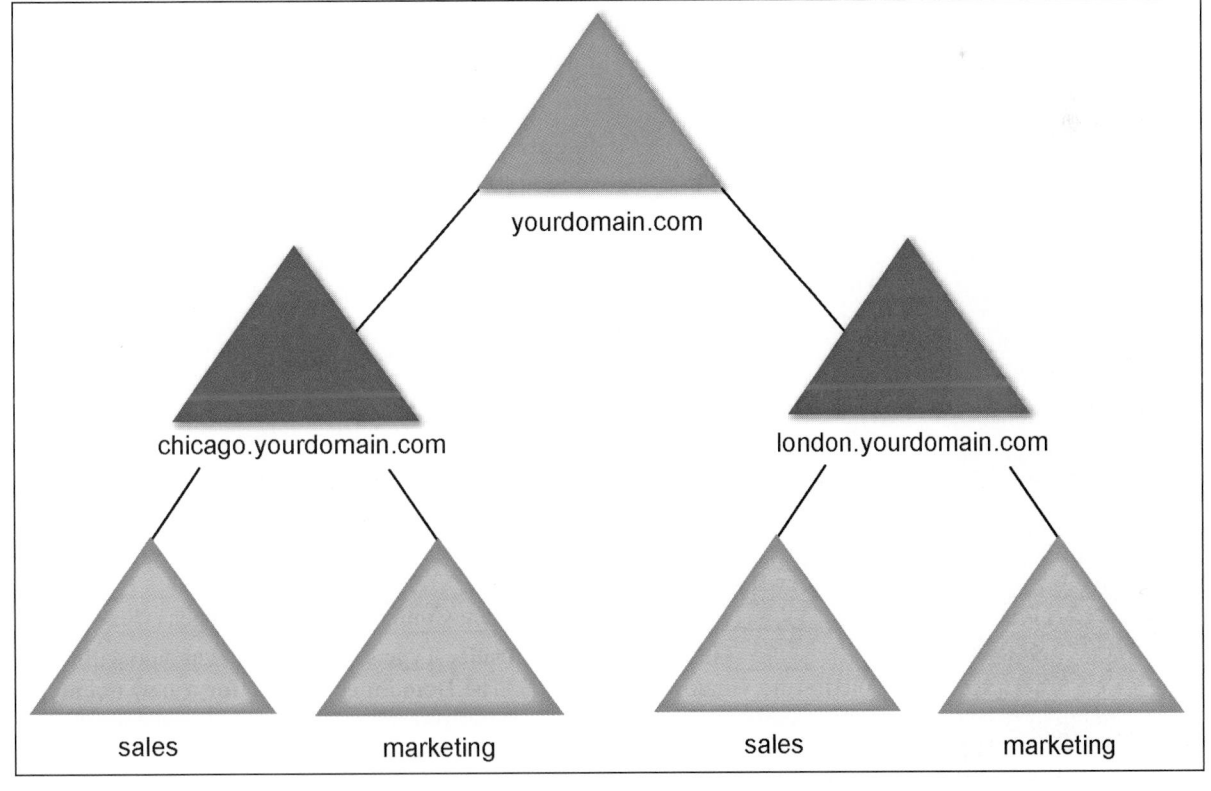

skill 6

Installing Active Directory

exam objective

Basic knowledge

overview

After you have planned the structure of the namespace, sites, and domains, you can install Active Directory on the Windows Server 2003 using the **Active Directory Installation Wizard (Dcpromo.exe)**. When you install Active Directory for the first time, the Active Directory forest is created and the first domain created in the forest is called the forest root. As a result of creating this first domain, the forest name is specified. The forest root comprises the first Active Directory tree and this first domain is called the root domain. Any domains created under the root domain are called child domains.

When you create a domain, by default, the domain is configured to run in **Windows 2000 mixed mode**. This mode allows the coexistence of Windows NT, Windows 2000, and Windows Server 2003 domains. If your domain consists of only Windows 2000 domain controllers, you can switch to **Windows 2000 native mode**. This mode supports Windows 2000 and Windows Server 2003 domains. If your domain has only Windows NT 4.0 servers, and you upgrade a server to Windows Server 2003, you can use **Windows Server 2003 interim mode**. This level is used when there are no Windows 2000 servers and you upgrade a Windows NT PDC (primary domain controller) to Windows Server 2003. Finally, if your domain consists of only Windows Server 2003 domain controllers, you can switch the domain to **Windows Server 2003 mode**, which supports the full Windows Server 2003 Active Directory implementation. Each of these modes has distinct benefits, as outlined previously in Table 2-3 in Lesson 2.

As a result of running the Active Directory Installation Wizard (Dcpromo.exe), the Windows Server 2003 computer becomes a domain controller. When you install Active Directory, some components, such as the database, database log files, and shared system volume, are created automatically. These components are described in **Table 3-6**.

tip

If you switch modes, the process is irreversible.

how to

Install Active Directory using the Active Directory Installation Wizard and create a domain on a Windows Server 2003.

1. Select **Start**, point to **Administrative Tools** and click **Configure Your Server Wizard**.
2. The **Welcome to the Configure Your Server Wizard** screen opens. Click **Next >**.
3. The **Preliminary Steps** screen appears. Verify that the steps outlined have been completed and click **Next >**. A message box appears informing you that the Configure Your Server Wizard will now detect your network settings **(Figure 3-15)**. Wait until the process is complete.
4. If the **Configuration Options** screen opens, select **Custom configuration** and click **Next >**.
5. The **Server Role** screen opens. Select **Domain Controller (Active Directory)** **(Figure 3-16)** and click **Next >**.
6. Review the **Summary of Selections** screen, and click **Next >** to initiate the **Active Directory Installation Wizard**.
7. Click **Next >**. The **Operating System Compatibility** screen opens **(Figure 3-17)**.
8. Click **Next >**. The **Domain Controller Type** screen opens. Here you will specify the role for the Windows Server 2003. The **Domain controller for a new domain** option button is selected by default. Note that if you are adding an additional domain controller to an existing domain, you would select the **Additional domain controller for an existing domain** option button **(Figure 3-18)**.

tip

You can also start the Configure Your Server Wizard from the Manage Your Server window by clicking Administrative Tools and selecting Configure Your Server Wizard.

tip

You can also start the Active Directory Installation Wizard by running the Dcpromo command from the command prompt.

Table 3-6 Components created automatically during Active Directory installation

Component	Description
Database and database log files	The database, Ntds.dit, and database log files are stored in the *%systemroot%*\Ntds folder, by default. However, during installation, you can specify a different storage location. The Ntds.dit file contains the schema information, global catalog, and all of the objects stored on the domain controller.
Shared system volume	The shared system volume, by default, is stored in the *%systemroot%*\Sysvol folder. This volume stores scripts and Group Policy objects for the new domain when you install Active Directory. You must store the shared system volume only on NTFS formatted volumes. Choose the location of Sysvol very carefully, as it cannot be changed later.

Figure 3-15 Detecting Local Area network settings

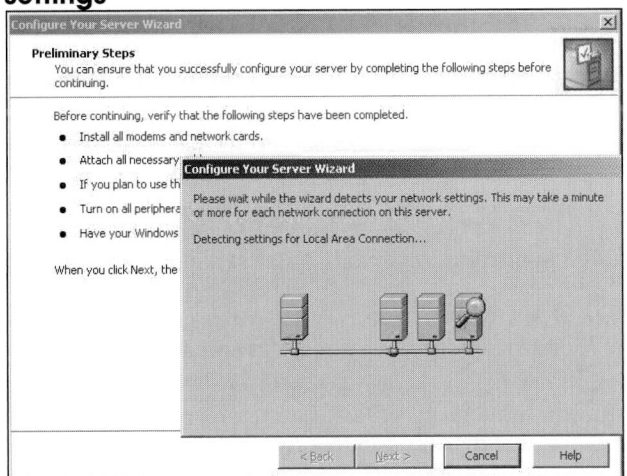

Figure 3-16 The Server Role screen

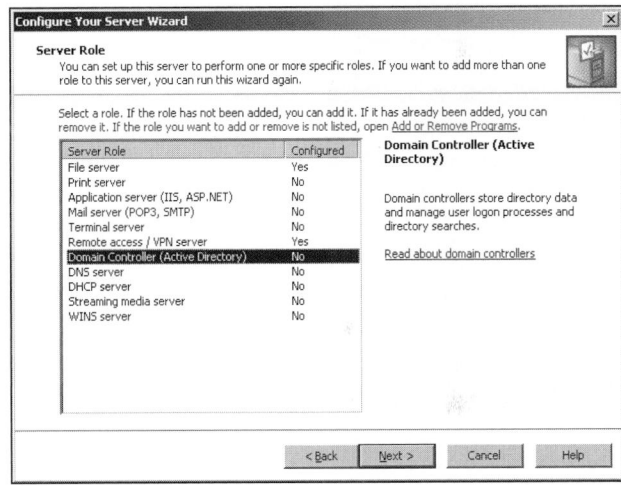

Figure 3-17 The Operating System Compatibility screen

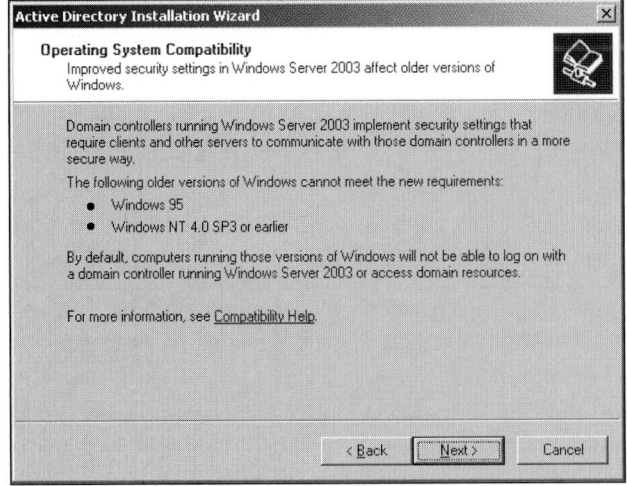

Figure 3-18 The Domain Controller Type screen

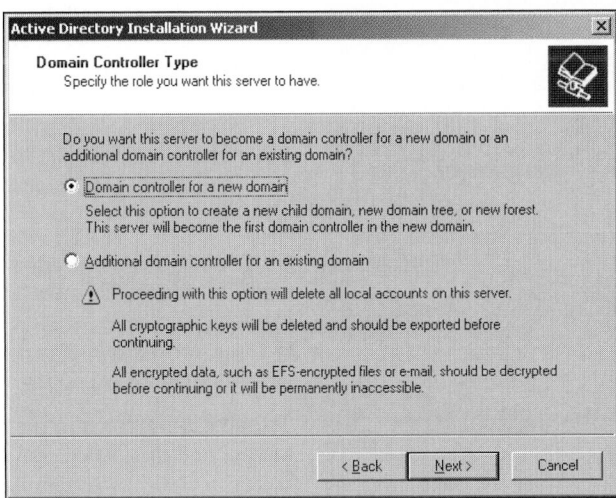

skill 6

Installing Active Directory (cont'd)

exam objective

Basic knowledge

how to

caution

Choose your domain name carefully. While Microsoft provides the new domain renaming tool for Windows 2003 domains, it is still somewhat difficult to change domain names, and doing so could have other consequences.

tip

To optimize Active Directory performance, you should place the database and log files on separate hard disks.

9. Click [Next >]. The **Create New Domain** screen opens. Here you must specify whether you want to create a new forest of domain trees, create a child domain in the existing tree, or place the domain tree in an existing forest. The **Domain in a new forest** option button is selected by default (**Figure 3-19**). To accept the default selection, click [Next >].

10. The **New Domain Name** screen opens. Type a domain name in the **Full DNS name for new domain** text box (**Figure 3-20**), and click [Next >].

11. The **NetBIOS Domain Name** screen opens with the NetBIOS equivalent name of the domain name (**Figure 3-21**). Accept the default domain NetBIOS name for users of earlier versions of Windows and click [Next >].

12. The **Database and Log Folders** screen opens with the default location, *%systemroot%\ NTDS*, in the **Database folder** and **Log folder** text boxes. To accept the default location, click [Next >].

13. The **Shared System Volume** screen opens with the default location, *%systemroot%\ SYSVOL*, already entered in the **Folder location** text box. Note that the Wizard reminds you that the Sysvol folder must be located on an NTFS volume. To accept the default location, click [Next >].

14. Next, the **DNS Registration Diagnostics** screen will open if the Wizard could not determine the name and address of the DNS server with which this domain controller will be registered. Select the **Install and configure the DNS server on this computer, and set this computer to use this DNS server as its preferred DNS server** and click [Next >].

15. The **Permissions** screen opens. Verify that **Permissions compatible only with Windows 2000 and Windows Server 2003 operating systems** is selected and click [Next >] (**Figure 3-22**).

16. The **Directory Services Restore Mode Administrator Password** page appears. Type a password into both the **Restore Mode Password** and **Confirm password** fields and click [Next >].

17. The **Summary** screen opens. Review the contents of this screen, and click [Next >].

18. The **Configuring Active Directory Installation** progress indicator displays as Active Directory is being installed. Note that this process takes several minutes.

19. When the **Completing the Active Directory Installation Wizard** screen appears, click [Finish]. The Windows Server 2003 computer is now a domain controller and Active Directory is installed on this domain controller for the domain. A message box requesting your confirmation to restart the computer opens.

20. Save any open work and click [Restart Now] to restart the computer. Any changes you made to the computer during the installation will be saved permanently on the hard disk. When you reboot the computer, the changes will be automatically applied to your computer.

21. After you reboot and log on using an Administrator account, click [Finish] to close the Configure Your Server Wizard.

more

In addition to creating a new domain, tree, and forest, the Active Directory Installation Wizard enables you to add more domains, trees, or replica domain controllers to your forest. For example, if a new division is added to your organization or your organization opens a new overseas branch, you can choose between creating either new domains or domain trees, depending upon the needs of you organization.

To add a child domain to a domain, select the **Domain controller for a new domain** option button, and then select the **Create a new child domain in an existing domain tree** option button. To add a domain tree to a forest, select the **Domain controller for a new domain** option button, then select the **Create a new domain tree** option button, and finally select the **Place this new domain tree in an existing forest** option button.

Figure 3-19 The Create New Domain screen

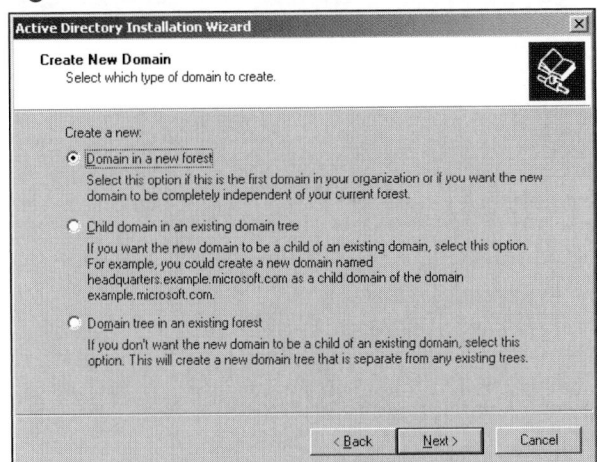

Figure 3-20 Specifying the full DNS domain name

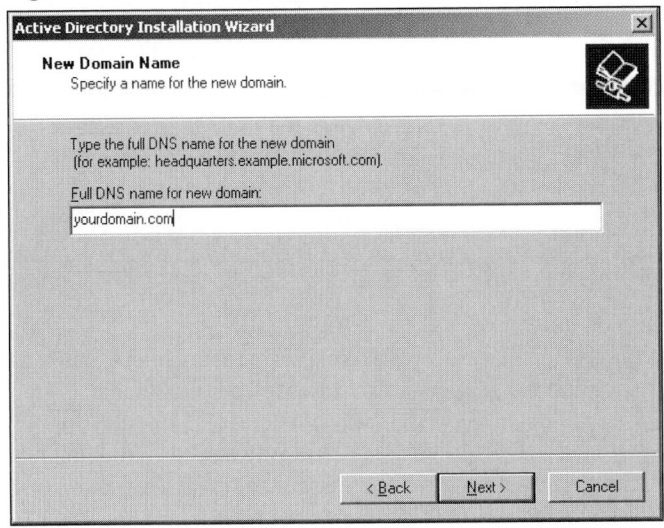

Figure 3-21 The NetBIOS Domain Name screen

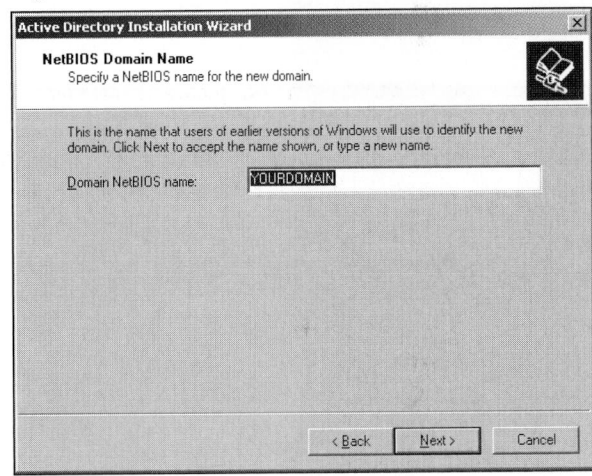

Figure 3-22 The Permissions screen

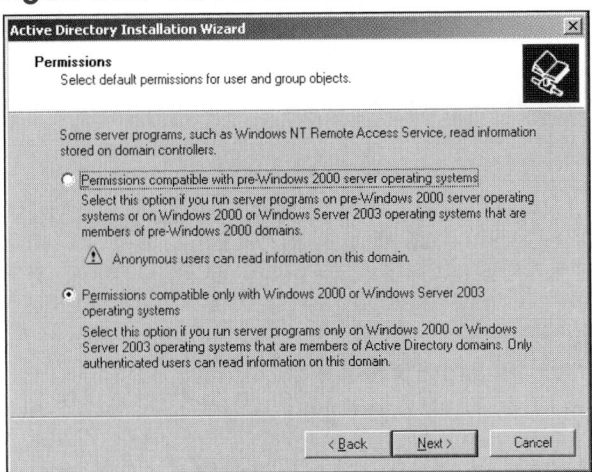

skill 7

Working with Microsoft Management Console (MMC) and Snap-Ins

exam objective

Basic knowledge

overview

Microsoft Management Console (MMC) is an ISV (Independent Software Vendor)-extensible, common console framework for management applications. MMC provides a common host environment for snap-ins, which provide the actual management behavior; MMC does not provide any management functionality by itself. The MMC is a packager of system tools (snap-ins) that can be used by designated users and groups to perform specific administrative tasks. The MMC has been enhanced in Windows Server 2003 to provide improved functionality within the interface. Improvements in the MMC snap-ins and the object picker component make the management of multiple objects easier. Using MMC snap-ins, administrators can do the following:

◆ **Edit multiple user objects.** Multiple object properties can be selected and edited.
◆ **Save queries.** Active Directory service queries can be saved for future use. Results are exportable in XML.
◆ **Quickly select objects using the improved object picker component.** The object picker component has been redesigned and enhanced to provide increased efficiency in finding objects in a large directory. More flexible query capability is also provided.

Snap-ins in an MMC are used to perform administrative tasks such as managing computers, services, and networks. For example, the System Information snap-in is used to collect and display system configuration data that can help technicians to resolve system problems which require input of specific information about your computer. You can combine snap-ins from various vendors such as Microsoft, ISVs, or in-house developers, into an MMC. An MMC acts as a common link between snap-ins provided by different vendors. You can select and combine different snap-ins to perform specific functions.

There are two types of snap-ins: stand-alone and extension. A **stand-alone snap-in** (often referred to simply as a snap-in) provides management functionality without requiring support from another snap-in and is used to perform administrative tasks even if no other snap-in is present in the console. **Extension snap-ins** (often referred to simply as an extension) require a parent snap-in above it in the console tree. Extension snap-ins extend the functionality provided by other snap-ins. For example, it may extend menus, toolbars, and wizards. An extension snap-in becomes functional only when you combine it with the parent snap-in (i.e., the snap-in for which it acts an extension).

Multiple snap-ins can be combined within the MMC interface and saved together as a file that can be distributed for administrative purposes. This combination of tools within a common MMC interface is called a **customized console**. When one of these custom consoles is sent to another person, that person can open the file, and the corresponding tool is loaded as configured. The advantages of using a customized console include:

◆ Administrative tasks can be centralized and customized.
◆ The reusability of the console is enhanced.
◆ Administrators can share a customized console with other administrators.
◆ The accessibility of the console is enhanced as a customized console can be accessed from any computer.

how to

Create a custom console called Active Directory and add the Active Directory Users and Computers snap-in, as well as the Computer Management snap-in, to it.

1. Click Start, then **Run** to open the **Run** dialog box.
2. Type **mmc** in the **Open** text box and click OK to open an empty console (**Figure 3-23**).
3. Open the **File** menu and click **Options** to open the **Options** dialog box. This dialog box displays the options configured for the MMC. Notice that **Author mode** is selected in the **Console mode** list box (**Figure 3-24**). Author mode is used to add or remove snap-ins, create new windows, and view all portions of the console tree.

Figure 3-23 An empty console window

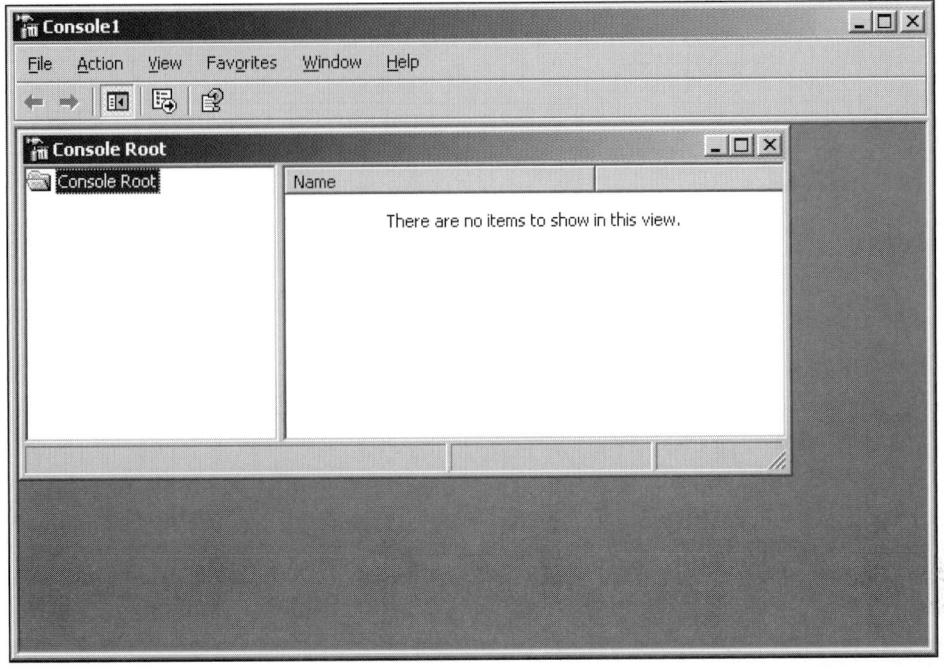

Figure 3-24 Setting the Author mode in the Console Options dialog box

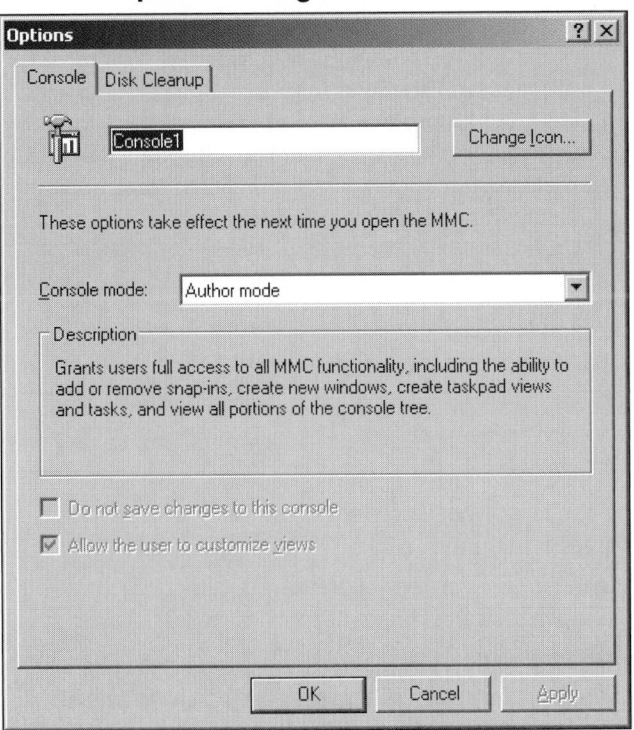

skill 7

Working with Microsoft Management Console (MMC) and Snap-Ins *(cont'd)*

exam objective   Basic knowledge

how to

tip

By default, Windows Server 2003 saves the customized console in the Administrative Tools folder.

4. Click OK to close the **Options** dialog box.
5. Open the **File** menu and select **Add/Remove Snap-in** to open the **Add/Remove Snap-in** dialog box.
6. Click Add... to open the **Add Standalone Snap-in** dialog box (**Figure 3-25**). The dialog box lists the snap-ins that are presently installed on your server and can be added to the console.
7. Select the **Active Directory Users and Computers** console snap-in and click Add... to add this snap-in to the Add/Remove Snap-in dialog box.
8. Repeat the previous step to add both the **Active Directory Sites and Services** and **Active Directory Domains and Trusts** snap-ins.
9. In the **Add Standalone Snap-in** dialog box, select the **Computer Management** snap-in and click Add...
10. The **Computer Management** dialog box opens. In the Computer Management dialog box, you can specify the computers you would like the snap-in to administer. By default, the **Local computer** option button is selected to manage the local computer (**Figure 3-26**). Click Finish to add the Computer Management snap-in to the **Add/Remove Snap-in** dialog box.
11. Click Close to close the **Add Standalone Snap-in** dialog box.
12. Click OK to close the **Add/Remove Snap-in** dialog box.
13. Open the **File** menu and click **Save** to open the **Save as** dialog box. Type **Active Directory.msc** in the **File name** text box. Consoles are saved as a file with an **.msc** extension.
14. Click Save to save the console.

Add and remove extensions from a snap-in.

1. In the Active Directory MMC, open the **File** menu and click **Add/Remove snap-in** to open the **Add/Remove Snap-in** dialog box.
2. Click the **Extensions** tab. Select **Computer Management** in the **Snap-ins that can be extended** list box. Clear the **Add All Extensions** check box.
3. Clear all of the check boxes, except the **Device Manager extension**, **Disk Management Extension**, and **Shared Folders Extension**, to display only these extensions in the Computer Management snap-in (**Figure 3-27**).
4. Your custom console now includes only the extensions you selected (**Figure 3-28**).

Figure 3-25 The Add Standalone Snap-in dialog box

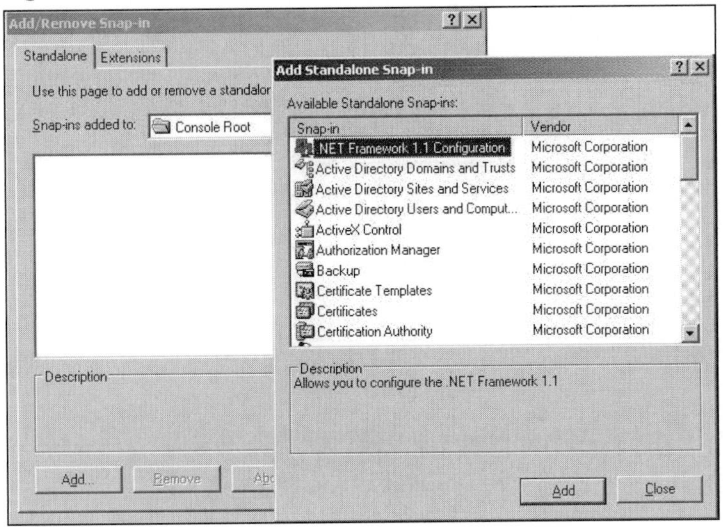

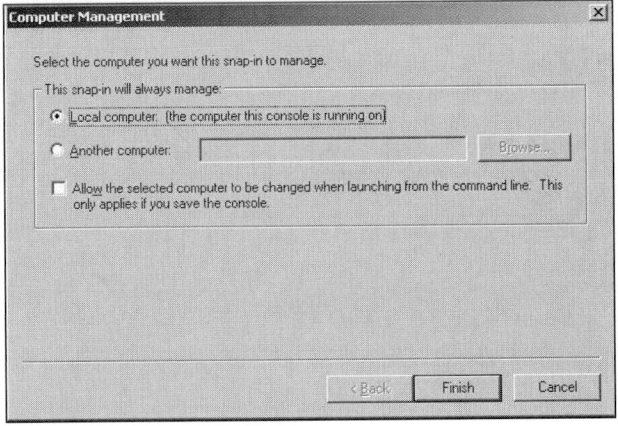

Figure 3-26 Using a snap-in to manage the local computer

Figure 3-27 Removing snap-in extensions

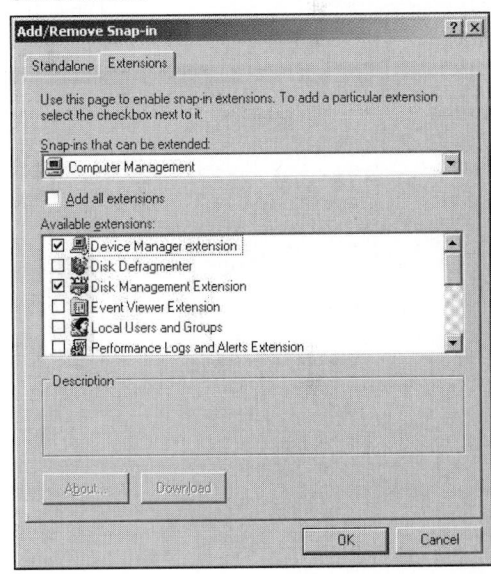

Figure 3-28 Console Root with selected extensions

Exam 70-290

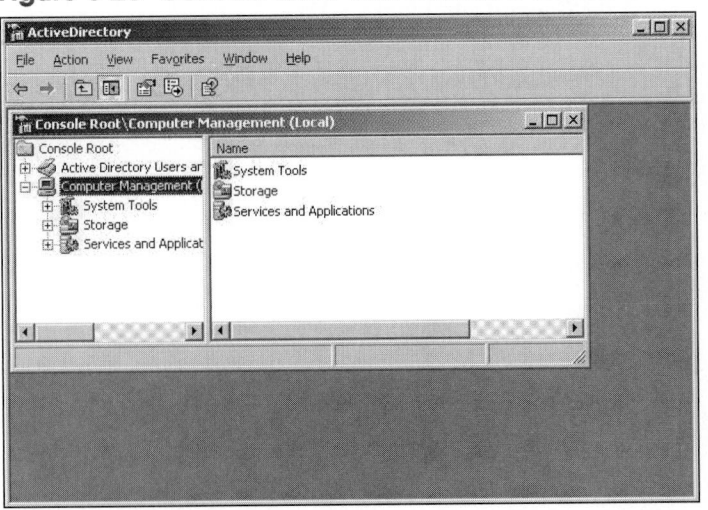

skill 8

Creating Organizational Units

exam objective

Basic knowledge

overview

You use the Active Directory Users and Computers console to create an organizational unit (OU) and to add objects to OUs. You can create an OU in a domain, in a domain controller object, or in another OU if you have been delegated permission to do so. By default, Windows Server 2003 grants permission to members of the Administrators group to create an OU.

how to

Create two OUs in the domain you created in Skill 6 and add a user object to an OU.

1. Log on as an **Administrator**.
2. Click start, point to **All Programs**, point to **Administrative Tools**, and then click **Active Directory.msc** to open the custom console you created in Skill 7.
3. Expand the Active Directory Users and Computers snap-in, if necessary.
4. In the console tree, double-click *<yourdomain.com>* (the domain you created in Skill 6). The contents of the domain display in the details pane.
5. Open the **Action** menu, point to **New**, and click **Organizational Unit (Figure 3-29)** to open the **New Object-Organizational Unit** dialog box.
6. Type **Marketing** in the **Name** text box. Click [OK] to close the dialog box. The Marketing OU is added to the console tree **(Figure 3-30)**.
7. Repeat steps 3-5 to create another OU called **Sales**.
8. Right-click the **Marketing** OU in the console tree, point to **New**, and click **User** to open the **New Object-User** dialog box.
9. Type **Jennifer** in the **First Name** textbox.
10. Type **Johnson** in the **Last Name** textbox.
11. Type **JJohnson** in the **User logon name** text box **(Figure 3-31)**.
12. Click [Next >] to move to the next screen of the New Object-User dialog box.
13. Type **ABcd1234** in the **Password** text box and retype the same password in the **Confirm password** text box.
14. Click [Next >]. The final screen of the **New Object – User** dialog box opens.
15. Click [Finish] to complete the process of creating a user object.
16. Double-click **Marketing** to display the contents of this OU in the details pane.
17. In the details pane, right-click the user object you just created and click [Properties] to open the **Properties** dialog box for the user object.
18. Type an email address, **JenniferJohnson@yourdomain.com**, in the **E-mail** text box on the **General** tab **(Figure 3-32)**.
19. Click [OK] to close the Properties dialog box.

Figure 3-29 Creating an Organizational Unit (OU)

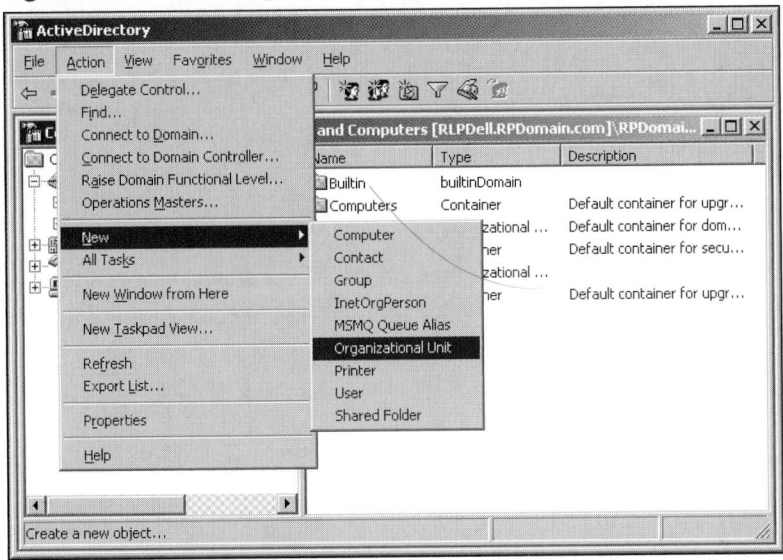

Figure 3-30 The Marketing OU added to the domain

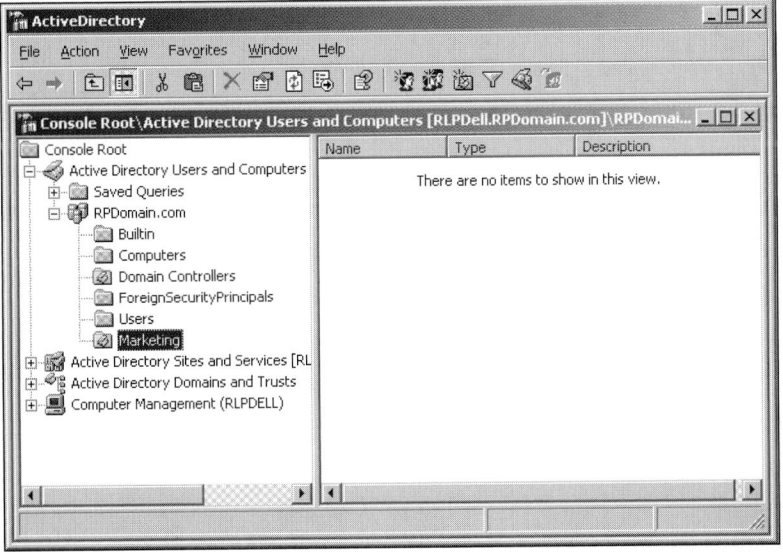

Figure 3-31 Creating a new user object

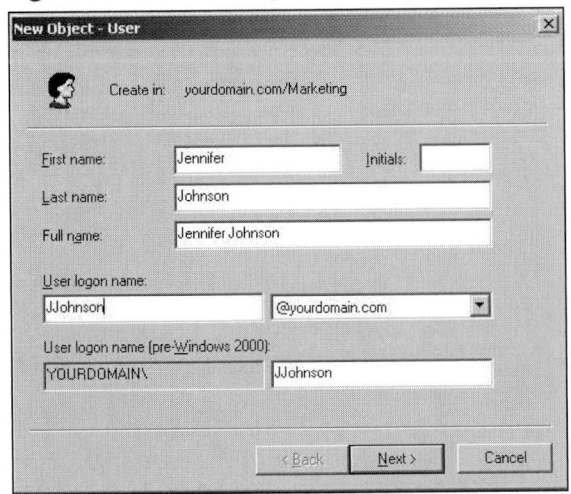

Figure 3-32 <User object> Properties dialog box

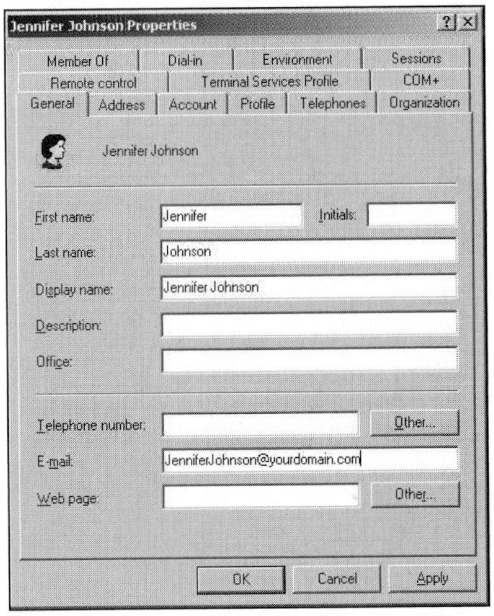

skill 8

Creating Organizational Units (cont'd)

exam objective

Basic knowledge

more

A number of objects are created by default when you install Active Directory. There are user objects that provide access to the system at several levels and group objects that allow administrators to delegate specific network tasks to others. **Table 3-7** lists the default objects created in Active Directory.

Table 3-7 Default Objects Created in Active Directory

Name	Description
Built in	
Account Operators	Members can administer domain user and group accounts.
Administrators	Administrators have complete and unrestricted access to the computer/domain.
Backup Operators	Backup Operators can override security restrictions for the sole purpose of backing up or restoring files.
Guests	Guests have the same access as members of the Users group by default, except for the Guest account which is further restricted.
Incoming Forest Trust Builders	Members of this group can create incoming, one-way trusts in this forest.
Network Configuration Operators	Members of this group can have some administrative privileges to manage configuration of networking features.
Performance Log Users	Members of this group have remote access to schedule logging of performance counters on this computer.
Performance Monitor Users	Members of this group have remote access to monitor this computer.
Pre-Windows 2000 Compatible Access	A backward compatibility group which allows Read access to all users and groups in the domain.
Print Operators	Members can administer domain printers.
Remote Desktop Users	Members in this group are granted the right to log on remotely.
Replicator	Supports file replication in a domain.
Server Operators	Members can administer domain servers.
Terminal Server License Servers	Terminal Server License Servers.
Users	Users are prevented from making accidental or intentional system-wide changes. Thus, Users can run certified applications, but not most legacy applications.
Windows Authorization Access Group	Members of this group have access to the computed tokenGroupsGlobalAndUniversal attribute on User objects.
Users	
Administrator	Built-in account for administering the computer/domain.
Cert Publishers	Members of this group are allowed to publish certificates to Active Directory.
Domain Admins	Designated administrators of the domain.
Domain Computers	All workstations and servers joined to the domain.
Domain Controllers	All domain controllers in the domain.
Domain Guests	All domain guests.
Domain Users	All domain users.
Enterprise Admins	Designated administrators of the enterprise (all domains in the forest).
Group Policy Creator Owners	Members in this group can modify Group Policy for the domain.
Guest	Built-in account for guest access to the computer/domain.
HelpServicesGroup	Group for the Help and Support Center.
RAS and IAS Servers	Servers in this group can access remote access properties of users.
Schema Admins	Designated administrators of the schema.
Support _388945a0	This is a vendor's account for the Help and Support Service.
TelnetClients	Members of this group have access to Telnet Server on this system.

skill 9 — *Managing Active Directory Objects*

exam objective

Basic knowledge

overview

After creating an OU and adding objects to it, you will periodically have to perform management tasks. Managing objects involves several tasks, including the following:

Searching for objects in Active Directory. Active Directory stores a partial replica of information about all objects in a forest in the global catalog. This central data repository is used to locate information anywhere in a forest. You can locate information in Active Directory using the **Find Users, Contacts, and Groups** dialog box in the **Active Directory Users and Computers** console.

Delegating administrative control. You can delegate the management of objects in Active Directory to other users or groups. This allows you to create OUs and assign permissions to other users to manage those OUs. You can either completely delegate administrative control or allow only partial control of an OU by using the **Delegation of Control Wizard**. To start this wizard, right-click the OU and click the **Delegate Control** command.

Modifying objects in Active Directory. You may need to modify the attributes of the objects in Active Directory to meet the changing needs of your organization. For example, the attributes for a user object will have to be modified when there is a change in telephone number or office location. You use the **Properties** dialog box for an object in the Active Directory Users and Computers console to change these attributes. To open the Properties dialog box, right-click the object and click **Properties**.

Moving objects within Active Directory. You can move an object from one location to another in Active Directory to meet the requirements of your organization. For example, if an employee in the Marketing department is transferred to the Sales department, you can move the user object from the Marketing OU to the Sales OU. The user will then inherit the group policies assigned to the Sales OU and lose the group policies assigned to the Marketing OU. You can move an object in Active Directory using the **Move** dialog box in the **Active Directory Users and Computers** console.

how to

Locate a user object in a domain and move it to another OU.

1. Open the **Active Directory.msc** console, if necessary.
2. In the console tree, select the **<yourdomain.com>** domain (the domain you created in Skill 6).
3. Click 🔍 (the **Find objects in Active Directory button**) to open the **Find Users, Contacts, and Groups** dialog box.
4. Make sure that **Users, Contacts and Groups** is selected in the **Find** list box and your domain name is selected in the **In** list box.
5. Type **Jennifer** in the **Name** text box (**Figure 3-33**).
6. Click the **Advanced** tab. On this page, you enter criteria for locating the user object.
7. Click Field ▼, point to **User**, and click **E-Mail Address**.
8. Type the e-mail address for the user object in the **Value** text box.
9. Click Add... to add the search criteria to the **Condition List**.
10. Click Find Now to search for the object in Active Directory. The name of the user object appears in the lower portion of the dialog box (**Figure 3-34**).

Figure 3-33 The Find Users, Contacts, and Groups dialog box

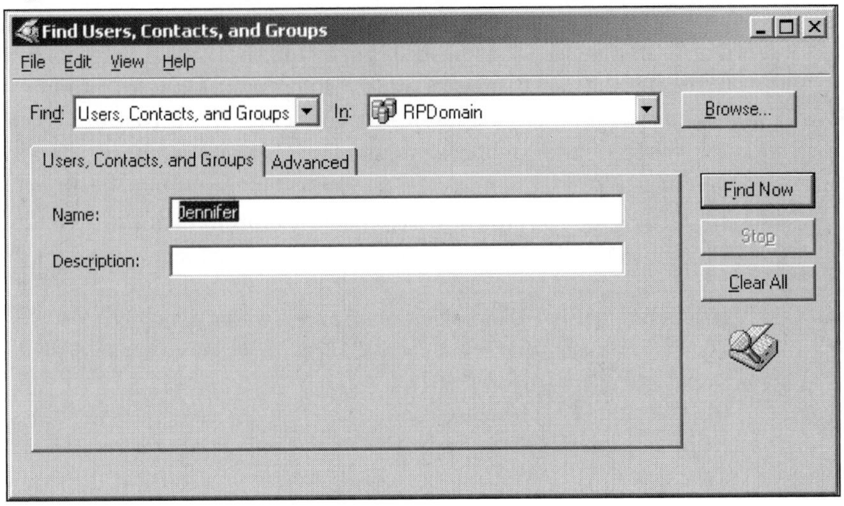

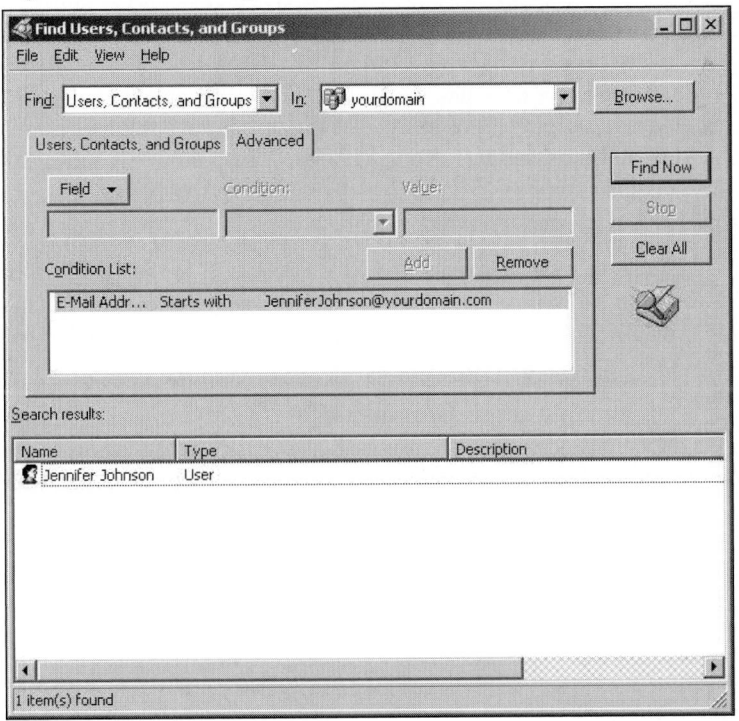

Figure 3-34 Finding a user in Active Directory

skill 9

Managing Active Directory Objects
(cont'd)

exam objective Basic knowledge

how to

11. To display the Distinguished Name of the user object in the search results, open the **View** menu and click **Choose Columns** to open the **Choose Columns** dialog box.
12. In the **Columns available** list box, click **X500 Distinguished Name** to display the details of the Distinguished Name for the object in the results window.
13. Click ⟨ Add >> ⟩ to include this option in the **Columns shown** list box.
14. Click ⟨ OK ⟩ to close the **Choose Columns** dialog box.
15. The X500 Distinguished Name of the user object appears in the lower portion of the dialog box **(Figure 3-35)**.
16. Close the **Find Users, Contacts, and Groups** dialog box.
17. In the details pane of the **Active Directory** custom console, double-click the **Marketing** OU to display its contents.
18. Click the user object to select it, and drag the object into the **Sales OU** in the console tree to move it.
19. Click the Sales OU in the console tree to confirm that the user object has been moved **(Figure 3-36)**.
20. Close the Active Directory.msc console.

more

After you have created domains and OUs and added objects to the OUs, you need to secure the resources in Active Directory from unauthorized access. Active Directory provides:

Object security: Active Directory provides a set of security descriptors for each object called a **Discretionary Access Control List (DACL)**. The DACL defines how that object can be accessed. For example, the DACL for a folder called **Budget Policies** may specify that only the user accounts **JJohnson** and **HNeale** can have full access to the share. In contrast, the permissions for the share, **BudgetPolicies**, may allow only full-control access for everyone in the organization.

Each file or folder on an NTFS drive has a DACL, and that DACL contains entries known as **Access Control Entries (ACEs)**. Each ACE in the DACL contains the SID of the user or group allowed or denied and the permissions associated with that user or group. By housing the list of ACEs, the DACL essentially controls access to the share.

Account logon security: Account logon security protects a computer and its resources from unauthorized access by restricting the ability of users to access a computer or a domain. Account authentication ensures that each user accessing network resources has a user account either in the local accounts database of the computer or on the domain controller. If the user is logging on to the computer using a domain account, the domain controller authenticates the user account by verifying the account name and password. After authentication, the user is granted access to network resources based on permissions associated with the user's access token. Access control is defined by the access control lists (ACLs), which designate the permissions for network resources.

Figure 3-35 Finding the Distinguished Name

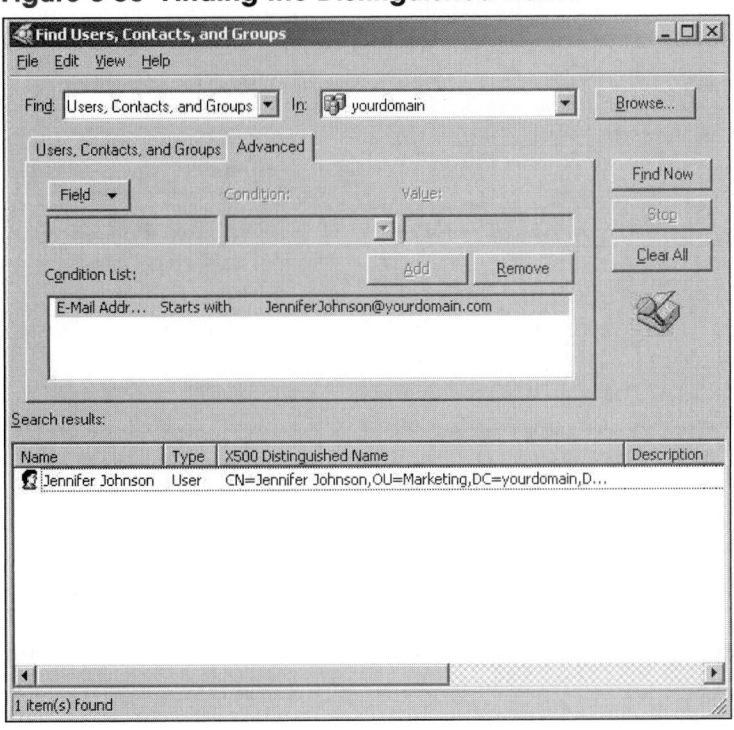

Figure 3-36 Moving a user object

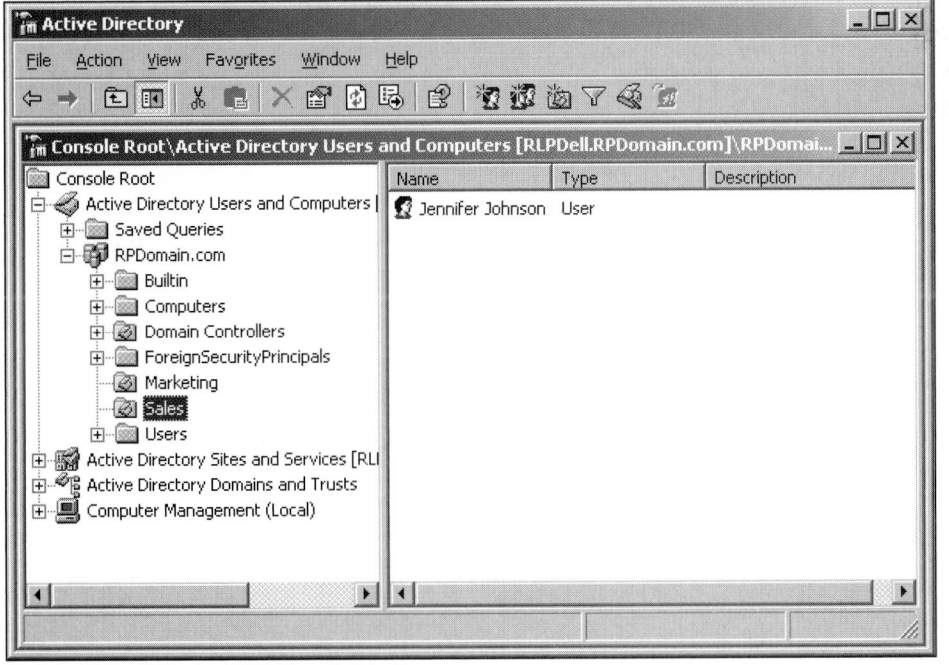

Summary

- Active Directory is a directory service for Windows Server 2003 that stores information about network objects in a logical and hierarchical manner.
- Active Directory provides many features such as centralized management, extensibility, scalability, and security.
- Active Directory architecture consists of three service layers (DSA, Database, and ESE), interfaces, the Data Store, and protocols to provide directory service.
- In order to understand how Active Directory functions, you must understand the following concepts: schema, global catalog, and namespace.
- The schema is the database design, which can be extended by adding new object classes or new attributes. For each class, the schema defines the permanent set of characteristics the class must have, as well as the optional attributes that it may have.
- A global catalog is created automatically on the initial domain controller in the first domain in the forest. A domain controller that hosts a global catalog is called a global catalog server. Using Active Directory multimaster replication, the information in the global catalog is replicated between global catalog servers in other domains.
- The global catalog stores a full replica of all object attributes in the directory for its host domain, and a partial replica of all object attributes contained in the directory for every domain in the forest. The partial replica stores the attributes most frequently used in search operations. It also stores commonly used logon and authentication data. Its functions are to respond to logon requests and search queries.
- DNS uses the Active Directory namespace to resolve a fully qualified domain name to an IP address. This process is called name resolution. Because Active Directory names are DNS names, you must carefully plan your DNS namespace implementation. There are two types of namespaces: contiguous and disjointed.
- Naming conventions used for objects stored in Active Directory are distinguished names (DN), relative distinguished names (RDN), globally unique identifiers (GUID), and user principal names (UPN).
- Active Directory divides a network into two types of structures: logical and physical.
    - The logical structure consists of forests, trees, domains, trust relationships, organizational units, and objects.
    - The physical structure consists of domain controllers and sites.
- An object is any "thing," either tangible or abstract, about which data is stored. It can be a network resource, such as a file, printer, or user, or a virtual object such as a forest, tree, domain, or organizational unit. An object consists of a unique set of attributes that defines its properties.
- A domain is a group of computers and devices on a network, which must follow a common set of rules and procedures, and which have the same security relationships with other domains. Domains are administered as a unit, although they can extend to more than one physical location.
- An organizational unit acts as a container that groups related objects within a domain.
- A tree consists of a set of one or more domains in a contiguous namespace.
- A forest consists of one or more domains that share a common schema, configuration, global catalog, and two-way, transitive trusts.
- A domain controller is a computer that stores a replica of the directory database for a single domain.
- A site is a set of subnets connected by high-speed, cost effective, reliable links. Sites are defined by creating subnets for each of the physical locations on the network.
- Before implementing Active Directory, you must first understand the business requirements of your organization, and then plan the namespace, sites, domain structure, and organizational units that will be used.
- The Active Directory Installation Wizard is used to install Active Directory on a Windows Server 2003 computer.
- Microsoft Management Console (MMC) is a console framework that provides a common host environment for snap-ins used to perform administrative tasks such as managing computers, services, and networks. There are two types of snap-ins: stand-alone snap-ins that provide management functionality without requiring support from another snap-in and extension snap-ins that extend the functionality provided by other snap-ins. An extension snap-ins require a parent snap-in above it in the console tree. Multiple snap-ins can be combined within the MMC interface as a customized console.
- You use the Active Directory Users and Computers console to create an organizational unit and add objects to an organizational unit (OU). An OU can be created in a domain, in a domain controller object, or in another OU. Members of the Administrators group have permission to create OUs by default in Windows Server 2003.
- Managing Active Directory objects involves tasks such as locating, modifying, and moving objects.
- To secure the resources in Active Directory from authorized access, Active Directory provides object security and account logon security.

Key Terms

Access Control Entry (ACE)
Active Directory
Active Directory Installation Wizard
Child domain
Customized console
Data Store (ntds.dit)
Database Layer
Directory service
Directory System Agent (DSA)
Discretionary Access Control List (DACL)
Distinguished Name (DN)
Domain
Domain controller
Extensible Storage Engine (ESE) Layer

Extension snap-in
Forest
Global catalog
Global catalog server
Globally Unique Identifier (GUID)
Lightweight Directory Access Protocol (LDAP)
Member server
Microsoft Management Console (MMC)
Multi-master replication
Namespace
Object
Organizational unit (OU)
Parent domain

Relative Distinguished Name (RDN)
Root domain
Schema
Site
Snap-in
Stand-alone snap-in
TCP/IP subnet
Tree
User Principal Name (UPN)
Windows Server 2003 mode
Windows Server 2003 interim mode
Windows 2000 mixed mode
Windows 2000 native mode

Test Yourself

1. In Active Directory, a _____ stores partial information about the replica of all objects in the domains in a forest.
   a. Global catalog
   b. Namespace
   c. Schema
   d. Site

2. Which of the following is a 128-bit number assigned to an object that is not changed even if you move or rename the object?
   a. Relative Distinguished Name (RDN)
   b. Distinguished Name (DN)
   c. User Principal Name (UPN)
   d. Globally Unique Identifier (GUID)

3. Which of the following is the core protocol of Active Directory?
   a. LDAP
   b. MAPI-RPC
   c. ADSI
   d. Windows Messaging

4. A formal set of definitions that describes the type of objects that can be created in Active Directory, as well as information about these objects such as the attributes, classes, and class properties:
   a. Global catalog
   b. Schema
   c. Namespace
   d. Class

5. You can use the external DNS namespace defined for your organization as the internal Active Directory namespace.
   a. True
   b. False

6. Which of the following connects a set of domain controllers by high-speed, cost effective links to represent a region of uniform network access in Active Directory?
   a. Domain controller
   b. Forest
   c. Site
   d. Organizational unit

7. Which of the following stores scripts and group policy objects for a domain?
   a. Database
   b. Shared system volume
   c. Database log files
   d. Mixed mode

8. _____ is a set of security descriptors that prevents unauthorized access to a shared resource.
   a. DACL
   b. DC
   c. GUID
   d. OU

9. By default, the ownership of an object in Active Directory belongs to the:
   a. User account that created it.
   b. Server administrator.
   c. Domain in which it was created.
   d. OU in which it was created.

10. Trees in a forest use:
   a. Different global catalogs.
   b. Same schema.
   c. Always use the same naming structure.
   d. One-way transitive trusts.

Exam 70-290

Projects: On Your Own

1. Create an OU called Purchasing in the yourdomian.com domain.
   1. Open the **Active Directory Users and Computers** console.
   2. Display the contents of the **yourdomain.com** domain.
   3. Open the **New User-Organizational Unit** dialog box.
   4. Specify the name of the OU.
   5. Close the New User-Organizational Unit dialog box.
2. Add a user object called **Dona Williams** to the Purchasing OU in the yourdomain.com domain. Specify **ABcd1234** as the password for this user object.
   1. Open the **Active Directory Users and Computers** console.
   2. Display the contents of the **yourdomain.com** domain.
   3. Select the **Purchasing** OU in the yourdomain.com domain.
   4. Open the **New Object-User** dialog box.

5. Specify the first Name and the last Name of the user object.
6. Display the next screen of the New Object-User dialog box.
7. Specify the password for the user object.
8. Display the final screen of New Object-user dialog box.
9. Close the New Object-user dialog box.
3. Find the Dona Williams user object in the yourdomain.com domain by specifying the name of the user object as the search criteria.
   1. Display the **Active Directory Users and Computers** console.
   2. Display the contents of the **yourdomain.com** domain.
   3. Display the **Find Users, Contacts, and Groups** dialog box.
   4. Specify the search criteria for locating **Dona Williams**.
   5. Search for the required object in Active Directory.

Problem Solving Scenarios

1. Your company, Wilson Media Arts Inc., has decided to implement Active Directory on its Windows Server 2003 network. Wilson Media (www.wilsonmedia.com) has 450 employees in five main organizational divisions: Logistics (warehousing and order fulfillment), Manufacturing, Finance, Marketing, and Sales. They have asked you to develop a plan for implementing Active Directory. Prepare a report that proposes a new namespace, designs the site, and plans a domain structure for the firm.

2. After implementing the Active Directory structure you proposed, Wilson Media now plans to expand its organization to include a Design department. Management would like to add a new organizational unit for the Design division to the network. Create a plan that will enable you to do so, and explain the steps required to implement the plan.

Organizing a Disk for Data Storage

Just like other operating systems, Windows Server 2003 allows you to store data on a hard disk so that you can save it for future reference and share it with others. However, before storing data in the Windows Server 2003 environment, you must set up the hard disk. Setting up a hard disk involves initializing it with a storage type, creating partitions or volumes, and formatting the hard disk with a file system.

When Windows Server 2003 is installed, you can use the Setup program to create and configure partitions. As your storage needs increase, you may need to change the storage type, change the file system, add more partitions, or exchange hard drives. You can initialize a hard disk with two types of storage: basic or dynamic. The default storage type is basic, and a basic disk is the same type of disk that all previous Microsoft operating systems have used. On a basic disk, you create partitions using the unallocated disk space. Partitions can be either primary or extended. You set up a primary partition to boot an operating system such as MS-DOS or Windows Server 2003. Dynamic disks are a new disk type first introduced in Windows 2000 Server. They are used when the simple administrative schemes available with a basic disk are not adequate for your purposes. A dynamic disk can comprise multiple volumes on a hard disk. The types of volumes that can be created on a dynamic disk include simple volumes, which are similar to the primary partitions on a basic disk, spanned volumes, striped volumes, mirrored volumes, and RAID-5 volumes. Virtual Disk Service (VDS) is new to Windows Server 2003. VDS enables disk management of different types of devices and is especially useful in simplifying the administration of multi-vendor storage devices.

After you have created partitions or volumes on a hard disk, you must format the hard disk with a file system in order to store data. You can use the Disk Management snap-in or command line tools, such as format and diskpart, to manage disks and partitions and optimize disk performance. You can use the snap-in to simplify the administration of your hard disks. In the Disk Management window, you can view disk properties and perform such functions as creating new partitions or volumes, setting an active partition, formatting drives, changing drive letters, and upgrading a disk from a conventional basic disk to a dynamic disk. You can also delete partitions or volumes and troubleshoot disk failures.

Goals

In this lesson, you will learn how to configure disk drives for use by Windows Server 2003. You will create a primary partition, an extended partition, and logical drives. You will also learn how to upgrade a basic disk to a dynamic disk, create volumes, and troubleshoot disks.

Lesson 4   Organizing a Disk for Data Storage

Skill	Exam 70-290 Objective
1. Introducing Storage Types	Manage basic disks and dynamic disks.
2. Creating a Primary Partition	Manage basic disks and dynamic disks.
3. Creating an Extended Partition and a Logical Drive	Manage basic disks and dynamic disks.
4. Upgrading a Disk from Basic to Dynamic	Manage basic disks and dynamic disks.
5. Creating a Simple Volume	Manage basic disks and dynamic disks.
6. Introducing Spanned, Striped and Mirrored Volumes	Optimize server disk performance.
7. Understanding and Implementing a RAID-5 Volume	Optimize server disk performance. Implement a RAID solution.
8. Defragmenting Volumes and Partitions	Optimize server disk performance. Defragment volumes and partitions.
9. Recovering from Disk Failures	Recover from server hardware failure.

Requirements

To complete this lesson, you will need administrative rights on a Windows Server 2003 computer set up for basic storage and at least 10 GB of unallocated disk space on two hard disks attached to the computer so that you can create partitions, upgrade a disk, and create volumes. To perform the optional exercise in Skill 7, you will also need unallocated space on three hard disks in order to create a RAID-5 volume.

skill 1

Introducing Storage Types

exam objective

Manage basic disks and dynamic disks.

overview

tip

An operating system is generally installed on a primary partition that is referred to as the C: drive.

There are two storage types used by Windows Server 2003: basic and dynamic. The storage type defines the structure of a hard disk. It also determines the fault tolerance of the disk. Traditionally, basic storage has been used by Microsoft and is supported by all Microsoft operating systems from MS-DOS to Windows Server 2003. Dynamic storage is supported by the Windows 2000, Windows Server 2003, and Windows XP networking operating systems.

The characteristics of the two types of storage are described below:

Basic storage: Basic storage divides a hard disk into partitions. A **partition** acts as a logical division for storing data in an organized manner. Partitioning creates sections on the hard disk to prepare it for formatting with a file system. The creation of partitions allows you to distribute the system files, data files, and other information in separate locations, enhancing the speed of your system. Any new disk added to a Windows Server 2003 computer is automatically created as a basic disk. Basic disks are included in Windows Server 2003 for backward compatibility with earlier versions of the operating system and with MS-DOS. Dual-boot systems with these earlier operating systems require basic disks. A basic disk supports the following types of partitions (**Figure 4-1**):

◆ **Primary:** A **primary partition** is a physical unit of storage created on a basic disk. A basic disk can consist of a maximum of four primary partitions. One of these four can be an extended partition. One of the primary partitions is marked as the active partition. The **active partition** stores the startup files, including all of the hardware-related files required to load the operating system. It is also referred to as the **system partition**. Another partition called the boot partition stores all of the Windows Server 2003 operating system files. It is important to make the distinction between the active or system partition and the boot partition. The active partition is where the files needed to *boot* the operating system are stored (Ntldr, Boot.ini and Ntdetect, for example). The **boot partition**, on the other hand, is the partition where the actual operating system files (typically \Windows) and the operating system support files (typically \Windows \System32) are stored. The boot partition can be the same partition as the system partition. Any partition can act as the boot partition. You can create up to four primary partitions on a basic disk. Note that up to 128 primary partitions can be created on one disk using the GUID partition table (GPT) disk-partitioning scheme. Because GPT doesn't limit you to four primary partitions, there is no need to create extended partitions or logical drives. GPT is available only on Itanium-based computers.

◆ **Extended: Extended partitions** are created from free space that has not yet been partitioned. They are created so that you can use more than the four drive letters on a basic disk. On all x86 computers, an extended partition cannot be the system partition, but it can be used to store the operating system files (i.e., it can be the *boot* partition). You can divide an extended partition into segments. Each segment acts as a **logical drive** to which you can assign a drive letter. You can also format each segment with a file system. For example, you can assign the drive letter E: to a logical drive and format it with the NTFS file system.

Dynamic storage: Dynamic storage enables you to escape the four partition limit imposed by basic disks. When you create a dynamic disk, you increase the number of segments the disk can support from 4 (using standard partitions) to 2000. Instead of partitions, a dynamic disk is divided into volumes. **Volumes** are essentially the same as partitions, with a few key differences. First, each volume can consist of a portion of a single hard disk or even portions of several hard disks. Second, when you convert to a dynamic disk, you can create fault-tolerant volumes. Fault tolerance provides redundancy in case of disk failure, and thus

Figure 4-1 Types of partitions on a basic disk

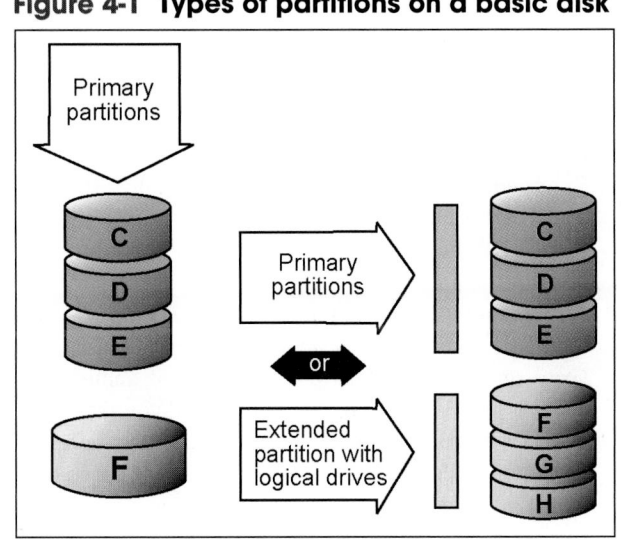

skill 1

Introducing Storage Types (cont'd)

Manage basic disks and dynamic disks.

overview

prevents data loss. Non-fault-tolerant volumes are subject to data loss because if you lose any piece of a volume, all data on the volume is lost. Another advantage of dynamic disks is that you can resize them dynamically. Dynamic disks support the following types of volumes (**Figure 4-2**):

◆ **Simple:** A **simple volume** consists of disk space from a single hard disk, an entire disk, or multiple regions on the same disk that are linked together. Regions are clusters of space on the same hard disk. If you do not use all of the available space on a disk to create one simple volume, later you can add all or some of the unallocated space to an existing simple volume to create an extended volume. A simple volume does not provide fault tolerance. You will often create a simple volume when there is only one hard disk on your computer. A simple volume is equivalent to a partition on a simple disk—you can format it and assign it a drive letter.

◆ **Spanned:** A **spanned volume** consists of disk space from multiple disks. You can create a spanned volume when there are a number of small hard disks—for example, if you have three 2 GB disks on your computer. You might also decide to create a spanned volume to combine small portions of free disk space that are scattered across the disk drives of the server. Finally, you can combine a number of smaller volumes to create a spanned volume. The benefit of spanned volumes is that they can be used to maximize the use of space on systems where small sections of unallocated space are distributed throughout several disks. Another benefit of spanned volumes is that a number of small disk drives or volumes can be combined for greater disk organization. When writing data to a spanned volume, Windows Server 2003 uses the disk space on the first available disk until it fills, and then writes data on other disks. This means that spanned volumes do not provide any improvement in speed over simple volumes. Also, like simple volumes, spanned volumes do not provide fault tolerance; in fact, if anything, they are *less* fault-tolerant, since a failure on any one drive in the spanned volume will take down the entire volume. In general, you will see spanned volumes used in situations where disk space became scarce, and rather than backing up the data, inserting a new, larger disk, and restoring the data, the administrator chose to simply insert a new disk and extend the existing simple volume across the new disk, thus increasing available space. In most situations this is a poor solution, as spanned volumes do not improve redundancy or speed.

◆ **Striped:** A **striped volume** (also known as **RAID-0**) combines areas of free disk space from two or more hard disks. Data in a striped volume is allocated alternately and evenly (in 64 KB stripes) across the disks, with the first 64KB written to the first disk, the next 64KB to the second disk, the third 64KB to the third disk and so on, but with a catch: Striping reads from and writes to all disks at the same time. This means striping offers the best possible performance, as it can maximize utilization of the disk controller's bandwidth. For example, if each disk is capable of 30MB per second of consistent throughput, you would need to read and write from no less than 6 disks at a time in order to completely utilize Ultra 160 SCSI's available 160MB per second of throughput. While a striped volume offers the best performance of all volume types in Windows Server 2003, it does not provide fault tolerance. You will lose all of your data if one of the disks in a striped volume fails.

◆ **Mirrored:** A **mirrored volume** (also known as **RAID-1**) is created using the free disk space on two physical hard disks. Mirrored volumes are tolerant of a single disk failure because all reads and writes to the mirrored volume are performed in duplicate on both disks. If one of the disks in a mirrored volume fails, data can be accessed from the other disk. To create a mirrored volume, you use free space on another disk to create a volume. If the second physical disk is larger than the original, the remaining space becomes free

caution

The disk space on both hard disks must be the same size because a mirrored volume simultaneously writes the same information on both hard disks.

Figure 4-2 How data is written to dynamic volumes

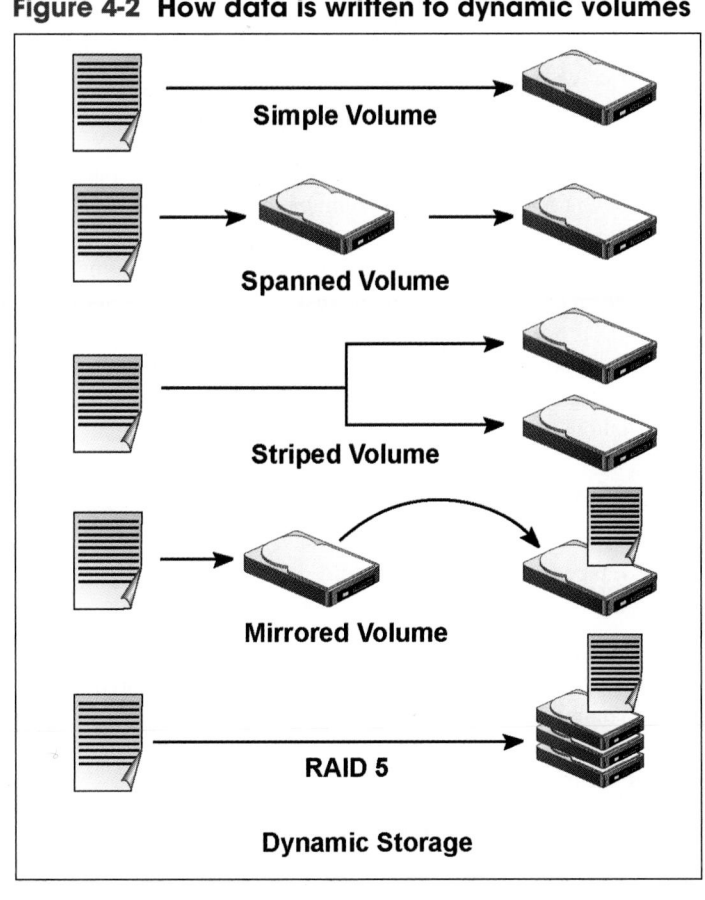

skill 1

Introducing Storage Types (cont'd)

exam objective

Manage basic disks and dynamic disks.

overview

space, and can be segmented with other volumes normally. Even the system and boot volumes can be mirrored onto another volume of the same size (or greater) on another disk (this is the only method of software redundancy allowed for the system and boot volumes). For best performance, you should use disks that are the same size, model, and manufacturer, but all that is really required is two separate physical disks. The same drive letter is used for both volumes. Mirrored volumes can be created only on dynamic disks running the Windows 2000 Server or Windows Server 2003 operating systems. You cannot extend mirrored volumes.

◆ **RAID-5:** A **RAID-5 volume** is a fault-tolerant, striped, dynamic volume that combines free disk space from 3 to 32 physical hard disks. Data and parity information is striped across all equal-sized portions of all disks. Parity is a calculated value that is used to recover data. If a portion of a physical disk fails, Windows Server 2003 can rebuild the lost data by performing calculations using the parity data. As mentioned previously, RAID-5 uses an equal amount of space on all disks. If the disks are not the same size, the amount of space used on each is equal to the smallest disk. Leftover space on the other disks may then be sectioned off into volumes normally. Software RAID-5 volumes can be created only on dynamic disks running the Windows 2000 Server or Windows Server 2003 operating systems. You cannot extend or mirror RAID-5 volumes. Additionally, software RAID-5 cannot host the system or boot volumes. RAID-5 is typically nearly as fast as RAID-0 on read operations, but is very slow on write operations, due to the calculations required to create the parity data.

more

In addition to basic and dynamic disks, you can use removable storage devices, such as floppy disks, tapes or cartridges, to store data. A removable storage device can have only a single primary partition and does not support dynamic storage.

On dynamic disks, the volume where the startup files (the files needed to boot the operating system, such as Ntldr, Boot.ini, and Ntdetect) are stored is referred to as the **system volume**. The volume where the Windows Server 2003 operating system files and the operating system support files are stored (typically \Windows and \Windows\System32) is referred to as the **boot volume**.

While dynamic disks have several advantages over basic disks, they have the following limitations (**Figure 4-3**):

◆ Dynamic storage is not supported by laptop and other portable computers, or by external FireWire or USB disks.

◆ You cannot create dynamic disks on computers that are set up for dual booting, in which two operating systems are installed on the hard disk. Only Windows 2000 and Windows Server 2003 support dynamic disks.

Note that in addition to software RAID, you can also use hardware RAID. Hardware RAID has many advantages over software RAID, such as ease of configuration and reconfiguration, hot-swappable drives in most cases, automatic data recreation in most hardware RAID-5 arrays, and perhaps most importantly, speed. Many hardware RAID-5 arrays are as fast as RAID-0 software arrays. The only real disadvantage to hardware RAID is the cost, but in most cases, it will be money well spent. Hardware RAID is discussed in more detail in Lesson 14.

Figure 4-3 Limitations of dynamic disks

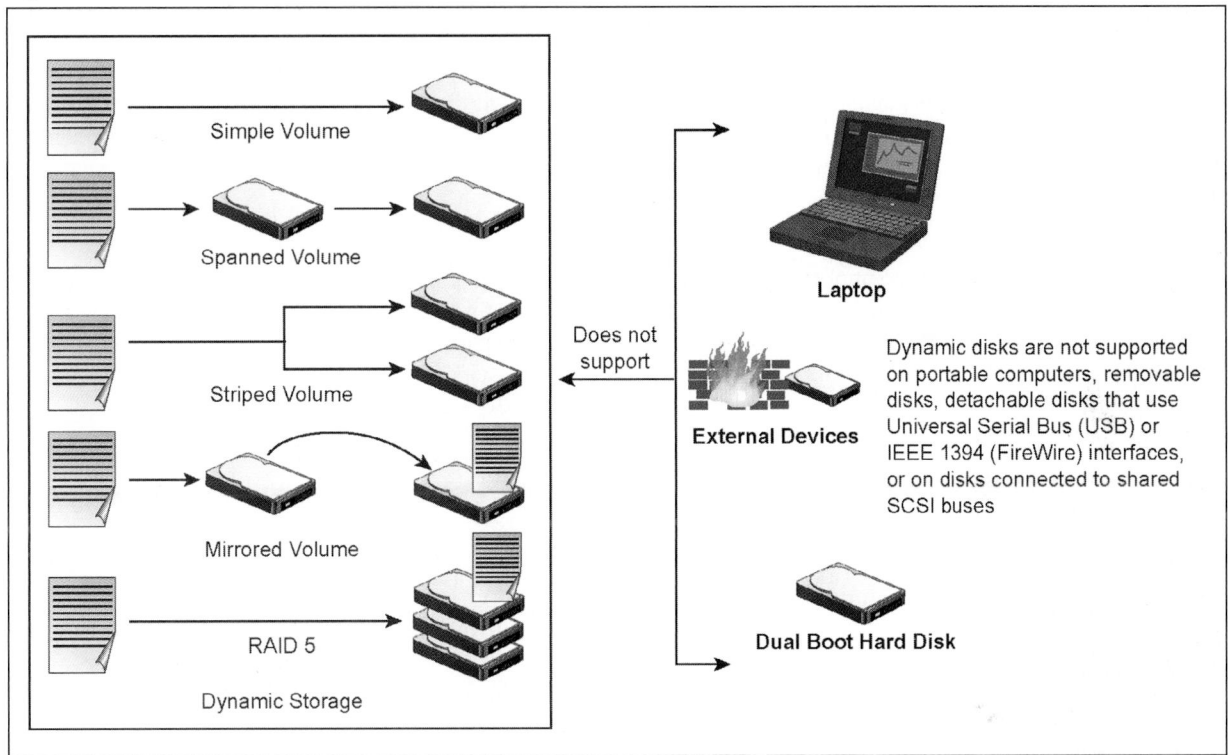

skill 2

Creating a Primary Partition

exam objective

Manage basic disks and dynamic disks.

overview

tip

You can also create a custom console that includes the Disk Management snap-in.

One primary partition on a basic disk stores the files required to boot your computer. The system files can be on an extended partition, but the boot files must reside on a primary partition or a volume. You use the **Disk Management snap-in**, or disport.exe to create additional primary partitions using unallocated space on the hard disk. You also use the Disk Management snap-in to initialize your hard disk with the selected storage type, format the hard disk, and optimize disk performance. The Disk Management snap-in is included in the pre-configured Computer Management console. Using the Disk Management snap-in, you can:

- Manage the hard disks on the local computer or on any computer on the network.
- Simplify administration of your hard disk and the partitions and volumes on the hard disks by creating shortcuts to tasks that you need to perform frequently.
- Use wizards to initialize a disk, create partitions or volumes, and upgrade a disk.

how to

tip

You can also use the command line utility **diskpart** to create a primary partition. However, this is a more complex process. Only use it if you are experienced with creating partitions in this manner.

Create a primary partition on your hard disk using the Disk Management snap-in.

1. Click ⟦ Start⟧, point to **Administrative Tools**, and click the **Computer Management** icon to open the **Computer Management** console.
2. If necessary, in the left pane of the Computer Management console, double-click the **Storage** node to expand it.
3. Click the **Disk Management** snap-in to display the disk configuration in the details pane **(Figure 4-4)**.
4. In **Disk 1**, or whichever disk has unallocated disk space, right-click the unallocated space and click **New Partition** to start the **New Partition Wizard**.
5. Click ⟦ Next >⟧ to open the **Select Partition Type** screen.
6. The **Primary partition** option button is selected by default. Accept the default and click ⟦ Next >⟧ to open the **Specify Partition Size** screen.
7. Type **500** in the **Partition size in MB** spin box to set the size for the primary partition.
8. Click ⟦ Next >⟧ to open the **Assign Drive Letter or Path** screen.
9. Select **F:** in the **Assign a drive letter** list box to assign a drive letter to the primary partition **(Figure 4-5)**.
10. Click ⟦ Next >⟧ to open the **Format partition** screen.
11. By default, the file system selected to format your primary partition is **NTFS**. Accept the defaults, and type **Primary** in the **Volume label** text box to specify a label for the primary partition.
12. Select the **Perform a quick format** check box.
13. Click ⟦ Next >⟧ to open the final summary page of the New Partition Wizard.
14. Click ⟦ Finish⟧ to complete the process of creating a primary partition. You can view the newly created primary partition in the details pane in the Disk Management snap-in **(Figure 4-6)**.

Figure 4-4 Available disk configuration

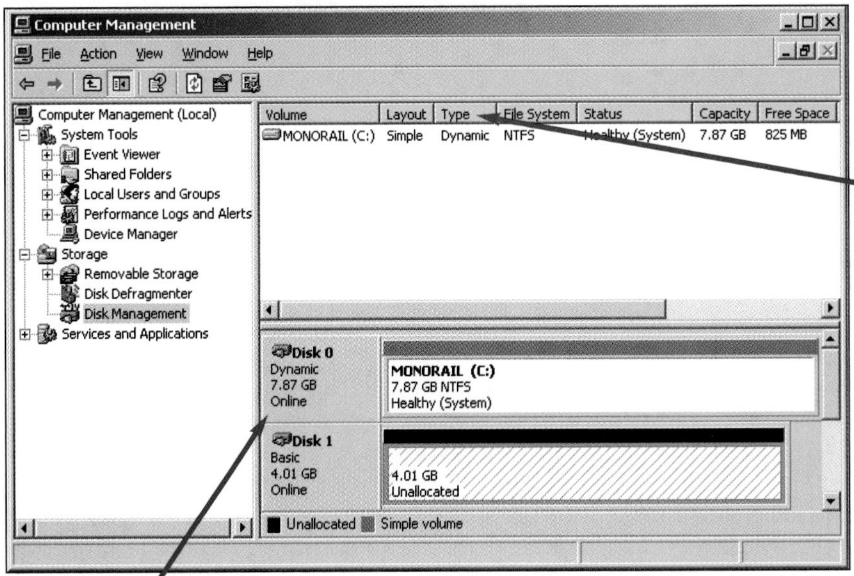

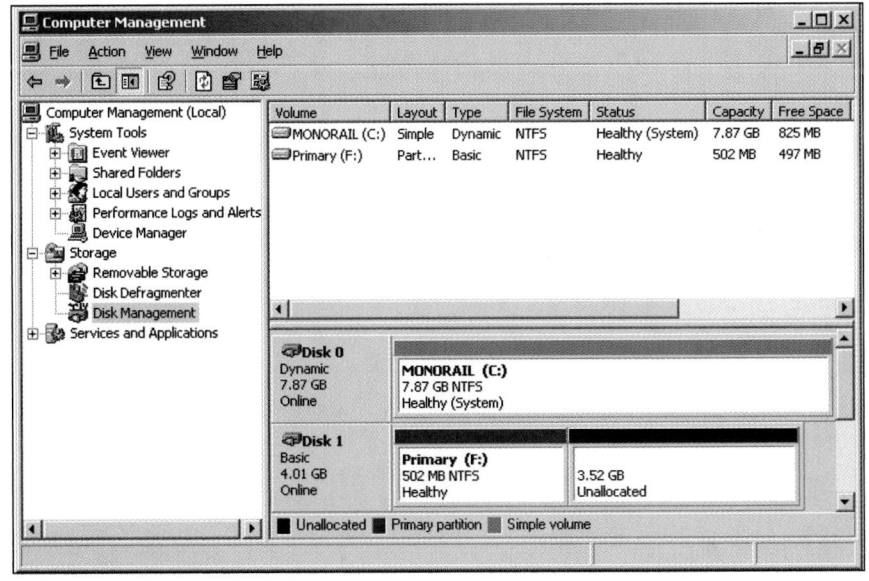

Computer Management
File Action View Window Help
Computer Management (Local)
System Tools
Event Viewer
Shared Folders
Local Users and Groups
Performance Logs and Alerts
Device Manager
Storage
Removable Storage
Disk Defragmenter
Disk Management
Services and Applications
Volume Layout Type File System Status Capacity Free Space
MONORAIL (C:) Simple Dynamic NTFS Healthy (System) 7.87 GB 825 MB
Disk 0
Dynamic
7.87 GB
Online
MONORAIL (C:)
7.87 GB NTFS
Healthy (System)
Disk 1
Basic
4.01 GB
Online
4.01 GB
Unallocated
Unallocated Simple volume

Provides information about the type of disk, the file system used to format the disk, the disk capacity, and the status of the disk

Provides information about each physical disk and the partitions or volumes on each disk

Figure 4-5 Assigning the drive letter

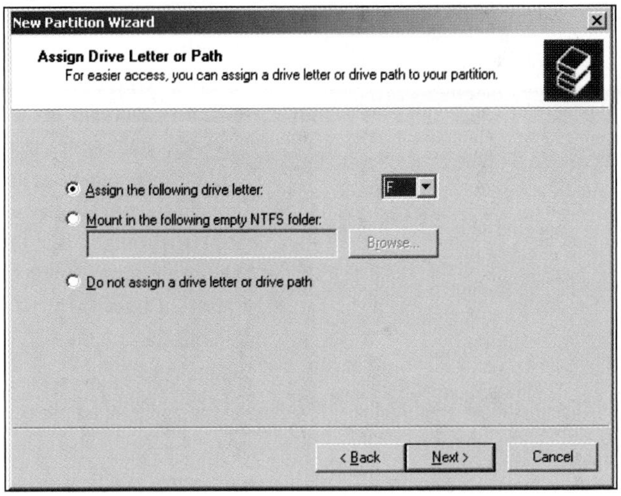

New Partition Wizard
Assign Drive Letter or Path
For easier access, you can assign a drive letter or drive path to your partition.
Assign the following drive letter:
F
Mount in the following empty NTFS folder:
Browse...
Do not assign a drive letter or drive path
< Back
Next >
Cancel

Figure 4-6 Formatting the partition and labeling the volume

Computer Management
File Action View Window Help
Computer Management (Local)
System Tools
Event Viewer
Shared Folders
Local Users and Groups
Performance Logs and Alerts
Device Manager
Storage
Removable Storage
Disk Defragmenter
Disk Management
Services and Applications
Volume Layout Type File System Status Capacity Free Space
MONORAIL (C:) Simple Dynamic NTFS Healthy (System) 7.87 GB 825 MB
Primary (F:) Part... Basic NTFS Healthy 502 MB 497 MB
Disk 0
Dynamic
7.87 GB
Online
MONORAIL (C:)
7.87 GB NTFS
Healthy (System)
Disk 1
Basic
4.01 GB
Online
Primary (F:)
502 MB NTFS
Healthy
3.52 GB
Unallocated
Unallocated Primary partition Simple volume

skill 2

Creating a Primary Partition (cont'd)

exam objective

Manage basic disks and dynamic disks.

more

caution

You must be careful when deleting a partition because all data on the partition will also be deleted.

In addition to creating a primary partition, you can use the Disk Management snap-in for the following tasks:

♦ **Mark the partition as active:** Right-click the partition and click **Mark Partition as Active** to create an active partition.

♦ **To view information about a disk:** Right-click the disk and click the **Properties** command on the context menu to open the **Properties** dialog box for the disk **(Figure 4-7)**. Various disk properties, such as the storage type, total disk capacity, status of the disk, and amount of free space available on the disk, can be viewed.

♦ **To update information for a disk:** Use the **Refresh** command on the **Action** menu to update the drive letter, file system, and volume information. You can also use this command to update removable media information and determine whether a volume is readable. You can use the **Rescan Disks** command to update the hardware information.

♦ **To view the volume properties:** Right-click the volume and select the **Properties** command on the context menu.

♦ **To change the drive letter for a partition:** Right-click the partition and click the **Change Drive Letter and Paths** command on the context menu **(Figure 4-8)** to open the **Change Drive Letter and Paths for (drive letter: volume name)** dialog box. Click Change... to open the **Change Drive Letter or Path** dialog box **(Figure 4-9)**. Here, you can choose a drive letter in the **Assign the following drive letter** list box.

♦ **Format a partition:** Right-click the partition and click the **Format** command to format the partition, change the partition label, change the allocation unit size, and/or enable file and folder compression.

♦ **Delete a partition:** Right-click the partition and click the **Delete Partition** command on the context menu.

Figure 4-7 Properties dialog box for the primary partition

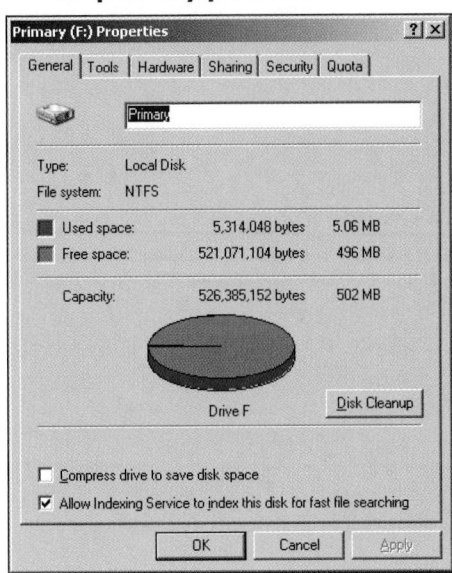

Figure 4-8 Changing the drive letter of a primary partition

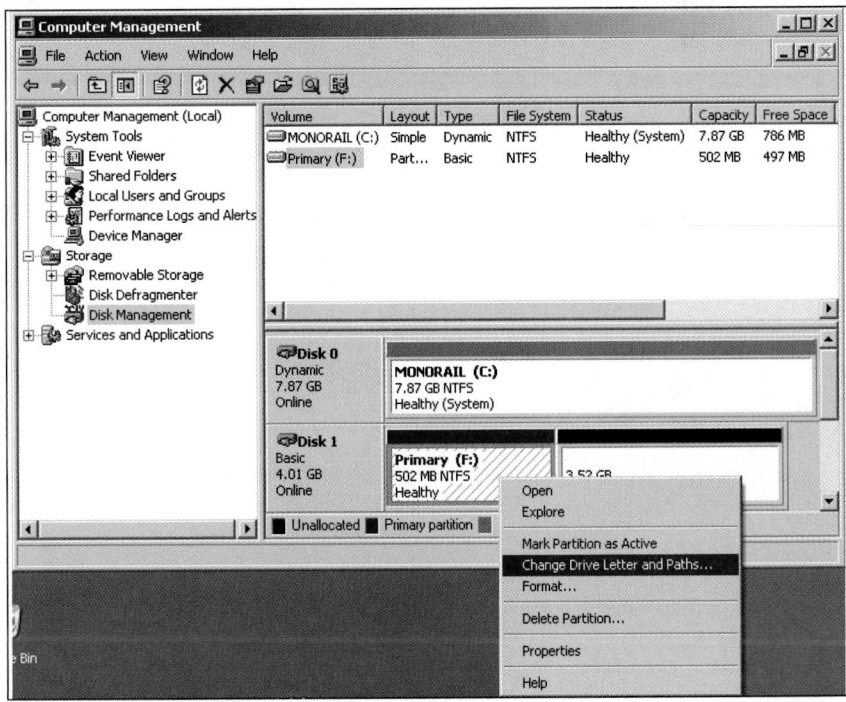

Figure 4-9 The Change Drive Letter or Path dialog box

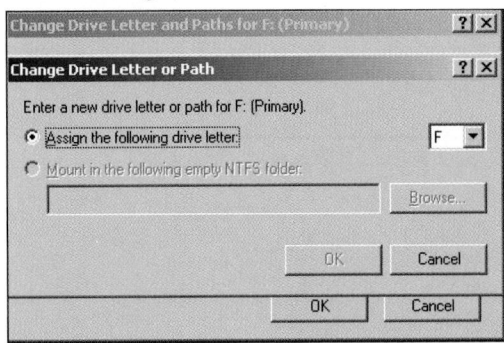

skill 3 | *Creating an Extended Partition and a Logical Drive*

exam objective

Manage basic disks and dynamic disks.

overview

Basic disks can have a maximum of four partitions per drive using the default master boot record (MBR) partitioning style. Only one MBR partition can be an extended partition. Therefore, you need to combine all available free disk space on your hard disk to create an extended partition. Extended partitions do not store data like primary or logical partitions. An extended partition acts as a container for logical partitions, where the data is actually stored. You can assign a drive letter to a logical partition and format it with a file system so that you can store and retrieve data.

how to

Create an extended partition, and then create a logical drive in the extended partition.

1. Open the **Computer Management** console, if necessary.
2. In the **Disk Management** snap-in, in **Disk 1**, or whichever disk has unallocated disk space, right-click the unallocated space and click **New Partition (Figure 4-10)** to open the first page of the **New Partition Wizard**.
3. Click ⟨ Next > ⟩ to open the **Select Partition Type** screen.
4. Select the **Extended partition** option button to create an extended partition **(Figure 4-11)**.
5. Click ⟨ Next > ⟩ to open the **Specify Partition Size** screen.
6. Type **300** in the **Partition size in MB** spin box to set the size for the extended partition **(Figure 4-12)**.
7. Click ⟨ Next > ⟩ to open the final summary screen of the New Partition Wizard.
8. Click ⟨ Finish ⟩ to complete the process of creating an extended partition. You can view the newly created extended partition in the Computer Management console.
9. To create a logical drive on this extended partition, right-click the free space in the extended partition, and click **New Logical Drive** to open the New Partition Wizard.
10. Click ⟨ Next > ⟩ to open the **Select Partition Type** screen. Note that the **Logical drive** option button is selected by default and the other options are inactive.
11. Click ⟨ Next > ⟩ to open the **Specify Partition Size** screen.
12. Type **300** in the **Partition size in MB** spin box to set the size for the logical partition.
13. Click ⟨ Next > ⟩ to open the **Assign Drive Letter or Path** screen.
14. Select **G:** in the **Assign the following drive letter** list box. You can also choose the **Do not assign a drive letter or drive path** option to forego this option at this time.
15. Click ⟨ Next > ⟩ to open the **Format Partition** screen.
16. By default, the file system selected to format your logical drive is **NTFS**. Accept the default file system and allocation unit size, and type **Logical** in the **Volume label** text box as the label for the logical drive.
17. Select the **Perform a quick format** check box. You can also choose **Do not format this partition** at this time and you can **Enable file and folder compression** on the partition if desired.
18. Click ⟨ Next > ⟩ to open the final summary screen of the wizard. Click ⟨ Finish ⟩ to create a logical drive on the extended partition. You can view the newly created logical drive in the Computer Management console **(Figure 4-13)**.

tip

The free space in an extended partition is enclosed in a box. An extended partition is dark green in color and the free space is lime green.

Figure 4-10 Starting the New Partition Wizard

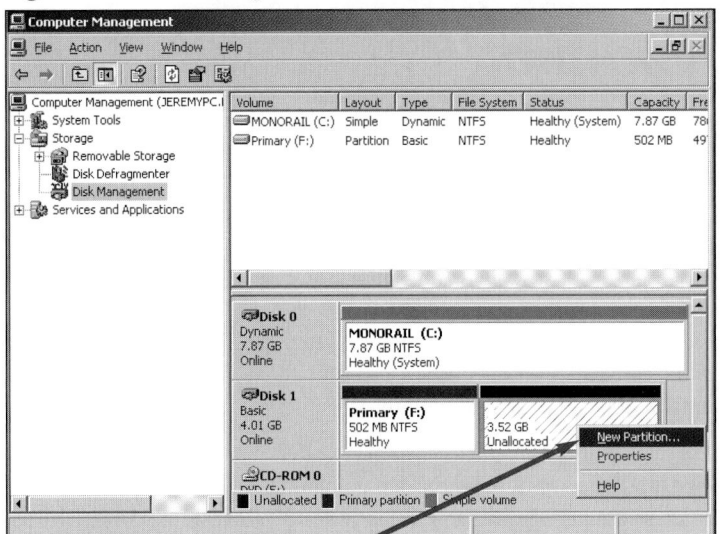

Figure 4-11 Creating an extended partition

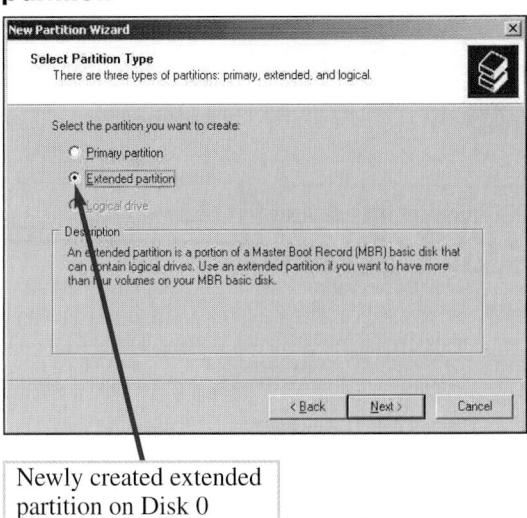

Newly created extended partition on Disk 0

Right click on the Unallocated disk area

Figure 4-12 Setting the size for the extended partition

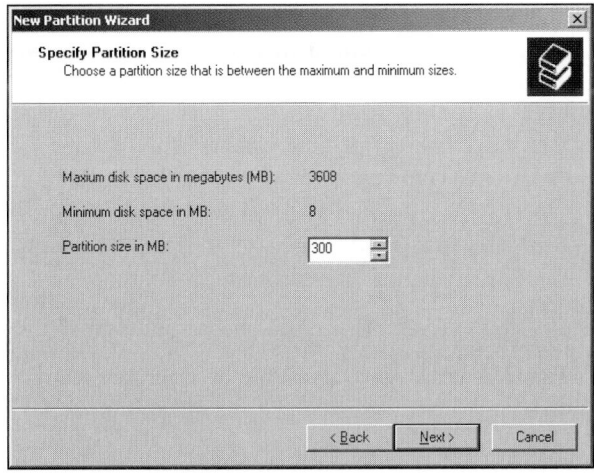

Figure 4-13 A logical drive on an extended partition

A logical drive has been created on Disk 1

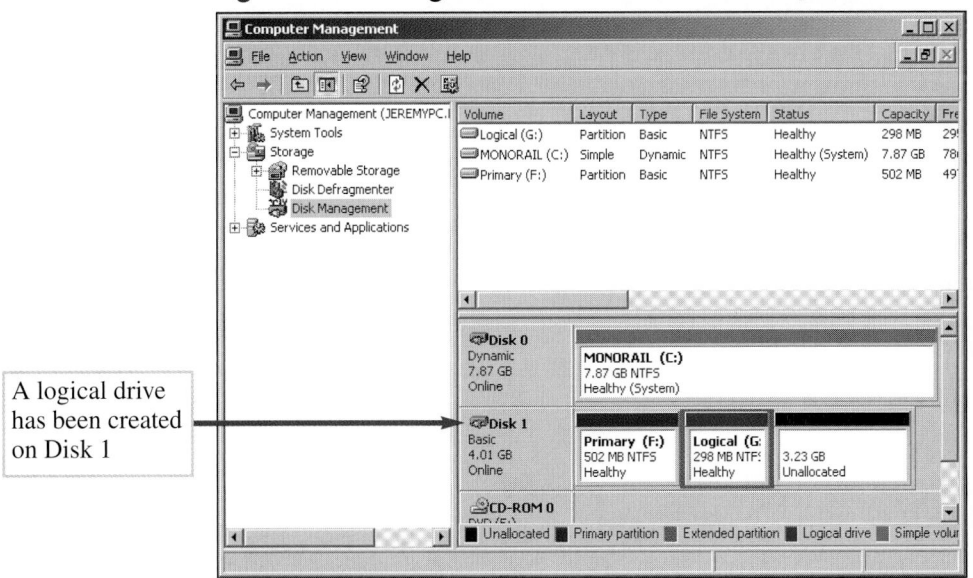

skill 4

Upgrading a Disk from Basic to Dynamic

exam objective

Manage basic disks and dynamic disks.

overview

caution

Before you upgrade a disk, close all running programs and back up your data to avoid data loss.

By default, the hard disk on a Windows Server 2003 computer is initialized with basic storage. Basic disks are sufficient for most typical configurations, but you will want to convert to dynamic disks in certain cases to take advantage of their enhancements. The main advantages of dynamic disks are that you can span volumes and create fault-tolerant volumes. There are two types of fault-tolerant volumes: mirrored and RAID-5. You use the Disk Management snap-in to upgrade a basic disk to a dynamic disk.

When you upgrade a basic disk, the existing partitions are converted into simple volumes. It is also important to remember that data on dynamic volumes cannot be accessed if you dual boot to MS-DOS or any other Windows operating systems prior to Windows 2000.

how to

tip

To upgrade a disk, you need at least 1 MB of free space on your hard disk.

Upgrade a disk from basic to dynamic.

1. Open the **Computer Management** console, if necessary.
2. In the left pane, expand the **Storage** node, if necessary, and click the **Disk Management** snap-in to display information about the disks and volumes on the system in the details pane.
3. Right-click **Disk 1**, or whichever disk you are going to convert, and click **Convert to Dynamic Disk** to open the **Convert to Dynamic Disk** dialog box. Make sure that the disk you want to upgrade is selected (**Figure 4-14**).
4. Click [OK]. The **Disks to Convert** dialog box opens (**Figure 4-15**).
5. Verify the disk or disks to convert and click [Convert]. The **Disk Management** message box warns you that if you convert disks to dynamic, you will not be able to start other installed operating systems from any volume on these disks (**Figure 4-16**).
6. Click [Yes] to confirm that you want to upgrade the disk.
7. The **Convert Disk to Dynamic** message box warns you that file systems on any of the disks to be converted will be dismounted (**Figure 4-17**).
8. Click [Yes] to confirm that you want to continue the operation. If you are converting a disk that includes the system volume, the boot volume, or a volume which contains the paging file, the **Confirm** alert box informs you that your computer will be rebooted (**Figure 4-18**).
9. If the Confirm message box does not open, the disks will automatically be converted to dynamic. If it opens, click [OK]. Your system will restart and the disk is upgraded from basic to dynamic. If you reboot, reopen the Disk Management snap-in to view the dynamic disk.

more

caution

You must back up your data before you revert to a basic disk, to avoid data loss.

You can revert a dynamic disk back to a basic disk. However, all information on the disk will be lost. First, you must delete all volumes from the dynamic disk to create unallocated space on the entire disk. When all volumes on the disk have been deleted, right-click the disk, and click **Convert To Basic Disk**.

Figure 4-14 The Convert to Dynamic Disk dialog box

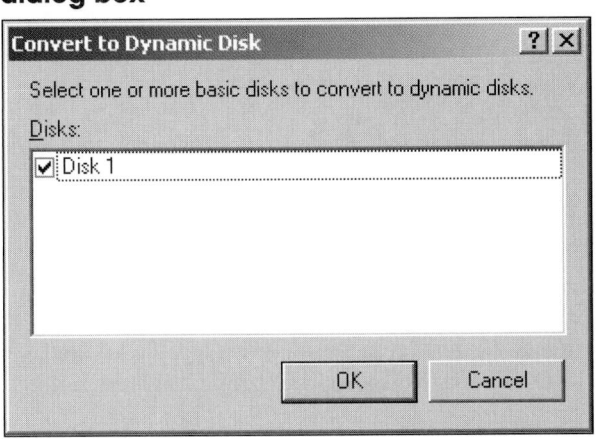

Figure 4-15 The Disks to Convert dialog box

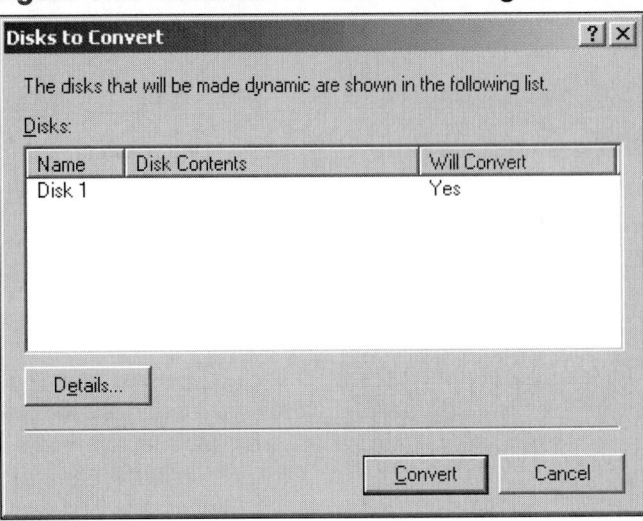

Figure 4-16 The Disk Management message box

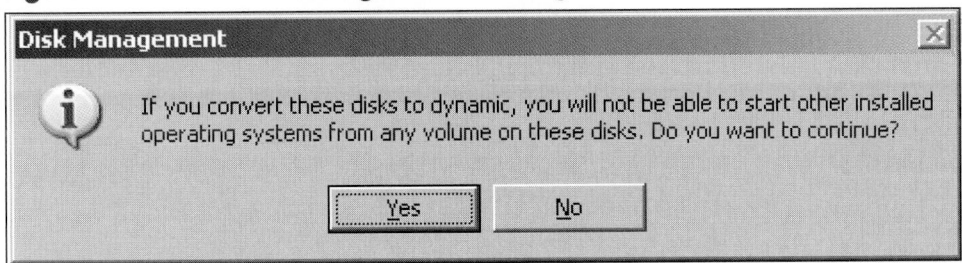

Figure 4-17 The Convert Disk to Dynamic warning message

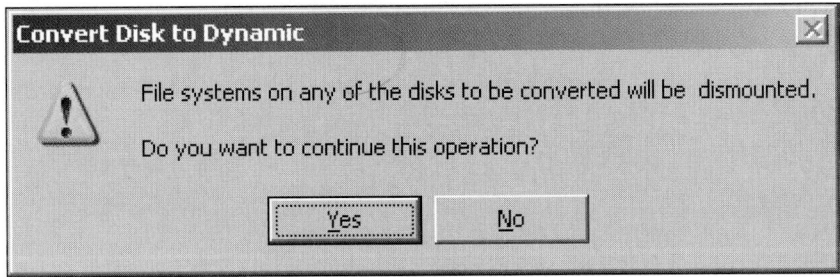

Figure 4-18 The Confirm message box

You will have to reboot if you are converting a disk that includes the boot volume, system volume or a volume that includes the paging file

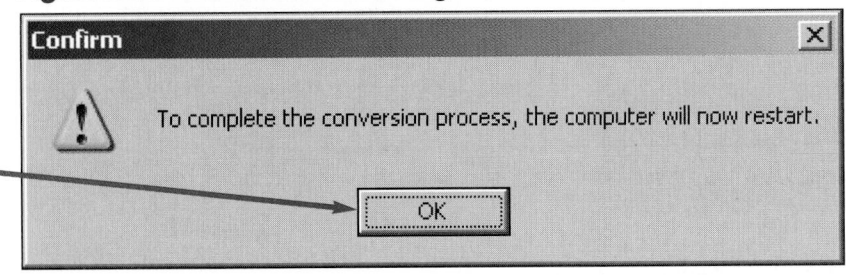

skill 5 | *Creating a Simple Volume*

exam objective   Manage basic disks and dynamic disks.

overview

When you upgrade a basic disk to a dynamic disk, any existing partitions are converted to volumes. Any free space that is left on the drive can be used to create additional volumes. A simple volume can be part of a disk or an entire disk and can be created only on a single dynamic disk. You often create simple volumes when you have only one disk drive on your computer. You can also increase the storage capacity of an existing simple volume by adding unallocated disk space that is left on your hard disk. This is referred to as extending the simple volume. You can extend a volume only if it is formatted using NTFS or if it is unformatted. FAT or FAT32 volumes cannot be extended; however, you can convert a FAT or FAT32 volume to NTFS, and then extend it. If you format a volume in the Disk Management snap-in, all data on the volume will be erased. However, you can use the Convert utility to convert a volume to NTFS while maintaining all of the files on the disk. At the command prompt, type **convert x: /fs:ntfs** (where **x** represents the letter of the volume) and press **[Enter]**.

However, it is recommended that you back up the drive before the conversion, just in case.

You can extend a simple or extended volume only if it was originally created on a dynamic disk. If you upgraded a basic disk with partitions to a dynamic disk, thereby upgrading the partitions to simple volumes, you cannot extend those volumes.

how to

Create a simple volume. (Remember that volumes are created on dynamic disks, while partitions are created on basic disks.)

1. Open the **Computer Management** console, if necessary, and open the **Disk Management** snap-in.
2. In the lower portion of the details pane, right-click the unallocated space on **Disk 1**, or whichever disk has unallocated disk space, and click **New Volume** to start the **New Volume Wizard**.
3. Click [Next >] to open the **Select Volume Type** screen (**Figure 4-19**). Under **Select the volume you want to create**, the **Simple** option button is selected by default.
4. Accept the default selection, and click [Next >]. The **Select Disks** screen displays all of the dynamic disks on the system. Select the disk on which you would like to create the simple volume, if necessary.
5. Type **300** in the **Select the amount of space in MB** spin box to set the size for the volume (**Figure 4-20**).
6. Click [Next >] to open the **Assign Drive Letter or Path** screen.
7. Select an unused drive letter in the **Assign the following drive letter** list box.
8. Click [Next >] to open the **Format Volume** screen.
9. By default, the file system selected to format your simple volume is **NTFS**. Accept the default file system and default allocation unit size, and type **Simple** in the **Volume label** text box as the label for the simple volume.
10. Select the **Perform a quick format** check box.
11. Click [Next >] to open the **Completing the New Volume Wizard** screen.
12. Click [Finish] to complete the process of creating a simple volume. You can view this volume in the Disk Management snap-in (**Figure 4-21**).

more

To extend an NTFS formatted simple volume, right-click the volume and click the **Extend Volume** command. The **Extend Volume Wizard** will guide you to use any unallocated disk space to extend the simple volume.

Figure 4-19 Creating a simple volume

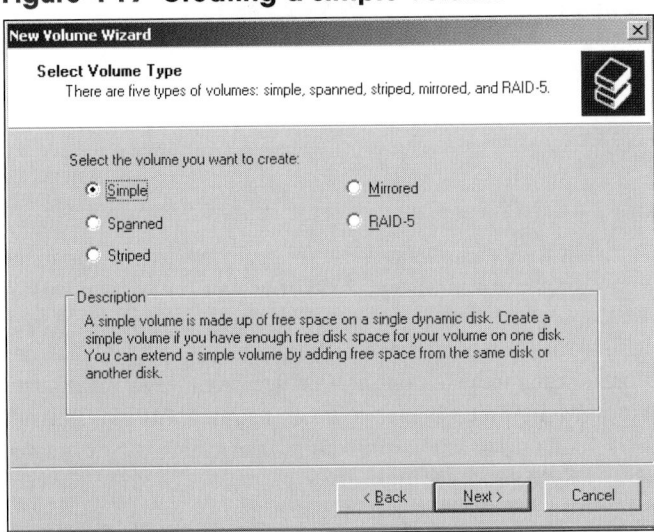

Figure 4-20 Setting the size for the simple volume

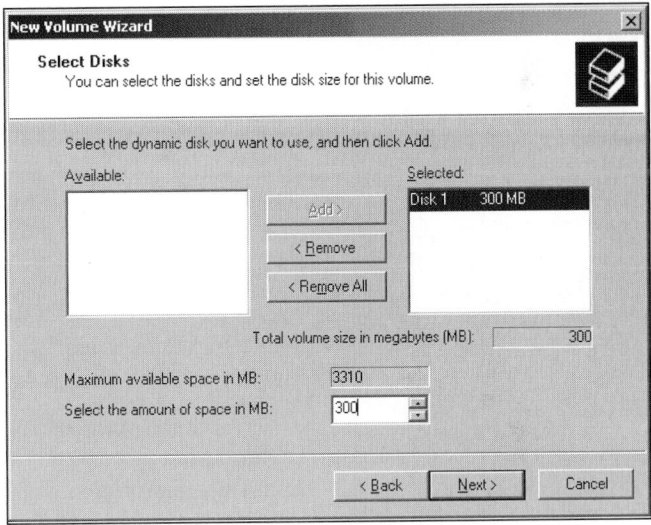

Figure 4-21 Newly created simple volume

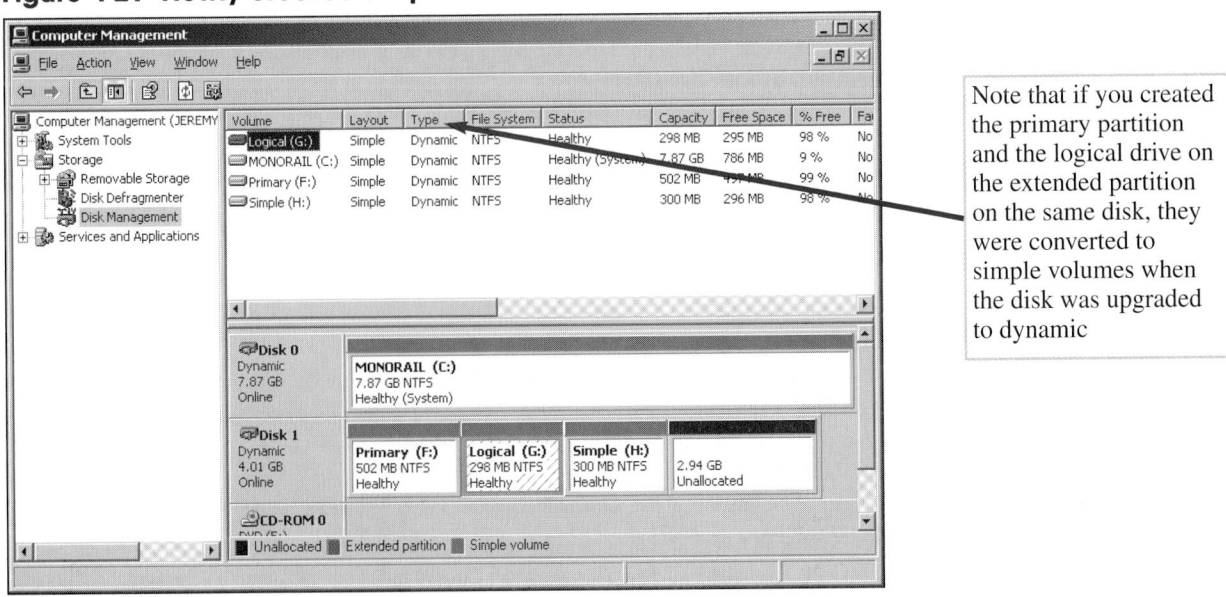

Note that if you created the primary partition and the logical drive on the extended partition on the same disk, they were converted to simple volumes when the disk was upgraded to dynamic

skill 6

Introducing Spanned, Striped and Mirrored Volumes

exam objective

Optimize server disk performance.

overview

caution

After you have extended a spanned volume, you cannot delete any portion without deleting the entire spanned volume.

caution

Neither spanned nor striped volumes provide fault tolerance. If one of the disks in a spanned or striped volume fails, the entire volume will fail.

caution

You cannot extend a mirrored volume.

If a disk is full, and you do not want to change its drive letter, you can create a spanned volume to combine the unallocated space on multiple disks into one logical volume. A spanned volume can organize disk space on up to a maximum of 32 disks. Windows Server 2003 starts data storage with the first disk. When that disk is full, it uses the second disk and so on, until all of the data has been accommodated on the spanned volume. Spanned disks allow you to combine the space used by multiple, smaller volumes, on multiple disks, into one spanned volume represented by a single drive letter. You can also extend NTFS formatted spanned volumes by adding free disk space from multiple disks.

As with spanned volumes, you can combine disk space from a maximum of 32 disks to create a striped volume. However, unlike spanned volumes, in striped volumes, the space allocated to the striped volume on each of these disks must be the same size. On a striped volume, data is divided in blocks of 64 KB across each segment of the volume. Data is simultaneously written across all of the disks so that it is added to the disks at the same rate. This enhances the performance of your hard disk subsystem because data is equally distributed among the disks.

A mirrored volume provides fault tolerance because you create two drives that are duplicates of each other. This ensures that if one of the hard disks fails, you can continue to use the data on the unaffected disk. However, mirrored volumes are inefficient in some respects because fifty percent of the available disk space is consumed by fault tolerance. This is the main disadvantage of mirroring. Two 20 GB mirrored hard drives will end up storing only 20 GB.

how to

Create a spanned volume. (In order to complete this exercise, you will need unallocated space on two dynamic disks.)

1. Open the **Computer Management** console, if necessary. Then, open the **Disk Management** snap-in.
2. In the lower portion of the details pane, right-click the unallocated space in **Disk 0** (or one of the dynamic disks with unallocated disk space) and click **New Volume**.
3. The **New Volume Wizard** opens. Click [Next >] to open the **Select Volume Type** screen.
4. Click the **Spanned** option button (**Figure 4-22**), and then click [Next >].
5. The **Select Disks** screen displays all of the dynamic disks on the system. Click **Disk 1** (or another disk with unallocated disk space) in the **Available** list box and click [Add >] to include Disk 1 in the **Selected** list box. There should be two disks in the Selected box.
6. Type **300** in the **Select the amount of space in MB** spin box to set the size for the spanned volume on Disk 1.
7. In the **Selected** box, select **Disk 0** and type **300** in the **Select the amount space in MB** spin box to set the size for the spanned volume on Disk 0. The spanned volume should now be configured to use 300 MB from each disk (**Figure 4-23**).
8. Click [Next >] to open the **Assign Drive Letter or Path** screen. Select an unused drive letter in the **Assign the following drive letter** list box, and click [Next >] to open the **Format Volume** screen.
9. By default, the file system selected to format your spanned volume is **NTFS**. Accept the default file system and the default allocation unit size, and type **Spanned** in the **Volume label** text box as the label for the spanned volume.
10. Select the **Perform a quick format** check box.
11. Click [Next >] to open the **Completing the New Volume Wizard** page (**Figure 4-24**).
12. Click [Finish] to create the spanned volume. The newly created spanned volume can be viewed in the Disk Management snap-in (**Figure 4-25**).

Figure 4-22 Creating a spanned volume

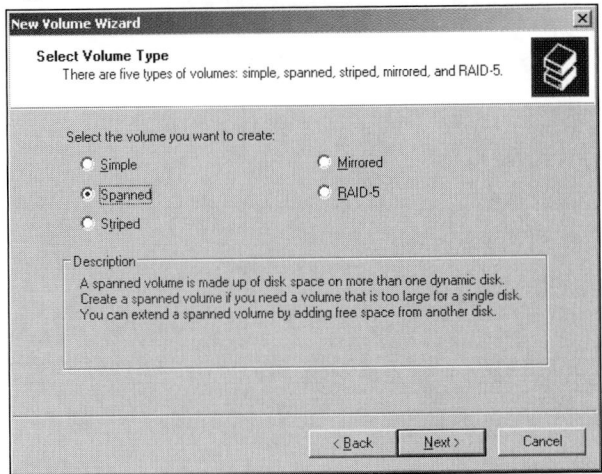

Figure 4-23 Selecting the disks to create a spanned volume

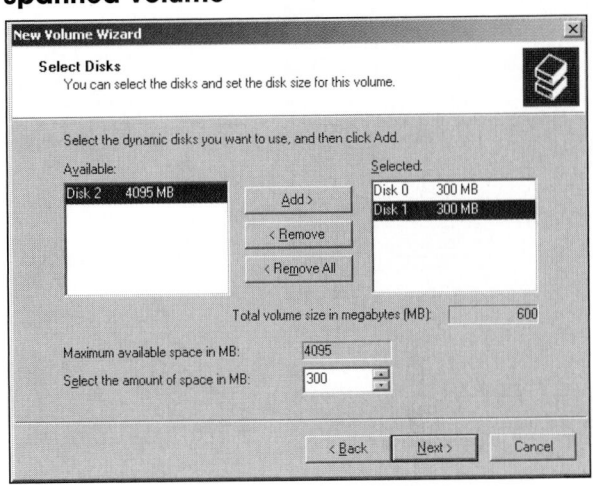

Figure 4-24 Details of the spanned volume

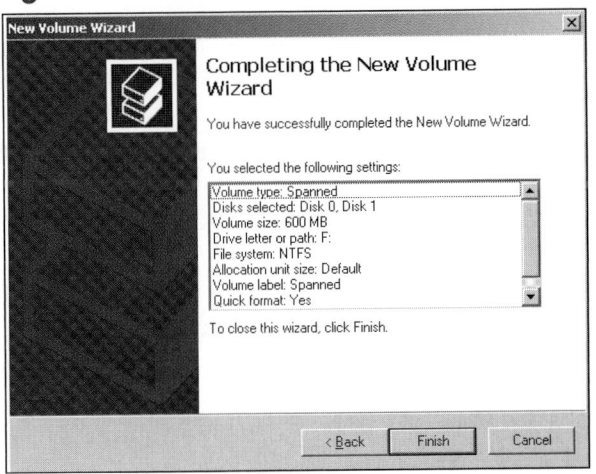

Figure 4-25 Newly created spanned volume

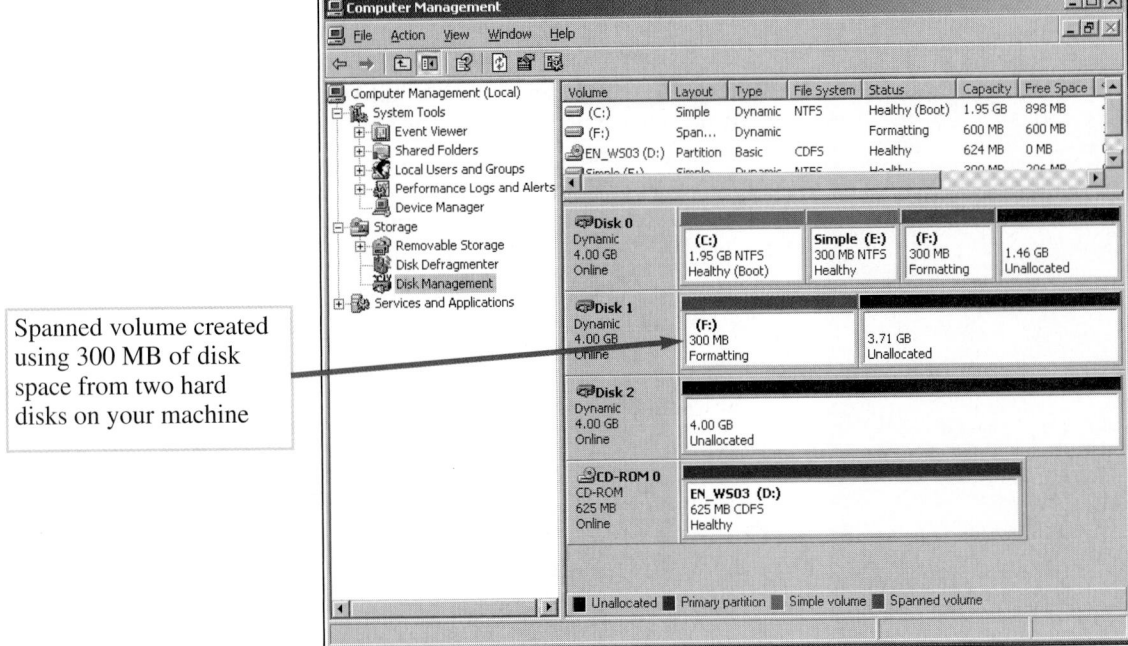

Spanned volume created using 300 MB of disk space from two hard disks on your machine

skill 6

Introducing Spanned, Striped and Mirrored Volumes (cont'd)

exam objective

Optimize server disk performance.

how to

Create a striped volume.

1. Perform steps 1–3 listed on page 4.20.
2. Under **Select the volume you want to create**, click the **Striped** option button.
3. Click Next > . The **Select Disks** screen displays all of the dynamic disks on the system.
4. Click **Disk 1** (or any second disk with unallocated disk space) in the **Available** list box and click Add > to include the second disk in the **Selected** list box.
5. Type **300** in the **Select the amount of space in MB** spin box to set the size for the striped volume. 300 MB will be used from each disk for a total of 600 MB.
6. Click Next > to open the **Assign Drive Letter or Path** screen.
7. Select an unused drive letter in the **Assign a drive letter** list box to assign a drive letter to the striped volume (**Figure 4-26**).
8. Click Next > to open the **Format Volume** screen.
9. By default, the file system selected to format your striped volume is **NTFS**. Accept the default file system and the default allocation unit size, and type **Striped** in the **Volume label** text box as the label for the striped volume.
10. Select the **Perform a quick format** check box.
11. Click Next > to open the **Completing the New Volume Wizard** screen.
12. Click Finish to create the striped volume. You can view the newly created striped volume in the Disk Management snap-in (**Figure 4-27**).

Create a mirrored volume.

1. Perform steps 1–3 listed on page 4.20.
2. Under **Select the volume you want to create**, click the **Mirrored** option button.
3. Click Next > . The **Select Disks** page displays all of the dynamic disks on the system.
4. Click **Disk 1** (or any second disk with unallocated disk space) in the **Available** list box and click Add > to include the second disk in the **Selected** list box.
5. Type **300** in the **Select the amount of space in MB** spin box to set the size for the mirrored volume (**Figure 4-28**). 300 MB from each disk will be used for a total of 300 MB of usable storage space (the other 300 MB is the mirror).
6. Click Next > to open the **Assign Drive Letter or Path** screen.
7. Select an unused drive letter in the **Assign a drive letter** list box.
8. Click Next > to open the **Format Volume** screen.
9. By default, the file system selected to format your mirrored volume is **NTFS**. Accept the default file system and the default allocation unit size, and type **Mirrored** in the **Volume label** text box as the label for the mirrored volume (**Figure 4-29**).
10. Select the **Perform a quick format** check box.
13. Click Next > to open the **Completing the New Volume Wizard** screen.
14. Click Finish to create the mirrored volume. The newly created mirrored volume can be viewed in the Disk Management snap-in (**Figure 4-30**).

tip

Note that you do not need to specify the size for each disk because the disk space for all disks in a striped volume will be identical.

tip

Note that you do not need to specify the size for each disk because the disk space from all disks in a mirrored volume is identical.

Figure 4-26 Assigning a drive letter to the striped volume

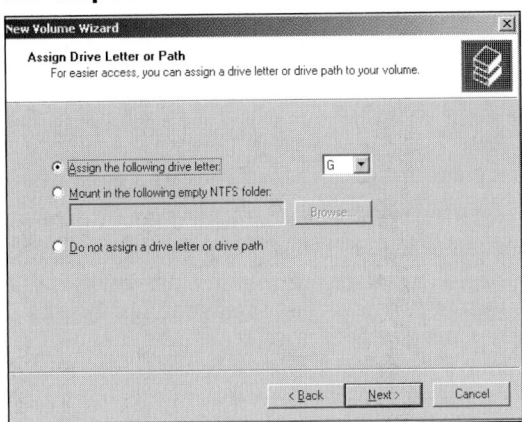

Figure 4-27 Newly created striped volume

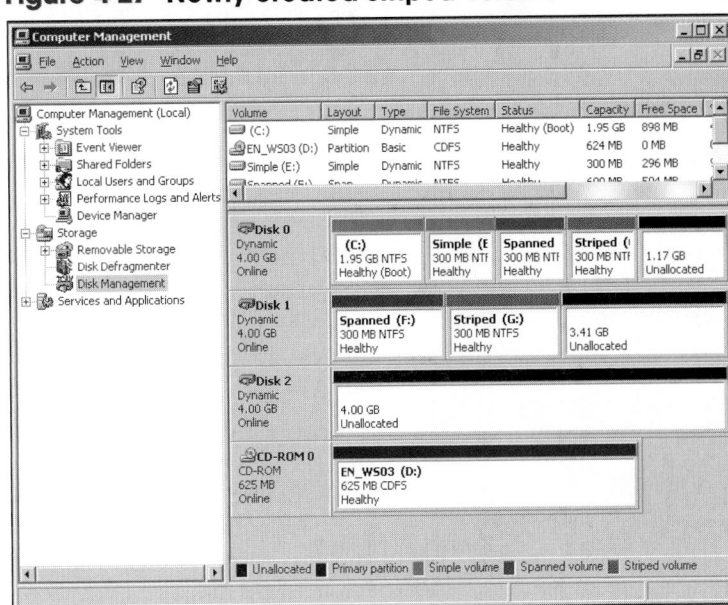

Figure 4-28 Selecting the disks for a mirrored volume

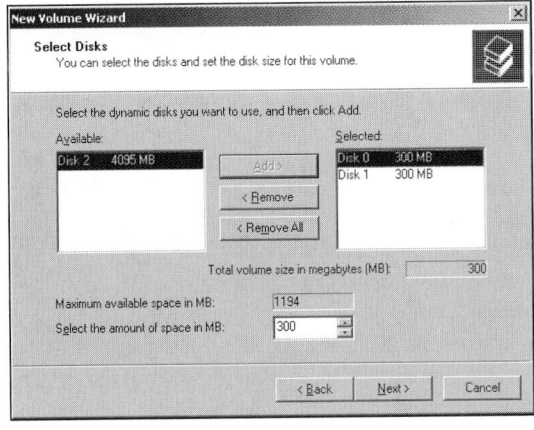

Figure 4-29 Selecting the file system, name, and format the volume

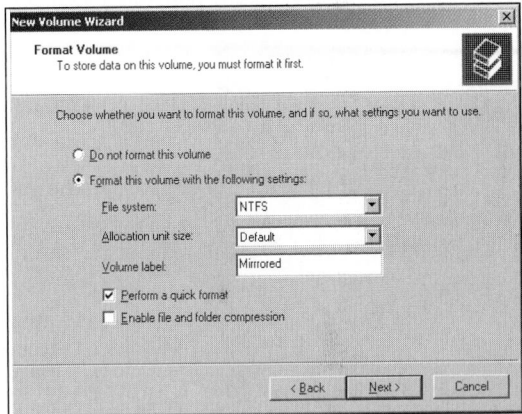

Figure 4-30 Newly created mirrored volume

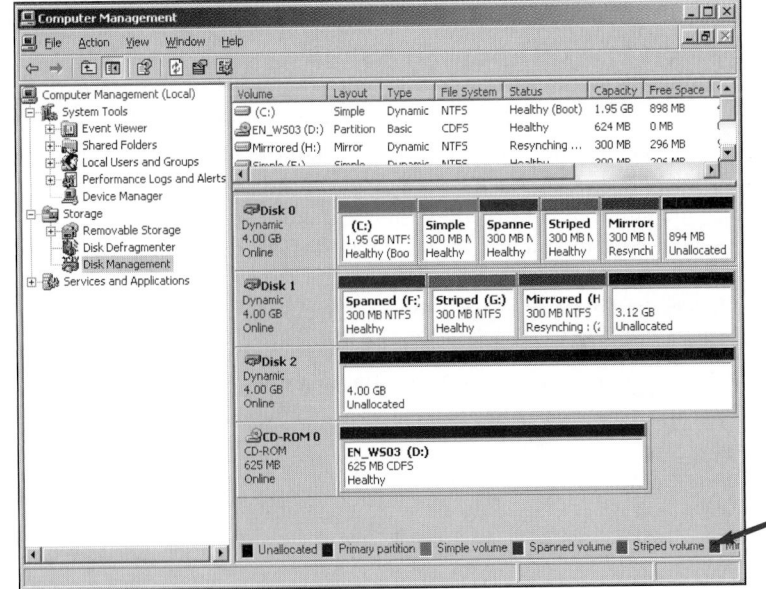

Mirrored volume created by combining free space from two hard disks

skill 7

Understanding and Implementing a RAID-5 Volume

exam objective

Optimize server disk performance. Implement a RAID solution.

overview

A RAID-5 volume consists of disk space on at least three physical hard disks. It provides fault tolerance by writing one block of parity information for each stripe of data. If a disk fails, the system uses the parity information and the data from the remaining disks and performs a logical XOR (Exclusive OR) operation to determine what the missing section of data should be.

Due to one parity block being written for each stripe of data, you will lose exactly one drive's worth of usable disk space in a RAID-5 array. While this leads to a rather large loss of space in small RAID-5 systems, it has the advantage of being more space efficient the larger the array is. For example, with three 10 GB drives in a RAID-5 array, you will lose 33% percent of your disk space, or 10 GB, to parity, leaving a total usable space of only 20 GB. However, with five 10 GB disks, you lose the same 10 GB (only 20%) of available disk space to parity, for a total of 40 GB of usable storage space.

For a slightly more technical explanation of how RAID-5 works, you can visit:

http://www.commodore.ca/misc/misc/raid5/raid5.htm

how to

Create a RAID-5 volume. (You will need unallocated space on three dynamic disks in order to complete this exercise.)

1. Open the **Computer Management** console, if necessary. Then, open the **Disk Management** snap-in.
2. In the lower portion of the details pane, right-click the unallocated space in **Disk 0** (or on one of the dynamic disks) and click **New Volume** to start the **New Volume Wizard**.
3. Click [Next >] to open the **Select Volume Type** screen.
4. Under **Select the volume you want to create**, click the **RAID-5** option button.
5. Click [Next >]. The **Select Disks** screen displays all of the dynamic disks on the system.
6. Click **Disk 1** (or another of the disks with unallocated space) in the **Available** list box and click [Add >] to include the disk in the **Selected** list box.
7. Click **Disk 2** (or another of the disks with unallocated space) in the **Available** list box and click [Add >] to include the disk in the **Selected** list box.
8. Type **300** in the **Select the amount of space in MB** spin box to set the size for the RAID-5 volume (**Figure 4-31**). 300 MB of space will be used from each disk for a total of 600 MB of usable storage space (300 MB will be used for parity data)
9. Click [Next >] to open the **Assign Drive Letter or Path** screen.
10. Select an unused drive letter in the **Assign the following drive** letter list box.
11. Click [Next >] to open the **Format Volume** screen.
12. By default, the **NTFS** file system is selected. Accept the default file system and the default allocation unit size, and type **RAID-5** in the **Volume label** text box as the label for the RAID-5 volume.
13. Select the **Perform a quick format** check box.
14. Click [Next >] to open the **Completing the New Volume Wizard** screen (**Figure 4-32**).
15. Click [Finish] to create the RAID-5 volume. You can view the newly created RAID-5 volume in the Disk Management snap-in (**Figure 4-33**).

tip

Note that you do not need to specify the size for each disk because the disk space for all disks in a RAID-5 volume will be identical.

Figure 4-31 Setting the size for a RAID-5 volume

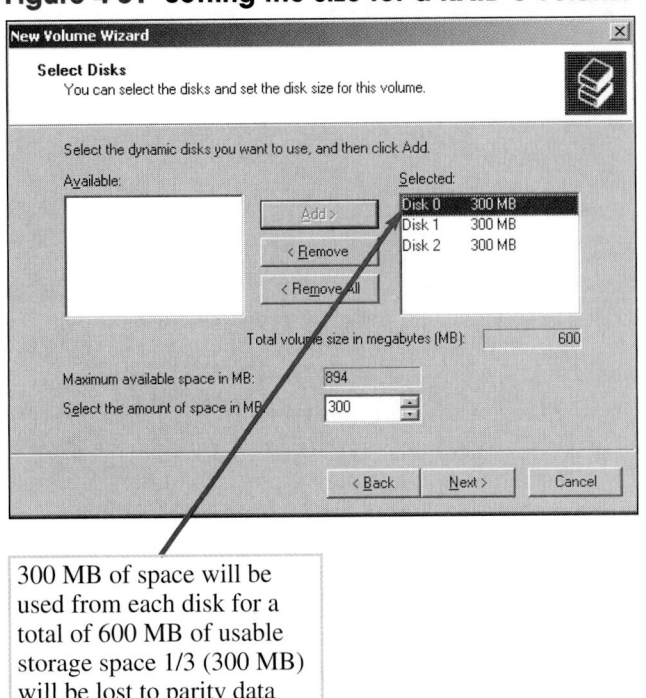

Figure 4-32 Details of the RAID-5 volume

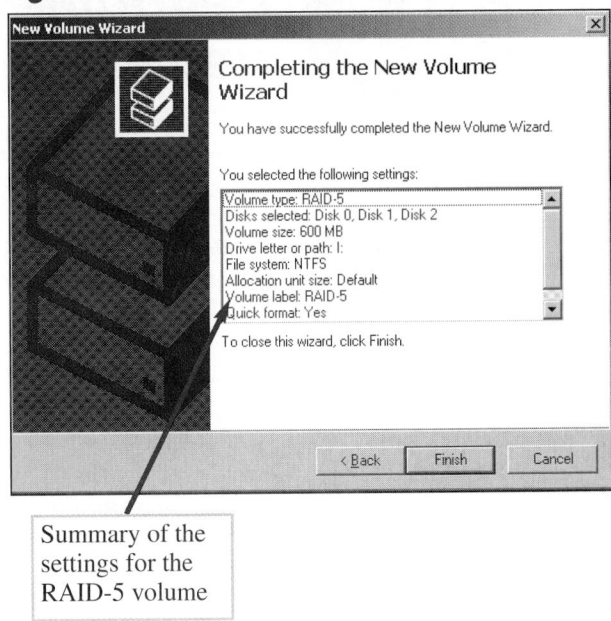

300 MB of space will be used from each disk for a total of 600 MB of usable storage space 1/3 (300 MB) will be lost to parity data

Summary of the settings for the RAID-5 volume

Figure 4-33 Newly created RAID-5 volume

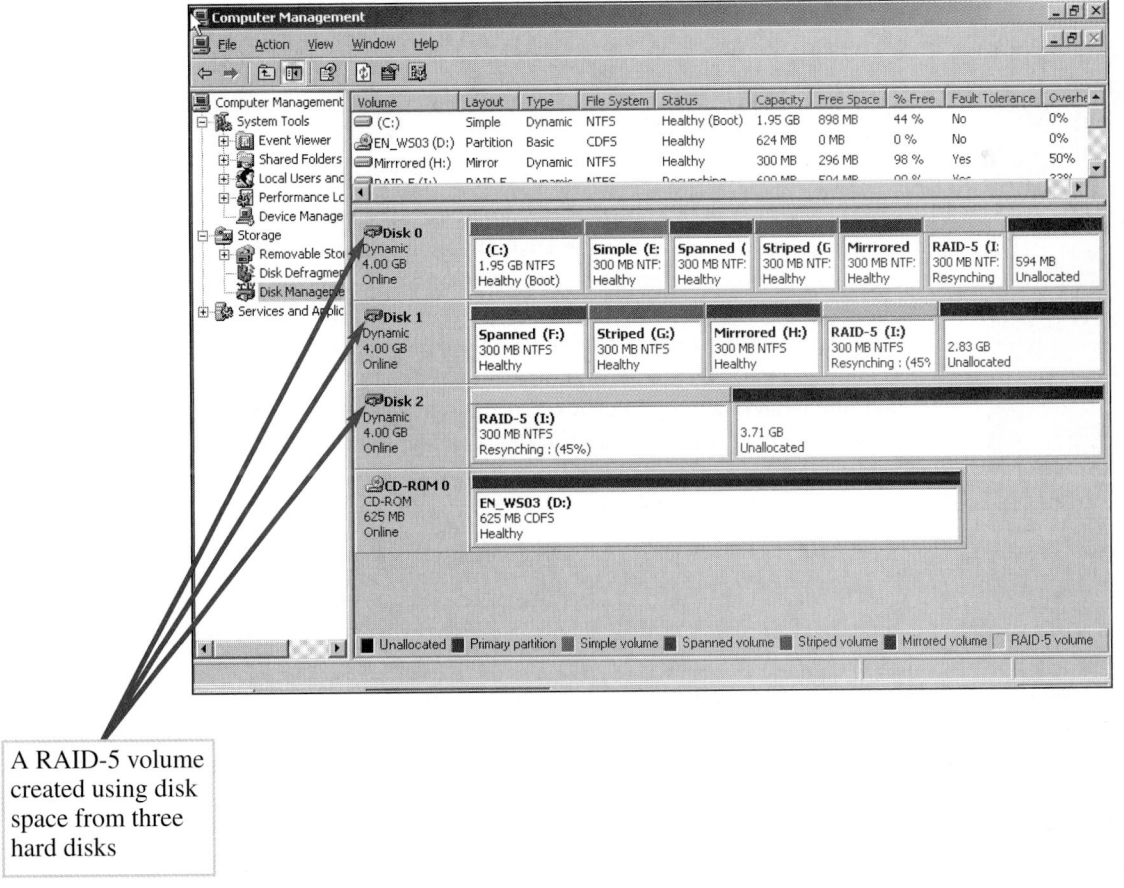

A RAID-5 volume created using disk space from three hard disks

skill 8

Defragmenting Volumes and Partitions

exam objective

Optimize server disk performance. Defragment volumes and partitions.

overview

Whenever files are created, deleted, or modified, Windows Server 2003 assigns a group of disk clusters depending on the size of the file. As file size fluctuates over time, so does the number of clusters assigned to the file. Eventually, you are likely to write a file to the disk that is large enough that a contiguous section of clusters on the disk capable of holding the entire file cannot be located. When this occurs, Windows writes the file in separate sections in available areas of free space. This will ultimately slow access times, as the disk has to "search" all over to reassemble all of the separate pieces of the files. Even though this process is more efficient when using NTFS than when using FAT16 or FAT32, the files will still become fragmented over time. As fragmentation levels increase, disk access slows. The system must take additional resources and time to find all the cluster groups in order to use the file. The **Disk Defragmenter** rearranges files and unused space, moving the segments of each file and folder to one location so that they occupy a single, contiguous space on the hard disk. This process has been improved in Windows Server 2003, particularly for NTFS volumes. In Windows 2000, you could not defragment volumes with cluster sizes larger than 4 KB. Furthermore, NTFS metadata files, for example, the Master File Table (MFT), were not defragmented. These limitations were mainly the result of the fact that the defragmenter was closely tied to NTFS support for compressed files. Compressed files are mapped into memory in 4 KB blocks using Cache Manager interfaces that do not support cluster sizes larger than 4 KB. In Windows XP and Windows Server 2003, file system defragmenter support has been rewritten so that it is no longer dependent on compressed file routines and the Cache Manager. The result is that the limitations on defragmenting volumes with cluster sizes larger than 4 KB and on moving single NTFS file clusters have been remedied. The Master File Table and most directory and file metadata can now be defragmented and defragmentation is also now supported for encrypted files, making the defragmentation utility far more robust and useful than its predecessors.

You can access the Disk Defragmenter in a several ways. You can open the **Computer Management** console, and select the **Disk Defragmenter** snap-in (**Figure 4-34**), open the **Properties** dialog box for a volume or partition on the **Tools** tab and select the **Defragment Now** button (**Figure 4-35**), or you can access it from the Start menu (Start-All Programs-Accessories-System Tools-Disk Defragmenter). You can also create a custom MMC and add the Disk Defragmenter console to it. Disk defragmentation is a time-consuming and memory-intensive process. You should set aside a block of idle time in which to defragment a hard disk. You can analyze the disk to determine the amount of fragmented files and folders on the disk before defragmenting it. When the analysis is complete, a dialog box will let you know if you need to defragment the disk (**Figure 4-36**).

The Disk Defragmenter window is divided into three parts:

◆ **Partitions to analyze and defragment:** Lists the volumes that you can view and defragment. It also provides details such as the type of **File System**, amount of **Free Space**, and drive **Capacity**.
◆ **Analysis display:** Provides a graphical depiction of how the selected volume is fragmented.
◆ **Defragmentation display:** Provides a constantly-updating representation of the volume during defragmentation.

Figure 4-34 The Disk Defragmenter utility in the Computer Management console

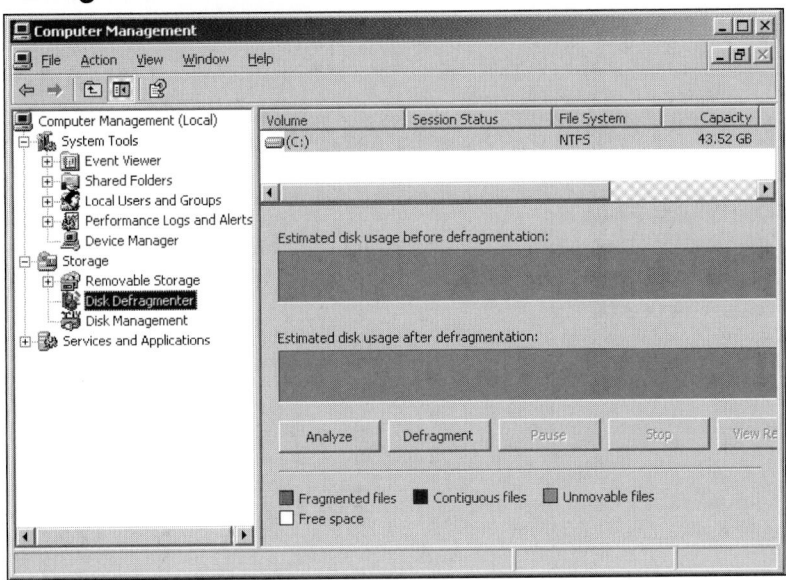

Figure 4-35 The Defragment Now button on the Tools tab

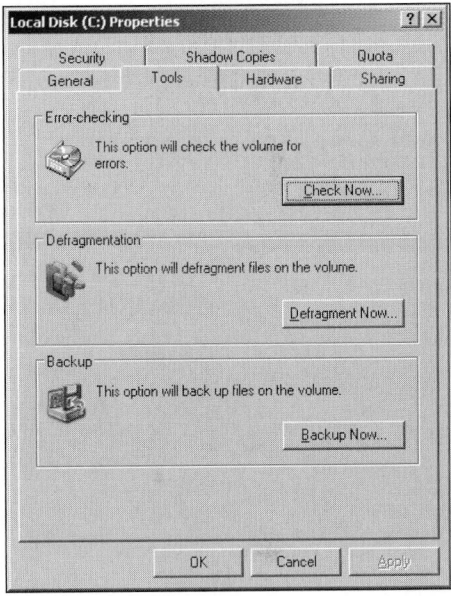

Figure 4-36 Analyzing a disk

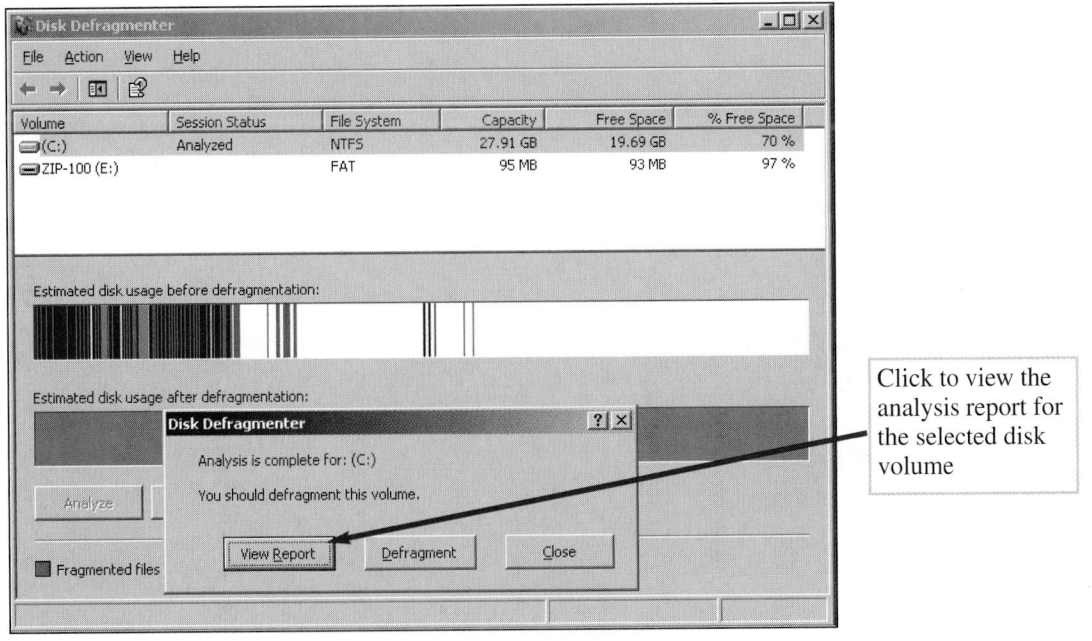

Click to view the analysis report for the selected disk volume

skill 8

Defragmenting Volumes and Partitions *(cont'd)*

exam objective

Optimize server disk performance. Defragment volumes and partitions.

overview

After defragmenting a disk, you can compare the Analysis display band and the Defragmentation display band in the Disk Defragmenter snap-in in order to determine the improved condition of the volume. In both bands, the following display colors indicate the condition of the volume (**Figure 4-37**):

- ◆ Red — fragmented files
- ◆ Blue — non-fragmented files
- ◆ White — free space
- ◆ Green — system files

To reduce disk fragmentation and improve performance, use Disk Defragmenter to defragment all volumes.

how to

Use Disk Defragmenter.

1. Choose **Start**, point to **All Programs**, point to **Accessories**, point to **System Tools**, and select **Disk Defragmenter**.
2. Select the drive that you wish to analyze and defragment.
3. Click [Analyze] to analyze the degree of fragmentation on your drive. When the analysis is complete, you will be prompted to either defragment the drive or to view a report of the drive status.
4. Click [View Report] to view a report concerning the status of the drive, as shown in **Figure 4-38**.
5. Or click [Defragment] to begin the defragmentation process. Note that if you select the Defragment button in the main window of the application, the program will automatically analyze the drive before proceeding with the defragmentation process.

Figure 4-37 **Viewing the status of a disk after defragmentation**

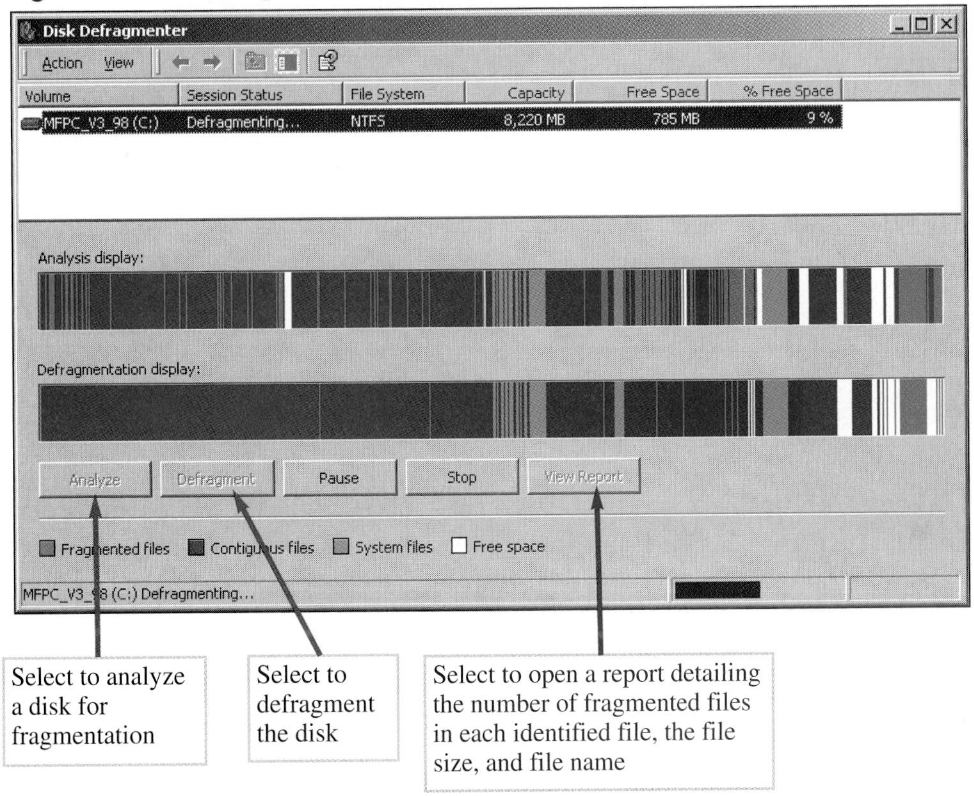

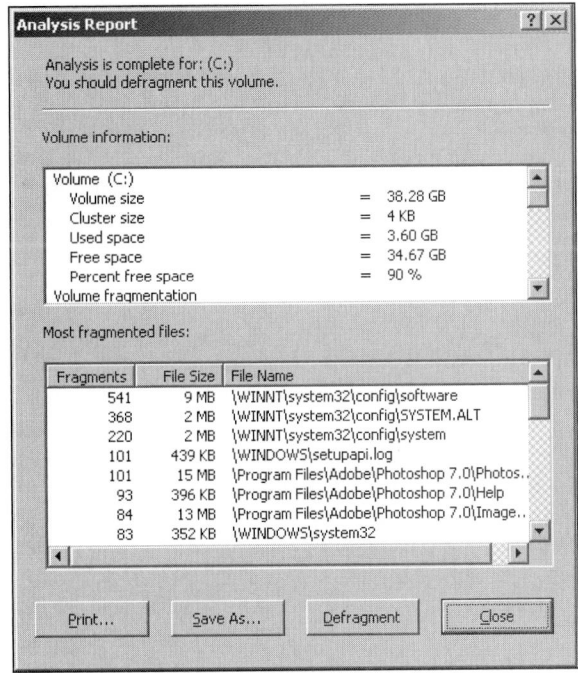

Select to analyze a disk for fragmentation

Select to defragment the disk

Select to open a report detailing the number of fragmented files in each identified file, the file size, and file name

Figure 4-38 **The Analysis Report**

skill 9   *Recovering from Disk Failures*

exam objective

Recover from server hardware failure.

overview

caution

You can only reactivate dynamic disks.

caution

You must reactivate the disk quickly because I/O errors can lead to total disk failure.

Disk or volume failures that result in data loss can happen for a variety of reasons. In such cases, it is important to repair the disk or volume as quickly as possible to minimize the damage. You can monitor the status of a disk or volume to determine if it is functioning normally in the Disk Management snap-in. You can review information about a disk including the type of disk, the file system used to format the disk, the disk capacity, and the status of the disk. The status of a disk or volume can be viewed in the **Status** column of the snap-in, or you can inspect the status on the graphical view **(Figure 4-39)**. A **Healthy** status indicates that a volume is working normally. Disks that are working normally are also displayed with the **Online** status. If a disk failure has occurred, the status of the disk will be Offline, Missing, Unnamed, or Online Disks (w/Errors).

If a volume fails, you must verify the status of the disk and take suitable corrective actions. A description of possible corrective actions is provided below:

Offline or Missing Status: If the status of a disk is Offline or Missing, first make sure that the disk is plugged in and attached to the computer. If Windows Server 2003 is able to locate the missing or offline disk, right-click it, and click the **Reactivate Disk** command on the context menu to bring the disk back online **(Figure 4-40)**. However, if you cannot repair the disk, you will have to replace the disk and add a new volume. The Reactivate Disk command should also be used if one of your volumes is displaying a status of **Healthy (At Risk)**.

Online Disks (w/Errors) Status: A disk with the Online Disks (w/Errors) status is accessible but it may contain I/O errors. In such a situation, you can try to reactive the disk to bring it back to Online status, but the best solution is to obtain a new disk, especially if this condition is accompanied by loud grinding noises.

Similarly, you can also recover data in the event of a RAID-5 volume failure. However, a RAID-5 volume failure is more serious than a mirrored volume failure because you do not have a complete copy of the data in a RAID-5 volume. Instead you need to regenerate the data on the failed disks using the parity information on the remaining disks in the volume. Regenerating a volume may take a long time, depending on several factors including the amount of data on the disk and the number of disks in the RAID-5 volume.

When a RAID-5 volume failure occurs, if the status of the failed disk is Offline or Missing, you can try the **Reactivate Volume** command **(Figure 4-41)**. This will be successful if the problem was caused by a simple interruption of power that temporarily knocked the drive offline. Select the physical disk on which you want to regenerate data, right-click, and choose **Reactivate Volume**. The status of the RAID-5 volume will change to **Regenerating** and finally, to **Healthy** after all of the data has been regenerated.

If reactivation does not work, first shut down the computer, if necessary, and replace the failed drive. If you are using hot-swappable disks, you will not have to shut down the computer. Hot swapping refers to the ability to replace a device without turning off the computer. If you are hot-swapping a drive in a software RAID-5 array, you will then need to rescan the disks in order for Windows to recognize the new drive. Do this by going to the **Action** menu and choosing **Rescan disks**. Then, right-click the new drive and select the **Repair Volume** command. Again, the status of the RAID-5 volume will change to **Regenerating** and finally, to **Healthy** after all of the data has been regenerated.

Figure 4-39 Failed Redundancy

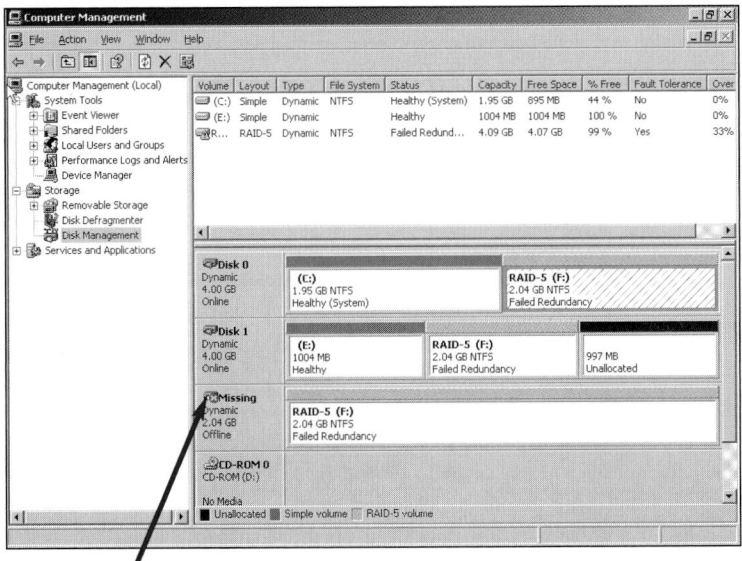

One disk in a 3-disk RAID array has failed because the disk is Offline, so redundancy has failed

Figure 4-40 Failed disks and Reactivating a Missing disk

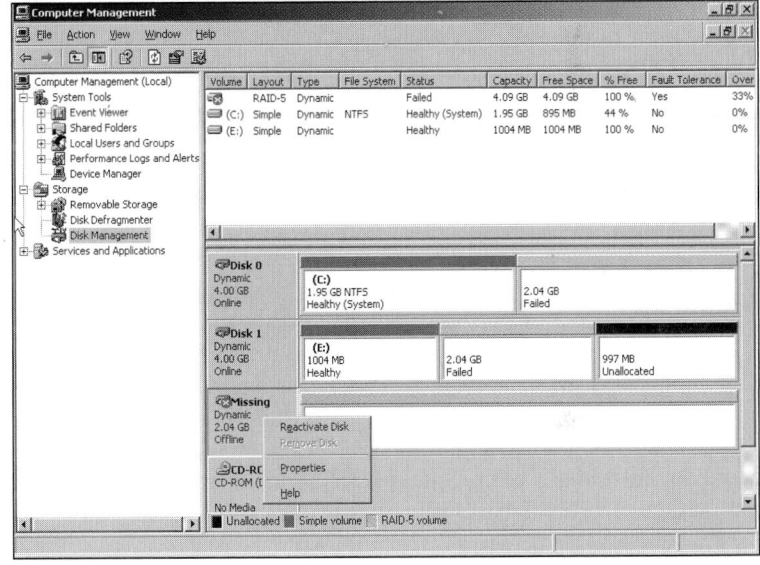

Figure 4-41 Reactivating a Volume

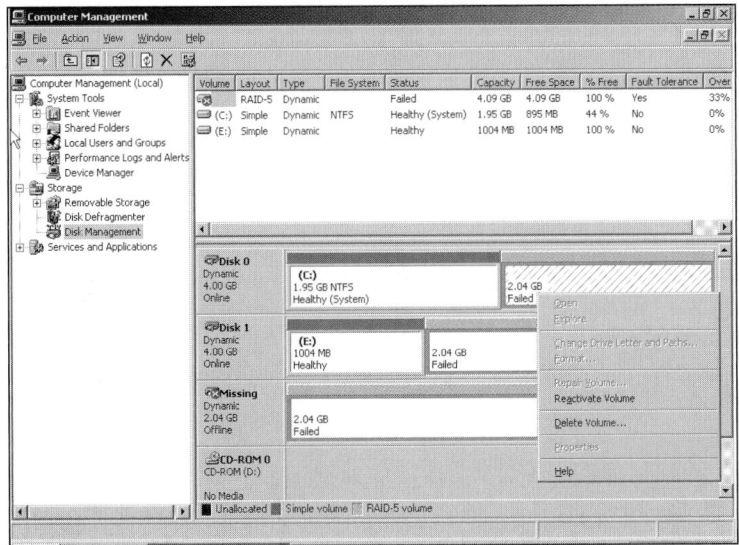

Summary

◆ You must set up a hard disk in order to store data. First, you need to choose a storage type, then you must create partitions or volumes, and finally you must format them with a file system.

◆ Windows Server 2003 uses two types of storage: basic and dynamic.

◆ Basic storage divides a hard disk into logical divisions, called partitions, which are used to store data.

◆ There are two types of partitions on a basic disk: primary and extended.

◆ A primary partition stores the startup files required to boot an operating system on your computer.

◆ Basic disks can have a maximum of four partitions per drive. Only one of these can be an extended partition.

◆ Extended partitions are created by combining un-partitioned free disk space on your hard disk in order to increase the available disk space.

◆ Extended partitions do not store data like primary or logical partitions. An extended partition acts as a container for creating logical partitions, where the data is actually stored.

◆ You can assign a drive letter to a logical partition and format it with a file system so that you can store and retrieve data.

◆ Dynamic storage does not use traditional partitioning. You can create as many volumes as you want on one disk and you can extend volumes to as many additional physical disks as you want. The main advantages of dynamic disks are that you can mount a drive within another folder, span volumes, and create fault-tolerant volumes.

◆ It is also important to remember that data on dynamic volumes cannot be accessed by computers running MS-DOS, or any other Windows operating systems prior to Windows 2000.

◆ A simple volume consists of disk space on a single hard disk. It can include a single expanse on a disk or multiple areas on the same disk that are linked together, and it can

be extended to a maximum of 32 regions on the same disk. Regions are contiguous clusters of free space on the same hard disk.

◆ You often create simple volumes when you have only one disk drive on your machine. A simple volume does not provide fault tolerance.

◆ If you do not use all of the available space on a disk to create one simple volume, later you can add all or some of the unallocated space to an existing simple volume to create an extended volume.

◆ A spanned volume combines unallocated space on multiple disks (up to 32) into one logical volume. Data storage is begun on the first disk. When that disk is full, the second disk is used, and so on, until all of the data has been accommodated on the spanned volume. Spanned volumes do not provide fault tolerance.

◆ A striped volume (also known as RAID level 0) uses two or more dynamic disks (up to 32), on which data is written in stripes across the disks. Striping equalizes disk load and increases disk performance. However, if one disk in a striped volume fails, you will generally lose all of your data.

◆ A mirrored volume provides fault tolerance by duplicating the data on two hard disks.

◆ A RAID-5 volume is a fault-tolerant striped volume that combines disk space from a minimum of three hard disks.

◆ Defragmentation is a process that rearranges files, programs, and unused space to ensure that all related components of the files and programs are placed in contiguous locations on the disk, enabling files to be located and opened more quickly. To reduce disk fragmentation and improve performance, use the Disk Defragmenter utility.

◆ You can recover from a disk failure using the Disk Management snap-in. In the Disk management snap-in, you can view information about the type of disk, the file system used to format the disk, the disk capacity, and the status of the disk.

Key Terms

Active partition (system partition)
Basic storage
Boot partition
Boot volume
Defragmentation
Disk Defragmenter
Disk Management snap-in

Dynamic storage
Extended partition
Logical drive
Mirrored volume (RAID-1)
Partition
Primary partition
RAID-5 volume

Simple volume
Spanned volume
Striped volume (RAID-0)
System volume
Volume

Test Yourself

1. You are installing Windows Server 2003 on your computer and you want to protect your system against the loss of data in the event of the failure of any of the disks on your machine. Which of the following volumes types should you select for this purpose?
   a. Spanned
   b. Mirrored
   c. Striped
   d. Simple

2. You open the Disk Management utility and you find that one of your volumes is showing a status of Healthy (At Risk) What should you do?
   a. The disk is healthy—you do not have to do anything.
   b. Use the Regenerate command.
   c. Use the Reactivate Disk command.
   d. Use the Repair Volume command.

3. A_____volume consists of disk space from a single hard disk and can be extended to a maximum of 32 regions on the same hard disk.
   a. Simple
   b. Spanned
   c. Striped
   d. Mirrored

4. Your Windows Server 2003 computer consists of four hard disks. You have combined disk space of 100 GB on three of the hard disks to create a single spanned volume. You want to add another disk to increase the available storage space. You also want to make the disk fault-tolerant; however, you want to do so using only the existing disks and do not want to use additional new disks. Which of the following methods should you use to achieve this?
   a. Convert the disk to a dynamic disk and restart the Windows Server 2003 computer.
   b. Back up the data on the spanned volume, and then delete the spanned volume. Create a RAID-5 volume by including free disk space on the four disks and finally, restore the data to the new RAID-5 volume.
   c. Back up the data on the spanned volume and delete the spanned volume. Create two separate striped volumes, with the first volume comprising the first two disks and the second volume comprising the last two disks.

5. How many extended partitions can be created on a basic disk using the MBR partition style?
   a. One
   b. Two
   c. Three
   d. None

6. You are creating a RAID-5 volume by including disk space from five 2 GB disks. In this RAID-5 volume, how much usable disk space will be available for storing data?
   a. Entire disk space
   b. 8 GB
   c. 7 GB
   d. 10 GB

7. One of the characteristics of dynamic storage is that it:
   a. Uses basic disks.
   b. Allows you to create mirrored/RAID-5 volumes that help provides fault tolerance.
   c. Divides a hard disk into partitions.
   d. Supports portable computers.

8. Your computer has been set up with a striped volume. One of the disks in the striped volume has failed and you have lost all of your data. Which of the following statements about recovering the lost data is applicable?
   a. You cannot recover the lost data because striped volumes do not provide fault tolerance.
   b. You must use the Disk Management snap-in to convert the remaining disks to simple volumes so that you can recover the lost data.
   c. You can use the parity information on the failed disk to restructure the data.
   d. You must replace the failed disk and then regenerate the lost data.

9. You can extend a FAT formatted simple volume on the unallocated disk space on your hard disk.
   a. True
   b. False

10. Which of the following types of partitions is used to store the startup files for Windows 2003, including Boot.ini, Ntdlr, and Ntdetect?
    a. Logical
    b. Extended
    c. Primary

11. If you have three 10 GB drives in a RAID-5 array, how much space is available for actual data storage?
    a. 75%
    b. 90%
    c. 66.6%
    d. 50%

12. On a dynamic disk, the *%systemroot%* folder is stored in the:
    a. boot volume
    b. system partition
    c. \Windows volume
    d. system volume

Projects: On Your Own

1. Upgrade a disk from basic to dynamic.
   a. Open the **Computer Management** console.
   b. Double-click the **Disk Management** snap-in.
   c. Open the **Convert to Dynamic Disk** dialog box for **Disk 0**.
   d. Make sure the disk you want to upgrade is selected and click **OK**.
   e. Verify the disk or disks to convert in the **Disks to Convert** dialog box and click **Convert**.
   f. Click **Yes** to confirm that you want to upgrade the disk in the **Disk Management** information box.
   g. Click **Yes** to confirm that you want to continue the operation in the **Convert Disk to Dynamic** warning box.
   h. If you are converting a disk that includes the system volume, the boot volume, or a volume which contains the paging file, the **Confirm** alert box informs you that your machine will be rebooted.
   i. If the Confirm alert box does not open, the disks will automatically be converted to dynamic. If it opens, click **OK**. Your system will restart and the disk is upgraded from basic to dynamic.
   j. If you reboot, reopen the Disk Management snap-in to view the dynamic disk.

2. Create a 1200 MB simple volume on your computer and set an used drive letter for the simple volume.
   a. Open the **Computer Management** window.
   b. Double-click the **Disk Management** snap-in.
   c. Right-click the unallocated space and start the **New Volume Wizard**.
   d. Display the next screen.
   e. Accept the default selection and display the next screen.
   f. Specify the volume size.
   g. Display the next screen.
   h. Assign a drive letter.
   i. Display the next screen of the Create Volume Wizard.
   j. Keep the default file system, and then display the final screen.
   k. Finish the New Volume Wizard.

3. Create a mirrored volume on a computer having two disks, Disk 0 and Disk 1. Specify 1200 MB as the volume size, G: as the drive letter, and NTFS as the file system for the mirrored volume.
   a. Open the **Computer Management** console.
   b. Right-click the unallocated space in **Disk 0** and start the **New Volume Wizard**.
   c. In the **New Volume Wizard**, display the **Select Volume Type** screen.
   d. Select the **Mirrored volume** option button.
   e. Display the next screen.
   f. Add **Disk 1** in the **Selected** list box.
   g. Set the volume size.
   h. Display the next screen.
   i. Assign an unused drive letter.
   j. Display the next screen of the New Volume Wizard.
   k. Keep the default file system and allocation unit size, and display the final screen.
   l. Close the New Volume Wizard.

4. Use the Disk Defragmenter to organize data on the **D:** drive of your member server after analyzing the disk for the amount of fragmentation.
   a. Open the **Disk Defragmenter** snap-in.
   b. Click the **D:** drive.
   c. Analyze the D: drive.
   d. Close the **Analysis Complete** dialog box.
   e. Initiate the defragmentation of the selected drive.
   f. Close the **Defragmentation Complete** dialog box.
   g. Close the **Disk Defragmenter** snap-in.

Problem Solving Scenarios

1. You are the administrator at a software development company, which makes AcWhiz Pro, a popular small business accounting package for Windows Server 2003. Your company has recently received a request from one of its customers to make AcWhiz Pro backward compatible with Windows 95. In order to accomplish this task, the development team needs to run the software on Windows 95 and test it for compatibility issues. Currently, all of the servers on your company's network run Windows Server 2003, Standard Edition. The client computers are all running either Windows 2000 Professional or Windows XP Professional. You have been asked to configure one of the computers to dual boot with Windows 2000 Professional and Windows 95. The computer currently has a dynamic NTFS 20 GB volume. Explain the steps you would take to configure the computer as desired. You are also required to safeguard the existing data while configuring the computer and to prevent any data loss.

2. Your Windows Server 2003 computer has two hard disks. The system and boot partitions are located on two primary partitions on Disk 0. Both of these partitions are mirrored on Disk 1. You now discover that Disk 1 has failed. List the steps you would perform to recover from this disk failure.

Working with File Systems

After creating partitions or volumes on a hard disk, you must format them with a file system. The file system defines how an operating system stores files by creating the filing structure. Windows Server 2003 supports three types of file systems: FAT (File Allocation Table) (also known as FAT16), FAT32, and NTFS. You choose a file system depending on your requirements, including security considerations and the number and size of the volumes or partitions. The FAT file system is suitable for formatting a small-sized partition where the folder structure is simple and file-level security is not required. FAT32 supports larger partitions and is more efficient at use of space, but does not support security. NTFS can be used for large-sized partitions and supports the advanced features of Windows Server 2003 such as file and folder level security.

After you have formatted a volume with a file system, you can store data on it. To improve data storage functionality, Windows Server 2003 provides features such as data compression and encryption on NTFS partitions. Compressing data enables you to create free space on a volume and thus increases storage capacity. Encryption of data allows you to ensure file security.

After a user has stored data, they will likely need to share it over the network. This exposes your data to security hazards. Windows Server 2003 enables you to control access to shared data using share and NTFS permissions. You can set permissions to specify which users can gain access to what shared data and the level of access they can have. For example, users may have permission only to read certain files, but may be allowed to modify and update others.

You can simplify the process of accessing shared resources over a network by using Distributed file system (Dfs). Dfs organizes shared folders on multiple servers into a single logical tree structure, so that they appear to users to reside in one location. This enables users on the network to access resources without having to specify the exact physical location of the files.

Goals

In this lesson, you will learn how to compress files and folders, and how to transfer compressed files and folders between volumes. In addition, you will learn how to assign shared folder permissions and NTFS permissions. Finally, you will learn about Dfs (Distributed file system).

Lesson 5   Working with File Systems

Skill	Exam 70-290 Objective
1. Introducing File Allocation Table (FAT)	Basic knowledge
2. Introducing NTFS	Basic knowledge
3. Compressing and Encrypting Data on an NTFS Volume	Basic knowledge
4. Assigning Shared Folder Permissions	Configure access to shared folders. Verify effective permissions when granting permissions. Manage shared folder permissions.
5. Setting NTFS Permissions	Configure file system permissions. Configure access to shared folders. Manage shared folder permissions. Verify effective permissions when granting permissions.
6. Setting Special Access Permissions	Configure file system permissions. Verify effective permissions when granting permissions. Change ownership of files and folders.
7. Troubleshooting Permissions	Verify effective permissions when granting permissions. Troubleshoot access to files and shared folders.
8. Introducing Distributed File System	Basic knowledge
9. Managing a Dfs Root	Basic knowledge

Requirements

To complete this lesson, you will need administrative rights on a Windows Server 2003 member server on a domain with an NTFS volume or partition and a domain user account.

skill 1

Introducing File Allocation Table (FAT)

exam objective

Basic knowledge

overview

tip
There is one other version of FAT, known as FAT-12; however, it is used only for floppy disks.

After you have created partitions or volumes on a hard disk, you must format them with a file system in order to store data. The file system determines how an operating system can store files on a volume or a partition and how disk space can be used efficiently. Windows Server 2003 supports three types of file systems: FAT (FAT16), FAT32, and NTFS.

FAT (File Allocation Table) is an older file system that can be read and accessed by most operating systems such as DOS, Windows 3.x, Windows 9.x, Windows NT, Windows 2000, Windows XP, and Windows Server 2003 **(Figure 5-1)**. It allocates storage space to files by setting up allocation units on a hard disk. An **allocation unit**, also known as a **cluster**, is the smallest unit for allocating storage space on a partition or volume. An allocation unit includes several sectors on a hard disk. **Sectors** are the base organizational units of the physical drive. They are the smallest units that can be used to transfer data to and from the disk and they hold 512 bytes of data.

FAT consists of a table or list that stores all of the information regarding the allocation units. This list is used to track the status of various segments of disk space that are used for file storage. FAT also provides information about the allocation units that are available to store new files. Each allocation unit has an entry in the file allocation table.

FAT can support up to a maximum of 64 KB of allocation units on a hard disk; however, the size of the allocation unit or cluster is variable. As the storage capacity increases, the size of the allocation unit also increases. For example, if the storage capacity of a disk partition is 32 MB or less, each allocation unit will be 512 bytes, by default. However, as the storage capacity increases, the size of the allocation units also increases. A 64 MB disk partition will have a default allocation unit size of 1024 bytes, while a 256 MB partition has a default cluster size of 4096 bytes.

Each file that you store on a FAT partition must occupy no less than one allocation unit. Therefore, as the allocation units become large, disk space can be wasted if you are storing small files. Large files, such as database files, are appropriately stored in several (preferably contiguous) allocation units. FAT also keeps a record of the set of attributes associated with each file, for example, hidden, archived, or read-only.

There are two primary versions of the FAT file system: FAT16 and FAT32 **(Figure 5-2)**. The **FAT16** file system is a 16-bit file system that was designed for computers with small disk storage capacity. The FAT16 file system:

◆ Supports partitions of up to 4 GB in size. However, only Windows NT, Windows 2000, Windows XP, and Windows Server 2003 support FAT16 partitions larger than 2 GB.
◆ Is efficient on small-sized partitions of up to 256 MB.
◆ Supports dual booting by all Microsoft operating systems.
◆ Provides only folder-level security.

The newer version of FAT, **FAT32**, is similar to FAT16, except for the fact that it supports large-sized partitions of up to 2 TB (2047 GB) in size. Although it supports larger partitions, it still does not support file security. It may be a viable choice for some desktop workstations, but it will rarely be the file system of choice for servers.

Figure 5-1 FAT file system

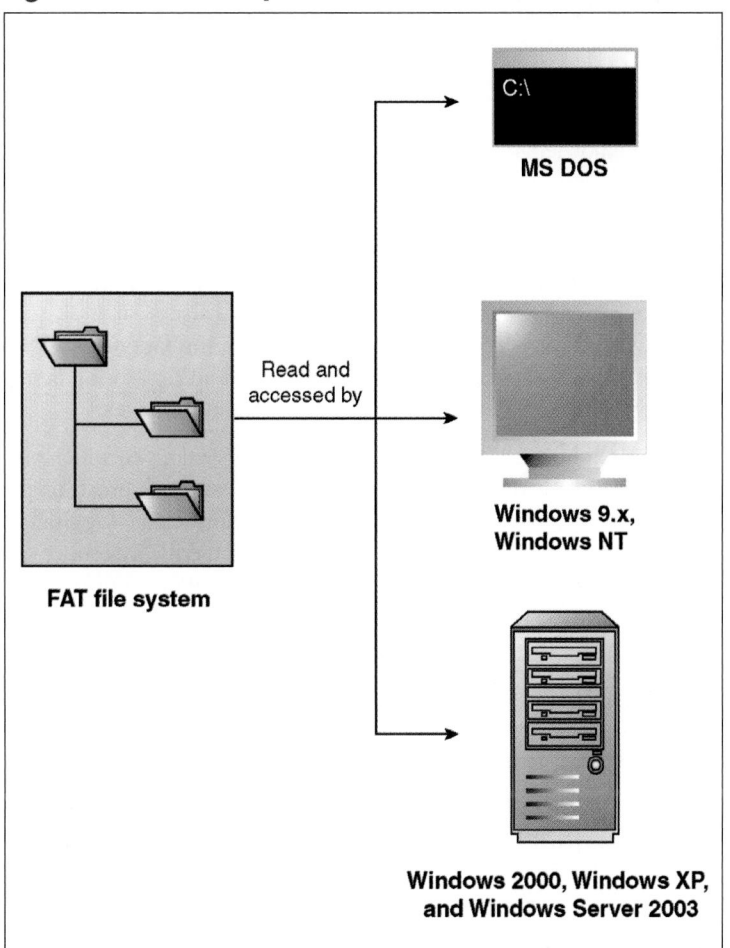

Figure 5-2 The FAT file system

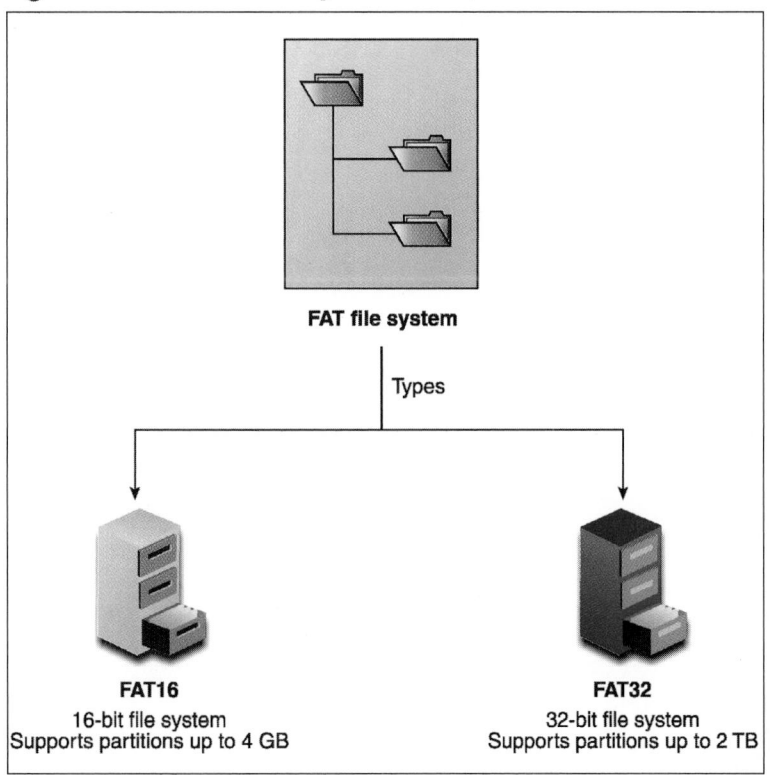

skill 2

Introducing NTFS

exam objective

Basic knowledge

overview

While FAT is supported by all Microsoft operating systems, it is a very old, limited and relatively simple file system. FAT does not support file security, nor does it have the capacity or reliability that is essential for high-end users such as servers and workstations in a networked environment. To overcome these limitations, **NTFS** was developed to provide a highly flexible, secure, and reliable file system for storing data. Formatting a partition with the NTFS file system provides the following advantages:

◆ **Reliability:** NTFS is a recoverable file systems in which volumes can be created that do not result in data loss in the event of a server crash or power failure. It implements specific features such as standard transaction logging and recovery techniques to automatically restore the consistency of the file system.

◆ **Security:** NTFS allows you to secure data by setting up permissions to control user access to files and folders. In contrast to share permissions, NTFS permissions are applied to all connections to the resource, whether local or remote. In addition, NTFS 5 supports Microsoft's Encrypting File System, which can be used to encrypt files and folders to prevent unauthorized access. If an unauthorized user attempts to open, copy, move, or rename an encrypted file or folder, an access denied message will appear.

◆ **Long file names:** NTFS natively allows file names to be up to 256 characters in length.

◆ **Efficiency:** NTFS is required in order to use certain features, such as Active Directory, which is used to store and manage network resources efficiently. NTFS also supports the compression of volumes, folders, and files. Data compression creates free space on a volume, enabling you to store a large amount of data.

◆ **Faster access:** NTFS minimizes the number of disk accesses required to find a file, thereby providing faster access speed than other file systems.

more

In addition to the advantages listed above, NTFS supports the Windows Server 2003 features described in **Table 5-1**.

Table 5-1 Features supported by the NTFS file system

Feature	Function
Disk quotas	Administrators use disk quotas to limit the amount of disk space available to users. Disk quotas allow you to track and control disk space usage.
Change Journal	The Change Journal feature creates a log file to keep track of file information, such as additions, deletions, and modifications, for each NTFS volume. It enables applications, such as file system indexing, replication managers, and remote storage, to monitor an NTFS volume.
Native Structured Storage (NSS)	Native Structured Storage (NSS) is a logical and structured storage method that improves the efficiency of storing ActiveX compound documents by storing them in the same multi-stream format that is used by ActiveX.
Line (link) tracking and Object Identifiers	The Line (link) tracking and Object Identifiers feature is used to maintain the integrity of shortcuts to file and OLE (Object Linking Embedding) objects by providing a line (link)-tracking service. This feature enables client applications to track linked sources that have been moved. For example, a client application will still be able to access a linked file, even if the location of the file has changed.
Reparse point	A reparse point is a file or directory containing a compilation of data, controlled by users, which is stored in the system-administered reparse attribute. The reparse attribute provides additional behavior to a file or directory in the underlying file system. This enables file system filters that interpret the data and process the file to add user-defined behavior to a file. For example, reparse points are used to implement the Microsoft Remote Storage Server (RSS). RSS moves files that are not used frequently to other storage devices such as a tape or CD-ROM. RSS uses reparse points to store information about the moved file in the file system.
Sparse files	Sparse files are used by applications to create large files that occupy only the minimal disk space necessary. NTFS supports sparse files for both compressed and uncompressed files.

skill 3

Compressing and Encrypting Data on an NTFS Volume

exam objective

Basic knowledge

overview

tip

Compressed folders are displayed in a different color in Windows Server 2003 by default.

Volumes formatted with the NTFS file system provide built-in features that are not supported by FAT such as **data compression,** which is used to increase available storage on a hard disk. You should compress data when you have large amounts that must be stored, but limited disk space. First, you can try to delete unnecessary data, but if this proves inadequate, you can use data compression to create free space on a volume. Some files, such as .jpg images and .zip files, are already compressed, so compressing them will not create any free space. Files that can be dramatically reduced in size include plain text files, most Office documents, and .bmp images, which can be decreased by 50 to 90 percent.

In NTFS volumes, you can compress only specific files and folders or the entire volume. When you add a new file or folder to a compressed folder, it will be compressed automatically. Other programs, such as any Windows or MS-DOS application, can read compressed files because they are automatically decompressed when they are requested. When you close or save the file, the server compresses it again.

Note that compressing files and folders might slow down the process of storing and retrieving data from the disk. This is because data must be compressed before it is stored, and uncompressed before you can retrieve it. Uncompressing a compressed file is not a particularly processor-intensive operation; however, re-compressing a file is a processor-intensive operation, so you should be careful to compress only those files that change rarely.

Any file copied to or from a compressed folder will inherit the folder's compression settings automatically. However, moving files to or from a compressed folder is a bit different. If the file is moved to another location on the same volume or partition, it retains its current compression state. Otherwise, it will inherit the compression state of the new parent folder. Details for moving and copying compressed files are shown in **Table 5-2**.

Compression and encryption are mutually exclusive. In other words, you cannot encrypt a compressed file, and vice versa. **Data encryption** is a security technique that attempts to ensure the confidentiality of a document by scrambling it using an encryption key. Without the correct key to decrypt the document, the file remains scrambled. Encryption in Windows Server 2003 is completely transparent to the user; files are encrypted and decrypted completely in the background. To encrypt a file, you simply set the encrypt data attribute on the file. To decrypt the file, you clear the attribute. However, since by default, only the user who originally encrypted the files and the designated recovery agent (none, by default, on a stand-alone server, and the domain administrator on a member server) has the proper keys for decrypting the file, and those are the only accounts that can decrypt the file. Note that when you encrypt a folder or even an entire volume, all files in that folder can also be encrypted.

The specifics of file encryption will be covered in Lesson 12.

how to

tip

You cannot compress encrypted files.

Compress a folder, then remove the compression and encrypt the folder.

1. Click [⊞ Start], then click **My Computer** to open the **My Computer** window.
2. Double-click the icon for an NTFS volume or partition on your system to display a list of the folders and files on the drive.
3. Click **File**, point to **New**, and click **Folder** to create a new folder with the default name, **New Folder (Figure 5-3)**.
4. Type a new name, such as **MktgPub**, to replace the default name.

Table 5-2   Change in the compression state when transferring a file across volumes

Transferring a file or folder	Compression state
Copy a file within an NTFS volume or between NTFS volumes	The copied file inherits the compression state of the destination folder.
Move a file or folder within an NTFS volume	A file or folder moved within an NTFS volume does not inherit the compression state of the destination folder. It retains its existing compression settings.
Move a file or folder between NTFS volumes	A file or folder moved between NTFS volumes inherits the compression state of the destination folder.
Copy or move a compressed file or folder from an NTFS volume to a FAT volume	Compressed files and folders that are moved or copied from an NTFS volume to a FAT partition are automatically uncompressed.
Copy or move a compressed file or folder from an NTFS volume to a floppy disk	Compressed files and folders that are moved from an NTFS volume to a floppy disk are automatically uncompressed.

Figure 5-3 Creating a new folder

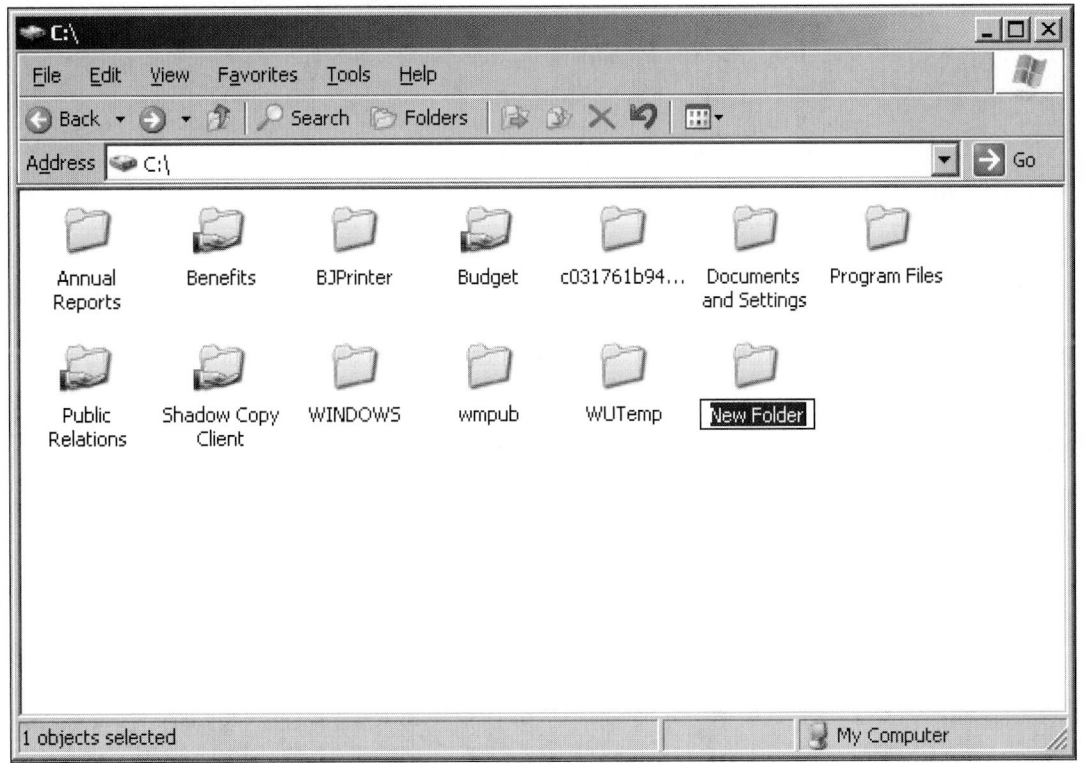

skill 3

Compressing and Encrypting Data on an NTFS Volume (cont'd)

exam objective   Basic knowledge

how to

5. Double-click the new folder to open it. Open the **File** menu, point to **New**, and click **Text Document**. Type a name for the new document, for example, **Reports.txt**, and press **[Enter]**.

6. Return to the list of files and folders for the drive. Right-click the folder and click **Properties** to open the **Properties** dialog box for the folder (**Figure 5-4**).

7. Click [Advanced...] to open the **Advanced Attributes** dialog box.

8. Select the **Compress contents to save disk space** check box in the **Compress or Encrypt attributes** section (**Figure 5-5**).

9. Click [OK] to close the **Advanced Attributes** dialog box.

10. In the **Properties** dialog box, click [Apply] to accept the changes. The **Confirm Attributes Changes** dialog box opens.

11. Select the **Apply changes to this folder, subfolders and files** option button to compress the current folder and all of the files and subfolders within it (**Figure 5-6**).

12. Click [OK] to close the **Confirm Attributes Changes** dialog box.

13. Click [OK] to close the **Properties** dialog box.

14. Right-click the folder again and click **Properties** to open the **Properties** dialog box for the folder.

15. Click [Advanced...] to open the **Advanced Attributes** dialog box.

16. Select the **Encrypt contents to secure data** check box in the **Compress or Encrypt attributes** section (**Figure 5-7**). Notice how the compression check box clears automatically.

17. Click [OK] to close the **Advanced Attributes** dialog box.

18. In the **Properties** dialog box, click [Apply] to apply the changes. The **Confirm Attributes Changes** dialog box opens.

19. Select the **Apply changes to this folder, subfolders and files** check box to compress the current folder and all of the files and subfolders within it, if necessary.

20. Click [OK] to close the **Confirm Attributes Changes** dialog box.

21. Click [OK] to close the **Properties** dialog box.

more

In addition to compression and encryption, you will also notice a check box in the Advanced Attributes dialog box labeled **For fast searching, allow Index service to index this folder**. This is the index attribute, and it determines whether or not the file or folder is indexed by the index service. After a file is indexed, you can search based on the contents of the file, rather than simply by name or type. While this can be useful in certain scenarios, many administrators choose to disable this feature due to the overhead it requires.

Figure 5-4 The Properties dialog box

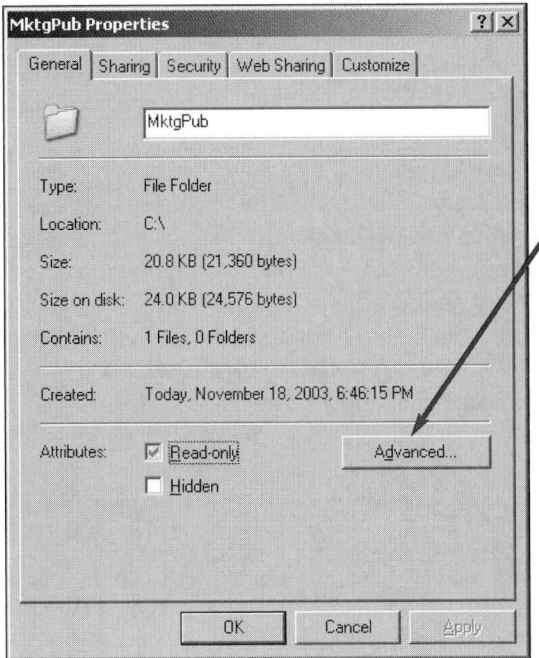

Click to open the
Advanced Attributes
dialog box

**Figure 5-5 Advanced Attributes dialog box with
compression enabled**

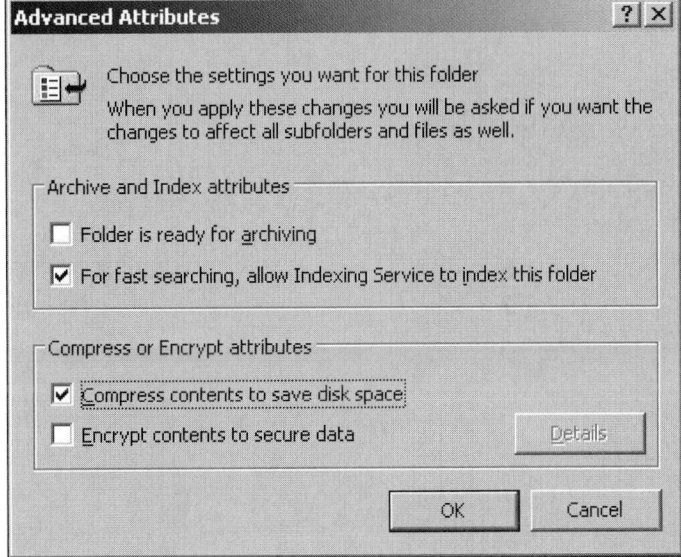

Figure 5-6 Confirm Attribute Changes dialog box

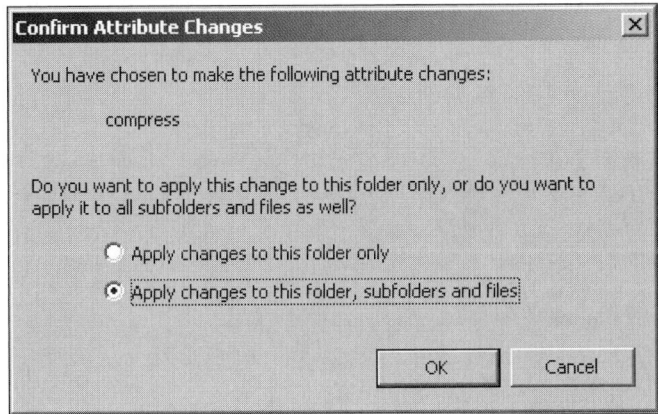

**Figure 5-7 Advanced Attributes dialog
box with encryption enabled**

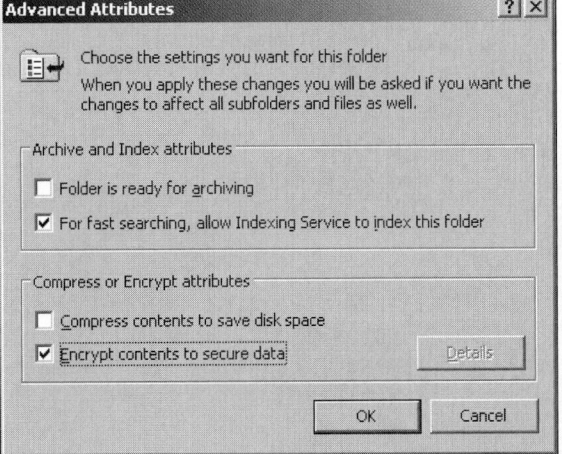

skill 4

Assigning Shared Folder Permissions

exam objective

Configure access to shared folders. Verify effective permissions when granting permissions. Manage shared folder permissions.

overview

One of the most important benefits of a well-managed network is the ability to share folders among users. However, when you share folders on a network, security concerns arise. You can prevent unauthorized access by assigning **shared folder permissions** (also sometimes called simply **share permissions**) to users. You can specify the type of access either an individual user or a group can have to a shared folder. You can also assign different shared folder permissions for different types of data. For example, the permissions assigned to a Registry key will necessarily be radically different from those assigned to Word files. You can assign the following types of shared folder permissions:

tip

A shared folder is represented with an icon of a hand holding the folder.

◆ **Read:** Allows users to view file and folder names, execute program files, and navigate within the shared folder.

◆ **Change:** Allows users to add files to the shared folder, create new folders within it, and modify the content and attributes of the files. Users can also delete files and folders and execute all of the tasks included in the Read permission.

◆ **Full Control:** Allows users to modify file permissions, take file ownership, and perform all of the tasks allowed by the Change permission.

how to

Create a shared folder and assign the Change shared folder permission to a user account.

1. Open **Windows Explorer**. Create a new folder named **Human Resources** on an NTFS volume or partition.
2. Right-click the **Human Resources** folder and click **Sharing and Security** to open the **Sharing** tab on the **Human Resources Properties** dialog box.
3. Click the **Share this folder** option button.
4. Accept the default share name and type **Documents and forms** in the **Comment** text box (**Figure 5-8**).
5. Click [Permissions...] to open the **Permissions for Human Resources** dialog box.
6. Click [Add...] to open the **Select Users, Computers, or Groups** dialog box.
7. Type the name for the user account you created in Lesson 3 (in our example, Jennifer Johnson) in the **Enter the object names to select** box (**Figure 5-9**).
8. Click [OK] to close the Select Users, Computers, or Groups dialog box and add the user account to the **Group or user names** box in the Permissions for Human Resources dialog box.
9. Select the **Allow** check box for the **Change** permission (**Figure 5-10**). Note that the **Read** permission is assigned to the selected user by default.
10. Select the **Everyone** group and click [Remove].
11. Click [OK] to close the Permissions for Human Resources dialog box.
12. Click [OK] to close the Human Resources Properties dialog box.
13. Following the above steps, create another shared folder named **Benefits**.

more

The characteristics common to all shared folder permissions are as follows:

◆ They can be applied only to shared folders and not to individual files.
◆ They restrict unauthorized access by users over the network only. A user can physically go to the computer and access the folder.
◆ They are the only method for securing data on a FAT volume, because FAT volumes do not support NTFS permissions.
◆ The Read shared folder permission is given to the Everyone group by default.

Figure 5-8 Sharing a folder

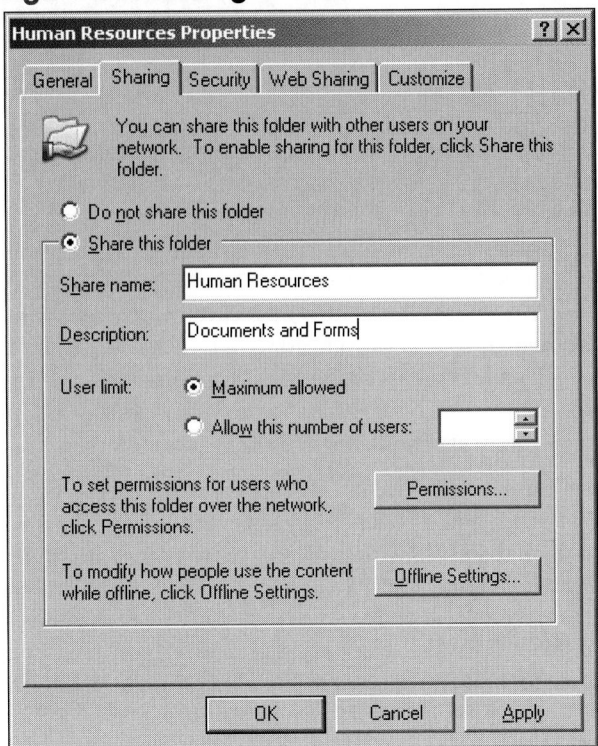

Figure 5-9 Adding a user account

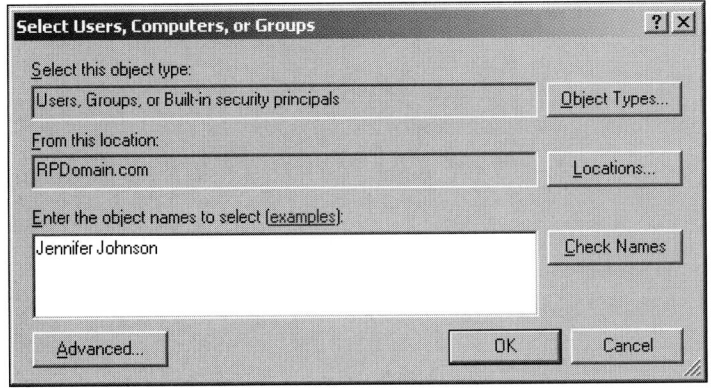

Figure 5-10 Assigning shared folder permissions

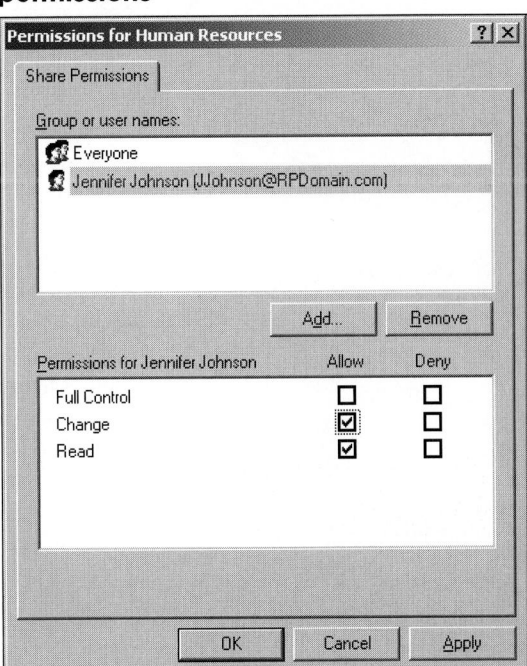

skill 5

Setting NTFS Permissions

exam objective

Configure file system permissions. Configure access to shared folders. Manage shared folder permissions. Verify effective permissions when granting permissions.

overview

In addition to shared folder permissions, you can assign **NTFS permissions** to restrict unauthorized access to shared files and folders. NTFS permissions enable you to secure network resources by controlling the level of access to files and folders for each user. For example, you can set up permissions to allow a user to read the contents of a file only or to modify the contents of the file. There are two types of NTFS permissions: NTFS folder permissions and NTFS file permissions. **Table 5-3** describes standard NTFS folder permissions while **Table 5-4** describes standard NTFS file permissions.

Note that when you apply permissions to a drive or folder, you are also applying those permissions to all files and folders underneath it, by default. If you want to change this, you must examine the **Advanced Security Settings for** *<file_name/folder_name>* dialog box **(Figure 5-11)** and deselect the **Allow inheritable permissions from parent to propagate to this object and all child objects. Include these with entries explicitly defined here** check box. A **Security** dialog box will open asking you to either copy or remove the permissions. If you choose **Copy**, the permissions that are currently being inherited will remain, but the check boxes for these permissions will no longer be grayed out, meaning that they can be changed. If you choose **Remove**, all inherited permissions will be immediately removed. Either way, any new permissions set on the folder's parent object will no longer be inherited by the folder or any child objects.

In addition to the standard NTFS permissions, you can assign special access permissions. These special NTFS permissions provide a more precise level of control over users' ability to access shared resources.

When assigning NTFS permissions, you should refer to the guidelines described below:

◆ Create folders to organize your data into categories. For example, you can create application folders, data folders, and a home folder for users to store their files on the file server. This will simplify the task of assigning permissions and of backing up data because all related data will be in one location.

◆ When you are defining the level of permission, always assign users the lowest level of permissions required for them to perform their jobs in order to protect data from being inadvertently changed or deleted.

◆ Assign the Read permission and the Write permission to the Users group. The Creator Owner group is assigned the Full Control permission by default. This will allow users to change and delete only those files and folders that they create and to read files created by other users.

◆ Avoid assigning the Full Control permission for a folder. Instead, you can assign other permissions such as Read & Execute or Modify to ensure that users do not accidentally delete any important data.

◆ Denying permissions should be used sparingly. The Deny condition is useful in cases where you must temporarily lock out particular users. As a general rule, however, you should assign the lowest level of permission that will allow a user to conduct his or her work efficiently and avoid using the Deny condition.

◆ Assign permissions to groups rather than to individual user accounts in order to simplify permission administration.

Table 5-3   Standard NTFS folder permissions

NTFS Folder Permission	Description
Read	Users can open and view the content of files, folders, and subfolders. They can also view the ownership of objects, permissions assigned to objects, and the various folder attributes such as Read-Only, Hidden, Archive, and System.
Write	Users can create new files and subfolders in a folder. This permission also allows users to view folder ownership, the assigned permissions, and to use the Properties dialog box to change folder attributes.
List Folder Contents	Users can only view the names of subfolders and files in a folder.
Read & Execute	This permission allows users to perform the tasks permitted by the Read and List Folder Contents permissions, and also gives users the ability to navigate through folders for which they do not have permission so that they can access files and folders for which they do have permission.
Modify	Users can view, create, delete, and modify the content of folders, as well as change attributes. This permission includes all tasks permitted by the Read, Write, and Read & Execute permissions.
Full Control	Users can change permissions and take ownership of folders. This permission includes all actions that are permitted by all other NTFS permissions and is usually granted only to administrators.

Table 5-4   Standard NTFS file permissions

NTFS File Permission	Description
Read	Users can read the file and view the file attributes, file ownership, and permissions.
Write	Users can change the file, change file attributes, and view file ownerships and permissions.
Read & Execute	Users can view the contents of files, file attributes, file ownership, and permissions, and can also run program applications.
Modify	Users can modify and delete the file, run applications, change attributes, and perform all other actions permitted by the Write and Read & Execute permissions.
Full Control	Users can change permissions, take ownership, and perform all actions permitted by the other NTFS permissions.

Figure 5-11 Advanced Security Settings dialog box

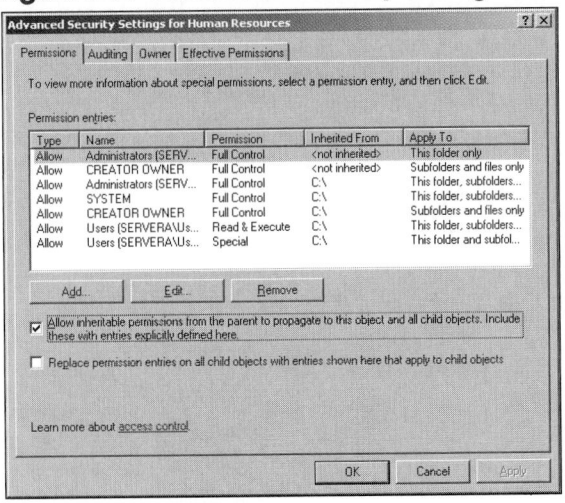

skill 5

Setting NTFS Permissions (cont'd)

Configure file system permissions. Configure access to shared folders. Manage shared folder permissions. Verify effective permissions when granting permissions.

overview

In addition, you must understand the following factors:

◆ **NTFS permissions can be inherited:** Files and folders inherit the permissions assigned to the parent folder by default. However, you can prevent this by setting permissions for individual files and folders that are different from those assigned to the parent folder.

◆ **Assign multiple NTFS permissions:** In addition to assigning permissions to a user account, you can assign permissions to the group to which the user belongs, thus giving them multiple permissions. To determine the permission level for a particular user, you must combine all of the permissions assigned. For example, if a user has been assigned the Change permission and belongs to a group having the Read permission, that user will have both the Read and the Change permissions for that file or folder.

◆ **NTFS file permissions override NTFS folder permissions:** If a user does not have access permissions to a folder, but has permissions to access files within that folder, then that user can open those files by typing the full universal naming convention (UNC). The syntax for specifying UNC is *\\server_name\share_name*, where *server_name* is the name of the server and *share_name* is the name of the shared resource.

◆ **A denied permission overrides an allowed permission:** When you deny a permission to a user, you restrict that permission from the user. For example, if you deny a user the Modify permission for a specific file, this will restrict the user from modifying the contents of the file, even if the user is a member of a group that is assigned the Full Control permission for the file.

how to

Assign the Write NTFS permission to a user account.

1. Right-click the **Human Resources** folder in **Windows Explorer** and click **Properties** to open the **Properties** dialog box for the folder.
2. Click the **Security** tab and then click [Add...] to open the **Select Users, Computers, or Groups** dialog box.
3. Type the name of the user account you created in Lesson 3 (in our example, Jennifer Johnson) in the **Select Users, Computers, or Groups** dialog box.
4. Click [OK] to close the Select Users, Computers, or Groups dialog box and add the user account to the **Group or user names** box on the Security tab in the Human Resources Properties dialog box.
5. Select the **Allow** check box for the **Write** permission (**Figure 5-12**). Note that by default, the **Read & Execute**, **List Folder Contents**, and **Read** NTFS permissions are assigned to the user account.
6. Click [OK] to assign the Write permission to the account.
7. Close Windows Explorer.

Figure 5-12 Assigning the Write Permission

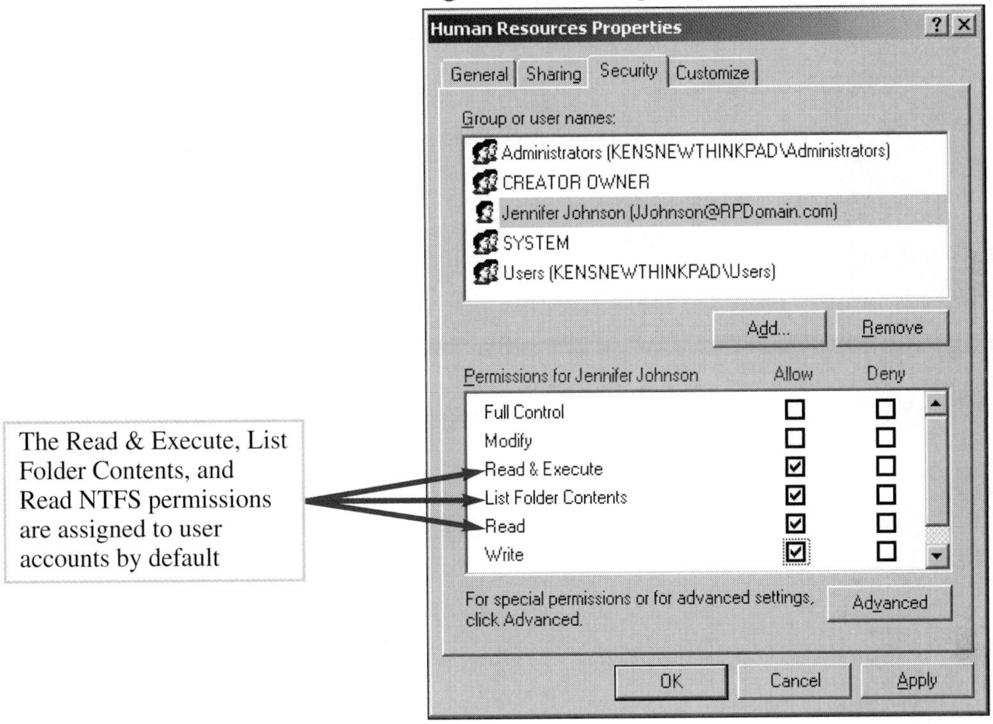

The Read & Execute, List
Folder Contents, and
Read NTFS permissions
are assigned to user
accounts by default

Human Resources Properties	? X

General | Sharing | Security | Customize |

Group or user names:

- Administrators (KENSNEWTHINKPAD\Administrators)
- CREATOR OWNER
- Jennifer Johnson (JJohnson@RPDomain.com)
- SYSTEM
- Users (KENSNEWTHINKPAD\Users)

Add...   Remove

Permissions for Jennifer Johnson	Allow	Deny
Full Control	☐	☐
Modify	☐	☐
Read & Execute	☑	☐
List Folder Contents	☑	☐
Read	☑	☐
Write	☑	☐

For special permissions or for advanced settings,
click Advanced.   Advanced

OK   Cancel   Apply

skill 6

Setting Special Access Permissions

exam objective

Configure file system permissions. Verify effective permissions when granting permissions. Change ownership of files and folders.

overview

The standard NTFS permissions should suffice in most cases, but occasionally, you may need to add a special level of permissions. For instance, you may require that a user have the ability to modify the attributes of a file, but not have the ability to read or write to the file. You can set and view special permissions in the **Advanced Security Settings for** *<file_name/folder_name>* dialog box from within the file properties. This dialog box gives you access to all possible permissions available for a file or folder.

It is typically recommended that you do not configure special permissions unless absolutely necessary because setting special permissions can make it difficult to determine the level of access assigned to a user. For example, if you configured only the **Write Extended Attributes** and **Change Permissions** permission for a user (such as Jennifer Johnson), you would not see any permissions listed for the user on the Security tab unless you scrolled down to see that the **Special Permissions** check box was selected (**Figure 5-13**). If you click **Advanced**, select the user account in the **Permission entries** box, and then click **Edit**, you can see the two special permissions the user (Jennifer Johnson, in this case) has been assigned (**Figure 5-14**).

The different special permissions available and their descriptions are listed in **Table 5-5**.

Figure 5-13 The Security tab in the Properties dialog box for a file or folder

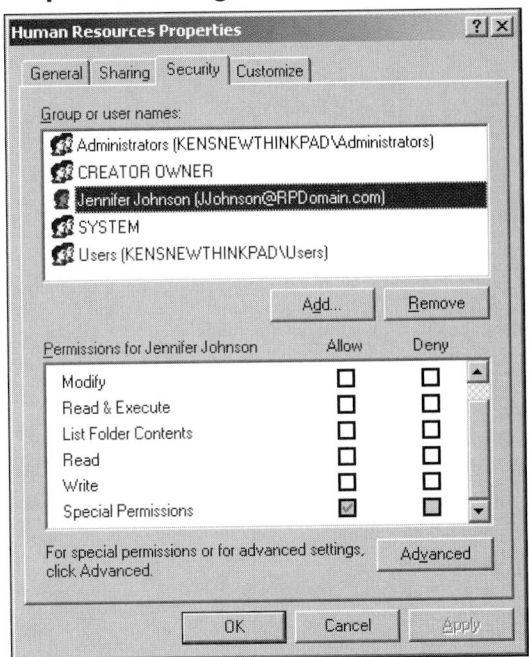

Figure 5-14 Jennifer Johnson's special permissions

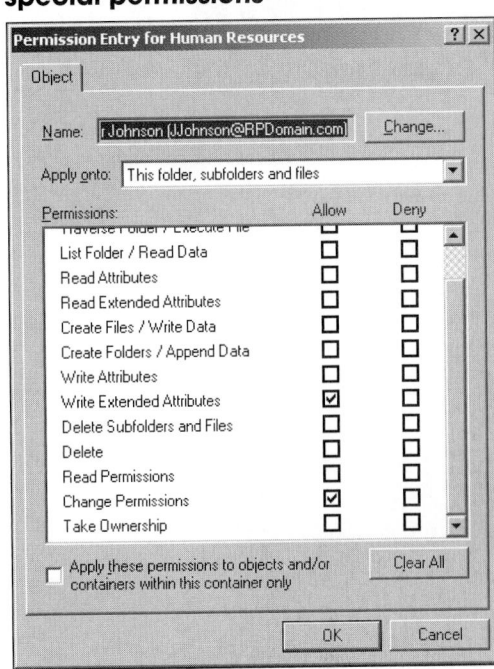

Table 5-5 Special NTFS file and folder permissions

NTFS Permission	Description
Traverse Folder/Execute File	Allows the user to traverse a folder in order to reach files and folders within it. When users are allowed this permission, it allows them to view files and folders within a folder, even if they cannot view the parent folder. This setting (for folders) only applies when the bypass traverse checking setting in Group Policy is disabled (by default it is enabled for the Everyone group). For files, this setting determines whether or not the user can execute the file (if the file is executable).
List Folder/Read Data	Allows the user to view all file and subfolder names in a folder, or to view data in files.
Read Attributes	Allows the user to view the standard attributes for a file or folder.
Read Extended Attributes	Allows the user to view the extended attributes for a file or folder. Extended attributes are typically application specific.
Create Folders/Append Data	Allows the user to add additional data to the end of a file, but does not allow the modification or removal of existing data. This permission will also deny deleting the file, as well as overwriting the file. For folders, this permission allows the user to create new subfolders.
Create Files/Write Data	Allows the user to create new files within the folder and modify or delete any files within the folder.
Write Attributes	Allows the user to modify the standard attributes for a file or folder.
Write Extended Attributes	Allows the user to modify the extended attributes for a file or folder.
Delete Subfolders and Files	Allows the user to delete any subfolder or file within the folder, even if the user does not have the Delete permission for the files or folders in question.
Delete	Allows the user to delete the file or folder.
Read Permissions	Allows the user to view the permissions for a file or folder.
Change Permissions	Allows the user to modify the permissions for a file or folder.
Take Ownership	Allows the user to take ownership of a file or folder, which also provides the ability to change permissions.
Synchronize	Allows a thread to act as a filing proxy of sorts for other threads that may wish to access the file. This permission is for multi-process and multi-threaded applications.

skill 6

Setting Special Access Permissions (cont'd)

exam objective

Configure file system permissions. Verify effective permissions when granting permissions. Change ownership of files and folders.

how to

Assign the Change Permissions special access permission to a user account.

1. Right-click the **Human Resources** folder in **Windows Explorer** and click **Properties** to open the **Properties** dialog box for the folder.
2. Click the **Security** tab and then click [Advanced] to open the **Advanced Security Settings for Human Resources** dialog box.
3. Select **Jennifer Johnson** in the **Permission entries** box, and click [Advanced] to open the **Permission Entry for Human Resources** dialog box (**Figure 5-15**).
4. Click the **Allow** check box beside the **Change Permissions** permission to give Jennifer this level of access (**Figure 5-16**).
5. Click [OK] to close the Permissions Entry for Human Resources dialog box and assign the permission to the account.
6. Click [OK] to close the Advanced Security Settings for Human Resources dialog box.
7. Click [OK] to close the Human Resources Properties dialog box.

Figure 5-15 The entry for Jennifer Johnson

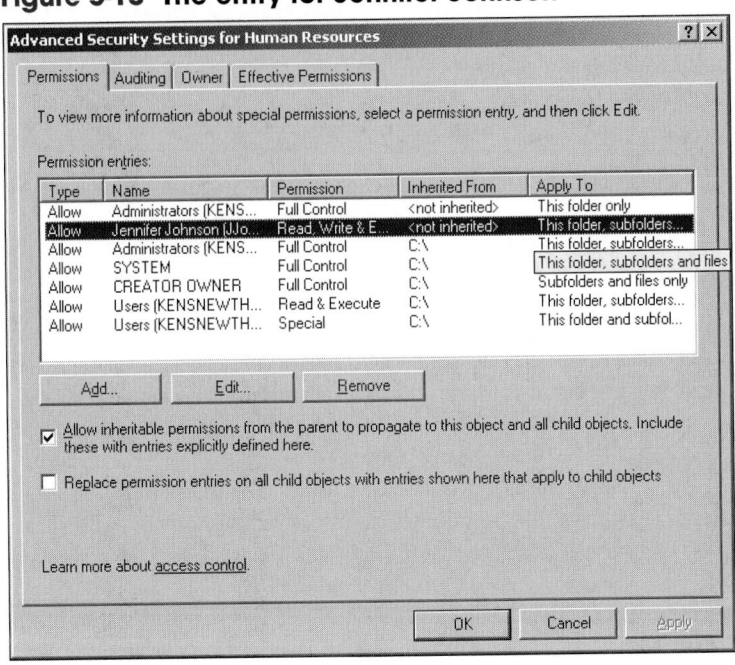

**Figure 5-16 Giving Jennifer the Change
Permissions permission**

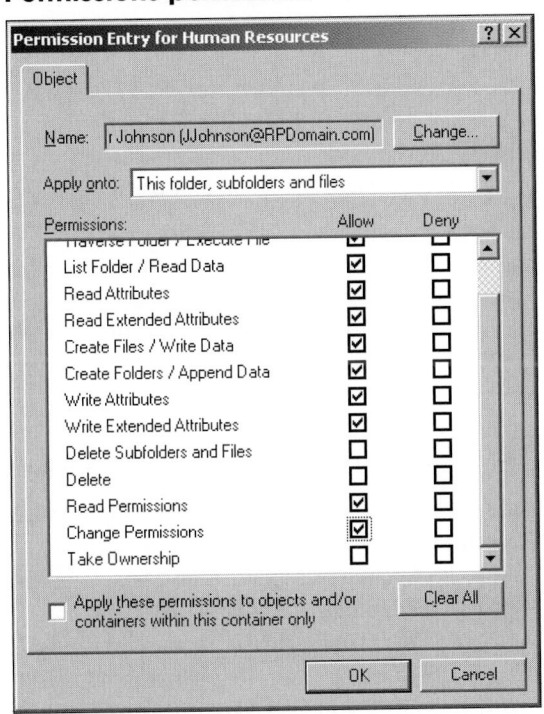

skill 7

Troubleshooting Permissions

exam objective

Verify effective permissions when granting permissions. Troubleshoot access to files and shared folders.

overview

When assigning permissions, you may encounter certain problems, which you can troubleshoot as follows:

If a user is not able to gain access to files and folders, you must do the following:

◆ Verify that permissions have been assigned to the user account and check to see if any permission denials, which are overriding the assigned permissions, have been entered. You must also check for permissions and denials assigned to the groups to which the user is a member.

◆ Sometimes permissions will change when files and folders are transferred across volumes because they inherit permissions from the folder to which they have been moved or copied.

◆ If a resource is local, shared permissions are irrelevant and only NTFS permissions must be checked. However, if the resource is remote rather than local, both shared folder and NTFS permissions apply, so you must check both the share-level and the NTFS permissions for the file or folder. In such cases, the most restrictive permissions will apply to the resource. One effective way to handle this is to create shared folders and set the share permissions to Full Control for the Everyone group. Then, use NTFS permissions to secure the resources. Since the most restrictive permission applies, as long as you have fine-tuned your NTFS permissions so that groups have the appropriate level of access, your resources will be secure. Additionally, since NTFS permissions operate locally, you can be confident that security for files and folders on the computers on which they are stored is effective when locally accessed.

◆ Sometimes a user will not be able to access a file or folder after you have added the user to a group. This problem can occur because the access token has not been updated. An access token stores data about the groups in which a user is a member and it is created each time he or she logs on. In order for the access token to be updated, have the user log off and log back on again.

◆ Remember that in Windows Server 2003, the default share permission is Read for the Everyone group, not Full Control. Similarly, the default NTFS permission is Read & Execute for the Users group, and the Everyone group is allowed only Read & Execute access to the root of the volume or partition, by default.

One new tool in Windows Server 2003 that is extremely helpful in troubleshooting NTFS permissions issues is the new **Effective Permissions** tab on the **Advanced Security Settings for <file_name/folder_name>** dialog box. On this page, you can query the file system and group memberships for a user to determine the effective permissions the user has, taking all of the user's group memberships into account.

how to

View the effective NTFS permissions for Jennifer Johnson for the Human Resources folder.

1. Right-click the **Human Resources** folder in **Windows Explorer** and click **Properties** to open the **Properties** dialog box for the folder.
2. Click the **Security** tab and then click [Advanced] to open the **Advanced Security Settings for Human Resources** dialog box.
3. Click the **Effective Permissions** tab (**Figure 5-17**).
4. Click [Select...] to open the **Select User, Computer, or Group** dialog box. Type **Jennifer Johnson** in the **Enter the object name to select** box.
5. Click [OK] to close the Select Users, Computers, or Groups dialog box.
6. Examine Jennifer's effective permissions (**Figure 5-18**).
7. Click [OK] to close the Advanced Security Settings for Human Resources dialog box.
8. Click [OK] to close the Properties dialog box.

Figure 5-17 The Effective Permissions tab

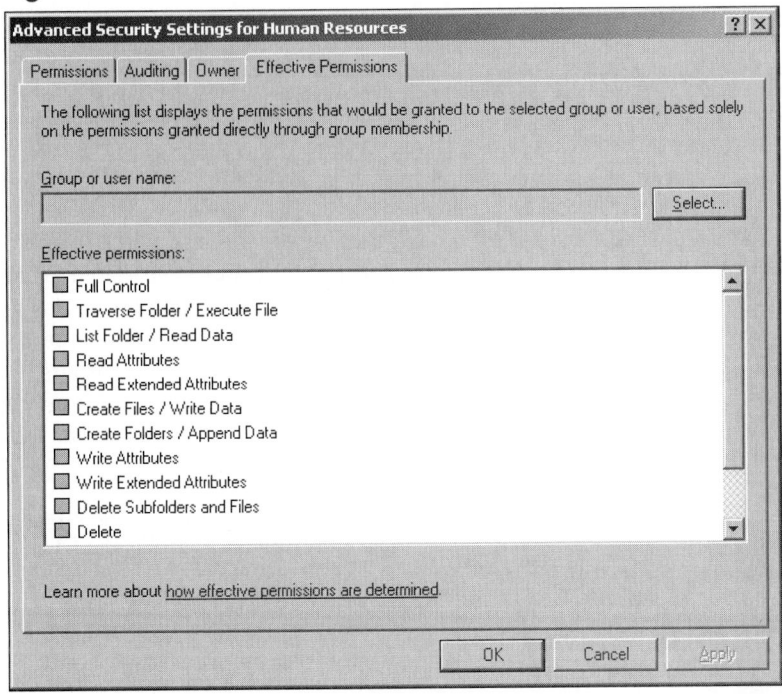

Figure 5-18 Jennifer Johnson's effective permissions

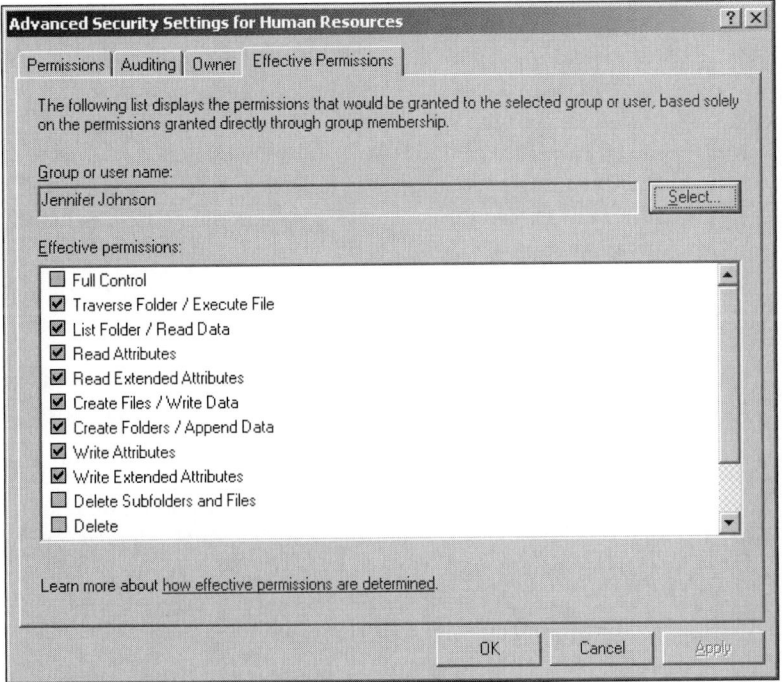

skill 8

Introducing Distributed File System

exam objective

Basic knowledge

overview

Distributed file system (Dfs) allows users to locate files and folders spread across the network quickly and easily. Files and folders distributed across multiple servers appear to users as if they are stored in one place on the network. To access these scattered files and folders you do not need to specify their actual physical location. For example, if you have Human Resources (HR) forms stored on multiple servers in a domain, you can set up a Dfs root for the Human Resource department. A single Dfs shared folder, called a **Dfs root**, can be used to coordinate all of the shared folders on multiple computers in the network. A single logical structure is created that makes it appear as though all of the forms reside on a single server. HR documents will be logically organized in the Dfs root rather than physically organized according to the server where they are stored. This effectively reduces the need for users to go to multiple locations on the network to find the data they need.

A Distributed file system (Dfs) topology consists of a hierarchical structure that includes a Dfs root, one or more Dfs links, and one or more Dfs shared folders, or replicas, to which each Dfs link points. One server or domain is chosen as the Dfs root. A Dfs root is stored on this physical server running the Dfs service. A Dfs root is a local share that acts as the starting point and host to other shared resources. A Dfs root can consist of one or more Dfs links (**Figure 5-19**). **Dfs links** point to shared folders on the network, and can refer to a shared folder with or without subfolders. You can add, modify or delete Dfs links from a Dfs root. A **replica** is a second instance of a Dfs link. Replicas are located on at least one other server, providing fault tolerance. When one Dfs link replica is unavailable, for example, because the server is down, Dfs clients automatically connect to the other replica, ensuring uninterrupted access.

You can configure the following two types of Dfs roots:

◆ **Stand-alone:** A **stand-alone Dfs root** is configured locally on a computer and stores all of the information in the local Registry. It consists of only a single level of Dfs links and does not provide data backup or replication.

◆ **Domain:** A **domain Dfs root** is also known as a fault-tolerant root and is integrated with Active Directory. Integration with Active Directory provides several enhanced features such as using a global catalog to retrieve the list of domains and servers, Automatic File Replication, and DNS naming based on the domain name. In addition, it is capable of using multiple levels of Dfs links.

The advantages of using Dfs are as follows:

◆ **Easy access to network resources:** Dfs provides easy access to network resources by providing a single point of entry for all resources. Even though the files may be spread across several servers, using Dfs, you only need to refer to one location on the network to access files.

◆ **Simplified network administration:** Dfs makes network administration easier by providing uninterrupted access to resources. For example, if you are unable to access network resources because of a server failure, you can modify the Dfs link by simply making the Dfs folder point to a new server. Users will not even know that the original Dfs server is down because they will continue to use the same Dfs path to access the resource from the new server.

◆ **Support for fault tolerance and load balancing:** Dfs provides fault tolerance and load balancing by distributing the load on multiple servers for a specific resource. For example, if a shared folder is accessed by a large number of users simultaneously, it may cause an overload on the server on which the folder is located. To prevent this, Dfs selects servers randomly from an available list.

tip

Windows Server 2003, Enterprise Edition and Datacenter Edition support multiple Dfs roots per server.

caution

You cannot remove Dfs from the operating system. However, you can start, stop, or pause this service.

Figure 5-19 Dfs links

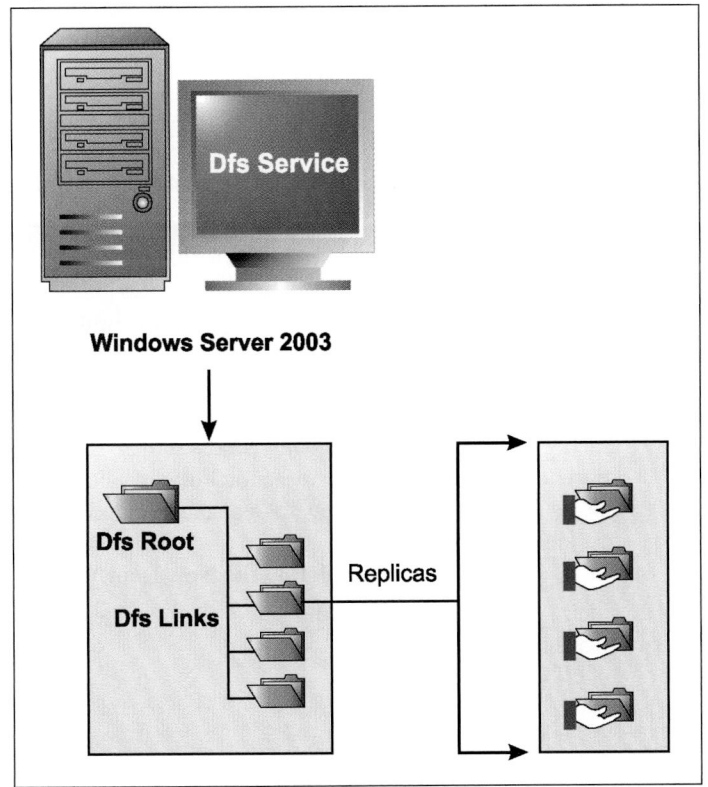

skill 8

Introducing Distributed File System
(cont'd)

exam objective

Basic knowledge

overview

◆ **Support for network permissions:** Dfs supports network permissions and existing Windows Server 2003 file and directory permissions. Therefore, you do not need any additional permissions or security configuration to access resources if you are using Dfs.

◆ **Integration with Internet Information Services (IIS):** Dfs can be integrated with IIS. This enables users to configure IIS to use file resources through Dfs, while taking advantage of the benefits of Dfs. For example, if you are moving a Web page from one server to another, you can select a Dfs root as the root for that Web site and move resources within the Dfs without breaking any HTML links. In this way, using a Dfs root precludes the need for updating links on the Web site.

how to

Create a stand-alone Dfs root.

1. Click [Start], point to **Administrative Tools**, and click **Distributed File System** to open the **Distributed File System** console.
2. Open the **Action** menu and click **New Root** to start the **New Root Wizard**.
3. Click [Next >] to open the **Root Type** screen.
4. Select **Stand-alone root** and click [Next >] **(Figure 5-20)**.
5. The **Host Server** screen opens. Type the name of your server **<server_name.your-domain.com>** and click [Next >].
6. The **Root Name** screen opens. Type **DFS** to name your root **(Figure 5-21)**.
7. Click [Next >] to open the **Root Share** screen. Click [Browse...] next to the **Folder to share** text box to open the **Browse for Folder** dialog box.
8. Locate the **Human Resources** folder, select it, and click [OK] to close the Browse for Folder dialog box.
9. Click [Next >]. The **Completing the New Root Wizard** screen opens **(Figure 5-22)**.
10. Click [Finish] and select the new Dfs root. The enabled Root Target displays in the details pane **(Figure 5-23)**.

tip

Only client computers with Dfs client software can gain access to Dfs resources. Computers running Windows Server 2003, Windows 2000, Window NT 4.0, and Window 98 include Dfs client software. You must download and install a Dfs client for Windows 95 computers. No DFS client is available for Windows NT 3.x, DOS, or Windows 3.x.

more

If you are not able to access a Dfs shared folder, you can check the status of the folder in the Distributed File System snap-in. Right-click the Dfs shared folder and click the **Check Status** command on the context menu. A fully connected and working Dfs shared folder will be displayed with a green check mark in a white circle on its folder icon **(Figure 5-24)**, while a disconnected shared folder (a folder from which the share has been removed), or a folder on a server that is unavailable, will display a white "x" in a red circle on its folder icon. You can also open the **Properties** dialog box for the Dfs shared folder and examine the physical resource to which you are connected, to find out if you are being blocked from the shared folder.

Figure 5-20 Selecting the root type

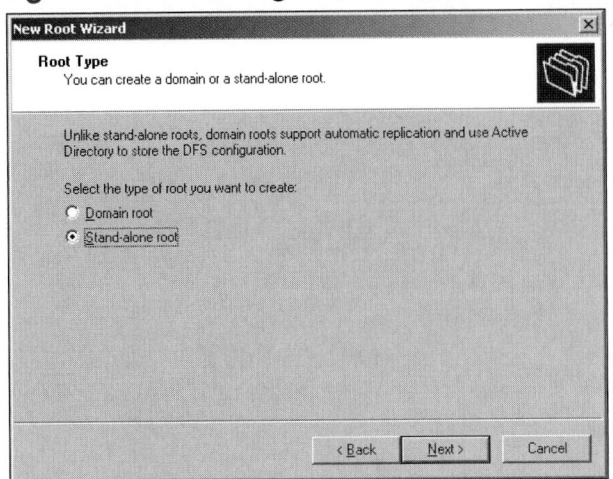

Figure 5-21 Specifying the Dfs root name

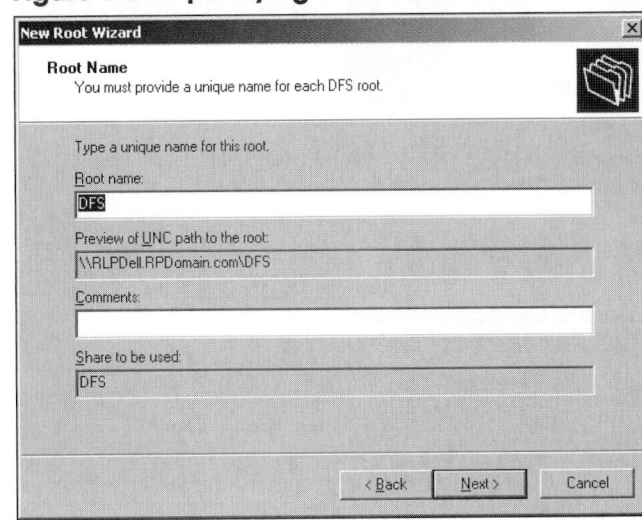

Figure 5-22 Completing the New Root Wizard

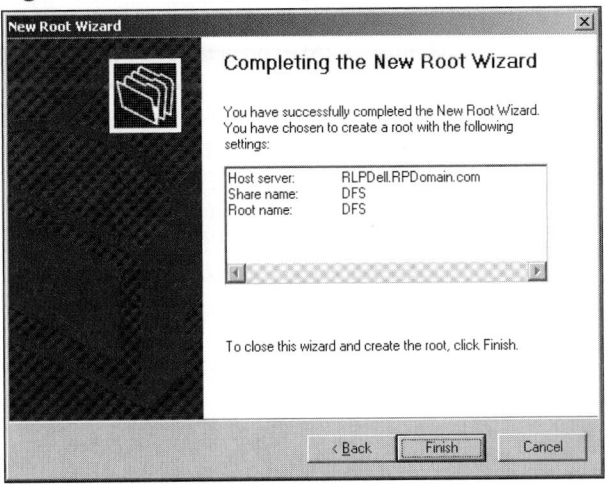

Figure 5-23 New Dfs Root in the Distributed File System console

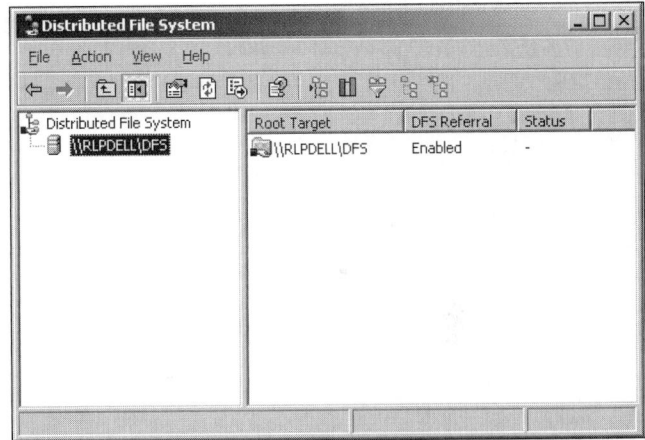

Figure 5-24 Checking the status of a Dfs root

A working Dfs shared folder will be displayed with a green check mark in a white circle on its folder icon, and a disconnected shared folder will be displayed with a white "x" in a red circle

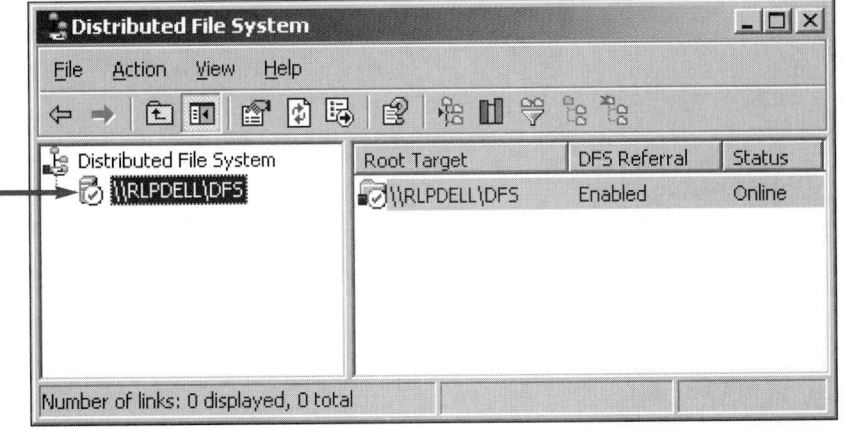

skill 9

Managing a Dfs Root

exam objective

Basic knowledge

overview

After you have created a Dfs root, you must manage it so that it continues to function properly. Network administrators will periodically need to perform the following functions:

Adding and removing Dfs links: You may be required to add more Dfs links to expand the Dfs topology. For example, to simplify access to shared folders on servers, you must include links to them on the Dfs root. You may also have to delete a Dfs link if the shared files that the Dfs link points to are redundant.

Disabling and enabling a Dfs link: Occasionally, you may need to disable a Dfs link when you do not need it for a period of time or if you must temporarily restrict users from accessing some shared files. You can reactivate the Dfs link whenever it is required.

tip

All permissions that you assign to the shared folder to which the Dfs link points apply to the Dfs link.

how to

Adding a Dfs link.

1. Open the **Distributed File System** console, if necessary.
2. Right-click the Dfs root and click **New Link (Figure 5-25)** to open the **New Link** dialog box.
3. Type **Benefits** in the **Link name** text box to specify the name of the Dfs link.
4. Type \\<*server_name*>**benefits** in the **Path to target (shared folder)** text box to specify the network path to the shared folder.
5. Type a brief description of the shared folder in the **Comment** text box.
6. Type **2500** in the **Clients cache this referral for** text box to specify the time duration for storing the Dfs link (**Figure 5-26**). After the referral time expires, a client computer queries the Dfs server to ask for the location of the link, even if the client computer has previously established a connection with the link.
7. Click [OK] to create the new link and close the New Link dialog box. The new Dfs link is added to the Distributed File System console (**Figure 5-27**).

tip

By default, 1800 seconds is the cache referral time for a Dfs link. You can extend the cache timeout value if the link seldom changes.

Figure 5-25 Creating a new Dfs link

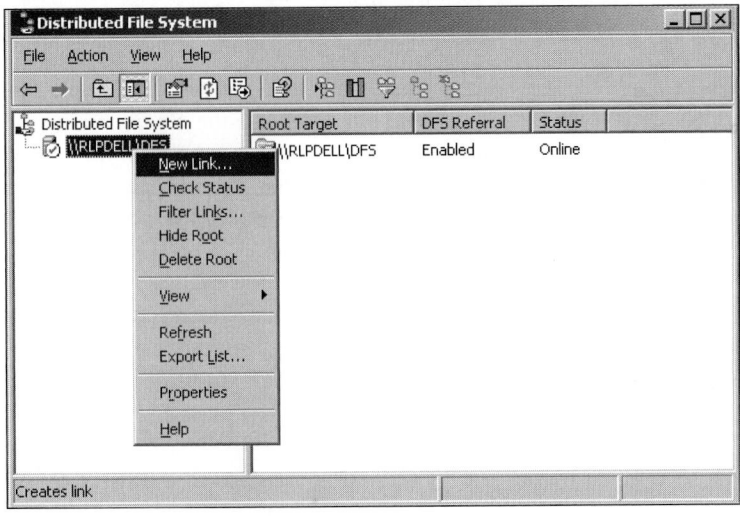

Figure 5-26 Specifying the time duration for storing the Dfs link

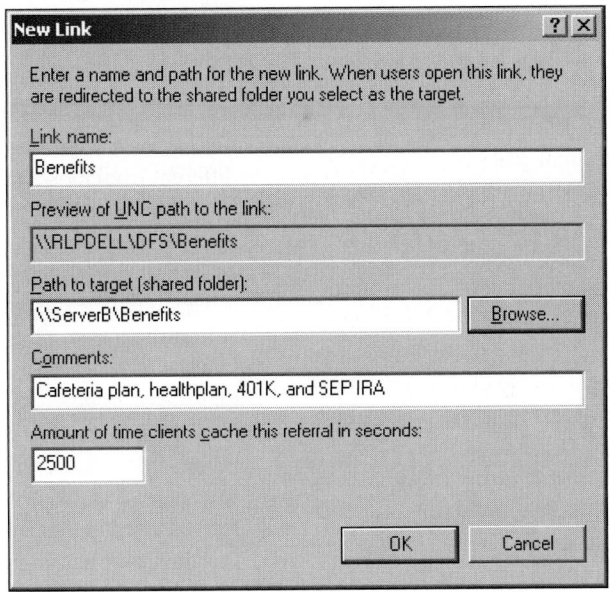

Figure 5-27 The new Dfs link

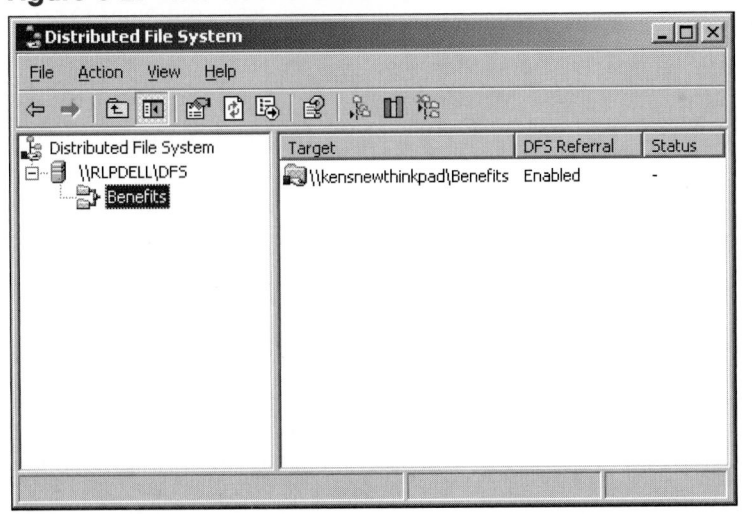

Summary

- FAT (File Allocation Table) is an older file system that can be read and accessed by most operating systems such as DOS, Windows 3.x, Windows 9.x, Windows NT, Windows 2000, Windows XP, and Windows Server 2003. FAT32 supports partitions of up to 2 TB (2047 GB).

- Formatting allocates storage space to files by setting up allocation units on a hard disk.

- An allocation unit, also known as a cluster, is the smallest unit for allocating storage space on a partition or volume.

- An allocation unit includes several sectors on a hard disk. Each allocation unit has an entry in the file allocation table.

- Sectors are the base organizational units of the physical drive. They are the smallest units that can be used to transfer data to and from the disk and they can hold 512 bytes of data.

- FAT can support up to a maximum of 64 KB of allocation units on a hard disk. However, the size of the allocation unit or cluster is variable. As the storage capacity increases, the size of the allocation unit also increases.

- The FAT16 file system is a 16-bit file system that was designed for computers having small disk storage capacity. It supports partitions of up to 4 GB in size, is efficient on small-sized partitions of up to 256 MB, supports dual booting, and provides only share-level security.

- FAT32 is similar to FAT16 except that it supports large-sized partitions of up to 2 TB (2047 GB) in size. Although it supports larger partitions, it still does not support file security. It may be a viable choice for some desktop workstations, but it will rarely be the file system of choice for servers.

- While FAT is supported by most Microsoft operating systems, it is a very old, limited, and relatively simple file system. FAT does not support file security, nor does it have the capacity or reliability that is essential for high-end users such as servers and workstations in a networked environment.

- NTFS was developed to provide a highly flexible, secure, and reliable file system for storing data.

- Formatting a partition with the NTFS file system provides reliability, security, efficiency, native support for long file names, and faster access. You can also enable data compression and encryption.

- You should compress data when you have large amounts that must be stored, but limited disk space. You can compress specific files or folders or the entire volume.

- When you add a new file or folder to a compressed folder, it will be compressed automatically.

- Other programs, such as any Windows or MS-DOS application, can read compressed files because they are automatically decompressed by NTFS when they are requested. When you close or save the file, NTFS compresses it again.

- Data encryption is a security technique that attempts to ensure the confidentiality of a document by scrambling it with secret encryption keys.

- Shared folder permissions enable you to secure shared resources by specifying the type of access granted to a user.

- Shared resources on a FAT volume can only be secured using shared folder permissions.

- The shared folder permissions are Read, Change, and Full Control.

- NTFS permissions restrict unauthorized access to files and folders.

- There are two types of NTFS permissions:
  - NTFS folder permissions
  - NTFS file permissions

- The NTFS folder permissions are Read, Write, List Folder Contents, Read & Execute, Modify, and Full Control.

- The NTFS file permissions are Read, Write, Read & Execute, Modify, and Full Control.

- Files and folders inherit the permissions assigned to the parent folder by default. However, you can prevent this by setting permissions for individual files and folders that are different from those assigned to the parent folder.

- You can also assign permissions to groups. To determine the permission level for a particular user, you must combine all of the permissions assigned. For example, if a user has been assigned the Change permission and belongs to a group having the Read permission, that user will have both the Read and the Change permissions for that file or folder.

- NTFS file permissions override NTFS folder permissions. If a user does not have access permissions to a folder, but has permissions to access files within that folder, then that user can open those files by typing the full universal naming convention (UNC) path.

- A denied permission overrides an allowed permission.

- The standard NTFS permissions should suffice in most cases, but occasionally, you may need to add special access permissions to provide a more precise level of control over users' ability to access shared resources.

- The special access permissions are Traverse Folder/Execute File, List Folder/Read Data, Read Attributes, Read Extended Attributes, Create Folders/Append Data, Create Files/Write Data, Write Attributes, Write Extended Attributes, Delete Subfolders and Files, Delete, Read Permissions, Change Permissions, Take Ownership, and Synchronize.

- If a user is not able to gain access to files and folders, first verify that permissions have been assigned to the user account and check to see if any permission denials have been entered that are overriding the assigned permissions. Then check for denials assigned to the groups to which the user is a member.

◆ Remember that permissions will change when files and folders are transferred across volumes because they inherit permissions from the folder to which they have been moved or copied.

◆ If a resource is local, shared folder permissions do not apply and only NTFS permissions must be checked.

◆ For remote resources, you can apply both shared folder and NTFS permissions, so you must check both the share-level and the NTFS permissions for the file or folder. In such cases, the most restrictive permissions will apply to the resource.

◆ Sometimes a user will not be able to access a file or folder after you have added the user to a group. This problem can occur because the access token has not been updated. Have the user log off and log back on again to update the access token.

◆ In Windows Server 2003, the default share permission is Read for the Everyone group.

◆ The default NTFS permission is Read & Execute for the Users group, and the Everyone group is allowed only Read & Execute access to the root of the volume or partition, by default.

◆ A new tool that can help you to troubleshoot access to resources is the Effective Permissions tab on the Advanced Security Settings for <file_name/folder_name> dialog box. Here, you can query the file system and group memberships for a user to determine the effective permissions the user has, taking all of the user's group memberships into account.

◆ Distributed file system (Dfs) allows users to easily locate files and folders spread across multiple computers on the network. Dfs enables users to browse files and folders in a logical structure rather than search the physical structure of the network.

◆ Dfs organizes network shares scattered on several servers in a logical tree structure. This logical tree structure consists of one or more Dfs roots.

◆ A Dfs root is a local share that acts as the starting point and host to other shared resources.

◆ There are two types of Dfs roots: stand-alone and domain.

◆ A stand-alone Dfs root allows a single level of Dfs links, while domain Dfs can have multiple levels of Dfs links.

◆ A domain Dfs root is also known as a fault-tolerant root and is integrated with Active Directory.

◆ A Dfs root can consist of one or more Dfs links. Dfs links point to shared folders on the network, and can refer to a shared folder with or without subfolders.

◆ Integration with Active Directory allows users to use a global catalog to retrieve the list of domains and servers. It also enables Automatic File Replication, DNS naming, and the ability to use multiple levels of Dfs links.

◆ A Distributed file system (Dfs) topology consists of a hierarchical structure that includes a Dfs root, one or more Dfs links, and one or more Dfs shared folders, or replicas, to which each Dfs link points.

◆ A replica is a second instance of a Dfs link. Replicas are located on at least one other server, providing fault tolerance. When one Dfs link replica is unavailable Dfs clients automatically connect to the other replica, ensuring uninterrupted access.

Key Terms

Allocation unit (cluster)	Domain Dfs root	Replica
Data compression	FAT (File Allocation Table)	Sector
Data encryption	FAT16	Shared folder permissions (Share
Dfs link	FAT32	permissions)
Dfs root	NTFS	Stand-alone Dfs root
Distributed file system (Dfs)	NTFS permissions	

Test Yourself

31. You are working in the Finance department of your company and you must create a shared folder that provides information about the finance policies of the company. However, you must restrict access so that all of the employees in the company can read the contents of the file but not make any changes or add any new files to the shared folder. To achieve this, which of the following is the best strategy to follow when assigning permissions?

a. Assign the Read permission at both the share level and the NTFS level for the folder.

b. Assign the NTFS Read permission and the Full Control share permission to the shared folder.

c. Assign the Read share permission and the Full Control NTFS permission to the shared folder.

d. Assign the Full Control permission at both the share level and the NTFS level for the folder.

2. Which of the following is a characteristic of a domain-based Dfs?
   a. It is integrated with Active Directory.
   b. It consists of only a single level of Dfs links.
   c. It stores Dfs topology in the local Registry.
   d. It does not provide fault tolerance.

3. You are an administrator working with a company called Global Net. You have created a Dfs root. Recently, you started receiving complaints from several employees that they are unable to find the required shared folders on the network. Which of the following is the first step you will take to troubleshoot this problem?
   a. Restart the File Replication Service.
   b. Delete the Dfs root.
   c. Verify that the server is working normally.
   d. Check the status of the Dfs root.

4. You can assign permissions at the file level on volumes formatted with the_____file system.
   a. NTFS
   b. FAT
   c. FAT32
   d. FAT16

5. Which of the following tabs on a folder's Property dialog box is used to assign NTFS permissions?
   a. Web Sharing
   b. Sharing
   c. Security
   d. General

6. A file does not inherit the compression state of the destination folder, when you:
   a. Copy it within an NTFS volume.
   b. Move it within an NTFS volume.
   c. Copy it between NTFS volumes.
   d. Copy it from an NTFS volume to a floppy disk.

7. Which of the following is a component of the Dfs topology? (Choose all that apply.)
   a. Root
   b. Link
   c. Disk Quotas
   d. FRS

8. Which of the following NTFS file permissions will you use to allow a user to display the contents of folders and run programs within a folder, but not change the file contents?
   a. Read & Execute
   b. Modify
   c. Read Attributes
   d. Write

9. You need additional permissions and security configuration to access network resources using a Dfs.
   a. True
   b. False

Projects: On Your Own

1. Deny a user account the Change share permission for the shared Budget folder.
   a. Create a new folder named **Budget** on an NTFS volume or partition.
   b. Open the **Properties** dialog box for the Budget folder.
   c. Share the Budget folder.
   d. Type **Data folder for XYZ Project** in the **Description** text box in the **Properties** dialog box for the Budget folder.
   e. Click the **Permissions** button.
   f. In the **Permissions for Budget** dialog box, click the **Add** button
   g. Select a user account.
   h. Click the **OK** button.
   i. Select the **Deny** check box for the **Change** permission.
   j. Click the **OK** button.
   k. Confirm the change.

2. Create and compress a new folder called HRPub.
   a. Open the **My Computer** window.
   b. Display the list of folders and files on an NTFS volume or partition on your system.
   c. Create a new folder called **HRPub.**
   d. Double-click the new folder to open it. Create a new text document in the folder.
   e. Return to the list of files and folders for the drive.
   f. Open the **Properties** dialog box for the HRPub folder and click the **Advanced** button (on the **General** tab).
   g. In the **Advanced Attributes** dialog box, select the **Compress contents to save disk space** check box.
   h. Click the **OK** button.
   i. Click the **Apply** button.
   j. In the Confirm Attributes Changes dialog box, select the **Apply changes to this folder, subfolders and files** check box.
   k. Click the **OK** button and close the **HRPub Properties** dialog box.

Problem Solving Scenarios

1. You are the network administrator for a Windows Server 2003 network. The Windows Server 2003 computer has a single 40 GB hard disk drive containing operating system files, as well as a shared folder. Only five users on the network have Write access to the shared folder that they use to store large Excel spreadsheet files, which they create every day. Due to the size of these files, disk space is being consumed very rapidly. How could you resolve the problem?

2. You are the system administrator for a company that has a centralized network with a Windows Server 2003 file server. Due to the lack of sufficient disk storage space, the company has requested you to add further disk capacity. You have also been asked to create a shared folder on this drive. All users are to be given the Write permission to this shared folder, but they should be denied permission to create any additional folders. They can, however, create subfolders within the shared folder. List the steps you would perform to set security permissions for the drive.

6 Administering User Accounts

Network users must be able to access resources on both their local computer and on the network. However, users may inadvertently delete or move data or perform unauthorized actions, such as installing unlicensed software. For security purposes, you can control user access to systems and networks by creating and managing user accounts and assigning permissions to prevent unauthorized access.

A user account serves as a form of identification for a user on a Windows Server 2003 network. It contains information about a user, such as the user name and password.

There are two types of user accounts: domain and local. A domain account allows a user to log on to and gain access to domain resources. A local account allows a user to log on only to the computer where the account was created and access resources on that computer.

In addition to these two types of user accounts, built-in user accounts are created, by default, during the installation of Windows Server 2003. Examples of built-in accounts are Administrator and Guest. The network administrator maintains user accounts by performing tasks such as enabling, disabling, and renaming the accounts.

For each user account, Windows Server 2003 automatically creates a user profile the first time the account is used to log on to a computer. The profile is created on the local computer and can also be replicated to a network location. User profiles contain settings that define the user environment and are applied when a user logs on to a system. The types of user profiles include local, roaming, and mandatory.

Goals

In this lesson, you will learn about the various types of user accounts and user profiles available in Windows Server 2003. You will also learn how to create local and domain user accounts, set account properties, manage user accounts, and create user profiles.

Lesson 6   Administering User Accounts

Skill	Exam 70-290 Objective
1. Introducing Local User Accounts	Create and manage user accounts.
2. Setting and Modifying Local User Account Properties	Create and manage user accounts. Troubleshoot user accounts. Diagnose and resolve issues related to user account properties. Troubleshoot user authentication issues.
3. Creating a Domain User Account	Create and manage user accounts. Create and modify user accounts by using the Active Directory Users and Computers MMC snap-in.
4. Setting Domain User Account Properties	Create and manage user accounts. Create and modify user accounts by using the Active Directory Users and Computers MMC snap-in.
5. Automating User Creation and Modification	Create and manage user accounts. Create and modify user accounts by using automation. Import user accounts.
6. Introducing User Profiles	Manage local, roaming, and mandatory user profiles.
7. Creating a Roaming User Profile	Manage local, roaming, and mandatory user profiles.

Requirements

To complete this lesson, you will need administrative rights on two computers, a Windows Server 2003 member server and a Windows Server 2003 domain controller with Active Directory installed. You will also need to create a domain user account.

skill 1

Introducing Local User Accounts

exam objective

Create and manage user accounts.

overview

A **user account** identifies a user on a network. It enables users to access both network resources, such as files, printers, and databases, and local resources on the computer where the user is logged on. A user account is used to authenticate the identity of a system or user through verification of the user logon name and password.

There are two types of user accounts in Windows Server 2003: domain and local. A **domain user account** is created in Active Directory and can be used to log on from any computer in the forest.

On the other hand, a **local user account** allows a user to log on only to a local computer and access the resources on that computer. The account information for a local account is not replicated to the domain controller. Local user accounts are stored in the security database of the computer where the account is created. This security database is also called the **local security database**. When a user logs on locally, the computer uses its local security database to authenticate the local user account. To administer a local user account, administrators must either log on or connect to the local computer.

Normally, you will not use local user accounts, other than on a workgroup network. On a domain, if users are using the local accounts database to log on to a workstation, each of them must have a user account on the local workstation. However, if you want them to be able to access resources on a server without having an additional Logon dialog box appear, a local account with the same name and password as the local account on their workstations must be created on the server. For example, you may want to create a local user account for a temporary employee, or perhaps a technical consultant or technician, so that he or she can access resources on a server in addition to their temporary workstation. You can create a local user account on a server so that he or she can access the resources on just that server.

Before you create your user accounts, you should determine how to organize the available information about your users. This will reduce the time it takes to create accounts, and simplify account management later on. When planning user accounts, you should consider the following factors:

◆ Naming conventions solidify an identification pattern for the users in a domain. You should follow a consistent naming convention so that users can easily remember and locate their logon names. For example, you may choose to use account names that are based on the actual names of the users or on the department to which they belong or a combination of both. Once users are aware of this pattern, they can easily remember and locate their accounts. You should follow the guidelines outlined in **Table 6-1**.

◆ Passwords play a very important role in protecting user access to a domain or a computer. Each user account is required to have a password. **Table 6-2** contains some guidelines and rules for setting passwords.

caution

It is not a good practice to create local user accounts on computers running Windows Server 2003 that are part of a domain because domains do not recognize local user accounts and local users may have difficulty accessing domain resources.

Table 6-1   Naming Convention Guidelines

Factors	Details
Local user accounts	Create unique local user account names for every user on the user's local computer when in a workgroup environment.
Domain user accounts	Create a unique logon name for every user in the directory. You must also ensure that the user's full name must be unique to the OU where you create the domain user account.
Character limit in user names	The user logon names you create should consist of 20 or less characters because Windows Server 2003 recognizes only the first 20 characters, even if more characters are entered.
Case-insensitivity	User logon names are not case-sensitive, so you can use a combination of alphanumeric and special characters to help uniquely identify user accounts.
Invalid characters	There are certain invalid characters that you cannot use in user logon names. These are: " [ ] / \ = , + ! * ? < > :
Employees with same names	The naming convention should include a method for differentiating between two users with the same name. For example, two users having the same name, Ryan Taylor, could use the logon names RTaylor and RBTaylor.
Employee type identification	In large organizations, you can also identify users by the division in which they work. For example, a user Michael Greg, who works in the Sales division, could have the user logon name MichaelG-Sales. If the division names change, the account will have to be renamed.
E-mail compatibility	Ensure the compatibility of the user principal name with e-mail accounts, as some e-mail applications do not accept characters such as spaces and parentheses.

Table 6-2   Password Guidelines

Factors	Details
Password for Administrator	An Administrator account should always have a password to prevent unauthorized access to the account.
Controlling passwords	As an administrator, you can decide whether you want to assign unique passwords for user accounts and prevent users from changing them, or allow users to decide their own passwords.
Creating passwords	Strong passwords contain characters from three of four possible groups: uppercase letters, lowercase letters, numbers, and the non-alphanumeric characters: ` ~ ! @ # $ % ^ & * ( ) _ + - = { }	[ ] \ : " ; ' < > ? , . /. Always create new passwords that are different from previously used passwords. Avoid using common words or names and do not use birth dates, children's names, street names and numbers, college names, or any other personally identifiable information. If your network includes Windows 95 or 98 computers, keep password length at 14 characters or less. These operating systems do not support passwords longer than this.
Maximum character limit	Passwords can contain up to 128 characters. Ideally, passwords should have at least eight characters.
Valid characters	To form a password, you can select characters from these groups: uppercase and lowercase letters, numerals, and non-alphanumeric characters.

skill 1

Introducing Local User Accounts
(cont'd)

Create and manage user accounts.

how to

Create a local user account.

1. Log on as an **Administrator** on a member server.
2. Click [Start], right-click **My Computer**, and click **Manage** to open the **Computer Management** console.
3. In the scope pane, double-click **Local Users and Groups** to expand it.
4. Right-click the **Users** folder and click **New User** to open the **New User** dialog box.
5. Type a name, such as **M.Jones**, in the **User name** text box to specify a user name for the user.
6. Type a name, such as **Maria Jones**, in the **Full name** text box.
7. Type a description, such as **Temporary Technician**, in the **Description** text box to specify the job title of the user.
8. Type a password, such as **password1**, in the **Password** field to set the password. Re-type the password in the **Confirm Password** box.
9. The **User must change password at next logon** check box is selected by default (**Figure 6-1**). The user will be required to change his or her password the first time he or she logs on using the new account.
10. Click [Create] to create the user account.
11. Click [Close] to close the **New User** dialog box. The new local user account is now shown in the details pane of the Computer Management console (**Figure 6-2**).
12. Close the Computer Management console.

more

In addition to local and domain user accounts, Windows Server 2003 provides several **built-in user accounts** that enable you to perform administrative tasks or gain access to network resources. The built-in accounts are created automatically during the installation of Windows Server 2003. You can rename built-in accounts, but you cannot delete them. There are two built-in accounts, Administrator and Guest. Both of these accounts can be disabled.

Administrator: The **Administrator account** is used to manage the overall functioning of a computer. You use it to manage and configure the local computer (on a workstation, stand-alone server, or member server) or a domain (on a domain controller). The Administrator account should always be renamed and you should not use it for any other work besides administrative tasks, so that you do not run the risk of inadvertently harming your system or allowing inappropriate access to your system. The Administrator account cannot be deleted and it cannot be locked out due to invalid logon attempts, though it *can* be disabled, which is generally a bad practice. You also cannot remove it from the Administrators local group to which it automatically belongs.

In a domain, the Administrator account is used to manage overall domain configuration. The network administrator can use this account to create user accounts and to set and monitor security policies. The Administrator account is also used to perform other networking tasks such as configuring printers and granting permissions to access shared resources on the network.

Guest: The **Guest account** is used for infrequent users who must log on to access shared resources for a short duration. Users who do not have a user account on a computer or a domain can also use it for logons.

tip
The Administrator account and the Guest account should always be renamed.

tip
By default, the Guest account is disabled.

Figure 6-1 Creating a local user account

New User
User name:
MJones
Full name:
Maria Jones
Description:
Human Resources Manager
Password:
Confirm password:
User must change password at next logon
User cannot change password
Password never expires
Account is disabled
Create
Close

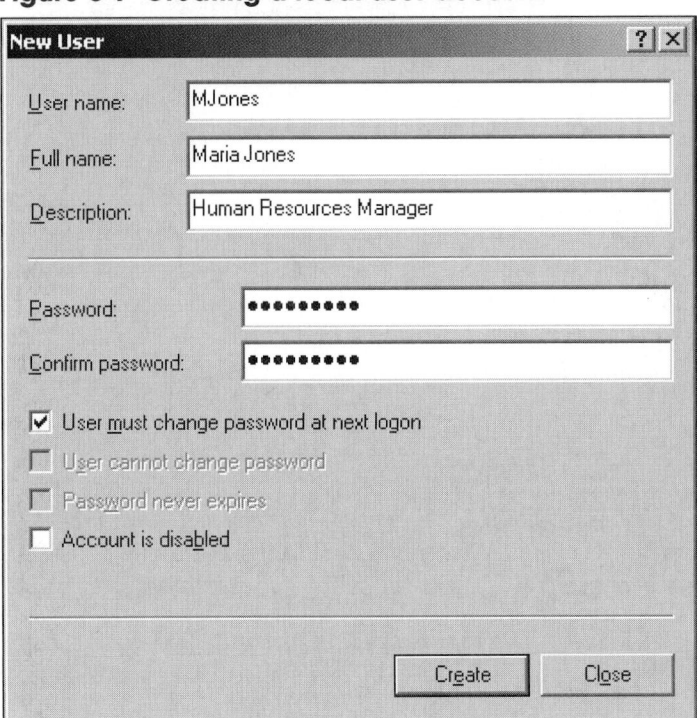

Figure 6-2 New local user account in the Users folder

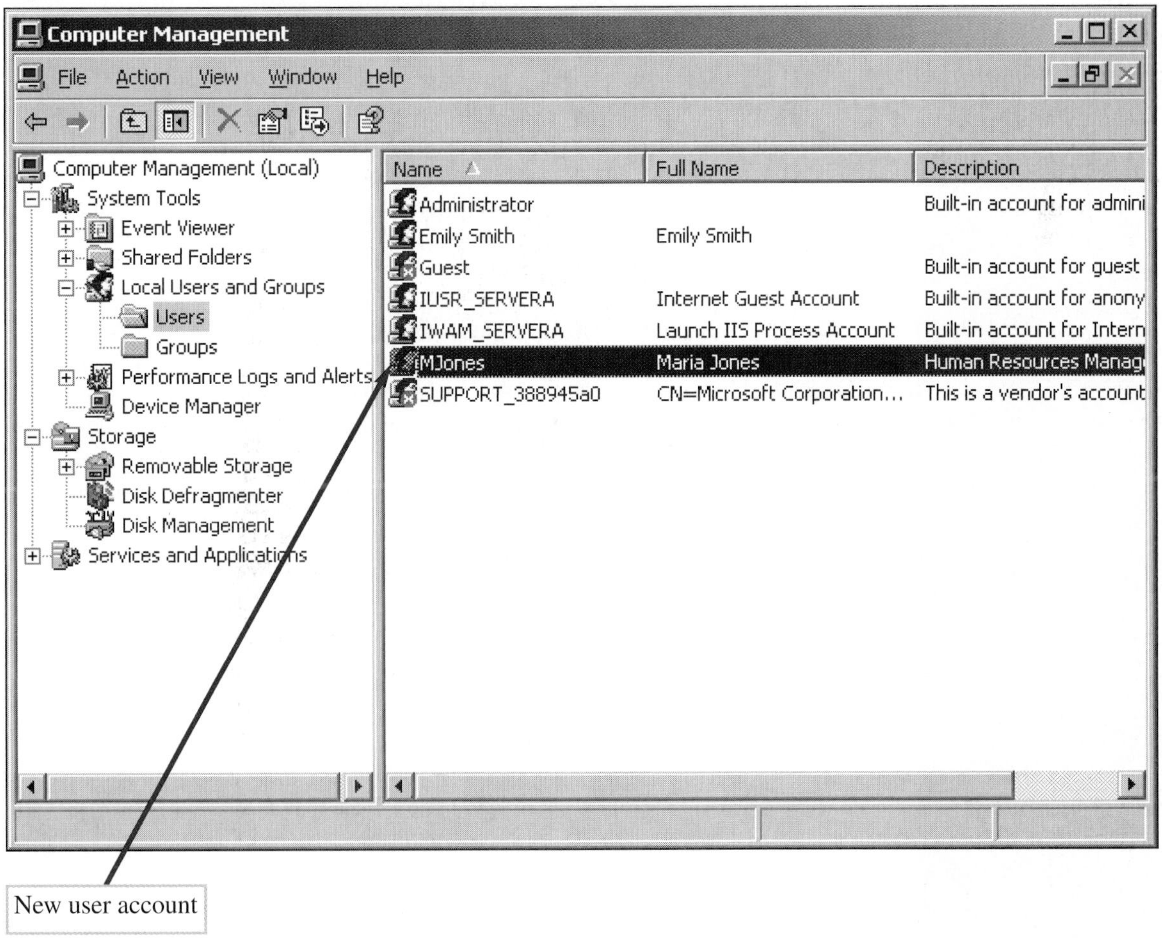

Computer Management
File Action View Window Help
Computer Management (Local)
System Tools
Event Viewer
Shared Folders
Local Users and Groups
Users
Groups
Performance Logs and Alerts
Device Manager
Storage
Removable Storage
Disk Defragmenter
Disk Management
Services and Applications
Name
Full Name
Description
Administrator
Built-in account for admini
Emily Smith
Emily Smith
Guest
Built-in account for guest
IUSR_SERVERA
Internet Guest Account
Built-in account for anony
IWAM_SERVERA
Launch IIS Process Account
Built-in account for Intern
MJones
Maria Jones
Human Resources Manag
SUPPORT_388945a0
CN=Microsoft Corporation...
This is a vendor's account
New user account

skill 2

Setting and Modifying Local User Account Properties

exam objective

Create and manage user accounts. Troubleshoot user accounts. Diagnose and resolve issues related to user account properties. Troubleshoot user authentication issues.

overview

Each local user account you create has a set of default properties associated with it, including the user name, password, and dial-in properties. You can configure the various properties for a user account using the Local Users and Groups snap-in.

By default, the following tabs are available in the Properties dialog box for a local user account (**Figure 6-3**):

◆ The **General** tab is used to enter personal information about the user, such as his or her full name, password properties, and a brief description of the user. The **Account is locked out** check box on the General tab is disabled by default and cannot be activated manually. The user account will be locked and the check box enabled when the user exceeds the Account lockout threshold policy specified by the administrator. The **Account lockout threshold policy** specifies the number of invalid logon attempts that will be tolerated before the account is locked out (see Lesson 12).

◆ The **Member Of** tab is used to designate the groups to which a user belongs. Adding users to groups simplifies network administration because the permissions you assign to a group are automatically applied to all group members.

◆ The **Profile** tab is used to specify the path to the user profile, the name of the logon script that should be run when the user logs on, and where the user's home folder is located (**Figure 6-4**). A user profile is a collection of directories and files that stores user-specific data. In earlier versions of Windows, logon scripts were used to set the desktop environment. User profiles have largely replaced them in this function. However, **logon scripts** are still used for other purposes, such as running custom VBScripts. A logon script is run each time the user logs on. A **home folder** is a private network location in addition to the My Documents folder where users can store personal files. It is stored in a shared folder on a network server. When you create the home folder on a network server, users can access it from any computer on the network. Administrators can use this centralized storage area to easily back up important network files instead of going from client computer to client computer to make sure that all relevant files are backed up. Users of client computers running any of the Microsoft operating systems, such as MS-DOS, Windows 95/98, or Windows 2000, can access the home folder.

◆ The **Dial-in** tab is used to set the dial-in properties for a user account. **Table 6-3** outlines the options you can choose on the Dial-in tab to set up how a user can make a dial-in connection to the local computer from a remote location. To gain access to a network, you must make sure that a dial-up connection is set for the server on the client computer. Only then can a user dial-in to a computer running Windows Server 2003 Remote Access Service (see Lesson 11).

tip

It is a good practice to store home folders on an NTFS volume in order to make use of NTFS permissions.

**Figure 6-3 Tabs on the Properties dialog
box for a local user account**

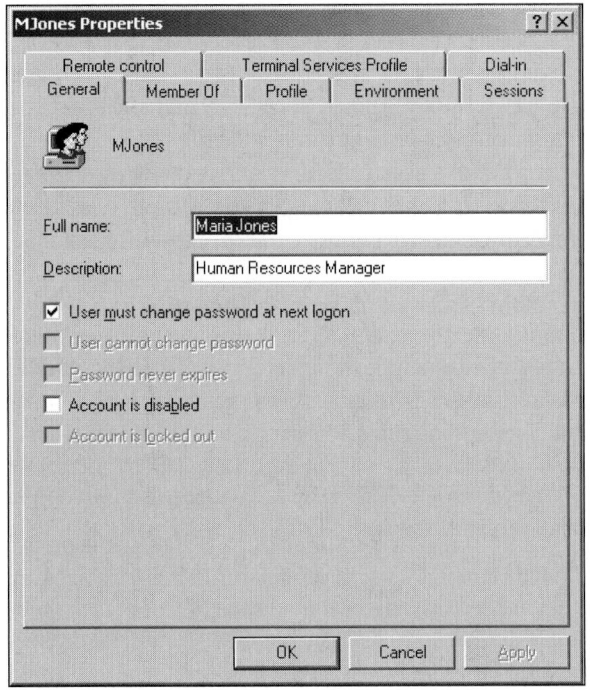

Figure 6-4 The Profile tab

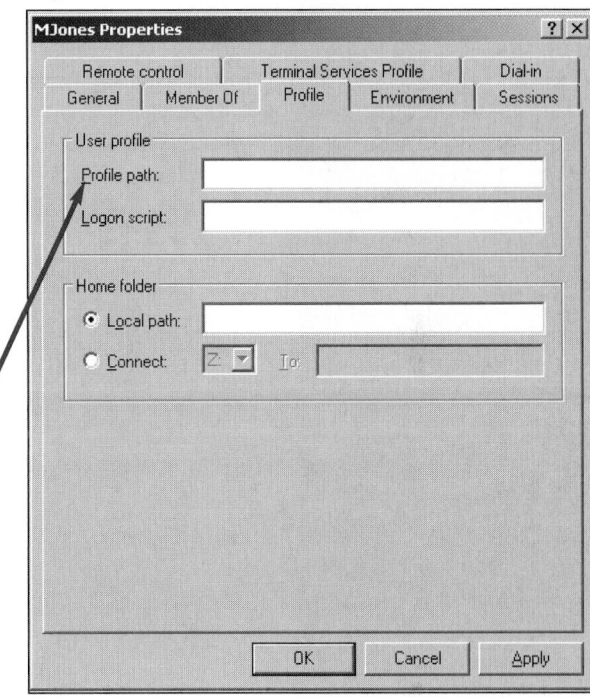

Used to specify
the path to the
user profile

Table 6-3   Options available on the Dial-in tab

Option	Description
Allow access	Activates the dial-in feature for the user account.
Deny access	Disables the dial-in feature.
Control access through Remote Access Policy	Specifies that remote access permission is controlled by a remote access policy.
Verify Caller-ID	Specifies the telephone number that must be used to dial-in to the server.
No Callback	Allows a user to call from any telephone number.
Set by Caller (Routing and Remote Access Service only)	Allows a user to specify a telephone number on which the RAS server will call back the user.
Always Callback to	Sets the callback telephone number. The RAS server will call back the user only on this specified number. It provides high security because the telephone number is pre-configured and this reduces the risk of an unauthorized person dialing in.
Assign a Static IP Address	Assigns a static TCP/IP address to the user.
Apply Static Routes	Allows you to set the routes to be followed once the connection is established.

skill 2

Setting and Modifying Local User Account Properties (cont'd)

exam objective

Create and manage user accounts. Troubleshoot user accounts. Diagnose and resolve issues related to user account properties. Troubleshoot user authentication issues.

overview

tip

When a user account is disabled, the context menu for the user account includes the Enable Account command.

◆ Finally, there are Terminal Services settings, which include the **Environment**, **Sessions** (**Figure 6-5**), **Terminal Services Profile, and Remote Control** tabs (**Figure 6-6**). Terminal Services provides the ability to connect to a server from a remote location, as well as run a session as if you were physically sitting at the computer. The Terminal Services client sends the equivalent of keystrokes and mouse movements (input events) to the terminal server, the terminal server runs applications in response to these events, and then the terminal server sends screenshots of the session back to the PC. For an overly simplified example, Terminal Services is similar to a server-based "PC anywhere" application. Terminal Services provides a multi-session environment that allows remote computers (or Windows terminals) access to Windows-based programs running on the server. To learn more about Terminal Services, see Lesson 15.

As a network administrator, you will have to modify user accounts to fulfill the changing requirements of your organization. For example, you may need to disable the user account of an employee who is on leave. This will temporarily disable the rights and permissions assigned to that employee. To modify local user accounts, you use the Local Users and Group snap-in. To modify domain user accounts, you use the Active Directory Users and Computers console.

You can manage user accounts by performing the following tasks:

◆ **Renaming a user account:** You can rename an account when you want to transfer a particular user account to a new user while keeping the rights, permissions, and group memberships of the previous user. For example, if a new HR employee is replacing a previous one, you can simply rename the account by changing the first name, last name, and user logon name for the previous HR user account to the information for the new HR member. This will assign the permissions and properties of the HR user account to the new user.

◆ **Resetting passwords:** Occasionally, you will need to reset passwords when a user's password has expired or has been forgotten. You do not need to know the old password in order to reset a password. After the administrator or the user sets a password, it is not visible to anybody, including the administrator. This is necessary to ensure security and prevent unauthorized access to user accounts. Be careful when modifying passwords, as Windows Server 2003 encrypts files using the password of the account, by default. You may lose access to your encrypted files if you change the password. However, Windows Server 2003 includes a password backup function, included in Windows Backup, that can be used to create backup copies of your password. If you are using EFS, you should ensure that the password for your account has been backed up.

◆ **Unlocking user accounts:** Windows Server 2003 can lock user accounts for users who violate the account lockout threshold policy. For example, if a policy is set to allow a maximum of ten failed logon attempts and a user exceeds the limit, Windows Server 2003 will lock the user account and the user will receive an error message to this effect. In such cases, the user can either wait until the lockout period expires (usually 30 minutes), or contact an administrator to unlock the user account.

Figure 6-5 The Sessions tab

Used to set Terminal Services timeout and reconnection settings

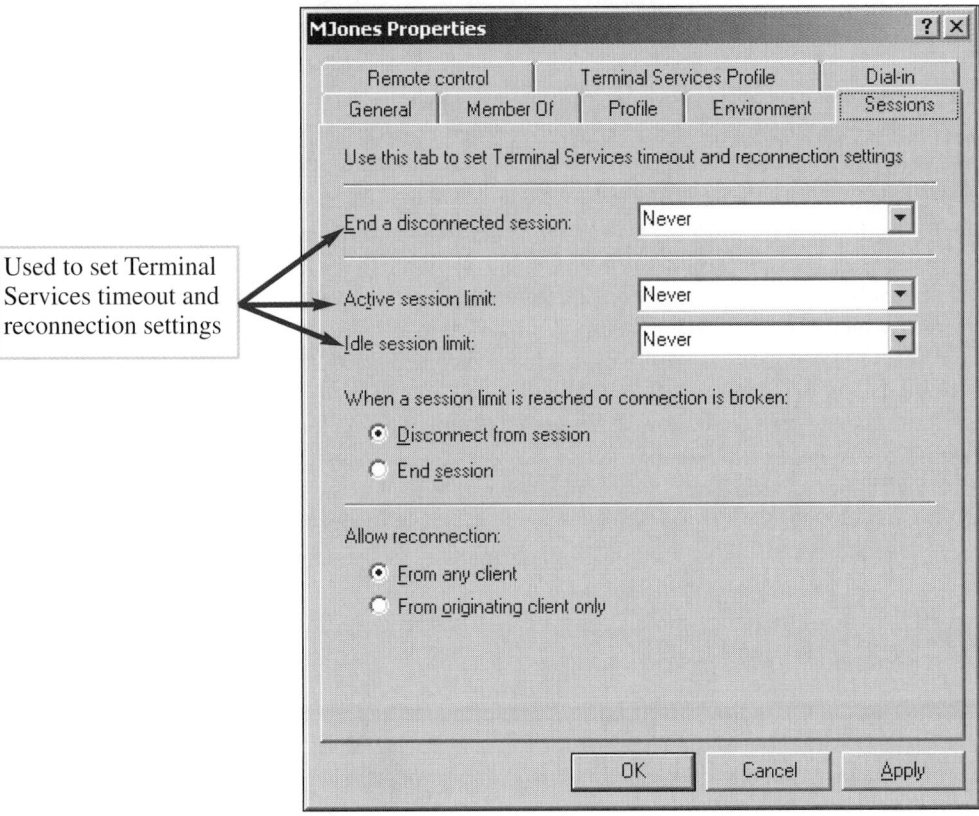

Figure 6-6 The Remote control tab

Used to configure settings for remotely observing or controlling a Terminal Services client session

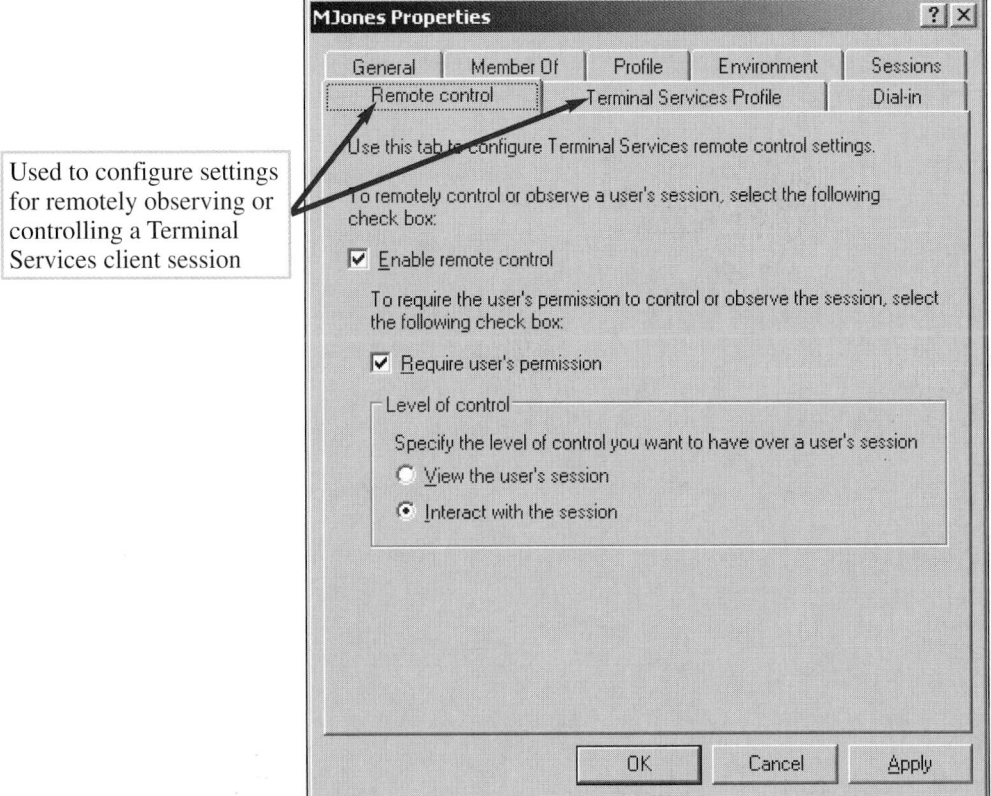

skill 2

Setting and Modifying Local User Account Properties (cont'd)

exam objective

Create and manage user accounts. Troubleshoot user accounts. Diagnose and resolve issues related to user account properties. Troubleshoot user authentication issues.

overview

◆ **Disabling and enabling a user account:** Disabling a user account will prevent a user from logging on to the network or to the local computer where the user account was created. You can disable a user account for security reasons and enable it again when required. For example, you can disable an account when a user goes on leave for a month and enable it again when the user returns so that the user can log on to the network again. It is a good practice to disable a user account when a user leaves the company, rather than deleting it. This way, if that user is replaced, you can simply rename and enable the old account to give the new user access to the correct resources.

◆ **Deleting a user account:** You can delete a user account when you no longer need it. For example, you can delete an account when a user leaves the company and you are sure that you cannot reuse the account by renaming it. Deleting user accounts will ensure that you do not have redundant accounts.

how to

Set the properties for a local user account.

1. Open the **Computer Management** console.
2. In the scope pane, double-click the **Local Users and Groups** snap-in to expand it, if necessary. Double-click the **Users** node to expand it, if necessary.
3. Right-click the user account you created in Skill 1 (in our example, **MJones**) and click the **Properties** command on the context menu.
4. Clear the **User must change password at next logon** check box. Note that the two other password-related check boxes are now enabled.
5. Select the **User cannot change password** check box to prevent the user from changing the password (**Figure 6-7**).
6. Click the **Dial-in** tab to set the dial-in properties for the user account.
7. Click the **Allow access** option button to enable the user to dial-in from a remote location (**Figure 6-8**).
8. Click [OK] to save the settings.
9. In the details pane, right-click **MJones** and click the **Set Password** command on the context menu (**Figure 6-9**).
10. A dialog box will open, warning you that changing the password for this user account could result in data loss (**Figure 6-10**). This is due to the new way EFS generates file encryption keys in Windows Server 2003. Since the keys are based partially on password, and since there is no default recovery agent, changing the password may result in the user being unable to access his or her files. Click **Proceed** to continue.

Figure 6-7 Preventing a user from changing the password

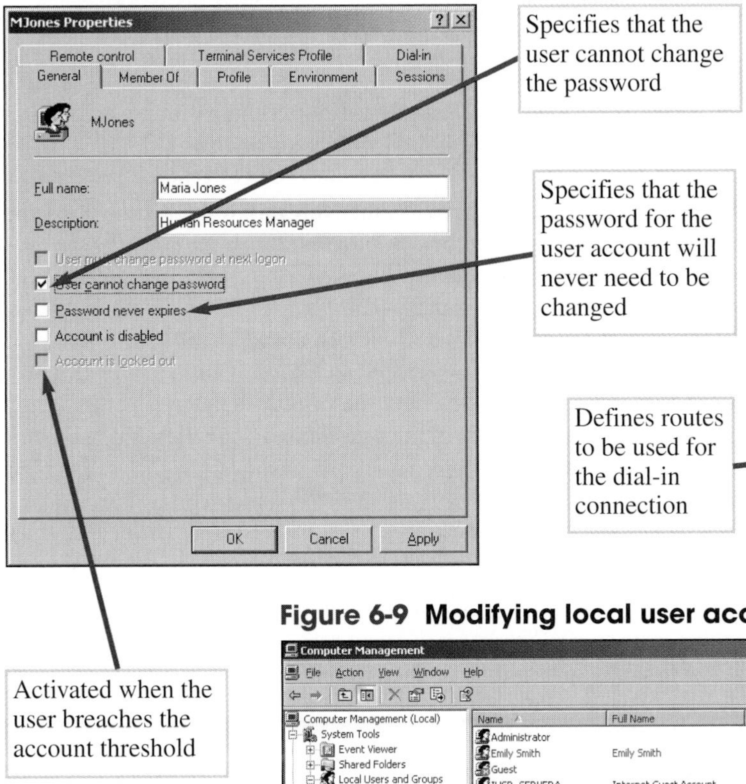

Specifies that the user cannot change the password

Specifies that the password for the user account will never need to be changed

Defines routes to be used for the dial-in connection

Activated when the user breaches the account threshold

Figure 6-8 Setting the dial-in properties

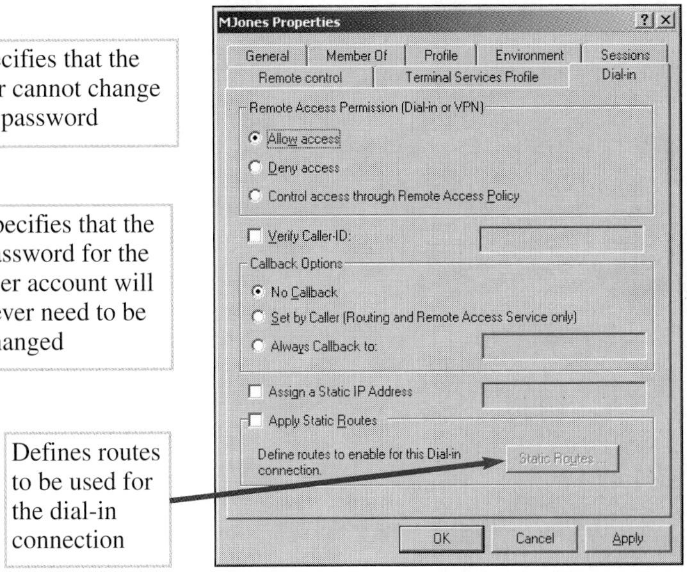

Figure 6-9 Modifying local user account properties

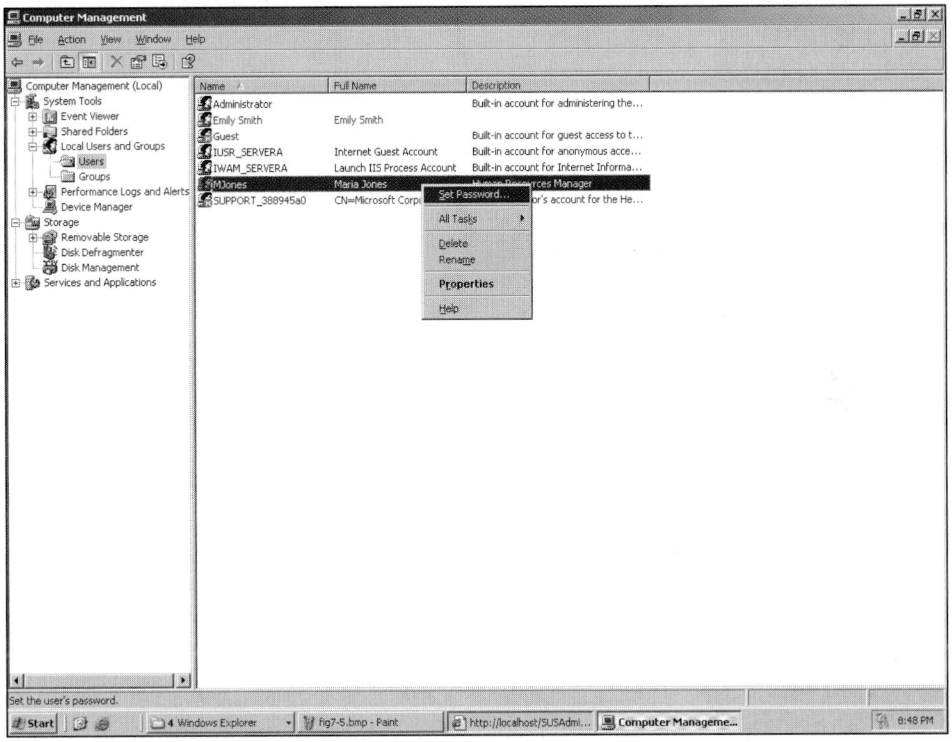

Figure 6-10 Setting a new password for a local user account

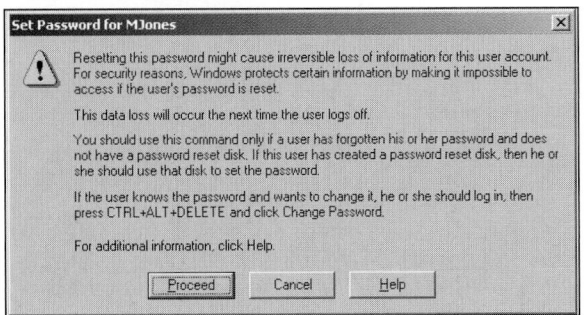

skill 2

Setting and Modifying Local User Account Properties *(cont'd)*

exam objective

Create and manage user accounts. Troubleshoot user accounts. Diagnose and resolve issues related to user account properties. Troubleshoot user authentication issues.

how to

11. Type a new password (for example, **password2**) in the **New password** text box. Retype the password in the **Confirm password** text box (**Figure 6-11**).
12. Click [OK]. The **Local Users and Groups** message box informs you that the password has been successfully changed (**Figure 6-12**).
13. Click [OK]. Right-click the user account and click **Rename**.
14. Type a new name (for example, **MDouglas**) and press **Enter**. This renames the user account (**Figure 6-13**). Note that this changes only the display name/user name for the user account. You must change the full name of the user in the **Properties** dialog box for the user account.
15. Close the Computer Management console.

more

When users are not able to log on, they will receive an alert telling them that the specified user account does not exist, the user name is unknown, or that an invalid password had been entered. First, the user should make sure that he or she has entered the user name and password correctly. Next, the user must make sure that he or she has chosen the correct authentication entity (either the local computer or the domain). After these errors have been checked, the administrator can check to make sure that the account name is valid and that the password is correct.

Figure 6-11 The Set Password for <user_name> dialog box

Set Password for MJones   ? X

New password: •••••••••

Confirm password: •••••••••

⚠ If you click OK, the following will occur:

This user account will immediately lose access to all of its encrypted files, stored passwords, and personal security certificates.

If you click Cancel, the password will not be changed and no data loss will occur.

OK   Cancel

Figure 6-12 Message confirming the changed password

Local Users and Groups   X

ⓘ The password has been set.

OK

Figure 6-13 Renaming a local user account

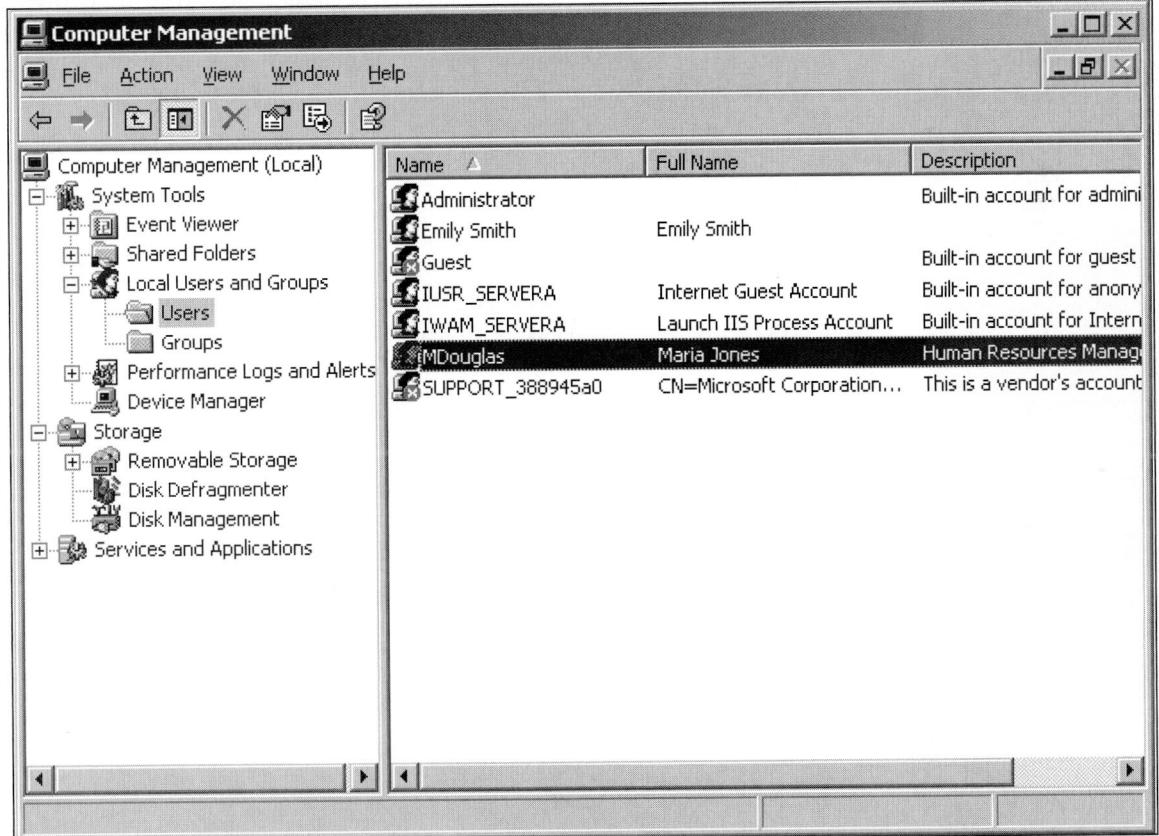

skill 3

Creating a Domain User Account

exam objective

Create and manage user accounts. Create and modify user accounts by using the Active Directory Users and Computers MMC snap-in.

overview

A user account is a form of identification for a user on a Windows Server 2003 network. A user account is used to build the user ticket (also known as a TGT, or Ticket Granting Ticket). The user ticket contains a list of the Security IDs (SIDs) associated with the user account and all domain groups in which the user account is a member. The user ticket is used to prove that the user account is valid and to construct session tickets. When the user wishes to access a resource, the operating system sends the user ticket to the domain controller with a special Kerberos request. The domain controller will then create two copies of the session ticket for the account, sending one copy to the resource server and the other copy to the user account. The requester will then present the session ticket to the specific computer controlling the resources (such as a file server, for example) as a form of identification. (For a more detailed explanation of Kerberos authentication, see Lesson 12.)

After the user is authenticated, the resource server will compare the SIDs in the ticket to a Discretionary Access Control List (DACL) on the resource. DACLs, as you learned in Lesson 3, are composed of Access Control Entries (ACEs). Each ACE contains the SID of a user account or group and the permissions that apply to it. Through this mechanism, a resource determines what level of access each user account should have, and grants an access token to the user for the user's specific access level.

You use a domain user account to log on to a domain and access network resources. You can create a domain user account in an OU on a domain controller, as shown in **Figures 6-14** and **6-15**. The domain controller then replicates the new user account information to all of the other domain controllers in the domain. After replication, all domain controllers in the domain will be able to authenticate the user during logon. In addition, all trusting domains can now allow the user account to gain access to their resources. You use the **Active Directory Users and Computers** console to create domain user accounts.

During the logon process, a user provides a logon name and password—or, alternately, inserts his or her smart card and provides a personal identification number (PIN). Windows Server 2003 uses this information to authenticate the user and build a user ticket that contains the user's identification and security settings. The purpose of the user ticket is to identify the user account in order to build session tickets, which are then used to identify the user to the domain member computers on which the user tries to access resources. An access token is then generated to allow the user specific levels of access. The access token remains available for the duration of the logon session.

Active Directory domain names are usually the full DNS name of the domain. However, for backward compatibility, each domain also has a pre-Windows 2000 name (the NetBIOS name of the domain) that is used by computers running pre-Windows 2000 operating systems. The pre-Windows 2000 domain name can be used to log on to a Windows 2000 or Windows Server 2003 domain from computers running pre-Windows 2000 operating systems. Thus, the same format can also be used to log on to a Windows Server 2003 domain from computers running Windows 2000 or XP.

Figure 6-14 Domain user account

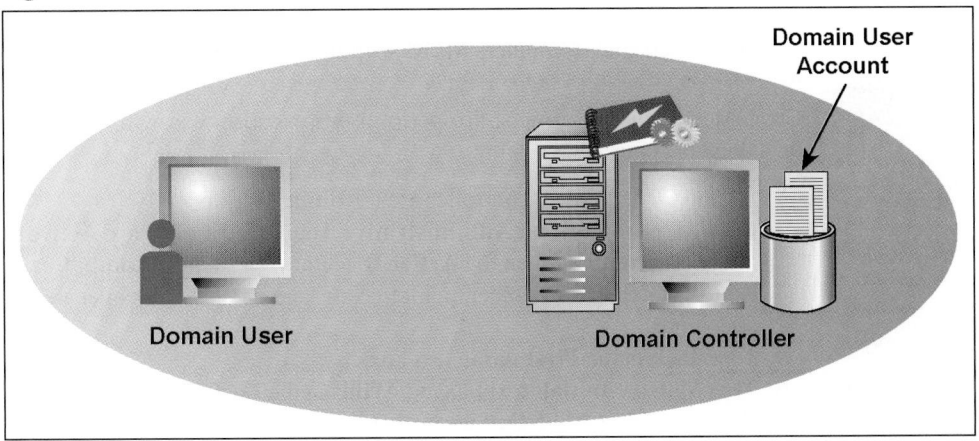

Figure 6-15 Creating a domain user account in an OU

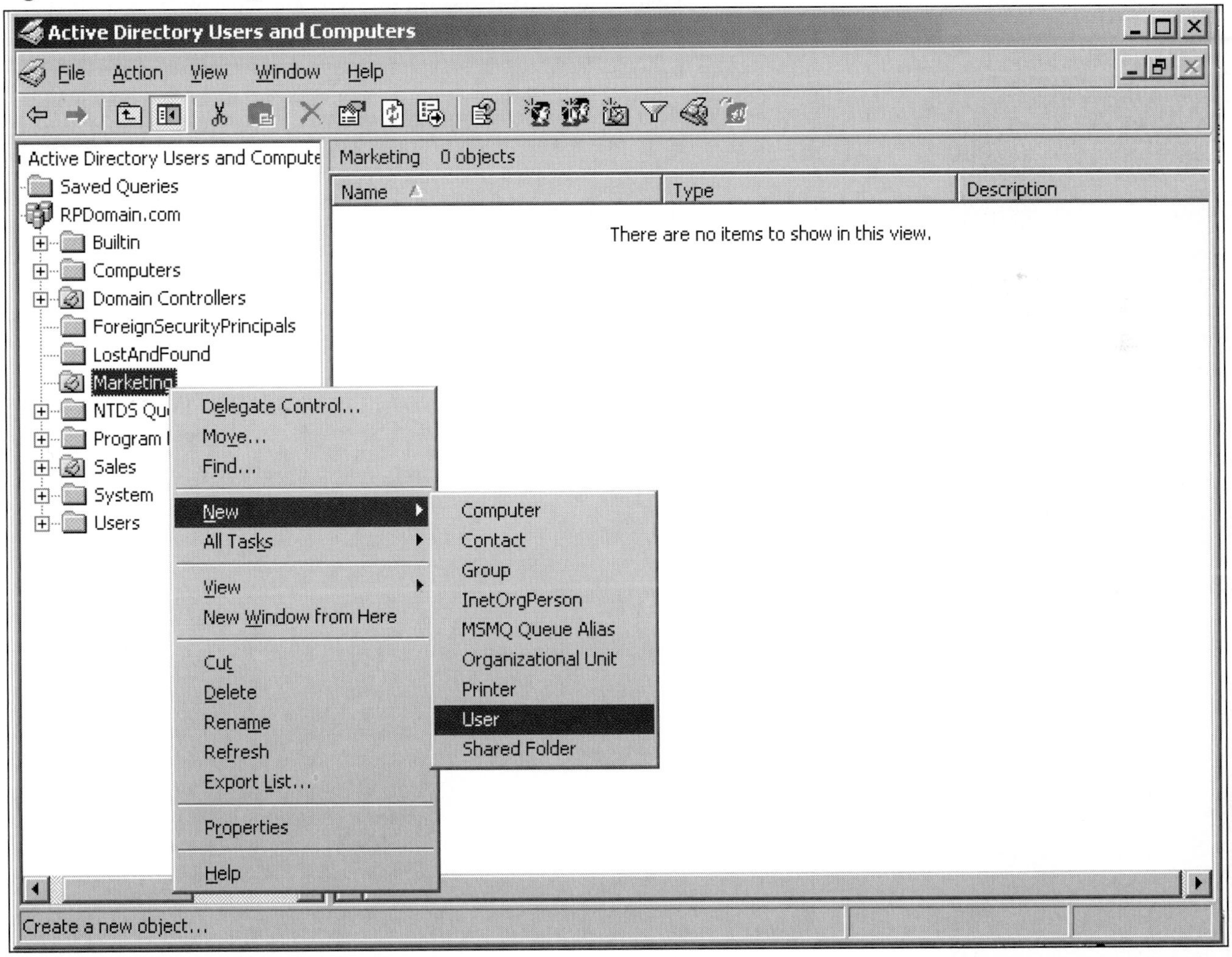

skill 3

Creating a Domain User Account
(cont'd)

exam objective

Create and manage user accounts. Create and modify user accounts by using the Active Directory Users and Computers MMC snap-in.

how to

Create domain user accounts. (To perform this exercise, you will need administrative rights on a domain controller.)

1. Log on to the domain controller as an **Administrator**.
2. Click **Start**, point to **Administrative Tools**, and then click **Active Directory Users and Computers** to open the **Active Directory Users and Computers** console.
3. Right-click the **Users** folder, point to **New**, and click **User** to open the **New Object-User** dialog box.
4. Type **Jack** in the **First name** text box.
5. Type **M** in the **Initials** text box and **Willis** in the **Last name** text box. Note that Jack's full name is filled into the **Full name** text box automatically.
6. Type **JWillis** in the **User logon name** text box. Note that a pre-Windows 2003 logon name is automatically created. This name is the same as the user logon name **(Figure 6-16)**.
7. Click **Next >** to display the options for specifying the user's initial password.
8. Type an appropriate password in the **Password** text box. On Windows Server 2003, the default password policy specifies that passwords must meet complexity requirements. According to this policy, passwords must be at least 6 characters long; however, the minimum password length policy on a domain controller requires seven characters. In addition, the complexity requirements stipulate that passwords must contain three of the four character types (uppercase letters, lower case letters, base 10 digits, or non-alphanumeric characters).
9. Retype the password in the **Confirm password** text box.
10. Select the **User must change password at next logon** check box **(Figure 6-17)**.
11. Click **Next >** . The **New Object-User** dialog box displays the options you have configured for this user account **(Figure 6-18)**.
12. Click **Finish** after verifying that the user account options are correct. You can click **< Back** to modify the user details and settings. The details pane of the **Active Directory Users and Computers** console displays the user account you have created **(Figure 6-19)**.
13. Follow the steps above to create another user account for **Barbara J. Clarke** with the user logon name **BClarke**.

Figure 6-16 Creating a domain user account

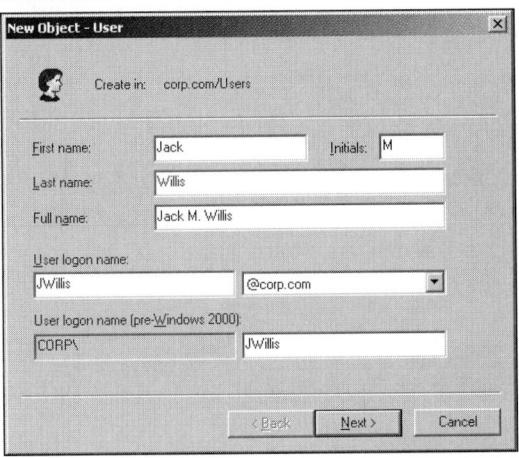

Figure 6-17 Specifying a password for a new domain user account

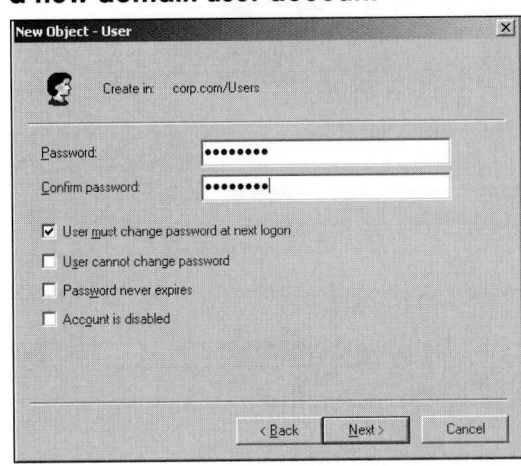

Figure 6-18 Summary screen for a new domain user account

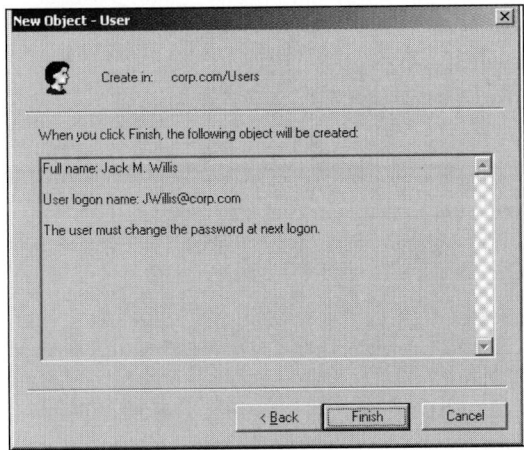

Figure 6-19 The new user in the Active Directory Users and Computers console

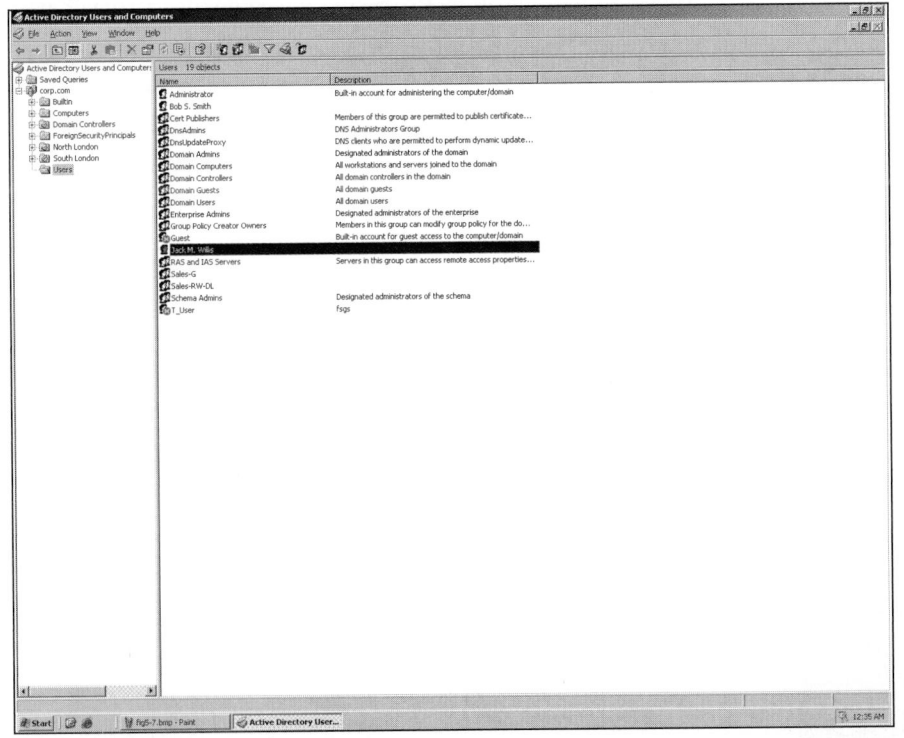

skill 4

Setting Domain User Account Properties

exam objective

Create and manage user accounts. Create and modify user accounts by using the Active Directory Users and Computers MMC snap-in.

overview

Every user account you create has a set of default properties associated with the account. You can configure personal information, logon settings, dial-in settings, and Terminal Services settings for a user.

The personal properties that you define for a domain user account are useful when searching for users. Therefore, if you want to be able to search for users based on very specific information, you should always provide as much detailed information for each domain user account as possible.

The logon settings are used to specify the logon hours for a user. As mentioned previously, this enables you to restrict the hours during which a user can remain logged on to the network.

You can also modify the dial-in settings for a user account. Dial-in settings for a user account specify if and how a user can make a dial-in connection to the network from a remote location.

Finally, you can specify Terminal Services settings for a user account. Terminal Services provides the ability to connect to a server from a remote location, as well as run a session as if you were physically sitting at the computer. As previously noted, the Terminal Services client sends the equivalent of keystrokes and mouse movements (input events) to the terminal server, the terminal server runs applications in response to these events, and then the terminal server sends screenshots of the session back to the PC. Windows Server 2003 includes Remote Desktop Connection client software to support 16- and 32-bit Windows-based Terminal Services clients.

Note that you can save a lot of time in a large environment by filling out the common fields shared between user accounts in a "template" account. A template account is a disabled account used as a template for creating other accounts. After filling out the appropriate fields, you can right-click the account and select **Copy** to create a new account with most of your pre-defined fields already filled in.

A description of the tabs of the **Properties** dialog box for a domain user account is provided in **Table 6-4**.

tip

Be aware that some user account settings (such as street address and description) are purely informational, while others (such as the user logon name) are functional.

Table 6-4   Tabs on the Properties dialog box of a domain user account

Tabs	Purpose
General	Stores the user's personal details, which include first name, last name, display name, description, office location, telephone numbers, e-mail address, home page, and additional Web pages.
Address	Stores the user's contact information, which includes street address, post office box, city, state or province, zip or postal code, and country or region details.
Account	Stores the user's account properties, such as user logon name, logon hours, account options, account expiration, and computers available for logging on.
Profile	Enables an administrator to set a profile path, logon script path, and home folder.
Telephones	Stores the user's home, pager, mobile, fax, and IP telephone numbers and any specific comments about these.
Organization	Stores the user's title, department, and company name, and the name of the user's manager.
Remote Control	Enables an administrator to configure the Terminal Services remote control settings.
Terminal Services Profile	Enables an administrator to configure the Terminal Services user profile.
Member Of	Stores the groups to which the user belongs.
Dial-in	Stores the dial-in properties for the user account such as access permissions and callback options.
Environment	Enables an administrator to configure the Terminal Services startup environment.
Sessions	Specifies the Terminal Services timeout and reconnection settings.

skill 4

Setting Domain User Account Properties (cont'd)

exam objective

Create and manage user accounts. Create and modify user accounts by using the Active Directory Users and Computers MMC snap-in.

how to

Set domain user account properties such as personal information and logon hours.

1. Click the **Users** folder in the **Active Directory Users and Computers** console. The list of user accounts is displayed in the details pane.
2. Right-click **Jack M. Willis** and click **Properties** to open the **Properties** dialog box for **Jack M. Willis**.
3. Type **ABC Consultants** in the **Office** text box.
4. Type **JWillis@abc.com** in the **E-mail** text box (**Figure 6-20**).
5. Click the **Account** tab to specify the logon hours for Jack (**Figure 6-21**).
6. Click [Logon Hours...] to open the **Logon Hours for Jack M. Willis** dialog box.
7. Click the **Logon Denied** option button to remove the default access times.
8. Drag the rectangle that corresponds to Monday 2 PM to the rectangle that corresponds to Friday 10 PM.
9. Click the **Logon Permitted** option button to specify Jack's logon hours as 2 PM through 10 PM, Monday through Friday (**Figure 6-22**).
10. Click [OK] to close the **Logon Hours for Jack M. Willis** dialog box.
11. Click [OK] to close the **Properties** dialog box and apply these settings.

tip

A blue rectangle corresponding to an hour indicates that the user can log on during that hour, and a white rectangle indicates that the user cannot log on during that hour.

Figure 6-20 Specifying user account properties

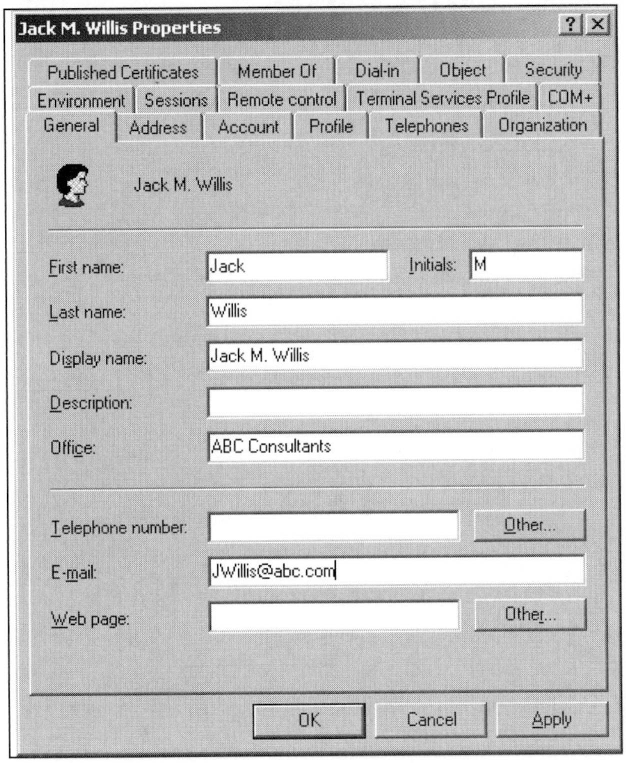

Figure 6-21 The Account tab for a domain user account

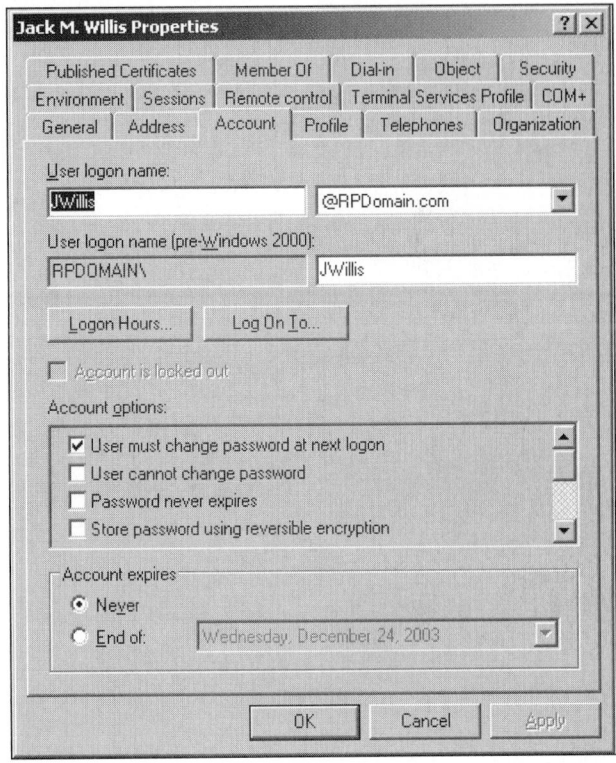

Figure 6-22 Specifying logon hours for a user account

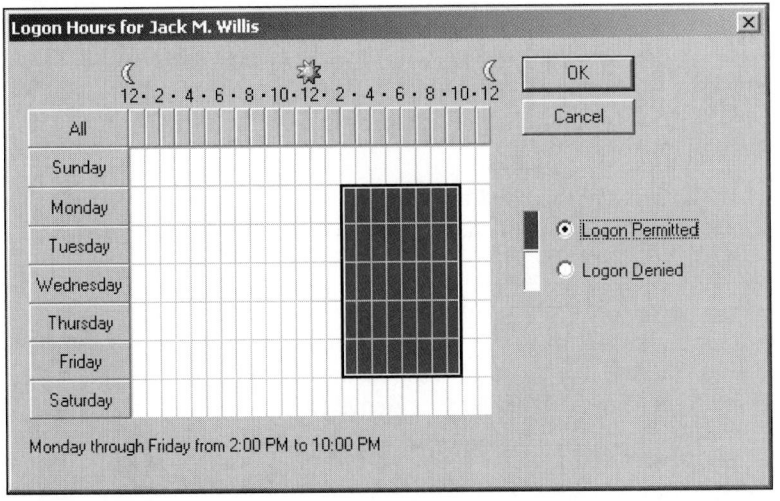

skill 5
Automating User Creation and Modification

exam objective

Create and manage user accounts. Create and modify user accounts by using automation. Import user accounts.

overview

Creating and modifying user accounts is tedious, time-consuming work. Luckily, Windows Server 2003 supports tools to automate this process, at least in a domain environment. The tools you can use to automate or partially automate the process of account creation are account templates, importation tools, and scripting. Tools you can use to automate account modification include scripting and importation tools. Let's examine each of these tools in turn, beginning with the simplest.

Templates are user accounts created specifically for copying. In other words, no one should be allowed to log on using the account. You create the account and fill out all of the information common to all users, and then simply copy it when creating new users. In large networks, this can save you significant time in account creation.

The following items are copied by default from the template account or accounts to new user accounts:

- Company
- Department
- Country/region
- City
- State/province
- Zip/Postal Code

- P.O. Box
- Manager
- Logon Hours
- Logon Workstations
- Account Expires
- Member of

- Primary Group
- Home Directory
- Profile Path
- Logon script
- Account options

While templates can significantly reduce the headaches involved with adding a small number of users, Windows Server 2003 ships with two other utilities that are immensely helpful in creating large batches of user accounts: **Csvde.exe** and **Ldifde.exe**. Csvde stands for **Comma separated value data exchange**. Csvde.exe is a utility designed to import and export objects into Active Directory using .csv files. .csv files can be used in Excel and most other spreadsheet programs, making it easy for your HR department to use a simple spreadsheet to fill out the information for your new users. All you must do is add a few fields to the spreadsheet and import the spreadsheet into Active Directory, creating the new user accounts. Additionally, you can export user accounts from Active Directory using Csvde.exe, modify the accounts, and re-import them, making mass user modifications relatively pain-free. For example, to export all objects of the user object class, which includes all user and computer accounts, to a .csv file named userlist, at the command prompt enter: **csvde.exe –f userlist.csv –r "(objectClass-user)"** (**Figures 6-23** and **6-24**), where –f is the filename parameter and –r is the export parameter for performing an LDAP search filter. To view all of the parameters for Csvde.exe, enter **csvde -?** at the command prompt.

Ldifde stands for **LDAP data interchange format data exchange**. Ldifde.exe is a utility that performs the same functions as Csvde.exe, only with .ldif files. .ldif files are specifically formatted text files supported by many third-party LDAP applications. The parameters used with Ldifde.exe are shown in **Figure 6-25**.

Both Csvde.exe and Ldifde.exe are installed by default with Windows 2003 Server, and should be run from a command prompt on the server itself.

In addition, there are scripting tools. Probably the most commonly used scripting interface for creating user accounts in Active Directory is Adsiedit.exe. Essentially, Adsiedit.exe is like a Registry editor for Active Directory. It allows you to make sweeping, low-level changes quickly. However, due to the power of this tool, it is recommended that it only be used by experienced administrators with a deep knowledge of Active Directory and some knowledge of scripting.

caution

When using Csvde.exe and Ldifde.exe, be aware that there are a few fields that are required to be in the spreadsheet for an import. If these fields are not present, you will receive an error on the import. For more information on using these utilities, see the Microsoft Knowledge Base articles 237677 and 327620.

tip

You can use many scripting languages, including **WSH (Windows Scripting Host)** to create and modify user accounts in Active Directory. However, be careful. Making a mistake on a single user account is bad enough, but making a mistake on 1,000 user accounts can be catastrophic.

tip

To learn more about ADSI scripting, visit the TechNet scripting center for ADSI Scriptomatic at **www.microsoft.com /technet/treeview/default .asp?url=/technet /scriptcenter/tools /admatic.asp**

Figure 6-23 Exporting user and computer accounts

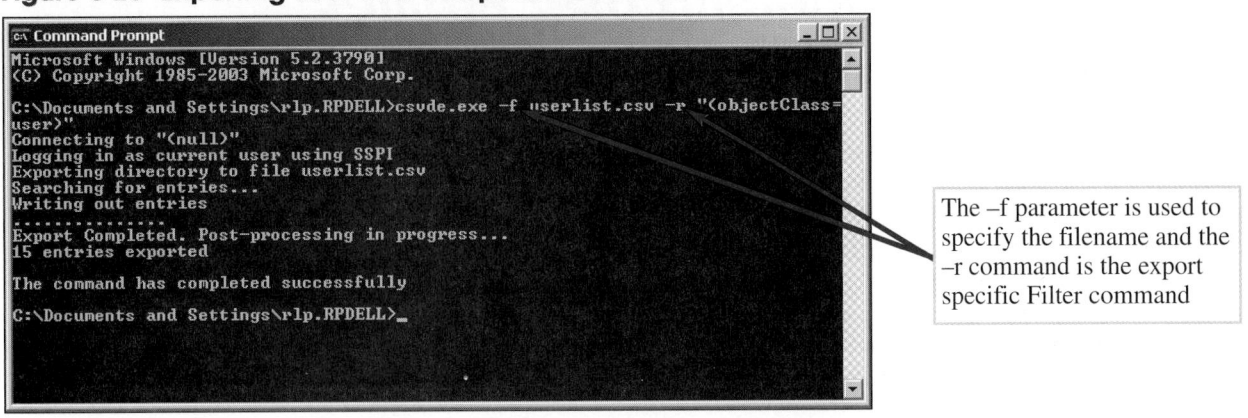

The –f parameter is used to specify the filename and the –r command is the export specific Filter command

Figure 6-24 Userlist.csv

All objects of the user object class have been exported to a .csv file that can be opened in Excel

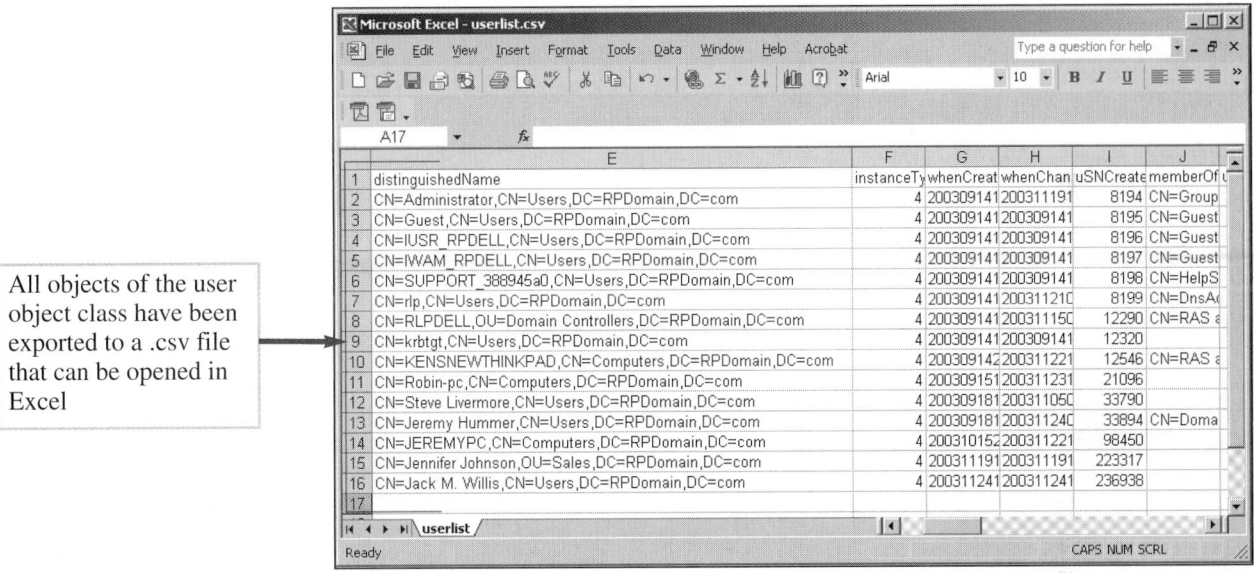

Figure 6-25 LDIF Directory Exchange parameters

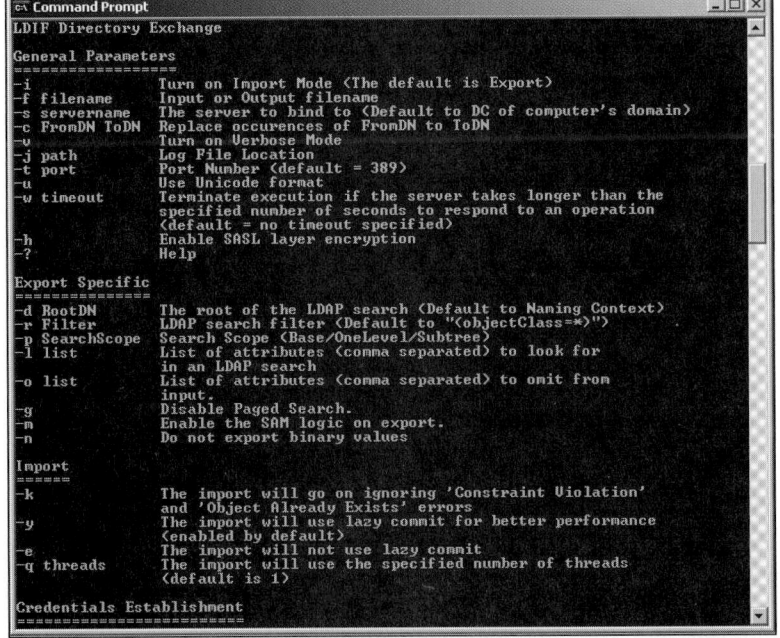

skill 6

Introducing User Profiles

exam objective

Manage local, roaming, and mandatory user profiles.

overview

A **user profile** is a collection of data that includes a user's personal data, desktop settings, printer connections, network connections that are established when the user logs on to the network, and other specified settings. In general, you can think of user profiles as collections of the user's settings. User profiles help in providing a consistent desktop environment each time you log on to the computer, which may be defined by you or your system administrator.

User profiles also enable multiple users to work from the same computer or a single user to work from multiple computers on a network without changing any of the settings. Even if multiple users use the same computer, the users can view their individual desktop settings whenever they log on. A user can customize the desktop environment without affecting another user's settings. Also, user profiles can be stored on a server so that users can use them on any computer running Microsoft Windows NT 4.0 or later. User profiles also store the application settings of applications that comply with Microsoft's Windows 2000 and Windows Server 2003 software development guidelines.

User profiles are stored in the Documents and Settings folder, by default, with the sole exception of servers and clients upgraded from Windows NT or Windows 9.x, in which case they are stored in a \Profiles folder. **Table 6-5** explains the configuration settings associated with a user profile along with the places where those settings are applied in Windows Server 2003. There are three types of user profiles: local user profiles, roaming user profiles, and mandatory user profiles.

A **local user profile**, as the name suggests, is limited to the computer you log on to and is stored on the system's local hard disk. It is created the first time you log on to a computer by copying the settings in the "default user" profile, and is the default type of profile. Any changes you make to your local user profile are also specific to the computer on which you made the changes. Local user profiles are stored in the **%*systemdrive%*:\Documents and Settings\<*user_logon_name*>** folder where *system drive* is the system drive name and *user_logon_name* is the name the user uses to log on to the system. For example, a user might add a picture to the My Pictures folder. Windows Server 2003 modifies the user profile accordingly to reflect the changes so that the next time the user logs on the picture will be present in the user's My Pictures folder. **Figure 6-26** displays the contents of a sample individual user profile folder.

Note that in some cases, your profile may be duplicated. Duplicates are named differently in order to avoid overwriting the previous copies. You can find out more information about the naming patterns in these cases at **http://support.microsoft.com/?kbid=314045**

A **roaming user profile** is a profile that is stored on a network server and retrieved at user logon. This makes them especially helpful when a user has to work on multiple computers on a network, because he or she can have a uniform desktop on all computers they use. To enable a roaming profile, you must configure a network path to the roaming profile in the Properties for the user account. The profile is then available to the user from all computers in the domain. Any changes the user makes to the roaming user profile are also updated on the server. Users can view their individual settings on any computer on the network, unlike a local user profile, which exists only on the computer on which it was created.

When the user logs on to a network computer for the first time, the operating system copies the roaming user profile from the network server to the local user profile and temporarily applies the roaming user profile settings to that computer. All roaming user profile files are copied to the local profile at logon and the changes are transferred back to the server at log off.

tip

If you want to ensure that all users get specific settings by default the first time they log on to a computer, you can configure a profile with the appropriate settings and copy those settings to the Default User profile in the User Profiles dialog box, which is accessed from the Advanced tab in the System Properties dialog box.

tip

If you are upgrading from a previous version of windows, profiles may be located in an alternate location such as *%systemroot%*\Profiles.

Table 6-5   Configuration settings associated with a user profile

Configuration settings stored in the user profile	Where those settings are applied
All user-definable settings	Windows Explorer, Control Panel
All user-specific program settings affecting the user's Windows environment, such as Calculator, Notepad, Clock, and Paint	Accessories
Per-user Program settings for programs written specifically for Windows Server 2003 and designed to track program settings	Windows Server 2003-based programs
Items stored on the Desktop and Shortcut elements	Desktop contents
All user-definable computer screen colors and display text settings	Display Properties
Application data and user-defined configuration settings	Application data and registry hive
Any user-created mapped network drives	Mapped network drive
Links to other computers on the network	My Network Places
Network printer connection settings	Printer settings
Any bookmarks placed in the Windows Server 2003 Help system	Online user education bookmarks

Figure 6-26 A sample user profile folder

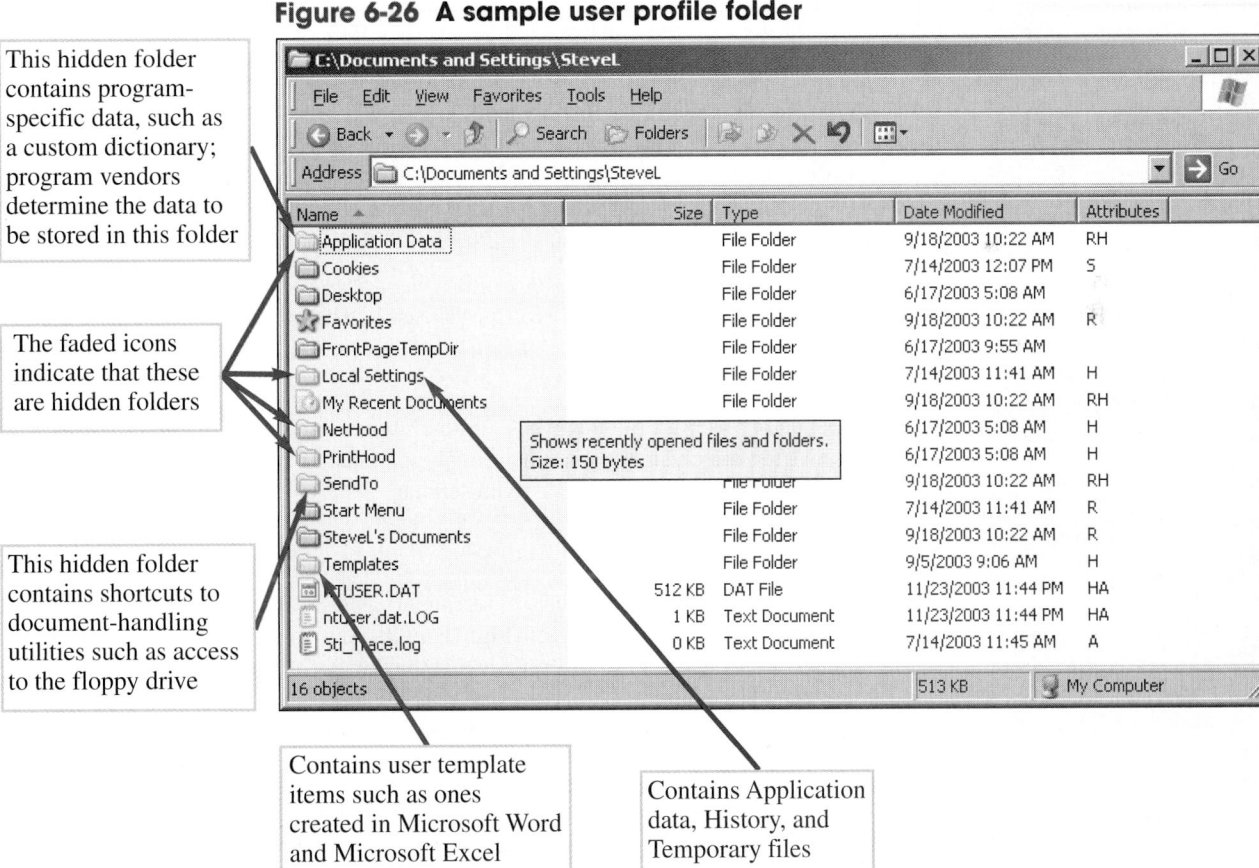

This hidden folder contains program-specific data, such as a custom dictionary; program vendors determine the data to be stored in this folder

The faded icons indicate that these are hidden folders

This hidden folder contains shortcuts to document-handling utilities such as access to the floppy drive

Contains user template items such as ones created in Microsoft Word and Microsoft Excel

Contains Application data, History, and Temporary files

skill 6

Introducing User Profiles (cont'd)

exam objective

Manage local, roaming, and mandatory user profiles.

overview

In the **User Profiles** dialog box on the local computer, which is accessed by clicking the **Change Type** button on the **Advanced** tab in the **System Properties** dialog box, the user's profile is automatically set to **Roaming (Figure 6-27)**. Subsequently, when that user logs on again, Windows Server 2003 compares the locally stored user profile files for the user, and the roaming user profile files on the server where they are stored, and copies only the files that have changed since the last time the user logged on. When the user logs off, Windows Server 2003 copies the changes made to the local copy of the roaming user profile back to the network server. Be aware that roaming profiles can, and typically do, consume large amounts of network bandwidth. This is due to users' habits, which typically include creating folder structures either on the desktop or in the My Documents folder and placing large quantities of data in these locations. Since both folders are part of the user profile, it is very easy for your users to create very large user profiles, which then use large amounts of bandwidth whenever they must be transferred.

A **mandatory user profile** is a type of roaming profile used to specify particular settings for individuals or a group. A mandatory user profile does not permanently save the desktop settings made by a user. Users can choose their own desktop settings for the computer they are logged on to, but none of these changes are saved when they log off. The mandatory profile settings are applied to the local computer each time the user logs on.

Mandatory user profiles can prove beneficial as an administrative tool because you can create a default user profile that is suited specifically for a user's tasks. For example, you can keep one user profile for all data entry operators. You can also specify the default user settings that will remain the same for all user profiles. However, you should realize that users typically do not appreciate mandatory user profiles. It is best to warn users before making their profiles mandatory.

You can set up a mandatory user profile for specific users. These users will be able to modify the desktop settings while they are logged on, but none of these changes will actually be retained when they log off.

Creating a mandatory user profile involves the same steps as creating a roaming profile, with one exception. After you create the roaming profile, you must go into the appropriate network share point and rename the ntuser.dat file to ntuser.man.

caution

Only system administrators can make changes to mandatory user profiles.

more

The All Users folder in *%systemdrive%*:\Documents and Settings is used to modify all profiles applied to an individual computer **(Figure 6-28)**. Any changes made to the All Users folder will apply to every profile of every user that logs on to that computer. For example, if you want to make a certain icon available on everyone's Start menu, you can simply add the icon to the Start Menu folder in the All Users folder.

Table 6-6 gives a brief explanation of each folder in an individual user profile. Notice that some folders in **Figure 6-28** appear shaded. This means that these folders are hidden and are not visible by default. You have to access the View tab on the Folder Options dialog box (Folder Options on the Tools menu in Windows Explorer or under Control Panel on the Start menu) to view hidden files and folders.

Figure 6-27 The Change Profile Type dialog box

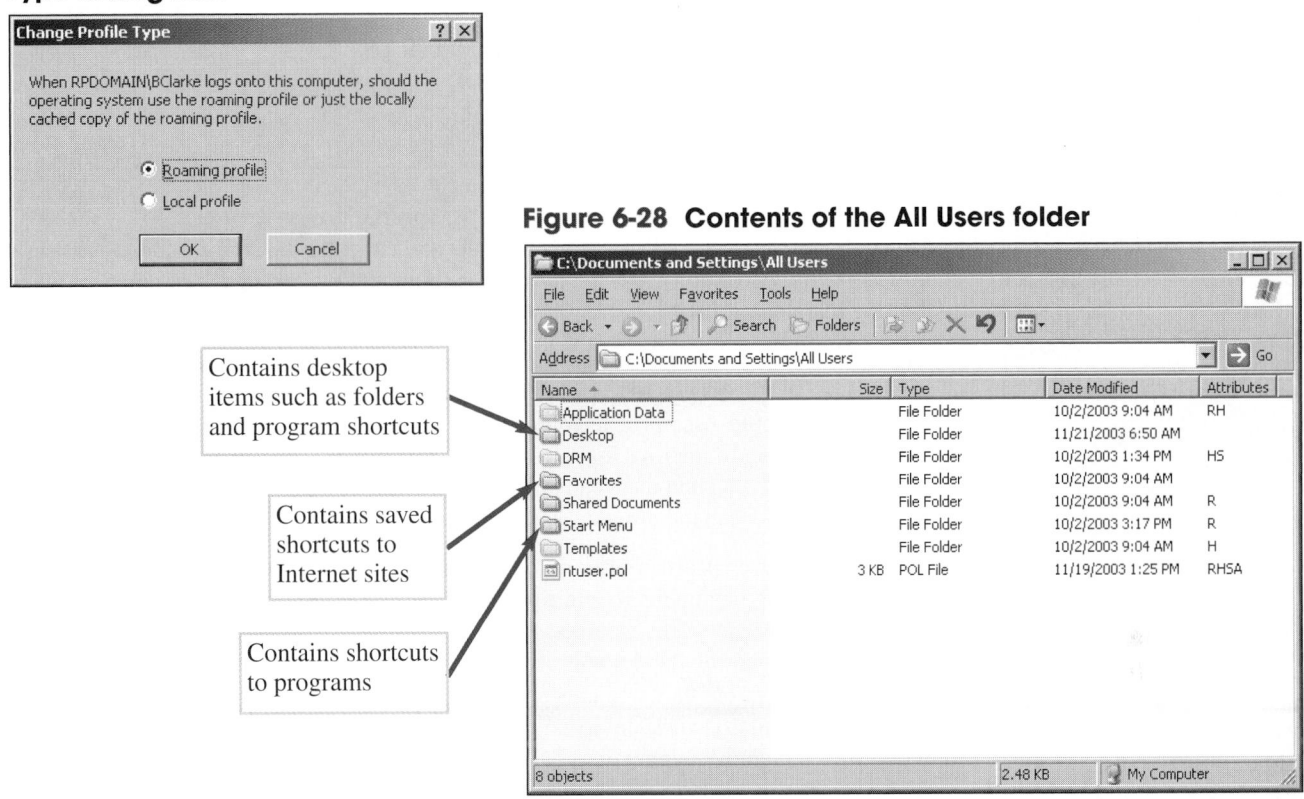

Figure 6-28 Contents of the All Users folder

Contains desktop items such as folders and program shortcuts

Contains saved shortcuts to Internet sites

Contains shortcuts to programs

Table 6-6	Contents of a sample user profile folder

Folder name	Contents
Desktop	Contains desktop items such as folders and program shortcuts.
Start Menu	Contains shortcuts to program items such as Microsoft Internet Explorer.
My Documents	Contains documents added or created by the user.
Favorites	Contains shortcuts to favorite sites on the Internet.
My Pictures	Contains the picture files stored by the user.
Local Settings	Contains Application data, History, and Temporary files.
Cookies	Contains user information and preferences such as logon data.
FrontPageTempDir	This is a temporary folder used by Microsoft FrontPage.
NetHood	Contains shortcuts to My Network Places items. This is a hidden folder.
PrintHood	Contains shortcuts to printer folder items. This is a hidden folder.
Recent	Contains shortcuts to the most recently used documents and accessed folders. This is a hidden folder.
SendTo	Contains shortcuts to document-handling utilities such as access to the floppy drive. This is a hidden folder.
Templates	Contains user template items such as ones created in Microsoft Word and Microsoft Excel.
Application Data	This is a hidden folder that contains program-specific data, such as a custom dictionary. Program vendors decide what data should be stored in this folder.
Ntuser.dat file	This is a hidden file that stores user registry settings. It also has a corresponding log file named ntuser.dat.log.

skill 7 | *Creating a Roaming User Profile*

exam objective | Manage local, roaming, and mandatory user profiles.

overview

You can create standard roaming user profiles for specific groups of users. To do this, you need to configure the desired desktop environment and copy the standard profile to the user's roaming user profile location. You should be aware of the following suggested practices when configuring roaming profiles:

caution

Removing applications from a user's profile will not remove the application from the user's hard disk. In some cases, the user may still be able to run the application by locating the executable for the application.

◆ Always create standard roaming user profiles on the file server you back up most frequently. This helps you to track copies of the latest roaming user profiles.

◆ Place the roaming user profile folder on a member server rather than on a domain controller in order to improve logon performance. Copying roaming user profiles between the server and client computers can tie up many system resources. Keeping profiles on the domain controller can therefore delay the authentication of users by the domain controller.

Standard roaming user profiles provide certain benefits. For example, you can provide a standard desktop environment to multiple users with similar job profiles. These users typically use the same network resources. For example, you can provide a standard desktop to all users in the Accounting department of an organization. These users can then modify the profile as they choose, but they will all start with a standardized profile. You can also provide users with the standard work environment that they require for performing their jobs. Similarly, you can remove applications and connections that some users do not require.

Standard roaming user profiles also help you to streamline troubleshooting. The system support team, for example, because they are familiar with the user profile settings, can identify solutions for problems more efficiently.

To create a standard roaming user profile, first create a shared folder on the server. Next, create a user profile template with the appropriate configuration. Then, copy the user profile template to the shared folder on the server and specify the users who will have access to the profile. Finally, specify the path to the profile template in the user account.

how to

Create a roaming user profile and set up a standard roaming user profile. (In order to perform this exercise, you will need to make sure that the accounts for Jack M. Willis and Barbara J Clarke [both created in Skill 3[are available.)

1. Log on to the domain controller as an **Administrator**.

2. Create a shared folder named TestProfiles in the C:\ folder and assign the **Full Control** share permission to the **Authenticated Users** group on the domain controller **(Figure 6-29)**. Remove the Everyone group for security reasons. The standard roaming user profile will reside in this shared folder.

3. Now, create a user profile template using the account of Jack M. Willis. To do this, click the **Users** folder in the **Active Directory Users and Computers** console.

4. Right-click **Jack M. Willis** and click **Properties** to open the **Properties** dialog box for Jack M. Willis.

caution

To create a roaming user profile for a user account, you either need administrative rights for the container in which the user account is stored, or the Write permission for the user account.

5. Click the **Member Of** tab, and click [Add...] to open the **Select Groups** dialog box.

6. Click [Advanced...] to expand the dialog box. Click [Find Now]. Select the **Print Operators** group in the **Search results list (Figure 6-30)**, and click [OK] to add the Print Operators group to the **Enter the object names to select** box in the Select Groups dialog box.

7. Click [OK] to close the Select Groups dialog box and make Jack a member of the **Print Operators** group so that he can log on to the domain controller. Domain controllers have enhanced security, and only allow administrative and operator groups the logon locally right. This step is not required when creating most user accounts.

8. Click [OK] to close the Properties dialog box for Jack Willis.

Figure 6-29 Assigning Full Control to the Authenticated Users Group

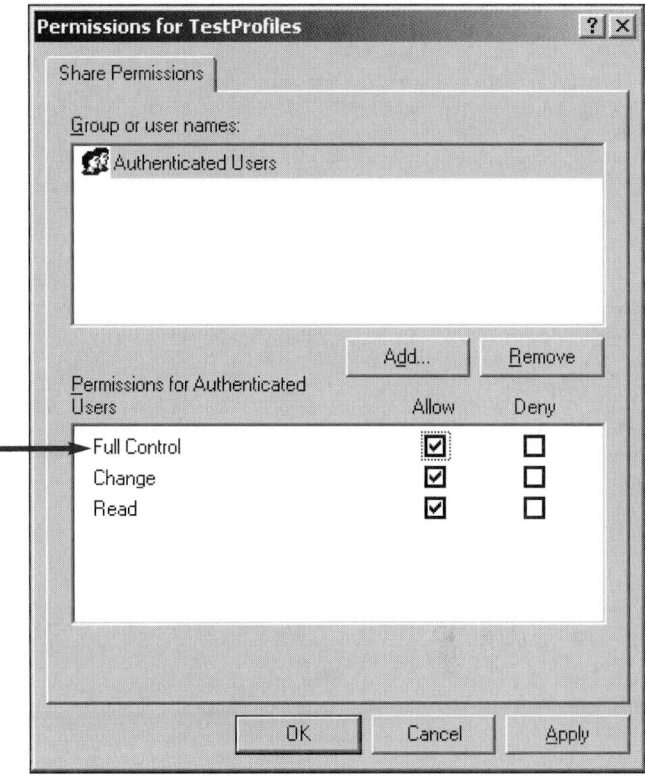

First, you must assign the Full Control share permission to the Authenticated Users group for the folder that will house the standard roaming user profile

Figure 6-30 Adding a user to the Print Operators group

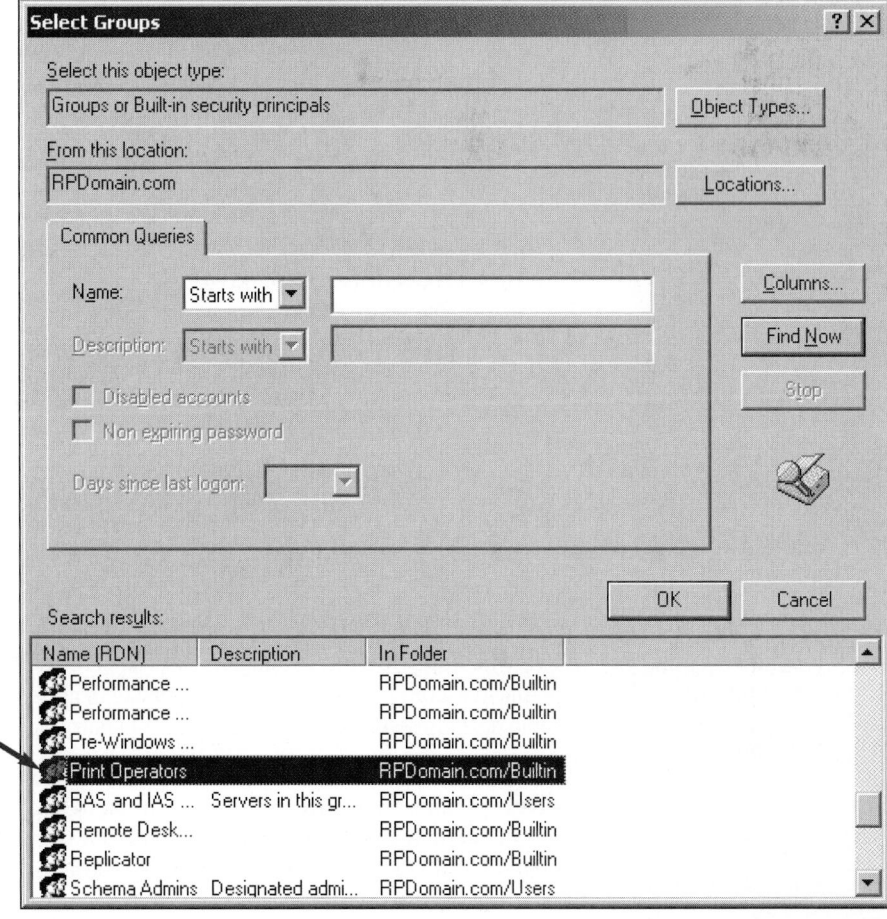

You must add the user account that will become the user profile template to the Print Operators group so that the user can log on to the domain controller and create a local user profile that can be copied; only the administrative and operator groups have the logon locally right by default

skill 7

Creating a Roaming User Profile
(cont'd)

exam objective

Manage local, roaming, and mandatory user profiles.

how to

9. Log off and log back on as **JWillis**. A local user profile is automatically created for Jack Willis. Change the current color scheme of the desktop from **Windows Standard** to **Spruce** by right-clicking the desktop and selecting **Properties** to open the **Display Properties** dialog box. On the **Appearance** tab, select **Spruce** in the **Color scheme** list box. Jack's user profile will be used as the user profile template for the standard roaming user profile.

10. Click [OK] to close the Display Properties dialog box and apply the change. Then, log off and log back on as **Administrator** and open the **Active Directory Users and Computers** console.

11. Add another user, **Barbara J. Clarke**, to the **Print Operators** group.

12. Click [Start], point to **Control Panel**, and click **System** to open the **System Properties** dialog box. Click the **Advanced** tab and then click [Settings] in the **User Profiles** section to open the **User Profiles** dialog box (**Figure 6-31**).

13. In the **Profiles stored on this computer** box, select *domain_name***JWillis**, where domain_name is the name of your domain, and click [Copy To] to open the **Copy To** dialog box.

14. Type **\\<*domain_controller_name*>\testprofiles\BClarke** in the **Copy profile to** text box. BClarke is the folder that will contain the roaming user profile for Barbara.

15. To specify Barbara as the user who will have access to the profile, click [Change] in the **Permitted to use** section (**Figure 6-32**). The **Select User or Group** dialog box opens.

16. In the **Select User or Group** dialog box, click [Advanced...], type **Barb** in the **Name** text box (**Starts with** should be selected in the list box) and click [Find Now] (**Figure 6-33**).

17. Select **Barbara J. Clarke** in the **Name** column, and click [OK] to close the dialog box. Barbara J. Clarke has now been specified as the user who is permitted to use the profile (**Figure 6-34**).

18. Click [OK] to close the Select User or Group dialog box. Click [OK] to close the **Copy To** dialog box.

19. Click [OK] to close the **User Profiles** dialog box. Click [OK] to close the **System Properties** dialog box.

20. Open the **Properties** dialog box for **Barbara J. Clarke** from the **Active Directory Users and Computers** console. Click the **Profile** tab to specify the path to the roaming user profile for Barbara J. Clarke.

21. Type **\\<*domain_controller_name*>\testprofiles\BClarke** in the **Profile path** text box (**Figure 6-35**), and click [OK].

22. Close the Active Directory Users and Computers console.

23. Log on as **BClarke** from another machine on the network to test the roaming profile.

tip

Using the variable **%username%** instead of the user's logon name automatically replaces the variable with the user account name and is useful when copying template accounts.

more

A mandatory user profile is a roaming user profile that is read-only (no changes can be saved). Although users might modify the desktop settings of the computer they are using, the changes are lost when they log off. Mandatory profile settings are applied to local client computers every time a user logs on. You can assign one mandatory profile to multiple users who require the same desktop settings — for example, data entry operators.

You can create a mandatory user profile using the hidden file **Ntuser.dat**. This file stores the Windows system settings (Registry entries in the HKEY_CURRENT_USER hive) that apply specifically to individual user accounts and user environment settings. To change the profile to read-only so that it becomes a mandatory user profile, rename the file **Ntuser.man**.

Figure 6-31 The User Profiles dialog box

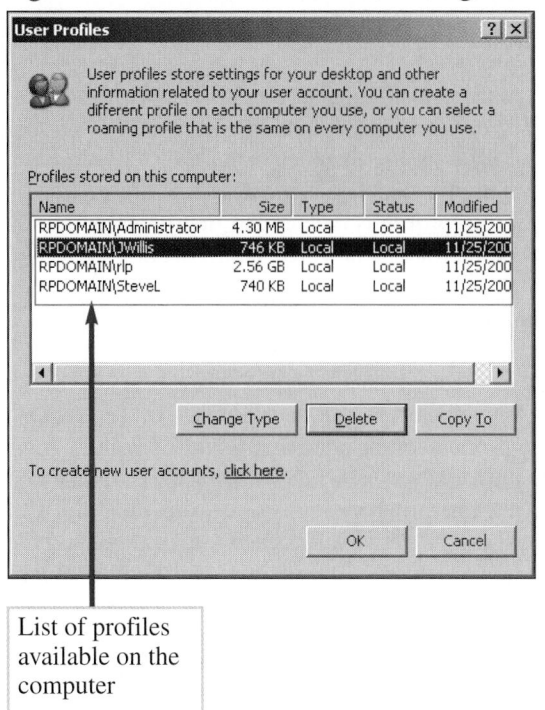

List of profiles available on the computer

Figure 6-32 Copying the user profile template to the shared folder

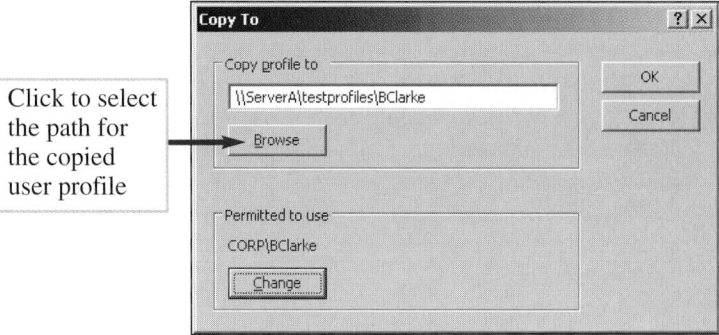

Click to select the path for the copied user profile

Figure 6-33 Selecting the user who will be permitted to use the profile

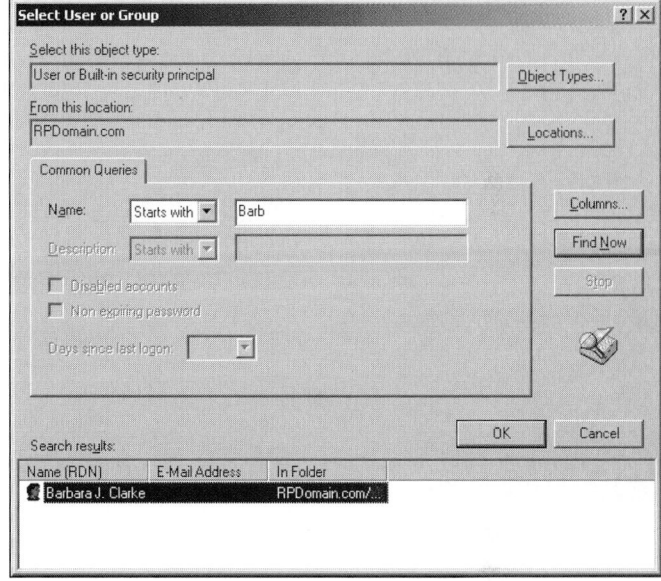

Figure 6-34 The user selected in the Select User or Group dialog box

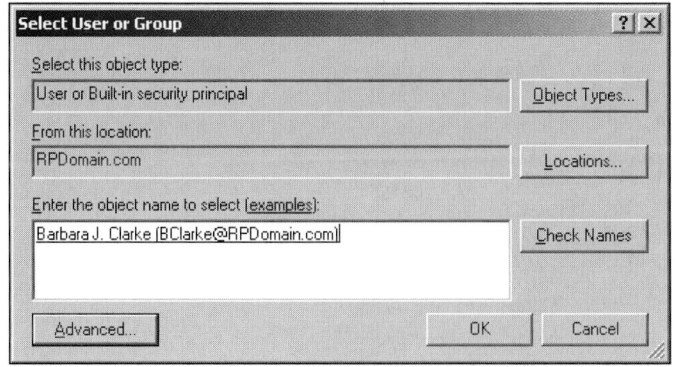

Figure 6-35 Specifying the path to the roaming user profile

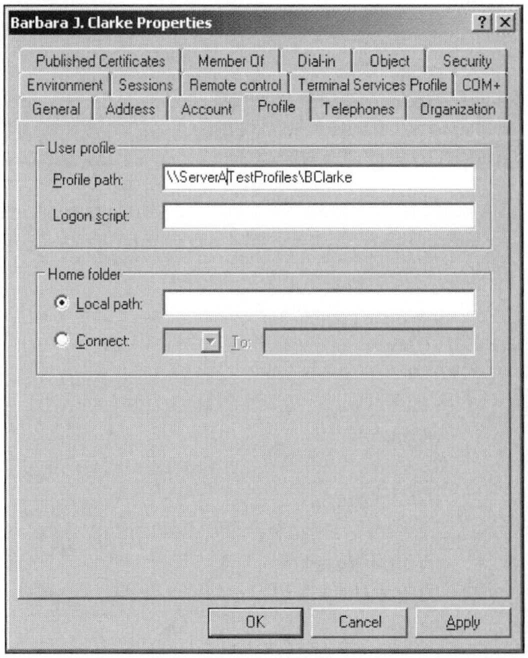

Summary

- A user account is a form of identification for a system or a user on a Windows Server 2003 computer.
- A user account includes information such as the user logon name, password, contact details, profile details, and dial-in settings.
- In Windows Server 2003, there are three types of user accounts: local user accounts, domain user accounts, and built-in user accounts.
- Local user accounts allow users to log on only to the computer on which the local user account is created. This means that users can gain access to the resources on the local computer. You use the Local Users and Groups snap-in in the Computer Management console to create local user accounts.
- Domain user accounts allow users to log on to the network from any computer in the domain and gain access to network resources. You use the Active Directory Users and Computers console to create domain user accounts.
- Built-in user accounts are created automatically during the installation of Windows Server 2003. These accounts are used to perform administrative tasks or to gain temporary access to network resources. Examples of such accounts are the Administrator and Guest accounts.

- User profiles contain settings that define the user environment and are applied when a user logs on to a system. Types of user profiles include local user profile, roaming user profile, and mandatory user profile.
- A local user profile is created the first time you log on to a computer and it is stored on a system's local hard disk.
- A roaming user profile is a profile that is stored on a network server and retrieved at user logon.
- You use roaming user profiles when users work on multiple computers so that their profiles will be available to them from all of the computers in the domain.
- When the user logs on to a network computer for the first time, the operating system copies the roaming user profile from the network server to the local user profile and temporarily applies the roaming user profile settings to that computer.
- All roaming user profile files are copied to the local profile at logon and the changes are transferred back to the server at log off.
- A mandatory user profile is a read-only roaming profile that can be used to specify particular settings for individuals or an entire group of users.

Key Terms

Account threshold lockout policy
Administrator account
Built-in user accounts
Domain user account
Guest account

Home folder
Local security database
Local user account
Local user profile
Logon script

Mandatory user profile
Roaming user profile
User account
User profile

Test Yourself

1. You are working as a system administrator. One of the employees, Susan Cally, has changed her name to Susan Cally Smith after marriage and wants this to be reflected in her logon name. What strategy would you follow to ensure that Susan can continue using network resources without any problem?
   a. Rename her user account and modify her group memberships.
   b. Rename her user account from SCally to SCallySmith.
   c. Rename her user account name and assign new permissions.
   d. Delete the SCally user account and create a new account called SCallySmith.

2. Which of the following user profiles are stored on a remote server?
   a. Mandatory and roaming
   b. Local and roaming
   c. Mandatory and local

3. One of the employees, Marriott, is leaving your organization. At the same time, a new employee is joining to take over Marriott's responsibilities. Which of the following strategies would you use to manage the user accounts and deny access to Marriott?
   a. Delete the user account for Marriott.
   b. Rename the user account for Marriott and set a new password.

c. Lock the user account for Marriott.

d. Change the password of the user account for Marriott.

4. You are working in the Web Design department of your organization. The members of your team are involved in creating Web designs and video compression. How can you ensure that all members of your team are using the same color scheme and display settings while working on different computers in the network?

   a. Create identical local user profiles for all users.

   b. Create both local and roaming user profiles for each user.

   c. Create a mandatory user profile for all users.

   d. Create a roaming user profile.

5. Which of the following options can you set on the Profile tab in the Properties dialog box for a user account?

   a. Add the user account to a group.

   b. Set a path for the home folder.

   c. Specify the details for the desktop settings.

   d. Specify the computers from which a user can log on to the network.

6. Which of the following statements about roaming user profiles is true?

   a. A mandatory user profile is a roaming user profile that can be changed by the user.

   b. Users can log on to only their computer to access their customized desktop settings.

c. User profiles are stored in the All Users folder.

d. Multiple users can log on to a single computer and access their own profiles.

7. The maximum number of characters that a user logon name can contain is _____ characters.

   a. 10

   b. 15

   c. 20

   d. 25

8. Which of the following tabs in the Properties dialog box for a domain user account is used to specify the Terminal Services timeout settings for the user account?

   a. Dial-in

   b. Terminal Services Profile

   c. Sessions

   d. Environment

9. To create a mandatory user profile, change the Ntuser.dat profile to read-only by renaming the file Ntuser.man.

   a. True

   b. False

10. On which of the following tabs would you to set the logon hours for a user to restrict his or her access to the network to a specific time period?

   a. Account

   b. General

   c. Remote Control

   d. Profile

Projects: On Your Own

1. Create a local user account for Mark Smith.

   a. Open the **Local Users and Groups** snap-in.

   b. Open the **New User** dialog box.

   c. Specify **MSmith** as the user name.

   d. Specify **Mark Smith** as the full name.

   e. Enter **Finance manager** in the **Description** text box.

   f. Specify the password as **Welcome2**.

   g. Specify the setting that requires the user to change the password at next logon.

   h. Save the settings and close the dialog box.

2. Set the password and dial-in property for Mark Smith's user account.

   a. Open the Properties dialog box for Mark Smith's user account.

   b. Clear the check box for **User must change password at next logon**.

   c. Prevent the user from changing the password.

   d. Activate the dial-in settings.

   e. Specify that the RAS server should not call back the user.

   f. Save the settings and close the dialog box.

3. Rename Mark Smith's user account.

   a. Right-click the **Mark Smith** user account and click the **Rename** command.

   b. Type **MSmith Rename** and press **Enter**.

Problem Solving Scenarios

1. You have just installed and configured a computer running Windows Server 2003 for your company's Accounts Receivable department. The Accounts Receivable manager needs to be able to log on to the computer. A stand-alone Windows Server 2003 machine is going to be shared by the Accounts Receivable manager and his intern. The Accounts Receivable manager will be the Administrator. He should be able to manage administrative tasks and reset passwords. He has asked you to create one user account for him and another named User1. List the steps describing how you will configure the stand-alone server.

2. Two new employees need to be added to your corporate network. The hours for the accounts must be restricted as follows:

   - Temp1: Monday through Saturday, 10 AM to 5 PM.
   - Temp2: Monday through Saturday, 5 PM to 1 AM.

   Both users should have logon rights to specific computers only. The desktop settings and home directory should be located on the domain controller. You have decided to create these user accounts as domain accounts. List the steps you will take to implement this plan.

LESSON 7

Introducing Group Accounts

I n the Windows Server 2003 environment, it is essential for network administrators to manage multiple users effectively. Groups are used to simplify the management of multiple user accounts. A group is a collection of user accounts that is assigned similar rights and permissions. This facilitates account management for administrators because it is much easier to assign permissions and rights to a group of users rather than assigning them on an individual basis. Permissions and rights are two different things. While rights give users the capability to perform certain actions such as changing the system time or shutting down the system, permissions give users a particular level of control over specific resources. Permissions determine whether a user can read only a particular file or modify and delete items from the folder.

You can create various types of groups. Local groups are used to assign permissions to users to access resources on a single local computer. Domain local groups are used to assign permissions to access resources in a single domain, and global groups are used to group users from the domain in which the group is defined to grant permissions for resources in any domain in the forest. When all domain controllers in a domain have been upgraded to Windows 2000 and Windows Server 2003 computers and Active Directory has been transferred to Windows 2000 native mode or Windows Server 2003 mode, you can also create universal groups, which can have members from many different domains, and permissions can be assigned for resources in any domain.

Windows Server 2003 also includes built-in groups that can be used to manage the accessibility of various resources on a computer or a network. Built-in groups are predefined groups that have a predefined set of rights and permissions. The concept behind all groups is the same: each user must have a unique account to identify the user, and account administration is made much simpler by grouping these user accounts into sets of users with similar needs, which can be given the same set of rights and permissions for accessing resources.

You can automate or partially automate the process of creating groups just as you automate the creation of user accounts, using group templates, the importation tools, Csvde.exe (Comma separated values data exchange) and Ldifde.exe (LDAP data interchange format data exchange), and scripting. On large networks, you reuse a group template to save time creating your groups. Csvde.exe is used to import and export group objects into and out of Active Directory, as is Ldifde.exe. Csvde.exe uses .csv files while Ldifde.exe uses .ldif files, which are supported by many third-party LDAP applications.

In the Windows Server 2003 environment, you manage components and applications available to users by using Group Policies. You can assign Group Policies to users to secure and enhance the work environment for users. Additionally, you can modify Group Policies to manage the desktop environment and to configure and manage software policies for the applications available to users in order to control unauthorized access.

The Group Policy Management Console (GPMC) is a comprehensive new tool in Windows Server 20003 which combines the functionality of Active Directory Users and Computers, Active Directory Sites and Services, the ACL Editor, the Delegation Wizard, and the Resultant Set of Policy tool. It can be used to control Group Policy administration on Windows 2000 and Windows Server 2003 domains.

Folder Redirection is a tool that administrators use to redirect the most common folders to a network server. Users will be able to browse the remote folder just as if they were browsing a network share. When a user opens an item in a redirected folder, the individual item is downloaded. This functionality saves considerable network bandwidth and can significantly

Goals

In this lesson, you will learn about the different types of group accounts and built-in groups in the Windows Server 2003 environment. You will also learn how to create domain local groups, as well as learn about the different types of Group Policies. Additionally, you will learn to manage software policies and utilize folder redirection policies.

Lesson 7 Introducing Group Accounts

Skill	Exam 70-290 Objective
1. Identifying the Types of Group Accounts	Create and manage groups. Manage group membership. Identify and modify the scope of a group.
2. Creating Local Groups	Create and manage groups. Manage group membership.
3. Introducing Built-in Groups	Create and manage groups. Manage group membership.
4. Creating and Modifying Groups by using the Active Directory Users and Computers MMC Snap-in	Create and manage groups. Create and modify groups by using the Active Directory Users and Computers Microsoft Management Console (MMC) snap-in. Manage group membership. Identify and modify the scope of a group. Create and modify groups by using automation.
5. Finding Domain Groups	Create and manage groups. Find domain groups in which a user is a member.
6. Creating Group Policy Objects	Basic knowledge
7. Identifying the Types of Group Policies	Basic knowledge
8. Modifying Software Settings Using GPO Software Policies	Basic knowledge
9. Redirecting Folders Using GPOs	Basic knowledge

Requirements

To complete this lesson, you will need administrative rights on a Windows Server 2003 member server and domain controller. You will also need the installation files for Microsoft Office and a local user account for MDouglas on the member server.

skill 1

Identifying the Types of Group Accounts

Create and manage groups. Manage group membership. Identify and modify the scope of a group.

overview

caution

To create groups, you must have administrative rights in your domain.

tip

Distribution groups cannot be listed in DACLs. They can be used only in e-mail applications.

caution

You can switch from Windows 2000 mixed mode to Windows 2000 native mode and from Windows 2000 native mode to Windows Server 2003 mode, but this process is irreversible. You should switch to Windows 2000 native mode only if all of your Windows NT domain controllers have been upgraded to Windows 2000, and you do not plan to add any more Windows NT 4.0 domain controllers. You should switch to Windows Server 2003 mode only when all of your domain controllers have been upgraded to Windows Server 2003 and you will not be adding any new Windows 2000 domain controllers. You can change the domain mode using the Active Directory Domains and Trusts or Active Directory Users and Computers consoles.

Users connected to a network must have appropriate rights and permissions to access various resources on a computer or on the network. It is the role of a network administrator to define permissions and assign rights to users. Administrators can categorize users into groups based on the functions they perform and the requirements of their jobs so that they can easily manage multiple users as a single entity. A **group** is a collection of user accounts or computers with similar rights and permissions. The users in a group are called **members**.

In the Windows Server 2003 domain environment, the groups you create are stored in Active Directory. There are two main types of groups, which are based upon their function, either security or distribution.

◆ **Security groups:** A **security group** is used to define the rights and permissions users will have to access resources on a computer or a network. When a user requests access to a network resource, the group memberships of the user are validated against the permissions assigned to verify whether or not the user is allowed access. You can also use a security group to distribute e-mail to multiple users because security groups have all of the same capabilities as distribution groups. Security groups are listed in **Discretionary Access Control Lists (DACLs)**. A DACL, as you have learned, is a list that defines the permissions that are allowed or denied to specific users and groups for resources and objects.

◆ **Distribution groups:** A **distribution group** is used only for the distribution of messages by applications such as Microsoft Exchange Server. It cannot be used to assign permissions to users.

When you create a group you must specify the group scope. The **group scope** determines whether the group can be used to access resources in a specific domain or across domains in a network.

There are three group scopes in a Windows Server 2003 environment. (**Figure 7-1**):

◆ **Domain local scope:** A **domain local group** is created in Active Directory on a domain controller. The scope of a domain local group is the domain in which the group was created. You can add members to a domain local group from any domain (**Table 7-1**). Domain local groups can be assigned permissions only for resources in the domain in which you create the domain local group.

◆ **Global scope:** A **global group** has members with common network access requirements. Members can be drawn only from the domain where the global group was created, but permissions can be assigned to members for resources in any domain. In Windows 2000 native mode and Windows Server 2003 mode, global groups can be nested in other global groups, and universal groups and global groups from any domain can be nested in domain local groups. In Windows 2000 mixed mode, global groups from any domain can be nested in domain local groups (**Table 7-2**). (For a further discussion of group nesting, see the More section.)

Figure 7-1 Group types and group scopes

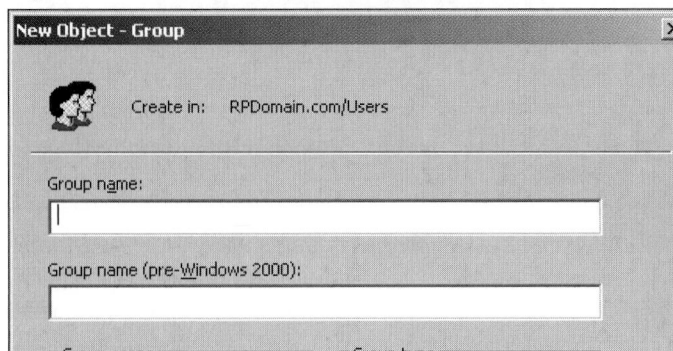

Table 7-1　Domain Local Groups

Group Scope	Parameters	Windows 2000 Mixed Mode	Windows 2000 Native Mode/Windows Server 2003
Domain local	Members include	Accounts and global groups from any domain	Accounts, global groups, and universal groups from any domain and domain local groups from the same domain
	Can be included as a member of	Not available	Other domain local groups in the same domain
	Used for	Assigning permissions to gain access to resources in the same domain	Assigning permissions in order to gain access to resources in the same domain
	Conversion to other group types	Not available	Universal group, provided that none of the members of the domain local group have domain local scope

---

Table 7-2　Global Groups

Group Scopes	Parameters	Windows 2000 Mixed Mode	Windows 2000 Native Mode/Windows Server 2003
Global	Members include	Accounts from the same domain	Accounts and other global groups from the same domain
	Can be included as a member of	Local groups in any domain	Global groups in its own domain, Universal and domain local groups in any domain
	Used for	Organizing user accounts	Organizing user accounts
	Conversion to other group types	Not available	Universal group, provided that the global group is not a member of any other group having global scope

skill 1

Identifying the Types of Group Accounts (cont'd)

exam objective

Create and manage groups. Manage group membership. Identify and modify the scope of a group.

overview

◆ **Universal Group Scope:** A **universal group** is used when there are multiple domains in a forest. Members can be drawn from many different domains and permissions can be assigned for resources in any domain. Universal groups are available only when Active Directory is running in Windows 2000 native mode or Windows Server 2003 mode. Remember that Active Directory has four modes: Windows 2000 mixed mode, Windows 2000 native mode, Windows Server 2003 interim mode, and Windows Server 2003 mode. Windows 2000 native mode is available only when all domain controllers in the domain are running either Windows 2000 Server or Windows Server 2003. Domains are configured by default to run in Windows 2000 mixed mode. Windows 2000 mixed mode allows the coexistence of Windows NT, Windows 2000, and Windows Server 2003 domain controllers in the same domain. If your domain consists of only Windows Server 2003 domain controllers, you can switch to Windows Server 2003 mode. You cannot create universal groups in a domain on which Active Directory is running in Windows 2000 mixed mode. Since Windows 2000 mixed mode is the default setup, to create universal groups you must change to Windows 2000 native mode after all domain controllers have been upgraded (**Table 7-3**). Other universal and global groups from any domain can be nested in universal groups in Windows 2000 native or Windows Server 2003 mode.

In Windows 2000 native or Windows Server 2003 mode, user accounts, computer accounts, other universal scope groups and groups with global scope from any domain can join a group with universal scope. Global groups can have as their members, accounts from the same domain and other groups with global scope from the same domain. Domain local scope groups can include user accounts, groups with universal scope, and groups with global scope from any domain. Other groups with domain local scope from the same domain can also be a member of a domain local group.

In Windows 2000 mixed mode, only user accounts can be members of domain groups with global scope. Groups with domain local scope can have as their members other groups with global scope and accounts.

more

You can add a group to another group in order to minimize the number of times you assign permissions to multiple groups. This process of adding groups to other groups is called **group nesting**. For example, if you create a group for users in the Finance department and groups for the Accounting and Accounts Receivable departments, some crossover needs may exist. The Accounting group and the Accounts Receivable group could be nested in the larger Finance group for some resource permissions so that you do not have to assign the same set of permissions twice (**Figure 7-2**).

Table 7-3 Universal Groups

Group Scopes	Parameters	Windows 2000 Mixed Mode	Windows 2000 Native Mode/Windows Server 2003
Universal	Members include	Not available	Accounts, global groups, and universal groups from any domain
	Can be included as a member of	Not available	Other Universal and Domain Local groups in any domain
	Used for	Not available	Assigning permissions to gain access to resources in any domain
	Conversion to other group types	Not available	Domain local and Global

Figure 7-2 Nested groups

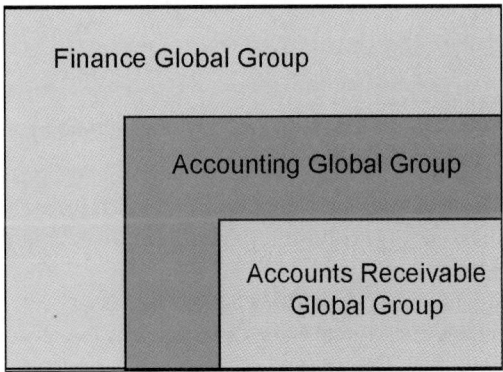

skill 2

Creating Local Groups

exam objective

Create and manage groups. Manage group membership.

overview

caution

You can put global and universal groups into a local group so that users can access resources on a single machine, but you cannot put local groups into any other type of group.

Local groups are mainly used in peer-to-peer or workgroup networks or on stand-alone computers that are not part of a domain. You populate local groups with user accounts that are stored in the local security database of a single computer. On a domain-based network, you can create global groups that belong to a local group so that domain users can be assigned rights and permissions for the resources on a particular workstation. However, local security groups should generally not be used on domain-based networks. Domain local security groups are used after you have installed Active Directory and they are used to manage resources in a domain.

Understand that there are two types of local groups:

Domain local groups: As noted in Skill 1, a domain local group is created and stored in Active Directory on a domain controller and is used to manage and access resources in a domain. Users in a domain local group can access any resources in the domain, and network administrators can perform their account management tasks in a single location. Domain local groups do not need to be created on multiple computers on the network because Active Directory serves as the central storage area for all account information on the network.

Local groups: You create a local group to group local user accounts on stand-alone servers, member servers, and Windows 2000 or XP Professional workstations. You use them to assign permissions to resources only on the local computer. A drawback to local groups is the lack of a central administration site. Therefore, their most common use is for workgroup networks.

In Windows Server 2003, you create local security groups (local groups) in the **Computer Management** console. Domain local groups, global groups and universal groups are created in the **Active Directory Users and Computers** console.

When you create a group, you assign a name that can contain up to 256 characters. This name cannot be the same as a name assigned to any other group or user. After setting the name and entering a description for the local group, you can add members to it.

how to

caution

Local group names cannot contain the characters / \ [ ] : ; | = , + * ? <>.

Create a new local group on your member server. (You will need to create a local user account named MDouglas on the server.)

1. Log on to your member server as an **Administrator**.
2. Click **Start**, right-click **My Computer** and click **Manage** to open the **Computer Management** console.
3. Expand the **System Tools** node, if necessary.
4. Double-click **Local Users and Groups** to view the subfolders in the details pane.
5. Right-click **Groups** and click **New Group** to open the **New Group** dialog box.
6. Type the name of the new group, **Managers**, in the **Group name** text box.
7. Type a description for the group, **Mid-level managers**, in the **Description** text box.
8. Click Add... to open the **Select Users, Computers, or Groups** dialog box.
9. Type **MDouglas** in the **Enter the object names to select** box (**Figure 7-3**).
10. If your server name is not selected in the **From this location box**, click Locations... to open the **Locations** dialog box (**Figure 7-4**). Select the name of your member server and click OK .
11. Click OK to close the **Select Users** dialog box. The **MDouglas** user account is added to the **Managers** group (**Figure 7-5**).

Figure 7-3 Selecting users in the Select Users, Computers, or Groups dialog box

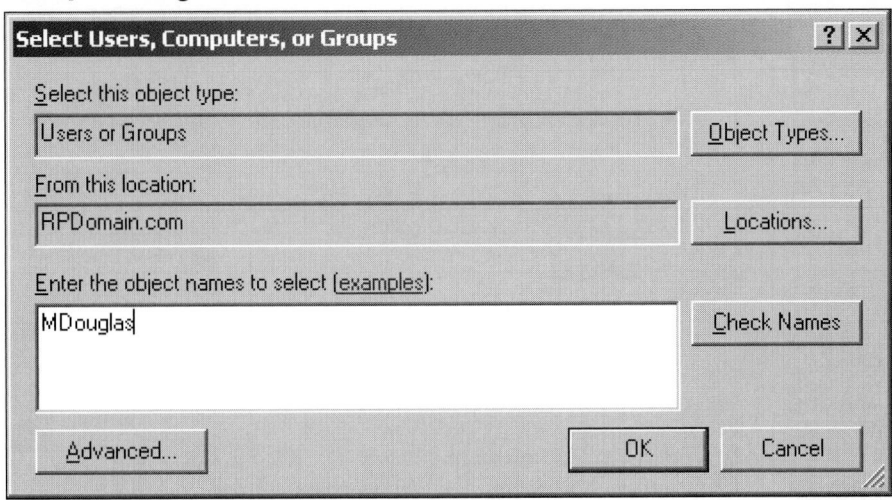

Figure 7-4 The Locations dialog box

To create a local group, select the name of your member server

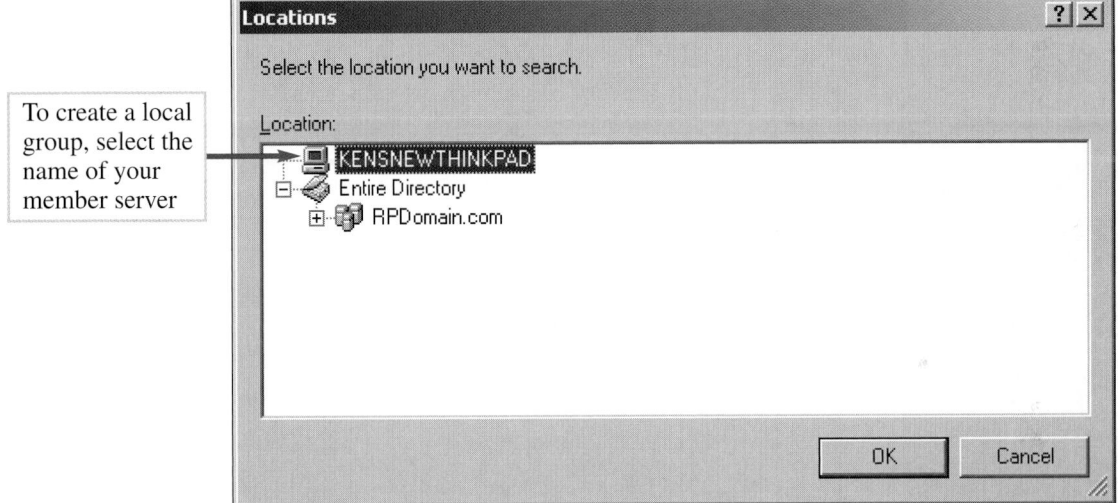

Figure 7-5 Adding members to the new group

skill 2

Creating Local Groups (cont'd)

exam objective

Create and manage groups. Manage group membership.

how to

12. Click [Create] to create the new local group on the member server.
13. Click [Close] to close the **New Group** dialog box. Double-click the **Groups** folder to view the new Managers group in the **Computer Management** console (**Figure 7-6**).
14. Close the Computer Management console.

more

The **Computer Management console** is a Windows Server 2003 tool that combines various administration utilities into a single console tree. You can view the list of users connected to a local or remote computer and manage the local or remote computer in the Computer Management console.

The Computer Management console has three nodes (**Figure 7-7**):

◆ **System Tools:** This node is used to monitor system events, view system information, view the hardware configuration, as well as manage shared folders, local users and groups.

◆ **Storage:** This node is used to view and manage the properties of a storage device such as a hard disk.

◆ **Services and Applications**: This node is used to view and manage the properties of a service, such as WINS, or an application running on your computer.

Figure 7-6 The new group displayed in the Computer Management console

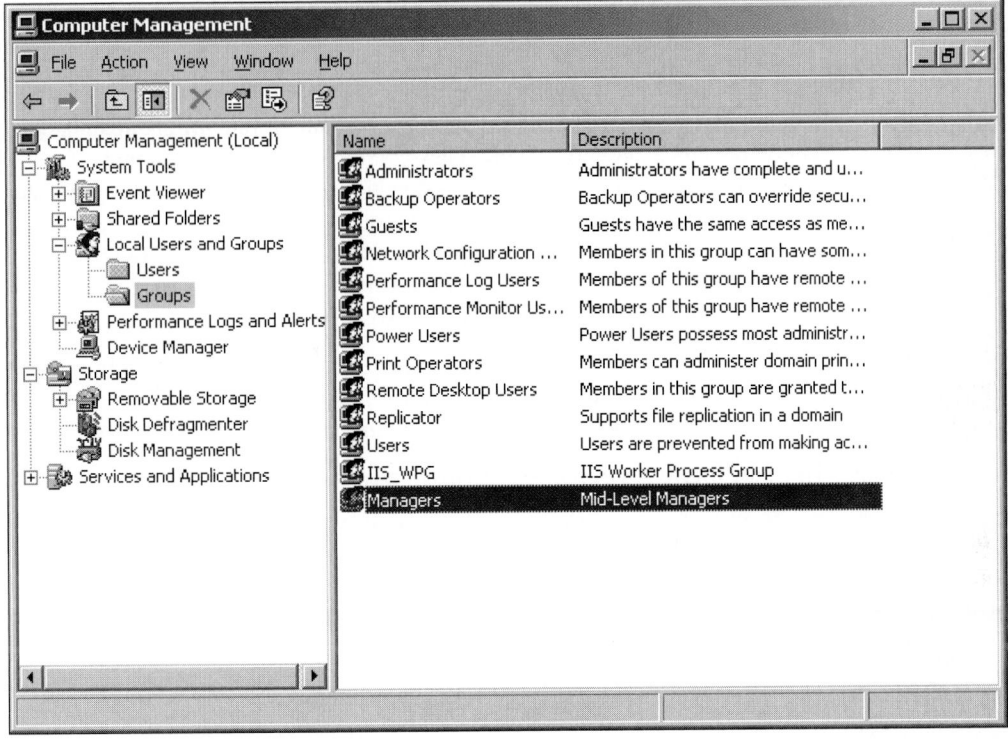

Figure 7-7 Nodes in the Computer Management console

Used to monitor system events, view system information, view the hardware configuration, and manage shared folders and local users and groups

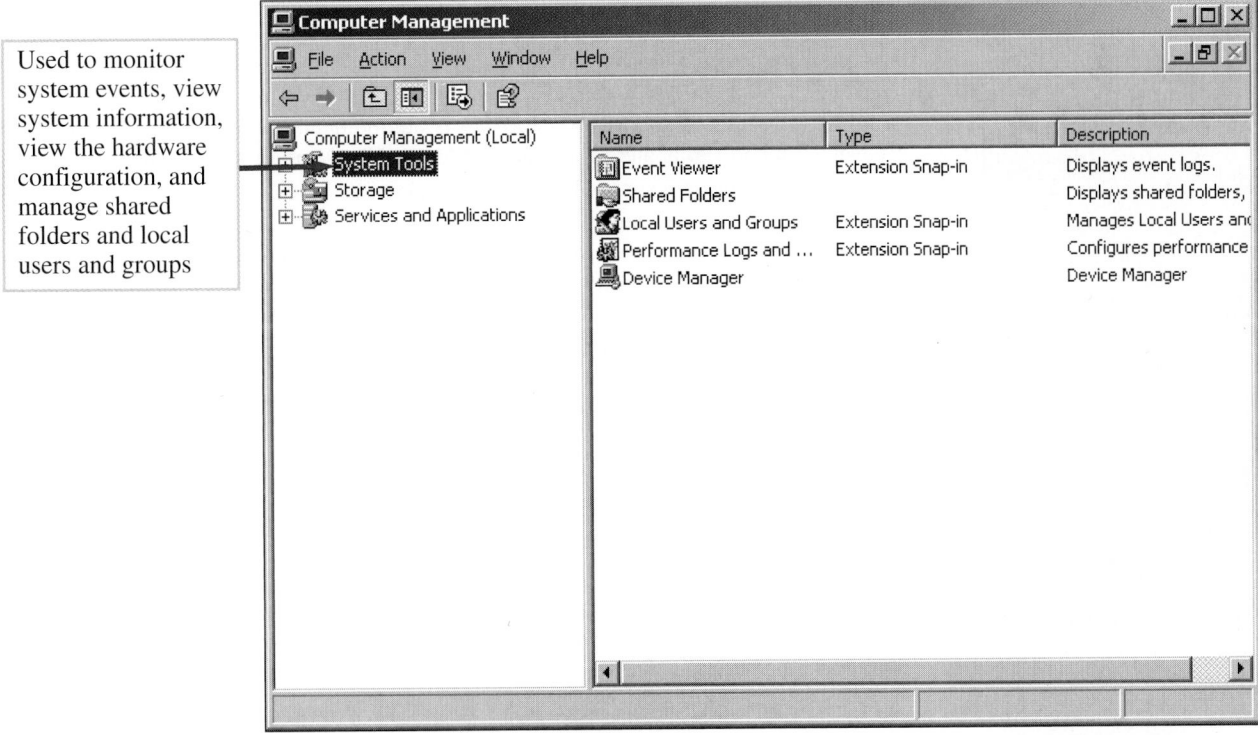

skill 3   *Introducing Built-in Groups*

exam objective

Create and manage groups. Manage group membership.

overview

Windows Server 2003 includes default groups called **built-in groups** that have a preset collection of rights and permissions. They can be used to manage common tasks performed by users. These built-in groups help you save time because they already have the set of permissions and rights you will need for certain groups of users. Instead of creating a new group, you can assign user accounts to the appropriate built-in group. For example, you can add a user account to the built-in Print Operator group to enable them to administer domain printers. Members are also added automatically to some of the built-in global groups.

In Windows Server 2003, built-in groups are created automatically when you install the operating system. When you install Active Directory on a Windows Server 2003 computer, another set of built-in groups associated with Active Directory is added.

There are four types of built-in groups:

◆ **Built-in local groups** are created on all Windows Server 2003 computers. They can be viewed in the **Groups** folder in the **Computer Management** console on all non-domain controllers (**Figure 7-8**). On domain controllers they are stored in the **Builtin** container in the Active Directory Users and Computers console (**Figure 7-9**). The built-in local groups in the Builtin container in the Active Directory Users and Computers console include:

- **Account Operators:** Members can administer domain user and group accounts, except for the operators and administrator groups.
- **Administrators:** The Administrator user account is automatically added to this group, which can perform all administrative tasks. If the computer joins a domain, the Domain Admins group will be nested in this local group. Administrators have complete and unrestricted access to the computer/domain.
- **Backup Operators:** This group can use Windows Backup to backup and restore the computer. Security restrictions are overridden so that files can be backed up or restored regardless of permissions settings.
- **Guests:** The disabled Guest account is automatically added to this group, which has limited rights and permissions. Members can temporarily change the desktop environment on a stand-alone server, but can do little else unless they are granted specific rights and permissions.
- **Incoming Forest Trust Builders:** This group, which has no members by default, is present only in the forest root domain. Members of this group are granted the **Create Inbound Forest Trust on the forest root domain** permission and can create one-way, incoming forest trusts with other forests for the forest root domain.
- **Network Configuration Operators:** Members of this group have the ability to modify the TCP/IP configuration of the domain controller. This group has no members by default.
- **Performance Log Users:** Members of this group can modify performance monitor settings, performance logs, counters and alerts on the server.
- **Performance Monitor Users:** Members of this group can monitor performance statistics in the Performance console for the server.
- **Pre-Windows 2000 Compatible Access:** This group was created for backward compatibility. Members have Read access for all users and groups in the domain.

tip

Administrators can modify the rights and permissions assigned to a built-in group.

Figure 7-8 Built-in local groups in the Computer Management console on a member server

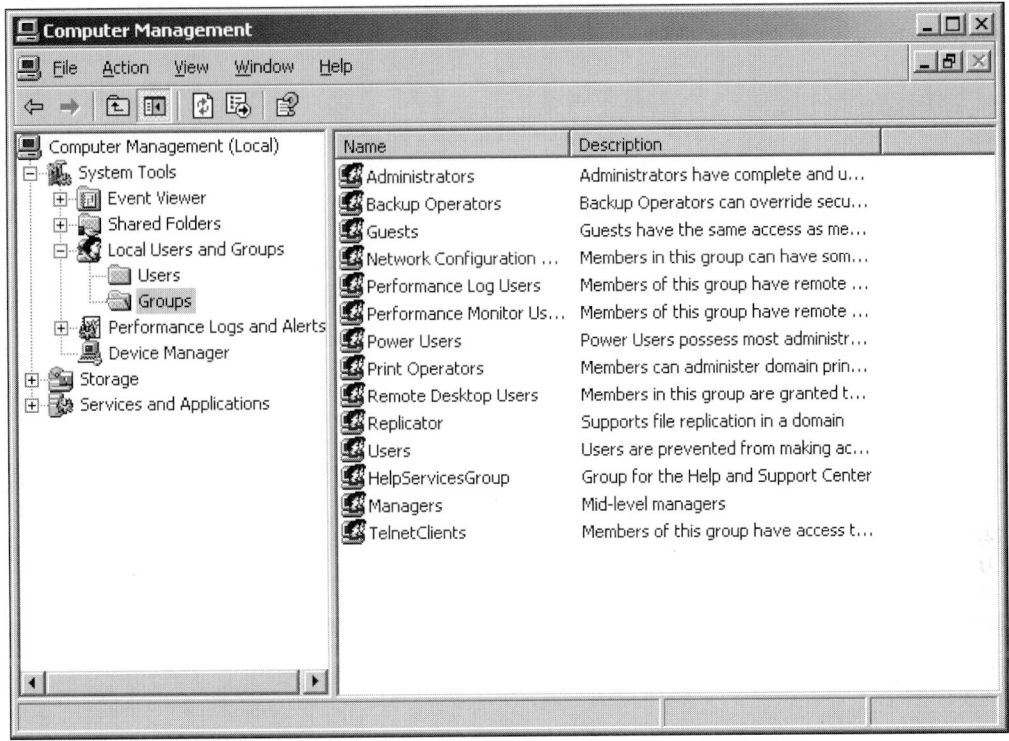

Figure 7-9 Built-in domain local groups in the Builtin container in the Active Directory Users and Computers console

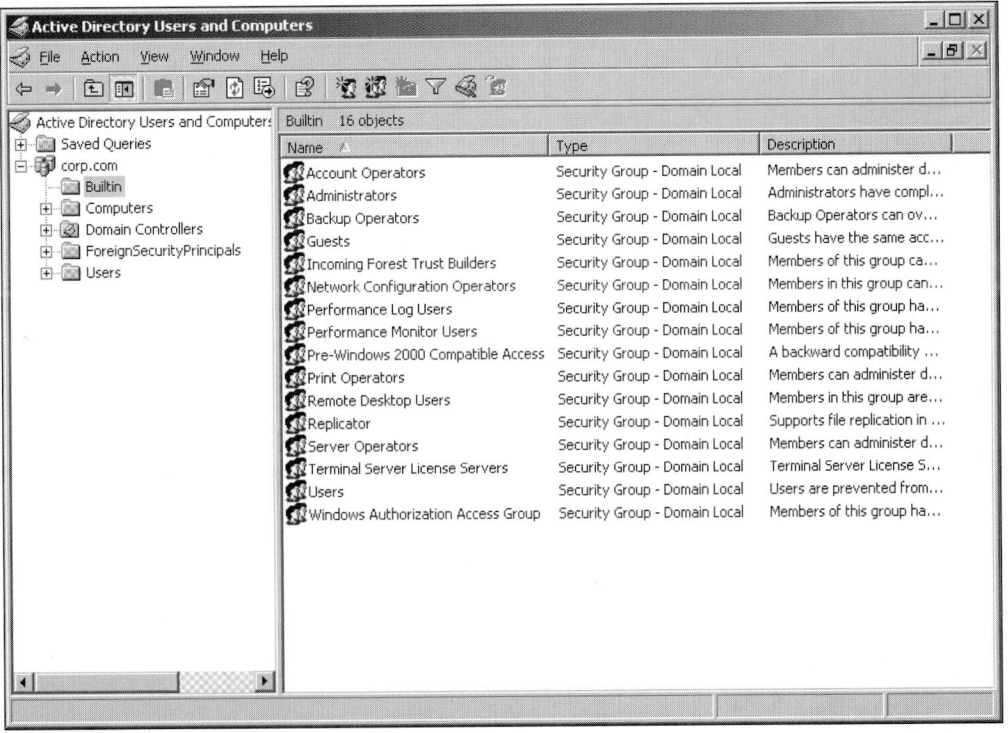

skill 3

Introducing Built-in Groups *(cont'd)*

exam objective   Create and manage groups. Manage group membership.

overview

- **Print Operators:** Members of this group can manage, create, share, and delete printers that are connected to domain controllers in the domain. They can log on to domain controllers locally, shut down domain controllers, install and uninstall device drivers on domain controllers, and manage Active Directory printer objects in the domain. There are no default users of this group. Since members have such extensive rights and privileges, you must add members to this group carefully.
- **Remote Desktop Users:** Members of this group can log on to the server remotely using Remote Desktop.
- **Replicator:** This group supports file replication in a domain. It is used by the File Replication service on domain controllers in the domain. There are no default members and you do not add users to this group.
- **Server Operators:** Members of this group can log on locally, create and delete shared resources, start and stop some services, back up and restore files, format hard disks, and shut down the computer. Since members have such extensive rights and privileges, you must add members to this group carefully.
- **Users:** All user accounts created in the domain are automatically added to this group. By default, the Domain Users global group, Authenticated Users built-in system group, and Interactive built-in system group will be nested in this group. You must assign specific rights and permissions so that members can perform tasks and access resources. Users are prohibited from making accidental or intentional changes to the system. They can run certified applications, but not most legacy applications.

◆ **Built-in domain local groups**, which cannot be deleted, are automatically created only on domain controllers. They are stored in the **Users container** in the Active Directory Users and Computers console. The number of domain local groups will be different on each domain controller, depending on the type of services the domain controller is running. The names generally identify the function of the group. For example, the DnsAdmins group is for users who can manage DNS servers in the domain. These groups have a set of predefined rights and permissions to perform various actions in Active Directory and on domain controllers (**Figure 7-10**). Examples of built-in domain local groups include the following:

- **Cert Publishers:** Members of this group, which has no default members, are permitted to publish certificates for users and computers.
- **DHCP Administrators:** Members have administrative access to the DHCP service.
- **DHCP Users:** Members have view-only access to the DHCP service.
- **DnsAdmins:** Members of this group have administrative access to the DNS Server service.
- **HelpServicesGroup:** This group is used by administrators to set rights that will be used for all support applications. The only default member is the account associated with Microsoft support applications such as Remote Assistance. Regular users are not added to this group.
- **IIS_WPG (installed with IIS):** The Internet Information Services 6.0 worker process group.
- **RAS and IAS Servers:** Members of this group are servers that are allowed to access the remote access Properties for users.
- **TelnetClients:** Members of this group have access to Telnet Server on this system.
- **WINS Users:** Members have view-only access to the WINS service.

Figure 7-10 Built-in domain local groups in the Users container in the Active Directory Users and Computers console

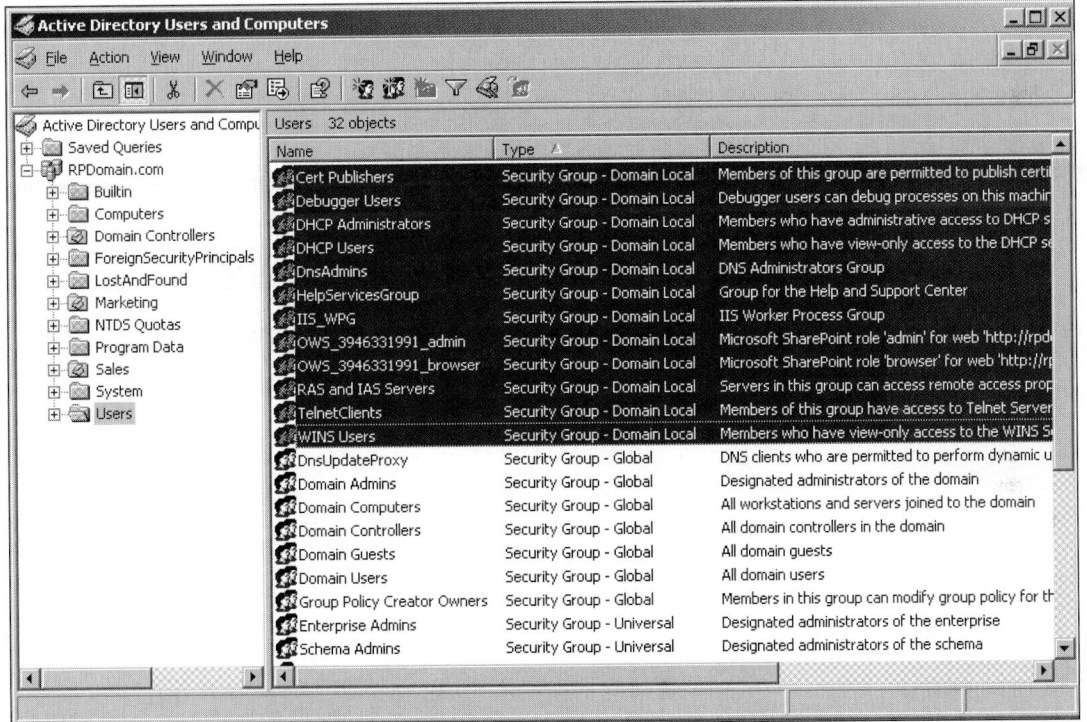

skill 3

Introducing Built-in Groups (cont'd)

exam objective

Create and manage groups. Manage group membership.

overview

◆ **Built-in global groups** are automatically created on domain controllers. They are also stored in the Users container in the Active Directory Users and Computers console **(Figure 7-11)**.

They include:

- **DnsUpdateProxy:** DNS clients who are permitted to perform dynamic updates on behalf of some other clients (such as DHCP servers).
- **Domain Admins:** Members of this group can access the domain controller from the network, adjust memory quotas for a process, back up files and directories, change the system time, create a pagefile, debug programs, enable computer and user accounts to be trusted for delegation, force a shutdown from a remote system, and more. They have full control over the domain. This group is a member of the Administrators group by default.
- **Domain Computers:** All workstations and servers joined to the domain.
- **Domain Controllers:** All domain controllers in the domain.
- **Domain Guests:** Used by network administrators to manage all guest accounts in a domain. The Guest account, which is disabled, is automatically added to this group.
- **Domain Users:** Members of this group include all user accounts in the domain. The Administrator account is a default member and every new domain user account becomes a member of the Domain Users built-in global group.
- **Group Policy Creator Owners:** Members in this group can modify Group Policy for the domain. The Administrator account is a member of this group by default.
- **Enterprise Admins:** This group, which is present only in the forest root domain, is used by network administrators to manage resources in an enterprise. The Domain Admins group and the Administrators user account are default members of this built-in global group, which has full control over all domains in the forest. The Administrators group is also a default member of this group. When Active Directory is running in Windows 2000 native or Windows Server 2003 mode this will be converted to a universal group.
- **Schema Admins:** Designated administrators of the schema. The Administrator account is a default member of this group. When Active Directory is running in Windows 2000 native or Windows Server 2003 mode this will be converted to a universal group.

◆ **Built-in system groups** are populated with users based upon how they access a computer or a resource. Network administrators cannot add, modify, or delete user accounts because the operating system does so automatically. For example, a user who connects to the network via a dial-up connection is automatically added to the Dial-up built-in system group. Since users cannot be added to built-in system groups, they are not shown when you are managing your user accounts, but they are available for selection when you are granting rights and permissions **(Figure 7-12)**. The built-in system groups include:

- **Anonymous Logon:** When Windows Server 2003 cannot validate a user account, it is added to the anonymous logon built-in system group.
- **Authenticated Users:** All users who have been authenticated either on the local computer or on the domain (those with valid user accounts in the local security database or in the domain database in Active Directory).
- **Creator Owner:** Every user who creates a resource or takes ownership of a resource is a member of this group.

Figure 7-11 Built-in global groups in the Users container

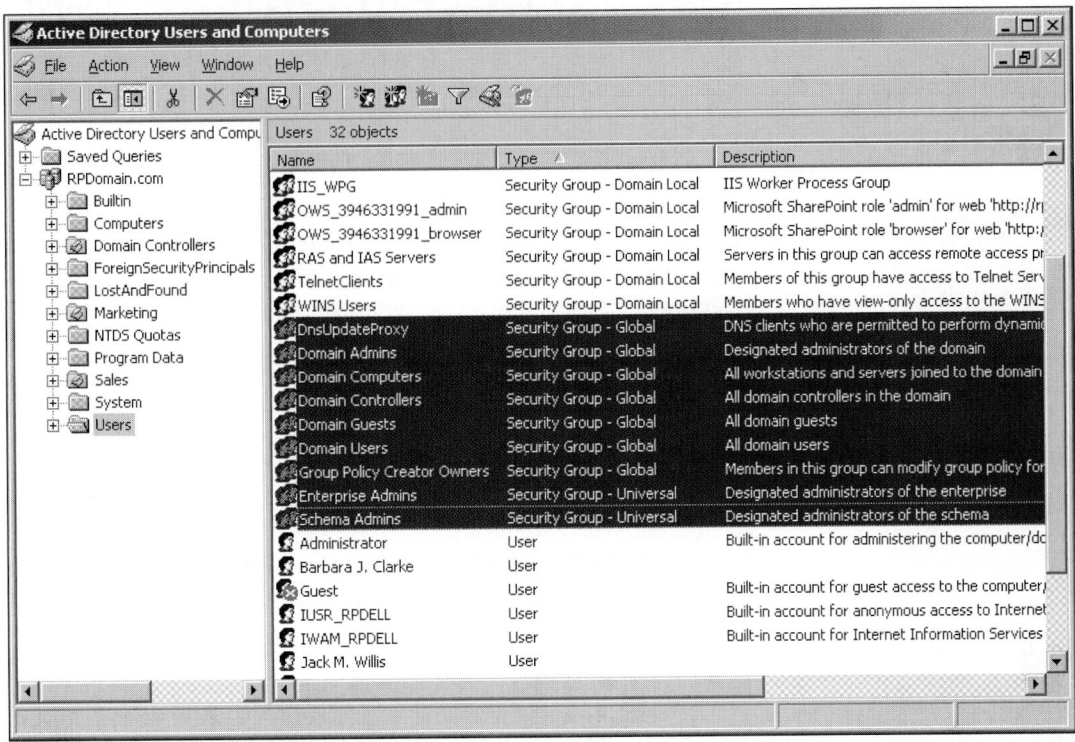

**Figure 7-12 Built-in system groups in the Select Users
or Groups dialog box**

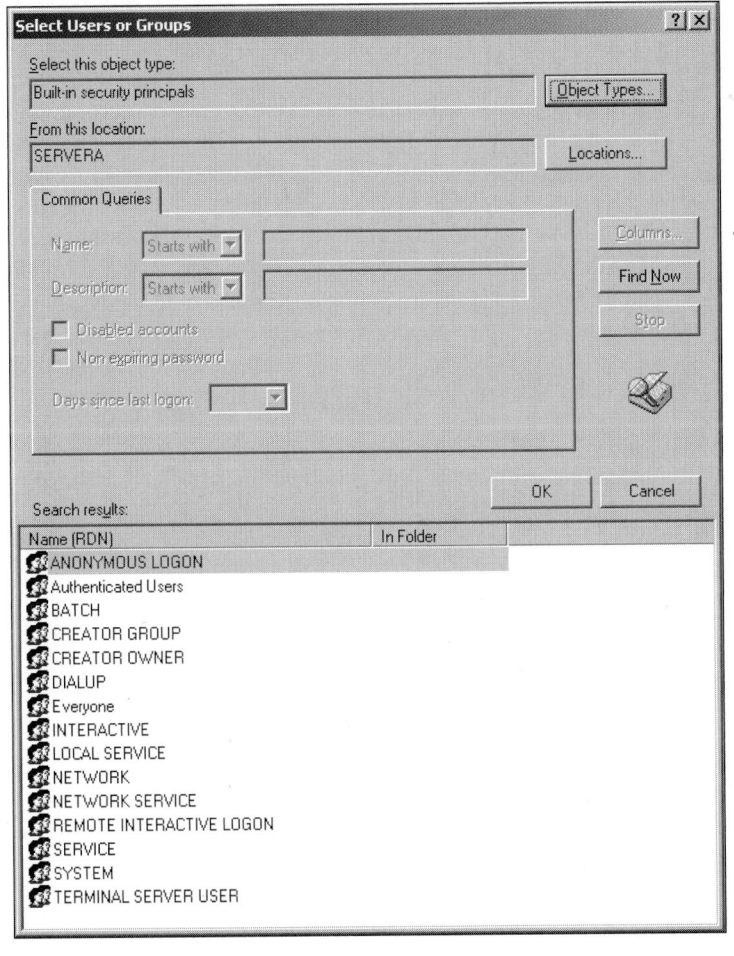

skill 3

Introducing Built-in Groups (cont'd)

exam objective

Create and manage groups. Manage group membership.

overview

- **Dial-up:** Users who are accessing a shared resource on a computer via a dial-up connection or a VPN (virtual private network).
- **Everyone:** All users who are accessing the computer including the Guest account. In contrast to previous versions of Windows, Windows Server 2003 does not include anonymous users as members of the Everyone group, by default.
- **Interactive:** Users who are accessing resources on the computer with which they are physically interacting. Anyone accessing the console is also a member of this group.
- **Network:** Users who are accessing a shared resource on a computer via a network connection.
- **Terminal Server Users:** Members of this group can run applications on the terminal server. All users who are currently logged in on the terminal server are members of this group.

more

In Windows 2000 mixed mode environments, the best practice is to use domain local and global groups following what is referred to as the **A-G-DL-P strategy**. You put user accounts (A) into global groups (G), put the global groups into domain local groups (DL), and grant permissions (P) to the domain local group.

First, you create domain user accounts for your users. Then, you create global groups to group your users according to department, function, location, or any other appropriate grouping. Next, you create domain local groups to grant the appropriate permissions for network resources so that you can control access to them. Finally, you place the global groups into domain local groups to give users access to shared resources. For example, if your company is constructed such that redhen.com is the root domain, and there are two child domains, publishing.redhen.com and finance.redhen.com, and you have printers in redhen.com that managers in the parent domain and the two child domains must access, the strategy would be to first create global groups for RedhenManagers, PublishingManagers, and FinanceManagers. Next, populate each global group with the appropriate domain user accounts from redhen.com, publishing.redhen.com, and finance.redhen.com. Then, create a domain local group PrintersRedhen in the redhen.com domain and assign permissions for the printers to it. Finally, add the three global groups to the PrintersRedhen domain local group **(Table 7-4)**.

In Windows 2000 native mode or Windows Server 2003 mode, universal groups can be used to organize global groups from multiple domains so that they fit between global and domain local, i.e., **A-G-U-DL-P**.

Table 7-4   A-G-DL-P strategy for redhen.com

Steps	Examples
1. Create global groups	RedhenManagers, PublishingManagers, FinanceManagers
2. Populate global groups with domain user accounts	bsmith@redhen.com (RedhenManagers), pcoast@publishing.redhen.com (PublishingManagers), ngesch@finance.redhen.com (FinanceManagers), shands@redhen.com (RedhenManagers)
3. Create a domain local group in redhen.com	PrintersRedhen
4. Assign permissions to the domain	
5. Add global groups to the domain local group	

skill 4

Creating and Modifying Groups by using the Active Directory Users and Computers MMC Snap-in

exam objective

Create and manage groups. Create and modify groups by using the Active Directory Users and Computers Microsoft Management Console (MMC) snap-in. Manage group membership. Identify and modify the scope of a group. Create and modify groups by using automation.

overview

Groups can be used effectively to manage large numbers of users and resources. In the following exercises, we will create a global distribution group and add members to this group using the Active Directory Users and Computers console. It is important to realize that creating any type or scope of group follows these same steps. However, even in small environments, it is advised that you follow the Microsoft rule for creating groups and assigning permissions. While it takes a little more work to set up, in the long run it reduces effort to such a large degree that the extra setup effort is worth it.

After you have created a group, you can set its properties in the **Properties** dialog box for the group. The tabs used to set the properties for a group include:

◆ **General:** Describes the scope and type assigned to the group.
◆ **Members:** Used to add members of the domain to the group. Members of a group can include user accounts, contacts, other groups, or computers.
◆ **Member Of:** Used to add the group to other groups in the domain or universal groups in other domains in the forest (**Figure 7-13**).
◆ **Managed By:** Used to specify the user or contact person managing the group.
◆ **Object:** Specifies the path to the group within the domain (**Figure 7-14**).
◆ **Security:** Used to specify permissions for members of the group.

Changes in the requirements of an organization may necessitate modifying the properties of groups. For example, when a network is restructured, it may become necessary for the administrator to change the scope of a group. You must keep two things in mind when you are planning the modification of group scopes. First, a domain local group can be converted to a universal group only if the domain local group does not contain another domain local group. Second, a global group can be changed to a universal group only if the global group is independent and not a member of another group.

Similarly, when you change the role of a group, you may also need to change its group type correspondingly. For example, a company hires trainees to work on a particular project and adds them to a distribution group so that they can communicate via e-mail. Later, when these trainees are transferred into various departments, they will need to access various resources on the network, depending on their roles. You can then change their distribution group to a security group and assign appropriate permissions to the group. This would call for a change in both the type and the scope of the existing group.

It is important to note here that group scopes and types can be changed only when the domain is operating in the Windows 2000 native mode or Windows Server 2003 mode. If your domain is in Windows 2000 mixed mode, you must first change the domain to Windows 2000 native mode or Windows Server 2003 mode before changing the group scope and type. Remember that this process is irreversible.

Figure 7-13 The Member Of tab in the Properties dialog box for a group

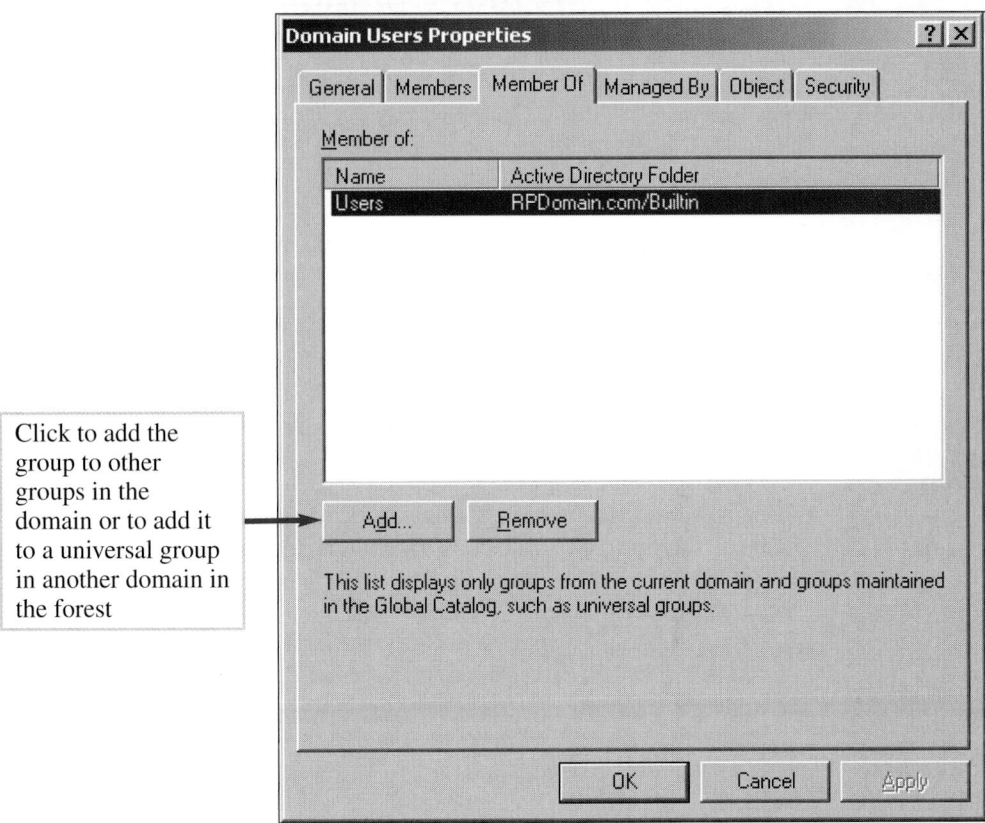

Click to add the
group to other
groups in the
domain or to add it
to a universal group
in another domain in
the forest

Figure 7-14 The Object tab

Displays the path
to the group in
the domain

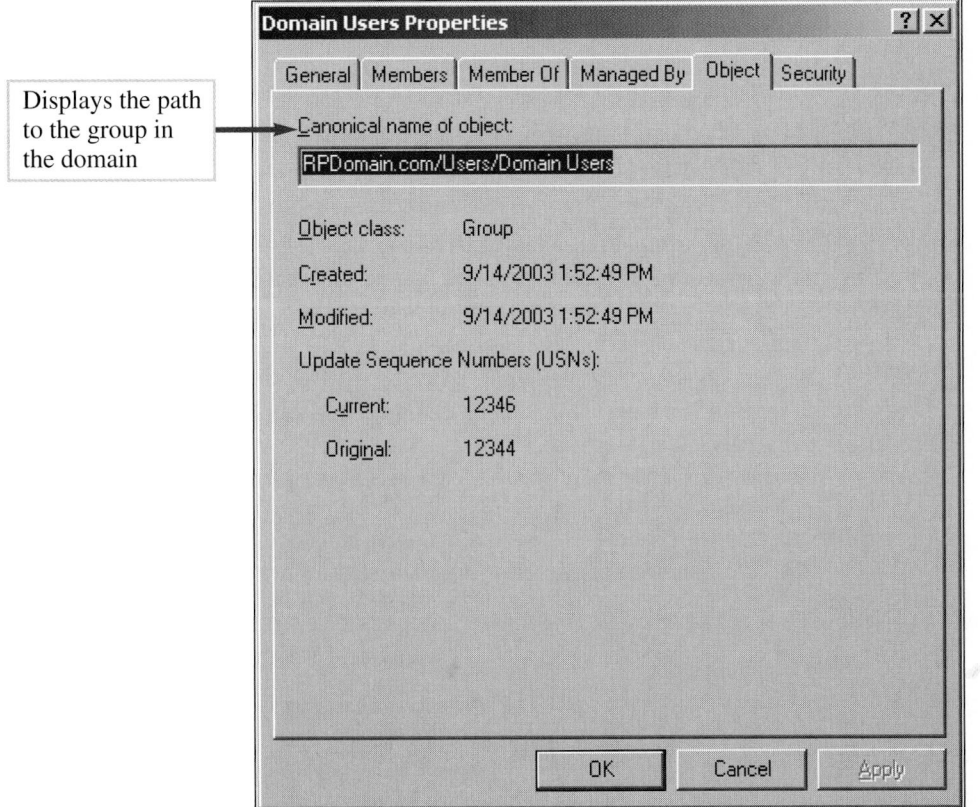

skill 4

Creating and Modifying Groups by using the Active Directory Users and Computers MMC Snap-in (cont'd)

exam objective

Create and manage groups. Create and modify groups by using the Active Directory Users and Computers Microsoft Management Console (MMC) snap-in. Manage group membership. Identify and modify the scope of a group. Create and modify groups by using automation.

how to

Create a group, add members to a group, specify a manager for the group, and change the type and scope of a group. (You can perform the final task only if your domain is in the Windows 2000 native mode or Windows Server 2003 mode.)

1. Log on to the domain controller as an **Administrator**.
2. Click **Start**, point to **Administrative Tools**, and click **Active Directory Users and Computers** to open the **Active Directory Users and Computers** console.
3. Right-click the **Users** container, point to **New**, and click **Group** to open the **New Object-Group** dialog box.
4. In the **Group name** text box, type **Group1**.
5. In the **Group scope** section, click the **Global** option button to create a global group.
6. In the **Group type** section, click the **Distribution** option button to create a distribution group **(Figure 7-15)**.
7. Click **OK** to complete the procedure for creating a group. **Figure 7-16** shows the new group in the **Active Directory Users and Computers** console.
8. Right-click **Group1** in the **Active Directory Users and Computers** console and click **Properties** to open the **Properties** dialog box for **Group1**.
9. Click the **Members** tab.
10. Click **Add...** to open the **Select Users, Contacts, Computers, or Groups** dialog box.
11. Click **Advanced...** to open the search dialog box.
12. Type **Barbara** in the **Name** text box (**Starts with** should be selected in the **Name** spin box) and click **Find Now**.
13. Select **Barbara J. Clarke** in the **Name (RDN)** column in the **Search results** list and click **OK** to close the search dialog box.
14. Click **OK** to close the Select Users, Contacts, Computers, or Groups dialog box and add this user to the group, Group1. The added member appears in the **Members** list **(Figure 7-17)**.
15. Click the **Managed By** tab to specify the manager for the group.
16. Click **Change** to open the **Select User or Contact** dialog box.
17. Click **Advanced...** to open the search dialog box.
18. Type **Admin** in the **Name** text box and click **Find Now**.
19. With **Administrator** selected in the **Name (RDN)** column in the **Search results** list, click **OK** to close the search dialog box.
20. Click **OK** to close the Select User or Contact dialog box. The **Name** box displays the group manager **(Figure 7-18)**.
21. Click the **General** tab. In the **Group scope** section, click the **Universal** option button to change the group scope.
22. In the **Group type** section, click the **Security** option button to change the group type **(Figure 7-19)**.
23. Click **OK** to close the **Properties** dialog box.
24. Close the **Active Directory Users and Computers** console.

Figure 7-15 The New Object-Group dialog box

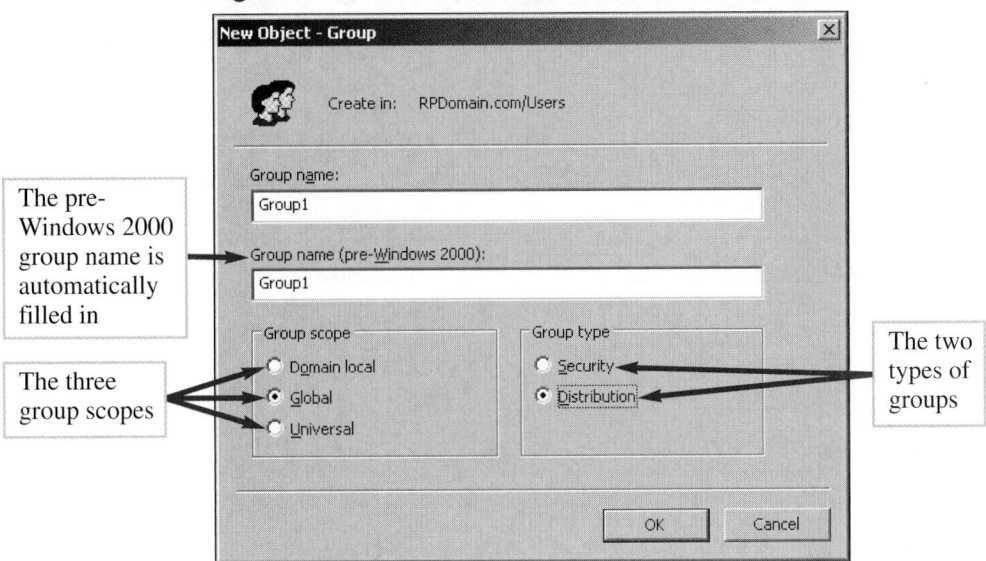

The pre-Windows 2000 group name is automatically filled in

The three group scopes

The two types of groups

Figure 7-16 The new group in the Active Directory Users and Computers console

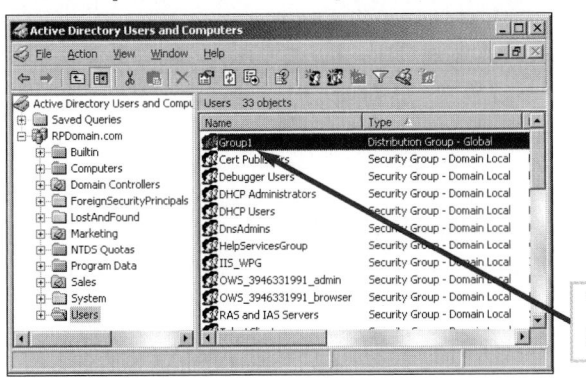

The new group

Figure 7-17 Adding a member to the group

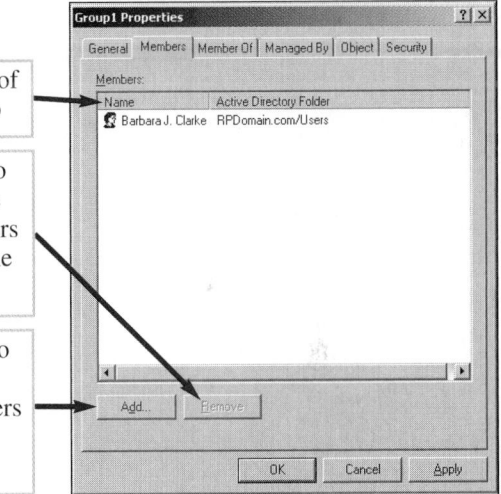

Member of the group

Click to remove members from the group

Click to add members to the group

Figure 7-18 Choosing the Manager for the group

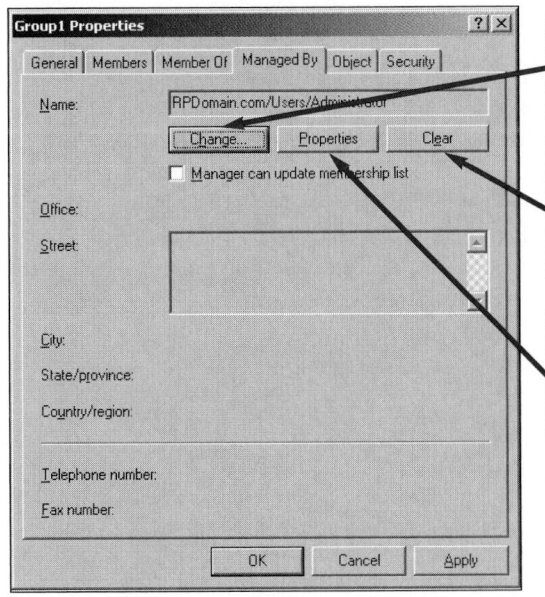

Click to select a new manager

Click to remove the existing manager of the group

Click to view the properties for the manager's account

The domain local group scope is disabled because a global group can be converted only to a universal group

Figure 7-19 Changing the properties for a group

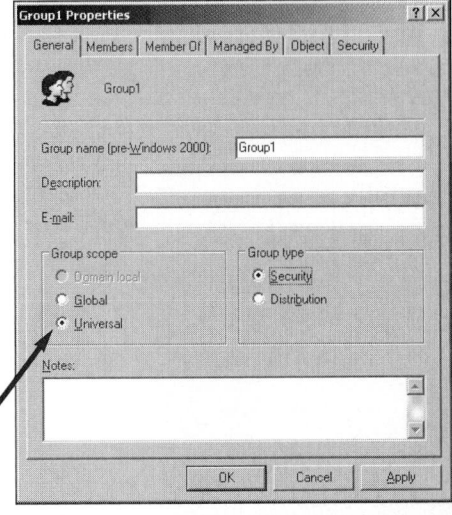

skill 4

Creating and Modifying Groups by using the Active Directory Users and Computers MMC Snap-in (cont'd)

exam objective

Create and manage groups. Create and modify groups by using the Active Directory Users and Computers Microsoft Management Console (MMC) snap-in. Manage group membership. Identify and modify the scope of a group. Create and modify groups by using automation.

more

caution

A group cannot be deleted if even a single member has the group set as his or her primary group. The default primary group for all users is Domain Users. Primary groups are relevant only to users who log on to the network through Macintosh Services or to users who run POSIX-compliant applications. You need to change the primary group only if you are using these services.

Some groups may become redundant as changes are instituted in an organization. It is important to delete groups that are no longer required in order to maintain security and avoid accidentally assigning permissions to groups and resources that are no longer required in your organization. Windows 2000 Active Directory uses the SID or Security Identifier to identify a particular group and assign permissions to it. The SID is a unique number that identifies each security object in Active Directory. When a group is deleted, the SID for that group is also deleted and will never be used again. Therefore, it is important to remember that after you delete a group you will not be able to recreate and restore the settings.

To delete a group, right-click the group in the details pane of the **Active Directory Users and Computers** console and click the **Delete** command. Then, click [Yes] in the **Active Directory** message box to confirm that you want to delete the group. You can also move and rename user groups based on changes in the organization structure.

You can use the same tools to automate or partially automate the process of group creation as you use to automate the process of user account creation: scripting and the importation tools. You can also use csvde.exe to import and export group objects into and out of Active Directory. For example, to export all objects in the users container with yourdomain.com as part of their distinguished name, including both users and groups, to a file named list.csv, at the command prompt type:

csvde.exe –f list.csv –d "cn=users,DC=yourdomain,DC=com"

–f is the filename parameter and –d is the export parameter used to specify the root of the LDAP search.

Or, to export just Group1 to a .csv file named Groups, use the command:

csvde.exe –f Group.csv –d "cn=Group1,cn=users,DC=yourdomain,DC=com" (**Figures 7-20** and **7-21**)

Be aware that when entering the Csvde paths, there should be no spaces after the commas.

You can also use Ldifde.exe to import and export group objects to and from .ldif files, which are supported by many third-party LDAP applications.

As you learned, the most commonly used scripting tool is Adsiedit.exe, which functions like a Registry Editor for Active Directory. ADSI Edit is an MMC snap-in that provides a means for adding, deleting, and moving Active Directory objects. Using this tool, you can view and change the attributes for an object. After you create the MMC, right-click ADSI Edit and connect to the domain. Then, you can open the Properties dialog box for an object and edit one or more attributes (**Figure 7-22**). However, this tool should used only by experienced administrators who have an in depth knowledge of Active Directory, as well as a working familiarity with scripting.

Figure 7-20 Using csvde.exe to export a group

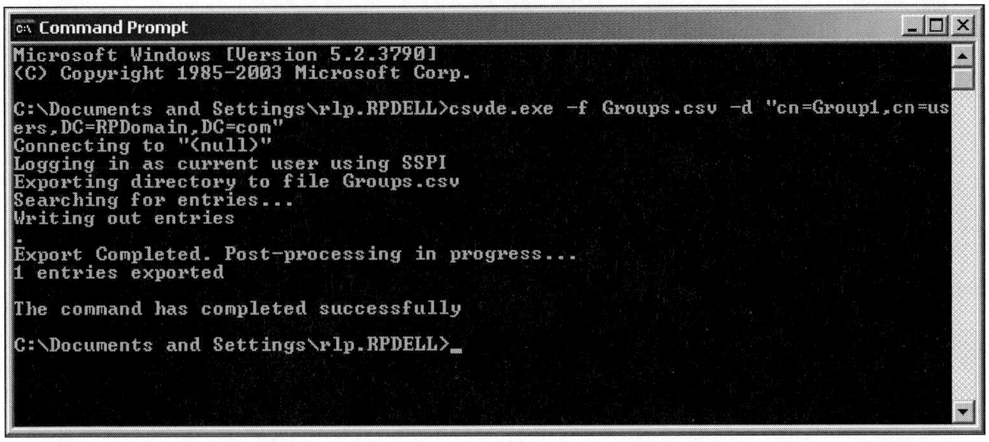

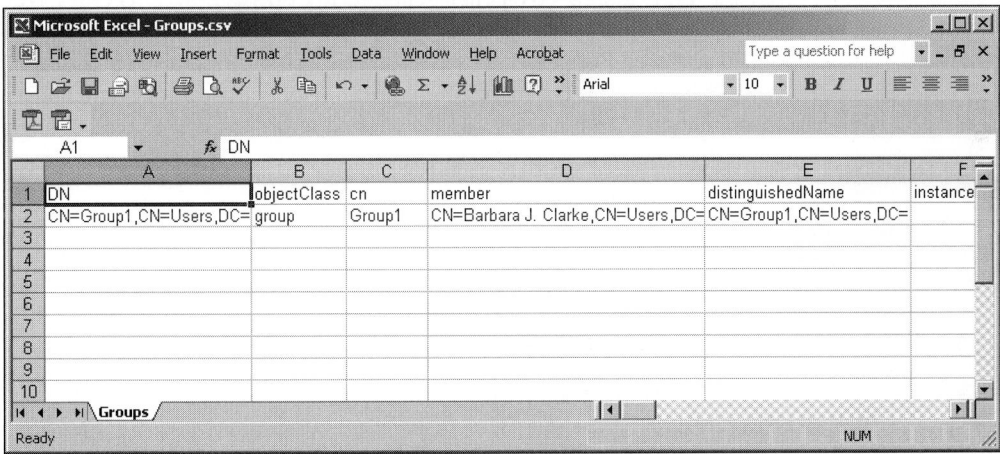

Figure 7-21 The Group1 group exported and opened in Excel

Figure 7-22 ADSI Edit

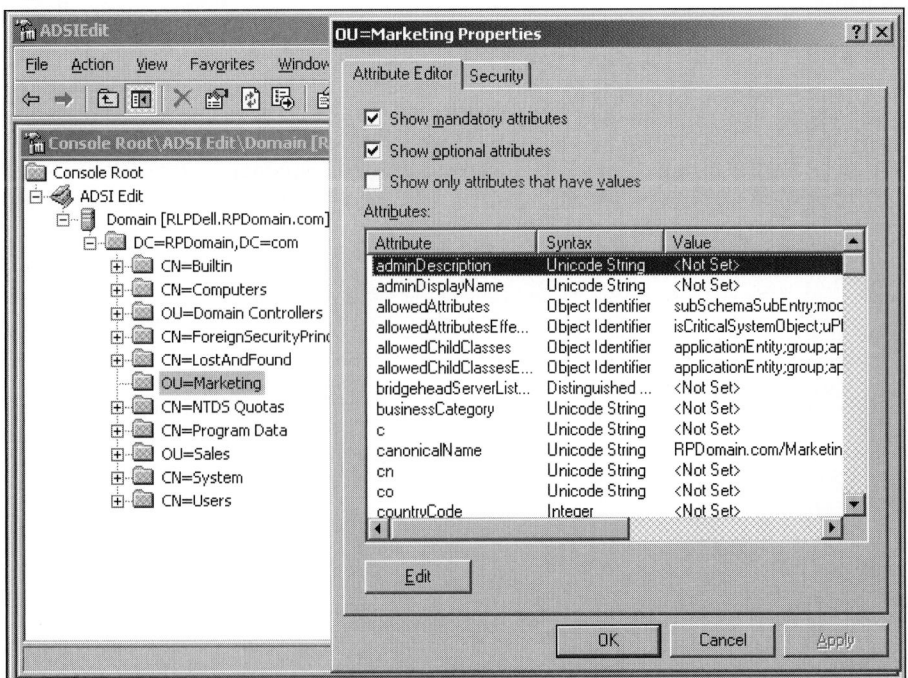

skill 5

Finding Domain Groups

exam objective

Create and manage groups. Find domain groups in which a user is a member.

overview

Active Directory contains information about all objects located on a network. Each Active Directory object has a unique set of attributes associated with it. For example, the attributes of a user account can include the user's address, telephone numbers, and organization details. On a network that has a large number of Active Directory objects, it becomes difficult for an administrator to remember the exact location of all of the objects. The administrator can then use the object attributes to locate the objects.

To locate objects in Active Directory, you use the **Find** dialog box in the Active Directory Users and Computers console. The Find dialog box provides you with various options that you can use to search for Active Directory objects. When you search Active Directory for an object, the Find dialog box helps generate a **Lightweight Directory Access Protocol (LDAP)** query. As you learned in Lesson 3, LDAP is the primary access protocol used to query and retrieve information about objects in Active Directory. The LDAP query searches the global catalog or the local domain (depending on the location listed in the **In** list box) for the specified object and then returns the queried information. The Find dialog box thus helps administrators in locating objects from the entire forest **(Figure 7-23)**.

When you use the Find dialog box, you can specify a single attribute or multiple attributes to locate an object. You can even specify partial values for the objects you are trying to locate. For example, to locate a computer named BIGPC, you can just specify the first two letters of the computer name 'BI'. Note that computer names are not case sensitive.

It is important to note that you can locate objects using Active Directory only if:

♦ You have the Read permission for the objects in question.
♦ Your computers have Windows Server 2003, Windows 2000, Windows XP, Windows NT with the Active Directory client, or Windows 95/98 with the Active Directory Client, IE 4.01 or later, and Active Desktop enabled.

tip

When you create an object, always supply the object's descriptive attributes. These attributes will help you to easily trace the object.

tip

Users should use the Search option on the Start menu, because, typically, users do not have access to the Active Directory Users and Computers console **(Figure 7-24)**.

how to

Locate the Group1 group.

1. Click **Start**, point to **Administrative Tools**, and click **Active Directory Users and Computers** to open the **Active Directory Users and Computers** console.
2. To initiate the search in the **Users** container in the domain, right-click the **Users** container and click **Find** to open the **Find Users, Contacts, and Computers** dialog box **(Figure 7-25)**.

Figure 7-23 The Find dialog box

The name of the Find dialog box will change according to the object type you select

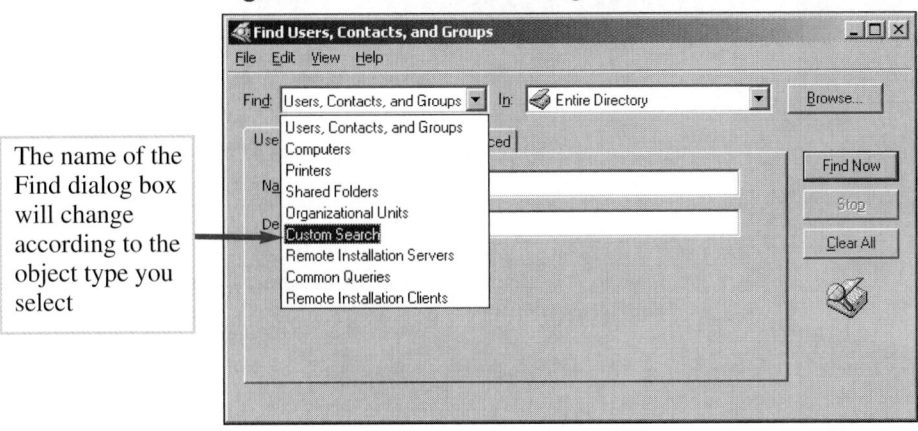

Figure 7-24 Searching for Printers, computers, or people using the Search tool on the Start menu

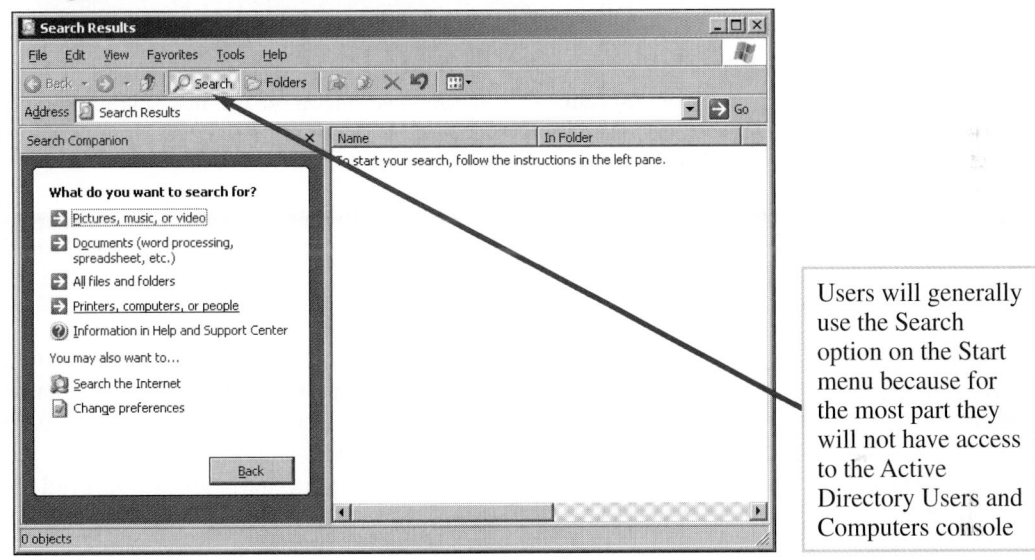

Users will generally use the Search option on the Start menu because for the most part they will not have access to the Active Directory Users and Computers console

Figure 7-25 Finding objects in the Users container

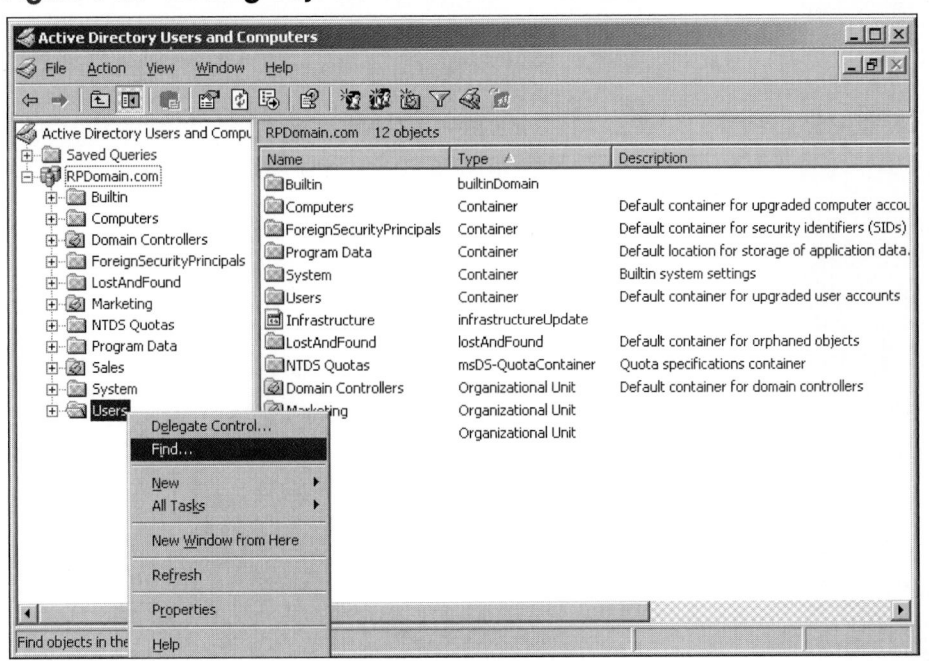

skill 5   *Finding Domain Groups (cont'd)*

exam objective

Create and manage groups. Find domain groups in which a user is a member.

how to

3. By default, the **Find** list box contains the object types **Users**, **Contacts**, and **Groups**. The **In** list box contains the name of the domain or OU where the search will be carried out. To specify the criteria for searching for the Group1 group, type **Group1** in the **Name** text box **(Figure 7-26)**.
4. Click [Find Now] to begin the search.
5. The Group1 group displays in the **Search results** list in the lower half of the **Find Users, Contacts, and Groups** dialog box **(Figure 7-27)**.
6. Close the Find Users, Contacts, and Groups dialog box but leave the Active Directory Users and Computers console open.

more

You can use the **Advanced** tab in the **Find** dialog box to make the search more specific. On this tab, you can search for an object based on multiple conditions. There are three search criteria you can specify:

◆ **Field:** Specifies the attribute you are searching against.
◆ **Condition:** You can specify various wildcards, such as **Starts with** and **Ends with**, to narrow the search.
◆ **Value:** Requires you to specify a value for the attribute.

When users search for Active Directory objects using the Search command on the Start menu, client programs use ADSI (Active Directory Services Interfaces). When you search for users, computers, or printers from the Start menu, or choose **Entire Directory** in the **In** list box in the Find dialog box in the Active Directory Users and Computers console, you are searching the global catalog. After you enter your search criteria and select **Find Now**, the search request is sent to the default global catalog port, 3268, and sent to the global catalog. It is the global catalog that allows users to search for directory information in all domains in a forest.

tip

The attributes listed in the Field button change according to the object type.

Figure 7-26 Specifying search attributes

Specify the object type you want to find

Specify the domain or OU you want to search: Entire Directory will search all domains in the forest

Specify the path to the container you want to search

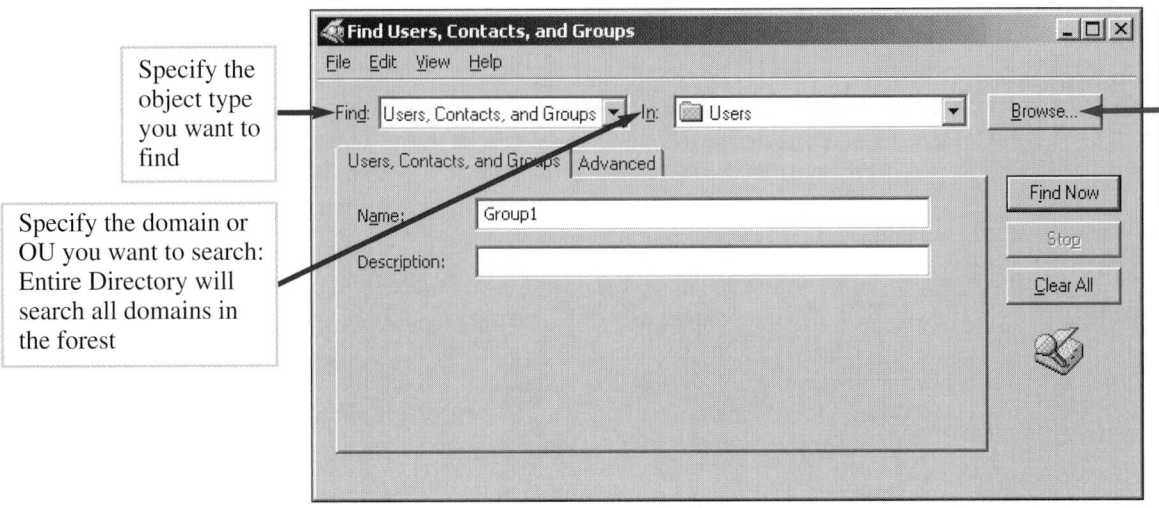

Figure 7-27 Filtering the search results

Results appear in the bottom white panel (Search results list)

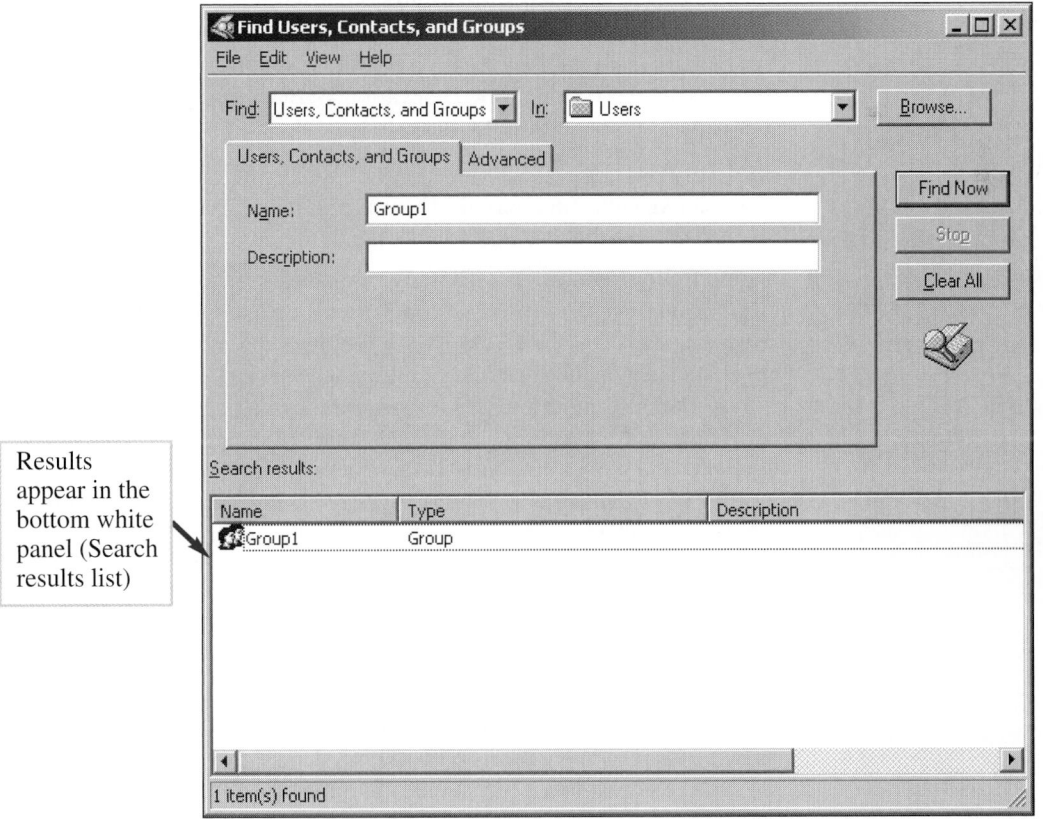

skill 6

Creating Group Policy Objects

Basic knowledge

overview

Group Policies are used to control the computer configuration, user environment, and account policies such as the minimum password length and length of time a password can be used. Network administrators apply Group Policies to centrally manage configuration settings for groups of users or computers and to control the distribution of software applications in a domain.

Group Policies are applied to objects in Active Directory to control how they and their child objects will function. There are both user settings and computer settings, which can also affect the rights that are given to user accounts and groups. The idea is to enforce uniform corporate policies on a portion of the network. For example, you can apply the **Remove My Documents icon from Start Menu** Group Policy to customize the Start menu so that the My Documents icon does not appear in the Start menu for all users logging on to the domain.

The Group Policy structure consists of the following components (**Table 7-5**):

tip

To install the GPMC, connect to the Internet and navigate to the Microsoft Download center: **www.microsoft.com/ downloads/search.asp**. Enter GPMC in the keywords text box to locate the GPMC download. When the download is complete, navigate to the location where you saved it and double-click gpmc.msi to install the tool.

tip

You can override local GPO settings with Active Directory-based GPO settings.

◆ **Group Policy Objects (GPO)**: All Group Policy settings that are applied to users and computers are stored in the GPO along with the properties associated with the objects in the Active Directory store. The policy settings for sites, domains, and organizational units are stored in GPOs. To create a GPO for a domain or an organizational unit, you use either the **Active Directory Users and Computers** console or the new **Group Policy Management console (GPMC)**, which must be downloaded from Microsoft (**Figure 7-28**). To create a GPO for a site, you use the **Active Directory Sites and Services** console or the GPMC which combines the functionality of Active Directory Users and Computers, Active Directory Sites and Services, the ACL Editor, the Delegation Wizard, and the Resultant Set of Policy tool. You can create two types of GPOs:

  • **Local:** These are stored on each Windows Server 2003 computer.
  • **Active Directory-based:** These are stored in Active Directory and are replicated to all domain controllers in the domain.

◆ **Group Policy Container (GPC):** The properties associated with a GPO are stored in a GPC. Group Policy settings for both users and computers that are small and for the most part static are stored in a GPC. Multiple GPCs can be associated with the same GPO and a single GPC can have multiple GPOs.

◆ **Group Policy Template (GPT):** Group Policy settings associated with administrative templates, security settings, scripts, and software settings are stored in GPTs. This data is dynamic and takes up more storage space, so it is stored in a folder structure in the *%systemroot%***\SYSVOL\Sysvol\<***yourdomain.com***>\Policies** folder on a domain controller.

how to

Create a GPO in a domain. (To perform this exercise, you must first download and install the Group Policy Management console.)

1. Click **Start**, point to **Administrative Tools**, and click **Group Policy Management** to open the **Group Policy Management** console.
2. Expand the **Forest** node. Expand the **Domains** node.

Table 7-5   Group Policy components

Component	Characteristics
Group Policy Objects (GPO)	Stores all Group Policy settings applied to users and computers. Stores properties associated with the objects in the Active Directory store. Must be created before Group Policies are created. Local GPOs stored on every Windows Server 2003 computer. Non-local GPOs stored on a domain controller in an Active Directory environment. Composed of a Group Policy Container and a Group Policy Template.
Group Policy Container (GPC)	Stores the properties associated with a GPO. Stores Group Policy settings for users and computers that are small and generally do not change. Not restricted to a one-to-one relationship with GPOs.
Group Policy Template (GPT)	Stores Group Policy settings associated with administrative templates, security settings, scripts, and software settings. Stored in a folder on a domain controller because data is dynamic and requires more storage space.

Figure 7-28 Download the GPMC

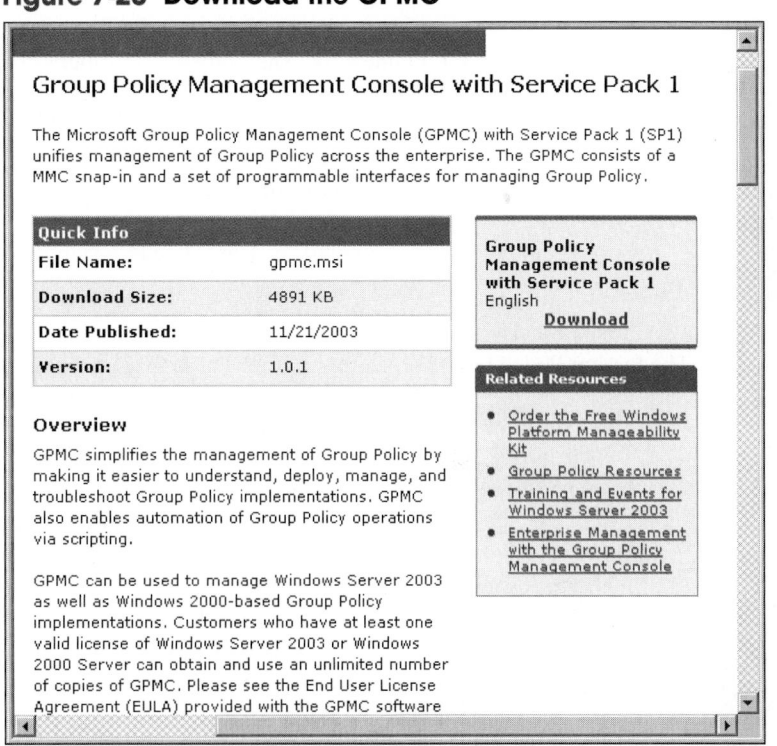

skill 6

Creating Group Policy Objects
(cont'd)

exam objective   Basic knowledge

how to

3. Right-click the domain name in the console tree and select **Create and Link a GPO Here** (Figure 7-29).
4. In the **New GPO** dialog box, type the Group Policy name, **Policy01**, in the **Name** text box and click ▢ OK ▢ (Figure 7-30).
5. **Policy01** is listed under the **Default Domain Policy** in the **GPO** column in the **Linked Group Policy Objects** list (Figure 7-31).
6. Close the **Group Policy Management** console.

more

The GPMC is designed as a comprehensive tool for Group Policy administration for Windows 2000 and Windows Server 2003 domains. It provides administrators with the ability to back up, restore, import, and copy/paste GPOs, as well as to create, delete, and rename them. You can use it to link GPOs, search for GPOs, and to delegate Group Policy-related features such as setting permissions on GPOs and for policy-related permission for sites, domains, and OUs. Although you can still create GPOs using the Active Directory Users and Computers console and the Active Directory Sites and Services console, if you have not installed the GPMC, it is recommended that you use the GPMC for all Group Policy management functions.

You can only install and run the GPMC on Windows Server 2003 or Windows XP Service Pack 1 or above computers. In order to run the GPMC on Windows XP Service pack 1 or above computers, you must also install the Quick Fix Engineering (QFE) update Q326469 and the Microsoft .NET Framework. The domain controllers must all be running Windows 2000 Service Pack 2 or later (Service Pack 3 or later is recommended). GPMC requires that all LDAP communications be signed and encrypted, so in order to access domain controllers in an external forest, they must be running Windows 2000 Service Pack 3 or later. If you want to access domain controllers in an external forest that are not yet running Service Pack 3 or later, you can edit the Registry on the computer running GPMC to relax LDAP signing and encryption requirements (See Knowledge Base Article 325465).

System policies are used for Windows 9.x and Windows NT. System policies were used in Windows 9.x and Windows NT to change Registry settings and control the user environment. The System Policy Editor (Poledit.exe) has been mostly replaced by Group Policy in Windows Server 2003; however, it can still be useful for managing Windows 9.x and NT computers. On a Windows 9.x computer, you can run the Poledit.exe version that is on the Windows 98 installation CD-ROM to create config.pol files. On Windows NT 4.0 Workstation or Server, you use poledit.exe that is included with Windows 2000 to create config.pol files. If you do not have a Windows 2000 Server CD, you can also download policy.exe, which contains poledit.exe, from **http://download.microsoft.com/download/5/d/3/5d3aaa79-8662-4ead-8fbe-97380c472dd0 /setuppol.exe**. However, if you create policy settings with the Windows 2000 version, you will not be able to edit them using the Windows NT 4.0 version. To manage a Windows 2000 or Windows Server 2003 computer that is not a member of a domain and not controlled by Group Policy settings, you modify settings in that computer's local computer policy, which applies to only that computer and all of its users.

tip

You cannot run the GPMC on 64-bit versions of Windows Server 2003.

tip

If QFE Q326469 is not already installed on a Windows XP machine on which you are attempting to install the GPMC, you will be prompted to install it. This QFE update is included in Windows XP Service Pack 2.

Figure 7-29 Creating a GPO

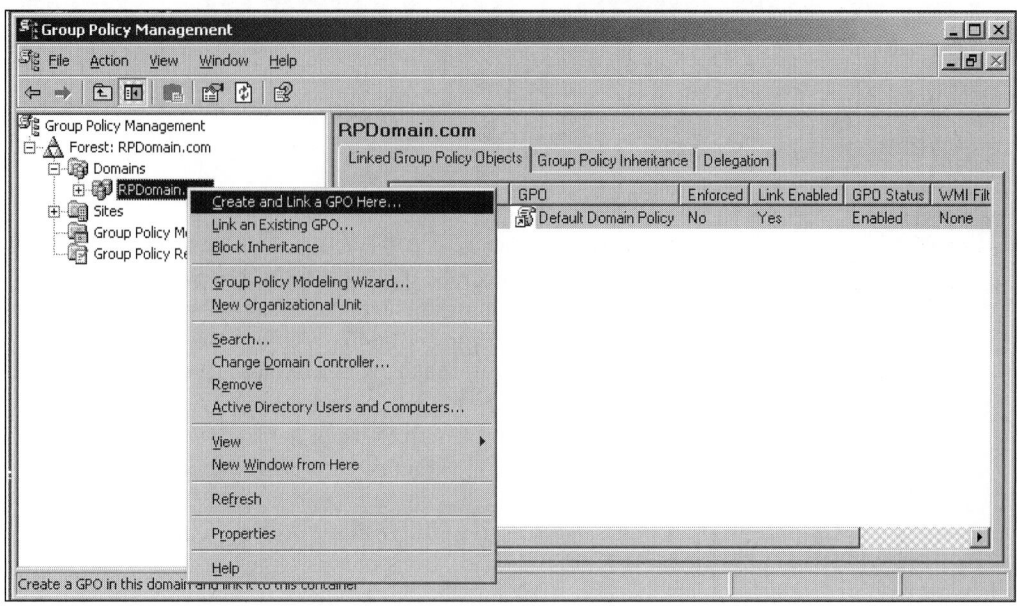

Figure 7-30 The New GPO dialog box

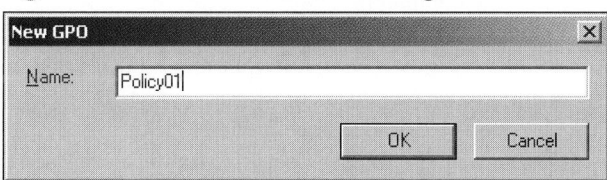

Figure 7-31 New Group Policy Object in a domain

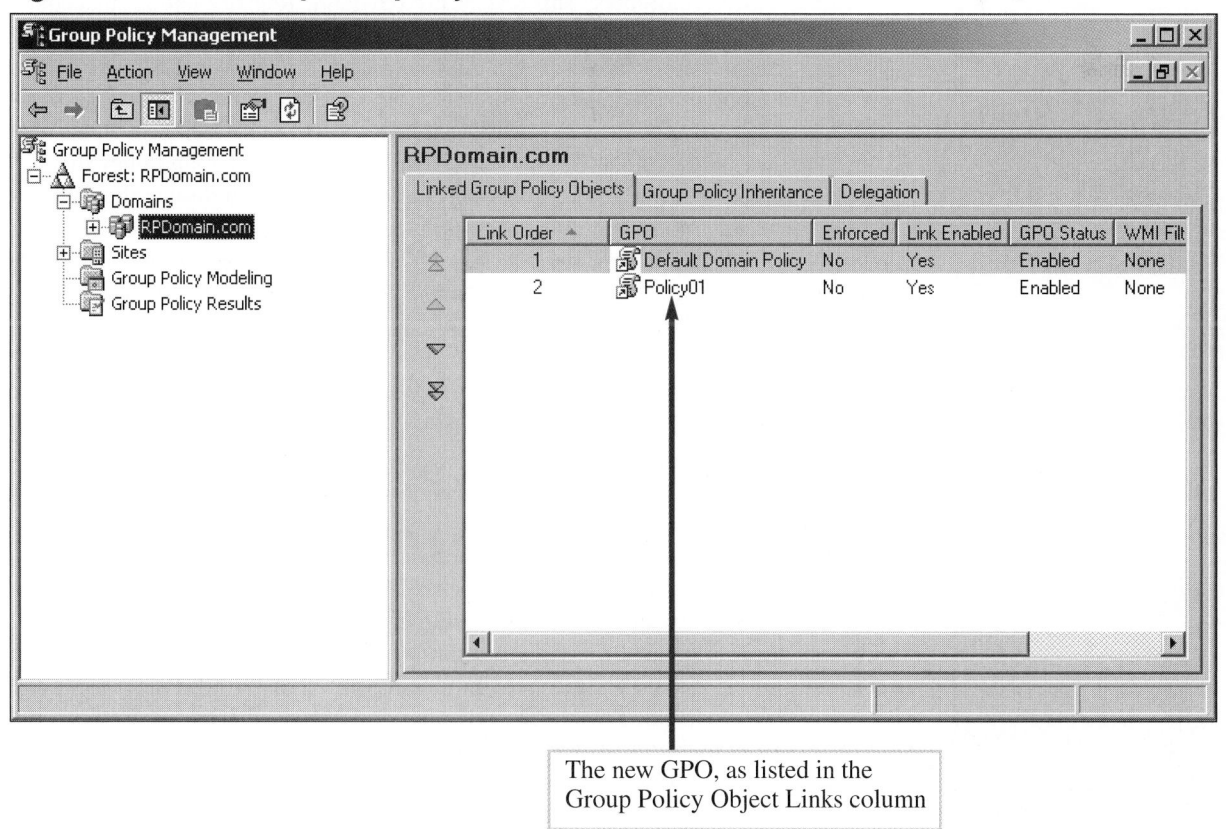

The new GPO, as listed in the
Group Policy Object Links column

skill 7

Identifying the Types of Group Policies

exam objective

Basic knowledge

overview

Group Policies are used to enhance and secure the work environment for users. Most Group Policy settings are associated with the Registry. You can create Group Policies to control the installation of applications on the user's computer. You can also use Group Policies to automate tasks when a user logs on to a computer. In the Windows Server 2003 environment, there are different types of Group Policies categorized according to the different network components and Active Directory objects they influence. Most Group Policies are used to update and manage Registry configuration data. Group Policies are modified in the **Group Policy Object Editor** snap-in, which you can use to modify the default settings for Group Policies according to your requirements. The Group Policy Object Editor is divided into a **Computer Configuration node** and a **User Configuration node**. Group Policy settings applied to the Computer Configuration node affect the computer objects to which they are applied. Some of the different Computer Configuration setting nodes for Group Policies are as follows:

◆ **Software Settings:** This configuration setting node is used to determine the applications that will be distributed to computers via a GPO. You use software settings to assign applications to computers.

◆ **Windows Settings:** This node contains two divisions for computers: Scripts and Security Settings **(Figure 7-32)**. Scripts are used to assign scripts and batch files that are configured to run at specific times, such as during system startup or shutdown. You can use scripts to automate repetitive tasks. Security Settings are used to configure computers on your network to use IP security and to specify settings for everything from user rights to system services. Account lockout policy, password policy, user rights, audit policy, public key access, Registry and Event Log access, and system services operation are all controlled in the Security Settings node **(Figure 7-33)**.

◆ **Administrative Templates:** This node is used to define Registry settings that control the behavior and appearance of the desktop, as well as other Windows Server 2003 components and applications. There are four folders under Administrative Templates: Windows Components, System, Network, and Printers. The Windows Components folder contains sub-folders for NetMeeting, Internet Explorer, Task Scheduler, Windows Installer, and others. In the NetMeeting folder, you can set a Group Policy that disables remote desktop sharing. In the Task Scheduler folder, you can disable the ability to run tasks on an individual computer or prohibit users from adding or removing tasks by moving or copying them in the Scheduled Tasks folder. In the System folder, there are sub-folders for Logon, Disk Quotas, Group Policy, Windows File Protection, and more. In the Logon subfolder, you can have the operating system notify users when a slow network link is detected. In the Network folder, you can set policies to control the use of Offline Files **(Figure 7-34)**. There are literally hundreds of Group Policy settings you can configure in this node.

Group Policy settings that affect the user environment include shortcuts, color schemes, access to Control Panel utilities, and other desktop settings. As with the Computer Configuration node, there are three main User Configuration setting nodes: Software Settings, Windows Settings, and Administrative Templates. Within the Windows Setting node, there are five folders: Internet Explorer Maintenance, Scripts, Security Settings, Remote Installation Services, and Folder Redirection. Remote Installation Services Group Policies are used to control the RIS installation options available to the user when the Client Installation Wizard is initiated. Folder Redirection Group Policies are used to relocate special folders such as My Documents, Start Menu, or Desktop. You can redirect these folders from their default locations in a user profile to alternate locations. They can be managed from a central location, accessed when the user is roaming, or made available in an Offline Folder when the user is not connected to the network.

Figure 7-32 Scripts Group Policy for computers

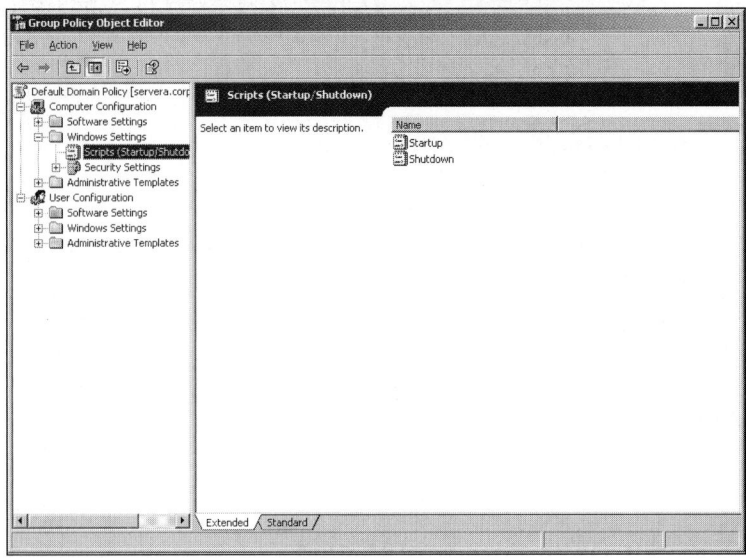

Figure 7-33 Security Settings for computers

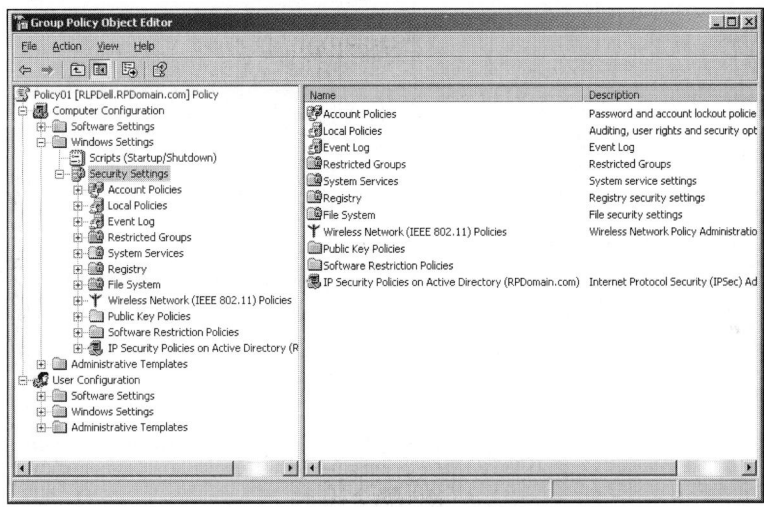

Figure 7-34 Group Policy settings for Offline Files

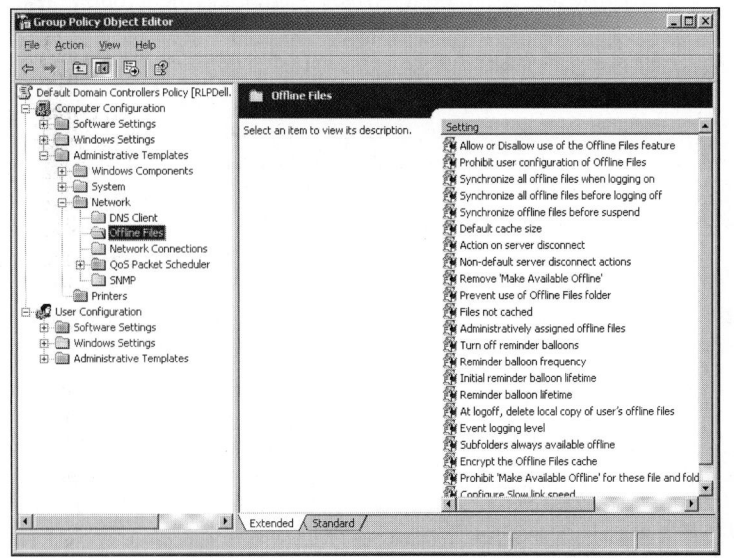

skill 7

Identifying the Types of Group Policies (cont'd)

exam objective   Basic knowledge

how to

Modify security settings to enable a user to log on to a server locally. (You will need to have a domain user account to complete this exercise.)

1. Open the **Group Policy Management** console. The **<*yourdomain.com*>** node should be selected in the console tree.
2. Double-click the **<*yourdomain.com*>** node to expand it. Then, expand the domain name node. Expand the **Domain Controllers** node. Select **Default Domain Controllers Policy**. The **Group Policy Management Console** dialog box opens to remind you that changes that you make to the GPO link are global to the GPO and will affect all other locations where the GPO is linked (**Figure 7-35**). Click ▭ OK ▭.
3. Right-click **Default Domain Controllers Policy** and select **Edit** to open the **Group Policy Object Editor** so that you can modify the Group Policy.
4. Click **Windows Settings** in the **Computer Configuration** node to display the Windows Settings policies.
5. Double-click **Security Settings** to view the list of Security Settings policies in the details pane.
6. Double-click **Local Policies**.
7. Double-click **User Rights Assignment** to view a list of the User Rights Assignment policies in the details pane.
8. Scroll down the **Policy** list and double-click **Allow log on locally** to open the **Allow log on locally Properties** dialog box. Here, you specify the users or groups to which the policy will be applied (**Figure 7-36**).
9. Click ▭ Add User or Group... ▭ to open the **Add User or Group** dialog box.
10. Click ▭ Browse... ▭ to open the **Select Users, Computers, or Groups** dialog box.
11. In the **Enter the object names to select** box, type **Barbara J. Clarke** (or the name of another domain user account you have created).
12. Click ▭ OK ▭ to close the **Select Users, Computers, or Groups** dialog box. The selected username is entered in the **User and group names** text box in the **Add User or Group** dialog box (**Figure 7-37**).
13. Click ▭ OK ▭ to close the **Add User or Group** dialog box.
14. The **Allow log on locally** user right has been assigned to Barbara J. Clarke (**Figure 7-38**).
15. Click ▭ OK ▭ to close the Allow log on locally Properties dialog box.
16. Close the Group Policy Object Editor and the Group Policy Management console.

Figure 7-35 Opening a link to the Default Domain Controllers Policy GPO

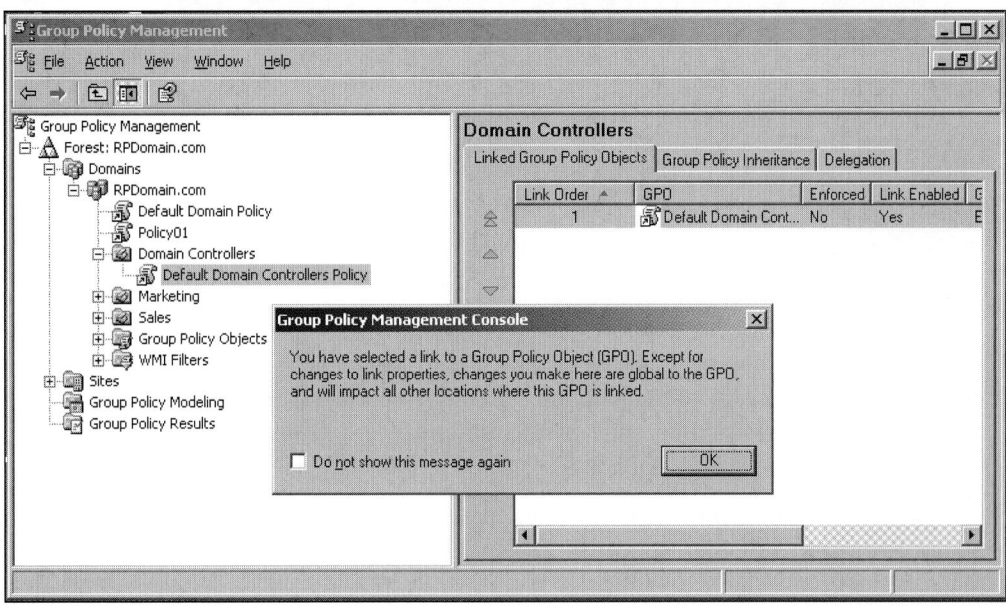

Figure 7-36 The Allow log on locally Properties dialog box

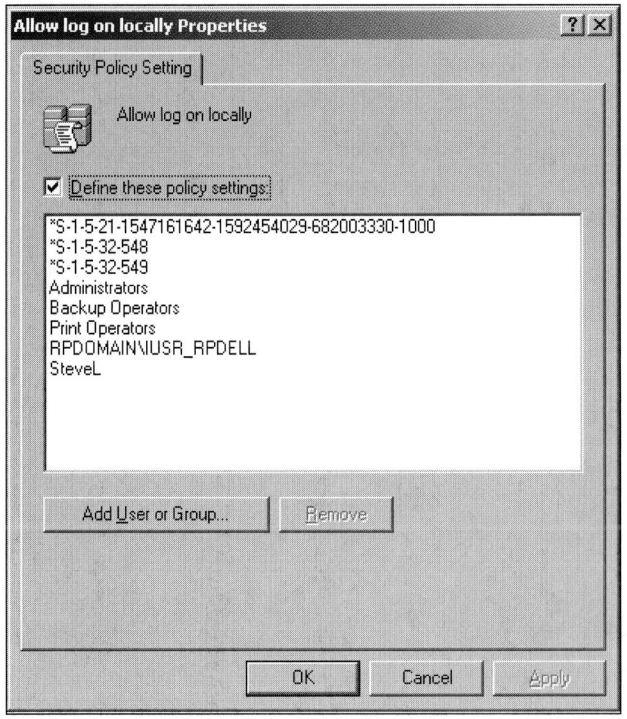

Figure 7-37 The Add User or Group dialog box

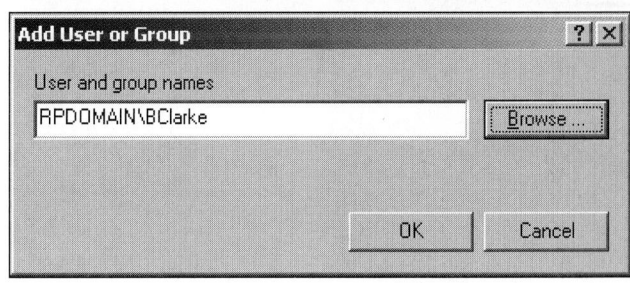

Figure 7-38 Allow log on locally user right assigned to a user

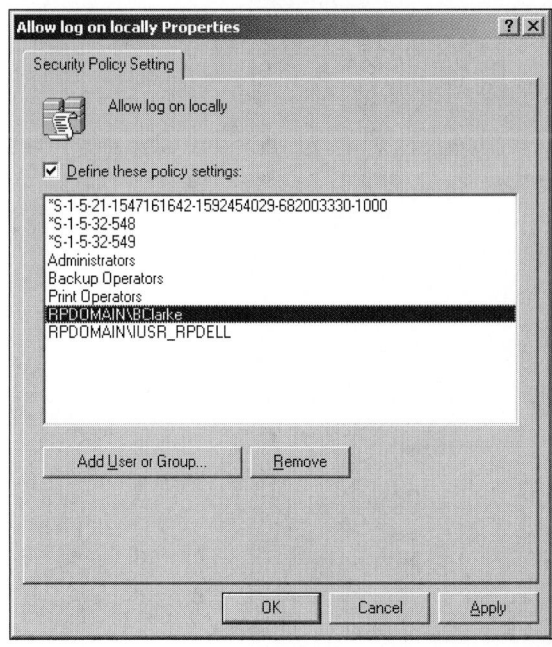

skill 7

Identifying the Types of Group Policies (cont'd)

exam objective

Basic knowledge

more

Group Policy can be applied to users and computers and it can be applied at the site, domain, or OU level. Every computer has one Group Policy Object that is stored locally. This Local Group Policy Object (LPGO) is applied first; then, GPOs assigned to the site will be processed. Next, policies assigned to the domain will be processed, and finally, policies assigned to OUs and child OUs will be processed. Policy settings are cumulative due to inheritance. You can link a single GPO to multiple sites, domains, or OUs. The Group Policy settings that are finally assigned to a computer or user is the cumulative effect of all GPOs assigned to the site, domain, and OU to which the user or computer belongs.

If a GPO is assigned to the parent container, but not the child container, the parent container GPO setting applies. If a GPO is assigned to both the parent container and the child container, and there is no conflict, both parent and child GPOs apply. If a GPO is assigned to both the parent container and the child container, and there is a conflict, the child container setting applies. These are the rules unless there is a conflict between a user setting and a computer setting. Then, the computer setting is applied. Computer settings take precedence over user settings when there is a conflict.

You can modify the default behavior or inheritance by using the **Block Inheritance** option, but this can make GPO administration more complicated and it should be used sparingly. You can block inheritance for the GPO links for an entire domain, for all domain controllers, or for a particular OU **(Figure 7-39)**. This prevents GPOs linked to higher sites, domains, or organizational units from being automatically inherited by the child container.

In addition to blocking inheritance, the default order for processing Group Policy settings is also affected by selecting the **Enforced** setting and by disabling the link. When you set a GPO link to Enforced, you are specifying that the policy settings in the GPO link will take precedence over the settings for any child object. This gives the parent GPO link precedence so that the default behavior (the child container settings override the parent container settings if there is a conflict) does not apply. This was formerly referred to as the **No override** option. The Enforced setting can also make GPO administration more complex and should not be used often. GPOs that are set to Enforced cannot have their inheritance blocked. When you disable a GPO link, you completely block that GPO from being applied for the selected site, domain, or OU. This disables the GPO only for the selected container object; it does not disable the GPO itself. If the GPO is linked to other sites, domains, or OUs, they will continue to process the GPO as long as their links are enabled. Processing is enabled for all GPO links by default. To disable a GPO link, right-click it and select the **Link Enabled** command, which will have a check mark by default to indicate that it is enabled. When you select the command, the check mark is removed and the link is disabled **(Figure 7-40)**.

When GPOs are linked to the same container object, for example, two GPOs for the same OU, the policies are evaluated based on the link order set on the Linked Group Policy Objects tab for the container object. The policy settings in the GPO with the lowest link order (link order 1) is processed last. It has the highest precedence and is used to settle a conflict. You can change the order of precedence on the **Linked Group Policy Objects** tab for the container object by using the ⊠ **(Move link to top)**, △ **(Move link up)**, ▽ **(Move link down)** and ⊠ **(Move link to bottom)** buttons **(Figure 7-41)**.

You can view the precedence order on the **Group Policy Inheritance** tab for a container object in the GPMC; however, GPOs linked to sites are not shown.

tip

In order to disable a GPO link or block inheritance, you must have the Link GPOs permission for the domain, site, or OU. If you do not have this permission, the Link Enabled command will be inactive.

tip

You can also disable a GPO link by right clicking the link in the Link section on the Scope tab in the GPMC.

Figure 7-39 Blocking Inheritance

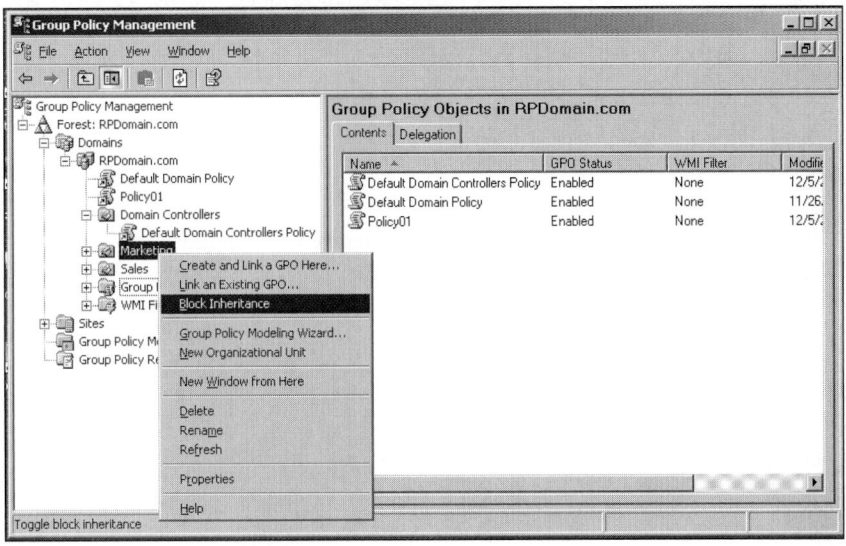

Figure 7-40 Disabling a GPO link

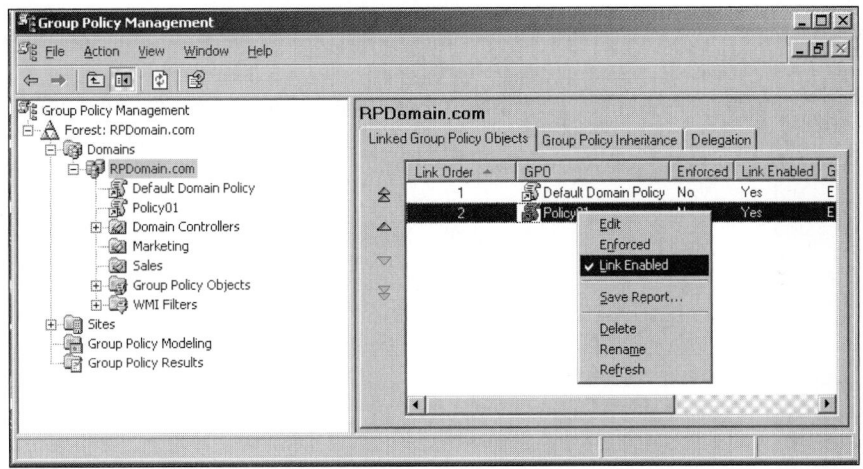

Figure 7-41 Changing the order of precedence

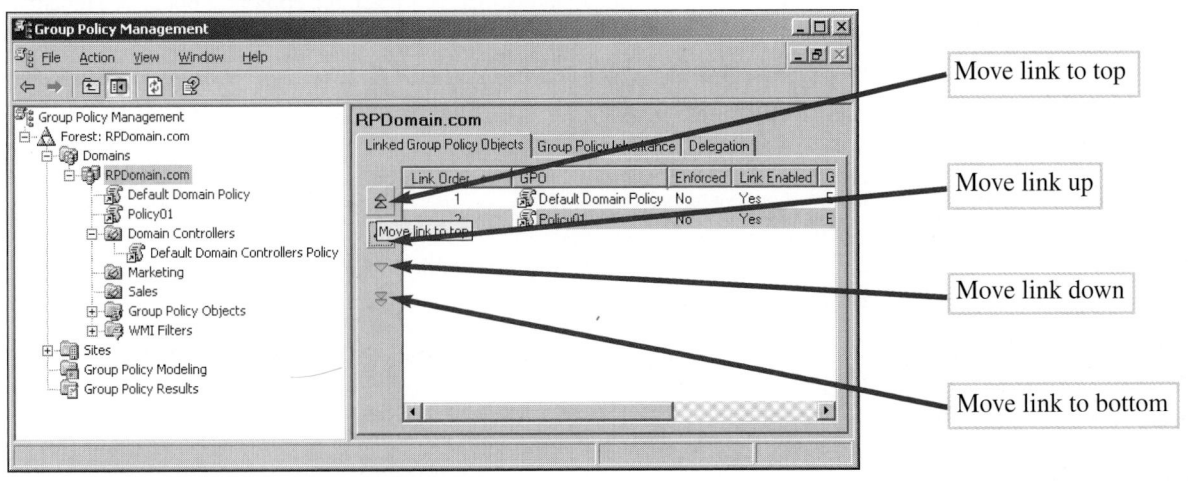

Move link to top

Move link up

Move link down

Move link to bottom

Exam 70-290

skill 8

Modifying Software Settings Using GPO Software Policies

exam objective

Basic knowledge

overview

Group Policies are used to assign and publish applications to groups of users or computers. Applications can be assigned to either users or computers, but they can be published only to users. After you have created the GPO, you can manage the software deployed to users and computers centrally in the **Group Policy Object Editor**. As you have learned, the Group Policy Object Editor has two parent nodes that are used to set Group Policies for users or computers (**Figure 7-42**):

◆ **User Configuration:** This node is used to set Group Policies for users, which are applied when the user logs on to the domain. You can use the User Configuration node to modify the settings for the desktop, applications, and for security. You can also assign and publish applications, set Group Policies to redirect folders, and set the scripts to be used for the logon and logoff processes.

  • If you assign an application to users, it will display in the Start menu for all of the users in the site, domain, or organizational unit, and may display a shortcut on the desktop, but will not actually install until the user invokes it. This functionality is called "advertising".

  • If you publish an application, it will appear in the Add/Remove Programs Wizard for all users in the domain, site, or organizational unit.

◆ **Computer Configuration:** This node is used to set Group Policies for computers that are members of the domain, OU, or site, depending on where the GPO is configured. These Group Policies are applied when the operating system initializes. You can use the Computer Configuration node to modify Group Policies related to the operating system, applications, and security controls for a computer. You can also set the scripts to be used in the computer startup and shutdown processes and assign applications in this node.

  • If you assign an application using the Computer Configuration node, the application installs automatically at boot for all computers in the domain, site, or organizational unit.

When an application is assigned to a user, it is announced to them when they log on. The application is installed when the user selects it on the Start menu or tries to open a document created with the program (known as document invocation). On the other hand, when an application is published to a user, it is listed as being available to install in **Add or Remove Programs**. The user can install the application using the Add or Remove Programs applet or by document invocation. Assigned applications also appear in Add or Remove Programs, but only assigned applications are advertised. If an application is assigned to a computer, it is not advertised; rather, it is immediately installed when the computer boots. Assigned applications are also resilient, which means that if part of the program is deleted, it will automatically reinstall the next time it is activated.

tip

In order to deploy and manage software using Group Policy, you must obtain Microsoft Windows Installer Packages (.msi) files from software vendors or developers, or you can create your own.

tip

You can uninstall applications that are published, but you cannot uninstall applications that are assigned.

Figure 7-42 The Computer Configuration and User Configuration nodes

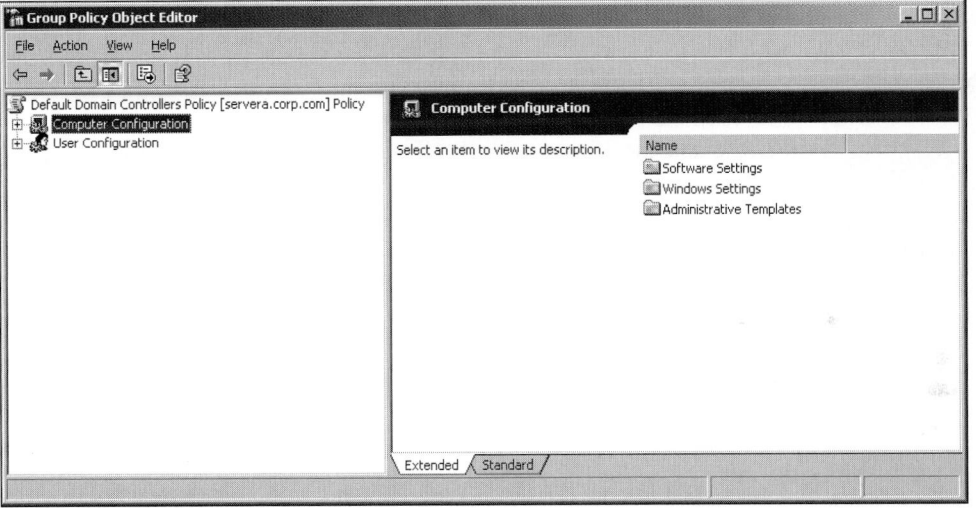

skill 8

Modifying Software Settings Using GPO Software Policies (cont'd)

exam objective

Basic knowledge

how to

Publish the Microsoft Office application to users on a server.

1. On the domain controller, click ⊞ Start, and then click **My Computer** to open the **My Computer** window.
2. Double-click **Local Disk (C:)** to view the list of the folders and files on the C: drive.
3. Click **File**, point to **New**, and click **Folder**. Name the new folder **Publish**.
4. Right-click the **Publish** folder and click **Sharing and Security** to open the **Publish Properties** dialog box on the **Sharing** tab.
5. Click the **Share this folder** option button, and click [Permissions...] to open the **Permissions for Publish** dialog box.
6. The **Read** permission is assigned to the **Everyone** group by default. Assign the **Full Control** permission to the **Administrators** group (**Figure 7-43**).
7. Click [OK] to close the **Permissions for Publish** dialog box.
8. Click [OK] to close the **Publish Properties** dialog box.
9. Insert the **Microsoft Office 2000** or **XP installation CD-ROM** in the **CD-ROM** drive.
10. Open the window for your CD-ROM drive and copy the entire contents of the **Microsoft Office CD-ROM** to the **Publish** folder.
11. Open the **Group Policy Management** console.
12. Expand the **Domains** node, if necessary. Expand the **<yourdomain.com>** node, if necessary. Select **Policy01** and click [OK] in the **Group Policy Management** dialog box to open the GPO link.
13. Right-click **Policy01** and select **Edit** to open the **Group Policy Object Editor**.
14. Double-click **Software Settings** in the **User Configuration** node and select **Software installation**.
15. Open the **Action** menu, point to **New**, and click **Package** to open the **Open** dialog box.
16. Open the **Look-in** list box, select **My Network Places**, and navigate through the **Entire Network** and the domain to locate the **Publish** folder on your server. Double-click it to place it in the Look-in list box and display the files in the Publish folder (**Figure 7-44**).
17. Double-click the **Proret.msi** file to open the **Deploy Software** dialog box. The **Published** option button is selected by default (**Figure 7-45**).
18. Click [OK] to accept the default selection, close the **Deploy Software** dialog box, and publish the application without modifications. The published application is added to the details pane in the **Group Policy Object Editor** (**Figure 7-46**).
19. Close the Group Policy Object Editor and the GPMC.

more

Every computer that runs Windows Server 2003 has one local policy. Local policy settings are the first to be overridden in an Active Directory network, but are available on all Windows 2000, Windows XP, and Windows Server 2003 computers. Local policies are modified in the Group Policy snap-in and stored in *%systemroot%*\System32\GroupPolicy folder. Computers that run Windows NT 4.0, Windows 9x, or earlier operating systems do not have local policies. Windows NT and Windows 9x use system policies, which have reduced functionality.

Figure 7-43 Assigning permissions to users

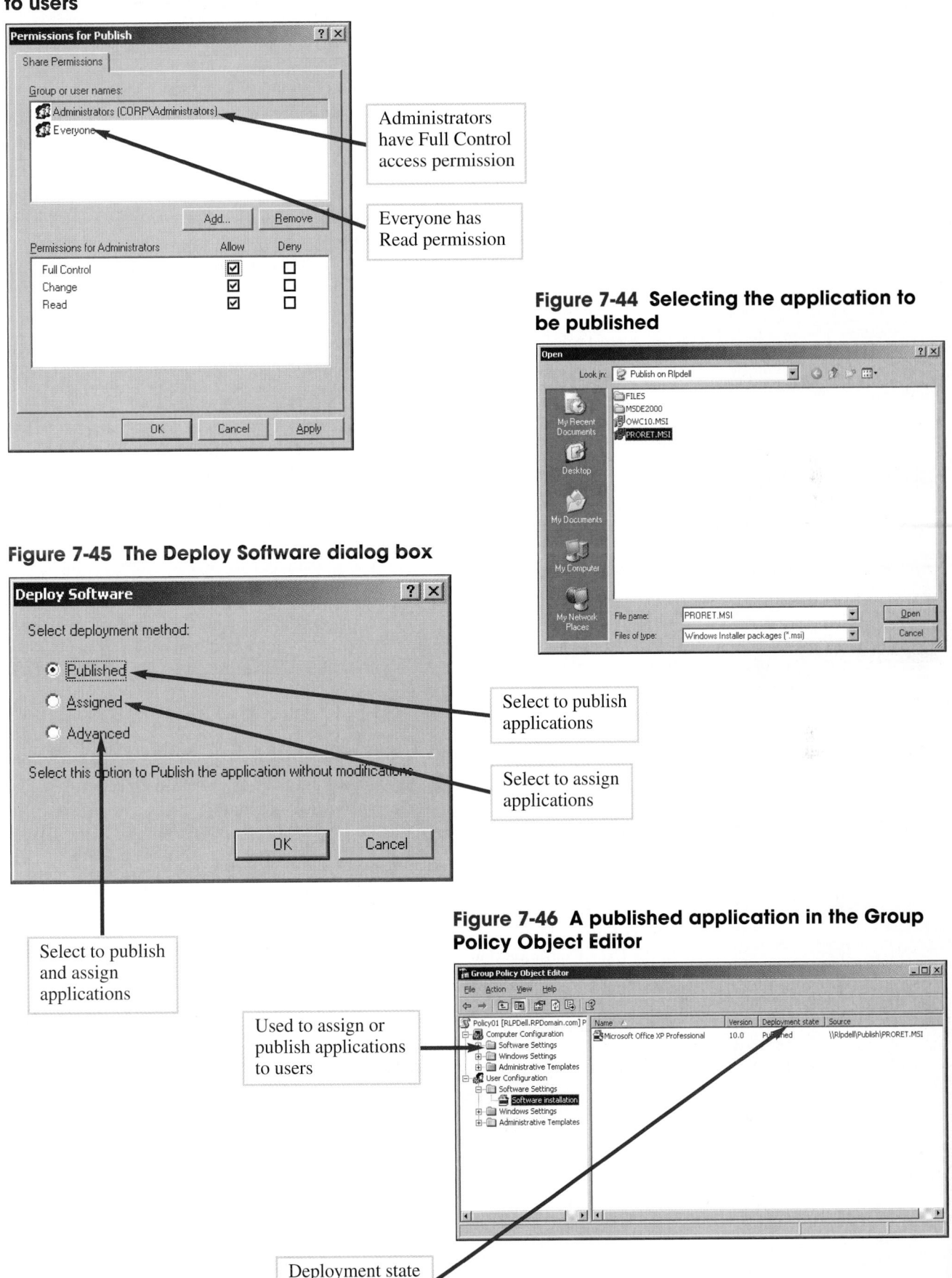

Administrators have Full Control access permission

Everyone has Read permission

Figure 7-44 Selecting the application to be published

Figure 7-45 The Deploy Software dialog box

Select to publish applications

Select to assign applications

Select to publish and assign applications

Figure 7-46 A published application in the Group Policy Object Editor

Used to assign or publish applications to users

Deployment state of the application

skill 9 | *Redirecting Folders Using GPOs*

exam objective

Basic knowledge

overview

Group Policy can also be used to help resolve the most common problem with roaming user profiles: network bandwidth waste. A feature in Group Policy called **Folder Redirection** allows you to take the most common folders and redirect them to a network server. This means that rather than downloading the full folder at logon, your users are instead browsing the remote folder, just as if they were browsing a network share. When a user opens an item in a redirected folder, the individual item is downloaded. This functionality saves considerable network bandwidth and can significantly reduce the logon time for users with large profiles.

You can redirect folders over a network using the **Folder Redirection** extension located in the **Windows Settings** folder. This folder resides in the **User Configuration** node in the Group Policy Object Editor, as shown in **Figure 7-47**.

Folder Redirection is especially beneficial to users. Users' documents, because they are on the network, are always available as long as the user is connected to the network, regardless of the computer the user logs on to. Also, systems that must be reconfigured at the system level or that require reinstallation of the operating system can redirect their data safely to a different location other than the local computer's hard disk. Folder Redirection does however, have one major drawback. Using roaming user profiles makes the process of logging on and off slower as compared to other operating systems, because roaming user profiles must download the entire folder structure at logon.

Backing up data on a shared network server can be scheduled as a routine system administrative task. The Folder Redirection feature is safer and less user-dependent than manually backing up data, because it does not involve any user action.

how to

Redirect the My Documents folder to a location for a user account, according to security group membership. (You will need a shared folder on your server named Documents, and a user account named Barbara J. Clarke, who is a member of Group1.)

1. Log on to the domain controller as an **Administrator**.
2. Click ⟦Start⟧, point to **Administrative Tools**, and click **Group Policy Management**.
3. Expand the **Domains** node, if necessary. Expand the *<yourdomain.com>* node, if necessary. Right-click **Default Domain Policy** and click **Edit** to open the **Group Policy Object Editor**.
4. In the **User Configuration** node, expand the **Windows Settings** folder, and select the **Folder Redirection** folder to view its contents.
5. In the details pane, right-click the **My Documents** folder and click **Properties** to open the **Properties** dialog box for the My Documents folder on the **Target** tab.
6. In the **Setting** list box, select **Advanced—Specify locations for various user groups** (**Figure 7-48**). This will allow you to specify different locations for redirection over the network for different user groups.
7. Click ⟦ Add... ⟧ to open the **Specify Group and Location** dialog box.
8. Click ⟦ Browse... ⟧ to open the **Select Group** dialog box.
9. Click **Advanced**, type **G** in the **Name** field, and click ⟦ Find Now ⟧.
10. Select **Group1** in the **Search results** list and click ⟦ OK ⟧ to specify the user group for Folder Redirection.
11. Click ⟦ OK ⟧ to close the Select Group dialog box. Group1 is inserted in the **Security Group Membership** text box (**Figure 7-49**).

Figure 7-47 Special folders available for redirection

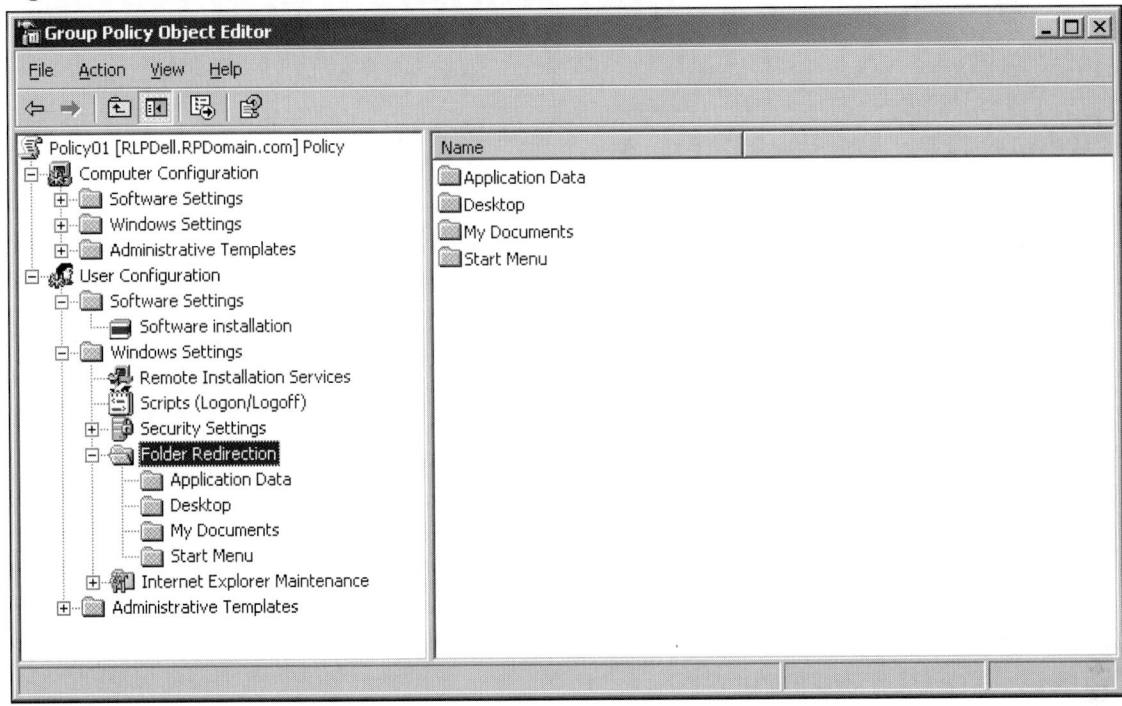

Figure 7-48 The Target tab

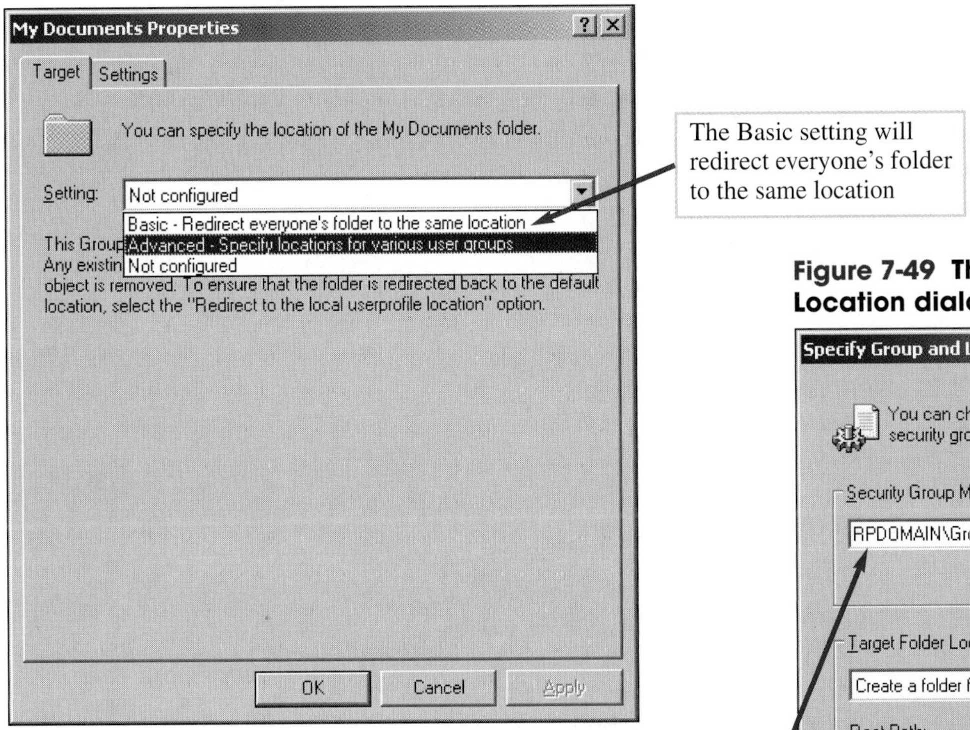

The Basic setting will redirect everyone's folder to the same location

Figure 7-49 The Specify Group and Location dialog box

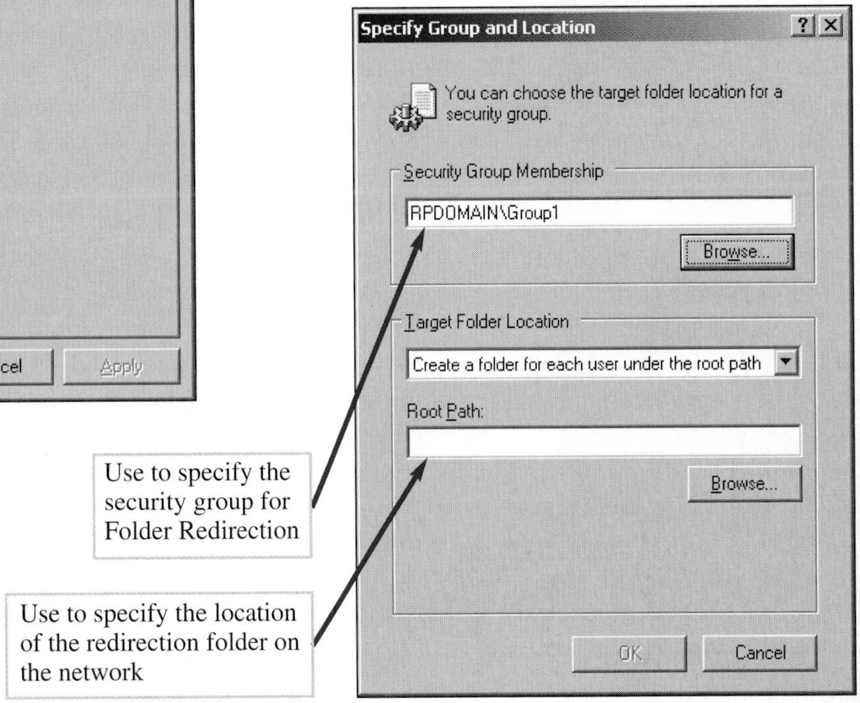

Use to specify the security group for Folder Redirection

Use to specify the location of the redirection folder on the network

skill 9

Redirecting Folders Using GPOs
(cont'd)

exam objective   Basic knowledge

how to

12. In the **Root Path** text box, type **\\Server\Documents**, where **Server** is the name of your server, to specify the location of the redirection folder on the network. The default settings in Windows Server 2003 create folders for each user under this location automatically.

13. Click [OK] to close the **Specify Group and Location** dialog box and return to the **Properties** dialog box. The Security group and the path to the redirection folder are entered in the **Security Group Membership** box (**Figure 7-50**).

14. Click the **Settings** tab to specify the redirection settings for the My Documents folder.

15. By default, the **Grant the user exclusive rights to My Documents** check box is selected. This makes the folder accessible exclusively to the user of the folder.

16. The **Move the contents of My Documents to the new location** check box is also selected by default. This will move the files from the local My Documents folder to the specified network location.

17. In the **Policy Removal** section, click the **Redirect the folder back to the local user profile location when policy is removed** option button in order to allow the folder contents to be moved back to the original location after the policy is removed (**Figure 7-51**).

18. Click [OK] to close the **Properties** dialog box.

19. Close the Group Policy Object Editor and the GPMC. You have now redirected the special folder My Documents for all users in Group 1 to a location on the network.

Figure 7-50 Entering the security group and the location of the redirection folder

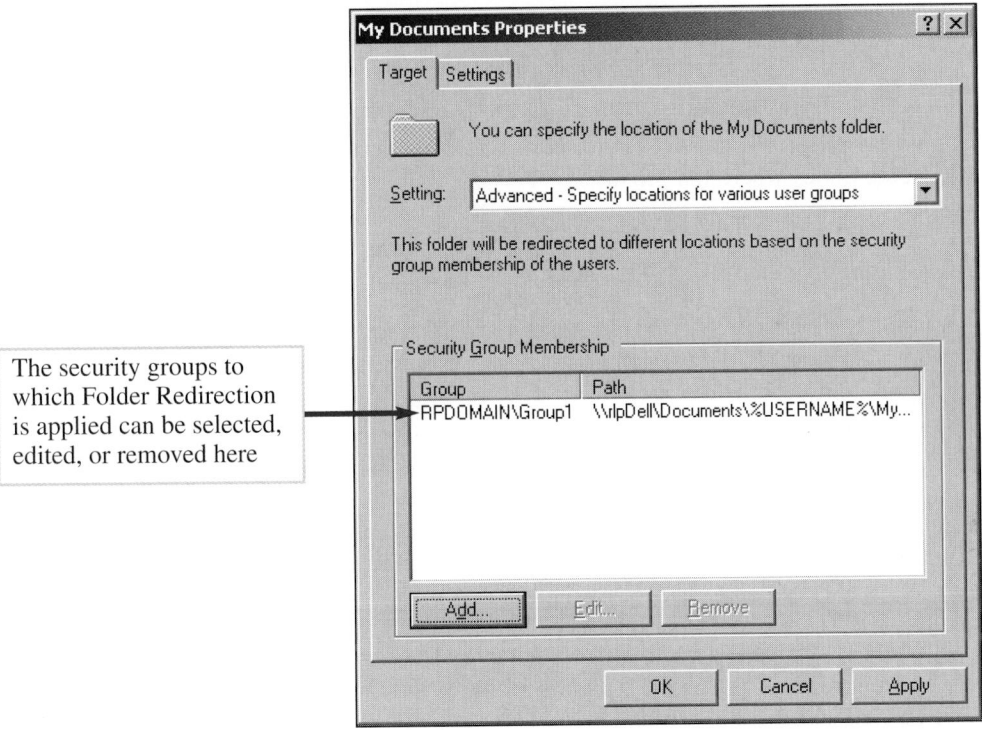

The security groups to which Folder Redirection is applied can be selected, edited, or removed here

Figure 7-51 The Settings tab

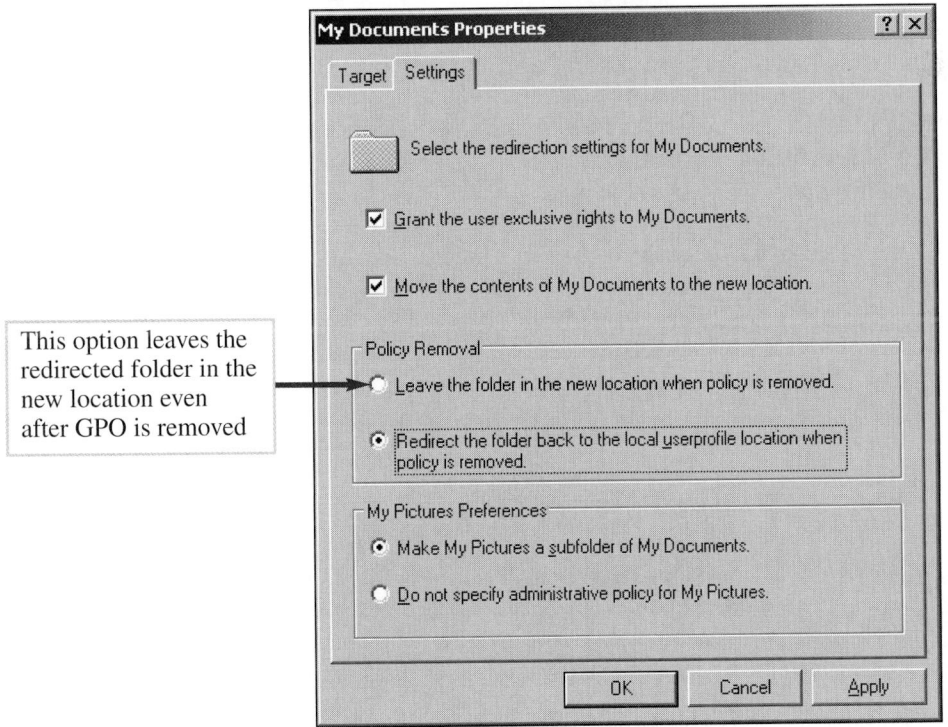

This option leaves the redirected folder in the new location even after GPO is removed

Summary

- Administrators can assign rights and permissions to groups in order to simplify the management of multiple user accounts.
- A group is a collection of user accounts requiring similar rights and permissions.
- In the Windows Server 2003 environment, you can create two types of groups: security and distribution.
- The group scope determines where the group can be used in the network.
- There are three different group scopes in the Windows Server 2003 environment: domain local, global, and universal.
- A local security group is a group that can be assigned permissions and rights only for the local computer.
- Built-in groups have a predefined set of rights and group memberships for users that can be modified if you have administrative rights. Windows Server 2003 has four types of built-in groups: built-in global, built-in domain local, built-in local, and built-in system groups.
- Built-in local groups are created on all Windows Server 2003 computers. They can be viewed in the Groups folder in the Computer Management console on all non-domain controllers. On domain controllers, they are stored in the Builtin container in the Active Directory Users and Computers console.
- Built-in domain local groups are automatically created only on domain controllers. They are stored in the Users container in the Active Directory Users and Computers console. The number of built-in domain local groups will be different on each domain controller, depending on the type of services the domain controller is running. The names generally identify the function of the group.
- Built-in global groups are automatically created on domain controllers. They are stored in the Users container in the Active Directory Users and Computers console.
- Built-in system groups are populated with users based upon how they access a computer or a resource. Network administrators cannot add, modify, or delete user accounts because the operating system does so automatically.
- In Windows 2000 mixed mode environments, the best practice for organizing groups is to use domain local and global groups following what is referred to as the A-G-DL-P strategy. You put user accounts (A) into global groups (G), put the global groups into domain local groups (DL), and grant permissions (P) to the domain local group.
- In Windows 2000 native mode or Windows Server 2003 mode, universal groups can be used to organize global groups from multiple domains so that they fit between global and domain local and the strategy becomes A-G-U-DL-P.
- To automate or partially automate the process of group creation you can use scripting or the Active Directory object importation tools.

- A template is simply a group that is specifically created for copying. The importation tools are Csvde.exe and Ldifde.exe. Csvde.exe is used to import and export Active Directory objects to .csv files, which can be opened and edited in Excel. Ldifde.exe is used to import and export Active Directory objects to and from .ldif files, which are supported by many third-party LDAP applications.
- The most commonly used scripting tool is Adsiedit.exe, which functions like a Registry Editor for Active Directory. ADSI Edit is an MMC snap-in that provides a means for adding, deleting, and moving Active Directory objects. Using this tool, you can view and change the attributes for an object.
- To locate objects in Active Directory, you use the Find dialog box in the Active Directory Users and Computers console. When you search Active Directory for an object, the Find dialog box helps generate a Lightweight Directory Access Protocol (LDAP) query. LDAP is the primary access protocol used to query and retrieve information about objects in Active Directory. The LDAP query searches the global catalog or the local domain (depending on the location listed in the In list box).
- When users search for Active Directory objects using the Search command on the Start menu, client programs use ADSI (Active Directory Services Interfaces). When you search for users, computers, or printers from the Start menu, or choose Entire Directory in the In list box in the Find dialog box in Active Directory Users and Computers, you are searching the global catalog. It is the global catalog that allows users to search for directory information in all domains in a forest.
- Group Policies are used to control the computer configuration, user environment, and account policies such as the minimum password length and length of time a password can be used.
- Network administrators apply Group Policies to centrally manage configuration settings for groups of users and computers and to control the distribution of software applications in a domain.
- Group Policies are a set of configuration settings applied by administrators to objects in the Active Directory store.
- A Group Policy Object (GPO) can contain Group Policy settings for sites, domains, or organizational units (OUs).
- A Group Policy Container (GPC) is an Active Directory object that stores the properties of a GPO and the sub containers for Group Policies that are associated with users and computers.
- Group Policy Template (GPT) is a folder structure used to store the Group Policy information for administrative templates, security settings, scripts, and software settings.

◆ The GPMC is a new Windows Server 2003 tool that combines the functionality of Active Directory Users and Computers, Active Directory Sites and Services, the ACL Editor, the Delegation Wizard, and the Resultant Set of Policy tool. GPMC is designed as a comprehensive tool for Group Policy administration for Windows 2000 and Windows Server 2003 domains. It provides administrators with the ability to backup, restore, import, and copy/paste GPOs, as well as to create, delete, and rename them.

◆ Every computer has one Group Policy Object that is stored locally. This Local Group Policy Object (LPGO) is applied first. GPOs assigned to the site will be processed next; then policies assigned to the domain will be processed, and finally, policies assigned to OUs and child OUs will be processed.

◆ Policy settings are cumulative due to inheritance. You can link a single GPO to multiple sites, domains, or OUs. The Group Policy settings that are finally assigned to a computer or user is the cumulative effect of all GPOs assigned to the site, domain, and OU to which the user or computer belongs.

◆ If a GPO is assigned to the parent container, but not the child container, the parent container GPO settings apply. If a GPO is assigned to both the parent container and the child container, and there is no conflict, both parent and child GPOs apply. If a GPO is assigned to both the parent container and the child container, and there is a conflict, the child container settings apply. However, if there is a conflict between a user setting and a computer setting, the computer setting is applied because computer settings take precedence over user settings when there is a conflict.

◆ You can block inheritance for the GPO links for an entire domain, for all domain controllers, or for a particular OU to prevent GPOs linked to higher sites, domains, or organizational units from being automatically inherited by the child container.

◆ The default order for processing Group Policy settings can also be changed by either enforcing the settings or by disabling the GPO link.

◆ When you set a GPO link to Enforced, you are specifying that the policy settings in the GPO link will take precedence over the settings for any child object. This gives the parent GPO link precedence so that the default behavior (the child container settings override the parent container settings if there is a conflict) does not apply. GPOs that are set to Enforced cannot have their inheritance blocked.

◆ When you disable a GPO link, you completely block that GPO from being applied for the selected site, domain, or OU. This disables the GPO only for the selected container object; it does not disable the GPO itself.

◆ When GPOs are linked to the same container object, the policies are evaluated based on the link order set on the Linked Group Policy Objects tab for the container object.

◆ The policy settings in the GPO with the lowest link order (link order 1) are processed last because it has the highest precedence and is used to settle a conflict.

◆ Group Policy can also be used to help resolve the most common problem with roaming user profiles: network bandwidth waste.

◆ Folder Redirection redirects local folders, such as My Documents, to a network share. Folder Redirection is especially beneficial to users because since their documents are on the network, they are always available as long as the user is connected to the network, regardless of the computer the user logs on to. Folder Redirection is also useful because systems that must be reconfigured at the system level, or that require reinstallation of the operating system, can redirect their data safely to a different location other than the local computer's hard disk.

◆ There are two Software Settings nodes: one under the User Configuration node and one under the Computer Configuration node.

Key Terms

A-G-DL-P strategy
Built-in domain local groups
Built-in global groups
Built-in groups
Built-in local groups
Built-in system groups
Computer Management console
Discretionary Access Control List (DACL)
Distribution group

Domain local group
Folder Redirection
Global group
Group
Group nesting
Group Policies
Group Policy Container (GPC)
Group Policy Management Console (GPMC)

Group Policy Object (GPO)
Group Policy Template (GPT)
Group scope
Local group
Members
Security group
Universal group

Test Yourself

1. A distribution group is used to:
a. Define permissions for resources and objects.
b. Manage and access resources on a domain.
c. Send e-mails to multiple users simultaneously.
d. Assign a predefined set of rights to users.

2. Multiple users in different locations need to access similar resources in multiple domains. Which is the best way to group these users?
a. Set the group scope to domain local.
b. Create a distribution group.
c. Set the group scope to universal.
d. Create a nondomain local group.

3. You are the domain controller of the cosmo.com domain. Multiple users access resources located on this domain. Which of the following groups can you create to manage the resources on the domain?
a. Domain local groups
b. Built-in global groups
c. Local groups
d. Built-in local groups

4. _____ groups are used to assign rights to users for performing tasks on a stand-alone server.
a. Built-in domain local
b. Built-in global
c. Built-in local
d. Built-in system

5. Windows Server 2003 has some predefined groups. The Server Operators built-in group can perform which of the following functions?
a. Modify user accounts and groups.
b. Share and backup disk resources.
c. Create OUs in Active Directory.
d. Modify GPOs.

6. Which of the following components or groups contain Group Policy settings for sites, domains, and OUs?

a. Group Policy Objects
b. Local groups
c. Group Policy Templates
d. Built-in groups

7. Which of the following is used to create Group Policy Objects for a domain?
a. Active Directory Sites and Services
b. Active Directory Domains and Trusts
c. Active Directory Users and Computers
d. Computer Management

8. You can modify software settings to:
a. Assign and publish applications.
b. Specify scripts and batch files.
c. Restrict user access to files and folders.
d. Regulate the Registry settings.

9. You want to restrict user access to the Registry and Event Log. Which of the following is the best way to restrict user access?
a. Apply Software Settings Group Policies.
b. Apply Administrative Templates Group Policies.
c. Apply Folder Redirection Group Policies.
d. Apply Security Settings Group Policies.

10. _____ are used to give users access to programs that they need on a Windows Server 2003.
a. Software policies
b. Security settings
c. Distribution groups

11. As the network administrator, you want to publish an application for all users in a domain. Which of the following components are used to publish an application?
a. The Computer Management console.
b. The Administrative Templates node in the Group Policy snap-in.
c. The User Configuration node in the Group Policy snap-in.

Projects: On Your Own

1. Create a local group on a member server with Domain Users as members.
a. Log on as an **Administrator** on a member server.
b. Open the **Computer Management** console.
c. Double-click **Local Users and Groups** to view the subfolders in the details pane.
d. Open the **New Group** dialog box.
e. Specify the name of the local group.
f. Specify the description of the local group.
g. Add the **Domain users** group to the local group.
h. Click the **Create** button to create the new group.
i. Close the Computer Management console.

2. Create a GPO on a server.
a. Log on to a server as an **Administrator**.
b. Open the **Group Policy Management** console.
c. Expand the **Forest** node. Expand the **Domains** node.
d. Right-click the domain name in the console tree and select **Create and Link a GPO Here**.
e. In the **New GPO** dialog box, type the Group Policy name, **Policy02,** in the **Name** text box and click **OK**.
f. **Policy02** is listed under the **Default Domain Policy** in the **GPO** column in the **Linked Group Policy Objects** list.
g. Close the **Group Policy Management** console.

3. Modify security settings to enable a user and the Administrators group to log on to servers locally.

a. Open the **Group Policy Management** snap-in.

b. Open the **Domains** node.

c. Right-click **Default Domain Policy** and click **Edit** to open the **Group Policy Object Editor**.

d. Open the **Windows Settings** node in the **Computer Configuration** node.

e. Double-click **Security Settings** to view the list of Security Settings policies in the details pane.

f. Double-click **Local Policies**.

g. Double-click **User Rights Assignment**.

h. Scroll down the **Policy** list and double-click **Allow log on locally**.

i. Select the **Define these policy settings** check box.

j. Click **Add User or Group** to open the **Add User or Group** dialog box.

k. Click **Browse** to open the **Select Users, Computers, or Groups** dialog box.

l. Click **Advanced**. Type **Jack** in the **Name** text box. Click **Find Now**.

m. The account you created for Jack M. Willis displays in the **Search results** list.

n. Click **OK** to close the **Select Users, Computers, or Groups** search dialog box.

o. The selected user is entered in the **Enter the object name to select** box.

p. Click **Advanced**. Click **Find Now**. Select **Administrators** in the Search results list.

q. Click **OK** to close the **Select Users, Computers, or Groups** search dialog box.

r. The **Administrators** group is added to the **Enter the object names to select** box.

s. Click **OK** to close the Select Users, Computers, or Groups dialog box.

t. The selected group and user are entered in the **User and group names** text box.

u. Click **OK** to close the **Add User or Group** dialog box.

v. The **Allow log on locally** user right has been assigned to **JWillis** and the **Administrators** group.

w. Click **OK** to close the **Allow log on locally Properties** dialog box.

x. Close the Group Policy Object Editor and the Group Policy Management console.

Problem Solving Scenarios

1. You are an administrator at Knowledge Charter Inc., an e-learning solutions company. The company's network has three Windows Server 2003 computers, 80 Windows XP Professional clients, and 20 Windows 98 clients. The designers in the company tend to use different computers in the network, depending on their assignment to different projects. To enable them to access their personal files, the designers have requested a shared folder on the network. The folder should allow them to store and access their personal design and artwork files from any computer on the network. Also, the folder should serve as a central repository for all design files created by the designers and should be backed up on a daily basis. Detail the steps you would take to implement this plan. [Hint: You need to create a shared folder named Design on the network file server and set up a Home folder in it. This folder should be accessible by all designers in the company.]

2. Pacifica Telecommunications Company employs temporary employees who take orders by telephone and enter customer data into a database. They use a proprietary call center software package for this purpose, which is installed on their computers. You are concerned about the security of the network and decide that you want to implement a Group Policy that enforces the following restrictions for the telemarketing users:

- Prevent users from mapping network drives.
- Prevent users from using My Network Places.
- Prevent users from making changes to the Taskbar and Start menu settings.
- Prevent users from accessing the Control Panel.
- Prevent users from right-clicking on the desktop and accessing the context menu.

List the steps you would take to create and implement this Group Policy as described above.

Introducing Computer Accounts

Computer accounts are an important and necessary part of Windows Server 2003 Active Directory. Just as user accounts are used to identify users, computer accounts are used to identify computers. They are also security principals. As a security principal, a computer account has a SID, which means it can be used to grant access to resources. When you give a computer account access to resources, either directly or through adding the account to a group, this gives all users who log on to the computer (except those who have been denied) access to those resources.

Additionally, computer accounts can be used to apply Group Policy. When you configure Group Policy settings in the Computer Configuration node, in the Group Policy Object Editor, those settings only apply to computer accounts. Therefore, you configure those settings for a Group Policy that is applied to a container (such as the entire domain or the domain controllers OU), which contains computer accounts. However, once applied, Computer Configuration Group Policy settings apply to all users logging on to those computer accounts, regardless of the OU the user account is in. This is an easy way to ensure that specific computers (such as kiosks) have specific settings, regardless of the user who logs on.

Each Windows Server 2003, Windows 2000, and Windows NT server computer in your environment must be given a computer account in order to participate in the domain. Similarly, each Windows XP Professional, 2000 Professional, and NT client computer must also be given a computer account.

Goals

In this lesson, you will learn how to create computer accounts using the Active Directory Users and Computers console, as well as how to create accounts automatically by joining the domain. You will also learn how to view and modify computer account properties using the Active Directory Users and Computers console. Next, you will learn how to find and move computer accounts using the Active Directory Users and Computers console. Finally, you'll learn how to avoid and correct common computer account difficulties, as well as how to reset computer accounts using the Active Directory Users and Computers console.

Lesson 8   Introducing Computer Accounts

Skill	Exam 70-290 Objective
1. Creating Computer Accounts	Create and manage computer accounts in an Active Directory environment.
2. Managing Computer Account Properties	Create and manage computer accounts in an Active Directory environment.
3. Locating and Moving Computer Accounts	Create and manage computer accounts in an Active Directory environment.
4. Troubleshooting Computer Accounts	Create and manage computer accounts in an Active Directory environment. Troubleshoot computer accounts. Diagnose and resolve issues related to computer accounts by using the Active Directory Users and Computers MMC snap-in. Reset computer accounts.

Requirements

To complete this lesson, you will need administrative rights on a Windows Server 2003 domain controller and a Windows XP Professional or Windows 2000 Professional client computer. You will also need an OU created in Active Directory called Marketing.

skill 1

Creating Computer Accounts

exam objective

Create and manage computer accounts in an Active Directory environment.

overview

tip

Windows 9.x, Windows 3.x, and DOS computers do not have computer accounts, as they do not support advanced security features.

As mentioned previously, a **computer account** is necessary for computers running the Windows Server 2003, Windows 2000, Windows XP, and Windows NT operating systems. The computer account in Active Directory is used to determine access rights for that computer and Group Policies applied to that machine, regardless of the user logged into the computer.

To create a computer account before the computer is added to the domain (i.e., preemptively), you use the Active Directory Users and Computers console. Right-click the destination container, point to **New**, and select **Computer** to create a new computer account in that container **(Figure 8-1)**. This will open the **New Object – Computer** dialog box, where you enter the computer name for the account and the Pre-Windows 2000 computer name for the account, also known as the NetBIOS name **(Figure 8-2)**.

Alternately, you can create a computer account in the default containers by simply joining a client or member server to a domain. Similarly, when installing Active Directory on a server, the new domain controller will have a computer account automatically created for it in the domain by the Dcpromo utility.

Note that in order to create computer accounts, your user account must be granted the **Add Workstations to Domain** right, or have the **Create computer objects** permission on the container that the account will be created in. By default, the Authenticated Users group has the Add Workstations to Domain right, which lets all users who have logged on to the domain create up to 10 computer accounts. However, if a user (or a group of which the user is a member) has the **Create computer accounts** permission in a container, the user can create an unlimited number of computer accounts in that specific container. Since the Enterprise Admins, Domain Admins, and Account Operators groups all have this permission for the entire domain by default, these groups can always create an unlimited number of computer accounts.

Figure 8-1 Using Active Directory Users and Computers to create a new computer account

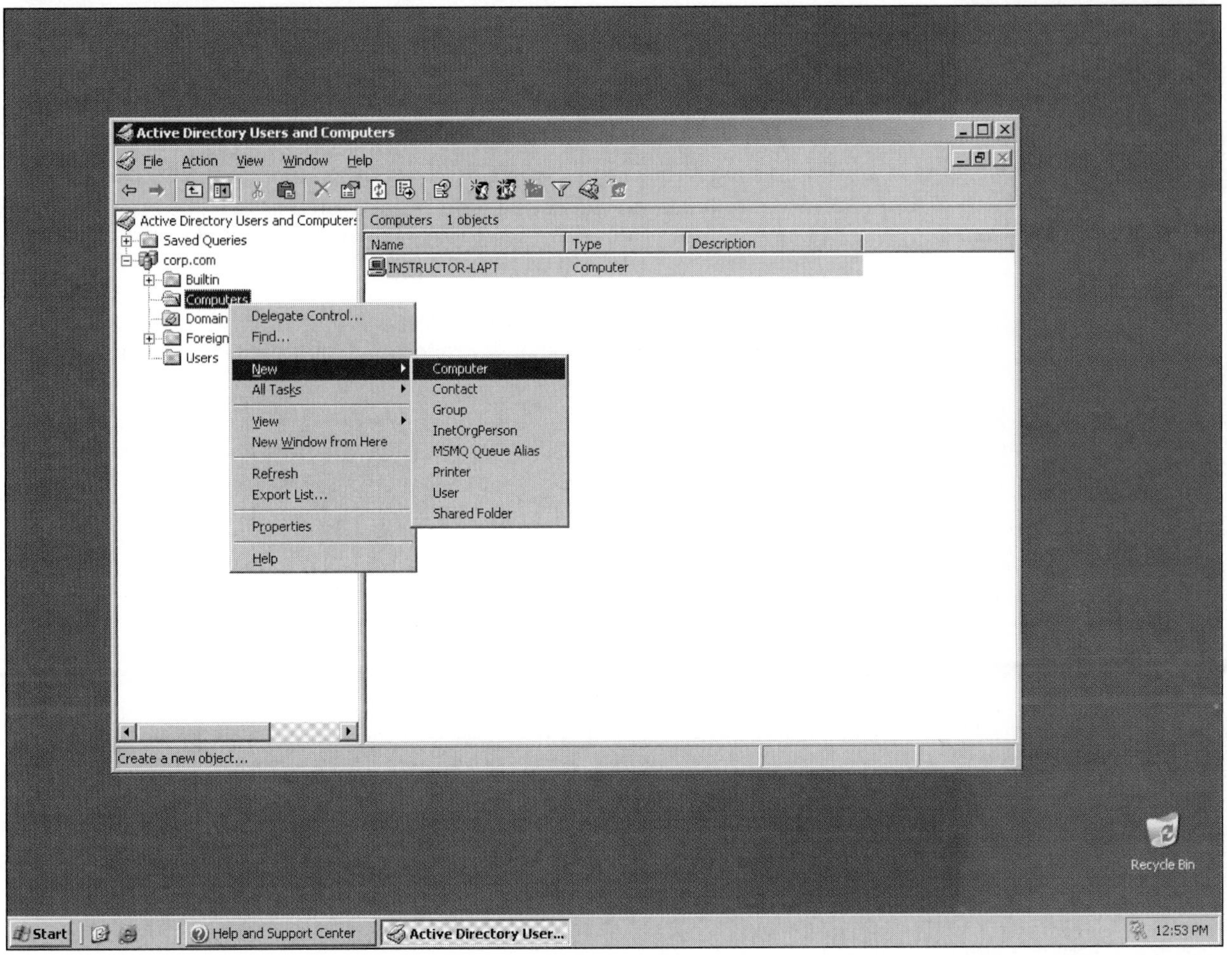

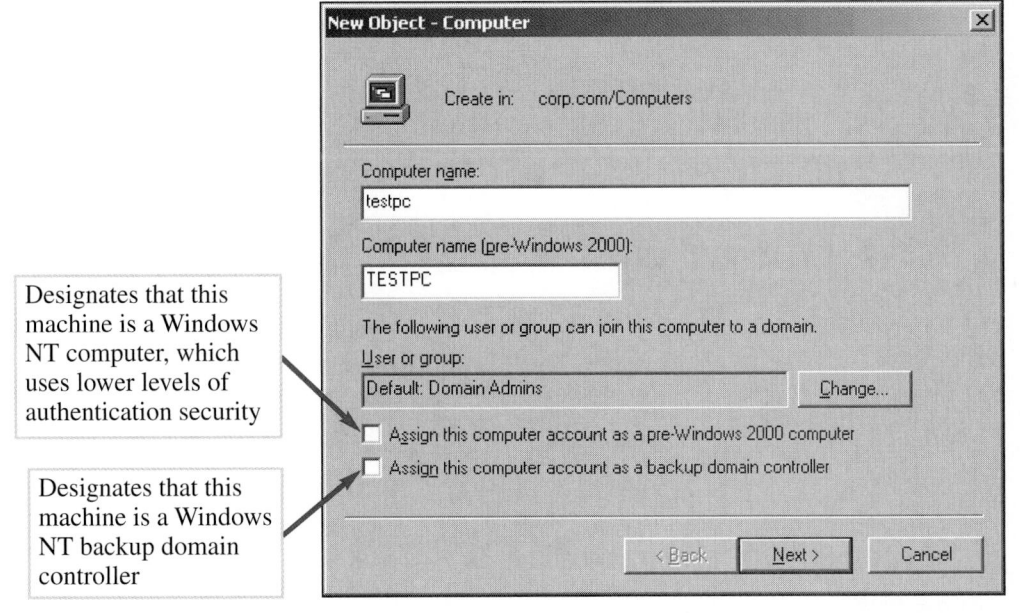

Figure 8-2 The New Object - Computer dialog box

Designates that this machine is a Windows NT computer, which uses lower levels of authentication security

Designates that this machine is a Windows NT backup domain controller

Exam 70-290

skill 1

Creating Computer Accounts (cont'd)

exam objective

Create and manage computer accounts in an Active Directory environment.

how to

Add a workstation to a domain and create its computer account automatically. (To perform this exercise, you will need to ensure that DNS is configured properly on your domain controller and that your workstation is configured to use the domain controller as its primary DNS server.)

1. Log on as an **Administrator** to your Windows 2000 Professional computer.
2. Right-click **My Computer** and choose **Properties** to open the **System Properties** dialog box.
3. Open the **Network Identification** tab (**Figure 8-3**).
4. Click [Properties] to open the **Identification Changes** dialog box (**Figure 8-4**).
5. Select the **Domain** option button and type the correct domain name in the text box.
6. Click [OK]. **The Domain Username and Password** dialog box will open, prompting you to enter a username and password for an account with rights to add a workstation to the domain (**Figure 8-5**). Type your Administrator account name and password, and click [OK].
7. A **Welcome to** *<domain_name>* dialog box will appear (**Figure 8-6**). Click [OK] to close the message box.
8. Click [OK] to close the System Properties dialog box. A message box will appear, telling you that you must restart the computer for the changes to take effect.
9. Click [OK] to restart the computer.

more

You can also preemptively create computer accounts using the command line application Dsadd.exe. To perform this operation, open a command prompt on the Windows Server 2003 computer and type **dsadd computer [distinguished name of computer]**, where the distinguished name is the full DN of the computer account. For example, the command **dsadd computer cn=pc1,cn=computers,dc=corp,dc=com** would add the PC1 computer account in the computers container of the corp.com domain.

Figure 8-3 The Network Identification tab on the System Properties dialog box (Windows 2000 Professional)

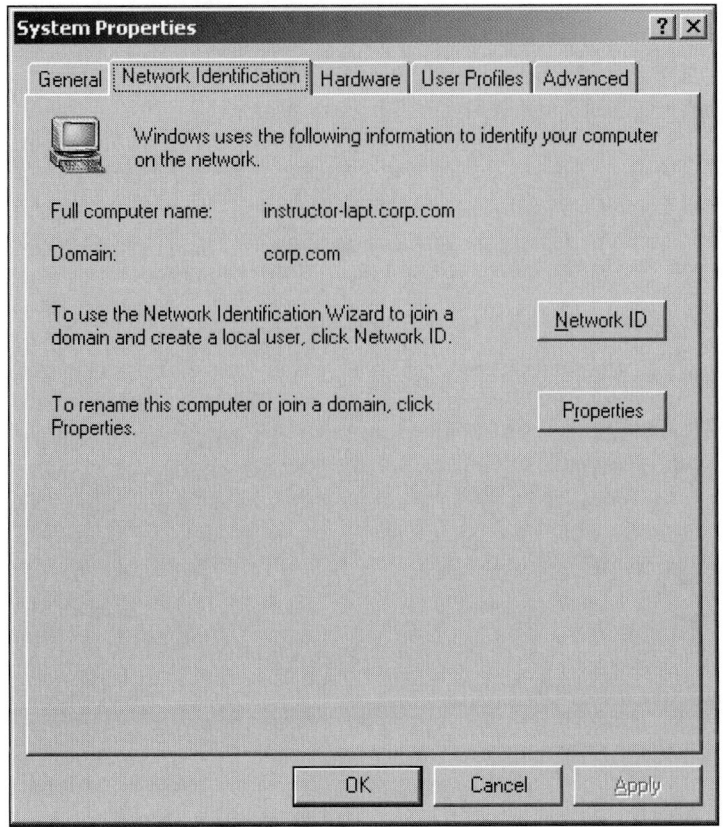

Figure 8-4 The Identification Changes dialog box (Windows 2000 Professional)

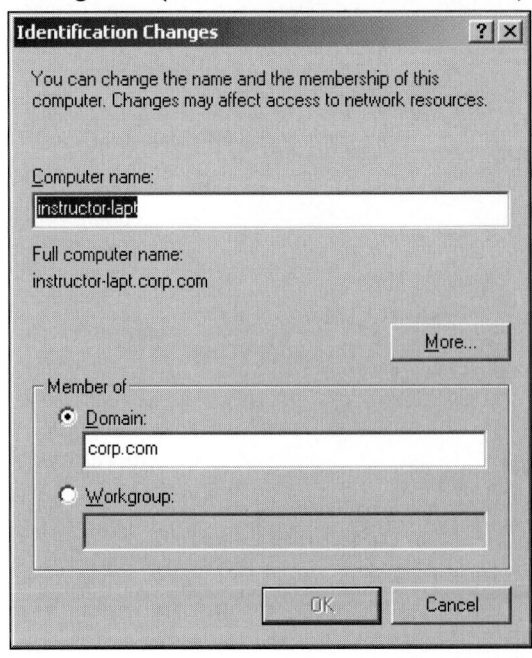

Figure 8-5 The Domain Username and Password dialog box

Figure 8-6 The Network Identification: Welcome to the domain message

skill 2

Managing Computer Accounts Properties

exam objective

Create and manage computer accounts in an Active Directory environment.

overview

After you create a computer account, you will be able to view and modify the properties of the account. Several of the account properties can be modified to allow for customization, while others are purely informative.

The Account Properties dialog box for a computer account includes the following tabs:

tip

In order to view the Object and Security tabs in the Properties dialog box for a computer account in the Active Directory Users and Computers console, open the View menu and select Advanced Features.

- ◆ **General:** Contains the basic information concerning the account such as the name, role, and description. On a Windows 2000 Native domain, this tab also includes the **Trust computer for delegation** check box, which allows you to define that this computer can perform services on other computers using the local system account. This option is typically used to allow servers to use the EFS encryption keys of clients to encrypt local files (needed when a client is encrypting a remote shared file on the server) (**Figure 8-7**).
- ◆ **Operating System:** This tab shows the operating system version and service packs used by the computer.
- ◆ **Member Of:** This tab shows the groups the computer is a member of and allows you to change the default group (only required in rare cases) (**Figure 8-8**).
- ◆ **Location:** This tab allows you to specify the location of the computer. Setting a location allows you to search for computer accounts based on the location field.
- ◆ **Managed By:** This is where you specify the manager responsible for the computer. This tab is informative only (the manager will gain no permissions over the account) (**Figure 8-9**).
- ◆ **Object:** On this tab, you can view object properties for the account, including the original and current **Update Sequence Numbers (USNs)**. This tab is only available when **Advanced Features** is enabled (**Figure 8-10**).
- ◆ **Security:** This allows you to configure the permissions associated with the account, thereby determining who can view and modify the account. This tab is only available when **Advanced Features** is enabled.
- ◆ **Dial-in:** Allows you to specify dial-in properties for the account, similar to the dial-in properties on a user account.
- ◆ **Delegation:** This tab is only available on Windows Server 2003 domains (**Figure 8-11**). After you have raised the functional level of your domain to Windows Server 2003, you select the **Trust this computer for delegation to any service (Kerberos only)** option to allow a computer to be trusted for delegation, and the option will no longer be included on the General tab. You must be a member of the Domain Admins or Enterprise Admins group or be delegated the appropriate authority in order to delegate trust. If you do not have a Delegation tab, you can register a **Service Principal Name (SPN)** for the computer account. You use the **Setspn** tool in the Support Tools folder on the Windows Server 2003 installation CD-ROM to register a service account. Only service accounts (not regular user accounts with User Principal Names [UPNs]) can perform delegation. SPNs are used to identify instances of a service. They often include the name of the computer that is running the service, in particular if there are multiple instances of a service running on multiple computers in a forest. SPNs can be used to request Kerberos tickets (See Lesson 12). They are required for mutual authentication.

**Figure 8-7 The General tab
(Windows 2000 Native domains)**

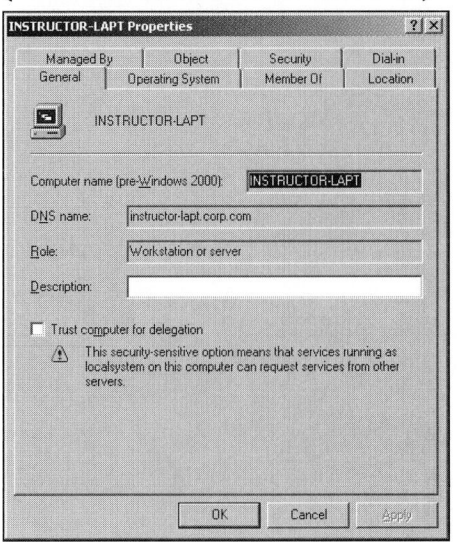

Figure 8-8 The Member Of tab

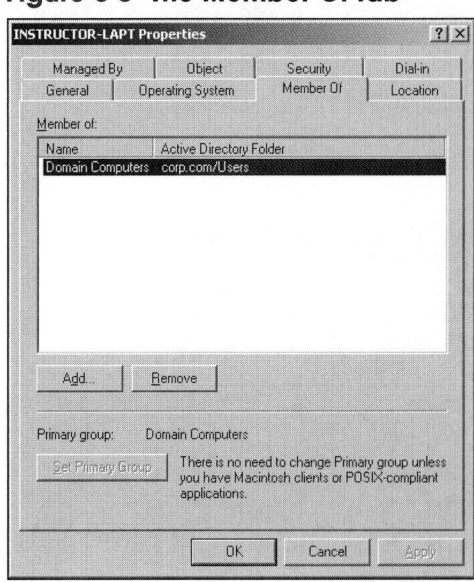

Figure 8-9 The Managed By tab

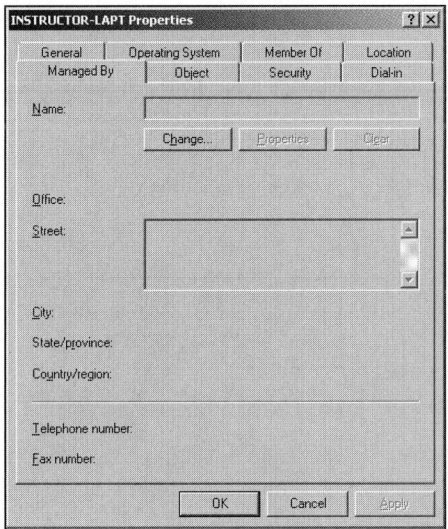

Figure 8-10 The Object tab

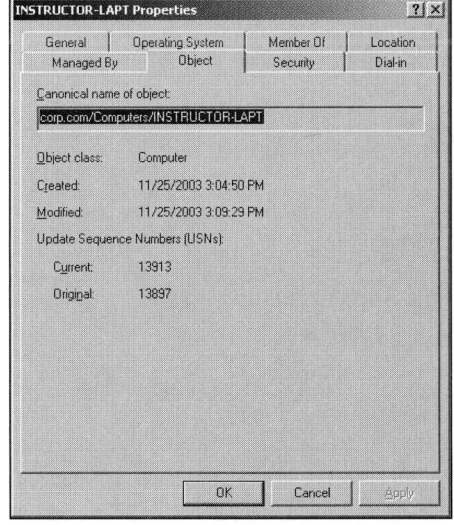

**Figure 8-11 The Delegation tab
(Windows Server 2003 domains)**

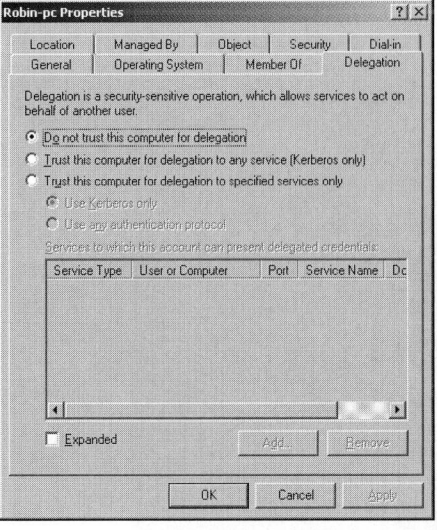

skill 3

Locating and Moving Computer Accounts

exam objective

Create and manage computer accounts in an Active Directory environment.

overview

By default, computer accounts for member servers and clients are created in the Computers container in the domain. Similarly, computer accounts for domain controllers are created in the Domain Controllers OU by default.

In some cases, you may find that it is advantageous to move these accounts to another location. For example, you may have custom Group Policies applied to your custom OU structure. In order for the computer accounts to inherit these Group Policies, they must be moved into the appropriate OUs.

You move computer accounts in the Active Directory Users and Computers console. Simply select the computer account or accounts that you wish to move, right-click them, and select **Move** to open the **Move** dialog box **(Figure 8-12)**. Then, select the appropriate OU. Alternatively, you can simply select the accounts and drag them into the appropriate OU.

You may also find that you are having difficulty finding a particular computer account. Windows Server 2003 Active Directory includes powerful search functionality that can help you in this case. Simply right-click the component of Active Directory that you wish to search in (such as a specific OU or the entire domain) and click **Find (Figure 8-13)**. Choose **Computers** in the **Find** list box and type the name (or partial name) of the computer in the **Computer name** text box. You can also search based on the role of the computer (Workstation/Server or Domain Controller) **(Figure 8-14)**.

how to

Move the previously created computer account into the Marketing OU and search for it.

1. Log on to your domain controller.
2. Click **Start**, point to **Administrative Tools**, and click **Active Directory Users and Computers**.
3. Click the **Computers** container and select the account you created in Skill 1.
4. Drag the account into the Marketing OU in the scope pane of the console. This will move the computer account into that OU.
5. Right-click your domain name and select **Find** to open the **Find Users, Contacts, and Groups** dialog box **(Figure 8-13)**.
6. Select **Computers** in the **Find** list box and type the name (or part of the name) of the computer in the **Computer name** text box.
7. Click **Find Now** to find the computer account **(Figure 8-14)**.
8. Close the **Find Computers** dialog box.

Figure 8-12 The Move dialog box

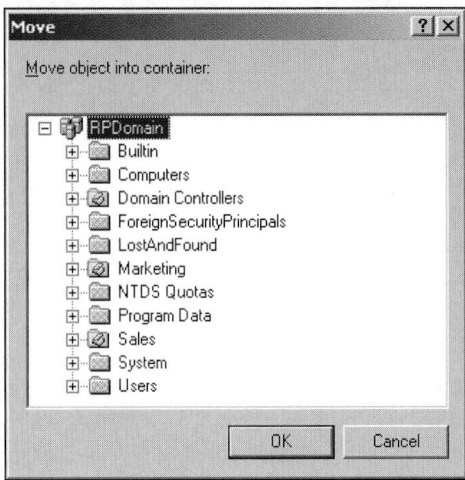

Figure 8-13 Opening the Find Computers dialog box

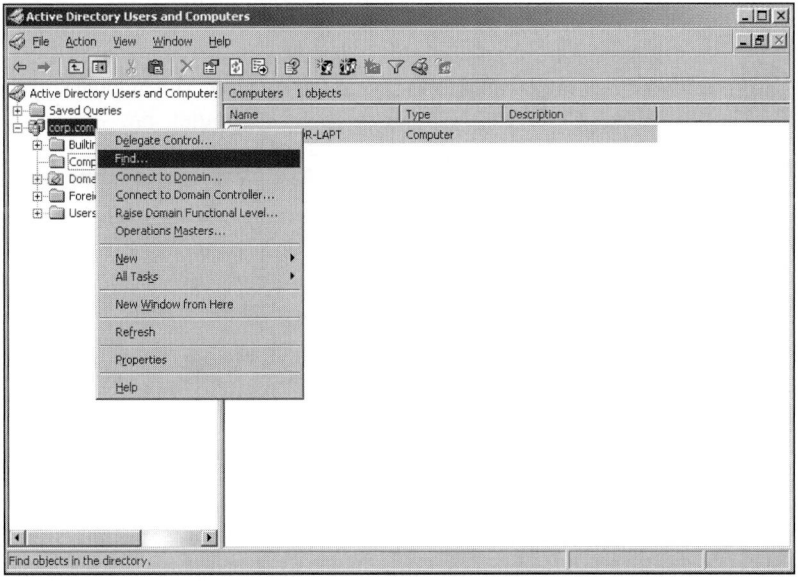

Figure 8-14 The Find Computers dialog box

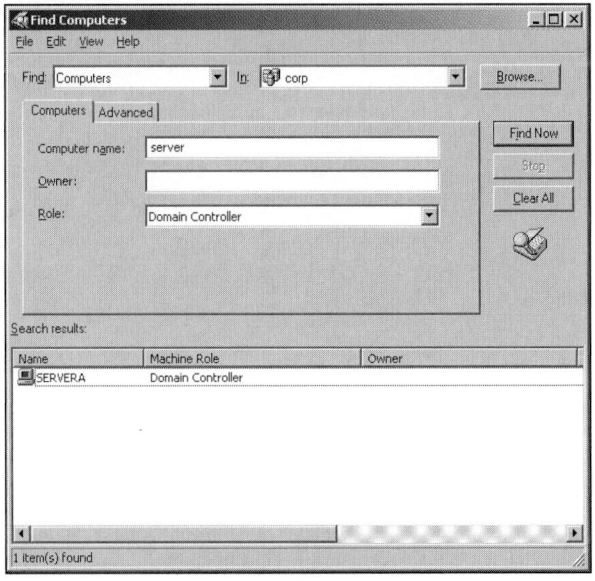

skill 4

Troubleshooting Computer Accounts

exam objective

Create and manage computer accounts in an Active Directory environment. Troubleshoot computer accounts. Diagnose and resolve issues related to computer accounts by using the Active Directory Users and Computers MMC snap-in. Reset computer accounts.

overview

Occasionally, you may have problems related to your computer accounts. While rare, these problems do sometimes occur. In most cases, the solution to the majority of computer account-related problems is simply to recreate the account. However, let's examine some of the more common issues and the methods used to resolve them.

First, you should understand that, like user accounts, computer accounts have passwords. The password for a computer account is used to establish secure communications between the computers in a domain. Therefore, while it is, for the most part, a hidden function, problems related to the computer account password can cause very real problems.

By default, the computer account password is changed by the Netlogon service every 7 days. When the service changes the password, it notifies the domain controller, ensuring that the correct password is propagated to the entire domain. One possible problem, then, is that a laptop computer that has been used offline for longer than 7 days may reconnect to the network and not be able to log on to the domain. This happens because the Netlogon service has changed the password for the local computer, but since it was not connected to the network at the time, the domain controllers are not aware of the change. Therefore, when they try to authorize the computer, they assume it must be an imposter, since it has an incorrect password. The simplest solution to this problem is, typically, to remove the computer from the domain (in the System Properties dialog box, as in Skill 1) and rejoin it (using the same process). This same problem can occur if you do not reboot the client within 10 minutes after changing its domain membership.

Other conditions that can cause these same problems include restoring the computer's configuration using an outdated (older than 7 days) System State backup, or Automated System Recovery (ASR) backup set (See Lesson 13), and the mistaken deletion of the computer account from the domain controller.

In all of these cases, simply recreating the computer account will resolve the problem. However, in some cases, this is not feasible (such as when this problem occurs on a domain controller). In these cases, you can reset the computer account password in Active Directory Users and Computers. Simply right-click the computer account and select **Reset** (**Figure 8-15**). This will force a password reset on the computer account, which should resolve the problem as long as the account was not deleted.

Figure 8-15 Resetting a computer account

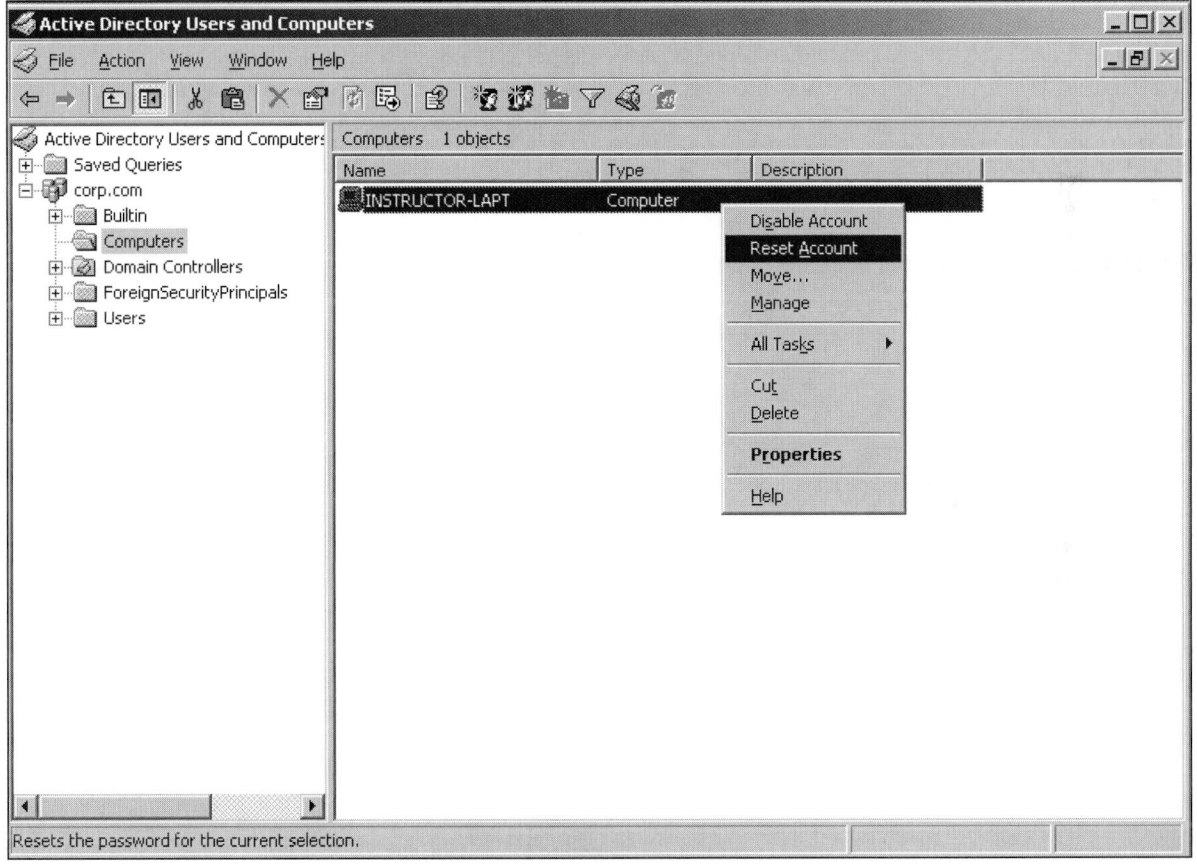

Summary

- Computer accounts are necessary for computers running the Windows Server 2003, Windows 2000, Windows XP, and Windows NT operating systems.
- The computer account in Active Directory is used to determine access rights for that computer and Group Policies applied to that computer, regardless of the user logged on to the computer.
- To create a computer account preemptively (before the computer is added to the domain), you use the Active Directory Users and Computers console.
- You can create a computer account in the default containers by simply joining a client or member server to the domain.
- To create computer accounts, your user account must be granted the Add Workstations to Domain right, or have the Create computer objects permission on the container that the account will be created in.

- After you create a computer account, you will be able to view and modify the properties of the account in the Active Directory Users and Computers console.
- By default, computer accounts for member servers and clients are created in the Computers container in the domain. Similarly, computer accounts for domain controllers are created in the Domain Controllers OU by default.
- Moving computer accounts can be accomplished using the Active Directory Users and Computers console.
- In most cases, the solution to computer account-related problems is simply to recreate the account or leave and rejoin the domain.
- The password for a computer account is used to establish secure communications between the computers in a domain.

Key Terms

Computer account
Service Principal Name (SPN)
Update Sequence Number (USN)

Test Yourself

1. You can create a computer account using: (Choose all that apply.)
   a. Dsadd.exe
   b. Server Manager
   c. The Active Directory Users and Computers console
   d. The Active Directory Domains and Trusts console

2. You allow a user to join his Windows XP workstation to the domain. A few hours later, the user calls back and complains that he cannot log on to the domain from that computer, but he can log on from other computers with no problem. What could be the cause of the problem? (Choose all that apply.)
   a. The user did not properly join the the computer to the domain.
   b. The user's workstation is not running SP1.
   c. The Name field on the Managed By tab has not been set properly for the computer account.
   d. The user waited longer than 10 minutes to reboot the workstation after joining the domain.

3. What do you need to do to display the Object tab on the Properties dialog box for a computer account?

   a. The Active Directory Schema console must be installed.
   b. The computer must be running either the Windows XP or Windows Server 2003 operating system.
   c. Advanced Features must be enabled in Active Directory Users and Computers.
   d. Dsadd.exe must be used to create the account.

4. Which of the following actions can cause computer account-related problems? (Choose all that apply.)
   a. Deleting the account on the domain controller.
   b. Moving the account out of the Computers container.
   c. Not rebooting within 10 minutes after joining the domain.
   d. Remaining offline for more than 7 days.

5. Which tab on the Properties dialog box for a computer account includes the Trust computer for delegation check box?
   a. The Object tab
   b. The Security tab
   c. The General tab
   d. The Member Of Tab

Test Yourself

6. By default, all authenticated users in the domain can create up to how many computer accounts?
a. Unlimited
b. None
c. 10
d. 15

7. Computer accounts are required for: (Choose all that apply.)
a. Windows 98 workstations
b. Windows Server 2003 servers
c. Windows NT 3.51 workstations
d. Windows 98 ME workstations

Projects: On Your Own

1. Preemptively create a new computer account using the Active Directory Users and Computers console.
a. Log on to your domain controller.
b. Open the **Active Directory Users and Computers** console.
c. In the **Computers** container, right click an empty area and choose **New > Computer**.
d. Name the computer account **TestPC**.
e. Close the **New Object – Computer** dialog box.

Problem Solving Scenarios

1. You are the administrator for Greenline Insurance, a small insurance agency. You have a single Active Directory domain, greenline.com, with a single site representing your company's only current office. Your company is expanding into new markets, and is creating four new satellite locations. New agents will be hired for these locations, and given laptops with Windows 2000 Professional installed. It is your job to create computer accounts for 20 new agents. Each computer account will need to be placed or moved into one of the four new OUs created to support the new locations. Explain how you would go about creating these accounts and configuring them to support the requirements. Make sure you think about potential problems that may arise along the way, and how to resolve them.

Installing and Configuring Network Printers

One of the most important, cost-saving advantages of a network is that it enables you to share print resources among multiple users. Shared print devices allow users on a network to print documents to the shared print device from their own machines, even though they are not physically connected to the printers. Thus, each client does not need its own expensive hardware device. Local printers spool to a location on the local hard disk. Network printers, on the other hand, spool to a location on the network print server.

A print server is a computer that handles requests for service for shared printers. A print server can administer these requests through either a print device physically connected to it via a COM, LPT, or USB port, or through a print device connected to the network using a built-in network card or a device interfacing the network to an LPT1 style connector. The print server receives the requests, spools them, uses a printer driver (software containing information used by operating systems to convert print commands for one model of print device into a printer language) to translate the digital documents into printer code, and sends those codes to the print device.

There are several ways you can connect to a network printer. One option is the Add Printer Wizard, which is also used to configure a logical printer on your computer when you connect a local print device to it. Another option is to browse My Network Places to locate the printer on the print server. The print server is the computer running Windows Server 2003 or other server software that controls the printer functions. A network printer can be configured to include the printer drivers for several versions of Windows that can be automatically down-loaded across the network. In this scenario, once you locate the network printer, you simply right-click on it and choose Connect. If available, the drivers will be automatically down-loaded and installed to the local computer. This feature is commonly known as Point and Print.

After you install a network printer, you can assign permissions to users or groups to control access. When there are many print devices on your network that can receive instructions from the same type of print driver, you can create a printer pool. A printer pool is a single printer that can queue print jobs to multiple ports and their associated print devices. Print pooling allows you to connect multiple print devices to a server and manage them as though they were a single print device. Print jobs will be allocated to the first available print device.

Printer priority is set when multiple configured printers use a common print device. You set printers as high-priority or low-priority to control the order in which their print jobs will be sent to the print device. You can use this functionality to give precedence to particular individuals or groups. By assigning a priority to a printer, you can make sure that critical documents print before other documents. For example, if you have two logical printers and only one print device, and you want one printer's documents to take priority, you can configure this printer to have a higher priority so that its print jobs will be completed first.

Managing printers also involves managing documents to be printed. For example, when one printer fails, you can transfer the print jobs to another print device. Printers, by default, are also published in Active Directory, which makes it easier for users to locate the different printers on a network and enables administrators to manage them from a central location. Users can also search to find printers based on their characteristics.

An administrator can use the System Monitor's Print Queue object and various counters to monitor printer performance. Statistics gathered by these counters can help administrators to identify network printing problems.

Goals

In this lesson, you will learn how to install and configure network printers using Windows Server 2003. You also will learn how to assign printer permissions, create a printing pool, manage printer priorities, and monitor the performance of a network printer. Finally, you will learn how to publish printers in Active Directory and troubleshoot printer-related problems.

Lesson 9 Installing and Configuring Network Printers

Skill	Exam 70-290 Objective
1. Introducing the Windows Server 2003 Network Printing Environment	Troubleshoot print queues.
2. Installing a Network Printer	Basic knowledge
3. Controlling Access to Printers	Basic knowledge
4. Creating a Printer Pool	Basic knowledge
5. Setting Printer Priorities	Basic knowledge
6. Monitoring Printer Performance	Monitor file and print servers. Tools might include Task Manager, Event Viewer, and System Monitor. Monitor print queues.
7. Publishing Printers in Active Directory	Basic knowledge
8. Troubleshooting Printer Problems	Monitor file and print servers. Tools might include Task Manager, Event Viewer, and System Monitor. Troubleshoot print queues.

Requirements

To complete this lesson, you will need administrative rights on a Windows 2003 member server.

skill 1

Introducing the Windows Server 2003 Network Printing Environment

exam objective

Troubleshoot print queues.

overview

Network administrators must manage network printing, printer availability, and printer security. A shared printer is an object, just like a folder, that can be shared with other network users. Print devices can be attached to servers, client workstations, or network printing devices that connect directly to the network with no attached computer. Network printing devices include both box-like devices that attach to the network on one end, and to one or more print devices on the other, and cards that are installed on a print device. Network interface print devices have their own NIC (network interface card) and network address, or an external network adapter connection.

Before you learn to install and configure network printers, you must first understand Microsoft's printing terminology.

- ◆ **Printer:** A **printer** is the software interface that delivers the request for service from the operating system to the physical print device. It is the configuration object that controls the connection to the print device, and it can be shared with other network users just like any other another resource stored on the hard drive.
- ◆ **Print device:** The term **print device** refers to the physical hardware that actually prints data.
- ◆ **Print server:** A **print server** is a computer, such as a Windows Server 2003 computer, that is connected to and sharing one or more print devices. It is used to print documents and to manage the printers on a network. The performance of your network printing depends largely on the print server. Therefore, it is essential that print servers satisfy memory and disk space requirements. **Table 9-1** describes the memory, disk space, disk speed, and network card requirements for a print server.
- ◆ **Printer driver:** A **printer driver** is the software that contains the information used by the operating system to convert the print commands for a particular model of print device into a printer language such as Printer Control Language (PCL) or PostScript. The driver translates a high-level view of the printed document, called a metafile, into the printer language understood by the print device. It tells the operating system what attributes the print device has and what print commands it follows so that documents can be properly printed.
- ◆ **Spooling:** The term **spooling** refers to the process of caching the print request to a hard disk, which releases the application quicker. For example, without spooling, when you print a document, the application can only send the document to the printer at the printer's pace. This means that the application will typically sit idle, basically unusable, until the printer completes the job. However, with spooling, the application is released as soon as the document finishes spooling. From here, the operating system will send the document to the printer in the background, allowing your application to resume normal functionality.
- ◆ **Spool:** A **spool** is a folder where converted print jobs are stored before they can be printed. The list of print jobs from different workstations stored on the spooler on the print server forms a print queue **(Figure 9-1)**.
- ◆ **Print queue:** A **print queue** is a list of print jobs from different workstations that is stored on the spooler of the print server. You can observe the status of the print queue by double-clicking the printer icon in the Printers and Faxes window or by clicking the printer icon that may appear in the system tray when you send a print command from your workstation. The printer window displays the print queue for a single printer only.

Table 9-1 Print Server Requirements

Requirements	Explanation
Memory	To make sure that a print server can process a large number of documents and manage several printers, you must make sure that it has enough random access memory (RAM). The amount of memory you need will depend on the number of print devices you connect to the server, and the number and complexity of the print jobs that are sent to the printer. If the print server does not have enough memory, the speed with which documents are printed will decrease considerably. In most cases, simply keeping an eye on the amount of available physical memory using either the Performance console or the Task Manager will be sufficient. When you reach 20% or less free physical memory, it is time to upgrade the amount of RAM in the server.
Disk space	To enable the print server to process print jobs, you must make sure that it has enough disk space to store documents until it sends them to a print device. For example, if the users in your organization send large numbers of large documents to be printed at the same time, your print server must have enough disk space to hold all of the documents. For instance, if the users sent a total of 200 documents, each 64 MB in size on average, your total disk space requirements, solely for spooling, would be 1.2 GB (64 MB times 200). If disk space is inadequate, errors will occur and users will not be able to print their documents.
Disk speed	Most high-performance print servers include a hardware RAID-5 array. When spooling is done to such an array, it can be considerably faster than it would be with a single disk (as much as 6 times faster).
Network Card	Depending on your print architecture, for network printers, the network can be a limiting factor. Where possible, use a high speed network card (100 Mbs or 1000 Mbps) and connect printers onto a switch. Additionally, consider ensuring that the network connecting the print server to the printing devices is as free from other traffic as possible.

Figure 9-1 Documents in a print queue

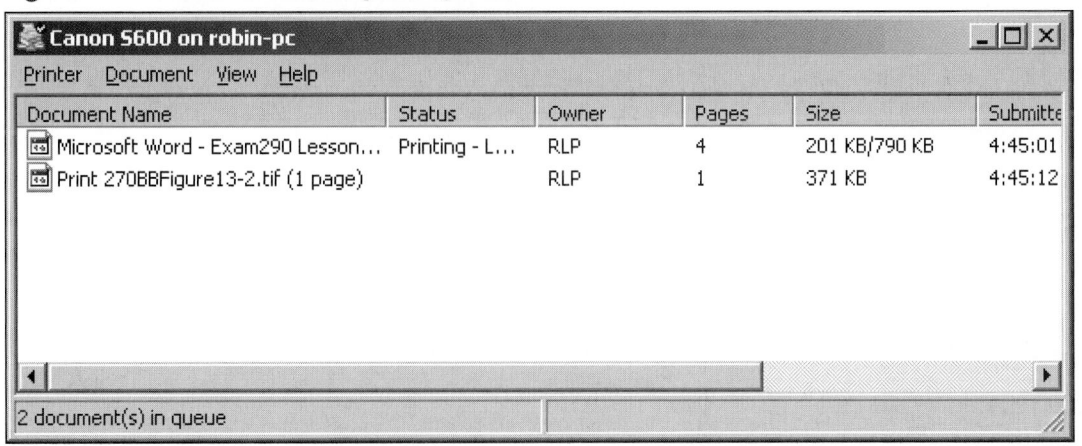

skill 1
Introducing the Windows Server 2003 Network Printing Environment (cont'd)

exam objective

Troubleshoot print queues.

overview

◆ **Graphics Device Interface (GDI):** The **GDI** controls the creation of any visual output for the operating system, either to the monitor or to the printer. The GDI must combine data such as the word-processing codes for the file, the embedded objects in the file, and the colors and fonts for the file with data that it gets from the printer driver on the client. This procedure is called **rendering**. The GDI must format the print file with control codes so that the correct graphics, color, and font attributes are configured. The rendering process produces a high-level view of the printed output called a metafile. The metafile is converted to the print output by the driver.

A print device can be accessed through a print server using one of the following methods:

◆ **Using a local print device:** A **local print device** is any device for which the spooling is done locally. The printer (software) is loaded locally on the computer, and all print functions are handled by the local computer.
◆ **Using network print devices:** A **network print device** is a device for which the spooling is done remotely. Workstations connect to these printers over the network, and all print jobs are sent from the workstation to the print server, which controls all printing to the print device. This allows for more expensive printers to be shared by multiple users. It also allows for centralized control of the print queue and printer permissions settings.

The principal distinction between network printers and local printers, in Microsoft terminology, is where the spooling takes place. Local printers spool to a location on the local hard disk. Network printers, on the other hand, spool to a location on the network print server.

When you plan the configuration of your network printing, you should attempt to provide all users with fast, convenient printing while using the fewest number of print devices. The criteria in **Table 9-2** will help in determining the placement and number of network printers.

more

As you learned above, spooling refers to the process in which documents, or metafiles, are stored on a disk until a printer is ready to accept them. First, the software application places the print file on the client's spooler by writing a spool file that is saved in a subfolder specifically for the spooling process. If the print server is ready to render to metafile, the print file is sent from the client's spooler folder to the Server Service on the Windows Server 2003 print server. Then, the Server Service contacts the Print Spooler service. The print router, a component of the Print Spooler service (Winspool.drv), sends the print file to the print provider, which stores it in the print server's spool file until the print device is ready to execute the print job. While the file is spooled on the print server, the print provider and the print processor make sure that it is formatted with the correct data type. The data type for a print job specifies if the print job must be modified and how it must be modified so that it will print correctly. This must be done because a Linux client and a Windows 2000 Professional client will not create a print job in the same way. The spool file will only be sent to the print device when it is completely formatted. After the file has printed, the print monitor removes the spool file from disk storage and transmits it to the print device.

Each new printer that you install is assigned to the spool directory by default. The path to the spool directory is **%systemroot%\System32\Spool\Printers**. You can move the spool directory to another location by specifying a different path in the **Spool folder** text box on the **Advanced** tab in the **Print Server Properties** dialog box **(Figure 9-2)**. To open the Print Server Properties dialog box, click the **Server Properties** command on the **File** menu in the **Printers and Faxes** window **(Figure 9-3)**. This is how you change the location of the spool

Table 9-2 *Criteria for determining number and placement of network printers*

Criterion	Explanation
Number of Users	As the number of users on a network increases, the workload on the print server and print devices increases. You may need to add more printers, print devices, or print servers to keep abreast of increasing demand.
Printing requirements of the organization	This will vary depending on both the volume of printing and the type of printing activities. Sometimes, even when there are few users on the network, an organization's printing requirements will be extensive. For example, a Sales department consisting of 5 users may need to bulk print invoices. You may need to have two or more print devices available for such a department. In contrast, a team of 15 Web designers may use printers rarely, because most of their work is saved on their workstations and they have very little need for printed output. This group of workers may only need one print device. In addition, you will need to select different types of print devices for different departments. For example, you will likely purchase a color printer for a Graphics department, whereas an Accounts Receivable department may only need a black-and-white laser printer for printing bills.
Location of print devices	Place print servers and print devices on the same segment as the workstations that will use them, when possible, to increase efficiency. Print devices should be positioned in convenient locations so that users can easily collect their documents.

Figure 9-2 The Advanced tab in the Print Server Properties dialog box

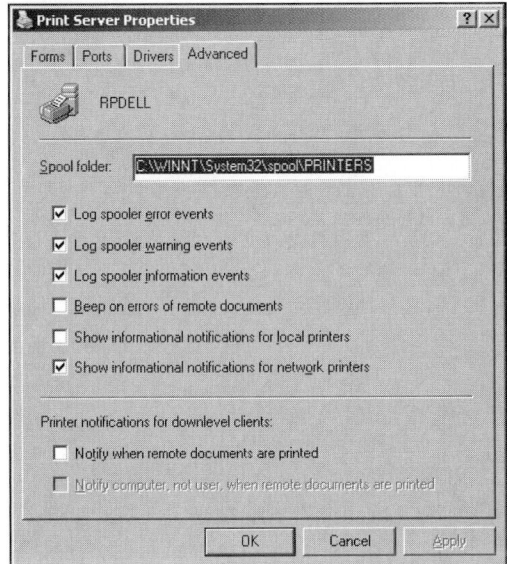

Figure 9-3 The Server Properties command on the File menu in the Printers and Faxes window

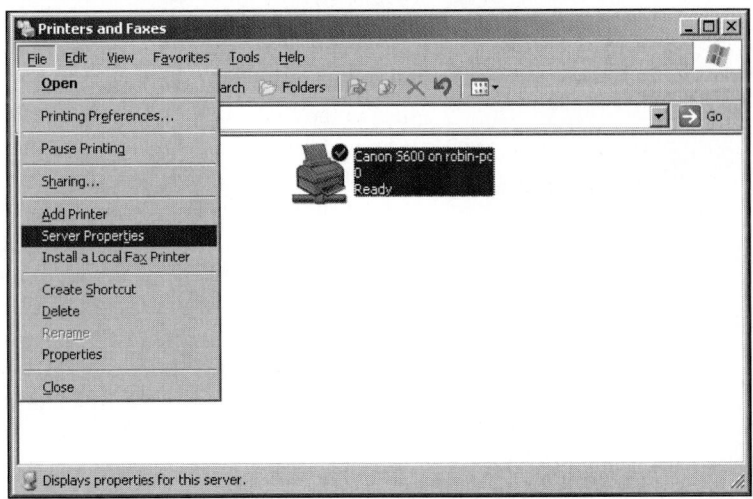

skill 1

Introducing the Windows Server 2003 Network Printing Environment (cont'd)

exam objective

Troubleshoot print queues.

more

folder for all printers on the print server. You will often want to move the spool folder to a different partition from the Windows system files if the print server supports many printers or if it must be able to handle large print jobs. By changing the location of the spool folder for all printers, you can increase free space on the system partition and improve operating system performance. When you specify a new location, do not use the root folder of a drive. For example, do not simply enter **F:**. Instead, you should always create a new folder, because if you use only the root of a drive, the default **%systemroot%\System32\Spool\Printers** folder will be used. Instead, always specify a new folder, for example, **F:\NewSpoolFolder**. After you change the spool folder location and click **OK**, a warning message will inform you that changes to the spool folder will occur immediately and any currently active documents will not print. Make sure that all documents have already printed before changing the location of the spool folder. Then, you can safely click **Yes** in the warning message box. Don't forget to make sure that users have NTFS permissions assigned to access the folder if you are moving it to an NTFS volume or partition. Then, stop and restart the Spooler service, or reboot the server.

To move the spool folder for a specific printer only, you must edit the Registry. First, you must create a new folder on the volume or partition you want to use. You must be logged on as an Administrator. Then, open the **Run** dialog box, enter **regedit** in the **Open** text box, and press **[Enter]**. In the Registry Editor, locate and select the Registry key: **HKEY_LOCAL_MACHINE\SOFTWARE\Microsoft\WindowsNT\CurrentVersion \Print\Printers\PrinterName** (where PrinterName is the printer whose spool folder you want to move). Locate the **SpoolDirectory** value in the details pane of the Registry Editor and double-click it to open the **Edit String** dialog box. In the **Value data** text box, enter the path to the new spool folder you created and click **OK (Figure 9-4)**. If you are moving a spool folder to an NTFS volume or partition, always make sure that users have NTFS permissions assigned to access the folder.

Sometimes a print job will not process correctly and this can create gridlock in the print queue. Occasionally, you may also not be able to delete the file in the usual way (right-click the job and select **Cancel** or select **Cancel All Documents** on the **Printer** menu in the print queue). When this happens, it usually means the job itself is corrupt and must be deleted manually. In this case you can stop the print spooler service, delete the document from the **%systemroot%\System32\Spool\Printers** directory (**Your Folder Options** must be set to view hidden and system files), and restart the spooler. You can either delete all .spl and .shd files in the folder or look for the files that were created at the date and time for the job you want to delete and delete only those files. After the spooler is restarted, users can resubmit the document for printing. To stop the print spooler, open the **Services** console (Start-Administrative Tools-Services) You can also open the Computer Management console; the Services snap-in is located in the Service and Applications node. Double-click **Print Spooler** in the details pane to open the **Print Spooler Properties (Local Computer)** dialog box. Click the **Stop** button to stop the service. You can also right-click **Print Spooler** in the details pane, point to **All Tasks**, and click **Stop**. Print commands, including **net stop** can also be run from the command prompt. The **net stop spooler** command will stop the print spooler. The other print commands you can run from the command prompt are shown in **Table 9-3** and demonstrated in **Figure 9-5**.

Table 9-3 Running Print commands from the Command Prompt

Command	Syntax	Function
print	print [/d:device] [drive:][path] filename Example: To print the text file unattend.txt in the Deploy folder on the C drive to a printer on parallel port LPT1: **print /d:LPT1 C:\Deploy\unattend.txt**	To print a text file or display the contents of a print queue.
net print	net print **\\computer\sharedprintername** use the /hold switch with the job #: net print **\\computer\sharedprintername** job # **/hold** use the **/release** switch with the job #: net print **\\computer\sharedprintername** job # **/release** use the **/delete** switch with the job # net print **\\computer\sharedprintername** job # **/delete**	To display or control print jobs and printer queues. To hold a print job so that it stays in the printer queue and other print jobs bypass it until you release it. To release a held print job. To remove a print job from the print queue.
net use	net use syntax examples: net use LPT1: **\\Server01\Printer1** net use LPT1: With no parameters, net use displays a list of all network connections	To connect to or disconnect from a shared printer or display information about computer connections. To redirect print output from the LPT1 port to Printer01 on the print server Server01. To display information about the LPT1 port.
net start	net start [service] Service names with two or more words must be enclosed in quotation marks. net start net start spooler	To start a service or display a list of started services. To display a list of running services. To start the print spooler service.
net stop	net stop [service] net stop spooler	To stop a service. Other dependent services may also need to be stopped. Dependent services will be listed and you will be prompted to confirm that you want them to stop also. To stop the print spooler service.

Figure 9-4 The Edit String dialog box

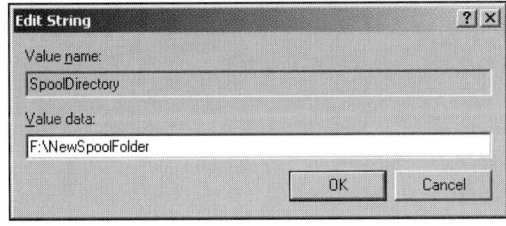

Figure 9-5 Running Print commands at the command prompt

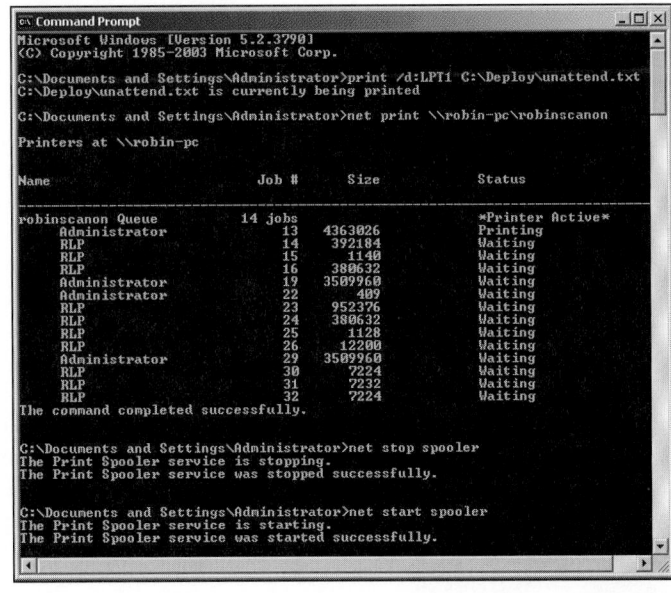

skill 2

Installing a Network Printer

exam objective

Basic knowledge

overview

tip

It is not necessary to physically connect the print device to set up the network printing infrastructure.

To create a network printer, you install the printer locally on the computer that is to become the print server. The printer is then shared to make it accessible to users over the network. First, you connect the print device to the local print server. Then, you must install the printer software (the printer). To install local printers, you use the **Add Printer Wizard** on your local computer (**Figure 9-6**). This wizard detects the print device and automatically configures the printer. Certain other settings, such as sharing the printer and publishing the printer in Active Directory, are also configured during the installation process. You can administer the printers you install in the Printers and Faxes window.

how to

tip

To start the Add Printer Wizard, you can also point to Control Panel, point to Printers and Faxes, and click Add Printer.

Install a local printer. (In this exercise, you will create a local HP 2500C Series printer and share it as Printer A. This will make the printer available to users over the network.)

1. Log on to a member server as an **Administrator**.
2. Click ⊞ **Start**, and click **Printers and Faxes** to open the **Printers and Faxes** window.
3. Double-click the **Add Printer** icon to initiate the **Add Printer Wizard** (**Figure 9-6**).
4. Click ⬛ **Next >** to open the **Local or Network Printer** screen.
5. Select the **Local printer attached to this computer** option button, if necessary.
6. Clear the **Automatically detect and install my Plug and Play printer** check box to disable automatic detection, since this is simply an exercise and you are not really installing an attached device.
7. Click ⬛ **Next >** to open the **Select a Printer Port** screen.
8. The **Use the following port** option button and the **LPT1** option are selected by default. Accept the default to use the LPT1 port for communication with the local printer (**Figure 9-7**).
9. Click ⬛ **Next >** to open the **Install Printer Software** screen.
10. Scroll down the **Manufacturer** list and select a manufacturer, in this case, **HP**.
11. Scroll down the **Printers** list and select a printer model, in this case **HP 2500C Series**. Note that all printer drivers that have been digitally signed are marked with a green check.
12. Click ⬛ **Next >** to open the **Name Your Printer** screen (**Figure 9-8**).
13. Accept the default name, **HP 2500C Series**, which has been automatically entered in the **Printer name** text box.
14. Click ⬛ **Next >** to open the **Printer Sharing** screen.
15. Click the **Share name** option button, if necessary, to share the printer over the network. Type **PrinterA** in the **Share name** text box (**Figure 9-9**). The shared printer name should follow a naming convention to help identify the printer on the network. Generally, you should keep the shared printer name short.
16. Click ⬛ **Next >** to open the **Location and Comment** screen.
17. Type **Office 508**, **Floor 7** in the **Location** text box to specify general information about the physical location of the printer.
18. Click ⬛ **Next >** to open the **Print Test Page** screen.
19. Click the **No** option button to specify that you do not want to print a test page for this exercise as you may not actually have the local printer attached to the computer. Normally, printing a test page is recommended.
20. Click ⬛ **Next >** to open the **Completing the Add Printer Wizard** screen. This screen provides a summary of the settings for the selected printer.
21. Click ⬛ **Finish** to complete the process of installing a local printer. After the printer is installed on the print server, users on the network can connect to it and send print jobs.

Figure 9-6 The Add Printer Wizard

Figure 9-7 Selecting a printer port

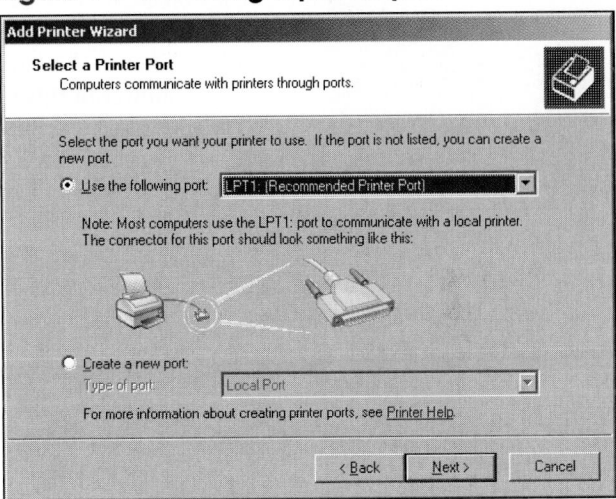

Figure 9-8 Assigning a printer name

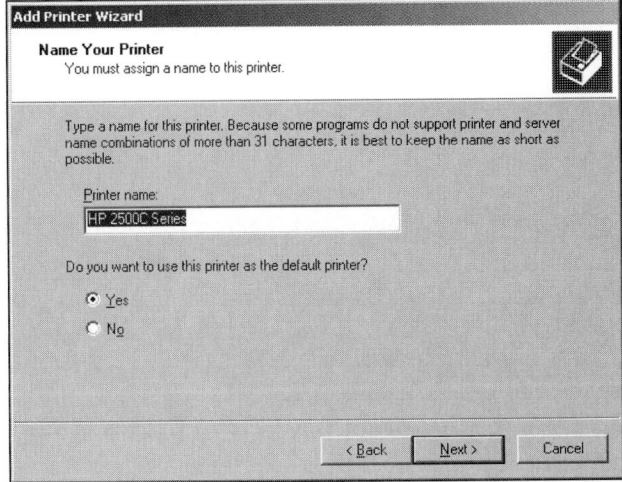

Figure 9-9 Sharing a printer

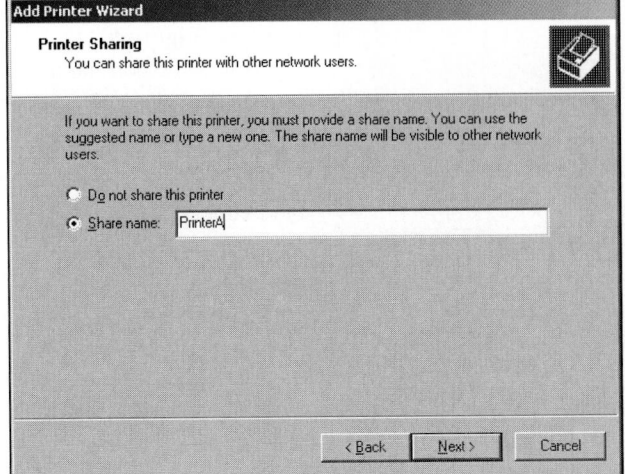

skill 2

Installing a Network Printer (cont'd)

exam objective   Basic knowledge

more

If you want your member server to connect to a print server on your network, you use the Add Printer Wizard to create the logical printer that will connect you to the shared print device. You will choose the **A network printer, or a printer attached to another computer** option button on the **Local or Network Printer** screen. The **Specify a Printer** screen will open next. If you are on an Active Directory network and the printer has been published, select the **Find a printer in the directory** option button to open the **Find Printers** dialog box, which you can use to search Active Directory for a printer based on its name, location, or model. You can also select the **Connect to this printer (or to browse for a printer, select this option and click Next)** option button and enter the UNC pathname for the shared printer, or simply click Next in order to browse the network to locate the *<printservername\sharename>* of your choice. Finally, you can select the **Connect to a printer on the Internet or on a home or office network** option button and enter the URL for a remote print device, such as a print device at a branch office of your company, to connect to it over the Internet or over your intranet. As long as you have permission for an Internet printer, you can connect to it using its URL.

You can also use My Network Places to locate and connect to a shared print device just as you would a shared folder. Alternatively, you can use the Run command on the Start menu and enter the UNC pathname in the Open text box.

If the client computers are running Windows Server 2003, Windows 2000, or Windows XP, the driver needed to deliver the requests for service from the operating system to the physical print device will be automatically installed. As long as a copy of the driver is stored on the print server, Windows 95, 98, Me, and NT 4.0 will also automatically download the appropriate driver. If there are any Windows 3.x clients or non-Windows clients, you will have to install the correct print drivers. Some non-Windows clients will also need print services, for example, Print Services for Macintosh.

Many organizations today have network-interface print devices which connect to the Internet using a network interface card (NIC). For these devices, which are not attached to a print server, you must configure a TCP/IP port to enable communication over the network. On the **Local or Network Printer** screen, you will select the **Local printer attached to this computer** option button. Then, on the **Select a Printer Port** screen, you will select the **Create a new port** option button, and select **Standard TCP/IP Port** in the **Type of port** list box **(Figure 9-10)**. When you click the Next button, the **Add Standard TCP/IP Printer Port Wizard** will open. On the **Add Port** screen, you will have to enter either the IP address or FQDN (fully qualified domain name) for the print device in the **Printer Name or IP Address** text box **(Figure 9-11)**. When you enter an IP address, the operating system automatically enters it as the port name in the **Port Name** text box. After you have created the new TCP/IP port, the Add Printer Wizard will resume so that you can complete the installation just as you did in the exercise for a local printer.

You can also configure a TCP/IP port for a network-interface print device on the **Ports** tab in the **Properties** dialog box for the print device. Simply click the **Add Port** button and select **Standard TCP/IP** port in the **Printer Ports** dialog box **(Figure 9-12)**. Click the **New Port** button to initiate the **Add Standard TCP/IP Port Wizard (Figure 9-13)**. Once again you will have to enter either the IP address or the FQDN name for the print device. In the final dialog boxes of the wizard, you will install and set up the port so that the logical printer will send its instructions to an IP address rather than a local port.

Figure 9-10 Creating a new standard TCP/IP port

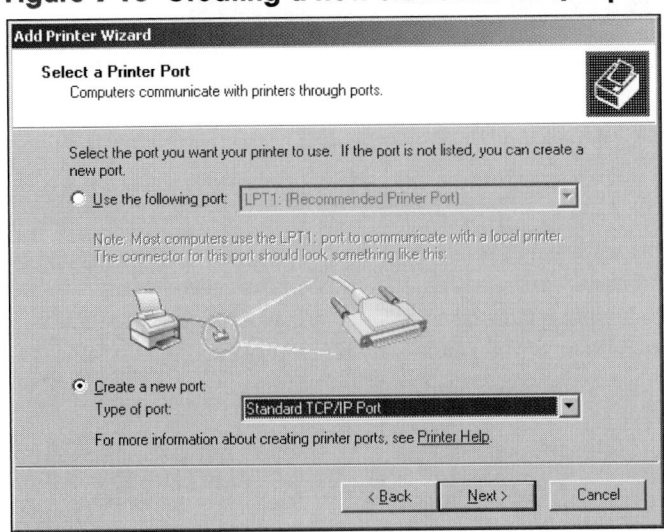

Figure 9-11 The Add Port screen

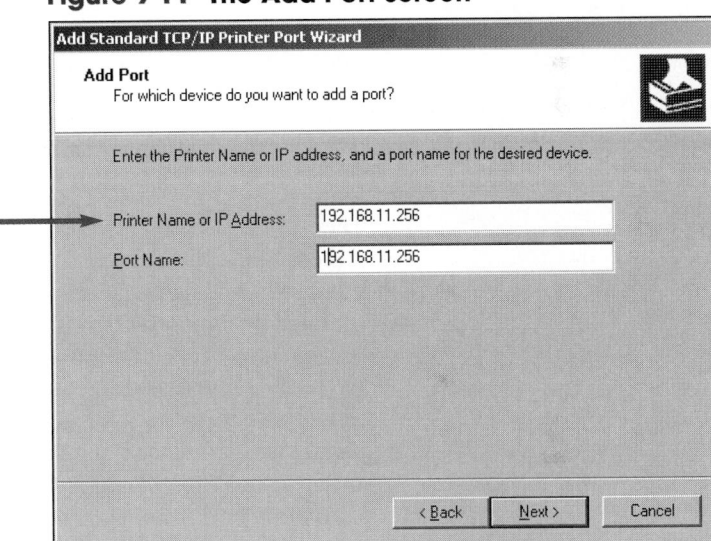

Enter either the IP address or FQDN for the print device

Figure 9-12 The Printer Ports dialog box

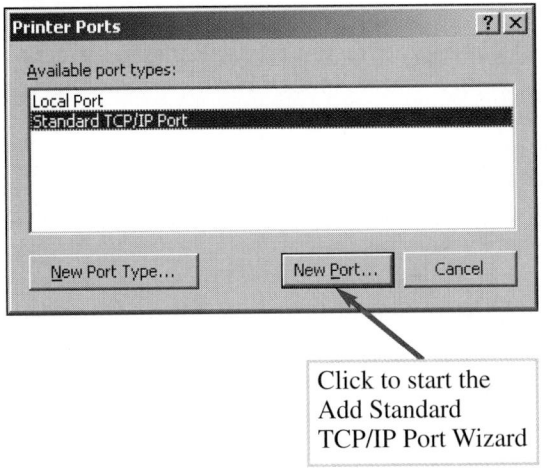

Click to start the Add Standard TCP/IP Port Wizard

Figure 9-13 The Add Standard TCP/IP Port Wizard

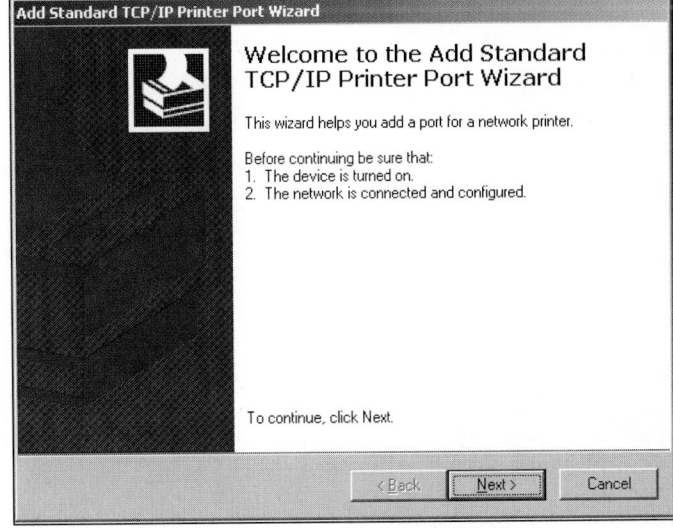

skill 3

Controlling Access to Printers

exam objective

Basic knowledge

overview

After you install a shared printer, it is ready for use. However, for security reasons, you may decide to restrict certain types of printer usage to certain users. For example, you may decide that only a Print Administrator should be allowed to monitor printer usage and troubleshoot printer problems. To control printer usage, you can modify the security settings for a printer by assigning permissions. Printer permissions can restrict:

◆ Who can print to a printer.
◆ Who can manage a printer.
◆ Who can manage the documents sent to a printer.

To prevent unauthorized access to a network printer, you must assign permissions. You can allow or deny printer permissions to a user or a group. Permissions that are denied override specifically allowed permissions for a user or group. When you deny a permission to a group, make sure that the group does not contain users who should be allowed that permission through membership in another group.

The types of printer permissions are listed below. Printer permissions are assigned on the **Security** tab in the Properties dialog box for the printer (**Figure 9-14**).

◆ **Print:** Users with the Print permission can connect to a printer and send it print jobs. They can also pause, resume, restart, or cancel their own print jobs. The Print permission is the lowest level of access. By default, the Print permission is assigned to the **Everyone** group, which includes all network users.

◆ **Manage Documents:** Users with the Manage Documents permission can pause, resume, restart, and cancel all other users' printing jobs. They can connect to a printer and control job settings for all documents, but they cannot control the status of the printer. They cannot share a printer, change printer properties, delete printers or change printer permissions. By default, the Manage Documents permission is assigned to the owner of each document (the **Creator Owner** group). Members of the **Print Operators**, **Server Operators** and **Administrators** groups can also manage documents because they are given all three permissions by default.

◆ **Manage Printers:** The Manage Printers permission, which is the highest level of access, grants a user administrative control over a printer. Users with this permission can pause and restart the printer, share a printer, change printer permissions, change printer properties, change printer drivers, or delete a printer. The Manage Printers permission is assigned to **Administrators**, the **Print Operators** group and the **Server Operators** group by default.

tip

To change printer permissions for a group or user, you must be either the owner of the printer or have the **Manage Printers** permission.

how to

Assign ownership of a printer and assign permissions to users and groups.

1. Click [Start], and then click **Printers and Faxes** to open the **Printers and Faxes** window.
2. Right-click the **HP 2500C Series** icon and select **Properties** to open the **HP 2500C Series Properties** dialog box. Alternatively, you can select the printer, open the **File** menu, and select the **Properties** command.
3. Open the **Security** tab, and click [Advanced...] to open the **Advanced Security Settings for HP 2500C Series** dialog box.
4. Click the **Owner** tab, and select [Other Users or Groups...] to open the **Select User, Computer, or Group** dialog box. Your domain name should be selected in the **From this location** box.

Figure 9-14 Assigning printer permissions

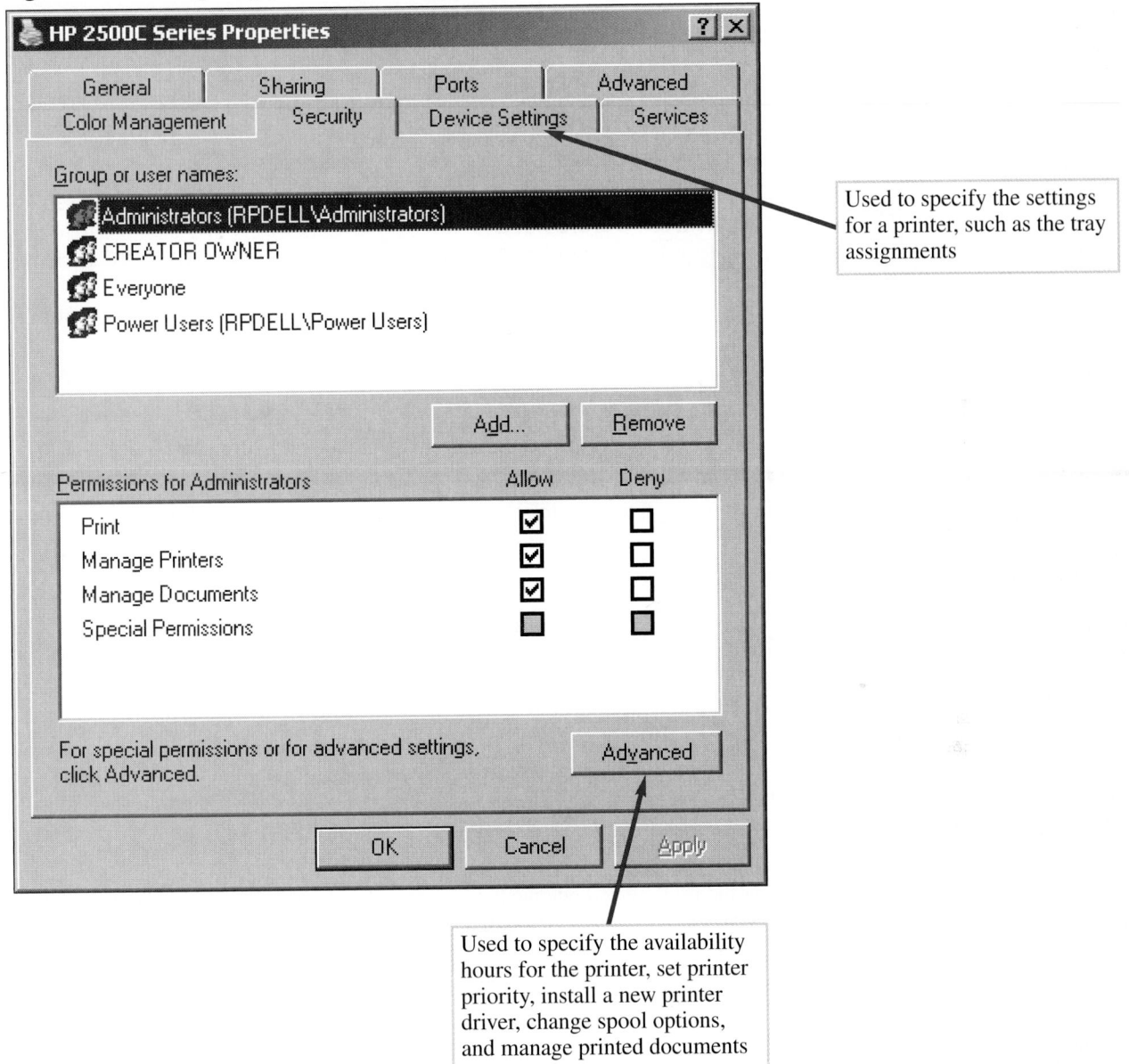

Used to specify the settings for a printer, such as the tray assignments

Used to specify the availability hours for the printer, set printer priority, install a new printer driver, change spool options, and manage printed documents

skill 3

Controlling Access to Printers (cont'd)

exam objective

Basic knowledge

how to

5. Click [Advanced...] to expand the dialog box. Click [Find Now] to list the users, groups, or built-in security principals in the domain.
6. Scroll down the search results list and select **Print Operators**. Click [OK].
7. **Print Operators** is added to the **Enter the object name to select** box. Click [OK].
8. Click [Advanced...] to reopen the **Advanced Security Settings for HP 2500C Series** dialog box. Open the **Owner** tab. **Print Operators** is now entered in the **Current owner of this item** box (**Figure 9-15**).
9. Click [OK] to close the Advanced Security Settings for HP 2500C Series dialog box.
10. In the HP 2500C Series Properties dialog box, click [Add...] on the Security tab to open the **Select Users**, **Computers**, **or Groups** dialog box.
11. Enter a user or group name in the **Enter the object names to select** box (**Figure 9-16**), and click [OK] to add the user to the **Group or user names** list in the Properties dialog box. The user or group is given the Print permission by default.
12. With this user's or group's name still selected, select the **Allow** check box for the **Manage Documents** permission in the **Permissions** list.
13. Click [OK] to close the HP 2500C Series Properties dialog box.

more

When a user installs a printer, he or she becomes the owner of the printer with rights to administer and assign permissions for the printer. In certain situations, administrators may need to take ownership of a printer (following the steps in the exercise above), for example, if the owner of a printer is transferred to another office. To take ownership of a printer, you must be a member of a group that has the **Manage Printers** permission for the printer. This permission is assigned by default to the **Administrators**, **Print Operators**, and **Server Operators** groups on a Windows Server 2003 printer, as well as to the **Administrators** and **Power Users** groups on a Windows XP Professional printer.

Users may also need to perform a variety of printing tasks such as pausing, resuming, and canceling the printing of documents. For example, if you send the wrong document to be printed, you can cancel the print job. If a printer is malfunctioning, you can pause it while you fix the problem and resume printing when the problem is resolved. To pause all print jobs, open the Printers and Faxes window, right-click the printer icon, and select the **Pause Printing** command. To resume all print jobs, select the **Resume Printing** command (**Figure 9-17**).

To pause a particular document, double-click the printer icon, right-click the document, and select **Pause (Figure 9-18)**. Use the [Shift] or [Ctrl] key to select multiple documents. To resume printing specific documents, double-click the printer icon, right-click the documents you want to resume and select **Resume**.

To cancel all documents, right-click the printer icon and select the **Cancel All Documents** command (**Figure 9-19**). To cancel one or more specific documents, double-click the printer icon, right-click the documents, and select the **Cancel** command. To restart a print job, right-click the documents and select the **Restart** command.

Figure 9-15 Changing the ownership of a printer

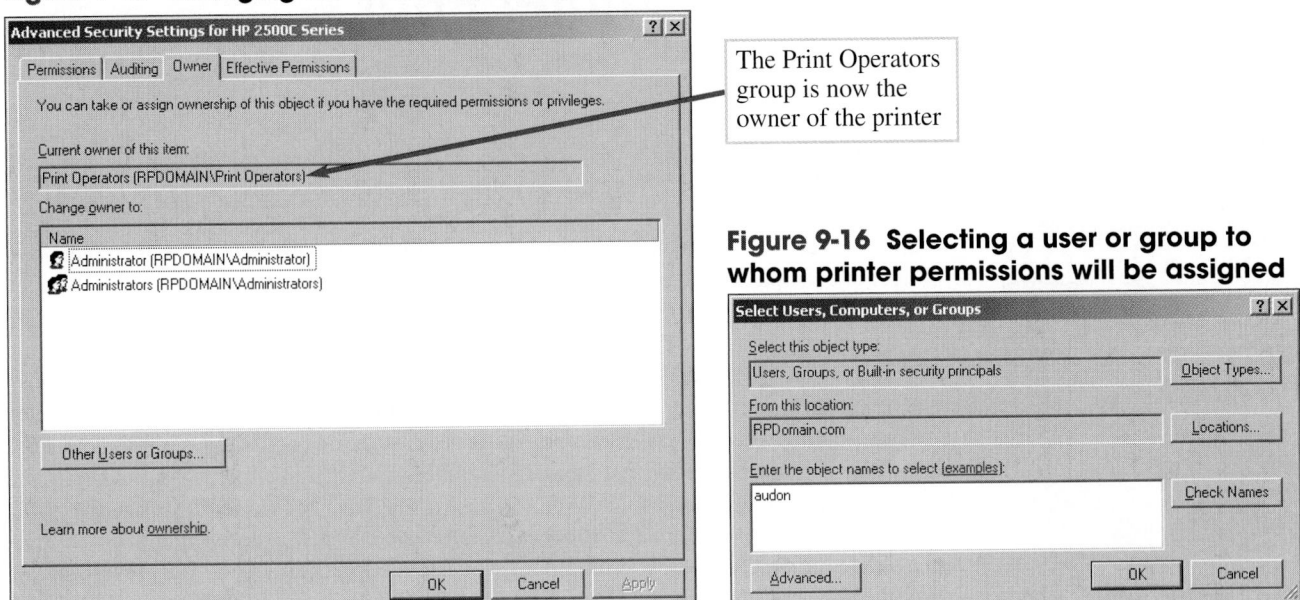

The Print Operators group is now the owner of the printer

Figure 9-16 Selecting a user or group to whom printer permissions will be assigned

Figure 9-17 Resuming all print jobs

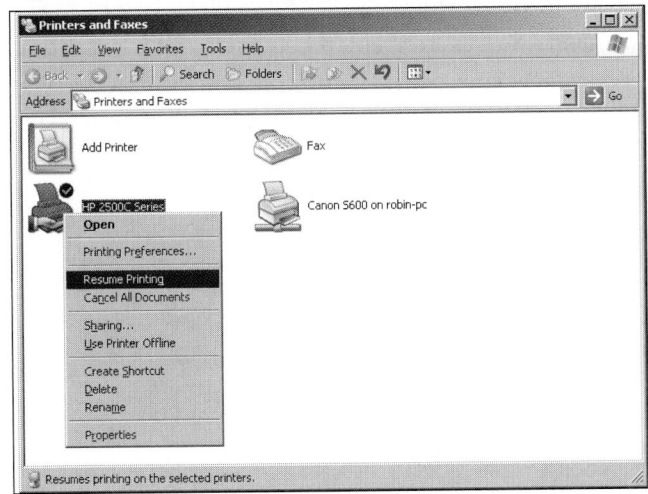

Figure 9-18 Pausing a single document

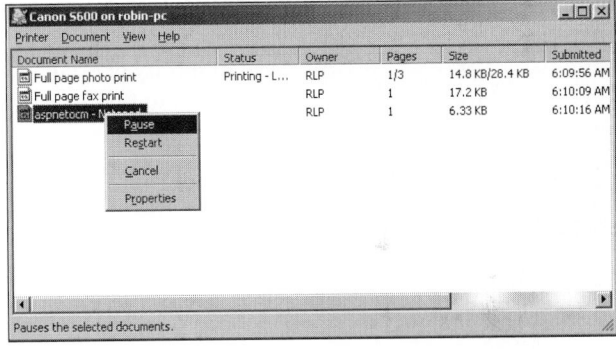

Figure 9-19 Canceling all documents

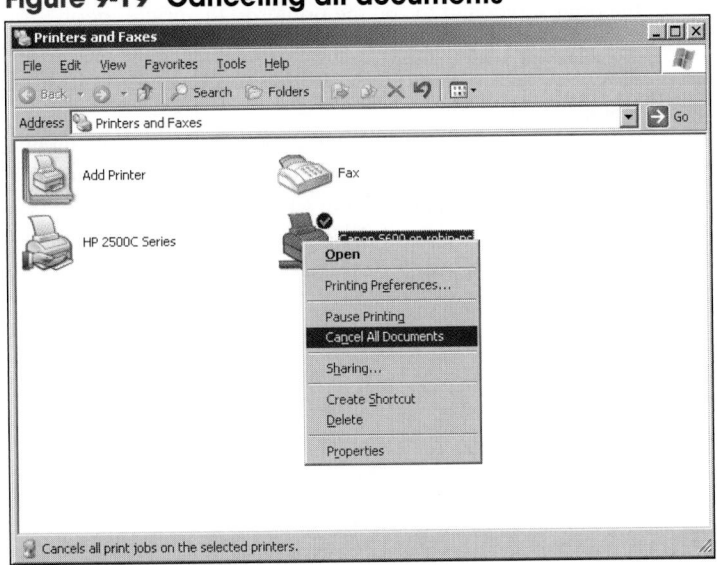

skill 4

Creating a Printer Pool

exam objective

Basic knowledge

overview

Windows Server 2003 offers various print server options that are used to manage network printing. For example, if you connect more than one print device to your print server, you may want the server to distribute print jobs automatically to the print devices so that no single print device becomes overloaded. You can create a **printer pool** so that all print jobs that the print server receives are distributed equally among the available print devices. A printer pool is a single printer on a print server that is associated with multiple physical print devices. You can use printer pooling when you have a number of the same type or similar types of print devices, which all use the same driver so that they can all understand the same sets of commands. Print jobs that are sent to a printer pool will be directed to the least busy print device in the pool. This is a benefit to the administrator because he or she can manage multiple print devices from a single printer. To create a printer pool, you use the **Ports** tab on the **Properties** dialog box for the printer. At the bottom of the tab, select the **Enable printer pooling** check box and select all of the ports to which you want the logical printer to print. When you enable printer pooling, you cannot control which print device will receive the job; therefore, it is helpful to have the print devices near each other so that your employees can easily find their documents.

A printing pool decreases the time spent by users waiting for their documents to print. Users can take advantage of a printer pool without any additional effort. In fact, the user does not need to specify or even be aware of the available print device. It is the job of the printer on the print server to find an available port and send the documents it receives to that port.

tip

When you create a printing pool, you can only add print devices that use the same printer driver.

tip

Using header pages will also help employees identify their documents.

how to

Create a printer pool using three printers.

1. Open the **Printers and Faxes** window, if necessary. Install the **HP2500C Series** printer on ports **LPT2** and **LPT3** as **HP 2500C Series (Copy 1)** and **(Copy 2)**. Do not make either of them the default printer, and share them as **PrinterB and PrinterC**.
2. Open the **HP 2500C Series Properties** dialog box.
3. Open the **Ports** tab to view a list of ports that can host a printer.
4. Select the **Enable printer pooling** check box to enable multiple printers to share print jobs equally **(Figure 9-20)**.
5. Select the **LPT2** check box to specify the port that will connect the second print device to the print server and to add the printer to the printer pool.
6. Select the **LPT3** check box to specify the port that will connect the third print device to the print server and to add the printer to the printing pool. Click [Apply] **(Figure 9-21)**.
7. Click [OK] to close the HP 2500C Properties dialog box.
8. The final step to create the printer pool would be to physically connect the additional print devices to ports LPT2 and LPT3. When a document is sent to the **HP 2500C Series** printer, the print server will search through ports 1, 2, and 3 until it finds an idle print device to send the print job to.

Figure 9-20 Enabling printer pooling

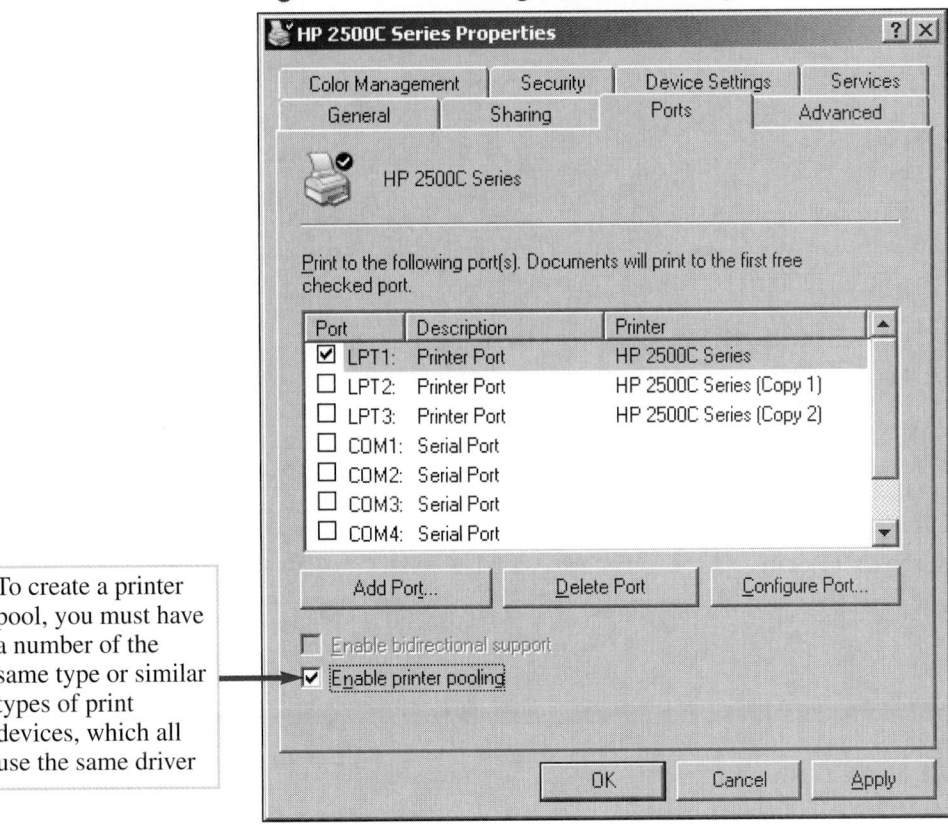

To create a printer pool, you must have a number of the same type or similar types of print devices, which all use the same driver

Figure 9-21 Adding printers to a printer pool

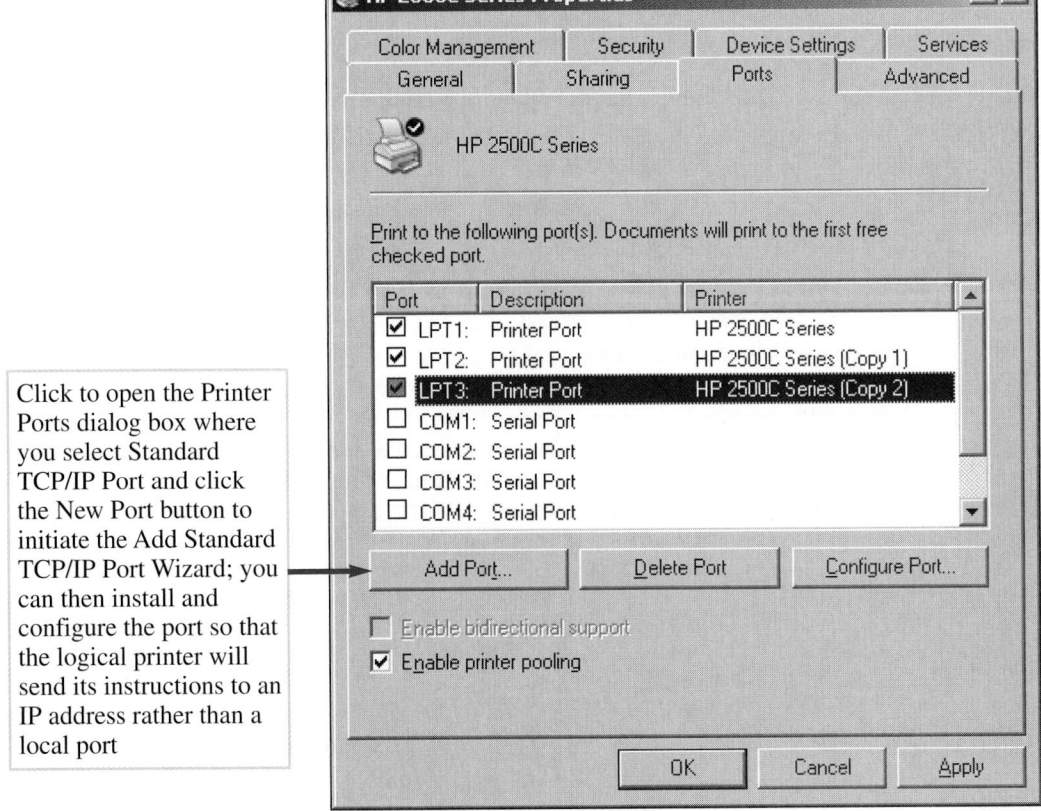

Click to open the Printer Ports dialog box where you select Standard TCP/IP Port and click the New Port button to initiate the Add Standard TCP/IP Port Wizard; you can then install and configure the port so that the logical printer will send its instructions to an IP address rather than a local port

skill 5

Setting Printer Priorities

exam objective

Basic knowledge

overview

Normally each print device has a corresponding printer associated with it. It is possible, however, to assign multiple printers to a single print device. You set printers as high-priority or low-priority to control the order in which their print jobs will be sent to the print device. When multiple printers have print jobs in the spool that require printing on the print device, the printer with the highest priority will print first. This can be particularly useful if you have one user or group whose print jobs are critical and must be printed as soon as they are ordered. For example, you can create two logical printers, HP 2500C Series and HP 2500 Series (Copy 1), that will both print to the same physical HP 2500C Series device. One group of users can be assigned to use the first logical printer, and a second group, whose jobs you want to take precedence, can be assigned to use the second logical printer. The second logical printer will be assigned a higher priority so that its print jobs will be completed first and the Print permission will be assigned to each group for the appropriate logical printer.

Print jobs sent by higher priority printers bypass the queue of documents in the lower priority printer spool and are sent to the print device first. To set the priority for a printer, you use the **Advanced** tab on the **Properties** dialog box for the printer. You can rank the priority of a printer from 1 through 99, with 1 being the lowest rank and selected by default. If you leave the default in place, any printer with a priority from 2-99 will have its jobs sent to the print device first. You can also use the **Available from** option button to make a printer available only at certain times. This can be useful if you have a user or group that has a large volume of low-priority printing jobs.

To understand how you can use printer priorities effectively, consider two user groups, Web Developers and Application Developers, who need to print documents on the same print device. If you want the print device to print documents that the Web Developers group generates before documents that the Application Developers group generates, first install two printers. Then, assign a priority value of 2 and the Print permission for one printer to the Web Developers group, and a priority value of 1 and the Print permission for the second printer to the Application Developers group. When the print server receives print jobs from both groups, it will print documents from the Web Developers group first because the printer assigned to it has the higher priority.

caution

Be aware that if a low priority document is printing when a high priority document is received, the low priority document *will not* be interrupted. Priority only controls the queue, it does not interrupt documents which are already printing.

how to

Assign print priority values to two printers. (For this exercise, you will need two domain local groups, Managers and Web Developers.)

1. Open the **Printers and Faxes** window.
2. Right-click the **HP 2500C Series** icon and select **Properties** to open the **HP 2500C Series Properties** dialog box (**Figure 9-22**).
3. Click the **Advanced** tab. This is where you set a priority value. Type **2** in the **Priority** spin box to specify a priority value for the printer (**Figure 9-23**).
4. Click the **Security** tab to change user permissions for the printer.
5. Select **Everyone** in the **Name** list, and click [Remove].
6. Click [Add...] to open the **Select Users**, **Computers**, or **Groups** dialog box.
7. Type the name for the group you have created, **Web Developers**, in the **Enter the object names to select box** (**Figure 9-24**).
8. Click [OK] to close the Select Users, Computers, or Groups dialog box.
9. The **Allow** check box for the **Print** permission is selected by default for the Web Developers group in the **Permissions for Web Developers** list.
10. Click [OK] to close the HP 2500C Series PCL Properties dialog box.

tip

The highest priority value is 99, and the lowest is 1.

Figure 9-22 The General tab in the <printer_name> Properties dialog box

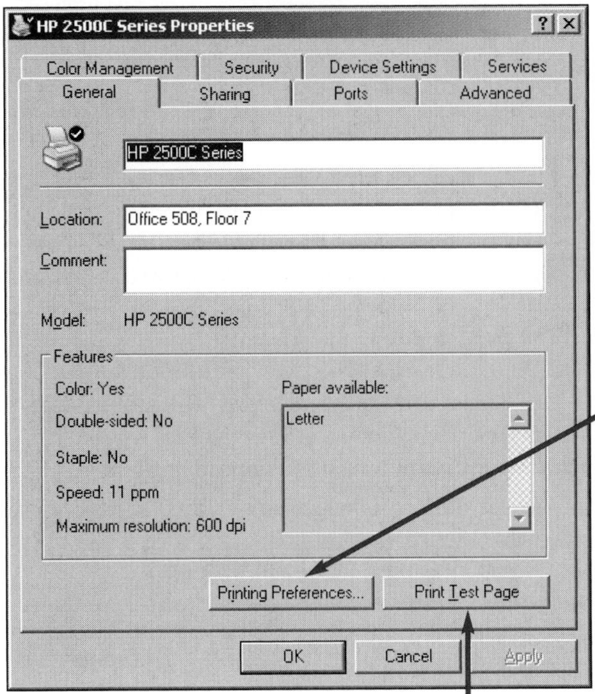

HP 2500C Series Properties
Color Management
Security
Device Settings
Services
General
Sharing
Ports
Advanced
HP 2500C Series
Location: Office 508, Floor 7
Comment:
Model: HP 2500C Series
Features
Color: Yes
Double-sided: No
Staple: No
Speed: 11 ppm
Maximum resolution: 600 dpi
Paper available:
Letter
Printing Preferences...
Print Test Page
OK
Cancel
Apply
Used to set additional properties for printing, such as setting portrait or landscape orientation as the default, printing on both sides of the paper by default, the default paper source if the printer supports special trays, and the color, print quality and effects settings, depending on the capabilities of the print device
Click to verify that the printer is working

Figure 9-23 Setting printer priority

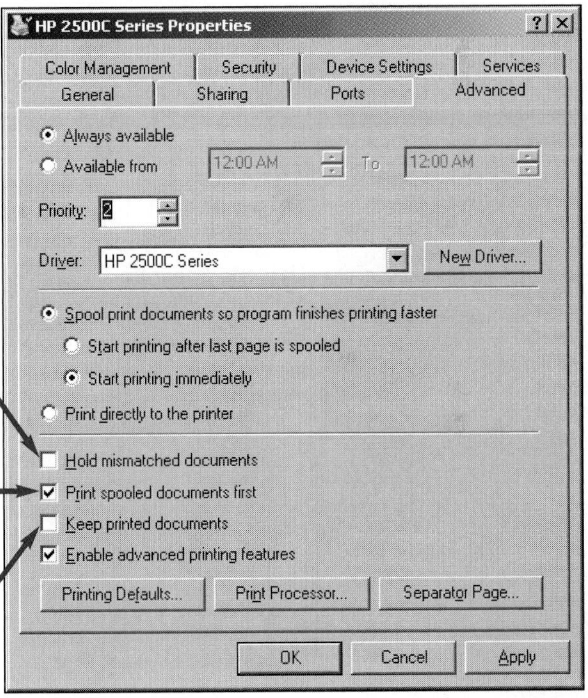

HP 2500C Series Properties
Color Management
Security
Device Settings
Services
General
Sharing
Ports
Advanced
Always available
Available from
12:00 AM
To
12:00 AM
Priority: 2
Driver: HP 2500C Series
New Driver...
Spool print documents so program finishes printing faster
Start printing after last page is spooled
Start printing immediately
Print directly to the printer
Hold mismatched documents
Print spooled documents first
Keep printed documents
Enable advanced printing features
Printing Defaults...
Print Processor...
Separator Page...
OK
Cancel
Apply
Makes the system compare the printer setup to the document setup to determine if they are compatible; if not, the print job will be put on hold
Allows jobs that have completed spooling to be printed, no matter what their priority is, which is useful in high-volume environments so that the printer will not be idle while waiting for lengthy jobs to spool
Keeps documents in the spooler after they have printed so that administrators can recreate a printout that has been damaged by a printer jam or other mishap

Figure 9-24 Setting printer permissions for a group

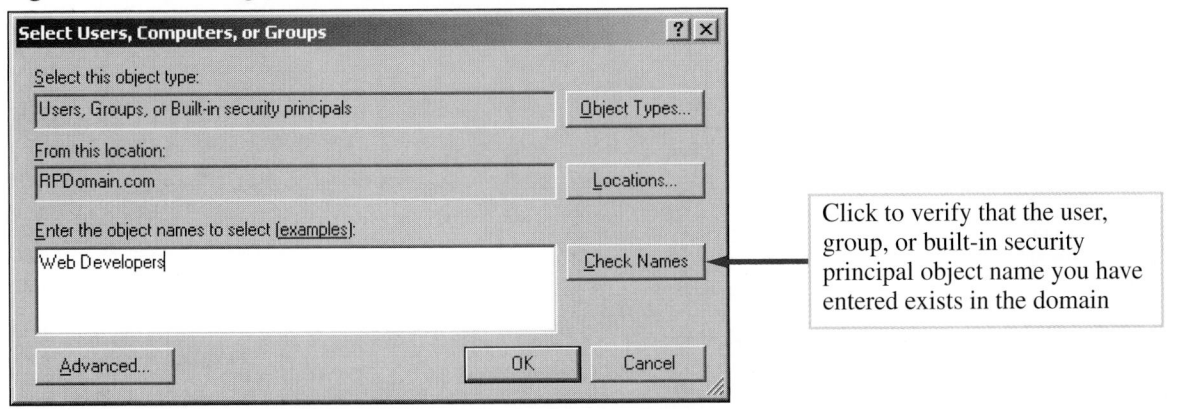

Select Users, Computers, or Groups
Select this object type:
Users, Groups, or Built-in security principals
Object Types...
From this location:
RPDomain.com
Locations...
Enter the object names to select (examples):
Web Developers
Check Names
Advanced...
OK
Cancel
Click to verify that the user, group, or built-in security principal object name you have entered exists in the domain

skill 5

Setting Printer Priorities *(cont'd)*

exam objective

Basic knowledge

how to

11. Right-click the **HP 2500C Series (Copy 1)** icon in the Printers window and click Properties to open the **HP 2500C Series (Copy 1) Properties** dialog box.
12. Open the **Advanced** tab. A value of 1 is entered by default in the **Priority** spin box (**Figure 9-25**).
13. Open the **Security** tab to change permissions for using the printer.
14. Select **Everyone** in the **Name** list, and click [Remove]. If you do not remove the Everyone group, users in the Web Developers and Managers groups will still be able to print to both printers as members of the Everyone group.
15. Click [Add...] to open the **Select Users, Computers, or Groups** dialog box.
16. Type **Managers** in the **Enter the object names to select** box. Click [Check Names] to verify that the object exists in the domain (**Figure 9-26**).
17. Click [OK] to close the Select Users, Computers, or Groups dialog box.
18. The **Allow** check box for the **Print** permission is selected by default for the **Managers** group in the **Permissions** for Managers list.
19. Click [OK] to close HP 2500C Series (Copy 1) Properties dialog box.

more

To install print drivers for down-level Windows clients, you use the **Additional Drivers** button on the **Sharing** tab in the Properties dialog box for the printer. In the **Additional Drivers** dialog box, you can install drivers for x86 computers that are running Windows 95, 98, and Me, and for x86 computers running Windows NT 4.0. You can also install drivers for Itanium machines running Windows XP and Windows Server 2003 (**Figure 9-27**). You will have to enter the path to the location of the driver files in the **Copy files from** text box in a dialog box for the drivers you are installing.

Figure 9-25 The Advanced tab in the Properties dialog box for a printer

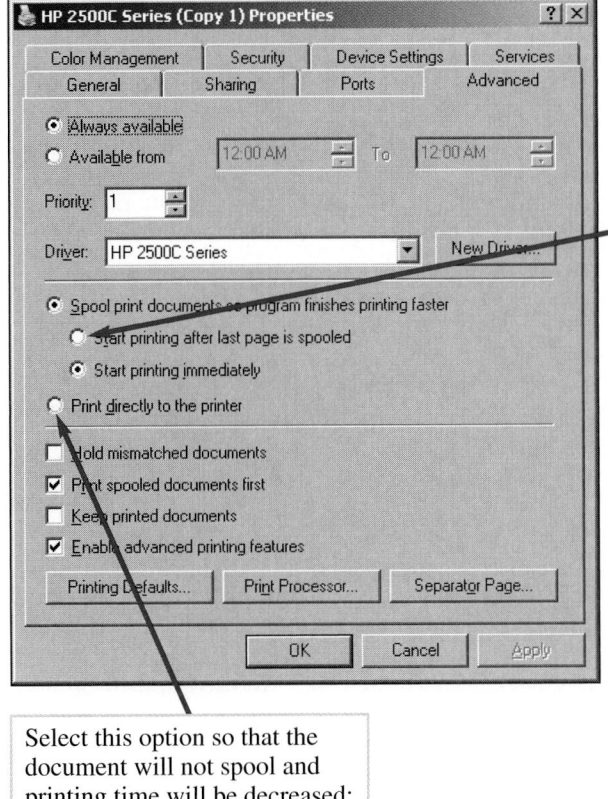

Select this option if you do not want documents to print until they are completely spooled; this option is used for documents that are assigned a low priority so that those with a higher priority will start printing right away

Select this option so that the document will not spool and printing time will be decreased; this option is used with programs that have their own spooling process

Figure 9-26 Verifying an object

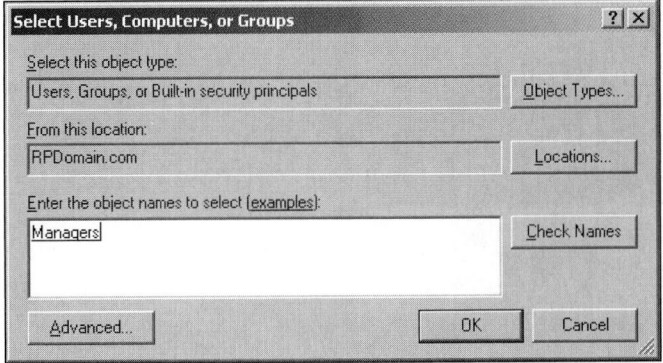

Figure 9-27 The Additional Drivers dialog box

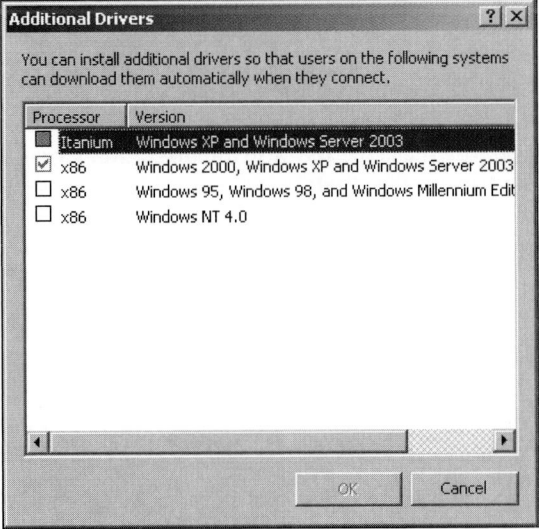

skill 6

Monitoring Printer Performance

exam objective

Monitor file and print servers. Tools might include Task Manager, Event Viewer, and System Monitor. Monitor print queues.

overview

Administrators must monitor the printers on a network so that they can judge their performance. This is done using the **System Monitor** to observe the performance and status of printers across a network. You use the System Monitor to view important data about the usage of hardware resources such as printers, as well as to monitor the activity of system services (**Figure 9-28**).

To use the System Monitor, you must specify performance objects and performance counters. A performance object is a system resource, such as a processor, disk, network interface, or memory, whose performance you can monitor. Counters are performance measures for the object that can be calculated and related as numeric figures. For example, if you want to monitor the performance of the processor object, you can monitor counters such as the percentage of time the processor is busy (%Processor Time) and the number of times each second that it is interrupted by service requests (Interrupts/Sec). Counters can have multiple instances. For example, if a computer has two processors, there will be three instances for the %Processor Time counter, one for each processor and one for the total processing time.

The main object you use to monitor printing is the **Print Queue object** because it is the key indicator of a printer's performance. You can choose different performance counters, such as **Bytes Printed/sec**, **Job Errors**, **Jobs**, and **Total Pages Printed** in order to monitor the speed, errors encountered, current workload, and total printed output, respectively. The Print Queue counters are reset when either the print server or the spooler service is restarted.

If you want to monitor and compare the performance of multiple printers simultaneously, you can specify each printer in separate instances.

tip

System Monitor's Print Queue object is used to monitor the performance of both local and network printers. The Total Pages Printed counter is the total number of print jobs printed on a print queue since the System Monitor was last restarted.

how to

tip

You can also open the Performance console by clicking Start, pointing to Administrative Tools, and then clicking Performance.

Monitor print queue performance.

1. Click **Start**, click **Run**, and type **perfmon** in the **Open** text box. Press **[Enter]** to open the **Performance** console.
2. Click the New Counter Set button on the **Performance** toolbar to clear the default counter set.
3. Click the **Add** button **+** on the **Performance** toolbar to open the **Add Counters** dialog box.
4. The **Select counters from computer** option button is selected by default and the name of the local computer is entered in the list box.
5. Select **Print Queue** in the **Performance object** list box.
6. The **Select counters from list** option button is selected by default.
7. Press and hold down the **[Ctrl]** key while you select the **Bytes Printed/sec**, **Job Errors**, **Jobs** and **Total Pages Printed** counters. Release the **[Ctrl]** key.
8. Click the **All instances** option button to monitor all printers on the print server (**Figure 9-29**).
9. Click **Add...** to add the specified instances for the counters for the Print Queue object to the System Monitor.
10. Click **Close** to close the Add Counters dialog box. The **System Monitor** displays the graph and data for the specified counters for all printer instances installed on the print server.
11. If one of the printer instances you are monitoring is attached to a print device, print several documents so that you can see the counters move.

Figure 9-28 Monitoring printer performance

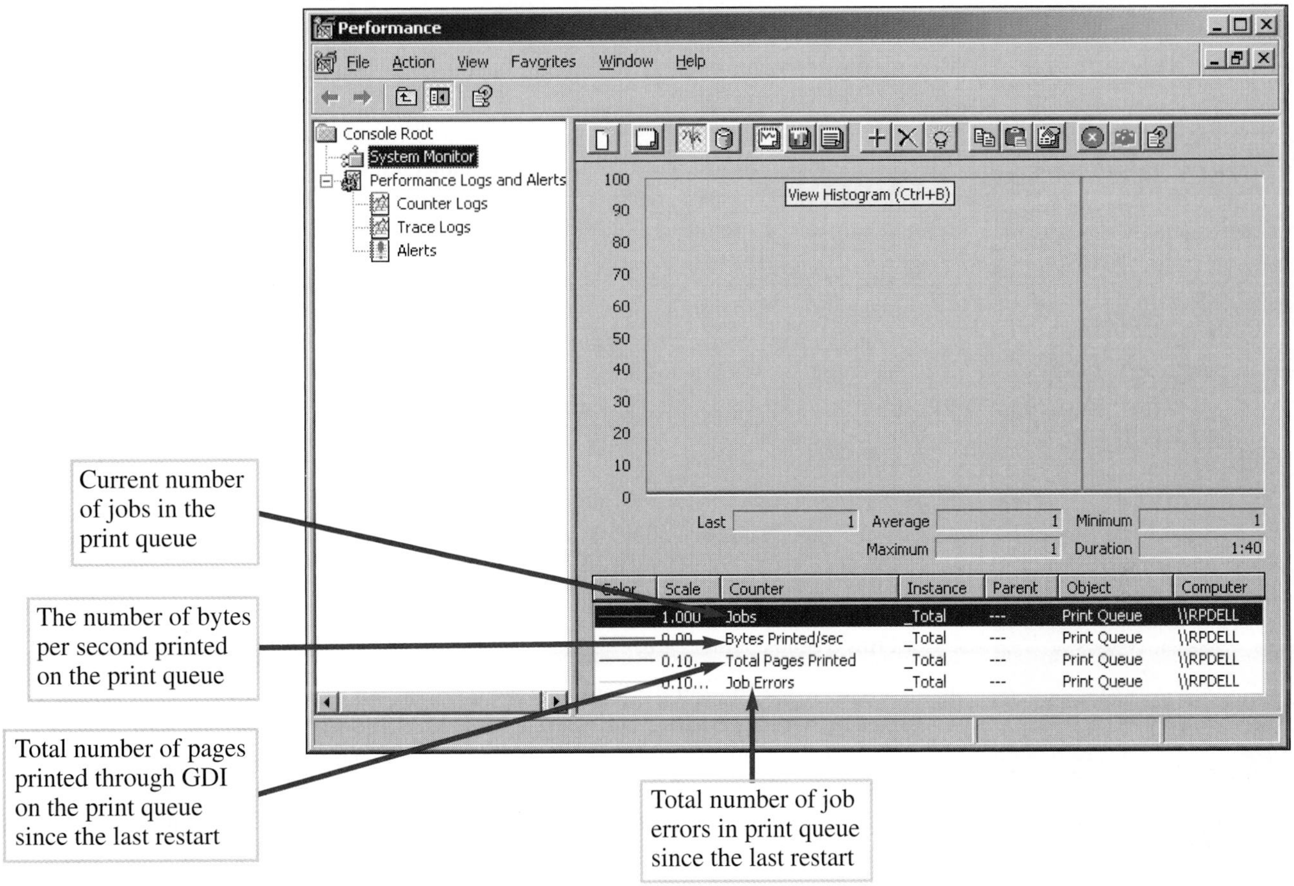

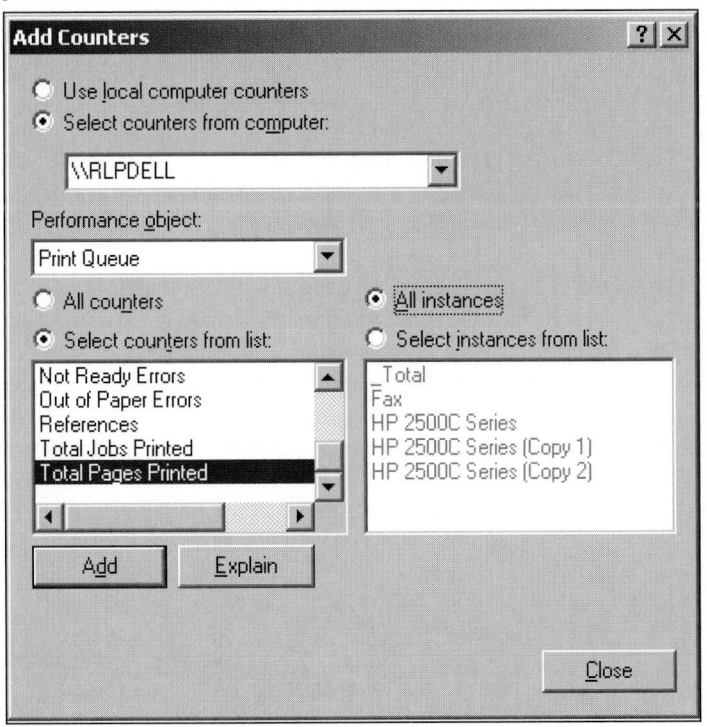

Current number of jobs in the print queue

The number of bytes per second printed on the print queue

Total number of pages printed through GDI on the print queue since the last restart

Total number of job errors in print queue since the last restart

Figure 9-29 Adding counters to monitor printer performance

skill 6

Monitoring Printer Performance
(cont'd)

exam objective

Monitor file and print servers. Tools might include Task Manager, Event Viewer, and System Monitor. Monitor print queues.

more

Windows Server 2003 includes many performance counters that can be used to identify possible bottlenecks that are hampering printer performance. The performance counters used in the exercise are explained below **(Figure 9-30)**:

◆ **Bytes Printed/sec:** If the System Monitor displays low values for this counter, it may indicate a printer throughput bottleneck. Keep in mind though, that the values for this counter depend on the type of printer. You must refer to your printer's documentation to find out the acceptable printer throughput values for your printer.

◆ **Job Errors:** If the System Monitor displays a high number of job errors, it is likely that the port configuration is incorrect. Check your port configuration and remove any invalid settings.

◆ **Jobs:** You use this counter to identify excessive use.

◆ **Total Pages Printed:** As the print file is created, the application communicates with the Graphics Device Interface (GDI). The Total Pages Printed counter tells you how many pages have printed through GDI on the print queue since the last restart.

Other Print Queue counters are:

◆ **Add Network Printer Calls:** Displays the total number of times other print servers called this print server to add shared network printers to it since the last time it was started. This is obviously a very specialized counter, and is therefore rarely used.

◆ **Enumerate Network Printer Calls:** Displays the total number of times browse clients have called this print server to request network browse lists since the print server was last started. Another specialized counter, this counter can tell you how many users are installing a newly shared printer.

◆ **Jobs Spooling:** Displays the number of print jobs that are currently spooling in the print queue. A constantly rising number in this counter is either an indicator of a paused or malfunctioning printer, or an indicator that you need to add additional printers to the pool.

◆ **Max Jobs Spooling:** Displays the maximum number of spooling jobs that have been held in a print queue since the print server was last started. This can be used to show you how active the spool has gotten at peak times.

◆ **Max References:** Displays the peak number of open handles the printer has had. This counter is very rarely used.

◆ **Not Ready Errors:** Displays the total number of "Printer not ready" errors the print queue has had since the print server was last started. This is used to detect malfunctioning printers.

◆ **Out of Paper Errors:** Displays the total number of "Out of paper" errors a print queue has had since the print server was last started.

◆ **References:** Displays the current number of open handles for a print queue. This can refer to a user or a program that is connecting to a printer and opening a print queue. This is another counter that is rarely used.

◆ **Total Jobs Printed:** The total number of jobs that were printed through the GDI for the print queue since the print server was last started. This can be used to statistically track how many documents are printed over a period of time.

Figure 9-30 Examining printer performance with the System Monitor

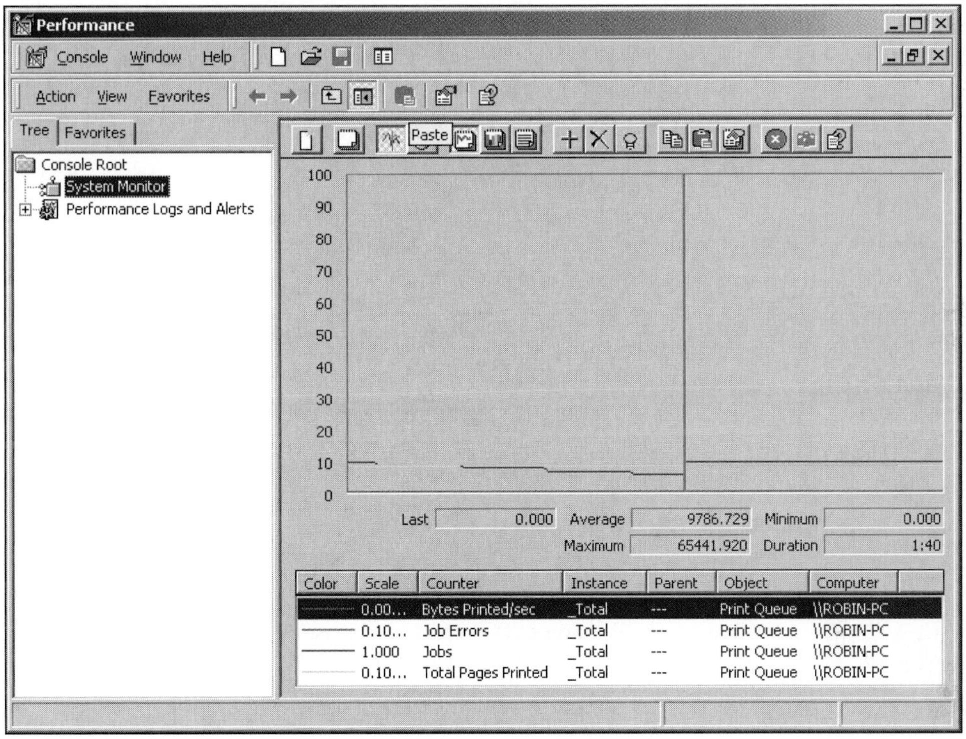

skill 7

Publishing Printers in Active Directory

exam objective

Basic knowledge

overview

On a Windows Server 2003 network, users and administrators often use Active Directory to locate and manage network printers. In Active Directory, all domain controllers can access and share printer information to allow users to access a network printer.

tip

Active Directory stores information about printer queues, sites, names, and addresses.

◆ Active Directory publishes a PrintQueue object for each printer that you install on a Windows 2000 Server or Windows Server 2003 print server in the directory by default. The PrintQueue object contains a subset of the information that the print server stores for a printer. If you change the printer configuration on the print server, the change propagates to Active Directory.

◆ The PrintQueue object is stored in the computer object for the print server. A computer object is an object containing information about a computer that is a member of the domain. However, when you open the Active Directory Users and Computers console, expand the Computers node, and select a computer object in the console tree, you do not see the PrintQueue objects in the details pane. The default view does not display computers as containers, and thus does not display the computers' sub-objects in the details pane. To view the PrintQueue objects and other sub-objects, open the **View** menu and select the **Users**, **Groups**, **and Computers as containers** command (**Figure 9-31**). Then, open the **Computers** folder and select any computer to display its sub-objects (**Figure 9-32**). After you do this, you can drag and drop the printer objects into other containers.

tip

Only shared printers are published in Active Directory.

◆ Active Directory deletes the printers associated with a server when you detach a print server from a network.

Active Directory publishes any printers that are installed on a domain print server that is running Windows Server 2003 or Windows 2000 Server by default. However, printers that are installed on pre-Windows 2000 print servers or on a Windows 2000 Professional print server are also not published in Active Directory by default and must have their printers manually published. You can manually publish a printer by creating a new PrintQueue object in Active Directory Users and Computers.

how to

Locate a published domain printer.

1. Open the **Active Directory Users and Computers** console.
2. Open the **View** menu and select **Users**, **Groups**, **and Computers as containers**.
3. Expand the **Computers** node. Select the name of the print server on which you installed the HP printers in Skills 2 and 4. The shared printers that you created earlier should display as published objects.
4. Right-click *<printservername>*-**HP 2500C Series** and select **Properties**. The properties listed here can be used to conduct a search for the printer object.
5. Select the **Double-sided** check box, and click [OK] (**Figure 9-33**).
6. Click [*Start*], and then **Search** to open the **Search Results** window.
7. In the **Search Companion** pane, scroll down, if necessary, and select **Other search options** (**Figure 9-34**).
8. Select **Printers**, **computers**, **or people**, and then select **A printer on the network** to open the **Find Printers** dialog box.
9. In the **In** list box, select your domain if it is not already selected, and select the **Features** tab.
10. Select the **Can print double-sided** check box. Click [Find Now].
11. The HP 2500C Series printer on the print server in your domain displays in the **Search results** pane (**Figure 9-35**).
12. Close the Find Printers dialog box and the Active Directory Users and Computers console.

Figure 9-31 The Users, Groups, and Computers as containers command

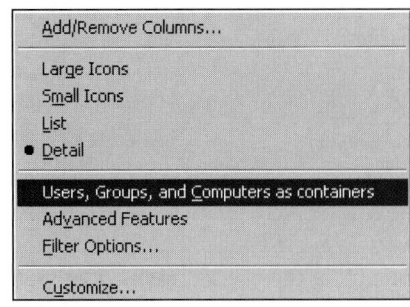

Figure 9-32 Viewing PrintQueue objects in Active Directory

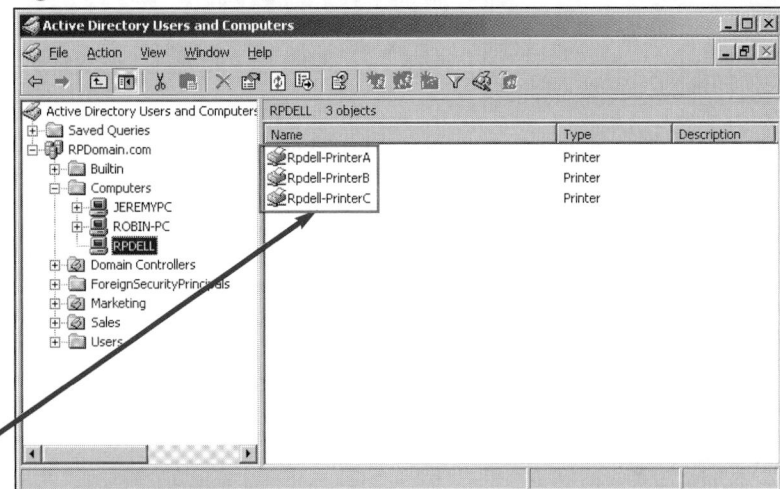

PrintQueue objects for published printers

Figure 9-33 The Properties dialog box for a published printer

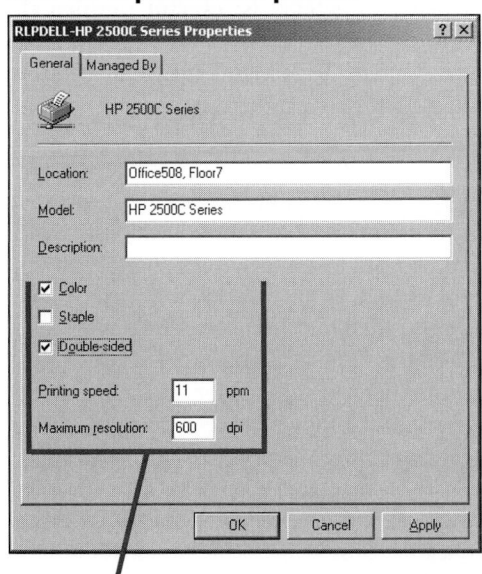

The features listed here can be used to conduct a search for the printer object

The published printer is located based on the capability to print double-sided

Figure 9-34 The Search Companion pane in the Search Results window

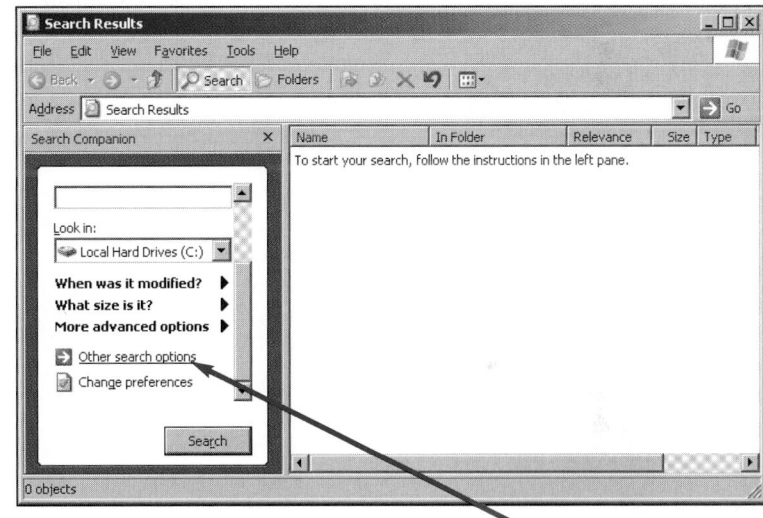

Click to display the Printers, computers, or people option, and then select A printer on the network to open the Find Printers dialog box

Figure 9-35 Finding a printer based on a feature

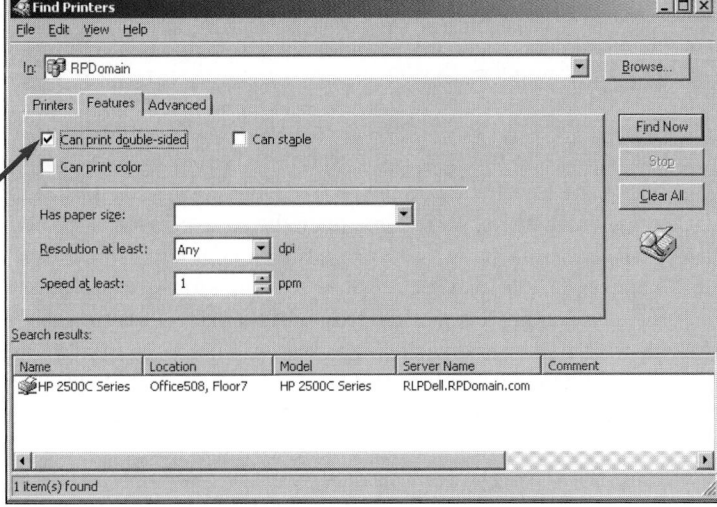

skill 7

Publishing Printers in Active Directory (cont'd)

exam objective

Basic knowledge

more

caution

You cannot use Pubprn.vbs to publish printers running on a Windows 2000 or Windows Server 2003 print server. This file is provided exclusively for backward compatibility with print servers that are running earlier versions of Windows.

To publish a pre-Windows 2000 printer that has been installed and shared, you can create a printer object the same way you create a user or group in the Active Directory Users and Computers console. A printer object is an object pointing to a printer on a server. In the Computers node in the Active Directory Users and Computers console, right-click the print server, point to **New** and select **Printer** to open the **New Object — Printer** dialog box. In the **Network path of the pre-Windows 2000 print share** text box, enter the UNC path to the printer (**Figure 9-36**).

You can also use the **Pubprn.vbs** script that is stored in the *%systemroot%*\System32 folder to publish a printer. Pubprn.vbs is a Windows Script Host file. This script is used on large networks to automate the process of manually publishing printers. It is run from the command prompt, using the cscript scripting host. The command must specify the container into which the printers should be published in LDAP format. The syntax is: **cscript pubprn.vbs** *servername* **dspath**. Dspath specifies the path to the target container. For example, the command to publish all printers on NTServ1 in the Printers OU in yourdomain.com is:

cscript *%systemroot%***system32\pubprn.vbd NTServer1 "LDAP://OU=Printers, DC= yourdomain, DC=com"**

There is also a set of Group Policies that apply to the Windows Server 2003 printing environment. One of these Group Policy settings is used to enable printer location-tracking. Printer location-tracking is used to search for and find printers at a specific location. It also provides you with flexibility in placing computers and printers following a convenient location scheme. When you enable printer location-tracking, it supersedes the standard method for locating and associating users and printers. The standard method uses the IP address and subnet mask of a computer to estimate its physical location and proximity to other computers. Location-tracking allows a user to browse for printers by location, without knowing their exact location or the location coding schema. With printer location-tracking enabled, the location is determined based on the user's subnet and a **Browse** button is added beside the **Location** field in the **Find Printers** dialog box and on the **General** tab in the **Properties** dialog box for the printer. Users can click the Browse button to browse for printers based on their location even if they do not know the location naming scheme.

You access the Find Printers dialog box either from the **Search Results** window, as in the exercise, or by clicking the **Find objects in Active Directory** button 🔍 on the Active Directory Users and Computers toolbar. This opens the **Find Users**, **Contacts**, **and Groups** dialog box. In the **Find** list box, select **Printers (Figure 9-37)**.

You use the Group Policy setting **Pre-populate printer search location text** to enable printer location-tracking for a group of computers. First, create the sites you want, if they are not already created, in the **Active Directory Sites and Services** console. Then, assign a subnet to each site. To do this, open the Active Directory Sites and Services console, then, open the **Sites** node, open the **Subnets** node, right-click the site name, and select **Properties**. In **Site**, select a site with which to associate this subnet. Next, right-click each subnet you created and click **Properties**. On the **Location** tab, enter the location of the subnet with a forward slash (/) between each part of the location string, for example, NewYork/Oneonta, and click OK. Now, you can apply the Group Policy setting to a site, OU, or domain in Active Directory Users and Computers or in the Group Policy Management console.

Figure 9-36 **Publishing a pre-Windows 2000 printer**

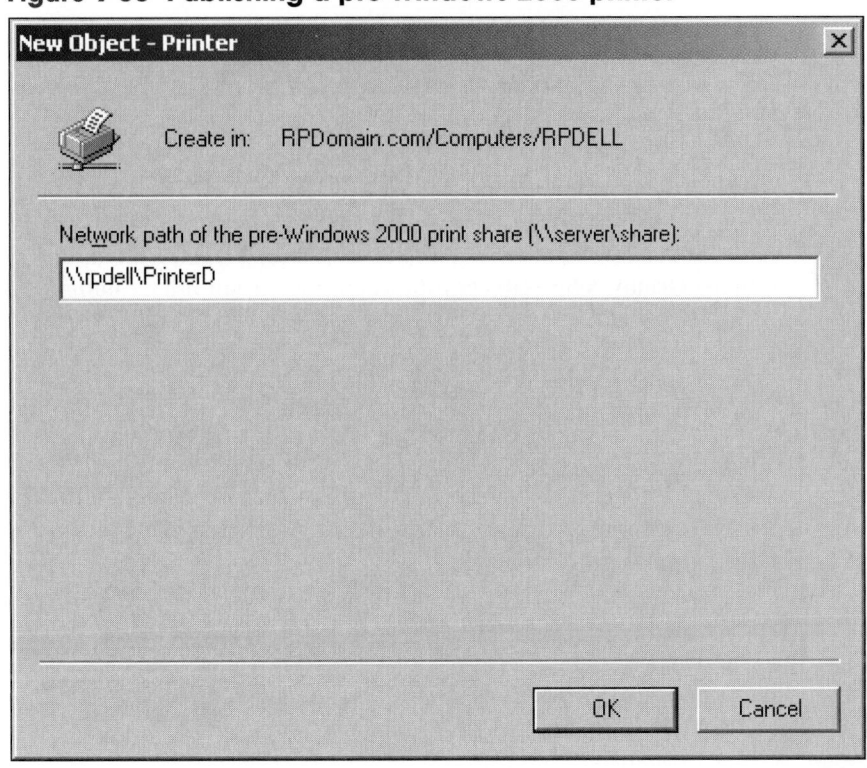

Figure 9-37 **The Find Printers dialog box**

When you enable printer location-tracking, a Browse button is added next to the Location field

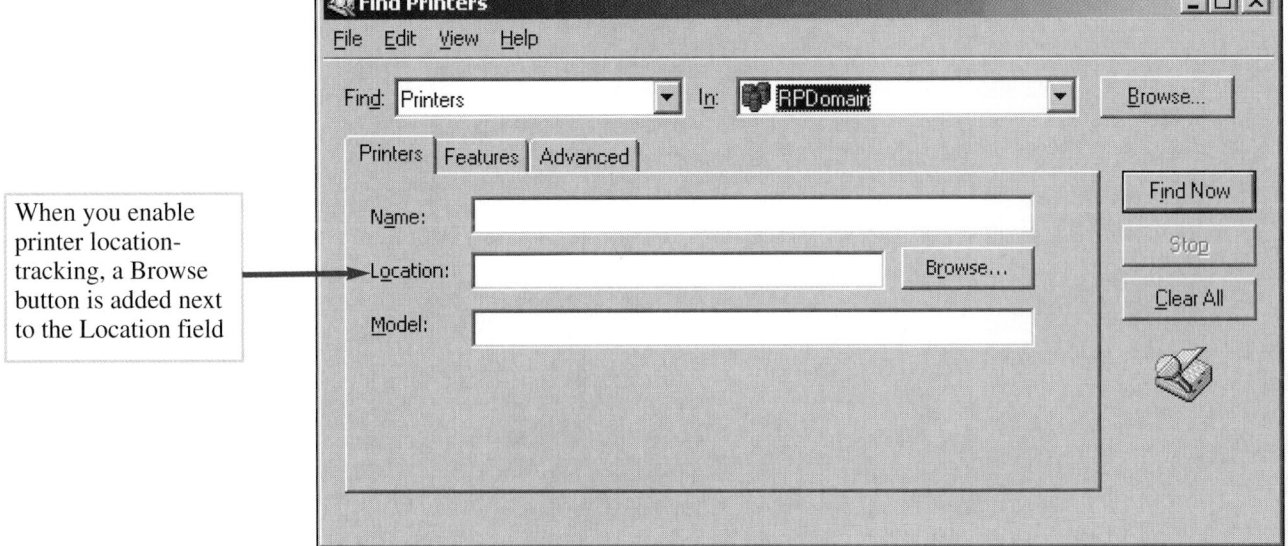

skill 7

Publishing Printers in Active Directory (cont'd)

exam objective   Basic knowledge

more

To enable printer location-tracking for a domain, in the Group Policy Management console, expand the domain name, right-click **Default Domain Policy**, and click **Edit** to open the **Group Policy Object Editor**. If you have not installed the Group Policy Management console, in the Active Directory Users and Computers console, right-click the domain and select **Properties**. On the **Group Policy** tab, select **Default Domain Policy** and click **Edit** to open the **Group Policy Object Editor**. Open the **Computer Configuration** node, open the **Administrative Templates** node, and select **Printers** to display the group policies for printers in the details pane **(Figure 9-38)**. Double-click **Pre-populate printer search location text** to open its Properties dialog box and select the **Enabled** option button **(Figure 9-39)**.

You then need to set a location for each printer in the Properties dialog box for the printer in the **Location** text box on the **General** tab. For example, for the subnet location NewYork/Oneonta, you might enter: NewYork/Oneonta/Bldg4/Floor5/Room263.

Now, when you search for printers, Windows uses the specified location and other search criteria, if you enter it, to find a printer nearby. When you click the **Find Now** button, the search will return a list of all printers that match the location. The search can be restricted by entering a name and/or model in the appropriate text boxes. It can be expanded by clearing the **Location** field or by clicking the **Clear All** button. If you do not configure printer tracking or you disable it, and the user does not enter a location, the operating system searches for a nearby printer based on the IP address and subnet mask of the user's computer.

To use printer location-tracking, Active Directory must be installed on the network and there must be more than one site and subnet. The IP addressing scheme must fairly closely match the physical network layout, and client computers must be able to query via LDAP 2 or later.

Figure 9-38 Enabling the Pre-populate printer search location text policy

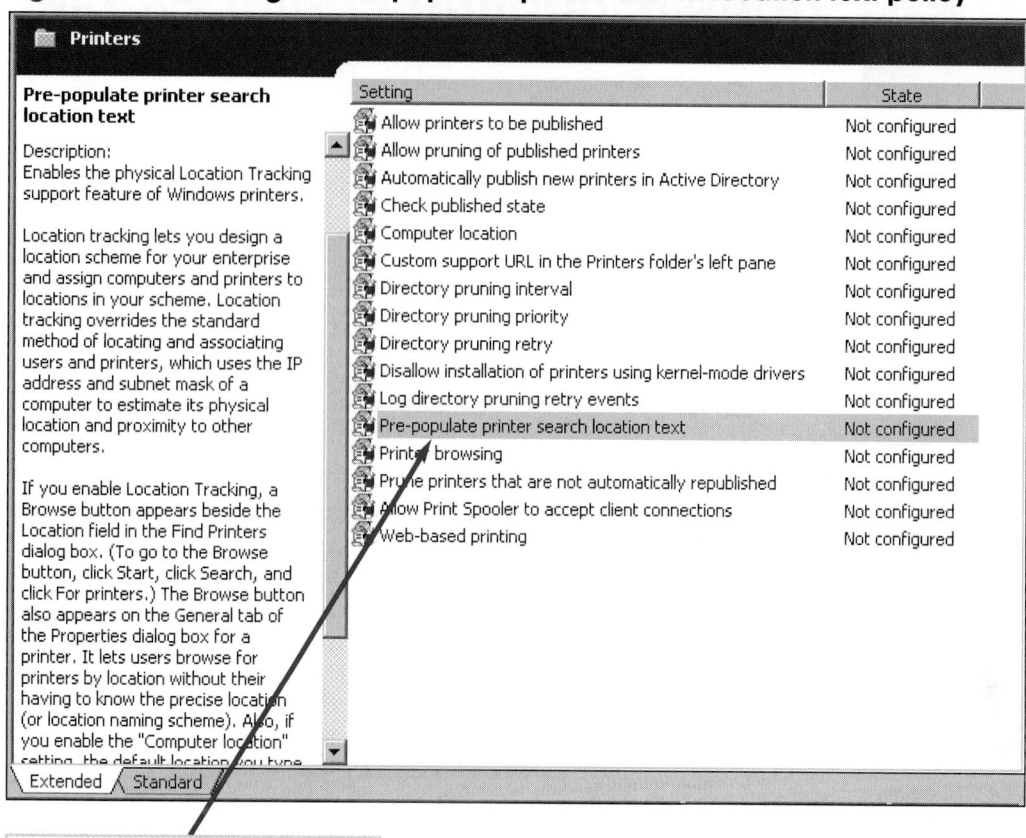

You enable this group policy to
enable printer location-tracking

Figure 9-39 Enabling printer location-tracking

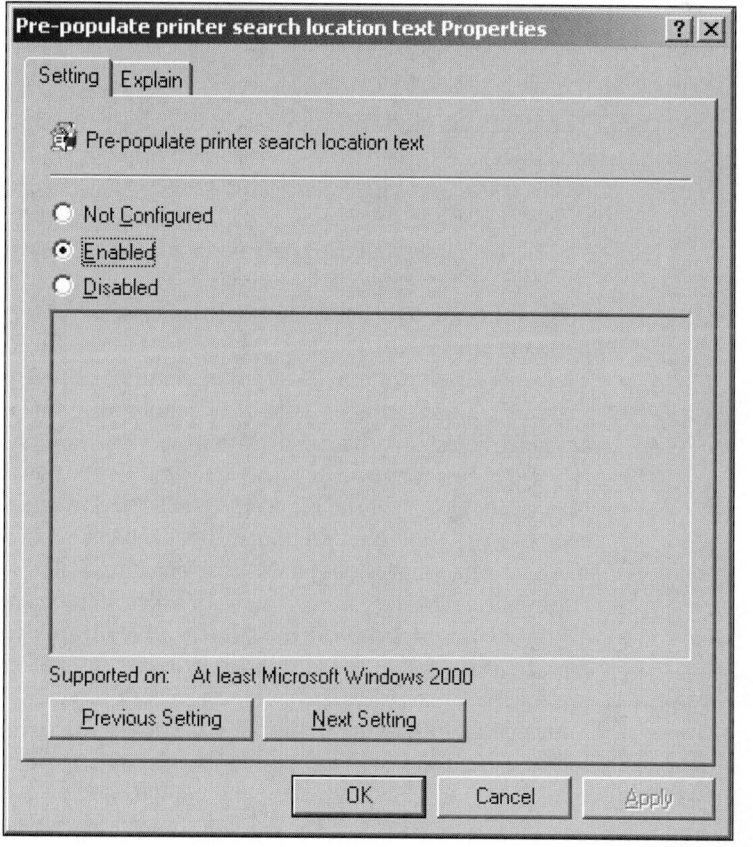

skill 8

Troubleshooting Printer Problems

exam objective

Monitor file and print servers. Tools might include Task Manager, Event Viewer, and System Monitor. Troubleshoot print queues.

overview

tip

When you encounter a printing problem, first check to make sure that the print device is online and connected to the print server. For a network print device, make sure that a network connection exists between the print device and the print server.

Problems in the network-printing environment may occur for various reasons ranging from a broken network connection to the installation of an incorrect printer driver. If a particular user is not able to access a printer but other users on the network have no problem accessing the same printer, the source of the problem is most likely at that user's workstation. This could be due to an incorrect printer driver on the user's workstation. Printing problems can arise on the user's workstation or can occur on the print server itself. To avoid printing problems, you must carefully plan your network printing structure and your permissions following the principles in the lesson (**Figure 9-40**).

The first thing you should check, as you would when troubleshooting any hardware device, is whether the local devices are plugged in and hooked up. You should check the cables, make sure the power is on, and check the paper and toner. Then, you can try printing a test page. If that is not successful, try recreating the printer on the client, reinstalling the print driver, and terminating and re-sharing the printer on the print server. Check the print queue for stalled print jobs (click Start, click Printers and Faxes and double-click the printer icon). If nothing is listed under **Status** (waiting, paused, or printing), it is likely the print job has stalled. You must also make sure that the print spool service is running (Open the **Services** snap-in in the **Administrative Tools** folder). Stop and restart the Print Spooler service (**Figure 9-41**). This will clear all print queues on the server. Make sure that there is enough disk space for spooling on the print server (75 MB or more is recommended). If the print device is operational and other users can print, the print server is probably not the problem. If other users also cannot print, make sure that the printer on the print server is using the correct driver and make sure that you have installed the correct drivers for other operating systems on the print server. If you are using a network-interface print device, you should first make sure that there is a network connection between the device and the print server. Make sure that you can see and connect to the print server from the workstation. Ping the IP address for a TCP/IP printer to make sure it is operational.

The following types of problems may occur when you are trying to print a document:
◆ **The print device is offline:** When the physical print device is not connected to the network, or is turned off or has gone offline, documents will not print and users will receive various error messages. The printer may issue an error message indicating that it cannot communicate with the print device, a red question mark will display on the printer icon in the System tray, and a **This document failed to print** warning may also display from the printer icon in the System tray. Usually there will be a light or an LCD message on the printer to tell you whether the printer is online. Press the Reset or Online button to cycle the printer into online mode.
◆ **The user receives an access denied, cannot access printer, or no access available message:** This is usually caused by improper permissions. A straightforward **Print** warning dialog box that informs the user that they do not have permission to use the selected printer may also display. Check the permissions assigned to both the user and the groups to which he or she is a member and check for any denied permissions. Sometimes a user will try to configure a printer from an older application and will receive this type of message when they do not have permission to change printer configurations. You must either change the user's permissions or ask an administrator to reconfigure the printer.
◆ **Your document prints incompletely or contains junk characters:** This problem typically occurs due to faulty printer drivers. Make sure the computer has the correct printer driver and that it is not corrupt.
◆ **Your documents do not print but other users can print their documents:** This usually indicates that the fault lies with your computer and not the print server. A possible solution would be to make sure your computer connects to the right printer. It could also indicate a driver issue, especially if accompanied by other errors.

Figure 9-40 Designing the network printing environment

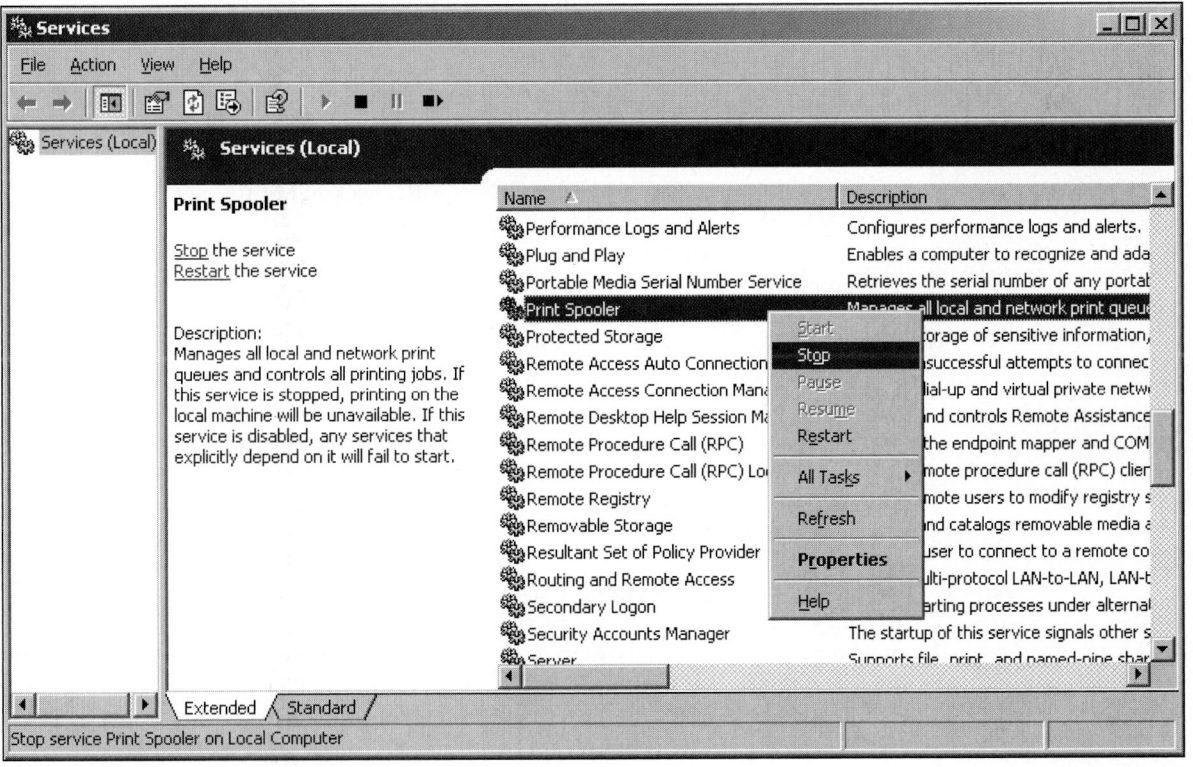

Figure 9-41 Stopping the Print Spooler service

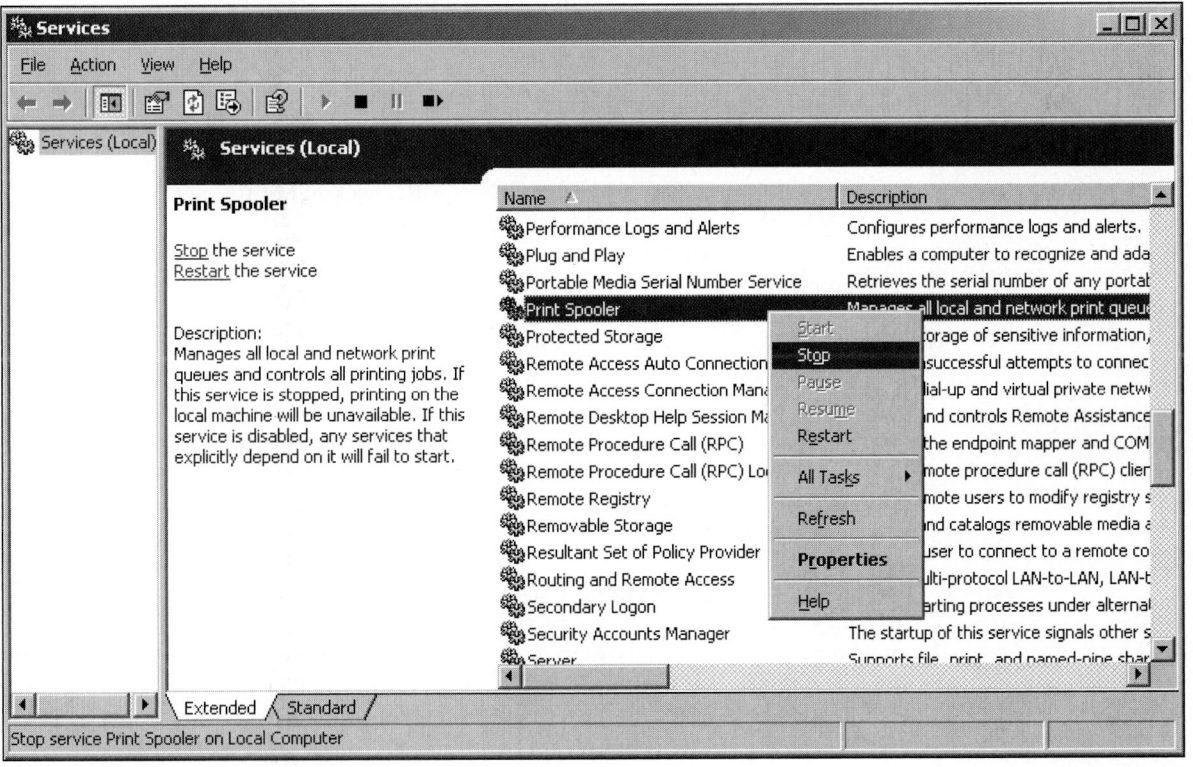

skill 8

Troubleshooting Printer Problems
(cont'd)

exam objective

Monitor file and print servers. Tools might include Task Manager, Event Viewer, and System Monitor. Troubleshoot print queues.

overview

tip

Nearly all printers respond to an HP LaserJet 4 or 5 driver.

◆ **Documents do not print correctly:** Documents may not print correctly on some printers in a printer pool when the print devices in the pool do not use the same driver. You must use either identical or similar print devices that use the same printer driver. If documents are not printing in the correct priority order in a printer pool, check and adjust the printer priorities as necessary.

◆ **Documents do not reach the print server:** This problem is most likely due to client-related network problems.

Troubleshooting Print Server Problems

If the problem is not with your workstation and other users are facing similar problems, then the problem is likely with the print server. Such problems may occur if the print server is not using the correct printer driver or if it does not have enough hard disk space for spooling. To troubleshoot print server problems, you can first open the Event Viewer on the print server and examine the error messages in the System log. You can also try opening the **Print Server Properties** dialog box from the Printers and Faxes window. Then, open the **File** menu and click the **Server Properties** command to configure properties such as forms, port settings, printer drivers, and the spool folder (**Figure 9-42**). By default, the spool folder path is **%systemroot%\System32\Spool\Printers**. However, if your print server is handling large volumes of printing, you can move the spool folder from the boot partition. If the drive fills up, the server will cease printing and the operating system may not perform smoothly. If a lengthy print job includes pages from other print jobs, set the **Start printing after the last page is spooled** option on the **Advanced** tab in the Properties dialog box for the printer. The printer will then only begin printing after all pages have spooled.

In brief, the print server is the source of the problem if the following problems arise:

◆ **The hard disk of the print server starts thrashing and documents do not reach the print device**: This problem could indicate too slow a hard disk for spooling, too much activity to the disk due to other factors (such as spooling), a fragmented hard disk, or insufficient space. A possible solution is to check to see if you need to defragment the disk or move the spool folder to a different physical drive.

◆ **When you install a printer on the print server, the test page does not print**: This problem may arise if you have configured the port incorrectly. A possible solution would be to configure the printer for the correct port. If you are using a network print device, make sure that you configure the network address correctly.

◆ **Several users receive error messages asking them to install a printer driver**: This problem is likely caused by the print server not installing the correct printer drivers for the operating systems that the client workstations are running. You can check the drivers installed on the print server and, if required, add the appropriate printer drivers for the client computers' operating systems. These drivers are installed in the Additional Drivers dialog box.

Windows Server 2003 includes a **Troubleshooting** section in the **Help and Support Center** to help you solve printer problems (**Figure 9-43**). You open the Windows Server 2003 Help and Support Center from the Start menu (**Start-Help and Support**). Next, click **Printers and Faxes** in the **Help Contents** list, click **Printing**, and click **Troubleshooting**. In the Troubleshooting section, click **Troubleshooting common printing problems** and an expandable list of common problems will appear. To view possible causes and solutions for a particular problem, simply click the **Plus** sign. For example, if you are having problems with a network printer, you can expand the **A printer connected to the network does not print** node to view a possible cause and solution for this problem.

Figure 9-42 The Drivers tab in the Print Server Properties dialog box

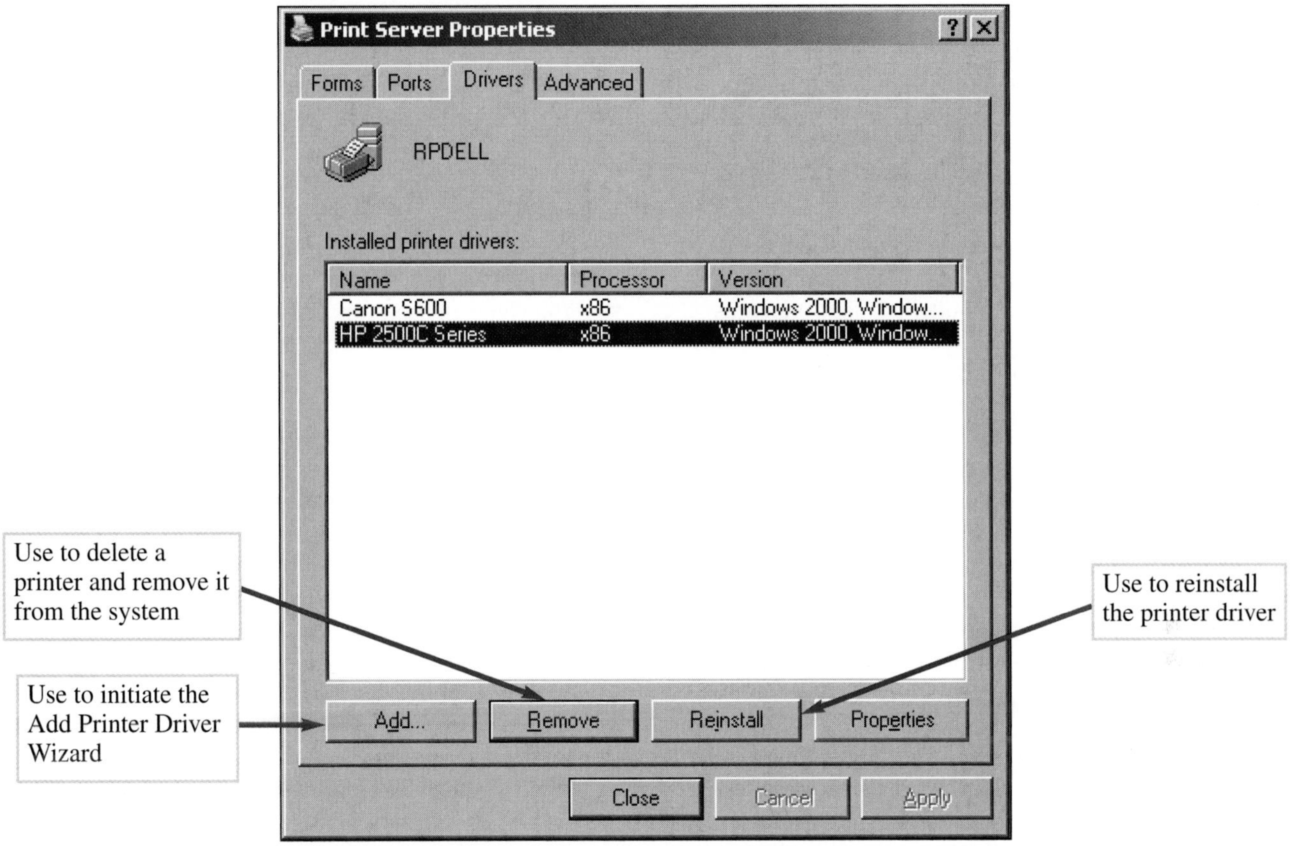

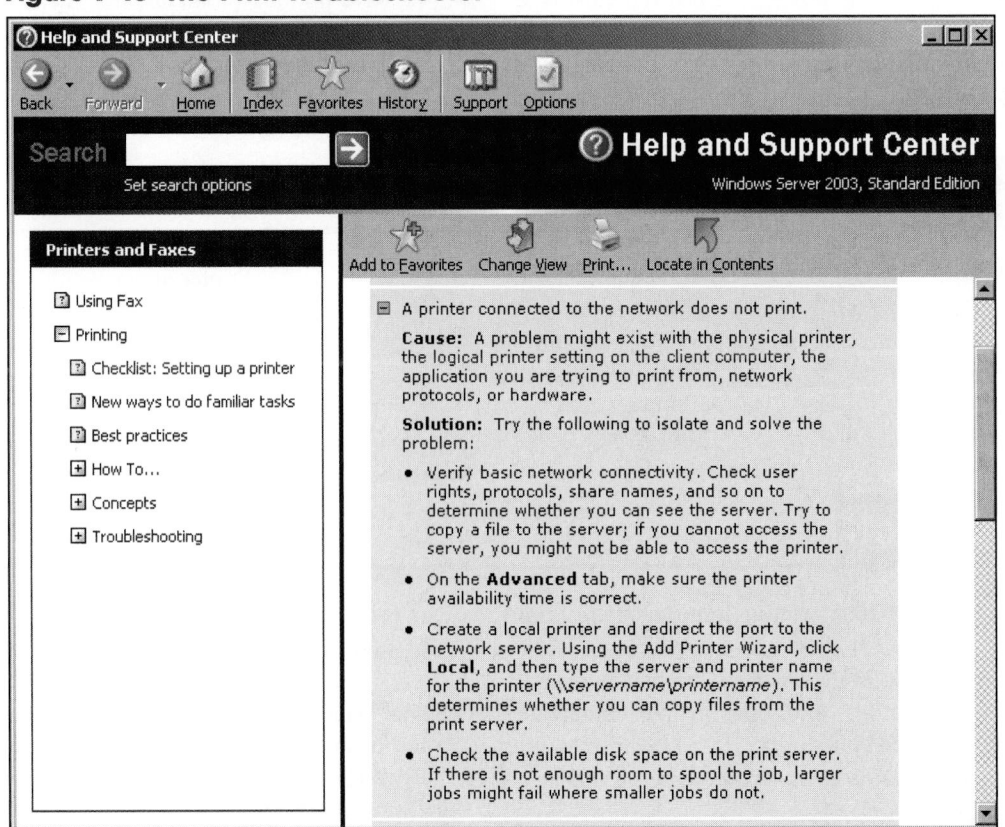

Use to delete a printer and remove it from the system

Use to reinstall the printer driver

Use to initiate the Add Printer Driver Wizard

Figure 9-43 The Print Troubleshooter

Summary

- In Windows Server 2003 printing terminology, a printer refers to a software interface that delivers the request for service from the operating system to the physical print device.
- A print device refers to the physical device that actually prints the data.
- A print server is a computer that is connected to and sharing one or more print devices.
- A print driver is the software that contains the information used by the operating system to convert the print commands for a particular model of print device into a printer language such as PostScript. It tells the operating system what attributes the print device has and what print commands it follows so that documents can be properly printed.
- Spooling is the process of caching the print request to a hard disk, which releases the application quicker. A spool is a folder where converted print jobs are stored before they can be printed.
- A local print device is any device for which spooling is done locally. A network print device is a device for which the spooling is done remotely.
- A print queue is a list of print jobs from different workstations that is stored on the spooler of the print server.
- The Graphics Device Interface (GDI) controls the creation of any visual output for the operating system, either to the monitor or to the printer. It "tells" the printer driver what type of print device is needed and what type of data must be used.
- Before you configure your network for printing, you should make sure that your print server satisfies memory and disk space requirements for your planned use.
- To plan an ideal network printing configuration, you should consider the number of users, your organization's printing requirements, and where the print devices should be located.
- You use the Add Printer Wizard to install printers on a print server and on client computers.
- You can assign print permissions on the Security tab in the Properties dialog box for a printer to control printer usage.
- You can take ownership of a printer on the Owner tab in the Advanced Security Settings for <*printername*> dialog box.
- To distribute print jobs automatically to one or more print devices, you can create a printer pool.
- If you want to prioritize groups of documents that print on the same print device, you can do so by first configuring several printers to point to the same print device, and then assigning them different priority levels.
- You can use the System Monitor to monitor the performance and status of printers across the network.
- You can manually publish a printer in Active Directory on the Sharing tab in the Properties dialog box for a printer, or by creating a new Print Queue object in the Active Directory Computers and Users console.
- To solve printing problems, first try to determine if the problem is with an application, a workstation, the print server, or the print device.

Key Terms

Add Printer Wizard
Graphics Device Interface (GDI
Local print devices
Network print devices
Rendering

Print device
Print queue
Print Queue object
Print server
Printer

Printer driver
Printer permissions
Printer pool
Spool
Spooler

Test Yourself

1. In Windows Server 2003 printing terminology, a print device:

a. Translates a high-level view of the printed document, called a metafile, into the printer language understood by the print device.

b. Enables you to print, change properties, and manage physical printers.

c. Prints data on paper or other hard copy media.

d. Stores print jobs from all workstations for printing.

2. Your Windows Server 2003 print server generates errors and print failures during office hours when multiple users must print their documents. However, after office

hours, it prints documents quickly and without errors. The cause of this problem could be:
a. Print device is not working properly.
b. Incorrectly installed printer driver.
c. The printer priority is set too low.
d. Insufficient hard disk space.

3. Nathan has been employed as the new assistant network administrator. He will need to be able to change permissions for a printer whenever necessary. To allow him to do so, you will assign him: (Choose all that apply.)
a. Print permission.
b. Manage Documents permission.
c. Manage Printers permission.

4. In your organization, there are two new departments: MIS and Developers. You want to restrict members of the Developers group from printing and allow the MIS members to change printer properties. To do this, you will:
a. Remove assigned Print permission for Developers, assign Print permissions for MIS.
b. Remove Print permission for the Everyone group, assign Manage Printers permissions for MIS.
c. Deny Print permissions for Developers, assign Manage Documents permissions for MIS.
d. Remove assigned Print permission for Developers, assign Manage Printers permissions for MIS.

5. Due to a heavy workload on your network printer, network users must wait a long time for their documents to be printed. To solve this problem, you add another print device that uses the same driver to the network. As the next step, to decrease users' waiting time and ensure maximum utilization of resources, you will:
a. Add the new printer as the default printer for all the user machines.
b. Divide users into two groups and assign each group rights to one printer.
c. Configure several printers to point to the same print device.
d. Create a printer pool with a printer pointing to several print devices.

6. When you create a printer pool you:
a. Configure several printers to point to the same print device.
b. Configure a printer to point to several print devices.

c. Must locate an idle print device and specify it for printing.
d. Can add any number and any type of printers to the pool.

7. In the Sales department of your organization, some employees need to print a few high priority documents on a daily basis. The other users of the company belong to the Web Developers department, which must continuously print a heavy workload of low priority documents. This affects print jobs from the Sales department. To solve this problem without increasing the cost overhead, you can:
a. Add another printer for the same print device, assign the Web Developers department the Print permission for one printer and assign the Sales department the Print permission for both printers.
b. Add another printer for the same device, assign different priorities to the printers, and assign the higher priority printer to the Sales department.
c. Add a print device and set the printer to point to the new printer to create a printer pool.
d. Add a print device, create Sales group, and assign the new printer exclusively to the Sales department.

8. Active Directory: (Choose all that apply.)
a. Automatically publishes a Windows NT 4.0 printer as soon as you share it.
b. Enables users across domains in the same forest to share a network printer.
c. Stores information in the Local Users and Groups snap-in.
d. Enables administrators to find and manage printers on the network.

9. You print a document from an application and the printed document contains junk characters. No other users are facing the same problem. This is because:
a. The wrong printer driver is installed on your computer.
b. Incorrect permissions for printing documents are assigned.
c. Your computer is connected to the wrong printer.
d. There is insufficient hard disk space for spooling on the print server.

Projects: On Your Own

1. Add a local HP OfficeJet K60 printer on your member server and share it using the Add Printer Wizard.
a. Open the **Printers and Faxes** window.
b. Initiate the **Add Printer Wizard**.
c. Select the **Local printer attached to this computer** option.
d. Use the LPT1 printer port.

e. Select **HP** in the **Manufacturer** list and **OfficeJet K60** in the **Printers** list box.
f. Share the printer, but do not make it the default printer.
g. Complete the process of adding a printer.
2. Create local user accounts named CEO and Manager on your print server. Assign ownership of an installed

printer (HP OfficeJet K60 in the exercise) to the CEO user account and assign the Manage Printers permission to the Manager user account.

a. Open the **Printers and Faxes** window.
b. Open the **HP OfficeJet K60 Properties** dialog box.
c. Open the **Advanced Security Settings for HP OfficeJet K60** dialog box.
d. Transfer ownership to the **CEO** user account.
e. Open the **Select Users or Groups** dialog box.
f. Add the user **Manager** to the list.

g. Assign the **Manage Documents** permission to the Manager user account.
h. Close the **HP OfficeJet K60 Properties** dialog box.

3. Create a printer pool using three printers (**HP 2500C Series** in the exercise).
a. Open the **Printers and Faxes** window.
b. Open the **HP 2500C Series** Properties dialog box.
c. On the **Ports** tab, activate the **Enable printer pooling** check box.
d. Select the **LPT2** and **LPT3** check boxes.
e. Close the **HP 2500C Series Properties** dialog box.

Problem Solving Scenarios

You are a network administrator with Art Ads, an advertising company. The company network consists of a single Windows Server 2003 computer and 35 Windows XP Professional client computers. The company also has a dedicated print server, with a single color laser printer, which handles all print jobs for the 35 network users. The accounts department has complained that it finds it difficult to get the bills and invoices printed on time, because the printer is always occupied with handling print jobs requested by the design department. The company has decided to purchase an additional inkjet printer and dedicate it to handling the printing of bills and invoices. You have been asked to set up the inkjet printer. You also need to share this printer and create a printer pool. Finally, you need to set permissions for the inkjet printer allowing exclusive access by the accounts department users alone. Explain in detail the steps you would take to set up the above printer pool and configure the permissions. Make sure you explain how the printer permissions will have to be assigned so that the appropriate group will be able to access the appropriate printer only.

Exploring TCP/IP and DHCP

A protocol is a set of rules and conventions for sending information over a network. These rules manage the content, format, timing, sequencing, and error control for messages exchanged among network devices. The protocol explains how the clients and servers on a network must arrange data in order to deliver it to other computers on the network and how they can interpret data that is delivered to them. Protocols are implemented in a layered architecture. This architecture is typically conceptualized in two alternative models: the DOD (Department of Defense) model and the OSI (Open Systems Interconnection) Reference Model.

The main networking protocol today is TCP/IP (Transmission Control Protocol/Internet Protocol), which is the core protocol for the Internet. TCP/IP is a scalable and routable protocol. It is scalable because it can be used for both large and small networks, and data can be transferred across networks and between computers using different operating systems and with widely varying structural designs. TCP/IP is a routable protocol because it is capable of transmitting data across a router, which is a special device used to transfer data between networks. In addition to TCP/IP, Windows Server 2003 supports several other protocols including NWLink and AppleTalk. NWLink enables computers running Microsoft operating systems to access resources on servers running a version of Novell Netware that predates Netware 4.0. Netware 4.0 servers and above support TCP/IP, while Netware 5.0 and above run TCP/IP as the native protocol suite. You can enable communication between computers running older versions of the Macintosh operating system and Windows Server 2003 by installing AppleTalk and File Services for Macintosh.

A computer using TCP/IP is assigned a unique IP address that identifies the computer on the network. You can assign an IP address manually or automate the process by using the Dynamic Host Configuration Protocol (DHCP) service. DHCP provides TCP/IP configuration information to client computers running Windows Server 2003, Windows 2000 Server, Windows XP and 2000 Professional, Windows 95, Windows 98, and many other types of client operating systems. The DHCP server's job is to dynamically assign IP addresses from a range of IP addresses to computers as they boot. This simplifies the administration of TCP/IP configuration because it automates the process of assigning IP addresses to clients.

Troubleshooting TCP/IP problems can consume a large portion of a network administrator's time. Windows Server 2003 provides you with utilities such as Ping, Ipconfig, Tracert, Netdiag, and Dcdiag to troubleshoot problems associated with TCP/IP. The Ping utility is used to verify the connectivity of a host computer to the TCP/IP network and also provides information about network problems such as incompatible TCP/IP configurations. The Ipconfig utility provides information about the host computer configuration, IP address, subnet mask, and default gateway. The Tracert utility enables you to identify the route being followed to transfer data between the communicating devices.

Goals

In this lesson, you will learn about the TCP/IP protocol and how to configure the IP address, subnet mask, and default gateway. You will also learn how to use troubleshooting utilities to diagnose network connectivity problems and how to install and configure the DHCP service.

Lesson 10 Exploring TCP/IP and DHCP

Skill	Exam 70-290 Objective
1. Introducing Networking Concepts	Basic knowledge
2. Introducing Network Protocols	Basic knowledge
3. Identifying the Fundamentals of TCP/IP	Basic knowledge
4. Configuring TCP/IP	Basic knowledge
5. Introducing IP Addressing in TCP/IP	Basic knowledge
6. Troubleshooting TCP/IP	Basic knowledge
7. Introducing Dynamic Host Configuration Protocol (DHCP)	Basic knowledge

Requirements

To complete this lesson, you will need administrative rights on a Windows Server 2003 member server and the Windows Server 2003 installation CD-ROM.

skill 1

Introducing Networking Concepts

exam objective

Basic knowledge

overview

To understand how communication occurs in a Windows Server 2003 network, you must first understand some basic networking concepts, including the definitions of the terms protocol, network interface card, and Network Driver Interface Specifications (NDIS).

A **protocol** provides a set of rules and standards for data transfer. Computers must share at least one common protocol to exchange data. A protocol defines the methods of formatting data into discrete units, called **packets** (also known as datagrams, segments, or frames), transfers these units across networks, and provides the rules for interpreting them. Packets are similar to the words that are combined to form a sentence. Words convey meaning only when they are arranged in a proper sequence. Similarly, a packet can only convey meaning when a complete set of packets is received and arranged in the proper sequence as defined by the application protocol.

An IP packet consists of three sections: header, data, and footer (also known as the trailer) **(Figure 10-1)**. The header contains information about the process of transmitting a packet from one computer to another. It stores the addresses of the computers sending and receiving the packet, options describing any special requirements for interpretation of the data within, the next layer protocol to be processed (known as the IP Protocol ID field), and a checksum, among other things. If the packet is not delivered to its destination, the address stored in the header is used to return it to the source. The data section stores the actual data to be transported, such as the contents of the message and any attachments, which is further encapsulated in other protocols (usually TCP at a minimum). The footer (trailer) contains an FCS, or Frame Check Sequence, which is a Cyclic Redundancy Check (CRC) used to determine if there are any bit errors in the transmission of the data. If an error is identified, the receiving device simply drops the packet. With TCP, it is the responsibility of the sending device to detect that an error has occurred due to the lack of a received ACK (Acknowledgement) of the sent data and to resend the data.

tip

A network interface card is also known as a network adapter.

Packets are sent and received through network media. **Network media** consists of physical wiring that can be made of copper, fiber-optic, or even wireless (radio wave-based or infrared) media. This wiring is connected to a **network interface card (NIC)** in the computer. A computer can have more than one NIC installed. Each NIC will have a unique address called the **media access control (MAC) address**, which is generally assigned by the manufacturer of the NIC. Some drivers will allow you to specify a different hardware MAC address, but in general, this should not be done. MAC addresses are supposed to be unique worldwide, but occasionally, manufacturers may repeat a MAC address by accident. In this case, you should either contact the manufacturer and get a new card, or change the default MAC address to a unique number. **Address Resolution Protocol (ARP)** resolves an IP address to a MAC address. This is necessary in order for any data transmission across an Ethernet network to occur. The MAC address, which is a unique 48-bit or 6-byte number, is also referred to as the hardware address, physical address, or Ethernet address. Each NIC has a set of software drivers that encodes data sent over the network media and decodes received data. These network interface adapter drivers must follow a set of Windows device driver specifications, called the **Network Driver Interface Specifications (NDIS)**. The main purpose of NDIS is to define a standard API (Application Programming Interface) for NICs so that a single NIC can support multiple network protocols. NDIS also provides a library of functions, which are commonly referred to as a "wrapper". The NDIS wrapper is used by MAC drivers and by higher level protocol drivers such as TCP/IP. The information about the hardware implementation for a NIC is wrapped by a MAC device driver so that a common programming interface can be used by all NICs for the same media. This makes the development of both MAC and protocol drivers easier for driver writers, who can all follow one set of standards (NDIS).

Figure 10-1 Packet Structure

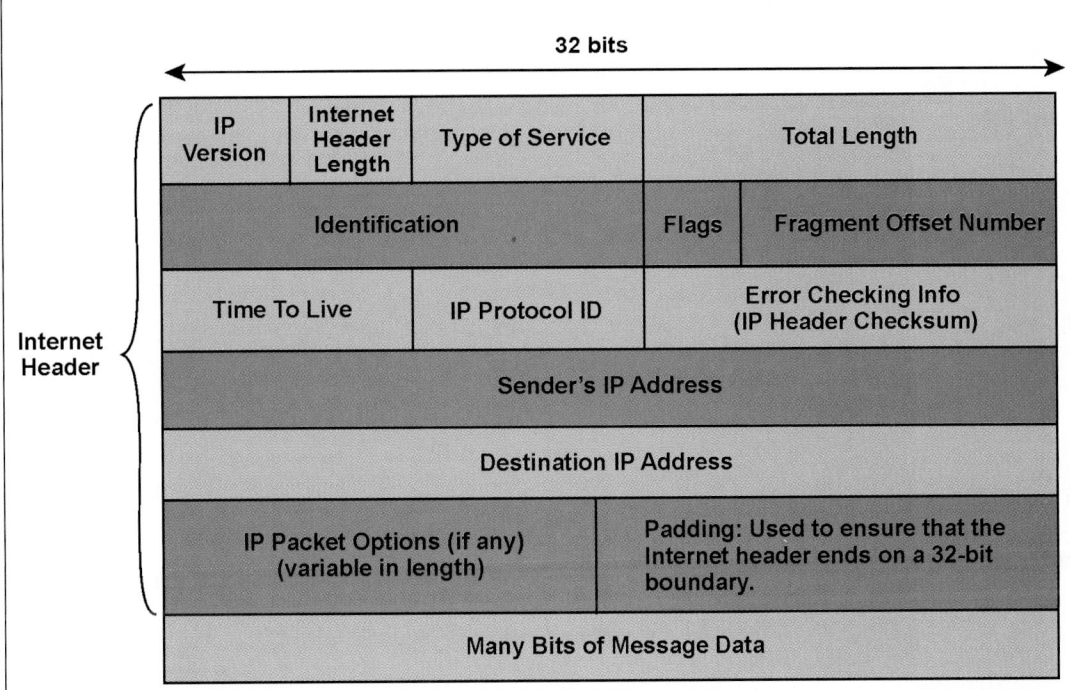

- **IP Version: (4 bits)** The Version field indicates the format of the Internet header, either IPv4 or IPv6
- **Internet Header Length: (4 bits)** The length of the Internet header in 32-bit words (x4 = length in bits). It points to the beginning of the data. The minimum value for a correct header is 5.
- **Type of Service: (8 bits)** Provides parameters for quality of service. In general there is a three-way tradeoff between low-delay, high-reliability, and high-throughput.
- **Total Length: (16 bits)** The length of the datagram, including Internet header and data, measured in octets. A datagram can be up to 65,535 octets long; however, datagrams this long are impractical for most hosts and networks. All hosts must be prepared to accept datagrams of up to 576 octets, either whole or in fragments.
- **Identification: (16 bits)** An identifying value assigned by the sender to aid in assembling the fragments of a datagram.
- **Flags: (3 bits)** Various control flags Bit 0: reserved, must be zero

  Bit 1: (DF) 0 = May Fragment, 1 = Don't Fragment. Bit 2: (MF) 0 = Last Fragment, 1 = More Fragments.
- **Fragment Offset: (13 bits)** Indicates where in the datagram this fragment belongs.
- **Time To Live: (8 bits)** The maximum time the datagram is allowed to remain in the Internet system. If this field contains the value zero, the datagram must be destroyed.
- **IP Protocol ID: (8 bits)** Indicates the next layer protocol used in the data portion of the IP datagram.
- **IP Header Checksum: (16 bits)** Checksum for the header only. Must be recomputed and verified each time the Internet header is processed because some header fields change (for example, Time To Live).

skill 1

Introducing Networking Concepts
(cont'd)

exam objective   Basic knowledge

overview

Binding is a process that configures a protocol to make use of a specific NIC. It provides information about available network services that client computers can use to make connections over a network. During the installation of Windows Server 2003, each protocol that is installed is bound to the NIC. NDIS allows you to bind multiple protocols to a NIC and enables each protocol to send information on the same network. However, you can manually change the binding order of the protocols to enhance network performance (**Figure 10-2**). The **binding order** establishes which protocol should be used first when a network connection is established. It is the client computer in an exchange that determines which protocol will be used to establish the connection. For example, if you frequently use a server to access data on other servers on a Microsoft network, and you must also occasionally locate files on an older Netware server, you will have both TCP/IP and NWLink configured on your network adapter. Since your most frequent tasks involve the use of TCP/IP, you will position the protocols so that TCP/IP is the protocol of choice for the Client for Microsoft Networks service. You do this in the Advanced Settings dialog box, which can be accessed from the Advanced menu in the Network Connections window.

Networks can be classified into three main types based on the location and proximity of the computers: local area network (LAN), metropolitan area network (MAN), and wide area network (WAN). A LAN is used to connect computers, printers, and other devices in the same physical location or within a limited geographic area, such as an office building. When you connect two or more LANs within the same city, the resulting network is known as a MAN. When you connect two or more geographically separated LANs or MANs, the resulting network is called a WAN. For example, you can connect the branch offices located in New Jersey, California, Alaska, and Los Angeles to form a WAN.

The cables that join computers in a network can have different layouts called network topologies. Network topologies are often separated into two types, logical, and physical. The physical network topology describes how the devices are cabled. A logical network topology describes the logical path each packet will take across the network. For instance, in a bus/bus (physical bus, logical bus) topology, such as 10Base-2 or Thin Ethernet, the **nodes** (all devices which are capable of communicating on the network) are wired in a bus, meaning they all connect to the same physical cable. This type of physical topology requires that each end of the bus be terminated, to prevent signals from rebounding at the end of each bus and causing signal errors (**Figure 10-3**). This is also a logical bus, because each data transmission must pass through each computer, regardless of the final destination.

In a physical ring topology, adjacent devices are connected and the nodes are arranged in a circular shape (**Figure 10-4**). Each device is connected directly to two other devices, one on either side of it, and no terminator is necessary. This is sometimes referred to as a closed loop configuration. Messages travel around the ring and each node will receive all messages, but each node only listens to messages that are addressed to it. While workstations that are next to each other are directly connected, the other workstations and devices are indirectly connected and data passes through one or more intermediate nodes in order to reach its destination.

You can use a **router** to connect LANs having different network topologies and to exchange data between computers and devices on different networks. For example, you could set up a router with both 10Base-T and 10Base-2 Ethernet and Token Ring. Routers must be strategically placed to efficiently distribute data traffic and provide the best path for transferring data.

Figure 10-2 Changing the binding order

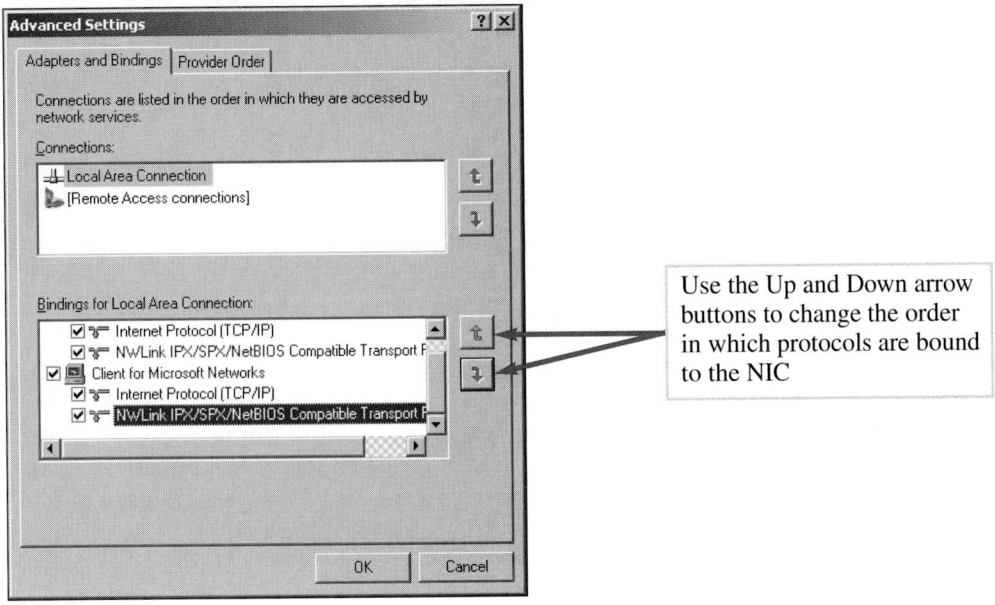

Use the Up and Down arrow buttons to change the order in which protocols are bound to the NIC

Figure 10-3 Bus network topology

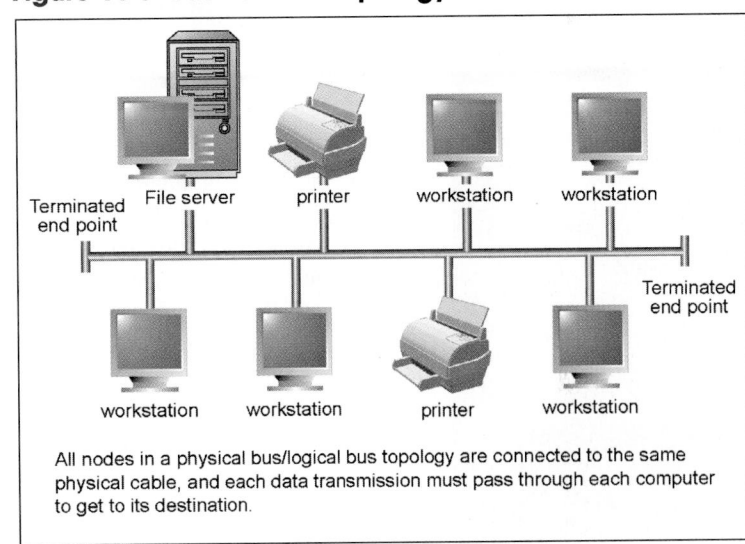

All nodes in a physical bus/logical bus topology are connected to the same physical cable, and each data transmission must pass through each computer to get to its destination.

Figure 10-4 Ring network topology

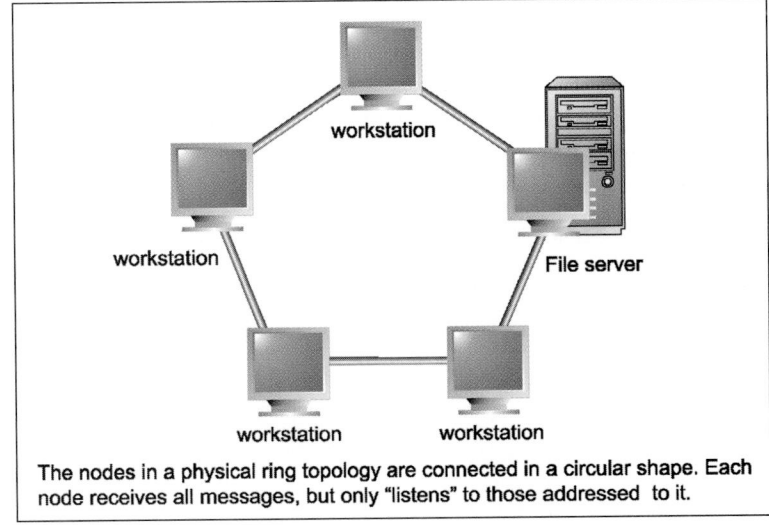

The nodes in a physical ring topology are connected in a circular shape. Each node receives all messages, but only "listens" to those addressed to it.

skill 1

Introducing Networking Concepts
(cont'd)

exam objective   Basic knowledge

more

Protocols that can route through LANs and WANs via a router are called **routable protocols**. Examples of routable protocols include TCP/IP and NWLink. **Non-routable protocols** can only be used on a local subnet. Examples of non-routable protocols include NetBEUI and Data Link Control (DLC), which are quickly becoming obsolete. NetBEUI, which was appropriate only for small LANs, is no longer supported by either Windows Server 2003 or Windows XP Professional. DLC, which was used to connect to IBM mainframes and to older network printers such as some Hewlett Packard printers, is no longer included as a network protocol that you can install in Windows Server 2003. You must now download the DLC Protocol for Windows XP, which is supported by Windows XP, Windows XP Professional, and Windows Server 2003, from the Microsoft Web site (**Figure 10-5**).

Some transport protocols are connection-oriented while others are connectionless protocols. A **connection-oriented protocol** establishes a confirmed connection with the destination computer. The transfer of data occurs in three steps: connection establishment, data transfer, and connection release (**Figure 10-6**). During the first step, a connection is established with the communicating computer; next, the data is transferred; and finally, the connection terminates. The concept of a connection-oriented protocol is similar to making a telephone call, where you dial a number to establish a connection, convey the message, and then terminate the call. TCP is a connection-oriented protocol.

On the other hand, with **connectionless protocols**, no connection is established between the communicating devices. Connectionless protocols are like delivering mail where a letter is dropped into the mailbox without confirming that the letter has reached its destination. Connectionless protocols, such as UDP, are used by hosts to send messages to a destination address, but there is no guarantee that they will reach their destination. There is no acknowledgement that the data packets have been received, so data is not retransmitted. Using the mailbox analogy, this means that if the address is incorrect, the sender will not be notified that the recipient has not received the message.

Figure 10-5 DLC Protocol for Windows XP

DLC Protocol for Windows XP

DLC is a transport protocol commonly used for communicating with mainframes. This DLC protocol is provided as is and is intended to be used only with Windows XP and Windows Server 2003 family operating systems.

Quick Info	
File Name:	dlc.exe
Download Size:	74 KB
Date Published:	12/15/2001
Version:	5.0.2195.2104

DLC Protocol for Windows XP
English
<u>Download</u>

Related Resources
- <u>Community Resources for Developers</u>
- <u>Developer Center for Windows XP</u>
- <u>Subscribe to MSDN and Stay Current with the Latest Updates</u>
- <u>Home Page for Driver Development Kits</u>

Overview

DLC is a transport protocol commonly used for communicating with mainframes. This DLC protocol is provided as is and is intended to be used only with Windows XP and Windows Server 2003 family operating systems. To use the DLC driver with SNA Server or Host Integration Server 2000 you must obtain it the from Microsoft Host Integration 2000 product CD.

System Requirements

- **Supported Operating Systems:** Windows XP
- Windows XP Professional or Windows Server 2003

Instructions

Supported by Windows XP, Windows XP Professional, and Windows Server 2003

Figure 10-6 Connection-oriented protocols

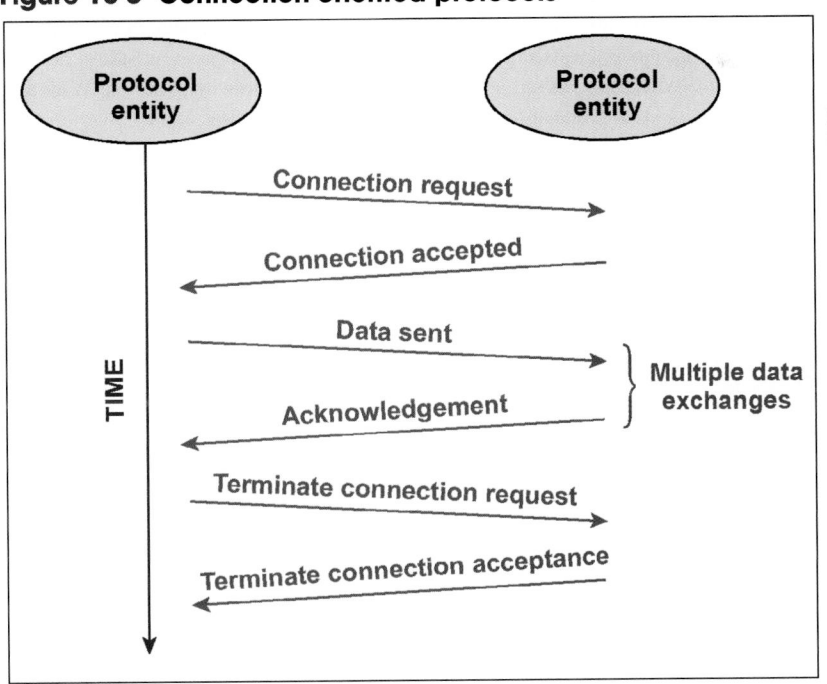

skill 2

Introducing Network Protocols

exam objective

Basic knowledge

overview

All editions of Windows Server 2003, Standard Edition support the installation of the following protocols:

TCP/IP: Windows Server 2003 uses **TCP/IP (Transmission Control Protocol/Internet Protocol)**, which includes IP version 4 (IPv4), as its default transport protocol. TCP/IP enables communication between computers on most networks, even when they include diverse hardware architecture and operating systems. Using TCP/IP, Windows Server 2003 can communicate with other Microsoft networking devices, as well as non-Microsoft systems, such as UNIX. TCP/IP is used by networks to access the Internet and the intranets in an organization by providing a standard suite of protocols that are designed for LAN and WAN environments **(Figure 10-7)**.

AppleTalk: AppleTalk is Apple Computer's protocol designed to allow communication between Apple Macintosh computers. AppleTalk allows applications and processes to exchange data and share resources such as printers and shares on file servers. You can enable communication between computers running the Macintosh operating system and Windows Server 2003 by installing AppleTalk and File Services for Macintosh. You can install Print Services for Macintosh so that Macintosh users can send print jobs to a print spooler on a Windows Server 2003 machine.

NWLink IPX/SPX/NetBIOS Compatible Transport protocol: IPX/SPX (Internetwork Packet Exchange/Sequenced Packet Exchange) is a connectionless protocol used for communication between computers on Novell NetWare and other networks. It consists of two protocols: IPX and SPX. The IPX protocol is used to transfer data over multiple networks. IPX provides unreliable communication, as it does not guarantee the delivery of data. On the other hand, SPX, which is layered on top of IPX just as TCP and UDP are layered on top of IP, is a connection-oriented protocol. It provides reliable transfer of application-specific data. **NWLink (NetWare Link)** is a protocol that emulates IPX/SPX within the Microsoft network architecture. NWLink enables computers running Microsoft operating systems to communicate with older NetWare servers and vice versa. However, NWLink does not permit direct access to the files and printers on a NetWare server. To access these resources from a Windows 2003 Server, you must install a service called Gateway Service for NetWare (GSNW). GSNW provides the client, or Workstation Service, required to log in to the Netware server to access resources.

Microsoft TCP/IP version 6: To date, TCP/IP using **IP version 6 (IPv6)** has mainly been used experimentally for testing purposes. It is the protocol of the future, designed to be more easily configured, more secure, and simpler for devices, in particular, routers, to process. It will also address the problem of a diminishing supply of unique IP addresses. When IPv6 is in widespread use, 128-bit IP addresses will be possible, greatly expanding the number of possible addresses on the Internet.

Network Monitor Driver: The **Network Monitor Driver** is used to obtain network performance statistics used by the System Monitor and the Network Monitor to observe and troubleshoot network events.

Reliable Multicast Protocol: Generally, User Datagram Protocol (UDP) is used to transmit multicast data streams rather than Transmission Control Protocol (TCP) because TCP is designed for unicast data streams. However, remember, with UDP there is no guarantee that data packets will reach their destination because there is no acknowledgement that the data packets have been received and no data retransmission. Therefore, reliable multicast protocols have been developed to support the dependable transmission of multicast data streams. **Pragmatic General Multicast (PGM)** is the reliable multicast protocol supported by Windows Server 2003. Although it cannot compete with TCP/IP in its capabilities and functionality, it does provide fundamental reliability for applications that support PGM. PGM operates at the Transport layer in the DOD (Department of Defense) model directly above IP, using neither UDP nor TCP to transmit messages in a multicast data stream. To use PGM, you must add the Reliable Multicast Protocol and create or use PGM-enabled applications.

tip

The Macintosh operating system has supported TCP/IP since OS 7.5 so, in reality, you can use TCP/IP to communicate with Mac clients. However, on the test, AppleTalk is the protocol used when connecting to Mac clients.

Figure 10-7 Windows Server 2003 network protocols

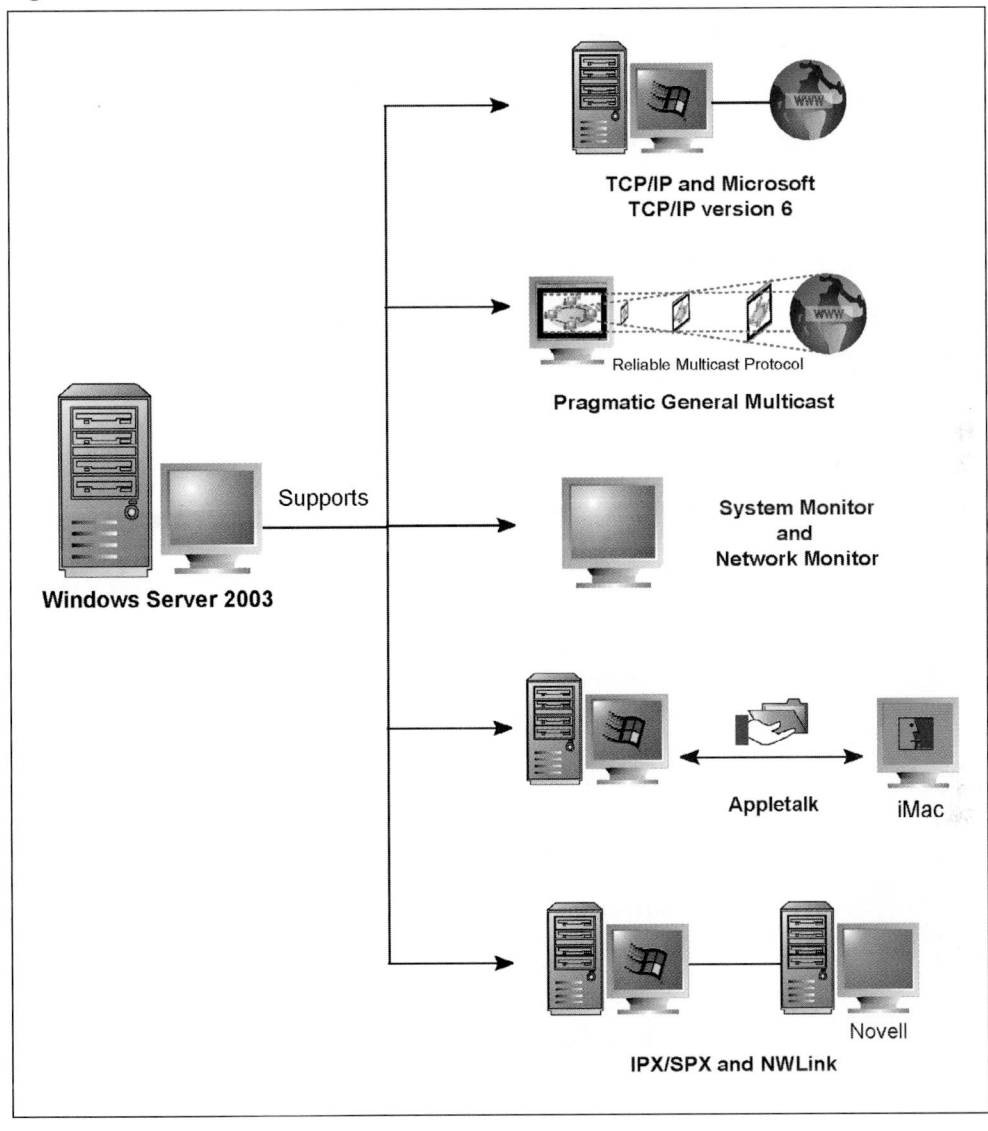

skill 3

Identifying the Fundamentals of TCP/IP

exam objective

Basic knowledge

overview

The TCP/IP protocol consists of a suite of protocols that are used to provide connectivity across operating systems and hardware platforms. TCP/IP is a scalable protocol. As a result, you can implement it in different types of networks, from small offices to large corporations. TCP/IP is the core protocol for the Internet and it provides reliable data transfer because it is a routable protocol.

The TCP/IP suite of protocols is based on a four-layered conceptual model called the **DOD (Department of Defense) model**. The four layers are the Network Interface, Internet, Transport, and Application layers **(Figure 10-8)**.

◆ **Network Interface:** This is the physical layer. The function of this layer is to place TCP/IP packets on the network medium and to receive them off of the network medium. Also known as the Network Access Layer, it is located at the base of the DOD model. TCP/IP can be used to connect different network types because it was specifically designed to be independent of the medium of connectivity. Thus, TCP/IP can be used to connect LAN technologies such as Ethernet or Token Ring and WAN technologies such as X.25 or Frame Relay. It also means that TCP/IP was modifiable as newer network technologies such as Asynchronous Transfer Mode (ATM) were developed.

◆ **Internet:** The Internet Layer is responsible for addressing and routing IP datagrams. Each packet that is being sent or received is called an IP datagram. An IP datagram contains information about the source and destination addresses that are used to transfer data between computers on a network and across networks. The Internet layer supports the following protocols:

   • **Internet Protocol (IP):** This is a connectionless protocol that is responsible for the delivery of packets, which includes the process of disassembling and reassembling them during the transmission process. However, IP is an unreliable protocol, as it does not always guarantee the delivery of packets and does not attempt to recover data if it is lost, duplicated, or delayed. All other network services in the TCP/IP suite are built on top of IP.

   • **Address Resolution Protocol (ARP):** The ARP protocol is responsible for resolving the IP address of a computer to its MAC address. When packets are transferred on a LAN, ARP broadcasts an inquiry packet that includes the IP address of the destination computer. All hosts are required to listen for ARP requests. The destination computer replies to this inquiry by sending its MAC address to the source computer. In order to improve network performance, this information is stored in the ARP cache for a short period, until it has timed out.

   • **Internet Control Message Protocol (ICMP):** ICMP supports packets containing error, control, and informational messages to IP hosts. This information, also called an ICMP packet, is used by higher-level protocols to solve transmission problems and by network administrators to discover where network problems are located. For example, ICMP sends a Destination Unreachable message to the source host if IP is unable to deliver a packet to the destination. ICMP packets are also used by the Ping, Pathping, and Tracert utilities to find out if an IP device on the network is working. Some common ICMP messages are described in **Table 10-1**.

   • **Internet Group Management Protocol (IGMP):** IGMP is responsible for the management of IP multicasting. IP multicasting is defined as the transmission of an IP datagram to a set of hosts called the IP multicast group, which is identified by a single IP multicast address. IGMP's primary job is to keep track of multicast groups and their memberships.

Figure 10-8 The DOD model

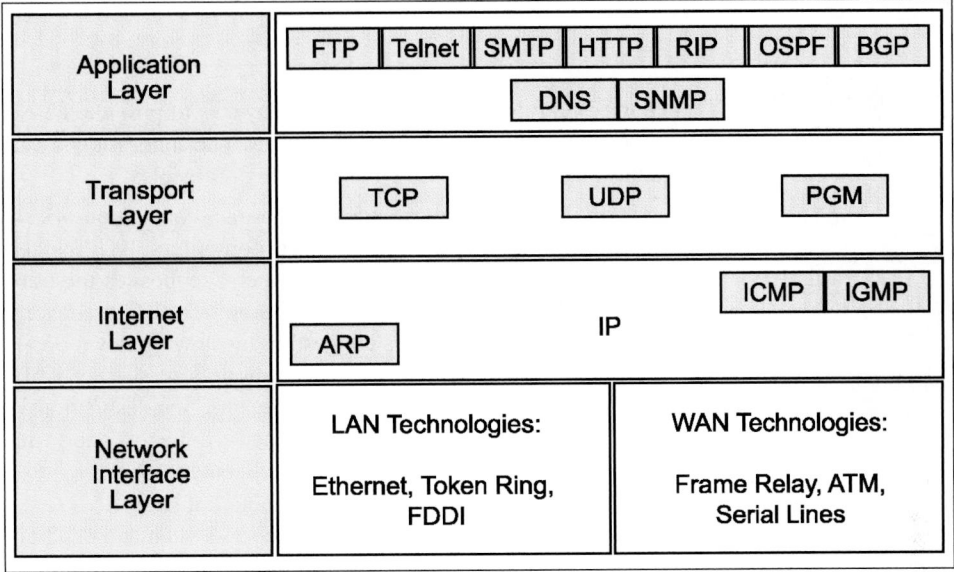

Application Layer	FTP	Telnet	SMTP	HTTP	RIP	OSPF	BGP
	DNS	SNMP					
Transport Layer	TCP		UDP		PGM		
Internet Layer	ARP		IP		ICMP	IGMP	
Network Interface Layer	LAN Technologies: Ethernet, Token Ring, FDDI			WAN Technologies: Frame Relay, ATM, Serial Lines			

Table 10-1   Common ICMP messages

ICMP Message	Function
Echo Request	Simple troubleshooting message used to check connectivity to the destination computer.
Echo Reply	Response to an ICMP Echo Request.
Redirect	Sent by a router to inform a sending host about a better path to a destination computer.
Source Quench	Sent by a router to inform a sending host that its IP datagrams are being removed due to congestion at the router. The sending host then lowers the transmission rate of the stream.
Destination Unreachable	Sent by a router or the destination computer to inform the sending host that a packet cannot be delivered.
Time Exceeded	Sent from a router to indicate to the client that its packet has been dropped due to the Time To Live field in the IP packet being reduced to zero.

skill 3

Identifying the Fundamentals of TCP/IP (cont'd)

exam objective

Basic knowledge

overview

◆ **Transport:** The function of the Transport layer is to provide the Application layer with session and datagram communication services. The connection is established between the communicating computers using the following protocols:

- **TCP:** This protocol provides one-to-one, connection-oriented, stream-oriented, reliable delivery of data between computers. TCP establishes a connection between the communicating computers, sequences the transfer of packets, and acknowledges the packets sent. Additionally, TCP recovers packets lost during transmission and handles congestion by slowing down or speeding up. It is used when you need to transfer large amounts of data reliably and it requires an acknowledgement that the data has reached the destination.
- **UDP:** This protocol provides a one-to-one or one-to-many connectionless communications service. UDP is unreliable as it does not guarantee the delivery of data. It is used when only a small amount of data needs to be transferred, such as data that can be sent in a single packet, and when the reliability of the transmission is not of primary importance.
- **Pragmatic General Multicast (PGM):** This is the TCP reliable multicast protocol supported by Windows Server 2003.

◆ **Application:** This layer is located at the top of the DOD model. The Application layer enables applications to access the services of the other layers and defines the protocols that applications must use to exchange data. The most common Application layer protocols are listed below:

- **Hypertext Transfer Protocol (HTTP):** This protocol is used to transfer the contents of a Web page into a browser in order to view HTML files. HTML files make up the Web pages of the World Wide Web.
- **File Transfer Protocol (FTP):** This protocol is used to download files and programs from a server to your computer, as well as to upload files from your computer to a server. FTP transfers the entire file from one computer to another.
- **Simple Mail Transfer Protocol (SMTP):** This protocol is used to transfer e-mail messages between computers.
- **Telnet:** This protocol is used to log on to network host computers from a remote location.

Another model that is used to conceptualize network communications is the **OSI (Open Systems Interconnection) Reference Model**. The OSI Reference Model uses a seven-layered networking framework. Just like the DOD model, the various networking protocols are implemented within this layered framework. During network communication, data management is transferred from one layer to the next. In the OSI model, data transmission begins at the Application layer in the sending device and moves layer by layer to the bottommost Physical layer. Each layer in this communication pipeline is responsible for specific functions. Data is then transmitted over a connection medium to the receiving device where it proceeds back up the data management chain from the Physical layer to the Application layer until finally it reaches the destination device. At each level, specific functions are performed. Each layer in the DOD model corresponds to one or more layers in the OSI model.

The seven layers in the OSI model are **(Figure 10-9):**

◆ **Application (Layer 7):** The Application layer is at the top of the conceptual model and provides various services to applications that are specifically written to run over the network. It enables access to network services that support applications and is responsible for network access, data flow control, and error recovery. It is also responsible for reconciling the

**Figure 10-9 The OSI (Open Systems Inter-
connection) Reference Model**

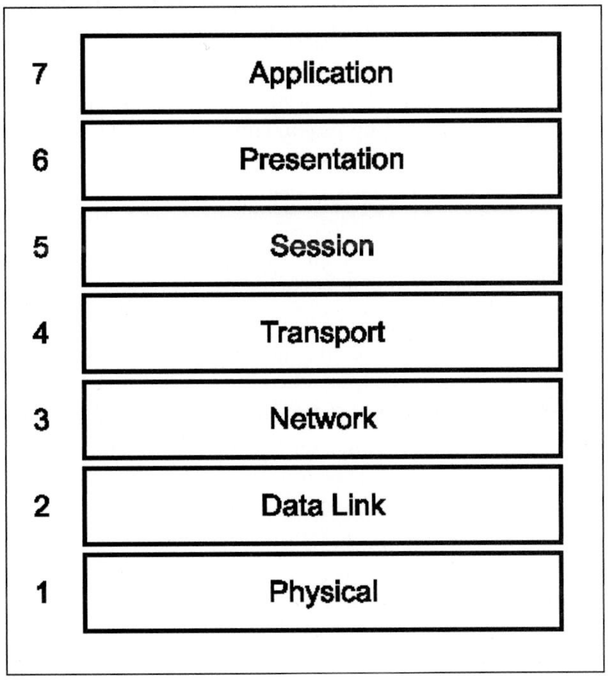

7	Application
6	Presentation
5	Session
4	Transport
3	Network
2	Data Link
1	Physical

skill 3 *Identifying the Fundamentals of TCP/IP (cont'd)*

exam objective   Basic knowledge

overview

differences in how files are transferred between systems that have different file naming conventions, different methods of characterizing text lines, and many other functions. E-mail, directory lookup, and numerous other services are also handled at this level.

◆ **Presentation (Layer 6):** The Presentation layer converts data. It is responsible for the syntax of data transmission, for example, making sure that data is encoded using a customary and agreed upon method. Different systems use different code to represent character strings, integers, floating point numbers, etc. These inconsistencies must be resolved in some manner in order for communication between different systems to take place. The Presentation layer handles converting data structures from the method used by the computer to a network standard that can be understood by all parties in a data transaction. It translates from the application to the network in data transmission and from the network back to the application as data is received. The Presentation layer is responsible for protocol conversion, character conversion, and expanding graphics commands. Data compression and cryptography are also handled at this level.

◆ **Session (Layer 5):** The Session layer is designed to deal with any problems that do not involve communication issues. It enables data transport by allowing users to establish sessions and by supplying services that are needed by certain applications. The Session layer is responsible for identifying the parties so that only the correct participants are included, and for managing who can send data and for how long they will be allowed to send it. Synchronization services at this level ensure that, for example, if a file transfer is interrupted, when the connection is reestablished, the file transfer will resume at the point at which it was broken off.

◆ **Transport (Layer 4):** The Transport layer supplies control for all communications from end point to end point. It controls the flow of data between parties across a network. Data is broken down into packets at this level on the sending computer and reassembled from the data packets at this level on the receiving computer. The Transport layer also supplies error-checking so that data will be delivered with no errors, no data loss, and no data duplication. Acknowledgement of successful data transmission and requests for retransmission if data packets do not arrive (or if they arrive with errors) also occurs at this level.

◆ **Network (Layer 3):** The Network layer is responsible for logical addressing and routing. If the router cannot send data frames as large as those it has received from the transmitting computer, at the network layer the frames will be broken down into smaller units. In the receiving computer, data packets will be reassembled at the Network layer.

◆ **Data Link (Layer 2):** The Data Link layer supplies error control between adjoining nodes and handles the data frames between the Network and Physical layers. It ensures that frames are transferred with no errors to other computers from the Physical layer. The Data Link layer converts data packets into frames for the Physical layer. At the receiving computer, it takes the raw data received from the Physical layer and packages it into data frames to send on the Network layer.

◆ **Physical (Layer 1):** The Physical layer, which is at the bottom of the conceptual model, connects the networking component to the media that will be used to transmit data. The raw bit stream is transmitted over the physical cables at this level. The physical structure is also defined at this level, including the cables, network cards, how the NICs attach to the hardware, how cable is attached to the NICs, and the techniques that will be used to transfer the bit stream to the cables. The Network Interface layer in the DOD model corresponds to the Data Link and Physical layers of the OSI model.

The data flow in the OSI model is illustrated in **Figure 10-10** and the protocols that operate at each level are illustrated in **Figure 10-11**.

Figure 10-10 Data flow in the OSI model

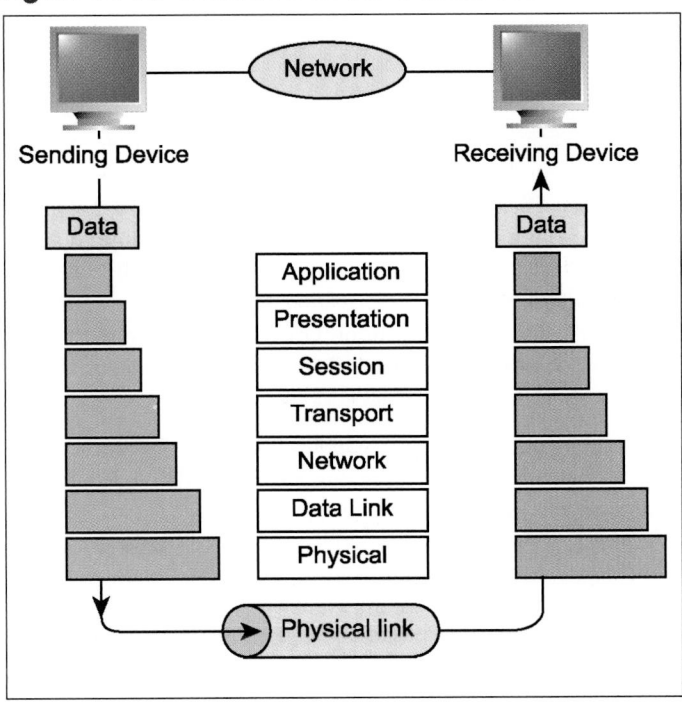

Figure 10-11 The OSI model and the TCP/IP protocol suite

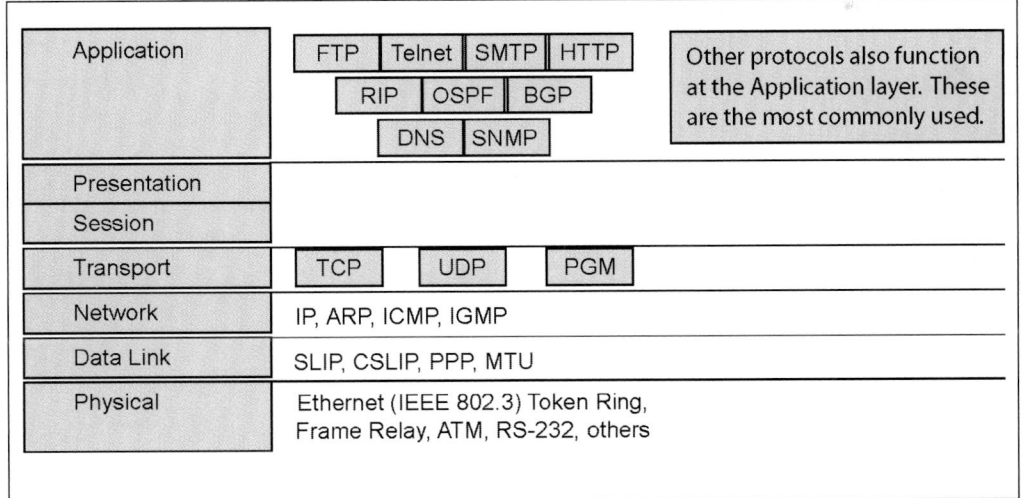

skill 3

Identifying the Fundamentals of TCP/IP (cont'd)

exam objective   Basic knowledge

more

The Application layer in the DOD model (Application, Presentation, and Session layers in the OSI model) also provides services that are used to access and manage resources on TCP/IP networks. These services are described in **Table 10-2**. DNS (Domain Name System) is the name resolution service used to resolve a host name to an IP address. Routers use routing protocols such as Routing Information Protocol (RIP) or Open Shortest Path First (OSPF) to send and receive routing information on an IP internetwork. Border Gateway Protocol (BGP) is used to exchange routing information for the Internet. It is the protocol used between ISPs. Simple Network Management Protocol (SNMP) is used to configure network devices for data collection that is used for network monitoring.

The Application layer allows applications to access the services provided by TCP/IP protocols through application programming interfaces (APIs). An API consists of a set of functions and commands that are called by an application code to perform network functions. Examples of the application programming interfaces provided by the Application layer are Windows Sockets (Winsock) and the .NET Framework classes. Windows Sockets provides a standard API for Microsoft Windows operating systems. Winsock allows a Windows program to send data over any network transport protocol. .NET framework classes are essentially the Windows API for .NET. Microsoft supplies core functionality that programmers can use when building applications in the .NET Framework classes. .NET is a new set of application technologies that are used to create and use Extensible Markup Language (XML)-based applications, processes, and Web sites. .NET applications can share information and combine data and functionality with one another. .NET is based on Internet functionality, but it is the new development model for Windows applications and will soon be a part of all Microsoft programs, servers, and tools **(Figure 10-12)**.

Table 10-2 · Application layer services (DOD model)

Service	Function
Domain Name System (DNS)	DNS is used to resolve a host name to an IP address.
Routing Information Protocol (RIP)	RIP is a routing protocol that routers use to exchange routing information on a network.
Open Shortest Path First	OSPF is a routing protocol developed for IP networks that is based on the SPF algorithm (sometimes called the Dijkstra algorithm, after its creator).
Border Gateway Protocol (BGP)	BGP is a routing protocol used to exchange routing information for the Internet. It is the protocol used between ISPs. Universities and corporations generally use an Interior Gateway Protocol (IGP) such as RIP or OSPF, while ISPs use BGP4.
Simple Network Management Protocol (SNMP)	SNMP is used to collect and exchange network management information such as the router used to connect computers.

Figure 10-12 The .Net framework

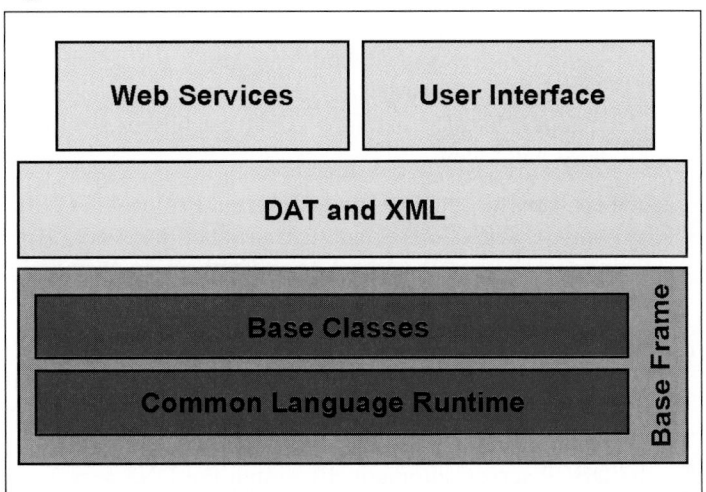

skill 4

Configuring TCP/IP

exam objective

Basic knowledge

overview

The TCP/IP protocol is installed by default during the installation of Windows Server 2003. However, in order to enable communication between hosts on your network, you will have to configure the TCP/IP parameters. You can either use a static IP addressing scheme, in which you will have to manually assign IP addresses to every network host, or you can use dynamic IP addressing, in which an IP address is assigned to a host each time it logs on to the network. In dynamic IP addressing, the DHCP service is installed on one of your servers to create a DHCP server, which will automatically assign IP addresses to network hosts as they boot up. Many, if not all, of the servers on your network will have to have static IP addresses so that there will be no difficulties in accessing them. For example, the DHCP server must have a constant IP address, and you may want each server running the WINS or DNS service to have a constant IP address. For these servers, you can either assign IP addresses manually or use client reservations. A client reservation refers to a specific IP address within a range of permanently reserved addresses that is only leased to a specific DHCP client (defined by the MAC address) to ensure that a particular host will always receive the same IP address.

When you configure static IP addressing, the TCP/IP parameters that you will need to configure are (**Table 10-3**):

◆ **IP address:** A 32-bit number divided into 4 octets. As you have learned, there are two parts: the network ID and the host ID. The **network ID** (also known as the network address) identifies all hosts on the network and the **host ID** identifies a specific host.

◆ **Subnet mask:** A **subnet mask** is a 32-bit value that distinguishes the network ID from the host ID, regardless of whether classful or classless IP addresses are being used. For example, consider the subnet mask for the class C IP address 205.220.195.235 with a subnet mask 255.255.255.0. In this example, 255.255.255.0 indicates that the network ID for the IP address is 205.220.195, and 235 is the host ID. The default subnet mask for class A IP addresses is 255.0.0.0, class B IP addresses use 255.255.0.0, and for class C it is 255.255.255.0.

◆ **Default gateway:** A **default gateway** is the default router for a TCP/IP host. It is the router that will be used to access any network that is not specifically defined in the host's routing table. The default gateway establishes a set route that communicating TCP/IP hosts will follow.

You configure IP addresses in the **Internet Protocol (TCP/IP) Properties** dialog box. In the **Network Connections** window, right-click the Local Area Connection icon and select **Properties** to open the **Local Area Connection Properties** dialog box. Select **Internet Protocol (TCP/IP)** in the **This connection uses the following items** box and click the **Properties** button (**Figure 10-13**).

If you are configuring a client to obtain an IP address automatically through a DHCP server, select the **Obtain an IP address automatically** option button. The client will contact a DHCP server on the network to be assigned an IP address. If you are also having the DHCP server automatically assign the DNS server, select the **Obtain DNS server automatically** option button. To statically configure an IP address, select the **Use the following IP address** option button and enter the IP address you are going to use. When you click in the **Subnet mask** text box, the default subnet mask for that class of IP address will be automatically assigned. If you are subnetting the base network, you will have to edit the subnet mask. Finally, enter the IP address for the default gateway, which is the IP address for the router that will link this computer with other networks (**Figure 10-14**).

Table 10-3 TCP/IP Settings

TCP/IP Parameter	Description
IP address	Used to identify a TCP/IP host: It is a 32-bit number expressed as 4 8-bit octets. Each octet, which is separated by a period, can be between zero and 255. Computers connected to a TCP/IP network are referred to as TCP/IP hosts. Each host must have a unique IP address for each network adapter card in a computer running TCP/IP. An IP address consists of a network ID and a host ID. The network ID identifies all hosts on the network, while the host ID represents a specific computer. For example, in the IP address 198.154.1.207, 198.154.1 is the network ID, and 207 is the host ID.
Subnet mask	Another 32-bit number, divided into four octets that is used to break up the IP address into the two parts: the network ID and the host ID. The subnet mask blocks or "masks" a part of the IP address in order to differentiate between the two. Companies generally either use the same subnet mask throughout their network or a VLSM (Variable Length Subnet Mask) subnetting scheme. Variable length subnet masking is a method of allocating sub-netted network IDs that use subnet masks of different sizes.
Default gateway	A 32-bit number written in dotted decimal notation that identifies the IP address of the router. Gateways or routers are used to connect different networks. A default gateway acts as an intermediate device between hosts on different network segments. TCP/IP sends packets to the router, which acts as a gateway to remote networks. The default gateway dispatches the data packets to the destination network. In most cases, you must configure an IP address with a default gateway in order to make remote communications possible. You do not need to configure a default gateway unless you are connecting to an external network. You also do not need to configure a default gateway if you wish to manually configure routing table entries to each remote network.

Figure 10-13 The Local Area Connection Properties dialog box

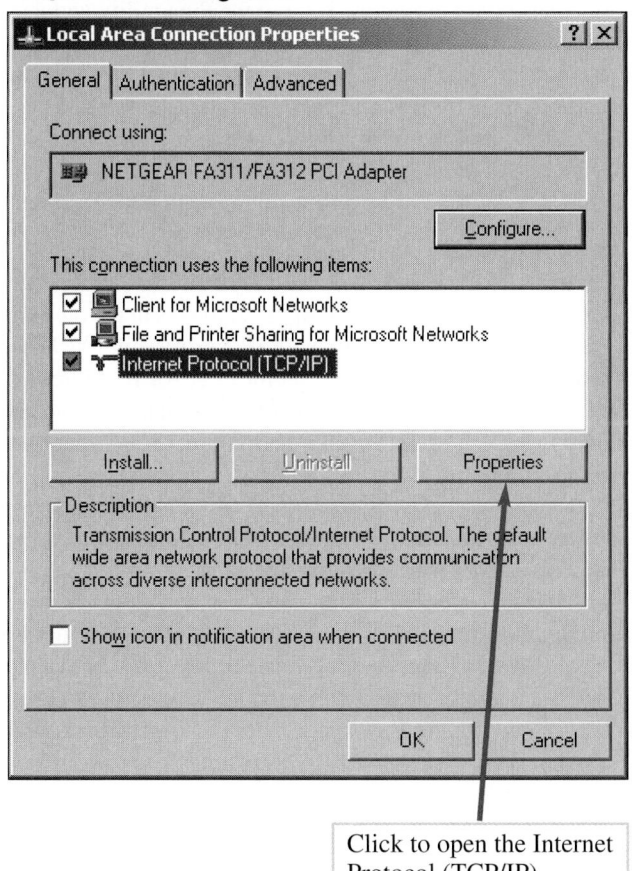

Click to open the Internet Protocol (TCP/IP) Properties dialog box

Figure 10-14 The Internet Protocol (TCP/IP) Properties dialog box

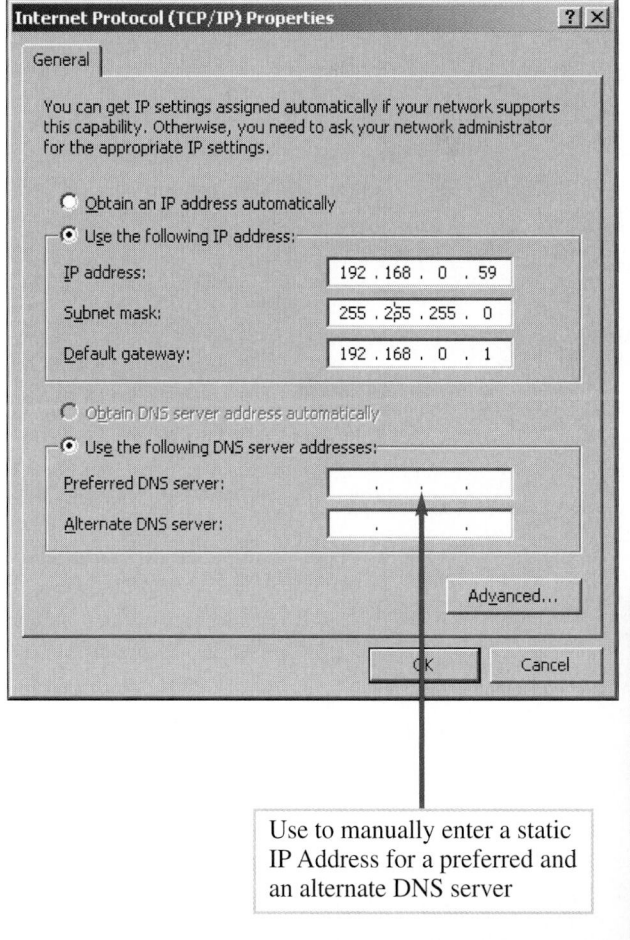

Use to manually enter a static IP Address for a preferred and an alternate DNS server

skill 4

Configuring TCP/IP (cont'd)

exam objective

Basic knowledge

more

Since people identify computers by their names, there must be a process for resolving names to IP addresses. There are two kinds of names associated with a computer: host names and NetBIOS names (also known as computer names). **Host names** are used on computers that use Domain Name System (DNS) naming convention. Host names can be up to 256 characters long and can contain letters, numbers, and special characters such as "_" and ".". **NetBIOS names** were used on older Windows networks and they are limited to 15 characters. The NetBIOS name is registered dynamically when computers or services start, or when users log on. A process known as name resolution is used to map computer names to IP addresses. Windows Server 2003 uses five different possible methods for name resolution, three of which are for NetBIOS name resolution, and two of which are for host name resolution. NetBIOS names can be resolved by using a broadcast (only useful in resolving names on the local segment), an LMHOSTS file (a static text file linking the NetBIOS names to IP addresses), or Windows Internet Naming Service (WINS), a server service that dynamically maps NetBIOS names to IP addresses. Host name resolution can be performed using a HOSTS file (similar to LMHOSTS, but only for host names) or Domain Name System (DNS), which is a server service that stores a hierarchical database containing the host names and IP addresses.

In order to plan the implementation of the IP addressing scheme for your network, you must understand several conventions. First, the IP address range 127.0.0.0 - 127.255.255.254 cannot be used on any network. This range has been set aside for the IP loopback function, which is used in diagnosing network connectivity problems. You use the Ping utility with any loopback address (or simply enter ping loopback, or *<host_name>* loopback) to determine if the local host is correctly configured to connect to a TCP/IP network. Second, there are several groups of reserved IP addresses that are referred to as private addresses. These addresses can only be used on private networks. They are most commonly used on private networks that use either Internet Connection Sharing (ICS) or Network Address Translation (NAT) or another NAT device, such as a proxy server, or a firewall, through which connections to the Internet are made. They cannot be used on the Internet.

The Internet Assigned Numbers Authority (IANA) has reserved the three blocks of the IP addresses outlined in **Table 10-4** for private networks. In addition, IP addresses in the range of 169.254.0.0 -169.254.255.255 are reserved for **Automatic Private IP Addressing (APIPA)**. APIPA is used by DHCP clients when no DHCP server can be located. An IP address is randomly chosen from the private APIPA address series, which is not in use on the Internet. In this way, computers on a LAN, where there is no DHCP server, or on a network where the DHCP server is down, can still be assigned an IP address and communicate with other computers on the same subnet. APIPA generates an address and broadcasts that address across the network. If no other computer responds to this address, the computer knows that it can assign the address to itself. The IP address will always be in the format 169.254.x.x and the subnet mask will always be 255.255.0.0. However, APIPA cannot assign a default gateway, so remote access, such as communication on the Internet or with outside networks, will not be possible. Computers that have used APIPA to assign themselves an IP address can usually only communicate with other computers on the same subnet that have also assigned themselves an IP address using APIPA. At present, most current versions of Unix, Linux, Mac OS, Windows 98, Windows ME, Windows 2000, Windows 2003, and Windows XP all support APIPA.

tip

On a subnet where there is no DHCP server, Windows 2000, XP, and Server 2003 computers can still use DHCP rather than APIPA if there is a router on the subnet that supports DHCP/BOOTP forwarding (also known as RFC 1542 Compliance), or if there is a Windows 2000, NT 4.0 Server, or Server 2003 computer running the DHCP Relay Agent service. Both RFC 1542 compliant routers and the DHCP Relay Agent can be configured with the IP address for the remote DHCP server.

Table 10-4   IANA Reserved IP addresses

Network ID		Subnet Mask	Address Range
10.0.0.0	(10.0.0.0/8)	255.0.0.0	10.0.0.0–10.255.255.255
172.16.0.0–172.32.0.0	(172.16.0.0/12)	255.240.0.0	172.16.0.0–172.31.255.255
192.168.0.0	(192.168.0.0/16)	255.255.255.0	192.168.0.0–192.168.255.25

◆   RFC 1918 specifies the reserved IP address ranges that are to be used only on private networks.
◆   These address ranges will not (should not) be routed out on the Internet.
◆   Internet Service Providers normally filter out these addresses for both outgoing and incoming data.
◆   If you are addressing a non-public intranet, a test lab, or a home network, these private addresses can be used rather than globally unique IP addresses.

skill 5

Introducing IP Addressing in TCP/IP

exam objective

Basic knowledge

overview

tip

Many students find a fully visual walkthrough of IP addressing exceptionally useful. Visit **www.learntosubnet.com,** for a free video which explains most of these concepts in a visual format.

Computers that use the TCP/IP protocol must have an IP address that identifies them on the network. As you have already learned, an IP address is a 32-bit number that is written as four octets separated by periods. Each octet is an 8-bit binary number, which represents a decimal number in the range 0-255. This is why the IP address format is referred to as the dotted decimal notation. For example, the binary number 11000000 10101000 00000011 00011000 is 192.168.3.24 in decimal format. To convert a dotted decimal notation IP address to a binary number that the computer can read, you simply must understand that each octet is written in base 10 and must be converted to base 2. First, remember what it means when you write a number in base 10. Each place is a power of 10, starting with 10^0 power (the "ones" place). You should recall from your math classes, that any number to the 0 power is 1. So, for example, the number 192 in base 10 is 1 10^2, 9 10^1, and 2 10^0. Likewise, each place in a binary number is a power of 2. The binary conversions for 1-15 are shown in **Table 10-5**. Notice that in the number before each power of 2, the places are all 1s. For example, 7 is 111, 15 is 1111, and 31 is 11111. Now you should understand why the highest decimal value for an octet is 255, which in binary is: 11111111. All eight places are filled. 256 is a nine-bit number.

For an eight-bit binary number:

bit 8 = 2^7 (128)
bit 7 = 2^6 (64)
bit 6 = 2^5 (32)
bit 6 = 2^4 (16)
bit 4 = 2^3 (8)
bit 3 = 2^2 (4)
bit 2 = 2^1 (2)
bit 1 = 2^0 (1)

Therefore, in base 2, 192 = 11000000: 1 2^7 + 1 2^6. There are no 2^5 thru 2^0 needed so only bit 8 and bit 7 are 1 and the remaining places are all 0.

Perhaps a simpler way to conceptualize writing decimal numbers in binary is to think of a place as either off or on: 1 is "on" and 0 is "off". So, for example, to convert the rest of the IP address 192.168.3.24 to binary:
In the second octet, bits 8, 6, and 4 must be "on" in order to yield: bit 8 (=128) + bit 6 (=32) + bit 4 (=8) = 168.
In the third octet, bits 1 and 2 must be "on" in order to yield: bit 2 (=2) + bit 1 (=1) = 3.
In the fourth octet, bits 4 and 5 must be "on" in order to yield:
bit 4 (=8) + bit 5 (=16) = 24 (**Figure 10-15**).

As you have learned, an IP address consists of two parts: a network ID and a host ID. The network ID identifies computers as being part of a particular network because all computers on the network use the same value. The host ID, on the other hand, is used to identify a server, workstation, or a router (node) on a network. It is also known as the host address. For example, in the IP address 192.168.3.24, the first three numbers 192.168.3 represent the network ID and the last number .24 represents the host ID. Each resource on a network has a different host ID (**Figure 10-16**).

Classful IP addressing was the first major addressing scheme used for the Internet. There are three main address classes: A, B, and C, which have 8-bit, 16-bit, and 24-bit network IDs respectively. An address belongs to an address class based on its first octet. In binary terms, this means that addresses beginning with a 0 are class A, addresses beginning 10 are class B, and addresses beginning 110 are class C. There are also two other classes: D, in which addresses begin with 1110, and E, in which addresses begin with 1111. Class D addresses are used for

Table 10-5   Decimal to Binary conversion

Base10 number	Base 2 number	Explanation
1	1	1 (2^0)
2	10	1 (2^1) and 1 (2^0)
3	11	1 (2^1) and 1 (2^0)
4	100	1 (2^2), 0 (2^1) and 0 (2^0)
5	101	1 (2^2), 0 (2^1) and 1 (2^0)
6	110	1 (2^2), 1 (2^1) and 0 (2^0)
7	111	1 (2^2), 1 (2^1) and 1 (2^0)
8	1000	1 (2^4), 0 (2^2), 0 (2^1), and 0(2^0)
9	1001	1 (2^4), 0 (2^2), 0 (2^1), and 1(2^0)
10	1010	1 (2^4), 0 (2^2), 1 (2^1), and 0(2^0)
11	1011	1 (2^4), 0 (2^2), 1 (2^1), and 1(2^0)
12	1100	1 (2^4), 1 (2^2), 0 (2^1), and 0(2^0)
13	1101	1 (2^4), 1 (2^2), 0 (2^1), and 1(2^0)
14	1110	1 (2^4), 1 (2^2), 1 (2^1), and 0(2^0)
15	1111	1 (2^4), 1 (2^2), 1 (2^1), and 1(2^0)

Figure 10-15 Converting Decimal to Binary

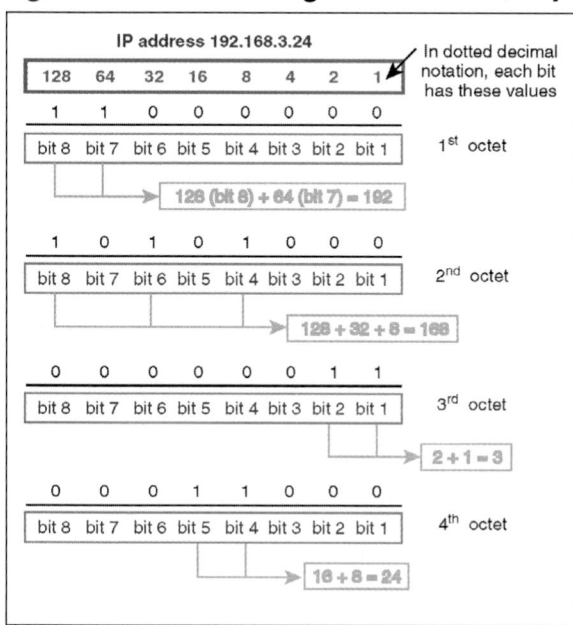

Figure 10-16 Each resource on a network has a different host ID

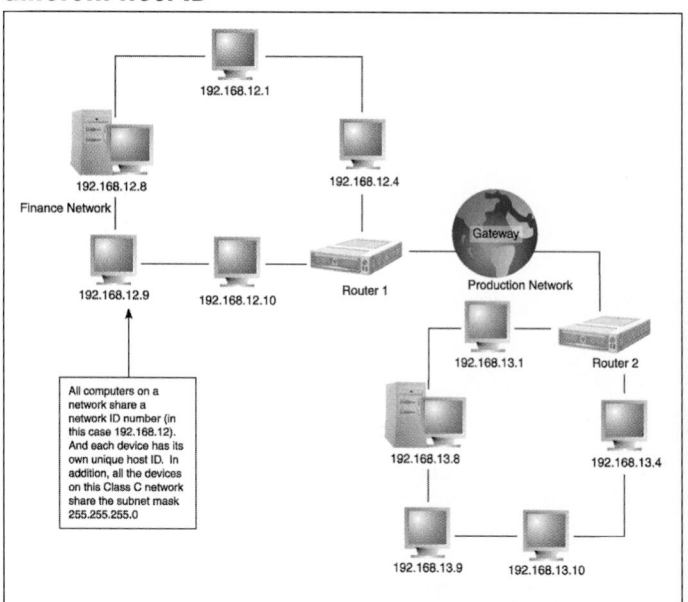

skill 5

Introducing IP Addressing in TCP/IP
(cont'd)

exam objective

Basic knowledge

overview

multicasting applications and class E addresses are used for experimental purposes. Classful addressing is presented in two different ways in Tables 10-6 and 10-7. In **Table 10-6**, an IP address is represented as w, x, y, z, where each letter represents an octet of the IP address in decimal format. For example, the IP address 128.3.68.2 is a Class B address, because the value for w is between 129 and 191. The first two octets, w and x, represent the network ID and the last two octets, y and z represent the host ID. In **Table 10-7**, an IP address is represented in binary format: **n** represents the portion of the address that is the network ID, and **h** represents the portion of the address that is the host ID. For example, 10.10.161.13 is a class A address, because the first octet begins with 0 (10 in eight-bit binary format is 00001010). The first octet is the network ID and the last three octets are the host ID. When a network is set up, the network administrator requests a Class A, B, or C network range from one of the regional number-assigning authorities appointed by the Internet Assigned Numbers Authority (IANA) (or more commonly now, from their ISP), depending on how large the network is expected to grow. The number-assigning authority or ISP assigns the network bits, and the local network administrator assigns the host bits.

To determine how many networks a class can have, raise 2 to the power of the number of bits in the network ID. For example, in a class A network, the network ID has seven bits because the first octet is the network ID, and bit 8 is always 0. Therefore, to calculate the number of possible networks: $2^7=128$. However, the maximum number of networks for Class A IP addresses is reduced by 2 to account for the reserved networks that begin with 01111111 (127 decimal) and 00000000. Addresses beginning in 127 decimal are reserved for loopback and 0.xxx.xxx.xxx is reserved for use as the default route. The x represents the host ID bits.

To calculate the number of hosts per network, raise 2 to the power of the number of bits in the host ID. In a class A network, the host ID is 24 bits long. Therefore, the number of possible hosts is: $2^{24} =16,777,216$. However, two of these cannot be used because one is the network address and one is the network broadcast address. The network address is the IP address in which all of the host ID bits are set to 0. It refers to the entire network. For example, 192.168.0.0 is used to identify the network 192.168 in routing tables. The general **broadcast address** is the IP address in which all bits are 1, that is, 255.255.255.255. Broadcasts are sent to all hosts on a network no matter what IP address they have. You cannot use this address to broadcast a message to external networks because routers block it, but datagrams with this address will broadcast to all hosts on the LAN. The **network broadcast address** for a specific network is the IP address in which all of the host ID bits are set to 1. For example, for the network 192.168, the network broadcast address is 192.168.255.255.

Thus, subtracting these two unusable addresses, there are 16,777,214 available hosts per network, and the formula for determining the number of hosts is ($2^n -2$), where n equals the number of bits in the host ID.

The subnet mask is another 32-bit number, divided into four octets, that is used to break up the IP address into the network ID and host ID (also called the node ID). The 1s in the subnet mask determine the network bits and the 0s determine the host or node bits. To determine the network ID, you perform what is referred to as a **logical AND operation** between the IP address and the subnet mask. The logical AND operation compares 2 bits and if they are both 1, the result is 1; otherwise, the result is 0. The default subnet masks for class A, B, and C IP addresses are as follows:

- **Class A** — 255.0.0.0   11111111 00000000 00000000 00000000
- **Class B** — 255.255.0.0   11111111 11111111 00000000 00000000
- **Class C** — 255.255.255.0 11111111 11111111 11111111 00000000

Table 10-6   IP address classes

Class	Value for w	Network ID	Host ID	Number of networks	Number of hosts per network	Possible range of IP addresses
A	1–126	w	x.y.z	126 (2^7–2)	16,777,214 (2^{24}–2)	0.0.0.0 through 127.255.255.255
B	128–191	w.x	y.z	16,384 (2^{14} because the first two bits are fixed at 10)	65,534 (2^{16}–2)	128.0.0.0 through 191.255.255.255
C	192–223	w.x.y	z	2,097,152 (2^{21} because the first three bits are fixed at 110)	254 (2^8–2)	192.0.0.0 through 223.255.255.255
D	224–239	N/A	N/A	N/A	N/A	224.0.0.0 through 239.255.255.255
E	240–254	N/A	N/A	N/A	N/A	240.0.0.0 through 247.255.255.255

Table 10-7   Classful addressing

Class	Leading bits and network ID/host ID configuration
Class A	0nnnnnnn hhhhhhhh hhhhhhhh hhhhhhhh
Class B	10nnnnnn nnnnnnnn hhhhhhhh hhhhhhhh
Class C	110nnnnn nnnnnnnn nnnnnnnn hhhhhhhh
Class D	1110mmmm mmmmmmmm mmmmmmmm mmmmmmmm
Class E	1111rrrr rrrrrrrr rrrrrrrr rrrrrrrr

m denotes multicast address bits, and **r** denotes reserved bits.

skill 5

Introducing IP Addressing in TCP/IP
(cont'd)

exam objective

Basic knowledge

overview

So, for example, performing the logical AND operation for the IP address 192.168.3.24, the network ID is 192.168.3, just as is outlined in the tables.

192.168.3.24	11000000 10101000 00000011 00011000
255.255.255.0	11111111 11111111 11111111 00000000
192.168.3	11000000 10101000 00000011 00000000

You can add additional bits to the default subnet mask for a particular class to subnet a network. When you subnet a network, you are simply splitting it up into smaller networks. For example, a company can partition one Class C network with 254 hosts to create several smaller networks, one for each department. This is frequently done to reduce network traffic by reducing the number of hosts that can populate a given segment.

It is important to realize that subnet masks must contain a continuous string of binary 1s. In other words, the binary 1s and 0s in a subnet mask must be contiguous and once you have a binary 0 in any octet, the rest of the octets will all be binary 0s. This rule does not simply apply to one octet; it applies to the entire subnet mask. This means each octet can only have 9 possible subnet values:

- 0 (Binary: 00000000)
- 128 (Binary: 10000000)
- 192 (Binary: 11000000)
- 224 (Binary: 11100000)
- 240 (Binary: 11110000)
- 248 (Binary: 11111000)
- 252 (Binary: 11111100)
- 254 (Binary: 11111110)
- 255 (Binary: 11111111)

When you use an IP address with a subnet mask that is not one of the defaults and you perform the logical AND operation, the result is that the host bits (the bits that identify the host ID) are broken up into two parts: a subnet ID and host ID. This type of IP addressing is called **classless IP addressing**. **Figure 10-17** demonstrates changing the default subnet mask for the IP address 192.168.3.24 to make it a classless address. Three 3 bits are "borrowed" from the host ID and used to create a subnet ID. An originally class C network is partitioned into smaller networks.

When you borrow bits from the host ID, you split the network up into a different number of sub-networks. In this example, three bits are borrowed and the network is partitioned into 8 smaller networks. To understand **Table 10-8**, think of the mathematical borrowing operation. When you borrow bit 8, you are borrowing the decimal equivalent of 128. When you borrow 2 bits, bit 8 and bit 7, you are borrowing the decimal equivalent of 192. When you borrow 3 bits, you are borrowing the decimal equivalent of 224, etc.

So, for example, the number of bits in the subnet ID for the IP address 10.165.143.6 with the subnet mask 255.248.0.0 is 5, because 10.65.143.6 is a class A address, which has an 8-bit network ID and normally, a 24-bit host ID. However, 5 bits (248 decimal) have been borrowed from the host ID for the subnet ID, as shown at the top of page 10.30:

Figure 10-17 Classless IP Addressing

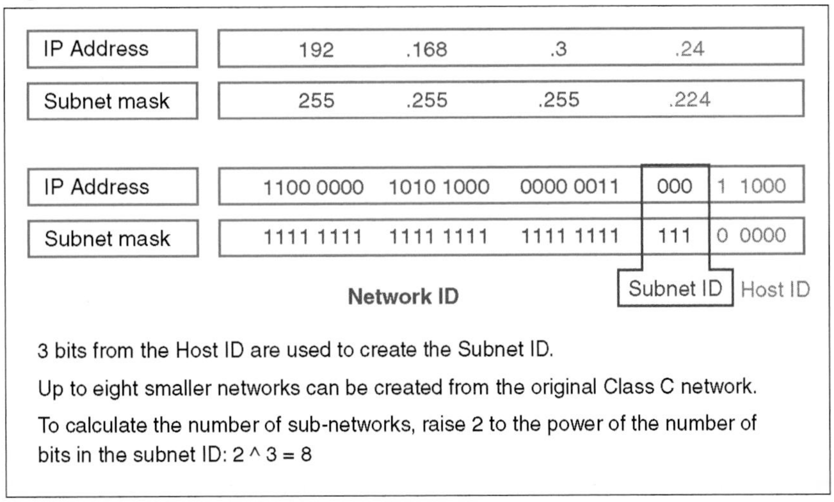

IP Address	192	.168	.3	.24
Subnet mask	255	.255	.255	.224

IP Address	1100 0000	1010 1000	0000 0011	000	1 1000
Subnet mask	1111 1111	1111 1111	1111 1111	111	0 0000

Network ID   Subnet ID   Host ID

3 bits from the Host ID are used to create the Subnet ID.

Up to eight smaller networks can be created from the original Class C network.

To calculate the number of sub-networks, raise 2 to the power of the number of bits in the subnet ID: $2 \wedge 3 = 8$

Table 10-8   Common Subnet masks

Number of bits	Class A	Class B	Class C
0 (default subnet mask)	255.0.0.0 (default subnet mask)	255.255.0.0 (default subnet mask)	255.255.255.0 (default subnet mask)
1	255.128.0.0 (default +1)	255.255.128.0 (default+1)	255.255.255.128 (default+1)
2	255.192.0.0 (default+2)	255.255.192.0 (default+2)	255.255.255.192 (default+2)
3	255.224.0.0 (default+3)	255.255.224.0 (default+3)	255.255.255.224 (default+3)
4	255.240.0.0 (default+4)	255.255.240.0 (default+4)	255.255.255.240 (default+4)
5	255.248.0.0 (default+5)	255.255.248.0 (default+5)	255.255.255.248 (default+5)
6	255.252.0.0 (default+6)	255.255.252.0 (default+6)	255.255.255.252 (default+6)
7	255.254.0.0 (default+7)	255.255.254.0 (default+7)	Unusable
8	255.255.0.0 (default+8)	255.255.255.0 (default+8)	Unusable

skill 5

Introducing IP Addressing in TCP/IP
(cont'd)

exam objective   Basic knowledge

more

Custom Mask:	1111 1111 **1111 1**000.0000 0000 0000 0000
Default Mask (Class A):	1111 1111 0000 0000 0000 0000 0000 0000

The number of bits in the subnet ID for the IP address, 192.168.34.112, with the subnet mask 255.255.255.252 is 6 because this is a Class C address, which has a 24-bit network ID, and normally, an 8-bit host ID. However, 6 bits (252 decimal) have been borrowed from the host ID for the subnet ID as shown below:

Custom Mask:	1111 1111 1111 1111 1111 1111 **1111 11**00
Default Mask (Class A):	1111 1111 1111 1111 1111 1111 0000 0000

To determine the number of subnets and hosts and the ranges for each of the eight new subnets in the example, you must look at the last octet, which contains the subnet ID and the host ID. In **Figure 10-18**, the last eight bits of the sub-netted network are examined. The binary value is incremented by one for each subnet so that the first three bits run from 000 to 111. Each subnet has 30 usable addresses. In the host ID portion (the last five bits) the first available host is 0 0001 (1 in decimal) and the last available host is 1 1110 (30 in decimal). This is because 0 0000 is reserved as the network address for the subnet and 1 1111 (31 in decimal) is the network broadcast address for the subnet.

The range of valid IP addresses tells you which IP addresses are valid on this subnet. That is: which addresses can communicate with each other on that subnet without using a router. To find the range of valid IP addresses, you simply find the network address and the broadcast address. The range of valid IP addresses is every IP address between the two.

To determine the network address for each subnet, you simply use the logical AND operation after converting an IP address to binary. For example, performing the logical AND operation for the IP address 192.168.3.76:

1100 0000 1010 1000 0000 0011 0100 1100	IP address (192.168.3.76)
1111 1111 1111 1111 1111 1111 1110 0000	Subnet mask (255.255.255.224)
1100 0000 1010 1000 0000 0011 0100 0000	Network address (192.168.3.64)

To determine the broadcast address, turn all of the host bits (identified by the section of the subnet mask that is all 0's) into binary 1's and convert the result into decimal (the **bold** bits are the host ID):

1100 0000 1010 1000 0000 1111 010**0 1100**	Network address (192.168.3.76)
1111 1111 1111 1111 1111 1111 111**0 0000**	Subnet mask (255.255.255.224)
1100 0000 1010 1000 0000 0011 010**1 1111**	Broadcast address (192.168.3.95)

All numbers between the network address and broadcast address are valid. This is because only the network address (the all binary 0s host address) and the broadcast address (the all binary 1s host address) are invalid on a given subnet. All addresses between the network address and broadcast address are valid.

In **Figure 10-19**, the subnet ID and the host ID are joined to determine the decimal number for the last octet, and the full range of IP addresses in each subnet is shown.

Remember, to calculate the number of subnets, use the formula 2^n, where n is the number of bits in the subnet ID. (2^n represents 2 raised to the nth power.) In many networking tutorials and documentation this formula is still shown as ($2^n - 2$), indicating that there are two

Figure 10-18 Determining Subnets

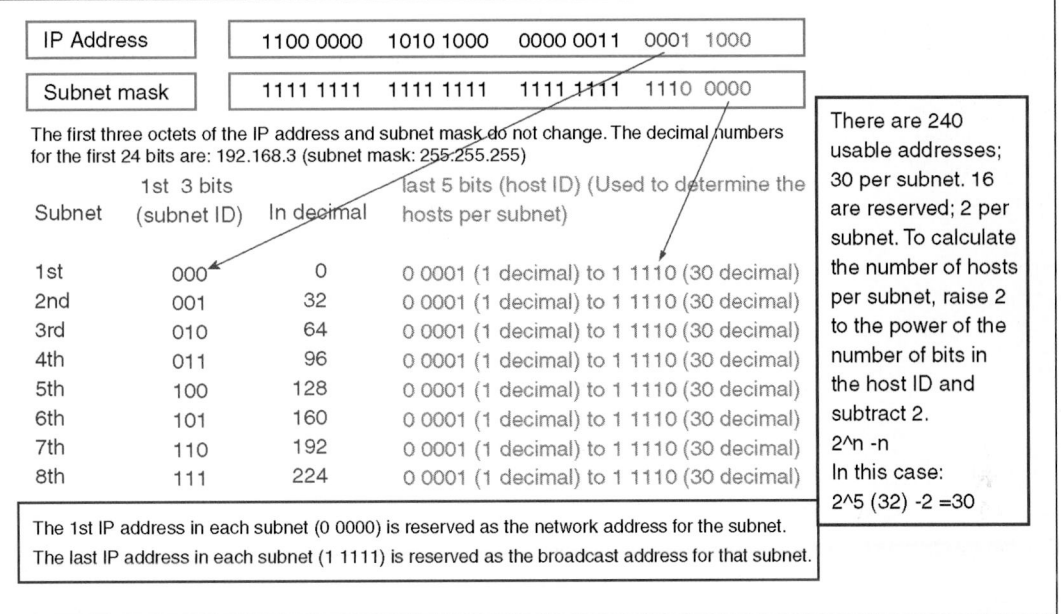

IP Address	1100 0000	1010 1000	0000 0011	0001 1000
Subnet mask	1111 1111	1111 1111	1111 1111	1110 0000

The first three octets of the IP address and subnet mask do not change. The decimal numbers for the first 24 bits are: 192.168.3 (subnet mask: 255.255.255)

Subnet	1st 3 bits (subnet ID)	In decimal	last 5 bits (host ID) (Used to determine the hosts per subnet)
1st	000	0	0 0001 (1 decimal) to 1 1110 (30 decimal)
2nd	001	32	0 0001 (1 decimal) to 1 1110 (30 decimal)
3rd	010	64	0 0001 (1 decimal) to 1 1110 (30 decimal)
4th	011	96	0 0001 (1 decimal) to 1 1110 (30 decimal)
5th	100	128	0 0001 (1 decimal) to 1 1110 (30 decimal)
6th	101	160	0 0001 (1 decimal) to 1 1110 (30 decimal)
7th	110	192	0 0001 (1 decimal) to 1 1110 (30 decimal)
8th	111	224	0 0001 (1 decimal) to 1 1110 (30 decimal)

There are 240 usable addresses; 30 per subnet. 16 are reserved; 2 per subnet. To calculate the number of hosts per subnet, raise 2 to the power of the number of bits in the host ID and subtract 2.
$2^n - n$
In this case:
$2^5 (32) - 2 = 30$

The 1st IP address in each subnet (0 0000) is reserved as the network address for the subnet.
The last IP address in each subnet (1 1111) is reserved as the broadcast address for that subnet.

Figure 10-19 Subnet Ranges

Subnet	1st IP address		Last IP address		Full IP Address Range
	Subnet ID	Host ID	Subnet ID	Host ID	
1st	0000	0000	0001	1111	192.168.3.0 — 192.168.3.31
2nd	0010	0000	0011	1111	192.168.3.32 — 192.168.3.63
3rd	0100	0000	0101	1111	192.168.3.64 — 192.168.3.95
4th	0110	0000	0111	1111	192.168.3.96 — 192.168.3.127
5th	1000	0000	1001	1111	192.168.3.128 — 192.168.3.159
6th	1010	0000	1011	1111	192.168.3.160 — 192.168.3.191
7th	1100	0000	1101	1111	192.168.3.192 — 192.168.3.223
8th	1110	0000	1111	1111	192.168.3.224 — 192.168.3.255

This demonstrates the full IP address range for each subnet. Don't forget that the 1st and last IP addresses in each subnet range (those with a host ID that is all 0s or all 1s) are reserved as the network address and the broadcast address respectively for that subnet.

skill 5

Introducing IP Addressing in TCP/IP
(cont'd)

exam objective   Basic knowledge

more

reserved subnets, those with all 0s or all 1s in the subnet ID. These two subnets are no longer reserved and can be used.

To calculate the number of hosts, use the formula (2^n-2), where n is the number of bits in host ID. Multiplying the number of subnets by the number of hosts available per subnet gives you the total number of hosts available per subnet.

Classless Inter-Domain Routing (CIDR) is the Internet routing method that uses classless IP addressing to allow for the more flexible and efficient allocation of IP addresses. By using a configurable, rather than static, subnet mask, the problems of wasted addresses and the diminishing capacity of Internet global routing tables are alleviated. CIDR was launched because a configurable subnet mask allows organizations to subnet a single network to meet their organizational needs, and they can be assigned only a portion of a Class A, B, or C network. This alleviates the problem of wasted addresses in the classful addressing scheme. For example, if a company needed more than 254 host addresses, but far fewer than 65,534, using classful IP addressing, they would still have to be assigned a Class B block of addresses, many of which would remain unused. A related problem was the rapidly increasing size of the Internet global routing tables. As the number of networks on the Internet increased, so did the number of routes. Before CIDR was introduced, experts were warning that global backbone Internet routers were quickly approaching the number of routes they could support. Using CIDR, a single routing table entry can replace hundreds or thousands of entries in a global routing table.

CIDR notation uses a slash followed by the number of bits in the network ID. For example, 192.168.1.0 /24 indicates a network ID of 24 bits. This is the same as the default subnet mask 255.255.255.0. The number following the slash notation is referred to as the **network prefix**. **Table 10-9** shows all of the CIDR network prefixes, the subnet mask each one uses, the number of IP addresses in each subnet, and an equivalent of the traditional classful addressing scheme. You may see this notation referred to alternatively as CIDR notation, prefix notation, or slash notation.

Let's examine an example to help you to understand how CIDR notation works. If you saw the IP address 202.12.30.38, you would immediately identify it as a Class C address with a 24-bit network ID (subnet mask: 255.255.255.0). However, if you use the /22 notation, the network ID is only 22 bits long. In CIDR, you quit worrying about the class of the address. Instead, you simply work within the confines of the address space you were given. In this example, the network address is 22 bits long, which means that you can further subdivide the network by borrowing bits from the host ID if necessary, but you cannot work backwards and "steal" bits from the network portion unless you have multiple contiguous /22 address spaces.

For example, if your ISP gives you a block of 128 IP addresses in the following format 64.1.1.128 (255.255.255.128), even though this is a class A address block, your organization does not have the entire class A IP block; the ISP owns that. You are simply being allowed to use one subnet of that block. So for your organization, the network section of the address would not be the first 8 bits, as in a typical class A, but rather, the first 25 bits (the part that was masked by the ISP, 11111111.11111111.11111111.10000000). We could subnet it further if we wanted (for instance, by changing the mask to 255.255.255.192), but we couldn't reduce the number of 1s in the mask. Modifying the mask used to include multiple, contiguous address spaces is also known as **supernetting**. Supernetting is basically the opposite of subnetting. Rather than making additional subnets, several addresses are combined to create a larger range of addresses. For example, if an organization needs 1000 addresses, it can be given 4 class C sized (/24) addresses. It can use this entire block of addresses for one supernet, use the standard four networks, or create more than four sub-networks using subnetting.

Table 10-9   CIDR

CIDR Network prefix	Subnet Mask	Number of IP addresses in a subnet (rounded)	Traditional class values
/1	128.0.0.0	2.1 billion	128 A
/2	192.0.0.0	1 billion	64 A
/3	224.0.0.0	536 million	32 A
/4	240.0.0.0	268 million	16 A
/5	248.0.0.0	134 million	8 A
/6	252.0.0.0	67 million	4 A
/7	254.0.0.0	34 million	2 A
/8	255.0.0.0	17 million (Class A)	1 A
/9	255.128.0.0	8.4 million	128 B
/10	255.192.0.0	4.2 million	64 B
/11	255.224.0.0	2.1 million	32 B
/12	255.240.0.0	1 million	16 B
/13	255.248.0.0	524 thousand	8 B
/14	255.252.0.0	262 thousand	4 B
/15	255.254.0.0	131 thousand	2 B
/16	255.255.0.0	65,534 (Class B)	1 B
/17	255.255.128.0	32,766	128 C
/18	255.255.192.0	16,382	64 C
/19	255.255.224.0	8,190	32 C
/20	255.255.240.0	4,094	16 C
/21	255.255.248.0	2,046	8 C
/22	255.255.252.0	1,022	4 C
/23	255.255.254.0	510	2 C
/24	255.255.255.0	254 (Class C)	1 C
/25	255.255.255.128	126	1/2 C
/26	255.255.255.192	62	1/4 C
/27	255.255.255.224	30	1/8 C
/28	255.255.255.240	14	1/16 C
/29	255.255.255.248	6	1/32 C
/30	255.255.255.252	2	1/64 C
/31	255.255.255.254	Unusable	1/128 C
/32	255.255.255.255	Loopback address This is only used as a host route in routing tables	

skill 6

Troubleshooting TCP/IP

exam objective

Basic knowledge

overview

Despite the precautions that you have taken when configuring TCP/IP, you may still encounter communication problems. For example, you may forget to add a default gateway, or the DNS service might fail to resolve a host name to its IP address. Windows Server 2003 includes utilities, such as Ping, Pathping, Ipconfig, Tracert, Arp, and Route, to troubleshoot such problems. All are run from the command prompt.

The troubleshooting utilities are described below:

♦ **Hostname:** This utility is used to display the host name for the local computer.
♦ **Ping:** The **Packet Internet Groper** utility is used to verify that the host computer can connect to the TCP/IP network and to diagnose network connectivity problems. You enter the IP address or the name of the computer you are testing for connectivity using the syntax **ping** *IP_address* or **ping** *host_name*. When you enter this command at the command prompt, the Ping command sends an ICMP Echo Request message to the TCP/IP host. By default, the Echo Request message is sent four times and, as a result, you will get four replies describing the RTT (round-trip time) required for the communication to travel to the destination and back. If you receive a message stating **unknown host** or **host unreachable**, there is a connectivity problem. **Figure 10-20** displays the Ping loopback command for a computer on which TCP/IP is bound to the NIC and properly functioning. **Table 10-10** describes the various Ping commands that you can use to test TCP/IP connectivity. There are also a number of other switches you can use with the Ping command. For example, you can control how many ICMP echo messages will be sent. Use **ping –t** *IP_address* to send a continuous ping to a host, and **ping –n (x)** *IP_address* (where x is a number) to specify the number of echo requests you want sent. You can use the **–l** switch to alter the size of the ICMP echo message. For example, enter **ping –l 64** *IP_address* to send echo requests that are 64 bytes rather than 32 bytes. To see the other switches that can be used with the Ping command, enter **ping /?**.
♦ **Arp:** This command is used to display and modify the IP address to physical address (MAC address) translation tables used by Address Resolution Protocol. You can use the **Arp** command with the **–a** switch to view the contents of the ARP cache **(Figure 10-21)**. The **–d** switch is used to reset the cache.
♦ **Ipconfig:** This utility provides information about the host computer configuration, IP address, subnet mask, and default gateway. You can display a summary of the TCP/IP configuration of your computer by typing **ipconfig** at the command prompt **(Figure 10-22)**. You can also display a detailed description of the TCP/IP configuration by typing **ipconfig /all** at the command prompt. The Ipconfig utility enables you to determine whether an IP address has been assigned to your computer and confirms that the TCP/IP protocol is running. You can also use the Ipconfig utility to renew the IP address for your computer (**ipconfig /renew**), or you can release an IP address manually by typing **ipconfig /release**. You can also register your computer's DNS name with a Dynamic DNS server using **ipconfig /registerdns**. This command is meant to be used to register host names with DNS, but it will also renew the IP address.
♦ **Tracert:** This utility is used to search the route taken when data is transferred between communicating devices. It also provides information about the links where communication failed. It displays the Fully Qualified Domain Name, if possible, and IP address of each gateway along the route to a remote host. The FQDN will only display if the host has specified reverse Domain Name System (rDNS). rDNS is a method of resolving an IP address to a domain name.
♦ **Pathping:** This utility is a combination of Ping and Tracert. It provides a statistical analysis of results over a period of time, generally around 25 seconds per hop. The time period can vary depending upon how many jumps must be analyzed. Pathping displays

tip

If you can ping the default gateway, but you cannot ping a remote host, it is likely that the problem lies with either the gateway itself, or with one of the routers between the default gateway and the remote host. Use Tracert to discover the route packets are taking to reach the destination. This will tell you at what point on the route between the local host and the remote host the packets are being dropped.

Table 10-10 Using the Ping command to test TCP/IP connectivity

Ping command	Description
ping 127.0.0.1	This command is also known as the loopback address. It is used to see if TCP/IP is correctly installed and configured on your computer. If there is no reply, it means that TCP/IP is not installed correctly and you must reinstall it.
ping *IP_address_of_hostcomputer* and ping *localhost*	This command is used to verify that the local computer is correctly added to the network. If the routing table is correct, this forwards the packet to the loopback address 127.0.0.1. Failure implies that the IP address is not bound properly, the routing table has errors, or that you have typed an incorrect IP address.
ping *IP_address_of _default_gateway*	This command enables you to determine whether you can reach the default gateway. If you fail to get a reply, either the network connection is not available, or there is a hardware or software problem preventing you from reaching the gateway.
ping *IP_address_of _remote_host*	This command is used to confirm that you can communicate through a router. Failure to receive a reply means that you have entered an incorrect default gateway address, that the remote system is offline, that one of the routers along the path is down, or that the routing table on one of the routers along the path is defective.
ping *name_of_remote_host*	This command is used to confirm that DNS name resolution is functioning.

Figure 10-20 The ping loopback command

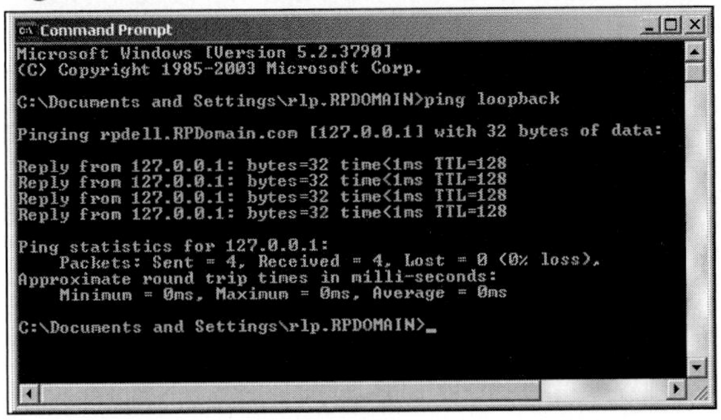

Figure 10-21 Using the arp -a command to view the contents of the ARP cache

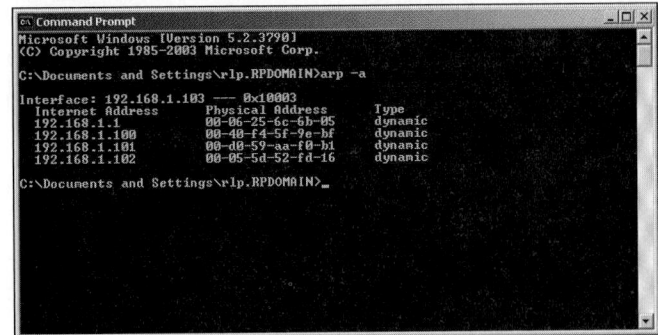

Figure 10-22 Using the Ipconfig command to display a summary of the TCP/IP configuration

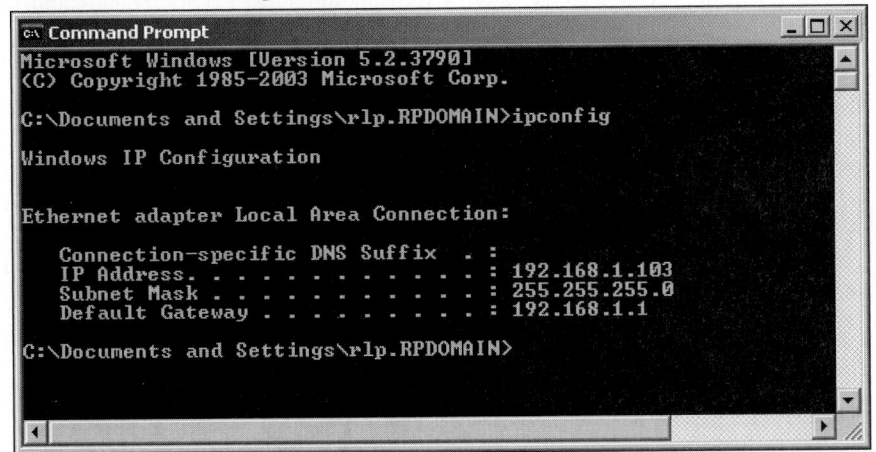

skill 6

Troubleshooting TCP/IP (cont'd)

exam objective

Basic knowledge

overview

the computer name and IP address for each jump and also calculates the percentage of lost/sent packets to each router, or link, making it easier for you to determine where the network problem is located.

◆ **Route:** This command is used to display and modify the local routing table. You can use it to set the route you want packets to take to a particular network, including the default gateway. To display the routing table on your computer, type **route print** at the command prompt (**Figure 10-23**). **Route delete** can be used to remove the routes from your routing table, while **route add** is used to add routes.

how to

Test network connectivity using the Ipconfig, Tracert, and Pathping commands.

1. Sign on to your computer as an **Administrator** and connect to the Internet.
2. Click ⊞Start, click **Run**, and type **cmd** in the **Open** text box. Press **[Enter]** or click ⌷ OK ⌷.
3. Type **ipconfig** and press **[Enter]**. The IP address, subnet mask, and default gateway for your computer display.
4. Type **ipconfig /all** and press **[Enter]** to display the host name, description of your network adapter, physical address, information about any DNS and WINS servers, and details about how your IP address is configured, such as whether it is static or dynamic, and other detailed information (**Figure 10-24**).
5. Type **tracert www.azimuth-interactive.com**. The time it takes to reach each router along the path is recorded, as well as the FQDN, if possible, and IP address for each router along the way. You will also be able to see how many hops it took to reach the destination. **Figures 10-25(a)** and **(b)** show two different paths to the same end host.
6. Type **tracert –h 3 www.azimuth-interactive.com**. The **–h** switch is used to set the number of hops to use to locate the destination host. The command will trace the route over a maximum of 3 hops. The destination host cannot be reached in only 3 hops.
7. Type **pathping www.azimuth-interactive.com**. An ICMP echo request message is sent to each router on the path between your computer and the destination host. First, the path to the destination host will be recorded similar to that displayed using Tracert, and then the percentage of lost/sent packets to each router is computed (**Figures 10-26(a)** and **(b)**).
8. Close the command prompt.

more

To find out how to use any of these commands, except Tracert and Hostname, type the command followed by **/?**. To view the switches for the Tracert command, simply type tracert at the command prompt. The Hostname command has no associated switches or parameters.

Another utility that you can use to diagnose network connectivity problems is **Netdiag**, the Network Connectivity Tester. This tool is included in the Windows Server 2003 Support Tools, which you can install by locating the **Suptools.msi** file in the **Support\Tools** folder on the Windows Server 2003 installation CD-ROM. It is used to evaluate the registration of DNS, DHCP, routing, and generally, to help network administrators to isolate connectivity problems. It performs a series of tests to determine if your network client is functional and displays significant network status information.

Dcdiag is a command line tool that you can use to troubleshoot problems with domain controllers. It can be used to analyze all domain controllers in an enterprise, all domain controllers in a site, or just one domain controller. Dcdiag includes a number of switches that you can use to run diagnostic tests with different options. With no switches, Dcdiag will run a standard test that includes DNS lookup and file replication checks. It can report on the status of connectivity, replication, topology integrity, user permissions, inter-site health, and more.

Figure 10-23 Using Route print to display the routing table on your computer

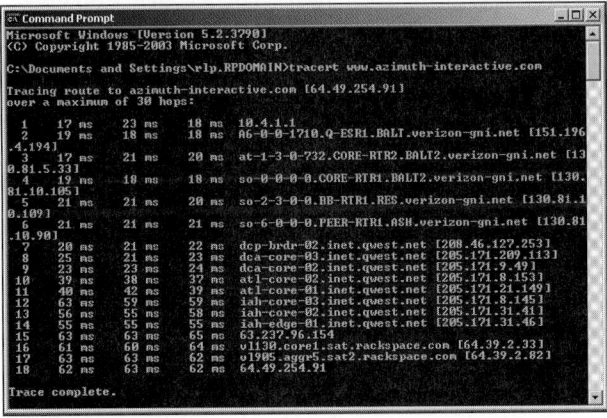

Figure 10-24 Ipconfig /all

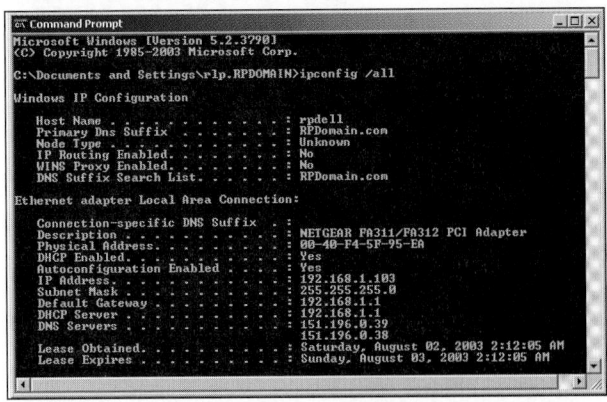

Figure 10-25(a) Using Tracert—two different paths to same end host

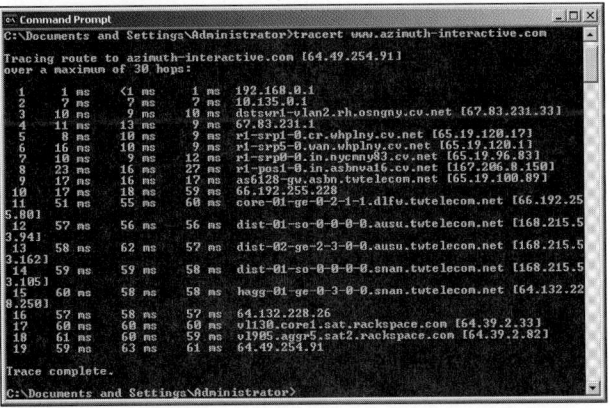

Figure 10-26(a) Using Pathping—two different paths to same end host

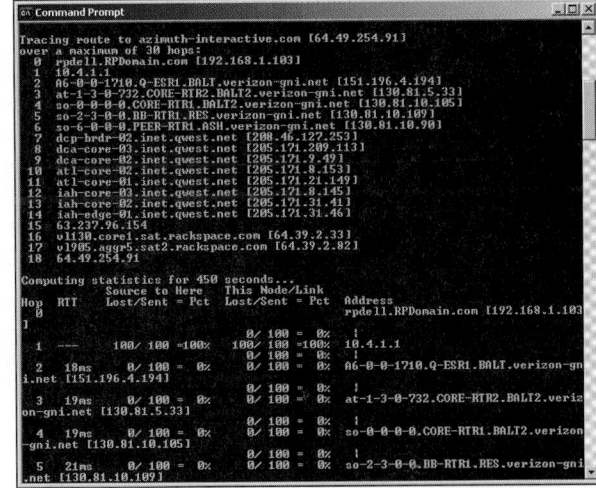

Figure 10-25(b) Using Tracert—two different paths to same end host

Figure 10-26(b) Using Pathping—two different paths to same end host

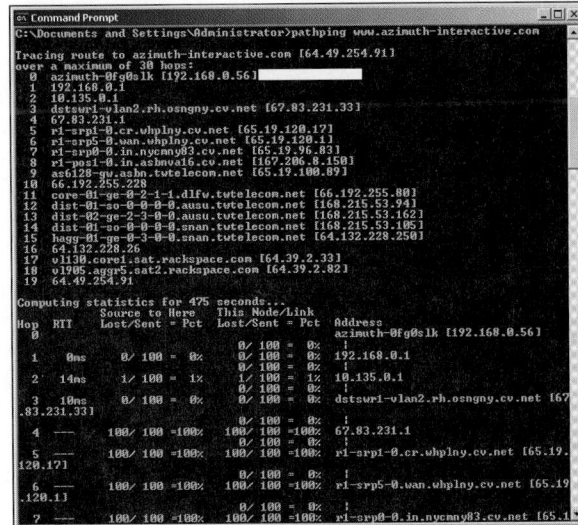

skill 7

Introducing Dynamic Host Configuration Protocol (DHCP)

exam objective

Basic knowledge

overview

Many network administrators prefer to automate the process of assigning IP addresses because the manual configuration of IP addresses has a number of disadvantages, such as the possibility of assigning duplicate IP addresses, and the sheer amount of time that it takes. You automate, centralize, and simplify the process of allocating IP addresses using **Dynamic Host Configuration Protocol (DHCP)**. A DHCP server has a database that stores the following information:

◆ Pool of IP addresses (the scope)
◆ Configuration parameters, such as the address of a default gateway, a DNS server, and a WINS server either for each scope, or for all scopes.
◆ Duration of the lease for each scope offered by the DHCP server. The lease defines the length of time during which the assigned IP address can be used by the DHCP client.

DHCP reduces the complexity of administering IP addresses. The network administrator configures one or more DHCP servers to automate the process of properly configuring DHCP client hosts with their IP configuration details so that the administrator does not have to manually configure each host.

You can configure a computer running Windows Server 2003 as a DHCP client by selecting the **Obtain an IP address automatically** option button in the **TCP/IP Properties** dialog box.

With a DHCP server installed and configured on your network, DHCP clients can obtain their IP address and related configuration parameters dynamically each time they boot up and when half of the DHCP lease time has expired. A **DHCP lease** is the amount of time that the DHCP server allows the DHCP client to use a particular IP address. The DHCP lease process occurs in four steps, as described in **Table 10-11**.

An IP address is assigned to a client for a particular period of time. However, a client will attempt to renew the IP address when half of the lease period has expired and every time the computer reboots. During the renewal process, a **DHCPREQUEST** message is sent to the DHCP server. If the lease can be renewed, the DHCP server sends a **DHCPACK** message, defines the new lease time, and updates the configuration parameters. You can also use the **ipconfig /renew** command at the command prompt to renew the IP address (**Figure 10-27**).

After installing the DHCP Server service, unless the DHCP server is a member of a workgroup, the DHCP server must be authorized in Active Directory. The DHCP server can either be a domain controller or a member server. To authorize a DHCP server in Active Directory, you must log on to the network with an account that is a member of the Enterprise Administrative group. Members of the Enterprise Administrative group have the rights needed to administer the entire network. After a DHCP server is authorized, the IP address of the DHCP server is added to the directory, which contains the IP addresses of all authorized DHCP servers in the network. Before the DHCP Server service starts, the DHCP server checks to make sure its IP address is on the authorized list of DHCP servers by requesting a DHCPInform packet. This packet will contain up to 25 DHCP servers that are authorized in the directory. If the DHCP server's IP address is not found in this packet, the DHCP Server service will not start. The DHCP Server service logs an event, indicating that the DHCP server could not service the request of the DHCP client because the DHCP server is unauthorized.

caution

Be aware that all DHCP messages sent by clients on initial boot are broadcasts. This means that these messages will not normally cross routers. In order for a client to obtain an IP address from a DHCP server across a router, the router must have BOOTP Forwarding (RFC 1542 compliance) enabled or there must be a DHCP relay agent configured on the client's subnet.

Table 10-11   The four steps in the DHCP lease process

Phase	Description	Purpose
DHCPDISCOVER	This is the first step of the DHCP lease process, in which the DHCP client sends a DHCPDISCOVER message. This message contains the hardware address (MAC address) and the name of the client computer.	This is how a client discovers the available DHCP server(s) that could provide an IP address.
DHCPOFFER	This is the second step of the DHCP lease process, in which the DHCP server broadcasts a message containing an IP address that is available for the client's use.	Each DHCP server that can provide an address responds with an offered address and other details.
DHCPREQUEST	This is the third step of the DHCP lease process, in which the client broadcasts a DHCPREQUEST message to the DHCP server in order to state that it has accepted the IP address. If multiple DHCPOFFERs are received, the client will send a DHCPREQUEST back for the first DHCPOFFER it receives and decline the rest.	The client will select one offer and will directly request the offered IP address.
DHCPACKnowledgment (DHCPACK)	This is the last step of the DHCP lease process, in which the DHCP server broadcasts a DHCPACK message to acknowledge that the IP address is now assigned to the client. If for some reason the IP address was taken by another client first, the DHCP server will send back a DHCPNACK (Negative ACKnowledgement), and the client will need to begin the lease process anew.	The DHCP server confirms the IP address lease and the associated configuration parameters.

Figure 10-27   Releasing and renewing an IP address

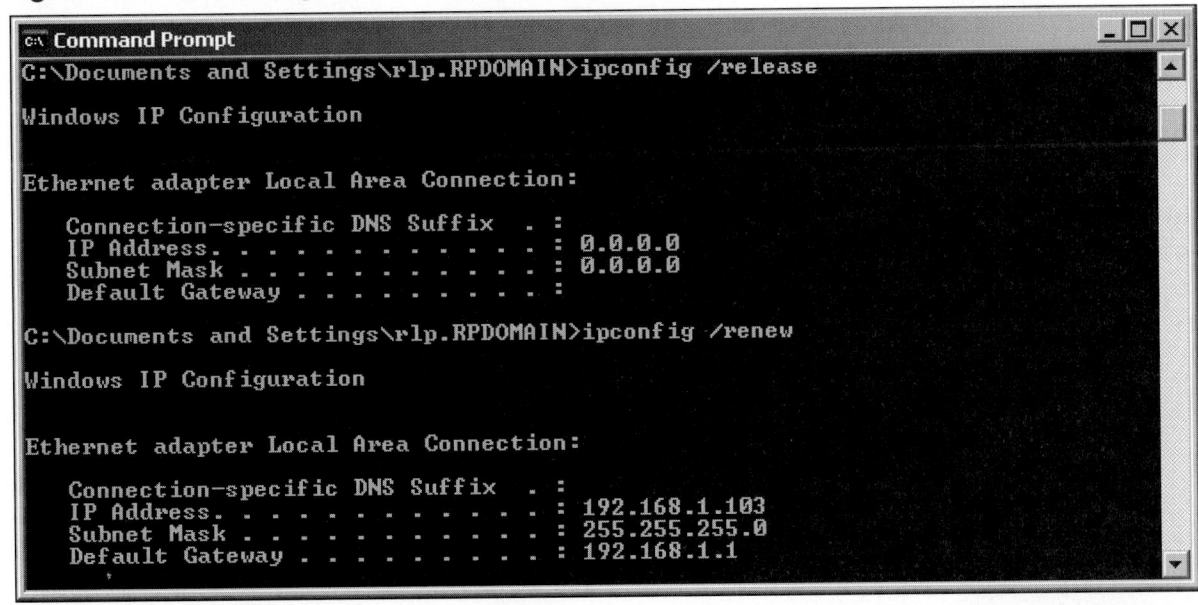

skill 7

Introducing Dynamic Host Configuration Protocol (DHCP) *(cont'd)*

exam objective

Basic knowledge

how to

Install the DHCP service and configure a DHCP server. (You must be signed on using an Administrator account and you will need the Windows Server 2003 installation CD-ROM.)

1. Click [Start], point to **Control Panel**, and click **Add or Remove Programs**.
2. Click the **Add/Remove Windows Components** button to open the **Windows Components Wizard (Figure 10-28)**.
3. Double-click **Networking Services** in the **Components** list to open the **Networking Services** dialog box.
4. Select the **Dynamic Host Configuration Protocol (DHCP)** check box, and click [OK] **(Figure 10-29)**.
5. Click [Next >]. If prompted, insert the Windows Server 2003 installation CD-ROM, and click [OK].
6. If your server has had a dynamically configured IP address, a message box will open to prompt you to change it to a static IP address.
7. After all of the components are configured, the **Completing the Windows Components Wizard** screen opens.
8. Click [Finish] and close the Add or Remove Programs window.
9. Click [Start], point to **All Programs**, point to **Administrative Tools**, and click **DHCP** to open the **DHCP** console.
10. Double-click **DHCP** to display the **DHCP** server name, if necessary. Then, select the DHCP server name. Information will display in the details pane about configuring the DHCP server.
11. Right-click the server name and select **New Scope** to start the **New Scope Wizard (Figure 10-30)**.
12. Click [Next >] to open the **New Scope** screen. Enter a name for the scope that will help you to easily identify it in the **Name** text box. Enter a description for the scope in the **Description** text box.
13. Click [Next >] to open the **IP Address Range** screen. Enter the start and end IP addresses, for example, 192.168.1.101 and 192.168.1.150 in the **Start IP address** and **End IP address** text boxes. To begin a new octet, press the period (.) key.
14. If you want to change the subnet mask from the default, 255.255.255.0, you can do so in the **Subnet mask** text box. If you change the subnet mask, click in the **Length** text box to automatically change the subnet mask length **(Figure 10-31)**.
15. Click [Next >] to open the **Add Exclusions** screen. Enter the start and end IP address for the range of addresses you want to exclude, and click [Add] to add the range to the **Excluded address range** list box. To exclude only one IP address, enter the same value in both the text boxes.
16. Click [Next >] to open the **Lease Duration** screen. The default lease duration is 8 days. You can reduce this for networks that include mainly portable computers and dial-up connections (from 8 to 24 hours), and increase it for networks that consist of desktop computers with stable connections (up to several weeks).
17. Click [Next >] to open the **Configure DHCP Options** screen. Select the **Yes, I want to configure these options now** option button, if necessary, to set the IP addresses for default gateways, DNS servers, and WINS servers.
18. Click [Next >] to open the **Router (Default Gateway)** screen. You will need to enter the IP address for a default gateway if access to the IP addresses in this scope must go through a router or default gateway.

caution

Do not install the DHCP service on a production network, for example, at your office. Your network may already have a DHCP server configured. Installing a new DHCP server would cause chaos, as some clients may get IP addresses from the wrong range or get duplicate IP addresses from the same range.

Figure 10-28 Adding a networking service

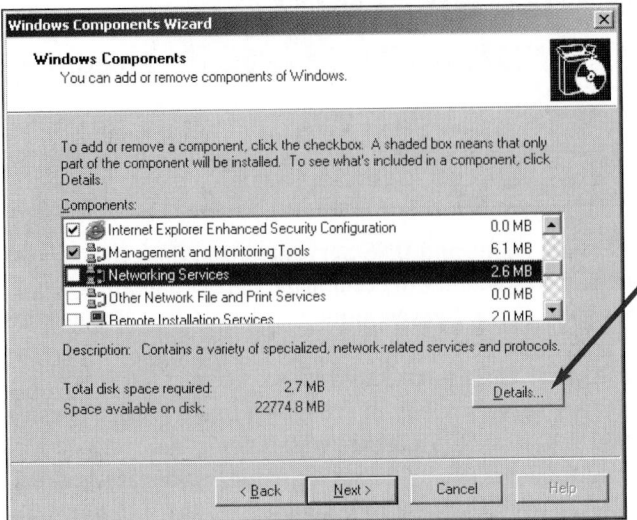

Click to open the Networking Services dialog box

Figure 10-29 Adding the DHCP service

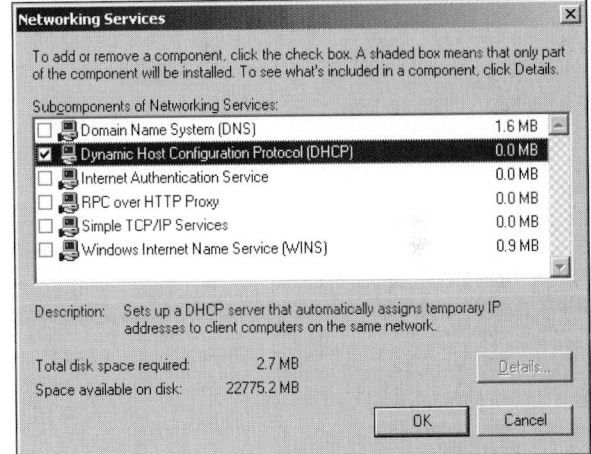

Figure 10-30 Creating a new scope

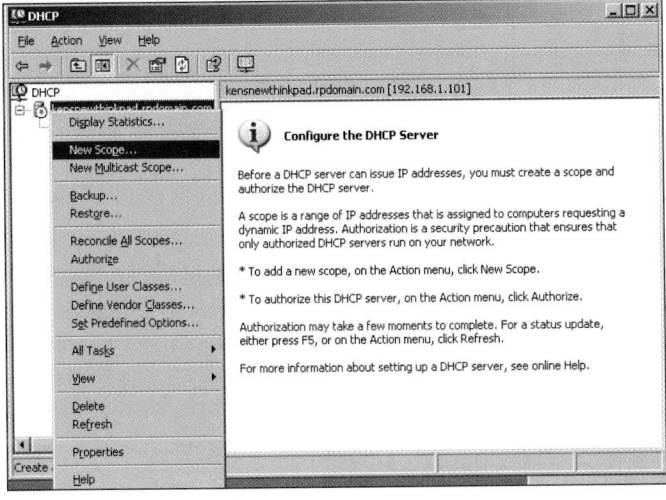

Figure 10-31 The IP Address Range screen

Enter the start and end IP addresses for the scope

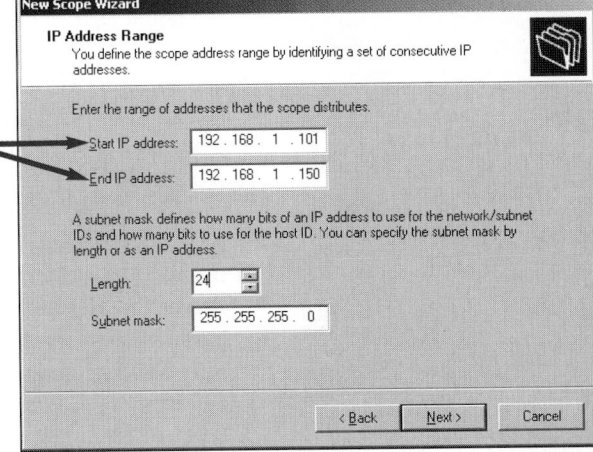

skill 7

Introducing Dynamic Host Configuration Protocol (DHCP) (cont'd)

exam objective

Basic knowledge

how to

19. Click [Next >] to open the **Domain Name and DNS Servers** screen. Enter the name of the parent domain where DNS name resolution will occur in the **Parent domain** text box. Enter the name of the **DNS server** in the **Server name** text box. Click [Resolve] to resolve the server name to its IP address. You can also simply enter the IP address for the DNS server in the **IP address** text box (**Figure 10-32**).

20. Click [Next >] to open the **WINS Servers** screen. If you are on a network that is using older Windows clients and NetBIOS name to IP address resolution is needed, you will enter the name of a WINS server for this scope in the **Server name** text box. Either click [Resolve] to enter the IP address, or manually enter the IP address for the WINS server.

21. Click [Next >] to open the **Activate Scope** screen. Select the **Yes, I want to activate this scope now** option button, if necessary, or click [Cancel] if you are doing this as an exercise only and are not going to create the scope (**Figure 10-33**).

22. Click [Next >] to open the **Completing the New Scope Wizard** screen.

23. Click [Finish]. In the details pane, instructions for authorizing the DHCP server appear.

24. Right-click the server name and select **Authorize** to authorize the DHCP server (**Figure 10-34**). Close the DHCP console.

more

A **scope** defines a range of IP addresses that can be leased for some duration, along with other IP configuration details, to DHCP clients.

Note that when creating scopes on multiple DHCP servers, you should ensure that the scopes do not conflict. This will ensure that unique IP addresses are assigned to all DHCP clients. You can also define scope options such as the default gateway address, the IP address of a DNS server, or the IP address of a WINS server. You can configure scope options at three levels:

◆ **Server:** Configuring scope options at the server level enables you to apply them to all scopes on the server so that all clients of this DHCP server use the same configuration information.

◆ **Scope:** Scope options are configured only for those DHCP clients that are assigned an IP address from a specific scope for a specific period of time. For example, if you create a new scope for each subnet, you must assign a unique default gateway for each subnet. Each DHCP client in a subnet will be assigned the scope created for that subnet and will use the default gateway assigned to that scope.

◆ **Class:** Class options are options that are set for a subset of users in a given scope. During the initial DHCPDISCOVER process, the client will tell the DHCP server which classes they are a member of. The DHCP server will then assign any options defined for that specific class to that client.

◆ **Reservation:** Configuring scope options at the reservation level enables you to assign reserved IP options to specific DHCP clients.

caution

Reservation options override Class options, Class options override Scope options, and Scope options override Server options.

The DHCP service provides the following advantages:

◆ Safe and reliable IP configuration because errors that might occur when entering values manually at each computer are prevented.

◆ Prevention of address conflicts that might occur when a previously assigned IP address is used on a new computer on the network.

◆ Reduced configuration management as servers can decrease the time spent configuring and reconfiguring network computers. DHCP servers can be configured to supply a full range of additional configuration values when assigning new address leases.

Figure 10-32 The Domain Name and DNS Servers screen

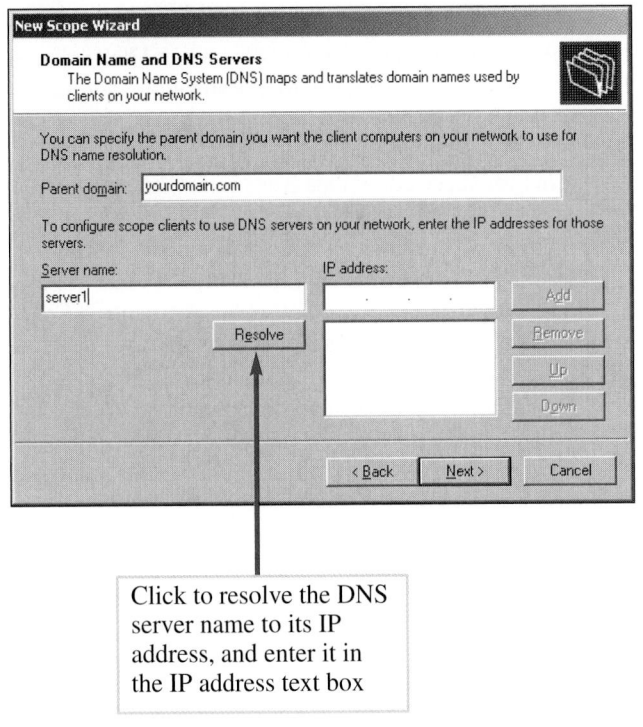

Click to resolve the DNS server name to its IP address, and enter it in the IP address text box

Figure 10-33 Activating a scope

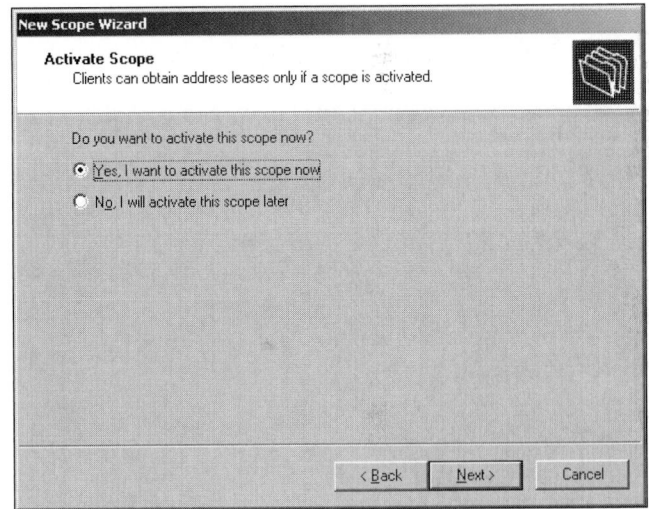

Figure 10-34 Authorizing the DHCP server

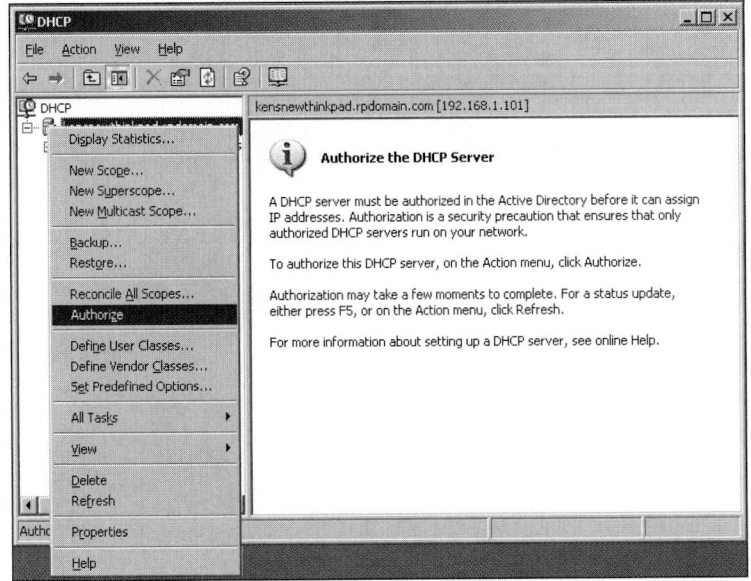

Summary

- A protocol provides a set of rules and standards for data transfer. Computers must share at least one common protocol in order to exchange data. Protocols define the methods of formatting data into discrete units called packets. They also transfer these packets across networks and provide guidelines for how packets are interpreted. In IP networks, packets are referred to as IP datagrams. The basic packet for Ethernet is called a frame.

- Protocols are implemented in a layered architecture. This architecture is conceptualized in two different models: The DOD (Department of Defense) model and the OSI (Open Systems Interconnection) Reference Model.

- Packets are sent and received through network media. Network media consists of physical wiring that can be made of coaxial cables, fiber-optic cables, or twisted-pair cables. This wiring is connected to a network interface card (NIC) in the computer.

- A computer can have more than one NIC and each one will have a unique address called the media access control (MAC) address, which is generally assigned by the manufacturer of the NIC. Some drivers will allow you to specify a different hardware MAC address.

- The MAC address is a unique 48 bit or 6 byte number. It is also referred to as the hardware address, physical address or Ethernet address.

- Each NIC has a set of software drivers that encodes data sent over the network media and decodes received data. These network interface adapter drivers must follow a set of specifications, called the Network Driver Interface Specifications (NDIS), so that a common interface is defined for communication between protocols and a NIC. NDIS is a wrapper around a driver designed to simplify the writing of each driver. It allows you to bind multiple protocols to a NIC and enables each protocol to send information on the same network.

- Binding is a process that configures a protocol to a specific NIC and provides information about available network services that client computers can use to make connections over a network. The binding order establishes which protocol should be used first when a network connection is established. It is the client computer in an exchange that determines which protocol will be used to establish the connection.

- Networks can be classified into three main types based on the location and proximity of the computers: local area network (LAN), metropolitan area network (MAN), and wide area network (WAN).

- A connection-oriented protocol establishes a confirmed connection with the destination computer. The transfer of data occurs in three steps: connection establishment, data transfer, and connection release.

- Connectionless protocols refer to standards in which no connection is established between the communicating devices. Connectionless protocols such as UDP are used by hosts to send messages to a destination address, but there is no guarantee that they will reach their destination. There is no acknowledgement that the data packets have been received, so data is not retransmitted.

- Windows Server 2003 supports the installation of TCP/IP (Transmission Control Protocol/Internet Protocol), AppleTalk, NWLink IPX/SPX/NetBIOS Compatible Transport protocol, Microsoft TCP/IP version 6, Network Monitor Driver, and Reliable Multicast Protocol

- The TCP/IP suite of protocols is based on a four-layered conceptual model called the DOD (Department of Defense) model. The four layers are the Network Interface, Internet, Transport, and Application layers.

- The Network Interface layer is the physical layer. The function of this layer is to place TCP/IP packets on the network medium and to receive them off of the network medium.

- The Internet layer is responsible for addressing and routing IP datagrams. Each packet that is being sent or received is called an IP datagram. An IP datagram contains information about the source and destination addresses that are used to transfer data between computers on a network and across networks. Protocols that operate at the Internet layer include IP, ARP, ICMP, and IGMP.

- The function of the Transport layer is to provide the Application layer with session and datagram communication services. The connection is established between the communicating computers using TCP, UDP, and Pragmatic General Multicast (PGM).

- The Application layer is located at the top of the DOD model. The Application layer enables applications to access the services of the other layers and defines the protocols that applications must use to exchange data. Application layer protocols include HTTP, FTP, SMTP, Telnet, RIP, OSPF, BGP, DNS, and SNMP.

- Another model that is used to conceptualize network communications is the OSI (Open Systems Interconnection) Reference Model. The OSI Reference Model uses a seven-layered networking framework. Just like the DOD model, the various networking protocols are implemented within this layered framework.

- The Application layer is at the top of the OSI model and it provides various services to applications that are specifically written to run over the network. It enables access to network services that support applications and is responsible for network access, data flow control, and error recovery.

- The Presentation layer converts data. It is responsible for the syntax of data transmission, for example, making sure that data is encoded using a customary and agreed upon method. The Presentation layer is responsible for protocol conversion, character conversion, and expanding graphics commands. Data compression and cryptography are also handled at this level.

◆ The Session layer is designed to deal with any problems that do not involve communication issues. It enables data transport by allowing users to establish sessions and by supplying services that are needed by certain applications. Protocols in this layer are responsible for identifying the parties so that only the correct participants are included and for managing who can send data and for how long they will be allowed to send it. Synchronization services at this level ensure that, for example, if a file transfer is interrupted, when the connection is reestablished, the file transfer will resume at the point at which it was broken.

◆ The Transport layer supplies control for all communications from end point to end point. It controls the flow of data between parties across a network. Data is broken down into packets at this level on the sending computer and reassembled from the data packets at this level on the receiving computer. The Transport layer also supplies error-checking so that data will be delivered with no errors, no data loss, and no data duplication. Acknowledgement of successful data transmission and requests for retransmission if data packets do not arrive (or if they arrive with errors) also occurs at this level.

◆ The Network layer is responsible for logical addressing and routing.

◆ The Data Link layer supplies error control between adjoining nodes and handles the data frames between the Network and Physical layers. It ensures that frames are transferred with no errors to other computers from the Physical layer. The Data Link layer converts data packets into frames for the physical layer. At the receiving computer, it takes the raw data received from the Physical layer and packages it into data frames to send on the Network layer.

◆ The Physical layer, which is at the bottom of the OSI model, connects the networking component to the media that will be used to transmit data. The raw bit stream is transmitted over the physical cables at this level. The physical structure is defined at this level, including the cables, network cards, how the NICs attach to the hardware, how cable is attached to the NICs, and the techniques that will be used to transfer the bit stream to the cables. The Network Interface layer in the DOD model corresponds to the Data Link and Physical layers of the OSI model.

◆ An IP address is a 32-bit number that consists of four octets separated by periods. These octets have values that are 8-bit binary numbers, each of which represents a decimal number in the range 0-255.

◆ There are two parts to a standard IP address: a network ID and a host ID. The network ID, also known as the network address, identifies computers as being part of a particular network because all computers on the network use the same value.

◆ The host ID identifies a server, workstation, or router on a network. It is also known as the host address.

◆ Classful IP addressing was the first major addressing scheme used for the Internet. There are three main address classes: A, B, and C, which have 8-bit, 16-bit, and 24-bit network IDs.

◆ Classless IP addressing is a newer IP addressing scheme in which any number for bits can be assigned to the network ID.

◆ When you use an IP address with a subnet mask that is not one of the defaults, bits are "borrowed" from the host ID and used to create a subnet ID. The host bits are broken up into two parts: a subnet ID and host ID.

◆ The network address is the IP address in which all of the host ID bits are set to 0. It refers to the entire network. For example, 192.168.0.0 is used to identify the network 192.168 in routing tables.

◆ The general broadcast address is the IP address in which all bits are 1(255.255.255.255). You cannot use this address to broadcast a message to external networks because routers block it, but datagrams with this address will broadcast to all hosts on the LAN.

◆ The network broadcast address for a specific network is the IP address in which all of the host ID bits are set to 1. For example, for the network 192.168, the network broadcast address is 192.168.255.255.

◆ Classless Inter-Domain Routing (CIDR) is the Internet routing method that uses classless IP addressing to allow for the more flexible and efficient allocation of IP addresses. By using a configurable, rather than static, subnet mask, the problems of wasted addresses and the diminishing capacity of Internet global routing tables are alleviated. Using CIDR, a single routing table entry can replace hundreds or thousands of entries in a global routing table.

◆ You can either use a static IP addressing scheme, in which you will have to manually assign IP addresses to every network host, or you can use dynamic IP addressing in which an IP address is assigned to a host each time it logs on to the network.

◆ In dynamic IP addressing, the DHCP service is installed on one of your servers to create a DHCP server, which will automatically assign IP addresses to network hosts as they sign on.

◆ The IP address range 127.0.0.0 - 127.255.255.254 cannot be used on any network. This range has been set aside for use in diagnosing network connectivity problems.

◆ The Internet Assigned Numbers Authority (IANA) has reserved three other blocks of the IP addresses for private networks: 10.0.0.0- 10.255.255.255, 172.16.0.0 - 172.31.255.255, and 192.168.0.0 - 192.168.255.255.

◆ In addition, IP addresses in the range of 169.254.0.0 - 169.254.255.255 are reserved for Automatic Private IP Addressing (APIPA). APIPA is used by DHCP clients when no DHCP server can be located.

- Windows Server 2003 includes utilities, such as Ping, Pathping, Ipconfig, Tracert, Arp, Route, Netdiag, and Dcdiag, to troubleshoot network problems. All are run from the command prompt.

- Ping, the Packet Internet Groper utility, is used to verify whether the host computer can connect to the TCP/IP network, and it provides information about network problems such as incompatible TCP/IP configurations.

- The Arp command is used to display and modify the IP address to physical address (MAC address) translation tables used by Address Resolution Protocol. You can use the Arp command with the –a switch to view the contents of the ARP cache and with the –d switch to reset the cache.

- Ipconfig provides information about the host computer configuration, IP address, subnet mask, and default gateway. The Ipconfig utility enables you to determine whether an IP address has been assigned to your computer and confirms that the TCP/IP protocol is running. You can also use the Ipconfig utility to release and renew the IP address for your computer.

- Tracert is used to search the route taken when data is transferred between communicating devices. It also provides information about the links where communication failed. It displays the Fully Qualified Domain Name and IP address of each gateway along the route to a remote host.

- Pathping is a combination of Ping and Tracert. It displays the computer name and IP address for each hop packets must make and also calculates the percentage of lost/sent packets to each router or link making it easier for you to determine where the network problem is located.

- Route is used to display and modify the local routing table. You can use it to set the route you want packets to take to a particular network, including the default gateway.

Key Terms

Address Resolution Protocol (ARP)
AppleTalk
Application layer (DOD model)
Application layer (OSI model)
Arp utility
Automatic Private IP Adressing (APIPA)
Binding
Binding order
Broadcast address
Classful IP addressing
Classless IP addressing
Classless Inter-Domain Routing (CIDR)
Connection-oriented protocol
Connectionless protocol
Data Link layer (OSI model)
Dcdiag
Default gateway
DHCP lease
DOD (Department of Defense) model
Dynamic Host Configuration Protocol (DHCP)
Host ID
Host name
Hostname

Internet Control Message Protocol (ICMP)
Internet Group Management Protocol (IGMP)
Internet layer (DOD model)
Internet protocol (IP)
IP address
IP version 6
Ipconfig
IPX/SPX
Logical AND operation
Media access control (MAC) address
NetBIOS name
Netdiag
Network broadcast address
Network Driver Interface Specifications (NDIS)
Network ID
Network Interface layer (DOD model)
Network layer (OSI model)
Network interface card (NIC)
Network media
Network Monitor Driver
Network prefix
Node
Non-routable protocol

NWLink
OSI (Open System Interconnection) Reference Model
Packet
Pathping
Physical layer (OSI model)
Ping
Pragmatic General Multicast (PGM)
Presentation layer (OSI model)
Protocol
Reliable Multicast Protocol
Routable protocol
Route
Router
Scope
Session layer (OSI model)
Subnet mask
Subnet ID
Supernetting
Transmission Control Protocol/ Internet Protocol (TCP/IP)
Tracert
Transport layer (DOD model)
Transport layer (OSI model)
User Datagram Protocol (UDP)

Test Yourself

1. In order to establish communication between network computers on the same segment, protocols must be bound to which of the following?
   a. NIC
   b. router
   c. packet
   d. terminator

2. Which of the following statements is true about TCP functions at the Transport layer?
   a. It resolves the IP address of a computer to its MAC address.
   b. It is used only when small amounts of data need to be exchanged between computers.
   c. It is an unreliable protocol as it does not guarantee the delivery of data.
   d. It is a connection-oriented protocol that acknowledges packets sent and resends packets lost during transmission.

3. Which of the following is a service that resolves a host name on a network to an IP address?
   a. ARP
   b. DNS
   c. SNMP
   d. DHCP

4. Which of the following protocols reports errors that might have occurred during the transmission of data?
   a. ARP
   b. IP
   c. ICMP
   d. IGMP

5. The_____ utility is used to identify the route taken when transferring data between two computers on a network.
   a. Ping
   b. Ipconfig
   c. Tracert
   d. Tracon

6. Which of the following commands is used to view a summary of the TCP/IP configuration of your Windows Server 2003 machine?
   a. ping *IP_address*
   b. tracert *IP_address*
   c. ping 127.0.0.1
   d. ipconfig

7. Which of the following ICMP messages is used to check IP connectivity to a host? (Choose all that apply.)
   a. Echo Request
   b. Source Quench
   c. Echo Reply
   d. Redirect

8. In which of the following layers in the DOD model does the PGM protocol operate?
   a. Network Interface
   b. Application
   c. Internet
   d. Transport

9. What is the binary conversion of the IP address 172.24.2.4?
   a. 10101000 0001000 00000010 00000100
   b. 10101100 0001000 00000010 00000100
   c. 10101100 0001100 00000010 00000100
   d. 10101010 0010000 00000010 00000100

10. If the IP address for your Windows Server 2003 computer is 143.210.8.16 and the subnet mask is 255.255.224.0, what subnet is it on?
    a. 143.0.0.0
    b. 143.210.0.0
    c. 143.210.8.0
    d. 143.210.4.0

11. During which of the following steps in the DHCP lease process is a message sent by a DHCP server to acknowledge the receipt of an IP address requested by the DHCP client?
    a. DHCPOFFER
    b. DHCPDISCOVER
    c. DHCPACK
    d. DHCPREQUEST

12. The loopback address is used to:
    a. Verify that TCP/IP is correctly installed and configured on your machine.
    b. Verify whether the local computer is correctly added to the network.
    c. Determine whether the default gateway is functioning.
    d. Make sure that you are able to communicate through a router.

13. You are attempting to access a resource on a TCP/IP-based network, but you cannot connect to the server. You discover that you cannot connect to any other network computers. You want to find out if DHCP is causing the problem so you decide to lease a new IP address from the DHCP server. What commands allow you to receive a new IP address? (Choose all that apply.)
  a. ipconfig /registerdns
  b. route /renew
  c. ipconfig
  d. ipconfig /renew

14. Where is a scope defined?
  a. Routing and Remote Access
  b. Active Directory Users and Computers
  c. DHCP Manager
  d. Computer Management

Projects: On Your Own

1. Test network connectivity
  a. Open the command prompt window.
  b. Make sure that TCP/IP is bound to the NIC in your machine and properly functioning.
  c. Display the IP address, subnet mask and default gateway for your computer.
  d. Display the host name, description of your network adapter, physical address, information about any DNS and WINS servers, and details about how your IP address is configured.
  e. Release and then renew the IP address for your computer.
  f. Display the time it takes to reach each router along the path to a remote host of your choice and the FQDN and IP address for each router along the way. Record the destination you chose and how many hops it took to reach the destination.
  g. Set the number of hops to use to locate the destination host. Can the destination host be reached in this number of hops?
  h. Send an ICMP echo request message to each router on the path between your computer and the destination host. Record the percentage of lost/sent packets to each router.
  i. View the contents of the ARP cache and reset the cache.
  j. Close the command prompt.

2. Install the DHCP service and configure a DHCP server.
  a. Open the **Add or Remove Programs** window.
  b. Start the **Windows Components Wizard**.
  c. Open the **Networking Services** dialog box.
  d. Install the **DHCP** service.
  e. Close the **Add or Remove Programs** window.
  f. Open the **DHCP** console.
  g. Start the **New Scope Wizard**.
  h. Create a name and enter a description for the new scope.
  i. Enter the start and end IP addresses for the new scope.
  j. Add at least one IP address to exclude from the scope.
  k. Set a lease duration. You can reduce the lease duration for networks that include mainly portable computers and dial-up connections (from 8 to 24 hours), and increase it for networks that consist of desktop computers with stable connections (up to several weeks).
  l. Set the IP addresses for the default gateway, DNS server, and WINS server.
  m. Activate the scope.
  n. Authorize the DHCP server.
  o. Close the DHCP console.

Problem Solving Scenarios

1. You are a network administrator at a rapidly growing independent book retailer, Boswell's Books. As the company has grown, problems have arisen with the static IP addressing system currently in use. The LAN uses Windows 2000 and Windows Server 2003 servers and Windows 2000 and XP Professional clients. DNS is operational on the network. Every time a client is issued an IP address, the related information must be updated on the DNS server. Boswell's has decided to move to automatic IP addressing. Prepare a document describing the actions you will take to implement automatic IP addressing while ensuring that users will always be able to access the Web server and application server on your LAN. Be sure to include the steps involved in setting up and configuring the DHCP server and the reasons why dynamic IP addressing will be an improvement over the current method. Who must authorize the DHCP server?

2. Bigelow Cleaning Supply has recently designed and implemented a new network that includes 20 Windows Server 2003 servers and 200 Windows XP Professional clients. A DHCP server has been installed and configured, but it is not functioning properly. Prepare a document detailing the troubleshooting methods you will use to attempt to discover the reason for the network communication breakdown.

LESSON

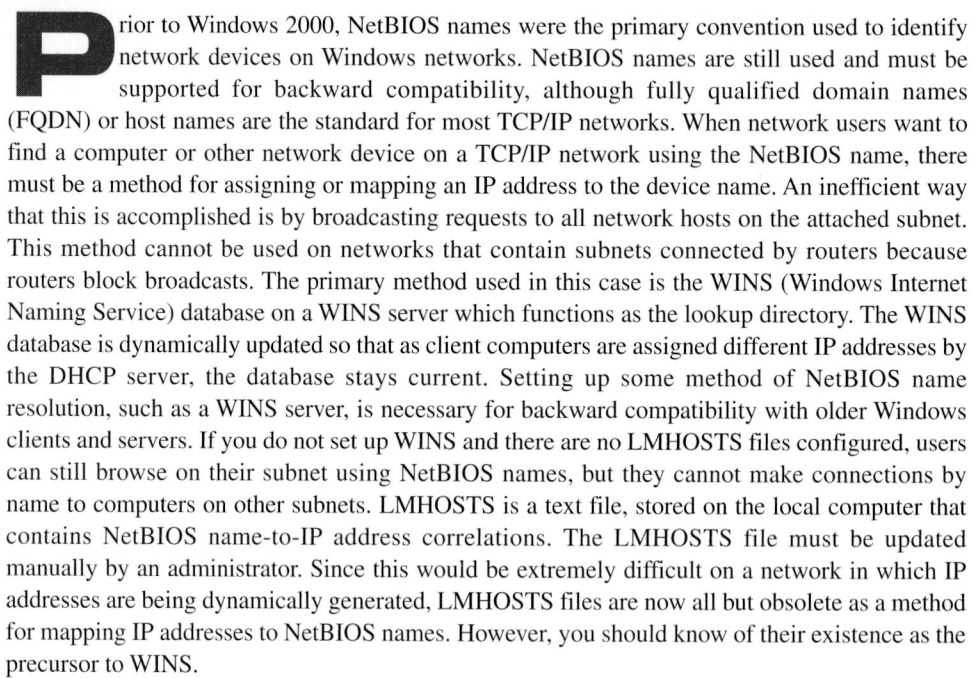

11

Introducing WINS, DNS, and RRAS

Prior to Windows 2000, NetBIOS names were the primary convention used to identify network devices on Windows networks. NetBIOS names are still used and must be supported for backward compatibility, although fully qualified domain names (FQDN) or host names are the standard for most TCP/IP networks. When network users want to find a computer or other network device on a TCP/IP network using the NetBIOS name, there must be a method for assigning or mapping an IP address to the device name. An inefficient way that this is accomplished is by broadcasting requests to all network hosts on the attached subnet. This method cannot be used on networks that contain subnets connected by routers because routers block broadcasts. The primary method used in this case is the WINS (Windows Internet Naming Service) database on a WINS server which functions as the lookup directory. The WINS database is dynamically updated so that as client computers are assigned different IP addresses by the DHCP server, the database stays current. Setting up some method of NetBIOS name resolution, such as a WINS server, is necessary for backward compatibility with older Windows clients and servers. If you do not set up WINS and there are no LMHOSTS files configured, users can still browse on their subnet using NetBIOS names, but they cannot make connections by name to computers on other subnets. LMHOSTS is a text file, stored on the local computer that contains NetBIOS name-to-IP address correlations. The LMHOSTS file must be updated manually by an administrator. Since this would be extremely difficult on a network in which IP addresses are being dynamically generated, LMHOSTS files are now all but obsolete as a method for mapping IP addresses to NetBIOS names. However, you should know of their existence as the precursor to WINS.

DNS (Domain Name Service) is the primary name resolution service for Windows 2000 and Windows Server 2003. It is a method of accessing computers on a TCP/IP network using the FQDN or host name. Fully qualified domain names consist of a host name and a domain name, including a top-level domain, which is the attached Internet suffix, for example, com, edu, gov, org, mil, net, info, coop, or a country code such as ca for Canada. They look like the URLs you use to access a Web page on the Internet, for example, www.azimuth-interactive.com. Although it is not required that TCP/IP networks use domain names, you cannot have an Active Directory domain-based network without a functioning DNS infrastructure. DNS is used to access computers on a TCP/IP network using the host name instead of an Internet Protocol (IP) address that, as you have learned, is a 32-bit number consisting of four octets. Name resolution is the translation of computer names to IP addresses and vice-versa. Name resolution is required so that a user can enter the name of the target computer, and the connection to the other computer can be established using computer language based on binary digits. Name resolution also allows the names of servers providing a service to be located. Previously this was done using NetBIOS.

To access resources on your organization's local area network (LAN) from a remote location, you use Windows Server 2003's Routing and Remote Access Service (RRAS). RRAS is installed by default when you install Windows Server 2003, but you must activate it and configure it to be used for a specific purpose before it is available for use. You can configure an RRAS server to perform the functions of a network router, to provide Remote Access Services, as a Virtual Private Network (VPN) server, or to provide shared Internet access.

Goals

In this lesson, you will learn about the DNS and WINS services and the processes used by these services to resolve name queries. In addition, you will be introduced to the fundamentals of the Routing and Remote Access Service.

Lesson 11   Introducing WINS, DNS, and RRAS

Skill	Exam 70-290 Objective
1. Understanding Windows Internet Naming Service (WINS)	Basic knowledge
2. Understanding the Domain Name System (DNS)	Basic knowledge
3. Understanding DNS Name Resolution	Basic knowledge
4. Installing and Configuring the DNS Service	Basic knowledge
5. Introducing Routing and Remote Access Service (RRAS)	Basic knowledge
6. Understanding Types of Remote Access Connections	Basic knowledge
7. Configuring Remote Access Services	Basic knowledge
8. Creating a Remote Access Policy	Basic knowledge
9. Creating a VPN Server	Basic knowledge
10. Introducing Internet Connection Sharing (ICS)	Basic knowledge
11. Introducing Network Address Translation (NAT)	Basic knowledge

Requirements

To complete this lesson, you will need administrative rights on a Windows Server 2003 member server on an Active Directory domain-based network and the Windows Server 2003 installation CD-ROM.

skill 1

Understanding Windows Internet Naming Service (WINS)

exam objective

Basic knowledge

overview

To enable TCP/IP hosts to communicate on a TCP/IP network using NetBIOS names, the NetBIOS name must be resolved to an IP address. The process of resolving a NetBIOS name to an IP address is known as NetBIOS name resolution. A **NetBIOS Name Server (NBNS)** is an application responsible for mapping NetBIOS names to IP addresses. Microsoft's implementation of an NBNS is **Windows Internet Naming Service (WINS)**. The computer running WINS is referred to as the **WINS server**. WINS allows clients on a network, which have been configured to use WINS (**WINS clients**), to dynamically register their NetBIOS name-to-IP address mappings in a database called the **WINS database**.

The following four methods are used by Microsoft WINS clients in the order listed to attempt to resolve NetBIOS names:

1. The **NetBIOS name cache** stores information about the most recently resolved NetBIOS names, and is maintained in client memory. When resolving a NetBIOS name, the client first refers to the NetBIOS name cache. If a mapping for the destination NetBIOS name is available, the name is resolved. If the name cannot be resolved using the NetBIOS name cache, the client tries the next available method. You can view the NetBIOS name cache on a computer by entering **nbtstat –c** at the command prompt.

2. **Windows Internet Naming Service (WINS):** The WINS service is the next method attempted because it is the one most likely to be used on a network and therefore the most likely to succeed. The process of resolving NetBIOS names using WINS **(Figure 11-1)** starts with a client sending a **name query request** to a WINS server. The WINS client asks the WINS server for the IP address for a NetBIOS name. The WINS server searches the WINS database for the IP address corresponding to the NetBIOS name of the computer. If the requested mapping exists, the WINS server sends a **name response message** back to the WINS client. The name response message contains the IP address. If the primary WINS server is not available or responds negatively, clients will try secondary WINS servers. Pre-Windows 2000 clients support two WINS server entries, while Windows 2000, Windows 2003, and Windows XP all support up to 12 WINS server entries. If the name has not been resolved after checking with all available WINS servers, the client will try the next method of resolution.

3. **Broadcast:** The basic method of NetBIOS name resolution is **broadcast**, which sends requests simultaneously to all network hosts on the attached subnet. If the previous methods fail, the client will broadcast a name resolution request on the local subnet. Upon receiving the broadcast, the destination host replies back with its IP address directly to the source host **(Figure 11-2)**. This method is inefficient due to the numerous broadcast requests. It will not work on large networks that contain subnets connected by routers because routers block broadcasts.

4. **LMHOSTS file:** An **LMHOSTS file** is a text file, stored on the local computer, which contains the static mappings of NetBIOS names to IP addresses for computers on remote networks only. NetBIOS resource mapping for the local network is not required in the LMHOSTS file because the name resolution process for local resources is accomplished via broadcasts. The LMHOSTS file is read from top to bottom. If an entry for the destination NetBIOS resource exists, the NetBIOS name is resolved **(Figure 11-3)**. Therefore, it is good practice to place the names of frequently accessed resources at the top of the entries in the LMHOSTS file. You open the LMHOSTS file in Notepad or another text editor in order to edit it. The LMHOSTS file is stored in the **%systemroot%\system32\drivers\etc** folder. By default, there is no LMHOSTS file, but a sample version of an LMHOSTS file, Lmhosts.sam, is also stored here. Lmhosts.sam provides detailed documentation of the format used in LMHOSTS files. To create an LMHOSTS file, you edit Lmhosts.sam and save it as "lmhosts" with no extension.

Figure 11-1 NetBIOS name resolution process using WINS

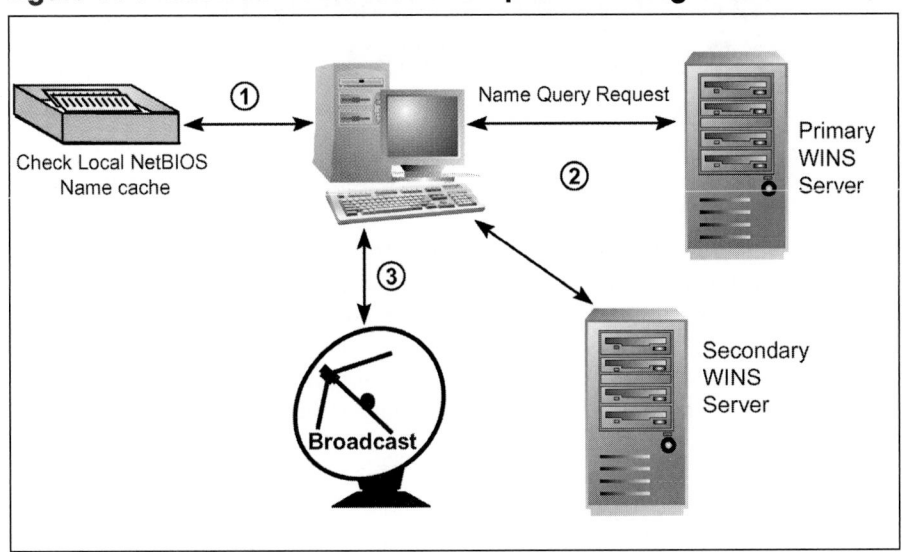

Figure 11-2 Resolving a NetBIOS name using a NetBIOS broadcast

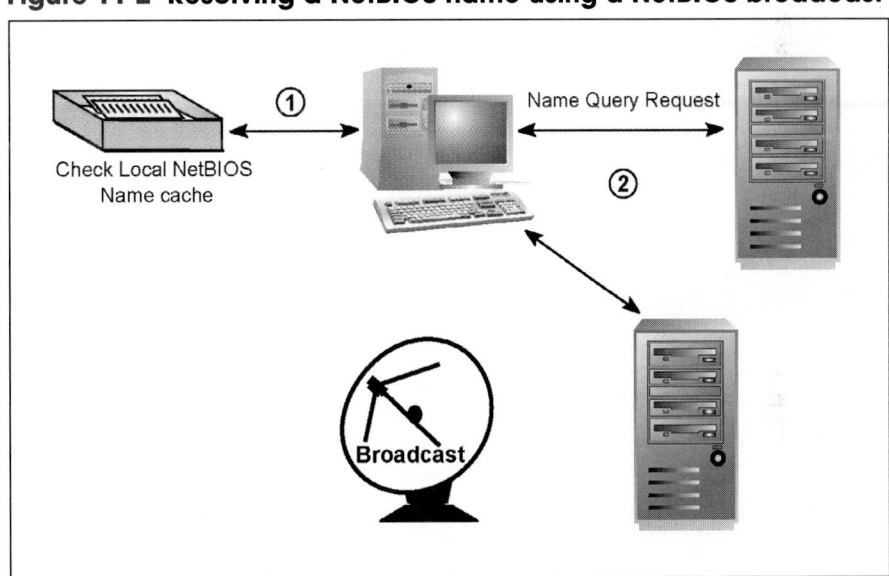

Figure 11-3 Resolving a NetBIOS name using the LMHOSTS file

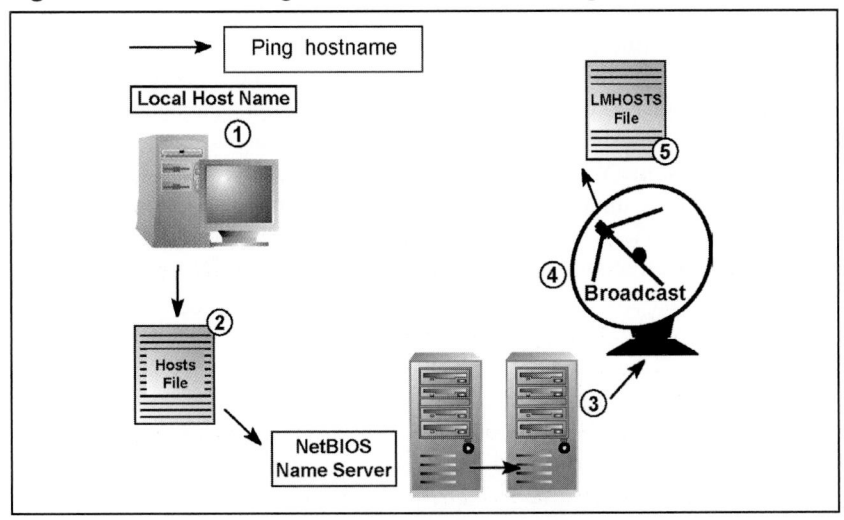

skill 1

Understanding Windows Internet Naming Service (WINS) *(cont'd)*

exam objective

Basic knowledge

overview

The resolution method and the order in which the methods will be used depend on the NetBIOS node type. The NetBIOS name cache is always checked first. You can find out what node type your machine is using by running **ipconfig /all**. Usually, the node type is configured as a DHCP option on the DHCP server. However, you can also change the **Node Type** key in the Registry (HKEY_LOCAL_MACHINE\SYSTEM\CurrentControlSet\Services\NetBT\ Parameters) to change the node type on individual machines **(Figure 11-4)**.

The node types and the corresponding Registry key values are listed and explained below.

◆ **B-node (Broadcast):** Broadcasts are used to resolve names on computers configured with a B-node type. On Windows computers, B-nodes are referred to as enhanced B-nodes because if the broadcast is not successful, the client will attempt to use the LMHOSTS file. This is the default node type if not using WINS (NodeType value 0x1).

◆ **P-node (Peer-to-Peer or Point-to Point):** The client queries a WINS server in order to resolve names. Broadcasts are never used (NodeType value 0x2).

◆ **M-node (Mixed):** Broadcasts are used first to attempt to resolve names. If this is unsuccessful, the client attempts to query a WINS server. This node type is usually used when the WINS server is located across a WAN link (NodeType value 0x4).

◆ **H-node (Hybrid):** The client attempts to query a WINS server first in order to resolve names. If this is unsuccessful, the B-node methods are used (i.e., broadcasts and then the LMHOSTS file). This is the default node type if using WINS (NodeType value 0x8).

If WINS is enabled, Windows 2000, XP Professional, and Windows Server 2003 computers are configured to use H-node by default. If WINS is not enabled, B-node is used by default.

The dynamic registration of NetBIOS name-to-IP address mappings works as follows: During the initial stages of a WINS client's boot process, it sends a **name registration request** to the WINS server. The WINS server checks its database for an existing entry that matches the request. If a matching record exists, this means that it is already registered by another host. The WINS server sends a challenge message to the currently registered host. If there is no response after three attempts, the NetBIOS name is registered to the new client and the new client is sent a **positive name registration response**. If the currently registered host responds, the new client will be turned down and will be sent a **negative name registration response**. At this point, a dialog box would appear on the offending client computer declaring "A duplicate name exists on the network". This informs the user of the computer that he or she should change the computer name.

If no matching records exist, the WINS server registers the NetBIOS name and sends a positive name registration response to the client. The positive name registration response includes the **time to live (TTL)** value for the registered name. As its name indicates, a TTL value indicates the time period during which the information will remain stored on the WINS server. Before the TTL ends, the WINS client must renew its name with the WINS server. To renew its name registration, the client must send a **name refresh request** to the WINS server, asking to refresh the TTL. When a WINS client no longer requires a registered name (i.e. during client shutdowns), it sends a **name release message** to the WINS server to release the name **(Figure 11-5)**.

caution

Be aware that even though LAN Manager 2.2c for MS-DOS is capable of using WINS, LAN Manager 2.2c for O/S 2 computers is NOT capable of using WINS.

Figure 11-4 The Node Type key

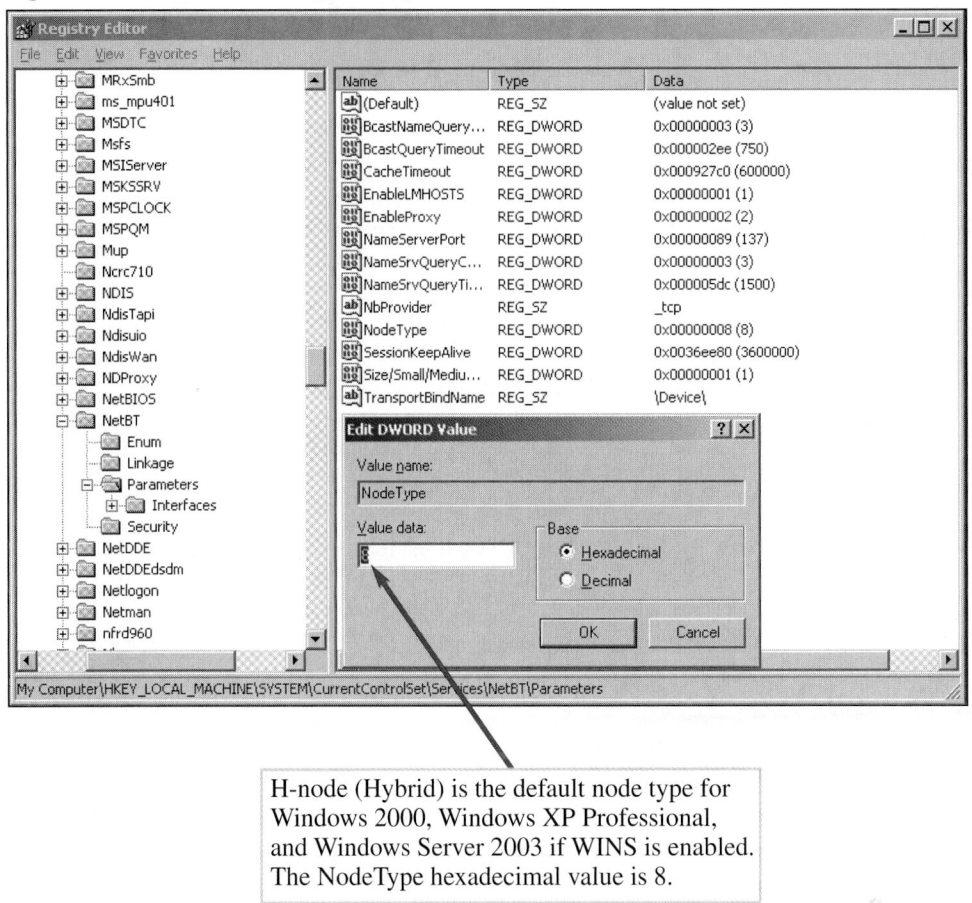

H-node (Hybrid) is the default node type for
Windows 2000, Windows XP Professional,
and Windows Server 2003 if WINS is enabled.
The NodeType hexadecimal value is 8.

Figure 11-5 The NetBIOS name registration process

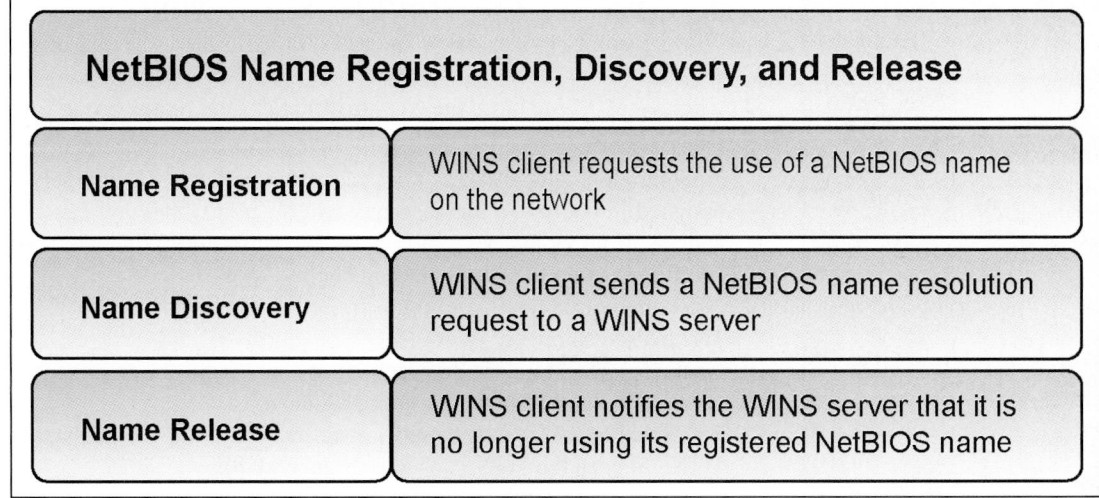

NetBIOS Name Registration, Discovery, and Release	
Name Registration	WINS client requests the use of a NetBIOS name on the network
Name Discovery	WINS client sends a NetBIOS name resolution request to a WINS server
Name Release	WINS client notifies the WINS server that it is no longer using its registered NetBIOS name

skill 1

Understanding Windows Internet Naming Service (WINS) *(cont'd)*

exam objective

Basic knowledge

overview

To begin using WINS, you must first install the WINS service on a Windows Server 2003 computer to create a WINS server. You must make sure that the computer on which you install the WINS service meets certain configuration requirements. On a TCP/IP network, the WINS service can only be installed on a Windows NT Server, Windows 2000 Server, or Windows Server 2003 computer, and the server must be configured with a static IP address, a subnet mask, a default gateway, and other TCP/IP parameters. Windows Server 2003 computers, Windows 2000 and XP, Windows 9.x, Windows NT 3.5 and later, Windows for Workgroups running TCP/IP driver and LAN Manager 2.2c for MS-DOS can all be WINS clients.

If speed is an issue, you should disable logging of database changes to make name registrations faster. You can set options in the Properties dialog box for a WINS server to disable detailed event logging.

After a WINS server has been configured, you must make sure that the clients on the network are configured so that they can access the WINS server, dynamically register their NetBIOS name-to-IP address mappings in the WINS database, and use the WINS server for name resolution services. The default setting is to use the NetBIOS setting from the DHCP server. A WINS client can also be configured manually in the **Advanced TCP/IP Settings** dialog box **(Figure 11-6)**. Click the **Add** button to enter the static IP address for the WINS server. If you configure a WINS client manually, the values that you enter will take precedence over the values that a DHCP server provides. Non-DHCP clients must be configured manually.

how to

Install and configure **WINS**.

1. Log on to your member server as an **Administrator**.
2. Click **Start**, point to **Control Panel**, and click **Add or Remove Programs** to open the **Add or Remove Programs** window.
3. Click the **Add/Remove Windows Components** button to start the **Windows Components Wizard**. A **Please wait** message appears while the Wizard is initiated.
4. Scroll down the **Components** list and select **Networking Services**.
5. Click **Details...** to open the **Networking Services** dialog box.
6. Select **Windows Internet Naming Service (WINS)** on the **Subcomponents of Networking Services** list **(Figure 11-7)**. All other selected boxes should be kept as they are.
7. Click **OK** to close the **Networking Services** dialog box.
8. Click **Next >** to open the **Configuring Components** screen while Setup makes the configuration changes. This may take a few minutes. If your server has a dynamically assigned IP address, a message box will open in which you can change it to a static IP address. If necessary, you will be asked to insert the Windows Server 2003 installation CD-ROM. Insert the CD-ROM and click **OK**.
9. After the components are configured, the **Completing the Windows Components Wizard** screen opens.
10. Click **Finish** to close the Completing the Windows Components Wizard screen.
11. Close the Add or Remove Programs window.
12. To configure the **WINS service**, click **Start**, point **Administrative Tools**, and click **WINS** to open the **WINS** console **(Figure 11-8)**.
13. To configure the server, right-click the server name and click **Properties** to open the *<server_name>* **Properties** dialog box.

Figure 11-6 The WINS tab in the Advanced TCP/IP Settings dialog box

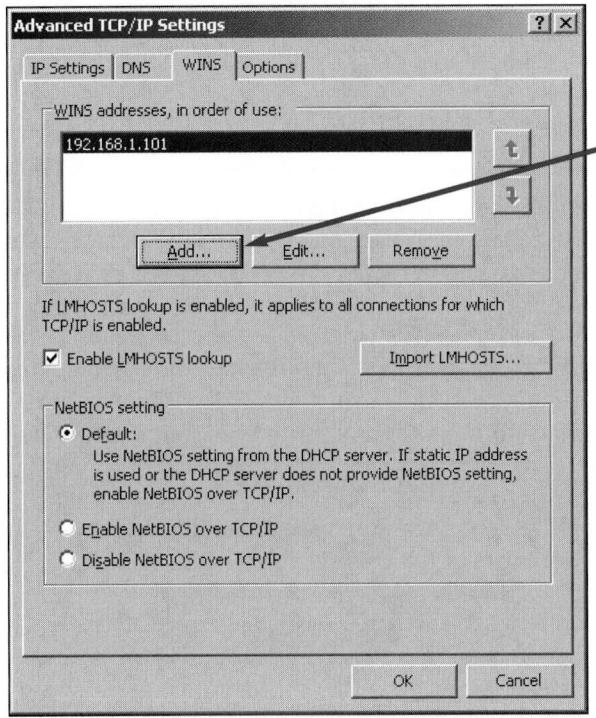

Click to open the TCP/IP WINS Server dialog box where you will enter the static IP address for a WINS server

Figure 11-7 The Networking Services dialog box

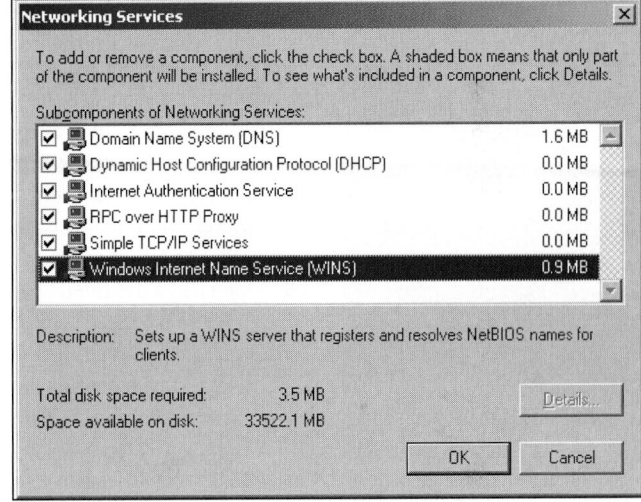

Figure 11-8 The WINS console

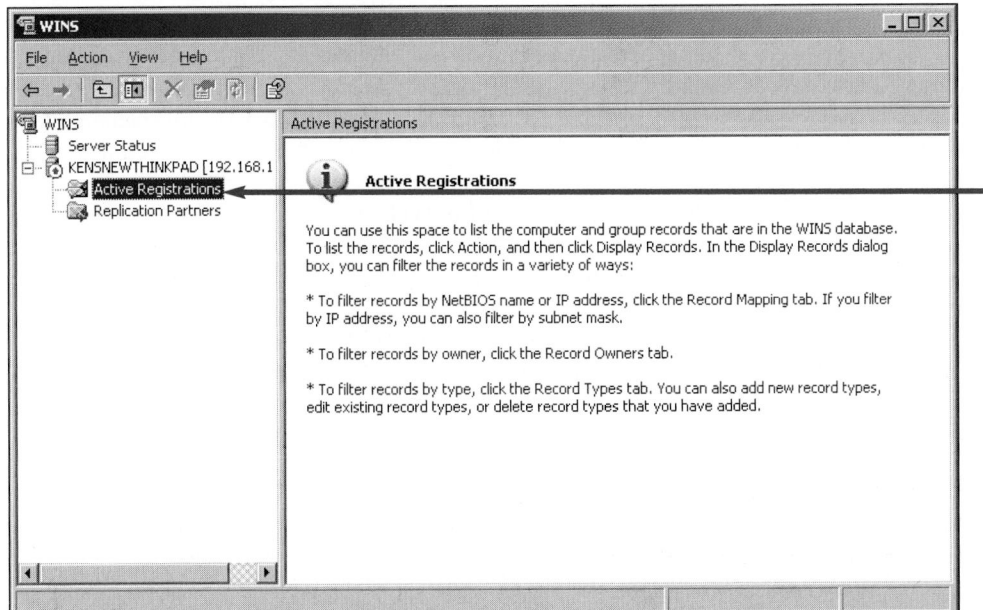

To view the content of the WINS database, right-click Active Registrations and select Display Records. Then, click the Find Now button to view all active registrations in the details pane. You can also create filters to search for records based on a name pattern, IP address, record owner, or record type.

skill 1

Understanding Windows Internet Naming Service (WINS) (cont'd)

exam objective   Basic knowledge

how to

14. The **Automatically update statistics every** option button is selected by default. The default setting is ten minutes and for the most part, this setting will not have to be changed. Unless you have a specific reason for doing so, you should probably leave the default in place (**Figure 11-9**). In order to make database backups of this server, you must enter the path to where the database backup will be stored on the server. Type the backup path in the **Default backup path** text box and select the **Backup database during server shutdown** check box.
15. Open the **Intervals** tab to specify the rate at which records will be renewed, deleted, and verified by the WINS server. The defaults are recommended (**Figure 11-10**). To restore the default settings, click Restore Defaults .
16. Open the **Database Verification** tab. Select the **Verify database consistency every** check box, and specify the time in hours in the **hours** text box (**Figure 11-11**). The recommended value is **24**, which is the default.
17. The default value in the **Maximum number of records verified each period** text box is **30000**, and the **Owner servers** option button is selected by default. The term "Owner servers" refers to servers that own particular records. This will allow the server to verify that its copy of the database is consistent with the copy that the record's owner has, for up to 30,000 records. The value used is 30,000 records because that equates to approximately 10,000 users, which is the typical load a single WINS server can support. Records can be verified against the owners of particular records or against randomly selected partners.
18. Open the **Advanced** tab to configure the event log settings, the number of requests for the server to handle, the database path, and the start version for the event log.
19. By default, the **Enable burst handling** check box is selected and set to **Medium**. If you have a slower server, you can change this setting to **Low**. The server must have good processing power to handle **High** or **Custom** settings (**Figure 11-12**).
20. Click OK to close the **Properties** dialog box for the server.
21. Close the WINS console.

more

If you decrease the default statistical update on the General tab in the Properties dialog box for a WINS server, you increase the number of server refreshes that must take place. Intervals that are too short can result in performance problems. Intervals that are too long will result in outdated data. It is a recommended practice to back up the WINS database every time the server shuts down (**Backup database during server shutdown** on the General tab). However, this increases the amount of shutdown time required. The default settings on the Intervals tab for the rates at which records are renewed, deleted, and verified are generally the best settings for your WINS server. The **Renew interval** refers to how often a client renews its name registration. The **Extinction interval** refers to the amount of time between marking a record released and marking it extinct for replication purposes. The **Extinction timeout interval** is the amount of time between marking a record extinct and deletion from the database. The **Verification interval** is the time after which the server will verify active records. The **Verify database consistency every** setting on the **Database Verification** tab corresponds to the **Verification interval** setting on the **Intervals** tab. A WINS server verifies the database every 24 hours by default.

Burst handling refers to a method for handling a high or burst period of WINS registration and renewal traffic. When burst handling is enabled, a burst queue size is set to a threshold value and if the burst of activity exceeds the threshold, burst handling is initiated. The WINS server begins to answer requests with an immediate affirmative response, but it assigns each

Figure 11-9 The General tab in the Properties dialog box for the WINS server

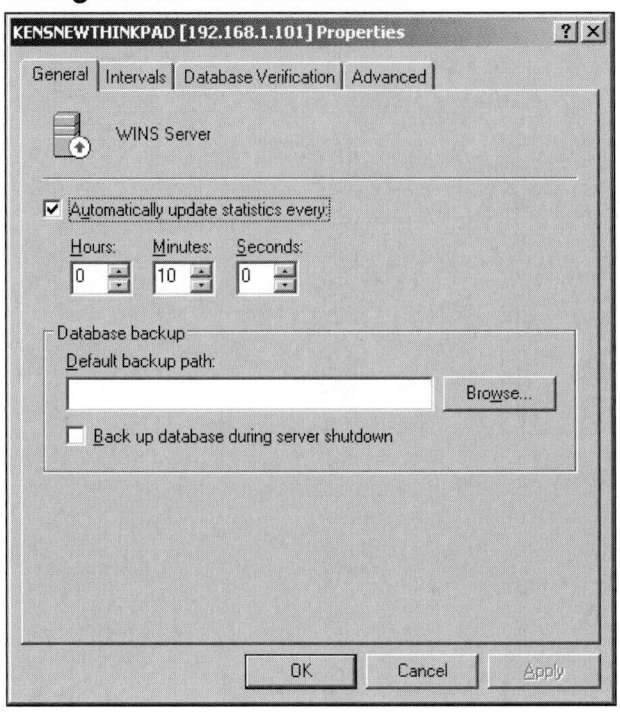

Figure 11-10 The Intervals tab

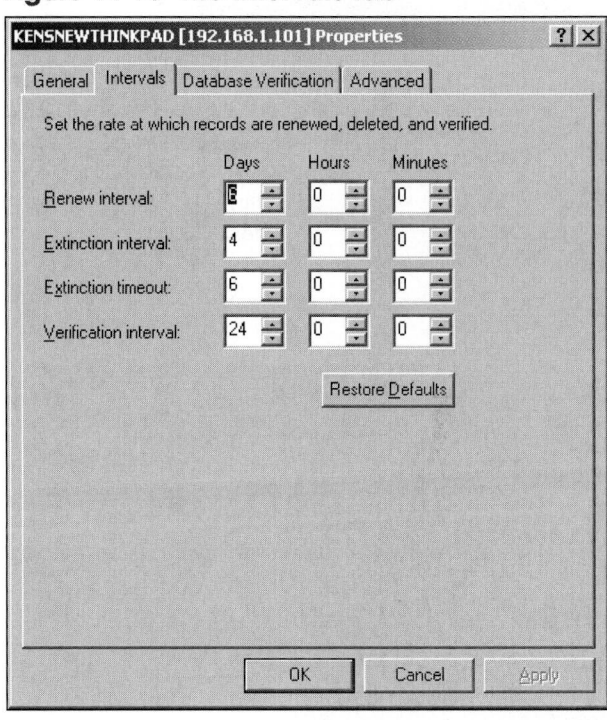

Figure 11-11 The Database Verification tab

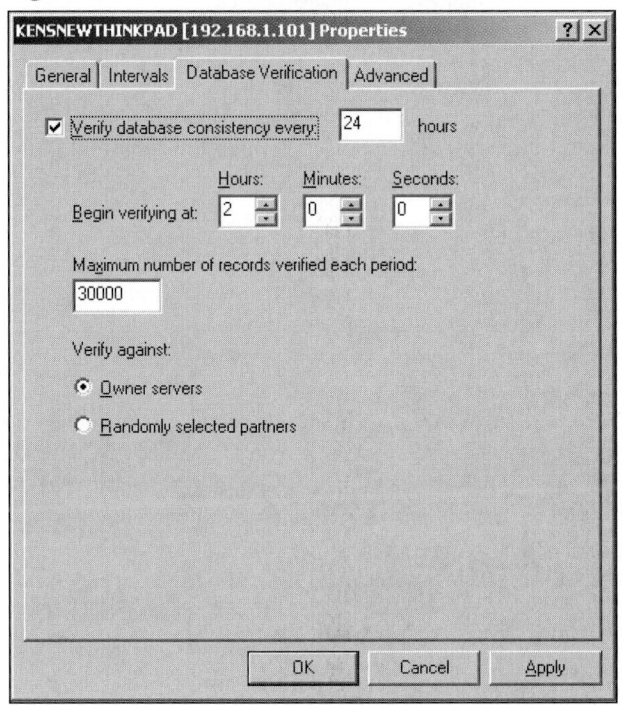

Figure 11-12 The Advanced tab

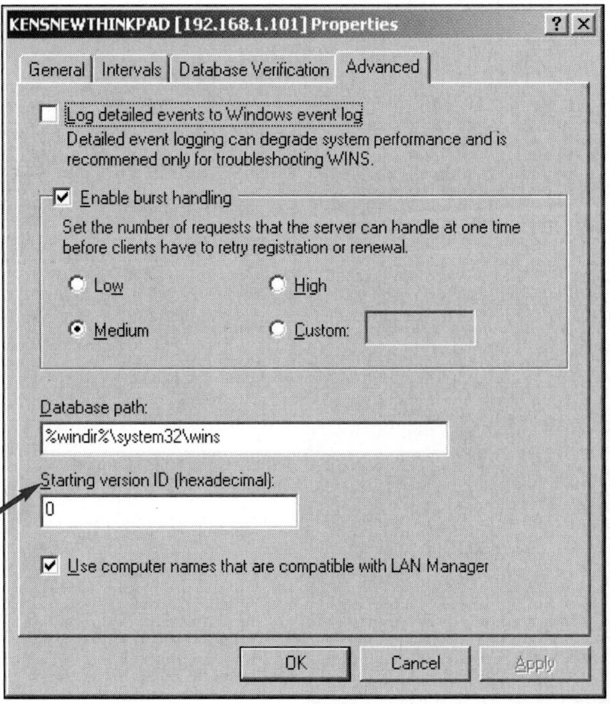

Used to force WINS replication when a new version of the WINS database has been created

skill 1

Understanding Windows Internet Naming Service (WINS) *(cont'd)*

exam objective   Basic knowledge

more

response a TTL (Time to Live) of between 5 and 50 minutes. This way the server has time to catch up to the backlog of requests before the TTLs expire and registration and renewal traffic does not simply halt. A setting of Low allows 300 name refresh and registration requests as the burst threshold. A setting of Medium allows 500 name refresh and registration requests as the burst threshold. A setting of High allows 1000 name refresh and registration requests as the burst threshold. If you select Custom you can assign your own value for the burst threshold.

The WINS replication process is how WINS servers on a network swap information with one another. You configure replication in the **Replication Partners** node in the WINS console tree. WINS replication is done through "partnering" with other WINS servers so that all WINS servers are interconnected and replication occurs between them. To enable automatic partner configuration, right-click the **Replication Partners** node and select **Properties** to open the **Replication Partners Properties** dialog box. On the **Advanced** tab, select the **Enable automatic partner configuration** check box **(Figure 11-13)**. When you enable automatic partner configuration, your WINS server uses IP multicast to identify the other WINS servers on the network, and they are automatically configured as Push/Pull replication partners (see page 11.14). Replication will occur every two hours. This simple configuration is appropriate for small or bounded LANs. All routers must support multicasts in order for this to work. The multicast address 224.0.1.24, which is reserved for WINS, is used for the automatic discovery of WINS servers on the network.

To configure new replication partners manually, right-click the **Replication Partners** node and select **New Replication Partner**. In the **New Replication Partner** dialog box **(Figure 11-14)**, you can either **Browse** to locate and select a partner, or you can enter the IP address of the WINS server you want to add as a partner. Select **Replication Partners** in the console tree to view the partners in the details pane. Right-click a partner name and click **Properties** to set replication properties for that server. On the **Advanced** tab, you can switch from the default, **Push/Pull** partner to just a **Push** or just a **Pull** partner (see page 11.14).

To set properties for all replication partners, right-click **Replication Partners** and click Properties. On the **General** tab, you can choose either **Replicate only with Partners**, which is the default configuration, or **Overwrite unique static mappings at this server (migrate on) (Figure 11-15)**. Normally, when you create a static mapping on a WINS server, it is permanently kept in the database, unless you remove it manually. Whereas dynamic records can be overwritten by the renewal process, or removed because they have become extinct, static mappings are permanent in order to guarantee that device mappings will always be available. However, this will cause dynamic name registration requests to be rejected when it is not appropriate, for example, when a static mapping replicated from another WINS server has incorrect name or address information. The (migrate on) setting is used to override this default behavior so that static mappings can be challenged. In the challenge process, the IP address for the static mapping is compared to any IP address the named client tries to dynamically register. If the two addresses do not match, WINS concludes that the static address is no longer active or in use, the IP address is changed from static to dynamic status, and the address is updated.

Figure 11-13 The Advanced tab in the Replication Partners Properties dialog box

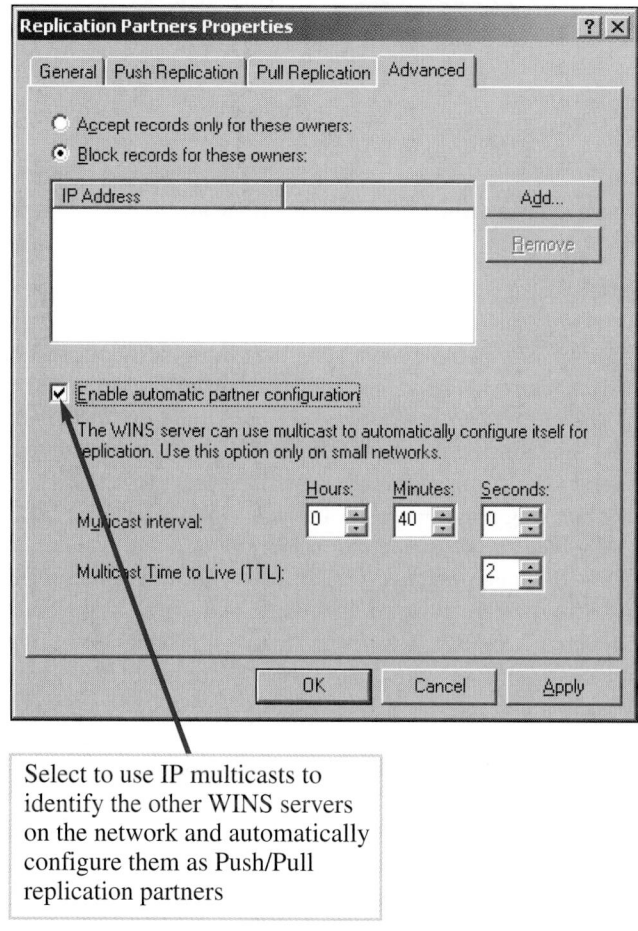

Select to use IP multicasts to identify the other WINS servers on the network and automatically configure them as Push/Pull replication partners

Figure 11-14 The New Replication Partner dialog box

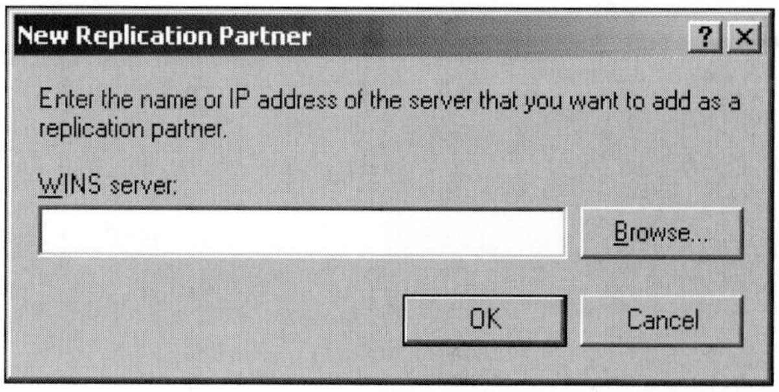

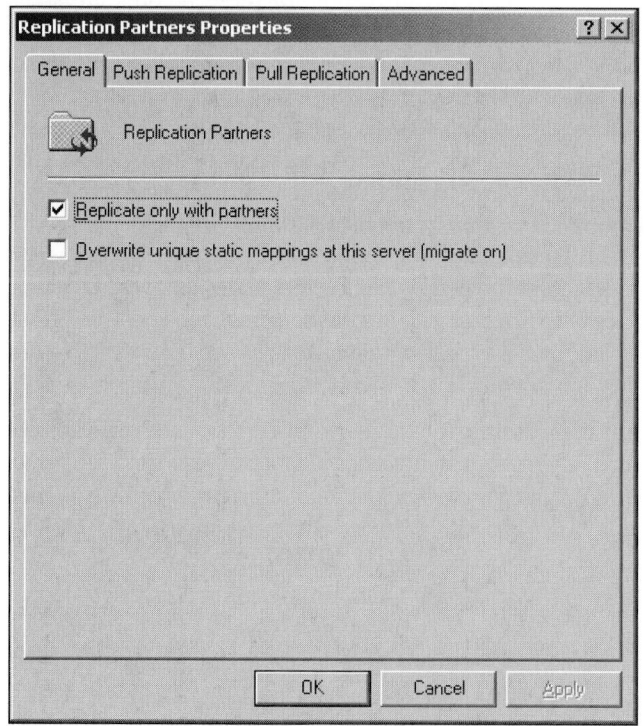

Figure 11-15 The Replication Partners Properties dialog box

skill 1

Understanding Windows Internet Naming Service (WINS) (cont'd)

exam objective

Basic knowledge

more

Generally, a combination of **Push Replication** and **Pull Replication** is configured. (**Figure 11-16**).

◆ **Push Replication:** When the service starts or when an address in the database changes, the server pushes replication by notifying its partners that changes have occurred. When the partners receive the notification, they pull the replication data from the WINS server (**Figure 11-17**). You can also set a threshold for the number of changes that must be recorded in the WINS database before push replication will be initiated (**Number of changes in version ID before replication**). Push replication is designed to ensure quick convergence, or quick propagation of changes made to the database. However, push replication cannot be scheduled, making it inefficient for use across WAN links.

◆ **Pull Replication:** You set a schedule for the partners to perform a pull replication. By default, this is set to occur every 30 minutes (**Figure 11-18**). Pull replication is designed around the efficient use of WAN bandwidth. However, in order to pull, the server's direct replication partner must be configured to push. This means that you cannot have a true pull/pull replication environment. To simulate pull/pull, you need to configure the servers to use both push and pull replication, but set the push interval to 0. A push interval of 0 means that the server will only push when the other side pulls.

You can configure both Push and Pull replication to **Use persistent connections** with their replication partners. This is designed to speed up replication because a new connection does not have to be created for each replication.

On the **Advanced** tab, you can create a list of servers which cannot replicate to your server. You set the **Block records to these owners** option to stop replication to your server from the servers on the list. The most common use for this setting is to block records from decommissioned servers which are still replicating to you, but their records are outdated. After a WINS server has been taken off the network, its records will continue to be replicated on the network between the partners. This is because some of these records are static mappings that must be removed manually or tombstoned and because dynamic mappings that were registered with the inactive WINS server are also not immediately deleted. **Tombstoning** marks records as extinct. The local WINS server immediately removes tombstoned records from use, but they remain in the database so that they can be replicated to the partners. The replication partners in turn apply the tombstone status to the records. After all WINS partners complete replication of these records, and after a designated time period has passed, the records will be removed. This time period is determined by the time intervals set for the replication cycle on the **Intervals** tab in the Properties dialog box for the server (**Figure 11-19**). These intervals also control when dynamic entries are removed. Dynamic entries cannot be removed unless the WINS server who owned them has been contacted. If the WINS server has been removed from the network, the replication partners retain the records because they cannot verify that they have expired.

Conversely, you can set the **Accept records only for these owners** option and create a list of servers whose name records your WINS server will accept. Name records from all WINS servers not on the list will be barred. You can only use one option or the other. It is a good idea, therefore, to choose the option that will need the fewest entries on the list.

Figure 11-16 WINS replication

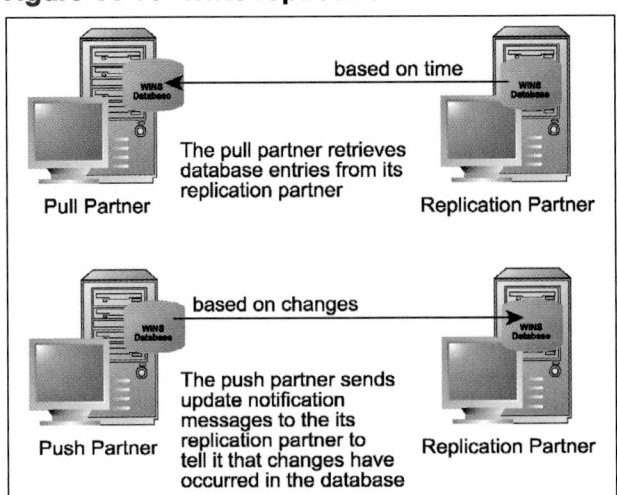

Figure 11-17 The Push Replication tab

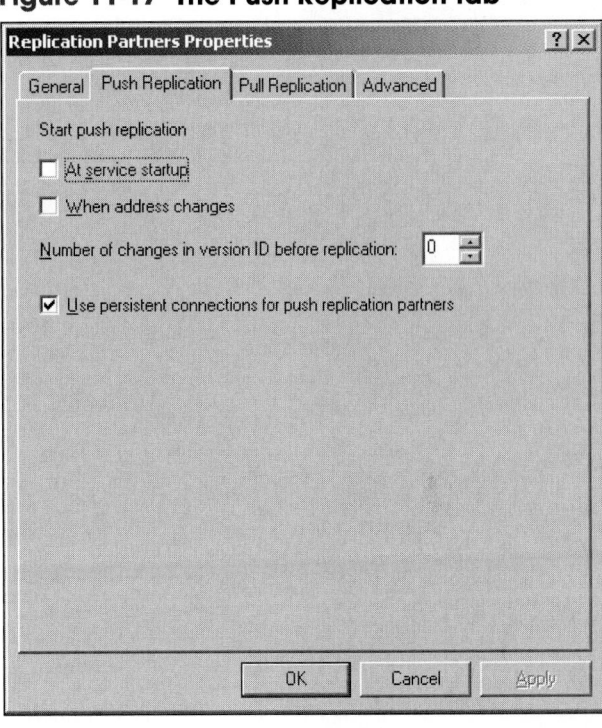

Figure 11-18 The Pull Replication tab

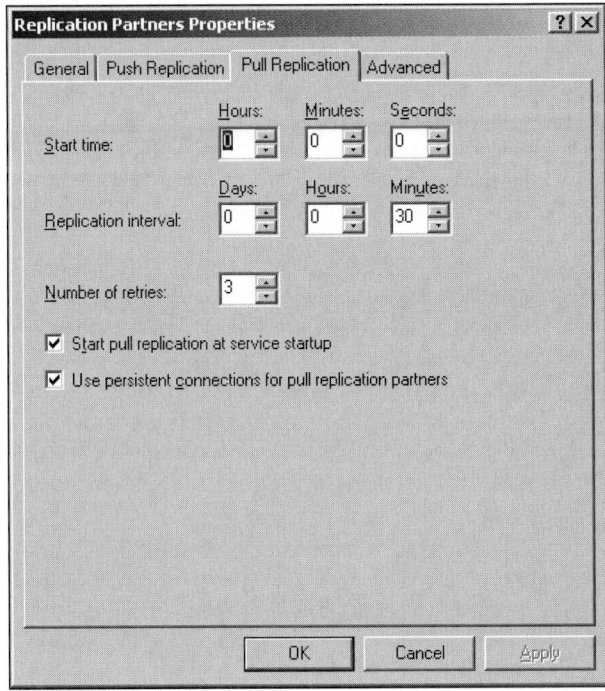

Figure 11-19 The Intervals tab on the Properties dialog box for a WINS server

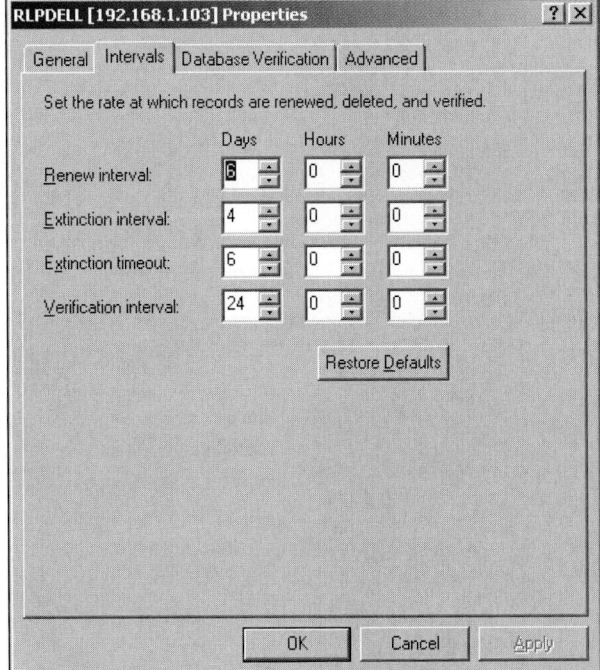

skill 2 *Understanding the Domain Name System (DNS)*

exam objective

Basic knowledge

overview

Domain Name System (DNS) is the main name resolution service for Windows Server 2003. **DNS servers**, also referred to as **DNS name servers**, perform the task of **name resolution** to convert host names to IP addresses and to resolve service names. The DNS server maintains a database containing IP addresses mapped to their corresponding names. To access a computer on the network, users need only specify its name.

DNS has a hierarchical structure. The nodes in this hierarchical structure are called **domains**. Each domain has a name associated with it, for example, domain1. As you add more domains to the DNS hierarchy, the name of the parent domain is added to the child domain or sub-domain. For example, in the domain name **exams.classes.com**, exams represents a sub-domain of the **classes.com** domain, and **classes** is a sub-domain of the **com** domain.

The domain at the top of the DNS hierarchy is called a **root domain**. The child domain of the root domain is called a **top-level domain**, and the child domain of a top-level domain is a **second-level domain**. The root domain is represented by the trailing full stop or period ("."). The top-level domains on the Internet are the two- and three-character names you are familiar with from surfing the Web, such as com, net, edu, org, gov, biz, info, museum, coop, pro, etc.; and the various country codes such as uk for Great Britain and ca for Canada. Second-level domains have two parts: a top-level name and a second-level name, for example, ebay.com, yale.edu, usmint.gov, and amazon.ca. A **host name** is at the bottom of the DNS hierarchy and it designates a particular computer, on either the Internet or a private network (**Figure 11-20**). The hierarchical structure of DNS is also referred to as the **DNS namespace (Table 11-1)**.

By default, TCP/IP in Windows Server 2003 sets the NetBIOS name (also known as the computer name) and the DNS host name to the same value, but you can set them to different names if you so desire. For example, if you knew the NetBIOS name of a computer was **classes**, and that computer was in the **domain1.com** domain, then by default, the FQDN for that computer would be **classes.domain1.com**. A **fully qualified domain name (FQDN)** includes a **domain name** in addition to the host name. It is a name that follows Internet naming conventions that use dots to separate parts of a name. For example, **server1** may be the alias for a computer on a TCP/IP network, whereas **server1.finance.redhen.com.** is the FQDN for the computer. The trailing stop or period means that this is an FQDN, but even if the trailing stop were missing, it is assumed to be there. Com is the top-level domain, designating on the Internet that this is a commercial organization. Redhen is the second-level domain, indicating the organization name. Finance is a sub-domain of Redhen.com (or third-level domain) indicating the Finance department, and server1 is the name of the computer in the Finance department. The host name is the leftmost part of a FQDN. The FQDN represents the exact location of the resource on the network, while the host name can be used by the user at this computer rather than typing the entire FQDN (**Figure 11-21**).

Keep in mind that DNS is fully integrated with Windows Server 2003. For example, redhen.com is a valid DNS name. It can also be used as a Windows Server 2003 domain name, and **TParks@redhen.com** can function as both an Internet e-mail address and a user name on your LAN. This way, your network users can locate things on the local network in the same way that they locate them on the Internet. Domain names are not case-sensitive and can be up to 63 characters long. A FQDN can have a maximum length of 255 characters. The standard characters supported by the DNS service are A-Z, a-z, 0-9, and the hyphen. The DNS service also supports the Unicode character set, which contains characters not included in the ASCII (American Standard Code for Information Interchange) character set to support languages other than English. You can use these characters only if all the DNS servers that

Table 11-1   The DNS namespace

Domain hierarchy	Description
Root domain	The primary domain in the DNS namespace. The root domain is represented by the trailing full stop or period (".").
Top-level domains	These domains are located below the root domain in the DNS namespace. They define the organization type or geographic location. Top-level domains are the two and three character codes such as com, used for commercial organizations; gov, used for government organizations; and org, used for non-commercial organizations. Other top-level domains (TLDs) include aero, biz, coop, info, museum, name, net, and pro, which is restricted to licensed professionals.
Second-level domains	These are placed below the top-level domains in the DNS namespace. For example, the .com top-level domain assigns and registers second-level domains to individuals and organizations such as Microsoft, Yahoo, MSN, etc.
Host names	The host name is the leftmost portion of a FQDN and is located below the second-level domains. It designates a particular computer or device, either on the Internet or on a private network.

Figure 11-20 The DNS hierarchy

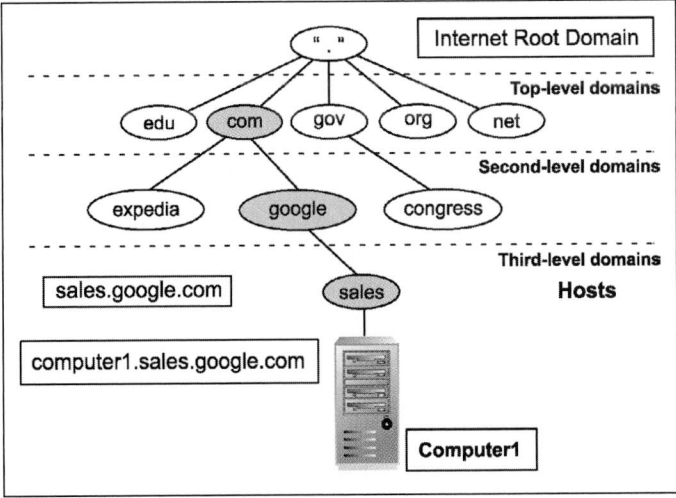

Figure 11-21 A FQDN

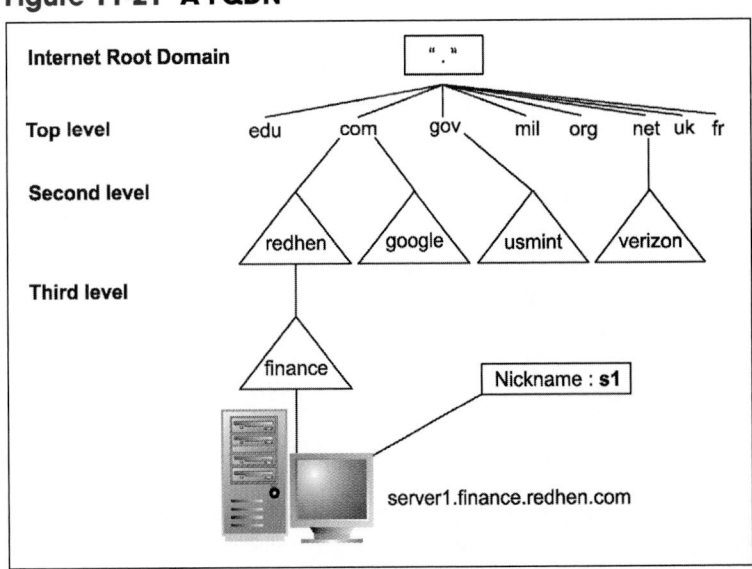

skill 2

Understanding the Domain Name System (DNS) *(cont'd)*

exam objective   Basic knowledge

overview

you are using to administer your site or network support Unicode. It is also advisable to restrict the FQDN to 3 or 4 domain levels. The more domain levels there are, the more administrative effort will be required to maintain them.

On a small network, a DNS server may contain just one database file that stores all of the name-to-IP-address resolution data. However, on larger networks, it becomes necessary to divide administrative control and DNS functions into zones. **Zones** are distinct, contiguous segments of the DNS namespace that make a large domain manageable by enabling different administrators to manage different zones. For example, if the resources in **domain1.com** are related to marketing and finance, the domain can be divided into the zones **marketing.domain1.com** and **finance.domain1.com**, respectively. This partitions or subdivides the DNS namespace and the responsibility for the contents is then delegated so that administrative responsibility can be shared. Servers in each zone store all records about the resources in that zone in a separate file called a **zone database file**. The zone database file contains various types of resource records as described in **Table 11-2**. A **resource record** is an entry in the DNS database. A resource record contains a TTL, the Record class (Internet, Hesiod, or Chaos), the record type (CNAME, PTR, A, etc), and finally the record data, which depends on the record type.

In standard DNS, when multiple DNS servers are created in a standard DNS zone, there are two kinds of DNS database files: primary and secondary. One DNS name server in the zone will store the **primary zone database file** and the others will store copies of it called **secondary zone database files**. Modifications and updates can only be made to the primary zone database file. **Zone transfers** occur to replicate any changes to the primary zone database file to the secondary zone database files. The server where the primary zone database file is housed is called the **authoritative server** because it has authority over the other DNS servers in the zone. The purpose of the secondary database file servers is to reduce the traffic and query load on the primary database zone server. Secondary database file servers also provide resolution redundancy; that is, if the authoritative server is down, the secondary database file servers can answer name resolution requests instead **(Figure 11-22)**.

You can also implement a caching-only DNS name server. **Caching-only name servers** use caching to store information collected during name resolution. Caching is a method of storing frequently requested information in memory so that clients can quickly access it when required. A caching-only name server has no database files. It simply forwards requests to a designated DNS server and caches the resolved result. This means that the next client to request resolution for that record will be answered from the cache, which reduces the load on the real DNS server, and can reduce WAN traffic caused by name resolution. Caching-only servers are not authoritative for any zone. They are used when you need to provide DNS services locally, but do not want to create a separate zone for this location. This situation may arise when the number of hosts that require DNS services at a location is small, or you do not want to increase administrative overhead by maintaining another zone. Another reason a caching-only name server is implemented rather than a primary or secondary name server is zone transfer traffic. Caching-only name servers do not participate in zone transfers, unlike primary and secondary name servers. This could be a critical design consideration when deciding to implement DNS at a remote location that is connected to your central intranet via slow WAN links. If you configure a primary DNS server at the central location and a secondary DNS server at the remote location, it may result in excessive zone transfer traffic. However, if you implement a caching-only name server at the remote location, you can provide DNS services without increasing zone transfer traffic. In fact, no zone transfer traffic will be generated at all.

Table 11-2 Types of resource records in a zone database file

Resource Record Type	Represented in a zone database file as	Description
Start of authority	SOA	First record in the DNS database file. Defines the general parameters for the DNS zone, including the name of the primary DNS server for the zone.
Name server	NS	Lists the additional name servers in the zone.
Address (Host name)	A	Associates a host name to its IP address. It maps a host name to a 32-bit IPv4 address.
IPv6 Address	AAAA	Associates the host name with the corresponding IP address. It maps a host name to a 128-bit IPv6.
Canonical name (Alias)	CNAME	States an alias to the name for a given computer. For example, nitrous.isp.net might be a Web server, but an alias is created to allow people to access the server using the name www.isp.net.
Pointer Record	PTR	Associates an IP address to a host name. Used in reverse lookup zones.
Mail exchange	MX	Specifies the mail exchanger host (e-mail server) for mail sent to the domain.
Service Location record	SRV	Identifies a server that offers a particular service such as HTTP, FTP or LDAP, with the information about how to contact the service.

Figure 11-22 The DNS namespace subdivided into zones

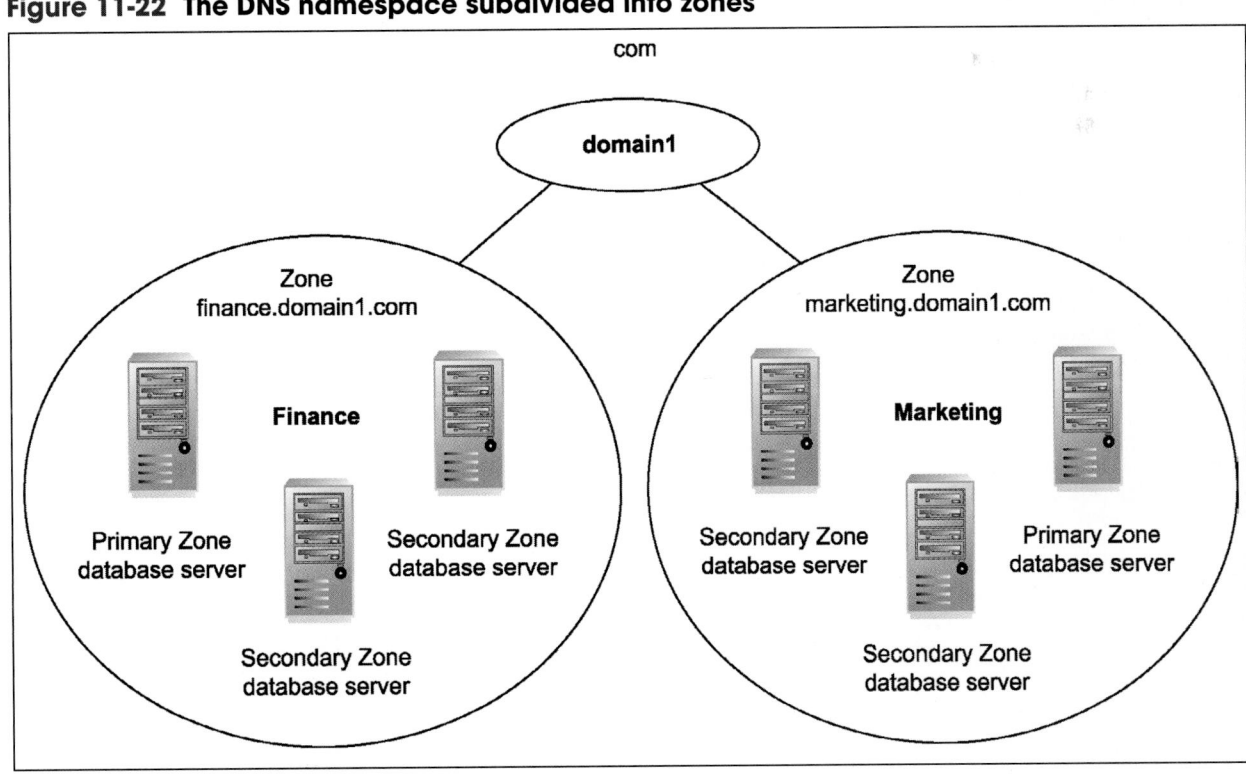

skill 2

Understanding the Domain Name System (DNS) *(cont'd)*

exam objective

Basic knowledge

overview

When you implement a caching-only DNS server on your network for the first time, the cache is empty. As the server starts to service client requests, information is cached and builds over time. Thus, during the initial phase of service, more requests must be forwarded to other DNS servers. As more name-to-IP-address resolution data is cached, the caching-only server will be able to resolve more frequently requested resources from cache rather than forwarding the request to other DNS servers for resolution (**Table 11-3**).

more

On a network such as the Internet, millions of queries are passed from one name server to another, causing a lot of network traffic. To reduce network traffic, DNS name servers cache query results. A query result can be cached for a specific amount of time called the **Time to Live (TTL)**, after which it is deleted. Updated information will not be sent in response to client requests until the TTL expires. Longer TTL values will increase network efficiency because requests will be able to be answered more quickly, but shorter TTL values ensure that current data is accessed. The default TTL in Windows Server 2003 DNS is 60 minutes. However, on the Internet, TTL values of 24 hours are common.

Table 11-3 Caching-only name servers

Definition	A DNS name server that is not authoritative for a zone. It responds to queries from a cached list of resolved names; for example, what is the IP address of http://www.ebay.com? Or on your intranet, where is the nearest domain controller for redhen.com? Such zone-less DNS servers are noted in the Event log under event ID 708, which mentions the caching-only trait.
Function	The sole function of a DNS name server is to look up names for clients and cache them. As it continues to look up and resolve names for clients, the cache is filled with query results and these name/address pairs are available for succeeding requests. If the caching-only server cannot answer a client request from it's cache, it forwards it to a designated DNS server and caches the resolved result.
When used?	At a site where DNS functionality is needed locally but you do not need a separate zone for that location. Since the DNS cache may be able to fulfill many requests locally, this can reduce DNS traffic on a WAN. You may decide to do this when the number of hosts that require DNS services at a location is small, or when you do not want to increase administrative overhead by maintaining another zone.
Why beneficial?	• Since they only supply a cached-query service, they do not keep zone database files like other secondary name servers must. This means that no network traffic is generated from zone transfers. When you are going to implement DNS at a remote location that is connected to your central intranet via slow WAN links, this could be an important design consideration. • Increased response time: Although during the initial phase of service, more requests must be forwarded to other DNS servers, as more name-to-IP-address resolution data is cached, the caching-only server will be able to quickly resolve more frequently requested resources from cache rather than forwarding the requests to other DNS servers.

skill 3

Understanding DNS Name Resolution

exam objective

Basic knowledge

overview

tip

IPv6 networks use the ip6.int domain to create reverse lookup zones.

There are two main aspects to understanding DNS name resolution. First, you must understand the types of queries that can be made. Second, you must understand the process by which names are resolved.

Client computers can make two standard types of queries to a DNS server: a forward lookup query and a reverse lookup query. A **forward lookup query** occurs when a client asks the DNS server to resolve a host name to an IP address **(Figure 11-23)**. A **reverse lookup query** involves resolving a known IP address to a host name. Since the DNS database is indexed by name and not by IP addresses, this process would be complex, involving an extensive search of all domain names if it were not for the reverse lookup zone **in-addr.arpa**. This second-level domain was expressly created to simplify this task. The sub-domains of in-addr.arpa are called reverse lookup domains. Reverse lookup domains are organized by IP address byte boundaries. A host with the IP address 10.68.12.8 will have the reverse host name, 8.12.68.10.in-addr.arpa **(Figure 11-24)**. This reverse host may belong to the reverse domain 12.68.10.in-addr.arpa if the network is assigned one or more class C networks (the IP address is greater than or equal to /24), or to 68.10.in-addr.arpa if the network is assigned a whole class B network (the IP address is /16), or it may be ISP dependent if the network is assigned less than a class C network (the IP address is less than /24). The reverse domain name must be correctly registered in in-addr.arpa or else the IP address-to-host name resolution will fail. After the in-addr.arpa domain is built, pointer (PTR) records are added to correlate IP addresses to their corresponding host names. PTR records generally correspond to an Address (host) (A) resource record for the DNS name for a host in its forward lookup zone.

During the process of DNS name resolution, first the client computer sends a **recursive query** to the designated DNS name server for the local network, asking to resolve a host name to an IP address. If this initial recursive query returns a "no such domain" response, resolution stops. If the designated DNS name server is unable to resolve the destination host name on its own because it is not authoritative for the domain, it sends an **iterative query** to another DNS name server to try to locate the DNS name server that is authoritative for the domain.

A recursive query is a type of forward lookup query that is used to request that a DNS name server provides the full and complete answer to the query. In other words, it is a request for the answer, not for a referral to another DNS server that may be able to answer the query. When a DNS server receives a recursive query, it must follow the query to its completion. This can include a "Not found" response.

A **resolver** is a host that can perform a recursive search to locate records that will answer a query. A resolver queries other DNS name servers, including the root servers, to look up DNS records on behalf of the client. If the local DNS server cannot resolve the host name to its IP address, it sends an iterative query on behalf of the client to assist in answering the recursive query. Iterative queries allow DNS servers to send back pointers or referrals. A DNS server that receives an iterative query can return a referral to the server that sent the iterative query if it does not have the answer.

Figure 11-23 Forward lookup queries

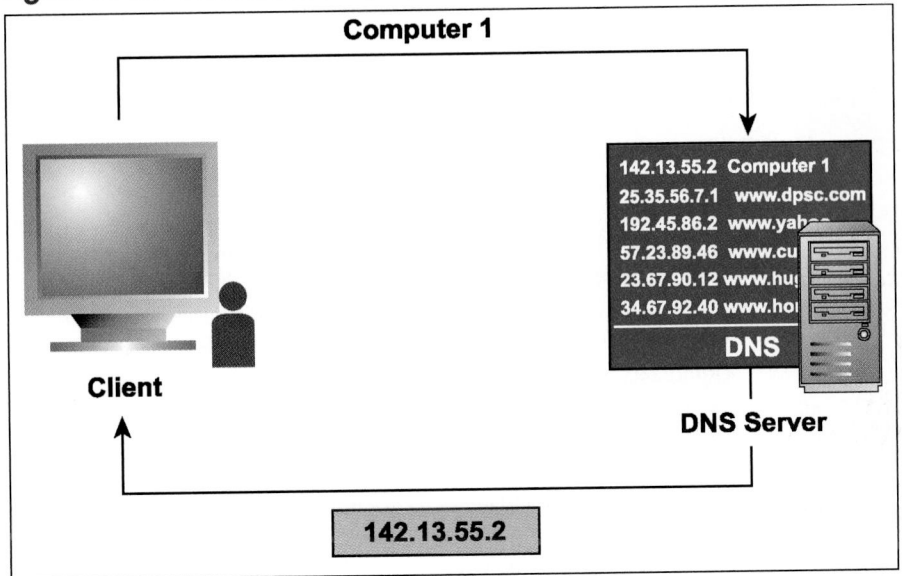

Figure 11-24 in-addr.arpa

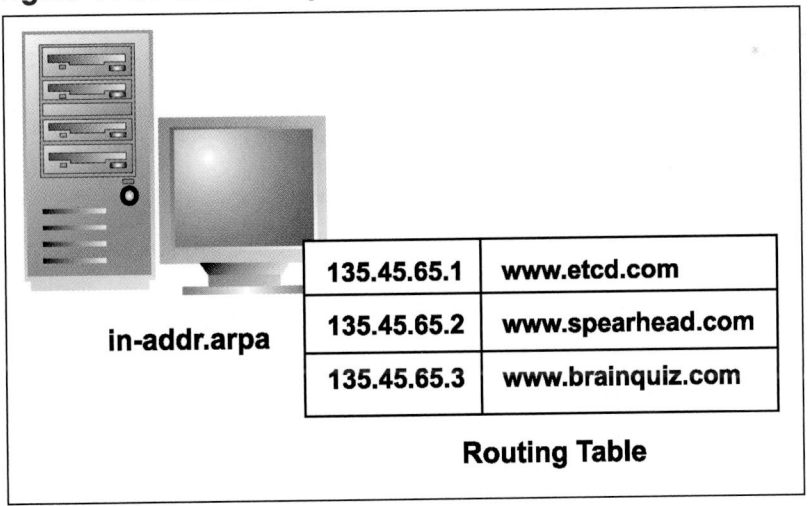

skill 3

Understanding DNS Name Resolution (cont'd)

exam objective

Basic knowledge

overview

Let's look at an example to understand the roles of the DNS name server and the resolver in the process of DNS name resolution. Suppose you are on an intranet and want to access a Web site, www.intergalaxy.com, on the Internet. In order for you to connect to the site, the Web site name must be resolved to its IP address. The name of the Web site will be resolved as follows **(Figure 11-25)**:

1. The client computer sends a recursive query to the designated name server for the local network asking to resolve www.intergalaxy.com to its IP address.
2. The designated DNS name server for the local network checks its database. If it is unable to find any information for the requested domain name, it sends an iterative query to the root name server on the Internet.
3. Root name servers often have names cached at the root, so the root name server first checks its cache, and, if it is able, returns the IP address of the name server for the intergalaxy.com domain. If it does not find the address in its cache, it replies back to the designated name server for the local network with the IP address of the DNS name server responsible for the com domain.
4. The designated name server for the local network sends an iterative query to the com name server for www.intergalaxy.com.
5. The com name server replies with the IP address of the name server for the intergalaxy.com domain.
6. The designated name server for the local network sends an iterative query to the intergalaxy.com name server for www.intergalaxy.com.
7. The intergalaxy.com name server replies with the IP address of www.intergalaxy.com.
8. The designated name server for the local network sends the IP address of www.intergalaxy.com to the client computer.

The DNS name resolution process is made more efficient because the DNS server caches the results at each point in the search. For example, if after connecting to www.intergalaxy.com, you want to connect to another .com server, the designated DNS server for the local network already has the address of the .com root name server, and if you want to connect to another computer in the www.intergalaxy.com domain, your DNS server already has the address for www.intergalaxy.com and will not have to send an iterative query for it again.

Figure 11-25 Resolving a host name to an IP address

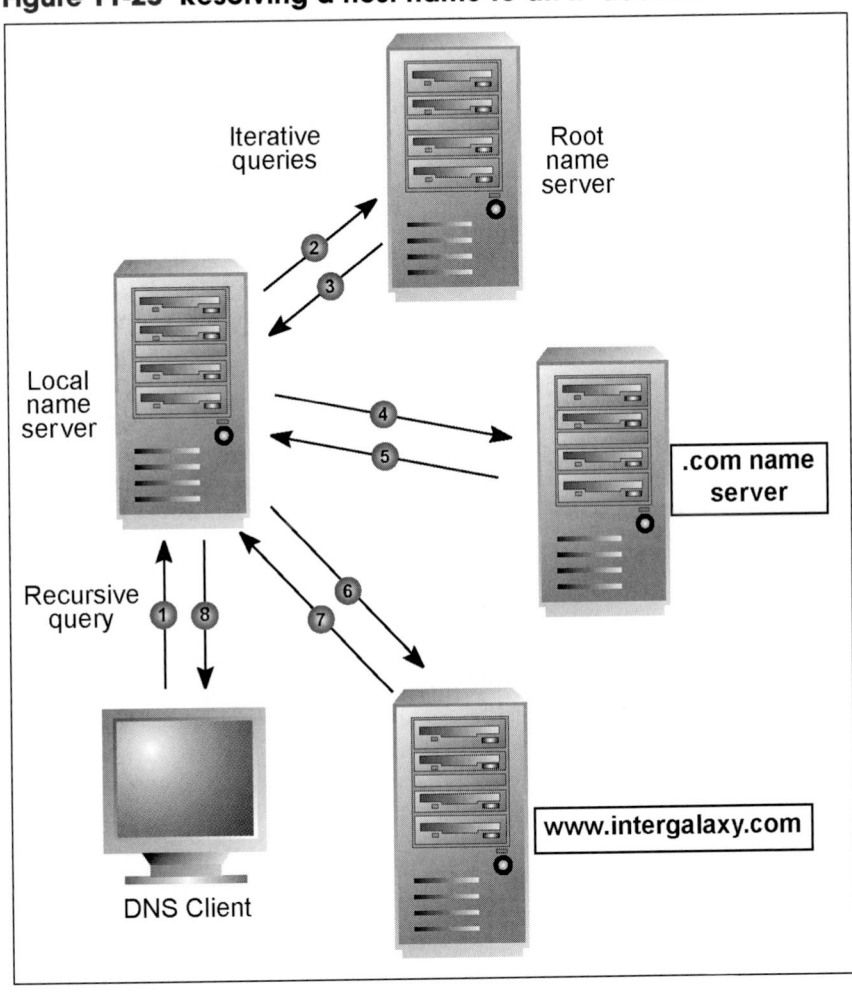

skill 4

Installing and Configuring the DNS Service

exam objective   Basic knowledge

overview

Before you begin to install and configure your DNS servers, you must plan and design your DNS infrastructure. You will almost always need to implement multiple DNS servers. Various factors will affect the DNS infrastructure, including the size of the network, network geography, security, bandwidth, and fault tolerance.

The size of your network is an important consideration because key implementation issues will vary for small, mid-sized, and large networks. On a small network, the main factor to consider is DNS resilience. **DNS resilience** refers to the hardiness of the DNS infrastructure, specifically its ability to continue operating when individual components have been damaged. To ensure DNS resiliency, the primary consideration is that you must have at least one primary and one secondary DNS server for a domain. When implementing DNS on a mid- to large-sized network, in addition to resiliency, you must take into account the quality of the connectivity between different locations, the available bandwidth, and future network modifications. You should answer questions such as how many DNS domains and sub-domains, how many zones, how many primary and secondary name servers, and how many DNS cache-only servers you will need to configure. Of course, in any sized environment where Active Directory will be implemented, it is also important to take the domain structure for your Active Directory domain design into consideration and to ensure that your DNS servers can support SRV records.

Another important factor is whether you will use DNS on an intranet, the Internet, or both. If you plan to use DNS to serve both the intranet and Internet requirements of your organization, you must decide whether you want to use the same domain name on your intranet and the Internet. If you implement the same namespace, users will be able to access resources on both the intranet and the Internet using a single domain name (**Figure 11-26**). If you are going to use the same namespace for both internal and external resources, in order to secure your intranet, you should create two separate DNS zones on two separate and unrelated servers. In effect, you should create two primary zones, one for each audience. One zone will allow Internet clients to access public resources and will not be configured to resolve internal resources. Since this DNS zone will not be configured to resolve internal resources, internal clients will not be able to access publicly available resources. You can overcome this problem by duplicating part of the content of the zone you created for Internet clients for use by internal clients. You can then configure hosts on your network to use this zone so that the internal clients can resolve external resources. This will solve the problem of security, but it will lead to more administrative overhead because you will have to manage two database files separately.

Two better alternatives are to use different domain names for the intranet and the Internet (e.g. company.local, or company.net), or to use a sub-domain of the Internet name (e.g. corp.company.com). The advantages of using different namespaces for internal and external resources are that you have added security if the internal namespace is not published externally, and you also have a clear demarcation between internal and external resources.

You must also determine the number of DNS servers you will need and their roles to ensure that DNS name resolution will proceed quickly and efficiently. Additionally, you will need to make sure that your DNS implementation is reliable and fault-tolerant. It is recommended that you implement at least two DNS servers, either one primary and one secondary or two Active Directory-integrated. Having multiple DNS servers will enhance reliability because if any one DNS server is unavailable, the other DNS server can handle client requests. Active Directory-integrated zones improve fault tolerance by allowing changes to the zone to be made on any available Active Directory-integrated DNS server, as opposed to the standard primary architecture, in which changes can only be made on the primary name server.

Figure 11-26 Same internal and external DNS namespace

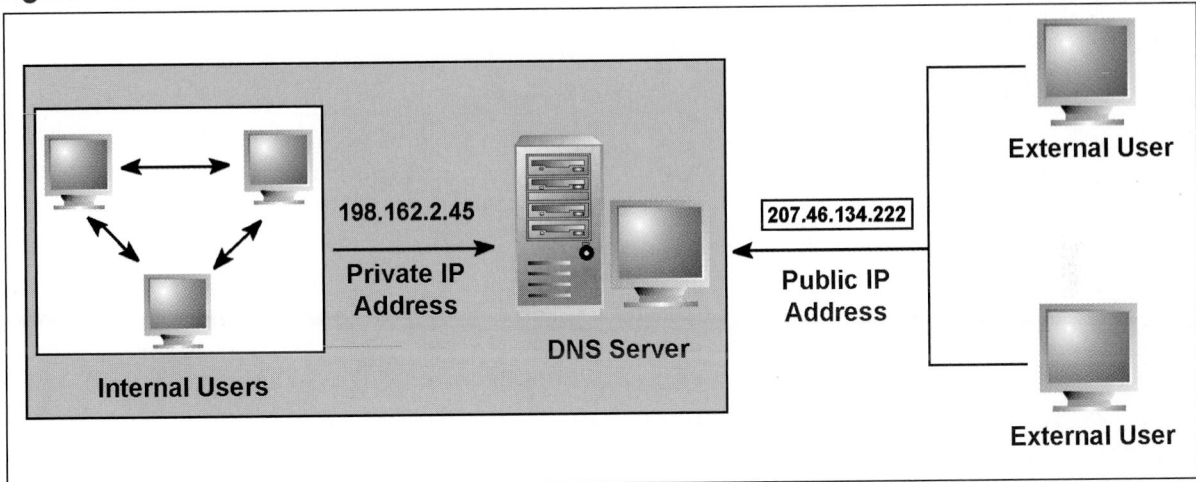

Internal Users

198.162.2.45
Private IP
Address

DNS Server

207.46.134.222
Public IP
Address

External User

External User

skill 4

Installing and Configuring the DNS Service (cont'd)

exam objective

Basic knowledge

overview

However, remember that the more DNS servers there are on the network, the more zone transfer traffic will be generated. It is important to schedule zone transfers in such a way that both the primary and secondary DNS servers have the latest data while the load on the name servers and the network is minimized.

If you plan to have an Internet presence, you must register your domain name with an Internet naming authority such as Network Solutions. The domain name you register is generally a second-level domain under a top-level domain, although in countries other than the United States, organizations' domains are often third-level domains. For example, in Great Britain, you register your domain name under co.uk, and in New Zealand you register under co.nz.

You typically have the authority to maintain domains that you register. However, various administrative bodies are assigned the task of managing the Internet root and top-level domains. The **Internet Corporation for Assigned Names and Numbers (ICANN)** is responsible for defining new top-level domains.

If you plan to implement DNS only on your intranet, you are not required to register the domain name with a naming authority; however, you should. Your Active Directory domain name should be based on a domain that you can, or already do, control. If the internal name you have chosen has already been registered by another organization, internal clients will not be able to distinguish between the internal name and the publicly registered DNS name. To avoid this situation, it is recommended that you register your internal DNS name even if you do not plan to use it on the Internet. You also should not use unregistered suffixes, for example, xyzcorp.internal. Although unregistered suffixes can work internally, they can become an issue in the future as your organization expands.

Before you implement your first DNS server, it is important that you understand the different types of zones and which zone type to use for the role your DNS server will perform on the network.

The DNS zones are listed below (**Table 11-4**):

tip

If you somehow delete or lose the Cache.dns file, or if the root hints list changes (which is rare), you can always get the most current copy at:
ftp://rs.internic.net/dom ain/named.root

◆ **Root zone:** A zone authoritative for the root domain. A root zone is either an Internet root, or an internal root (also known as a "fake root" or "empty root"). An internal root is rarely implemented.
◆ **Forward lookup zones:** Used to resolve host names to IP addresses.
◆ **Reverse lookup zones:** Used to resolve IP addresses to host names.

It is only appropriate to configure an internal root zone if you are configuring DNS solely for an intranet, but even then it is not necessary. The current records for all root name servers on the Internet are stored in the **Cache.dns** file in the **%systemroot%\System32\dns** folder on your DNS Server (**Figure 11-27**).

If you determine that your network will need to support an internal root zone, this file must contain the names of DNS servers that are authoritative for the root domain on your network in order for the correct resolution of DNS intranet names to take place. The **root name server** is a DNS server that has authority for the top-most domain in the DNS namespace hierarchy, the root domain. The root domain is the starting point of reference for all domains under it. You configure a DNS server in the role of an internal root name server by creating the root zone. The internal root zone can either be an Active Directory-integrated or standard primary zone. The root zone contains the Start of Authority (SOA) record for the root domain. The SOA record is the first record in the zone and indicates the root name server for the zone.

Table 11-4   DNS zones

Root	Zone that is authoritative for the root domain. A root zone is either an Internet root, or an internal root. An internal root is rarely implemented by corporate customers.
Forward lookup	Zone in which forward lookup queries are performed. Forward lookup queries are searches that begin with the DNS name of a host as it is stored in an address (A) resource record. The resource data returned will be an IP address.
Reverse lookup	Zone in which reverse lookup queries are performed. Reverse lookup queries start with a known IP address and search for a host name based on its address. Since DNS was not designed to support reverse lookup queries, the only way to do this would be to search in all domains in the DNS namespace, which would be time exhaustive. This is why the in-addr.arpa domain was defined in the DNS standards. in-addr.arpa is set aside in the Internet DNS namespace to provide a practical and dependable way to perform reverse queries. Sub-domains within the in-addr.arpa domain are created by reversing the order of the IP address octets so that the host name will be read first. When they are read from left to right, the IP host address (which normally would be contained in the last octets) will be read first, and the IP network address (which normally would be contained in the first octets) will be read last. IPv6 networks use the ip6.int domain to create reverse lookup zones.

Figure 11-27 The DNS Cache file opened in Microsoft Word

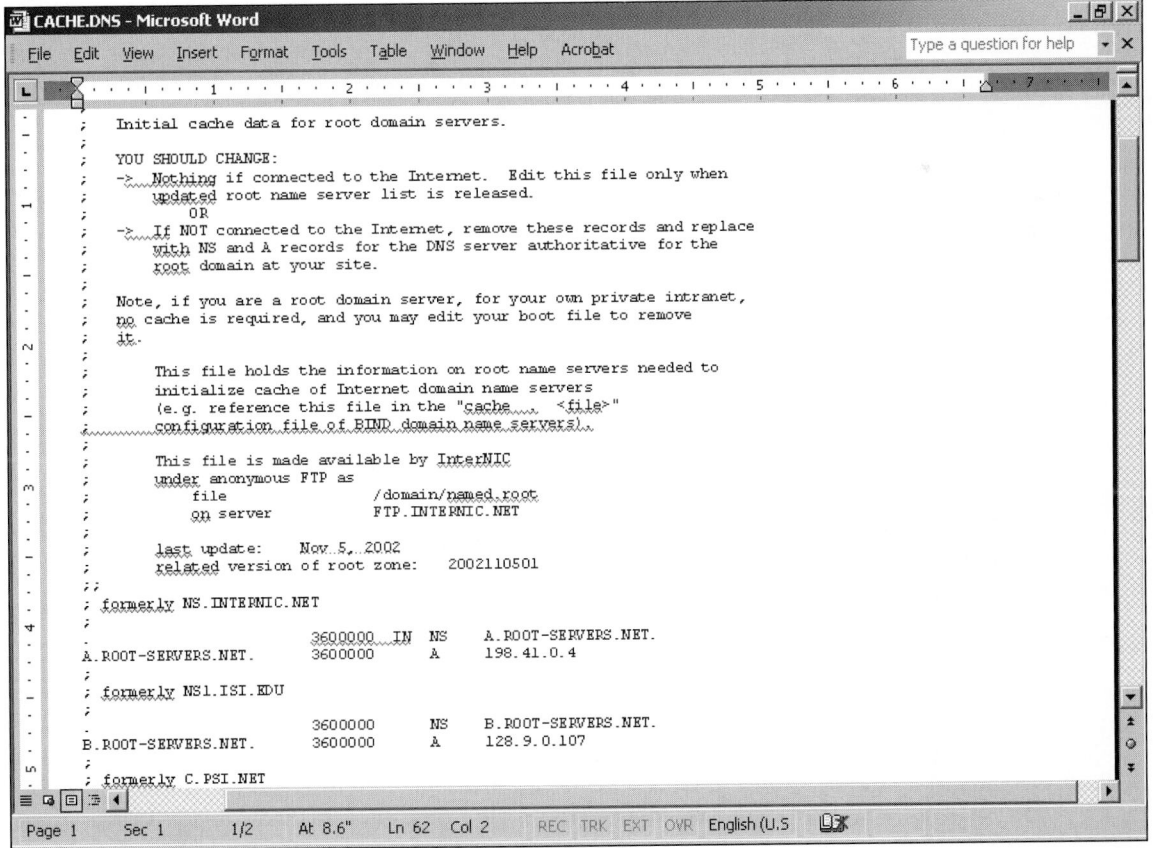

skill 4

Installing and Configuring the DNS Service (cont'd)

exam objective   Basic knowledge

overview

tip

It is a relatively common practice to point all resolvers (clients and other DNS servers) to the secondary zones, rather than the primary. This has a number of advantages, but the largest is that it helps secure the database against unauthorized additions.

On the Internet, there are thirteen root name servers that control the DNS name resolution process for the entire world. The ICANN DNS Root Server System Advisory Committee coordinates and regulates these thirteen name servers, but they are actually maintained by a number of different organizations (**Table 11-5**). The Internet root name servers are responsible for the top-level domain (TLD) registries, including the global registries such as .com and .org and the 244 country registries.

There are four zone types (**Table 11-6**):

Standard Primary: This is the first zone to be created and it is authoritative for one or more domains. All DNS records are created here, and it is the only copy of the zone file that can be edited. This zone is responsible for all updates such as resource record (RR) additions or deletions. It is a read-write text file that is usually stored locally on the hard disk of the DNS server. The DNS name server that maintains the primary zone is called the **primary DNS server** or the **primary name server**. A primary zone maintains the original copy of all information related to that part of the DNS namespace. This data is then replicated to other dependent DNS servers during the zone transfer process.

Standard Secondary: This zone maintains a read-only copy of another zone on the network. The DNS name server that maintains the secondary zone is called the **secondary DNS server** or the **secondary name server**. Secondary zones are created after the primary zone to provide redundancy for the primary name server. The secondary name server contains a copy of the primary zone database so that client requests can be answered when the primary name server is not available; however, you cannot edit the records in the secondary zone because they are only copies. When configuring a standard secondary zone, you must specify the IP address for the primary name server.

Stub: Stub zones are an enhancement to delegated sub-domains that were added as a new feature in Windows Server 2003's DNS Server service. A delegated sub-domain is when a parent domain (corp.com) delegates a specific sub-domain of its namespace (such as sales.corp.com) to another server or group of servers. Delegated sub-domains are required because when someone in research.corp.com queries for sales.corp.com, the research.corp.com DNS servers would forward that query to the parent servers (corp.com). The parent DNS servers in corp.com would then need to contain either the zone information for sales.corp.com or a delegation pointing to the DNS servers that do contain that information. The problem with a basic delegated sub-domain, however, is that the servers in the parent zone are never updated when new DNS servers for the child domain are added, meaning that the parent zone's list of servers that have been delegated control for the child domains can become outdated. Stub zones resolve this problem by replicating the SOA, NS, and core A records from the delegated child domain to the parent domain. This way, when a new secondary DNS server is added to the child domain, the parent domain is already aware of it.

Active Directory-integrated: The zone information for a standard primary and standard secondary zone is stored in a text file. When you create an **Active Directory-integrated zone**, information about the zone is stored in Active Directory. Since an Active Directory-integrated zone is a part of Active Directory, it inherits all security features of Active Directory. This allows for the secure storage and transfer of zone information. One of the advantages of creating and maintaining an Active Directory-integrated zone rather than a standard DNS zone is the management of zone transfers. When you use standard DNS zones, zone transfers can be performed in one of two ways: Incrementally (IXFR) or Completely (AXFR). Complete zone transfers copy the entire database whenever a change occurs. For instance, if your database contained 50,000 records, and a single record changed, AXFR would transfer

Table 11-5 The 13 Worldwide Root Name Servers

Server	Operator	Location	IP Address
A.ROOT-SERVERS.NET	Network Solutions Inc. (NSI)	Herndon, VA	198.41.0.4
B.ROOT-SERVERS.NET	University of Southern California, Information Sciences Institute (USC-ISI)	Marina del Rey, CA	IPv4: 128.9.0.107 IPv6: 2001:478:65::53
C.ROOT-SERVERS.NET	PSINet	Herndon, VA	192.33.4.12
D.ROOT-SERVERS.NET	University of Maryland	College Park, MD	128.8.10.90
E.ROOT-SERVERS.NET	NASA (Ames Research Center)	Mountain View, CA	192.203.230.10
F.ROOT-SERVERS.NET	Internet Software Consortium	Palo Alto, CA	IPv4: 192.5.5.241 IPv6: 2001:500::1035
G.ROOT-SERVERS.NET	U.S. Defense Information Systems Agency (DISA)	Vienna, VA	192.112.36.4
H.ROOT-SERVERS.NET	ARL (U.S. Army Research Laboratory)	Aberdeen, MD	IPv4: 128.63.2.53 IPv6: 2001:500:1::803f:235
I.ROOT-SERVERS.NET	NORDU Net	Stockholm, Sweden	192.36.148.17
J.ROOT-SERVERS.NET	VeriSign Global Registry Services	Herndon, VA	192.58.128.30
K.ROOT-SERVERS.NET	RIPE (Réseaux IP Européens) Network Coordination Centre	London, England	193.0.14.129
L.ROOT-SERVERS.NET	ICANN (Internet Corporation for Assigned Names and Numbers)	Marina del Rey, CA	198.32.64.12
M.ROOT-SERVERS.NET	WIDE (Widely Integrated Distributed Environment) Project	Tokyo, Japan	202.12.27.33 IPv6: 2001:dc3::35

Table 11-6 Zone types

Zone Type	Description
Standard primary zone	This zone type maintains the original copy of zone data in a standard text file and stores it locally on the server. This is the only copy that can be edited (read-write).
Standard secondary zone	This zone type maintains a read-only copy of an existing zone. It is created only after the primary zone has been configured on the server. Secondary zones provide redundancy and fault tolerance to ease the strain on a primary zone name server.
Stub zone	Enhancement to delegated sub-domains: When you use basic delegated sub-domains, servers in the parent zone are not updated when new DNS servers for the child domain are added. Thus the parent zone's list of servers that have been delegated control for the child domains can become outdated. Stub zones resolve this problem by replicating the SOA, NS, and core A records from the delegated child domain to the parent domain. This way, when a new secondary DNS server is added to the child domain, the parent domain is already aware of it.
Active Directory-integrated zone	This zone type uses Active Directory to store and replicate zone database files. It provides integrated storage and secure updates of all zone database files.

skill 4

Installing and Configuring the DNS Service (cont'd)

exam objective   Basic knowledge

overview

all 50,000 records. AXFR is typically reserved for backwards compatibility with older DNS servers, but it is also used when there are major database errors and when a secondary server is first brought online (since it needs a full copy of the database). Incremental transfers, on the other hand, only transfer the record that has changed, making IXFR much more efficient than AXFR. Standard primary and secondary DNS servers are limited to using AXFR or IXFR, but Active Directory-integrated DNS servers improve upon IXFR by inserting the DNS database into Active Directory and using attribute level AD replication techniques. When you create Active Directory-integrated zones, the information is updated and replicated automatically across the domain as part of the Active Directory replication cycle. An Active Directory-integrated zone appears as an object in the Active Directory. You can create an Active Directory-integrated zone only if the DNS server is a domain controller.

There are two places where DNS zones can be stored in Active Directory: the domain directory partition or an application directory partition. The **domain directory partition** is where data pertaining to a particular Active Directory domain is stored. This includes data about objects such as users and computers. Data stored in the domain directory partition is replicated to all domain controllers in an Active Directory domain, but it cannot be replicated to domain controllers in other Active Directory domains. Thus, even if they are not DNS servers, all domain controllers in the domain will receive copies of the zone. Unnecessary Active Directory synchronization will occur and network traffic will be needlessly increased. However, the advantage here is that you will always have a valid copy of the DNS database as long as you have at least one domain controller up, even if all of your DNS servers fail. If one of the servers where an Active Directory-integrated zone is stored is a Windows 2000 server, you must store the zone in the domain directory partition, as application directory partitions are a new feature in Windows Server 2003.

Application directory partitions were implemented to improve replication efficiency in situations where only a subset of the domain controllers needs a copy of the application data. You can use them to store data in Active Directory that will only be replicated to a specific group of domain controllers. Domain controllers where an application directory partition is stored do not have to be in the same Active Directory domain, but they must be in the same Active Directory forest. Data can be replicated to any domain controller in the same Active Directory forest. In an application directory partition, you can store DNS zones on all DNS servers in the Active Directory forest, on all DNS servers in the Active Directory domain, or on all servers designated in a scope that you create for the partition. Synchronization will only occur between servers which actually use the DNS data, unlike if you used a domain directory partition.

In Windows Server 2003, you have four options regarding how to replicate the application directory partition. You can select to replicate to all DNS servers in the forest (**Figure 11-28**), to all DNS servers in the domain (**Figure 11-29**), to all domain controllers in the domain, or to all domain controllers specified in a custom scope. While most of these choices are self-explanatory, the last option, "all domain controllers in a custom scope", is a bit complicated. It is designed to allow increased flexibility for advanced administrators who need more flexibility in scope than the default application data partitions allow. When choosing a scope, keep in mind that in general, the wider the scope, the larger the quantity of traffic generated for DNS replication.

Figure 11-28 Creating an application directory partition for a forest

DNS zone data will be replicated to all domain controller/DNS servers in the Active Directory forest

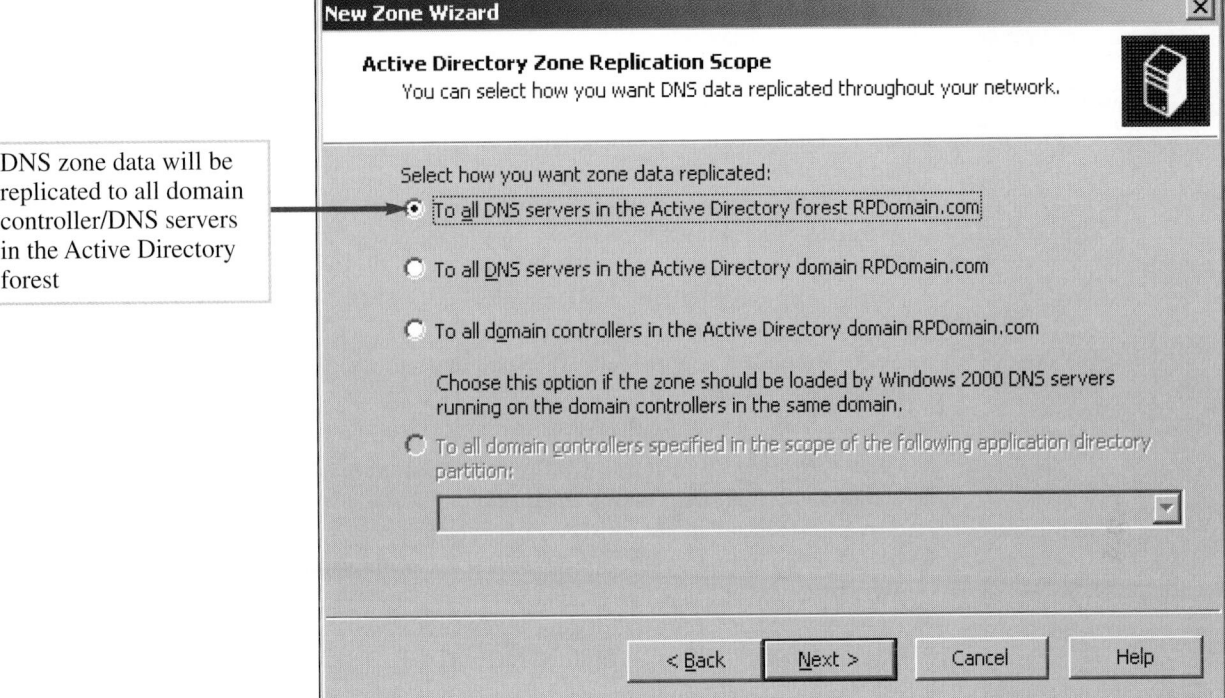

Figure 11-29 Creating an application directory partition for a domain

DNS zone data will be replicated to all domain controller/DNS servers in the Active Directory domain

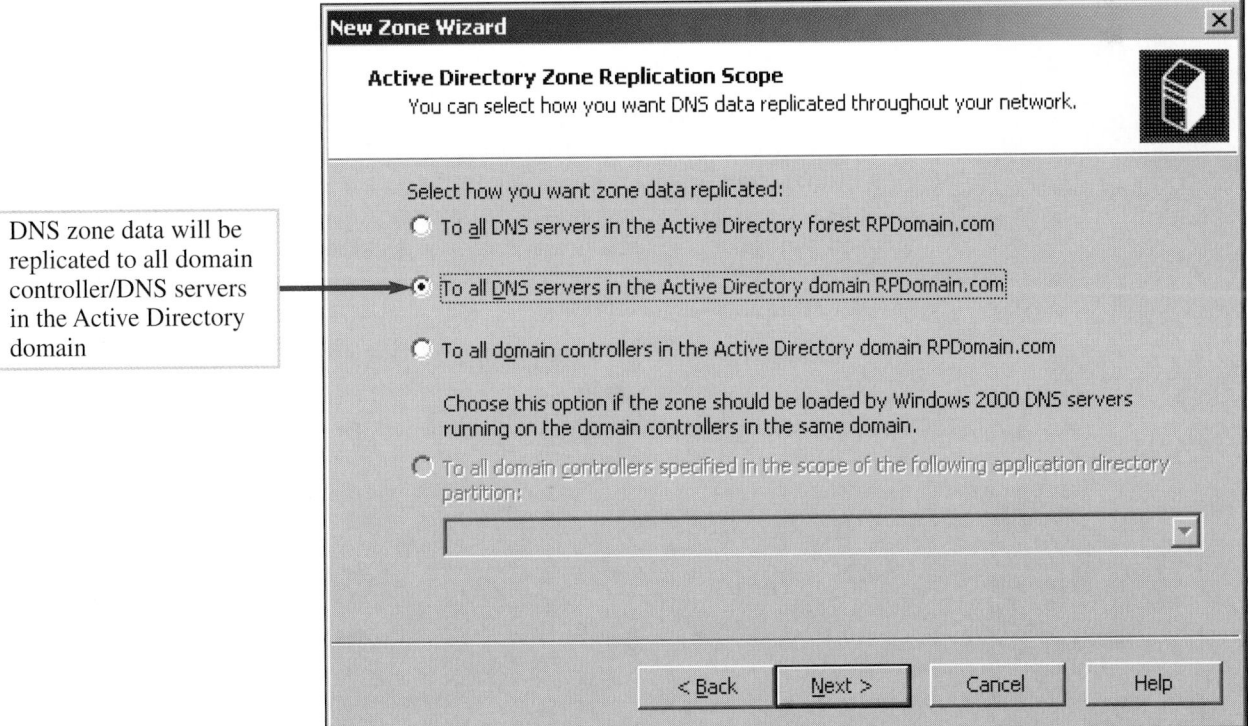

skill 4

Installing and Configuring the DNS Service (cont'd)

exam objective   Basic knowledge

how to

Install the DNS service and create a forward lookup zone.

1. Log on as an **Administrator**.
2. Click **Start**, point to **Control Panel**, and click **Add or Remove Programs** to open the **Add/Remove Programs** window.
3. Click **Add/Remove Windows Components** to open the **Windows Components Wizard**. A **Please wait** message appears on the screen while the **Windows Components Wizard** is loaded.
4. Scroll down the **Components** list and double-click **Networking Services** to open the **Networking Services** dialog box.
5. Select **Domain Name System (DNS)** on the **Subcomponents of Networking Services** list **(Figure 11-30)**.
6. Click **OK** to close the **Networking Services** dialog box.
7. Click **Next >** to open the **Configuring Components** screen. Setup configures the components. This will take a few minutes. If you are prompted, insert the Windows Server 2003 installation CD-ROM, and click **OK**.
8. After the components are configured, the **Completing the Windows Components Wizard** screen opens. Click **Finish**.
9. Close the Add or Remove Programs window.
10. Click **Start**, point to **Administrative Tools**, and click **DNS** to open the DNS Management console.
11. Click the plus sign to the right of the DNS server name to display the **Forward Lookup Zones** and **Reverse Lookup Zone** folders and the **Event Viewer** snap-in **(Figure 11-31)**.
12. Right-click the DNS server name and select **Configure a DNS server** to start the **Configure a DNS Server Wizard**.
13. Click **Next >** to open the **Select Configuration Action** screen. Select the **Create forward and reverse lookup zones (recommended for large networks)** option button **(Figure 11-32)**.
14. Click **Next >** to open the **Forward Lookup Zone** screen. The **Yes, create a forward lookup zone now (recommended)** option button is selected by default **(Figure 11-33)**. Click **Next >** to accept the default and open the **Zone Type** screen.
15. The **Primary zone** option button is selected by default. If the DNS server is a domain controller, the **Store the zone in Active Directory (available only if DNS server is a domain controller)** option button will also be selected by default. This will make the zone an **Active-Directory-integrated** zone, and all zone and database data will be stored in Active Directory **(Figure 11-34)**.
16. Click **Next >** to open the **Zone Name** screen. Enter the name of the zone, and click **Next >** to open the **Zone File** screen.
17. Review the settings, and click **Next >** to open the **Dynamic Update** screen.

Figure 11-30 Installing the DNS service

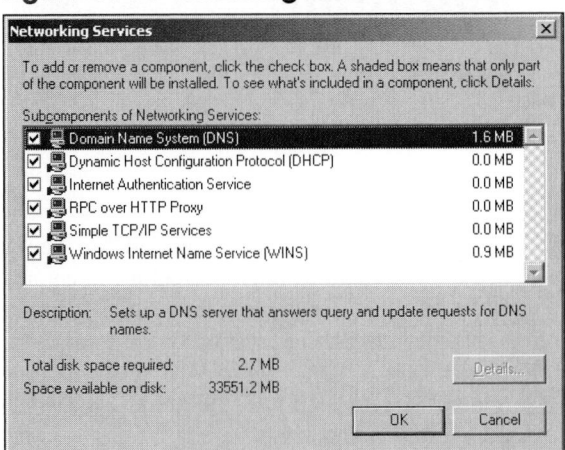

Figure 11-31 The dnsmgmt console

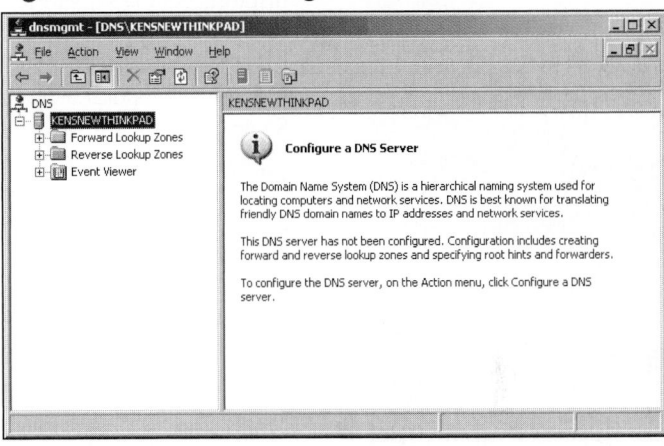

Figure 11-32 The Select Configuration Action screen

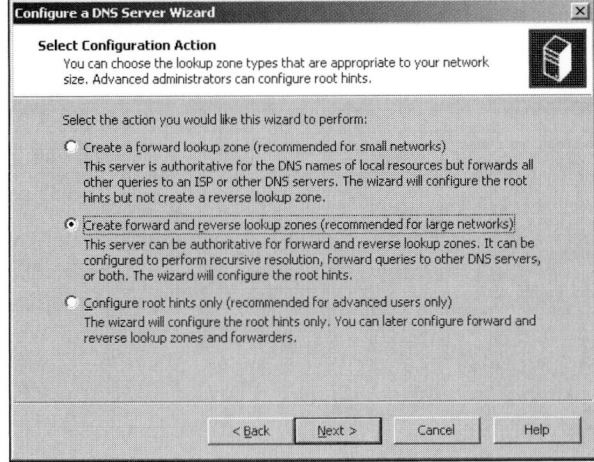

Figure 11-33 The Forward Lookup Zone screen

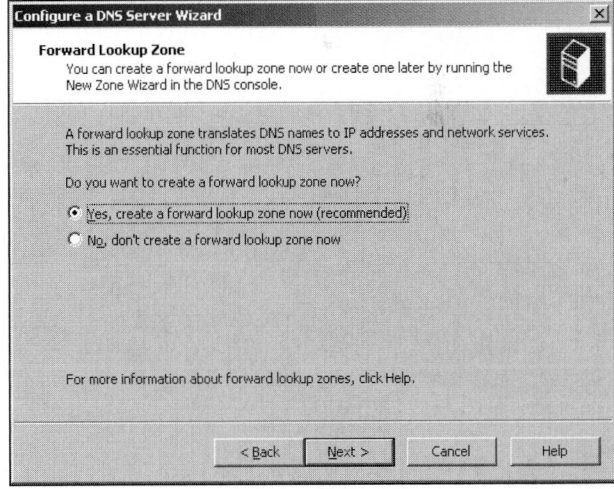

Figure 11-34 The Zone Type screen

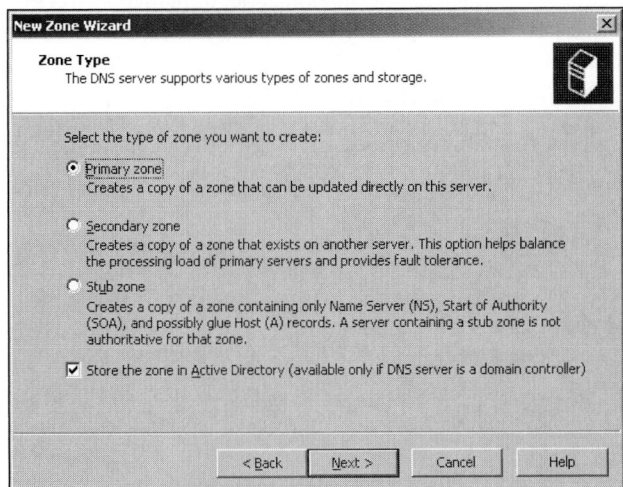

skill 4

Installing and Configuring the DNS Service (cont'd)

exam objective   Basic knowledge

how to

18. The first option, **Allow only secure dynamic updates (recommended for Active Directory)**, will only be available if you are creating an Active Directory-integrated zone, which you can only do if the DNS server is a domain controller. If you are installing the DNS service on a member server, the **Do not allow dynamic updates** option button is selected by default **(Figure 11-35)**.
19. Click [Next >] to open the **Reverse Lookup Zone** screen. The **Yes, create a reverse lookup zone** option button is selected by default **(Figure 11-36)**.
20. Select the **No, don't create a reverse lookup zone now** option button, and click [Next >] to open the **Forwarders** screen.
21. If you want the DNS server to forward queries, select the **Yes it should forward queries to DNS servers with the following IP addresses** option button and enter the IP addresses in the text boxes provided.
22. Click [Next >]. The **Searching for Root Hints** dialog box will appear, and then the **Completing the Configure a DNS Server Wizard** screen will open. A summary of the configuration options can be viewed here.
23. Click [Finish].

more

To create a reverse lookup zone, right-click **Reverse Lookup Zones** in the console tree and select **New Zone** to start the New Zone Wizard. The first reverse lookup zone you create will be a primary zone. If your DNS server is a domain controller and you are creating an Active Directory-integrated zone, you will have to configure the settings for how you want zone data to be replicated. You do this on the **Active Directory Zone Replication Scope** screen. The default configuration is for zone data to be replicated to all domain controllers in the Active Directory domain (domain directory partition). As noted earlier, in Windows Server 2003, you can also replicate all zone data to all DNS servers in the Active Directory forest or to all DNS servers in the Active Directory domain by creating application directory partitions. Next, you will have to enter the network ID for the reverse lookup zone. The network ID is the first two or three octets in the IP address which are used to identify the network. The subnet mask that you are using will determine whether it is the first two or the first three octets. If the zone network ID is 151.196, the in-addr.arpa reverse lookup zone will be 196.151.in-addr.arpa. The in-addr.arpa design will be built by the Wizard based on the network address you enter.

After you create and configure the zones, you can add information about domain resources by creating resource records. A zone must contain the resource records for all resources in the domain for which it is responsible. When a zone is created, DNS automatically adds an SOA (Start of Authority) resource record and a NS (Name Server) resource record. To add a resource record, such as a forward lookup zone host address (A), in the DNS Management console, right-click the name of the zone in which you want to create the record, and click **New Host (A)**. Enter the name of the host and its IP address in their appropriate fields in the **New Host** dialog box **(Figure 11-37)**, and click the **Add Host** button.

To configure a Windows XP Professional computer as a DNS client, right-click the **My Network Places** icon and click **Properties** to open the **Network Connections** window. Right-click **Local Area Connection** and click **Properties** to open the **Local Area Connection Properties** dialog box. Select **Internet Protocol (TCP/IP)** and click **Properties**. Select the **Use the following DNS server address** option button and type the IP address of the primary DNS server for the client in the **Preferred DNS server** text box. If another DNS server is available on the network, you can type its IP address in the **Alternate DNS server** text box. This DNS server is used if the primary DNS server is not available.

Figure 11-35 **The Dynamic Update screen**

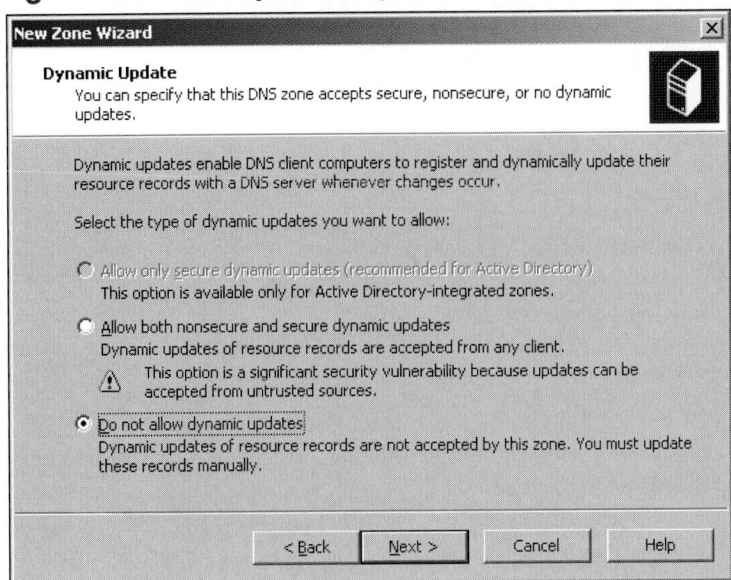

Figure 11-36 **The Reverse Lookup Zone screen**

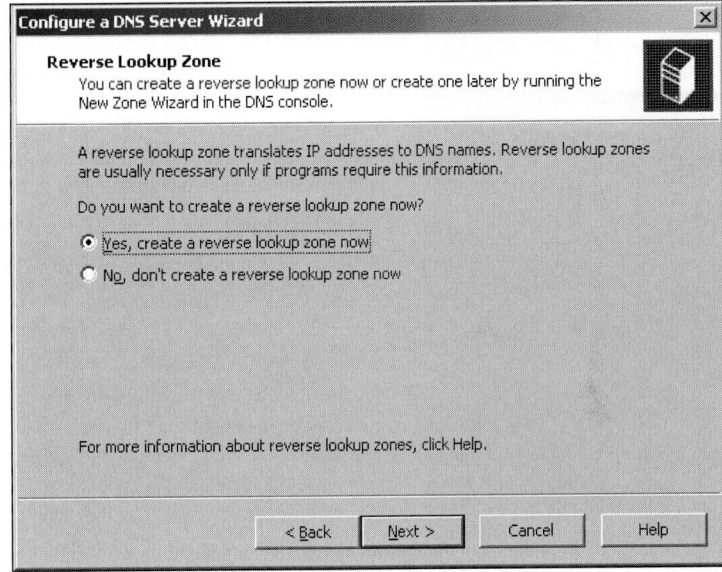

Figure 11-37 **Adding a resource record**

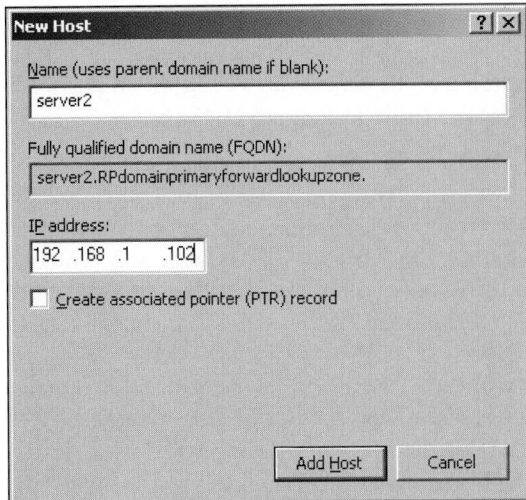

skill 5

Introducing Routing and Remote Access Service (RRAS)

exam objective   Basic knowledge

overview

Routing and Remote Access Service (RRAS) can be configured on a Windows Server 2003 computer to manage hundreds of concurrent dial-up connections or to receive Virtual Private Network (VPN) connections on the internal network. It can also be configured to provide shared Internet access using Network Address Translation (NAT) or to create a secure connection between two servers on the Internet to connect two LANs.

When you configure RRAS to function as a dial-in remote access server (RAS), telecommuters, employees whose jobs involve traveling, and other remote employees can connect to their office networks and access resources. A **remote access server** is a computer running Windows Server 2003 and the RRAS service that is configured specifically to function using a modem, or a modem pool, to allow users to dial-in from laptops or any other remote computers that are also configured with a modem. Users can then access their e-mail, scheduling, and file and printer sharing services. A VPN server is another type of remote access server (**Figure 11-38**).

The two connection methods used by clients are either dial-up or VPN (connecting to a VPN over the Internet). These are described below:

Dial-up: A **dial-up connection** establishes a non-permanent connection between a remote access server and a remote access client using telecommunications services such as an analog phone line or ISDN. Using a dial-up connection, a remote access server provides connectivity with a remote access client by answering the call, authenticating and authorizing the caller, and then transferring data (**Figure 11-39**).

To establish a dial-up connection, Windows Server 2003 uses either the **Point-to-Point Protocol (PPP)** or the **Serial Line Internet Protocol (SLIP)** WAN protocols (**Figure 11-40**). The PPP protocol allows remote clients to access network resources and provides error-checking to detect possible problems prior to data transfer. SLIP is an older remote communications protocol that is used by UNIX computers. It does not provide security and transfers data without checking for errors. PPP provides a more efficient, but slower method of transferring data due to the error-checking. SLIP has, for the most part, been replaced by PPP, because although error-checking may slow PPP down somewhat, it is still more efficient. This is because if there are problems, they are detected much sooner and thus solved more quickly. SLIP also does not support dynamically assigned IP addresses and can only be used on TCP/IP networks. The updated CSLIP (Compressed SLIP) uses header compression to reduce transmission overhead; however the header must be decompressed when the data packets are received. SLIP is also not supported by Windows Server 2003 for clients dialing in, though it can still be used by the server to establish connections to remote Unix RAS servers. PPP, which can support many networking protocols besides TCP/IP (IPX, NetBEUI, etc.), can use a variety of authentication protocols (**Table 11-7, page 11.41**):

◆ **Password Authentication Protocol (PAP):** PAP is the least secure authentication protocol used with PPP connections. It uses plain text passwords for authentication. However, PAP is used when a more secure authentication method cannot be used, and this protocol may be necessary for creating dial-up connections with non-Windows networks that do not encrypt passwords. Finally, you may choose to use PAP when attempting to troubleshoot connection problems, and PAP is the most compatible of all authentication protocols.

◆ **Shiva Password Authentication Protocol (SPAP):** SPAP is an authentication protocol that is used if you are connecting to a Shiva server. This protocol is more secure than PAP but less secure than CHAP or MS-CHAP. Data encryption is not supported with SPAP.

Figure 11-38 RAS

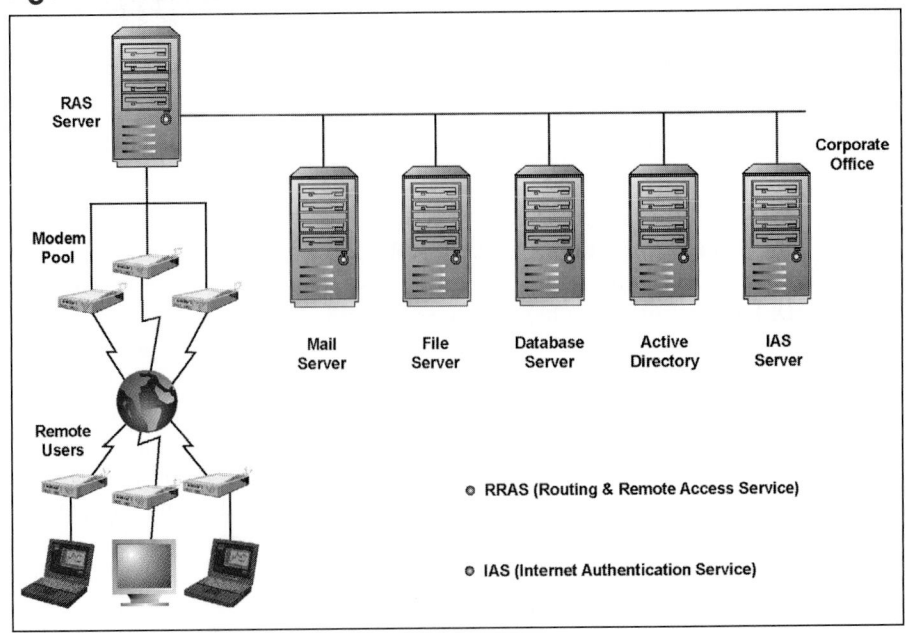

o RRAS (Routing & Remote Access Service)

o IAS (Internet Authentication Service)

Figure 11-39 Dial-up connections

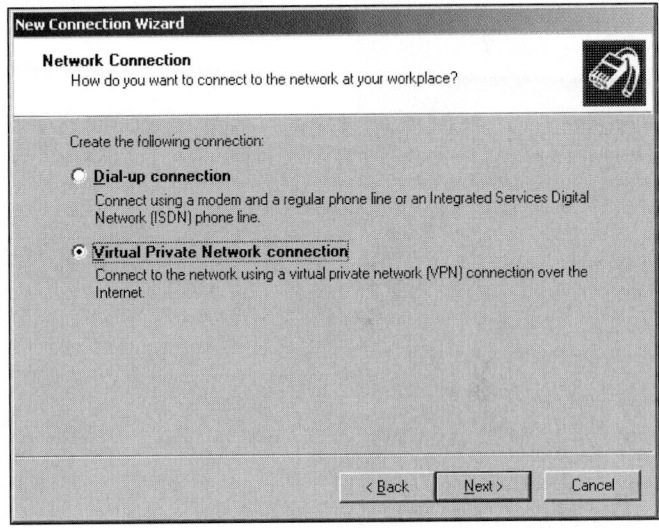

Figure 11-40 SLIP and PPP

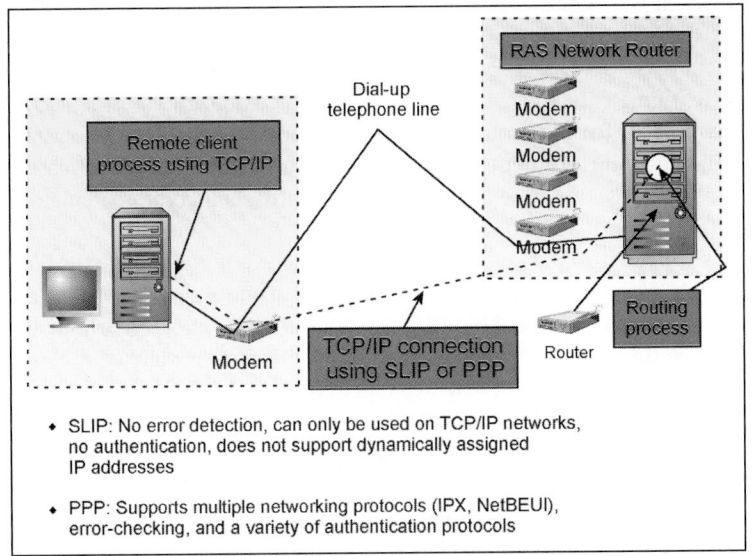

- SLIP: No error detection, can only be used on TCP/IP networks, no authentication, does not support dynamically assigned IP addresses

- PPP: Supports multiple networking protocols (IPX, NetBEUI), error-checking, and a variety of authentication protocols

skill 5

Introducing Routing and Remote Access Service (RRAS) *(cont'd)*

exam objective   Basic knowledge

overview

♦ **Challenge Handshake Authentication Protocol (CHAP):** CHAP is a protocol that provides authentication on the basis of a one-way hash created by seeding the Message Digest 5 (MD5) encryption algorithm with the password. Algorithms are mathematical formulas with a clearly defined endpoint that are used to solve a particular problem. They can be written in any language, from English to programming languages. MD5-CHAP uses the Message Digest 5 (MD5) one-way hashing algorithm to encrypt user names and passwords. Hashing algorithms take a variable length string and change it into a fixed length string, which is referred to as a hash value. The hash value has no correlation to the original data, and even small changes to the original variable length string will produce an entirely different result. The MD5 algorithm produces a 16-byte hash, which can be used to verify the integrity of a block of data by comparing two hash values of the same data, one created on the sending end, and the other recreated on the receiving end. In CHAP authentication, essentially, the user sends his or her user name to the RAS server in plain text form, but does not send the password. The server then creates a challenge message and sends this challenge to the client. The client computer then uses the MD-5 algorithm, seeded with the user's password, to encrypt the challenge. When the client sends this challenge to the server, the server will compare the client's hash to the hash it expected to receive (based on the password it has listed for the client). If the values match, the client is allowed to connect, and if not, the client is dropped. It is important to note that for CHAP to function properly, the password that CHAP uses must be in plain text. In Windows Server 2003, this requires that you store domain passwords in a reversibly encrypted format. This means that the password's encryption can be quickly and easily reversed, which is a major security consideration. For this reason, the use of CHAP is not generally recommended.

♦ **Microsoft CHAP (MS-CHAP):** MS-CHAP is Microsoft's version of CHAP. The challenge message is specifically designed for Windows operating systems and one-way encryption is used. MS-CHAP is used with Windows 9.x and NT and only the client is authenticated. In the extended version, **MS-CHAP2**, both the client and the server are authenticated. Windows 9.x clients can now be modernized so that they are compatible with MS-CHAP2 by downloading the patch for Dial-up networking that upgrades it to version 1.3. MS-CHAP2 also uses a different encryption key for transmitting data and for receiving data. MS-CHAP v1 CPW and MS-CHAP v2 CPW are updated versions of these protocols in which the user can change an expired password. Both versions of MS-CHAP support data encryption using the Microsoft Point-to-Point Encryption (MPPE) algorithm, but only MS-CHAP 2 supports mutual authentication.

♦ **Extensible Authentication Protocol (EAP):** EAP is used to customize your method of remote access authentication for PPP connections. It is a general authentication system that extends the Point-to-Point Protocol (PPP) by supporting multiple authentication methods including token cards, one-time passwords, smart cards, and crypto-calculators. EAP supports authentication using either TLS (Transport Layer Security) or MD5-CHAP. TLS supports smart cards and certificates. It is composed of two layers: the TLS Record protocol, which uses symmetric data encryption to ensure that connections are private, and the TLS Handshake protocol, which negotiates an encryption algorithm and cryptographic key before the application protocol can transmit or receive any data. Smart cards store user certificates and public/private keys that are used for authentication purposes in conjunction with a PIN number. Certificates are digital signatures that validate users and networks. EAP-MD5 CHAP uses the same challenge handshake protocol as CHAP, but the challenge and response messages are sent as EAP messages. EAP-MD5 CHAP is commonly used to authenticate remote access clients by using user name and password security systems.

Table 11-7　Authentication protocols

Name	Description
PAP	The least secure of all authentication protocols because it sends all information in a clear text format. PAP has no provision for authenticating the client and the server to each other. Therefore, PAP is only used when minimal security is required.
SPAP	Provides more security than the PAP protocol. SPAP is an authentication protocol that is used if you are connecting to servers manufactured by Shiva.
CHAP	Considered a more secure protocol than PAP or SPAP. Used by Unix-based and other non-Microsoft clients to communicate with a RRAS server. CHAP provides authentication on the basis of a value that is calculated using an algorithm. CHAP sends a challenge message to the client when the client dials in. The client applies an algorithm to the message to calculate a hash value (a fixed-length number), and sends the value to the server. The server also calculates a value and compares this value to the value sent by the client. If the value matches, the connection is established and the user can access shared resources on the server.
MS-CHAP	Microsoft's version of CHAP. There are two versions: MS-CHAP version 1 and MS-CHAP version 2. MS-CHAP version 1, also known commonly as MS-CHAP, supports only a one-way authentication process. MS-CHAP version 2 supports a two-way authentication process known as mutual authentication.
EAP	An extension to the Point-to-Point (PPP) protocol. EAP provides support for authentication mechanisms such as smart cards, token cards, and certificates to validate remote access server connections. Using EAP, a RAS client and a RAS server negotiate and agree upon an authentication method that both of them support. For example, when a RAS client uses a generic token card, the RAS server separately sends queries to the remote access client to obtain information about the user. As each query is asked and answered, the remote access client passes through another level of authentication. After all questions have been answered, the RAS client is authenticated.
IEEE 802.1X:	New authentication protocol supported by Windows Server 2003 for wireless and Ethernet LAN connections.

skill 5 — *Introducing Routing and Remote Access Service (RRAS)* (cont'd)

exam objective   Basic knowledge

overview

♦ **IEEE 802.1X:** New in Windows Server 2003 is support for IEEE 802.1X, allowing wireless and Ethernet LAN connections.

VPN: In this type of connection, a secure point-to-point connection is established across private networks or a public network such as the Internet. A VPN creates a logical link, called a tunnel, between a remote user and a private network. Secure connections in VPNs are created using either Point-to-Point Tunneling Protocol (PPTP) or Layer Two Tunneling Protocol (L2TP). **Point-to-Point Tunneling Protocol (PPTP)** is an extension of the Point-to-Point (PPP) protocol. It is installed by default during the installation of RRAS. **Layer 2 Tunneling Protocol (L2TP)** is also an extension of the PPP protocol. It combines features from PPTP and Cisco Systems' Layer Two Forwarding (L2F) protocol.

When using PPTP, encryption is always provided using Microsoft Point-to-Point Encryption (MPPE), though you can doubly encrypt PPTP in Windows 2000 and Server 2003 by using IPSec to re-encrypt the data stream. L2TP, on the other hand, does not have built in encryption; it relies solely on IPSec **(Figure 11-41)**. Both of these protocols work over dial-up lines, public TCP/IP networks (the Internet), local network links, and WAN links. If you use L2TP, a tunnel will be created, but data will not be encrypted. L2TP must be used in conjunction with IPSec, which will provide data encryption. When you use L2TP, the message header is compressed, while PPTP does not use header compression. Furthermore, PPTP does not tunnel (or encrypt) the authentication information, so use of an encrypted authentication protocol with PPTP is almost a necessity. L2TP does tunnel the authentication, however, making L2TP more secure.

tip

In general, L2TP is the more secure of the two tunneling protocols. However, when communicating with Windows 9x or Windows NT 4 machines, you will be forced to use PPTP.

more

Bandwidth Allocation Protocol (BAP) is another network protocol used with remote networks that use dial-in connections. It is often referred to as Multilink PPP because it is used with PPP to augment the use of multilinked devices. The term multilinked devices refers to combining several ISDN (Integrated Services Digital Network) lines or modem links to obtain greater bandwidth. (ISDN simply refers to the international data transfer format for sending voice, video, and data over digital telephone lines or normal telephone wires.) Multilinking means that multiple physical links are combined to create one logical link. All of the links are pooled and the load is balanced among the physical connection components. BAP is used to dynamically add or drop links on demand so that only as much bandwidth as is required for the current network traffic is used. BAP dynamically provides optimum bandwidth and helps in reducing connection costs. However, as the price of broadband has decreased, multilinking has become increasingly less cost effective because the cost of extra phone lines and modems exceed the cost of broadband access, which typically yields many times the bandwidth **(Figure 11-42)**.

Bandwidth Allocation Control Protocol (BACP): BACP is the control protocol for BAP. For the most part, you can think of BAP and BACP as the same thing. However, if you would like a more technical explanation, you can examine the RFC for BAP at **http://www.ietf.org/rfc/rfc2125.txt**

Figure 11-41 Tunneling

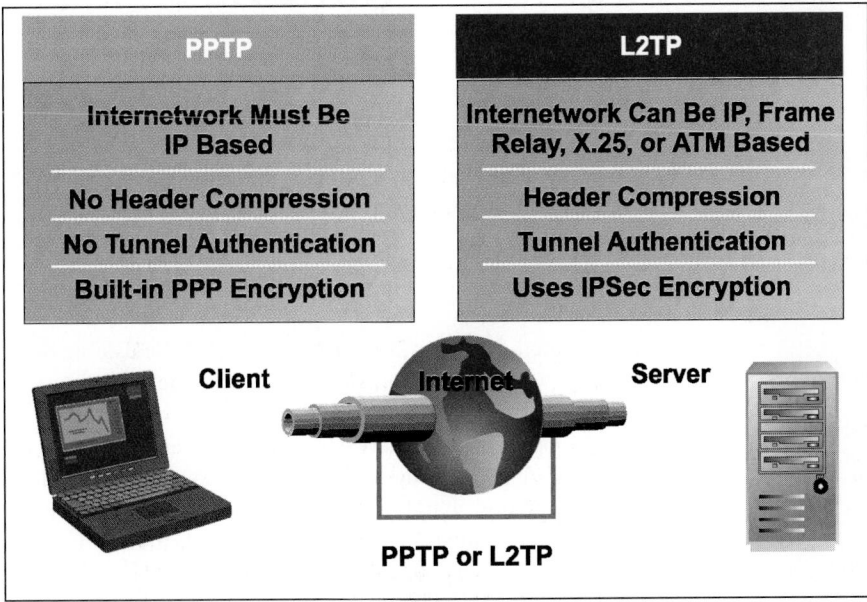

Figure 11-42 Configuring BAP and BACP

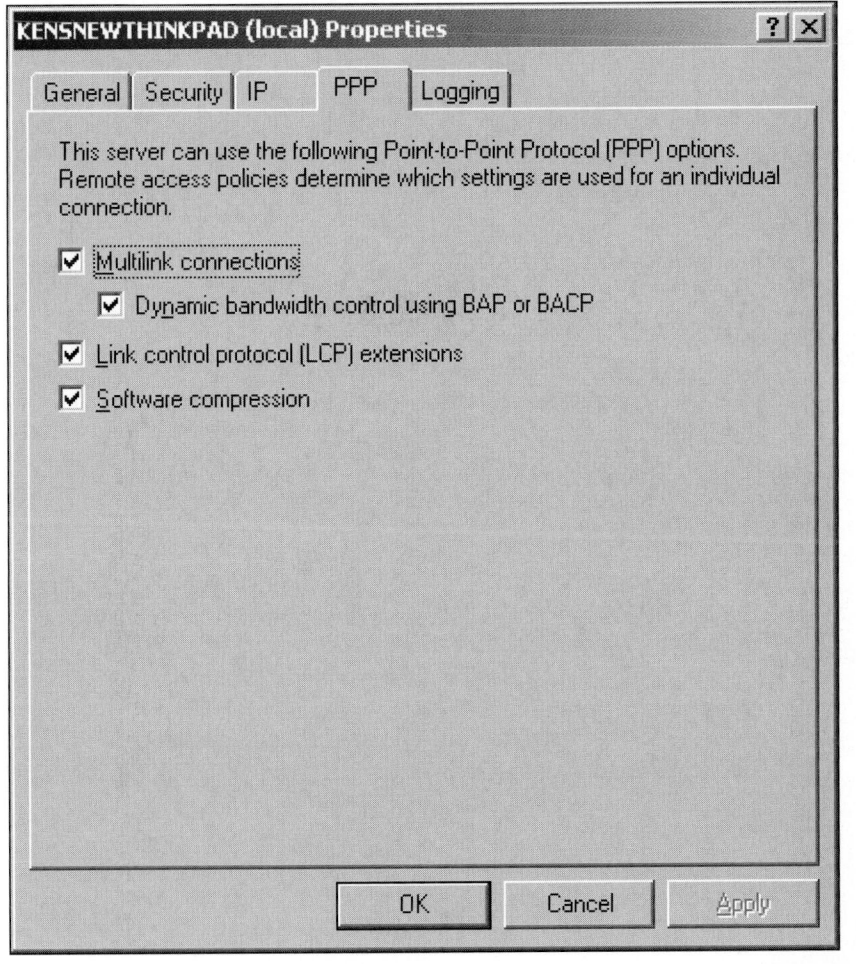

skill 6

Understanding Types of Remote Access Connections

exam objective

Basic knowledge

overview

To establish a connection between a remote network and a remote access client, you use the following types of dial-up equipment, as well as those described in **Table 11-8**:

◆ **POTS:** The Plain Old Telephone System (POTS) establishes an end-to-end analog connection between your computer and a remote network using normal modems and phone lines.

◆ **ISDN:** Integrated Services Digital Network (ISDN) establishes an end-to-end digital connection between your computer and a remote network using digital telephone lines. These telephone lines transmit data at a speed of 64 kilobits per second (Kbps) to 1.544 Mbps. ISDN also provides other services such as fax, voice, and data transmission.

◆ **DSL:** Digital Subscriber Line (DSL) is a special communication line that uses copper wires to transfer high-bandwidth data such as audio and video to homes and small offices. DSL uses modulation technology to encode digital or analog signals into a carrier signal. The carrier signal adapts the digital or analog signal to a frequency range that is different from that of the original. Upon reaching the destination, the original signal is separated from the carrier signal using an inverse process called demodulation. DSL runs digital signals over Plain Old Telephone System (POTS) lines.

◆ **Cable modem lines:** Cable modem lines use the coaxial cables originally designed for carrying cable television signals, and in some cases, both fiber optic and coaxial cable, to transfer data.

◆ **Frame relay:** Frame relay was developed for WANs. Frame relay uses packet-switching technology. Transmission speeds range between 56 Kbps and 45 Mbps.

◆ **Leased telecommunication lines:** Usually, leased telecommunication lines are T-carrier lines. T-carrier lines are digital lines that use multiplexing to send multiple signals over a single communications line. A device called a multiplexer is used to combine two or more input signals from various devices into a single data stream that is transmitted over a single transmission medium.

tip

Both the client and the remote access server must have an ISDN adapter.

tip

A Windows 2000, Windows XP, Windows NT 3.5 or higher, or a Windows 95/98 computer can act as a remote access client.

more

The number of dial-up remote callers who can connect to a Windows Server 2003 RAS server at one time is not limited. VPN connections are limited by the type of hardware in use, up to a maximum of 2,000 connections (1,000 PPTP and 1,000 L2TP). Virtually all Microsoft operating systems including Windows 3.1 and 3.11 (Windows for Workgroups), all versions of Windows NT, Windows 9.x, ME, 2000, and XP can be configured as RAS clients. Even MS-DOS machines can be RAS clients.

The first step to creating a RAS server on a small network is to install several modems in the Windows Server 2003 computers that you are going to configure as the RAS server. On larger networks, a network device called an access server is used. Access servers can accommodate multiple modems, ISDN line connections, T-carrier line connections, or E-carrier line connections (in Europe). You must use an access server that is compatible with Windows Server 2003 so that the software and drivers work properly with the operating system to synchronize IP routing and other communication capabilities.

Table 11-8	*Communication Equipment Supported by Windows Server 2003 RAS*
Device	**Description**
Asynchronous modem	The most common modem type, it uses a special signal or data bit to transmit each unit of data. This data bit displays the start and end of each unit during transmission.
Synchronous modem	This type of modem, which is not in wide use, uses a clocking technique to denote the start and end point of each unit of data during transmission.
Null modem communications portable	Null modem communications use a specially designed cable to directly connect two computers via their serial communications ports (RS-232 ports). Null modem cables are most often used with computers.
Regular dial-up telephone lines	The Plain Old Telephone System (POTS) establishes an end-to-end analog connection between your computer and a remote network using modems and phone lines.
ISDN lines	The international data transfer formats for sending voice, video, and data over digital telephone lines or normal telephone wires. There are several styles of ISDN (EURO, US). ISDN uses 64 Kbps channels in conjunction with different types of services. The ISDN basic rate interface has three channels: two 64 Kbps channels used to send data, voice, and graphics, and one 16 Kbps channel used to transmit communications signaling.
X.25 lines	Not widely used in the U.S. and Canada, but still used in Europe and other parts of the world, X.25 is an older WAN communication method that originally could only transmit data at speeds up to 64 Kbps, but was upgraded in 1992 so that it can now provide data transfer rates up to 2.048 Mbps.
DSL (Digital Subscriber Line) lines	DSL runs digital signals over Plain Old Telephone System (POTS) lines. DSL uses modulation technology to encode digital or analog signals into a carrier signal. The carrier signal adapts the digital or analog signal to a frequency range that is different from that of the original. Upon reaching the destination, the original signal is separated from the carrier signal using an inverse process called demodulation.
Frame relay	Frame relay is a WAN technique. It is used on packet-switching networks, depends on virtual connection techniques, and can transmit data at speeds between 56 Kbps and 45 Mbps.
Leased telecommunication lines	This term most commonly refers to T- carrier lines, which are digital lines that use multiplexing to send multiple signals over a single communications line. T-1 lines, which are the most commonly used in the U.S., can carry 24 separate signals at a transmission rate of 64 Kbps each, making the total transmission rate 1.544 Mbps. A T-3 line can send 672 separate signals at 64 Kbps each, creating a total transmission speed of 43 Mbps. It can match the transmission speed of 28 T-1 lines. The Internet backbone uses T-3 lines, as well as optical carrier circuits (OC1, OC3, OC12, OC24, and OC48). However, these types of lines are cost-prohibitive and only large enterprises can afford the initial investment. Multiplexing refers to using a device called a multiplexer to combine two or more input signals from various devices into a single data stream that is transmitted over a single transmission medium.

skill 7

Configuring Remote Access Services

exam objective

Basic knowledge

overview

Routing and Remote Access Service (RRAS) is installed automatically during the installation of Windows Server 2003. However, by default, RRAS is not enabled. You must manually enable and configure RRAS to either set up a RAS server, a VPN, Network Address Translation (NAT), a secure connection between two servers, or a network router.

When you configure a remote access server, inbound connections can be accepted from users who simply dial-in to the RAS server and provide their user account name and password. Since security is an important consideration when you are going to provide remote access to your network, you must secure RAS connections so that only authorized users can access network resources. When a user dials-in to a RAS server, the connection is accepted only after it is authenticated and authorized. During the authentication process, the information provided by the user is verified using one of the authentication protocols outlined earlier. After the information is authenticated, it must be authorized by the RAS server. During the authorization process, the RAS server verifies that the connection attempt is allowed.

how to

Install and configure a RAS server.

1. Click [Start], point to **Administrative Tools**, and select **Routing and Remote Access** to open the **Routing and Remote Access** console.
2. Select the server on which you want to activate RRAS. If the server you want to configure is not listed, right-click **Routing and Remote Access** and click **Add Server**. In the **Add Server** dialog box, select the **This computer** option button to add the local computer. Select the **The following computer** option button and enter the name of the server to configure a different server (**Figure 11-43**).
3. Right-click the server name and select **Configure and Enable Routing and Remote Access** to start the **Routing and Remote Access Server Setup Wizard**.
4. Click [Next >] to open the **Configuration** screen. To set up a network router, you would select the **Custom configuration** option. Select the **Remote access (dial-up or VPN)** option button, if necessary (**Figure 11-44**).
5. Click [Next >] to open the **Remote Access** screen. Select the **Dial-up** check box (**Figure 11-45**).
6. Click [Next >] to open the **IP Address Assignment** screen. If there is more than one network connection configured on the server, the **Network Selection** dialog box will open so that you can select the correct network interface (**Figure 11-46**). If you have a DHCP server on your network, select the **Automatically** option button. The DHCP server will assign IP addresses to the remote access clients. This exercise will assume that you have a DHCP server. (If you do not have DHCP enabled on your network, select the **From a specified range** of IP addresses option button and enter the range of addresses to be assigned to remote access clients on the **Address Range Assignment** screen.)

Figure 11-43 The Add Server dialog box

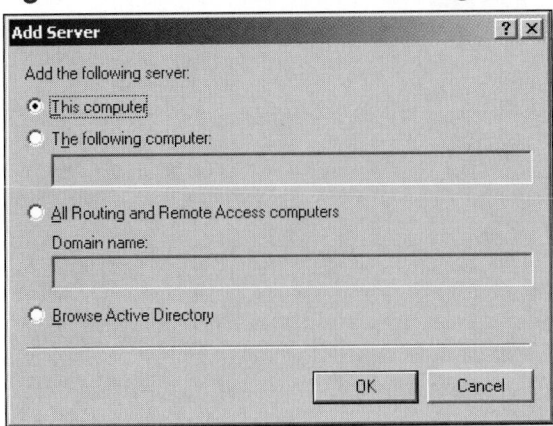

Figure 11-44 The Configuration screen in the RRAS Setup Wizard

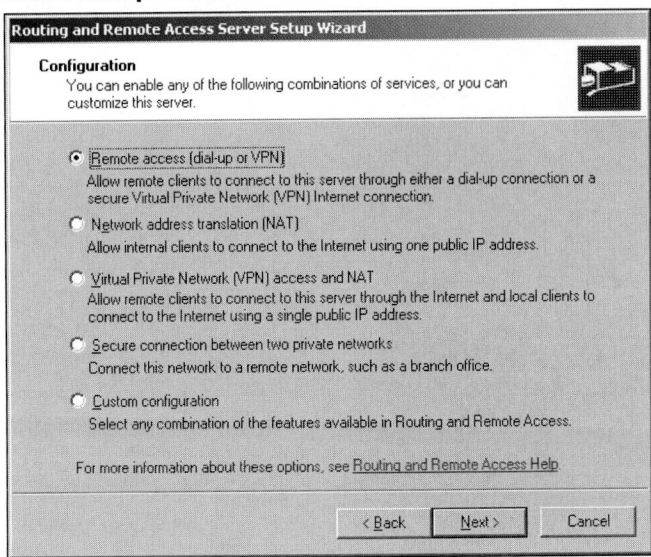

Figure 11-45 The Remote Access screen

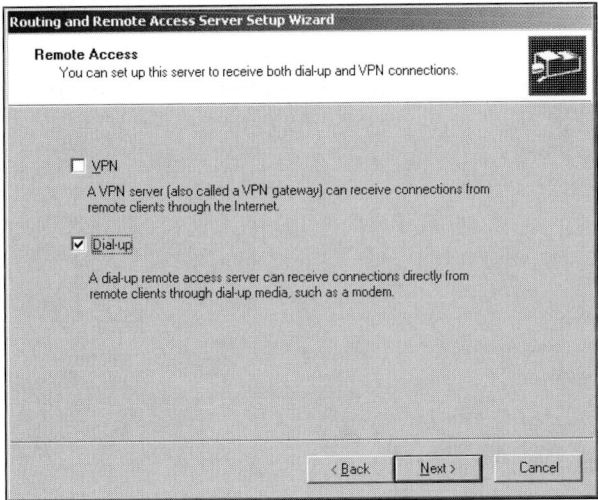

Figure 11-46 The Network Selection screen

If there is more than one network connection configured on the server, this screen will open so that you can select the correct network interface

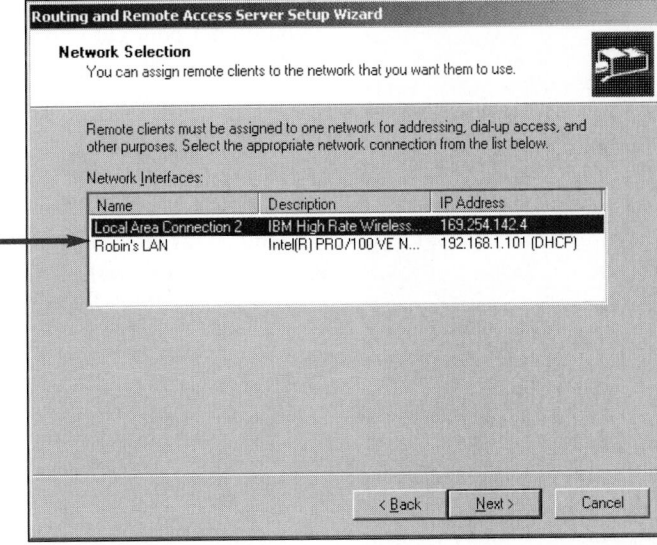

skill 7

Configuring Remote Access Services (cont'd)

exam objective   Basic knowledge

how to

7. Click [Next>] to open the **Managing Multiple Remote Access Servers** screen. Networks that have multiple RAS servers will often use a **Remote Authentication Dial-In User Service (RADIUS)** server to provide centralized authentication. For example, many ISPs use a RADIUS server so that users from geographically disparate locations will all be routed to the RADIUS server for authentication. Having a RADIUS server on your network can be convenient because when you change a password it is immediately updated, and when you delete a user, the user will be immediately locked out of the entire system. Replication delays, or any other holdups, are not a factor because the new authentication data takes effect immediately. If you have a RADIUS server on your network, select **Yes, set up this server to work with a RADIUS server**. Next, you will have to enter the names of a primary and an alternate RADIUS server, as well as a shared secret (password) that will be used to contact these RADIUS servers **(Figure 11-47)**. This exercise will assume that you do not have a RADIUS server.

8. Select the **No, use Routing and Remote Access to authenticate connection requests** option button, if necessary **(Figure 11-48)**.

9. Click [Next>] to open the **Completing the Routing and Remote Access Server Wizard** screen.

10. Click [Finish]. A message box may open to inform you that the next task you need to perform is configuring DHCP relay agent properties. Click [OK].

11. Select the plus sign to the left of the RAS server name, if necessary. The Routing and Remote Access console now includes nodes for configuring Remote Access Clients, Ports, IP Routing, Remote Access Policies, and Remote Access Logging **(Figure 11-49)**.

more

As you saw in Step 6, if you already have a DHCP server providing IP addressing information to your internal network clients, you can also use the server to assign IP addresses to your RAS clients. When you choose this option, you should make the RAS server a DHCP Relay Agent. To do this, open the **IP Routing** node, right-click **DHCP Relay Agent**, and select **Properties** to open the **DHCP Relay Agent Properties** dialog box. In the **Server address** text box, enter the IP address for the DHCP server if it has not already been entered and click **Add (Figure 11-50)**. You can add the IP addresses for several DHCP servers if you have several DHCP servers on your network.

If you do not configure your RAS server as a DHCP relay agent, clients will receive an IP address and subnet mask, but will not receive any option information, such as DNS server IP address. This, in general, means that the client will only be able to access the RAS server by name.

After you install the DHCP relay agent, you can double-click the **Internal** interface in the **Interface** column in the details pane to set the Hop count threshold and the Boot threshold. The **Hop count** threshold controls the maximum number of Relay Agents that will service a request. The **Boot** threshold is the number of seconds that the Relay Agent will wait before it relays a request. By default, both values are set to **4**.

Figure 11-47 The RADIUS Server Selection screen

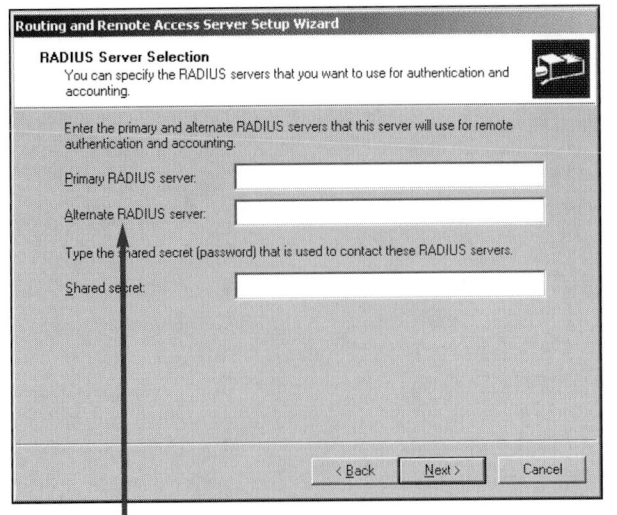

Figure 11-48 The Managing Multiple Remote Access Servers screen

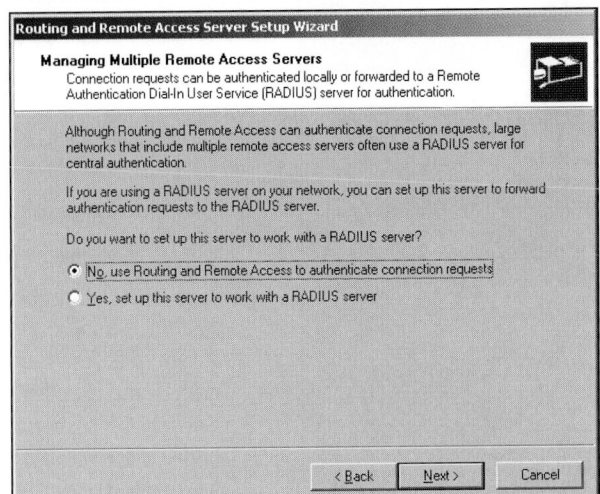

RADIUS servers are used to provide centralized authentication

Figure 11-49 The Routing and Remote Access console

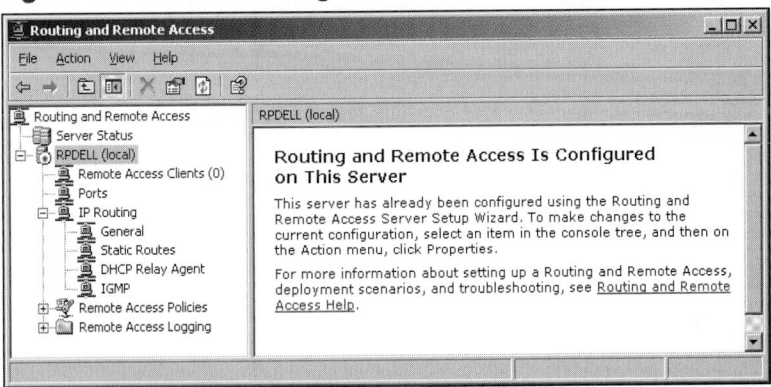

Figure 11-50 The DHCP Relay Agent Properties dialog box

Enter the IP address for the DHCP server in the Server address text box and click Add

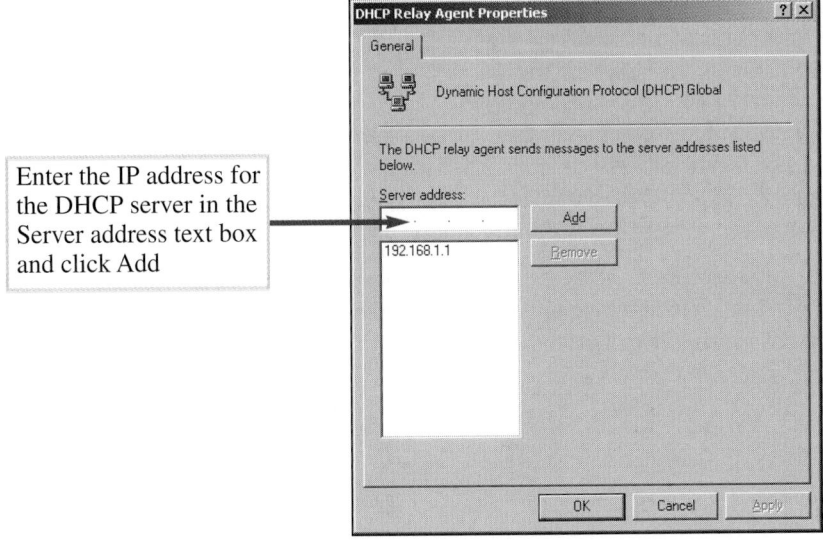

skill 7

Configuring Remote Access Services (cont'd)

exam objective   Basic knowledge

more

You configure your RAS server in its Properties dialog box. The default tabs on the Properties dialog box are described below:

◆ **General:** This tab is used to specify whether your computer will be configured as a router for the local area network only, as a router for a LAN and demand-dial routing, as a remote access server, or as both a router and a RAS (**Figure 11-51**). You can also clear both of the check boxes to disable RAS. Since there are a number of excellent dedicated routers on the market that are designed specifically for routing functionality and include high-level firewalls, most networks prefer to use them rather than configuring the RAS as a router too. Adding router functionality to the RAS increases the overhead on the server. However, the RAS must be configured as a router if it is directly connected to the Internet or the WAN. The most common reason for this is when either a digital modem (linking to an ISDN line) or a DSL adapter (linking to a digital subscriber line) is directly connecting the server to the Internet or WAN.

◆ **Security:** This tab is used to choose one of two types of authentication providers to validate remote access clients (**Figure 11-52**).

   • **Windows authentication** is the built-in authentication provider for Windows Server 2003. It authenticates connection attempts from remote users using one of several authentication methods that verify both the identity of the user and the network.

   • **RADIUS authentication** sends authentication requests to a RADIUS server, which runs the Internet Authentication Service (IAS). IAS authenticates clients using information stored in either the local accounts database or from the domain database. On the Security tab, you can also set the authentication protocols that will be used to verify user credentials by clicking the **Authentication Methods** button.

◆ **IP:** This tab is used to specify settings for the IP protocol such as the method for distributing IP addresses to remote clients. There are two methods for distributing IP addresses:

   • Using the DHCP server.
   • Assigning static IP addresses to remote clients.

◆ **PPP:** This tab is used to configure PPP (Point-to-Point Protocol) to specify whether a remote client can establish multilink connections. A multilink connection combines multiple physical links into one logical link. For example, you can combine two or more ISDN (Integrated Services Digital Network) lines or modem links to obtain greater bandwidth. The PPP tab also allows you to specify whether a client and server can dynamically add and remove physical links using either Bandwidth Allocation Protocol (BAP) or Bandwidth Allocation Control Protocol (BACP).

◆ **Logging:** This tab is used to manage and monitor an RRAS server by selecting the types of events you want to record for accounting and security purposes.

Other tabs will appear on the Properties dialog box depending on the protocols installed on your Windows Server 2003 computer. For example, if you have installed the Internetwork Packet Exchange (IPX) protocol on your computer, a tab for IPX will be available; otherwise, the tab for IPX will be absent.

Figure 11-51 The General tab in the <RAS_servername> Properties dialog box

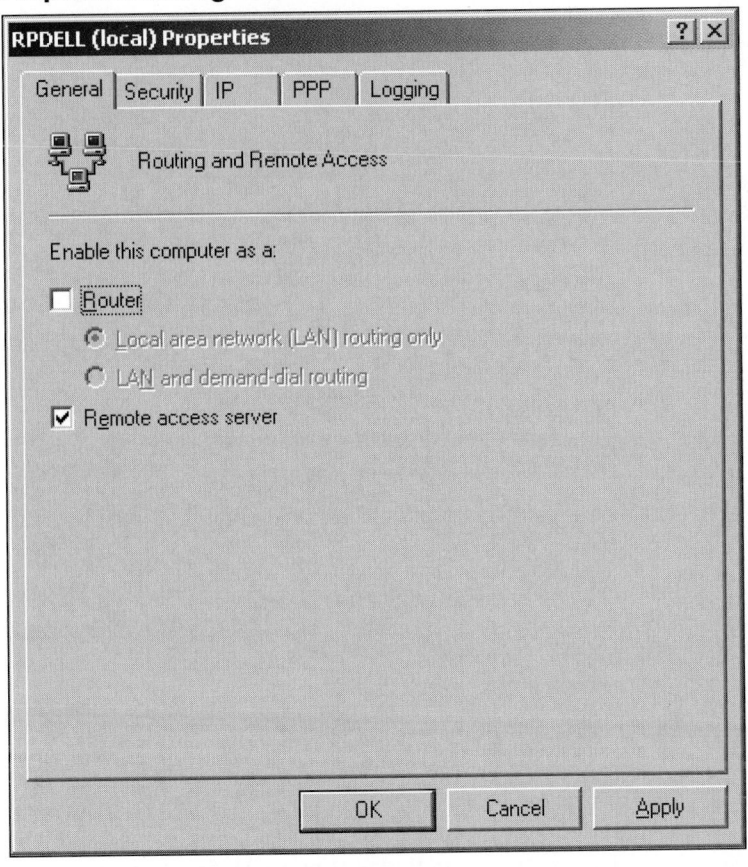

Figure 11-52 The Security tab

Click to open the
Authentication Methods
dialog box to set the
authentication protocols

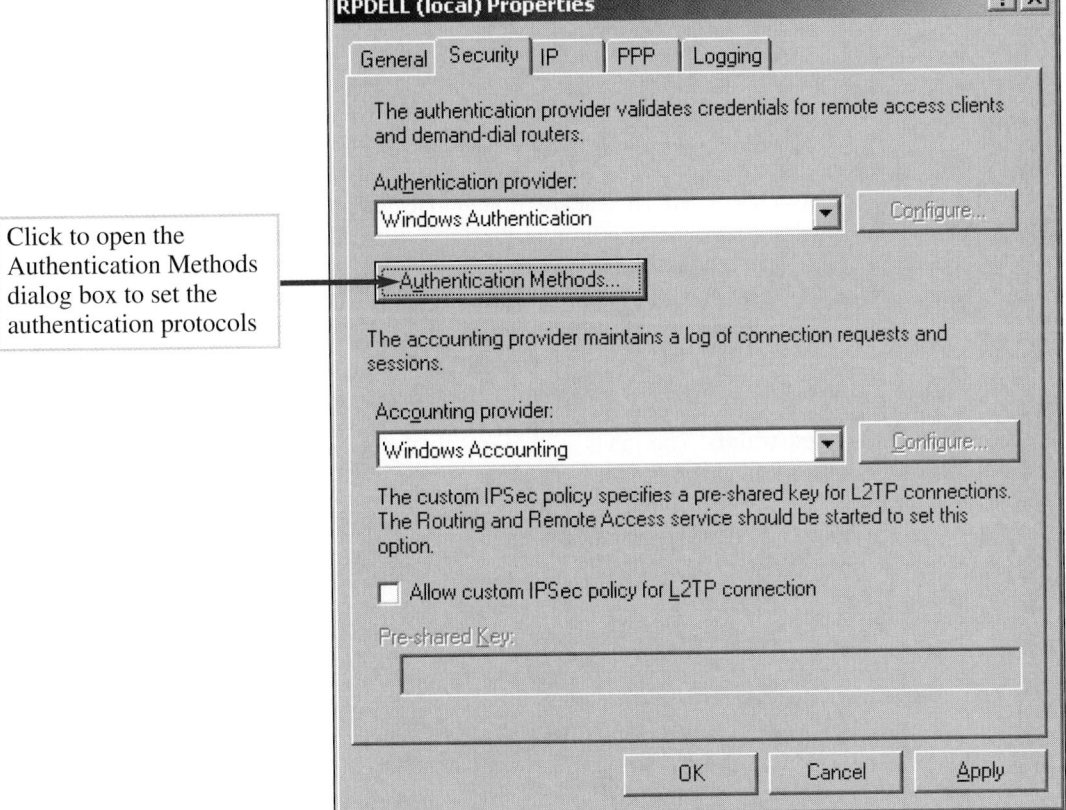

skill 8   *Creating a Remote Access Policy*

exam objective   Basic knowledge

overview

tip

To gain access to network resources through a RRAS server, all conditions in a single remote access policy must be satisfied.

tip

The Control access through Remote Access Policy option will only be available if your domain is in either Native mode or Windows Server 2003 mode.

Remote access policies are used to control what connection attempts will be rejected or accepted by the RRAS server. You create them to determine which users can access the network and to prevent unauthorized access. A **remote access policy** consists of a set of rules and conditions that must be met by a connection before a user can gain access. The criteria, which can include parameters such as the time, groups, and connection type, are evaluated one by one when a user connects to the RRAS server. For example, you can create a policy that allows employees in the Marketing department to access network resources between 9 AM and 6 PM. Remote access policies are either stored locally on the RRAS server or they can be stored and managed using RADIUS. They are not stored in Active Directory.

There are actually three components of a remote access policy: conditions, permissions, and a profile.

Conditions are a set of criteria that the user must match in order for the policy to apply to them. Conditions include specifications such as time of day, day of the week, number dialed, and Windows group membership (**Figure 11-53**). If the user does not match all of the conditions in a given policy, then a match is attempted against the next policy. If the user doesn't match any policies, they are disconnected. When a user matches all of the conditions in a given policy, the permissions section of their user account is consulted.

Permissions are located on the **Dial-in** tab in the user account **Properties** dialog box. There are three settings for user account dial-in permissions: **Allow**, **Deny**, and **Control access through Remote Access Policy (Figure 11-54)**. If the user account permissions are set to Deny, the caller is dropped. If they are set to Allow, the permissions section in the remote access policy is skipped, and the remote access profile is applied. If the user account dial-in permissions are set to Control through Remote Access Policy, the permissions configured in the remote access policy are checked. If they are set to **Grant remote access permission**, the profile is applied. If they are set to **Deny remote access permission**, the caller is disconnected.

Regardless of whether the caller is allowed to connect through the user account permissions or through remote access policy permissions, the last thing to apply is the profile. The **remote access profile** is a list of settings that are offered to the client. These settings include allowed dial-in days and times, connection limits, allowed dial-in media and phone numbers, authentication settings, encryption settings, and so forth. The settings in the profile are offered to the client, and if the client cannot support the offered settings, they are disconnected. For example, if the profile offers EAP as the only authentication method and the client does not support EAP, the client will be disconnected. You configure a remote access profile in the **Edit Dial-in Profile** dialog box, which contains the following tabs:

◆ **Dial-in Constraints:** This tab is used to specify the dial-in number and the type of media to be used for connection. For example, you can specify that a dial-in connection can only use a modem to connect to the RRAS server. You can also set day and time restrictions for connections and the idle time period that will be permitted. When the maximum idle time has been reached, the user will be disconnected (**Figure 11-55**).

◆ **IP:** This tab is used to set the IP properties for a connection. You can specify the method a client will use to obtain an IP address. For example, you can specify either that the RRAS server must provide the IP address or that a client can request a specific IP address. You can also enhance security by defining IP packet filters. Using IP packet filters, you can control which TCP and UDP ports a client can use, the allowed upper-layer protocols, and the remote IP addresses they are allowed to communicate with. There are two kinds of IP packet filters: input and output (**Figure 11-56**). You use

Figure 11-53 The Select Attribute dialog box

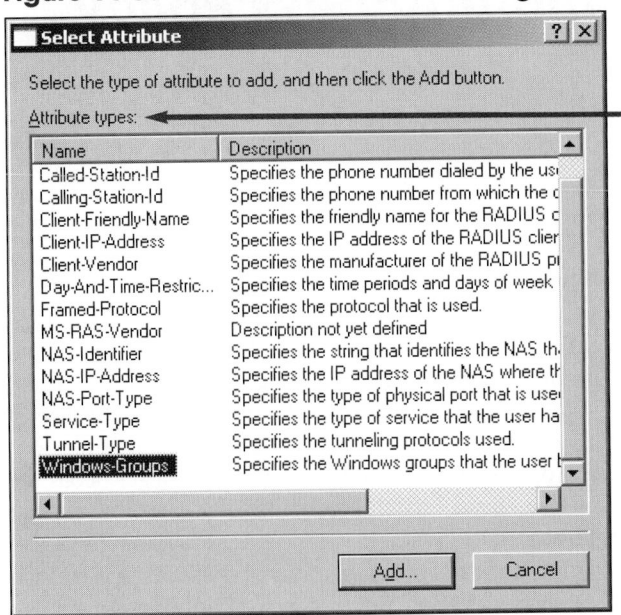

Attributes that can be set as conditions for a remote access policy

Figure 11-54 The Dial-in tab in the Properties dialog box for a user

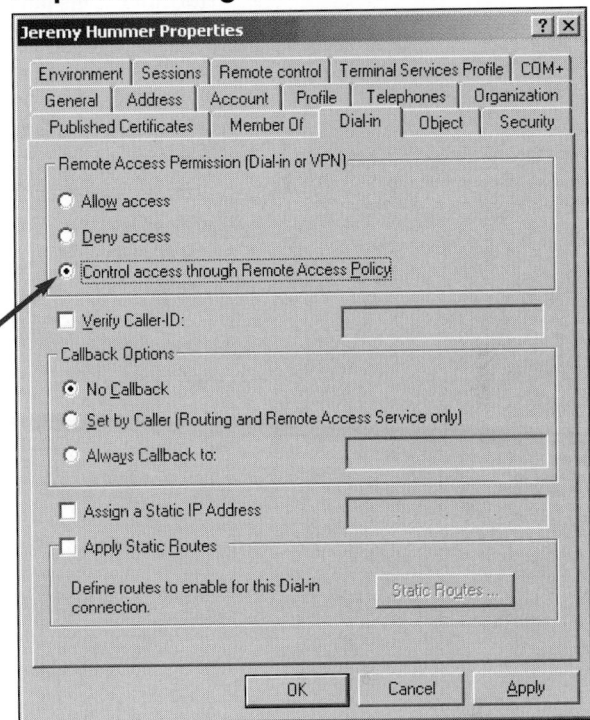

Only available in Windows 2000 native mode or Windows 2003 mode domains. When this option is set, the permissions configured in the remote access policy are checked. If they are set to Grant, the profile is applied. If they are set to Deny, the caller is disconnected.

Figure 11-55 The Dial-in Constraints tab on the Edit Dial-in Profile dialog box

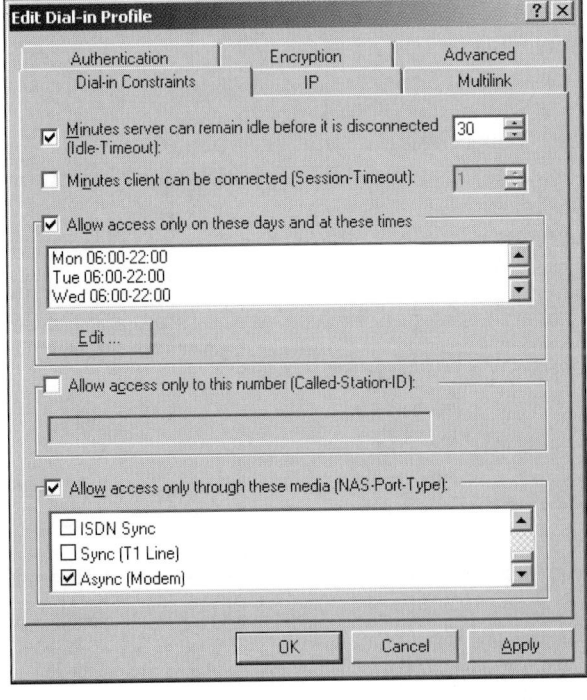

Figure 11-56 The Inbound Filters dialog box

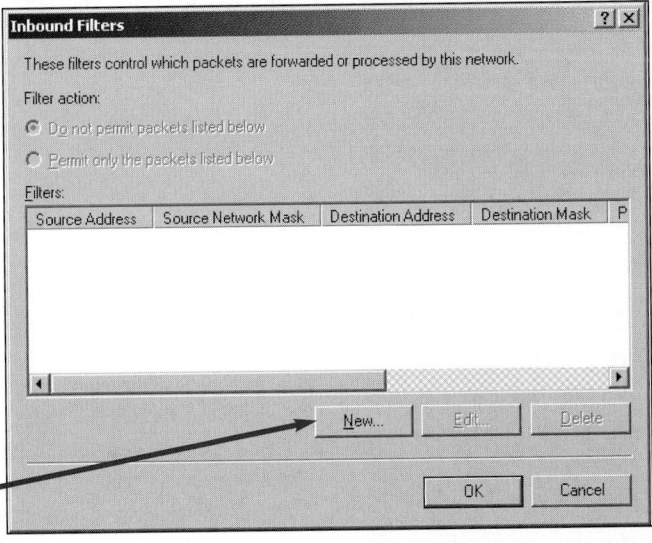

Click to open the Add IP Filter dialog box

skill 8

Creating a Remote Access Policy
(cont'd)

exam objective

Basic knowledge

overview

input filters to filter packets sent to your server and output filters to control packets your server sends to the RAS client. Input filters are more commonly used for the RRAS server in order to control the types of connections users can establish (**Figure 11-57**).

◆ **Multilink:** This tab is used to configure the RRAS server to handle multilink calls and to specify the number of ports that a single remote client can use at one time. You can also specify Bandwidth Allocation Protocol (BAP) settings. BAP settings are used to specify the actions to be taken if the bandwidth usage by remote clients drops below a set threshold. For example, you can drop a multilink line if the client no longer needs the increased bandwidth so that you use only as much bandwidth as is required for the current network traffic (**Figure 11-58**).

◆ **Authentication:** This tab is used to set the authentication protocols that can be used such as PAP, SPAP, CHAP, MS-CHAP, MS-CHAP v2, and EAP. If multiple protocols are selected, they will all be attempted in order from most secure (the top of the list) to least secure (the bottom of the list) until a match is found. If no match is found, the caller will be disconnected.

◆ **Encryption:** This tab is used to specify the type of encryption for your remote access clients: no encryption, basic, strong, or strongest. Like authentication, if multiple levels of encryption are selected, they will all be tried in order, from most secure to least secure, until a match is found.

  • **No encryption** allows clients to connect without using data encryption.
  • **Basic** allows clients to connect using 40-bit encryption key MPPE (Microsoft Point-to-Point Encryption) for dial-up or PPTP connections, or 56-bit DES encryption for L2TP/IPSec connections. MPPE, which is included in Windows operating systems, is a point-to-point encryption technique that uses encryption keys between 40 and 128 bits.
  • **Strong** allows clients to connect using 56-bit encryption key MPPE for dial-up or PPTP connections or 56-bit DES for L2TP/IPSec connections.
  • **Strongest** allows clients to connect using 128-bit encryption key MPPE for dial-up or PPTP connections, or Triple DES (3DES), which uses three 56-bit keys, for L2TP/IPSec connections.

◆ **Advanced:** This tab is used to configure connection attributes such as RADIUS, frame types, AppleTalk zones, special filters, Ascend attributes, and many more.

In order to use IPSec encryption, you have to configure IPSec as a TCP/IP property on the RRAS server in the Network Connections window. In order to use MPPE, the client must have MS-CHAP, MS-CHAP v2, or EAP authentication support.

how to

Create a remote access policy.

1. Open the **Routing and Remote Access** console, if necessary.
2. Double-click the RRAS server name to expand the node, if necessary. Select the **Remote Access Policies** node. Note that there is a default policy named **Allow access if dial-in permission is enabled** (**Figure 11-59**). By default, this policy does not allow remote access. Day and Time restrictions are in place 24 hours a day, seven days a week.
3. Right-click **Remote Access Policies** and select **New Remote Access Policy** to start the **New Remote Access Policy Wizard**.
4. Click [Next >] to open the **Policy Configuration Method** screen. Enter a name for the remote access policy such as **Marketing group RAS policy** in the **Policy name** text box. Select the **Set up a custom policy** option button (**Figure 11-60**).

Figure 11-57 The Add IP Filter dialog box

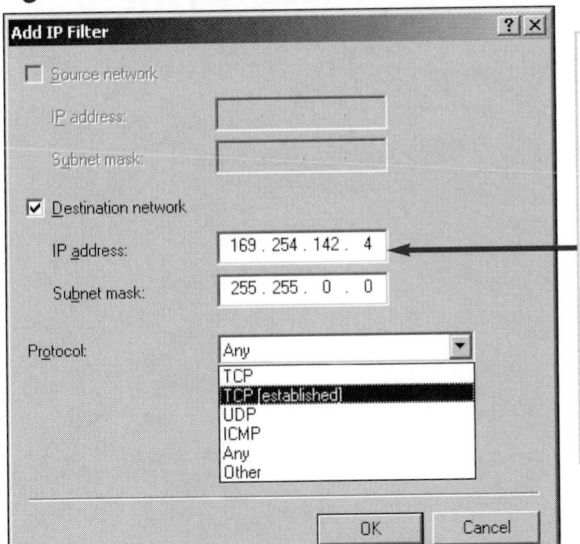

You can create an IP packet filter to control the allowed upper-layer protocols, and the remote IP addresses with which clients are allowed to communicate

Figure 11-58 The Multilink tab

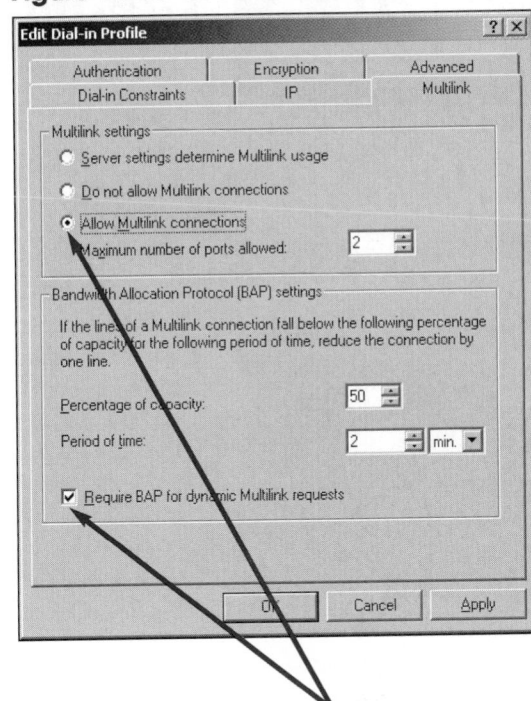

Select to set Bandwidth Allocation Protocol (BAP) settings; you can dynamically drop a link if bandwidth usage by remote clients drops below a certain threshold

Figure 11-59 The Routing and Remote Access console

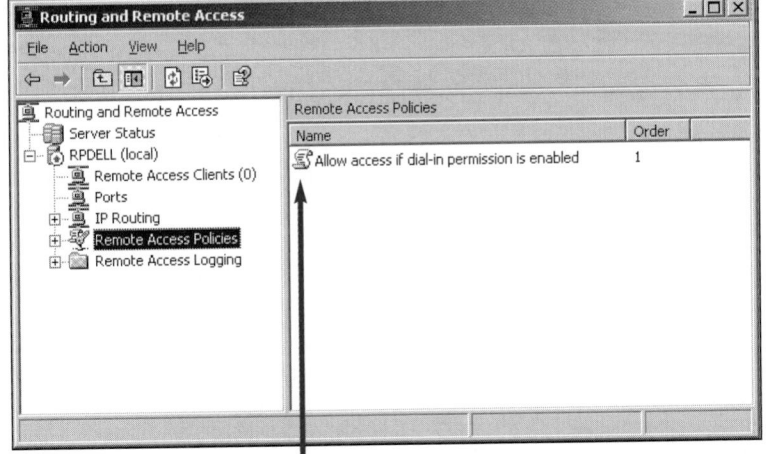

The default remote access policy denies remote access

Figure 11-60 The Policy Configuration Method screen

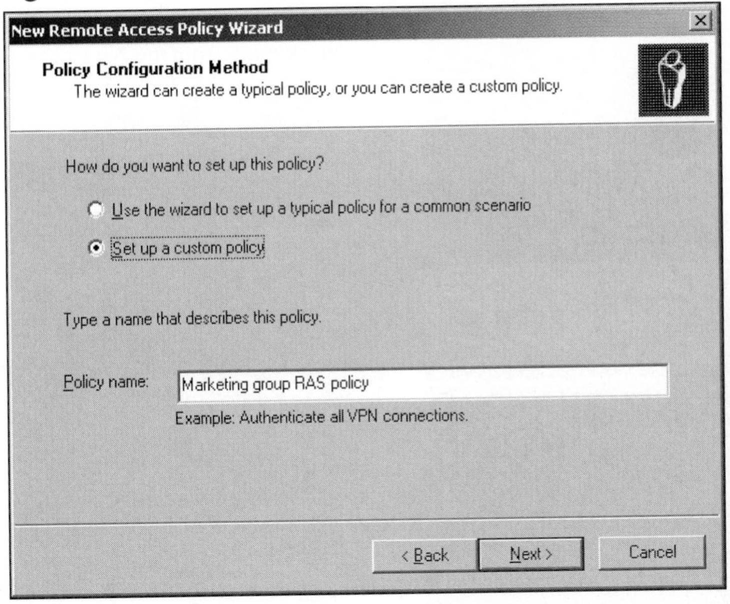

skill 8

Creating a Remote Access Policy
(cont'd)

exam objective

Basic knowledge

how to

tip

In the Time of day constraints dialog box, a blue rectangle designates a permitted logon hour and a white rectangle designates a denied logon hour.

5. Click [Next >] to open the **Policy Conditions** screen. Click [Add] to open the **Select Attribute** dialog box.

6. Double-click **Day-and-Time Restrictions** in the **Name** column (**Figure 11-61**) to open the **Time of day constraints** dialog box.

7. By default, all dates and times are **Denied**. Click the rectangle that corresponds to **Monday 8AM** and drag down and to the right diagonally to create a rectangle that extends to **Friday 6 PM** to specify the permitted connection hours. Click the **Permitted** option button (**Figure 11-62**).

8. Click [OK] to add the constraint to the **Policy conditions** box on the Policy Conditions screen.

9. Click [Add] to reopen the **Select Attribute** dialog box. Double-click **Windows-Groups** to open the **Groups** dialog box.

10. Click [Add] to open the **Select Groups** dialog box. Type **Marketing** in the **Enter object names to select** box, and click [OK]. The *<domain_name>*\Marketing group is added to the **Name** column in the **Groups** box in the Groups dialog box.

11. Click [OK] to close the Groups dialog box. The Windows-Groups matches *<domain_name>*\Marketing condition is added to the Policy conditions box (**Figure 11-63**).

12. Click [Next >] to open the **Permissions** screen.

13. Select the **Grant remote access permission** option button (**Figure 11-64**).

14. Click [Next >] to open the **Profile** screen.

15. Click [Edit Profile...] to open the **Edit Dial-in Profile** dialog box.

16. Select the **Minutes server can remain idle before it is disconnected (Idle-Timeout)** check box and type **30** in the spin box.

17. Click the **IP** tab. Click the **Client may request an IP address** option button in the **IP address assignment (Framed-IP address)** section (**Figure 11-65**).

18. Click the **Authentication** tab. Make sure that **MS-CHAP v2** and **MS-CHAP** are selected. You can use one or a combination of authentication protocols. If you select several different authentication methods, the RRAS server will negotiate with the client to find an authentication method that will work.

19. Click the **Encryption** tab. All levels of encryption are selected by default. Clear the check mark from the **No Encryption** check box. If No Encryption is checked, encryption will not be used for any client no matter what functionality the client has (**Figure 11-66**).

20. Click [OK] to apply the changes and close the **Properties** dialog box for the policy.

21. Click [Next >] to open the **Completing the New Remote Access Policy Wizard** screen. The conditions you set are outlined so that you can check them.

22. Click [Finish] to close the Wizard and set up the remote access policy.

more

If you have created multiple remote access policies, the RRAS server evaluates them in the order in which they are listed in the **Routing and Remote Access** console. However, you can change the order by right-clicking a policy and clicking the **Move Up** and **Move Down** commands on the context menu. To configure a new condition, right-click the policy and click **Properties** to open the Properties dialog box for the policy. Click **Add** to open the **Select Attribute** dialog box. Select a new attribute type in the **Name** column and click **Add**. In the dialog box for the attribute, configure the attribute and click **OK**. To change the configuration of an existing condition, select the condition and click **Edit**. In the attribute dialog box, configure the settings and click **OK**.

Figure 11-61 Setting Day and Time Restrictions

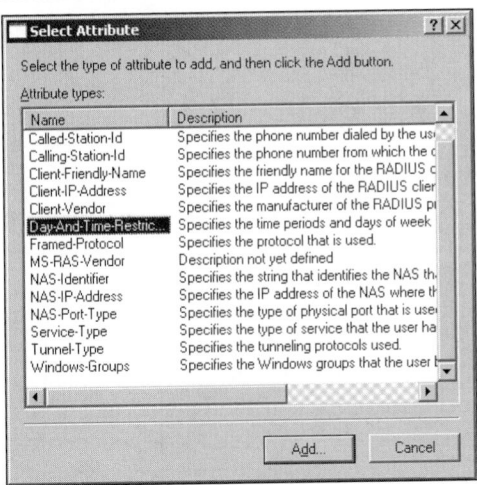

Figure 11-62 The Time of day constraints dialog box

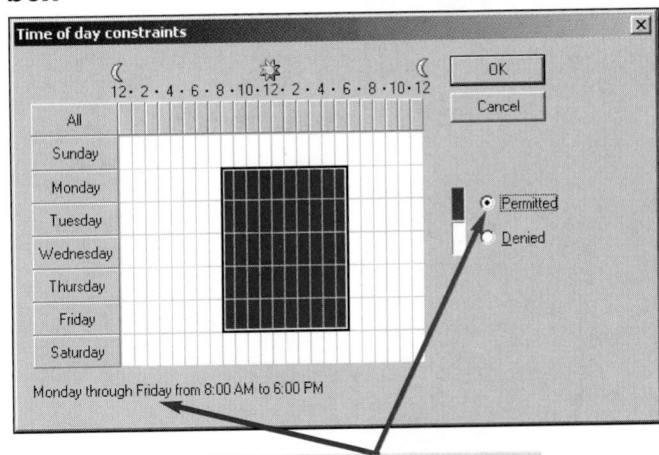

Time during which the policy will permit users to connect to the remote access server

Figure 11-63 The Policy Conditions screen

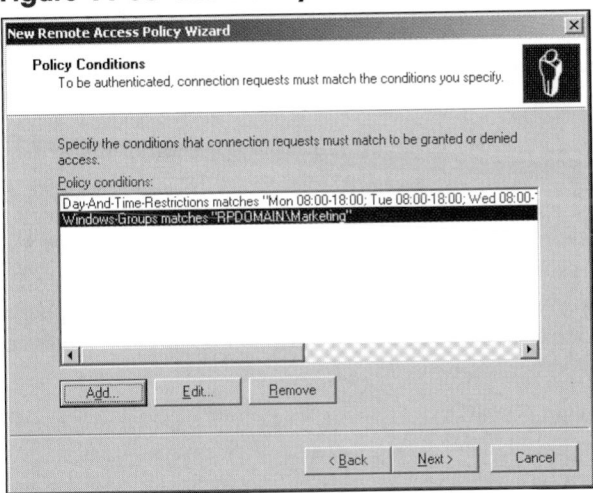

Figure 11-64 The Permissions screen

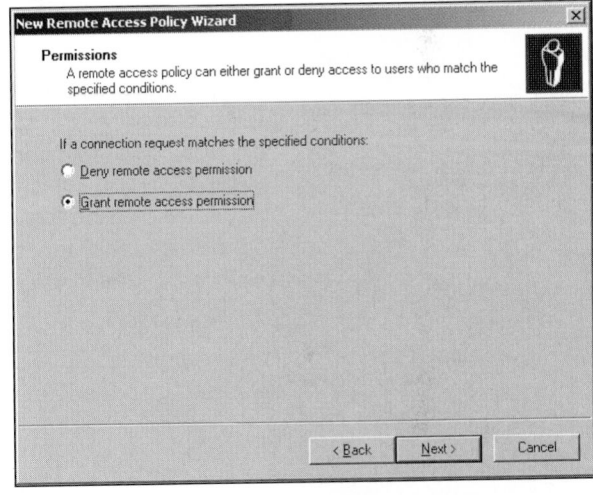

Figure 11-65 The IP tab

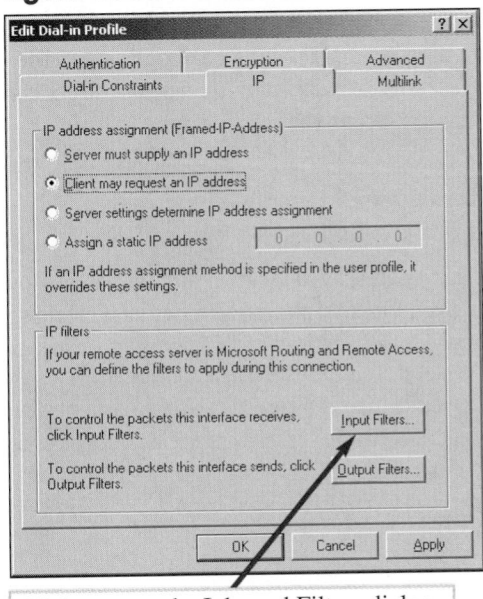

Click to open the Inbound Filters dialog box to deny or permit particular IP packets to be processed by the network

Allows clients to connect using 40-bit encryption key MPPE or IPSec encryption

Allows clients to connect using 56-bit encryption key MPPE or IPSec encryption

Allows clients to connect using 128-bit encryption key MPPE or IPSec encryption

Allows clients to connect without using data encryption

Figure 11-66 The Encryption tab

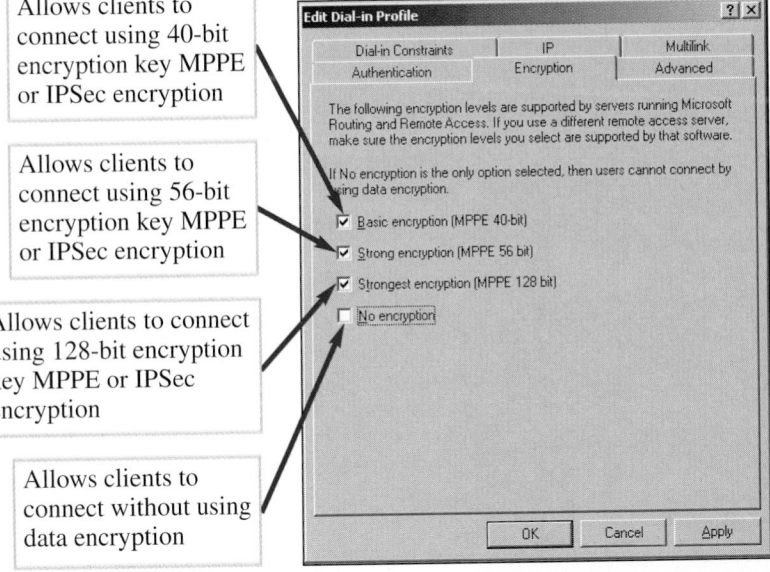

skill 8

Creating a Remote Access Policy
(cont'd)

exam objective

Basic knowledge

more

In RRAS, either the properties of individual user accounts or the RRAS policy is used to set which users can access the RRAS server. Your domain must be in Windows 2000 native mode or Windows Server 2003 mode in order to use RRAS policies to control permissions. The biggest advantage of using RRAS policies to control access is simply ease. Rather than configuring permissions for each individual user account, you can simply use RAS policies to specify permissions for groups of users. Permissions in RAS policies are controlled within the policy itself. The permission location is set at the bottom of the policy Properties dialog box. The settings are simply **Grant remote access permission** or **Deny remote access permission**. If you choose Grant, all users who meet the conditions, have **Control access through remote access policy** set on the Dial-in tab in their user account Properties dialog box, and can accept the settings in the profile, will be allowed access.

User properties are stored in Active Directory and can be viewed in the Active Directory Users and Groups console on a domain controller. The options you can set on the Dial-in tab are described in **Table 11-9**.

Callback options can also be set for each user on the **Dial-in** tab on the Properties dialog box for a user account. If you set a callback number, the server will authenticate the incoming user, disconnect, and call him or her back at the number you specify. This enhances security because, if an unauthorized user calls in, this number will be called back to establish the connection, not the number of the unauthorized user. You can also use callback options to avoid long distance charges for the connection. The bill will be charged to the local phone number where the server is located, rather than to the client who is calling in. There are three callback options that define how a computer responds when a user dials in:

◆ **No callback:** If you select this option, there will be no callback. Once the connection is established, the computer stays connected and allows the user to access resources.

◆ **Set by Caller (Routing and Remote Access Service only):** If you select this option, the server disconnects as soon as a user dials-in and calls them back on the number that they indicate. This setting is useful when users need to dial-in from different locations because they can indicate a different number to call back each time they connect (**Figure 11-67**).

◆ **Always Callback to:** If you select this option, the computer calls back only a specified number. Selecting this option enhances the security of your network because users can establish a connection to the computer using only one number.

If you are in a Windows 2000 mixed mode domain, some of the options on the Dial-in tab will not be available. These include the **Control access through Remote Access Policy**, **Verify Caller ID**, **Assign a Static IP address**, and **Apply Static Routes** options.

In order for client computers to access the RAS server, you must create a dial-up connection on each computer that will be dialing in to the server. On a Windows XP computer, you use the **Connection Manager** (Start-Connect To-Show All Connections). Click the **Create a new connection** link to start the **New Connection Wizard**. On the **Network Connection Type** screen, select **Connect to the network at my workplace**. On the **Network Connection** screen, choose **Dial-up connection**. On the **Connection Name** screen, enter the name of your company. On the **Phone Number to Dial** screen, enter the number for the RAS server. Finally click **Finish** on the **Completing the New Connection Wizard** screen to create the dial-up connection.

Table 11-9 Options on the Dial-in tab in the Properties dialog box for a user account

Option	Description
Allow access	Activates the dial-in feature for a user account.
Deny access	Disables the dial-in feature.
Control access through	Only available in Windows 2000 native mode. Specifies that remote access is controlled by a remote remote access policy access policy.
Verify Caller-ID	Specifies the telephone number that must be used to dial-in to the server.
No Callback	Allows a user to call from any telephone number; however, it does not allow an RAS server to call back the user. This provides a low level of security.
Set by Caller (Routing and Remote Access Service only)	Allows a user to specify a telephone number on which the RAS server will call back the user. This provides a medium level of security.
Always Callback to	Sets the callback telephone number. The RAS server will call back the user only on this number. It provides high security because the telephone number is pre-configured, reducing the risk of an unauthorized person dialing in.
Assign a Static IP Address	Assigns a static TCP/IP address to a user.
Apply Static Routes	Allows you to specify routes to be followed to facilitate a dial-in connection.

Figure 11-67 Dial-in properties for a user account

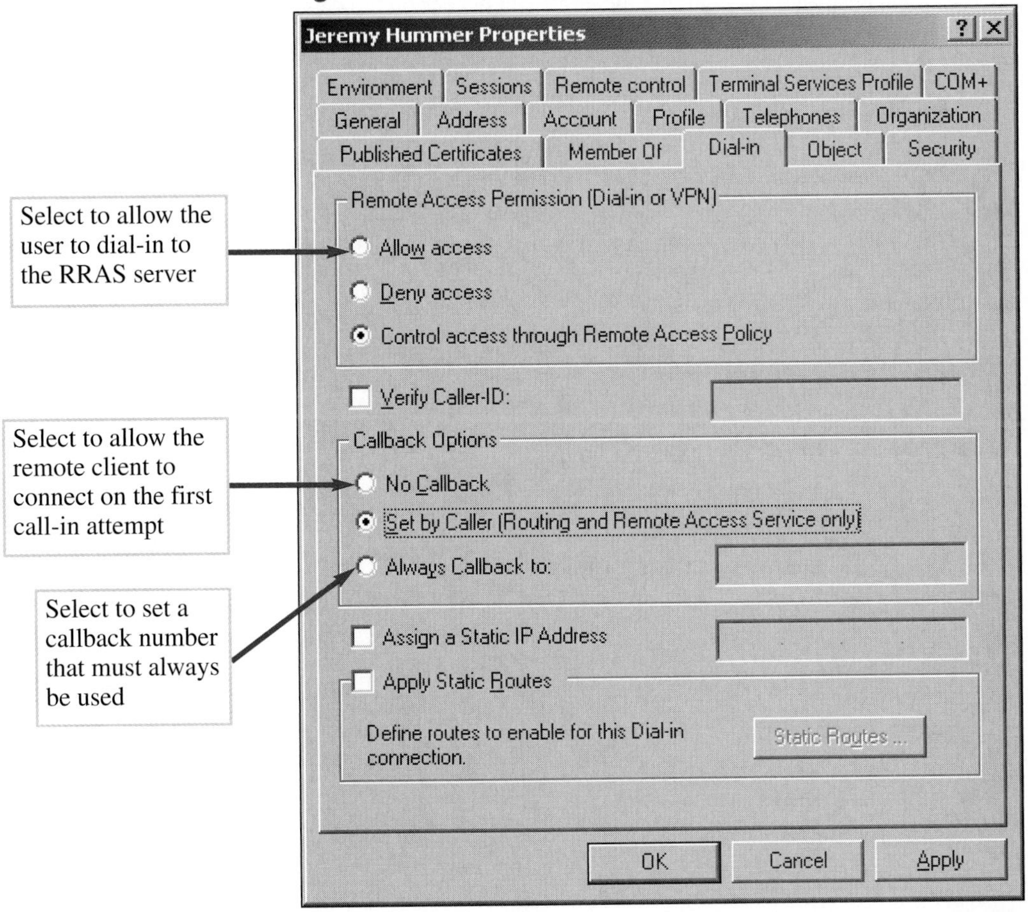

Select to allow the user to dial-in to the RRAS server

Select to allow the remote client to connect on the first call-in attempt

Select to set a callback number that must always be used

skill 9

Creating a VPN Server

exam objective

Basic knowledge

overview

A **virtual private network (VPN)** is a method of using the public telecommunication infrastructure to securely connect two or more subnets. Access is restricted to only certain clients who are authenticated by their user account, subnet, or IP address. You can use a VPN to access resources on a private network remotely through the Internet or through a private network. Most commonly, VPN connections involve a remote client creating a connection to the Internet through a dial-up connection, modem, cable, or digital subscriber line (DSL). Then, tunneling and encryption protocols are used to establish a secure channel through the established infrastructure of the Internet to the LAN. The protocols keep the data flow private even though it is traveling through the public Internet (**Figure 11-68**).

Before VPN technologies were introduced, in order to connect two distant offices, you had to create a wide area network (WAN), which is expensive. Using a VPN, the cost is greatly reduced because you can use the existing infrastructure. Remote users can make a local call to an Internet Service Provider (ISP), connect to the Internet, and then connect to a remote access server running Windows Server 2003. Since the ISP is responsible for managing the modems and communications lines required for dial-up access, organizations do not have to maintain expensive hardware configurations. The VPN connection is secure because the remote access server enforces authentication and encryption protocols so that packets that are intercepted on the shared or public network are indecipherable without the encryption keys.

A VPN encapsulates, authorizes, and routes data by creating tunnels. A **tunnel** is a secure, logical link that is established between a remote user and a private network. Data is encapsulated by including an additional header on the data packets or frames. The additional header provides routing information so that the data packets can reach the destination. The encapsulated packets are transferred through the tunnel endpoints and de-encapsulated upon reaching the destination. This process of encapsulating and transferring packets is known as tunneling.

As you learned in Skill 5, secure connections in VPNs are created using either Point-to-Point Tunneling Protocol (PPTP) or Layer Two Tunneling Protocol (L2TP) with IPSec. Both of these protocols work over dial-up lines, public TCP/IP networks (the Internet), local network links, and WAN links. If you use L2TP, the tunnel is created, but data is not encrypted. L2TP must be used in conjunction with IPSec, which will provide data encryption. When you use L2TP, the message header is compressed, while PPTP does not use header compression. PPTP uses Microsoft Point-to-Point Encryption (MPPE) to furnish encryption.

The Routing and Remote Access service can be used to configure a computer to be a VPN server which can accept both remote access and demand-dial VPN connections from remote access clients. First, the VPN server must have two network interfaces installed, one for a permanent connection to the Internet, and one for the connection to the LAN. After that, configuring a VPN server is very similar to configuring a RAS server. If you have already configured a RAS server, you simply right-click **Ports**, choose **Properties**, select either PPTP or L2TP WAN Mini-ports, and increase the number. If you have not already configured RRAS, then you simply start the Remote Access Server Setup Wizard, as in Skill 7. The only differences are that on the **Remote Access** screen, you will select **VPN** (**Figure 11-69**), and then, on the **VPN Connection** screen, you will select the network interface that connects the server to the Internet (**Figure 11-70**). Next, you will configure how IP addresses will be assigned and whether you will use a RADIUS server to manage multiple RAS servers just as you did when you set up a RAS server. After the VPN server is configured and enabled, you can set its properties just as you did for a RAS server on the General, Security, IP, PPP, and Logging tabs in the Properties dialog box for the server. You can configure multilink capabil-

tip

If you have configured your RAS server only as a router for the local area network (LAN), you will not have a Ports node.

Figure 11-68 Creating a VPN

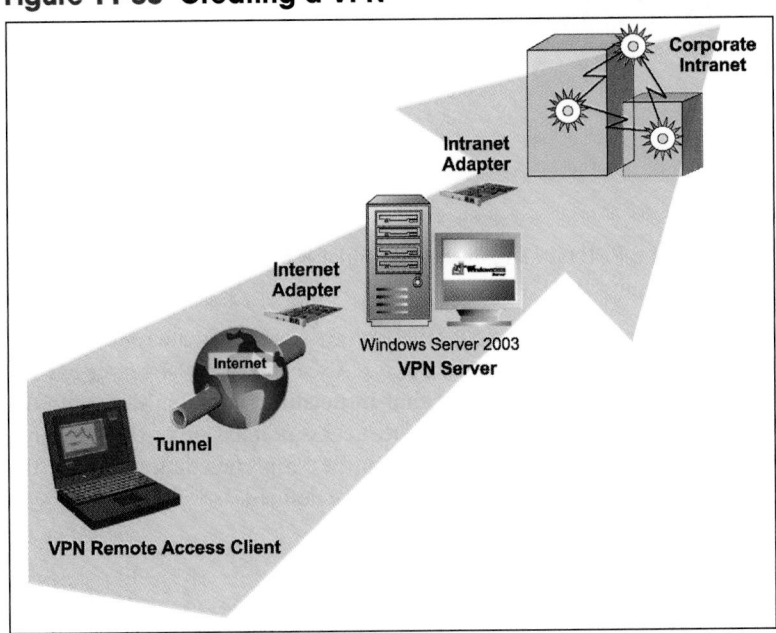

Figure 11-69 Creating a VPN server

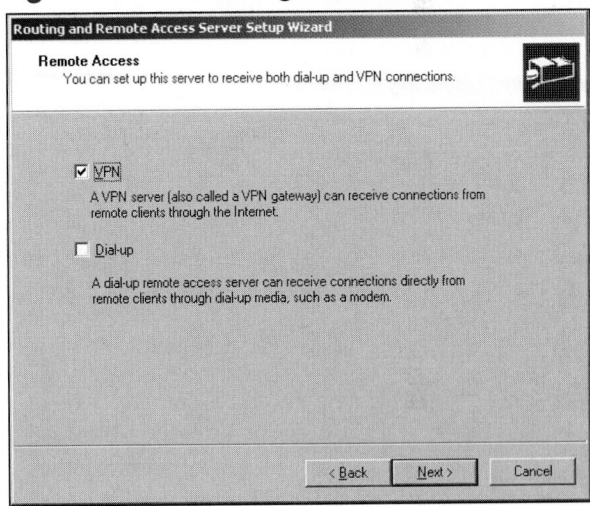

Figure 11-70 Selecting the network interface that connects to the Internet

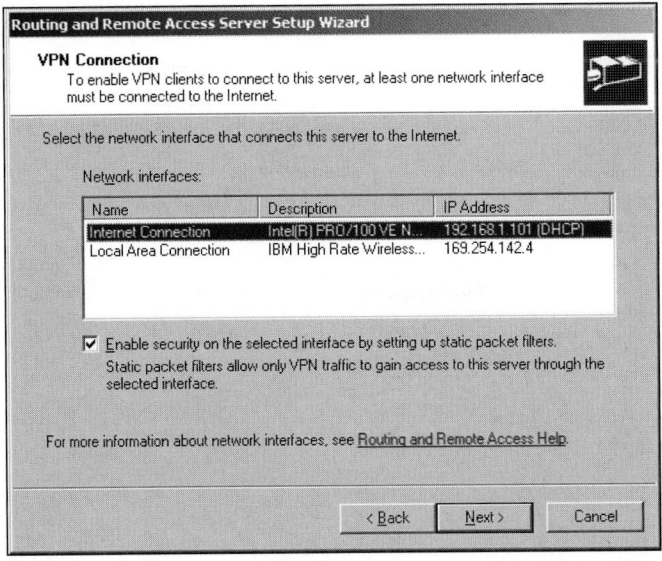

skill 9

Creating a VPN Server (cont'd)

exam objective

Basic knowledge

overview

ities using BAP or BACP on the PPP tab. VPN servers, unlike RAS servers, must be configured as a router on the General tab.

After you have configured the properties for your VPN server, you can create remote access polices and a remote access profile just as you did for a RAS server. A VPN server has the same default remote access policy, **Allow access if dial-in permission is enabled**, with the same configuration as a RAS server. Either **Grant remote access** permission or **Deny remote access** permission must be selected on the Settings tab in the Properties dialog box for the remote access policy to correspond to the conditions you have defined.

more

By default, if configured to support VPN connections, Windows Server 2003 automatically creates 128 PPTP and 128 L2TP ports for incoming VPN connections. Otherwise, it automatically creates only 5 PPTP and 5 L2TP ports. Either way, you can change the number of ports if your VPN server needs to support more clients for either protocol. If you are not going to allow PPTP clients, you can clear the **Allow Remote Access Connections** check box in the Port Properties dialog box, or likewise, if you are not going to accept L2TP connections, you clear the same check box in the L2TP Port Properties. You can also reduce the number of ports to zero, but this only works for L2TP, as Windows Server 2003 must always have at least one PPTP port. To modify the number of ports, right-click the **Ports** node in the **Routing and Remote Access** console and click **Properties** to open the **Ports Properties** dialog box **(Figure 11-71)**. Then, select either **WAN Miniport (PPTP)** or **WAN Miniport (L2TP)**, and click [Configure...] to open the **Configure Device** dialog box **(Figure 11-72)**. Type the required number of ports in the **Maximum ports** spin box.

To configure VPN clients, rather than entering a phone number as you did for RAS clients, you must enter the FQDN or IP address for the VPN server in the New Connection Wizard. This is all you will need to specify for clients that have a dedicated Internet connection. To configure a VPN connection for a client that must first dial-in to an ISP to connect to the Internet, you enter the dial-up connection to be established first before the VPN connection is initiated, as well as the FQDN or IP address for the VPN server. The connection can then be seamlessly instituted in one step.

Figure 11-71 The Ports Properties dialog box

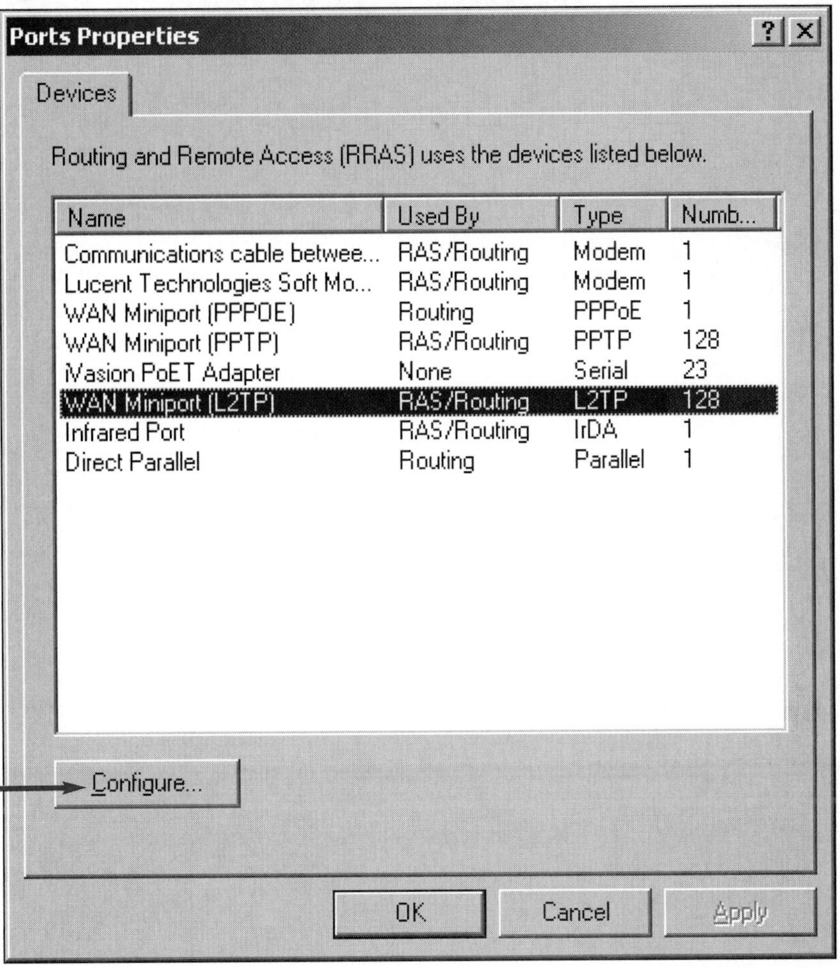

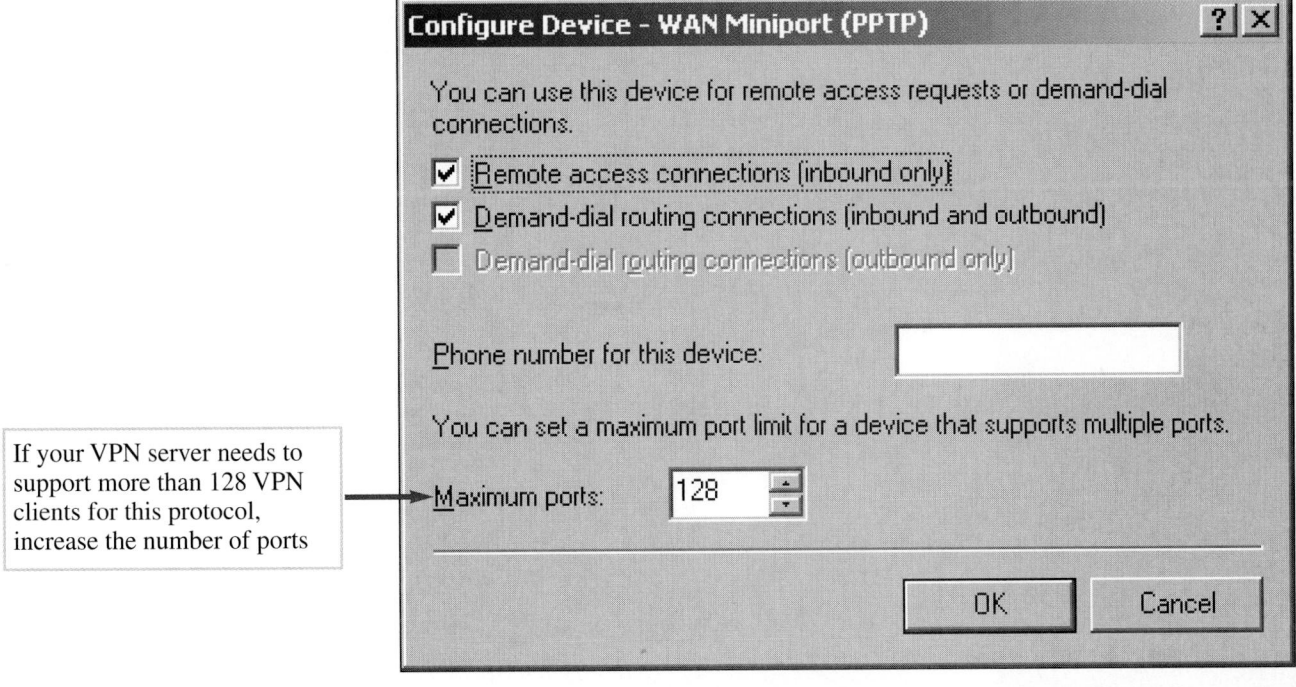

Click to open the
Configure Device
dialog box

Figure 11-72 The Configure Device dialog box

If your VPN server needs to
support more than 128 VPN
clients for this protocol,
increase the number of ports

skill 10

Introducing Internet Connection Sharing (ICS)

exam objective

Basic knowledge

overview

tip

The ICS clients must be configured to obtain their IP addresses automatically.

Using **Internet Connection Sharing (ICS)**, you can share a single point of access to the Internet with other computers on your home or small network. The other computers on the network will use the share to access the Internet. The connection to the internal network is configured so that all of the computers sharing the connection are assigned an IP address from a private address range. The ICS-enabled computer has both a public IP address and a private IP address. The clients sharing the connection request Internet access from the ICS-enabled computer, which accesses the Internet for them and passes the information to them. There are actually two methods you can use to share an Internet connection. You can use ICS, which configures the internal network range of private IP addresses automatically, and doesn't allow for advanced configuration, or you can use NAT, which is described in Skill 11.

ICS is only suitable for small networks because only a certain limited range of private IP addresses can be used and it cannot be extended across subnets **(Figure 11-73)**. To set up ICS on a Windows Server 2003 computer, you need two network connections: one for the LAN and one for the Internet. The local area network (LAN) connects to the computers on your home or small office network. The other connection can use a modem, ISDN, DSL, or cable modem to connect the home or small office network to the Internet. ICS cannot be enabled on a computer on which RRAS has been enabled. To enable ICS, you must first disable RRAS. To do this, right-click the server name in the Routing and Remote Access console and select **Disable Routing and Remote Access (Figure 11-74)**.

Internet Connection Sharing automatically assigns unregistered non-routable private IP addresses to the client computers on the network in the Class C subnet range 192.168.0.2-192.168.0.254. These addresses cannot be changed by the user. The address for the ICS computer will always be the Windows Server 2003 internal address 192.168.0.1 with a subnet mask of 255.255.255.0. A DHCP allocator is included with ICS in order to assign IP addressing to the ICS clients.

Public IP addresses are assigned by a registrar and are unique on the Internet. There are four regional registries:

- ◆ **APNIC** (Asia Pacific Network Information Centre): Asia Pacific region.
- ◆ **ARIN** (American Registry for Internet Numbers): Americas and Southern Africa.
- ◆ **LACNIC** (Regional Latin-American and Caribbean IP address Registry).
- ◆ **RIPE** (Reseaux IP Europeans Network Coordination Center): Europe and surrounding areas.

Routes are already entered into the routers in the Internet to reach the destination public addresses. In contrast, any packets destined for private network addresses will be dropped by routers on the Internet. This is the purpose of Network Address Translation (NAT), a service provided by both ICS and the NAT service in RRAS. NAT translates private IP addresses used on the private LAN into public IP addresses to be used on the Internet.

Figure 11-73 ICS

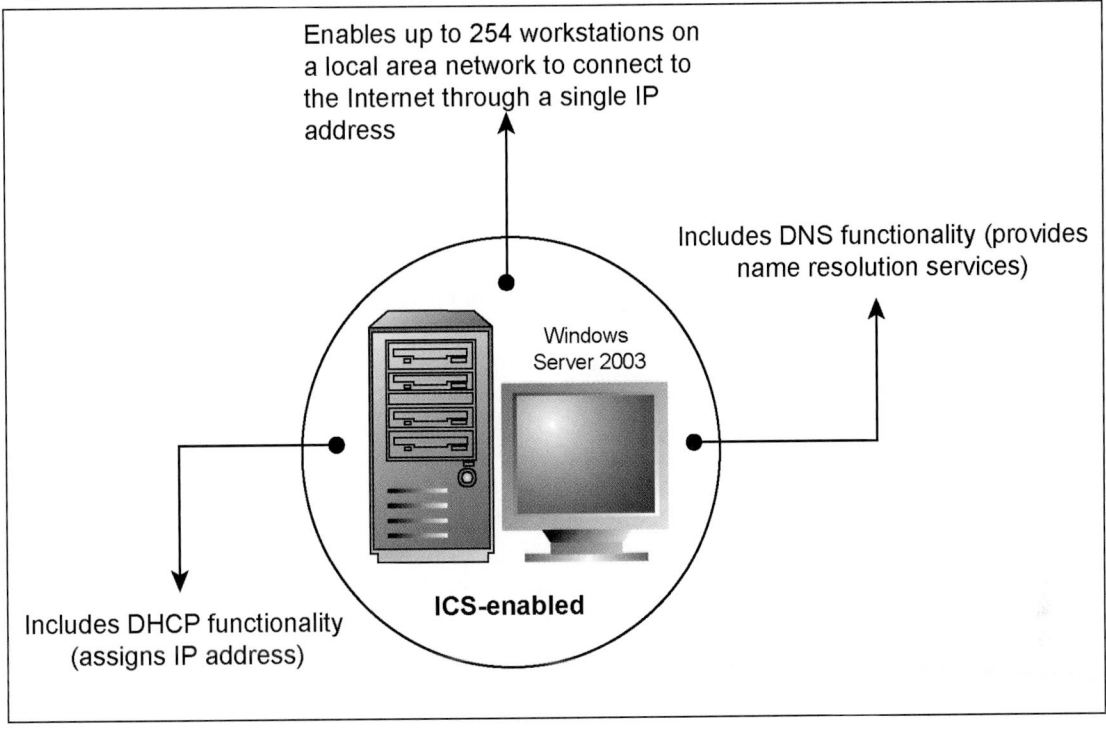

Enables up to 254 workstations on a local area network to connect to the Internet through a single IP address

Includes DNS functionality (provides name resolution services)

Windows Server 2003

Includes DHCP functionality (assigns IP address)

ICS-enabled

Figure 11-74 Disabling RRAS

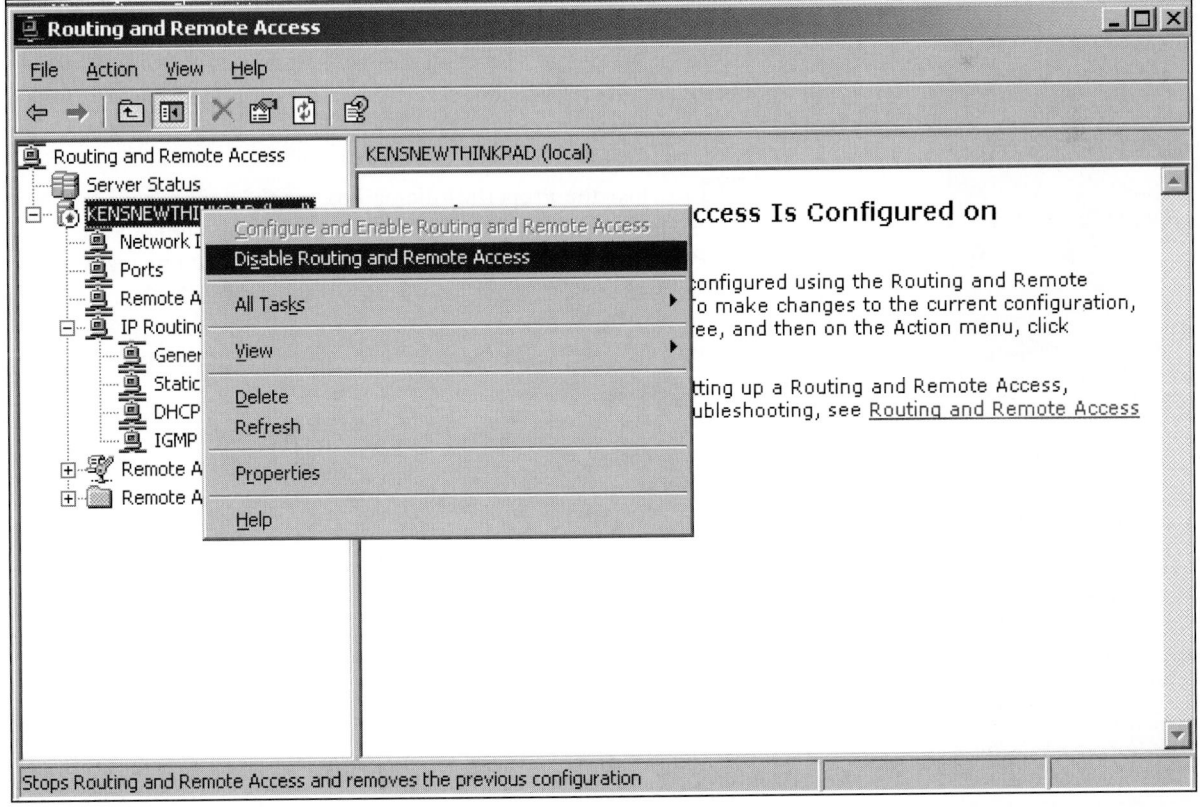

skill 10

Introducing Internet Connection Sharing (ICS) *(cont'd)*

exam objective

Basic knowledge

how to

Enable ICS for a dial-up Internet connection on a Windows Server 2003 computer.

1. Click **Start**, point to **Control Panel**, and double-click **Network Connections** to open the **Network Connections** window.
2. Right-click the dial-up Internet connection you want to share and click **Properties** to open the **Properties** dialog box for the connection.
3. Click the **Advanced** tab. Select the **Allow other network users to connect through this computer's Internet connection** check box to enable ICS.
4. The **Establish a dial-up connection whenever a computer on my network attempts to access the Internet** check box will be activated and selected by default. This will instruct the ICS machine to call the ISP when any computer on the network attempts to access a resource on the Internet and this connection is not currently active **(Figure 11-75)**.
5. The **Network Connections** dialog box may open to remind you to save your user name and password for all users in the **Connect** dialog box so that automatic dialing will be enabled. Otherwise, ICS will only be able to dial the connection when you are logged on. Click **OK**.
6. Click **Settings...** to open the **Advanced Settings** dialog box. On the **Services** tab, you can configure services on the internal network to be accessed from the Internet and you can add your own service **(Figure 11-76)**. For example, to route packets to an **Internet Mail Server (SMTP)** on the internal network, click the **Internal Mail Server (SMTP)** service check box. The **Service Settings** dialog box opens. In the dialog box, the description of the service and the ports are automatically entered. Enter the IP address or the FQDN name of the server to which you are enabling access to complete the configuration **(Figure 11-77)**.
7. Click **OK** to enable Internet access to the internal service (or click **Cancel** if you are not setting up an internal network service) and close the **Services Settings** dialog box.
8. Click **OK** to close the **Advanced Settings** dialog box.
9. Click **OK** to close the Properties dialog box for the connection. The **Network Connections** message box informs you that, with ICS enabled, your LAN adapter will be set to use the IP address 192.168.0.01, and that you may lose connectivity to other computers on your network if they have static IP addresses **(Figure 11-78)**. Click **Yes**.
10. Close the Properties dialog box for the connection and close the Network Connections window.

caution

Be careful not to configure ICS on a production network that contains another DHCP service. Conflicting and/or incompatible IP addresses may be handed out by both services if you do so.

Figure 11-75 Enabling ICS on the Advanced tab

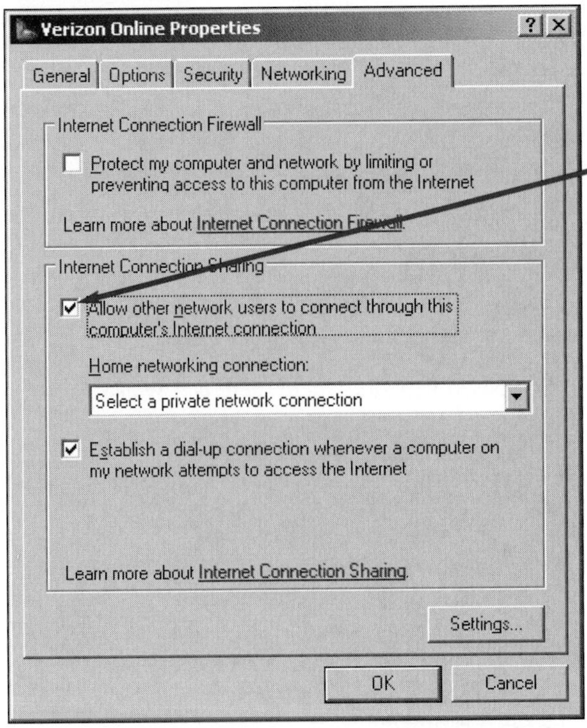

Verizon Online Properties

General | Options | Security | Networking | Advanced

Internet Connection Firewall

☐ Protect my computer and network by limiting or preventing access to this computer from the Internet

Learn more about Internet Connection Firewall.

Internet Connection Sharing

☑ Allow other network users to connect through this computer's Internet connection

Home networking connection:

Select a private network connection ▼

☑ Establish a dial-up connection whenever a computer on my network attempts to access the Internet

Learn more about Internet Connection Sharing.

Settings...

OK | Cancel

> Allows multiple users to connect through a single connection

Figure 11-76 The Advanced Settings dialog box

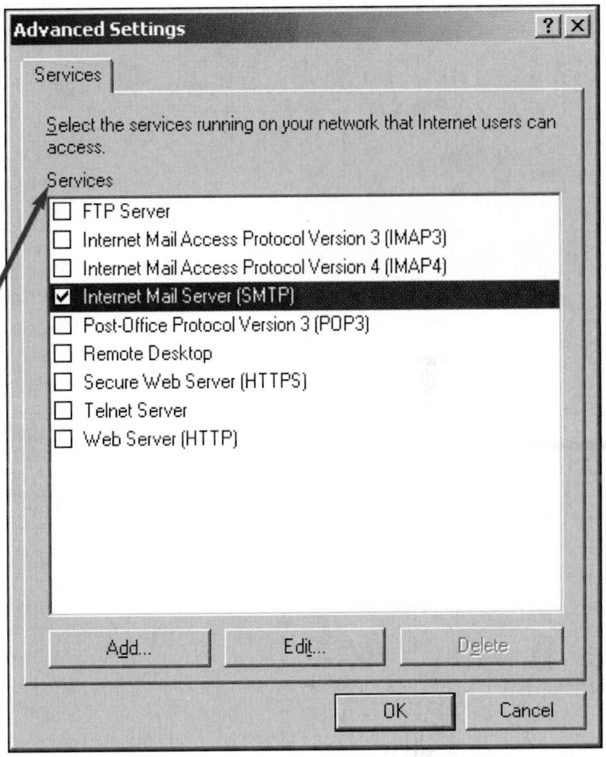

Advanced Settings

Services

Select the services running on your network that Internet users can access.

Services

☐ FTP Server
☐ Internet Mail Access Protocol Version 3 (IMAP3)
☐ Internet Mail Access Protocol Version 4 (IMAP4)
☑ Internet Mail Server (SMTP)
☐ Post-Office Protocol Version 3 (POP3)
☐ Remote Desktop
☐ Secure Web Server (HTTPS)
☐ Telnet Server
☐ Web Server (HTTP)

Add... | Edit... | Delete

OK | Cancel

> Select services configured on the internal network that can be accessed from the Internet

Figure 11-77 The Service Settings dialog box

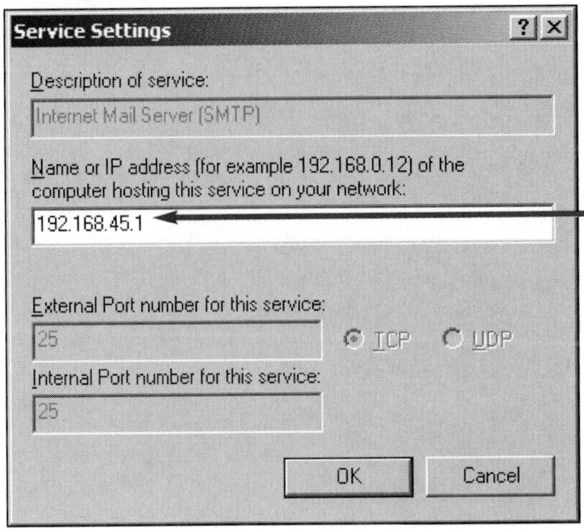

Service Settings

Description of service:

Internet Mail Server (SMTP)

Name or IP address (for example 192.168.0.12) of the computer hosting this service on your network:

192.168.45.1

External Port number for this service:

25   ◉ TCP ○ UDP

Internal Port number for this service:

25

OK | Cancel

> Enter the IP address or FQDN of the server to which you are enabling access

> The address for the ICS computer will always be the Windows internal address 192.168.0.1; unregistered non-routable private IP addresses in the Class C subnet range 192.168.0.2-192.168.0.254 will be assigned to the client computers on the network

Figure 11-78 Network Connections message box

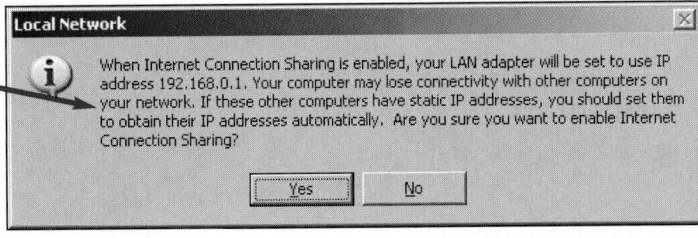

Local Network

ⓘ When Internet Connection Sharing is enabled, your LAN adapter will be set to use IP address 192.168.0.1. Your computer may lose connectivity with other computers on your network. If these other computers have static IP addresses, you should set them to obtain their IP addresses automatically. Are you sure you want to enable Internet Connection Sharing?

Yes | No

skill 10

Introducing Internet Connection Sharing (ICS) *(cont'd)*

Basic knowledge

more

If you are on a LAN, the NIC on the computer on which ICS is configured is assigned a static IP address; thus, any previously established TCP/IP connections will be lost and will have to be reconfigured. The ICS server will assign IP addresses and subnet masks to the other computers on the LAN just like a DHCP server. The default gateway for the other computers on the LAN will be the IP address for the ICS enabled network interface.

ICS is generally not suitable for a domain-based network where there is a WINS server, a DNS server, or any other computer with a static IP address. The WINS and DNS servers will have to work within the ICS range of IP addresses. If there is a DHCP server on the network, the DHCP service should be stopped because it may interfere with the DHCP allocator functionality included with ICS.

The ICS service also includes a DNS Proxy service. This is what enables clients on the network to use ICS to connect to the Internet. Neither the DHCP allocator nor the DNS Proxy service can be configured when you enable ICS. They start when ICS is enabled. You cannot have either DNS or DHCP running on the same computer as ICS because the DHCP allocator and the DNS Proxy services in ICS will bind to the same TCP ports that a DDNS or DHCP server uses and there will be conflicts after ICS is running.

To check to make sure that ICS has been properly configured, you can use the ipconfig command to confirm that the ICS-enabled network interface has been assigned the Windows internal address 192.168.0.1 and a subnet mask of 255.255.255.0. You can also use ipconfig to confirm that ICS clients are being assigned IP addresses in the Class C subnet range 192.168.0.2- 192.168.0.254 with a subnet mask of 255.255.255.0. The default gateway for all ICS clients should be the IP address for the ICS enabled network interface, 192.168.0.1 (**Figure 11-79**).

The other computers on the LAN must be configured to get their IP addresses automatically (in the Internet Protocol (TCP/IP) Properties dialog box). Furthermore, if they have previously established an Internet connection, you will have to open the **Tools** menu in **Internet Explorer** and select the **Internet Options** command to open the Internet Options dialog box. On the **Connections** tab, you will have to select the **Never dial a connection** option button (**Figure 11-80**).

Figure 11-79 ICS

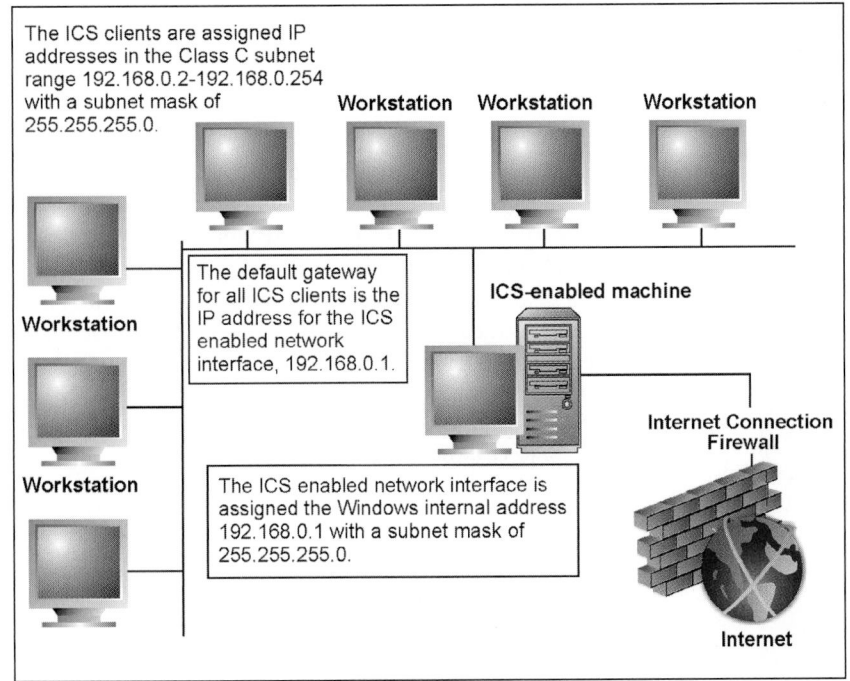

The ICS clients are assigned IP addresses in the Class C subnet range 192.168.0.2-192.168.0.254 with a subnet mask of 255.255.255.0.

Workstation   Workstation   Workstation

Workstation

The default gateway for all ICS clients is the IP address for the ICS enabled network interface, 192.168.0.1.

ICS-enabled machine

Workstation

The ICS enabled network interface is assigned the Windows internal address 192.168.0.1 with a subnet mask of 255.255.255.0.

Internet Connection Firewall

Internet

Figure 11-80 The Internet Options dialog box

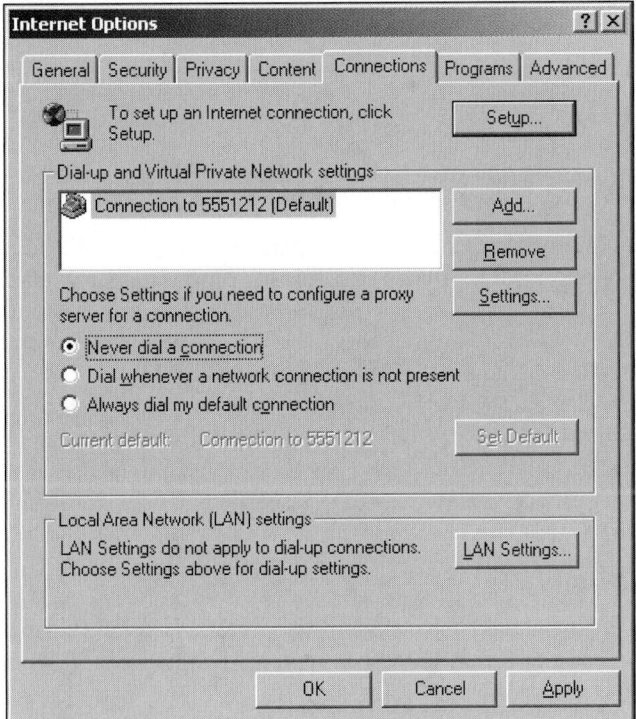

skill 11

Introducing Network Address Translation (NAT)

exam objective

Basic knowledge

overview

Similar to ICS, **Network Address Translation (NAT)** also allows computers on a network to share a single Internet connection, but with greater flexibility. NAT is a service that can translate private IP addresses to public IP addresses and vice versa as they are being forwarded from client computers to a server or from the server to client computers. One of the most significant distinctions between NAT and ICS is that with NAT you can determine your own client IP address range; whereas with ICS, the IP addresses are predetermined within the Class C subnet range 192.168.0.2 - 192.168.0.254, with the server having 192.168.0.1. NAT is extendable for a larger network that has multiple subnets over a routed network. Windows Server 2003 Network Address Translation also includes simple firewall functionality to protect your network **(Figure 11-81)**.

This is how NAT works:

◆ The client sends a data packet to the RRAS server configured with a NAT router.
◆ The server modifies the packet header, replacing the source IP address with the IP address of the router's external surface. The source port number is also changed. A new source port number is randomly generated on the router's external surface. The data packet is then ready to be sent over the Internet to a Web server.
◆ The NAT table stores the original source IP address, the original source port number, and the new source port number. This data is referred to as the translation data.
◆ The Web server that received the data packet sends the reply to the RRAS server addressed to the external interface on the router (destination IP address and port number). When the NAT router receives the reply, the port number is looked up in the NAT table. The IP address of the client is inserted in place of the destination IP address, and the port number for the client is inserted in place of the destination port.
◆ After the RRAS server modifies the packet header and determines the destination, it sends the packet to the client.

NAT translates the private IP addresses in the IP packet headers to a public address in order to supply address translation for the internal network clients. The clients do not need any additional software. The RRAS server acts as a NAT router, which can translate both TCP and UDP ports for the clients. The RRAS server also runs a DHCP allocator to assign IP addressing to NAT clients just as ICS does. The NAT clients are configured as DHCP clients so that the RRAS server can allocate IP addresses and subnet masks to them. Just as with ICS, the IP address for the RRAS server is the default gateway for all of the NAT clients. In addition, the RRAS server can be configured to function as a DNS proxy server for the clients just like ICS. In this case, DNS queries will be forwarded to a DNS server on the Internet and returned to the client through the RRAS server. NAT also now includes a basic firewall to help protect clients from intrusions from the Internet. When you enable the basic firewall, you can configure static, stateless packet filters to designate the kinds of traffic you will allow to both enter and leave the internal network. NAT is installed using the **Routing and Remote Access Server Setup Wizard**. It can also be installed as an extra service on an existing RRAS server.

caution

Before installing NAT, you must make sure that ICS is not enabled on the same computer. You can disable ICS by clearing the Allow other network users to connect through this computer's Internet connection check box on the Advanced tab in the Properties dialog box for the connection.

tip

Even though NAT can function as a simplistic firewall, it is always recommended that you choose a dedicated firewall product with stateful functionality to protect any sensitive data.

how to

Install and configure NAT.

1. First disable ICS if necessary. Click [🏁 start], point to **Administrative Tools**, and select **Routing and Remote Access** to open the **Routing and Remote Access** console.
2. Right-click the server name and select **Configure and Enable Routing and Remote Access** to start the **Routing and Remote Access Server Setup Wizard**.
3. Click [Next >] to open the **Configuration** screen. Select the **Network address translation (NAT)** option button **(Figure 11-82)**.

Figure 11-81 NAT

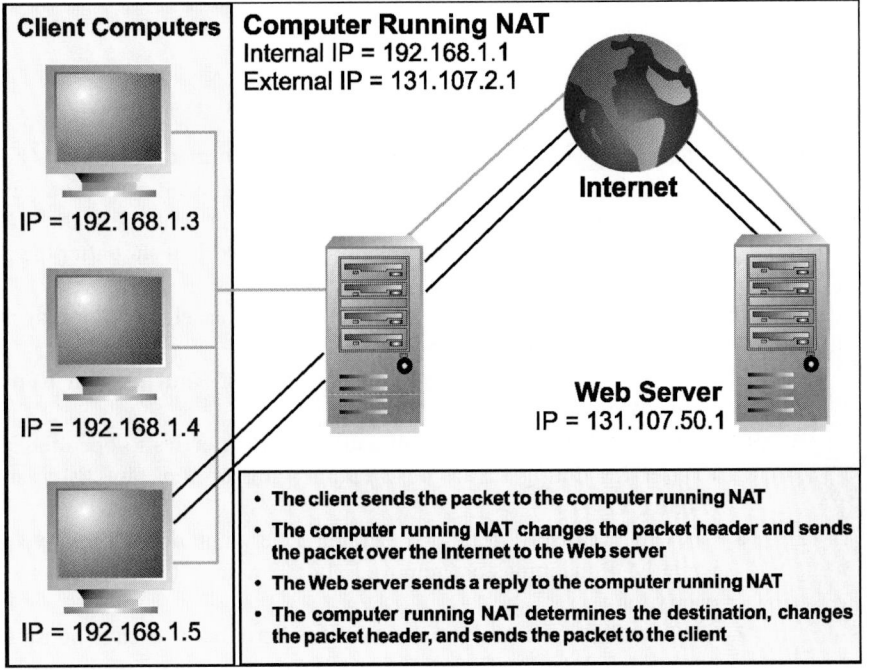

Figure 11-82 Installing NAT

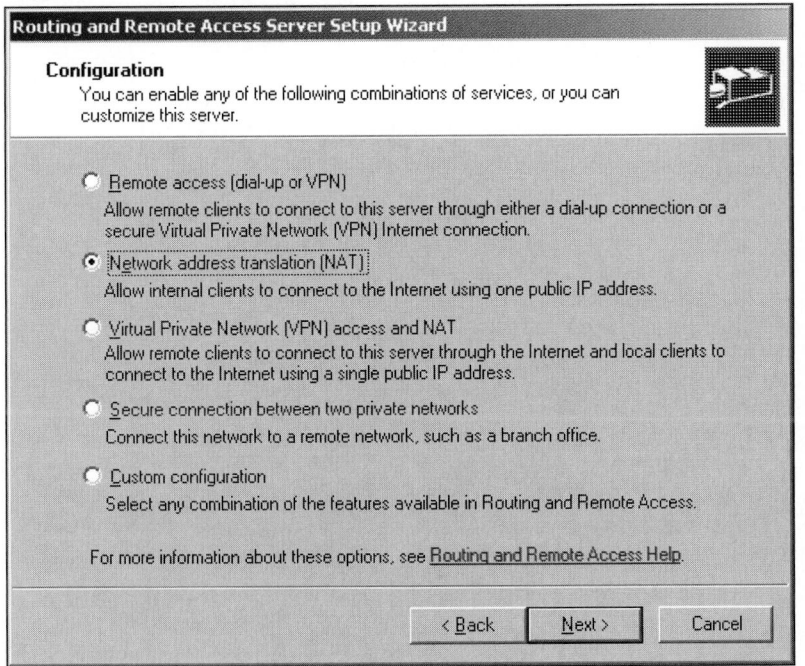

skill 11

Introducing Network Address Translation (NAT) *(cont'd)*

exam objective   Basic knowledge

how to

4. Click [Next >] to open the **NAT Internet Connection** screen (**Figure 11-83**). Select the interface that will be used to connect to the Internet. You can also create a new demand-dial interface to be activated when a client accesses the Internet. If you choose this option, the **Demand-Dial Interface Wizard** will start after the Routing and Remote Access Server Setup Wizard has finished.

5. Notice that by default the **Enable security on the selected interface by setting up Basic Firewall** check box is selected.

6. Click [Next >] to open the **Completing the Routing and Remote Access Server Setup Wizard** screen. Click [Finish].

7. Right-click **Nat/Basic Firewall** and select **Properties** to open the **NAT/Basic Firewall Properties** dialog box. The event logging options are listed on the **General** tab (**Figure 11-84**).

8. Click the **Translation** tab. By default, TCP mappings are removed after 1440 minutes while UDP mappings are removed after 1 minute. For TCP connections, this might be overly long.

9. Click the **Address Assignment** tab. It is here that you can choose to enable the DHCP allocator and configure the range of IP addresses that you want to be assigned to NAT clients (**Figure 11-85**). Select the **Automatically assign IP addresses by using DHCP allocator** check box to automatically assign IP addresses to the client computers on the network using the DHCP allocator included when you install NAT.

10. Click the **Name Resolution** tab. Here you can configure the NAT server to function as a DNS proxy. This is another major difference between ICS and NAT. When ICS is enabled, the DNS proxy is automatically configured and cannot be disabled. When you use NAT, you can choose whether or not to use the DNS proxy. Select the **Client using Domain Name System (DNS)** check box so that DNS queries will be forwarded to the DNS server configured for the router (**Figure 11-86**).

11. Click [OK] to close the NAT/Basic Firewall Properties dialog box.

Figure 11-83 The NAT Internet Connection screen

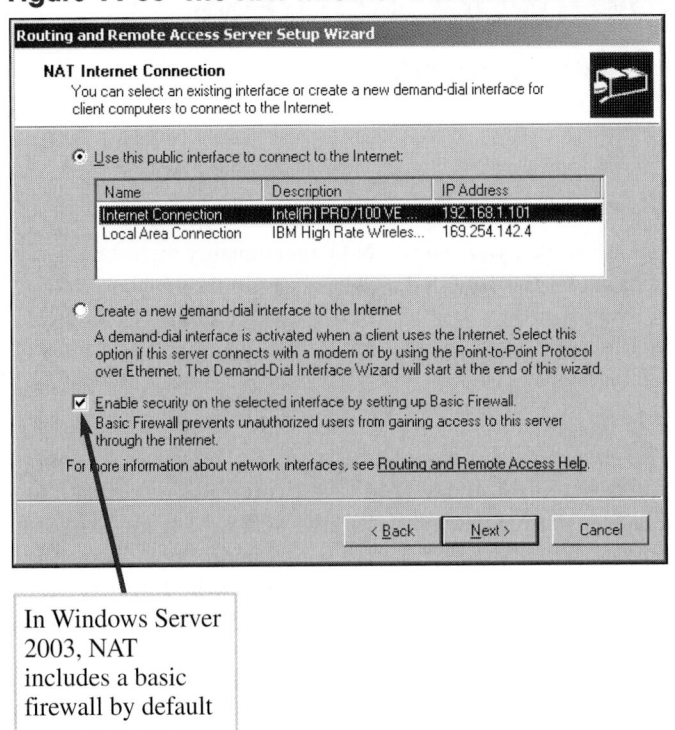

In Windows Server 2003, NAT includes a basic firewall by default

Figure 11-84 The General tab on the NAT/Basic Firewall Properties dialog box

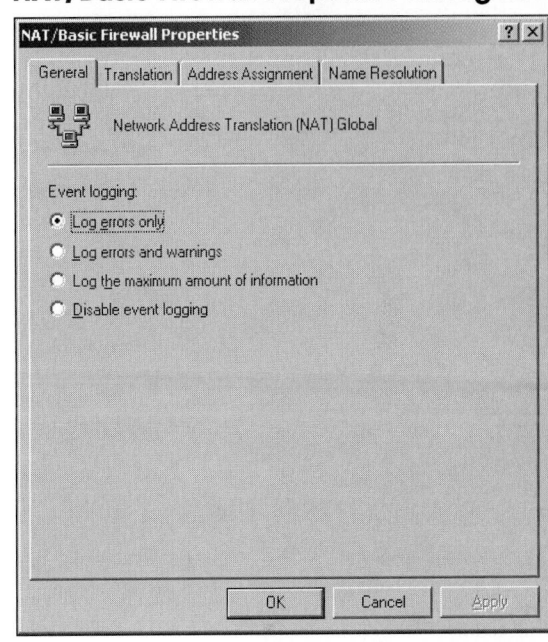

Figure 11-85 The Address Assignment tab

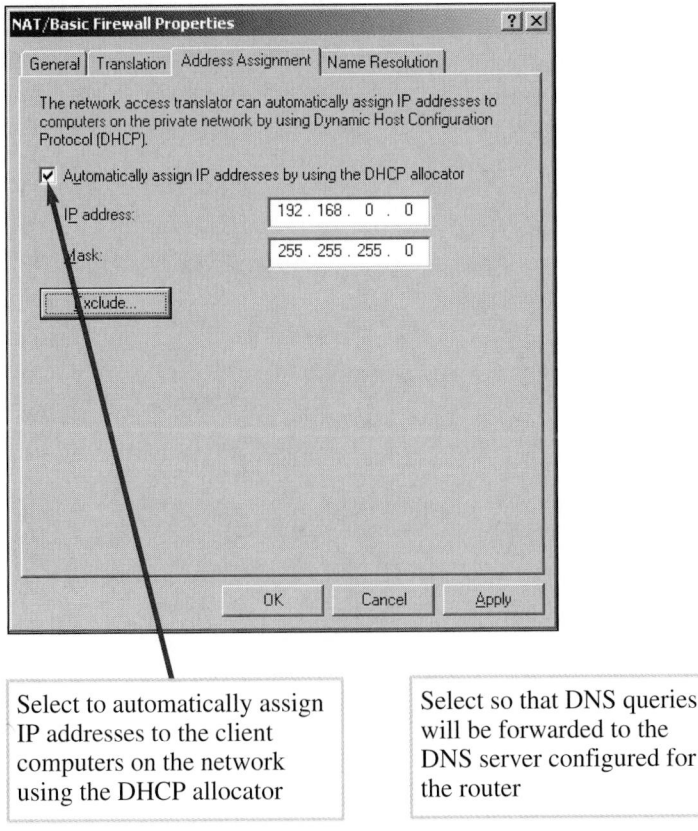

Select to automatically assign IP addresses to the client computers on the network using the DHCP allocator

Select so that DNS queries will be forwarded to the DNS server configured for the router

Figure 11-86 The Name Resolution tab

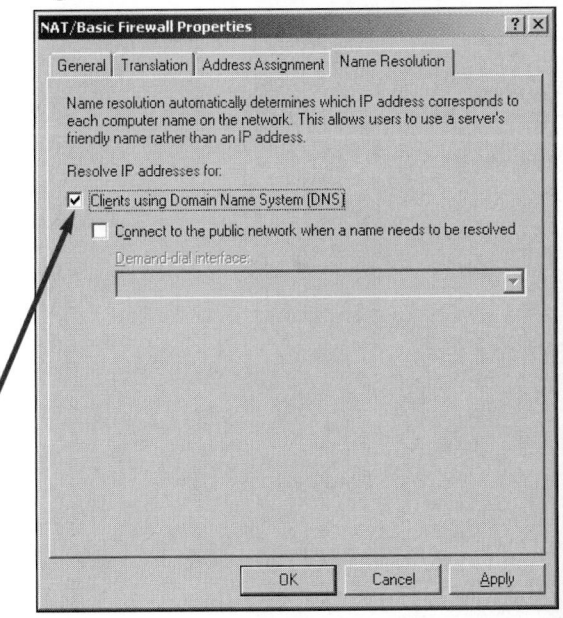

skill 11

Introducing Network Address Translation (NAT) *(cont'd)*

exam objective

Basic knowledge

more

If you have already enabled a RRAS server, you can add NAT functionality by installing and configuring the NAT protocol. In the **IP Routing** node, right-click **General** and select **New Routing Protocol** to open the **New Routing Protocol** dialog box **(Figure 11-87)**. Select **NAT/Basic Firewall** in the **Routing protocols** box and click **OK**. The NAT/Basic Firewall node will be added to the IP Routing node.

Next, you must add interfaces to the protocol to make it functional. This was done for you using the Wizard, although you should still check these to make sure that they have been properly configured. Right-click **NAT/Basic Firewall** and select **New Interface** to open the **New Interface for Network Address Translation** dialog box. Select **Local Area Connection** and click **OK**. The **Network Address Translation Properties — Local Area Connection Properties** dialog box opens. Select the **Public interface connected to the Internet** option button. The IP address of the public interface is the one that will be used as the source address for outbound packets. There must be one public interface and at least one private interface. Next, click the **Enable a basic firewall on this interface** check box. Now you can configure static packet filters **(Figure 11-88)**. You must create one rule to allow outbound traffic to exit and one rule to allow inbound responses to enter. The Wizard also automatically configures the appropriate packet filters for VPN traffic. Additional rules can be added as required.

Click the **Outbound Filters** button to open the **Outbound Filters** dialog box. Click the **New** button to open the **Add IP Filter** dialog box. You create IP filters to control data traffic based on the IP address of the source or the destination, the source or destination port number and the type of data packet. For example, to prevent internal NAT clients from Web browsing, you can create an IP filter that blocks access to external Web servers that use the destination port 80.

Figure 11-87 The New Routing Protocol dialog box

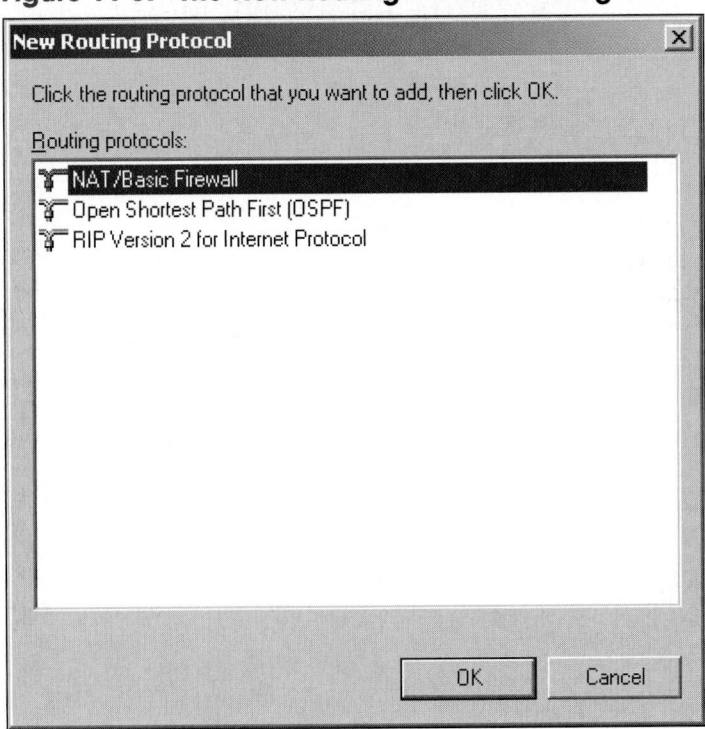

Figure 11-88 The Network Address Translation Properties dialog box

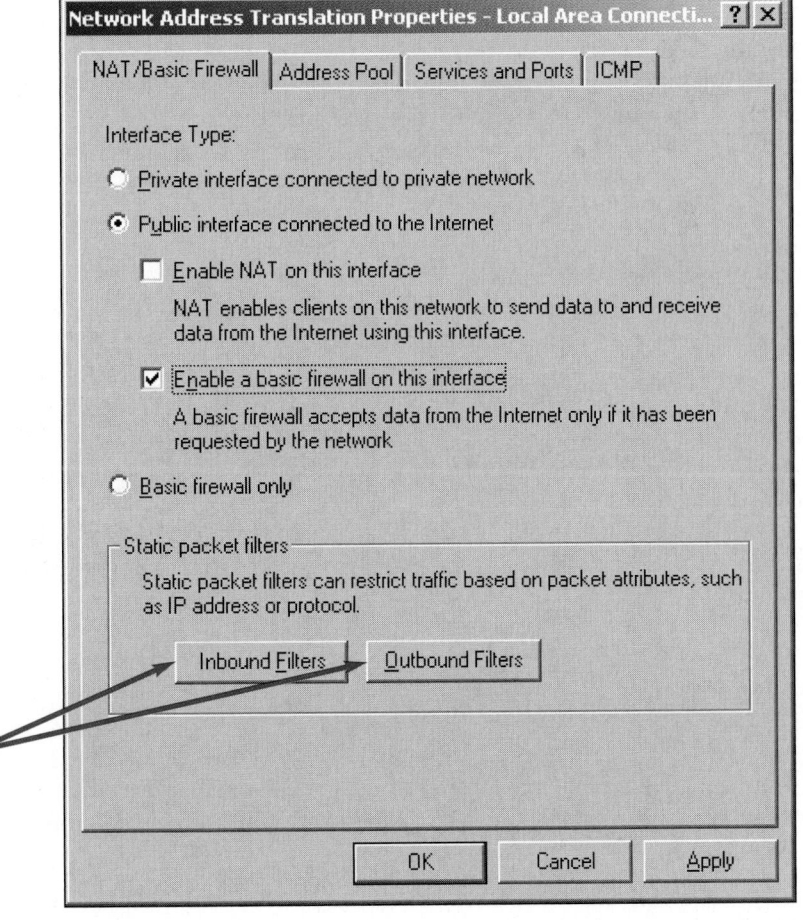

Use to create IP filters to control data traffic based on the IP address of the source or destination, the source or destination port number, and the type of data packet

Summary

- A NetBIOS Name Server (NBNS) is an application responsible for mapping NetBIOS names to IP addresses. Microsoft's implementation of an NBNS is Windows Internet Naming Service (WINS).

- The computer running WINS is referred to as the WINS server. WINS allows clients on a network, which have been configured to use WINS (WINS clients), to dynamically register their NetBIOS name-to-IP address mappings in a database called the WINS database.

- There are four methods used by Microsoft clients to attempt to resolve NetBIOS names: the NetBIOS name cache, WINS, broadcasts, and the LMHOSTS file.

- The basic method of NetBIOS name resolution is broadcast, which sends requests simultaneously to all network hosts. If no WINS server has been configured on the network, or if the client is incorrectly configured, the NetBIOS name of the destination host is broadcast to all other hosts on the network.

- An LMHOSTS file is a text file, usually stored on the local computer in *%systemroot%*\system32\drivers\etc, which contains the static mappings of NetBIOS names to IP addresses for computers on remote networks only. NetBIOS resource mapping for the local network is not required in the LMHOSTS file because the name resolution process for local resources is accomplished via broadcasts.

- The NetBIOS name cache stores information about the most recently resolved NetBIOS names. It is maintained in the WINS client's memory. When resolving a NetBIOS name, the client first refers to the NetBIOS name cache.

- The resolution method used next and the order in which the other methods will be used depend on the NetBIOS node type.

- There are 4 node types: B-node, P-node, M-node, and H-node.

- B-nodes use broadcasts to resolve names. On Microsoft machines B-nodes are referred to as enhanced B-nodes, because if the broadcast is not successful, the client will attempt to use the LMHOSTS file.

- If a machine uses the P-node (Peer-to-Peer) type, it queries a WINS server in order to resolve names. Broadcasts are never used.

- If M-node (Mixed) is used, broadcasts are used first to attempt to resolve names. If this is unsuccessful, the client attempts to query a WINS server. This node type is usually used when the WINS server is located across a WAN link.

- If a machine uses an H-node (Hybrid), the client attempts to query a WINS server first in order to resolve names. If this is unsuccessful, the B-node methods are used (i.e., broadcasts and then the LMHOSTS file).

- If WINS is enabled, Windows 2000, XP Professional, and Windows Server 2003 computers are configured to use H-node by default. If WINS is not enabled, B-node is used by default.

- The WINS replication process is how WINS servers on a network swap information with one another. WINS replication is done through "partnering" with other WINS servers so that all WINS servers are interconnected and replication occurs between them.

- WINS Push Replication occurs when the service starts or when an address in the database changes. The server pushes replication by notifying its partners that changes have occurred. When the partners receive the notification, they can pull the replication data from the WINS server.

- WINS Pull Replication is controlled by setting a schedule for the partners. By default, this is set to occur every 30 minutes.

- Domain Name System (DNS) is the main name resolution service for Windows Server 2003. DNS servers, also referred to as DNS name servers, perform the task of name resolution to convert host names to IP addresses.

- The DNS namespace has a hierarchical structure. The nodes in this hierarchical structure are called domains. As you add more domains to the DNS hierarchy, the name of the parent domain is added to the child domain or sub-domain.

- The domain at the top of the DNS namespace hierarchy is called a root domain. The child domain of the root domain is called a top-level domain, and the child domain of a top-level domain is a second-level domain.

- The root domain is represented by the trailing full stop or period ("."). The top-level domains are the two- and three-character names such as com, net, edu, org, gov, aero, biz, coop, info, museum, pro, etc., and the country codes.

- Second-level domains have two parts: a top-level name and a second-level name; for example, ebay.com.

- The host name is the leftmost part of a FQDN. It designates a particular computer or device either on the Internet or on a private network.

- On a small network, a DNS server may contain just one database file that stores all of the name-to-IP-address resolution data.

- In standard DNS, when multiple DNS servers are created in a standard DNS zone, there are two kinds of DNS database files: primary and secondary. One DNS name server in the zone will store the primary zone database file and the others will store copies of it called secondary zone database files.

◆ In a standard primary zone, modifications and updates can only be made to the primary zone database file. Zone transfers occur to replicate any changes to the primary zone database file to the secondary zone database files.

◆ The purpose of the secondary database file servers is to reduce the traffic and query load on the primary database zone server and to provide redundancy so that if the authoritative server is down, the secondary database file servers can service requests instead.

◆ Caching-only name servers use caching to store information collected during name resolution. They are not authoritative for any zone. They are used when you need to provide DNS services locally, but do not want to create a separate zone for this location. They do not participate in zone transfers.

◆ To reduce network traffic, DNS name servers cache query results. A query result can be cached for a specific amount of time called the Time to Live (TTL), after which it is deleted.

◆ A forward lookup query occurs when a client asks the DNS server to resolve a host name to an IP address.

◆ A reverse lookup query resolves a known IP address to a host name. in-addr.arpa is a second-level domain created for this purpose that contains name-to-IP address mappings indexed by IP addresses.

◆ A recursive query is a type of forward lookup query that is used to request that a DNS name server provides the full and complete answer to the query. It is a request for the answer, not for a referral to another DNS server that may be able to answer the query.

◆ A resolver is a host that can perform a recursive search and can issue iterative queries. A resolver queries other DNS name servers, including the root servers, to look up DNS records on behalf of the client.

◆ An iterative query is performed by a resolver on behalf of the client to assist in answering the recursive query. Iterative queries allow DNS servers to send back pointers or referrals.

◆ The three main types of DNS zones are: standard primary, standard secondary and Active Directory-integrated. The standard primary zone is the first zone to be created and it is authoritative for one or more domains. Standard secondary zones are read-only copies of another zone on the network. Secondary zones are created after the primary zone to provide redundancy for the primary name server. Active Directory-integrated zone data is stored in Active Directory and these zones have all security features of Active Directory, allowing for the secure storage and transfer of zone information.

◆ Routing and Remote Access Service (RRAS) can be configured to create a remote access service (RAS) server that can manage hundreds of concurrent connections or to receive Virtual Private Network (VPN) connections on the internal network. It can also be configured to provide shared Internet access using Network Address Translation (NAT) or to create a secure connection between two servers on the Internet to connect two LANs.

◆ To establish a dial-up connection, either the Point-to-Point Protocol (PPP) or the Serial Line Internet Protocol (SLIP) network protocols are used.

◆ SLIP is an older remote communications protocol that is used by UNIX computers as well as Windows clients. It does not provide security and transfers data without checking for errors. SLIP has, for the most part, been replaced by PPP. It does not support dynamically assigned IP addresses and can only be used on TCP/IP networks.

◆ PPP can support many networking protocols besides TCP/IP (IPX, NetBEUI, etc.). It also supports a variety of authentication protocols including PAP, CHAP, MS-CHAP, EAP, and SPAP.

◆ Password Authentication Protocol (PAP) is the least secure authentication protocol. It uses plain text passwords for authentication.

◆ Challenge Handshake Authentication Protocol (CHAP) sends a challenge message to the client, the client applies an algorithm to the message in order to calculate a hash value (a fixed-length number), and sends the value to the server. The server also calculates a value and compares this value to the value sent by the client. If the value matches, the connection is established.

◆ MS-CHAP is Microsoft's version of CHAP. The challenge message is specifically designed for Windows operating systems and one-way encryption is used. Only the client is authenticated.

◆ MS-CHAP2 authenticates both the client and the server and a different encryption key is used for transmitting data and for receiving data.

◆ Extensible Authentication Protocol (EAP) is used to customize your method of remote access authentication. It supports authentication using either TLS (Transport Layer Security) or MD5-CHAP.

◆ TLS supports smart cards and certificates. Smart cards store user certificates and public/private keys that are used for authentication purposes in conjunction with a PIN number. Certificates are digital signatures that validate users and networks.

◆ MD5-CHAP uses a Message Digest 5 (MD5) algorithm to encrypt user names and passwords.

◆ Shiva Password Authentication Protocol (SPAP) is the authentication protocol used to connect to a Shiva server.

- Windows Server 2003 supports IEEE 802.1X, allowing wireless and Ethernet LAN connections.
- A virtual private network (VPN) creates a secure point-to-point connection across private networks or a public network such as the Internet. A VPN creates a logical link called a tunnel between a remote user and a private network.
- Secure connections in VPNs are created using either Point-to-Point Tunneling Protocol (PPTP) or Layer Two Tunneling Protocol (L2TP) along with IPSec, which provides encryption.
- Bandwidth Allocation Protocol (BAP), often referred to as Multilink PPP, is used with PPP to augment the use of multilinked devices. Multilinked devices are several ISDN lines or modem links combined to obtain greater bandwidth. BAP is used to dynamically add or drop links on demand so that only as much bandwidth as is required for the current network traffic is used.
- Bandwidth Allocation Control Protocol (BACP) is the control protocol for BAP. For the most part, you can think of BAP and BACP as one and the same.
- Remote access policies, along with user properties in some cases, are used to control what connection attempts will be rejected or accepted by an RRAS server. You create them to determine which users can access the network and to prevent unauthorized access.
- There are three components of a remote access policy: conditions, permissions, and a profile.
- Conditions are the criteria a user must meet in order to be granted access. Conditions can depend on group membership, time of day, IP address, and many other criteria.
- Permissions are located on the Dial-in tab in the <user account> Properties dialog box. There are three settings for user account dial-in permissions: Allow, Deny, and Control access through Remote Access Policy.
- If the user account dial-in permissions are set to Control through Remote Access Policy, the permissions configured in the remote access policy are checked. If they are set to Grant remote access permission, the profile is applied. If they are set to Deny remote access permission, the caller is disconnected.
- Regardless of whether the caller is allowed to connect through the user account permissions or through remote access policy permissions, the last thing to apply is the profile.
- The remote access profile is a list of settings that are offered to the client. These settings include allowed dial-in days and times, connection limits, allowed dial-in media and phone numbers, authentication settings, encryption settings, and so forth.
- Administrators can use IP packet filters to set conditions for accepting or rejecting a connection such as the protocols, IP addresses, and ports clients must use.

- There are two kinds of IP packet filters: input and output. You use input filters to filter packets sent to your server and output filters to control packets your server sends to other hosts on the network. Input filters are more commonly used for the RRAS server in order to control the types of connections users can establish.
- Administrators can also specify the type of encryption for the remote access clients: no encryption, basic, strong, or strongest.
- You also create remote access polices and a remote access profile for a VPN server.
- Internet Connection Sharing (ICS) is used to create an Internet connection access point with other computers on a home or small network.
- The ICS-enabled computer has both a public IP address and a private IP address. The clients sharing the connection request Internet access from the ICS-enabled computer, which accesses the Internet for them and passes the information to them.
- To set up ICS, you need two network connections: one for the LAN and one for the Internet. The local area network (LAN) connects to the computers on your home or small office network. The other connection can use a modem, ISDN, DSL, or cable modem to connect the home or small office network to the Internet.
- ICS automatically assigns unregistered non-routable private IP addresses to the client computers on the network in the Class C subnet range 192.168.0.2-192.168.0.254. The address for the ICS computer will always be the Windows Server 2003 internal address 192.168.0.1 with a subnet mask of 255.255.255.0.
- Network Address Translation (NAT) also allows computers on a network to share a single Internet connection, but with greater flexibility. NAT is a service that can translate private IP addresses to public IP addresses and vice versa as they are being forwarded from client computers to a server or from the server to client computers.
- Using NAT, you can determine your own IP address range, making NAT extendable for a larger network that has multiple subnets over a routed network.
- Network Address Translation is also used to create a firewall to protect your network. You can configure static packet filters to designate the kinds of traffic you will allow to both enter and leave the internal network.
- The NAT-configured RRAS server also runs a DHCP allocator to assign IP addressing to clients. The NAT clients are configured as DHCP clients so that the RRAS server can allocate IP addresses and subnet masks to them.
- The IP address for the RRAS server is the default gateway for the NAT clients.
- A NAT-configured RRAS server can also be configured to function as a DNS proxy server for the clients. DNS

Key Terms

Active Directory-integrated zone
Application directory partition
Authoritative server
Bandwidth Allocation Protocol (BAP)
Bandwidth Allocation Control
    Protocol (BACP)
B-node (Broadcast)
Broadcast
Burst handling
Caching-only DNS name server
Challenge Handshake Authentication
    Protocol (CHAP)
Dial-up connection
DNS namespace
DNS server
Domain
Domain directory partition
Domain Name System (DNS)
Extensible Authentication Protocol
    (EAP)
Forward lookup query
Forward lookup zone
Fully qualified domain name (FQDN)
H-node (Hybrid)
Host name
Internet Corporation for Assigned
    Names and Numbers (ICANN)
IEEE 802.1X
In-addr.arpa
Internet Connection Sharing (ICS)
Iterative query
Layer Two Tunneling Protocol (L2TP)

LMHOSTS file
Microsoft CHAP (MS-CHAP)
M-node (Mixed)
MS-CHAP2
Name query request
Name refresh request
Name registration request
Name release message
Name resolution
Name response message
Negative name registration
NetBIOS name cache
NetBIOS Name Server (NBNS)
Network Address Translation (NAT)
Password Authentication Protocol
    (PAP)
Point-to-Point Protocol (PPP)
Point-to-Point Tunneling Protocol
    (PPTP)
Positive name registration response
P-node (Peer-to-Peer)
Primary DNS server (Primary name
    server)
Primary zone database file
Pull replication
Push replication
Remote access server
Remote Authentication Dial-in User
    Service (RADIUS)
Recursive query
Remote access policy
Remote access profile

Resolver
Resource record
Reverse lookup query
Reverse lookup zone
Root domain
Root name server
Root zone
Routing and Remote Access Service
    (RRAS)
Secondary DNS server (Secondary
    name server)
Secondary zone database file
Second-level domain
Shiva Password Authentication
    Protocol (SPAP)
Serial Line Internet Protocol (SLIP)
Standard primary zone
Standard secondary zone
Stub zone
Time to live (TTL)
Tombstoning
Top-level domain
Tunnel
Virtual private network (VPN)
Windows Internet Naming Service
    (WINS)
WINS client
WINS database
WINS server
Zone
Zone database file
Zone transfer

Test Yourself

1. An Active Directory-integrated zone can be:
   a. A Reverse lookup zone
   b. A Forward lookup zone
   c. Both a and b

2. Which DNS server has authority for the top-most domain in the DNS hierarchy?
   a. Primary name server
   b. Secondary name server
   c. Caching-only name server
   d. Root name server

3. When resolving an IP address to its corresponding host name, the client queries the DNS server for a(n)_____ record for that IP address:
   a. SOA
   b. PTR

   c. SRV
   d. NS

4. What protocol does the tunneling protocol L2TP depend on for data encryption?
   a. EAP
   b. PAP
   c. MS-CHAP v2
   d. IPSec

5. What are the advantages of using different namespaces for internal and external resources? (Choose all that apply.)
   a. Added security if the internal namespace is not published externally.
   b. Increased administrative demands for DNS record management.

c. A clear separation between internal and external resources.

d. An additional layer of security because the internal zone is not published to the outside world.

6. In the domain name review.networks.com., which of the following is the root domain?

a. review

b. .com

c. "."

d. networks.com

7. Internet Assigned Numbers Authority (IANA) manages the _____ level of Internet accessible domains

a. root

b. top-level

c. second-level

d. sub-domain

8. The in-addr.arpa domain namespace is used to conduct:

a. Forward lookup queries

b. Reverse lookup queries

9. Which of the following messages is sent by a WINS client to create a NetBIOS name-to-IP address mapping?

a. Name registration response

b. Name refresh response

c. Name query request

d. Name registration request

10. Which of the following would you use to provide an Internet connection to employees on a small network so that they can check their e-mail and access resources from a remote location with just one modem and a phone line?

a. WINS

b. DHCP

c. DNS

d. ICS

11. Which of the following protocols will you use to dynamically add or remove links to an RRAS server? (Choose all that apply.)

a. CHAP

b. BAP

c. PAP

d. BACP

12. Which of the following protocols is used to establish a dial-up connection? (Choose all that apply.)

a. SLIP

b. PPP

c. PPTP

d. L2TP

e. BACP

f. MS-CHAPv2

13. Your network administrator has contacted you about some WINS issues on the network. He also sent you an LMHOSTS file, which he wants you to use until the configuration problems are resolved. Where do you need to store this file on the workstations on the network so that they can be used for NetBIOS name resolution respectively?

a. %systemroot%\system32

b. %systemroot%\system32\drivers\etc

c. %systemroot%\system32\tcpip

d. %systemroot%\system32\dns

14. You can grant remote access to clients at a specific time by:

a. Creating a remote access policy.

b. Setting authentication options for the RRAS server.

c. Setting options while enabling RRAS on a computer.

d. Creating a static address pool containing IP addresses of specific clients.

15. When using the CHAP authentication protocol, when is the user's password transmitted across the network?

a. During both challenge and response

b. During the response

c. Never

d. During the challenge

Projects: On Your Own

1. Create a remote access policy and profile

a. Open the **Routing and Remote Access** console.

b. Make sure that you can view all of the nodes in the console tree. Double-click to open the nodes as necessary.

c. Right-click **Remote Access Policies** and click **New Remote Access Policy**.

d. Click **Next** and type **Domain RAS policy** in the Policy name text box.

e. Select the **Set up a custom policy** option button.

f. Click **Next**. Click **Add** to open the **Select Attribute** dialog box.

g. Double-click **Authentication Type**.

h. Select **MS-CHAP v1**. It is compatible with most versions of Windows. Click **Add**.

i. Add **MS-CHAP v2** and **EAP** to the **Selected types** box as well and click **OK**.

j. Click **Add** in the Policy Conditions dialog box.

k. Double-click **Day and Time Restrictions**. Allow domain users to access the RAS server from Monday thru Friday from 10 AM to 6 PM. Click OK.

l. Click **Add** in the Policy Conditions dialog box.

m. Double-click **Framed Protocol**.

n. Double-click **PPP** in the **Available types** list box. Click OK.

o. Click **Next** and select the **Grant remote access permission** option button.
p. Click **Next** and click the **Edit Profile** button.
q. Check the **Authentication** tab to make sure that MS-CHAP and MS-CHAP v2 are selected.
r. Open the **Encryption** tab. Use only Strong encryption (MPPE 56-bit) Click **OK**.
s. Click **Next**, and then **Finish**.
t. Close the Routing and Remote Access console.

2. Configure a Dial-up connection
   a. Click **Start**, point to **Control Panel**, point to **Network Connections**, and select **New Connection Wizard**.
   b. Click **Next** and select the **Connect to the network at my workplace** option button.
   c. Click **Next** and select the **Dial-up connection** option button.
   d. Click **Next** and select the dial-up device you will use if you have more than one dial-up device on your computer.
   e. Click **Next** and enter your company name in the text box.
   f. Click **Next** and enter the telephone number of the RAS server to which you connect.
   g. Click **Next** and select the **Anyone's use** option button so that other users can use this connection.
   h. Click **Next**, and then **Finish**.
   i. Close the Connect dialog box.

3. Create a reverse lookup zone on a domain controller.
   a. Open the **dnsmgmt** console.
   b. Expand the nodes in the console tree if necessary.
   c. Right-click **Reverse Lookup Zones** and select **New Zone** to start the **New Zone Wizard**.
   d. Click **Next** and select the **Primary zone** option button, if necessary.
   e. Select the **Store the zone in Active Directory (available only if DNS server is a domain controller)** check box.

f. Click **Next** and select the **To all domain controllers in the Active Directory domain <*domain_name.com*>** option button, if necessary.
g. Click **Next** and enter the network ID for the reverse lookup zone. This is the first two or three octets depending on the subnet mask in use. If your network ID is 128.45, the in-addr.arpa reverse lookup zone will be 45.128.in-addr.arpa.
h. Click **Next** and select the **Allow only secure dynamic updates (recommended for Active Directory)** option button, if necessary.
i. Click **Next**, make sure everything is configured correctly, and click **Finish**.

4. Create a DNS Host A Address Resource Record.
   a. Open the **dnsmgmt** console, if necessary.
   b. Expand the **Forward Lookup Zones** node, if necessary.
   c. Select the domain name.
   d. Open the **Action** menu and select **New Host (A)**.
   e. Type the name of a host computer in the domain in the **Name** text box.
   f. Notice that the FQDN is automatically entered in the **Fully qualified domain name (FQDN)** label.
   g. Enter the IP address for the host computer in the **IP address** text box.
   h. Select the **Create associated pointer (PTR)** record check box.
   i. Select the **Allow any authenticated user to update DNS records with the same owner name** check box. Windows 2000, XP, and Server 2003 machines will all be able to update along with DHCP. This is a secure method because an ACL will be linked with the Host A record.
   j. Click **Add Host**.
   k. Click **OK** to confirm that the host record was successfully created.
   l. Click **Done** and close the dnsmgt console.

Problem Solving Scenarios

1. Employees in the Sales and Marketing division of your company connect to the company's LAN remotely through dial-up access. The company has issued smart cards to these users, which will be used to authenticate them when they attempt to connect to the company's LAN. As the administrator of the network, you have been asked to configure the Windows Server 2003 network and provide dial-up access to these users. You must also set up the authentication mechanism. List the steps you will take to configure your Remote Access Server for this capability.

2. Your company, Info Aggregators Inc., has a small network of seven users. To access the Internet, the company has subscribed to a local cable service. You want to implement Internet Connection Sharing so that all of the computers on the network can share the same connection. Explain the steps you would take to configure the Internet connection on one of the computers, and to set up ICS on your network.

3. Your CEO has asked you to prepare a report for him on the feasibility of setting up a VPN server for your network. He is particularly interested in allowing upper-level managers who travel frequently to access the corporate LAN over the Internet. Prepare a report that outlines the steps that would have to be followed to set up a VPN server. Also include the steps that would need to be taken on the client laptop computers of the executives to configure them as VPN clients.

Implementing Security in Windows Server 2003

The security of data is a major area of concern on any network. An unauthorized intruder can change data, delete data, or add malicious content. Windows Server 2003 provides native support for the Public Key Infrastructure (PKI) and a set of security tools that you can use to combat threats from unauthorized users. PKI supports and augments the basic security functions of network authentication and encryption. Microsoft Certificate Services enables an organization to use digital certificates by providing a Certification Authority (CA). A CA issues and revokes certificates. CAs can either be internal, making use of Certificate Services, or they can be outside companies—such as VeriSign, Entrust, and Equifax—that sell certificates to companies and organizations.

IPSec is used for both internal and external security. It can be used for authentication purposes, for encryption, for simple packet filtering in data transmission, and for tunneling. It was developed by the Internet Engineering Task Force (IETF) and is used to allow computers exchanging data to verify each other's identity before data is sent. IPSec operates at the Network layer, making it application independent. As you learned in Lesson 11, it is also widely used in conjunction with L2TP (Layer 2 Tunneling Protocol) to encrypt VPN tunnels.

The Kerberos protocol is used to enable a server to carry out user authentication. Kerberos issues a ticket, which contains information about the user, when authentication is requested. This ticket, known as a user ticket or TGT, is then presented to the Key Distribution Center whenever access to a particular resource is necessary. The TGT allows the user to receive a session ticket for the particular resource. A user who has a session ticket can then access a server or a service on a network that trusts the Kerberos service for authentication.

Account policy consists of Account Lockout, Password, and Kerberos policies, which are used to control the logon process. Account lockout policy designates the number of invalid logon attempts that will be allowed, the time duration for the account lockout, and the amount of time that must pass after an invalid logon attempt before the bad logon attempt counter is reset to 0. Password policy is used to specify how users must manage their passwords, for example, when a password must be changed. Kerberos policies are applied on a domain controller to designate logon ticket lifetimes and logon restriction enforcement.

Account lockout troubleshooting in Windows Server 2003 is accomplished using a group of tools called the Account Lockout package (ALTools.exe) that can be downloaded from Microsoft. These tools include AcctInfo.dll, which adds a new property page to user objects in the Active Directory Users and Computers console. The new property page can be used to locate and troubleshoot account lockouts. Another tool, LockoutStatus.exe, displays information about a locked out account that it has obtained from Active Directory. ALockout.dll helps administrators to determine what program or process is sending incorrect credentials, and ALoInfo.exe is used to find out which users' passwords are about to expire.

The Security Template and Security Analysis and Configuration tools can be used to configure and manage security settings. You can use a security template to apply a group of security settings all at once. You apply a security template to a Group Policy object so that all of the settings are put into operation on a site, a domain, or an OU (organizational unit). A security template can include account policies and local security policies, as well as group membership information and access controls.

Goals

In this lesson, you will learn about the various security services provided by Windows Server 2003. You will be introduced to Certificates Services and Kerberos authentication. You will also learn how to configure account policy, how to diagnose and troubleshoot account lockouts, and how to configure Security Options and User Rights Assignments. Finally, you will learn how to use Administrative Templates to implement client-side security and how to configure and analyze the security settings on a system.

Lesson 12   Implementing Security in Windows Server 2003

Skill	Exam 70-290 Objective
1. Introducing Public Key Infrastructure	Basic knowledge
2. Identifying the Features of Public Key Cryptography	Basic knowledge
3. Working with IPSec	Basic knowledge
4. Introducing Certification Authorities	Basic knowledge
5. Authenticating User Identity Using Kerberos Protocol	Basic knowledge
6. Implementing Account Policy	Basic knowledge
7. Diagnosing and Resolving Account Lockouts	Diagnose and resolve account lockouts.
8. Implementing Security Options	Basic knowledge
9. Configuring User Rights Assignments	Basic knowledge
10. Configuring Client Security	Basic knowledge
11. Working with Security Tools and Templates	Implement, configure, manage and troubleshoot security by using the configuration tool set.

Requirements

To complete this lesson, you will need administrative rights on a Windows Server 2003 member server on a domain network and access to Active Directory, as well as access to a Windows Server 2003 domain controller. You will also need a Windows Server 2003 installation CD.

skill 1

Introducing Public Key Infrastructure

exam objective

Basic knowledge

overview

The Public Key Infrastructure (PKI) enables users of unsecured networks to securely exchange data. It supports and enhances authentication and encryption.

Windows Server 2003 supports a variety of PKI-based security technologies that can help you to enhance the security of your network. The fundamental security concepts you will have to understand are: private and public key cryptography, certificates, Certification Authorities, Encrypting File System (EFS) and the related security service, IPSec.

Table 12-1 lists additional security technologies offered by PKI that can be used to make your network secure and reliable.

Digital encryption scrambles messages so that they are unreadable should a recipient, other than the one intended, intercept it. Usually, a session key is used to encrypt and decrypt the data. The session key must be secured so that unauthorized users cannot obtain it. In **symmetric key** (also known as **single key** or **secret key**) **encryption**, both the sender and the recipient must share the same session key. This presents a dilemma in that in order to communicate securely, the two parties must somehow exchange the key. Sending it over the network is obviously not safe because the e-mail message could be intercepted. One solution to this problem has been **public key cryptography** (also known as asymmetric key cryptography), which uses a key pair called a public key and a private key. The keys in the pair are mathematical opposites so that messages encrypted with the public key can only be decrypted by the corresponding private key and vice versa. However, they are so complex that it is very difficult to determine the formula for one key from analyzing the other. The **public key** is widely disseminated, while the **private key** is only issued to an authorized user and must be kept secure **(Figure 12-1)**. Authentication methods can include a public key cryptography component so that one user can send a message to another user that has been signed with a digital signature. A **digital signature** is a way of validating that the message actually came from the user who claims to have sent it, and also ensures that the message has not been tampered with in any way.

Digital signatures, which are also used in e-commerce transactions, are created by applying a one-way hashing algorithm. One-way hashing algorithms transform data in such a way that the resulting data is unique and cannot be converted back to its original form. The hashing algorithm is applied to the message to reduce it to a fixed length, which is called the **message digest**. The digital signature is created by encrypting the message digest using the user's private key. By encrypting the message with the sending user's private key, you allow anyone who has that user's public key (which could be everyone) to decrypt the message, so this doesn't provide true encryption. However, since the only person who could have encrypted the message with the private key is that one specific user, by decrypting the message with that user's public key, you have verified the identity of the sender. If a message is intercepted and modified, the digital signature becomes corrupt and the receiver will be alerted that the message may have been altered during transmission **(Figure 12-2)**.

Certificates are used for a number of things including authenticating servers to clients in e-commerce, authenticating clients to servers in some remote access situations, signing software to prove that it has been certified by a particular developer, encrypting or digitally signing e-mail, and encrypting IP network traffic between IPSec clients and servers. A **certificate** is a digitally signed document that functions as a component of PKI. The certificate contains the name of the subject, which can be a directory name, e-mail name, and/or a DNS name, validation information (such as valid to and valid from dates), and a public key. The **Certification Authority (CA)** signs the certificate to confirm that the private key that is linked to the public key in the certificate is owned by the subject named in the certificate. The CA acts as the center of trust—i.e., if you trust the CA, you automatically trust all certificates issued by the CA.

EFS (Encrypting File System) uses certificate/key pairs to encrypt files on NTFS volumes and partitions. To fully understand EFS, you must understand the benefits and drawbacks associated with symmetric key and asymmetric key encryption.

Table 12-1 PKI Services

Service	Description
Smart card	A credit card-sized device that stores an encrypted copy of the public and private key values of the user certificate. The user has to insert the card into a supported smart-card reader, and then log on to the computer by supplying his or her PIN. The PIN provides the seed required to decrypt the user's certificate. The certificate, which is mapped to the user account in Active Directory, is then used by Windows as the authentication entity.
Authenticode digital signature	Verifies the authenticity and integrity of software downloaded from the network. It verifies that software is being downloaded from a valid host. Windows Internet Explorer makes use of this service.
Secure Socket Layer (SSL)	HTTP uses SSL3.0 to transfer data through a secure route by ensuring the authentication, integrity, and confidentiality of data. Windows Server 2003 implements SSL and TSL through the SChannel authentication package.
Transport Layer Security (TSL)	The TSL or TLS protocol is composed of two layers: the TLS Handshake protocol and the TLS Record protocol. It must be used in conjunction with a connection-based transport protocol, such as TCP, which is the norm. It enables client/server applications to recognize message interference, interception, and falsification. The TLS Handshake protocol establishes or resumes a secure session. The server must validate its identity to the client, and sometimes the client must also prove its identity to the server. It uses a PKI-based authentication, which is decided upon by negotiating a cipher suite. The keys that are created during the Handshake are used by the TLS Record protocol to secure application data and validate its integrity and origin. The TLS Record protocol divides outgoing messages into blocks and reconstructs them upon arrival, encrypts outgoing messages and decrypts incoming ones, and can also optionally compress outgoing blocks and decompress incoming blocks. It also adds a message authentication code (MAC) to outgoing messages and uses the MAC to authenticate incoming ones. Finally the TLS Record protocol sends data to the TCP layer to be transmitted after it has completed its functions.

Figure 12-1 Public key cryptography

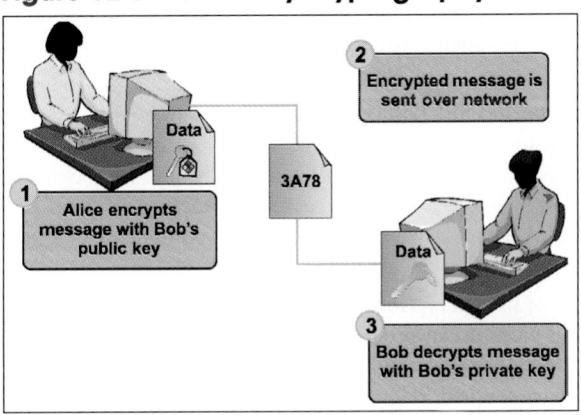

Figure 12-2 Digital signatures

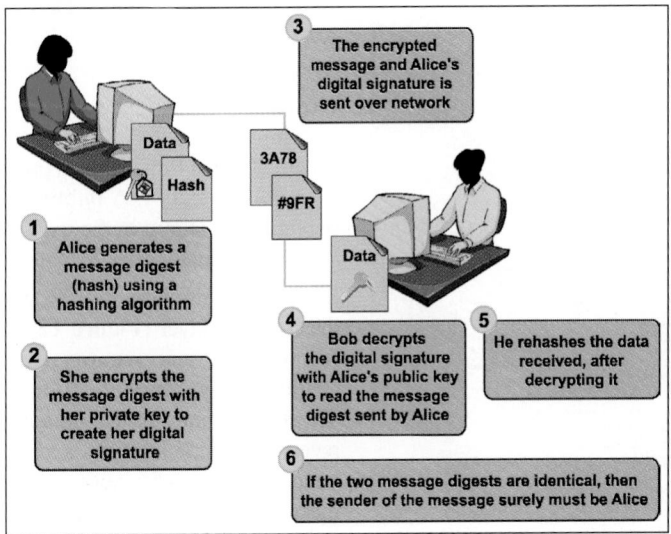

skill 1

Introducing Public Key Infrastructure (cont'd)

exam objective

Basic knowledge

overview

The disadvantage of symmetric key encryption is quite simply that it isn't very secure. The same key is used for both encryption and decryption, making it semi-public. For example, if Bob uses a symmetric key to encrypt an e-mail sent to Mary, then he must give Mary that key in order for her to decrypt the file. However, now that Mary has the key, she can also decrypt anything that Bob has encrypted with that key, including things Bob might have sent to other users. This leads to a dilemma of trust; as Benjamin Franklin so eloquently put it, "Three may keep a secret, if two of them are dead."

The advantage of symmetric key encryption, however, is that the formulas involved are very simple, making encryption using a single key relatively quick. This also helps conserve the processor resources used in processing the encryption. Asymmetric key encryption, on the other hand, has one major advantage: It is highly secure. However, due to its complexity, it is slow and processor intensive. For this reason, many modern encryption techniques, including EFS, work off of a rather elegant technique which combines the best of both types of encryption.

In EFS, files are encrypted using a **file encryption key (FEK)**, which is a randomly generated symmetric key. Since it is randomly generated, it will never be used again, thus nearly eliminating the possibility of the key becoming public. Windows then makes two copies of the FEK, and encrypts each copy. One copy is encrypted using the public key of the user who encrypted the document. This copy is placed in a special section of the file header known as the Data Decryption Field (DDF). The other copy of the FEK is encrypted using the recovery agent's public key, and is placed in a similar field in the file header known as the Data Recovery Field (DRF). The file is now securely encrypted. To open the file, a user must possess one of the corresponding private keys: either the private key of the recovery agent at the time of the encryption, or the private key of the user at the time of encryption. The file cannot be opened in any other way.

When a user encrypts a file or folder, EFS first tries to find the user's certificate in the user's personal certificate store. If the user does not have a certificate that has been authorized for use with EFS and there is a CA on the network, the CA will be asked to supply a certificate. If no CA is available, EFS creates its own self-signed certificate for the user. Similarly, the system also attempts to find the recovery agent's public key in the certificate store. If it is not available, EFS will check with the CA, and if that fails, it will generate a self-signed key for the recovery agent. In order to encrypt, EFS requires at least one recovery agent. The default recovery policy for a domain designates that the Domain Administrator on the first domain controller (the first Domain Administrator to sign on) will receive the self-signed certificate, making him or her the recovery agent for the domain.

The use of self-signed certificates is the default behavior for EFS; however, this is not recommended on a domain network. Instead, it is recommended that you either configure certification authorities (CAs) to provide EFS certificates to users, or disable EFS entirely using Group Policy. A public key/private key pair is always created for each certificate. The public key is stored in the user's certificate. The user's certificates are stored in the user's personal certificate stores. Private keys are stored in user profiles.

IPSec works similarly to EFS, but instead of file encryption, IPSec is designed to secure traffic at the Network layer (**Figure 12-3**). The services it can provide emphasize the four fundamental functions of any security system: authentication, integrity, anti-replay protection, and confidentiality. **Authentication**, as you have learned, refers to the process of verifying the identity of a computer or user in a communication exchange. **Integrity** refers to the accuracy of the received data. If integrity services are provided by a security method, data is protected from tampering or modification in transit. **Confidentiality** refers to putting protections in place to make sure that data is revealed only to the designated recipients. **Anti-replay** protection refers to safety measures so that data packets are not retransmitted. Since each datagram sent over a network is unique, it cannot be re-sent, helping to prevent others from intercepting messages and impersonating one of the clients.

Figure 12-3 IPSec

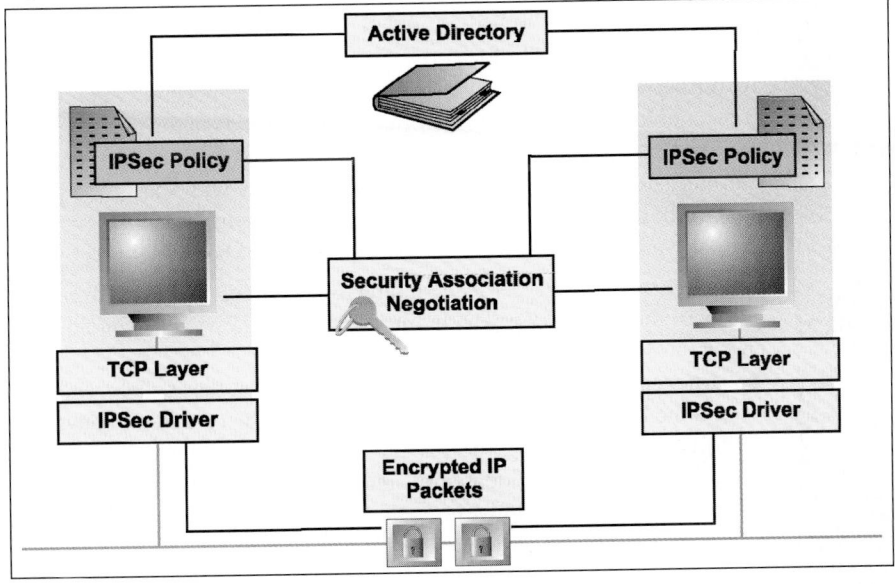

skill 2

Identifying the Features of Public Key Cryptography

exam objective

Basic knowledge

overview

PKI uses public key cryptography as one of the main techniques for securing network data. The set of instructions used by the public key/private key pair uses mathematical calculations, called **algorithms**, to encrypt and decrypt data. Rivest, Shamir and Aldeman (RSA) is the most commonly used algorithm. **Table 12-2** lists some other commonly used algorithms. The public and private key pair is used to encrypt and decrypt data.

Symmetric key cryptography, which uses a single key (often referred to as a secret key) to both encrypt and decrypt data, is most often used to encrypt data on hard drives. The user who encrypts the data simply keeps the key and distribution is not an issue.

For example, you can arrange a NetMeeting session with your employees and provide all employees who will attend the meeting with a secret key that will only be used for this one meeting. An unauthorized user will not be able to access the secret key and will, therefore, not have access to the NetMeeting. Authorized users who have the secret key will only be able to use it while the meeting is in progress. They cannot use the secret key for any other purpose or for the next NetMeeting.

To further enhance secret key security, you can encrypt a secret key with a public key. For example, if a user named Caroline wants to send a message to another user, Alan, she will encrypt the secret key with Alan's public key. Similarly, if Alan were sending a message to Caroline, Alan in turn would encrypt the secret key with Caroline's public key. As mentioned previously in our discussion of EFS, combining symmetric key encryption with asymmetric key encryption in this manner gives you the best of both worlds.

You can issue a public key using a directory service, such as Active Directory, or through the owner of the private key. The public and private key pair technology uses two processes to encrypt user data, as listed below:

◆ **Encryption** is the process of converting data at the sender's end with a combination of a public key and an algorithm. **Decryption** is the process of converting the data back to its original form using the private key and the same algorithm. Encryption provides authentication, confidentiality, and integrity. For example, if a user named Martha needs to send a file named Investments.xls to Mary, before sending the file, Martha will request Mary's public key. Martha will encrypt Investments.xls with Mary's public key and send the file to Mary. In order for Mary to open the file, she simply has to decrypt it using her own private key (**Figure 12-4**).

◆ **Digital message signing** is a way of authenticating a sender and receiver and ensuring data integrity. The sender uses a one-way hashing algorithm (also referred to as a one-way hash function) to create a message digest. A message digest, as noted in the previous skill, is a shortened version of a text message. The message is compressed into is a single fixed string of digits, generally 128, 160, 192, or 224 bits long. A message digest functions as a kind of "digital fingerprint" for a message. If you look at the message digest, the original message contents are not disclosed. If even a single bit on the message is altered, a completely different output value will result. It is impossible to come up with an identical message digest for two different messages. The sender then uses his or her private key to encrypt the message digest. The result is the digital signature. The digital signature is appended to the message, thus digitally signing the message. On the recipient's end, first, the digital signature is decrypted using the sender's public key. If this is successful, the recipient knows that the message came from the correct sender because only that sender holds that particular private key. When the digital signature is decrypted it is changed back into the message digest. Then, the recipient recreates the message digest (rehashes the original message). The two message digests are compared. If they are identical, the recipient knows that the message was not tampered with in transit and that it came from the owner of the private key.

Table 12-2 Algorithms used for data encryption

Category of Algorithm	Name	Description
General	Rivest, Shamir, Adleman (RSA)	Applied in certificates and secret key agreements using a public key.
	Digital Signature Standard (DSA)	Applied in producing digital signatures to authenticate users.
Public Key Cryptography	Diffie-Hellman	Supports secret key exchange for certificates.
Secret key	Hash Message Authentication Code (HMAC)	Services provided include integrity, authentication, and anti-replay. HMAC uses hash functions to create secure hashes.
	Data Encryption Standard-Cipher Chaining (DES-CBC)	A secret key algorithm used to ensure the confidentiality of data. DES generates a random number and uses the number with the secret key in order to block the encrypted data.
Hash	HMAC-Message Digest function 5 (MD5)	MD5 applies four hashes to the data to produce a 128-bit digital signature. Provides integrity, authentication, and anti-replay.
	HMAC-Secure Hash Algorithm (SHA)	SHA is very similar to MD5 but it provides a 160-bit digital signature and is considered more secure. Provides authentication, integrity, and anti-replay.

Figure 12-4 The data encryption process

Exam 70-290

skill 2

Identifying the Features of Public Key Cryptography (cont'd)

exam objective

Basic knowledge

more

Windows Server 2003 includes digital code signing, which is used to digitally sign the drivers and system files on your system. Microsoft uses digital signatures to assure users that the drivers they are using have been tested for quality and are safe for installation. A digital signature on a file certifies that the file has not been altered or overwritten by another program's installation process. There are several ways to protect digitally signed files.

The **Windows File Protection utility** prevents the replacement of system files in protected folders, some of which end in .sys, .dll, .ocx, .ttf, .fon, and .exe. It detects any attempt by other programs to replace or move a protected system file and looks up the file signature in a catalog file (.cat) to determine if the correct Microsoft version is being installed. If an attempt is made to replace the correct Microsoft version of a file, an event is written to the event log to record the replacement attempt and the file will be replaced from the Dllcache folder or the distribution media. Windows File Protection is enabled by default and will only allow system files to be replaced if they are included in signed Windows Server 2003 service packs, upgrades, or hot fixes, or if they are obtained from the Windows Update Web site.

The **System File Checker utility** scans and verifies the versions of all protected system files. If a protected file has been overwritten, the correct version of the file is retrieved from the **%systemroot%\system32\dllcache** folder. The **sfc** command can be run from the command prompt. The syntax for the System File Checker is as follows:

sfc [/scannow] [/scanonce] [/scanboot] [/cancel] [/quiet] [/enable] [/purgecache] [/cachesize=x] (Figure 12-5).

The parameters for the syntax are described in **Table 12-3**.

The **File Signature Verification utility** is used to identify unsigned files on your computer and display the related information such as the file's name, location, last modification date, file type, and the file's version number **(Figure 12-6)**. You can run this utility by entering **sigverif** (or **sigverif.exe**) in the **Open** text box in the **Run** dialog box. To start a complete scan of all Windows Server 2003 system files, click **Start**. To configure advanced settings such as scanning to find other files that are not digitally signed, click **Advanced** to open the **Advanced File Signature Verification Settings** dialog box. Unsigned files can be installed on your system quite easily if you leave your driver signing options set to the default, **Warn— Display a message before installing an unsigned driver**. You may have installed an unsigned driver that is now causing system instability. You can run the File Signature Verification utility to locate and identify unsigned files that have been installed, which may now be causing a problem with the system. You can also use it to check driver files that you have downloaded before you install them. You simply have to point the utility to the location of the uninstalled file or search the computer for a particular type of file to verify that the file has been digitally signed on the **Search** tab. On the **Logging** tab, you can configure the program to save the results to a log file. You can either append the data to an existing log file or overwrite an existing log file.

Figure 12-5 The System File Checker

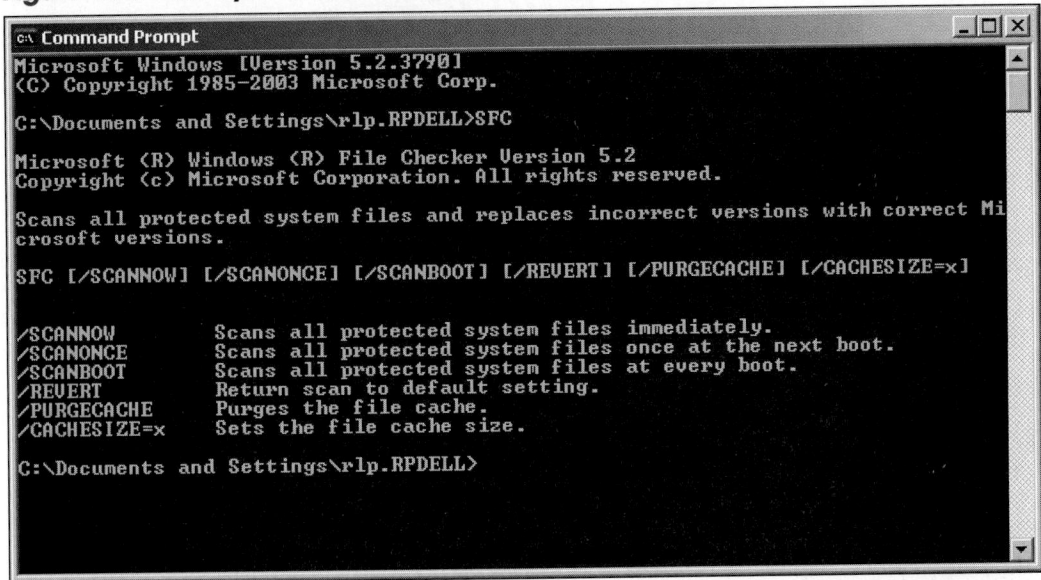

```
Command Prompt                                                    _ □ X
Microsoft Windows [Version 5.2.3790]
(C) Copyright 1985-2003 Microsoft Corp.

C:\Documents and Settings\rlp.RPDELL>SFC

Microsoft (R) Windows (R) File Checker Version 5.2
Copyright (c) Microsoft Corporation. All rights reserved.

Scans all protected system files and replaces incorrect versions with correct Mi
crosoft versions.

SFC [/SCANNOW] [/SCANONCE] [/SCANBOOT] [/REVERT] [/PURGECACHE] [/CACHESIZE=x]


/SCANNOW       Scans all protected system files immediately.
/SCANONCE      Scans all protected system files once at the next boot.
/SCANBOOT      Scans all protected system files at every boot.
/REVERT        Return scan to default setting.
/PURGECACHE    Purges the file cache.
/CACHESIZE=x   Sets the file cache size.

C:\Documents and Settings\rlp.RPDELL>
```

Table 12-3 Syntax for System File Checker

Parameter	Description
/scannow	Scans all protected system files immediately.
/scanonce	Scans all protected system files once.
/scanboot	Scans all protected system files every time the computer restarts.
/cancel	Cancels all pending scans of protected system files.
/quiet	Replaces all incorrect file versions without prompting the user.
/enable	Returns Windows File Protection to default operation. When the System File Checker detects an incorrect version of a file, it prompts the user to restore protected system files.
/purgecache	Purges the Windows File Protection file cache and scans all protected system files immediately.
/cachesize=x	Sets Windows File Protection file cache size.

Figure 12-6 The File Signature Verification utility

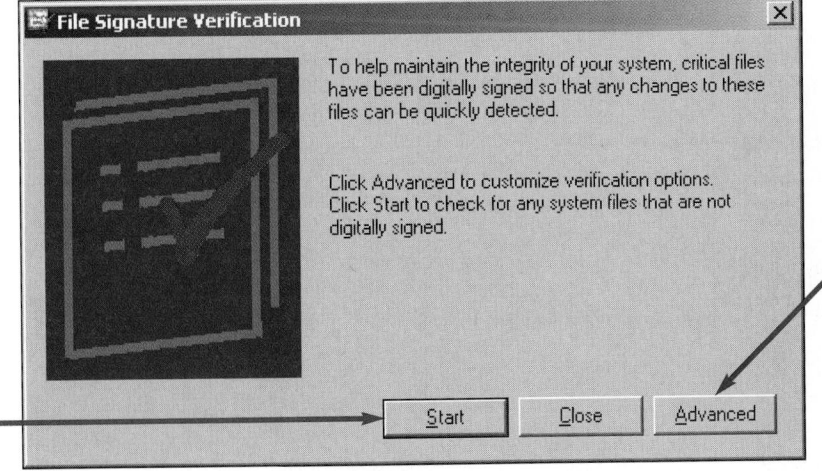

Click to scan all Windows Server 2003 system files

Click to open the Advanced File Signature Verification Settings dialog box to configure searches for unsigned files

skill 3

Working with IPSec

Basic knowledge

overview

IP Security (IPSec) policies use both asymmetric and symmetric encryption to secure data transmitted across a network. IPSec can be used both on your intranet and to secure Internet communications. It performs three main functions: authentication, packet filtering, and tunneling or encapsulation. For authentication purposes it can be used so that the sender and the receiver in a data transmission can verify each other's authenticity before any data is sent. Because standard IP packets are used, only the sender and the receiver must support IPSec. IPSec is put into operation using IPSec policies, which can be applied to the local computer. Alternatively, you can create a GPO (Group Policy object) to implement them at the domain, or OU level or to apply them to a group of computers. Since IPSec is not a proprietary Microsoft protocol and is supported by many hardware and application developers, it is compatible with many systems, making its implementation feasible both on an internal mixed network and with external networks.

IPSec policies use two main security mechanisms: Authentication Header and Encapsulating Security Payload. These two security mechanisms are used in conjunction to provide data authentication, data integrity, and encryption.

♦ **Authentication Header (AH)** is used for authentication and data integrity purposes but does not provide encryption. It uses the HMAC-MD5 and HMAC-SHA hashing algorithms previously described in **Table 12-2** to create digital signatures. AH ensures that the correct, unmodified data is sent to the recipient. Using AH, you know that a packet originated from the anticipated source; it does not come from an impersonator and it was not modified in transit.

♦ **Encapsulating Security Payload (ESP)** is used to transmit encrypted data. It uses the encryption algorithm DES to encrypt the packet and the HMAC algorithm to digitally sign the data in the packet. ESP guarantees the confidentiality of data packets.

IPSec can only be configured by administrators. IPSec policies can apply to the local computer or be configured for a site, OU, or domain. To set IPSec policy at the local level, you use the Local Security Settings console, a custom MMC to which you have added the Group Policy Object Editor snap-in, or a custom MMC to which you have added the IP Security Policies snap-in. The IP Security Polices on Local Machine node is readily viewable in the Local Security Settings console. In the Local Computer Policy node, expand the Computer Configuration node, expand the Windows Settings node, and expand the Security Settings node to locate it **(Figure 12-7)**. You use the Group Policy Object Editor from the Active Directory Users and Computers console to set IPSec policies at the domain or OU level and from the Active Directory Sites and Services console to set them at the site level. If you have installed the Group Policy Management console, you can open the Group Policy Object Editor for the appropriate object from there. You can also add the IP Security Policies snap-in to a custom MMC and specify that it will manage the Active Directory domain of which the local computer is a member **(Figure 12-8)**, manage another Active Directory domain, or simply manage another computer.

There are three preconfigured policy templates you can choose from: **Client (Respond Only)**, **Server (Request Security)**, and **Secure Server (Require Security)** **(Figure 12-9)**. You set IPSec policies based on whether your computer is performing the role of a client or a server. Of the three policy options, the **Client (Respond Only)** policy is used to provide maximum flexibility when negotiating security. By default, this policy sends data packets without applying security measures such as encryption; however, if specifically requested by a server, the policy ensures that data will be encrypted before it is sent. The client does not request a secure session, but it will provide one if asked.

Figure 12-7 The IP Security Policies on Local Computer node in the Group Policy snap-in

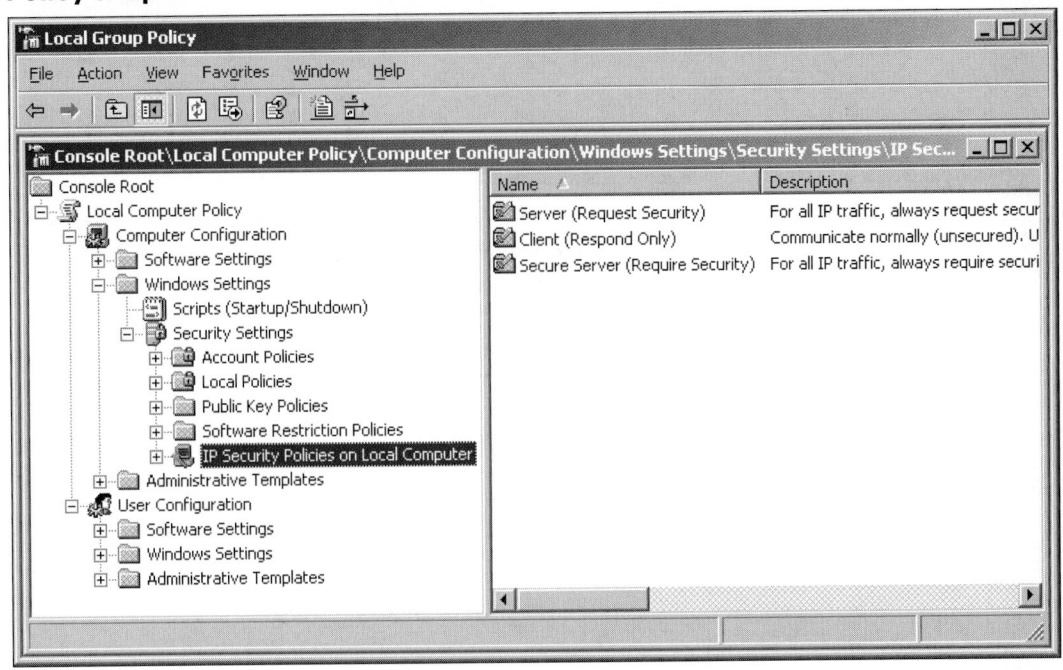

Figure 12-8 The IP Security Policies snap-in

The IP Security Policies snap-in configured to manage the Active Directory domain of which the computer is a member

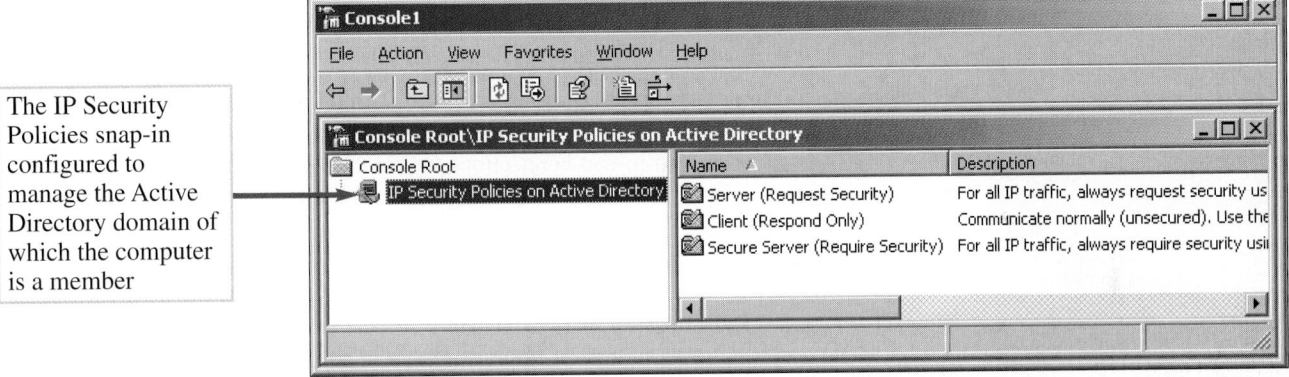

Figure 12-9 The predefined IPSec policies

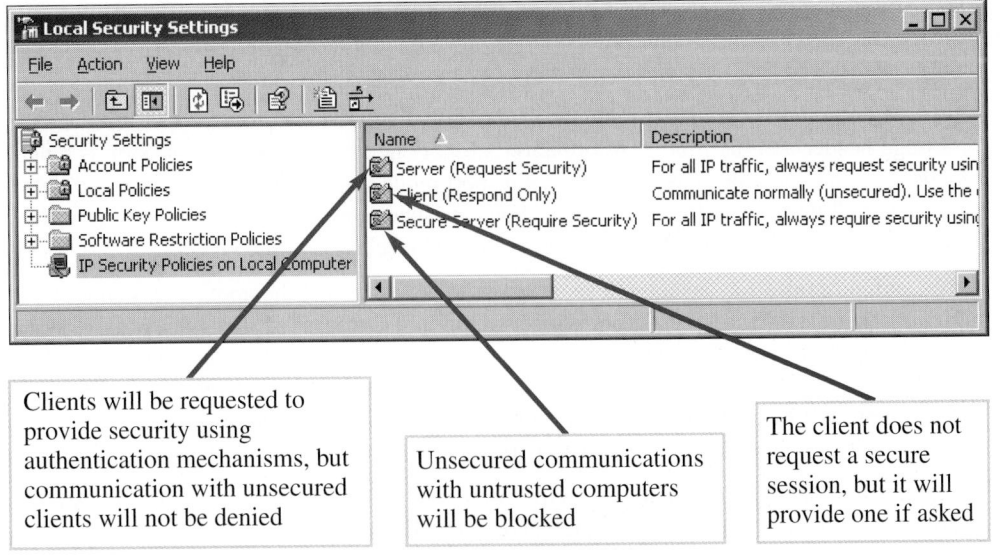

Clients will be requested to provide security using authentication mechanisms, but communication with unsecured clients will not be denied

Unsecured communications with untrusted computers will be blocked

The client does not request a secure session, but it will provide one if asked

skill 3

Working with IPSec (cont'd)

exam objective   Basic knowledge

overview

The **Server (Request Security)** option always attempts to provide secure communication by requesting security using Kerberos trust from other computers. This means that, for all IP traffic, clients will be requested to provide security using authentication mechanisms, but communication with unsecured clients will not be denied. Data packets will still be exchanged, even if the other side is not IPSec capable. Previous versions of Windows did not include support for IPSec; therefore, if you must communicate with Windows NT 4.0 or earlier computers, you should use this policy or the Client (Respond Only) policy. Communications with other Windows Server 2003 computers and with all other systems that support IPSec will be secured, but you will still be able to conduct unsecured communications with computers that do not support IPSec.

The **Secure Server (Require Security)** option ensures that all communication is encrypted, which may minimize the number of client computers with which you can communicate over a network, because all communications must be secured. When you set this policy, unsecured communications with un-trusted computers are blocked. Whether or not a computer is trusted is determined by the authentication mechanism used by the client. Windows Server 2003 provides several authentication mechanisms, but the default mechanism for IPSec is Kerberos V5.

It is important to note that none of the IPSec policy options are assigned to a computer by default. You can assign any of these three policies without modification, or you can modify a policy option by either adding a new IP security rule or editing an existing IP security rule in the *<policy name>* **Properties** dialog box **(Figure 12-10)**.

IPSec operates in either tunnel mode or transport mode. **Tunnel mode** is used to create a secure IPSec tunnel through which data can travel from one end to the other. Although it was chiefly designed to create secure end-to-end connections over public networks, such as the Internet, many private corporate networks also use IPSec to secure communications channels because they are beginning to realize that shortcomings in their own private networks make them vulnerable as well. In tunnel mode, the message, the message header, and the routing information are all encrypted. Only communications between the computers configured as the end points are secure. No other computers on the network share the tunnel. You can create a local IPSec tunnel between two computers with static IP addresses. Each computer is configured with the Secure Server (Require Security) policy, which is modified to set each computer as a tunnel endpoint. The IP address for each computer is entered on the **Tunnel Setting** tab in the **Edit Rule Properties** dialog box, which you access by opening the Properties dialog box for the Secure Server (Require Security) dialog box and clicking **Edit**. The IPSec tunnel mode policy is set for all IP traffic between the two endpoints. Public key cryptography is the foundation for IPSec VPNs. IPSec can either use a shared key, Kerberos, or certificates to encrypt and sign communications.

In **transport mode**, which is the default mode, only the data itself is encrypted. Because the message header and the routing information are not encrypted, it is not as secure as tunnel mode. You can configure IPSec policy in transport mode for an entire network depending on your network makeup and security needs. You can divide the computers on the network into 2 or more groups and apply IPSec policies at the OU level by creating GPOs.

You configure rules for IPSec Policies to regulate how they will be applied and under what circumstances. The Tunnel endpoint is one example of a rule: it applies only when you are configuring IPSec policy in tunnel mode. Other rules, each of which also have a tab in the Edit Rule Properties dialog box, include the **Authentication Methods**, **Connection Type**, **IP Filter List**, and **Filter Action** rules **(Figure 12-11)**. You can apply an IPSec rule to just a LAN, to remote access traffic, or to all network traffic.

You can use one of three authentication methods: Kerberos V5, which is the default, certificates from a trusted CA, or a pre-shared key **(Figure 12-12)**. Pre-shared keys are the

tip

In general, you want to be as specific as possible with your filter list, because encryption consumes processor resources and additional bandwidth. Use filters to pinpoint the specific traffic you wish to encrypt.

Figure 12-10 Editing an existing IP security rule

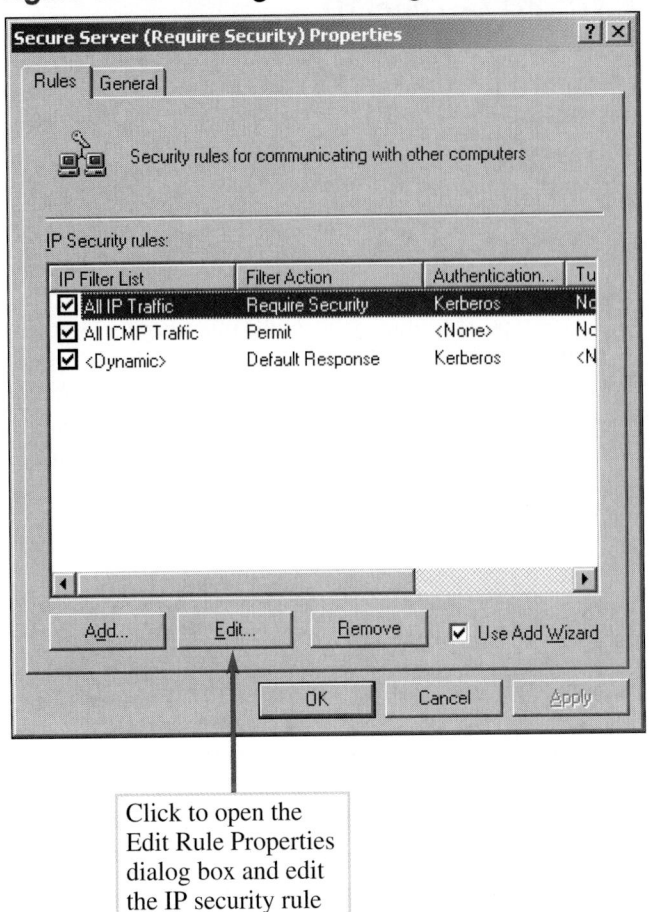

Figure 12-11 The Edit Rule Properties dialog box

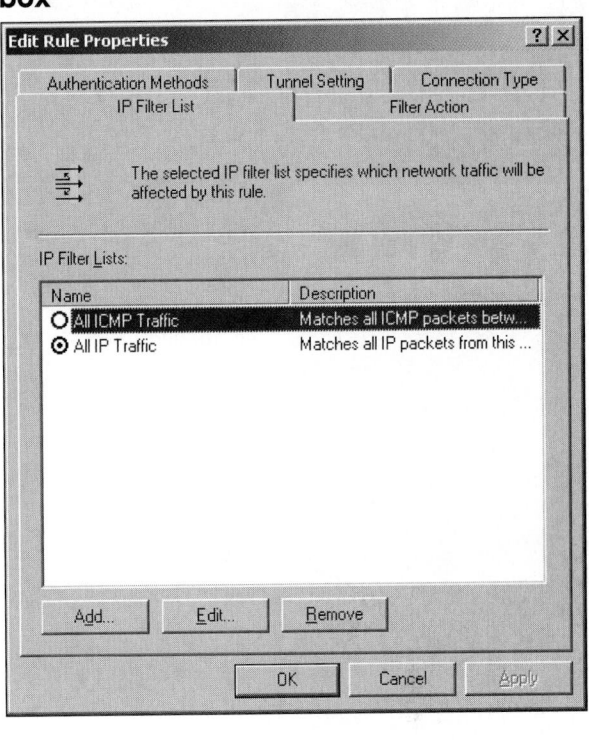

Click to open the Edit Rule Properties dialog box and edit the IP security rule

Figure 12-12 The New Authentication Method Properties dialog box

Kerberos is the default authentication method, but you can also use a certificate from a trusted CA or a pre-shared key

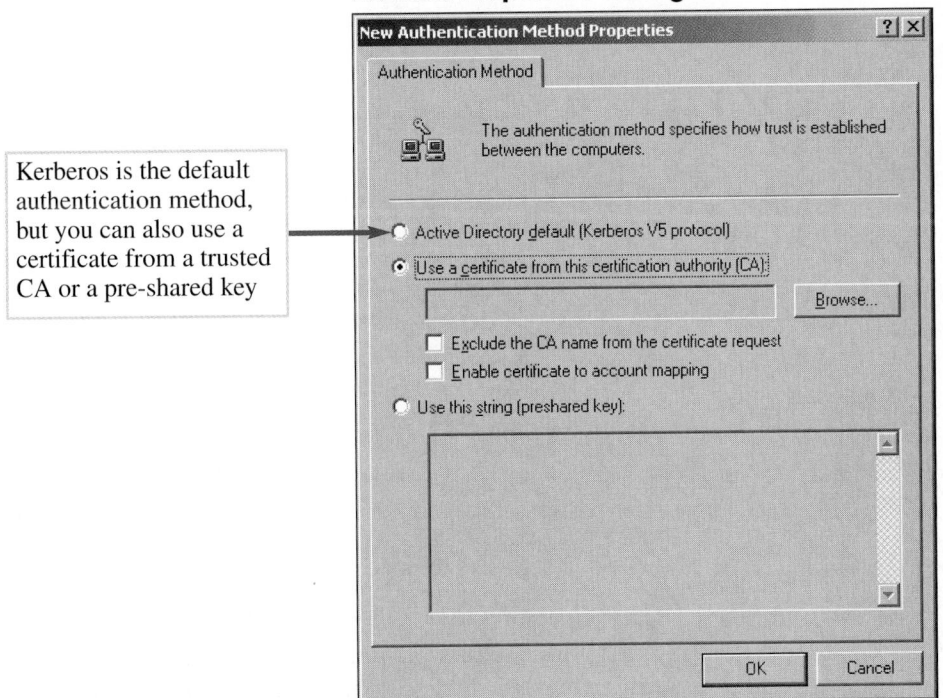

skill 3

Working with IPSec (cont'd)

exam objective

Basic knowledge

overview

least secure because they can be viewed in the Properties dialog box for the IPSec policy. If you use certificates, you must setup a CA on the network.

The IP filter list is used to designate what type of traffic you want the rule to apply to. It can be applied to all IP traffic, to all ICMP traffic, or you can create custom filters for certain kinds of IP traffic. The filter action is the security method that will be applied when the traffic matches one of the three main policies. On the **Filter Action** tab, **Permit**, **Request Security (Optional)**, or **Require Security** will be selected depending on which policy you are modifying (**Figure 12-13**). Click **Edit** to **Permit**, **Block**, or **Negotiate security** for the IP filter (**Figure 12-14**). Permit allows traffic, Block denies traffic, and when you choose Negotiate security, security will be negotiated for the connection.

You can choose one or more security methods, which are placed in preference order. The security methods use AH (Authentication Header) and ESP (Encapsulating Security Payload). These are referred to as negotiation policies and they designate which security services will be provided. For example, AH will provide authentication, integrity, and anti-replay, but not confidentiality (encryption).

more

The security cycle for IPSec communications uses the IPSec Policy Agent service, Internet Key Exchange (IKE) protocol, and IPSec driver components to secure data in transit (**Table 12-5**). The IPSec Policy Agent service receives the policies from Active Directory and passes them to the Registry, IPSec network driver, and the Internet Key Exchange protocol. The Internet Key Exchange (IKE) protocol negotiates and establishes the Security Association used to authenticate a user or transfer data. The IPSec driver checks the IP Filter criteria.

Figure 12-13 The Filter Action tab

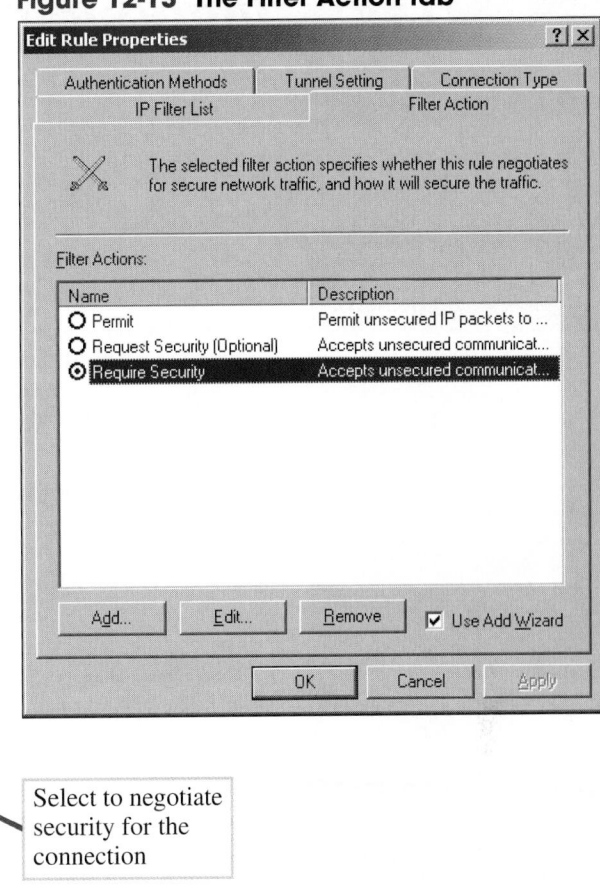

Figure 12-14 The Require Security Properties dialog box

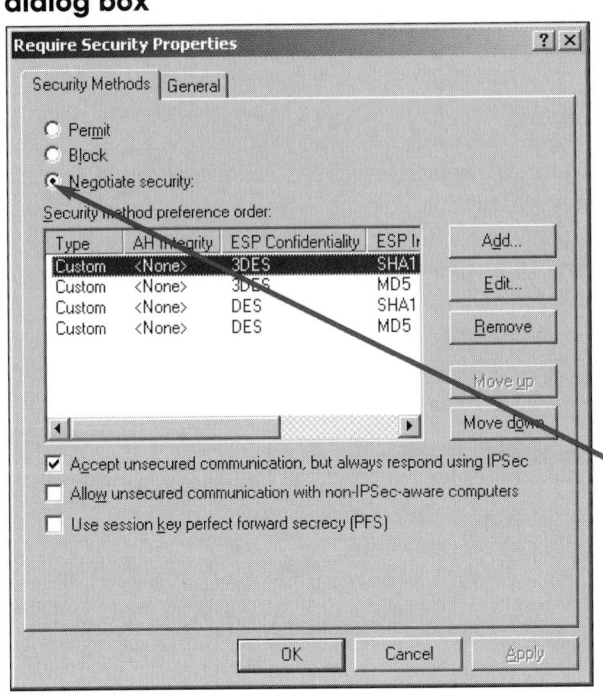

Select to negotiate security for the connection

Table 12-5   Components of IPSec

Component	Function
IPSec Policy Agent service	Used to retrieve IPSec polices from Active Directory and pass it to the Registry, IPSec driver and the Internet Key Exchange (IKE) protocols (which are started by the agent) after checking it against the IPSec policies.
Internet Key Exchange (IKE) protocol (formerly called Internet Security Association and Key Management Protocol (ISAKMP)/Oakley Key Management protocol)	Negotiates and establishes a Security Association between computers using the configured authentication method for the communicating computers and sends the Security Association and key information to the IPSec driver.
IPSec driver	Screens the criteria set by the IP Filter in order to check to make sure that the IP datagram meets the requirements of the security policy. If the data fulfills the criteria, the driver holds the IP datagrams in a queue and notifies Internet Key Exchange (IKE) to begin security negotiations with the destination IP address of the packet. After a successful security negotiation has been reached, among other tasks, the IPSec driver signs the packets, encrypts them, if called for, and sends them to the IP layer to be forwarded to the destination computer.

skill 4

Introducing Certification Authorities

exam objective

Basic knowledge

overview

When you install Microsoft Certificate Services on a Windows Server 2003 computer, you create the first Certification Authority (CA). Certificates are issued and revoked by a CA. The purpose of a CA is to act as a trusted third-party in a communication exchange or other digital transactions. Certificates contain a unique public key and identifying data about the entity to which it is being issued. Certificates can be issued to user accounts, computers, and services (**Figure 12-15**). The CA signs each certificate that it issues to guarantee its authenticity and to pledge that the public key belongs to the certificate owner. You can view the CAs that are trusted by default by Internet Explorer (IE), which is a PKI-enabled application. Launch IE, open the **Tools** menu, and click **Internet Options** to open the Internet Options dialog box. Open the **Content** tab and click the **Certificates** button to open the **Certificates** dialog box. Select the **Trusted Root Certification Authorities** tab to view the list of IE-trusted CAs (**Figure 12-16**). These are established external CA companies that are in the business of selling certificates to businesses and organizations. Other programs that must function with PKI will have lists similar to this one. To see this list for the entire computer, create a new MMC console and load the Certificates snap-in. This list will show up under the Trusted Root Certification Authorities container.

An internal CA can be configured so that all of the computers on the local network trust it. Network users, computers, and services can then make requests to the CA to issue them a certificate. The CA must confirm the information sent by the requester. Each CA has a policy module that dictates how the process of verification takes place and a private key that it uses to digitally sign the certificate prior to issuance. The policy module may require a company letterhead, or corporate seal, or any type of identifying information from the user to verify who they are, such as a driver's license or other ID card, a credit card number, or simply a list of physical attributes for the user.

CAs generally belong to a hierarchical system in which one CA certifies another CA to manage certificates over a part of a network. Trust relationships are at the core of this hierarchy, which is also referred to as CA chaining. The trust relationships begin with the **root CA**, which is the most highly trusted CA in the CA organizational structure. The root CA must be kept secure, because if a security breach occurs at the root CA level, all certificate-based security on the network is in jeopardy. The root CA has the authority to issue certificates to other CAs. There are two classes of CAs: either enterprise or stand-alone. Within each class there are root CAs and subordinate CAs. **Table 12-6** describes each of the types of CA: **Enterprise Root CA**, **Enterprise Subordinate CA**, **Stand-alone Root CA**, **and Stand-alone Subordinate CA**.

CA functions also include revoking certificates and keeping a record of those revoked certificates in the **Certificate Revocation List (CRL)**. The CRL also includes certificates that have expired or have been removed by the CA. Revocation is the process of taking back a certificate from a user who no longer needs to access a network, either because he or she has left the organization or because his or her privileges have changed.

Certificates store information in a particular syntax and format. The content of all certificates includes the certificate version, serial number or SID, issuer name, validity period, user name, user public key information, issuer unique identifier, user unique identifier, and extensions.

tip

Both Windows 2000 and Windows Server 2003 certificates follow the X.509 standard, which is based on the International Telecommunication Union Telecommunication (ITUT) standard.

Figure 12-15 Creating a certificate

Figure 12-16 IE-trusted CAs

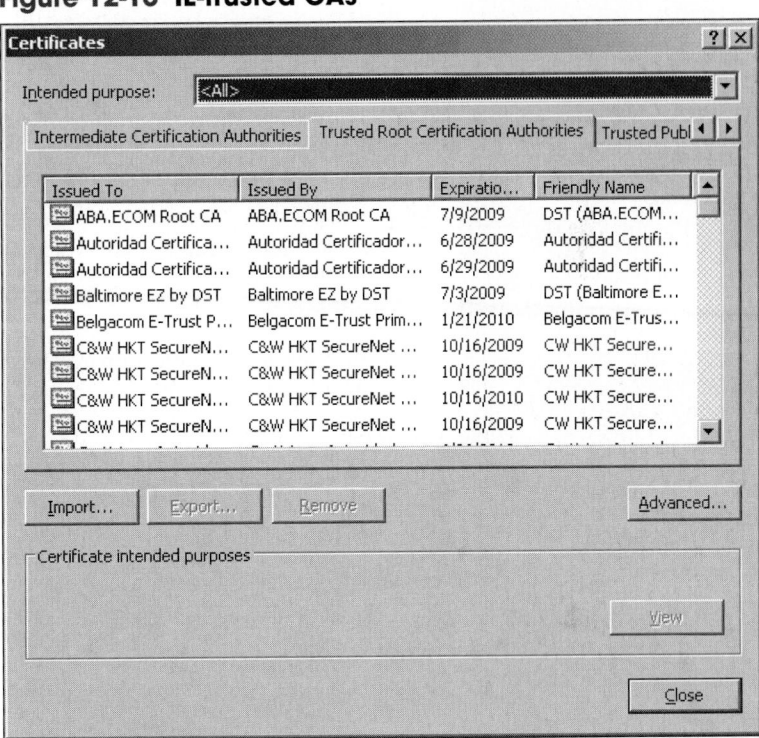

Certificate Type	Description
Table 12-6 CA Roles	
Enterprise Root CA	Root CA for the hierarchy that requires Active Directory. Enterprise CAs can be used to issue certificates for smart card log on to Active Directory.
Enterprise Subordinate CA	A subordinate CA requests a certificate from the Enterprise Root CA. Enterprise Subordinate CAs also require Active Directory, because they are integrated with Active Directory. Enterprise CAs can be used to issue certificates for smart card log on to Active Directory.
Stand-alone Root CA	Root CA for a hierarchy of CAs that does not require Active Directory. Stand-alone CAs cannot issue certificates for Active Directory-related functions.
Stand-alone Subordinate CA	A Subordinate CA requests a certificate from the Stand-alone Root CA and does not need Active Directory to work as the CA is not integrated with Active Directory. Stand-alone CAs cannot issue certificates for Active Directory-related functions.

skill 5

Authenticating User Identity Using Kerberos Protocol

exam objective

Basic knowledge

overview

Kerberos, which is named after the mythological three-headed dog, Cerberos, that guards the underworld of Hades, is a network authentication protocol. It was designed in the 1980s at the Massachusetts Institute of Technology (MIT). It uses strong cryptography to validate the identity of a client to a server and vice versa.

Kerberos is generally used when a user wants to access a network service on a network server and the service is set up for security reasons to require verification of the client's identity. The user must present a ticket that was issued by a Kerberos Authentication Service (AS) in order to access the server. A **ticket** is the identifying data that verifies that the user has been authenticated. The server inspects the ticket, verifies the user's identity, and allows the user to access the resource or service. In order to perform its function, the ticket must include some type of information that can unambiguously identify the user. This information is the password, which (theoretically) only the user and the directory service will know. The ticket must also be protected so that it cannot be appropriated and used by an imposter. Kerberos keeps the password secure by building an Authenticator from the password data and a time stamp. The Authenticator is encrypted and hashed, so any modification to it will void it. In addition, since it is time stamped, it cannot be replayed. Finally, since it is encrypted, the password is still confidential.

Kerberos uses an authentication system with three parties: the client or party that needs to be authenticated, the party that has the resource or service (the server), and the party that stores the credentials for the others. Both the user and the server are required to have keys that are registered with the authentication server. The user's password (the password field for the Active Directory user object) is used to calculate his or her key. The server's key is chosen at random.

First, there are some terms you should understand. The party that needs to be authenticated (the user or computer) is called the **security principal**. The database holding the credentials for the security principals is called the realm. The **realm** is the set of systems, servers and users that the Key Distribution Center (KDC) recognizes.

The ticket is a key component of Kerberos. It stores all of the information, which is encrypted, that will be used by the 3-party authentication system. The **Key Distribution Center (KDC)** is the ticket issuer. The KDC is comprised of two services: the **Authentication Service (AS)** and the **Ticket Granting Service (TGS)**. First, the AS must verify the credentials of any security principal that is requesting a ticket. The AS must make sure that the ticket will be issued to a legitimate party in the realm. Then, it issues a **Ticket Granting Ticket (TGT)**. The TGT is used to verify the identity of the user and grant admission to the Ticket Granting Service. It is valid for seven days from the initial time of authentication, by default. Finally, the Ticket Granting Service issues the ticket. This ticket will be used in all communications between the party and the KDC in the future. The Ticket Granting Service also issues tickets that will arrange communication sessions between a security principal and a Validation Server. The **Validation Server** is the server that the security principal wants to access. It must be in the same domain (realm) as the KDC **(Figure 12-17)**.

If a user is logging on to a stand-alone Windows Server 2003 computer or a workgroup, Kerberos is not used, **NTLM (NT LAN Manager)** is. The NTLM protocol was the default network authentication method for Windows NT 4.0, and it has been kept in Windows Server 2003 for backward compatibility. On a Windows 2000 or Windows Server 2003 Active Directory domain, Kerberos is generally used to access domain resources, although NTLM can also be used.

tip

NTLM is used in any situation in which a Windows 9x or Windows NT client needs to authenticate. NTLM V2, a much stronger version of NTLM authentication, is available for these clients by downloading SP4 for Windows NT systems, and by installing the Directory Services Client on Windows 9x systems.

Figure 12-17 Primary components of Kerberos

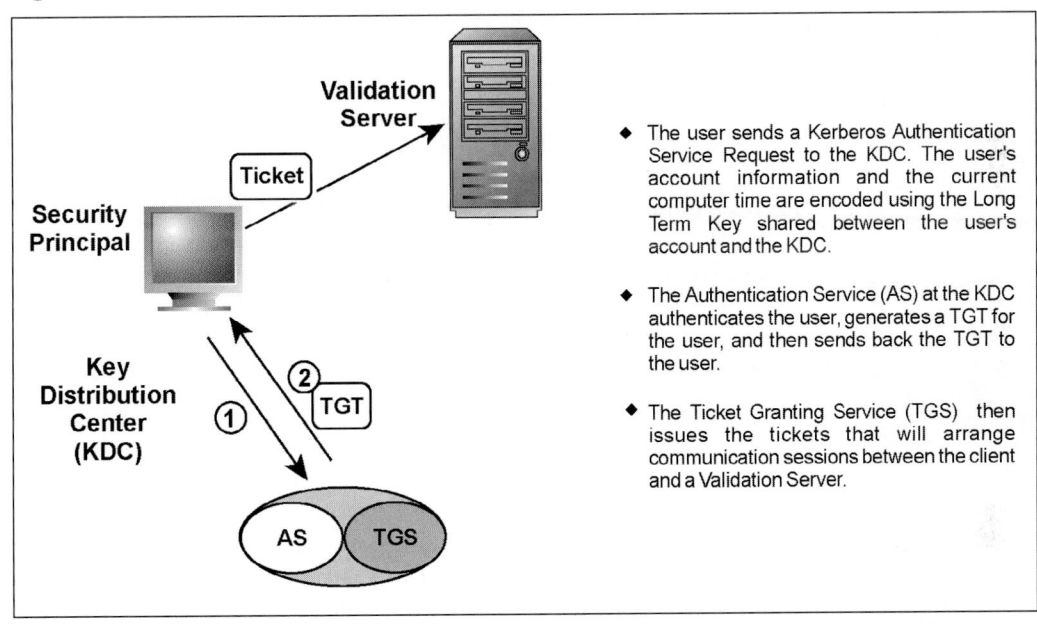

The user sends a Kerberos Authentication Service Request to the KDC. The user's account information and the current computer time are encoded using the Long Term Key shared between the user's account and the KDC.

The Authentication Service (AS) at the KDC authenticates the user, generates a TGT for the user, and then sends back the TGT to the user.

The Ticket Granting Service (TGS) then issues the tickets that will arrange communication sessions between the client and a Validation Server.

skill 5

Authenticating User Identity Using Kerberos Protocol (cont'd)

exam objective

Basic knowledge

overview

When a user logs on to the domain, the Local Security Authority Subsystem, Lsass, using the Kerberos protocol, encrypts the password, creates a Hash, and caches it. The Hash, which is referred to as the user's Long Term Key, will function as an encryption key. NetLogon then creates a request for the Ticket Granting Service. The Kerberos Security Provider is also involved in this process. The request to TGS contains the user's account name, the Key Distribution Center's name, a random number called a nonce that is obtained from the timestamp, and the type of ticket that is being requested. The nonce is encrypted using the user's Long Term Key. The KDC tries to decrypt the nonce using the hashed password for the user that is stored in Active Directory. If it is unable to, the request is denied. If it can decrypt it, the Authentication Service (AS) sends a Ticket Granting Ticket (TGT), which will grant admission to the TGS. The NetLogon process at the client computer must then decrypt the TGT to make sure that it matches the nonce. After the TGT for the Ticket Granting Service is received and decrypted, NetLogon queries the DNS server to locate a domain controller with an open Kerberos port. After the name and IP address for a domain controller are received, NetLogon sends a second TGT, requesting admission to the particular server, to the domain controller. Now, NetLogon on the domain controller receives the TGT request and moves it on to the LSA subsystem. The user account name must be looked up in Active Directory, and Lsass uses the **Kerberos Key Distribution Center Service (KDCSVC)** to do this. Thus, KDCSVC is a service that all domain controllers must and do have. If the user account name is found in Active Directory, the user's Long Term Key is returned. KDCSVC must then decrypt the TGT request, most importantly the nonce. If this is successful, the user's SID is located, as are the SIDs of any groups to which he or she belongs.

Because the nonce is derived from the timestamp, time services are an important part of the logon process. If the timestamp on the TGT request (the time it was created) varies too much from the timestamp on the DC, the TGT request will be denied. From a security standpoint, this leaves only a short time period during which a hacker might have a chance to tamper with the original TGT request, making Kerberos a secure authentication protocol. The time differential is five minutes by default. (This means that the window is five minutes on either side of the KDC's clock.) This is useful for administrators who have to deal with users being unable to log on to the domain over slow WAN links.

After the user and group SID information is located, the KDCSVC Authentication Service on the domain controller, now being in possession of all of the data it needs, creates the service ticket. The TGT usually includes a timestamp and TTL (Time to Live interval) during which the TGT is legitimate, a session key that uniquely identifies the ticket, and the authorization data which includes the user's credentials and a nonce. Now, the AS encrypts a copy of the session key, the timestamp, the authorization data, and the TTL data using the Long Term Key for the account that controls KDCSVC on the domain controller. The client's hashed password from Active Directory is used to encrypt another copy of the session key, the client's nonce, and a CRC (cyclic redundancy check). Theses two items, called the Logon Session Ticket and the Logon Session Key, are sent back to the client by the Lsass and NetLogon on the domain controller (**Figure 12-18**).

Other Kerberos security features are listed in **Table 12-7**.

more

The Kerberos protocol does not communicate directly with the client. The client interacts with the Kerberos protocol through the Local Security Authority (LSA) using the Kernel Mode Security Support Provider Interface on the Windows Server 2003 computer. When both the local and domain logons are simultaneously active, the domain logon will be implemented.

Figure 12-18 The Kerberos Authentication process

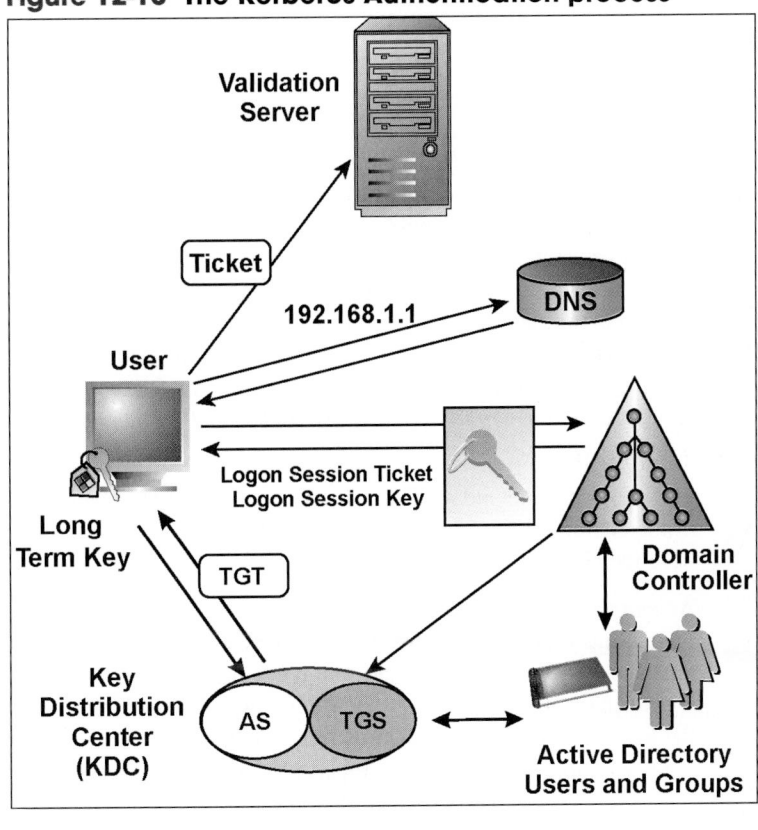

Table 12-7   Features of Kerberos

Feature	Description
Inter-operability with Platforms	Kerberos can communicate with servers using many platforms other than Windows. For example, a UNIX server can be authenticated using Windows Server 2003 Kerberos. If the platform parameters do not match, Kerberos tries to match the user name in the ticket to the users in the Windows environment.
Enhanced Connection Speed	The server does not need to query the client or the Kerberos protocol to authenticate the client. This is because the client has already obtained the ticket with which the server can give the access token to the client. When and if the workload on the server reduces, it can respond to more requests in shorter periods of time.
Server Authentication	Kerberos authenticates both the client and the server.
Delegation	A user can access the services of an application server such as a Web server or database server by obtaining a ticket to access both servers. In this scenario, the Web server can use the ticket of the user to authenticate itself and access the services from the database server.
Common Standard	After the Kerberos system issues a ticket, the same ticket will be valid for any other Kerberos system because the ticket standards for all Kerberos systems are the same.

skill 6

Implementing Account Policy

exam objective

Basic Knowledge

overview

Account policies are used to set the user account properties that control the logon process. They include password policies and account lockout policies. Password policies are used to supplement the security of your system by requiring users to change their passwords at specific time intervals, requiring passwords to be a certain length, and by making users keep a password history so that they cannot simply switch back and forth between two passwords. Locking an account will ensure that further logon attempts will not be permitted until a specified time period has passed. In this way, you can help to secure your system from unauthorized access. You can set the number of invalid logon attempts that will be permitted and the time period during which the account will be locked out after this number has been exceeded, or you can lock the account indefinitely until an Administrator unlocks it.

There are three types of account policies: **Account Lockout**, **Password**, and **Kerberos**. You can configure and manage these policies using the **Group Policy Object Editor** snap-in or the **Group Policy Management console (GPMC)**. The three types of account policies are described below:

Account Lockout: Account Lockout policy is used to enhance the security of your system by preventing users from trying to guess passwords. If a user repeatedly attempts to log on unsuccessfully, the system can automatically lock out the user account according to the specifications that you set. You can set the number of invalid logon attempts you will tolerate, the time duration for the account lockout, and the time duration that must pass after an invalid logon attempt before the bad logon attempt counter is reset to 0. There is immediate replication of Active Directory data between Windows Server 2003 domain controllers when an account is locked out. Account Lockout Policy is configured by setting the following three policies:

tip

All three account policies are unique in that they cannot be configured anywhere but on the entire domain in a domain environment. If you set these policies at any other level (such as for an OU, for example) they will simply not apply.

◆ **Account lockout threshold:** The Account lockout threshold is used to specify the number of invalid logon attempts a user can make after which the account will be locked and the user will be prevented from making further logon attempts. The default value for this option is 0, meaning that the account will never be locked no matter how many invalid logon attempts are made. You can set the account lockout threshold between 0 and 999. In order to reduce the number of account lockouts that occur due to simple user error, on Windows Server 2003 domain controllers, before a logon attempt is counted as bad (i.e., before an addition is made to the **badPwdCount** Registry value), the invalid password is checked against the password history. If the password matches one of the last two entries in the password history, it will not be added to the invalid count for both NTLM and the Kerberos protocol.

◆ **Account lockout duration:** The Account lockout duration (the **LockoutDuration** Registry value) is used to set the time duration (minutes from 0 to 99999) during which you want the account to be disabled. You can set the value to 0 to lock the account indefinitely until the Administrator unlocks it.

◆ **Reset account lockout counter after:** The Reset account lockout counter after setting (the **ObservationWindow** Registry value) sets the time duration that must elapse after an invalid logon attempt before the account lockout counter is reset to 0 (i.e., the number of minutes after which the badPwdCount Registry value is reset). You can reset the bad logon attempt counter between 1 and 99999 minutes.

Password: Allows you to specify how users must manage their passwords by specifying options such as requiring passwords to follow complexity rules or defining when a password needs to be changed. You can set the options described in **Table 12-8** for a password policy.

Kerberos: As you have learned, the Kerberos V5 authentication protocol is implemented through a Key Distribution Center (KDC) that runs on each Windows Server 2003 domain

Table 12-8 Password policies

Option	Description
Enforce password history	Used to set the number of passwords that will be stored in the password history. You can store up to 24 old passwords so that users will not be able to reuse them until they drop off the list. The default setting is 24 passwords remembered.
Maximum password age	Used to set the maximum number of days users can keep a particular password. You can set this option as high as 999, although Windows allows you to use a password for 42 days by default. Setting a value of 0 indicates that a password will never expire.
Minimum password age	Used to set the minimum number of days during which users must keep the same password. This option can also be set as high as 999 days. Setting a value of 0 indicates that a password can be changed on the same day on which it is set. This setting is particularly useful when a user is compelled to change his or her password by the system so that you can prevent that user from immediately changing it back. The default setting is 1 day.
Minimum password length	Used to set the minimum number of characters a password must have. You can set the minimum password length as high as 14 characters. The default setting is 7 characters.
Passwords must meet complexity requirements	This option is enabled by default. Password complexity requirements stipulate that passwords contain characters that include at least three of the following four different types of characters: upper case letters, lower case letters, digits, or non-alphanumeric characters (such as !,$,#,%). The password also cannot include all or part of the user's account name.
Store password using reversible encryption for all users in the domain	Used by network administrators so that a reversibly encrypted password is stored for all users in a domain. This policy is only enabled if support is required for applications that use protocols that need to use the user's password for authentication. It is nearly as bad, from a security standpoint, as storing plaintext versions of passwords. It should not be enabled unless application requirements are more important than password protection. This policy is required when using CHAP authentication through remote access or IAS services. It is also required when using Digest Authentication on Internet Information Services (IIS).

skill 6

Implementing Account Policy (cont'd)

overview

controller. Kerberos policies are only applicable to domain user accounts or computer accounts and they define such settings as ticket lifetimes and logon restriction enforcement. They are not present in local computer policy. Generally, the default Kerberos policy values that are set by the Default Domain Policy are suitable for most networks and it is not recommended that they be changed. However, in some situations, you may want to decrease the lifetime of the tickets to reduce the possibility of a hacker stealing passwords, but keep in mind that this will increase the authorization process overhead.

The Kerberos policies are explained below (**Figure 12-19**):

◆ **Enforce user logon restrictions:** The default setting for this policy is Enabled, which requires that the KDC check the user account to verify that it is still valid, as well as check the user rights policy on the target computer to confirm that the user has the right either to log on locally or to access the computer from the network before a session ticket will be issued.

◆ **Maximum lifetime for service ticket:** This policy sets the maximum length of time that the Logon Session Ticket can be used before it must be renewed. This policy is set in minutes; it must be more than ten minutes and less than the setting for the Maximum lifetime for user ticket policy. The default setting is 600 minutes (10 hours).

◆ **Maximum lifetime for user ticket:** This policy sets the maximum length of time that the Ticket Granting Ticket (TGT) will be valid. The TGT must be renewed when this threshold has been met. The default value is 10 hours.

◆ **Maximum lifetime for user ticket renewal:** This policy sets the maximum lifetime for both the Ticket Granting Ticket (TGT) and the Logon Session Ticket, even though the policy only specifies that it is for the user ticket. After the default time period of 7 days, neither ticket can be renewed.

◆ **Maximum tolerance for computer clock synchronization:** This policy sets the maximum number of minutes that the clock on the KDC can be different from the clock on the Kerberos client. If this threshold, which is by default set to 5 minutes, is exceeded, tickets will not be issued to the client. This is a deterrent to replay attacks.

how to

Set password, account lockout, and Kerberos policies.

1. On a domain controller, click [🏁 start], point to **Administrative Tools** and click **Group Policy Management** to open the Group Policy Management console.
2. Expand the node for the forest that your domain is in, if necessary.
3. Expand the **Domains** node.
4. Double-click the name of your domain.
5. Right-click **Default Domain Policy**, and click [Edit...] to open the **Group Policy Object Editor** snap-in.
6. In the console tree, in the **Computer Configuration** node, double-click the **Windows Settings** node to expand it.
7. Double-click **Security Settings**.
8. Double-click **Account Policies**, and then double-click **Account Lockout Policy** to list the options in the details pane.
9. In the details pane, double-click **Account lockout threshold** to open the **Account lockout threshold Properties** dialog box.
10. Select the **Define this policy setting** check box, if necessary.

Figure 12-19 The Kerberos policies

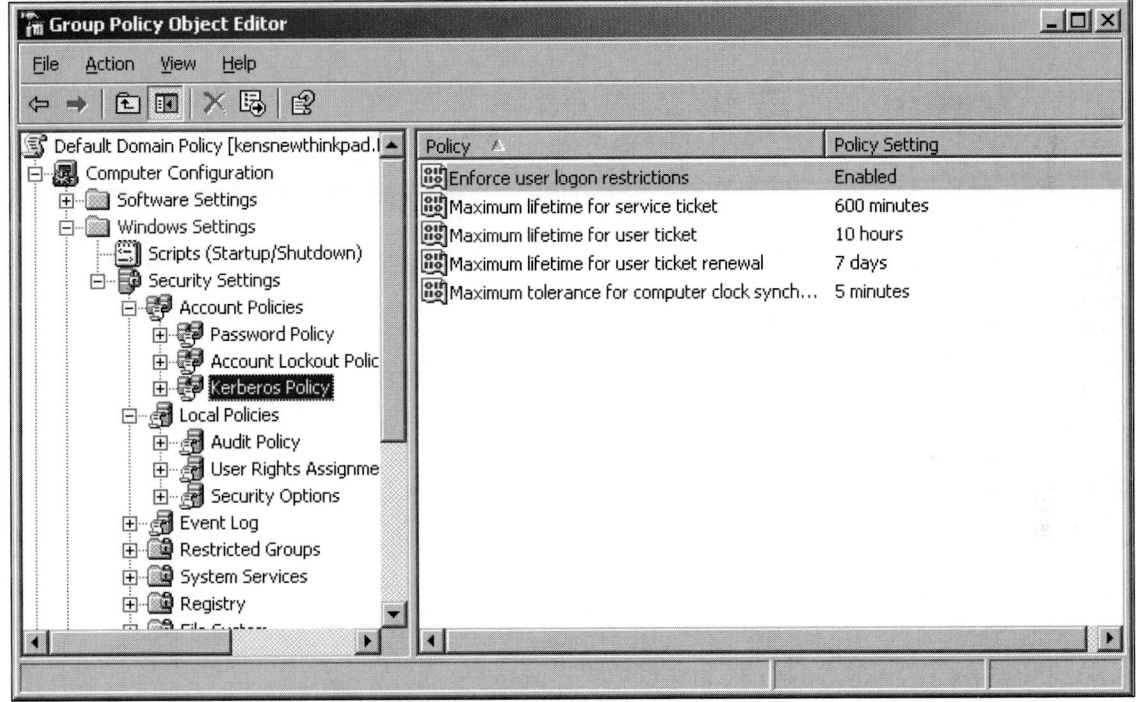

skill 6

Implementing Account Policy (cont'd)

exam objective

Basic knowledge

how to

tip

The Suggested Value Changes window opens each time the Account lockout threshold or Account lockout duration is changed to or from zero [0]. It will also open when the Account lockout duration is set to a number lower than the Reset lockout counter after value, or when the Account duration or Reset lockout duration after value is changed from Not Defined.

11. Type **10** in the **Account will lock out after** spin box **(Figure 12-20)**. This is the recommended account lockout threshold for medium to high security environments.
12. Click [OK]. The **Suggested Value Changes** dialog box opens with the recommended values for the **Account lockout duration** and **Reset account lockout counter after** policies **(Figure 12-21)**.
13. Click [OK] to accept the new values.
14. In the console tree, double-click **Password Policy** to list the policies in the details pane.
15. Double-click the **Enforce Password History** option to open the **Enforce Password History Properties** dialog box.
16. Make sure that the **Define this policy setting** check box is selected.
17. Type **6** in the **Keep password history for** spin box to specify the number of passwords you want your system to remember **(Figure 12-22)**.
18. Click [OK] to apply the new settings.
19. Double-click **Maximum password age**. Select the **Define this policy setting** check box, if necessary. Type **60** in the **Password will expire in** spin box. Click [OK].
20. The **Suggested Value Changes** dialog box will open if the **Minimum password age** policy has not been set. The Suggested Setting for the Minimum password age value is 30 days. Click [OK] to accept the suggested value.
21. Double-click **Minimum password length**. Select the **Define this policy setting** check box, if necessary. Type **8** in the **Password must be at least____characters** spin box **(Figure 12-23)**. Click [OK].
22. Double-click **Kerberos Policy** in the console tree to display the Kerberos policies in the details pane.
23. Double-click **Maximum lifetime for service ticket**. Select the **Define this policy setting check box**, if necessary. Type **720** in the **Ticket expires in____minutes** spin box **(Figure 12-24)**. Click [OK].
24. The **Suggested Value Changes** dialog box opens with a recommended change for the **Maximum lifetime for user ticket** value **(Figure 12-25)**. Click [OK] to set the maximum lifetime for the user ticket to **12**.
25. Close the **Group Policy Object Editor** snap-in and the **Group Policy Management** console.

Figure 12-20 The Account lockout threshold Properties dialog box

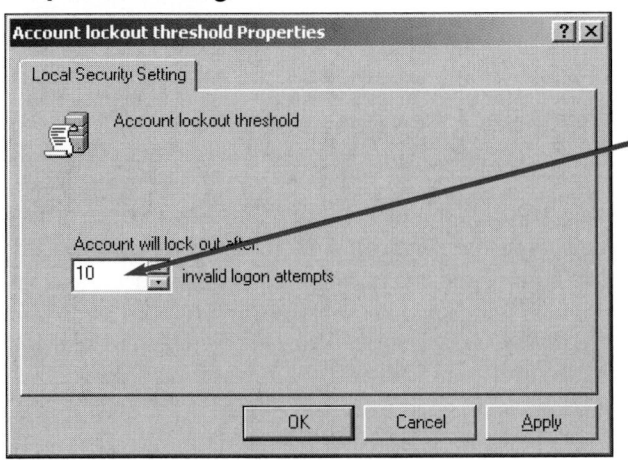

Set the number of unsuccessful logon attempts that will be allowed

Figure 12-21 The Suggested Value Changes dialog box

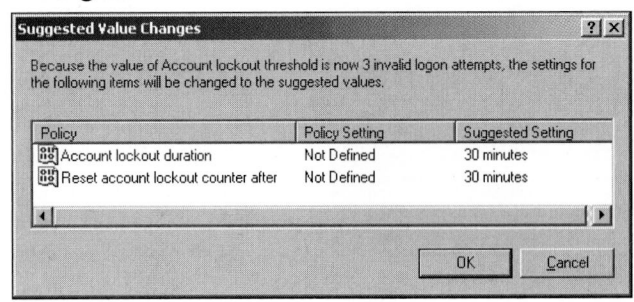

Figure 12-22 The Enforce password history Properties dialog box

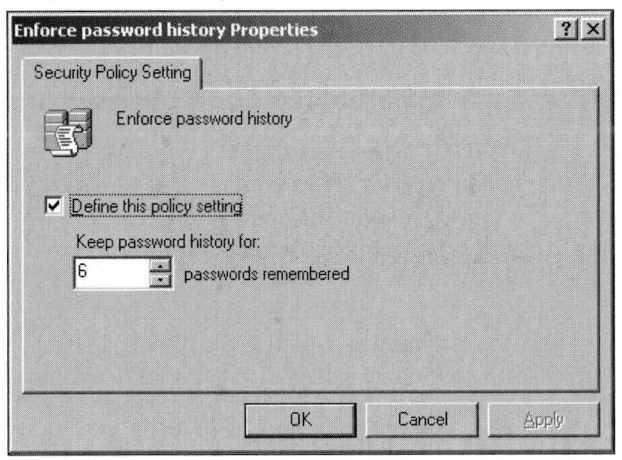

Figure 12-23 The Minimum password length Properties dialog box

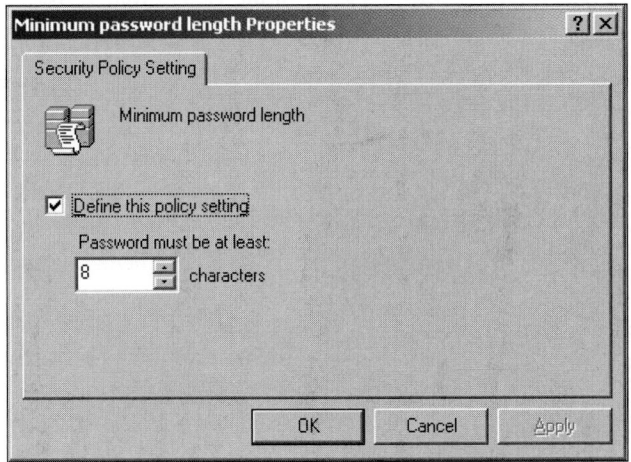

Figure 12-24 The Maximum lifetime for service ticket Properties dialog box

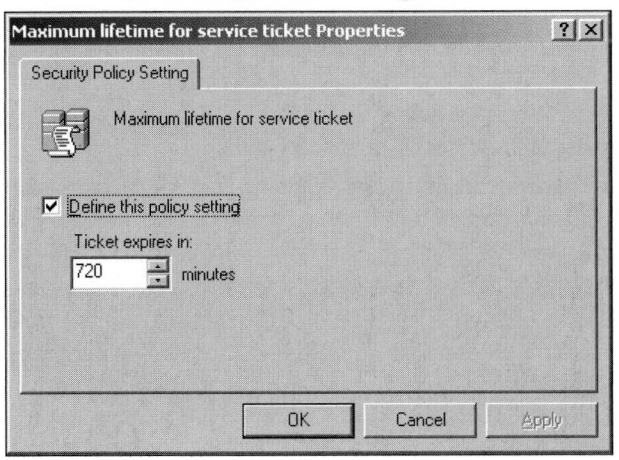

Figure 12-25 The Suggested Value Changes dialog box

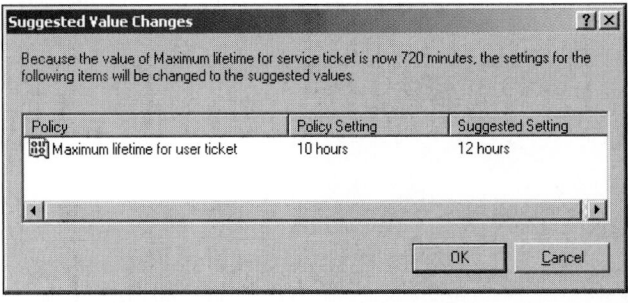

skill 7

Diagnosing and Resolving Account Lockouts

exam objective

Diagnose and resolve account lockouts.

overview

On some networks, after you institute an account lockout policy, you may have a problem with an excessive amount of lockouts. In order to diagnose and resolve these difficulties, you must first determine if the lockouts are occurring due to user errors or if an intruder is attempting to attack the network. The first thing you should do is make sure that all domain controllers and client computers have had the latest service packs and hot fixes applied. Next, you can configure auditing at the domain level (See Lesson 14) for Account Logon Events (Failure), Account Management (Success), and Logon Events (Failure).

You should also configure Kerberos and Netlogon logging to track both Kerberos logon attempts and NTLM authentication attempts. When a server or service attempts to authenticate a client, Kerberos authentication will be tried first. However, if Kerberos authentication does not succeed, the client will then try NTLM. You enable Netlogon logging on any domain controllers that are involved in user authentication. You can determine the authenticating domain controller by typing **set l** at a command prompt. To enable Netlogon logging type **nltest /dbflag:2080ffff** at the command prompt (**Figure 12-26**). Nltest is a command line utility that can be used on x86-based systems to display information about Active Directory objects, get a list of the domain controllers on the network, check and test trust relationships, and configure some logging options.

The Netlogon.log file is created in *%systemroot%*\Debug (**Figure 12-27**). If the log file is not in the Debug folder, use **net stop netlogon** and **net start netlogon** to stop and restart the Netlogon service. The total disk space used by Netlogon logging is never more than 40 MB because when the log becomes 20 MB, it is renamed Netlogon.bak and a new Netlogon.log is started. When the new Netlogon.log becomes 20 MB, Netlogon.bak is condensed by deleting the oldest data, and the active Netlogon.log file is renamed Netlogon.bak. Netlogon logging increases system overhead and performance can deteriorate, so you should disable it after you have diagnosed the problem. To disable Netlogon logging, type **nltest /dbflag:0** and press **[Enter]**, then use **net start netlogon** to restart the service.

To enable Kerberos logging for Windows 2000 or later Kerberos clients, open the Registry Editor on the client (**Start—Run**, type **regedit** in the **Open** text box and press **[Enter]**) and navigate to the **HKEY_LOCAL_MACHINE\SYSTEM\CurrentControlSet\Control\Lsa\ Kerberos\Parameters** key. Right-click **Parameters**, point to **New**, and select **DWORD Value**. Name the new Registry value, **LogLevel** (**Figure 12-28**). Right-click the new Registry value and select **Modify** to open the **Edit DWORD** value dialog box. Enter **0x1** in the **Value data** text box. If the Parameters key is not present you will have to create it first (right-click **Kerberos**, point to **New** and select **Key**). Kerberos logging can also negatively impact system performance so you should disable it after you have diagnosed the problem. To disable Kerberos logging, delete the LogLevel Registry value. You must restart the computer after you enable or disable Kerberos logging in order to change the log settings.

Finally, you will have to analyze the Security and System event logs for all of the computers that are involved with the client's lockout to attempt to discover where the lockouts are occurring and why they are occurring.

When faced with excessive account lockouts, check the computers on which the lockouts are occurring for programs and service accounts that cache credentials. Many programs will cache credentials or maintain an active thread with old credentials after a user has changed their password. Furthermore, the Service Control Manager caches service account passwords on client computers that use the account. You cannot reset the password for a service unless you also reset the account in the Service Control Manager, because when the computers that use the account are denied access, they will continue to attempt to log on using the former password. You can examine the Netlogon log files and the event log files on client computers to find out if this is occurring, and then set the Security Control Manager to use the new password.

Figure 12-26 Enabling Netlogon logging

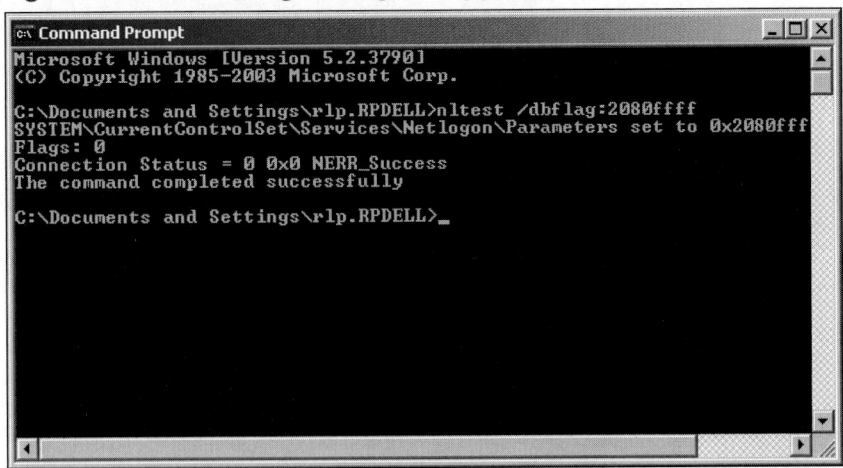

Figure 12-27 Netlogon.log startup

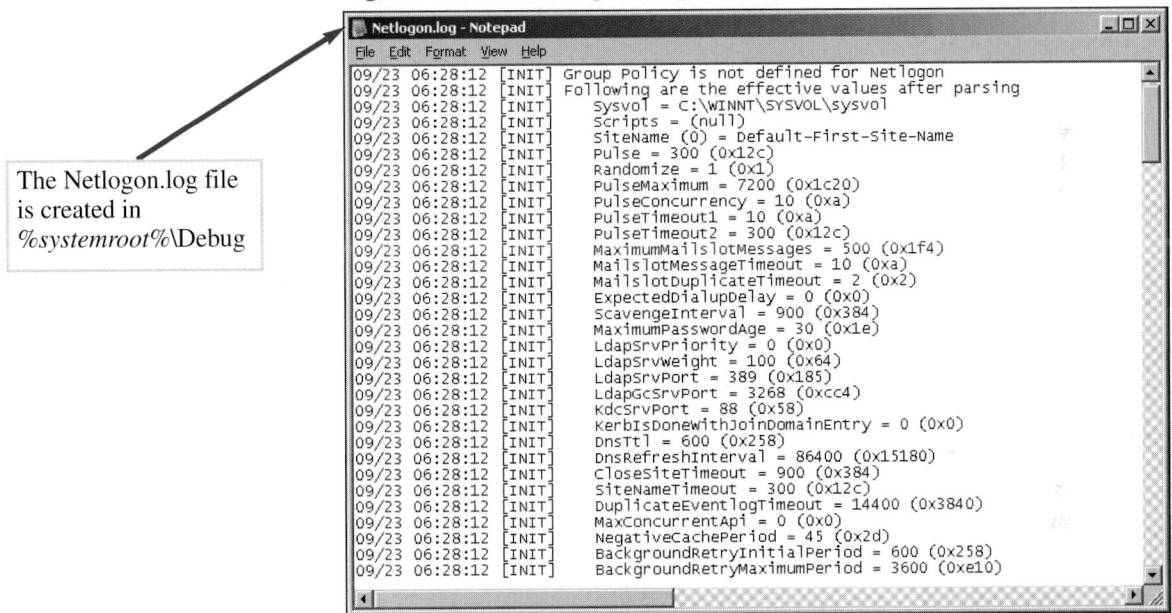

The Netlogon.log file is created in %systemroot%\Debug

Figure 12-28 Adding the LogLevel Registry value

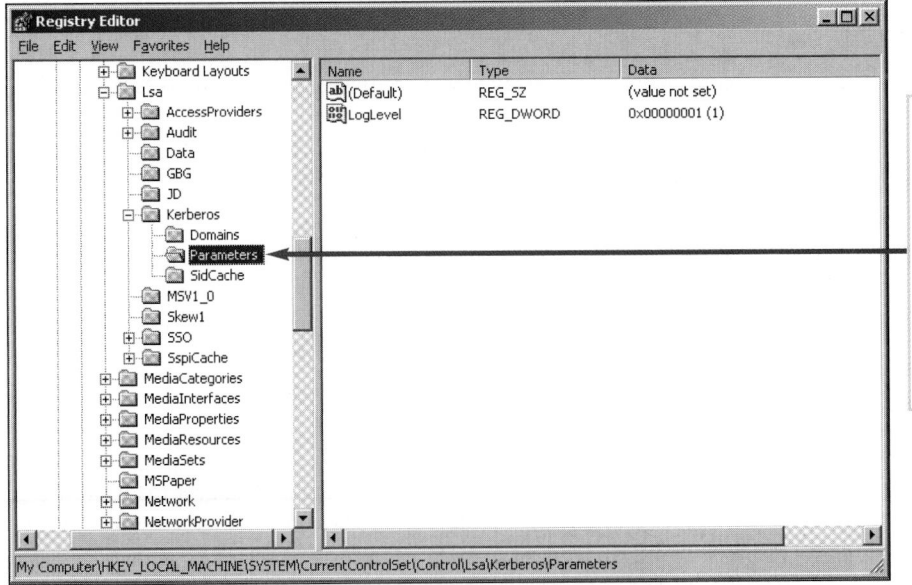

To enable Kerberos event logging on a computer, add a Registry value named LogLevel to the HKEY_LOCAL_MACHINE\SYSTEM\CurrentControlSet\Control\Lsa\Kerberos\Parameters Registry key; it must be the REG_DWORD Value type with a Value data of 0x1

skill 7

Diagnosing and Resolving Account Lockouts (cont'd)

exam objective

Diagnose and resolve account lockouts.

overview

Probably the most common reason for excessive account lockouts is that the account lockout threshold has been set lower than the recommended 10 invalid logon attempts. False lockouts will occur when programs or services automatically retry passwords that have changed. For instance, if you configure a scheduled task to run under a particular user context, you must enter the password for the user. If you then change that user's password, the scheduled task will fail. If the scheduled task runs very often, or if it is set to continually retry, it may inadvertently lock the account out.

Users may also be logging on to several computers at once and running programs that are accessing network resources using the account name and password they used to log on. If the user changes the password on one of these computers, those programs will continue to use the invalid password when they attempt to access another network resource, which will lead to an account lockout. On Windows XP Professional and Windows Server 2003 computers, the change will be detected and the user will be prompted to lock and unlock the computer to get the new password. However, network users should be instructed to log off of all computers before they change their password to avoid this situation on older systems. Saved credentials should also be deleted in the **Stored User Names and Passwords** applet in the Control Panel if they are the same as the logon credentials. This applet is used to store logon information that is used to authenticate for different resources **(Figure 12-29)**. The operating system tries the current logon credentials when there are no explicitly saved credentials in Stored User Names and Passwords.

You can also check for scheduled tasks that have been set using credentials that are no longer current and for persistent drive mappings that were established using credentials that have expired or been deleted. If a user enters a user name and password to connect to a share, those credentials are not persistent unless they have been saved in Stored User Names and Passwords. When the user logs off or on the network, or reboots the computer, Windows tries to restore the connection using stored credentials and authentication fails. You can prevent this from happening by entering **net use /persistent:no** at the command prompt to stop persistent connections, or you can disconnect and reconnect the persistent drive. You should also make sure that Active Directory replication is occurring to ensure that user properties are being replicated between domain controllers. Terminal Server sessions (See Lesson 15) that are disconnected can also be running processes that access network resources using expired credentials. This can have the same effect as a user who is logged on to multiple computers, except that the lockout source is solely the computer that is running Terminal Services.

A group of tools called the ALTools.exe package is used to diagnose and troubleshoot account lockouts. These tools can be downloaded from the following Web page: **http://www.microsoft.com/downloads/details.aspx?FamilyId=7AF2E69C-91F3-4E63-8629-B999ADDE0B9E&displaylang=en**

After you download and save ALTools.exe, navigate to the location where you have saved it and double-click the icon to install it. You will be asked for the location where you want to store the extracted files. ALTools.exe includes LockoutStatus.exe, ALockout.dll, AcctInfo.dll, ALoInfo.exe, EventCombMT.exe, and NLParse.exe.

LockoutStatus.exe displays information about a locked out account that it has obtained from Active Directory. It displays all domain controllers in a domain **(DC Name)**, the sites where the domain controllers are located **(Site)**, the status of the user and whether the account is locked out **(User State)**, the number of bad logon attempts recorded on each domain controller **(Bad Pwd Count)**, the time of the last bad logon attempt **(Last Bad Pwd)**, the value of the last good password or the time when the computer was unlocked **(Pwd Last Set)**, the time when the account was locked out **(Lockout Time)**, and the domain controller that locked the account **(Orig Lock)**.

Figure 12-29 The Stored User Names and Passwords dialog box

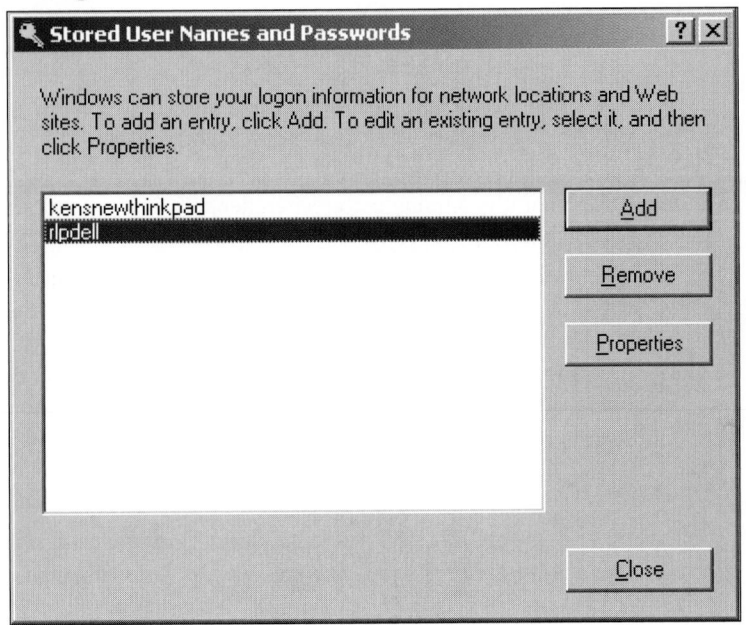

skill 7 | *Diagnosing and Resolving Account Lockouts (cont'd)*

exam objective

Diagnose and resolve account lockouts.

overview

To run LockoutStatus.exe, simply double-click it, open the **File** menu, and choose **Select Target**. In the **Select Target & Credentials** dialog box **(Figure 12-30)**, enter the name of the user account that you want lockout information about and click **OK**. The information related to the locked out account, which is received from the domain controllers in the domain, displays in a window titled with the user's name **(Figure 12-31)**.

ALockout.dll is a logging tool that is used to find out what program or process is sending incorrect credentials. You use it after you have enabled Netlogon and Kerberos logging and logon auditing on the local computer. ALockout.dll can attach to a number of different function calls that might be used by a process for authentication. It saves data about the process or program making the function calls in **%systemroot%\Debug\Alockout.txt**. Each event is time stamped. You can then locate events with the same time stamp in the Security event log or in Netlogon.log to get more information. The Appinit.reg script must first be used to initialize the ALockout.dll file. This tool should not be installed on servers that host any network programs or services and it should not be enabled on Exchange servers, as it may prevent the Exchange database from loading. Generally, you will install it on a client computer after you have examined the Netlogon.log file and the Security event log, and determined that it is sending incorrect credentials. It is a good practice to make a full backup of all data and the operating system before you install Alockout.dll.

Before you can use the Appinit.reg script to initialize the ALockout.dll file, you must copy both ALockout.dll and Appinit.reg to the **%systemroot%\system32** folder on the computer that has generated account lockout error messages in the Security event log. Then, double-click Appinit.reg to run the script and add the dll to the Appinit_DLL Registry key (i.e., register the dll). You must then reboot the computer to complete the installation. When an account locks out on the computer, **Alockout.txt** will be created in the **%systemroot%/Debug** folder **(Figure 12-32)**. You can then compare event time stamps in ALockout.txt with the time stamps in Netlogon.log and the Security event log to determine what process is causing the lockouts.

To remove ALockout.dll, first delete it from the **%systemroot%\system32** folder. Then, open the command prompt and type **regsvr32 /u alockout.dll**. Finally, open the Registry Editor and navigate to **HKEY_LOCAL_MACHINE\Software\Microsoft\Windows NT\Current Version\Windows**. Double-click the **AppInit_DLLs** Registry key and delete the **Alockout.dll** value data so that the Registry key is blank. Then, reboot the computer.

AcctInfo.dll is used to add a new property page to user objects when you display them in the Active Directory Users and Computers console. The property page supplies extensive data about user password attributes that can be used to isolate and troubleshoot account lockouts. You can also use the property page to reset the user's passwords on a domain controller in the user's site. AcctInfo.dll displays the last time the password was set, when it will expire, the time the account was locked out, the SID (security identifier) and SIDHistory for the account, the GUID (globally unique identifier) for the account, and the User Account Control Raw Value and Decode values. It also provides the Last Logon, Last Logoff, Last Bad Logon Time, Logon Count, and Bad Password Count account properties. Remember that replication may not always be up-to-date on all domain controllers, and AcctInfo.dll will display the data from only domain controller.

To install AcctInfo.dll, first copy it to the **system32** folder on the domain controller where you are going to run Active Directory Users and Computers. Next, open a command prompt and type **regsvr32 acctinfo.dll**. Press **[Enter]** to register the dll. Click **OK**. In order to use the **Account Lockout Status** button in the tool, LockoutStatus.exe must also be in the **%systemroot%\system32** folder. Open the Active Directory Users and Computers console. Right-click the user name, select **Properties**, and select the **Additional Account Info** tab **(Figure 12-33)**. Click the **Domain PW Info** button to view the password policy for the domain **(Figure 12-34)**. To reset the user's password on a domain controller in the user's site, click the

Figure 12-30 The Select Target & Credentials dialog box

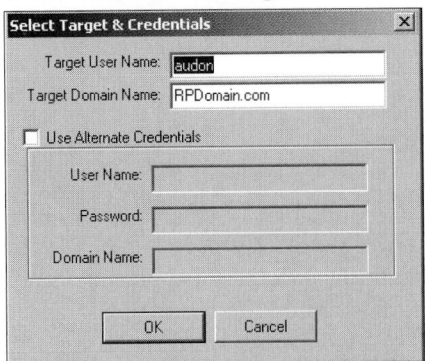

Figure 12-31 Displaying information with the LockoutStatus.exe tool

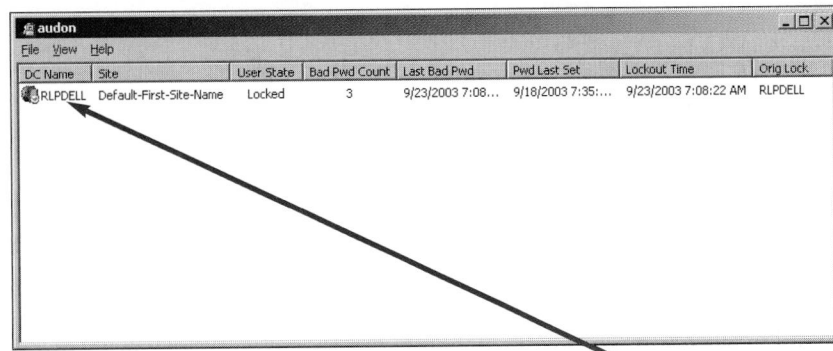

LockoutStatus.exe displays information about a locked out account that it has obtained from Active Directory

Figure 12-32 Alockout.txt

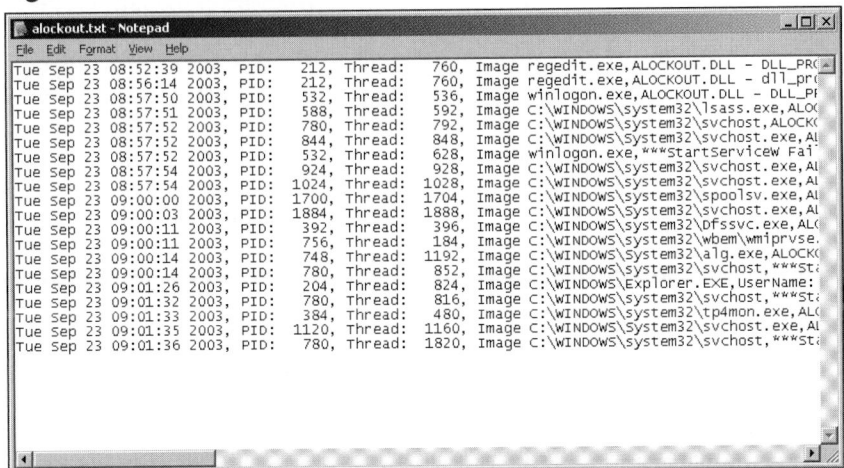

Figure 12-33 The Additional Account Info tab

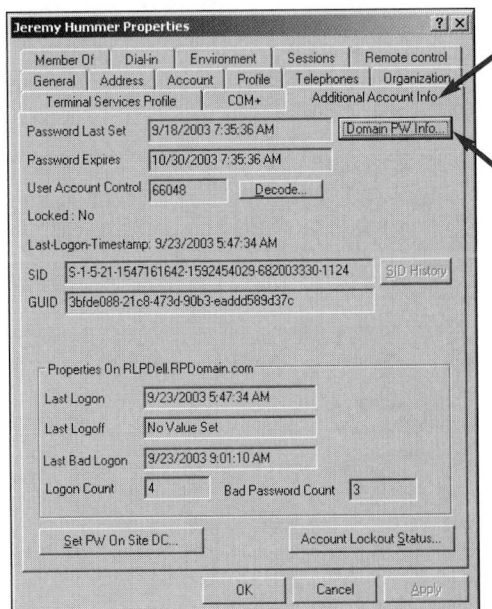

The new Additional Account Info property page provides detailed information about a user account that can be used to isolate and troubleshoot account lockouts

Click the Domain PW Info button on the Additional Account Info tab to view the password policy for the domain

Figure 12-34 The Domain Password Policy dialog box

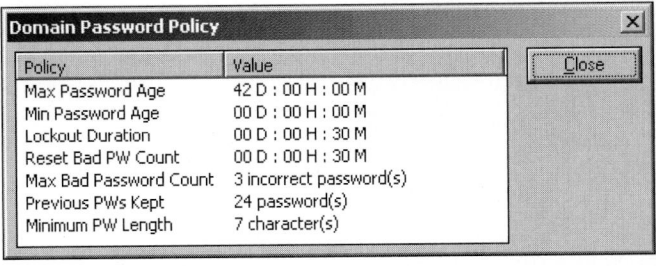

skill 7

Diagnosing and Resolving Account Lockouts (cont'd)

exam objective

Diagnose and resolve account lockouts.

overview

Set PW On Site DC button. Enter the name of the user's computer and enter and confirm the new password (**Figure 12-35**). To remove AcctInfo.dll, first delete the AcctInfo.dll file from the *%systemroot%*/**system32** folder. Then, open the command prompt and type the following: **regsvr32 /u acctinfo.dll.**

ALoInfo.exe is used to determine which users' passwords are about to expire. You use it when you have determined that account lockouts are often occurring on your network after users have been forced to change their passwords. ALoInfo.exe displays all user account names and their password age. You can also use it to view a list of all local services and their startup account information.

To install ALoInfo.exe, you simply have to install the ALTools.exe package on your domain controller. To display the account password ages on a domain controller in descending password age order, type **aloinfo /expires /server:<*domain_controller_name*>**, at the command prompt. To display all local service startup account information and the mapped drive information for a user who is currently logged on, at the command prompt, type **aloinfo /stored /server:<*computer_name*>**. You can also send the output from ALoInfo.exe to a text file, which you can sort to try to figure out which users are involved in the account lockout or save for future analysis.

EventCombMT.exe is a tool with specific built-in search categories that is used to collect events from the event logs of several different computers. Searching for account lockouts is one of the built-in search capabilities. The events that you can use EventCombMT.exe to locate are explained in **Table 12-9**. The events are consolidated in one place and you can designate that you want to search for specific events and computers.

To run EventCombMT.exe, simply locate and double-click **EventCombMT.exe**, open the **Searches** menu, point to **Built in searches**, and select **Account lockouts**. Events will be compiled from the event logs from all of the domain controllers in your site. You can also search for other events, such as event **12294**, by adding them to the **Event IDs** box. Click the **Search** button to start the search. The results will display in the **Status** box (**Figure 12-36**), and can be saved to the EventCombMT.txt file. Security_LOG.txt files will also be created for each domain controller searched (**Figure 12-37**).

NLParse.exe is used to parse Netlogon log files, which can grow to up to 20 MB in size, in order to locate specific data. You can specify that you want to view only particular Netlogon return status codes, for example, 0xC000006A and 0xC0000234, which are for account lockouts. You can save the results in a comma-separated values (.csv) file that can be opened in Excel and sorted.

Table 12-9 Events you can locate using EventCombMT.exe

Event #	Description
644	Generated when an account is locked out.
675	Generated on a Key Distribution Center (KDC) when a user types in an incorrect password.
676	Generated on pre-Windows XP and Windows Server 2003 computers when an Authentication ticket request has failed.
529	Generated when a logon attempt was made with an unknown user name or a known user name with a bad password.
681	Generated when a logon failure using a domain account logon on a pre-Windows XP and Windows Server 2003 computer has occurred.

Figure 12-35 The Change Password On a DC In The Users Site dialog box

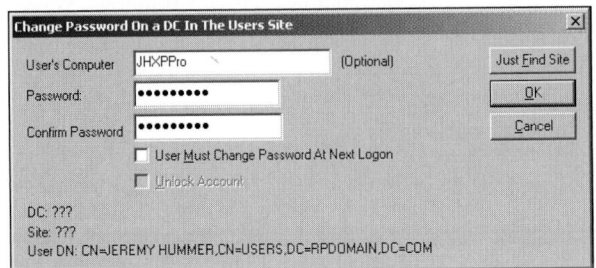

Figure 12-36 EventCombMT

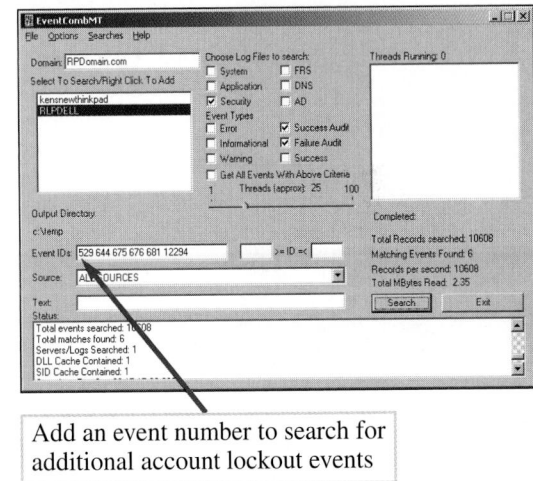

Add an event number to search for additional account lockout events

Figure 12-37 Results from EventCombMT

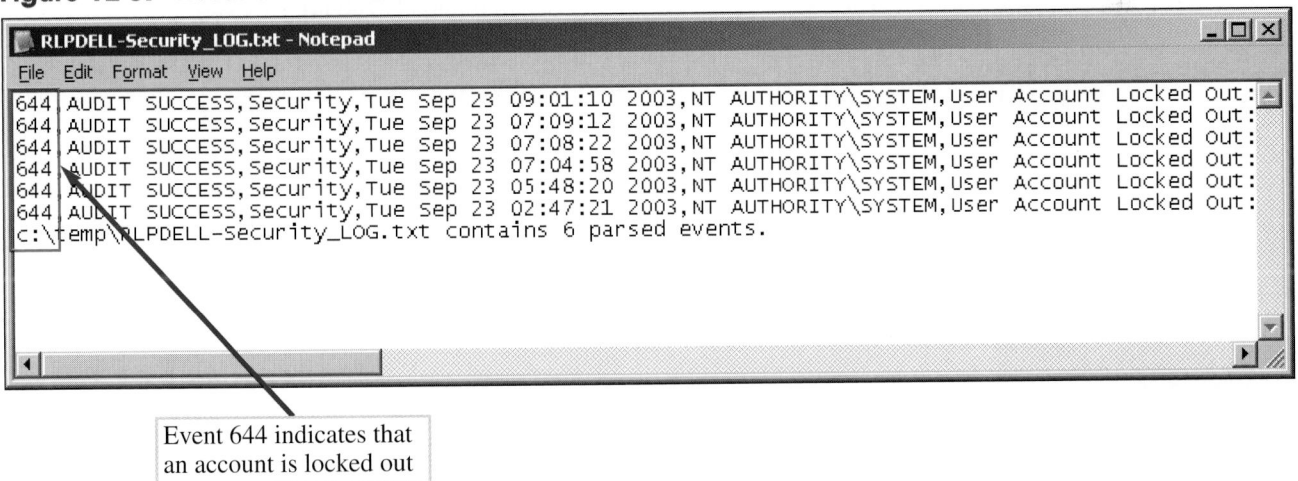

Event 644 indicates that an account is locked out.

skill 7 · *Diagnosing and Resolving Account Lockouts (cont'd)*

exam objective

Diagnose and resolve account lockouts.

overview

To run NLParse.exe, simply locate and double-click **Nlparse.exe**, and click the **Open** button. Use the **Open** dialog box to locate and open the Netlogon.log file that you want to parse. Then, select the appropriate check boxes to configure the search. After you have selected the status codes that you want to search for, click the **Extract** button **(Figure 12-38)**. The output goes to a CSV file, Netlogon.log -Out.csv, that will open in Excel and can be sorted further, if necessary.

FindStr.exe, a command line tool, can also be used to parse Netlogon log files. It is more versatile because it can be used to parse several Netlogon.log files at the same time. It is included with the default installations of Windows 2000, Windows XP, and Windows Server 2003. First, you must collect the Netlogon,log files from several domain controllers, rename them, and save them all in the same folder. Then, at the command prompt, type **FindStr /I** *"User1"* ***netlogon*.log >c:*user1.txt***. You can extract data about a particular user account, computer account, or error code from the Netlogon.log files.

more

One thing you must keep in mind when dealing with account lockouts is that replication latency can delay when changes that you have instituted, such as unlocking an account, will take effect. The first thing you can do to counteract replication latency is to make changes to a user's account only in the user's local site. Do this by ensuring that the Active Directory Users and Computers console is focused on a domain controller located in the user's site. Right-clicking on the root of the console allows you to change the focus.

You can also use the Replmon and Repadmin utilities to verify that Active Directory replication is taking place. Replmon and Repadmin are included in Support.cab in the Support\Tools folder on the Windows Server 2003, Standard Edition CD-ROM.

Type **replmon** at the command prompt to open the Replication Monitor. First, right-click **Monitored Servers**, select **Add Monitored Server**, and add the servers you want to monitor. In the Replication Monitor you can view the "low-level" status of Active Directory replication between all domain controllers in a single site. For example, you can see which partitions are being replicated on each domain controller and who the replication partners are for each partition. You can also find out if the domain controller is a global catalog server and you can force synchronization between domain controllers and across site boundaries.

Type **repadmin /showrepl** at the command prompt to display the replication partners for each naming context.

Figure 12-38 Netlogon-Parse

The return codes specific to account lockouts are 0xC000006A and 0xC0000234

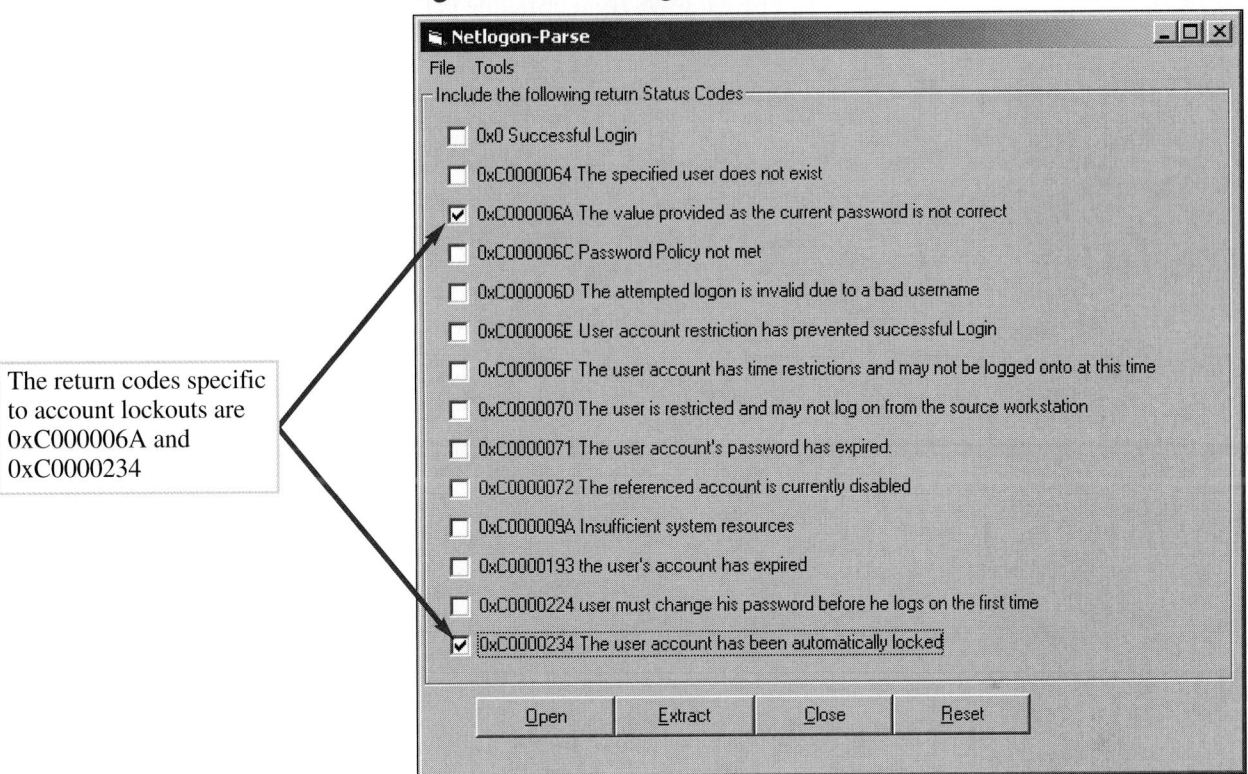

skill 8

Implementing Security Options

exam objective

Basic knowledge

overview

There are many Security Options you can use to further enhance the security of your network. For example, you can **Restrict CD-ROM (or floppy) access to the locally logged-on user only**, or you can **Prevent users from installing printer drivers**.

You can also set the behavior for installing unsigned drivers (**Unsigned driver installation behavior**). You can either set the system to **Silently succeed**, to **Warn but allow installation**, or to disallow the installation of unsigned drivers (**Do not allow installation**). Other security options include allowing automatic administrative log on to the Recovery Console (**Recovery Console: Allow automatic administrative logon**) and shutting down the system immediately if the system is unable to log security audits.

The **Security Options** node, which is found under the **Local Policies** node in the Local Security Policy console or in the Computer Configuration\Windows Settings\Security Settings\Local Policies node in the **Group Policy Object Editor**, is used to set 67 types of security options for a computer, OU, domain, or site (**Figure 12-39**).

Security Options are divided into 14 general categories depending on their function:

- Accounts
- Audit
- Devices
- Domain controller
- Domain member
- Interactive logon
- Microsoft network client
- Network access
- Network security
- Recovery Console
- Shutdown
- System cryptography
- System objects
- System settings

how to

Configure Security Options.

1. On a domain controller, click ![Start], point to **Administrative Tools**, and click **Group Policy Management** to open the **Group Policy Management** console.
2. Expand the node for the forest your domain is in, if necessary.
3. Expand the **Domains** node.
4. Double-click the name of your domain.
5. Right-click **Default Domain Policy** and click **Edit** to open the **Group Policy Object Editor** snap-in.
6. In the console tree, in the **Computer Configuration** node, double-click the **Windows Settings** node to expand it.
7. Double-click **Security Settings**.
8. Double-click **Local Policies**.
9. Double-click **Security Options**.

Figure 12-39 Security Options

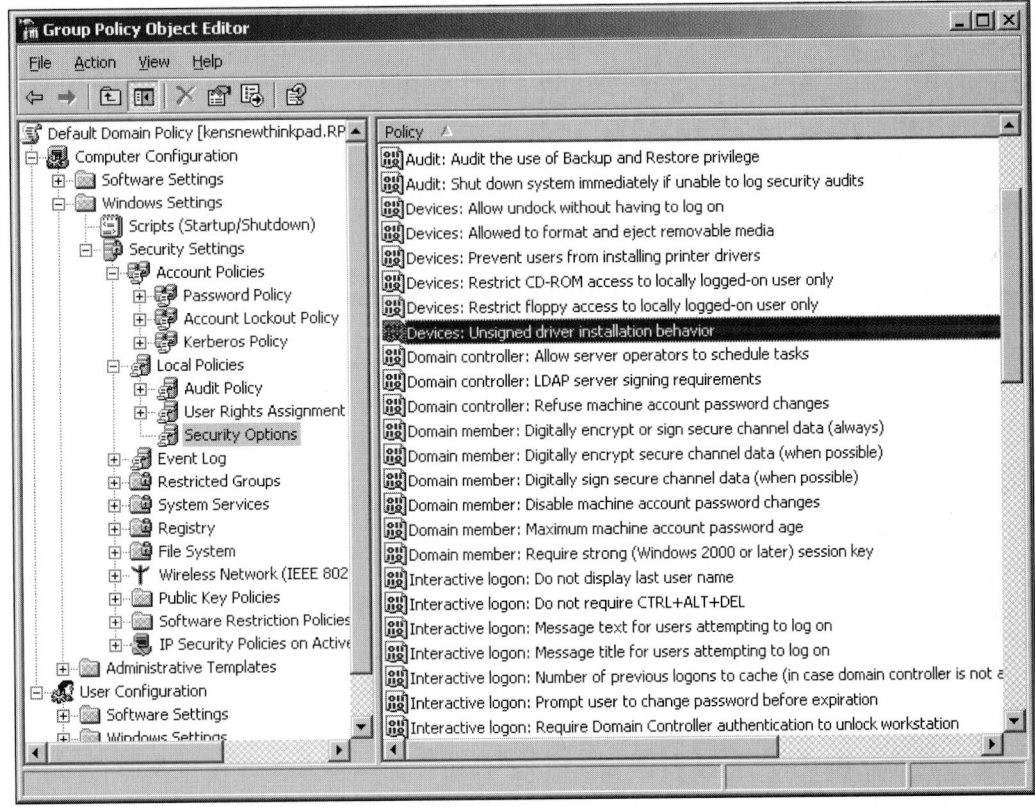

skill 8

Implementing Security Options (cont'd)

exam objective

Basic knowledge

how to

10. Double-click **Accounts: Rename Guest Account**.
11. Select the **Define this policy setting** check box.
12. Type **Corporate** in the **Define this policy setting** text box (**Figure 12-40**). Click [OK].
13. Double-click **Interactive Logon: Do not display last user name**.
14. Select the **Define this policy setting** check box. Click the **Enabled** option button (**Figure 12-41**).
15. Click [OK]. The last user name who logged on will no longer appear in the logon dialog box.
16. Double-click **Shutdown: Allow system to be shutdown without having to logon**.
17. Select the **Define this policy setting** check box. Select the **Disabled** option button (**Figure 12-42**). Click [OK]. No one will be able to shut down a computer unless he or she has logged on.
18. Close the **Group Policy Object Editor** and the **Group Policy Management** console.

Figure 12-40 The Accounts: Rename guest account Properties dialog box

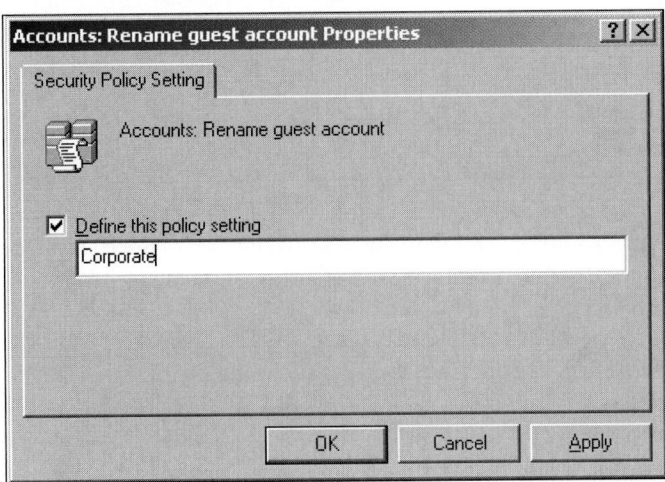

Figure 12-41 The Interactive logon: Do not display last user name Properties dialog box

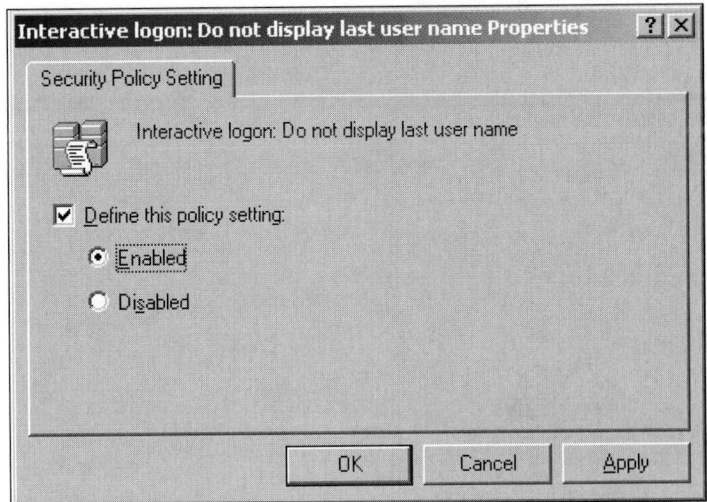

Figure 12-42 The Shutdown: Allow system to be shut down without having to log on Properties dialog box

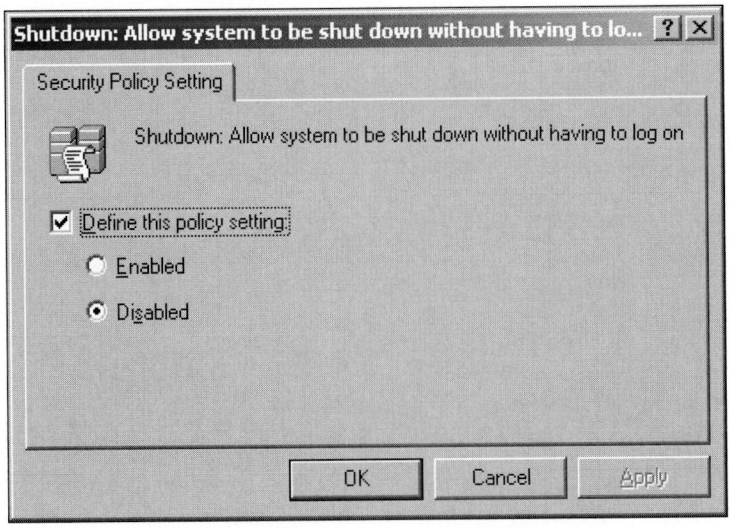

skill 9

Configuring User Rights Assignments

Basic knowledge

overview

User rights assignments are configured to designate the tasks a user or group is allowed to perform either on an individual system or on a domain. User rights are divided into two categories: logon rights and privileges. **Logon rights** are assigned to designate who can log on to a computer and how they can log on. For example, the **Access this computer from the network** user right lets a user connect to a computer from the network, and the **Allow log on locally** user right allows a user to log on interactively at a computer at which the user is physically located.

By default, on workstations and servers, members of the Administrators, Backup Operators, Power Users, Users, and Everyone groups can connect to the computer from the network. On domain controllers, members of the Administrators, Authenticated Users, and Everyone groups can connect over the network.

By default on workstations and servers, Administrators, Backup Operators Power Users, Users, and Guest can log on interactively to the computer. On domain controllers, Account Operators, Administrators, Backup Operators, Print Operators, and Server Operators can log on interactively. Logons that are begun by pressing the [Ctrl]+[Alt]+[Del] sequence require this right, and some service or administrative applications may need this right if they have the ability to log on users. For security purposes, you may want to restrict who can log on interactively to a domain controller or server, or you may need to assign this right to a certain group to allow them local access.

Privileges permit users to interact with the operating system and with system-wide resources. For example, the **Add workstations to domain** user right allows a user to add up to ten computers to a specific domain. This privilege must be assigned to a user as part of the Default Domain Controllers policy for the domain. Other examples of privileges are the **Shut down the system** and **Change the system time** user rights. The Change the system time privilege is assigned to users so that they will be able to change the time on the internal clock for a computer. The Shut down the system privilege allows a user to shut down the local computer. Other user rights include performing volume maintenance, generating security audits, creating and changing the size of a page file, taking ownership of files or other objects, and much more.

how to

Set user rights assignments.

1. On a domain controller, click **Start**, point to **Administrative Tools**, and click **Group Policy Management** to open the **Group Policy Management** console.
2. Expand the node for the forest your domain is in, if necessary.
3. Expand the **Domains** node.
4. Double-click the name of your domain.
5. Right-click **Default Domain Policy** and click **Edit** to open the **Group Policy Object Editor** snap-in.
6. In the console tree, in the **Computer Configuration** node, double-click the **Windows Settings** node to expand it.
7. Double-click **Security Settings**. Double-click **Local Policies**.
8. Double-click **User Rights Assignment** to display the policies in the details pane (**Figure 12-43**). Scroll through the list and examine the policies that can be set.
9. Double-click **Access this computer from the network**. Select the **Define these policy settings** check box, if necessary. Select the **Everyone** group if it is included in the list, and click **Remove**.

Figure 12-43 User Rights Assignment

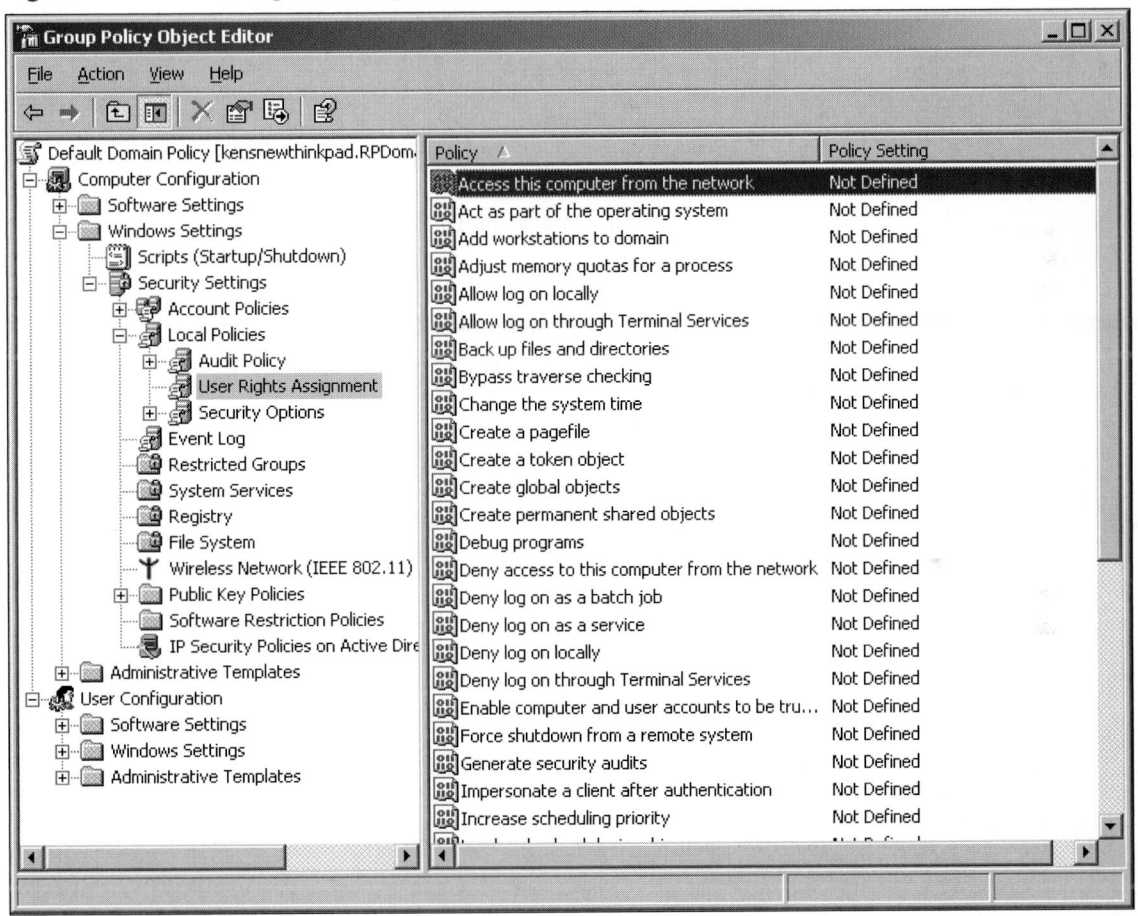

skill 9

Configuring User Rights Assignments (cont'd)

exam objective

Basic knowledge

how to

10. Click | Add User or Group... | to open the **Add User or Group** dialog box.

11. Click | Browse ... | to open the **Select Users, Computers, or Groups** dialog box. Click | Advanced... |. Click | Find Now |.

12. Hold down the **[Ctrl]** key and select the **DNSAdmins** and **Domain Admins** groups **(Figure 12-44)**. Click | OK |.

13. Click | OK | to close the Select Users, Computers, or Groups dialog box.

14. Click | OK | to close the Add User or Group dialog box.

15. The two groups have been added to the **Access this computer from the network Properties** dialog box **(Figure 12-45)**. Click | OK |.

16. Double-click **Shut down the system**. Select the **Define these policy settings** check box, if necessary. Click | Add User or Group... |.

17. Click | Browse ... |. Click | Advanced... |. Click | Find Now |.

18. Double-click **Administrators** and click | OK | to close the Select Users, Computers, or Groups dialog box.

19. Click | OK | twice to close the open dialog boxes.

20. Close the Group Policy Object Editor snap-in, the Properties dialog box for the domain, and the Active Directory Users and Computers console.

Figure 12-44 The Select Users, Computers, or Groups dialog box

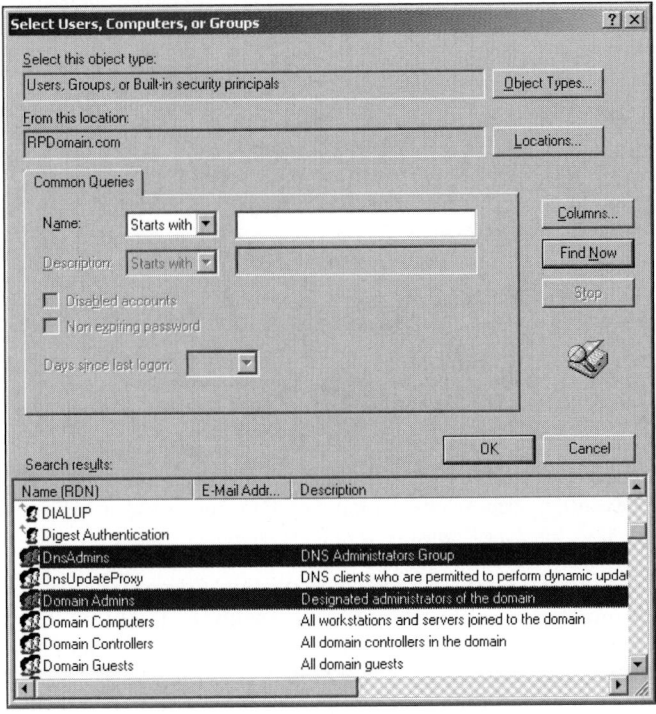

Figure 12-45 The Access this computer from the network Properties dialog box

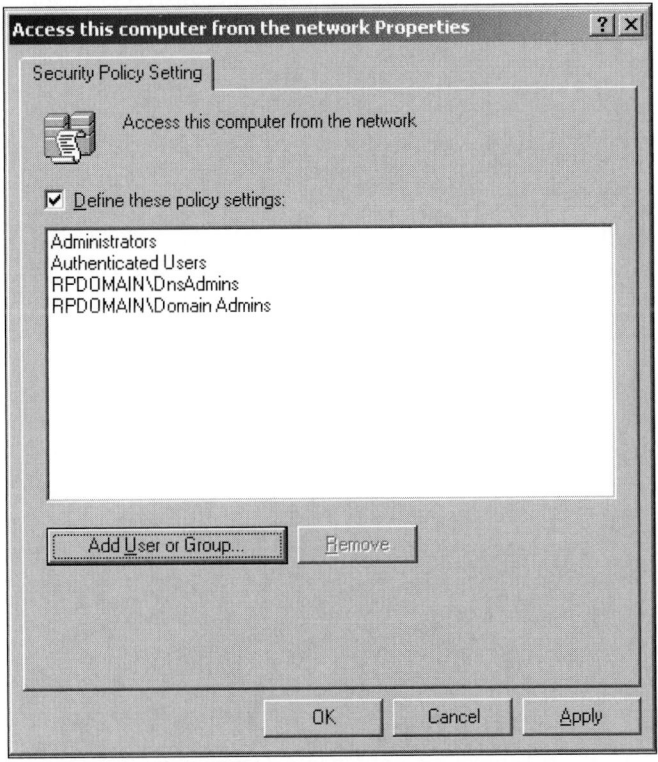

skill 10

Configuring Client Security

exam objective

Basic knowledge

overview

You can use Administrative Template policy settings to customize the settings used by the clients that access a Windows Server 2003 network. The two main reasons these policies are used are to improve security and to supply a consistent working environment for all clients. These policies are generally put into effect when the client logs on to the server, although they can also be set for the local computer. For example, you can disable the entire Control Panel or particular elements of the Control Panel for all clients who log on to the network or for a particular group of clients.

As you have learned, you use the Group Policy Object Editor to configure policies for clients that can apply at the site, domain or OU level, although not all policies can be applied at all levels. Administrative Templates are commonly used to manage the user environment, such as preventing users from accessing certain functions, or to control the use of particular software such as Internet Explorer or objects such as printers.

The nodes in the User Configuration\Administrative Templates node are: **Windows Components**, **Start Menu and Taskbar**, **Desktop**, **Control Panel**, **Shared Folders, Network**, and **System (Figure 12-46)**. The types of policies you can set from each of these nodes are outlined in **Table 12-10**.

One aspect of working with the numerous policy settings in the User Configuration\ Administrative Templates node that eases the burden somewhat is that in **Extended** view, when you select a policy, a detailed explanation appears to the left of the list of policies in the details pane. This description generally includes not only an explanation of what the policy setting will accomplish, but also the minimum software and system requirements if applicable. In addition, after you have configured policies, you can use the **show** links for a particular node on the **Settings** tab in the Group Policy Management console to expand the nodes and view the configured policies. You can select a policy, for example, User Configuration\Administrative Templates\Control Panel, Prohibit access to the Control Panel, to read an explanation of what the policy will do.

The settings available in the Administrative Templates node are based on .adm template files. These settings designate Registry entry modifications that change aspects of the user environment. The preconfigured administrative templates determine what the groups of configurable settings will be. They are stored in *%systemroot%* \inf. The preconfigured administrative templates are explained in **Table 12-11**. The group of settings that can be configured can also be extended by creating custom .adm files.

how to

Configure Group Policy for Windows Server 2003 clients and install an administrative template.

1. On a domain controller, click ![Start], point to **Administrative Tools**, and click **Group Policy Management** to open the **Group Policy Management** console.
2. Expand the node for the forest your domain is in, if necessary.
3. Expand the **Domains** node.
4. Double-click the name of your domain.
5. Right-click **Default Domain Policy** and click **Edit** to open the **Group Policy Object Editor** snap-in.
6. Expand the **User Configuration** node. Expand the **Administrative Templates** node.
7. Select **Windows Components**. Double-click **Internet Explorer**.

**Figure 12-46 The User Configuration\
Administrative Templates node**

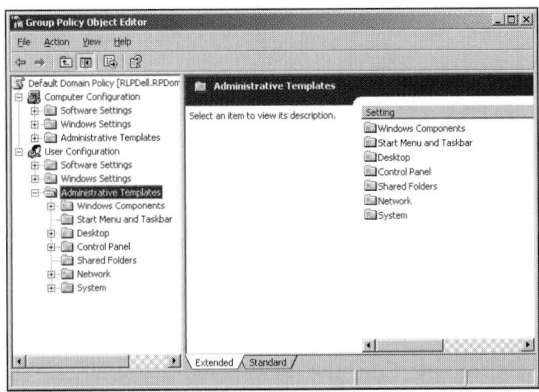

Table 12-10 User Configuration\Administrative Templates

Node	Types of Policies
Windows Components	Policies to control installed software such as Internet Explorer, Windows Installer, Windows Messenger, Windows Update, the Help and Support Center, and more.
Start Menu and Taskbar	Policies that will affect the ability of users to change the configuration of the Start menu and to use Start menu options.
Desktop	Policies that will affect the ability of users to access desktop utilities such as Internet Explorer, My Computer, the Recycle Bin, and My Network Places, and how they will be able to conduct Active Directory searches.
Control Panel	Policies to control access to Control Panel applets including the Add/Remove Programs utility, the Display Properties and Regional and Language Options dialog boxes, and the Printers and Faxes window.
Shared Folders	Policies that enable users to publish shared folders or Dfs roots in Active Directory.
Network	Policies that affect users' ability to access offline files and to configure network connections in the Network Connections window.
System	Policies that control user access to system functions, such as which domain controller the Group Policy Object Editor snap-in uses, the use of the Task Manager, and whether users will be able to change their passwords at will.

Table 12-11 Windows Server 2003 Administrative Templates

Template	Explanation
Common.adm	Used to control the desktop settings for Windows 9.x and NT clients. It is used with the System Policy Editor (Poledit.exe).
Conf.adm	Used to set NetMeeting policies used by client computers for common communications.
Inetcorp.adm	Used to set dial-up properties, language and temporary Internet files settings for Internet Explorer.
Inetres.adm	Used to configure Internet Explorer policies for Windows 2000 clients.
Inetset.adm	Used to control advanced settings and additional Internet properties in Internet Explorer.
System.adm	The default settings used to manage desktop settings for Windows 2000 and XP Professional clients.
Windows.adm	Used to set user interface options specific to Windows 95 and Windows 98. It is used with the System Policy Editor (Poledit.exe).
Winnt.adm	Used to control user interface options specific to Windows NT 4.0. It is used with the System Policy Editor (Poledit.exe).
Wmp.adm	Used to manage Windows Media Player 6.4 configuration on client computers.
Wmplayer.adm	Used to control Windows Media player settings for Windows 2000 and Windows XP clients.
Waua.adm	Used to control how systems can use Windows Update to auto-update over the Internet.

skill10

Configuring Client Security *(cont'd)*

exam objective

Basic knowledge

how to

8. Double-click **Disable changing history settings**. Open the **Explain** tab. When you enable this policy setting, users will not be able to change the settings in the History area in the Internet Options dialog box **(Figure 12-47)**.
9. Return to the **Setting** tab. Select the **Enabled** option button **(Figure 12-48)**.
10. Click [Next Setting] to open the **Disable changing color settings Properties** dialog box. Click the **Enabled** option button. Users will not be able to change the default Web page colors. Click [OK].
11. Double-click **Internet Control Panel**.
12. Double-click **Disable the Security Page**. Click the **Enabled** option button.
13. Click [Next Setting] twice. In the **Disable the Connections page Properties** dialog box, click the **Enabled** option button.
14. Click [Next Setting] three times. In the **Disable the Advanced page Properties** dialog box, click the **Enabled** option button. These policy settings will prevent users from making any changes to Internet Explorer's Security, Connections, and Advanced Properties pages. Click [OK].
15. In the console tree, select **Control Panel** (in the Administrative Templates node)
16. In the details pane, double-click **Prohibit access to Control Panel**.
17. Select the **Explain** tab and read the explanation of the policy setting **(Figure 12-49)**.
18. Return to the Setting tab and select the **Enabled** option button. Click [OK].
19. Right-click **Administrative Templates** and select **Add/Remove Templates** to open the **Add/Remove Templates** dialog box. The files listed here are the loaded .adm files.
20. Click [Add...] to open the **Policy Templates** dialog box **(Figure 12-50)**. Double-click **inetcorp.adm**. This template is used to set dial-up properties, language and temporary Internet files settings for Internet Explorer.
21. Click [Yes] if the **Confirm File Replace** dialog box opens because the template is already installed. When you load an administrative template, the .adm file is copied to *%systemroot%*\SYSVOL\Sysvol\<*domain_name*>\Policies\GUID\Adm.
22. Click [Close].
23. Close the **Group Policy Editor** and the **Group Policy Management** console.

Figure 12-47 Display changing history settings Properties dialog box-Explain tab

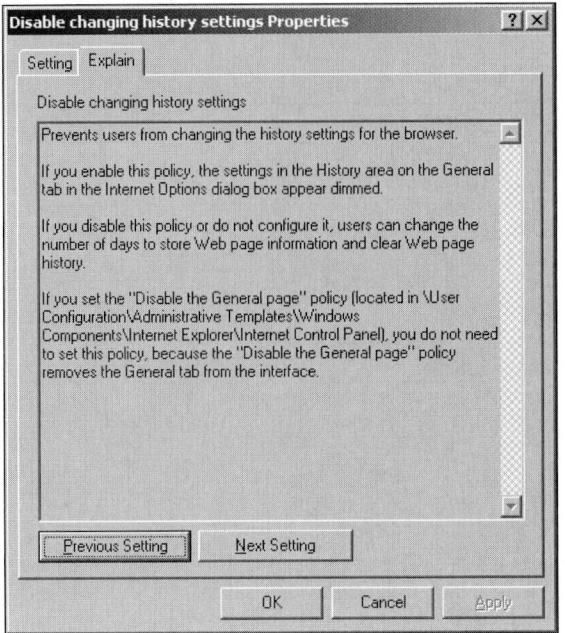

Figure 12-48 Display changing history settings Properties dialog box- Setting tab

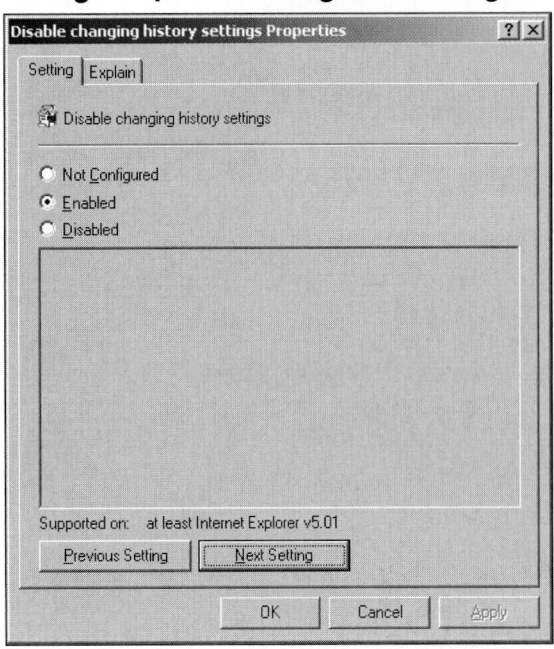

Figure 12-49 Prohibit access to the Control Panel Properties dialog box

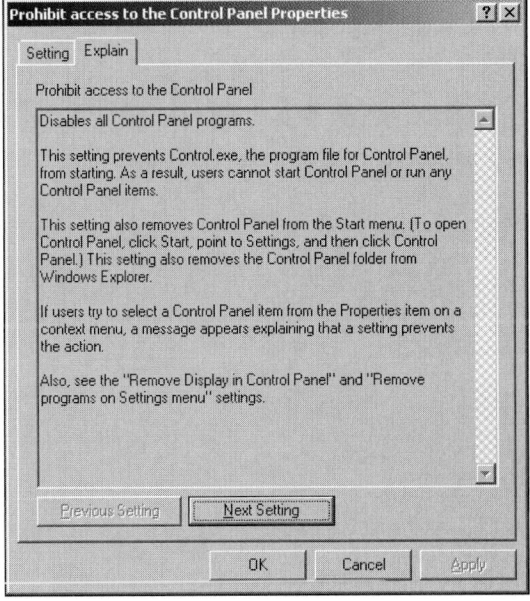

Figure 12-50 The Policy Templates dialog box

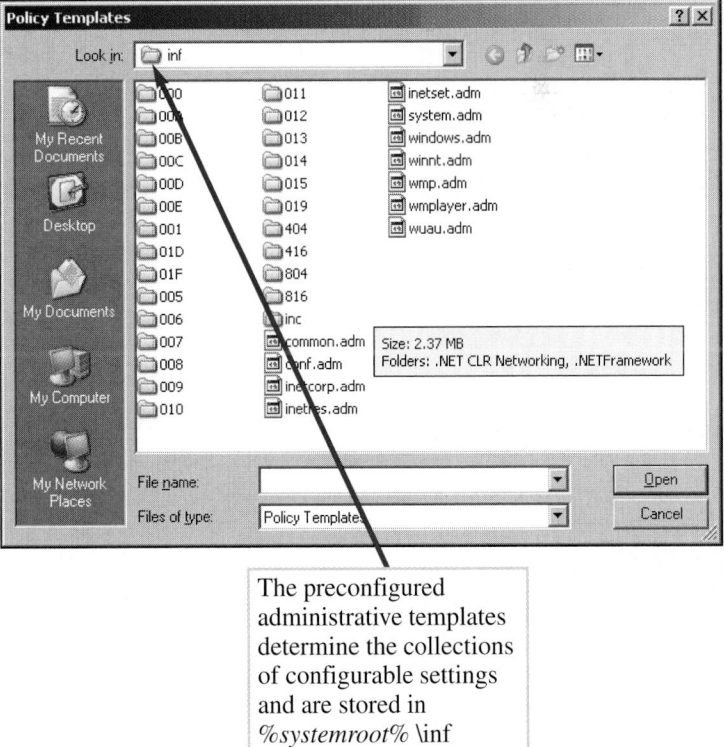

The preconfigured administrative templates determine the collections of configurable settings and are stored in %systemroot% \inf

skill 11 *Working with Security Tools and Templates*

Implement, configure, manage and troubleshoot security by using the configuration tool set.

You can create a custom MMC with the **Security Templates** and **Security Configuration and Analysis** snap-ins to provide a centralized tool where many of the security attributes are organized in one place, and you can analyze the security configuration of a computer. A security template can include password and account lockout policies, local security policies, user rights assignments, Registry key security, group memberships, and permissions for the local file system. On a domain-based network, you can import a security template into a Group Policy object so that all of the settings are put into operation on a site, a domain, or an OU. You use the **Import Policy** command on the context menu for the **Security Settings** node in order to import a security template to a Group Policy object. You import a security template to a Group Policy object in order to configure the security settings for multiple computers at one time. Security templates are saved as .inf files. You can copy, paste, import, and export some or all of the security settings from these text files to apply them to a Group Policy object. All security attributes, except IPSec and Public Key policies, can be stored in a security template. In a workgroup environment, you can use Security Configuration and Analysis to configure security on each computer, and then ensure that they retain their security settings by scheduling the command line version of Security Configuration and Analysis, secedit.exe, to apply the template at logon. Secedit.exe is discussed further in the More section at the end of this skill.

The Security and Configuration Analysis snap-in is used to compare the current security configuration of the computer to one of the security templates, to create custom templates, and to apply a template to either the local computer or to a Group Policy object. The predefined templates are explained in **Table 12-12**.

When you open a database, you are creating a database that you will work with to analyze settings, make changes, and apply the new configuration. You can also simply use all of the database settings to apply the complete configuration outlined in one of the templates. The templates are .inf files.

When you install the operating system, a template file, **Setup Security.inf**, is created in the *%systemroot%*\security\templates folder to store the default security settings for the computer. These settings are determined by the original configuration of the computer. Upgraded computers will retain any security settings already applied. Setup Security.inf is created so that an administrator can return the computer to its original security settings, if necessary. This template should not be applied to a Group Policy object because it includes settings that may critically impede the performance of Group Policy processing.

Create a custom Security Templates console and use the Security and Configuration Analysis tool to analyze the current security configuration of a member server, customize one of the predefined security templates, and apply it to the local computer.

1. Click **Start** and click the **Run** command to open the **Run** dialog box.
2. Type **mmc** in the **Open** text box and press **[Enter]** to open the **Console Root** window.
3. Open the **File** menu and click **Add/Remove Snap-in** to open the **Add/Remove Snap-in** dialog box.
4. Click **Add...** to open the **Add Standalone Snap-in** dialog box. Scroll down the **Available Standalone Snap-ins** list to locate and select the **Security Templates** snap-in. Click **Add...**.
5. Select the **Security Configuration and Analysis** snap-in and click **Add...** (Figure 12-51).
6. Close the **Add Standalone Snap-in** dialog box.

Table 12-12   The Predefined Security Templates

Template	Explanation
compatws	Compatible workstation. Used on workstations or servers that must be compatible with older applications. Increased security in Windows Server 2003 can cause compatibility issues with legacy applications, particularly for older non-certified applications that must access the Registry. When you apply this template, Users group access controls are made less stringent for certain files, folders, and Registry keys that older applications often need to access so that they can be run with no problem by members of the Users group. You can apply this template to reduce the default security level and allow older applications to run in Windows Server 2003. (Other options are to make the user a member of the Power Users group or increase the permissions level for the Users group.)
hisecws	The template for a high security workstation or server. It should be applied only to computers running Windows 2000 or above, all computers in the domain must be configured, and all of the domain controllers in the domain to which the client belongs must run Windows 2000 or above, or network connectivity problems may ensue. This template increases security levels for network communication protocols. It will cause servers to reject connections from both LAN Manager and NTLM responses and requires server-side SMB packet signing.
hisecdc	The template for a high security domain controller. It should be applied only to domain controllers running Windows 2000 and above, and all domain controllers in the domain must run Windows 2000 or above.
rootsec	This template contains the original permissions assigned to the root of the system drive. It is used if the security permissions for the root directory have been accidentally changed and must be reapplied. It can also be modified and used to apply the same root permissions to other volumes.
securedc	The template for a secure domain controller. It will increase the security levels for Registry permissions, audit settings, and account policy (stronger password and lockout settings), which are the least likely to impact application compatibility. It will cause servers to reject connections from LAN Manager responses and enables server-side SMB packet signing, but does not require it.
securews	The template for a secure workstation or server. It will increase the security levels for Registry permissions, auditing, and account policy. These security settings are the least likely to impact application compatibility. It will cause servers to reject connections from LAN Manager responses and enables server-side SMB packet signing, but does not require it.
setup security	The template created during installation, which will vary depending on whether the installation was a clean installation or an upgrade. The default security settings for the root of the system drive, which were applied during installation, including the file permissions, are stored here. It can be applied only to servers and client computers, not to domain controllers. In disaster recovery situations, you can also just apply parts of this template.

Figure 12-51 The Add Standalone Snap-in dialog box

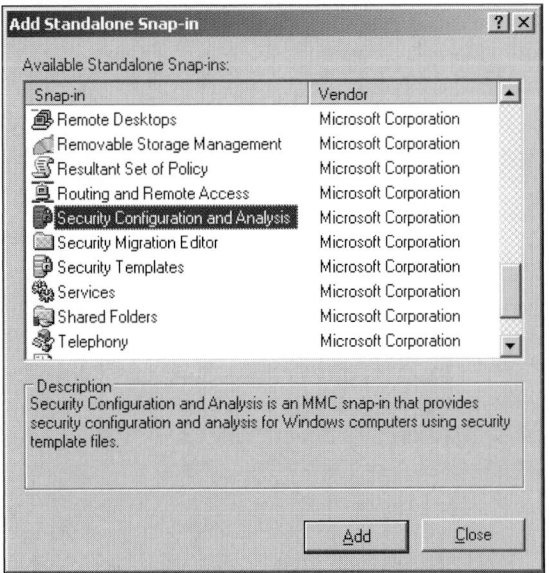

skill 11

Working with Security Tools and Templates (cont'd)

exam objective

Implement, configure, manage and troubleshoot security by using the configuration tool set.

how to

7. Close the **Add/Remove Snap-in** dialog box.
8. Open the **File** menu and click **Save** to open the **Save As** dialog box.
9. Type **Security Templates** in the **File name** text box, and click [Save]. By default, the console will be saved in the Administrative Tools folder.
10. Expand the **Security Templates** node. Expand the **%systemroot%\security\templates** node. The pre-configured security templates appear (**Figure 12-52**).
11. Right-click the **Security Configuration and Analysis** node and select **Open database** to open the **Open database** dialog box.
12. Type **Secure server** in the **File name** text box and click **Open** to open the **Import Template** dialog box.
13. Select **securews.inf** in the contents window and click **Open** to open the template for a secure workstation or server.
14. Right-click the **Security and Configuration Analysis** node and select **Analyze Computer Now**. Click [OK] in the **Perform Analysis** dialog box to confirm the path to the log file.
15. When the analysis is complete, open the **Security Configuration and Analysis** node.
16. Open the **Account Policies** node and select **Password Policy**. Policies with a green check mark indicate that the policy meets the requirements for a secure server. Policies with a red X do not (**Figure 12-53**).
17. Double-click **Enforce password history** to open the **Enforce password history Properties** dialog box. The database setting for a secure server is 24. Click [OK] to maintain this database setting for the template and close the dialog box.
18. Double-click **Minimum password length**. The database setting for a secure server is 8. In the **characters** spin box, enter **10** to change this database setting for the template (**Figure 12-54**). Click [OK].
19. Click the **Account Lockout Policy** node. Double-click **Account lockout threshold**.
20. The database setting for a secure server allows 5 invalid logon attempts. Click [OK] to maintain the database setting for the template.
21. Expand the **Local Policies** node and select **Audit Policy**. Open the **Audit account logon events Properties** dialog box. Remove the check mark from the **Define this policy in the database** check box, and click [OK] to remove this policy setting from the database.
22. Select the **Security Option**s node. Double-click **Interactive logon: Do not display last user name**. Click the **Enabled** option button, and click [OK] to define this policy in the database. Note that there are a number of security options that do not meet the requirements for a secure server.
23. Right-click the **Security Configuration and Analysis** node and select **Configure Computer Now**. In the **Configure System** dialog box, click [OK] to confirm the path to the log file (**Figure 12-55**). The system is configured with the custom template you designed in the exercise.
24. Right-click the **Security and Configuration Analysis** node and select the **Analyze Computer Now** command. Click [OK] in the **Perform Analysis** dialog box to confirm the path to the log file. You will now be able to view the information in the database and compare it with the new computer settings.
25. Expand the **Account Policies** node and select **Password Policy.** Notice that now the current computer settings match the database settings for all of the password policies.
26. Select **Account Lockout Policy**. All of the current computer settings now match the database settings.

**Figure 12-52 The default security templates in the
Security Templates snap-in**

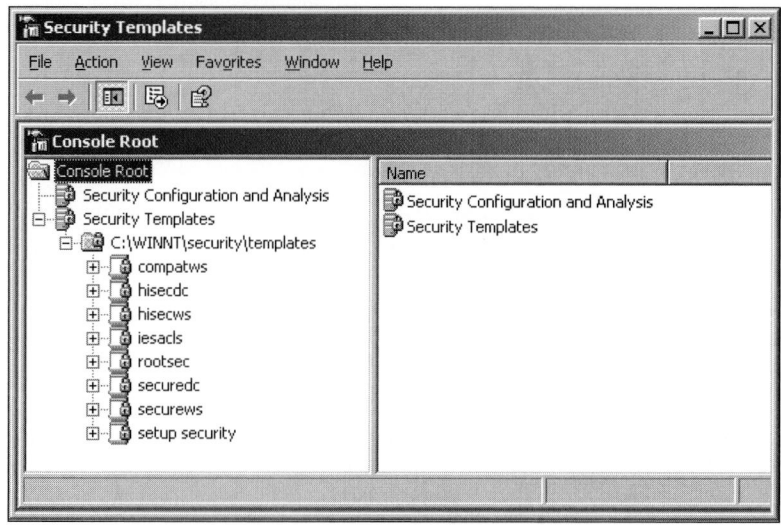

Figure 12-53 Analyzed Password Policy

Policies with a green
check mark meet the
requirements for a
secure server; policies
with a red X do not

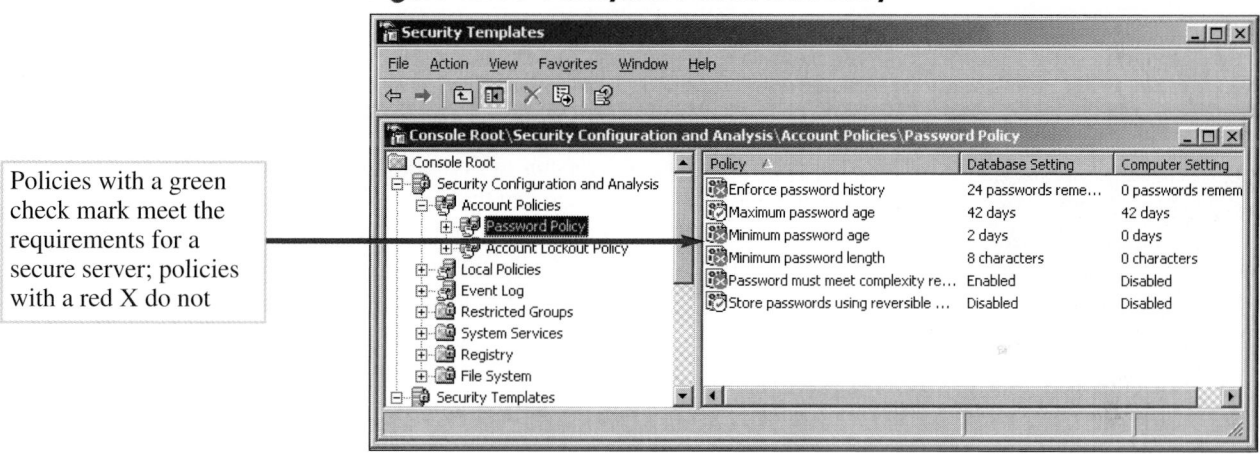

**Figure 12-54 The Minimum password length
Properties dialog box**

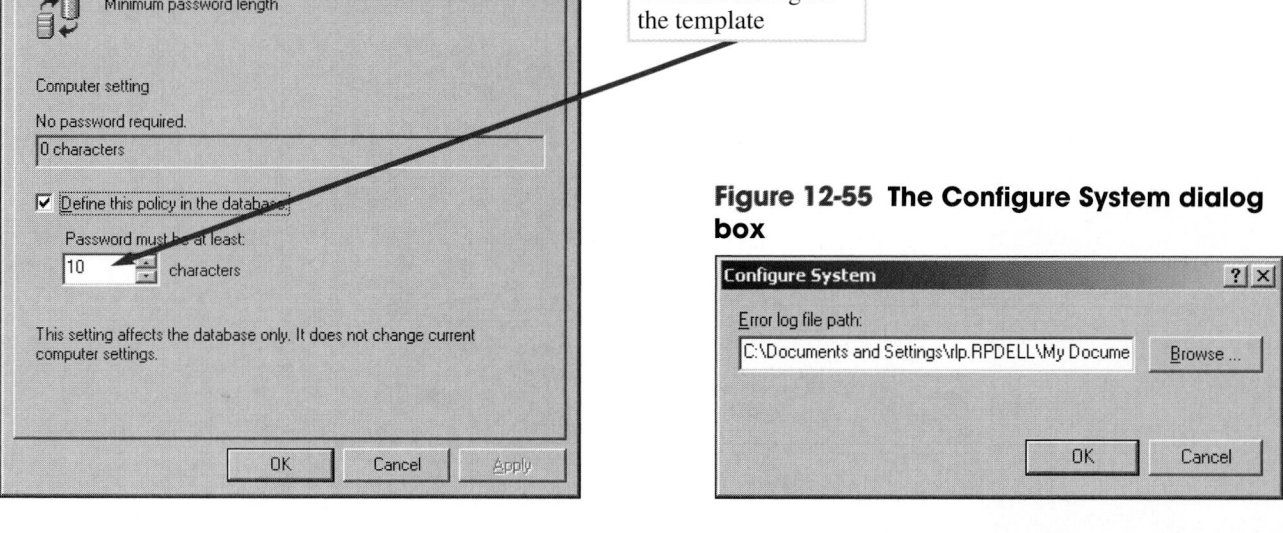

Use to change the
database setting for
the template

**Figure 12-55 The Configure System dialog
box**

skill 11
Working with Security Tools and Templates (cont'd)

exam objective

Implement, configure, manage and troubleshoot security by using the configuration tool set.

how to

27. Expand the **Local Policies** node and select **Security Options**. Scroll through the policies and notice which policies have been enabled in addition to the Do not display last user name policy (**Figure 12-56**).
28. Close the Security Templates console and save the console settings.

more

There is also a command line tool called Secedit.exe that you can use to perform most of the same functions as the Security Template and Security Configuration and Analysis snap-ins. This utility works from a batch file, script, or automatic task scheduler; for example, you can use a Secedit command in a logon script that is used for the entire system. Secedit can also be run from the command line to create templates, analyze security, and apply a security template. The Secedit tool is particularly useful on a domain-based system to perform analyses on a large number of computers at the same time. The results of the analysis can either be viewed in the Security Configuration and Analysis snap-in or from the command line. Some of the most commonly used command parameters for Secedit are explained in **Table 12-13**.

A new command line utility, Gpupdate, replaces the refreshpolicy command that was provided with the Windows 2000 version of Secedit. Gpupdate can be used to refresh both local group policy settings and those applied through a GPO on an Active Directory network. The parameters for the Gpupdate utility are explained in **Table 12-14**. Gpupdate allows you to instantly refresh group policy settings on a computer, instead of waiting the standard 90-120 minutes for the refresh interval to expire, making it extremely useful.

Security templates can be applied only to Windows 2000, XP Professional, and Windows Server 2003 computers as some of the security settings are not compatible with earlier versions of the operating system, particularly those related to encryption. This means that when you use one of the secure or high security templates, you may not be able to communicate with computers that are running versions of Windows below 2000. Use either the default or compatible workstation template on a network that includes Windows 9.x or Windows NT computers.

Figure 12-56 The configured Security Options policies

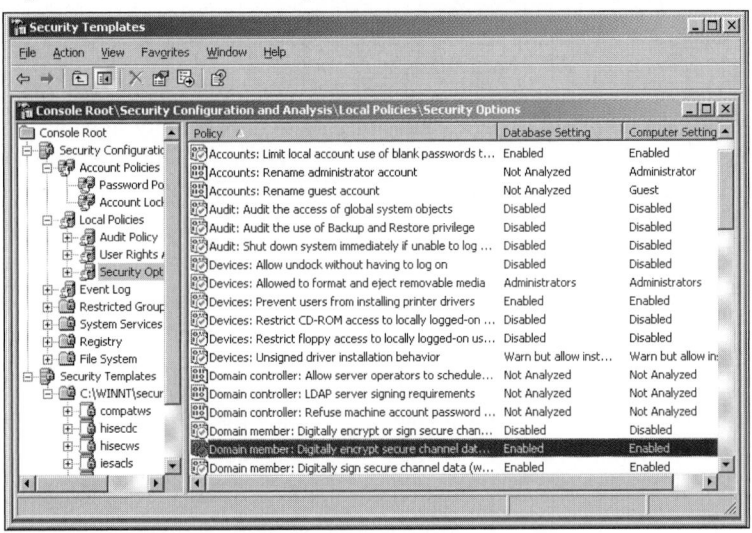

Table 12-13   Secedit Command Parameters

Variable	Explanation
/analyze	Analyzes the current security settings against the /DB and /CFG parameters you enter. (See below.)
/configure	Configures the security settings on the computer based on the /DB and /CFG parameters you enter.
/export	Exports a template from a security database to an .inf template file using the /DB and /CFG parameters you enter.
/import	Imports a .inf template into a security database in order to perform an analysis.
/DB *filename*	The path to the database that contains the security configuration settings you want Secedit to use to perform the analysis or that you want to be applied.
/CFG *filename*	The path to the security template that you want Secedit to use to analyze or configure the database you specified with the /DB parameter. You can use this argument only in conjunction with the /DB parameter. If you do not specify a security template, the template that is already stored in the database will be applied, or the analysis will be performed against the configuration settings that are already stored in the database.
/validate *filename*	Validates the syntax of a security template that you want to import into a database for analysis or apply to the system.
/GenerateRollback	Creates a template of the current security settings. This template can be reapplied if the settings are changed and you want to return to a particular security setting configuration.

Table 12-14   Gpupdate Command Parameters

Variable	Explanation
/target:{computer|user}	Used to designate that you only want computer settings or current user settings to be updated. User settings will be updated depending on the switch that is specified.
/force	Used to designate that you want to ignore all processing optimization settings for GPOs. All security configuration settings are reapplied.
/logoff	Used to log off after the update has completed. This is useful because some Group Policy settings do not automatically refresh as a background process, but will update only when a user logs on. In particular, new Folder Redirection and Software Installation policies will update only when a user logs back on.
/boot	Used to reboot the computer after the update. This is useful because some Group Policy settings do not automatically refresh as a background process, but will update only when the computer boots.

Summary

- The Public Key Infrastructure (PKI) enables users of unsecured networks to securely exchange data. It supports and enhances authentication and encryption.
- Key security concepts include public key cryptography, certificates, Certification Authorities, Encrypting File System (EFS), and Internet Protocol Security (IPSec).
- Public key cryptography uses a key pair called a public key and a private key. The key pair is mathematically related so that messages encrypted with the public key can be decrypted only by the corresponding private key. The public key is widely disseminated, while the private key is issued only to an authorized user and must be kept secure.
- A digital signature is an attached certificate that is encrypted using the sender's private key. The recipient authenticates the sender by decrypting the digital signature with the sender's public key.
- EFS (Encrypting File System) uses certificate/key pairs to encrypt files on NTFS volumes and partitions. Either the user who encrypted the file or a user who has been designated as the recovery agent can recover an encrypted file. Files are encrypted using file encryption key (FEK) and the FEK is then encrypted using both the user's public key and the recovery agent's public key. The FEK will later be decrypted using the user's private key. The recovery agent has a file recovery certificate and his or her own private key that corresponds to and is contained in the certificate.
- IPSec is designed to secure traffic in the IP layer. The services it can provide emphasize the four fundamental functions of any security system: authentication, integrity, anti-replay protection, and confidentiality.
- Symmetric key cryptography uses a single key, often referred to as a secret key, to both encrypt and decrypt data.
- To further enhance secret key security, you can encrypt a secret key with a public key. The message sender encrypts the secret key with the recipient's public key. Combining symmetric key encryption with asymmetric key encryption provides the best of both types of encryption.
- Digital message signing is another way of authenticating a sender and receiver. The sender uses a hashing algorithm to create a message digest, which is a shortened version of a text message. The sender then uses his or her private key to encrypt the message digest. The recipient decrypts the message digest using the sender's public key. Then, the recipient recreates the message digest and the two message digests are compared. If they are identical, the recipient knows that the message was not tampered with in transit and that it came from the owner of the private key.
- Windows Server 2003 includes code signing, which is used to digitally sign the drivers and system files on your system. Digital signatures certify that the file has not been altered or overwritten by another program's installation process.
- The Windows File Protection utility prevents the replacement of system files in protected folders, some of which end in .sys, .dll, .ocx, .ttf, .fon, and .exe. It detects any attempt by other programs to replace or move a protected system file and looks up the file signature in a catalog file (.cat) to determine if the correct Microsoft version is being installed. If an attempt is made to replace the correct Microsoft version of a file, an event is written to the event log to record the replacement attempt and the file will be replaced from the dllcache folder or the distribution media.
- The System File Checker utility scans and verifies the versions of all protected system files. If a protected file has been overwritten, the correct version of the file is retrieved from the *%systemroot%*\system32\dllcache folder or is requested from the installation CD-ROM.
- IP Security policies ensure the use of both asymmetric and symmetric encryption to secure data transmitted across a network.
- IPSec uses two main security mechanisms: Authentication Header and Encapsulating Security Payload. IPSec policies can apply to the local computer or be configured for a site, OU, or domain.
- IPSec operates in either tunnel mode or transport mode. Tunnel mode is used to create a secure IPSec tunnel.
- In IPSec tunnel mode, the message, the message header, and the routing information are all encrypted. Only communications between the computers configured as the end points are secure. No other computers on the network share the tunnel. You can create a local IPSec tunnel between two computers with static IP addresses.
- In IPSec transport mode, which is the default, only the data itself is encrypted. Because the message header and the routing information are not encrypted, it is not as secure as tunnel mode. You can configure IPSec policy in transport mode for an entire network or you can divide the computers on the network into 2 or more groups and apply IPSec policies at the OU level by creating GPOs.
- You configure rules for IPSec policies to regulate how they will be applied and under what circumstances. Each rule has a tab in the Edit Rule Properties dialog box: Authentication Methods, Tunnel Setting, Connection Type, IP Filter List, and Filter Action.
- You can apply an IPSec rule to just a LAN, to remote access traffic, or to all network traffic.

◆ When you install Certificate Services on a Windows Server 2003 computer, you create the first Certification Authority (CA).

◆ CAs issue and revoke certificates, issue and revoke keys, and encrypt and decrypt data.

◆ Certificates contain a public key and identifying data about the entity to which it is being issued. Certificates can be issued to user accounts, computers, and services.

◆ CAs often belong to a hierarchical system in which one CA certifies another CA to manage certificates over a part of a network. Trust relationships are at the core of this hierarchy, which is also referred to as CA chaining.

◆ The trust relationships begin with the root CA, which is the most highly trusted CA in the CA organizational structure. The root CA must be kept secure, because if a security breach occurs at the root CA level, all certificate-based security on the network is in jeopardy.

◆ Root CAs issue certificates only to subordinate CAs. Subordinate CAs are classified as either intermediate or issuing CAs. Intermediate CAs issue certificates only to other CAs. Issuing CAs issue certificates to users or computers.

◆ An Enterprise root CA is at the top of the CA hierarchy and Enterprise root CAs sign their own CA certificates. Active Directory must be accessible to install and configure an Enterprise CA. Many organizations install an Enterprise CA on a computer that will be kept off the network and in a secure location, except when it is needed to issue certificates to enterprise subordinate CAs.

◆ A stand-alone root CA is a top-level CA just like an enterprise root CA; however, it does not necessarily have to be a member of a domain. Since domain membership is not required, neither is Active Directory access.

◆ Enterprise subordinate CAs are located underneath either an Enterprise root, stand-alone root, or another Enterprise subordinate CA in the hierarchy. They issue certificates within an organization either to lower level issuing CAs or directly to users and computers. They cannot be created until after either an initial Enterprise or stand-alone root CA has been created.

◆ A stand-alone subordinate CA can function all by itself, or it can be part of a CA hierarchy. It does not necessarily need a parent stand-alone root CA on the network, although it can have one. It can also have an external commercial CA as its parent.

◆ Kerberos uses an authentication system with three parties: the client or party that needs to be authenticated, the party that has the resource or service (the server), and the party that stores the credentials for the others.

◆ The ticket is the identifying data that is used to authenticate a user. It is a key component of Kerberos.

◆ The Key Distribution Center (KDC) is the ticket issuer. The KDC has two parts: the Authentication Service (AS) and the Ticket Granting Service (TGS).

◆ First, the AS must verify the credentials of any security principal that is requesting a ticket. Then, it issues a Ticket Granting Ticket (TGT). The TGT is used to verify the identity of the user and grant admission to the Ticket Granting Service. The Ticket Granting Service issues a ticket which will be used in all communications between the party and the KDC in the future. The TGS also issues tickets that will arrange communication sessions between a security principal and a Validation Server. The Validation Server is the server that the security principal wants to access. It must be in the same domain (realm) as the KDC.

◆ Account policies are used to set the user account properties that control the logon process. There are three types of account policies: Account Lockout, Password, and Kerberos.

◆ Account lockout policy is used to prevent users from trying to guess passwords. If a user repeatedly attempts to log on unsuccessfully, the system can automatically lock out the user account according to specifications set by a network administrator.

◆ Kerberos policies apply only to domain user accounts, and they define such settings as ticket lifetimes and logon restriction enforcement.

◆ Account lockout troubleshooting in Windows Server 2003 is accomplished using a group of tools called the Account Lockout Tools package (ALTools.exe), which can be downloaded from Microsoft. These tools include LockoutStatus.exe, AcctInfo.dll, AloInfor.exe, EventCombMT.exe, NLParse.exe, and FindStr.exe.

◆ Security Options are used to set over 65 types of security policy settings for a computer, OU, domain, or site. You can set restrictions such as denying unknown connections to a computer, logging off users when the logon time expires, and prompting users to change passwords before the password expires.

◆ Administrative Template policy settings are used to customize the settings used by the clients that access a Windows Server 2003 network.

◆ The settings available in the Administrative Templates node are based on .adm template files. These settings designate Registry entry modifications that change aspects of the user environment.

◆ The preconfigured Administrative Templates, which are stored in *%systemroot%* \inf, determine what the groups of configurable settings will be.

◆ User rights assignments include such actions as accessing a computer from the network, allowing local logons, changing the system time, performing volume maintenance, generating security audits, and much more.

◆ Security templates can include password and account lockout policies, local security policies, user rights assignments, Registry key security, group memberships, and permissions for the local file system.

◆ On a domain-based network, you can apply a security template to a Group Policy object so that all of the settings are put into operation on a site, a domain, or an OU.

◆ All security attributes, except IPSec and Public Key policies, can be stored in a security template.

◆ The Security and Configuration Analysis snap-in is used to compare the current security configuration of the computer to one of the security templates, to create custom templates, and to apply a template to either the local computer or to a Group Policy object.

Key Terms

Account Policies	Enterprise Subordinate CA	Realm
Algorithm	File Encryption Key	Recovery Agent
Anti-replay	File Signature Verification utility	Root CA
Authentication	Integrity	Security principal
Authentication Header (AH)	IPSec	Secure Server (Require Security)
Authentication Service (AS)	Kerberos	Server (Request Security)
Certificate	Kerberos Key Distribution Center	Standalone Root CA
Certification Authority (CA)	Service (KDCSvc)	Stand-alone Subordinate CA
Certificate Revocation List	Key Distribution Center (KDC)	Symmetric key encryption
Client (Respond Only)	Logon rights	System File Checker utility
Confidentiality	Message digest	Ticket
Decryption	Microsoft Certificate Services	Ticket Granting Service (TGS)
Digital message signing	NT LAN Manager (NTLM)	Ticket Granting Ticket (TGT)
Digital signature	Private key	Transport mode
Encapsulating Security Payload (ESP)	Privileges	Tunnel mode
Encryption	Public key	User rights assignments
Encrypting File System (EFS)	Public key cryptography	Windows File Protection
Enterprise Root CA	Public key infrastructure	

Test Yourself

1. You want to send your pay stub to Mr. Morris, who is the Accounting department head. To make sure that the document is accessible to Mr. Morris only, which security property would you look for in a security tool?
   a. Integrity
   b. Authenticity
   c. Confidentiality
   d. Anti-Replay

2. In order for encryption and decryption to be successful, data should be encrypted with the: (Choose all that apply.)
   a. Recipient's private key.
   b. Recipient's public key.
   c. Secret key.
   d. Sender's private key.
   e. Sender's public key.

3. Microsoft Certificate Services follows the _____ standard for formatting certificates.
   a. X.509
   b. SSL
   c. TSL
   d. IPSec

4. Which of the following types of CAs would be the first to be created on a network?
   a. Enterprise Root CA
   b. Issuing CA
   c. Enterprise Subordinate CA
   d. Standalone Subordinate CA

5. The command used to analyze the security of all the computers on a particular domain is:
   a. secedit /analyzo
   b. cipher /a
   c. certutil
   d. cipher /h

6. You open a security template called Setsecure.inf. Then, you make some changes to it and save it as mysecure.inf to configure the security in the system. What happens to the setsecure.inf security template?
   a. Setsecure has changed content.
   b. Setsecure is renamed mysecure.
   c. Setsecure does not change.
   d. The Setsecure template is deleted.

7. Which administrative template is used by default to manage desktop settings for Windows 2000 and XP Professional clients?
   a. Windows.adm
   b. Winnt.adm
   c. System.adm
   d. Common.adm

8. You have a Windows Server 2003 domain on which you have configured Group Policy. The Default Domain policy has been configured with Password and Account Lockout policy settings. You have also created the Accounting OU in the domain. It has been configured with User Configuration\Administrative Templates policy settings to prevent users from changing the security zone settings in Windows Explorer, to enforce the same security zone and proxy settings for all users, and to prevent users from downloading offline content to their workstations. Stephanie uses a Windows XP Professional workstation in the Accounting OU. Which Group Policy settings will be applied to her computer by default?
   a. Only the User Configuration\Administrative Templates policy settings.
   b. Only the Password and Account Lockout policy settings.
   c. The Password and Account Lockout policy settings and the User Configuration\Administrative Templates policy settings.
   d. None of the policy settings will apply to Stephanie's computer.

9. You are having a problem on your network with users reusing passwords from previous months. You consider this to be a security risk because users have been known to store their passwords on post-it notes stuck to various places at their workstations and to share them with other users on occasion. How can you stop users from reusing old passwords?
   a. Set the passwords must meet complexity requirements policy.
   b. Set the User must change password at next logon option for all users.
   c. Set the Enforce password history policy.
   d. Send a memo to all employees prohibiting the practice of sharing or reusing passwords with the threat of disciplinary action.

10. You are the network administrator for a large financial institution. You have recently upgraded all of your servers and all are running either Windows 2000 Server or Windows Server 2003. You want to institute site-wide security settings that will provide the maximum amount of security for your domain controllers. Since backward compatibility is not an issue, which of the following templates can you apply to accomplish this goal?
    a. hisecdc
    b. securedc
    c. rootsec
    d. setup security

Projects: On Your Own

1. Configure user rights.
   a. Open the **Group Policy Object Editor** for the **Default Domain Policy**.
   b. Expand the **Computer Configuration** node. Expand the **Windows Settings** node.
   c. Expand the **Security Settings** node. Expand **Local Policies** and select **User Rights Assignment**.
   d. Double-click **Allow log on locally**.
   e. Select the **Define these policy settings** check box.
   f. Click the **Add User or Group** button.
   g. Click **Browse**.
   h. Click the **Advanced** button.
   i. Click **Find Now**.
   j. Hold down the [Ctrl] key and select **Administrator**, **Administrators**, and **Server Operators**. Click **OK**.
   k. Click **OK** to close the Select Users, Computers, or Groups dialog box.
   l. Click **OK** to close the Add User or Group dialog box.
   m. The user and groups you selected are added to the policy settings box in the **Allow log on locally Properties** dialog box. Click **OK**.
   n. Double-click **Back up files and Directories**.
   o. Select the **Define these policy settings** check box.
   p. Click the **Add User or Group** button.
   q. Click **Browse**.
   r. Click the **Advanced** button.
   s. Click **Find Now**.
   t. Hold down the [Ctrl] key and select **Backup Operators**, **Administrators**, and **Server Operators**. Click **OK**.
   u. Click **OK** to close the Select Users, Computers, or Groups dialog box.
   v. Click **OK** to close the Add User or Group dialog box.
   w. The groups you selected are added to the policy settings box in the **Back up Files and Directories Properties** dialog box. Click **OK**.
   x. Close the Group Policy Editor and all other open windows.

2. Configure Security Options.
   a. Open the Group Policy Object Editor for the Default Domain Policy.
   b. Expand the **Computer Configuration** node. Expand the **Windows Settings** node.

c. Expand the **Security Settings** node. Expand **Local Policies** and select **Security Options**.

d. Double-click **Devices: Restrict CD-ROM access to locally logged on-user only**.

e. Select the **Define this policy setting** check box.

f. Select the **Enabled** option button. Click **OK**.

g. Double-click **Devices: Restrict floppy access to locally logged-on user-only**.

h. Select the **Define this policy setting** check box.

i. Select the **Enabled** option button. Click **OK**.

j. Double-click **Interactive logon: Message text for users attempting to log on**.

k. Select the **Define this policy setting in the template** check box.

l. Enter a message in the box, for example, **Welcome to <domain_name.com>**.

m. Click **OK**. The message you entered is entered in the **Policy Setting** column in the details pane.

n. Close the Group Policy Editor and any other open windows.

3. Configure client security.

a. Open the Group Policy Object Editor for the Default Domain Policy.

b. Expand the **User Configuration** node. Expand the **Windows Settings** node.

c. Double-click **Administrative Templates**.

d. Select **Windows Components**.

e. In the details pane, double-click **Internet Explorer**.

f. Double-click **Disable changing homepage settings**.

g. Open the **Explain** tab and read about the policy setting.

h. Return to the **Setting** tab and select the **Enabled** option button. Click **OK**.

i. In the console tree, select **Help and Support Center**.

j. Select **Do not allow "Did you know" content to appear**. If the **Extended** tab is not already active, select it and read the description.

k. Right-click **Do not allow "Did you know" content to appear** and select **Properties**.

l. Select the **Enabled** option button. Click **OK**.

m. Select **Windows Installer** in the console tree.

n. Select **Prevent removable media source for any install** and read the description. This policy setting will prevent users from installing software from a CD-ROM, floppy or DVD.

o. Enable the policy and close the Properties dialog box.

p. Double-click **Control Panel** in the console tree. Select **Add or Remove Programs**.

q. Double-click **Hide the "Add a program from CD-ROM or floppy disk" option**.

r. Click the **Enabled** option button. You have now instituted policies to prevent users from installing software. Click **OK**.

s. Close the Group Policy Editor and all other open windows.

Problem Solving Scenarios

1. Pacifica Telecommunications Company employs temporary employees who take orders by telephone and enter customer data into a database. They use a proprietary call center software package for this purpose, which is installed on their computers. You are concerned about the security of the network and decide that you want to implement a Group Policy that enforces the following restrictions for the telemarketing users:

   1. Prevent users from mapping network drives.
   2. Prevent users from using My Network Places.
   3. Prevent users from making changes to the Taskbar and Start menu settings.
   4. Prevent users from accessing the Control Panel.
   5. Prevent users from right-clicking on the desktop and accessing the context menu.

   List the steps you would take to create and implement this Group Policy.

2. Pacifica Telecommunications has also decided that Internet access by employees must be made more secure. They have asked you to set up security zones in IE and to make sure that users will not be able to change these settings. You decide that you must also make sure that IE uses the same security zones and proxy settings for all users and that you do not want users to be able to make any changes to the Security, Connections, or Advanced Properties pages in IE. Outline the steps you will take to implement this new domain-wide policy.

3. Senior Management at Techtonics Inc. is very concerned about the security of data on the company's network. They want you to deploy a stringent password protection and account lockout policy package. Outline the policies you will implement and explain why you have chosen them and what they will accomplish. Also explain the steps you will take to deploy these new policies. Management wants the policies to apply to the three domains in the site for the local LAN.

Implementing Data and System Recovery

There are several tools and utilities that are used to protect your data and system in the event of a catastrophe such as a disk drive crash, a virus, or a power outage. The Windows Server 2003 Backup utility (Ntbackup) includes the Backup Wizard, the Restore Wizard, and the Automated System Recovery Wizard. You use the Backup Wizard to create copies of vital enterprise data that are either stored in a backup file on a different hard disk, a Zip or Jaz drive, or magnetic tape. If data is lost or damaged, you can use the Restore Wizard to recover it from the backup copies. You must also back up all system files, the startup environment files, the partition boot sector, and the Registry, because they can also be accidentally deleted or become corrupt. The Automated System Recovery Wizard will be used to back up the operating system files, configuration settings, and System State data so that you can rebuild your system if the system files become corrupt or the operating system will not start.

Before making backups, you should create a backup plan so that you can retrieve lost data quickly and efficiently. First, you must identify the data that needs to be backed up and the medium you are going to use. Then, you must decide upon a backup schedule and a backup type. Backup types differ depending on how the *archive attribute* or *backup marker* (also referred to as the archive bit) is treated. The archive attribute is set on a file when it has changed. Some backup types will remove the archive bit when the file has been backed up, while others will ignore it.

When you are booting a server and a problem occurs that prevents the operating system from starting, you can try to boot the computer in Safe Mode. When you start up in Safe Mode, only a set of basic drivers and files are loaded. You can use Safe Mode to remove corrupt drivers, fix driver conflicts, or uninstall and reinstall applications to resolve possible Autostart difficulties. The Last Known Good Configuration can be useful if you have incorrectly edited the Registry, added a new driver that is either not compatible with your hardware or is defective, or if you have disabled a critical device driver. If Safe Mode and the Last Known Good Configuration do not work, you can try the Recovery Console. It provides you with a set of administrative command-line tools that can be used to repair the operating system installation.

Redundant Array of Inexpensive Disks (RAID) implementation using RAID-5 volumes is used to store data on multiple dynamic disks. If one hard disk fails, data can be reconstructed from the existing data and from error correction and checksum verification information called parity information stored on the other hard drives. You can use either the software implementation or the hardware implementation of RAID. Software RAID implementation is used to manage the RAID process through the operating system, whereas hardware implementation is used to control disk management through the disk controllers.

The Volume Shadow Copy Service (VSS) provides two new services in Windows Server 2003. You can configure VSS so that previous versions of saved files that are stored on a share on a particular volume can be recovered if they are accidentally deleted or overwritten. VSS can also be used by applications to access locked files or files that are in use by other services or applications. The Backup utility in Windows Server 2003 uses the API for VSS so that all files, including those that are open or locked, can be backed up.

Goals

In this lesson, you will learn to use the Windows Backup utility. You will also learn to use Safe Mode, the Last Known Good Configuration, and the Recovery Console to repair system files. Finally, you will learn how to create and apply an Automated System Recovery backup set and how to configure and use the Volume Shadow Copy service.

Lesson 13   Implementing Data and System Recovery

Skill	Exam 70-290 Objective
1. Understanding the Windows Backup Utility	Manage backup procedures. Manage backup storage media. Verify the successful completion of backup jobs.
2. Scheduling a Backup	Manage backup procedures. Back up files and System State data to media. Schedule backup jobs.
3. Restoring System Data	Manage backup procedures. Recover from server hardware failure. Restore backup data. Verify the successful completion of backup jobs.
4. Understanding Fault Tolerance in Hard Disk Volumes	Recover from server hardware failure.
5. Restoring Your System Using Safe Mode	Managing and implementing disaster recovery. Perform system recovery for a server.
6. Using the Last Known Good Configuration	Perform system recovery for a server.
7. Working with the Recovery Console	Perform system recovery for a server. Recover from server hardware failure.
8. Implementing Automated System Recovery	Perform system recovery for a server. Recover from server hardware failure. Implement Automated System Recovery (ASR).
9. Configuring the Volume Shadow Copy Service	Restore data from shadow copy volumes.

Requirements

To complete this lesson, you will need administrative rights on a Windows Server 2003 computer, a folder named Reports stored on the C: drive on your member server, between 300 and 400 MB of space on your storage medium for the System State data, a tape or enough Zip disks to store 1.5 or more GB of system files, and a floppy disk to create the ASR backup set.

skill 1

Understanding the Windows Backup Utility

exam objective

Manage backup procedures. Manage backup storage media. Verify the successful completion of backup jobs.

overview

tip

The System State data on a domain controller includes the Sysvol folder and the Active Directory database.

The data stored on any computer can be categorized as either user data or System State data. **System State data** consists of several key components related to the operating system or applications. Loss of System State data can render a computer non-operational. Since user data can be the most important asset of an organization, you must make sure that it is protected from losses due to viruses, disk drive failures, or user deletion. You can safeguard data by creating **backups**, or copies, of the files and folders saved on network file servers or on a local computer. Lost or damaged data can be retrieved if you have conscientiously designed and implemented a comprehensive backup plan. You can use the Windows Backup utility to perform backups and to schedule backups to be performed at a specified date and time. However, it is not considered to be an enterprise solution.

The Restore utility is used to retrieve lost data from the backup copies. An Automated System Recovery (ASR) is a backup of your system configuration including critical system files and the Registry. The ASR backup set includes a backup of all system files needed to start your system and a floppy disk that lists the Windows system files installed on your computer. It is used to repair your system partition in the event of a complete malfunction due to a hard drive issue or corrupt system files.

Before you perform a backup, you must decide whether you want to back up user data or System State data, or both. If you are backing up user data, you can either back up all the files and folders on a computer or only specific files and folders. You back up the System State data so that you can restore the operating system to its original state in the event of a system failure. The System State data on a member server contains the Registry, the COM+ Class Registration database; the system boot files and all system files (all files under Windows File Protection), as shown in **Table 13-1**; the Certificate Services database if the member server is a certificate server; and the DNS zones, if DNS is installed. A System State backup will also include both the IIS Metadirectory if IIS is installed and the Cluster service if the server is part of a cluster (**Table 13-2**).

A System State restore is performed on a clean installation of the operating system to recover all of the configuration changes. System State backups should frequently be part of the backup process because the System State will change when system components, such as the Registry, change, which can happen quite often. Using Ntbackup, you cannot back up the System State data on a remote computer and you cannot back up individual components of the System State data, as all of the components of the System State data are dependent on each other. However, some third-party utilities such as Veritas Backup Exec can back up individual components.

In order to back up data, you must have the necessary user rights to access the data being backed up. Any user can back up files and folders that they have created (files they own) and files for which they have the **Read**, **Read & Execute**, **Modify**, or **Full Control** permission. Local **Administrators** and **Backup Operators** can back up any file or folder on the local computer. **Domain Administrators** and members of the built-in **Backup Operators** group on a domain controller can back up any file or folder in the domain or in other trusted domains because they are granted the **Back up files and directories** user right by default. Similarly, to restore a backed up file or folder, you must have the appropriate user rights and permissions. File or folder owners can restore the backup copy. Other users can restore files or folders if they have the **Write**, **Modify**, or **Full Control** permission. Members of the local Administrators and Backup Operators groups can restore any file or folder on the local computer. Administrators and Backup Operators on the domain controller have the **Restore**

Table 13-1 System Startup files backed up in a System State backup

File	Location	Function
Ntldr	Root of the system partition	The boot loader. It initiates the startup procedure, operating system selection, and hardware detection.
Bootsect.dos	Root of the system partition	Provides the DOS boot information for computers that are configured for dual-booting.
Boot.ini	Root of the system partition	Provides the boot menu information and the location of the operating systems to Ntldr.
Ntdetect.com	Root of the system partition	Detects the hardware attached to the computer.
Ntbootdd.sys	Root of the system partition	Driver for SCSI adapters if they present. It allows the operating system to access the SCSI driver on a computer on which the onboard BIOS is disabled.
Ntoskrnl.exe	%systemroot%\system32	The Windows Server 2003 kernel.
Hal.dll	%systemroot%\system32	The hardware abstraction layer.

Table 13-2 Elements of a System State backup

Component	Type of Computer
Registry	All
COM+ Class Registration database· ◆ Installed COM+ applications	All
Boot and system files	All
Windows File Protection system files	All
Active Directory database	Domain controllers
Sysvol folder ◆ Group Policies and logon scripts	Domain controllers
Certificate Services database	Certificate servers
DNS zones	DNS servers
Cluster service database information	Servers that are part of a cluster
IIS Metadirectory	Web application servers

skill 1

Understanding the Windows Backup Utility (cont'd)

exam objective

Manage backup procedures. Manage backup storage media. Verify the completion of backup jobs.

overview

files and directories user right by default and can restore any backup file or folder on the domain.

Next, you must decide on the media you will use. You can back up files to Zip or Jaz drives, to tape, or to the hard drive on a remote file server. A backup to a file on the file server can then be backed up to a Zip, Jaz, or tape drive. Magnetic tape has been the most widely used backup medium because it is inexpensive and you can store large amounts of data on it; however, tape can deteriorate over time. **Table 13-3** lists types of backup media and their advantages and disadvantages.

There are five different backup types from which you can choose either in the Backup Wizard or on the Backup Type tab in the Options dialog box. The different types of backup and their characteristics are explained in **Table 13-4**. In order to choose one of these types, you must first understand what the archive attribute or archive bit is and how each backup type handles it. The **archive attribute** is a property for files and folders that is used to identify them when they have changed. When a file has changed, the archive attribute, which is actually an attribute of the file header, is automatically selected. This can be viewed on the General tab in the Properties dialog box for a file or folder on a FAT32 partition. On an NTFS partition, this can be viewed in the Advanced Attributes dialog box. To access the Advanced Attributes dialog box, click the Advanced button on the General tab in the Properties dialog box for a file or folder.

Some backup types remove the archive attribute to mark files as having been backed up, while others do not. For example, in a **Normal backup**, the archive attribute is removed to denote that the file has been backed up, but in a **Copy backup**, the archive attribute is not removed. Copy backups are used between Normal and Incremental or Normal and Differential backups so that when they take place the backup process will not be affected by the removal of the archive bit. The Copy backup type essentially "ignores" the archive attribute, creating a representation of your data at a particular point in time. An **Incremental backup** backs up only selected files and folders that have the archive attribute and the archive attribute is then removed. Thus, if a file has not changed since the previous backup, it will be skipped during the next Incremental backup. A **Differential backup**, on the other hand, backs up only selected files and folders with the archive attribute, and it is not removed. Therefore, even if a file has not changed since the previous Differential backup, it will be backed up again because it still has the archive attribute. A **Daily backup** is used to back up all selected files and folders that have changed on that day, but the archive bit is not removed.

Table 13-3   Storage media

Media	Description
Online	Used to back up data onto a server. Beneficial only if the Internet connection is fast and you have few files to store. If the Internet connection is slow or you have a large amount of data to backup, this can take a long time. It allows you to avoid the management of storage media because you can have the Web server back up data on a regular basis, and in case of any type of natural calamity, your backed up data is safe, because it is stored at another location.
Magnetic Tape Drives	Used to store backup data sequentially. This traditional backup media is often still the best choice because of its high capacity and low cost. Since hard disk size on new computers now averages several gigabytes, tape is generally the only media you can use to completely back up a hard disk without having to change media. However, you must carefully mark and store the tapes, and tapes can deteriorate over time. DLT (Digital Linear Tape) drives are the most common backup devices. They are single-spindled and use magnetic tapes that can hold 20 GB to 40 GB of data and they transfer data at approximately 5 MB/sec. Super DLT drives have an average transfer rate of 11 MB/sec and can store up to 110 GB per tape, uncompressed. DLT and SDLT units are often not compatible. Mid-range and low-end systems generally use 8mm helical scan technology because of their high capacity. A disadvantage is that a complex tape path puts a lot of pressure on the tape. Low-end systems that have less demanding backup requirements can use 4mm helical scan digital audio tape (DAT) and quarter-inch cartridge (QIC) linear tape.
Optical	This category of media includes CD-R, CD-RW, DVD-R, and DVD-RAM. CD-R and CD-RW media can store up to 700 MB of data per CD, and DVD-R and DVD-RAM media can store up to 9.4 GB per DVD (4.7 GB per side). While this is a cheap and easy method for many to use, it requires the purchase of additional software, as the Windows Server 2003 Backup utility does not support the use of this media type.
DAT	Originally a format for storing music on magnetic tape, DAT was adopted for general data storage through an ISO (International Organization for Standardization) standard. You can sequentially store between 4 and 40 GB of backup data on a 120 meter tape depending on the standard and compression. Compression is designated from DDS-1 through DDS-4 (Digital Data Storage). DAT is a cost efficient choice for tape backups because the tapes and the drive are generally far less expensive than DLT, but because the sustained transfer rate is still considerably slower than DLT, DAT is generally only used in small network or workgroup environments.
Flash RAM	Flash RAM storage devices encompass any device based on solid-state electronic storage, including many models of USB "thumb drives", PC-Card based Flash RAM, Smart Media, Multi-Media cards, and so forth. Capacities range from 4 MB to 1 GB. This method of storage is not typically used for system backups; rather, it is commonly used for backups of selected user data. The advantages of this media type include ease, speed, and portability, but the disadvantage of this type of storage is the comparatively astronomical cost per MB.

Table 13-4   Types of backups

Backup Type	Criteria for Backing Up Files	Archive Attribute
Normal	All selected files/folders are backed up whether or not they have the archive attribute set.	Archive attribute is cleared
Differential	Only the selected files/folders with the archive attribute set are backed up.	Archive attribute is not changed
Incremental	Only the selected files/folders with the archive attribute set are backed up.	Archive attribute is cleared
Copy	All selected files/folders are backed up whether or not they have the archive attribute set.	Archive attribute is not changed
Daily	All selected files/folders that have been modified that day are backed up.	Archive attribute is not changed

skill 1

Understanding the Windows Backup Utility *(cont'd)*

exam objective

Manage backup procedures. Manage backup storage media. Verify the successful completion of backup jobs.

how to

Back up and restore the Reports folder. (You can back it up to a Zip or Jaz drive or even store it on a floppy disk for this exercise.)

tip

You can also run the Backup utility by typing the ntbackup command in the Run dialog box.

1. Click **Start**, point to **All Programs**, point to **Accessories**, point to **System Tools**, and click **Backup** to open the **Backup or Restore Wizard** (**Figure 13-1**).
2. Click the **Advanced Mode** link to open the **Backup Utility Advanced Mode** window (**Figure 13-2**).
3. Click the **Backup** tab.
4. Click the **+** button next to **Local Disk (C:)** to expand its contents.
5. Scroll down the list of folders to locate the **Reports** folder. Click in the check box to the left of the Reports folder to select it.
6. In the **Backup media or file name** text box, type **x:\Backup-Reports.bkf** (where x represents the drive letter you are using) (**Figure 13-3**).
7. Click **Start Backup**.
8. The **Backup Job Information** dialog box opens. Check the information entered in the dialog box, and click **Start Backup** (**Figure 13-4**).

Figure 13-1 The Backup or Restore Wizard

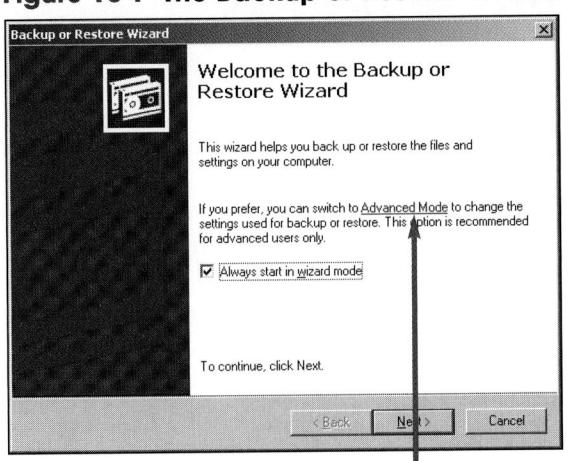

Click to open the Backup
Utility Advanced Mode
window

Figure 13-2 The Backup Utility Advanced Mode

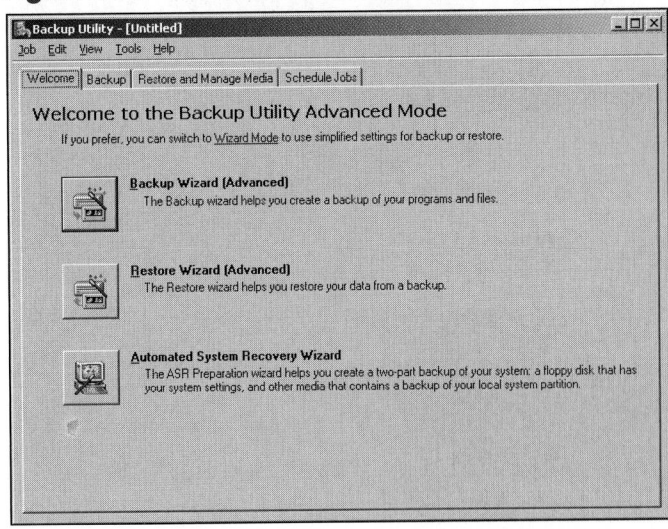

Figure 13-3 Selecting the folders and files to backup

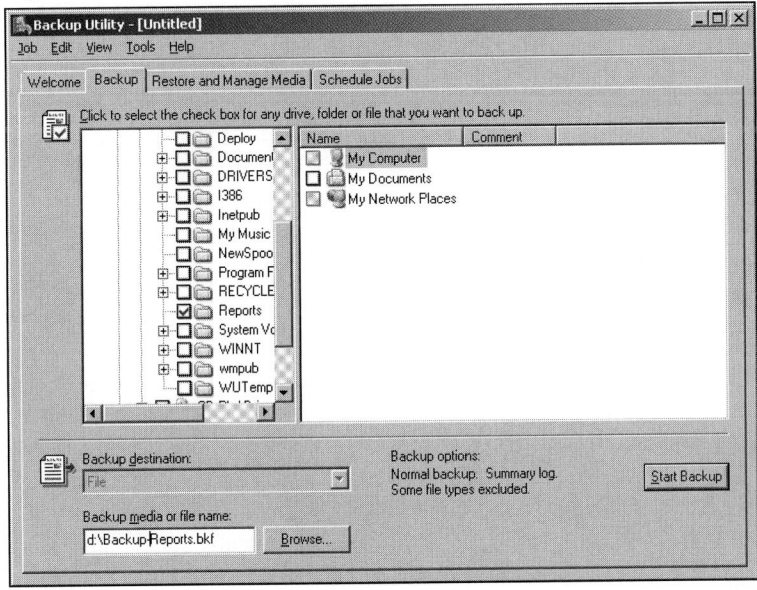

Figure 13-4 The Backup Job Information dialog box

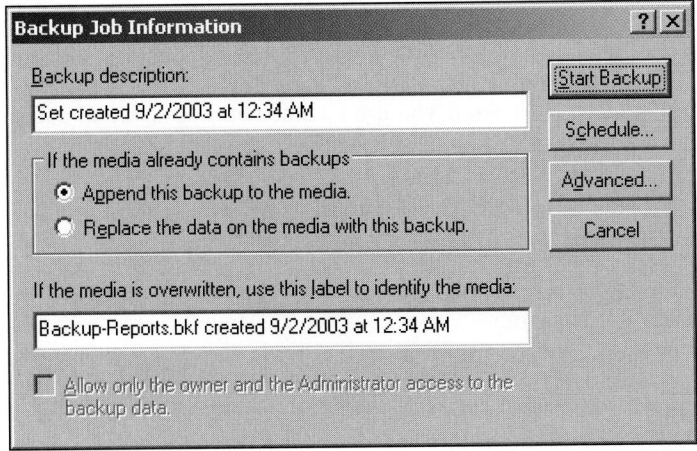

skill 1
Understanding the Windows Backup Utility (cont'd)

exam objective

Manage backup procedures. Manage backup storage media. Verify the successful completion of backup jobs.

how to

9. The **Backup Progress** dialog box opens and displays the status of the backup process including the backed up files, the time taken by the backup process, and the backup media used. After the backup is complete, the **Status** text box will show **Completed**, as shown in **Figure 13-5**.
10. Click [Report...] to open the text file, which contains the details of the backup process **(Figure 13-6)**.
11. Close the report. Close the Backup Progress dialog box.
12. Click the **Restore and Manage Media** tab.
13. Click the [+] button to the left of the **File** icon.
14. Click the [+] button next to the C: icon.
15. Click the check box next to the Reports folder. Select the Reports folder to view the contents of the folder.
16. In the **Restore files to** list box, select **Alternate location**. Type **x: \Reports-Backup** in the **Alternate location** text box **(Figure 13-7)**.
17. Click [Start Restore]. In the **Confirm Restore** dialog box, click [OK].
18. The **Restore Progress** dialog box opens. When the job is complete, close the Restore Progress dialog box and the Backup Utility window.
19. Click [*Start*]. Click **My Computer**. Locate the drive on which you backed up and restored the Reports folder.
20. Verify that both Backup-Reports.bkf and Reports-Backup have been saved on the backup media.
21. Close all open windows.

more

Organizations use a blend of the different backup types in order to optimize the time spent on both the backup and the restore processes. For example, a Normal backup will take longer than an Incremental backup because with a Normal backup, all selected files are backed up whether or not they have the archive attribute; however, you can quickly restore all of your files using the most recent copy of the backup file or tape. On the other hand, if you used only Incremental backups you would likely need to restore numerous backup files or tapes in order to recover all of your data. Since an Incremental backup only backs up files and folders with the archive attribute, you would not be starting with a full set of files. Furthermore, you would have to restore a whole series of backup tapes in order to recapture all of your files because each backup would only include changed files. Therefore, although the backup process would be quick, the restore process would be unwieldy, if not impossible. For these reasons, you should use a combination of Normal and other backup types to effectively manage your backup and restore times and ensure that all lost data can be recovered. For example, if you create a backup schedule that uses a combination of the Normal and Differential backup types, you will only have to restore the last Normal backup and the last Differential backup. On the other hand, if you use a combination of Normal and Incremental backups, you will have to restore the last Normal backup and all Incremental backups in the interim. A Normal/Incremental strategy will take less time to back up files because each Incremental backup will only capture changed files, whereas each Differential backup will capture all files that have changed since the last Normal backup. However, a Normal/Incremental strategy will take more time to restore files.

In most modern networks, however, the strategy is much simpler. Since tape drive speeds and capacities have increased so rapidly in the past few years, most large companies simply perform a full Normal backup of the servers nightly.

Figure 13-5 The Backup Progress dialog box

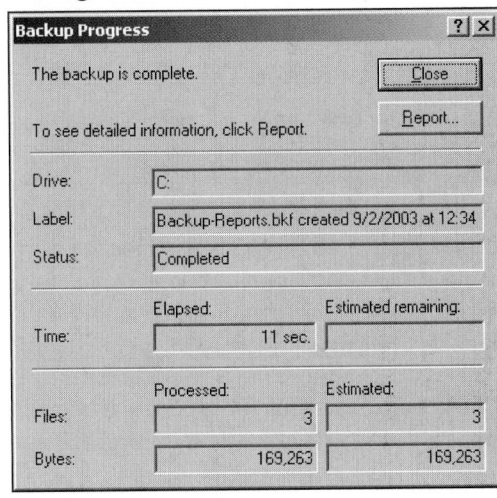

Figure 13-6 The backup log file

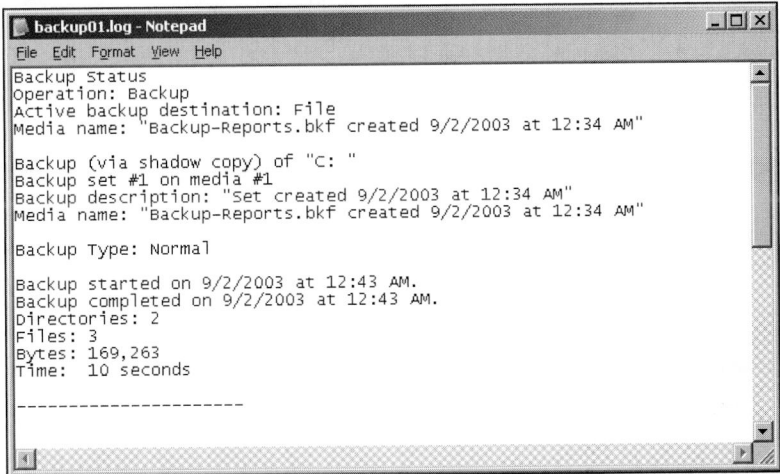

Figure 13-7 The Restore and Manage Media tab

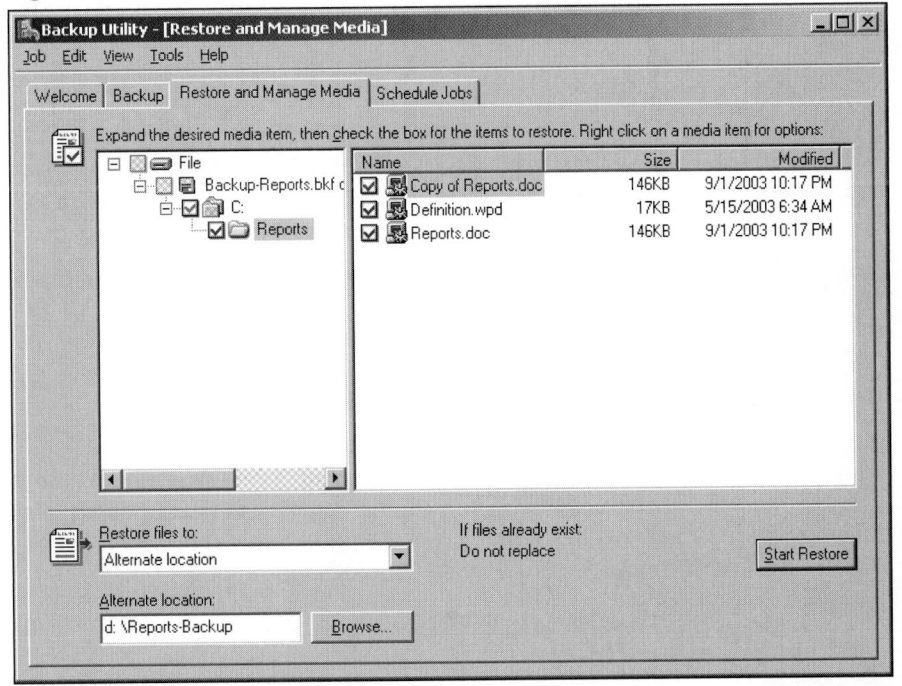

skill 2 *Scheduling a Backup*

exam objective

Manage backup procedures. Back up files and System State data to media. Schedule backup jobs.

overview

The System State changes when any system component, such as the Registry, changes, which can happen quite frequently. For example, when you install new software or hardware on your Windows Server 2003 computer, if the application makes Registry entries, the System State data will change. To keep up-to-date with these changes, you should perform a backup of the System State data regularly, typically, every night. It is critical to back up this data because it will allow you to restore the Registry data, the system startup files, all files under Windows File Protection, the Component Service Class Registration (COM +) database, and the Certificate Services database (if it is installed) to its most recent state using the latest backup.

You can use the Backup utility to schedule backups to run at specified dates and times. Ntbackup then uses the **Task Scheduler** to schedule the backup. For example, if you want to back up the System State data on your member server twice a week at 7:00 PM, you can specify the two days along with the start time in the **Schedule Job** dialog box, which you can access from the Backup Wizard. The Task Scheduler will then automatically initiate the backup operation at the scheduled date and time. You can also set the number of weeks, months, or years that you want this schedule to continue. The backup job will be put on the calendar on the Schedule Jobs tab in the Backup window. If the server you are backing up is running Certificate Services, you must also schedule Certificate Services to stop before the backup is run. The backup will not succeed if Certificate Services is running. You can also use the Task Scheduler to restart Certificate Services when the backup job is complete.

To schedule Certificate Services to stop, in the **Scheduled Tasks** window (Start-All Programs-Accessories-System Tools-Scheduled Tasks), click **Add Scheduled Task** to start the **Scheduled Task Wizard**. On the second screen in the Wizard, choose the command prompt as the program you want Windows to run. Name the task appropriately and set the schedule so that it is just prior to the scheduled System State backup. Next, you will have to enter the name and password for the user account under which the task will run. Open the Properties dialog box for the task when you have finished. Enter **net stop certsvc** in the **Run** dialog box after the task path. When you click OK you will have to confirm the user account name and password. To schedule Certificate Service to restart after the System State backup is complete, enter **net start certserv** in the Run dialog box after the task path.

how to

Schedule an Incremental backup of the System State data on your member server to occur three times a week for three weeks at 11:00 PM on a Zip or Jaz drive. (You will generally need between 300 and 400 MB of space on your storage medium for the System State data.)

1. Click ⊞ Start, point to **All Programs**, point to **Accessories**, point to **System Tools**, and click **Backup** to open the **Backup or Restore Wizard**.
2. Click the **Advanced Mode** link to open the **Backup Utility Advanced Mode** window.
3. Click the **Schedule Jobs** tab. Click Add Job to start the **Backup Wizard**.
4. Click Next > to open the **What to Back Up** screen. Select the **Only back up the System State data** option button (**Figure 13-8**).
5. Click Next > to open the **Backup Type, Destination, and Name** screen. Select the drive you are using for your backup media in the **Choose a place to save your backup** list box, or use the **Browse** button to locate the drive. In the **Type a name for this backup** text box, type **BackupSSD.bkf** (**Figure 13-9**).

Figure 13-8 Backing up the System State data

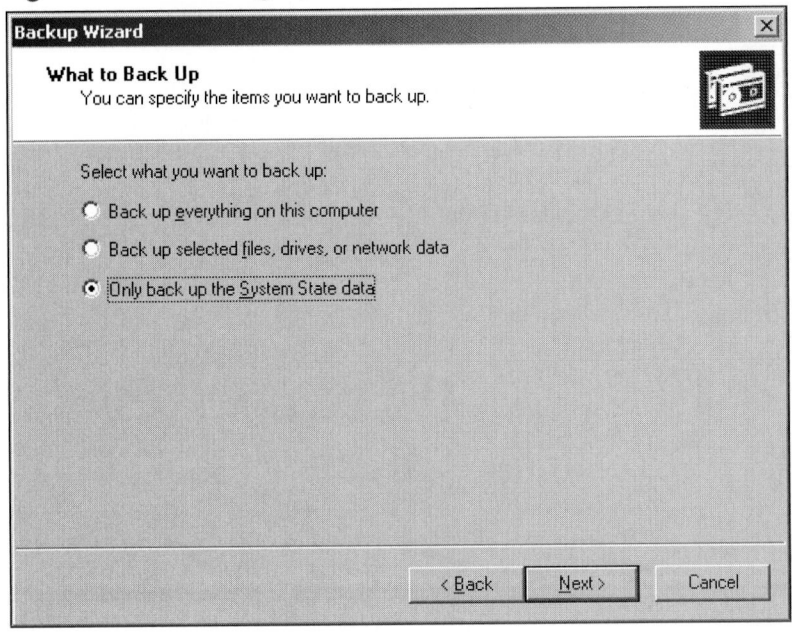

Figure 13-9 The Backup Type, Destination, and Name screen

Enter the
location to save
the backup file

Enter a name for
the backup file

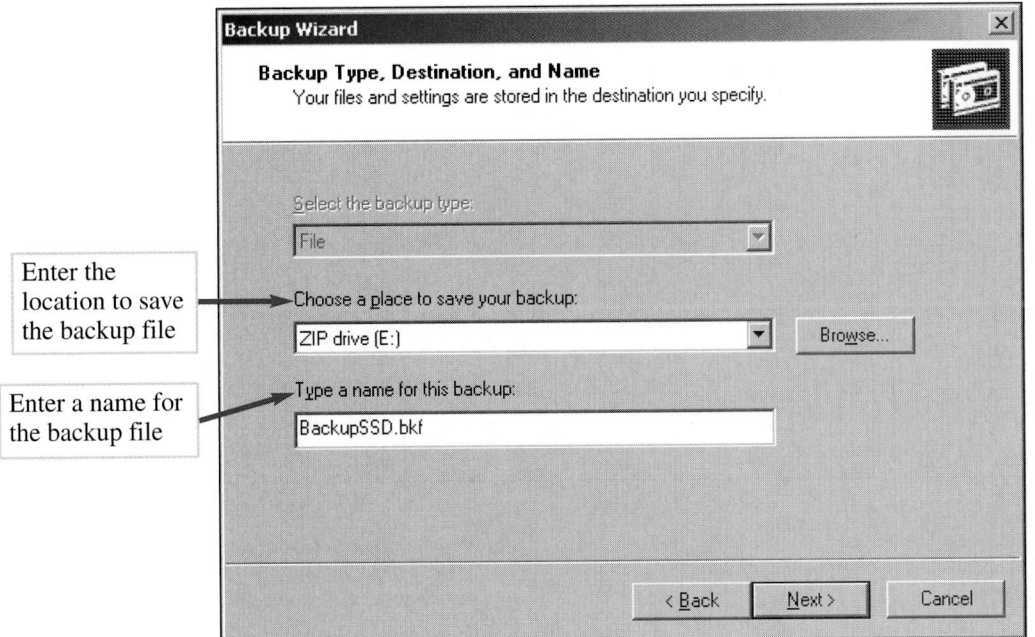

skill 2

Scheduling a Backup (cont'd)

exam objective

Manage backup procedures. Back up files and System State data to media. Schedule backup jobs.

how to

6. Click [Next >] to open the **How to Back Up** screen. Select the **Verify data after backup** check box to make sure that data is checked for consistency after the backup operation.

7. Click [Next >] to open the **Backup Options** screen. Select the **Replace the existing backups** option button. Select the **Allow only the owner and the Administrator access to the backup data and to any backups appended to this medium** check box.

8. Click [Next >] to open the **When to Back Up** screen. Select the **Later** option button, if necessary. In the **Job name** text box, type **SSD Backup**.

9. Click [Set Schedule...] to open the **Schedule Job** dialog box.

10. Select **Weekly** in the **Schedule Task** list box.

11. Select the check box for the day of the week you are currently on (**Mon**, **Tue**, **Wed**, etc.).

12. Type the time that is 2 minutes beyond the present time on the computer's clock in the **Start time** spin box to specify a start time that is two minutes from now (**Figure 13-10**).

13. Click [Advanced...] to open the **Advanced Schedule Options** dialog box. You use this dialog box to specify the start and end dates for the job. By default, the current date appears as the start date.

14. Select the **End Date** check box. Click the list arrow on the **End Date** list box. A calendar for the current month appears (**Figure 13-11**).

15. To schedule the backup operation to continue for three weeks, select a date that is 21 days from the start date. Click [OK] to apply the settings and return to the Schedule Job dialog box.

16. Click [OK] to apply the settings and return to the **When to Backup** screen. The **Set Account Information** dialog box opens. In this dialog box, you must enter a valid account name and password for a user who is a member of either the Administrators or Backup Operators group. By default, **<computername>\administrator** is entered in the **Run as** text box if you are logged on using the Administrator account.

17. Type the administrator password in the **Password** and **Confirm Password** text boxes (**Figure 13-12**), and click [OK].

Figure 13-10 The Schedule Job dialog box

Used to set power
management and
idle time settings

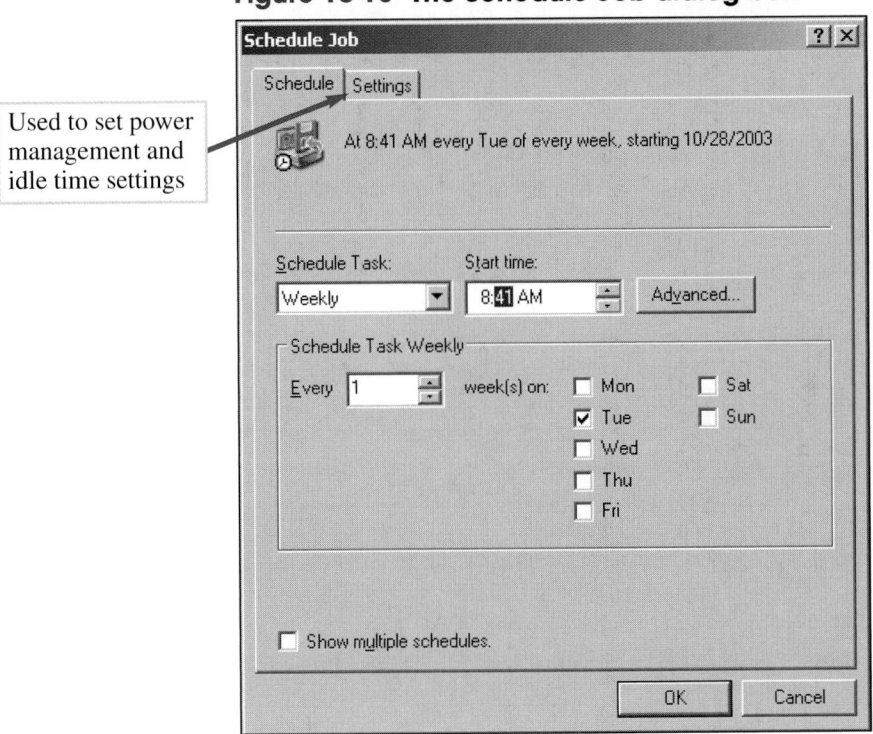

**Figure 13-11 The Advanced Schedule
Options dialog box**

Used to set the
repetition cycle for
the backup operation
within a specified
time frame

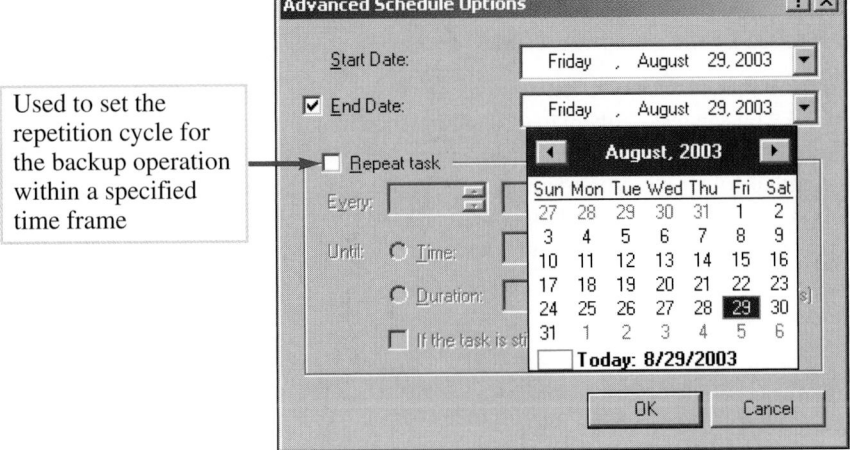

**Figure 13-12 The Set Account Information
dialog box**

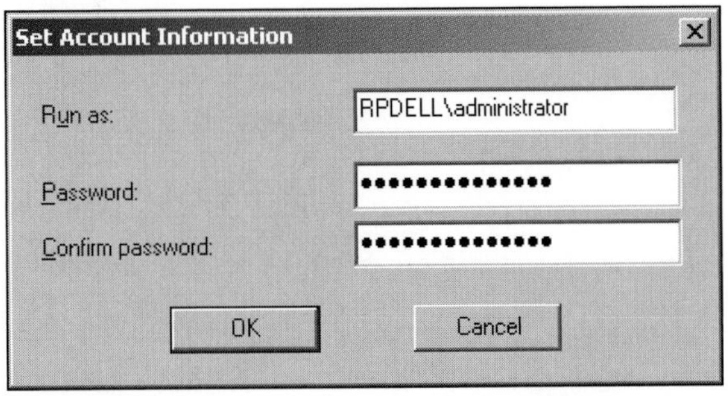

skill 2

Scheduling a Backup (cont'd)

Manage backup procedures. Back up files and System State data to media. Schedule backup jobs.

how to

18. Click [Next >] to open the **Completing the Backup Wizard** screen.
19. Click [Finish] to complete the Backup Wizard and return to the Schedule Jobs tab in the Backup Utility window. The System State backup you configured displays on the calendar for the next three weeks (**Figure 13-13**).
20. Close the Backup Utility window.
21. Click [Start], point to **All Programs**, point to **Accessories**, point to **System Tools**, and click **Scheduled Tasks** to open the **Scheduled Tasks** window. The presence of the SSD Backup task in the Scheduled Tasks folder verifies the successful creation of the backup operation (**Figure 13-14**).
22. Double-click the **SSD Backup** icon to open the **SSD Backup** dialog box. Click the Schedule tab to verify the schedule details.
23. Click [OK] to close the SSD Backup dialog box.
24. Close the Scheduled Tasks folder. The Task Scheduler will initiate the backup operation in 2 minutes.

more

On the Schedule Jobs tab in the Backup Utility window, you can click the icon for a scheduled job to open the **Scheduled Job Options** dialog box. Here you can change the job name on the **Schedule data** tab and view the job details on the **Backup details** tab. The **Job summary** section displays the backup type and the properties that were set for the backup job such as whether **Verify data** has been set, whether hardware compression is to be used, and if access is restricted to the owner or administrator. Here, you can also find out the media name that will be used for the job and the set description.

When you restore files, you have three choices as to the location where you want them to be restored. You can restore them to the original location, restore them to an alternate location, or restore them to a single folder. If you restore to the original or an alternate location, you retain the original folder structure. However, if you restore the backup file to a single folder, the original folder structure is no longer kept and the single folder will contain all of the files that were in all of the folders that were backed up.

Figure 13-13 Scheduled jobs on the calendar on the Schedule Jobs tab

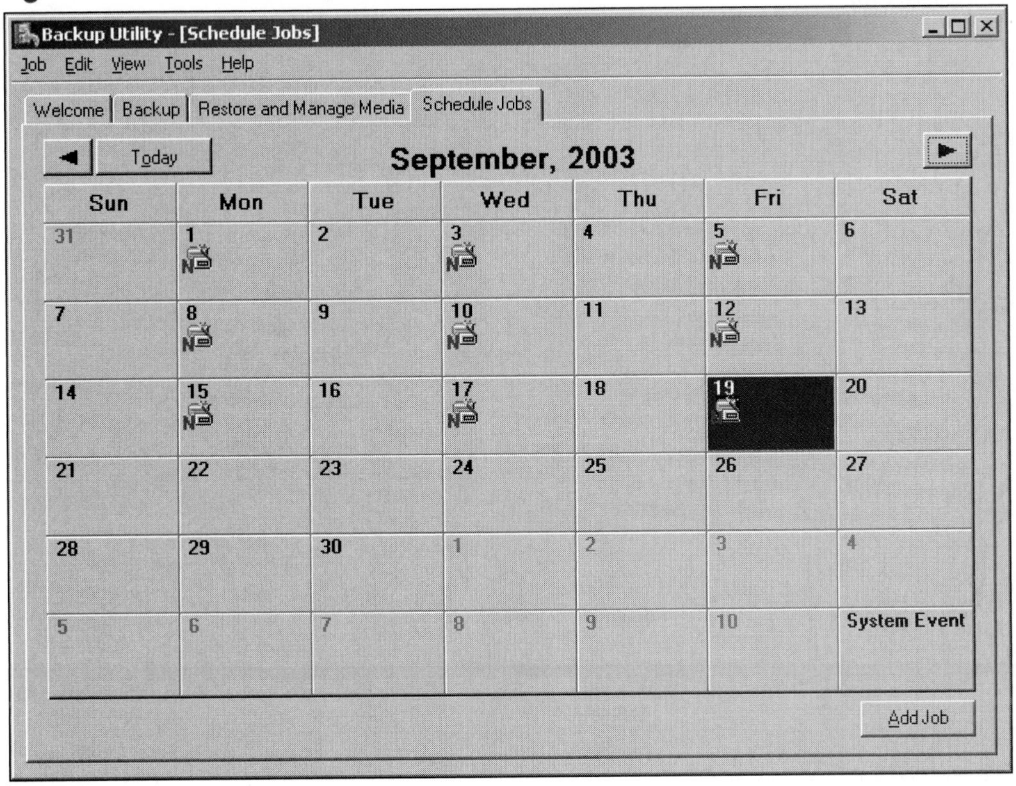

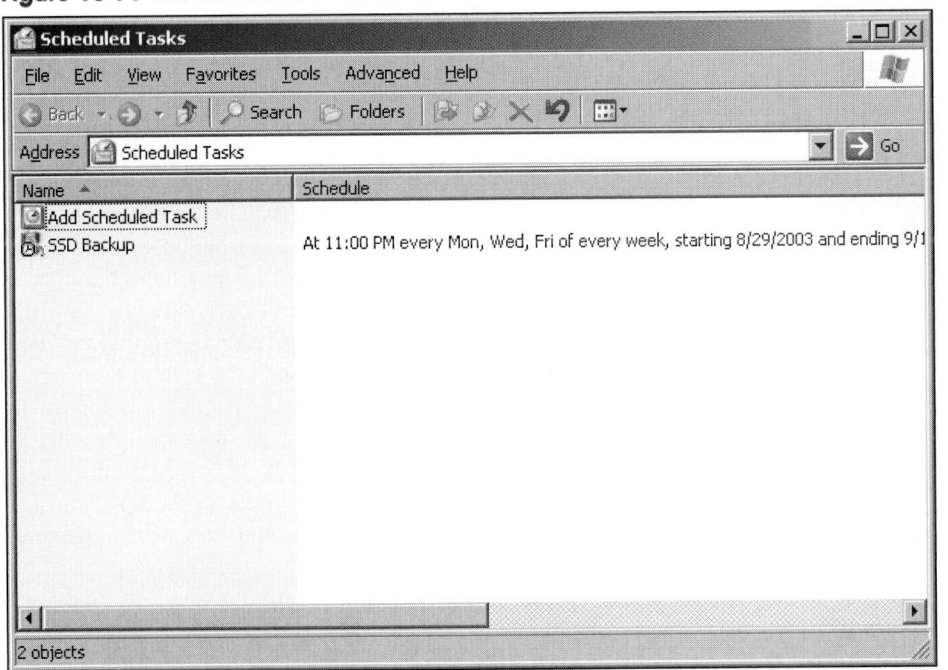

Figure 13-14 The Scheduled Tasks window

skill 3

Restoring System Data

exam objective

Manage backup procedures. Recover from server hardware failure. Restore backup data. Verify the successful completion of backup jobs.

overview

tip

You can also specify an alternate location for the Restore Wizard to restore data.

The purpose of backing up data, of course, is to allow you to retrieve it in the event of a virus attack, a system or disk failure, or for other reasons. To retrieve data from an existing backup, you can either use the **Restore Wizard** in Ntbackup, or you can use the **Restore** tab in the Backup Utility window to manually run the restoration process. You should test the restoration process regularly to ensure that you will be able to restore your data to its original state in the event of a catastrophe. You should restore data to an alternate location and compare the restored data with the original data on the hard disk. Your restore strategy is often based on the backup strategy you chose. For example, if you used a combination of Normal and Incremental backups, you will have to restore the last Normal backup you made along with all Incremental backups taken since that date. If you used a Normal/Differential strategy, you will have to restore the last Normal backup and the last Differential backup. It is also important to keep records of each backup job that is performed. Good recordkeeping may allow you to restore only tapes from a specific date, depending on what you need to restore. You should create and print a backup log for each job that will detail all backed up files and folders and which tape, disk, or other storage media the job is stored on.

By default, the Restore Wizard restores data to its original location. For example, if you back up the My Documents folder, which is stored in the **C:\Documents and Settings** *user_account_name***\My Documents** folder, when you restore the My Documents folder, the Restore Wizard will automatically restore the folder to the correct folder for the user account in **C:\Documents and Settings**. If you restore files that are already on your system, you must decide whether you want to replace the existing files with the files from the backup set. When you back up a file, the security settings, such as the user permissions, are preserved with the file. If you must restore the file, you have the option to restore the original security settings, but you do not have to restore security. Thus, if you restore a file from an NTFS partition to an NTFS partition, the security settings for the file can optionally be retained. Even when you restore files to a different directory, they can retain the full NTFS permissions set when the file was backed up because they are set not to inherit permissions from the parent folder. However, if you restore an NTFS file or folder to a FAT partition, you will lose the security settings because a FAT partition does not support NTFS security settings.

If you are restoring System State data, including Active Directory objects on a domain controller, you can perform one of the following types of restores (**Table 13-5**):

◆ **Non-authoritative (Normal) restore:** You use this method when you need to recover a domain controller from hardware failure or replacement and you are sure that the data on the other domain controllers in the forest is correct. Under these circumstances, all you must do is restore the most recent backup of the domain controller. Restored data, including Active Directory objects, will have their original update sequence number (USN). The update sequence number is used to detect and propagate Active Directory changes among the servers on the network. The Active Directory replication system will view data that is restored non-authoritatively as old data, and it will thus not be replicated to the other servers. If more recent data is available on other servers, the Active Directory replication system will use this to update the restored data. You must use an authoritative restore in order to replicate restored data to other servers. After the non-authoritative restore, Active Directory replication will begin and any changes that occurred on the other domain controllers will be automatically propagated to the domain controller that has come back online.

◆ **Authoritative restore (Figure 13-5):** You use this option when an Active Directory object or group of objects has been accidentally deleted. When an object is deleted in Active Directory, it is not truly deleted. Rather, it is tombstoned, which essentially marks

Table 13-5   Methods for restoring data

Method	Function	When Used
Non-authoritative restore	Data is synchronized with data on other domain controllers	When you want the restored System State data to be updated with newer data replicated from the domain controllers replication partners.
Authoritative restore	Data is authoritative in relation to the domain – Use Ntdsutil – Recover deleted directory objects – Restore objects changed since backup	When you have multiple domain controllers and you need the restored System State data to be replicated to the domain controller's replication partners.
Primary restore	A new FRS (File Replication System) database is built by loading the present data in the Sysvol folder from backup	When the domain controller that you need to restore is the only functioning server for a replicated data set. Usually performed only when all domain controllers in the domain are lost and you must rebuild the domain.

Figure 13-15 Authoritative restore

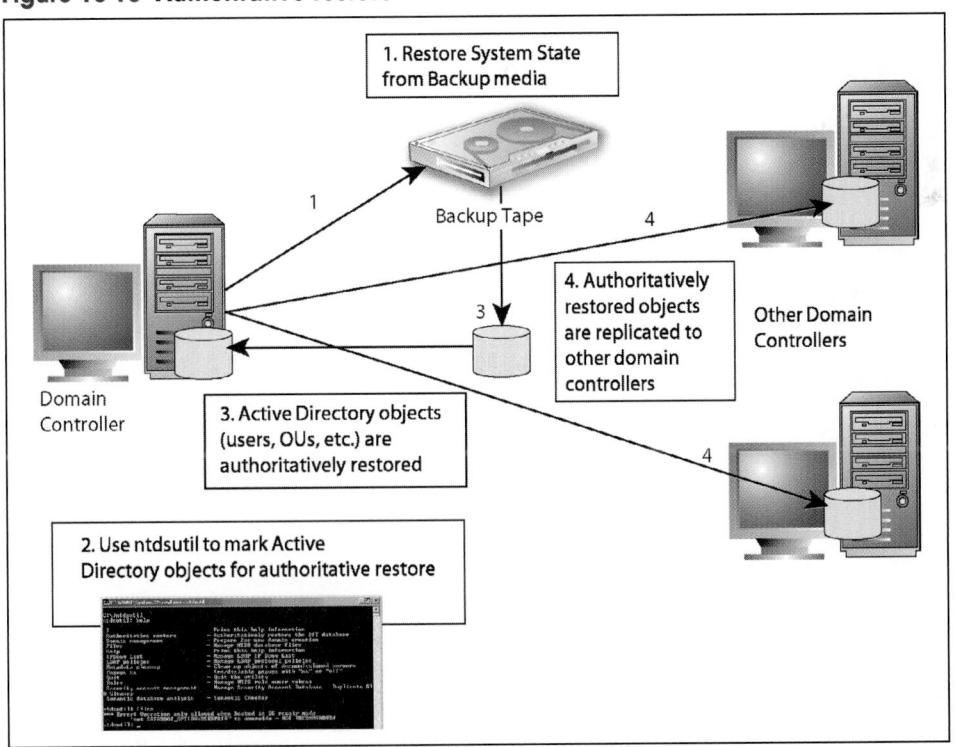

skill 3

Restoring System Data (cont'd)

exam objective

Manage backup procedures. Recover from server hardware failure. Restore backup data. Verify the successful completion of backup jobs.

overview

the object as "dead," making it unusable, and updates the object's version number (the update sequence number, or USN). This is done so that the "deletion" is properly replicated to all domain controllers. Once per night, a process known as Garbage Collection runs on all domain controllers, and any object that has been tombstoned for more than 60 days (by default) is actually deleted. Because of the tombstoning process, in order to effectively restore a deleted object, you need to increment the USN of that object subsequent to the actual restore process, thereby making the restored copy the "more up-to-date" version. You perform an authoritative restore by executing the Ntdsutil command on a domain controller. You run the Ntdsutil command after you have restored the System State data and before you restart the server. **Ntdsutil** is a command-line utility, stored in *%systemroot%*\System32 that supplies a number of other directory management features not found in any of the graphical tools (**Figure 13-16**). Using Ntdsutil, you mark Active Directory objects for authoritative restore, which modifies the update sequence number making it higher than any other update sequence number in the Active Directory replication system. Thus, objects that you mark as being authoritatively restored are considered to be the most current copy of those objects, and are properly replicated or distributed to the other servers on the network.

◆ **Primary restore:** You do a primary restore when you must rebuild the domain from backup because all domain controllers in the domain have been lost. You perform a primary restore on the first domain controller and non-authoritative restores on all of the other domain controllers.

When restoring System State data on a domain controller, first you must reboot the domain controller and press F8 during startup to access the Windows Advanced Options Menu. Select **Directory Services Restore** mode. In Directory Services Restore mode, you can restore the Sysvol directory and the Active Directory database. The domain controller will be off line while the restore takes place.

how to

Restore the System State data on your member server. (If the task you created in the previous skill has not yet run, open the Scheduled Tasks window, right-click SSD Backup, and click Run. You will have to wait until the System State data has been backed up before you can perform this exercise.)

1. Click [Start] and click the **Run** command to open the **Run** dialog box.
2. In the **Open** text box, type **ntbackup**, and click [OK] to open the **Backup or Restore Wizard**.
3. Click [Next >] to open the **Backup or Restore** screen. Select the **Restore files and settings** option button.
4. Click [Next >] to open the **What to Restore** screen. Insert the disk with your System State backup into the appropriate drive.
5. In the **Items to restore** box, click the [+] button next to the **File** folder.
6. In the File node, click the [+] button next to the **BackupSSD.bkf created on mm/dd/yyyy** node.
7. Click in the check box next to **System State** to insert a check mark (**Figure 13-17**).
8. Click [Next >] to open the **Completing the Backup or Restore Wizard** screen.
9. Click [Advanced...] to open the **Where to Restore** screen. Keep the default **Original location** in the **Restore files to** list box.

Figure 13-16 First level of commands for Ntdsutil

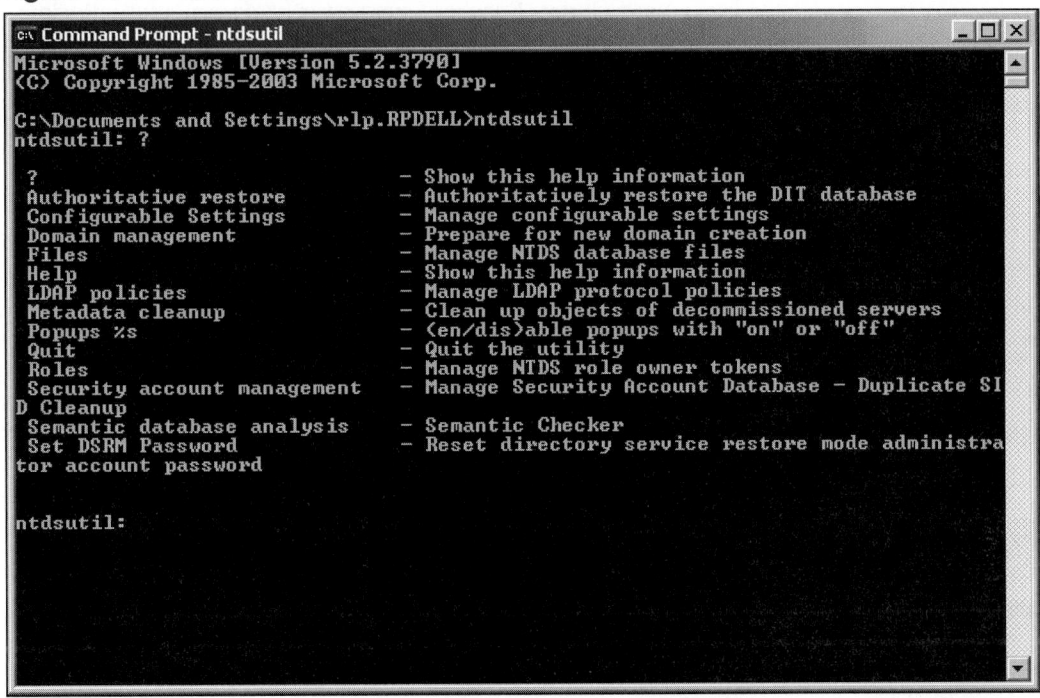

Figure 13-17 Restoring the System State data

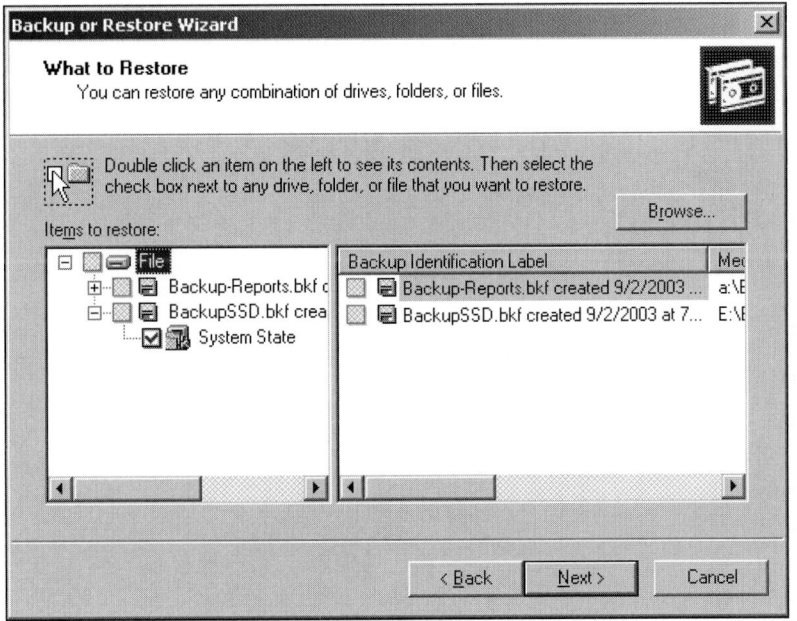

skill 3

Restoring System Data (cont'd)

exam objective

Manage backup procedures. Recover from server hardware failure. Restore backup data. Verify the successful completion of backup jobs.

how to

10. Click [Next >]. In the warning dialog box, click [OK] to overwrite the current System State. The **How to Restore** screen opens. Select the **Replace existing files** option button.

11. Click [Next >] to open the **Advanced Restore Options** screen. By default, the security settings will be restored. Security settings include permissions, audit entries, and ownership. This option is available only if you have backed up data from an NTFS volume used in the Windows Server 2003 family of operating systems, and you are restoring it to an NTFS volume used in Windows Server 2003 family of operating systems. All junction points will also be restored by default, but not the folders and file data they reference. With this option selected, junction points are restored, but you may not be able to access the data they point to. Junction points are locations on a hard disk that point to data in another location. This can be another location on the hard disk or on another storage device. Junction points are created when you create a mounted drive, so you should clear this option when you are restoring a mounted drive. Mounted drives are drives attached to an empty folder on an NTFS volume that are assigned a label or name rather than a drive letter. Existing volume mount points will also be preserved by default. Volume mount points are directories on a volume that an application can use as a gateway to a volume. The application can be set up for use at a location that a user specifies (**Figure 13-18**).

12. Click [Next >] to open to the **Completing the Backup or Restore Wizard** screen. Click [Finish].

13. The **Restore Progress** dialog box opens, showing the status of the operation, the estimated and actual amount of data being restored, the time that has passed, and the time left until the operation is complete (**Figure 13-19**).

14. When the operation is complete, click [Report...] in the Restore Progress dialog box to view information on the restore process. The restore log, which will open in Notepad, shows the number of files that have been restored, the duration of the restore process, the total size of the files restored, the start and end time for the restore operation, the restore destination, and the media type and label. This information will be appended to the backup log (**Figure 13-20**). The restore log can prove useful at a later date to confirm what files were restored.

15. Close the log file. Close the Restore Progress dialog box. You will be prompted to restart the computer.

Figure 13-18 The Advanced Restore Options screen

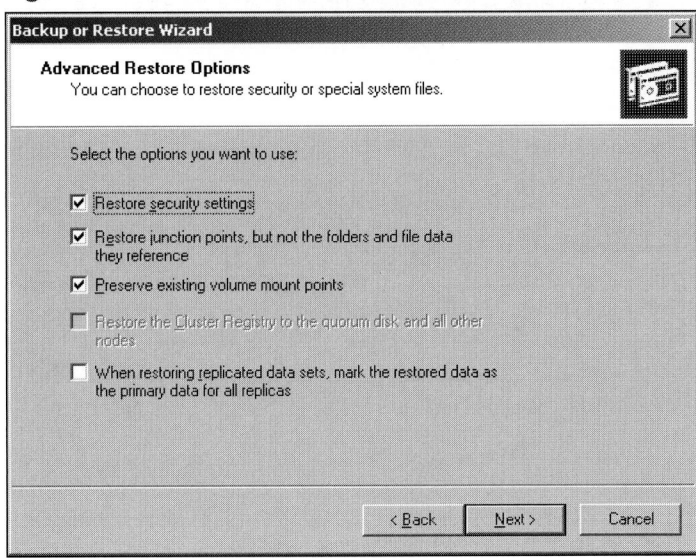

Figure 13-19 The Restore Progress dialog box

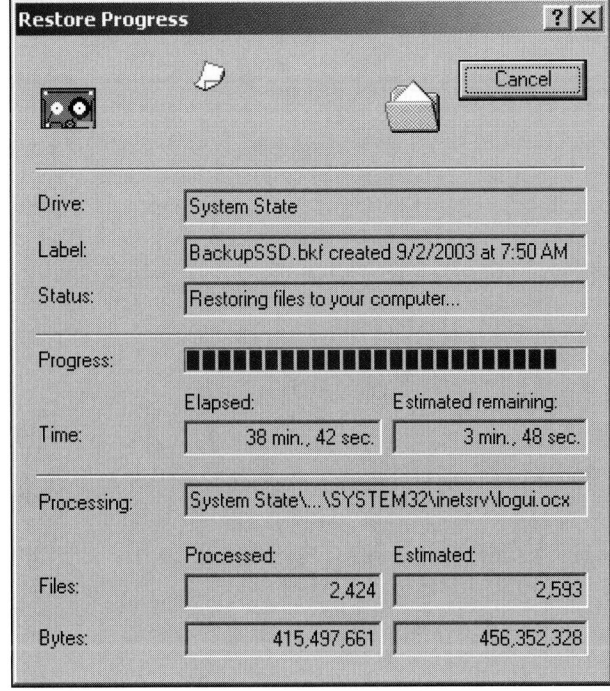

Figure 13-20 The restore log

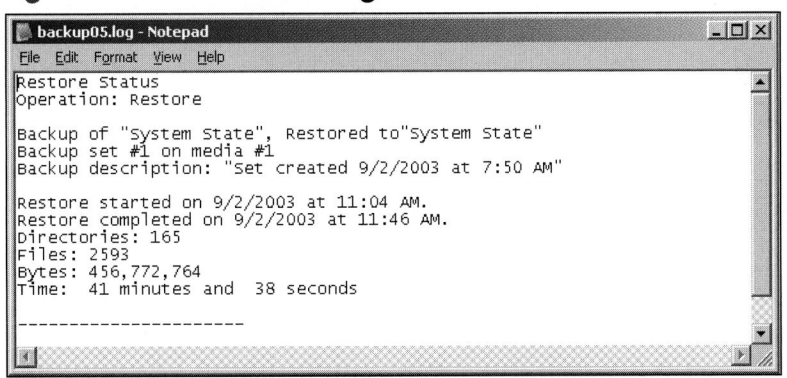

skill 4   *Understanding Fault Tolerance in Hard Disk Volumes*

Recover from disk failures. Recover from server hardware failure.

overview

Hard disk failure can occur as a result of a power failure, or just from every day wear and tear, causing information loss. You can improve the odds against losing data due to a disk failure by using fault-tolerant disk arrays. However, even though data that is stored on fault-tolerant disk arrays is recoverable when a hard disk fails, you must still back up both System State and user data. In order to recover data that has been accidentally deleted, stolen, or been in a fire, you will still need your backup files.

To maintain data access when you experience hard disk failure, Windows Server 2003 supports several disk redundancy technologies known as RAID, or redundant array of inexpensive (or independent) disks. These disk redundancy technologies are the software implementation of RAID. RAID is used to increase disk life and prevent the data loss. There are eight levels of software RAID, only 3 of which (0, 1, and 5) are supported by Windows Server 2003.

RAID level 0 involves the use of striped volumes, which distribute data evenly in stripes across the disks in the volume. There can be up to 32 disks. RAID level 0 provides extremely fast read and write access; however, if one disk in a striped volume fails, you will lose all data on that Raid 0 volume (**Figure 13- 21**).

RAID level 1, or mirrored volumes, is a fault-tolerant solution that duplicates data on two disks: a primary disk and a secondary disk. If one disk fails, data can be "restored" in the sense that it will be resynchronized with the mirror when a replacement drive is installed (**Figure 13-22**). Windows Server 2003 supports disk mirroring, which can include disk duplexing. In **disk duplexing**, instead of having two disks which are both attached to the same disk controller (SCSI adapter), the mirrored disk is attached to a disk controller (SCSI adapter) that is separate from the one used for the primary disk. The use of redundant disk controllers ensures that if one disk controller fails, data will still be accessible (**Figure 13-23**). Disk duplexing is accomplished in Windows Server 2003 using the fault-tolerance driver Ftdisk.sys. Mirrored volumes in Windows Server 2003 use the Ftdisk driver to write data to physical disks. The drawback to using mirrored volumes is the amount of disk space required. In order to store 4 GB of data, you must have 8 GB of storage space. Furthermore, because data must be written twice, write access is usually slightly slower than when using a single disk. Read access, however, is unaffected.

The other RAID standard supported by Windows Server 2003 is RAID-5. In RAID-5, data blocks are written in stripes across a set of at least three (up to 32) physical disks. Error correction and checksum verification information are also written in blocks that are spread across all of the disks in the array. This data is called a **parity block**. Each stripe contains 1 parity block and **n-1** data blocks. The parity blocks in RAID-5 are mathematical calculations using logical XORs (Exclusive OR) against the data contained in the stripe. This allows

tip

When a RAID hard disk fails, the failed hard disk is called an orphan. The fault-tolerant driver "figures out" that the orphaned member is no longer useable and it directs all new reads and writes to other volumes in the fault-tolerant volume.

Figure 13-21 RAID level 0

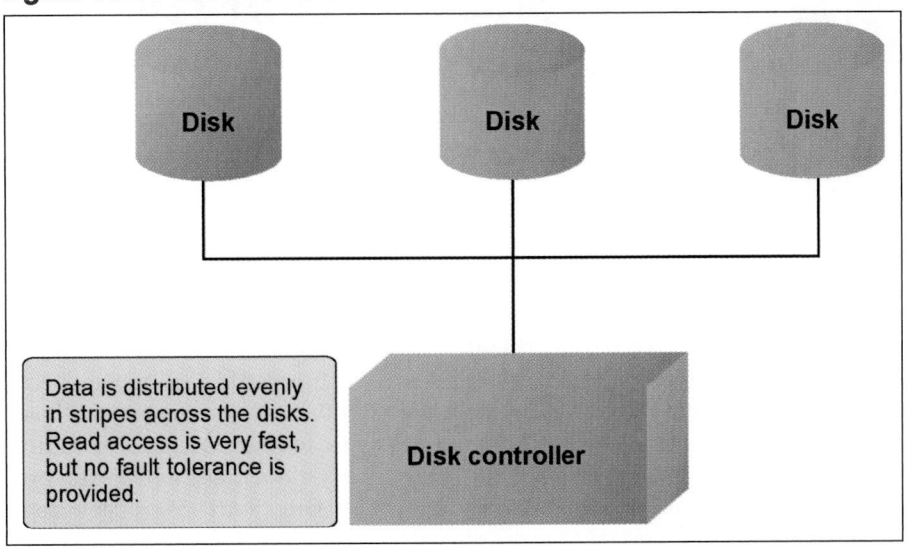

Figure 13-22 RAID level 1

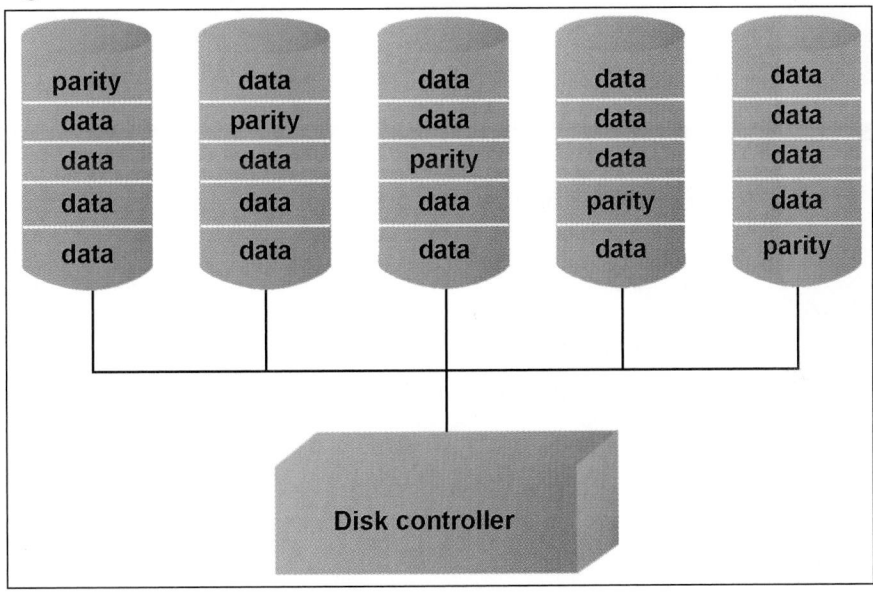

Figure 13-23 Disk Duplexing

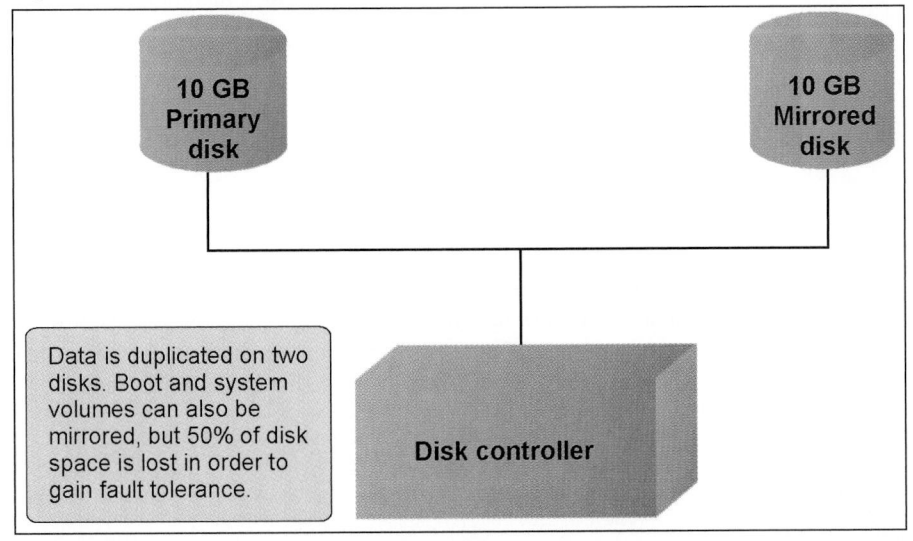

skill 4
Understanding Fault Tolerance in Hard Disk Volumes (cont'd)

Recover from disk failures. Recover from server hardware failure.

overview

RAID-5 to remain functional in the event of the failure of any single disk, as the parity blocks are simply calculated against the remaining data, which effectively recreates the lost data blocks. RAID-5 volumes are thus often referred to as striped volumes with parity or striping with distributed parity **(Figure 13-24)**. Because of this extra parity information on every disk, RAID-5 requires at least three disks and at least 16 MB of additional memory for system functions. Data redundancy is achieved at the cost of a number of MB equal to one additional disk per volume. RAID-5 has much faster read access than disk mirroring. However, write access on a RAID-5 volume is necessarily slower, due to the extra overhead involved with parity calculation. Additionally, if a disk fails, RAID-5 will slow considerably, due to the significant overhead imposed on the system by the calculations necessary to recreate the lost data in RAM.

RAID volumes can be formatted with either the FAT32 or NTFS file system. Neither mirrored volumes nor RAID-5 volumes are supported in the Windows 2000 Professional or XP Professional client operating systems. However, you can use a Windows XP Professional computer to create mirrored or RAID-5 volumes on remote Windows 2000 Server and Windows Server 2003 machines.

Boot and system files can be stored on a mirrored volume, but they cannot be stored on a RAID-5 volume. If you use RAID-5 volumes, you must store the boot and system files on a separate disk or on a separate mirrored volume, unless you are implementing hardware RAID. It is best to use RAID-1 (mirrored volumes) for the boot and system volumes if using software RAID.

You can use either the software or the hardware implementation of RAID.

Software RAID implementation: In the software implementation of RAID, fault tolerance is handled by the server's operating system. Any of the RAID levels supported by Windows Server 2003 (levels 0, 1 and 5), as discussed above, are configured in the Disk Management snap-in. The server hardware identifies and configures the drives independently and the operating system examines them and connects them in a single logical array. In the software implementation of RAID, you can tolerate a single disk failure.

Hardware RAID implementation: In the hardware implementation of RAID, fault tolerance is independent of the operating system and is implemented through the server's hardware. The disk controller (SCSI adapter) includes a chip on which the RAID setup is stored. This chip often has a battery so that it will not lose power and the RAID setup will not be lost during a power outage. Hardware RAID implementation is more expensive than software implementation, but it has faster read and write access, and you can store the boot and system volumes at any RAID level supported by the hardware. In the hardware implementation of RAID, hot swapping can often be performed because many hardware RAID controllers support it. Hot swapping means that you can replace a failed RAID-5 hard disk without turning off your computer, and the operating system will automatically recognize the change. Thus, you can recreate lost data using the parity information without turning off your computer. There are also more options for recovering lost or damaged data in the hardware implementation, and you may be able to support additional levels of RAID, such as RAID-10 (striping across mirrored volumes), depending on the manufacturer. You may have to buy the adapter, cable, and disk drives from the same hardware RAID vendor.

Figure 13-24 RAID 5

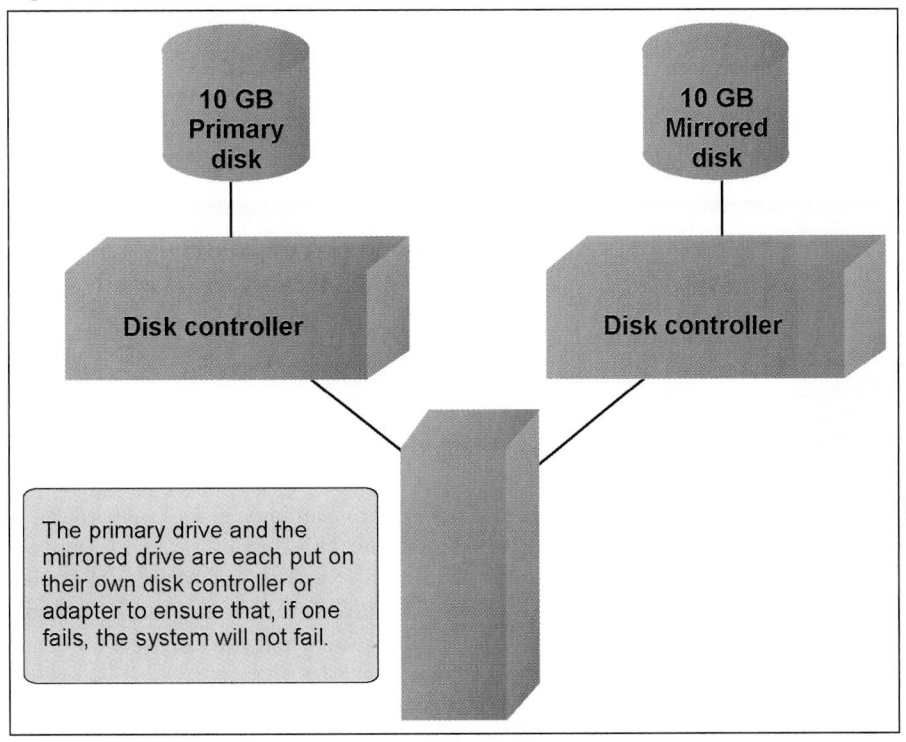

10 GB
Primary
disk

10 GB
Mirrored
disk

Disk controller

Disk controller

The primary drive and the
mirrored drive are each put on
their own disk controller or
adapter to ensure that, if one
fails, the system will not fail.

skill 5

Restoring Your System Using Safe Mode

exam objective

Perform system recovery for a server.

overview

Servers can fail to start or load the operating system for a variety of reasons, including incompatibility between a device driver and the existing hardware configuration of the computer. If this happens, you can start the computer in **Safe Mode** to attempt to restore it to a functional state. When you boot in Safe Mode, the computer starts up with a basic set of drivers that are needed to boot the system and make it accessible. Safe Mode is used to resolve problems that result from faulty device drivers, faulty programs, system service failures, or services that start automatically. In Safe Mode, the operating system will only load the files and drivers for the keyboard, mouse, basic VGA monitor, default system services, and disk. While in Safe Mode, you can remove corrupt drivers, fix driver conflicts, remove applications that automatically load from the startup folder or Registry, or uninstall and reinstall applications to resolve problems associated with those programs. **Safe Mode with Networking** includes networking drivers and services if you must have network access to fix the problem, and **Safe Mode with Command Prompt** opens the command prompt instead of the Graphical User Interface (GUI) environment. The other options on the menu are listed below:

◆ **Enable Boot Logging:** This option records the loading and initialization of drivers and services in the **Ntbtlog.txt** log file, which is located in the *%systemroot%* folder. Data pertaining to drivers and services that load successfully, as well as those that do not load or initialize, will be stored here, creating a constructive foundation for your troubleshooting efforts. This option is automatically enabled when you start the computer in any of the Safe Modes.

◆ **Enable VGA Mode:** This option boots the operating system with only a basic VGA driver and is useful when your display driver has been configured at a setting that your monitor does not support.

◆ **Last Known Good Configuration:** This option starts the computer using the Registry information that Windows saved after the last successful logon. This option is useful in correcting problems that arise after installing a new device driver.

◆ **Directory Services Restore Mode:** This option is available only on domain controllers. You use this option to restore the System State data on a domain controller, which includes the Sysvol folder and Active Directory database. You must also use this option when performing an authoritative restore and you can use it for other tasks such as offline defragmentation of Ntds.dit.

◆ **Debugging Mode:** In this mode, when the system restarts, it sends information about the boot process to another computer through a serial cable so that you can track the error and repair it.

how to

Start your member server in Safe Mode.

1. Click ![Start] and select **Shut Down**. The **Shut Down Windows** dialog box opens.
2. Select **Restart** in the **What do you want the computer to do?** list box.
3. Select **Hardware: Maintenance (Planned)** in the **Option** list box in the **Shutdown Event Tracker** section (**Figure 13-25**).
4. Click ![OK].
5. As soon as the computer boots, press the **[F8]** key to open the **Windows Advanced Options Menu** screen.
6. Use the **[Up]** or **[Down]** arrow key to select **Safe Mode** (**Figure 13-26**), and press the **[Enter]** key to start the boot process.
7. Select **Windows Server 2003, Standard** as the operating system and press **[Enter]** to open a screen showing a list of drivers used in the Safe Mode (**Figure 13-27**).
8. Press **[Ctrl]+[Alt]+[Del]** and log on as an **Administrator**.

Figure 13-25 The Shut Down Windows dialog box

Shut Down Windows
Microsoft
Windows Server 2003
Standard Edition
Copyright © 1985-2003 Microsoft Corporation
Microsoft
What do you want the computer to do?
Restart
Ends your session, shuts down Windows, and starts Windows again.
Shutdown Event Tracker
Select the option that best describes why you want to shut down the computer
Option:
Planned
Hardware: Maintenance (Planned)
A restart or shutdown to service hardware on the system.
Comment:
OK
Cancel
Help

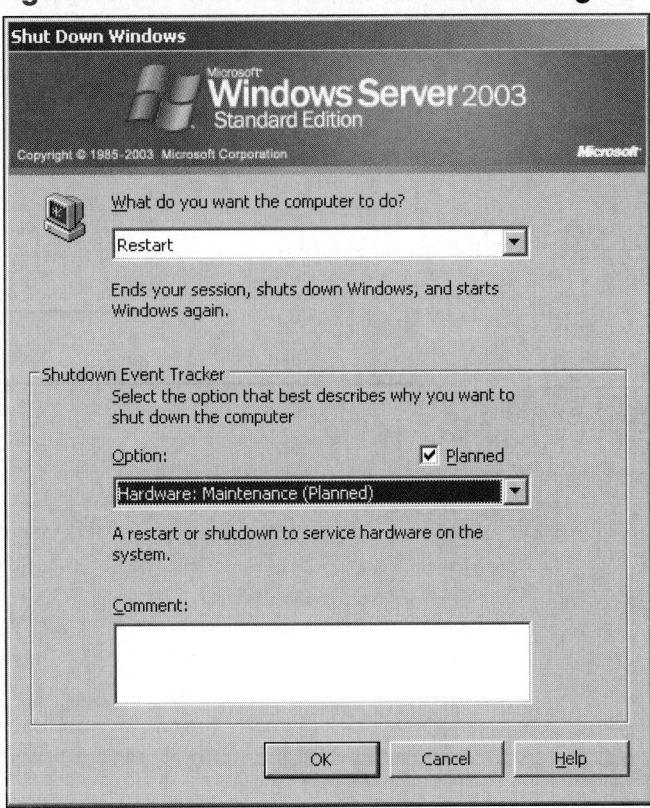

Figure 13-26 The Windows Advanced Options Menu

Windows Advanced Options Menu
Please select an option:
Safe Mode
Safe Mode with Networking
Safe Mode with Command Prompt
Enable Boot Logging
Enable VGA Mode
Last Known Good Configuration (your most recent settings that worked)
Directory Services Restore Mode (Windows domain controllers only)
Debugging Mode
Start Windows Normally
Reboot
Return to OS Choices Menu
Use the up and down arrow keys to move the highlight to your choice.

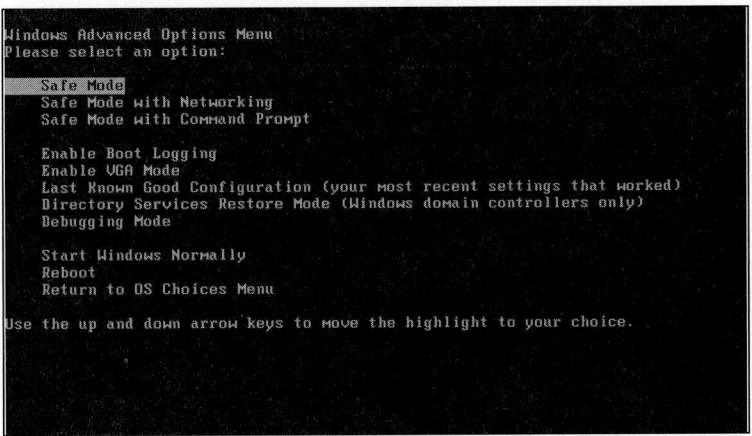

Figure 13-27 List of drivers loaded in Safe Mode

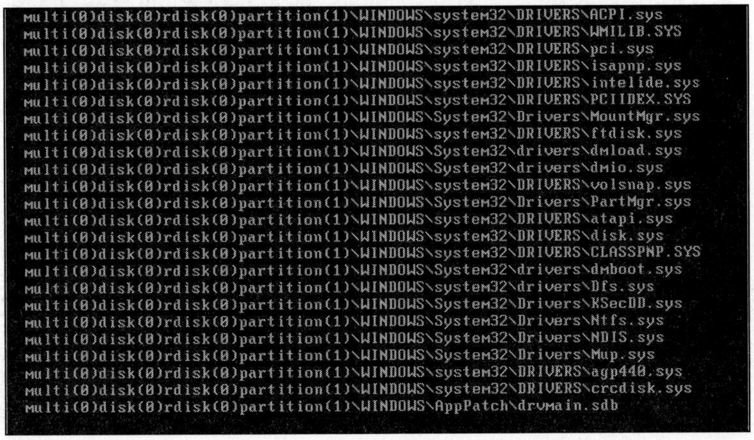

multi(0)disk(0)rdisk(0)partition(1)\WINDOWS\system32\DRIVERS\ACPI.sys
multi(0)disk(0)rdisk(0)partition(1)\WINDOWS\system32\DRIVERS\WMILIB.SYS
multi(0)disk(0)rdisk(0)partition(1)\WINDOWS\system32\DRIVERS\pci.sys
multi(0)disk(0)rdisk(0)partition(1)\WINDOWS\system32\DRIVERS\isapnp.sys
multi(0)disk(0)rdisk(0)partition(1)\WINDOWS\system32\DRIVERS\intelide.sys
multi(0)disk(0)rdisk(0)partition(1)\WINDOWS\system32\DRIVERS\PCIIDEX.SYS
multi(0)disk(0)rdisk(0)partition(1)\WINDOWS\System32\Drivers\MountMgr.sys
multi(0)disk(0)rdisk(0)partition(1)\WINDOWS\system32\DRIVERS\ftdisk.sys
multi(0)disk(0)rdisk(0)partition(1)\WINDOWS\System32\drivers\dmload.sys
multi(0)disk(0)rdisk(0)partition(1)\WINDOWS\System32\drivers\dmio.sys
multi(0)disk(0)rdisk(0)partition(1)\WINDOWS\system32\DRIVERS\volsnap.sys
multi(0)disk(0)rdisk(0)partition(1)\WINDOWS\System32\Drivers\PartMgr.sys
multi(0)disk(0)rdisk(0)partition(1)\WINDOWS\system32\DRIVERS\atapi.sys
multi(0)disk(0)rdisk(0)partition(1)\WINDOWS\system32\DRIVERS\disk.sys
multi(0)disk(0)rdisk(0)partition(1)\WINDOWS\system32\DRIVERS\CLASSPNP.SYS
multi(0)disk(0)rdisk(0)partition(1)\WINDOWS\System32\drivers\dmboot.sys
multi(0)disk(0)rdisk(0)partition(1)\WINDOWS\system32\drivers\Dfs.sys
multi(0)disk(0)rdisk(0)partition(1)\WINDOWS\System32\Drivers\KSecDD.sys
multi(0)disk(0)rdisk(0)partition(1)\WINDOWS\System32\Drivers\Ntfs.sys
multi(0)disk(0)rdisk(0)partition(1)\WINDOWS\System32\Drivers\NDIS.sys
multi(0)disk(0)rdisk(0)partition(1)\WINDOWS\System32\Drivers\Mup.sys
multi(0)disk(0)rdisk(0)partition(1)\WINDOWS\system32\DRIVERS\agp440.sys
multi(0)disk(0)rdisk(0)partition(1)\WINDOWS\system32\DRIVERS\crcdisk.sys
multi(0)disk(0)rdisk(0)partition(1)\WINDOWS\AppPatch\drvmain.sdb

skill 5

Restoring Your System Using Safe Mode (cont'd)

exam objective

Perform system recovery for a server.

how to

9. A **Desktop** message box informs you that the computer is running in safe mode (**Figure 13-28**).
10. Click [OK] to continue with the startup process. **Safe Mode** appears in all four corners of the screen.
11. Reboot the computer.

more

A local power failure can corrupt disk drives, memory, and other key server components requiring you to reinstall the operating system. A **UPS** (**uninterruptible power supply**) is the best way to avoid data loss and component damage from sudden power outages. A UPS is a hardware device that supplies power from capacitance cells to a computer full-time. When there is a loss of power, the UPS device takes over. Thus, UPS devices enable you to save your data and shut down in a systematic way when a power failure occurs. Most UPS devices also include power surge protection. There are two kinds of UPS systems, loosely referred to as either online or offline. Online UPS systems supply power directly from their capacitance cells, which are continually charging while the electrical power is intact. Offline UPS systems, which are also referred to as SPS (standby power systems), have battery backups. They monitor the electrical line to the equipment until there is a sudden decrease in power. Then, they use a switching mechanism to switch from electrical outlet power to battery power. Offline UPS systems are less expensive and last longer, but they may not switch over to battery power in time to avoid all damage from a sudden power outage. Most UPS systems supply power for around 10 to 20 minutes, although top-of-the-line devices can supply power for hours. During this time, you can decide whether or not to shut down. If it looks as if the power outage is going to last for an extended period, all work can be saved, and the system can be shut down. Battery output time will depend on how much equipment and what kinds of devices are attached to the UPS device. Some offline UPS devices have additional circuits for handling brownouts, as well as full outages, and online UPS systems can almost always adjust the power supply to handle brownouts.

UPS communications options are set on the UPS tab in the Power Options dialog box. You open the Power Options dialog box from the Power Options command on the Control Panel sub-menu on the Start menu. To configure the UPS service, first you must click the **Select** button to open the **UPS Selection** dialog box, where you select the manufacturer and model, and the COM port to which the UPS device is connected (**Figure 13-29**). Then, you can click the **Configure** button to open the **UPS Configuration** dialog box, where you can set the number of seconds between the power failure and the first notification, the seconds between subsequent power failure notifications, and the minutes on the battery before a critical alarm will sound. You can also configure the system to run a specific program just before the UPS runs out of power (**Figure 13-30**).

When a UPS is attached to your system, the UPS service will prompt your system to send a notification in the following cases:

◆ Main-power failure detection: When the power supply fails, the UPS will alert you that your system is running on the UPS.
◆ Low-battery detection: When the battery for the UPS is low, it will alert you.
◆ UPS shutdown: When the UPS wants to shut down due to low battery power, it will prompt you to shut down your system. If you do not shut down your system, the UPS automatically closes all of your applications, notifies other users on the network about the system shutdown, and shuts down the system.

Always make sure that the UPS device you are going to install is listed in the Windows Server Catalog.

tip

Often, in order to enable the UPS alert system, you will have to install the UPS software that comes with the UPS.

Figure 13-28 The Desktop message box

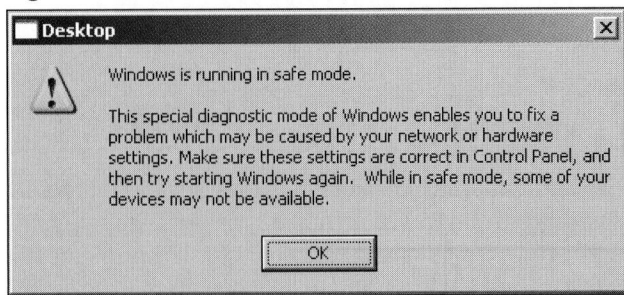

Figure 13-29 The UPS Selection dialog box

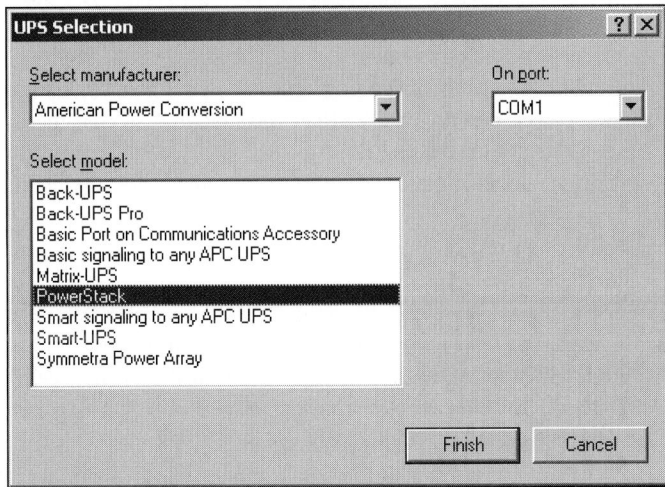

Figure 13-30 The UPS Configuration dialog box

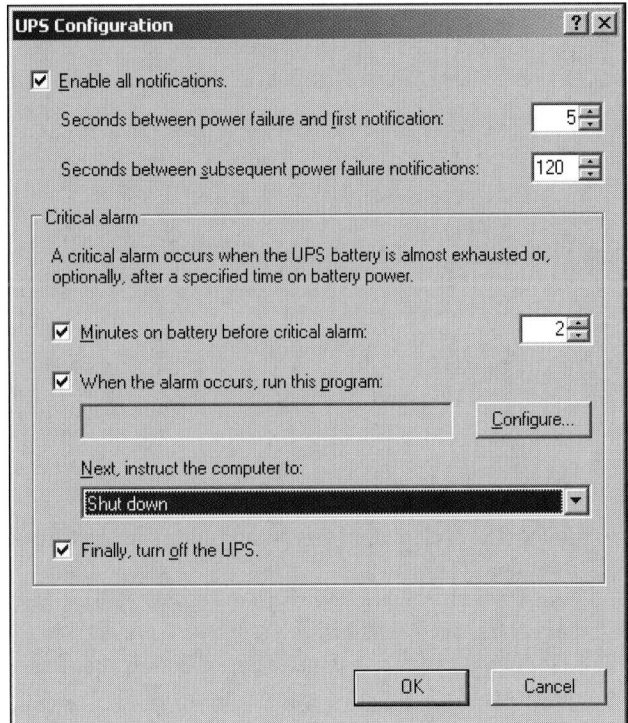

skill 6

Using the Last Known Good Configuration

exam objective

Perform system recovery for a server.

overview

The **Last Known Good Configuration** contains settings saved in the Registry the last time a user successfully logged on to the computer. After every successful logon, the data used for configuring the computer, is copied to the LastKnownGood value entry in the Registry **(Figure 13-31)**. When you start your computer, there are usually only two configurations that can be used: the default configuration or the Last Known Good Configuration. The configuration information that is saved when a computer shuts down normally is contained in the default configuration, and the configuration data that was saved just after the last successful logon is saved in the Last Known Good Configuration. The default configuration includes any changes made during the last logon session before the reboot process was initiated. Sometimes these configuration changes, for example, installing an incompatible device driver, can adversely affect the machine so that the computer will not boot. In these cases, you can try to use the Last Known Good Configuration to boot the computer and reverse the detrimental configuration change, although this may not always be successful.

The Last Known Good Configuration can be useful if you have incorrectly edited the Registry, added a new driver that is either not compatible with your hardware or is defective, or if you have disabled a critical device driver (such as the SCSIPORT driver).

However, the Last Known Good Configuration cannot help you to restart the computer if there are corrupt or missing files, or if a new driver has been copied onto an old driver that is still active. In this case, the configuration does not change and reverting to the Last Known Good Configuration will not help.

The Last Known Good Configuration also will not work if there are any improper operating system modifications that are not related to the Registry settings (for example, incorrectly configured user profiles or improper file permissions).

Furthermore, if a hardware device problem is occurring and you forget to choose Last Known Good Configuration, and then you successfully log on, the Last Known Good Configuration will be updated and you will no longer be able to revert to a pre-configuration change state.

caution

If you run into difficulties due to a configuration change on your computer and you forget to use the Last Known Good Configuration when you reboot, **do not** log on. The LastKnownGood Registry value entry will be overwritten if you log on.

how to

Use the Last Known Good Configuration to resolve configuration problems.

1. Click **Start** . Right-click **My Computer** and select **Manage** to open the Computer Management console.
2. Double-click **Device Manager**.
3. Double-click **Network adapters**. Right-click the NIC icon and select **Disable** **(Figure 13-32)**.
4. A warning message will inform you that disabling this device will cause it to stop functioning. Click Yes .
5. The network adapter icon now has a red x on top. Close the Computer Management console.
6. Connect to the Internet if you are not using an always connected method. Open your browser.
7. Type **www.ebay.com**. You will not be able to open the search page because the network adapter has been disabled.
8. Click OK to close the message dialog box if necessary. Close the browser.
9. Click **Start** and select **Shut Down**. Select **Restart** in the **What do you want the computer to do?** list box.
10. Type **TEST** in the **Comment** box. Click OK .

Figure 13-31 LKG and Default value entries in the Registry

Contains
configuration
information
that is saved
when a
computer
shuts down
normally

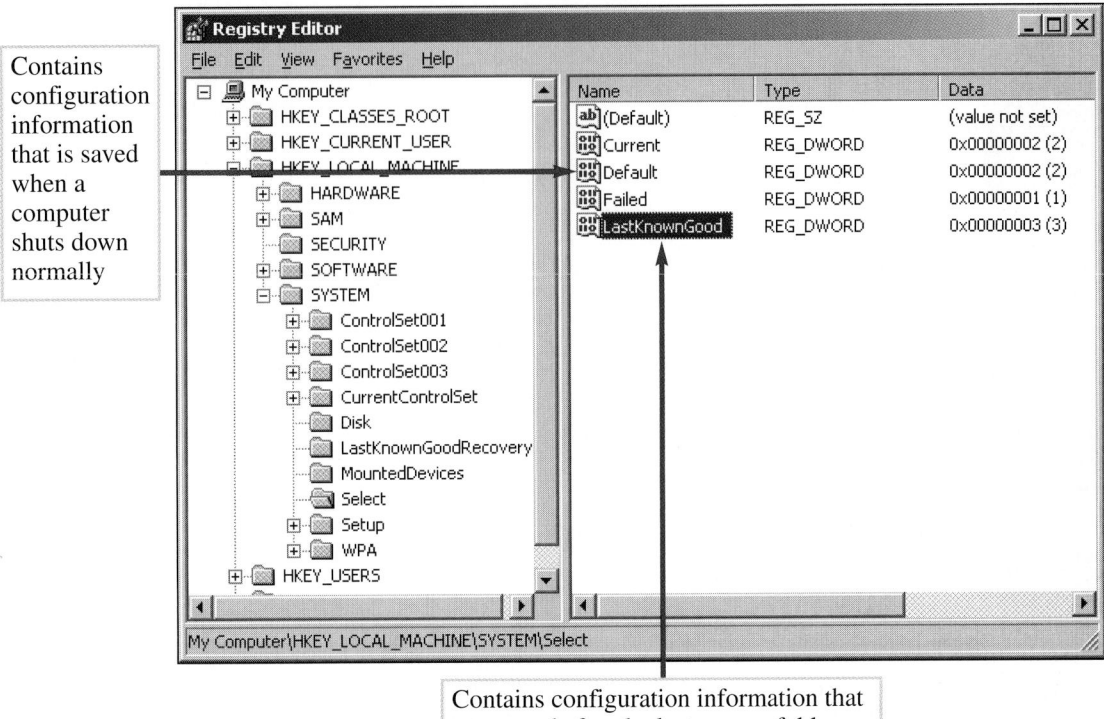

Contains configuration information that
was saved after the last successful logon

Figure 13-32 Disabling the network adapter

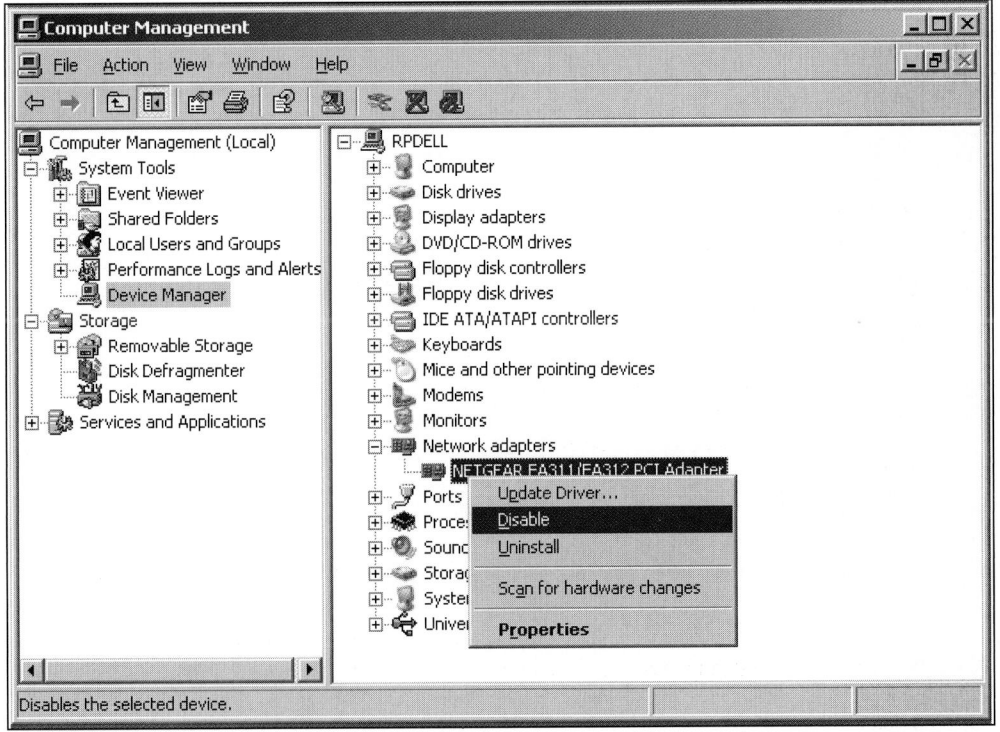

skill 6

Using the Last Known Good Configuration (cont'd)

exam objective

Perform system recovery for a server.

how to

11. As soon as the computer boots, press the **[F8]** key to open the **Windows Advanced Options Menu**.
12. Use the **[Up]** or **[Down]** arrow key to select **Last Known Good Configuration (your most recent settings that worked)** (**Figure 13-33**), and press **[Enter]**.
13. Select **Windows Server 2003, Standard** on the Boot Selection menu (**Please select the operating system to start**), and press **[Enter]**.
14. Log on as an **Administrator**.
15. Click ⊞Start. Right-click **My Computer** and select **Properties** to open the **System Properties** dialog box.
16. Open the Hardware tab and select [Device Manager...] (**Figure 13-34**).
17. Double-click **Network adapters**. Confirm that the NIC is not disabled (It does not have a red **x**).
18. Close the Device Manager and the System Properties dialog box.

more

Remember, the Last Known Good Configuration cannot be used to solve problems caused by missing or corrupt drivers or files. It is also very important to understand that any changes made since the last successful startup can be reversed only if the user has not logged on again and overwritten the old control set in the Registry.

Figure 13-33 Last Known Good Configuration

Windows Advanced Options Menu
Please select an option:
Safe Mode
Safe Mode with Networking
Safe Mode with Command Prompt
Enable Boot Logging
Enable VGA Mode
Last Known Good Configuration (your most recent settings that worked)
Directory Services Restore Mode (Windows domain controllers only)
Debugging Mode
Start Windows Normally
Reboot
Return to OS Choices Menu
Use the up and down arrow keys to move the highlight to your choice.

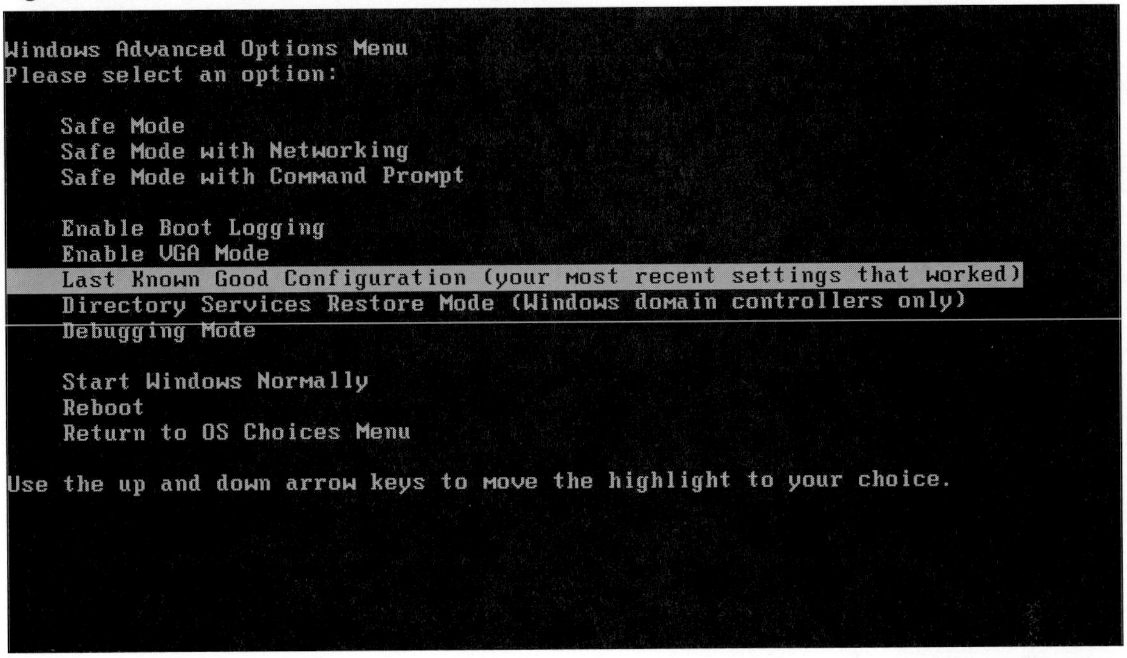

Figure 13-34 The Hardware tab in the System Properties dialog box

System Properties
Advanced
Automatic Updates
Remote
General
Computer Name
Hardware
Add Hardware Wizard
The Add Hardware Wizard helps you install hardware.
Add Hardware Wizard
Device Manager
The Device Manager lists all the hardware devices installed on your computer. Use the Device Manager to change the properties of any device.
Driver Signing
Device Manager
Hardware Profiles
Hardware profiles provide a way for you to set up and store different hardware configurations.
Hardware Profiles
OK
Cancel
Apply

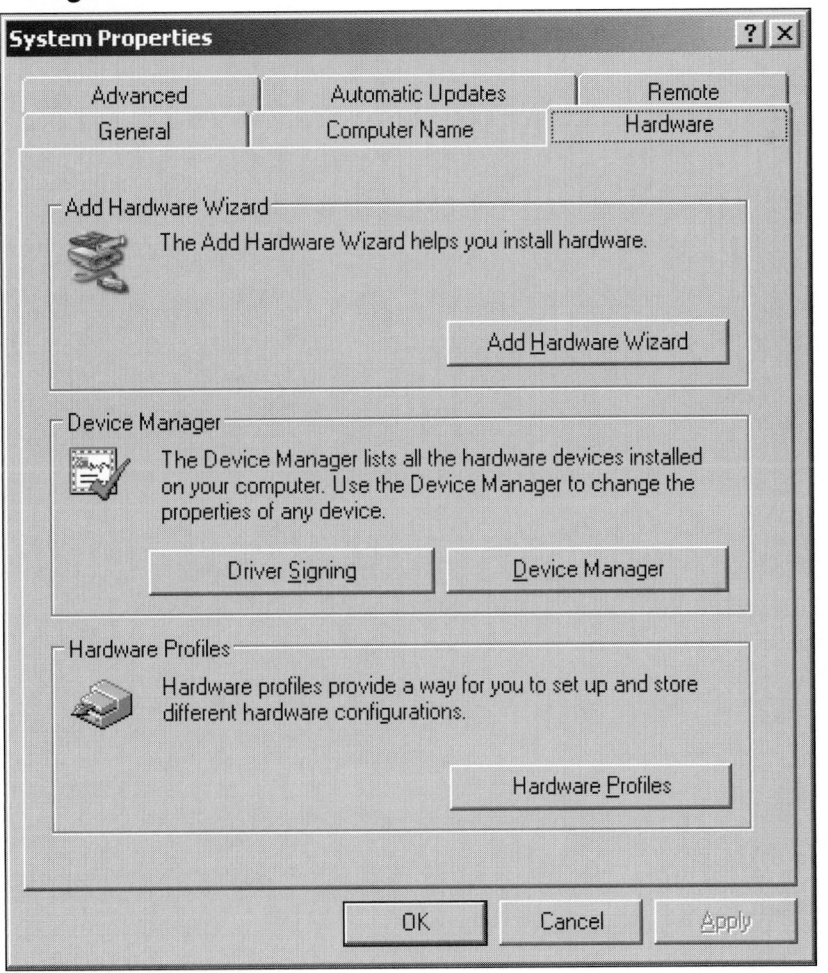

skill 7

Working with the Recovery Console

exam objective

Perform system recovery for a server. Recover from server hardware failure.

overview

tip

The Recovery Console
prompts you for an
administrative password
to verify your identity
before allowing you to
view hard disk details.

If you are unable to boot your server using either the Last Known Good Configuration or Safe Mode, you may be able to use the **Recovery Console** to recover the system. It allows you to start the operating system so that you can stop the specific software or driver that is causing the problem. The Recovery Console does not start the Registry, so you can use it to copy a Registry backup that you have made to *%systemroot%*\System32\Config to restore the Registry, if necessary. The Recovery console is a command-line interface that you can use to:

◆ Troubleshoot, enable, disable, and reconfigure services
◆ Copy, rename, or replace operating system files and folders
◆ Format hard disks,
◆ Repair the file system, boot sector, or the Master Boot Record (MBR)
◆ Read and write data on a local drive

You can also use the Recovery Console to obtain limited access to the hard disk of your computer to view and repair the following files and folders:

◆ %systemroot%
◆ Windows Server 2003 installation subfolders
◆ %systemdrive%
◆ CD-ROM drive
◆ Floppy drive

You repair files using the commands listed in **Table 13-6**. You can access the Recovery Console window only when you log on as a local administrator.

To use the Recovery Console, you can launch it from the installation CD, if your computer supports booting from the CD-ROM drive, or you can install it from the Windows Server 2003 installation CD-ROM so that it will be included on the boot menu. You will need the password for the built-in Administrator account.

Table 13-6	*Recovery Console Commands*
Command	**Used to:**
Attrib	Change the attributes of a file or directory
Batch	Execute commands specified in a text file
Bootcfg	Configure and recover the boot file (boot.ini)
Chdir (CD)	Display the name of the current directory or to change the current directory
Chkdsk	Check a disk and display a status report
Cls	Clear the screen
Copy	Copy a single file to another location
Delete (Del)	Delete one or more files
Dir	Display a list of files and subdirectories in a directory
Disable	Disable system services or devices
Diskpart	Create, delete, and manage partitions on the hard drives
Enable	Enable system services or devices
Exit	Close the Recovery Console and restart the computer
Expand	Extract a file from a compressed file
Fixboot	Write a new partition boot sector to the system partition
Fixmbr	Write a new Master Boot Record to the hard drive
Format	Format a disk
Help	Display the list of commands that can be used in the Recovery Console
Listsvc	List the services and drivers on the computer
Logon	Log on to an installation of Windows Server 2003
Map	Display a mapping of drive letters to physical device names
Mkdir (Md)	Create a directory
More (Type)	Display a text file
Rename (Ren)	Rename a directory
Rmdir (Rd)	Delete a directory
Set	Display and set environment variables
Systemroot	Set the current directory to the *%systemroot%* folder

skill 7

Working with the Recovery Console
(cont'd)

exam objective

Perform system recovery for a server. Recover from server hardware failure.

how to

Install the Recovery Console and use the fixboot command to repair the boot sector on your member server.

1. Insert the Windows Server 2003 installation CD in the CD-ROM drive.
2. Open the command prompt. Type **x:** (where x represents the letter for your CD-ROM drive) to switch to the CD-ROM drive.
3. Type **\i386\winnt32.exe /cmdcons (Figure 13-35)**.
4. A Windows Setup message box tells you about installing the Recovery Console as a startup option **(Figure 13-36)**.
5. Click [Yes] to install the Recovery Console. The files are copied onto your computer. When the process is complete, a message box will inform you that the Recovery Console has been successfully installed and you will be prompted to restart the computer **(Figure 13-37)**.
6. Click [OK] and reboot. Click [Start] and select **Shut Down**.
7. In the **Shut Down Windows** dialog box, select **Restart** in the **What do you want the computer to do?** list box.
8. Select **Application: Maintenance (Planned)** in the **Option** list box in the **Shutdown Event Tracker** section.
9. In the **Comment** box, type **Testing**. Click [OK].
10. When the computer restarts, the **Microsoft Windows Recovery Console** will be listed on the **Please select an operating system to start** screen (the Boot Selection menu). Use the down arrow key to select it and press **[Enter]**.
11. When the Recovery Console opens, you will be asked which Windows installation you would like to log on to; usually there will only be one installation. Type **1**, and press **[Enter]**.
12. You will be prompted to type the Administrator password. Type the Administrator password you set, and press **[Enter]** to receive the **C:\WINNT** command prompt.
13. Type **listsvc** and press **[Enter]** to list the services and drivers on the server. Use the **[Enter]** key to scroll line-by-line and the space bar to scroll page-to-page to view the list **(Figure 13-38)**.
14. Press **[Esc]** to return to the command line.
15. Type **fixboot** and press **[Enter]**. **The target partition is C: Are you sure you want to write a new boot sector to the partition C:?** message appears.
16. Type **y** to start fixing the errors in boot files.
17. First, the file system on the startup partition will be identified. Then, the message **FIXBOOT is writing a new boot sector will display**. Finally, you will be notified that the new boot sector was successfully written **(Figure 13-39)**.
18. Type **cls** and press **[Enter]** to clear the screen.
19. Type **Help** and press **[Enter]** to view the list of the commands you can use.
20. Type **Exit** and press **[Enter]** to close the Recovery Console.
21. Reboot to the Windows Server 2003, Standard Edition installation.

tip

You can only install the Recovery Console on x86-based computers. You can not install it on Itanium-based computers.

more

Once you install the Recovery Console, it is included on the boot menu as one of the boot options. As a result, it could provide a method for unauthorized users to access a computer. Booting to the Recovery Console bypasses many of the normal safety measures in the logon process. Since this is a possible security hazard, even though access to data volumes is not allowed using the Recovery Console, you may not want to install the Recovery Console unless the server is maintained in a secure environment, in which physical access is controlled.

Figure 13-35 Accessing the Recovery Console installation files

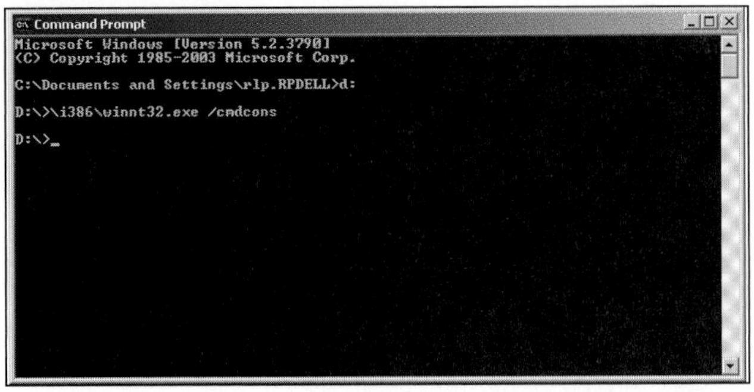

Figure 13-36 Windows Setup message box: Installing the Recovery Console as a startup option

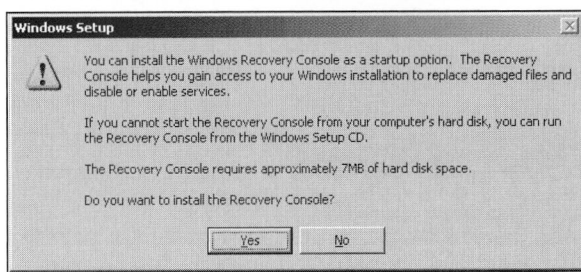

Figure 13-37 Windows Setup message box: Recovery Console has been installed

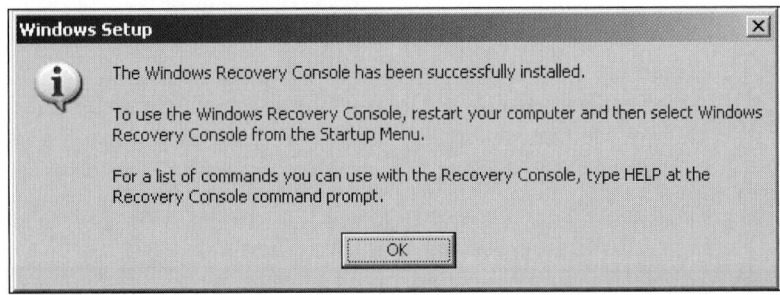

List of services and drivers installed on the computer

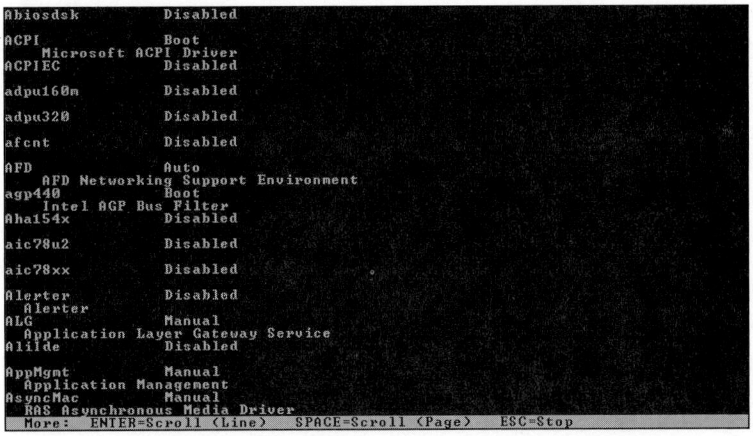

Figure 13-38 Recovery Console: Listsvc command

```
Abiosdsk          Disabled
ACPI              Boot
     Microsoft ACPI Driver
ACPIEC            Disabled

adpu160m          Disabled

adpu320           Disabled

afcnt             Disabled

AFD               Auto
     AFD Networking Support Environment
agp440            Boot
     Intel AGP Bus Filter
Aha154x           Disabled

aic78u2           Disabled

aic78xx           Disabled

Alerter           Disabled
  Alerter
ALG               Manual
     Application Layer Gateway Service
Alilde            Disabled

AppMgmt           Manual
     Application Management
AsyncMac          Manual
     RAS Asynchronous Media Driver
More:  ENTER=Scroll (Line)    SPACE=Scroll (Page)    ESC=Stop
```

Figure 13-39 Recovery Console: Fixboot command

Fixboot command

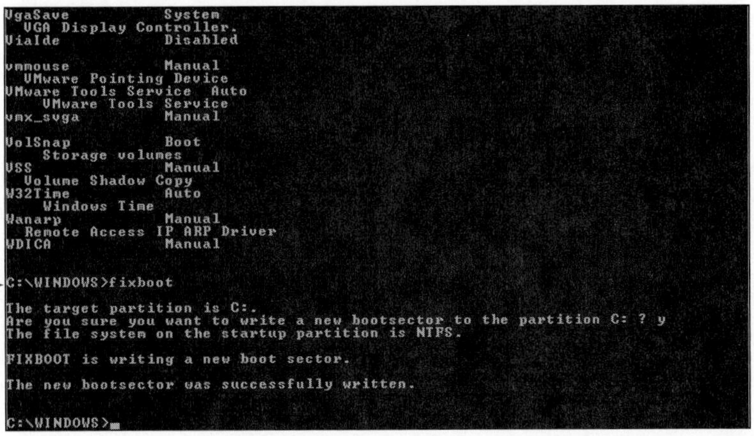

```
VgaSave           System
  VGA Display Controller.
ViaIde            Disabled

vmmouse           Manual
  VMware Pointing Device
VMware Tools Service  Auto
        VMware Tools Service
vmx_svga          Manual

VolSnap           Boot
   Storage volumes
VSS               Manual
  Volume Shadow Copy
W32Time           Auto
   Windows Time
Wanarp            Manual
  Remote Access IP ARP Driver
WDICA             Manual

C:\WINDOWS>fixboot

The target partition is C:.
Are you sure you want to write a new bootsector to the partition C: ? y
The file system on the startup partition is NTFS.

FIXBOOT is writing a new boot sector.

The new bootsector was successfully written.

C:\WINDOWS>
```

skill 8

Implementing Automated System Recovery

exam objective

Perform system recovery for a server. Recover from server hardware failure. Implement Automated System Recovery (ASR).

overview

If you cannot start your server using Safe Mode, the Last Known Good Configuration, or the Recovery Console, you can try using the **Automated System Recovery (ASR)** backup. ASR is a backup of your system configuration information including key system files and the Registry that is designed to enable you to repair your system partition. You use ASR to recover a failed server in the event of a complete break down.

When you use the **Automated System Recovery Preparation Wizard**, the configuration of your system drive and boot volume are saved to whatever backup medium you choose. There are two parts to the ASR backup. First, all system files are backed up, which can require 1.5 or more GB of storage space. Second, the system settings needed for an ASR recovery are backed up, which only requires 1.44 MB of storage space. An ASR backup should be performed immediately following the successful installation of the operating system and updated whenever you modify the system configuration, such as adding a new device driver, adding a protocol, or using Windows Update to install a patch or service pack.

When an ASR restore is performed, it formats the system drive. All user data on the system partition will be lost, so you will have to restore all user data as well as all system partition data.

To perform an ASR backup you will need one floppy disk and a backup storage medium sufficient in size to store the operating system files, configuration settings, and System State data.

To perform an ASR restore, you will need the bootable Windows Server 2003 CD-ROM, the most recent copy of the ASR backup set, which is generally saved on tape or another removable storage medium, and your most recent backup media set.

The ASR floppy cannot be used to boot a Windows Server 2003 system, but if you can boot the computer using the installation CD-ROM, you can use the ASR floppy and the ASR backup set to repair the system partition. The ASR floppy replaces the Emergency Repair Diskette (ERD) that was used in Windows 2000 to perform the emergency repair process.

how to

Create an ASR backup set. (You will need several Zip disks, depending on their size, or a tape to store 1.5 or more GB of system files. You will also need a floppy disk for the system settings backup.)

1. Click [Start] and then click the **Run** command to open the **Run** dialog box.
2. In the **Open** text box, type **ntbackup** and click [OK] to open the **Backup or Restore Wizard**.
3. Click the **Advanced Mode** link to open the **Backup Utility** window.
4. Click the **Automated System Recovery Wizard button** [ ] to open the **Automated System Recovery Preparation Wizard (Figure 13-40)**.
5. Click [Next >] to open the **Backup Destination** screen. In the **Backup or media file name** text box, enter the path to the tape or Zip drive you are using, for example, **E: \ASRBackup.bkf**.
6. Click [Next >] to open the **Completing the Automated System Recovery Preparation Wizard** screen **(Figure 13-41)**.

Figure 13-40 The Automated System Recovery Preparation Wizard

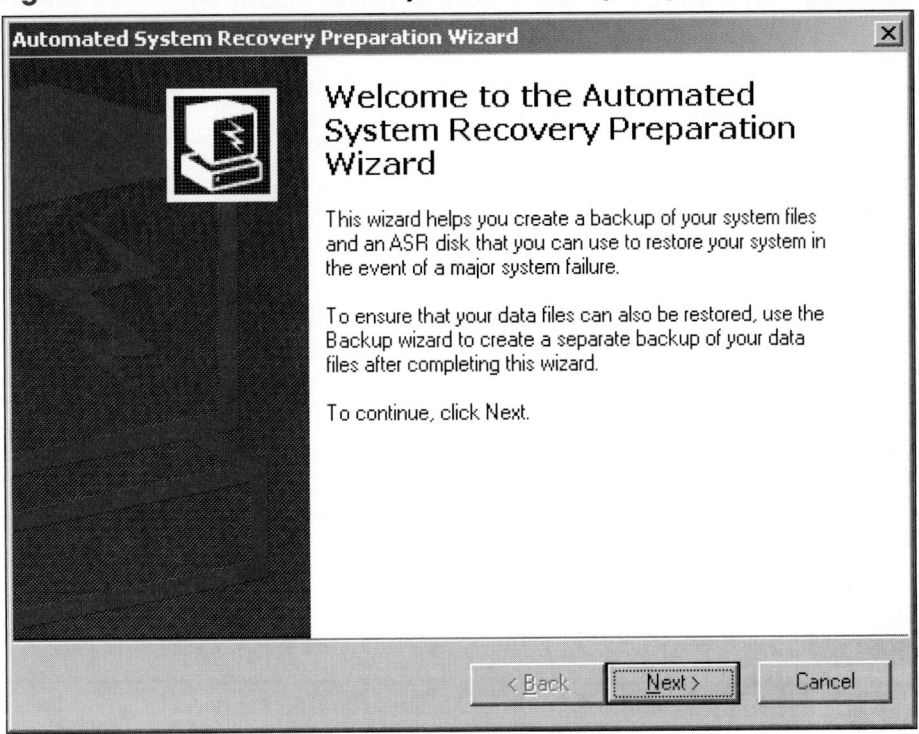

Figure 13-41 Completing the ASR Preparation Wizard

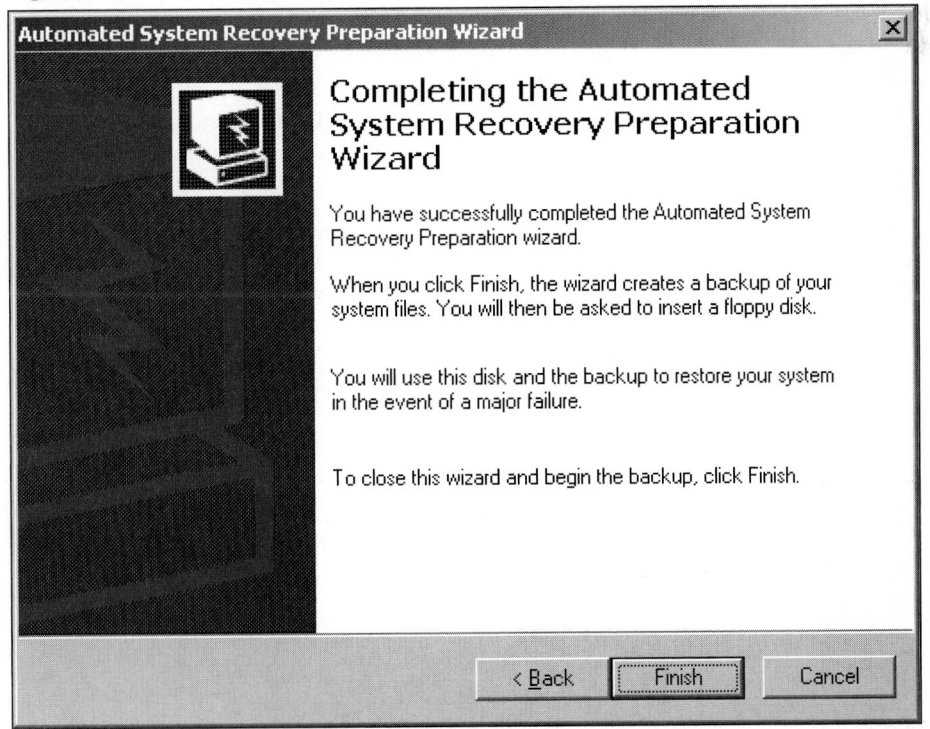

skill 8

Implementing Automated System Recovery (cont'd)

exam objective

Perform system recovery for a server. Recover from server hardware failure. Implement Automated System Recovery (ASR).

how to

7. Click [Finish].The backup files will be written to the tape or Zip drive. The **Windows Automated System Recovery** message box opens first **(Figure 13-42)**.
8. Next, the **Selection Information** message box **(Figure 13-43)** and the **Backup Progress** message box will display.
9. Click [Cancel] if you do not have any removable media available.
10. Insert additional Zip disks as prompted. The entire process can take quite some time. When it is complete you will be prompted to insert a floppy disk to create the ASR floppy disk **(Figure 13-44)**. Click [OK].
11. Remove the floppy disk and the Zip disk or backup tape, and click [OK].
12. Mark your ASR backup set appropriately.
13. Close the Backup Progress dialog box and the Backup Utility window.
14. The backup set and the floppy disk together will be used to restore your system in the event of a complete system failure.

more

You use the ASR backup set when you cannot solve your boot problem using the options on the Windows Advanced Options Menu or the Recovery Console. An ASR restore can be useful in cases where you are recovering from a single boot disk failure or when you need to move the system to a larger disk. You will need the set of disks or the tape you created in the exercise and your most recent backup media sets. You will also need a Windows Server 2003 CD-ROM.

First, shut down the computer, if possible, or turn the computer off. Then, insert the Windows Server 2003 CD-ROM in the CD-ROM drive. You will have to boot the computer from the installation CD-ROM. You may have to adjust the system BIOS to make this possible. After the text-mode segment of Windows Setup begins, press **[F2]** to enter the ASR bootstrap program. You will be prompted to insert the ASR floppy disk. The ASR code in Windows Setup can read the ASR floppy disk to reconfigure the storage system on the server. ASR will automatically call the restore program to restore the rest of the data from the ASR backup. On-screen instructions will then guide you through the rest of the ASR restore process.

The ASR backup set is read and the disk signatures, volumes, partitions, and system files that are needed to boot the computer are restored. After this has been accomplished, a basic version of the operating system is installed. Finally, you can restore the system using the backup media you created earlier.

Figure 13-42 The Windows Automated System Recovery message box

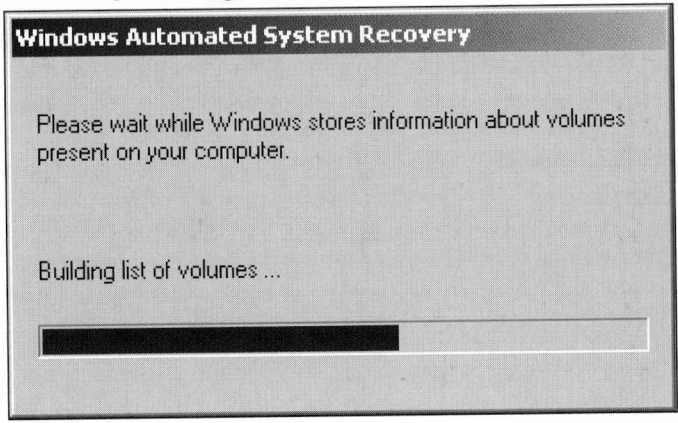

Figure 13-43 The Selection Information message box

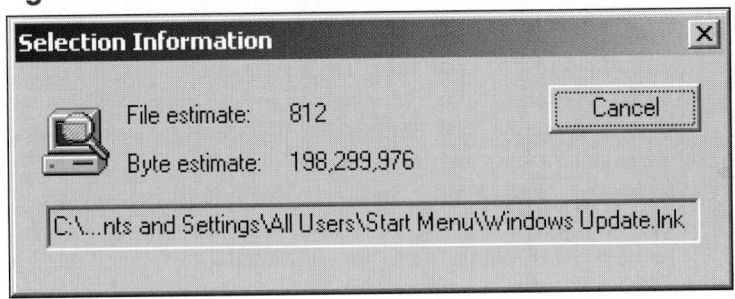

Figure 13-44 The Backup Utility message to create the ASR floppy

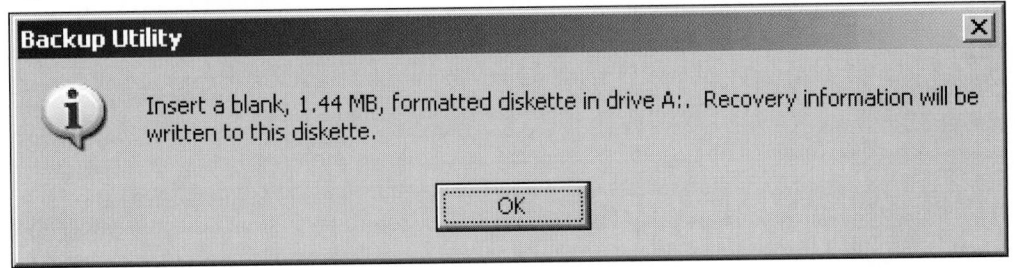

skill 9
Configuring the Volume Shadow Copy Service

exam objective

Restore data from shadow copy volumes.

overview

tip

The minimum amount of storage space that you can set for shadow copies of stored folders is 100 MB. By default, it will be set to 10% of the volume size.

The Volume Shadow Copy Service (VSS) provides two new services in Windows Server 2003. First, it can be used by applications to access locked files or files that are in use by other services or applications. For example, the Backup utility makes use of VSS technology. The default volume shadow copy backup mode enables you to create exact backup copies at a particular point in time of all files, including those that are open. In previous versions of Windows, this was not the case. Open or locked files would be excluded from the backup process. Applications can now be writing data to a volume or partition during the backup process, and open files are no longer skipped. This also means that backups can be performed at any time, and users need not be locked out during the process.

This is how volume shadow copy backup mode works: a reference copy of the volume that is being backed up is immediately created using Volume Shadow Copy Technology (VSCT). The reference copy is really just a pointer to the data. The Backup utility then backs up the selected files and folders from the shadow copy rather than from the original. Data that is being written to the volume after the shadow copy is created is not included in the backup. The Backup utility "sees" these open files as closed because it is viewing the shadow copy, and open files are halted at a fixed point in time when the shadow copy is created.

Second, you can configure the service so that previous versions of saved files that are stored on a network share on a particular volume can be accessed and restored from shadow copies, which are created at scheduled intervals. You enable and configure VSS on the **Shadow Copies** tab on the **Local Disk Properties** dialog box or the Properties dialog box for the volume (**Figure 13-45**). Previous versions of files that users have inadvertently deleted or overwritten can be recovered on the file server. Windows Server 2003 and Windows XP Professional users can recover lost files by locating the shadow copies on the **Previous Versions** tab on the **Properties** dialog box for a shared network file or folder (**Figure 13-46**). The Previous Versions client is stored on the server in the **%systemroot%\system32\clients\twclient folder**. There are three versions of the client: one for x86-based computers, one for computers based on the AMD64 architecture, and one for computers based on the IA-64 architecture. Each client version has its own folder; however, depending on the version of Windows Server 2003, all of the clients may not be present (**Figure 13-47**).

When VSS is enabled on a volume, a snapshot is taken of the entire volume and all of its files. This snapshot records the "state" of the volume. Initially, it does not create copies. When a file is updated by a user and then saved, it is "recognized" as having changed by VSS and at that point the changed sections of the file as it existed at the last scheduled shadow copy run time are copied and saved. This is the copy of the file that will become available on the Previous Versions tab. Since only the changes are copied, previous versions of files generally do not take up as much disk space as the current file. However, the amount of disk space consumed will vary depending on the program used to modify the file.

Shadow copying can be enabled on a volume and scheduled to occur at regular intervals so that snapshots of all shares on the volume will be created at set intervals of time. The snapshots and the log files will be stored in a new hidden folder, **System Volume Information**, which is created on the root of the volume. You can set a maximum size for this storage folder. Once the maximum storage size has been reached, older versions of shadow copies will be deleted, and will therefore no longer be available.

Figure 13-45 The Shadow Copies tab on the Properties dialog box for a disk

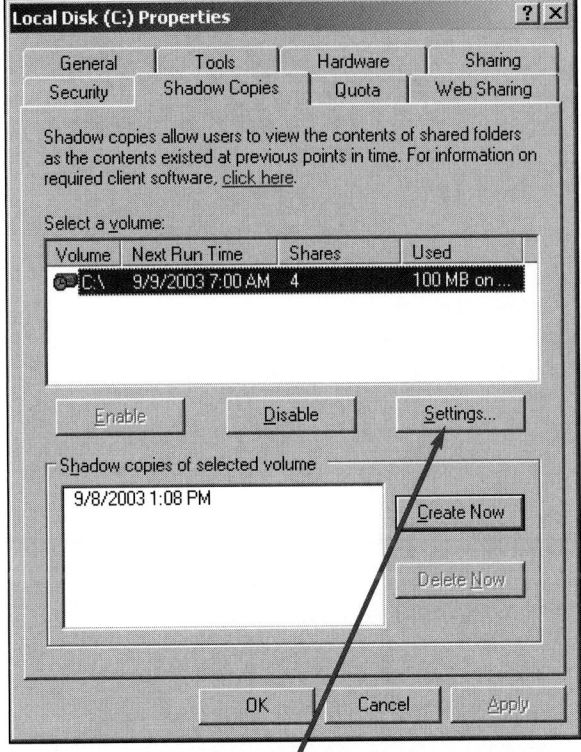

Click to configure the settings for which drive to store the shadow copies on, and the maximum amount of space to use for the shadow copies

Figure 13-46 The Previous Versions tab on the Properties dialog box for a folder

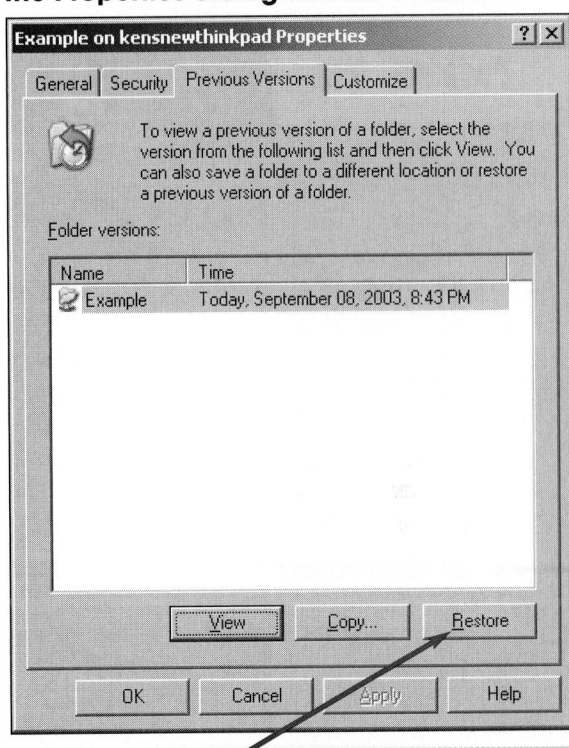

Click to restore a previous version of the file or folder; this will roll back the file or folder to its state at the date and time you select; changes made since that time will be lost

Figure 13-47 The three versions of the Previous Versions client

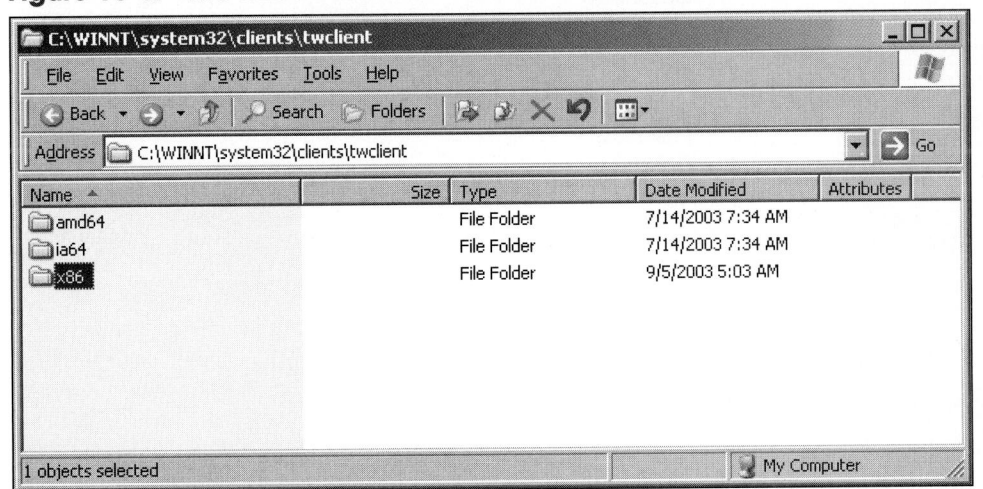

skill 9

Configuring the Volume Shadow Copy Service (cont'd)

exam objective

Restore data from shadow copy volumes.

how to

tip

You can also right-click **Shared Folders**, select **All Tasks**, and click **Configure Shadow Copies** to enable VSS.

Enable the Volume Shadow Copy Service (VSS).

1. Click ⏁Start. Right-click **My Computer** and select **Manage** to open the **Computer Management** console.
2. Select the **Disk Management** snap-in. Right-click the drive you are going to configure, for example C:\, and select **Properties**.
3. Open the **Shadow Copies** tab.
4. In the **Select a volume** box, select the volume for which you want to enable Shadow Copies.
5. Click Settings to open the **Settings** dialog box.
6. In the **Volume** text box, change the drive on which you want VSS to store the shadow copies, if possible. This is the recommended practice. You want the storage folder to be located on a volume on which VSS has not been enabled, not on the one on which you are enabling the service. This will provide better performance and will remove the danger that high input/output load will cause shadow copies to be deleted. You can specify only the drive, not the folder.
7. In the **Maximum size** spin box, enter the maximum size for the storage folder. This must be at least 100 MB. By default, it will be set to 10% of the VSS enabled volume. If you are storing the shadow copies on a separate volume, modify the default so that it is consistent with the available space on the storage volume (**Figure 13-48**).
8. Click Schedule... . The default schedule is 7:00 am and 12:00 noon Monday through Friday (**Figure 13-49**).
9. Click New to create a new schedule. In the **Schedule Task** list box, select **Weekly**.
10. In the **Start time** spin box, enter **2:00 PM**. Select the **Mon**, **Tues**, **Wed**, **Thu**, and **Fri** check boxes.
11. Click Advanced... to open the **Advanced Schedule Options** dialog box. Select the **End date** check box.
12. In the **End date** list box, select a date one month from today's date on the calendar (**Figure 13-50**).
13. Click OK to close the Advanced Schedule dialog box. VSS will now create shadow copies at 2:00 PM Monday through Friday for one month in addition to the default schedule.
14. Click OK to close the <C:\> volume dialog box.
15. Click OK to close the Settings dialog box. VSS is now enabled. As you can see, the Enable button is inactive. You can optionally click Create Now to create a starting snapshot.
16. Close the Local Disk Properties dialog box and the Computer Management console.

Figure 13-48 The Settings dialog box

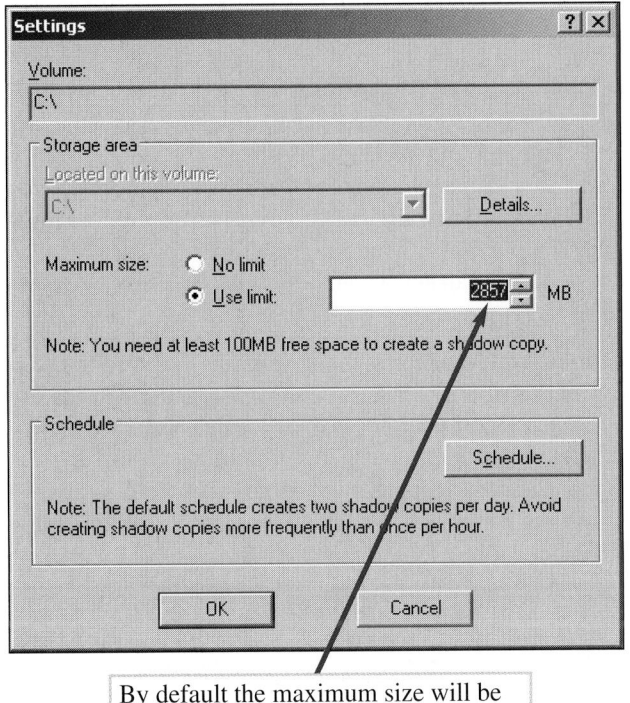

By default the maximum size will be set to 10% of the VSS enabled volume

Figure 13-49 The Schedule tab

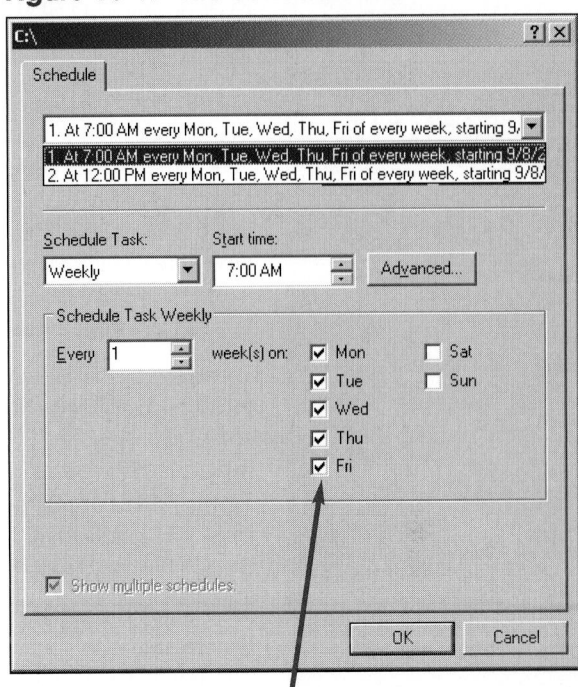

The default shadow copy schedule is 7:00 am and 12:00 noon Monday through Friday

Figure 13-50 The Advanced Schedule Options dialog box

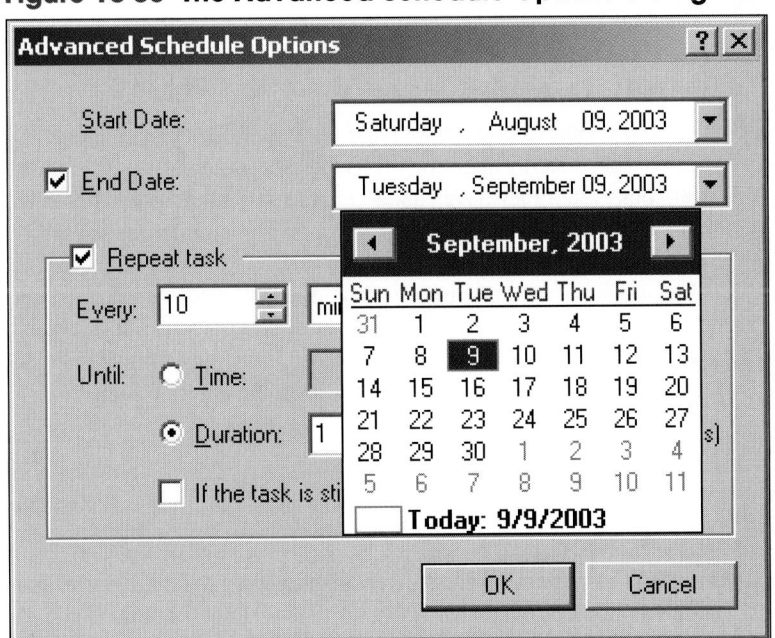

skill 9

Configuring the Volume Shadow Copy Service *(cont'd)*

exam objective

Restore data from shadow copy volumes.

more

tip

You cannot install the Previous Versions client (twcli32.msi) on computers running operating systems below Windows XP.

The Previous Version client is a built-in function of Windows Server 2003 and Windows XP. You do not need to install it. Windows 2000 Server with SP3 and above applied, Windows 2000 Professional with SP3 and above applied, and Windows 98 clients can access shadow copies only after the Shadow Copies of Shared Folders client software has been installed. You can download the Shadow Copy Client from **www.microsoft.com/windowsserver2003/ downloads/shadowcopyclient.mspx**. You must have Windows Installer 2.0 or later installed in order to install the Shadow Copy Client. You can download the correct version of Windows Installer 2.0 from the same Web page.

To deploy the Shadow Copy Client to down-level clients you have three choices. First, you can simply place the **ShadowCopyClient.msi** file in a shared network folder and users can access and install the client from the share **(Figure 13-51)**. Second, you can use Group Policy to assign the client to users on the network, or third, you can use the Systems Management Server (SMS) or another software management application to deploy the client as an .msi package. The Shadow Copy Client installs a Previous Versions tab on the Properties dialog box for files and folders on network shares.

After emphasizing that VSS can be used to restore point-in-time copies of deleted files, it is important to also point out that the user must know the file name for the file they have inadvertently deleted and the folder in which it was stored. To recover a deleted file, navigate to the folder in which the deleted file was stored, right-click a blank space in the folder, and select **Properties**. On the **Previous Versions** tab, select the version of the folder that contains the file before it was deleted and click the **View** button to open the date and time-stamped folder window **(Figure 13-52)**. Select the file you want to recover, and drag and drop or cut and paste the shadow copy to the desktop or a folder on your local computer. To recover an overwritten or corrupt file, right-click the file and select **Properties**. On the **Previous Versions** tab, select the version you want to recover and click **View** to make sure this is the correct version. To copy the shadow copy version to another location, click **Copy**. To replace the current version with the older version, click **Restore**.

Shadow copies of compressed and encrypted files can be created. The permissions that were set for the shared folders or files when the shadow copies were taken apply to the previous versions even if they have changed in the current version. These old ACLs control which users can read files on the shadow copy as well as which users can restore them. They are not restored when you restore a previous version to its original location if the file still exists. Even though the restored previous version overwrites the current version, the permissions assigned to the current version are assigned. However, if you restore a previous version to its original location and the file no longer exists, or if you copy a previous version to another location, the restored file will inherit permissions from the parent folder.

Some limitations of VSS are that only 64 shadow copies can be stored and that the schedule can only be set for the entire volume. Administrators cannot set different schedules for folders on the same volume, and after 64 shadow copies have been created, the oldest ones will be deleted. This may prove inadequate for folders that are heavily accessed and updated.

It is also important to stress that VSS technology should never be thought of as a replacement for a comprehensive network backup plan. However, it does allows users to recreate lost data within minutes rather than requiring perhaps hours for an IT professional to locate and restore a file from backup tapes. Thus, VSS may allow you to re-examine your backup strategy and schedules.

It is also important to understand that changes made between the scheduled run times are not saved, so users will not have the ability to fully recover updated files.

Figure 13-51 ShadowCopyClient.msi on a network share

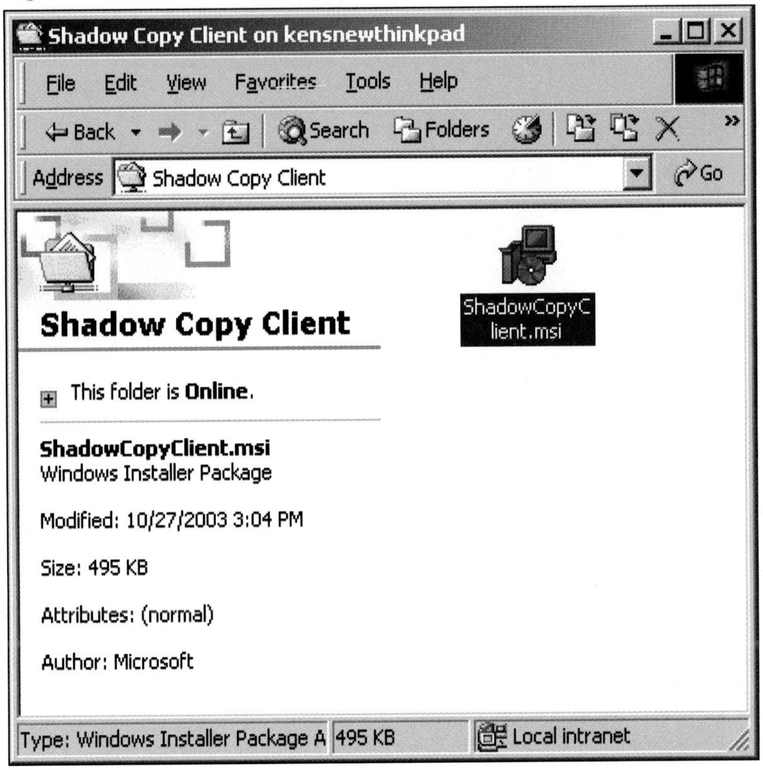

Figure 13-52 The Previous Version contents list for a folder

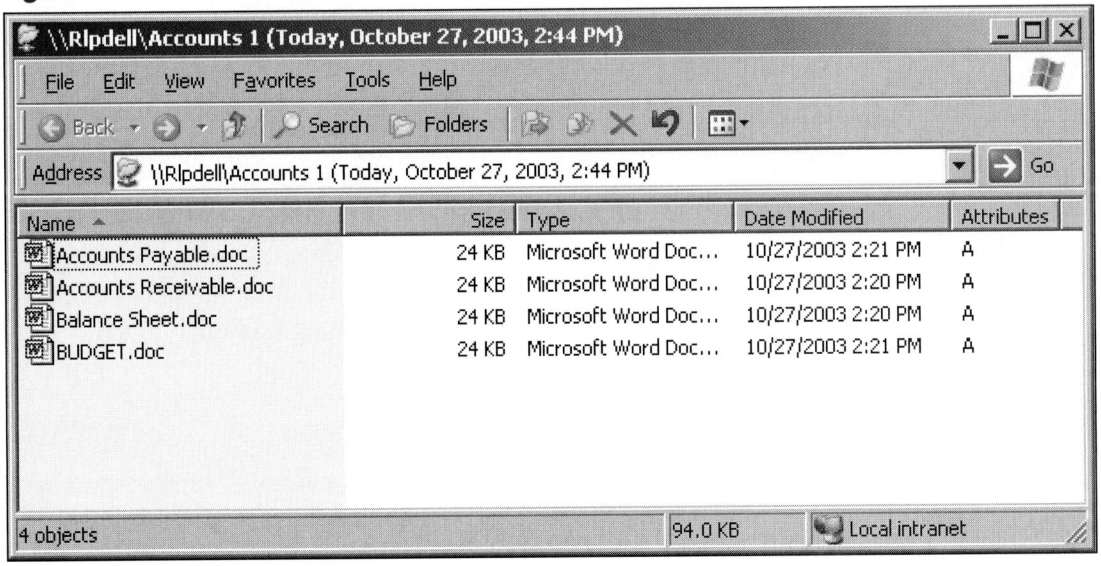

Summary

- You can categorize the data stored on any computer as either user data or System State data.
- System State data consists of files related to the operating system. Loss of System State data can render a computer non-operational.
- The System State data on a member server contains the Registry, the COM+ Class Registration database, the system boot files and all system files (all files under Windows File Protection), the Certificate Services database if the member server is a certificate server and the DNS zones if DNS is installed. A System State backup will also include the IIS Metadirectory if IIS is installed and the Cluster service if the server is part of a cluster. The System State data on a domain controller includes the Sysvol folder and the Active Directory database.
- There are five different backup types, which are identified according to how they handle the archive attribute.
- The archive attribute is a property for files and folders that is used to identify them when they have changed.
- In a Normal backup, all selected files and folders are backed up whether or not they have the archive attribute and the archive attribute is removed.
- In a Differential backup, only the selected files and folders with the archive attribute are backed up and the archive attribute is not removed.
- In an Incremental backup, only the selected files and folders with the archive attribute are backed up and the archive attribute is not removed.
- In a Copy backup, all selected files and folders are backed up whether or not they have the archive attribute and the archive attribute is removed.
- In a Daily backup, all selected files and folders that have been modified that day are backed up and the archive attribute is not removed.
- To retrieve data from an existing backup, you can either use the Restore Wizard or you can use the Restore tab in the Backup Utility window to manually run the restoration process.
- Your restore strategy is often based on the backup strategy you chose. If you used a combination of Normal and Incremental backups, you will have to restore the last Normal backup you made along with all Incremental backups taken since that date. If you used a Normal/Differential strategy, you will have to restore the last Normal backup and the last Differential backup.
- When you back up a file, the security settings, such as the user permissions, are preserved with the file. If you must restore the file, you have the option to restore the original security settings, but you do not have to restore security.
- If you restore a file from an NTFS partition to an NTFS partition, the security settings for the file can optionally be retained. Even when you restore files to a different directory, they can retain the full NTFS permissions set when the file was backed up because they are set not to inherit permissions from the parent folder. However, if you restore an NTFS file or folder to a FAT partition, you will lose the security settings because a FAT partition does not support NTFS security settings.
- Safe Mode is used to resolve problems that result from faulty device drivers, faulty programs, system service failures, or services that start automatically. In Safe Mode, the operating system will only load the files and drivers for the keyboard, mouse, basic VGA monitor, default system services, and disk. While in Safe Mode, you can remove corrupted drivers, fix driver conflicts, or uninstall and reinstall applications to resolve possible Autostart difficulties.
- The Last Known Good Configuration contains settings saved in the Registry the last time a user successfully logged on to the computer. After every successful logon, the data used for configuring the computer, is copied to the LastKnownGood value entry in the Registry.
- When you start your computer, there are usually only two configurations that can be used: the default configuration or the Last Known Good Configuration. The configuration information that is saved when a computer shuts down normally is contained in the default configuration, and the configuration data that was saved after the last successful logon is saved in the Last Known Good Configuration.
- The default configuration includes any changes made during the last logon session before the reboot process was initiated. Sometimes these configuration changes (for example, installing an incompatible device driver) can adversely affect the computer so that it will not boot. In these cases, you can use the Last Known Good Configuration to boot the computer, reversing the detrimental configuration change.
- A UPS (uninterruptible power supply) is the best way to avoid data loss and component damage due to sudden power outages. A UPS is a hardware device that supplies power from capacitance cells to a computer full-time. When there is a loss of power, the UPS device takes over. Thus, UPS devices enable you to save your data and shut down in a systematic way when a power failure occurs.
- Hard disk failure can occur as a result of a power failure or just from every day wear and tear. Fault-tolerant disk arrays can be used to ensure that data is protected in these types of disasters.

- RAID level 0 involves the use of striped volumes to distribute data evenly in stripes across up to 32 disks in a volume. However, if one disk in a striped volume fails, you will generally lose all of your data.
- RAID level 1, or mirrored volumes, is a fault-tolerant solution that duplicates data on two disks: a primary disk and a secondary disk. If one disk fails, data can be "restored" in the sense that it will be resynchronized with the mirror when a replacement drive is installed.
- Disk duplexing means that rather than having two mirrored disks, which are both attached to the same disk controller or SCSI adapter, the mirrored disk is attached to a different disk controller than the primary disk. The use of redundant disk controllers ensures that if one disk controller fails, data will still be accessible. Disk duplexing is accomplished using the fault tolerance driver Ftdisk.sys.
- The other RAID standard supported by Windows Server 2003 is RAID 5. In RAID 5, data is written in stripes across a set of at least three (up to 32) physical disks and error correction and checksum verification information are written in blocks that are spread over all of the disks in the array. RAID 5 volumes are often referred to as striped volumes with parity.
- A parity bit is used by the system to reconstruct data after a disk failure.
- Due to the extra parity information on every disk, RAID 5 requires at least three disks and at least 16 MB of additional memory for system functions.
- RAID volumes can be formatted with either the FAT or NTFS file system.
- The system and boot volumes can be stored on a mirrored volume, but they cannot be stored on software RAID 5 volumes. If you use RAID 5 volumes, you must store the boot and system volumes on a separate disk or on a separate mirrored volume, unless you are implementing hardware RAID. It is best to use RAID-1 for the boot and system volumes if using software RAID.
- In the software implementation of RAID, fault tolerance is handled by the server's operating system. In the hardware implementation of RAID, fault tolerance is independent of the operating system and is implemented through the server's hardware. The hardware implementation of RAID supports hot swapping, which means that you can replace a failed RAID 5 hard disk with a new hard disk without turning off the computer.
- You can use the Recovery Console to troubleshoot and to copy, rename, or replace operating system files and folders, format hard disks, repair the file system boot sector and/or the Master Boot Record (MBR), and to read and write data on a local drive.

- If you cannot start your server using Safe Mode, the Last Known Good Configuration, or the Recovery Console, you can try using the Automated System Recovery backup.
- ASR is a backup of your system configuration that is designed to enable you to repair your system or boot volume. Using the ASR backup set, you will be able to restart the operating system in the event of a complete malfunction due to a hard drive issue or corrupt system files.
- An ASR backup should be performed immediately following the successful installation of the operating system and updated whenever you modify the system configuration such as adding a new device driver, adding a protocol, or using Windows Update to install a patch or service pack.
- There are two parts to the ASR backup. First, all system files are backed up, which can require 1.5 or more GB of storage space. Second, the system settings needed for an ASR recovery are backed up, which only requires 1.44 MB of storage space.
- To perform an ASR restore, you will need a bootable Windows Server 2003 CD-ROM, the most recent copy of the ASR backup set that is generally saved on tape or another removable storage medium, and your most recent backup media set.
- When an ASR restore is performed, it formats the system drive. All user data on the system partition will be lost, so you will have to restore all user data as well as all system partition data.
- The Volume Shadow Copy Service (VSS) provides two new services in Windows Server 2003. First, it can be used by applications to access locked files or files that are in use by other services or applications. Second, you can configure the Volume Shadow Copy Service so that previous versions of saved files that are stored on a share on a particular volume can be accessed and restored from shadow copies that are created at scheduled times.
- After the Previous Versions client software is deployed, users can recover lost files by locating the shadow copies on the Previous Versions tab on the Properties dialog box for the shared file or folder.
- Some limitations of VSS are that only 64 shadow copies can be stored and that the schedule can only be set for the entire volume. Administrators cannot set different schedules for different folders on the same volume, and after 64 shadow copies have been created, the oldest ones will be deleted. Users must know the file name for the file they have inadvertently deleted and the folder in which it was stored.

Key Terms

Archive attribute
Authoritative restore
Automated System Recovery (ASR)
Backup
Copy backup
Daily backup
Differential backup
Disk duplexing

Hardware RAID implementation
Incremental backup
Last Known Good Configuration
Non-authoritative (normal) restore
Normal backup
Ntdsutil
Parity bit
Primary restore

Recovery Console
Safe Mode
Software RAID implementation
System State data
UPS (uninterruptible power supply)
Volume Shadow Copy Service (VSS)

Test Yourself

1. You are working as an administrator at DataNet Inc. One of your duties is to back up large data files three times per week on magnetic tape drives. The time taken to perform the Normal backup is about 6 hours. Which of the following backup options will you use on Wednesdays and Fridays if reducing the amount of time it takes to perform the backup on those days is your top priority?
   a. Incremental backup
   b. Normal backup
   c. Copy backup
   d. Differential backup

2. Which of the following is true of software RAID 5 volumes?
   a. Used to recreate boot files.
   b. Data is duplicated on multiple disks.
   c. Parity information is used to recreate data.
   d. Use Disk duplexing to add fault tolerance for disk controllers or adapters to fault tolerance for disks.

3. You cannot boot your server using either the Last Known Good Configuration or Safe Mode because some of the boot files on your system are corrupt due to a virus infection. Which of the following options will you use to repair your system boot files to restart your computer?
   a. Enable VGA Mode
   b. Recovery Console
   c. Restore Wizard
   d. Service pack

4. Which of the following items do you need to backup in order to restore the Registry and make it functional?
   a. Registry
   b. System State data
   c. %systemroot% folder
   d. System Startup files

5. You have installed a new display adapter on your system. When you restart your system, the system hangs

at the logon prompt. Which of the following Safe Mode options would you use to boot your system?
   a. Video Card Mode
   b. Debugging Mode
   c. Enable VGA Mode
   d. Directory Services Restore Mode

6. A Windows Server 2003 compatible UPS shows an alert message and then automatically:
   a. Makes a backup of your data.
   b. Restarts your system in Safe Mode.
   c. Shuts down your system.
   d. Repairs corrupt system files.

7. Users who have the _____ permission for a file or folder, or who have Backup Operator rights, will be able to back up and restore other user's files.
   a. Read
   b. Write
   c. Read and Execute
   d. Modify

8. The Automatic System Recovery Wizard: (Choose all that apply)
   a. Is used to enable previous versions of saved files that are stored on a share on a particular volume to be accessed and restored.
   b. Creates a backup of your system configuration that is designed to enable you to repair your system partition so that you can restart the operating system in the event of a complete malfunction.
   c. Creates a backup set that includes the operating system files, configuration settings, and System State data.
   d. Creates a backup set that is used if you cannot start your server using Safe Mode, the Last Known Good Configuration, or the Recovery Console.

9. How do you start the Recovery Console? (Choose all that apply.)

a. Install it on the computer and select it on the Boot Selection menu (Please select the operating system to start).

b. Reboot the computer and press F8 during startup to access the Windows Advanced Options Menu. Select Recovery Console.

c. Click Start, Administrative Tools, Services to open the Services console. Select Recovery Console.

d. Insert the installation CD-ROM in the CD-ROM drive and reboot the computer from the CD-ROM. When the text-based portion of Setup begins, press R to select the repair or recover option.

10. Which of the following statements is true about the archive attribute? (Choose all that apply)

a. The archive attribute is also called the backup marker or the archive bit.

b. In a Normal backup, all selected files and folders are backed up whether they have the archive attribute or not, and the attribute is removed to denote that a file has been backed up.

c. The archive attribute is used to mark files that have been modified since the last backup.

d. In a Copy backup, all selected files and folders with or without the archive attribute are backed up and the archive attribute is removed.

e. A Differential backup backs up all selected files and folders and the attribute is not removed.

Projects: On Your Own

1. Schedule a Normal backup of the My Documents folder three times a week.

a. Click **Start**, point to **All Programs**, point to **Accessories**, point to **System Tools**, and click **Backup**.

b. Click the **Advanced Mode** link.

c. Open the Backup tab.

d. Select the **My Documents** folder for backup.

e. Click **Start Backup**.

f. Enter the backup description, select how to write on the media if it already contains backups, and enter a label for the backup.

g. Click the **Schedule** button.

h. Click **Yes** to save the backup selections.

i. Enter a filename for saving the selection parameters for the backup job and click **Save**.

j. Enter and confirm the password for the account from which the job will be run and click **OK**.

k. In the **Scheduled Job Options** dialog box, enter the **job name** in the Job name text box.

l. Click **Properties**.

m. Select **Weekly** in the Scheduled Task list box.

n. Select the **Mon**, **Wed**, and **Fri** check boxes.

o. Enter the **Start time** of your choice.

p. Click **OK** to close the **Schedule Job** dialog box.

q. Click **OK** to close the **Scheduled Job Options** dialog box.

r. Close the Backup Utility window.

2. Back up the System State data and system protected files.

a. Click **Start**, point to **All Programs**, point to **Accessories**, point to **System Tools**, and click **Backup**.

b. Click the **Advanced Mode** link.

c. Open the **Backup** tab.

d. Click the **System State** check box in the left pane.

e. Click **Start Backup**.

f. In the **Backup Job Information** dialog box, click **Advanced**.

g. Make sure the **Automatically backup System Protected Files with the System State** check box is selected.

h. Close the **Advanced Backup Options** dialog box.

i. Click **Start Backup**.

j. When the backup is complete, click **Report** to view the backup log file.

k. Close the log file, the **Backup Progress** dialog box, and the Backup Utility window.

3. Use VSS to recover a deleted file.

a. Open Windows Explorer.

b. Create a new folder named **Budget** on the C: drive.

c. Double-click the new Budget folder to open it.

d. Create a new text file or Word document named **Accounts**.

e. Click the **Back** button to return to the C: drive.

f. Share the **Budget** folder. Click the **Permissions** button to set permissions for users who access the folder over the network. Give the **Everyone** group **Full Control**.

g. Right-click the C: drive icon (Local Disk [C:]) and select **Properties**.

h. On the **Shadow Copies** tab, enable VSS, if necessary. You can simply click the **Enable** button to initiate shadow copies using the default schedule and settings and to create a copy of the volume now if VSS has not yet been enabled.

i. If VSS has already been enabled for the volume, click the **Create Now** button to create a new shadow copy of volume that will include the new Budgets folder.

j. When the process is complete, click **OK** to close the Properties dialog box.

k. Open the **Budget** folder. Delete the **Accounts** folder.

l. Click **Yes** to confirm the deletion.

m. Select **My Network Places** in the folder tree.

n. Add a network place for the Budget folder (*server_name***Budget**).

o. When you have finished, the Budget folder will open and you can confirm that it is empty.

p. Close the *server_name***Budget** window to return to **My Network Places**.

q. Right-click the **Budget on <*server_name*>** folder network place and select **Properties**. You must open the folder using its UNC path rather than opening it locally because the **Previous Versions** tab is only available when you are connected to a network share over the network.

r. On the **Previous Versions** tab, select the shadow copy in the **Folder versions** list and click the **Restore** button.

s. Click **Yes** to restore the previous version of the folder

t. Click **OK** to confirm that the folder has been successfully restored to the previous version.

u. Click **OK** to close the Budget on <server_name> Properties dialog box.

v. Open the **Budget on <*server_name*>** folder network place to confirm that the previous version of the Budget folder has been restored with the deleted Accounts file recovered.

Problem Solving Scenarios

1. You are the system administrator for a garden tools and supplies company. The CEO has asked you to confirm for her that a comprehensive backup plan has been designed and implemented on the network LAN. Prepare a report for her explaining how you have provided for backing up the file server on which users save their daily reports, backing up the domain controller, and backing up four shared folders that contain sales data that will be imported into a database for analysis and archival.

2. You are a system administrator at an engineering design firm. This morning, one of the users in your company was changing his display settings and inadvertently chose a refresh rate unsupported by his monitor. His display is now scrambled and he is unable to restore the original display settings. He cannot work until the problem is fixed. List the steps you would take to start the computer in Safe Mode and restore his original display settings.

An important part of the job of a network or systems administrator is to make sure that the servers on the network are functioning optimally. This includes optimizing the hard disk performance of the servers on your network and monitoring systems so that you can anticipate and resolve resource problems such as components that need to be upgraded or replaced. By first establishing a baseline performance level, you can determine what the normal operating parameters for the server are. This is referred to as establishing a baseline or benchmarking the system. The idea is that in order to detect anomalous system behavior, you must first know what level of performance you have during normal usage and under typical workloads. In particular, you should establish baseline behavior when a server first begins to run on the network and when the hardware or software configuration has been modified. The baseline performance level can include statistics about the CPU, disks, and memory. You can also determine and keep records for the performance of the server during slow, average, and peak periods. This way, you can determine the effect when you add new software, when more users come online, or when users begin to access the system more often. You use the System Monitor either to establish a baseline or to diagnose a bottleneck. A bottleneck refers to any resource, such as memory or disk space, which causes other resources to delay while it completes its assigned function. For example, if your server has insufficient memory, the server will begin paging out to disk, which causes a reduction in overall performance. In this case, memory is the bottleneck that is holding up system functions. The solution to bottlenecks in most situations is to upgrade your system. You may need to add more RAM, get a faster network interface card, buy a more powerful processor, or upgrade your drives.

The Task Manager is used to manage system processes and performance. You can use it to stop malfunctioning applications or stalled processes or to increase the priority of a process so that more CPU resources will be allocated to it than were designated by default.

The Check Disk and Disk Defragmenter tools are used to improve hard disk performance. The Check Disk tool inspects your hard disk for errors or bad sectors and repairs them when possible, while the Disk Defragmenter rearranges files and unused disk space to enable a system to access files more quickly and increase the speed with which programs can run.

NTFS compression is used to conserve disk space, while disk quotas are used to allocate a specified amount of disk storage space to users on the server's hard disks.

Auditing is used to observe and record the events that occur on the network, including logons (both successful and unsuccessful) and access to files, folders, the Registry, and printers. These events are recorded in the Security event log, which you can view using Event Viewer. These tools are used to keep administrators informed of events such as a user who attempts to access a computer by repeatedly guessing account names and/or passwords, users who are accessing files at unusual times of the day, and users who are accessing resources that they should not have access to.

You can use the Network Monitor Driver to obtain network performance statistics that are used by the System Monitor and the Network Monitor to monitor specific network events and troubleshoot networking problems. You can also manage some network activities using the Simple Network Management Protocol (SNMP) service. You can monitor from a central location using an SNMP network management station and respond to errors.

Goals

In this lesson, you will learn to use the Check Disk tool, the Disk Defragmenter, NTFS data compression, and disk quotas to optimize disk performance. Next, you will learn how to monitor the performance of applications and the network using the Task Manager. Then, you will learn how to monitor the performance of system components and processes such as the processor, memory, hard disks, and paging file using the System Monitor. You will also learn how to monitor network resources in the System Monitor and how to monitor application and system processes that are currently running. You will learn how to implement and configure audit policy, audit access attempts to various components on a network, and use the Event Viewer to view the Security log where the success and failure audits are recorded. Finally, you will learn the basics of network monitoring including using the Network Monitor Driver, Network Monitor, and SNMP service.

Lesson 14   Monitoring Windows Server 2003 Performance

Skill	Exam 70-290 Objective
1. Optimizing Hard Disk Performance	Optimize server disk performance. Defragment volumes and partitions.
2. Optimizing Disk Storage Performance	Optimize server disk performance. Monitor and optimize a server environment for application performance. Monitor disk quotas.
3. Working with the Task Manager	Monitor file and print servers. Tools might include Task Manager, Event Viewer, and System Monitor. Monitor system performance. Monitor and optimize a server environment for application performance. Monitor server hardware for bottlenecks.
4. Working with the System Monitor	Monitor file and print servers. Tools might include Task Manager, Event Viewer, and System Monitor. Monitor server hardware for bottlenecks. Monitor system performance. Monitor and optimize a server environment for application performance. Monitor disk performance objects.
5. Working with Performance Logs and Alerts	Monitor file and print servers. Tools might include Task Manager, Event Viewer, and System Monitor. Monitor and analyze events. Monitor server hardware for bottlenecks. Monitor system performance. Monitor and optimize a server environment for application performance. Monitor memory performance objects.
6. Creating Trace Logs	Monitor file and print servers. Tools might include Task Manager, Event Viewer, and System Monitor. Monitor and optimize a server environment for application performance. Monitor server hardware for bottlenecks. Monitor system performance.
7. Monitoring Network and Process Performance Objects	Monitor file and print servers. Tools might include Task Manager, Event Viewer, and System Monitor. Monitor and analyze events. Tools might include Event Viewer and System Monitor. Monitor server hardware for bottlenecks. Monitor and optimize a server environment for application performance. Monitor network performance objects. Monitor process performance objects.
8. Tracking Windows Server 2003 Activities with Audit Policy	Basic knowledge
9. Viewing the Security Log	Basic knowledge
10. Working with the Network Monitor	Monitor and optimize a server environment for application performance. Monitor network performance objects.
11. Introducing Simple Network Management Protocol (SNMP) Services	Monitor and optimize a server environment for application performance. Monitor network performance objects.

Requirements

To complete this lesson, you will need administrative rights on a Windows Server 2003 member server with an NTFS volume or partition. You will also need a folder named Annual Reports saved on the NTFS partition.

skill 1   *Optimizing Hard Disk Performance*

exam objective

Optimize server disk performance. Defragment volumes and partitions.

overview

caution

Before running the Check Disk tool, close all applications or files on the disk that you want to check so that the utility can automatically fix file system errors.

You can optimize the performance of a server's hard disk using the following tools.

Check Disk (Error-checking) tool: Use this tool to check the hard disk for file system errors and bad sectors on volumes that have been formatted with the FAT, FAT32, or NTFS file system. Check Disk identifies errors and fixes them automatically. On an NTFS volume, all file transactions are logged, bad clusters are replaced, and copies of essential information for all files are stored on the volume. To use this tool, open the **Properties** dialog box for the disk volume. Open the **Tools** tab and click the **Check Now** button to open the **Check Disk** dialog box. You can select the check boxes to **Automatically fix file system errors** and **Scan for and attempt recovery of bad sectors**. Then, click the **Start** button to initiate the disk checking process **(Figure 14-1)**. If you are currently on the volume that you want to check or if there are any applications running, you will receive a message informing you that exclusive access to the drive could not be obtained, and asking if you want to schedule the disk check to occur the next time you restart the computer.

You can also run the Check Disk utility from the Run dialog box by typing **chkdsk** in the Open text box **(Figure 14-2)**. Chkdsk also automatically runs when you boot if the boot process detects file corruption or corruption in a file allocation table. On a FAT volume or partition, it checks the file allocation table, folders, files, disk sectors, and disk allocation units. On an NTFS volume or partition, it checks files, folders, indexes, security descriptors, user files, and disk allocation units **(Figure 14-3)**. If you suspect that one of your disks is damaged, you can use the /r switch to identify bad sectors. It is not unusual to find some bad sectors on a disk. However, if you continually get bad sectors, or you have a large number of sectors marked as bad, a physical problem with the disk is likely. The other switches you can use with chkdsk are outlined in **Table 14-1**.

If chkdsk locates lost allocation units or chains, you will be prompted to answer either Y or N to the question: Convert lost chains to files? If you answer Yes, the lost data will be saved to files named Filexxx.chk. These files can be read and edited in Notepad to determine the contents. If chkdsk locates a damaged area on the disk, you can also try to recover the files in that sector using the Recover command in the command prompt window. The Recover command reads the file, sector by sector, and attempts to rebuild as much of the file as possible. The syntax for the Recover command is **Recover [drive letter and path]** *file_name*. You must use the Recover command on one file at a time.

Always run chkdsk when there are no users on the server so that you can lock the disk from use, as well as fix errors using the /f switch. If the server has large disks, you will need to set aside a block of idle time to run the process.

Figure 14-1 Using the Check Disk tool

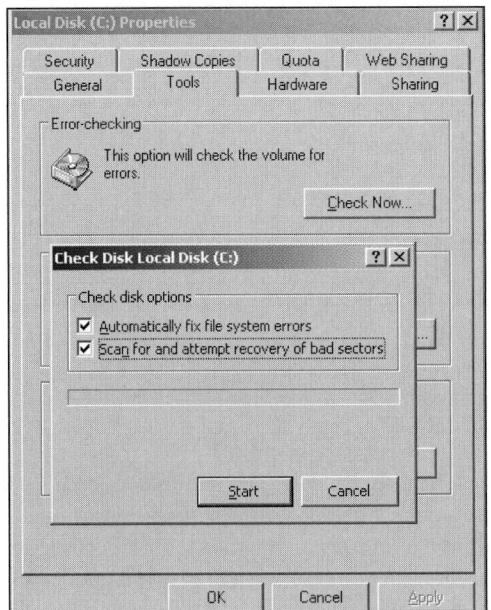

Figure 14-2 Running the chkdsk utility

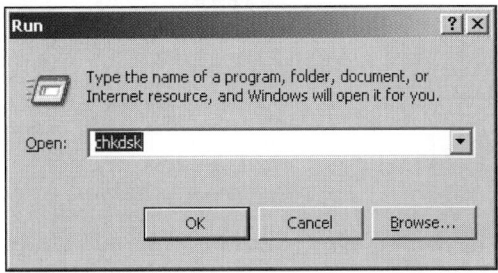

Figure 14-3 Running chkdsk in read-only mode

A warning is shown because the
disk has not been locked from use
so that errors that are located can
be automatically fixed

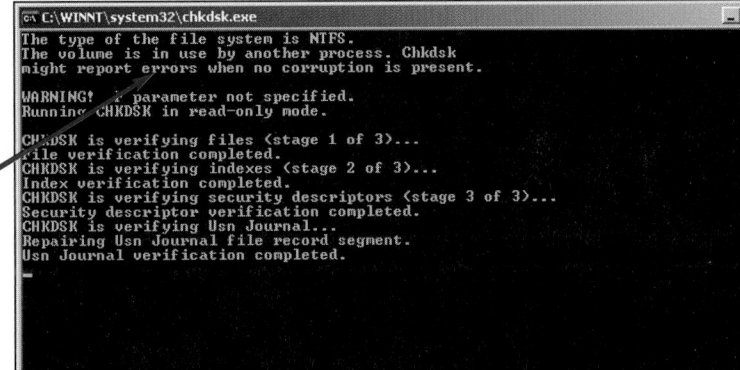

Table 14-1	Parameters for the chkdsk utility
Switch/ Parameter	**Function**
[volume]	Used to run chkdsk only on the volume you enter.
[file_name]	Used to run chkdsk only on the specified file or file type.
/c	Used on an NTFS volume or partition to run only a check of the folder structure.
/f	Used to tell chkdsk to fix errors it finds. This switch locks the disk from use until the process is complete, which means it cannot be used on the disk containing the operating system files.
/i	Used on an NTFS volume or partition to run a less rigorous set of tests on the indexes.
/L:size	Used on an NTFS volume or partition to specify the size for the log file that chkdsk creates.
/r	Used to search for bad sectors, fix any problems, and recover data. When data cannot be recovered using the /r command, use the Recover command on a per-file basis at the command prompt.
/v	Used on a FAT volume or partition to display the entire path name for files. On an NTFS volume or partition, it displays the cleanup messages for errors.
/x	Used to dismount or lock a volume before chkdsk begins. The /f switch also dismounts or locks a volume.

skill 1

Optimizing Hard Disk Performance
(cont'd)

exam objective

Optimize server disk performance. Defragment volumes and partitions.

overview

caution

You can only defragment local file system volumes, and you can only run one Disk Defragmenter console at one time.

Disk Cleanup: Use this utility (Start>All Programs>Accessories>System Tools>Disk Cleanup) to clean out old files on the hard disk in order to create more storage space. Disk Cleanup locates files you are likely to want to delete such as Temporary Internet files, Temporary files, and Downloaded Program Files. It also selects files that you have not accessed for some time in order to target them for compression **(Figure14-4)**. When the calculations are complete, you are presented with a list of files you can choose to delete or compress **(Figure 14-5)**.

Disk Defragmenter: As you learned in Lesson 4, when you save files and folders on a FAT partition, they are saved in the first available space on the hard disk by the hard disk controller. This causes file and folder fragmentation as pieces or fragments of large files are stored on different parts of the hard disk. As data becomes increasingly scattered over different parts of the hard disk, the computer takes longer to access files, leading to a general deterioration in system performance. The computer also takes longer to create new files and folders because free space is also scattered on the hard disk. NTFS partitions always attempt to save files in contiguous clusters. However, when you modify a file by adding additional data to it, the additional data is likely to be placed on a different section of the disk, which causes fragmentation. You can use the Disk Defragmenter to reorganize the files on any partition or volume. Refer to Lesson 4 for more information about the Disk Defragmenter utility.

Page file placement: Another important aspect of optimizing disk performance involves the placement of the page file. The page file is used to hold temporary data, which is swapped in and out of physical memory in order to provide a larger virtual memory set. This is called paging. Paging affects disk performance because data must be moved out of RAM and to the hard disk. The page file (also referred to as the swap file), **pagefile.sys**, is created during Setup in the root of the boot drive as a hidden system file. In order to view it, you must select the **Show hidden files and folders** option on the **View** tab in the **Folder Options** dialog box. By default, pagefile.sys is approximately 1.5 times the system RAM, which is Microsoft's recommendation if RAM is less than 4 GB. If RAM is 4 GB or more, pagefile.sys should be set to at least 2050 MB so that it is large enough to capture a kernel memory dump.

Disk access is measured in milliseconds, while RAM access is measured in nanoseconds, underscoring the significantly slower speed of disk access. When you return to an application whose memory has been swapped out to the page file, that memory must be returned to RAM. In order to make room for it in RAM, memory for another application will have to be swapped out to the page file on the hard disk. This means that time is expended and the system is slowed down. If you do not have enough physical RAM to run all processes, you can optimize the use of pagefile.sys by relocating it to a less active disk, if you have more than one disk. The disk you move pagefile.sys to should be a fast drive that is not used very often and one that has high throughput. Avoid having the page file on the same drive as the system files (as that disk will already be heavily used), and do not place page files on multiple partitions on the same physical hard drive. Another technique for page file placement is to place it on a hardware RAID-5 array or a striped volume. Placing the page file on a mirrored volume or a software RAID-5 array will generally slow down its performance (due to the overhead present during writes), but a hardware RAID-5 array or a striped volume will improve performance.

You can set the initial and maximum sizes for the page file in the **Virtual Memory** dialog box **(Figure 14-6)**. To access this dialog box, right-click My Computer either on the desktop or on the Start menu and select **Properties** to open the **System Properties** dialog box. Open the **Advanced** tab and click the **Settings** button in the **Performance** section to open the

Figure 14-4 Calculating files to be deleted and compressed

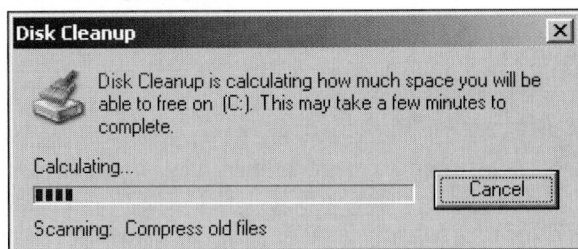

Figure 14-5 Disk Cleanup

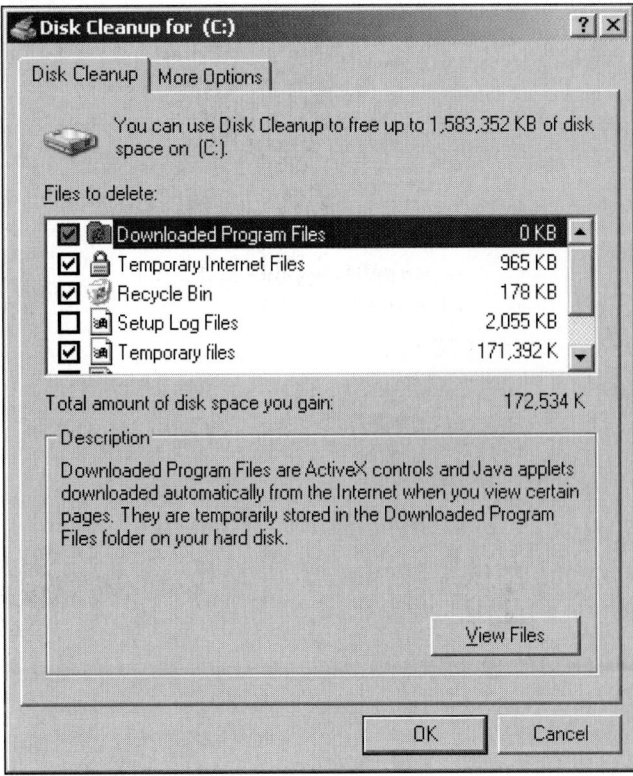

Figure 14-6 The Virtual Memory dialog box

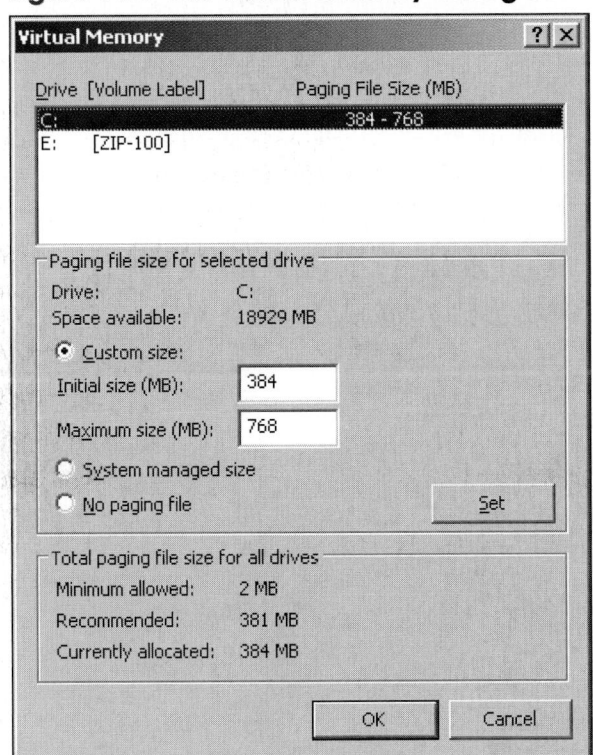

skill 1

Optimizing Hard Disk Performance
(cont'd)

Optimize server disk performance. Defragment volumes and partitions.

Performance Options dialog box. On the **Advanced** tab, click the **Change** button to open the Virtual Memory dialog box. Select the drive from the provided list and enter the amount of space you want dedicated to the swap file in the text boxes. It is recommended that you use the same value for both the initial and maximum size in order to improve performance, as well as cut down on possible fragmentation. This is particularly important on large memory systems (RAM greater than 4 GB) so that the page file will not become fragmented on the hard drive, which can create difficulties when the kernel memory dump is written to disk. As noted above, the minimum recommended paging file size on computers with more than 4 GB of RAM is 2050 MB, if you wish to store memory dumps. You must reboot the system for changes to the page file to take effect.

You can also choose to let Windows manage the page file by selecting the **System managed size** option. On systems with more than 2 GB of physical RAM that are not using a memory dump, you can typically disable the page file entirely, by selecting the **No paging file** option. This is only recommended, however, when both of those conditions are true.

Table 14-2 summarizes the various methods you can use to optimize hard disk performance.

Dr. Watson is an error debugger utility that logs program errors. You can use the log file generated by Dr. Watson, **drwtsn32.log**, to diagnose and solve system problems. When a program error occurs, Dr. Watson stops the program and records some diagnostic statistics. It is automatically started by the system when a program has an unhandled exception. An unhandled exception means that the program itself does not contain any code for handling the error, and there are no other debuggers installed and configured to handle it. To configure options for Dr. Watson, type **drwtsn32** in the Open text box in the Run dialog box to open the **Dr. Watson for Windows** dialog box (**Figure 14-7**).

Table 14-2 Optimizing hard disk performance

Tool or Strategy	Function
Check Disk	Checks the hard disk for file system errors and bad sectors on volumes and fixes errors automatically. On a FAT volume or partition, it checks the file allocation table, folders, files, disk sectors, and disk allocation units. On an NTFS volume or partition, it checks files, folders, indexes, security descriptors, user files, and disk allocation units. All file transactions are logged, bad clusters are replaced, and copies of essential information for all files are stored on the volume.
Disk Cleanup	Cleans out old files on the hard disk in order to create more storage space. Locates files you are likely to want to delete such as Temporary Internet files, Temporary files, and Downloaded Program Files and files that you have not accessed for some time so that you can select them for compression.
Disk Defragmenter	Reorganizes fragmented files on any partition or volume. On FAT partitions, files and folders are saved in the first available space on the hard disk. Over time, both data and free space become scattered over different parts of the hard disk and it takes longer to both access and create new files. On NTFS partitions, the hard disk controller always tries to save files in contiguous clusters, but when you add data to a file, the additional data is often placed on a different section of the disk causing fragmentation.
Page file placement	Optimize the use of pagefile.sys by relocating it to a less active disk This should be a high throughput, fast drive that is not used very often. Do not keep pagefile.sys on the system drive. Do not place page files on multiple partitions on the same physical hard drive. Consider storing the page file on a hardware RAID-5 array or a striped volume. Set the initial and maximum sizes for the page file to the same value to cut down on possible fragmentation (especially on systems where RAM > 4 GB) and avoid problems when the kernel memory dump is written to disk.

Figure 14-7 Dr. Watson for Windows

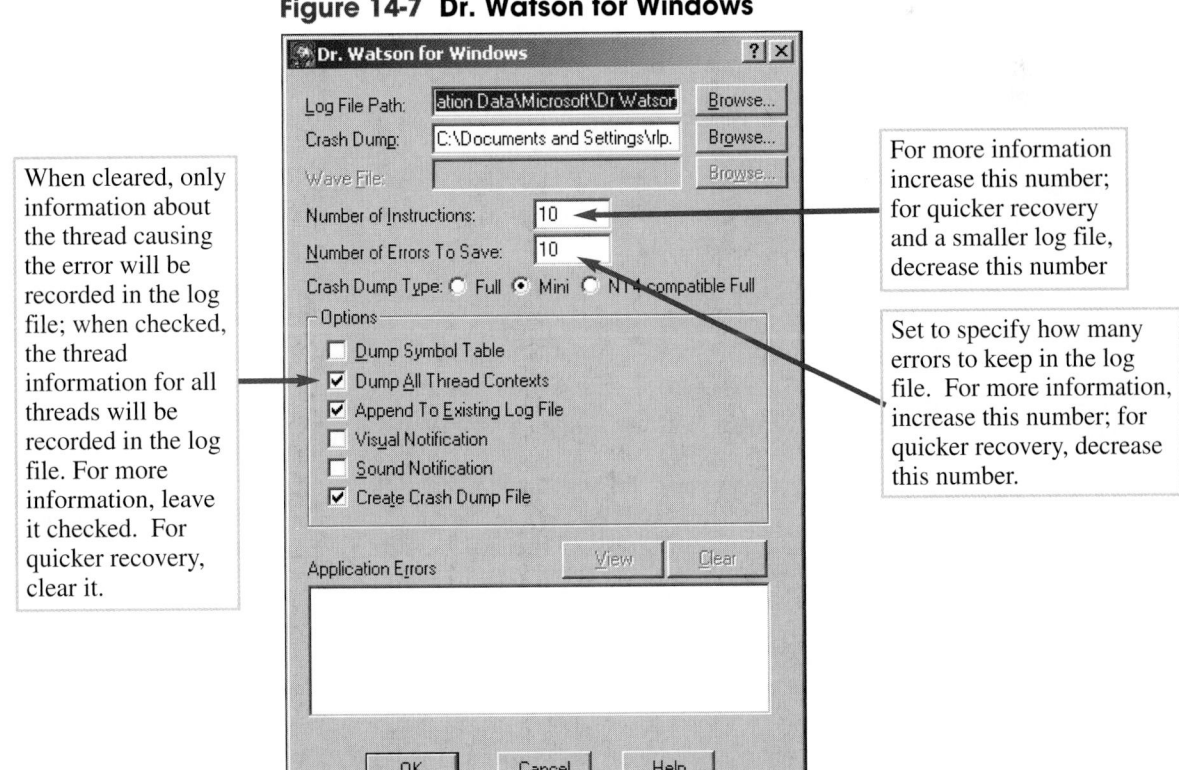

When cleared, only information about the thread causing the error will be recorded in the log file; when checked, the thread information for all threads will be recorded in the log file. For more information, leave it checked. For quicker recovery, clear it.

For more information increase this number; for quicker recovery and a smaller log file, decrease this number

Set to specify how many errors to keep in the log file. For more information, increase this number; for quicker recovery, decrease this number.

skill 2

Optimizing Disk Storage Performance

exam objective

Optimize server disk performance. Monitor and optimize a server environment for application performance. Monitor disk quotas.

overview

The overall functioning of a computer is dependent upon the state of its hard disks, where data is stored. As the number of users on your network increases, you will have to manage the greatly increasing amount of data that users store or retrieve from the file servers. To help you optimize disk storage, you can use the following tools:

NTFS Data compression: On NTFS partitions, you can store files and folders in a compressed state. You can compress files and folders such as Word or other Office documents and bitmaps to conserve disk space. Compression can reduce some types of files and folders by 50% to 90%. However, many files can only be reduced by 5% or less. All NTFS files and folders have a compression state, either compressed or uncompressed. After you have compressed a file, you do not have to manually uncompress it. It is uncompressed when you open and edit it, and recompressed when you close it again. If you create a new file in a compressed folder, the file will be automatically compressed. However, NTFS allocates disk space based on the uncompressed file size. If there is enough space on the NTFS volume for you to store a compressed file (but not enough space to store that file in the uncompressed state), when you try to copy the file to the disk, you will receive an error message stating that there is not enough disk space available for the file.

You set the compression attribute for a file or folder in the **Advanced Attributes** dialog box, which you can access from the **Properties** dialog box of that file or folder **(Figure 14-8)**. You can also compress an entire drive in the Properties dialog box for the drive so that you do not have to explicitly compress each file or folder on an NTFS volume **(Figure 14-9)**. However, this is not a good idea on the system or boot drives. Compressing the boot volume may result in significantly increased processor overhead. In the Advanced Attributes dialog box, you can also set the encryption attribute. However, compression and encryption are mutually exclusive attributes. You cannot both encrypt and compress a file or folder.

By default, compressed files and folders are displayed in a different color to distinguish them from uncompressed files and folders. To change the default behavior, open Windows Explorer, open the **Tools** menu, and select **Folder Options** to open the Folder Options dialog box, or point to **Control Panel** on the **Start** menu and click **Folder Options**. On the **View** tab, clear the **Show encrypted or compressed NTFS files in color** check box **(Figure 14-10)**.

When compressing files and folders, choose appropriate file types. For example, .zip, .cab, .gif, .mpg, and .jpg files are already compressed. Trying to compress these and other already compressed files is a waste of time, as Windows compression cannot improve upon most specific compression techniques. On the other hand, bitmap files can be compressed to less than 50 percent of the original size, and text files can often be compressed to less than 75 percent of their original size. You can compress static data, but do not compress files that are frequently changed, because compressing files is processor intensive, while uncompressing files is much less so. Copying a compressed file may affect the performance of the system because the operating system must first uncompress the file, copy it, and then compress it again, consuming valuable system resources.

When you copy or move a file, the compression state of the file depends on whether you are copying or moving the file from a different location within the same NTFS volume, between two NTFS volumes, or between NTFS and FAT volumes. The state of compression follows the same rules as for permissions. That is, when moving a file on the same NTFS partition, the compression state of the file will remain unchanged. In all other cases, the file will inherit the compression state of the parent folder. This is because, when a file is moved to another location on the same partition, the file is not actually modified in any way. The pointer in the

tip

In general, you should avoid compressing any file that uses internal compression, such as .zip, .jpg, .mpg, .mp3, .gif, .tif, and many other multimedia file types. The compression routines in Windows Server 2003 are intelligent enough not to increase the size of these files by recompressing them, but it wastes processor cycles while attempting to.

tip

You can also compress and uncompress files and folders from the command line using the utility compact.exe. This is extremely useful in compressing all files of a particular type on a disk. For example, the command: **compact /c /s *.doc** will compress all Word documents (.doc file extension) on the drive, regardless of the directory, but will not affect the state of other files.

Figure 14-8 Setting the compression attribute

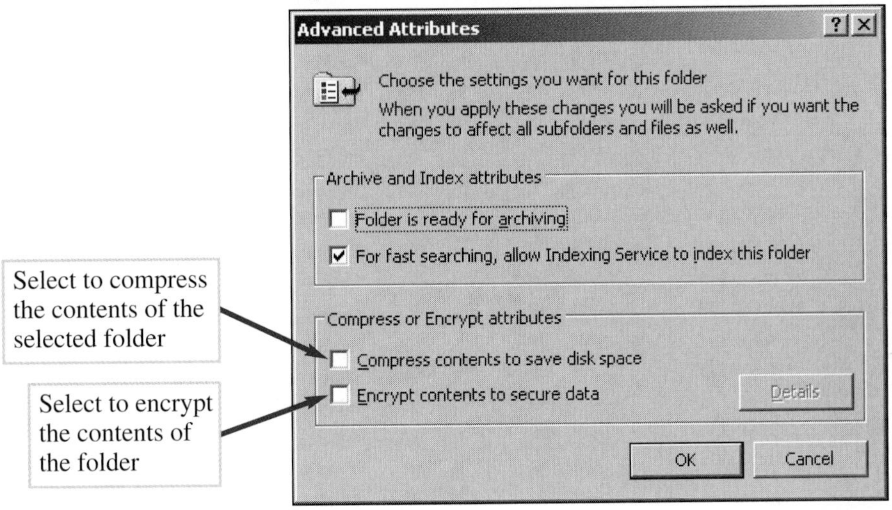

Select to compress the contents of the selected folder

Select to encrypt the contents of the folder

Figure 14-9 Compressing a drive to save disk space

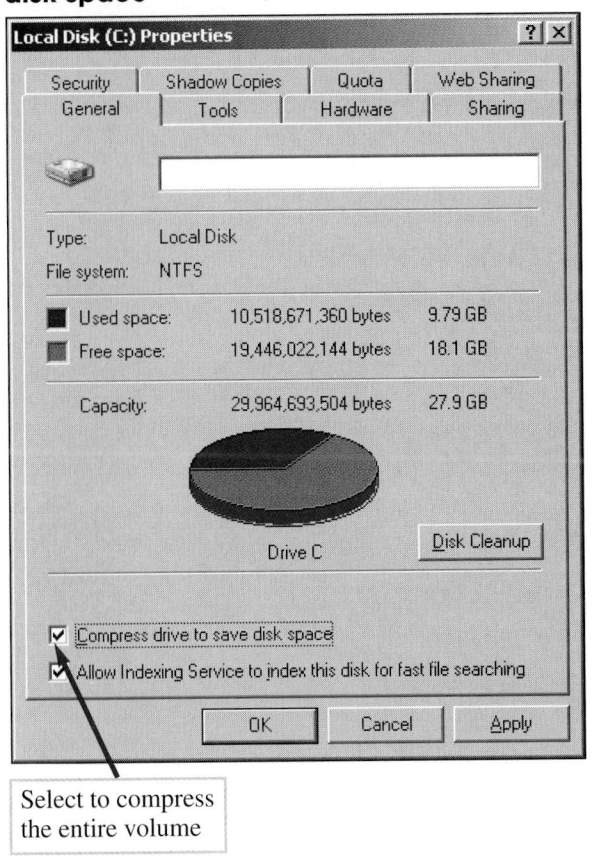

Select to compress the entire volume

Figure 14-10 The Folder Options dialog box

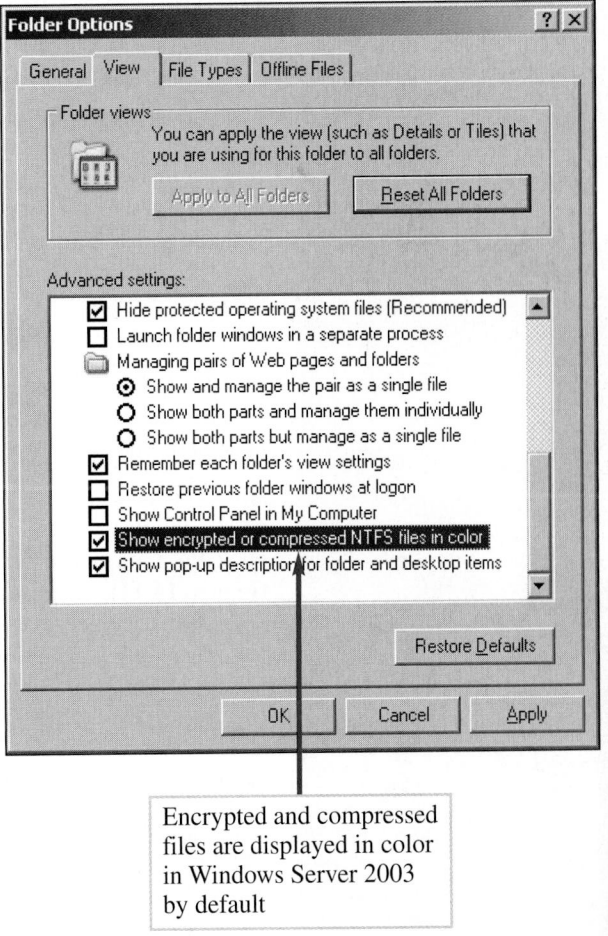

Encrypted and compressed files are displayed in color in Windows Server 2003 by default

skill 2

Optimizing Disk Storage Performance (cont'd)

exam objective

Optimize server disk performance. Monitor and optimize a server environment for application performance. Monitor disk quotas.

overview

caution

NTFS is not usable on most removable media smaller than 40 MB. This is due to the considerable overhead involved in the NTFS file system. For this reason, NTFS compression is not supported on standard (1.44 MB) floppy disks.

caution

Disk quotas are partition or volume (in other words, drive letter) specific. You cannot configure quotas for individual folders.

MFT (Master File Table) is simply modified to indicate the new logical location of the file. Therefore, if the file was already compressed, it will remain so. However, any copy operation creates a brand new file, which will inherit its compression state from the parent folder. This means that files moved to another partition will inherit their compression state as well, since moving a file to another partition involves making a copy of the file on the destination partition and then deleting the original file from the source partition. A new file is created through the copy process; therefore, the file inherits the compression attribute from this location. Finally, since FAT partitions do not support compression, any operation (copy or move) to a FAT partition removes compression.

Disk quotas: You can also use disk quotas to optimize disk storage by allocating a specific amount of disk space to each user. You set disk quotas on the **Quota** tab in the **Properties** dialog box for an NTFS volume. You can set two values: the disk limit and the warning level. The **disk limit** designates the amount of space a user is allowed to use, and the **warning level** sets the storage level at which a warning will be issued to the user. For example, if a user's disk space requirement generally does not exceed 60 MB, you can set the disk limit for a particular volume to 60 MB and the warning level to 55 MB. When the user's storage capacity exceeds 55 MB, a warning will be issued. The user can then either delete some files to create space or ask the Administrator to increase the quota limit. By default, only members of the Administrators group can view and modify quota settings. The disk quotas you assign are based on the sizes of uncompressed files, so take this into account when determining the appropriate storage requirement for a user. If a user has been allotted 60 MB of storage space, compression does not allow the user to store more than 60 MB. In effect, disk quotas encourage users to delete outdated or unnecessary files. Quotas are assigned based on file ownership, not the location of the files. Therefore, if you restore data for a user from a backup to a volume on which disk quotas have been set, you must restore the user's files and folders with the correct ownership by choosing the Advanced restore option **Restore security** during the restore operation. You must also carefully think about where you store the spool folder and the user profile folders. Files generated from these sources are owned by the user generating them and will be debited against the user's disk quota.

You can also use disk quotas simply to track disk usage without denying disk space to users who exceed their quota limit. In this case, you can enable quota logging so that an event will be logged when users exceed their limit, when users exceed their warning level, or both.

After you have enabled quotas on a volume and chosen the options you want to impose, you must configure quota entries for the users of the volume. To apply disk quotas for users, click the **Quota Entries** button on the **Quota** tab to open the **Quota Entries** window (**Figure 14-11**). Then open the **Quota** menu and click the **New Quota Entry** command to open the user list from Active Directory or the local accounts database so that you can select the user for whom you want to apply a quota (**Figure 14-12**).

how to

Set disk quotas to monitor and track disk usage by users on a volume on your member server.

1. Click [Start] and click **My Computer** to open the **My Computer** window.
2. Right-click the **(x:)** icon, where x is the drive letter for an NTFS volume on your system, and click **Properties** to open the **(x:) Properties** dialog box.
3. Click the **Quota** tab. If quotas have not yet been enabled on the volume, to the left of a traffic light, **Status: Disk quotas are disabled** is shown (**Figure 14-13**).

Figure 14-11 The Quota Entries for (volume) window

Shows if a user is above limit, has been issued a warning, or is OK

Lists the username for the quota entry

Lists the amount of disk space used by the user

Displays the warning level for the disk quota

Displays the disk quota for the user on the volume

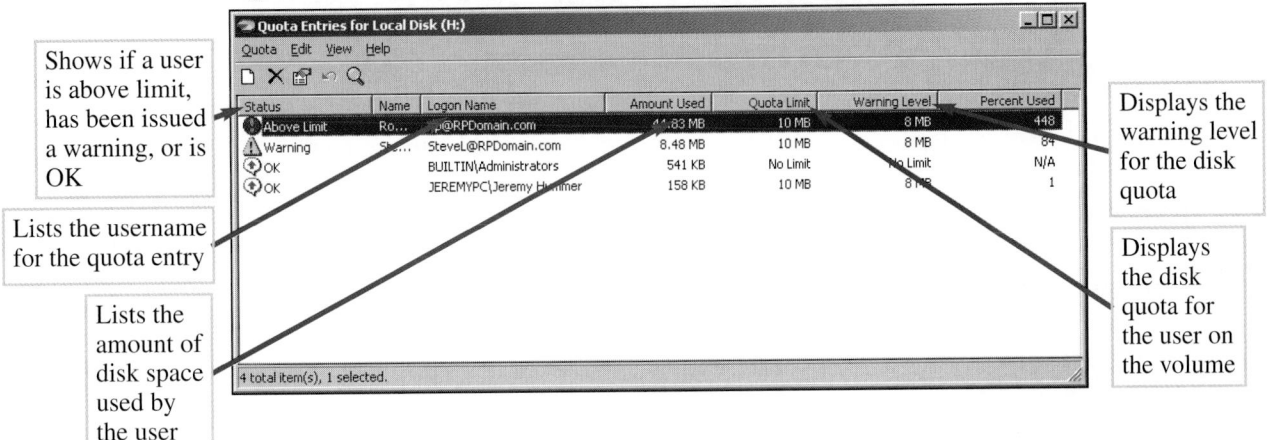

Figure 14-12 Adding a New Quota entry

Click to open the Select Users dialog box

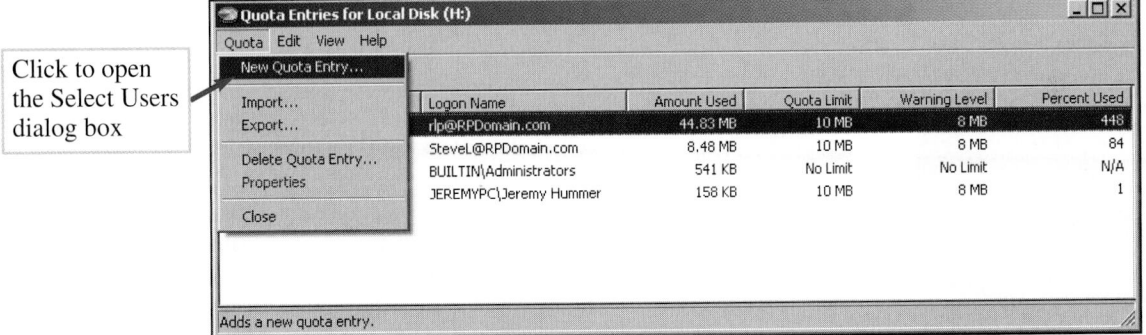

Figure 14-13 The Quota tab

Tells you whether disk quotas have been enabled for the volume or not

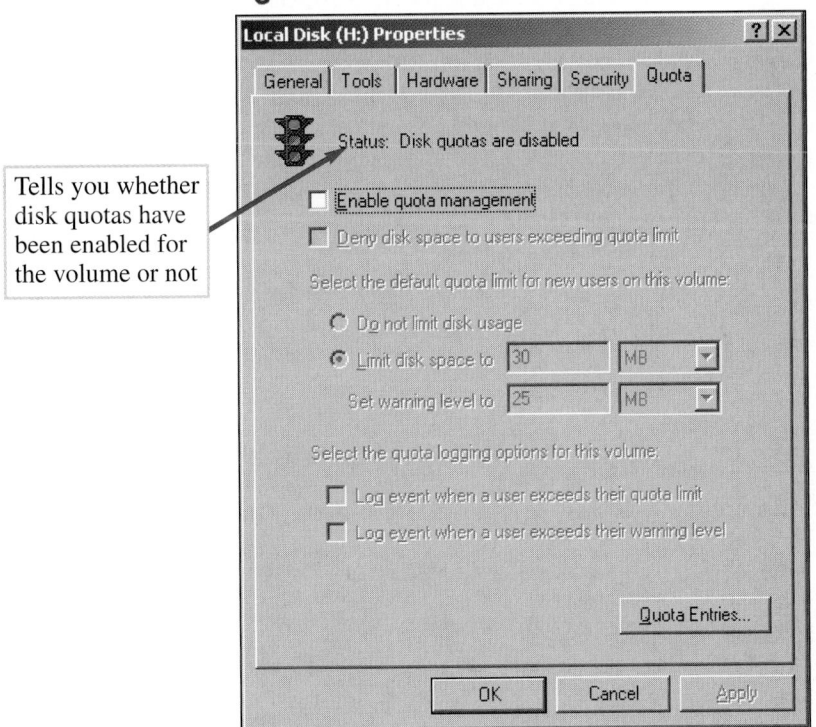

skill 2

Optimizing Disk Storage Performance *(cont'd)*

exam objective

Optimize server disk performance. Monitor and optimize a server environment for application performance. Monitor disk quotas.

how to

4. Select the **Enable quota management** check box, and select the **Limit disk space to** option button.
5. Type **30** in the **Limit disk space to** text box and select **MB** as the disk space limit unit for new users on the volume.
6. Type **25** in the **Set warning level to** text box and select **MB** as the warning level for new users on the volume (**Figure 14-14**).
7. Click [Apply] to enable disk quotas on the volume. The **Disk Quota** message box appears to warn you that you should only enable the disk quota system if you intend to use quotas on the volume, as well as to tell you that the volume will be rescanned to update disk usage statistics (**Figure 14-15**).
8. Click [OK] to close the Disk Quota message box.
9. Click [Quota Entries...] to open the **Quota Entries for (x:)** window.
10. Open the **Quota** menu and select **New Quota Entry** to open the **Select Users** dialog box. You can also click the **New quota entry** button [ ] on the toolbar to open the Select Users dialog box. Select the name of a user to whom you wish to apply a quota and click [Add]. Click **OK** to close the Select Users dialog box.
11. The **Add New Quota Entry** dialog box opens (**Figure 14-16**).
12. Type **50** in the **Limit disk space to** text box and select **MB** as the unit size.
13. Type **45** in the **Set warning level to** text box and select **MB** as the unit size.
14. Click **OK** to close the Add New Quota Entry dialog box. Close the Quota Entries for (x:) window, the Properties dialog box for the volume, and the My Computer window.

more

You can edit any quota entries you have configured by selecting the user in the Quota Entries for (volume) window and clicking the Properties button [ ] on the toolbar, or by right-clicking the user and clicking **Properties**. This will open the **Quota Settings for <*user_name*>** dialog box where you can view **Quota used** and **Quota remaining** statistics, as well as change the **Limit disk space to** and **Set warning level to** settings (**Figure 14-17**). You cannot delete a quota entry unless all of a user's files and folders have been either moved or deleted from the volume, or unless another user with a quota entry on the volume has taken ownership of them. If you have many users with quota entries on the volume you can use the **Find quota entry** [ ] button on the toolbar in the **Quota Entries for (volume)** window to open the **Find Quota Entry** dialog box. You locate quota entries by entering the user name in the **Logon Name** text box.

Figure 14-14 Enabling disk quotas

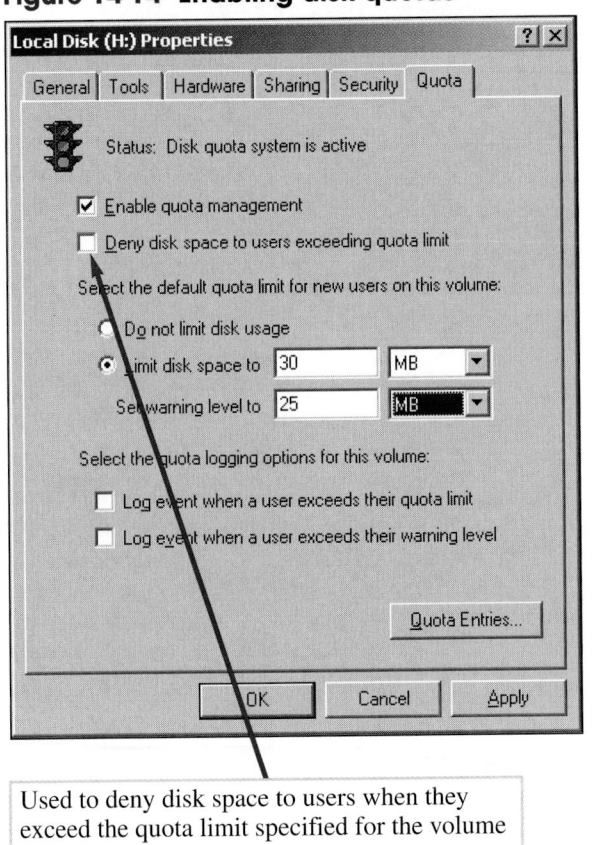

Figure 14-15 The Disk Quota warning message

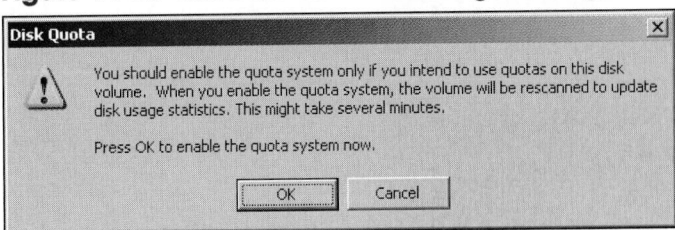

Used to deny disk space to users when they exceed the quota limit specified for the volume

Figure 14-16 The Add New Quota Entry dialog box

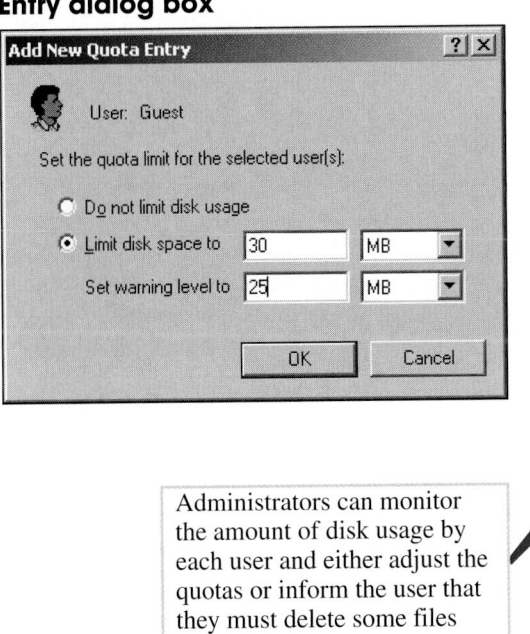

Figure 14-17 The Quota Settings for <user_name> dialog box

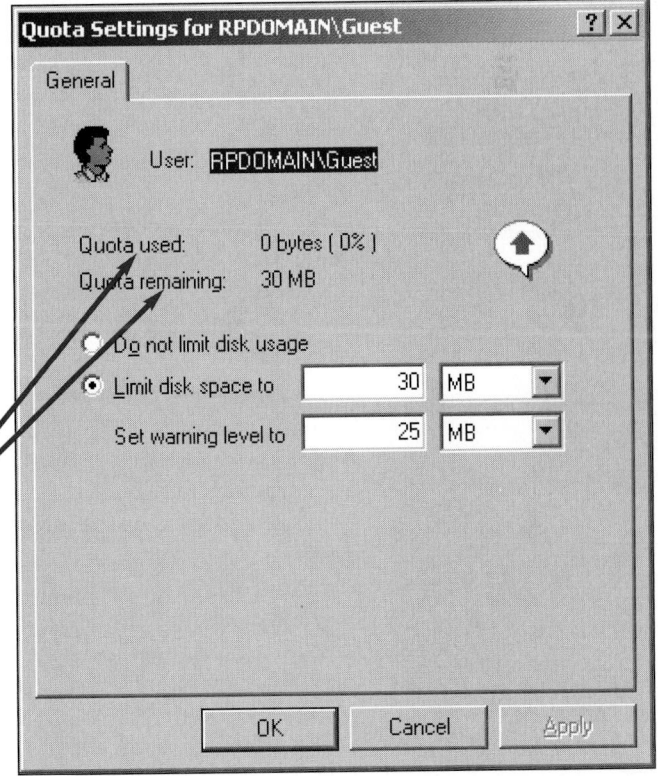

Administrators can monitor the amount of disk usage by each user and either adjust the quotas or inform the user that they must delete some files

skill 3

Working with the Task Manager

Monitor file and print servers. Tools might include Task Manager, Event Viewer, and System Monitor. Monitor and optimize a server environment for application performance. Monitor server hardware for bottlenecks.

overview

One important utility you can use to manage system processes and performance on a server is the Task Manager. You can use the **Task Manager** to view running applications to determine if they are placing unnecessary demands on the server or generating unnecessary network traffic. Unfortunately, some applications may place a disproportionate burden on the server, causing degenerating system performance. When this happens, sharp increases in the amount of processor, memory, or disk resource utilization may point to an inefficient program as the source of the problem.

tip

You can also open Task Manager, by right-clicking an empty space on the Taskbar and selecting Task Manager.

To open the Task Manager, press **[Ctrl]+[Alt]+[Del]** to open the **Windows Security** dialog box. You must be logged on as an Administrator (or as a member of the Server Operators group). Then, click the **Task Manager** button to open the Windows Task Manager dialog box where you can perform the following tasks:

View the status of, and stop and start programs: On the **Applications** tab (**Figure 14-18**), you can view the status of all applications that are currently running, use the **End Task** button to end an application that is malfunctioning, or use the **New Task** button to open the **Create New Task** dialog box, which you can use to start an application. The Create New Task dialog box works just like the Run dialog box (**Figure 14-19**). In most cases, a **Not responding** status on the Applications tab indicates that an application is stalled and you should end the task in order to stop the execution of the program. The status bar at the bottom of the dialog box displays data on how many processes are currently running, the percentage of CPU currently being used, and the current memory usage out of the total memory available.

View information about processes: On the **Processes** tab, you can view a list of all processes currently running. You can select any process and click the **End Process** button to terminate the process. A **process** in Task Manager refers to an executable program or an application running as a component of the primary application. When a process is running, it may initiate other processes. The main process and its offshoot processes are referred to as a process tree. The additional processes will be displayed directly under and indented from the main process. For example, when running a DOS 16-bit application, the NTVDM (NT Virtual DOS Machine) process is the primary process, and the application itself would be shown as a child process.

To stop an entire process tree, right-click the main process and click **End Process Tree**. This would be required in a situation where a DOS or 16-bit Windows application failed, as 16-bit applications use shared memory. This means that when a single 16-bit process fails, there is a good chance that all processes running under the same NTVDM will also fail. Therefore, when a 16-bit application has problems, you should end the entire process tree.

The **Image Name** column tells you the name of the process such as explorer.exe for Windows Explorer or ntbackup.exe. The **User Name** column tells you the user account under which the process is running. The **CPU** column tells you the percentage of processor resources used by the process and the **Mem Usage** column tells you the amount of memory the process is using (**Figure 14-20**). These are the default performance statistics. You can also view other statistics by opening the **View** menu and clicking the **Select Columns** command. In the **Select Columns** dialog box, you can choose alternative statistics (**Figure 14-21**). If you are concerned about a particular program and think that it may be causing a **bottleneck** (a resource that causes other resources to delay while it completes its assigned function), right-click the program on the Applications tab and select the **Go To Process** command. The Processes tab will open with the process or processes for that application highlighted. The CPU column will let you know if the process is using too many processor resources and the Mem Usage column can point out a memory bottleneck. You can then stop the program until you can determine the cause of the difficulty.

Figure 14-18 The Applications tab in the Task Manager

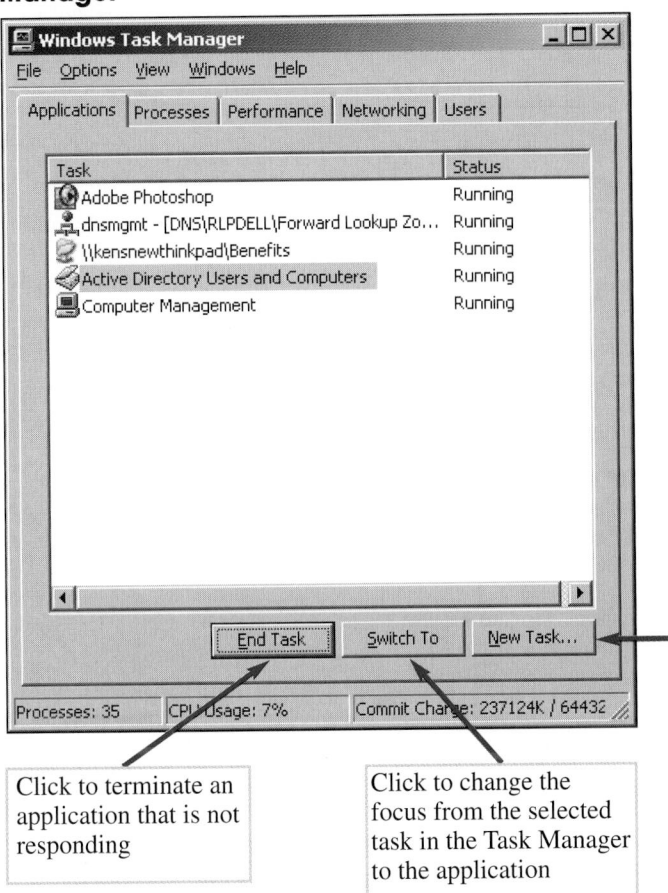

Figure 14-19 The Create New Task dialog box

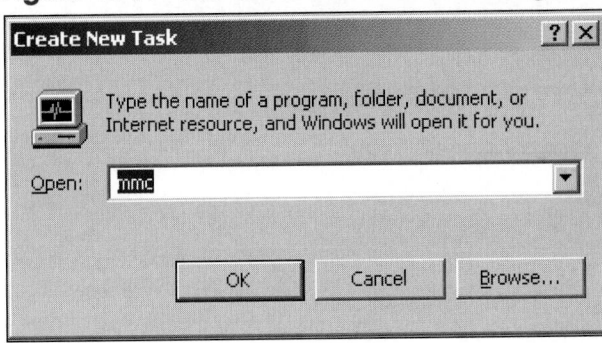

Click to open the Create New Task dialog box and start a new application

Click to terminate an application that is not responding

Click to change the focus from the selected task in the Task Manager to the application

Figure 14-20 The Processes tab

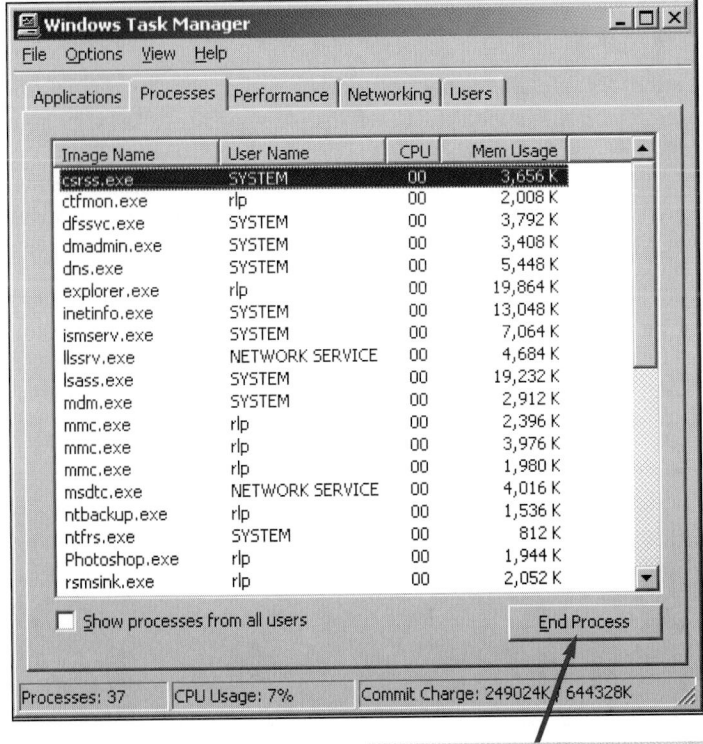

Click to end a selected process

Figure 14-21 Performance Statistics in the Select Columns dialog box

Select Columns

Select the columns that will appear on the Process page of the Task Manager.

☑ Image Name	☐ Page Faults Delta
☐ PID (Process Identifier)	☐ Virtual Memory Size
☑ CPU Usage	☐ Paged Pool
☐ CPU Time	☐ Non-paged Pool
☑ Memory Usage	☐ Base Priority
☐ Memory Usage Delta	☐ Handle Count
☐ Peak Memory Usage	☐ Thread Count
☐ Page Faults	☐ GDI Objects
☐ USER Objects	☐ I/O Writes
☐ I/O Reads	☐ I/O Write Bytes
☐ I/O Read Bytes	☐ I/O Other
☐ Session ID	☐ I/O Other Bytes
☑ User Name	

OK   Cancel

skill 3

Working with the Task Manager
(cont'd)

exam objective

Monitor file and print servers. Tools might include Task Manager, Event Viewer, and System Monitor. Monitor and optimize a server environment for application performance. Monitor server hardware for bottlenecks.

overview

You can also increase the priority of a process so that it will take precedence over other processes that are demanding CPU attention. Right-click the process for which you want to change the priority and click **Set Priority**. The priority assigned to a process is either set by program code in the application or Windows assigns it the **Normal** priority. The server administrator can change the priority to **Realtime**, **High**, **AboveNormal**, **BelowNormal**, or **Low (Figure 14-22)**. Processes assigned the Low priority will have to wait in a queue for processor time, disk access, memory access, or another system resource until all processes with higher priorities are serviced first. Realtime priority is generally unused, as realtime processes can be given precedence over system processes, which can cause serious failures. A process assigned the Realtime priority can overwhelm the server and block all other processes from running. If you have installed a debugging program, you can also run it from the context menu for a running process.

Monitor CPU and page file usage: On the **Performance** tab, graphs of the CPU and memory usage are displayed to provide a dynamic overview of the performance of your server **(Figure 14-23)**. The **CPU Usage** and **PF Usage** bar charts display the current use of the processor and the page file. The graphs to the right of each bar chart display the recent history of CPU and page file usage. At the bottom of the dialog box, detailed statistics tell you the total number of handles and threads used. A **handle** is any resource, such as a file, that is used by an application. It has its own identification so that the program can access it. A **thread** is a block of program code. You can also display the amount of CPU resources consumed by kernel operations by opening the **View** menu and selecting **Show Kernel Times**. A red line will be added to the CPU Usage bar chart and to the **CPU Usage History** graph. This red secondary graph line displays the CPU activity dedicated to the operating system in kernel mode. The difference between the green and red lines demonstrates the CPU activity dedicated to user mode activities such as applications.

Monitor Network Performance: On the **Networking tab**, you can monitor all of the NICs installed on the server **(Figure 14-24)**. Total network utilization is represented on a graph for each NIC to indicate the approximate percentage of network bandwidth in use. At the bottom of the dialog box, each **Adapter Name** (connection name) is listed as well as the percentage of **Network Utilization**, the **Link Speed**, and the **State** of the connection. The information on the Networking tab can alert you to a problem that is causing high network utilization for an extended period of time or simply let you know if a particular network adapter is working.

Monitor Users: On the **Users** tab, you can view a list of currently logged-on users. You can also use the **Logoff** button at the bottom of the dialog box or the Logoff command on the context menu when you right-click a user's name, to close any files a user has open and log the user off. If this does not work, you can use either the **Disconnect** button or command to disconnect a user whose connection is hung.

On each of the tabs in the Windows Task Manager, you can select the **Refresh Now** command on the **View** menu to refresh the data and information that it displays. You can also use the **Update Speed** command to increase or decrease the rate at which data is automatically displayed.

Figure 14-22 Setting the priority for a process

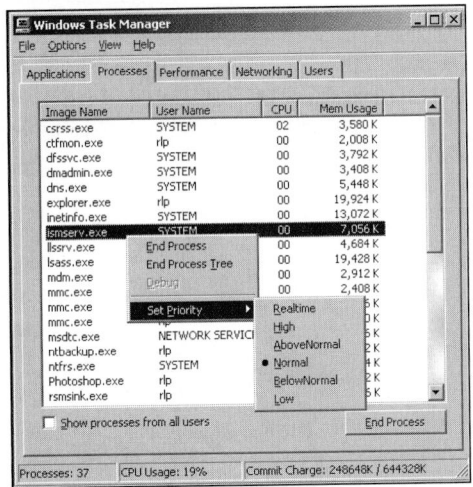

Figure 14-23 The Performance tab

The current number of handles, threads, and processes in use on the system

Total indicates the total amount of virtual memory currently committed to all processes; Limit, the total physical and page file size minus the amount of non-paged memory used by the system; Peak, the peak amount of memory that has been used during the current Task Manager monitoring session

The total amount of physical memory (RAM) on the computer, the currently available RAM, and the amount of RAM used for file caching

The total amount of memory being used by the kernel, divided into paged (virtual memory) and non-paged (RAM) memory

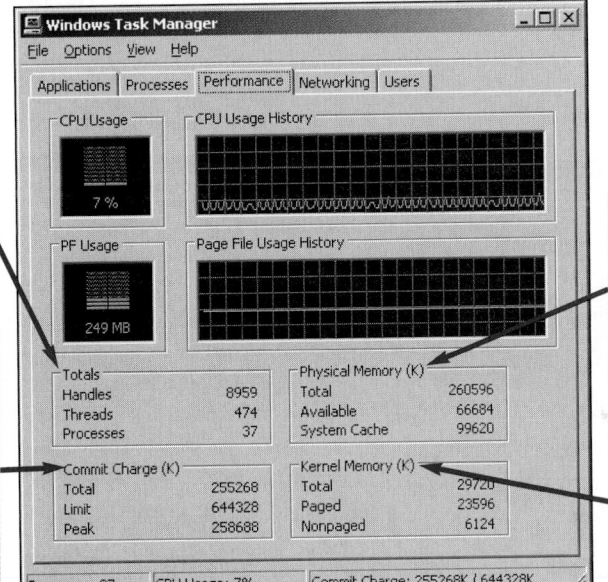

Figure 14-24 The Networking tab

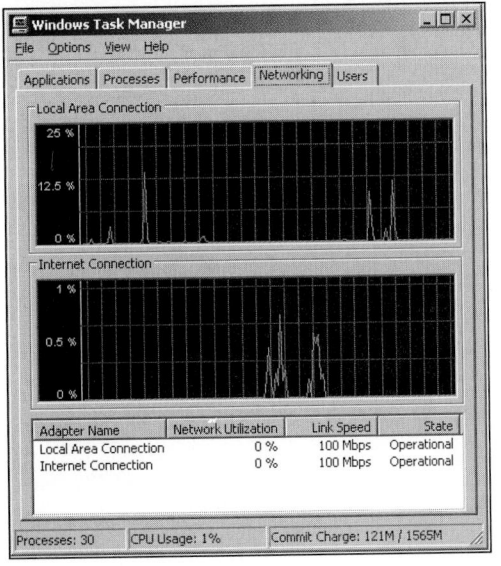

skill 3

Working with the Task Manager
(cont'd)

exam objective

Monitor file and print servers. Tools might include Task Manager, Event Viewer, and System Monitor. Monitor and optimize a server environment for application performance. Monitor server hardware for bottlenecks.

how to

Work with the Task Manager.

1. Click [Start], point to **All Programs**, point to **Accessories**, and click **Notepad**.
2. Press **[Ctrl]+[Alt]+[Del]** to open the **Windows Security** dialog box. Click the **Task Manager** button.
3. Open the **Applications** tab, if necessary.
4. Right-click **Untitled—Notepad** and select **Switch To** to open the blank Notepad document.
5. Click **Windows Task Manager** on the Taskbar to return to the Task Manager.
6. Select **Untitled—Notepad** if necessary, and click [End Task].
7. Click [Start], point to **All Programs**, point to **Accessories**, and click **Paint**.
8. Right-click **untitled—Paint** and select **Go To Process (Figure 14-25)**. The **Processes** tab opens with the process used by the Paint program highlighted.
9. Right-click **mspaint.exe**, point to **Set Priority** and select **AboveNormal**.
10. The **Task Manager Warning** message box informs you that changing the priority class can cause undesired results **(Figure 14-26)**. Click [Yes] to change the priority class.
11. Open the **Performance** tab.
12. Resize the Paint window and position the Task Manager dialog box and the Paint window so that they are side by side.
13. Open a file in Paint. You should be able to observe a small increase in CPU usage and a small spike should appear on the **CPU Usage History** graph.
14. Open the **View** menu and select **Show Kernel Times**. A red line is added to the **CPU Usage** and **CPU Usage History** graphs.
15. Open the **Networking** tab. Minimize Task Manager.
16. Click [Start] and click the **Run** command to open the Run dialog box. Type **cmd** in the **Open** text box and press **[Enter]** or click [OK].
17. Type **ping -t -1 1000 <*IP_address*>**. Use the IP address of a computer on your LAN. You may recall from Lesson 10 that the **-t** switch pings the host until stopped and the **-l** (lowercase **L**) switch is used to designate the size of the ICMP echo request. This command will ping the destination host continuously with echo requests that are 1000 bytes.
18. Restore the Task Manager. You should be able to see a small increase in network utilization **(Figure 14-27)**.
19. Close the Task Manager and the command prompt window.

Figure 14-25 Using the Go To Process command

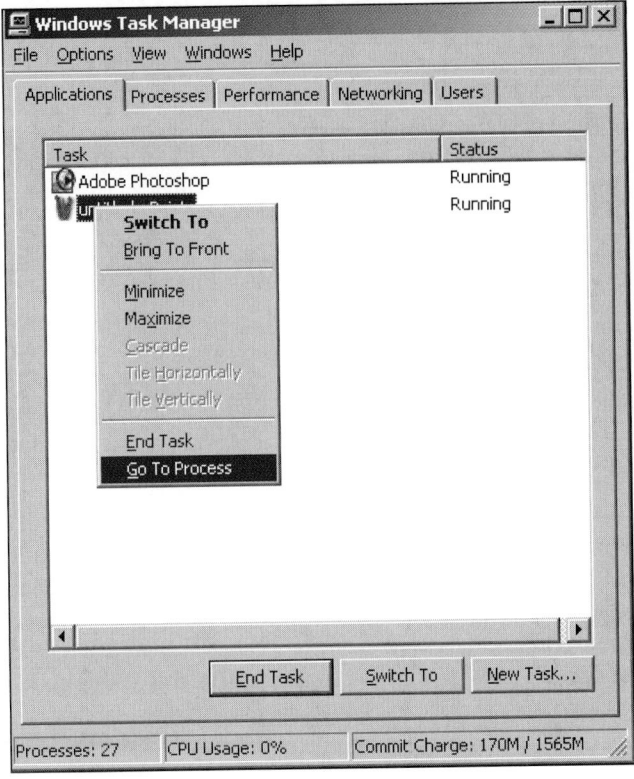

Figure 14-26 The Task Manager Warning message box

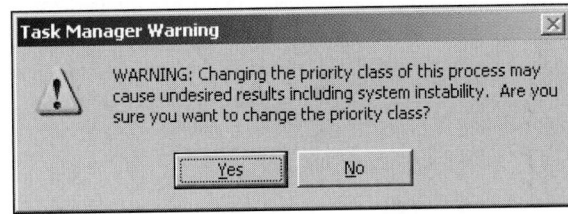

Figure 14-27 Viewing network utilization for the Local Area Connection

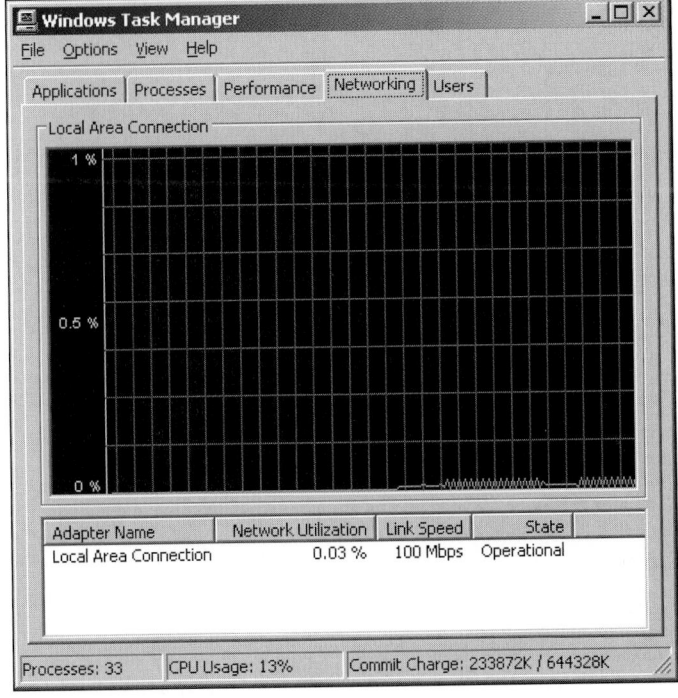

skill 4

Working with the System Monitor

exam objective

Monitor file and print servers. Tools might include Task Manager, Event Viewer, and System Monitor. Monitor server hardware for bottlenecks. Monitor system performance. Monitor and optimize a server environment for application performance. Monitor disk performance objects.

overview

You can monitor the resources on your server, either to establish a baseline or to diagnose a bottleneck, in the **Performance** console. The Performance console consists of the System Monitor and the Performance Logs and Alerts tools. The **System Monitor** is used to view a graphical real-time representation of the performance of the resources on your computer. The data captured by the System Monitor is displayed as a chart, a histogram, or a report. The **Performance Logs and Alerts** tool is used to record the performance of resources in logs and to configure alerts, which are activated based on threshold values that you set, to perform specific actions.

When you open the Performance console, the System Monitor appears by default with the default set of counters configured: Memory—Pages/sec, PhysicalDisk—Avg. Disk Queue Length, and Processor—%Processor Time **(Figure 14-28)**. Performance is measured based on objects and counters. A **performance object** is a system resource, such as memory, a disk, a processor, or a network interface, whose performance you can monitor. **Performance counters** are performance measures for the object that can be calculated and related as numeric figures. For example, the Pages/sec counter for the Memory object measures the number of pages written to or read from virtual memory per second. The Avg. Disk Queue Length counter for the Physical Disk object measures the average number of read and write requests that were queued for the selected disk. A large queue (typically, a sustained queue of over 2) could indicate that the disk subsystem is a bottleneck. The % Processor Time counter for the Processor object measures the percentage of time that the processor is busy processing instructions. Threads, which are the basic unit of execution in the CPU, execute instructions, and processes control the threads.

Counters can have multiple instances. For example, if a computer has two processors, there will be three instances for the %Processor Time counter, one for each processor, and one for the total processing time. Processors are not frequently the cause of a bottleneck, but if the values are consistently above 80%, then you should determine the cause of the high processor usage. Be aware that almost any activity in the system (including paging) can affect processor usage. Also, spikes are of no concern, but prolonged peaks are.

You can also use the Processor-Interrupts/sec counter to determine the average number of times the processor is interrupted by hardware device requests for attention. When the system is not in use, the only interrupts are caused by the processor hardware timer, which will produce approximately 66 to 100 interrupts per second. First, establish a baseline for normal workloads. This value will depend on the number of disk I/0 operations per second and the number of network packets per second. Interrupts/sec is primarily used to determine when a device is failing. In general, an increase in this counter with no corresponding increase in activity indicates a failing hardware component.

Figure 14-28 System Monitor

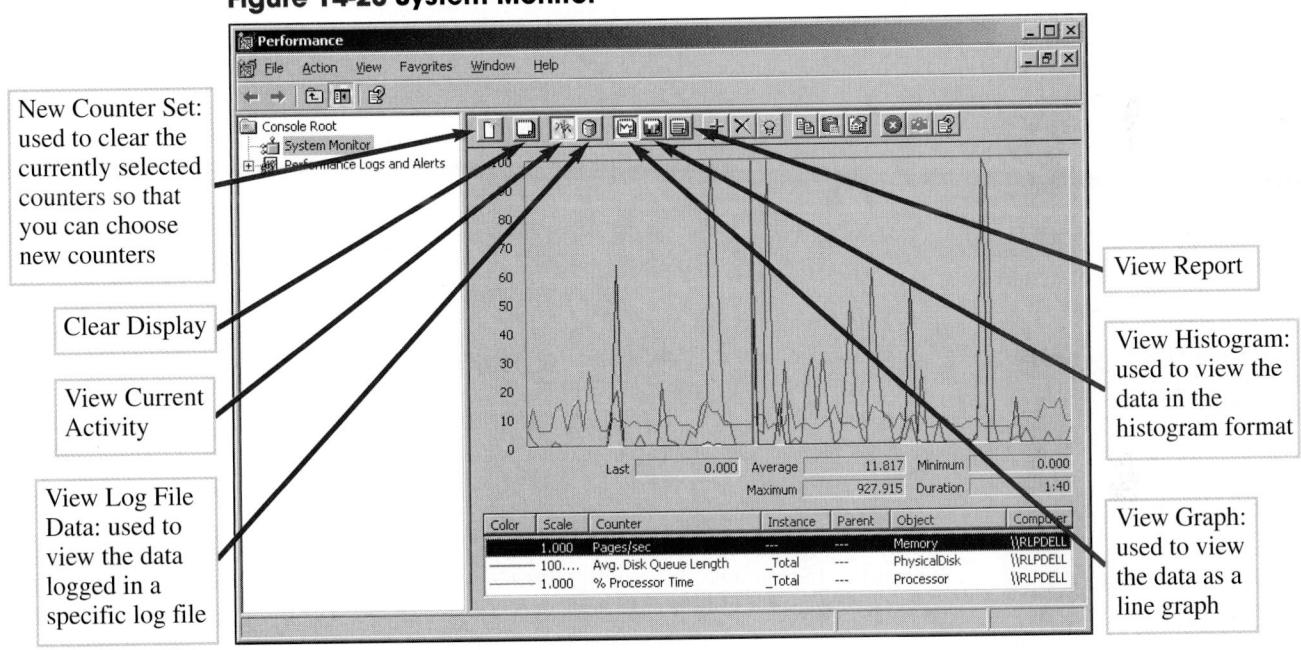

New Counter Set: used to clear the currently selected counters so that you can choose new counters

Clear Display

View Current Activity

View Log File Data: used to view the data logged in a specific log file

View Report

View Histogram: used to view the data in the histogram format

View Graph: used to view the data as a line graph

skill 4

Using the System Monitor (cont'd)

exam objective

Monitor file and print servers. Tools might include Task Manager, Event Viewer, and System Monitor. Monitor server hardware for bottlenecks. Monitor system performance. Monitor and optimize a server environment for application performance. Monitor disk performance objects.

how to

Monitor processor usage.

1. Click **Start**, point to **Administrative Tools**, and click **Performance** to open the **Performance** console.
2. Click the **New Counter Set** button on the **Performance** toolbar to clear the default counter set.
3. Click the **Add** button on the **Performance** toolbar to open the **Add Counters** dialog box.
4. The **Select counters from computer** option button is selected by default and the name of the local computer is entered in the list box. To monitor another computer on the local area network, enter the UNC path, \\<*computer_name*>.
5. Select **Processor** in the **Performance object** list box to specify the resource you want to monitor.
6. Click the **Select counters from list** option button, if necessary, and select the **% Processor Time** counter. This counter is a primary indicator of processor activity. It measures the percentage of time the processor spends executing non-idle threads.
7. Click the **All instances** option button to monitor all instances of the counter **(Figure 14-29)**.
8. Click **Add** to add the % Processor Time counter to System Monitor.
9. Select **Interrupts/Sec** in the **Select counters from list** box. Select the **All instances** option button and click **Add**.
10. Select **%Interrupt Time**. This counter measures the amount of time the processor is servicing hardware requests from devices such as the disk, CD-ROM drive, devices plugged into the serial and parallel ports, and the network interface card (NIC). If the %Interrupt Time is high as compared to the baseline you have established, you may have a malfunctioning hardware device or NIC. Click **Add**.
11. Select **System** in the **Performance object** list box.
12. Select **Processor Queue Length** in the **Select counters from** list box. This counter measures the number of execution threads waiting to access a CPU. A Processor Queue Length value that frequently exceeds 3 for a single processor indicates processor congestion. You will either have to distribute some of the load to other servers, add another CPU, or upgrade the server or its motherboard. If the value is over 2 per CPU on a multiprocessor system, you probably need to add another CPU or increase processor speed. Click **Add**.
13. Click **Close** to close the Add Counters dialog box. The data is displayed as a line graph by default **(Figure 14-30)**.
14. Click the **View Histogram** button to display the captured data as a histogram **(Figure 14-31)**.
15. Click the **View Report** button to view the output statistics **(Figure 14-32)**.
16. Close the Performance console.

Figure 14-29 The Add Counters dialog box

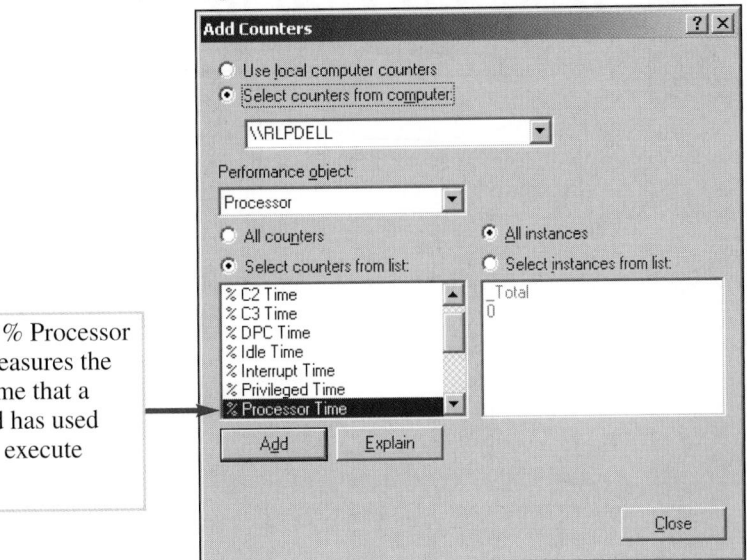

The Processor - % Processor Time counter measures the percentage of time that a particular thread has used the processor to execute instructions

Figure 14-30 Monitoring processor performance

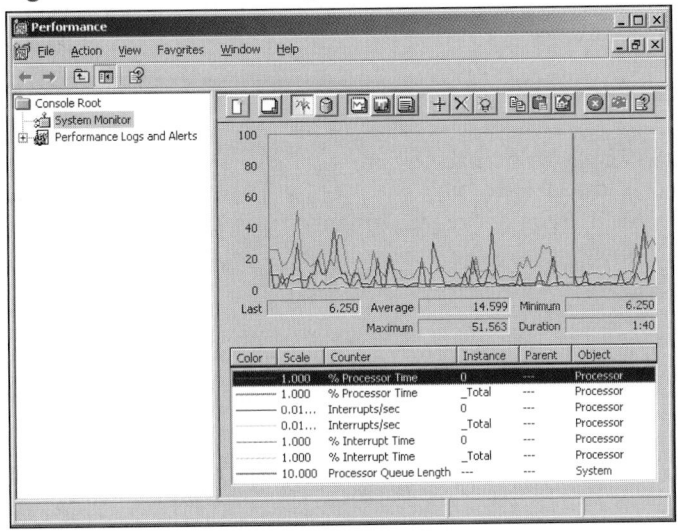

Figure 14-31 Histogram view

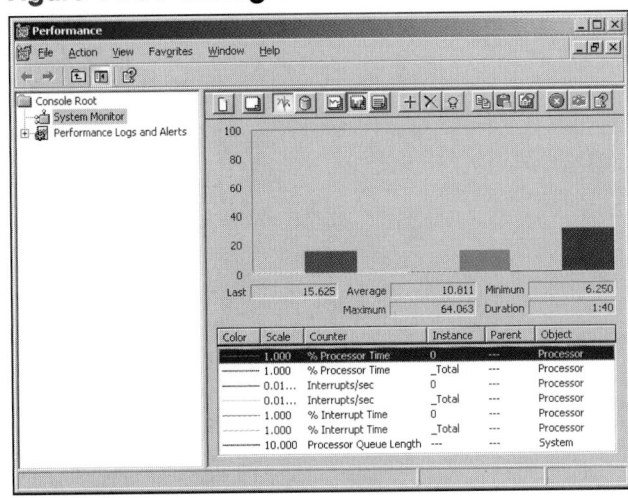

Figure 14-32 Report view

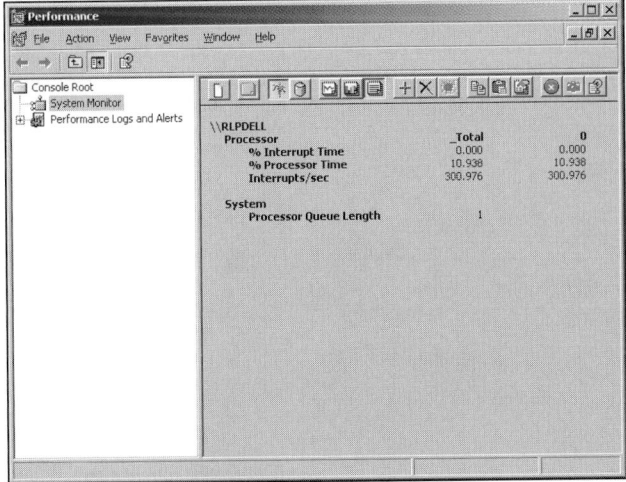

skill 4

Working with the System Monitor
(cont'd)

exam objective

Monitor file and print servers. Tools might include Task Manager, Event Viewer, and System Monitor. Monitor server hardware for bottlenecks. Monitor system performance. Monitor and optimize a server environment for application performance. Monitor disk performance objects.

more

In Windows Server 2003, both the physical hard disk (PhysicalDisk) and the LogicalDisk are automatically System Monitor performance objects. Performance counter data for physical disks and for logical drives, or storage volumes, is collected using the **Disk Performance Statistics Driver**. If either the PhysicalDisk or the LogicalDisk object has been disabled, you can run the **Diskperf** utility from the command prompt. If the counters for both objects are already enabled, the message shown in **Figure 14-33** will be displayed. Diskperf, which is located in the *%systemroot%\system32* folder, is used to enable or disable the counters for both physical and logical disk monitoring. The switches used with the Diskperf command are outlined in **Table 14-3**.

The Physical Disk counters %Disk Time and Avg. Disk Queue Length can be used to look for bottlenecks at the disk level. The %Disk Time counter measures the percentage of time the selected disk drive was busy servicing read or write requests during the monitoring period. Remaining general, you would like to ensure that it remains under 60% on a sustained basis. The Avg. Disk Queue Length measures the average number of read and write requests that were queued for the selected disk during the sample time period. It should be less than 2 for any physical disk. You can also use the Avg. Disk Read Queue Length and Avg. Disk Write Queue Length counters to break this reading up into its individual components.

There are many other counters you can track with the System Monitor. Since it would be difficult to memorize the purpose of each one, you can select the counter you want to find out about in the Add Counter dialog box and use the **Explain** button to open the **Explain Text** section, which provides a description of what the counter measures (**Figure 14-34**).

Services and protocols running on your Windows Server 2003 system, such as TCP, UDP, Terminal Services, the Server Service, DNS, the Browser, WINS, and Network Monitor Driver, etc., are also listed as objects in the System Monitor. When these services are installed on your server, you can also monitor their performance. For example, you can monitor the number of bytes transmitted and received per second by the Server Service; the number of errors in logons; the number of logged-off, errored out, and forced off sessions; and the number of errors for access permissions (**Figure 14-35**).

Figure 14-33 The diskperf command

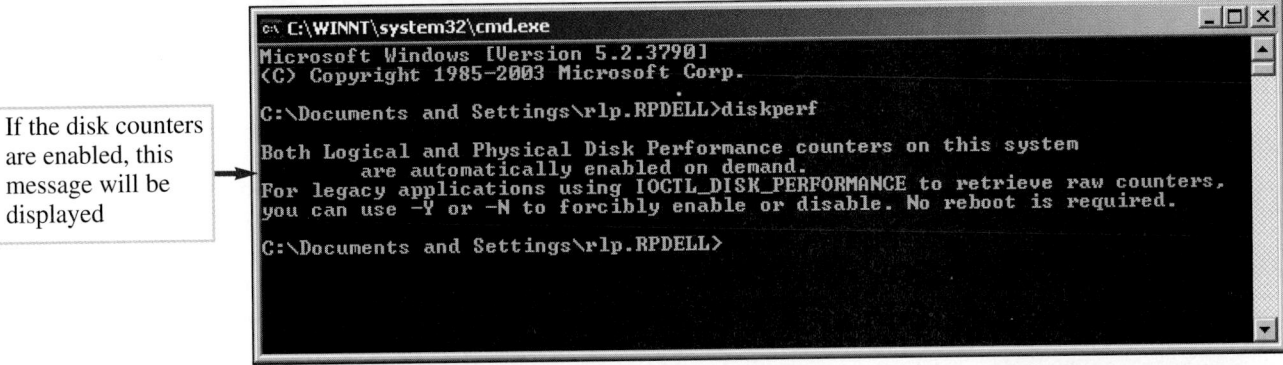

If the disk counters are enabled, this message will be displayed

Table 14-3   Parameters used with Diskperf

Diskperf	Tells you if the PhysicalDisk and LogicalDisk performance counters are on the system and are automatically enabled on demand.
-y	Sets the system to start all disk performance counters when the system is rebooted.
-yd	Enables the counters for monitoring physical drives when the system is rebooted.
-yv	Enables the counters for monitoring logical drives or storage volumes when the system is rebooted.
-n	Disables both PhysicalDisk and LogicalDisk performance counters when the system is rebooted.
-nd	Disables the disk performance counters for physical drives.
-nv	Disables the disk performance counters for logical drives.
\\computer_name	The name of the server on which you want to set disk counters.
/?	Displays the diskperf switches.

Figure 14-34 The Explain Text dialog box for the Avg. Disk Queue Length counter

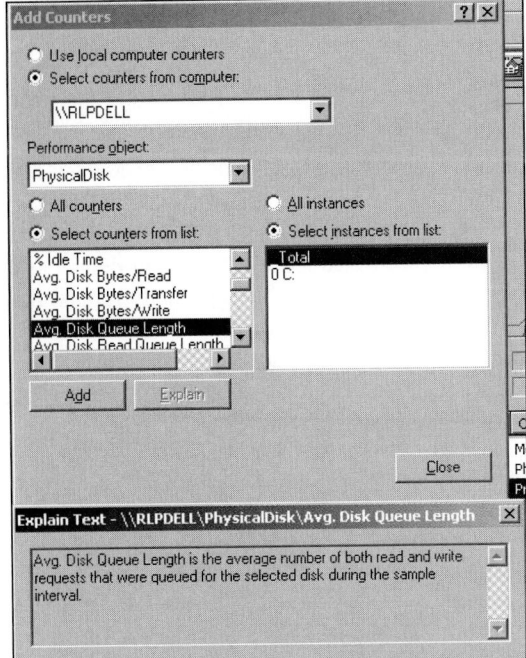

Figure 14-35 The Explain Text dialog box for the Access Permissions counter

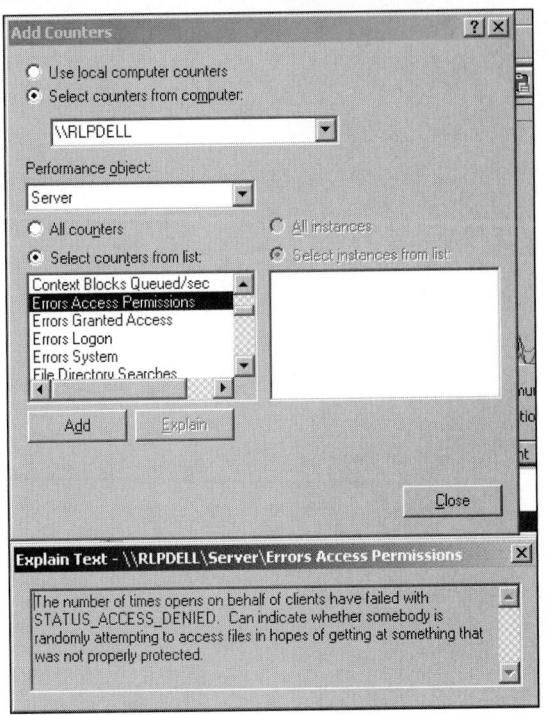

skill 5

Working with Performance Logs and Alerts

Monitor file and print servers. Tools might include Task Manager, Event Viewer, and System Monitor. Monitor and analyze events. Tools might include Event Viewer and System Monitor. Monitor server hardware for bottlenecks. Monitor system performance. Monitor and optimize a server environment for application performance. Monitor memory performance objects.

overview

While the System Monitor displays graphical real-time representations of the performance measures for various objects, Performance Logs and Alerts are used to store the data for future reference. You can create two types of logs: Counter logs and Trace logs. **Counter logs** use the GUI data from the System Monitor to create a log file, which is by default in the *.blg format (Binary LoG) (**Figure 14-36**). They record the state of object counters at specific intervals of time that you set, for a specified time period (**Figure 14-37**). Counter logs can rapidly become large and quickly consume a lot of disk space. This can degrade system performance. To keep this under control, it is recommended that you monitor at intervals more frequent than 15 seconds only if you are going to take measurements for four hours or less. Microsoft recommends that you only take measurements every five minutes or longer if you are going to monitor system performance for 8 hours or more. You can also control the size to which you will allow the log file to grow, but you must make sure that it is large enough to store data for all intervals within the monitored time period. You should also realize that the act of logging data does affect system performance and the corresponding data collected to a degree.

You should establish baseline behavior when a server first begins to run on the network and when the hardware or software configuration has been modified. For example, to determine the baseline behavior for the processors, you can create a counter log using the Processor-%Processing Time counter and the System-Processor Queue Length counter, which you should run for a few weeks to a month. This way, at a later date when you make system modifications, you will have a benchmark range of values to evaluate against the new range of values you get post-modification. Sporadic spikes in the values recorded by a counter are generally discarded. The idea is to get a reliable range of values against which future performance can be compared. As a general rule, baselines should be established for all of the important servers on the network.

Based on the performance of resources on your server, you will have to take precautions or make upgrades in order to maintain or enhance its performance. For example, the most frequent cause of system bottlenecks is memory. There are several counters you can use to evaluate how much memory your system is using. The Available MBytes counter calculates how much physical memory is left to run a process after all other running processes and the cache are taken care of. The Memory\Available Mbytes counter should optimally remain above 10% of RAM, for example, above 25 MB on a system with 256 MB of RAM.

The Pages/sec counter measures the number of times the processor had to ask for data that was not in RAM (physical memory), but rather had been stored in the page file. The page file, as you have learned, is a logical memory location on the root drive where the operating system was installed. If the page file is habitually being called upon, system delays are most likely already perceptible. The Memory\Pages/sec counter should optimally remain between 0-20 on a sustained basis. Values over 80 indicate a severe problem. Excessive swapping to the page file will degrade system performance and must be addressed by either reducing the load on the server or by adding additional RAM. The Paging file counter, %Usage, will tell you how much of the page file is currently being used.

tip

You can export your log files to .csv and .tsv files for importation into a spreadsheet or database application.

You can use these three counters to create a counter log to monitor the memory on your system (**Figure 14-38**). Then, you can configure an alert to send you a message when the value is either under or over certain thresholds. For example, if the available megabytes of memory dips below 25 MB on a system with 256 MB of RAM, the paging file usage is consistently more than 99 percent, or if you see frequent peaks over 20 being recorded by the Pages/sec counter, it is probably time to add more memory to your system. The average number of times

Figure 14-36 The Counter Logs node

The default counter log, System Overview, is a pre-defined sample counter log file that uses the Memory—Pages/sec, PhysicalDisk - Avg. Disk Queue Length, and Processor—% Processor Time counters

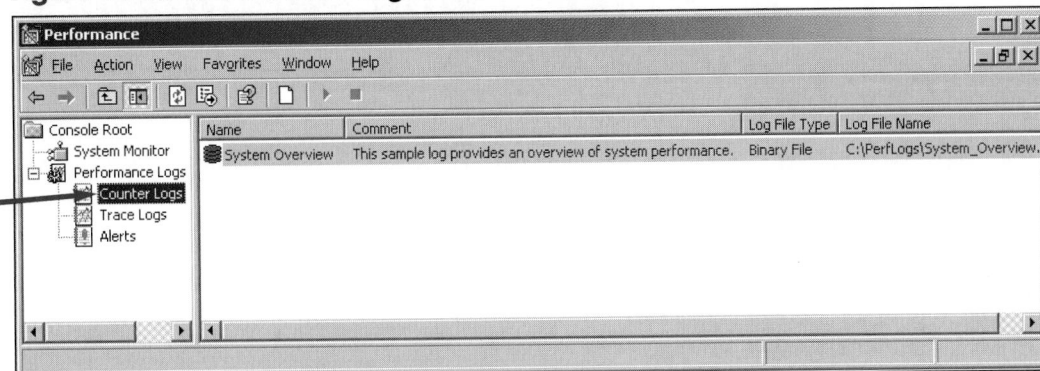

Figure 14-37 The System Overview Properties dialog box

The System Overview counter log is set to begin recording data at 8:00 AM on 9/30/03 and to stop after 8 hours

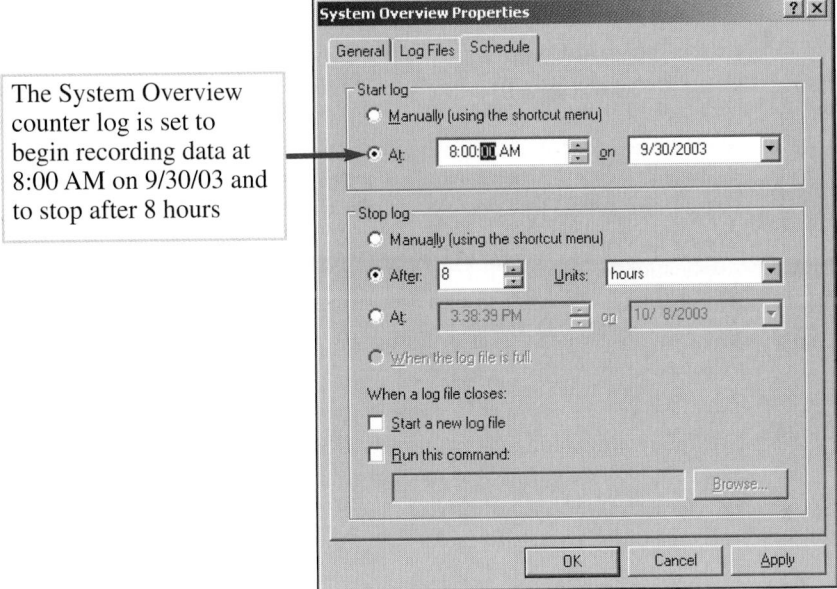

Figure 14-38 A Counter log

A counter log using the Memory\Available MBytes, Memory\Pages/sec, and Pagingfile\%Usage counters saved in the Text File (Comma delimited) log file type opened in Excel

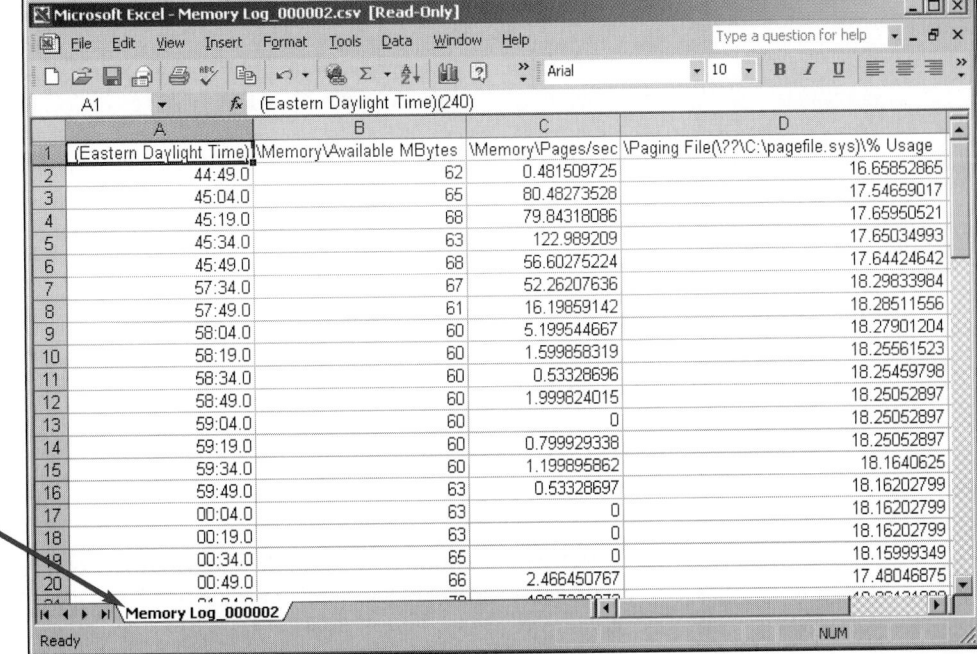

skill 5

Working with Performance Logs and Alerts (cont'd)

exam objective

Monitor file and print servers. Tools might include Task Manager, Event Viewer, and System Monitor. Monitor and analyze events. Tools might include Event Viewer and System Monitor. Monitor server hardware for bottlenecks. Monitor system performance. Monitor and optimize a server environment for application performance. Monitor memory performance objects.

overview

per second that the processor has to ask for data that is not in physical RAM should not exceed 80. You can also automate actions to be performed when the value of a counter surpasses the threshold value for that particular counter, and you can configure an alert to monitor a particular counter at a scheduled time or when you manually start the scan. You can configure alerts to perform the following actions:

Send a message: Alerts can send messages to computers that are connected to the computer being monitored. For example, you can set up an alert on a computer on your network to send a message to your computer when the available disk space is less than a certain value.

Run a program: Alerts can be programmed to run a program. For example, you can configure an alert to run a pager program in order to page you when the available disk space is below a certain limit.

Start a new log: Alerts can be configured to create a new log to record events when the counter value is either under or over the threshold you have set. Starting a new log enables you to view events that occur after the alert has been triggered.

Create an entry in the Application log: Alerts can create an entry in the Application log. The Application log records events that occur when an application is run. Logging an entry in the Application log enables you to determine the time when an alert was triggered.

You can also export server performance data from counter log files to spreadsheet programs or databases to analyze and report the performance of the server.

how to

Create a counter log and an alert to evaluate how much memory your system is using at particular points in time and to send a message to another computer when certain thresholds are crossed (the available memory falls below **25 MB**, the **Pages/sec** exceeds **20**, or the **%Usage** of the page file reaches **99%**).

1. Click [*Start*], click **Run**, and type **perfmon** in the **Open** text box. Press **[Enter]** or click [OK] to open the **Performance** console.
2. Expand the **Performance Logs and Alerts** node.
3. Right-click **Counter Logs** and click **New Log Settings** to open the **New Log Settings** dialog box.
4. Type **Memory Log** in the **Name** text box in order to name the new log (**Figure 14-39**).
5. Click [OK] to close the **New Log Settings** dialog box and open the **Memory Log** dialog box.
6. Click [Add Counters...] to open the **Add Counters** dialog box.
7. In the **Performance object** list box, select **Memory**.
8. Make sure that the **Select counters from list** option button is selected.
9. Hold down the **[Ctrl]** key and select the **Available MBytes** and **Pages/sec** counters (**Figure 14-40**).
10. Click [Add] to add the selected counters to the counter log file.
11. In the **Performance object** list box, select **Paging File**.
12. In the **Select counters from list** box, select **%Usage** and click [Add].
13. Close the Add Counters dialog box.
14. To set the time interval at which the log will record data from the selected counters, type **30** in the **Interval** spin box and select **seconds** in the **Units** list box (**Figure 14-41**).
15. Click the **Log Files** tab. The location where the log file will be saved, **C:\PerfLogs**, is entered in the **Example** label.
16. Select **yyyymmddhh** in the **End file names with** list box to append the year, month, day, and hour of the day to the name of the log file. You can also add the month, day, and hour; month, day, hour, and minute; or the year and day; year and month, etc.; or a serial number to the name of the log file.

Figure 14-40 Adding counters for the Memory object

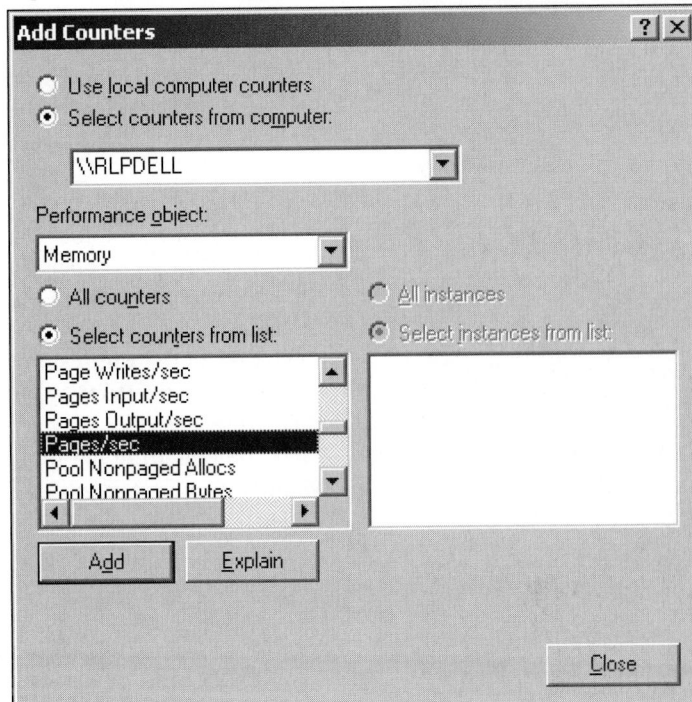

Figure 14-39 Creating a new log file

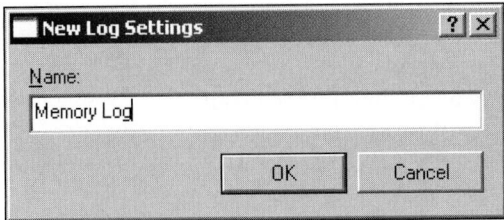

Figure 14-41 Setting the time interval for recording data in the log

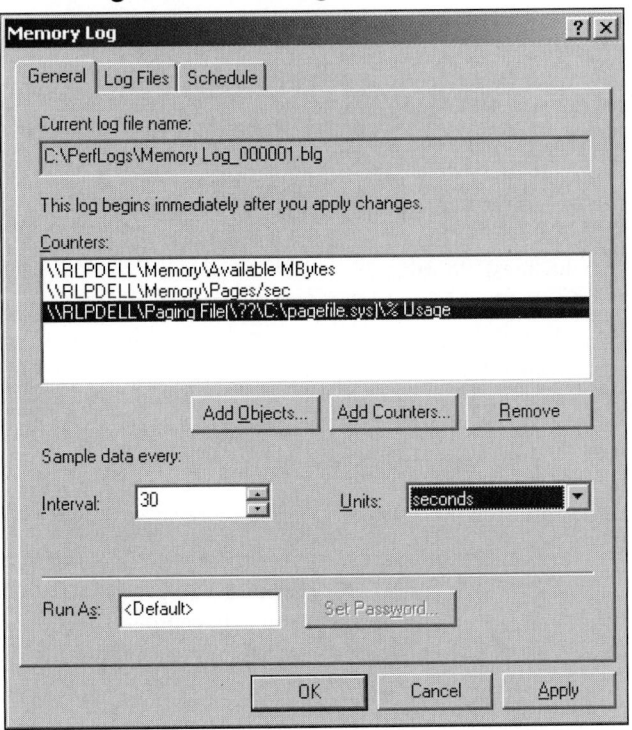

skill 5

Working with Performance Logs and Alerts (cont'd)

exam objective

Monitor file and print servers. Tools might include Task Manager, Event Viewer, and System Monitor. Monitor and analyze events. Tools might include Event Viewer and System Monitor. Monitor server hardware for bottlenecks. Monitor system performance. Monitor and optimize a server environment for application performance. Monitor memory performance objects.

how to

17. Select **Text File (Comma delimited)** in the **Log file type** list box to make the log file a comma-separated text file.
18. Click [Configure...] to open the **Configure Log Files** dialog box. You can change the default location for the log file in the **Location** text box.
19. Select the **Limit of** option button to specify a size limit for the log file.
20. Type **2028** in the **Limit of** text box (**Figure 14-42**). Click [OK]. Click [OK] again to create the **PerfLogs** folder if you receive a warning stating that C:\PerfLogs does not exist.
21. Click the **Schedule** tab to access the options for scheduling the log file. Select the **Manually** option button in the **Start log** section to indicate that you will manually start the log.
22. Select the **Manually** option button in the **Stop log** section, if necessary, to indicate that you will manually stop the log.
23. Click [OK] to save the configuration and close the Memory Log dialog box. To start the counter log, right-click **Memory Log** and click **Start**.
24. Right-click the **Alerts** node, and click **New Alert Settings** to open the **New Alert Settings** dialog box.
25. Type **Memory Alert** in the **Name** text box. Click [OK] to open the **Memory Alert** dialog box.
26. In the **Comment** text box on the **General** tab, enter the message that you want the alert to send. For example, type **You must add memory**.
27. Click [Add...] to open the **Add Counters** dialog box.
28. In the **Performance object** list box, select **Memory**. Make sure that the **Select counters from list** option button is selected. Hold down the [Ctrl] key, and select the **Available MBytes** and **Pages/sec** counters in the scrolling list box.
29. Click [Add] to add the selected counter to the alert.
30. In the **Performance object** list box, select **Paging File**.
31. In the **Select counters from list** box, select **%Usage** and click [Add].
32. Close the Add Counters dialog box.
33. Select the **Memory\Available MBytes** counter in the **Counters** scrolling list box. In the **Alert when the value is** list box, select **Under**, if necessary. In the **Limit** text box, enter the threshold value **25**.
34. Select the **Memory\Pages/sec** counter in the **Counters** list box. In the **Alert when the value is** list box, select **Over**. In the **Limit** text box, enter the threshold value **20** (**Figure 14-43**).
35. Select the **Paging File\%Usage** counter in the Counters list box. In the **Alert when the value is** list box, select **Over**. In the **Limit** text box, enter the threshold value **99**.
36. Click the **Action** tab to display the check boxes that you use to specify the action the alert should perform.
37. Select the **Send a network message to** check box.
38. Enter the name of the computer to which you want the alert to send a message. For example, type **\\Server1** (**Figure 14-44**).
39. Click the **Schedule** tab to display the options for starting the alert scan.
40. Select the **Manually (using the shortcut menu)** option button to indicate that you will manually start monitoring. **Manually** should also be automatically selected in the **Stop scan** section (**Figure 14-45**).
41. Click [OK] to save the configuration and close the Memory Alert dialog box. To start the alert, right-click Memory Alert and select **Start**.
42. Close the Performance console.

Figure 14-42 The Configure Log Files dialog box

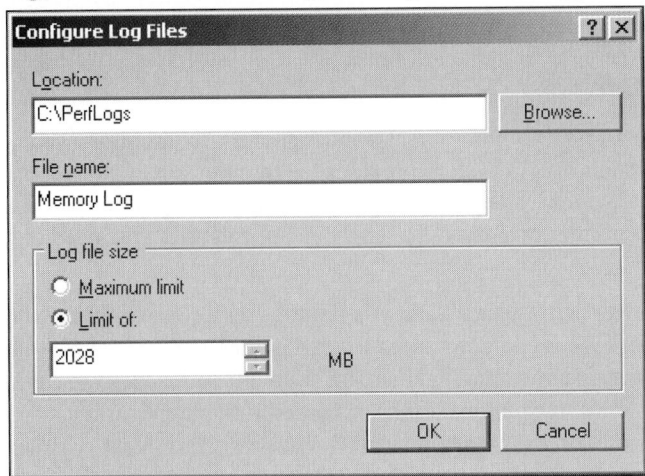

Figure 14-43 Setting threshold values

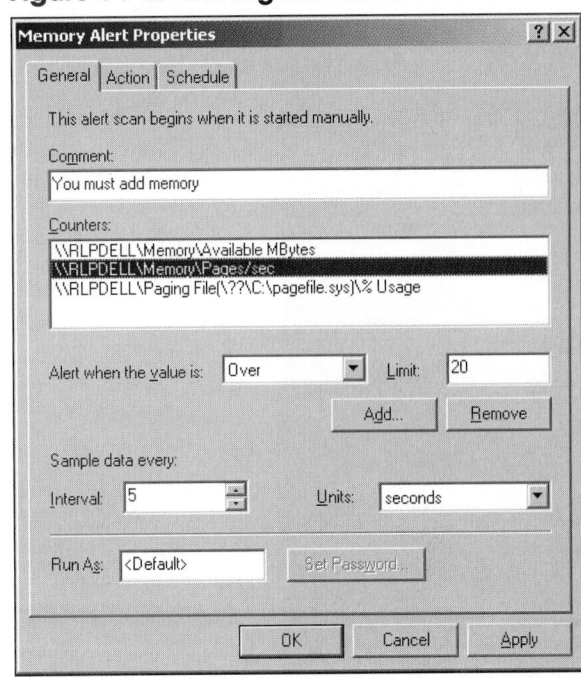

Figure 14-44 Sending an alert message

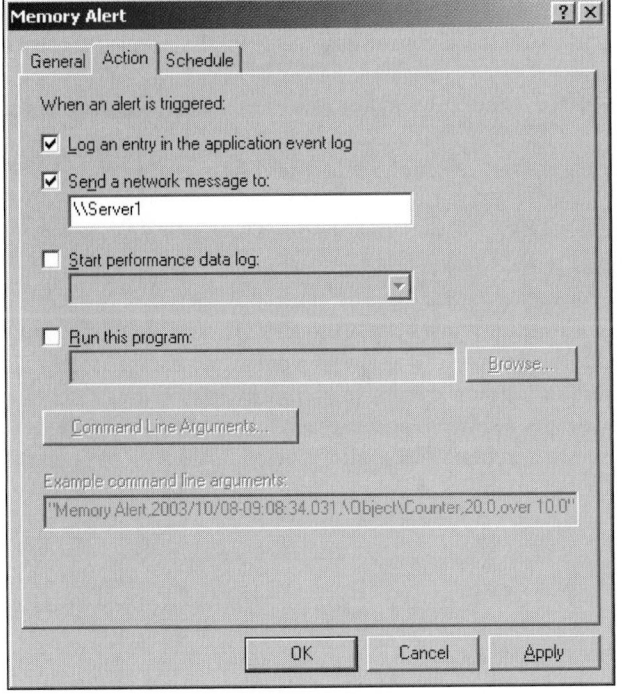

Figure 14-45 Scheduling the scan

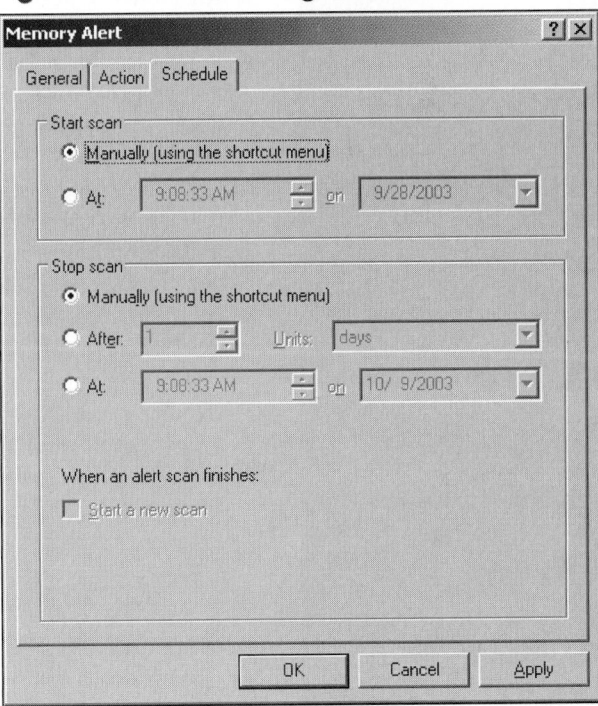

skill 6

Creating Trace Logs

exam objective

Monitor file and print servers. Tools might include Task Manager, Event Viewer, and System Monitor. Monitor and optimize a server environment for application performance. Monitor server hardware for bottlenecks. Monitor system performance.

overview

While counter logs use the System Monitor objects and counters to monitor system performance, **trace logs** use system or non-system providers to monitor a particular event over a period of time. A source provider is an operating system or application service that has traceable events. There are two system source providers on a domain controller: the operating system and Active Directory.

caution

Collecting page faults and file detail events increases system overhead and the log file can quickly increase in size. You should only collect page faults and file details for a short period of time.

Since trace logs do not track object performance data, you do not select counters when you configure them. Instead, trace logs record only instances when a particular event, such as an Active Directory Kerberos security event, a page fault, or disk input/output activity, occurs. As with a counter log, you can store trace log data for a specified time period. You can set begin and end times or you can start and stop them manually. However, you do not set time intervals at which to collect data. Trace logs monitor a particular event continuously, from start time to end time, and record data only when the event for the source provider occurs. Trace logs are typically used only in very specific situations, such as when debugging a custom application.

how to

Create a trace log.

1. Click ![Start], click **Run**, and type **perfmon** in the **Open** text box. Press [Enter] or click ![OK] to open the **Performance** console.
2. Right-click **Trace Logs** and click **New Log Settings**.
3. Type **Disk Input Output** in the **Name** text box and click ![OK].
4. In the Disk Input Output dialog box on the **General** tab, select the **Events logged by a system provider** option button.
5. Clear the checks from all of the other check boxes except **Disk input/output** (**Figure 14-46**).
6. Click the **Schedule** tab. Leave the default selection in the **Start Log** section, which will be the present time and date.
7. In the **Stop Log** section, select the **After** option button. In the **After** spin box, enter **2**. In the **Units** list box, select **hours** (**Figure 14-48**).
8. Click the **Log Files** tab. When you create a trace log, you can choose between two log file types: **Sequential Trace File** or **Circular Trace File**. A sequential trace file writes events as they occur up to the maximum log file size if you have set one. If no maximum log file size has been set, it will continue logging events sequentially. A circular trace log overwrites old events with new events when the log file reaches a specified size limit.
9. In the **Log file type** list box, select **Circular Trace File**. Click ![Configure...] to open the **Configure Log Files** dialog box.

tip

To choose a non-system provider, with the Non-system providers option button selected, click the Add button to open the Add Nonsystem Providers dialog box (**Figure 14-47**).

Figure 14-46 The General tab for a trace log

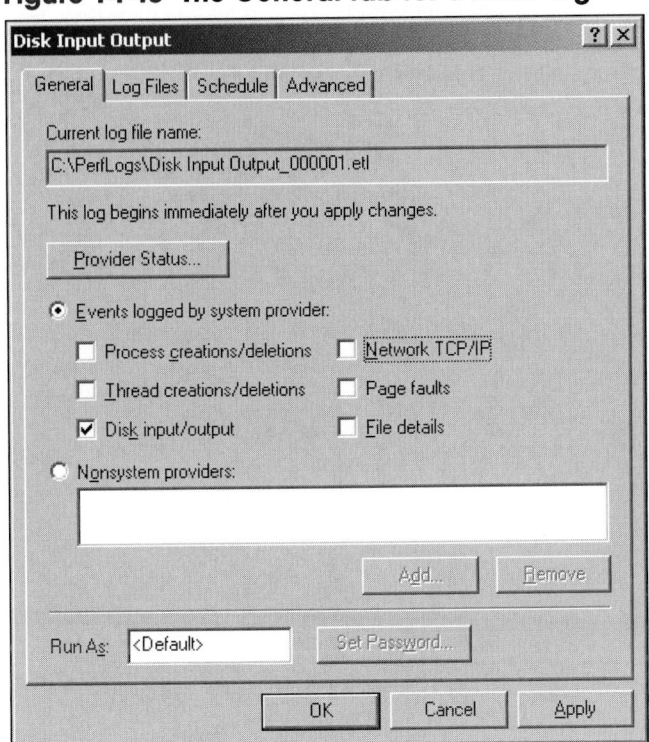

Figure 14-47 The Nonsystem Providers dialog box

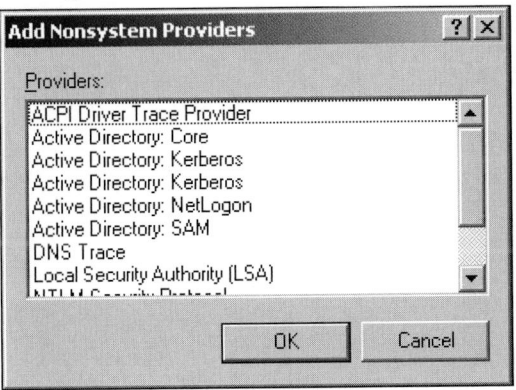

Figure 14-48 Setting the schedule for a trace log

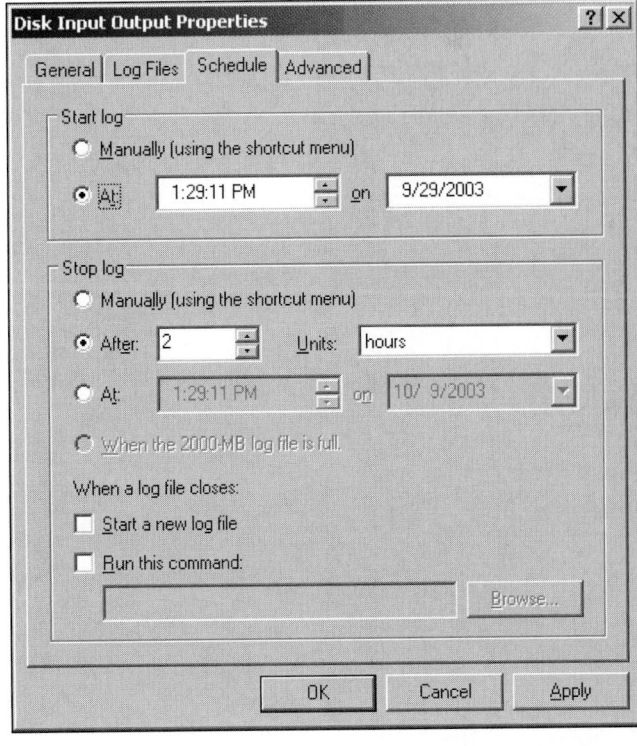

skill 6

Creating Trace Logs *(cont'd)*

Monitor file and print servers. Tools might include Task Manager, Event Viewer, and System Monitor. Monitor and optimize a server environment for application performance. Monitor server hardware for bottlenecks. Monitor system performance.

how to

10. In the **Limit of** spin box, enter **2000**. The maximum size is 4095 MB. Click [OK].
11. In the **End file names with** list box, select **yyyymmdd (Figure 14-49)**.
12. Click the **Advanced** tab. This is the only tab that is different from the dialog box for a counter log. Trace logs store data in memory buffers until the buffers are full. This is in contrast to counter logs, which log data in real-time. On the Advanced tab for a trace log, you can change the default settings to make the buffers larger or smaller. You can also set the number of seconds between transfers to force the buffers to write to the trace log at a set interval rather than waiting until the buffers are full (**Figure 14-50**).
13. Keep the default settings and click [OK] to close the Disk Input Output dialog box.
14. Close the Performance console.

more

Tracerptp.exe, which is included with Windows Server 2003, is a command-line tool that can be used to create a readable summary of trace log data. It uses the output from the buffers in the trace log file and parses it into a form that is readable. Using Tracerpt you can view trace log data in either summary .txt or .csv (Text file [comma delimited]) form. You can also perform real-time tracing by instructing Tracerpt to read directly from the buffers rather than from the trace log file.

Figure 14-49 Setting the file name ending

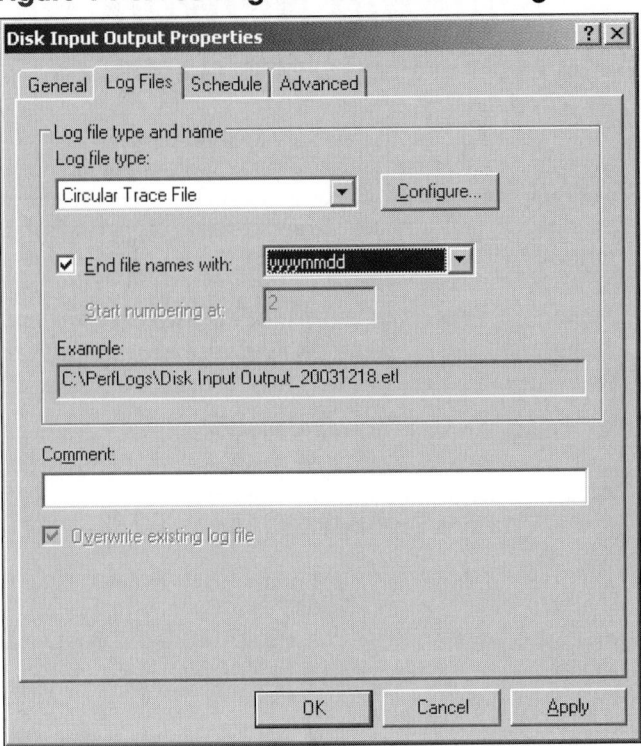

Figure 14-50 The Advanced tab for a trace log

Select to set the
number of seconds
between transfers
from the buffers to
the trace log file

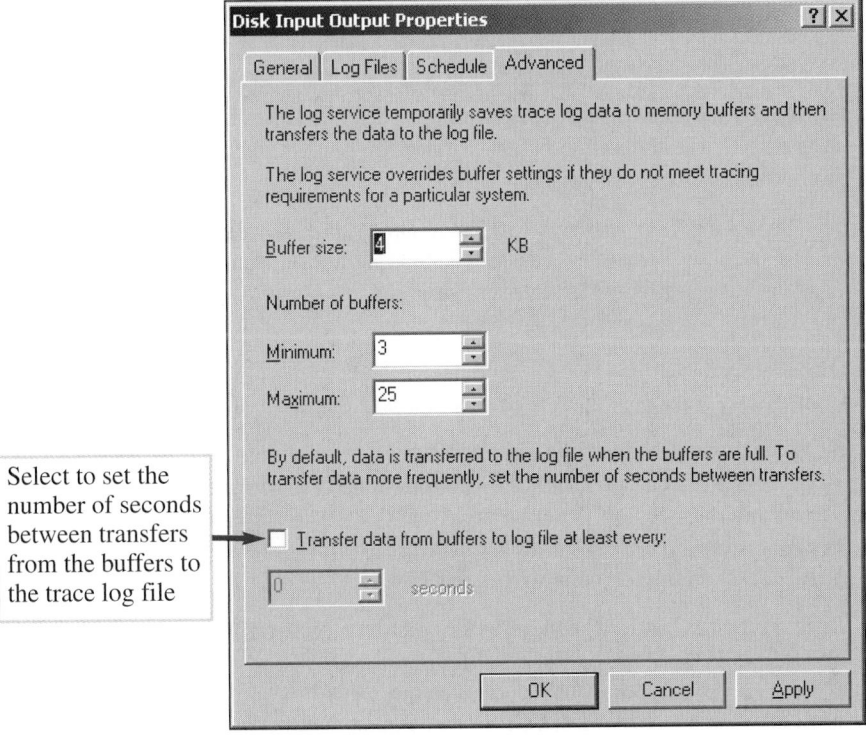

skill 7

Monitoring Network and Process Performance Objects

exam objective

Monitor file and print servers. Tools might include Task Manager, Event Viewer, and System Monitor. Monitor and analyze events. Tools might include Event Viewer and System Monitor. Monitor server hardware for bottlenecks. Monitor and optimize a server environment for application performance. Monitor network performance objects. Monitor process performance objects.

overview

Monitoring network performance has two components: monitoring servers to examine resource utilization and assessing overall network traffic. Microsoft recommends using the following objects and counters to fully monitor resource utilization (**Figure 14-51**).

Disk: Physical Disk\ Disk Reads/sec
       Physical Disk\ Disk Writes/sec
       Logical Disk\ % Free Space
       Physical Disk\ % Disk Time

These counters measure disk usage. The Total instance of the Physical Disk % Time must be analyzed along with the % Idle Time counter in order to accurately interpret disk usage on multi-disk systems. The Physical Disk\ Avg. Disk Queue Length (all instances) counter should also be used to monitor for disk bottlenecks.

Memory: \Available Bytes
         \Cache Bytes
         \Pages/sec
         \Page Reads/sec
         \Transition Faults/sec
         \Pool Paged Bytes
         \Pool Nonpaged Bytes
Paging File\% Usage object (all instances)
Cache\Data Map Hits %
Server\Pool Paged Bytes
Server\Pool Nonpaged Bytes

To monitor memory usage, the Memory\ Available Bytes and Memory\ Cache Bytes should be watched. The remaining object counters on the list above are used to monitor for memory bottlenecks.

Processor: Processor\ % Processor Time (all instances)
            System\Processor Queue Length (all instances)
            Processor\Interrupts/sec
            System\Context switches/sec

The Processor\%Processor Time counter is used to monitor processor usage. The other three counters are used to monitor for processor bottlenecks.

Assessing overall network traffic should be done in conjunction with some of these counters. In particular, when you configure network counters, you should watch them along with the Processor\% Processor Time, Physical Disk\% Disk Time, and Memory\Pages/sec counters because abnormal network counter values can indicate memory, processor, or disk bottlenecks rather than network bottlenecks.

To monitor for bottlenecked network resources, you can observe the Network Interface— Bytes Total/sec, Bytes Sent/sec, and Bytes Received/sec counters for each network adapter (NIC). The Bytes Received/sec counter measures the rate at which bytes are received from each network adapter over a TCP/IP connection and the Bytes Sent/sec counter measures the rate at which bytes are sent over each network adapter. Network Interface - Bytes Total/sec is the sum of the Bytes Sent/sec and Bytes Received/sec values. The Network Interface performance object also includes counters that monitor connection errors. The Network

Figure 14-51 Monitoring Server Resource Utilization

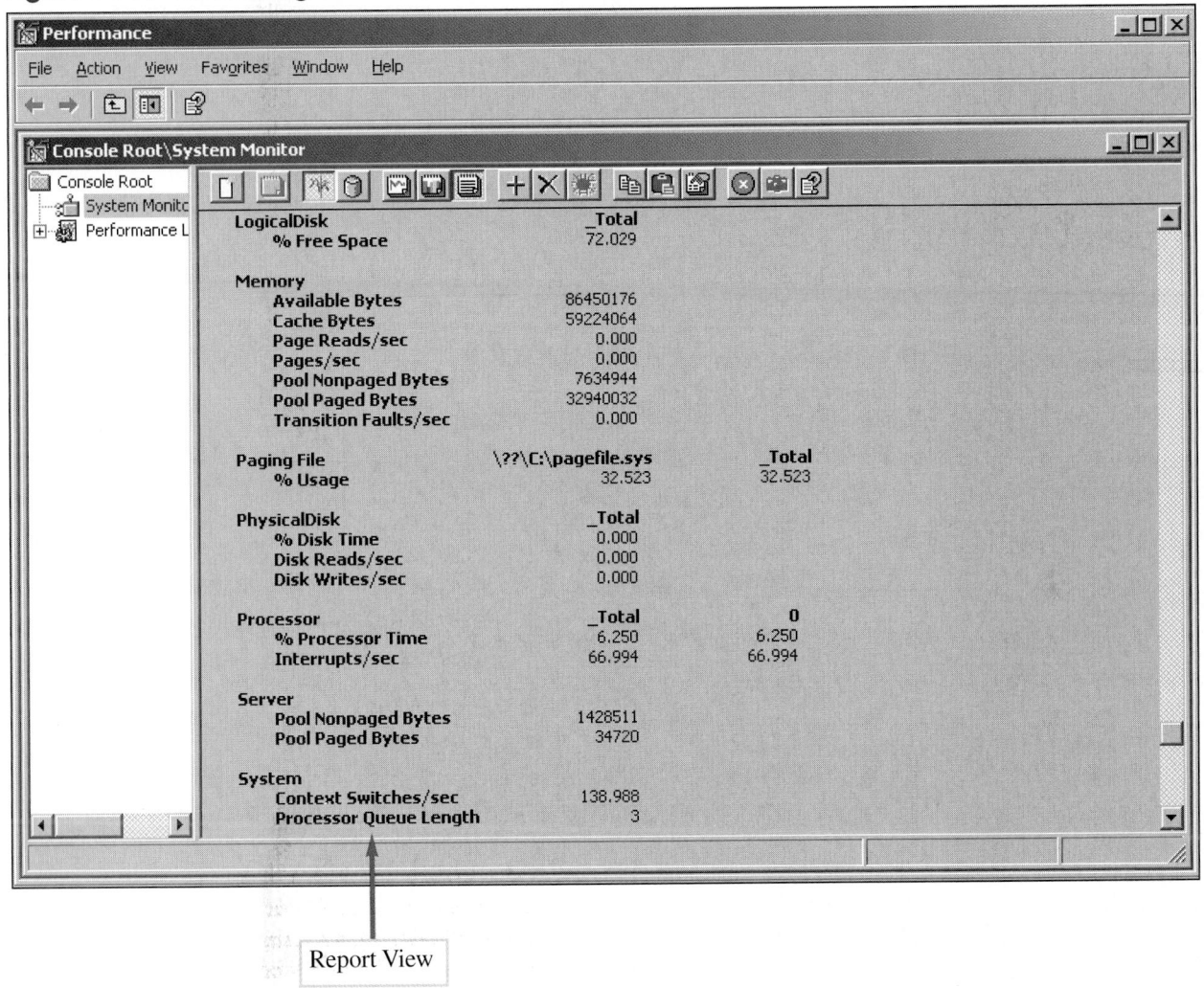

Report View

skill 7

Monitoring Network and Process Performance Objects (cont'd)

exam objective

Monitor file and print servers. Tools might include Task Manager, Event Viewer, and System Monitor. Monitor and analyze events. Tools might include Event Viewer and System Monitor. Monitor server hardware for bottlenecks. Monitor and optimize a server environment for application performance. Monitor network performance objects. Monitor process performance objects.

overview

Interface counters are described in **Table 14-4**. In the System Monitor, Instance 1 of the Network Interface object is for the loopback, which is the local path through the protocol stack. Each instance after that is for a NIC installed on the server. Monitoring counters for the Network Interface object represents monitoring the Data-Link layer of the OSI model.

In addition, you can monitor protocol objects, for example IPv4 (or IPv6), to examine network performance at the Network layer, and TCPv4 (or TCPv6) to examine network performance at the Transport layer. Among the important IP object counters are: Datagrams Forwarded/sec, Datagrams Received/sec, Datagrams Sent/sec, and Datagrams/sec. The IP-Datagrams Received/sec counter measures the rate at which IP datagrams are received from the network adapters excluding datagrams in error. The IP-Datagrams Sent/sec counter measures the rate at which IP datagrams are sent for transmission by local IP user-protocols, including ICMP datagrams, but excluding any datagrams counted by the IP- Datagrams Forwarded/sec counter. The Datagrams/sec counter measures the rate of both datagrams sent and received, including datagrams in error, but excluding forwarded datagrams.

At the Transport layer, the protocols you monitor will depend on the network protocol being used. On a TCP/IP network, you use the TCPv4 (or TCPv6) object counters: Segments Received/sec, Segments Retransmitted/sec, Segments/sec, and Segments Sent/sec. High values for the Segments Retransmitted/sec counter indicate a possible hardware problem.

To perform more in-depth analysis of TCP/IP network transmissions, you can use the ICMP (Network layer) and UDP (Transport layer) performance object counters. In addition to many other measurements, the ICMP (or ICMPv6) counters measure the rate at which Internet Control Message (ICMP) messages are sent and received and the number of ICMP protocol errors, both outbound and inbound. The UDPv4 (or UDPv6) object counters measure the rate at which UDP datagrams are sent and received, and the number of UDP errors received.

You can monitor the percentage of network bandwidth in use on a network segment using the Network Segment - % Network Utilization counter. The network utilization level that indicates a problem depends on the network infrastructure and topology. For example, if network utilization is above 30 to 40 percent on a 10 Mb un-switched, half-duplex Ethernet network segment, it is likely that collisions are causing network performance deterioration.

In general, network performance will deteriorate if network capacity is not sufficient to handle the volume of network traffic. You can monitor network-wide traffic levels using the counters for the Network Segment performance object so that this does not happen. The other two important Network Segment object counters are: Broadcast Frames Received/sec and Total Frames Received/sec. The Broadcast Frames Received/sec counter can be monitored over a period of time to establish a baseline level. If large increases in broadcast levels occur, network performance will deteriorate. When a network administrator observes that broadcast levels are significantly above the baseline levels, the problem can be explored to try to determine the cause. The Total Frames Received/sec counter can be used in conjunction with the Broadcast counter to determine the percentage of broadcasts in total frames. A high number of broadcasts in your total frame count either indicates a poorly written network application or a problem with a machine that is sending out too many broadcasts (known as a broadcast storm). It can also be an indicator that your network segment has grown too large and should be split into separate broadcast domains using a router or layer-3 switch. The Network Segment performance object is installed in Windows Server 2003 when you install

Table 14-4 Network Interface Object Counters

Counter	Description
Bytes Received/sec	Displays number of bytes/second received by each NIC. This includes framing characters and is a subset of Bytes Total/sec.
Bytes Sent/sec	Displays the number of bytes/second sent by each NIC. This includes framing characters and is a subset of Bytes Total/sec.
Bytes Total/sec	Displays the number of bytes both sent and received per second by each NIC. Sum of Bytes Received/sec + Bytes Sent/sec.
Current Bandwidth	Estimates the current bandwidth of a network interface in bits/second (bps). When no accurate estimate can be determined, or on interfaces that have no bandwidth variation, this will display the bandwidth assigned to the interface (nominal bandwidth).
Output Queue Length	Displays the number of packets in the output packet queue. A value greater than 2 indicates a bottleneck. The network I/O adapter is waiting for the network and cannot keep up with server requests to move data onto the network. Theoretically, since requests are queued by Network Driver Interface Specification (NDIS), this value should always be 0.
Packets Outbound Discarded	Displays the number of outbound packets that were discarded even though no errors were found. Sometimes packets that can be transmitted are discarded because buffer space must be freed up.
Packets Outbound Errors	Displays the number of outbound packets that have errors and thus cannot be transmitted.
Packets Received Discarded	Displays the number of inbound packets that were discarded even though no errors were found. Packets may not be delivered to a higher-level protocol because buffer space must be freed up.
Packets Received Errors	Displays the number of inbound packets that have errors and thus cannot be transmitted to a higher-layer protocol.
Packets Received Non-Unicast/sec	Displays the number of non-unicast packets received/second. This includes both broadcast and multicast packets on the subnet that were delivered to a higher-layer protocol.
Packets Received Unicast/sec	Displays the number of unicast packets on the subnet that were delivered to a higher-layer protocol per second.
Packets Received Unknown	Displays the number of packets that were discarded because they used an unknown or unsupported protocol.
Packets Received/sec	Displays the number of packets received by the network interface per second.
Packets Sent/sec	Displays the number of packets sent by the network interface per second.
Packets Sent Non-Unicast/sec	Displays the number of packets that were requested to be sent to non-unicast addresses by higher-level protocols. This consists of both broadcast and multicast packets on the subnet and includes discarded packets.
Packets Sent Unicast/sec	Displays the number of packets per second that were requested to be transmitted by a higher-layer protocol, including discarded packets.

skill 7

Monitoring Network Performance Objects (cont'd)

exam objective

Monitor file and print servers. Tools might include Task Manager, Event Viewer, and System Monitor. Monitor and analyze events. Tools might include Event Viewer and System Monitor. Monitor server hardware for bottlenecks. Monitor and optimize a server environment for application performance. Monitor network performance objects. Monitor process performance objects.

overview

Network Monitor Tools, and it is the Network Monitor that is used to analyze network segment statistics (See Skill 10).

Finally, to get a general picture of how busy the server is, you can use the Server—Bytes Total/sec, Bytes Received/sec and Bytes Transmitted/sec counters. If the sum of the Server—Bytes Total/sec counter for all network servers is approaching the maximum transfer rates (i.e., 10 MB/sec or 100 MB/sec), you may need to segment the network **(Figure 14-52)**. Monitoring Server object counters represents monitoring the server at the Session, Presentation, and Application layers in the OSI model. The Server object counters collect data about requests received by the Server service.

If you want to monitor network connections that originate from a client computer, you use the Redirector object counters on the client. The Redirector object counters collect data about requests transmitted by the Workstation service.

more

In order to monitor application and system processes that are currently running, you use the Process performance object counters. Within a single process, all threads are assigned the same address space and can access the same data. Some of the important Process object counters include % Privileged Time, % User Time, and % Processor Time. Privileged Time refers to a processing mode that allows direct access to hardware and memory. Privileged time indicates processor resources used by the operating system. User Time refers to a processing mode that is used by applications, environment subsystems, and integral subsystems. Application threads must be switched from user mode to privileged mode so that they can access operating system services. The % Privileged Time counter measures the percentage of non-idle processor time spent executing code in privileged mode. The % User Time counter measures the percentage of processor time spent executing code in user mode. Applications, environment subsystems, and integral subsystems execute in user mode. The Windows Executive, the kernel, and the device drivers are protected from code executing in user mode. A high value for the %Privileged Time counter could indicate a faulty device that is generating a large number of interrupts.

Windows Server 2003 system services often run in privileged mode so that they can access private system data that is protected from user mode thread access. The protection of privileged mode from user mode has traditionally been a feature of Windows operating systems. In the Windows 2000 and Windows Server 2003 operating systems, additional protection is provided by process boundaries, which supply protection for subsystem processes. Thus, some operating system processes performed for an application may not be included in privileged time.

The % Processor Time counter for the Process object measures the percentage of time the processor spends executing a non-idle thread (in effect, the percentage of time the processor is busy). Every processor has an idle thread that uses processor cycles when no other threads are ready to run. %Processor Time is measured by subtracting the time period during which the idle thread is active from 100% to determine the amount of time the processor is active during the measurement period.

Some of the other counters for the Process performance object are outlined in **Table 14-5**.

Figure 14-52 Finding Network Bottlenecks

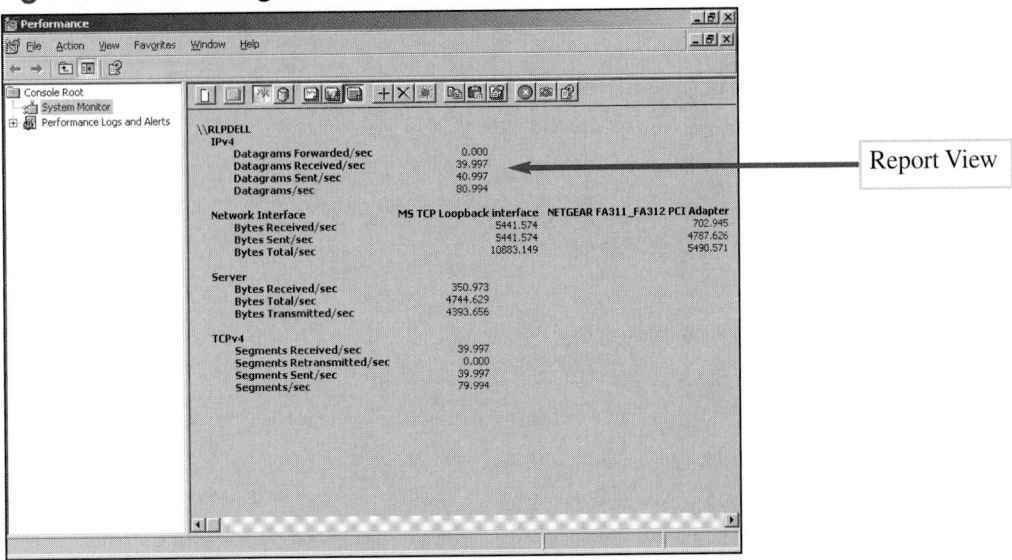

Report View

Table 14-5 Process Object Counters

Counter	Description
Page Faults/sec	Displays the number of page faults per second handled by the operating system. Page faults are classified as either hard or soft faults. Hard faults require disk access and can cause system delays. Soft faults occur elsewhere in physical memory and the CPU can handle many of them. Page faults are caused when a process needs code or data that is not in its working set. The working set is the set of pages in memory that were recently touched by the threads in the process.
Page File Bytes	Displays the number of bytes of virtual memory a process has reserved for use in the paging file/files. Pages of memory used by a process are stored in paging files, which are shared by all processes. If the paging files do not have enough space, other processes may not be able to allocate memory. If there is no paging file, this counter measures the current amount of virtual memory set aside for use by the process in RAM.
Page File Bytes Peak	Displays the maximum number of bytes in virtual memory that a process has reserved for use in the paging file/files. If there is no paging file, this counter measures the maximum amount of virtual memory set aside for use by the process in RAM.
Priority Base	Displays the current base priority of this process, which is the priority at which all of the threads for this processes will begin. In a single process, threads can raise and lower their base priority compared to the base priority for the process.
Private Bytes	Displays the number of bytes allocated by this process that it cannot share with other processes. This counter is mainly used for debugging.
Working Set	Displays the number of bytes in the working set for this process. If the computer has unused memory above a certain threshold, pages in the working set will be kept there even if they are not in use, but when unused memory drops below the threshold level, pages will be removed from the working set. If the removed pages are needed, soft faults will be generated to replace them before leaving main memory.
Elapsed Time	Displays the number of seconds this process has been running.
Handle Count	Displays the total number of handles this process currently has open. It is the sum of the number of handles each thread in this process currently has open.
Thread Count	Displays the number of active threads in this process.
Virtual Bytes	Displays the number of bytes of virtual address space the process is using. If a process is using too much virtual address space, it may not be able to load libraries.
Virtual Bytes Peak	Displays the maximum number of bytes of virtual address space a process has used at any time.
Working Set Peak	Displays the maximum number of bytes in the working set for a process.

skill 8

Tracking Windows Server 2003 Activities with Audit Policy

exam objective

Basic knowledge

overview

caution

Auditing increases the overhead on a computer. File system reads take place frequently, which can overload the Security event log and cause both disk space and performance shortfalls. Therefore, you must decide which events are important to track to meet the needs of your network.

Each time a user logs on to a computer or to a network, he or she performs a number of activities, including accessing files, folders, printers, and the Registry and the logon process itself. These activities are called events. As a network administrator, you will want to track and monitor some of these events on a regular basis in order to ensure the security and seamless functioning of the computers on the network. Auditing is used to track user activities and object access on the computers on a network. First, you will need to determine which events need to be audited. Auditing can be used to track exactly who logged on to a computer or a domain and when, what files were accessed or folders were created, what printers were used, what Registry keys were accessed when, and by whom, and what actions the users attempted to perform on them. In order to audit who is accessing which objects and what actions they are performing on those objects, you must first activate the audit object access policy. No auditing is set up for either servers or workstations by default, with the sole exception of Windows Server 2003 domain controllers, which have a minimal auditing level. Then you configure the audit object access policy in the Properties dialog box and the System ACL editor for the object.

At this point, it might help to distinguish between a System ACL (SACL) and a Discretionary ACL (DACL). A System ACL (SACL) is used to allow the system administrator to log any attempts to gain access to an object. The list of ACEs (access control entries) in the SACL will determine which users and groups will be audited. A discretionary ACL (DACL), which is used to set permissions, determines which users and groups can and cannot access the object, and is controlled by the owner of the object or anyone who has been granted the right to change permissions for the object.

You can audit local users or local groups, and if the computer is in a domain, domain users, and domain groups. After you select who you are going to audit, you must choose what file system actions you want to monitor in the SACL editor for the file or folder. For example, you can audit who is viewing a folder, creating a file, changing permissions, or viewing permissions. You can also specify whether or not the subfolders within a folder should inherit the auditing settings. If you are enabling auditing for a subfolder, you can specify whether or not it should inherit the auditing settings of its parent folder.

In an organization, auditing is used to help prevent security breaches by allowing you to track unauthorized attempts to log on or access folders. Auditing is also used to help conduct resource planning for the computers on your network. For example, you may discover that too many users are accessing a particular printer on the network, and that this printer is overtaxed. Based on this finding, you may decide to install another printer.

tip

You can configure an audit policy for any Group Policy, not just the Default Domain Policy. For example, to implement audit policy for domain controllers, you configure audit policy settings in the Default Domain Controllers Policy for the Domain Controllers OU.

In order to monitor a particular event, you must define an audit policy. To configure audit policy on non-domain, stand-alone workstations or servers, access the **Audit Policy** folder under the **Local Policies** node in the **Local Security Settings** console. On a domain controller, you can modify the Default Domain Policy to configure audit policy for the domain. In the **Group Policy Management** console, open the node for the domain for which you want to modify the policy, right-click **Default Domain Policy** and click **Edit** to open the **Group Policy Object Editor**. Under **Computer Configuration**, expand the **Windows Settings** node, double-click **Security Settings**, double-click **Local Policies**, and double-click **Audit Policy** to view the available audit policies (**Figure 14-53**). Only Domain Administrators and Enterprise Administrators can configure auditing at the domain level, and set up and modify the SACL on a domain controller.

The audit policy tells the operating system what to record in the Security log on each computer. The events you can audit are explained in **Table 14-6**. When you define an audit policy, you select the events you want to track and decide whether to track the success or failure, or

Figure 14-53 Modifying the default domain audit policy

If you change audit policy in the Default Domain Policy GPO, which links to the root of the domain, the same audit policy will be applied to every computer in the domain unless a higher priority GPO or a GPO linked to a lower OU has a conflicting audit policy

The audit policies that can be configured on all computers

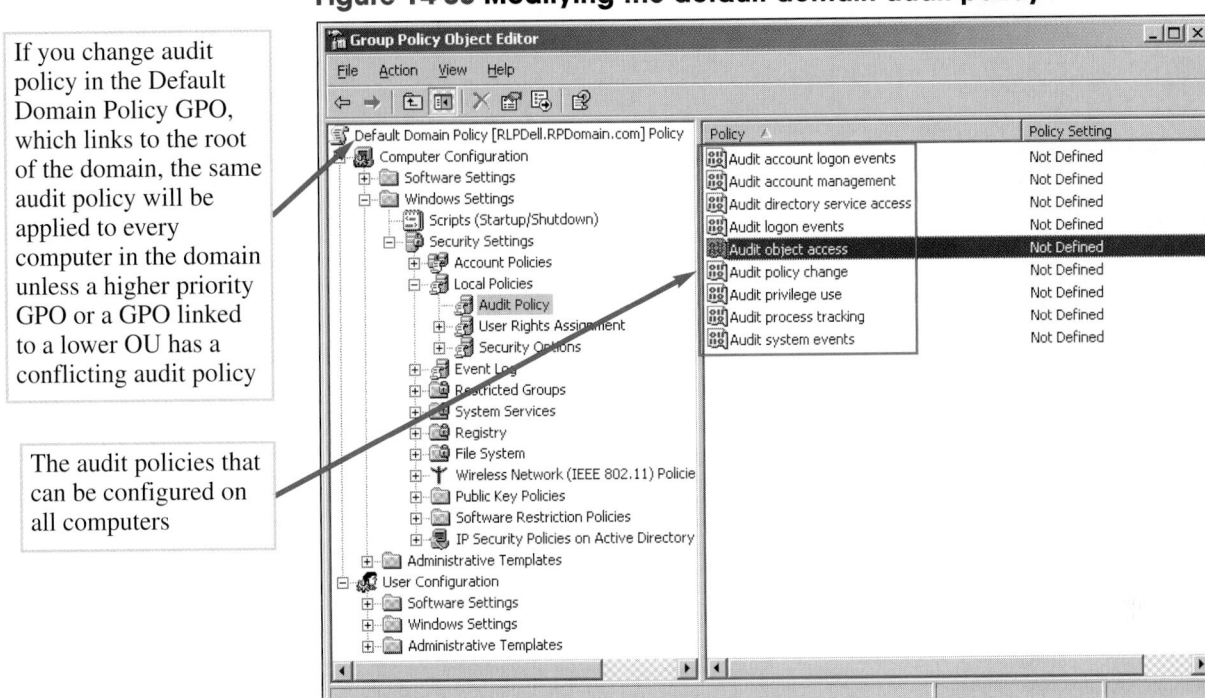

Table 14-6   Events that can be audited

Event	Description
Account Logon Events	The computer has joined a domain and a request to log on to the domain is sent to the domain controller.
Account Management	An account or group is created, deleted, or modified, or a user account is renamed, has a new password set, or is activated or disabled.
Directory Service Access	The computer has joined a domain and an Active Directory object, such as a computer or domain, is accessed.
Logon Events	Users log on or off a computer, or make or cancel a network connection.
Object Access	A file, folder, Registry key, or printer is accessed.
Policy Change	User rights, audit policies, or user security options are changed.
Privilege Use	A user successfully exercises a right, such as Take Ownership or Print, or when a user unsuccessfully tries to use a right that has not been assigned to them.
Process Tracking	A program is executed by a user. Process tracking allows you to monitor what each process is doing in the foreground and the background, as well as how long the program ran. However, a huge Security log will be generated, so this is generally only used for application development purposes.
System Events	A computer is shut down or restarted, or some event that concerns the Security log has taken place, such as clearing an event log.

skill 8

Tracking Windows Server 2003 Activities with Audit Policy (cont'd)

exam objective

Basic knowledge

overview

both, for the event. For example, if you want to audit the system events that occur on your computer, such as when a user restarts or shuts down their computer, you will activate the **Audit system events** policy and specify whether to audit successes or failures or both. Audited events are stored in the **Security log** (also called the Security event log). You can view the Security log using the **Event Viewer** snap-in in the Computer Management console.

how to

Configure audit policies and monitor object access for a folder on an NTFS volume or partition on your member server.

1. Click [Start], point to **Administrative Tools**, and click **Local Security Policy** to open the **Local Security Settings** console.
2. Double-click **Local Policies**. Click **Audit Policy** to view the list of audit policies in the details pane.
3. Double-click **Audit logon events** to open the **Audit logon events Properties** dialog box.
4. Select the **Failure** check box to track failed logon attempts (**Figure 14-54**).
5. Click [OK] to save the settings and close the Audit logon events Properties dialog box.
6. Double-click **Audit object access** to open the **Audit object access Properties** dialog box.
7. Select the **Success** check box to track successful object access attempts and the **Failure** check box to track failed object access attempts (**Figure 14-55**).
8. Click [OK] to close the Audit object access Properties dialog box.
9. Close the **Local Security Settings** console.
10. Right-click [Start] and click **Explore** to open Windows Explorer. Locate and double-click the NTFS partition where you have created the **Annual Reports** folder.
11. Right-click the **Annual Reports** folder and click **Properties** to open the **Annual Reports Properties** dialog box.
12. Click the **Security** tab, and click [Advanced...] to open the **Advanced Security Settings for Annual Reports** dialog box.
13. Click the **Auditing** tab. The **Allow inheritable auditing entries from parent to propagate to this object and all child objects**. The **Include these with entries explicitly defined here** check box is selected by default. This default means that the auditing settings for the parent folder are inherited by this folder.
14. Select the **Replace auditing entries on all child objects with entries shown here that apply to child objects** check box. Any pre-existing auditing settings on the subfolders in the **Annual Reports** folder will be reset and will now inherit the settings you are configuring for the Annual Reports folder (**Figure 14-56**).
15. Click [Add...] to open the **Select User, Computer, or Group** dialog box.
16. Click [Advanced...] to expand the dialog box. Click [Find Now] to display the groups and users in the domain in the **Search results** pane.
17. Scroll down and select the **Everyone** group. Click [OK] to enter the Everyone group in the **Enter the object name to select** box in the Select User, Computer, or Group dialog box.
18. Click [OK] to close the Select User, Computer, or Group dialog box.
19. The **Auditing Entry for Annual Reports** dialog box opens.
20. Select the **Successful** check box for the **Create Files/Write Data** access.

tip

The Audit account logon events policy is used to monitor either successful or failed attempts to log on to a domain.

tip

Audit policy is also activated through policy refresh, which by default occurs every 90-120 minutes on each workstation.

Figure 14-54 Tracking failed logon attempts

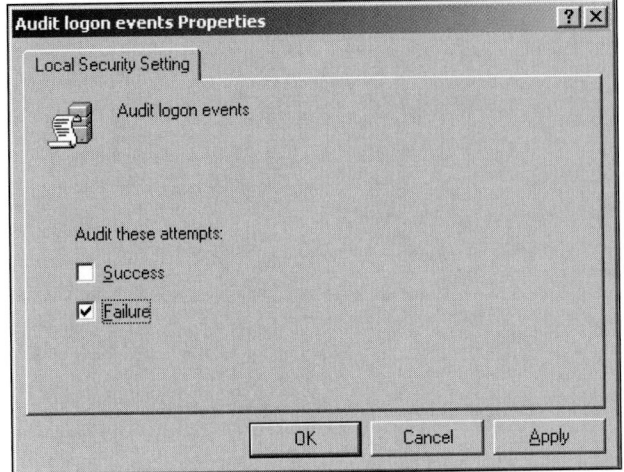

Figure 14-55 Tracking both successful and failed object access

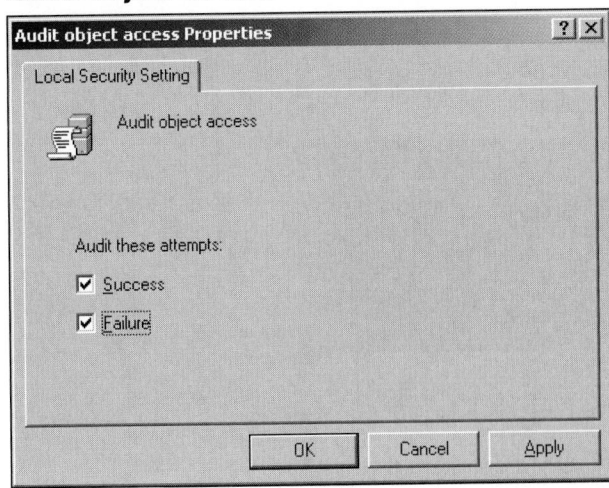

Figure 14-56 Advanced Security Settings for Annual Reports dialog box

Click to open the Select User, Computer, or Group dialog box where you can choose who or what to audit

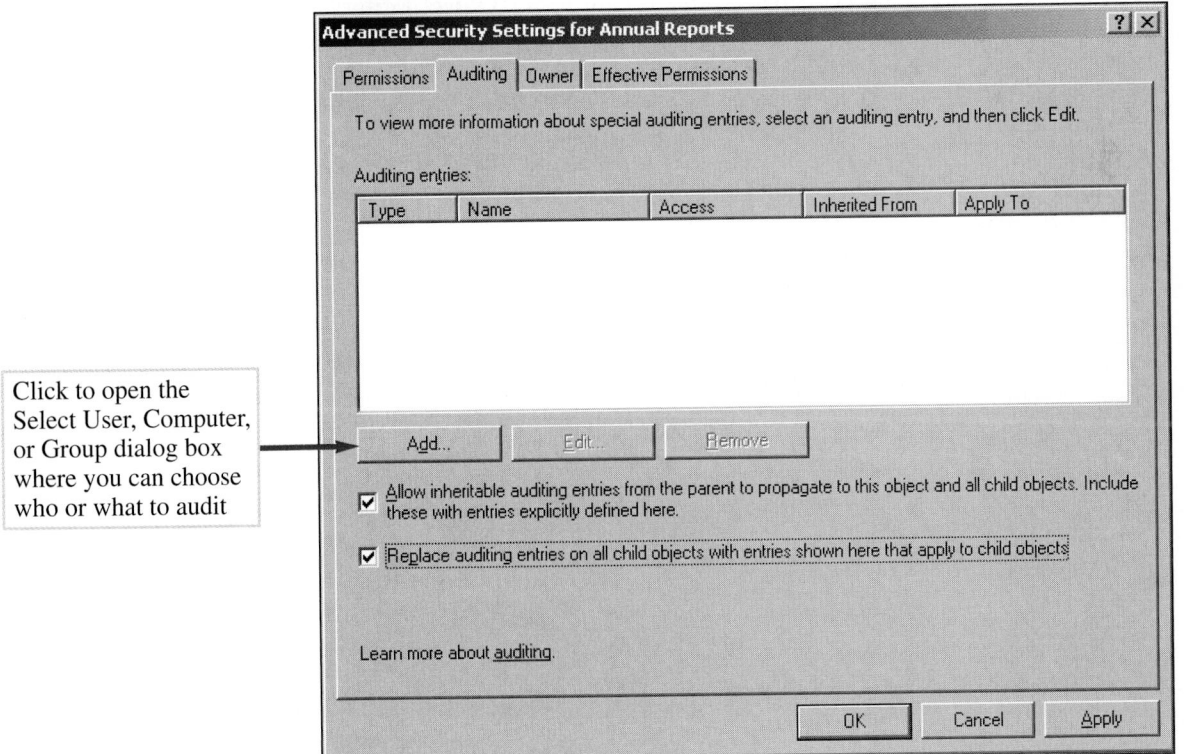

skill 8

Tracking Windows Server 2003 Activities with Audit Policy (cont'd)

exam objective

Basic knowledge

how to

21. Select the **Successful** check box for the **Delete Subfolders and Files** access (**Figure 14-57**).

22. Click [OK] to close the **Auditing Entry for Annual Reports** dialog box.

23. Click [OK] to close the **Advanced Security Settings for Annual Reports** dialog box.

24. Click [OK] to close the **Annual Reports Properties** dialog box. Close Windows Explorer.

more

You can enable or change audit entries only if you are an Administrator on the computer on which you are configuring the policy or if you have the **Manage auditing and security log** permission, which is granted to the Administrators group by default. You can only audit folders and files on NTFS volumes or partitions.

You can use the **Computer Management** console to view the Security log on a remote computer if you have administrative privileges. Open the **Action** menu and select **Connect to another computer** (**Figure 14-58**). Choose a computer in the **Select Computer** dialog box to connect to it and view the audit entries in the Security log (**Figure 14-59**).

To configure auditing for Active Directory objects, you must first enable the **Audit directory service access** policy in the **Group Policy Object Editor**. Then, in the **Active Directory Users and Computers** console, open the **View** menu and select **Advanced Features**. Select the appropriate folder, Computers, Domain Controllers, Users, etc., and select the object you want to audit. Open the **Security** tab in the **Properties** dialog box for the object. Click the **Advanced** button and configure auditing for the object on the **Auditing** tab just as you did in the exercise.

Figure 14-57 Selecting the actions to be audited

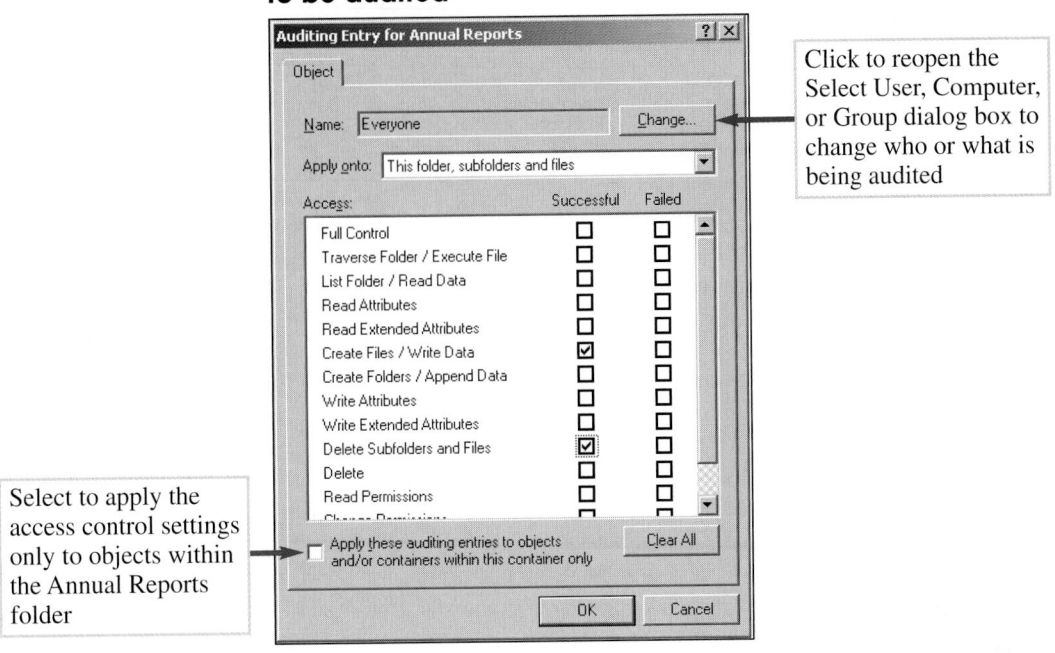

Click to reopen the Select User, Computer, or Group dialog box to change who or what is being audited

Select to apply the access control settings only to objects within the Annual Reports folder

Figure 14-58 Connecting to a remote computer

In the Computer Management console, you can view the audit entries in the Security log on a remote computer if you have administrative privileges

Figure 14-59 The Select Computer dialog box

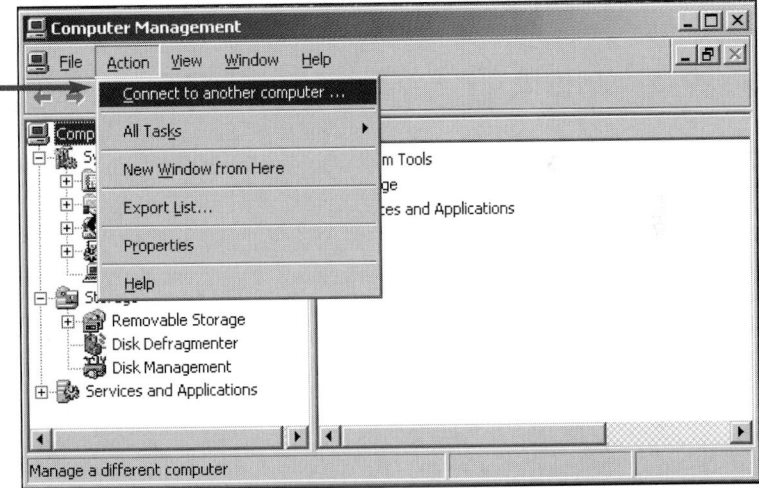

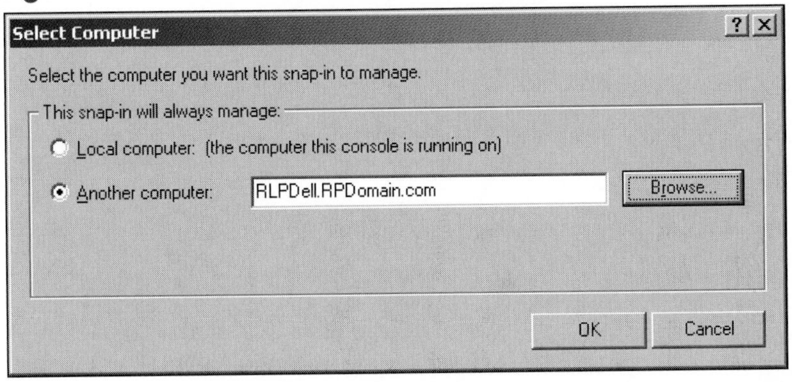

skill 9

Viewing the Security Log

exam objective

Basic knowledge

overview

When you implement audit policies, remember that auditing increases the overhead on a computer. The CPU will be frequently reading file systems and the Security event log can become inundated with entries, which can cause problems with both disk space and performance. This underscores the importance of deciding which events are important to track for your circumstances. Once you have carefully chosen the events you think are important to monitor, for whom you want to monitor them, and what actions you want to track, you must set a schedule for yourself to check the Security log regularly. You can also maintain the size of the Security log by specifying a maximum file size. When the Security log reaches the maximum file size, you can choose to either overwrite old events as needed, set a specific age for the events you want to be overwritten, or prevent events from being overwritten. If you choose the first option, you could lose data if the log becomes full before you archive it. If you choose the second option, you could lose data that is at least as many days old as you have chosen if you do not archive the log soon enough. If you choose the final option, you must make sure that you monitor the Security log often enough to archive or clear the log before it becomes full, because when the log is full the operating system will stop recording events **(Figure 14-60)**. Archiving is the process you use to save a history of the Security events you are auditing so that you can track trends in resource usage. You use the Event Viewer to view the Security log and to archive old log files and store them for future reference.

When you open the Security log, by default, all events that have been recorded are shown. However, you can change what is shown in the log viewer and locate specific events on the **Filter** tab. To open the Properties dialog box for the Security log on the Filter tab, use the **Filter** command on the **View** menu. You can also locate specific events using the **Find** command. To filter events, you must specify one or more of the following criteria **(Figure 14-61)**:

◆ **Event type:** You can choose to view events of a certain type: Information, Warning, Error, or Success or Failure audit.

◆ **Event source:** You can choose to view events logged from a particular source, for example the Spooler, LSA (Local Security Authority), or SC (Service Control) Manager.

◆ **Category:** You can choose to view a particular category of event after choosing an event source. For example, you can view Account Logon, Account Management, Directory Service Access, Privilege Use, Object Access, and other events.

◆ **Event ID:** You can enter an event ID number to view only events of that type.

◆ **User:** You can enter a specific user name to view Security events that have been logged for that user.

◆ **Computer:** You can enter a specific computer name to view Security events that have been logged for that computer

◆ **Specific time periods:** You can enter beginning and end dates and times to view events in a certain time period.

Figure 14-60 The Security (log) Properties dialog box

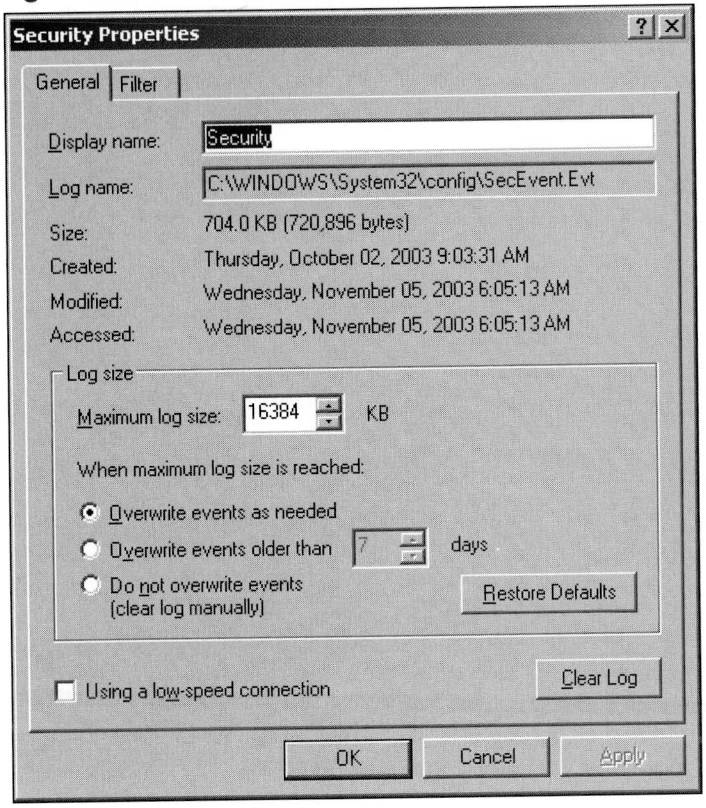

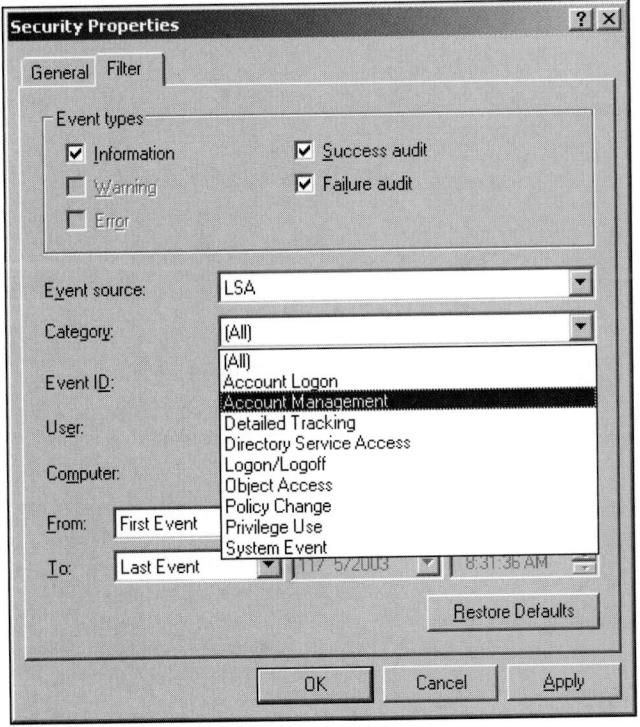

Figure 14-61 The Filter tab in the Security Properties dialog box

Exam 70-290

skill 9

Viewing the Security Log (cont'd)

exam objective

Basic knowledge

how to

Use Event Viewer to view the Security log on your member server, and use the **Filter** command to view only failed and successful file object access.

1. Log off of the **Administrator** account. Attempt to log back on using any user account you have created on the computer. Enter an incorrect user name on your first logon attempt. Enter an incorrect password on your second logon attempt. Log on successfully on your third attempt.
2. Create a file named **Balance Sheet** and save it in the **Annual Reports** folder. Close the file.
3. Log off of the user account and log back on as an Administrator.
4. Click [*Start*], point to **Administrative Tools**, and click **Event Viewer** to open the **Event Viewer** snap-in.
5. Click **Security** in the left pane to list the events recorded in the Security log in the details pane (**Figure 14-62**).
6. Open the **View** menu and click **Filter** to open the **Security Properties** dialog box on the **Filter** tab.
7. Clear the **Information**, **Warning**, and **Error** check boxes to filter out these event types.
8. Type the user name you used in the **User** text box to specify that events related only to this user should appear in the Security log.
9. Select **Security** in the **Event source** list box. Select **Object Access** in the **Category** list box (**Figure 14-63**).
10. Click [OK] to close the Security Log Properties dialog box. The Security log now lists only object access attempts by the User account name that you used in steps 1 and 2. Success audits are recorded with a key icon and failure audits are recorded with a lock icon.
11. Double-click the first event in the Security log to open the **Event Properties** dialog box. Click [↓] to scroll down the list of events until you locate the success object access audit in which MKane saved the Balance Sheet file to the Annual Reports folder (**Figure 14-64**).
12. Click [OK] to close the Event Properties dialog box.
13. Close the Event Viewer.

more

Do not forget to examine the Security event log regularly. Configuring auditing will not warn you if security infringements are occurring. Your sensitive files should always be monitored by first setting an audit policy and then following up to see if unauthorized users are either attempting to access them or succeeding in accessing them. Do not audit events that are not essential either for enhancing the security of your system or for tracking developments in system usage.

You can set the size of the Security log from as low as 64 KB to as high as 4,194,240 KB (4GB).

Viewing the Security log in the Event Viewer requires the **Manage auditing and security** log right, the same right needed for configuring auditing, which is granted to the Administrators group by default.

Figure 14-62 The Security log

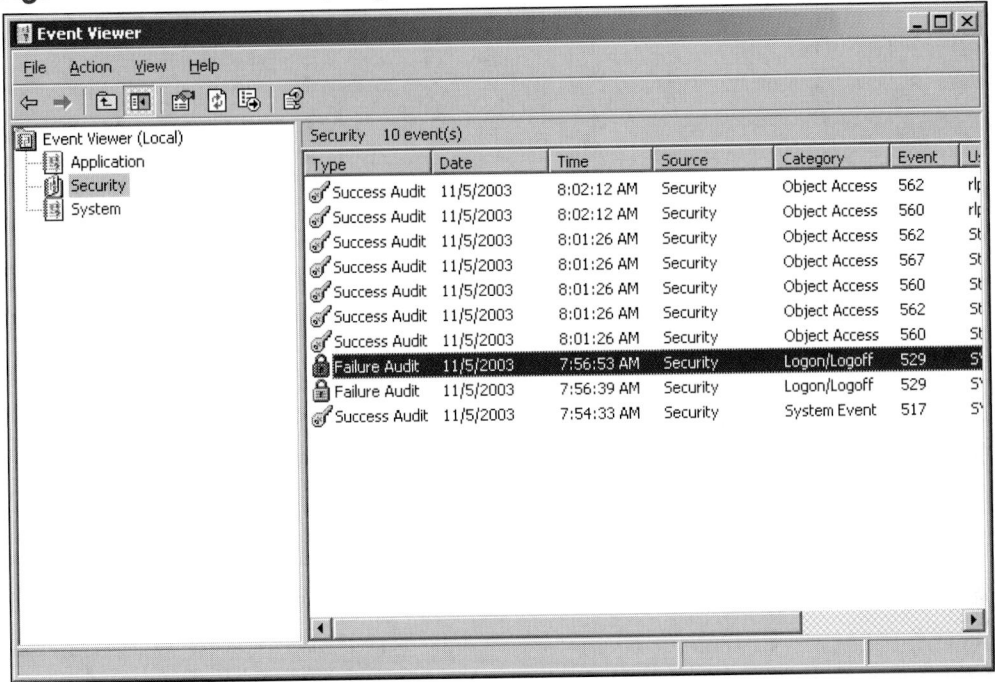

Figure 14-63 Filtering the Security log

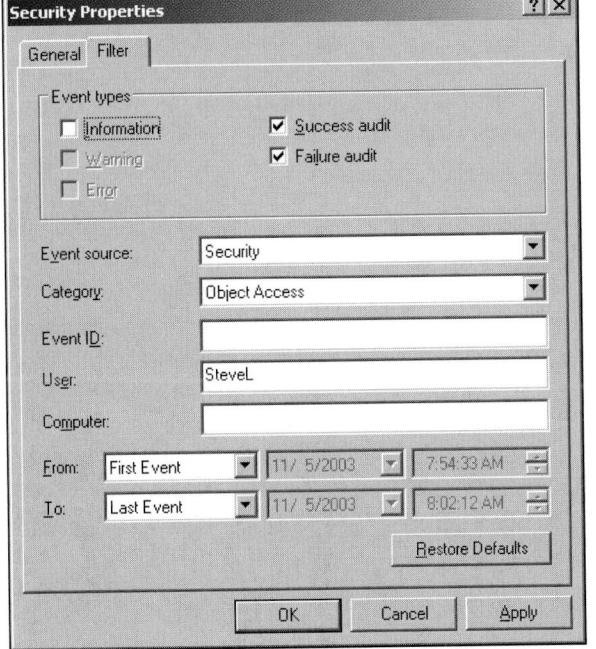

Figure 14-64 Viewing event details

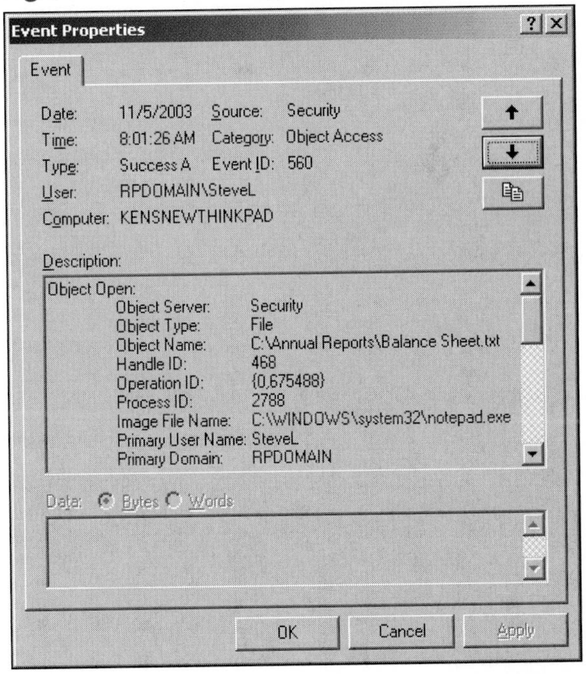

skill 10

Working with the Network Monitor

exam objective

Monitor and optimize a server environment for application performance. Monitor network performance objects.

overview

Changing network conditions will frequently necessitate administrative intervention, whether it is to proactively preempt slowdowns or to respond to an immediate crisis. For example, network performance can degrade due to increased user activity, a NIC on a server or a workstation that is causing a bottleneck by constantly broadcasting over the network (known as a broadcast storm), or a NIC on a server that is not fast enough to handle the number of client requests it is receiving. An inadequate processor on a server and numerous other causes can be at the root of a network problem. In order to effectively monitor your network, you must first lay the groundwork, just as you would when monitoring key network servers. Establishing benchmark behavior for the network is the key to identifying and solving problems as they emerge.

First, you will want to ascertain the pattern of network activity on your network. For example: When is your network the busiest, when is it the least busy, and what are the average workloads? You may also want to determine other network benchmarks, including network activity attributable to particular subnets, servers, workstations, applications, and protocols. Network benchmarks used in conjunction with server benchmarks can help you to optimize network performance and discover the causes of network difficulties when they occur.

In addition to the System Monitor, the other tools you can use to monitor the network include the Network Monitor Driver, Network Monitor, and SNMP service. The **Network Monitor Driver** works in conjunction with **Network Monitor** to make it possible for you to analyze frames (data packets) sent by and received from a NIC. You can use it to obtain network performance statistics that are used by System Monitor and Network Monitor to troubleshoot networking problems and monitor for specific network events.

The Network Monitor Driver protocol is used to collect statistics about the activity detected by the network card. These statistics are reported to, and can be viewed on, a Windows Server 2003 computer that is either running the Network Monitor Agent Service or Systems Management Server. After the Network Monitor Driver is installed, you can monitor the number of packets sent and received by a computer. The NIC gathers information about broadcasts, unicasts, and multicasts, as well as data regarding protocol traffic and network activity. Broadcasting refers to sending data to everyone on the network, while multicasting refers to sending messages only to a select group. Multicasting is a transmission method for sending identical data to a select group of recipients. The server can transmit a single stream, regardless of how many clients have requested it. A unicast transmission sends one copy of each data packet to the destination computers, which is inefficient when compared with multicasting. Multicasting sends a single data stream that can be received by multiple computers, whereas a unicast transmission requires that a data packet be sent to each recipient **(Figure 14-65)**. **Table 14-7** describes the functionality of broadcasts, unicasts, and multicasts in more depth.

Either a workstation or a server that is equipped with the Network Monitor can connect to a machine that is running the Network Monitor Driver to collect frames from the NIC. Remote computers that are connected to your network via RAS can also be configured to perform network analysis. The Network Monitor Driver is installed just like any other protocol in the Properties dialog box for the network connection.

Figure 14-65 Broadcast, multicast, and unicast

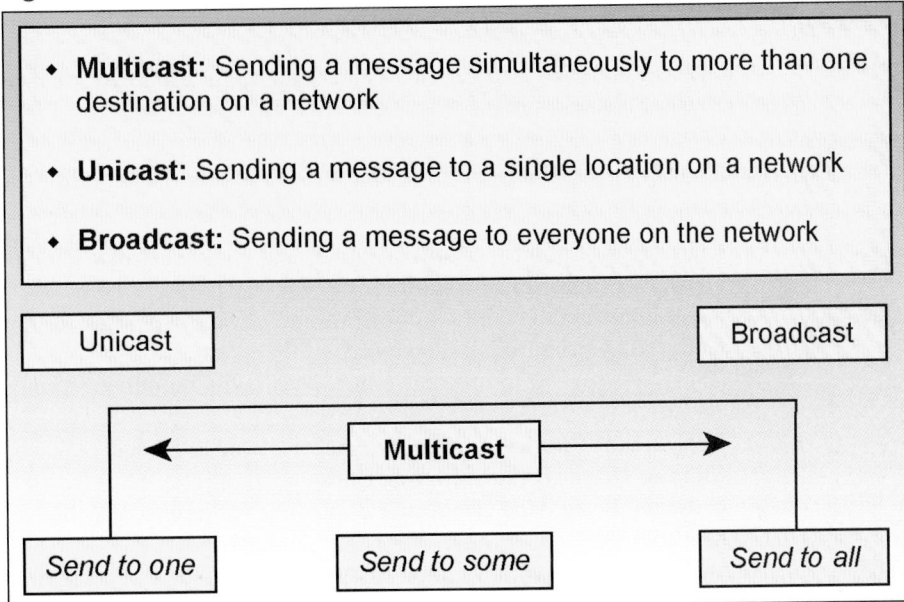

Table 14-7 Transmission types

Type	Functionality
Unicast	Communication between a single sender and a single receiver. A packet is sent from a single source to a specified destination. The standard unicast applications include HTTP, FTP, SMTP, and Telnet, which all use the TCP transport protocol. TCP only supports unicast transmissions. If the same data must be sent to multiple receivers, the sending computer must send a different copy of the data to each recipient. This makes unicast transmissions inefficient and bandwidth intensive for multipoint communications.
Multicast	Communication method in which data is sent simultaneously to more than one destination on a network. In IP multicasting, a group of hosts is identified by a single IP address (the multicast IP address). The multicast address is a class D IP address. When data reaches the destination identified by the multicast IP address, it is distributed through routers only to those hosts that requested it. There can be more than one sender and data is distributed to a set of receivers (referred to as many-to-many connectivity). The set of receivers is called a multicast group. Clients must specifically join the multicast group identified by the multicast group IP address. Since multicasting sends a single data stream that can be received by multiple computers, significant bandwidth savings can be gained for communications that a group of clients must all receive at the same time or when clients can receive and cache common data until they need it. UDP and reliable multicast protocols such as Pragmatic General Multicast (PGM) are used to transmit multicast data streams.
Broadcast	Communication method in which data is sent from one point to all other points on a LAN. There is only one sender, but data is sent to all connected hosts. Packets must be forwarded to all hosts in order to make sure that they reach their intended recipients. Address Resolution Protocol (ARP) uses broadcasts to send address resolution queries to all computers on a LAN and IP also supports broadcasts so that the same packet can be sent to all hosts on a subnet. The last IP address in a subnet is the IP broadcast address. Broadcasting is bandwidth intensive.

skill 10

Working with the Network Monitor
(cont'd)

exam objective

Monitor and optimize a server environment for application performance. Monitor network performance objects.

how to

Install the Network Monitor Driver, the Network Monitor, and SNMP and start the Network Monitor.

1. Click **Start**, point to **Control Panel**, and click **Network Connections** to open the **Network Connections** window.
2. Right-click **Local Area Connection** and click **Properties** to open the **Local Area Connection Properties** dialog box.
3. Click **Install...** to open the **Select Network Component Type** dialog box (**Figure 14-66**).
4. Double-click **Protocol** to open the **Select Network Protocol** dialog box. Select **Network Monitor Driver (Figure 14- 67)**. Click **OK**.
5. Close the Local Area Connection Properties dialog box and the Network Connections window.
6. To install the Network Monitor, first, insert the Windows Server 2003 installation CD in the CD-ROM drive. Then, click **Start**, point to **Control Panel**, and click **Add or Remove Programs**.
7. Click **Add/Remove Windows Components**.
8. Scroll down the **Components** list to locate and select **Management and Monitoring Tools**.
9. Click **Details...** to open the **Management and Monitoring Tools** dialog box. Check **Network Monitor Tools** and **Simple Network Management Protocol (Figure 14-68)**.
10. Click **OK**. Click **Next >**. After the configuration changes are complete, click **Finish**.
11. Close the Add or Remove Programs window.
12. Click **Start**, point to **Administrative Tools**, and click **Network Monitor** to open **Microsoft Network Monitor**.
13. The **Microsoft Network Monitor** message box prompts you to select the network on which you want to capture data. If you do not select a network, by default the local area network will be selected (**Figure 14-69**).
14. Click **OK** to open the **Select a network** dialog box (**Figure 14-70**). Expand the **Local Computer** node to view a list of all of the NICs installed on the server.
15. Select the connection you want to monitor and click **OK**. If there are several NICs on the server and you do not know what you have named the connection you want to monitor, run **ipconfig /all** at the command prompt to locate the Physical Address for the NIC.
16. The **Capture Window (Station Stats)** window for the NIC opens in the Microsoft Network Monitor window (**Figure 14-71**). Maximize both windows.
17. Click the **Start Capture** button ▶. In the **Graph pane** of the Capture window you can view bar graphs for the **% Network utilization**, **Frames per second**, **Bytes per second**, **Broadcasts per second**, and **Multicasts per second**.
18. The **Total Statistics pane** on the right side of the window displays the **Time Elapsed** and **Network statistics**, **Captured statistics**, **Per Second statistics**, **Network Card (MAC)**

tip

If the number of frames per second has significantly increased compared to your baseline levels, you may have a bridge or switch that is malfunctioning and must be replaced or reconfigured.

Figure 14-66 **The Select Network Component Type dialog box**

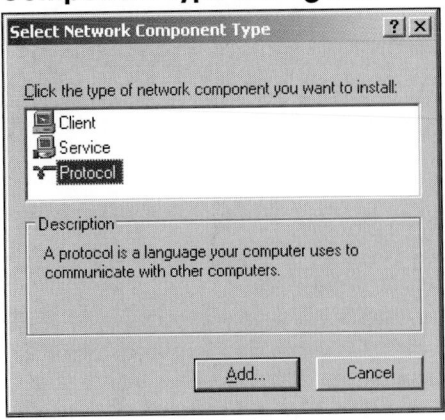

Figure 14-67 **Installing the Network Monitor Driver protocol**

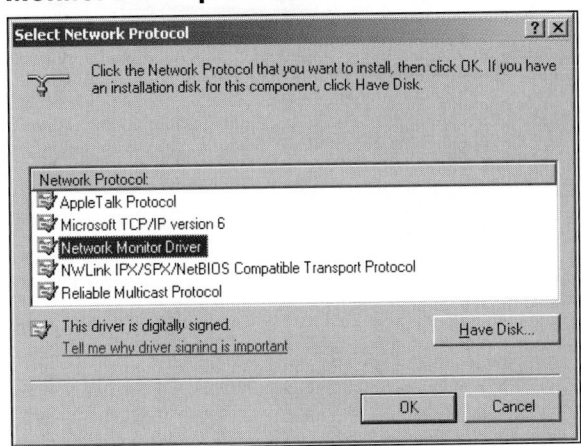

Figure 14-68 **Installing Network Monitor and SNMP**

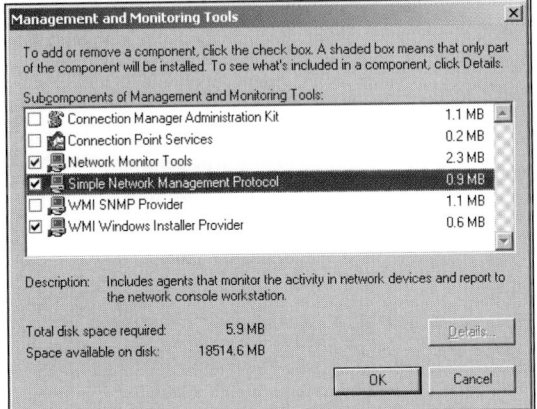

Figure 14-69 **The Microsoft Network Monitor message box**

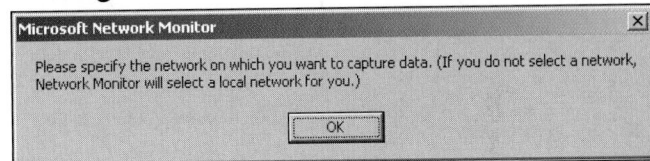

Figure 14-70 **The Select a network dialog box**

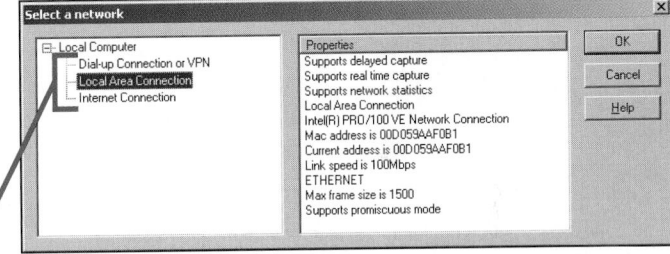

Select the connection that you want to monitor

Figure 14-71 **The Capture window in Network Monitor**

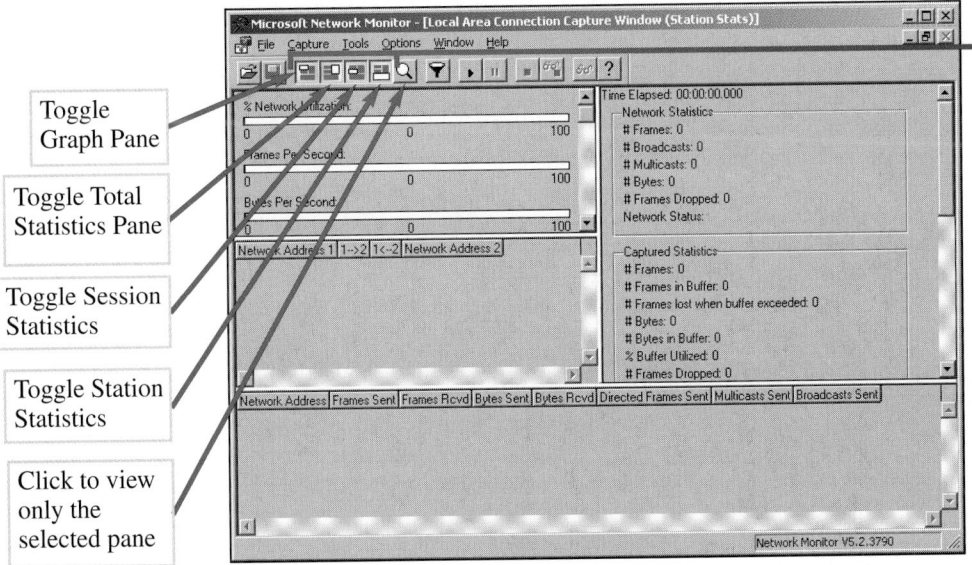

Toggle Graph Pane

Toggle Total Statistics Pane

Toggle Session Statistics

Toggle Station Statistics

Click to view only the selected pane

The toggle buttons toggle the pane either open or closed. All panes are open by default

skill 10

Working with the Network Monitor
(cont'd)

exam objective

Monitor and optimize a server environment for application performance. Monitor network performance objects.

how to

statistics, and **Network Card (MAC) Error statistics**. You will have to use the scroll bars to view the bottom statistics (**Figure 14-72**).

19. The **Session Statistics pane** just below the Graph pane displays statistics for the traffic from other computers on the network. You can also view the MAC address for the NIC of each computer and statistics for the number of frames sent by and received from each computer.

20. The bottommost section is the **Station Statistics pane**. Here, you can view total statistics on all communicating network stations. The **Network Address, Frames Sent, Frames Received, Bytes Sent, Bytes Received, Directed Frames Sent, Multicasts Sent**, and **Broadcasts Sent** can all be monitored.

21. Click the **Pause/Continue Capture** button ｜｜ to temporarily stop capturing data. Toggle it back on to resume.

22. Click in the **Station Statistics pane**. Click the **Zoom Pane** button 🔍 to view only the selected pane. Toggle the Zoom Pane button off.

23. Click the **Stop and View Capture** 🔬 button to view a report of all of the captured data (**Figure 14-73**). You can save the captured summary data to a file. The default location for saving captured data is *%systemroot%*\System32\Netmon\Captures.

24. Close the Capture Summary window. Click ▶ to resume capturing data. A message box will ask if you want to save the capture. Click No .

25. Click the **Stop Capture** button ■ . Close Network Monitor. A **Microsoft Network Monitor** message box asks if you want to save the capture. To save the captured data in the **Captures** folder by default, click Yes . Enter a file name and click Save in the **Save As** dialog box. Otherwise, click No .

more

Using the Network Monitor, like auditing and using the System Monitor, increases the overhead on a computer. If you are using these tools on a busy network file or application server, you must run them only to establish your baseline readings and later to monitor and diagnose network problems. You do not want statistic gathering activities to impede everyday server activities. One strategy for keeping server overhead reasonable while using this tool is to gather network data from the NIC on a Windows 2000 Professional or XP Professional workstation.

tip

A large number of Frames dropped or CRC (cyclic redundancy check) errors in the Network Card MAC Error Statistics section in the Total Statistics pane probably means you must replace your NIC or repair damage to the network connection.

The Graph pane is particularly useful for collecting your baseline data. You can collect data on the percentage of network bandwidth in use (% Network Utilization), the total traffic frames for broadcasts, multicasts, and unicasts (Frames Per Second), and find out how much network traffic is caused by broadcasts from servers and workstations (Broadcasts Per Second). You can also monitor the amount of network traffic attributable to multimedia servers by collecting the statistics from the Multicasts Per Second graph. You can collect data over a few weeks time to construct a representative view of your network during peak periods, as well as under slow and average workloads. Network utilization percentages that run over 40%, especially on an un-switched, half-duplex network, may indicate a bottleneck that you need to address. If this figure rises above 70%, it is likely that you need to address network design concerns such as the need to add more subnets or boost network speed. One possible problem is a malfunctioning NIC on either a workstation or a server. If Network utilization and Broadcasts per second numbers have significantly increased, you can try to isolate the computer with the faulty NIC in the Station pane. If the Frames per second value seems excessive compared to your benchmark, while the Broadcasts per second and Multicasts per second figures remain in the normal range, you may have a multimedia application that is using unicasts. It may be possible to adjust the application so that it will use multicasts instead. If both the Multicasts per second and Network utilization numbers look high and your multimedia applications all use multicasts, it is likely that you need to look at the network segments involved to see if you can increase their speed.

Figure 14-72 Viewing network statistics

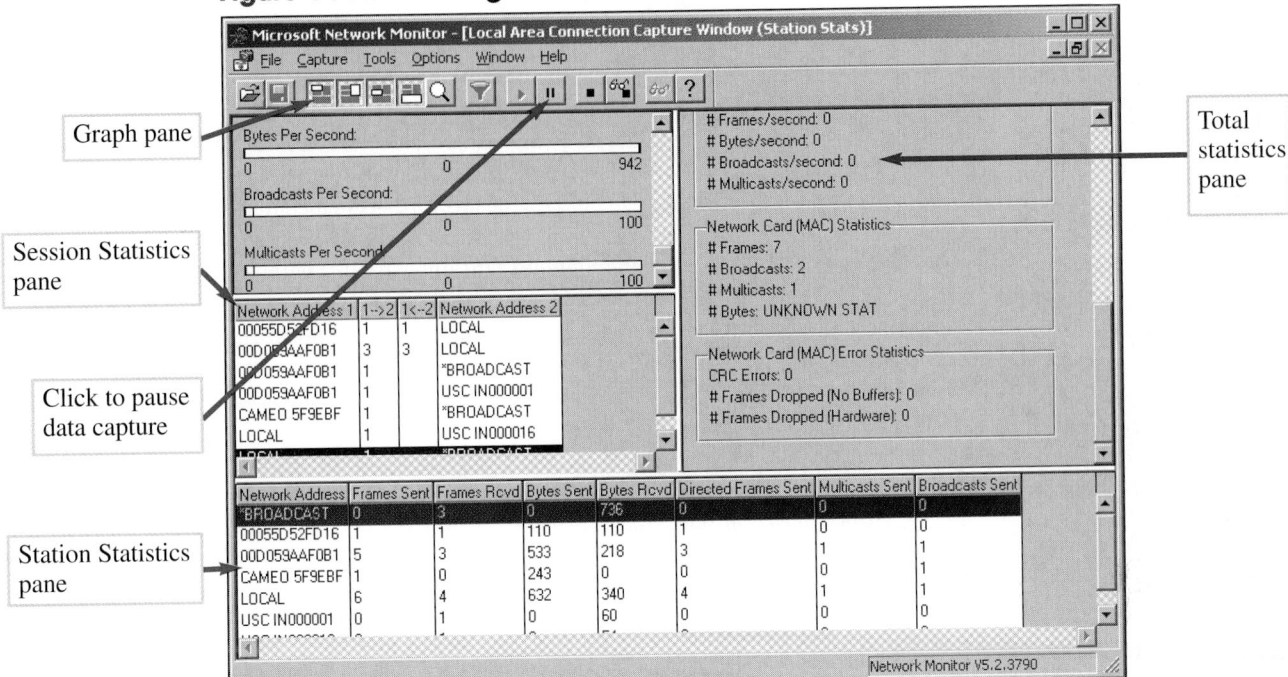

Graph pane

Session Statistics pane

Click to pause data capture

Station Statistics pane

Total statistics pane

Figure 14-73 A Capture summary

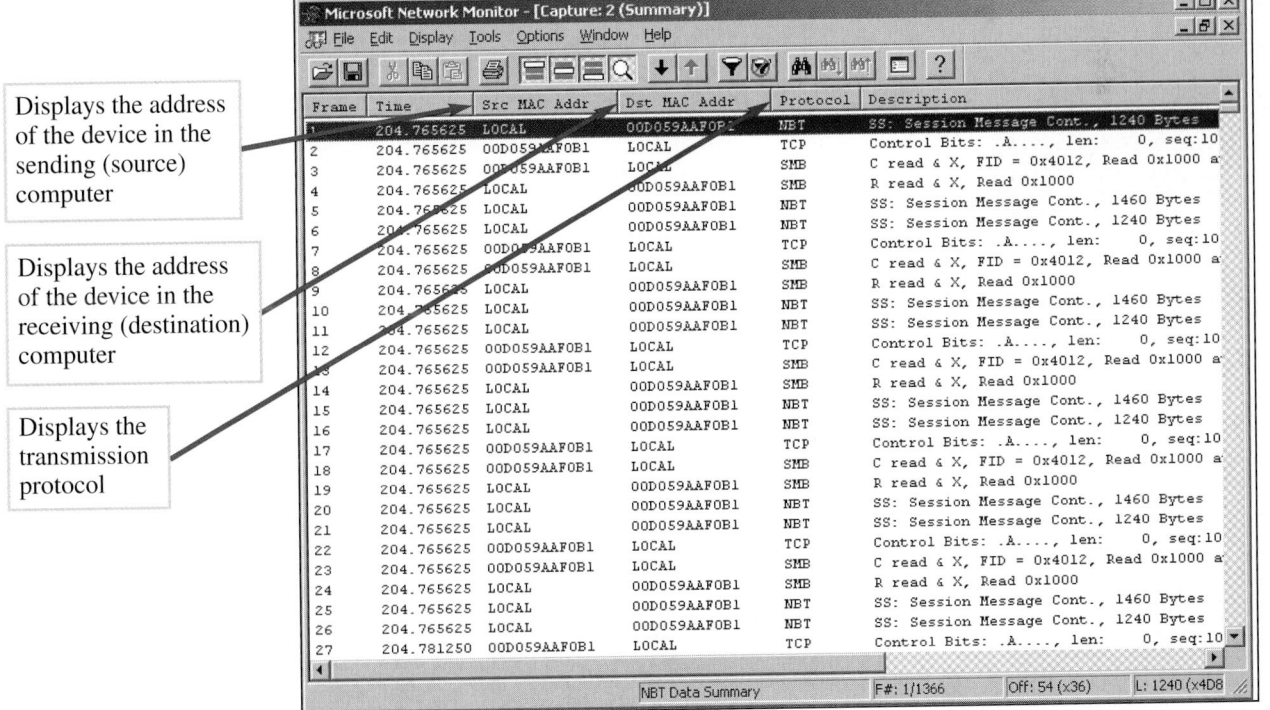

Displays the address of the device in the sending (source) computer

Displays the address of the device in the receiving (destination) computer

Displays the transmission protocol

skill 11

Introducing Simple Network Management Protocol (SNMP) Services

exam objective

Monitor and optimize a server environment for applications performance. Monitor network performance objects.

overview

Another way to capture network data is to use the SNMP service. **SNMP (Simple Network Management Protocol)**, which is part of the TCP/IP protocol suite, is used to configure network devices and computers to compile network performance data. When you install the **SNMP service** on a computer, your computer becomes an **SNMP agent** that can communicate with an SNMP **network management station (NMS)**. The NMS can monitor SNMP-enabled TCP/IP network devices to examine network performance, detect network malfunctions, and audit network usage. Windows Server 2003 does not include NMS software. In order to set up a network management station, you must purchase software from a third-party vendor such as Solstice Site Manager or Solstice Enterprise Manager from Sun Microsystems or SNMPc from Jade Communications.

The components of the SNMP service are listed below:

◆ **Network management station (NMS):** The NMS is centrally located and is used by administrators to manage remote network devices. The NMS can request information from SNMP agents such as network protocol identification and statistics, dynamic identification of devices attached to the network, hardware and software configuration data, device performance and usage statistics, device error and event messages, and program and application usage statistics.

◆ **SNMP agent**: A device running the SNMP agent software, such as the SNMP service, is called an SNMP agent. SNMP agents are used to provide information about activities that occur on the network. They provide data to the NMS and respond to messages sent by the NMS. **Table 14-8** describes the types of SNMP messages communicated between the management station and the SNMP agents.

◆ **Management information base (MIB):** Network performance information is stored in a MIB on a network agent, which gathers data for the NMS. The parameters stored in the MIB can be remotely configured. The NMS can obtain or change the data in the MIB using an assortment of different commands.

The NMS and the SNMP agents belong to an **SNMP community**, which is a collection of computers grouped for administrative and security purposes. Defining communities is a security feature, similar to creating a password. Only an NMS configured to be a member of the same community as the agents can poll the agents. However, since the community name is transmitted in clear text across the network, it is weak security at best. The best method of enforcing SNMP security on a network (using the SNMP 2.0 specification) is to define NMS IP addresses. This prevents agents from responding to a rogue NMS, since its IP is not in the allowed list.

Administrators assign community names. An NMS can belong to multiple communities, but an SNMP agent cannot receive requests from an NMS that is not on a list of acceptable community names. For example, if there are two communities, Comm1 and Comm2, and Agent1 and NMS1 belong to Comm1, while Agent2, Agent3, and NMS2 belong to Comm2, Agent1 can receive requests from NMS1 because they are both in the same community, Comm1. Similarly, Agent2 and Agent3 can communicate with NMS2 because they are in the Comm2 community.

You configure the properties for the SNMP service in the **SNMP Service Properties (Local Computer)** dialog box. **Table 14-9** describes the tabs on the SNMP Service Properties (Local Computer) dialog box.

Even without an NMS on your network, installing the SNMP service can be useful because you can monitor SNMP traffic in the Network Monitor. You may decide to do this to discover whether any unauthorized users are using NMS software to tamper with security on network devices such as routers.

Table 14-8 SNMP Messages

SNMP Messages	Explanation
GET	This is a basic SNMP message. It is sent by the network management station to request information about a MIB entry on the SNMP agent, such as a device error.
Get-next	This is an extended request message used to browse all management objects. When a Get-next request for the object is processed, the SNMP agent sends the identity (the person or entity that has been authenticated) and the value of the object following the previous information request.
Set	This message is used to send and assign an updated MIB value to an SNMP agent. It can be used only if Write access is permitted on the network.
Getbulk	This message is used to request that data transferred by the SNMP agent be within a maximum message size. This reduces the number of protocol exchanges that must be used to obtain a large amount of information from the MIB.
Trap/Notify	This is a message sent by an SNMP agent to an SNMP network management station. The message is sent when the SNMP agent identifies that an event has occurred locally. The SNMP management system that receives a trap message is called a trap destination.

Table 14-9 Tabs on the SNMP Service Properties dialog box

Name	Description
General	Used to start or stop the SNMP service and to specify the startup type and start parameters for the SNMP service.
Log On	Used to specify how the SNMP service logs on to the system. You can also enable or disable the SNMP service for a hardware profile on this tab.
Recovery	Used to set the response from the computer if the service fails. Additionally, it enables the SNMP service to recover from an abnormal failure of the service or the system.
Dependencies	On this tab, you can view a list of the services upon which the SNMP service depends. By default, the SNMP service depends on the Event log. You can also view a list of the services that depend on the SNMP service.
Agent	Used to configure the SNMP agent properties. You can also specify the name and location for the contact person, such as the administrator, for access by Internet management systems.
Traps	Used to specify one or more community names if traps are required. Trap destinations can be host names, IP addresses, or IPX addresses.
Security	Used to configure SNMP security. You can either accept requests from any IP address or from only specified IP addresses. You can also add or remove communities here and send authentication trap messages for events such as when a received request does not have a valid community name.

skill 11

Introducing Simple Network Management Protocol (SNMP) Services (cont'd)

exam objective

Monitor and optimize a server environment for applications performance. Monitor network performance objects.

how to

Configure the SNMP service on a Windows Server 2003 member server. (If you did not install the SNMP service in the previous skill, you must first use the Windows Components Wizard to install it.)

1. Click ⊞Start, point to **Administrative Tools**, and click **Services** to open the **Services** snap-in.
2. Scroll down the **Name** list to locate the **SNMP Service**. Make sure that the **Status** column says **Started** and the **Startup** Type column says **Automatic**.
3. Double-click **SNMP Service** to open the **SNMP Service Properties (Local Computer)** dialog box. If you need to start the service, click [Start]. To set the service to start automatically, select **Automatic** in the Startup type list box (**Figure 14-74**).
4. Click the **Security** tab to configure SNMP security. If you purchase network management software and set up an NMS, you will create community names and set community rights in the **Accepted community** names box. There is no default community name, so the service will not respond to any community names that are presented by default. If an SNMP request is received from a community name that is not on the list, an authentication trap will be generated. The community name, Public, should not be used because it is a security risk. Community rights are determined by the permission level that you assign to a community. The permission level designates how the SNMP agent processes requests from a particular community.
5. Click [Add...] to open the **SNMP Service Configuration** dialog box. Open the **Community rights** list to view the permission levels you can assign to a community (**Figure 14-75**).
6. Click [Cancel] since you are not going to set up a community yet.
7. Click the **Accept SNMP packets from these hosts** option button. This option enables an SNMP agent to receive data only from specific computers. The list you create here will designate the acceptable SNMP management systems. There is one host configured by default, localhost. This is the loopback interface on the local computer. If you use the Accept SNMP packets from any host option, no SNMP packets will be rejected based on the name or address of the source host.
8. Click [Add...] to open the **SNMP Service Configuration** dialog box.
9. Type the IP address of the host, for example **192.168.1.45**, in the **Host name, IP or IPX address** text box (**Figure 14-76**).
10. Click [Add...] to close the **SNMP Service Configuration** dialog box. The accepted host IP address is added to the lower box on the Security tab (**Figure 14-77**).
11. The **Send authentication trap** check box is selected by default. When the SNMP agent receives a request from a community name that is not accepted or that is not on the list of acceptable hosts, the SNMP agent sends an authentication trap message to one or more NMS.
12. Click the **Traps** tab. A trap is an event that you want to be notified about. For example, you may want to be warned when the NMS detects that a network device is offline or if a request for data is sent by an unrecognized NMS. You must enter a **Community name** and a **Trap destination**. The trap destination is the IP address (or IPX address because SNMP is compatible with both IPX/SPX and AppleTalk) for the NMS (**Figure 14-78**).
13. Click [OK] to close the SNMP Service Properties (Local Computer) dialog box.
14. Close the Services snap-in.

tip

If you set up an NMS and you configure traps to capture events, you must also start the SNMP Trap Service. The SNMP Trap Service will receive traps from the SNMP agent and forward them to the NMS.

**Figure 14-74 The SNMP Service
Properties dialog box**

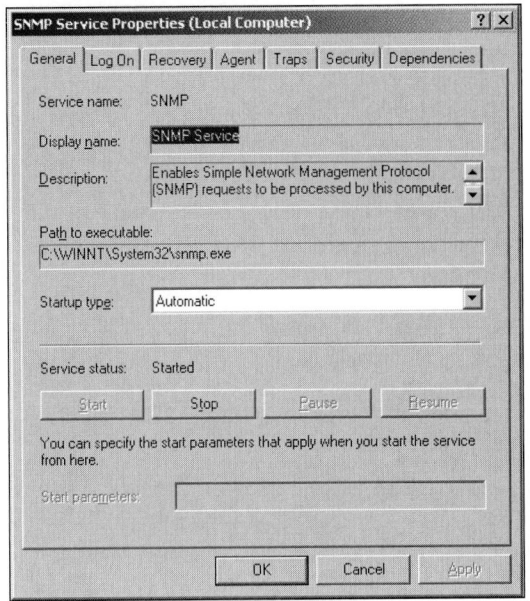

**Figure 14-75 SNMP Service
Configuration dialog box**

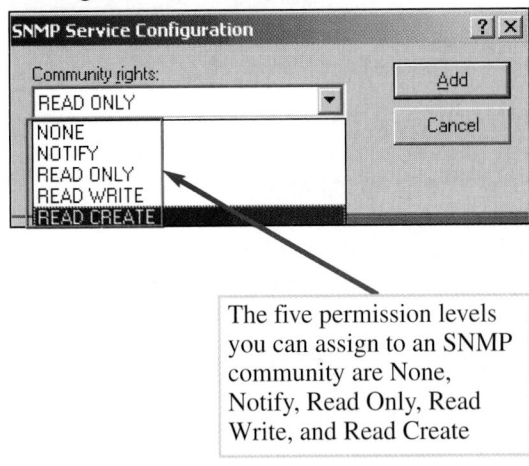

The five permission levels
you can assign to an SNMP
community are None,
Notify, Read Only, Read
Write, and Read Create

Figure 14-76 Configuring SNMP security

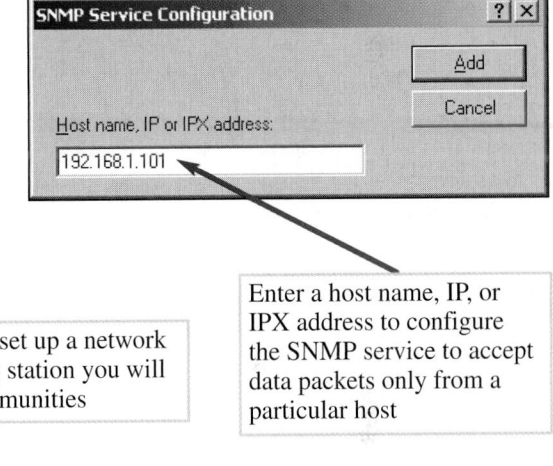

Enter a host name, IP, or
IPX address to configure
the SNMP service to accept
data packets only from a
particular host

**Figure 14-77 Security tab—SNMP
Service Properties dialog box**

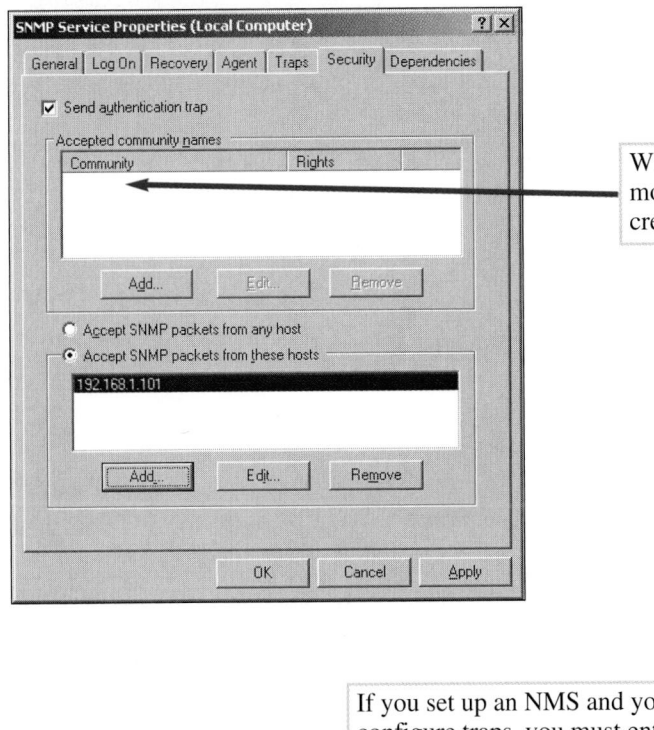

When you set up a network
monitoring station you will
create communities

**Figure 14-78 The Traps tab - SNMP
Service Properties dialog box**

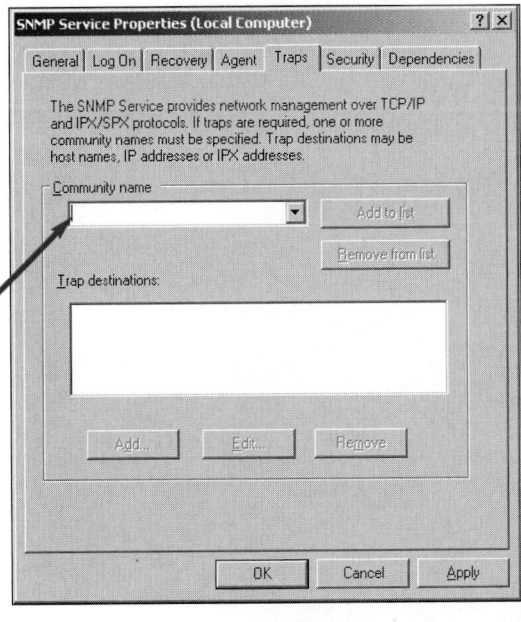

If you set up an NMS and you
configure traps, you must enter
a Community name and a Trap
destination (IP or IPX address
or host name) to which the
traps will be forwarded

skill 11

Introducing Simple Network Management Protocol (SNMP) Services (cont'd)

exam objective

Monitor and optimize a server environment for applications performance. Monitor network performance objects.

more

As you saw in this skill, SNMP security is configured by creating lists of acceptable community names or lists of acceptable hosts and through the use of authentication traps. The SNMP security properties are described in further detail in **Table 14-10**.

Some general problems that may occur after configuring the SNMP service and their solutions are listed below:

◆ **The SNMP service does not function properly:** While the SNMP service is gathering status information, it may connect with an unknown network, causing the SNMP service to malfunction. To solve problems related to the functioning of the SNMP service, SNMP error handling has been integrated with the Event Viewer. You can create a View filter to see System log information related to SNMP only.

◆ **The SNMP time-out period is not adequate for communicating with the WINS server:** In order to receive status information, the NMS may also have to communicate with the WINS server. If some WINS queries work, but others time out, the SNMP time-out period on the NMS must be increased.

◆ **An Error 3 occurs when an IPX address is entered as a trap destination and the computer is restarted:** If you have entered an IPX address as a trap destination and it is not entered correctly, you will receive an Error 3 message. To solve this, the IPX trap destination must follow the 8.12 format for the network number and MAC address. The Windows Server 2003 SNMP service will not accept addresses that contain hyphens or commas between the network number and the MAC address, although this is acceptable in other SNMP management software.

The format is xxxxxxxx.yyyyyyyyyyyy where xxxxxxxx is the network number and yyyyyyyyyyyy is the MAC address.

In Windows Server 2003, there are also several new Group Policy settings you can use to set the acceptable SNMP communities, and permitted network management stations, and to configure traps for public for the SNMP agent. These new policies are located in the **Computer Configuration\Administrative Templates\Network\SNMP** folder. As always, if you set Group Policy, it overrides the local settings **(Figure 14-79)**.

Table 14-10 SNMP security properties

Property	Description
Accepted community names	There is no default community name. No SNMP message from any community name will be responded to by default. You can add, delete, and change community names. An authentication trap will be generated when an SNMP request is received from a community not on the list. You can define community rights for a community name in the SNMP Service Configuration dialog box. These permission levels designate how the SNMP agent will process requests from that community. The community name Public should never be used.
Accept SNMP packets from any host	If you choose this option, SNMP messages will not be rejected from any host. The list of acceptable hosts will not be consulted.
Accept SNMP packets from these hosts	If you keep this default option, you create a list of the SNMP management systems from which you will accept messages. One host is configured by default: localhost. This is the loopback interface on the local computer. SNMP packets will be accepted only from localhost. If any other host sends an SNMP message, it will be rejected. This will generate an authentication trap. Setting this option and defining NMS IP addresses is more secure than using a community name, because a community can include multiple hosts.
Send authentication trap	When the SNMP agent receives a request from a community name that is not on the list of acceptable community names or the list of acceptable hosts, the SNMP agent sends an authentication trap message to one or more network management stations. The trap message reports that the community or host was not valid and was thus not authenticated. This option is selected by default.

Figure 14-79 SNMP Group Policy

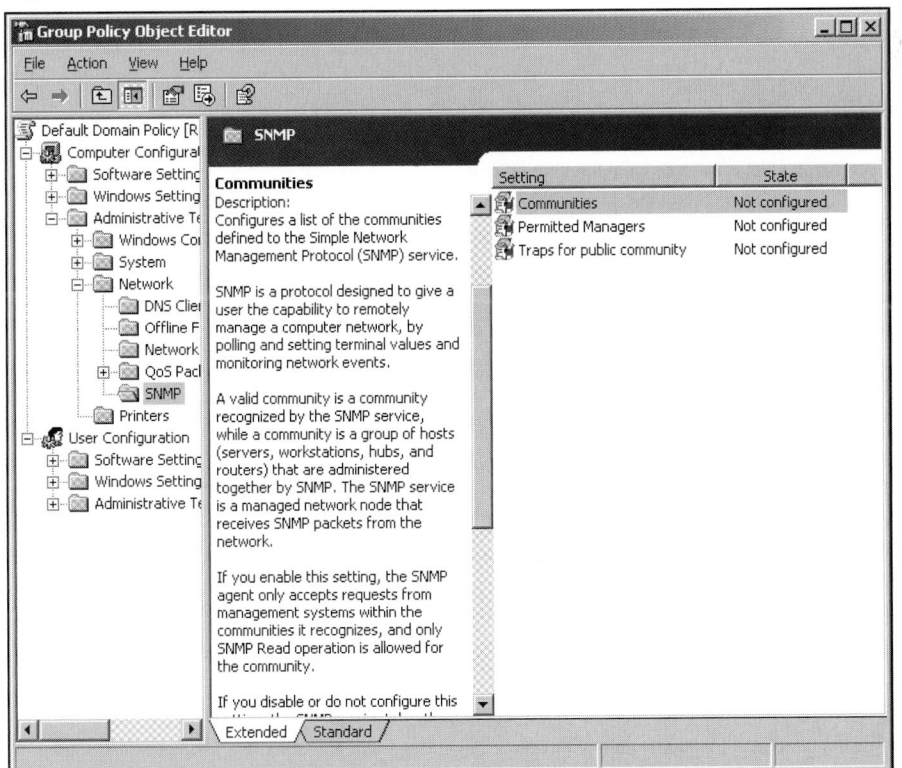

Summary

- The Check Disk tool is used to check the hard disk for file system errors and bad sectors on FAT, FAT32, or NTFS volumes. Chkdsk automatically runs when you boot if the boot process detects file corruption or corruption in a file allocation table.

- The Disk Defragmenter rearranges files and unused space, moving the segments of each file and folder to one location so that they occupy a single, contiguous space on the hard disk, enabling the system to access files more quickly and programs to load faster.

- NTFS data compression is used to compress files and folders such as Word or other Office documents and bitmaps to conserve disk space. Compression can reduce some types of files and folders by 50% to 90%; however, many files can be reduced by only 5% or less.

- Copying a compressed file may affect the performance of the system because the operating system must first uncompress the file, copy it, and then compress it again, using valuable system resources.

- You can also use disk quotas to optimize disk storage by allocating a specific amount of disk space to each user.

- The Task Manager is used to view applications that are running on the server in order to determine if they are placing unnecessary demands or generating unnecessary network traffic.

- On the Task Manager's Applications tab, you can view the status of all applications that are currently running, end an application that is malfunctioning, or start a new application.

- On the Task Manager's Processes tab, you can view a list of all processes currently running and terminate a process. A process in the Task Manager refers to an executable program that is run from within the main application, such as a Help utility, in an Office program.

- On the Task Manager's Performance tab, you can view graphs of the CPU and Page file usage. Detailed statistics tell you the total number of handles and threads used. A handle is any resource, such as a file, that is used by an application. It has its own identification so that the program can access it. A thread is a block of program code.

- On the Task Manager's Networking tab, you can monitor all of the NICs installed on the server. Total network utilization is represented on a graph for each NIC to indicate the approximate percentage of network bandwidth in use.

- You monitor the resources on your server in the Performance console, either to establish a baseline or to diagnose a bottleneck. The Performance console consists of the System Monitor and the Performance Logs and Alerts tools.

- The System Monitor is used to view a graphical representation of the performance of the resources on your computer.

- The Performance Logs and Alerts tool is used to record the performance of resources in logs and to configure alerts, which are activated based on threshold values that you set, to perform specific actions.

- You configure the display in the System Monitor and create counter logs by choosing objects and counters. An object is a system resource, such as a processor, disk, network interface, or memory, whose performance you can monitor. Counters are performance measures for the object that can be calculated and related as numeric figures.

- In Windows Server 2003, both the physical hard disk (PhysicalDisk) and the LogicalDisk are automatically System Monitor performance objects.

- Performance counter data for physical disks and for logical drives, or storage volumes, is collected using the Disk Performance Statistics Driver.

- If either the PhysicalDisk object or the LogicalDisk object is not enabled, you can run the Diskperf utility at the command prompt.

- Services and protocols running on your Windows Server 2003 system, such as TCP, UDP, Indexing Services, the Server Service, the Workstation Service, the Browser, WINS, and Network Monitor Driver, etc., are also objects whose performance you can monitor.

- Performance Logs and Alerts are used to store the data for future reference. You can create either Counter logs or Trace logs. Counter logs use the GUI data from the System Monitor to create a log file, which is by default in the *.blg format (Binary LoG). Trace logs survey events that take place on the system. You choose the events logged by a system provider or you add a non-system provider to log system events. Counter logs record the state of object counters at specific intervals of time that you set and Trace logs monitor a particular value continuously.

- You should establish baseline behavior when a server first begins to run on the network and when the hardware or software configuration has been modified.

- You can configure alerts to send messages to other computers, run a program, start a new log to record events when the counter value is either under or over the threshold you have set, or to create an entry in the Application log.

- Auditing is used to track user activities and object access on the computers on a network. Auditing must be set up for each computer individually.

- When you define an audit policy, you select the events you want to track and decide whether to track the success or failure, or both, for the event.

- Auditing can be used to track exactly who logged on to a computer and when, what files were accessed or folders were created, what printers were used, and what

Registry keys were accessed when and by whom and what actions the users attempted to perform on them.

◆ Auditing is used to help prevent security breaches by allowing you to track unauthorized attempts in order to log on or access folders. Auditing is also used to help conduct resource planning for the computers on your network.

◆ The audit policy tells the operating system what to record in the Security event log on each computer.

◆ Auditing increases the overhead on a computer, so you must carefully choose what events you think are important to monitor.

◆ You can enable or change audit entries and view the Security log only if you are an Administrator on the computer on which you are configuring the policy or if you have the Manage auditing and security log permission, which is granted to the Administrators group by default.

◆ You can only audit folders and files on NTFS volumes or partitions.

◆ You can change what is shown in the log and locate specific events using the Filter command. You can also locate specific events using the Find command.

◆ The Network Monitor Driver works in conjunction with Network Monitor to make it possible for you to analyze frames (data packets) sent by and received from a NIC.

◆ The System Monitor and Network Monitor are used to troubleshoot networking problems and to monitor for specific network events.

◆ The Network Monitor Driver protocol is used to collect statistics about the activity detected by the network card. These statistics are reported to, and can be viewed on, a Windows Server 2003 computer that is either running the Network Monitor Agent Service or the Systems Management Server.

◆ SNMP (Simple Network Management Protocol), which is part of the TCP/IP protocol suite, is used to configure network devices and computers to compile network performance data.

◆ When you install the SNMP service on a computer, you make it an SNMP agent that can communicate with an SNMP network management station (NMS).

◆ The NMS can monitor SNMP-enabled TCP/IP network devices to examine network performance, detect network malfunctions, and audit network usage.

◆ Windows Server 2003 does not include NMS software. In order to set up a network management station, you must purchase software from a third-party vendor.

Key Terms

Alert	Management information base (MIB)	SNMP (Simple Network Management Protocol)
Bottleneck	Network Monitor	
Check Disk	Network Monitor Driver	SNMP agent
Counter log	NMS (network management station)	SNMP community
Disk Cleanup	pagefile.sys	SNMP service
Disk Defragmenter	Performance counter	System Monitor
Disk quota	Performance Logs and Alerts	Task Manager
Dr. Watson	Performance object	Thread
Event Viewer	Process	Trace log
Handle	Security log	

Test Yourself

1. The Task Manager can be used to: (Choose all that apply.)
   a. Log performance data in a file.
   b. Track users trying to access a server resource.
   c. Change the priority of a running program.
   d. Monitor processes occurring on the system using objects and counters.

2. What tool can you use to have a message sent to your computer to inform you when a performance counter is over or under a threshold value?
   a. Counter Logs
   b. Task Manager
   c. Trace Logs
   d. Alert

3. You are having problems with one of the hard disks on your computer. You decide to create a counter log so that you can examine the read and write times to the disk. What performance object will you choose in the Add counters dialog box?
   a. Processor
   b. Memory
   c. Paging file
   d. Physical Disk

4. You seem to be having a lot of paging occurring on your system. You decide to create a counter log file to examine the memory usage on your system. Which counters will you choose? (Choose all that apply.)
   a. Memory/Available MBytes
   b. Memory/Pages/sec
   c. Paging File/%Usage
   d. Network Segment /% Network Utilization

5. When you add the Processor Queue Length performance counter in the System Monitor, you are monitoring:
   a. The percentage of time the processor spends in servicing interrupts.
   b. Whether your computer needs a better hard disk.
   c. The percentage of time the CPU is handling non-idle threads.
   d. Whether there is a processor bottleneck on your computer.

6. You can use the System Monitor to:
   a. Measure the performance of local computers only.
   b. View performance data of both local and remote computers.
   c. Import data to spreadsheet programs.
   d. Create trace logs when a disk I/O operation or a page fault occurs.

7. You are using the Memory\Available MBytes counter to monitor the memory on your system, which has 256 MB of RAM. What value indicates that you need to add more RAM?
   a. Consistent values between 30 and 35 MB
   b. Consistent values below 25 MB
   c. Consistent values over 25 MB
   d. Consistent values between 25 MB and 30 MB

8. When you use Event Viewer to view audit activity, you can:
   a. Filter events on the basis of the resource or object for which you have enabled auditing.
   b. Add performance counters and performance objects for monitoring the resource.
   c. Configure the properties of the Security log to specify its size and the behavior for overwriting events.
   d. View data that the Security log obtains from the system when a particular time interval elapses.

9. _____ is a collection of computers that are grouped for administrative and security purposes when SNMP network data gathering has been configured.
   a. NMS community
   b. SNMP community
   c. SNMP agents
   d. SNMP protocol

10. You have formatted the D: volume of a server with the FAT32 file system. On this volume you can: (Choose all that apply.)
   a. Use the Disk Defragmenter to analyze the D: volume to determine the number of fragmented files and folders.
   b. Use the Check Disk tool to check the hard disk for file system errors and bad sectors.
   c. Set disk quotas.
   d. Set a compression state for files and folders.

Projects: On Your Own

1. Use Task Manager:
   a. Click **Start** and then click **My Computer**.
   b. Press **[Ctrl]+[Alt]+[Del]** to open the **Windows Security** dialog box.
   c. Click the **Task Manager** button.
   d. Open the **Applications** tab, if necessary.
   e. Select **My Computer**, if necessary.
   f. Click the **Switch To** button to move the **My Computer** window to the foreground.
   g. Click the **Windows Task Manager** button on the Task bar.
   h. Click the **End Task** button to close the My Computer window.
   i. Open the **Processes** tab.
   j. Right-click **snmp.exe** and select **End Process**.
   k. Click **Yes** in the **Task Manager Warning** dialog box to terminate the process. This will stop the SNMP service on your server.
   l. Right-click **tskmgr.exe**, point to **Set Priority** and select **Above Normal**.
   m. Click **Yes** in the **Task Manager Warning** dialog box to change the priority class for the Task Manager process.
   n. Open the **Performance** tab.
   o. Open the **View** menu and select the **Show Kernel Times** command. A new red line indicating the percentage of processor usage by the kernel rather than the processes is added to both the CPU Usage and PF Usage graphs.
   p. Open the **Networking** tab.
   q. Open the command prompt.
   r. Type: **ping -t -1 1500 <*IP_address*>**. Use the IP address of a computer on your LAN. This command will ping the destination host continuously with echo requests that are 1500 bytes.
   s. Return to the Task Manager window and view the Local Area Connection graph and the Network Utilization column.
   t. Close the Task Manager and the command prompt window.

2. Monitor the processor usage of your member server.
   a. Open the **Performance** console.
   b. Open the **Add Counters** dialog box.
   c. Select the computer \\<*server _name*> in the **Select counters from computer** list box.
   d. Select **Processor** in the **Performance object** list box.
   e. Select the **% Processor Time** and the **Interrupts/sec** counters.
   f. Select the **All instances** option button.
   g. Add the counters to the Performance console.
   h. Create a counter log to record the real-time data you are now viewing in the Performance console.

3. Configure auditing for a folder on an NTFS volume on your member server in order to audit successful modifications to the folder.
   a. Open the **Local Security Settings** console.
   b. Access the audit policies. Open the **Audit object access Properties** dialog box. Configure audit object access for both successes and failures.
   c. Create a folder named **Bank Accounts** and open the **Bank Accounts Properties** dialog box.
   d. Open the **Advanced Security Settings for Bank Accounts** dialog box.
   e. Open the **Select User**, **Computer**, **or Group** dialog box. Choose the users you want to audit.
   f. Select the **Successful** check box for **Create Files/Write Data**.
   g. Apply the audit policy and close all open dialog boxes and windows.

Problem Solving Scenarios

1. ForgeAhead International Co., a manufacturing firm, has a multiprocessor Windows Server 2003 system that runs a number of proprietary applications. These applications monitor and control the manufacturing process, and therefore require a dedicated processor. The administrator has asked you to explain to him graphically the average time each processor spends servicing requests from these applications and how often they are interrupted by device requests. You must also make a list of the devices that are causing these interrupts so that these can be minimized. Explain the steps you would take to monitor system performance and display the data as a histogram.

15

Configuring a Windows Server 2003 Application Server

Terminal Services is the Windows Server 2003 implementation of a centralized computing architecture that lets users execute Windows-based applications on a remote server. With Terminal Services, clients need not fit the typical Windows Server 2003 client/server model in which each user works from an independent client that is responsible for its own application processing, local storage, and operating system management. Terminal Services supports a full range of clients, including so-called "thin clients," as well as Windows 98, NT, CE, 2000, and XP Professional computers. With the help of third-party software, it will also support Unix, Unix-based X-terminals, and Macintosh computers. All processing is remotely performed on the server. The Terminal Server client software is installed on the client, the client receives the Windows Server 2003 GUI from the Terminal Server, users enter keystrokes and mouse clicks, the commands are sent to the Terminal Server for execution, and the server then refreshes the local terminal screen. Compaq, IBM, and Wyse have each developed thin client product lines in response to the newest implementations of Terminal Services. Other benefits for the typical "fat client" network include the ability to run applications on older PCs and on clients using legacy hardware (as long as they meet the hardware requirements), thus reducing hardware expenses. Implementing Terminal Services can also lead to improved application performance over slow network connections. Terminal Services also provides an easier way to update software. There are also two important Terminal Services-based tools: Remote Desktop for Administration and Remote Desktop Assistance. Remote Desktop for Administration is used to manage a computer from nearly any computer on your network and Remote Assistance is used to allow a trusted party to remotely access your system. This expert can be allowed to either just view your system or to both view and interact with your system.

Internet Information Services (IIS) 6.0 is a component you can install to make your Windows Server 2003 server a Web server. If you install all of the components, IIS includes the World Wide Web Publishing (WWW), File Transfer Protocol (FTP), Network News Transfer Protocol (NNTP), and Simple Mail Transfer Protocol (SMTP) services, the Background Intelligent Transfer Service (BITS) server extension, and FrontPage 2002 Server Extensions. The BITS server extension provides functionality for transferring files using spare bandwidth and for resuming data transfers if a session has been disconnected or if the computer reboots. FrontPage 2002 Server Extensions provide functionality for Microsoft FrontPage and Visual InterDev FrontPage and services for creating, configuring, and managing the Web environment. IIS 6.0 management and security features help you to ensure the reliability of the content on the Web server, as well as enhance the security of the Web environment so that users can safely publish and share information over an intranet or the Internet.

Goals

In this lesson, you will learn how to install, configure, and troubleshoot Terminal Services and how to use Remote Desktop for Administration and Remote Assistance. You will also learn about Internet Information Services (IIS) 6.0 and how to configure, manage, and troubleshoot the Web environment.

Lesson 15   Configuring a Windows Server 2003 Application Server

Skill	Exam 70-290 Objective
1. Introducing Terminal Services	Manage servers remotely.
2. Working with Remote Desktop for Administration	Manage servers remotely. Manage a server by using Terminal Services remote administration mode. Manage a server by using available support tools.
3. Using Remote Assistance	Manage servers remotely. Manage a server by using Remote Assistance. Manage a server by using available support tools.
4. Configuring Terminal Services	Manage a server by using available support tools.
5. Troubleshooting Terminal Services	Troubleshoot Terminal Services. Diagnose and resolve issues related to Terminal Services security. Diagnose and resolve issues related to client Terminal Services.
6. Introducing Internet Information Services 6.0	Manage a Web server. Manage Internet Information Services (IIS).
7. Examining IIS Configuration Changes	Manage a Web server. Manage Internet Information Services (IIS).
8. Managing IIS	Manage a Web server. Manage Internet Information Services (IIS). Manage a server by using available support tools.
9. Configuring IIS Security	Manage a Web server. Manage Internet Information Services (IIS). Manage security for IIS.
10. Administering the Web Environment	Manage a Web server. Manage Internet Information Services (IIS). Manage security for IIS.
11. Creating Application Pools	Manage a Web server. Manage Internet Information Services (IIS).
12. Troubleshooting the Web Environment	Manage a Web server. Manage Internet Information Services (IIS). Manage security for IIS.

Requirements

To complete this lesson, you will need administrative rights on a Windows Server 2003 member server, a Windows XP or 2000 Professional client, and the Windows Server 2003 installation CD-ROM. If you do not have access to two computers, simply perform the steps listed on your member server; however, you will not be able to create the Remote Desktop, Remote Assistance, or Terminal Services connections.

skill 1

Introducing Terminal Services

Manage servers remotely.

overview

Terminal Services is an application service that enables clients to access a server remotely to execute, process, and store data on the server **(Figure 15-1)**. When Terminal Services is set up, each workstation runs Windows sessions on the server, all programs are executed on the server, and all processing and data storage takes place on the server. The PC merely displays the work done by the Terminal Server. Since the Terminal Server is handling the bulk of the work, PCs that might otherwise be obsolete can be given a second life as a terminal. An Application layer protocol called **Remote Desktop Protocol (RDP)** handles communication between the Terminal Server client and Terminal Server. RDP, which is designed to handle the transmission of graphical data, supports automatic disconnection, remote configuration, and three levels of session encryption. Terminal Services works with Windows terminals, handheld PCs that use RDP, and PC clients. On PC clients, you must install the Remote Desktop client.

Terminal Services offers numerous benefits, as described below:

◆ **Support for thin clients:** Terminal Services enables thin clients to access a Windows Server 2003 computer. A **thin client** has fewer system resources, such as RAM, and only the minimal operating system required for connecting to a server. A thin client is usually a small computer that runs embedded Linux or Windows CE. Examples of thin clients, which can save organizations several hundred dollars per purchase over a new PC, include Maxspeed's MaxTerm, Wyse Technology's Winterm and Hewlett-Packard's Netstation **(Figure 15-2)**.

◆ **Centralized access to applications:** Applications can be executed and stored at a central location so that administrators can control access to them from a single location. Terminal Services can also greatly reduce the amount of network and workstation maintenance. In many offices, both large and small, some PCs are still running Office 97, while others are running Office 2000 or XP. Upgrading each client workstation to the most recent versions can be a time-consuming task, both from the administrative perspective of updating records and from the perspective of the network technicians commissioned to perform the job. Using Terminal Services, only the server must be upgraded. When users next log on, they will be "supplied" with the new program, in the sense that the new application display will be transmitted to them from the server. Deploying new applications is likewise simplified and control over how applications are used is consolidated.

◆ **Remote administration of Windows Server 2003:** Administrators can manage the resources on a Windows Server 2003 computer remotely. Furthermore, remote administration can be performed over any network, from any type of client. The Active Directory Users and Computers console, Computer Management console, and DHCP and DNS snap-ins (in fact, all tools in the Administrative Tools folder, as well as custom MMCs) can be accessed remotely.

◆ **Interoperability:** Terminal Services allows clients with all down-level Windows operating systems to connect to a Windows Server 2003 computer for the purpose of executing applications and services on the server. With the help of additional third-party software, you can also use Terminal Services to connect Macintosh-based clients or UNIX clients to a Windows Server 2003 server.

◆ **Low bandwidth Access to Data:** Using Terminal Services you can significantly reduce network bandwidth requirements for remote access users. Users can run applications over low bandwidth dial-up connections or shared WAN links much more efficiently because data is not transmitted; the PC merely displays the work done by the server.

Figure 15-1 Terminal Services

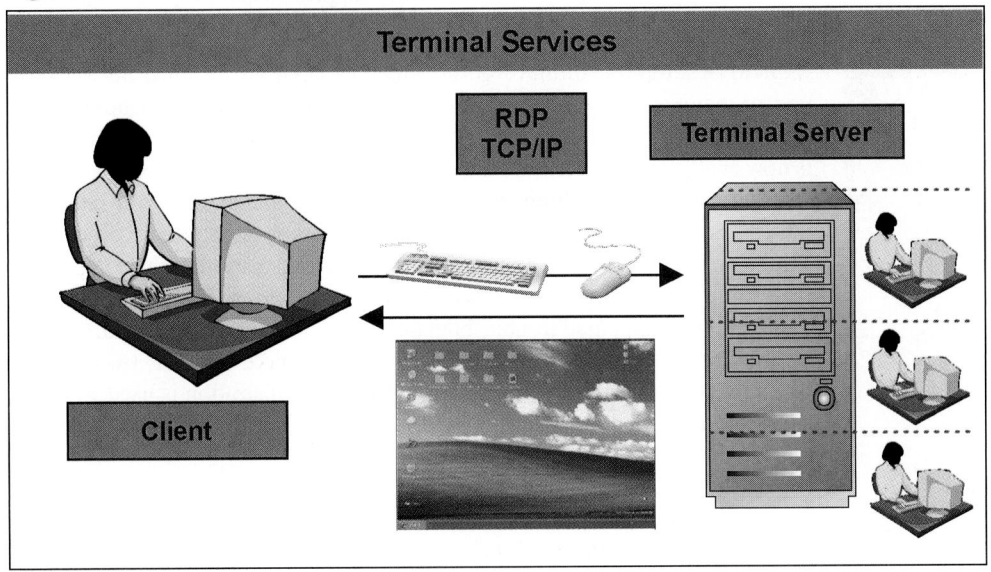

Figure 15-2 Terminal Services Architecture

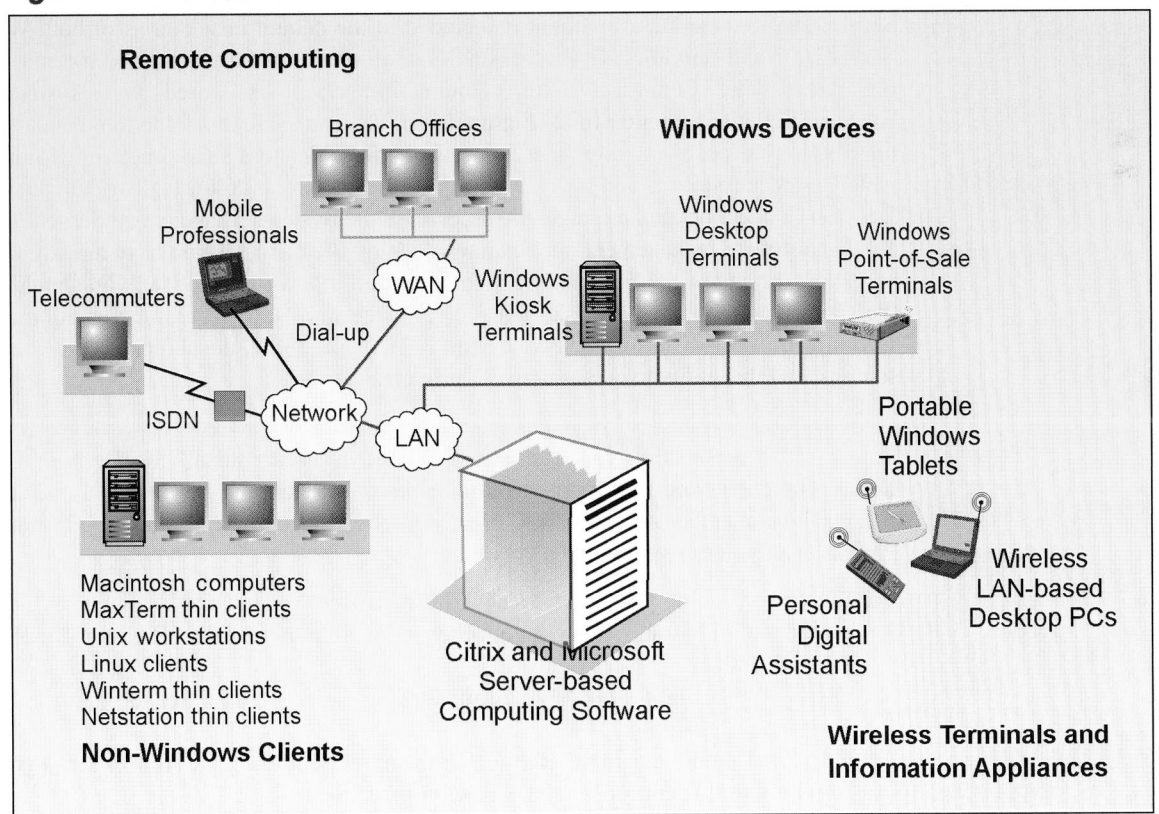

skill 2

Working with Remote Desktop for Administration

exam objective

Manage servers remotely. Manage a server by using Terminal Services remote administration mode. Manage a server by using available support tools.

overview

Remote Desktop for Administration, which is based on Terminal Services technology, allows you to manage a computer from nearly any computer on your network. This technology, previously installed as Terminal Services in Remote Administration mode in Windows 2000, is now enabled on the **Remote** tab in the System Properties dialog box **(Figure 15-3)**. You use Remote Desktop for Administration to access and manage a server remotely from anywhere on the network. You can perform almost any task remotely that you could while physically logged on to the server, including shutting down and restarting the computer. Remote Desktop for Administration works with almost any kind of connection, so an administrator can even configure, maintain, and troubleshoot a server from home or the road. A server configured for Remote Desktop administration supports a maximum of two simultaneous remote administration sessions. Remote Desktop for Administration is used when you want to allow administrators to access a server for configuration or troubleshooting purposes using a Terminal Server session. No additional licensing is required. Servers that are not domain controllers are configured by default to allow Terminal Services connections by the Remote Desktop Users group. If the Terminal Server is a domain controller, you must also configure the Default Domain Policy GPO to allow the Remote Desktop Users group to connect through Terminal Services; only the Administrators group is granted the **Allow logon through Terminal Services** user right by default on a domain controller. Windows XP Professional includes an equivalent version of Remote Desktop for Administration called simply Remote Desktop.

Remote Desktop Connection is the client software that is used to connect to a Terminal Server. The Remote Desktop client is included in the default installations of both Windows Server 2003 and Windows XP Professional. For all other operating systems, you must install the client. The Remote Desktop Connection client is stored in *%systemroot%*\system32\clients\tsclient\win32 **(Figure 15-4)**. You can share this folder on the network for distribution purposes (or copy the contents of the folder to a shared network folder from which users can access and install the client), configure Group Policy to distribute the Remote Desktop Connection .msi package, or you can use the Systems Management Server (SMS) or another software management application to deploy the client. If you have already installed an earlier version of the Terminal Services client on a down-level client, you should update the software so that you can take advantage of the newest features such as alternate port selection (the default Terminal Services port is TCP port 3389), the ability to save connection settings, and the ability to access network printers.

tip

Remote Desktop for Administration is disabled by default in Windows Server 2003.

tip

For security reasons, all Terminal Servers, including servers configured for Remote Desktop for Administration, should be behind a firewall and all users who make remote desktop connections should be required to use strong passwords.

how to

Enable Remote Desktop for Administration on a server, install the Remote Desktop Connection client, and start a remote administration session. (To perform this exercise, you will need one member server and one client computer. If your client is running Windows XP Professional, you can skip step 8.)

1. Log on to your member server as an **Administrator**. You must be logged on as a member of the Administrators group in order to enable or disable Remote Desktop for Administration.
2. Click ![Start], right-click **My Computer**, and select **Properties** to open the **System Properties** dialog box.
3. Open the **Remote** tab. In the **Remote Desktop** section, select the **Allow users to connect remotely to this computer** check box **(Figure 15-3)**.
4. The **Remote Sessions** message box opens to warn you that all accounts used for remote connections must have passwords and that the correct port must be open if you are using Internet Connection Sharing or a personal firewall **(Figure 15-5)**. Click [OK].

Figure 15-3 The Remote tab in the System Properties dialog box

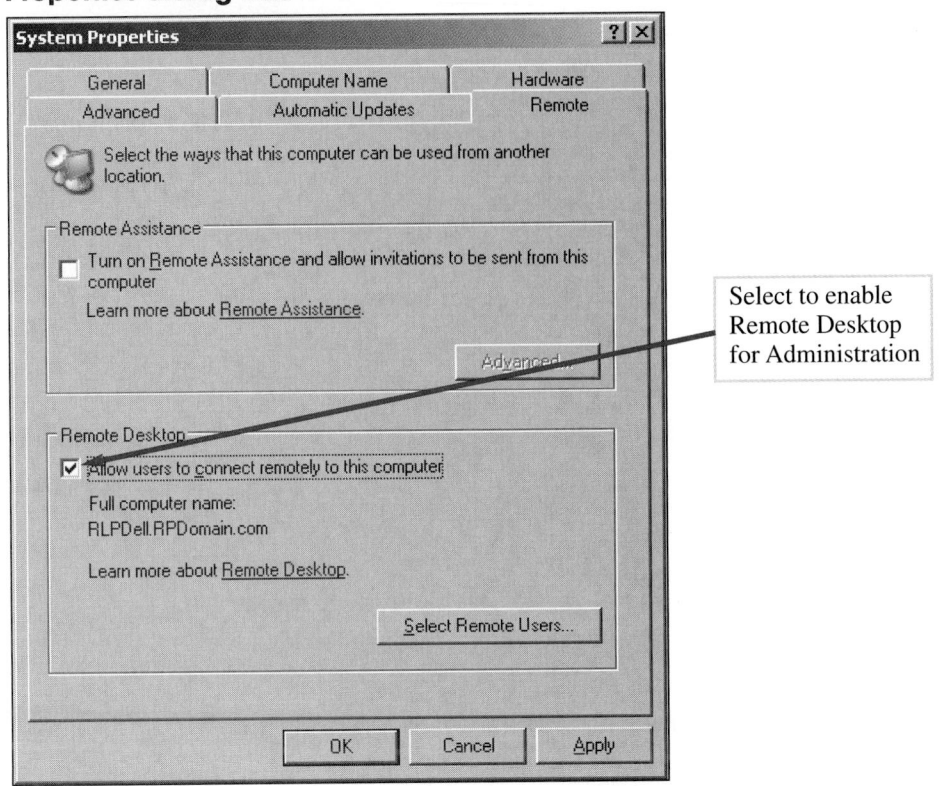

Select to enable
Remote Desktop
for Administration

Figure 15-4 Locating the Remote Desktop Connection client

The Remote Desktop
Connection .msi package
in the
%systemroot%\system32
\clients\tsclient\win32
folder

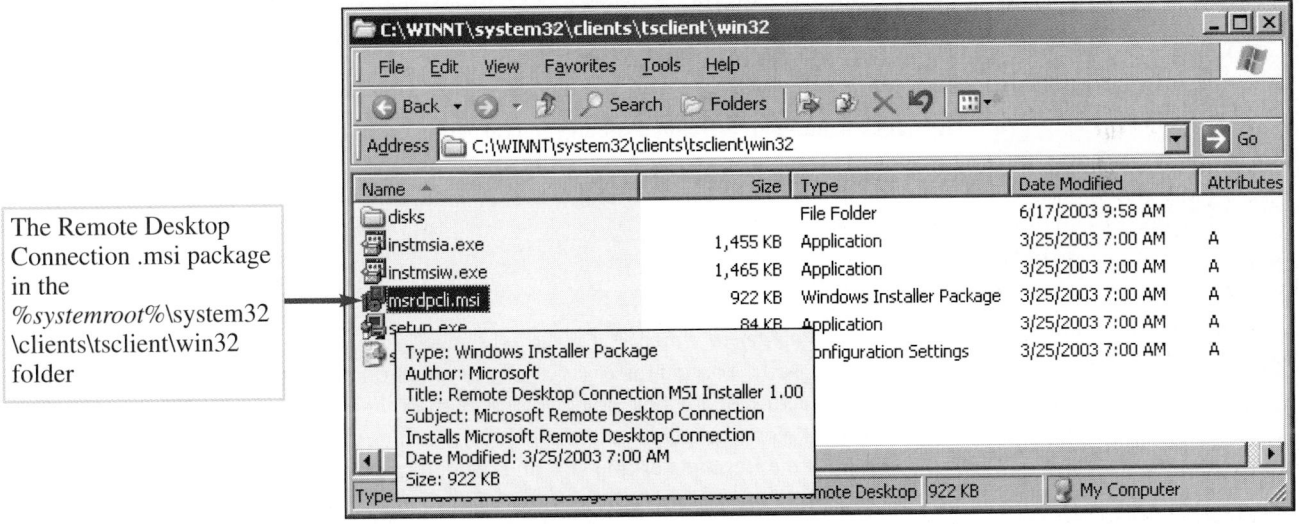

Figure 15-5 The Remote Sessions message box

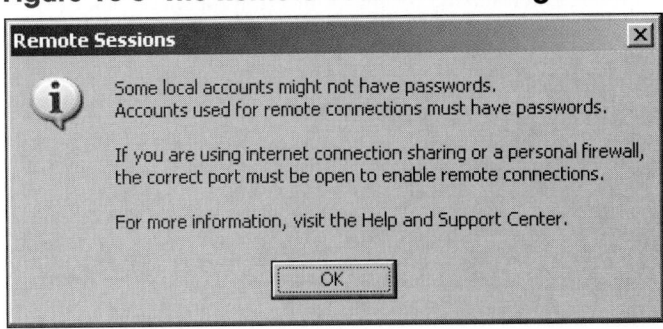

skill 2

Working with Remote Desktop for Administration (cont'd)

exam objective

Manage servers remotely. Manage a server by using Terminal Services remote administration mode. Manage a server by using available support tools.

how to

5. Click [OK] to close the System Properties dialog box.
6. Click [Start], click **My Computer**, and open your boot volume (the volume where the Windows Server 2003 operating system files and the operating system support files are stored). Navigate to **system32\clients\tsclient\win32**.
7. Right-click the **win32** folder and select **Sharing and Security**. Click the **Share this folder** option button. In the **Share name** text box, type **Remote Desktop Connection Installation**. Click [OK] to close the win32 Properties dialog box. Close the **%systemroot%\system32\clients\tsclient** window.
8. Log on to your client computer. Access the **Remote Desktop Connection Installation** folder over the network. Double-click the **setup.exe** program and follow the steps in the Remote Desktop Connection InstallShield Wizard to install the client.
9. On the client computer, click [Start], point to **Programs** (or **All Programs**), point to **Accessories**, point to **Communications** and click **Remote Desktop Connection** to open the **Remote Desktop Connection** dialog box (**Figure 15-6**).
10. In the **Computer** list box, type **<server_name>** and click [Connect].
11. The **Log On to Windows** dialog box opens. Type your administrative user name, password, and domain in the appropriate text boxes and click [OK].
12. You can now remotely administer your member server from your client computer. On the server monitor you are not logged on; however, on the client computer you are logged on to the member server.
13. Click [Start], point to **Programs** (or **All Programs**), point to **Administrative Tools**, and click **Services**. You can start, stop, and configure any services on your member server.
14. Close the Services window. Click the close button on the Remote Desktop console toolbar.
15. The **Disconnect Windows session** dialog box opens (**Figure 15-7**). Click [OK] to end the session.

more

To reestablish a previous Remote Desktop for Administration session, in the **Remote Desktop Connection** dialog box, click the list arrow on the **Computer** list box and select the name of the computer to which you want to connect. Then, follow the rest of the procedure outlined in the skill. You can also save your connection settings to a file. In the **Remote Desktop Connection** dialog box, click [Options <<] to expand the dialog box (**Figure 15-8**). On the **General** tab, you can specify automatic logon settings for the connection. On the **Display** tab, you can set the Remote desktop size and the color settings. On the **Local Resources** tab, you can specify keyboard and remote computer sound settings and specify which local resources, such as disk drives and printers, you want to automatically connect to when logged on the remote computer. When you have finished configuring the connection settings, click the **Save As** button on the General tab, enter a name for the connection file, and click **Save**.

tip

On the Programs tab in the expanded Remote Desktop Connection dialog box you can set a program to start when you connect to the remote computer.

Figure 15-6 The Remote Desktop Connection dialog box

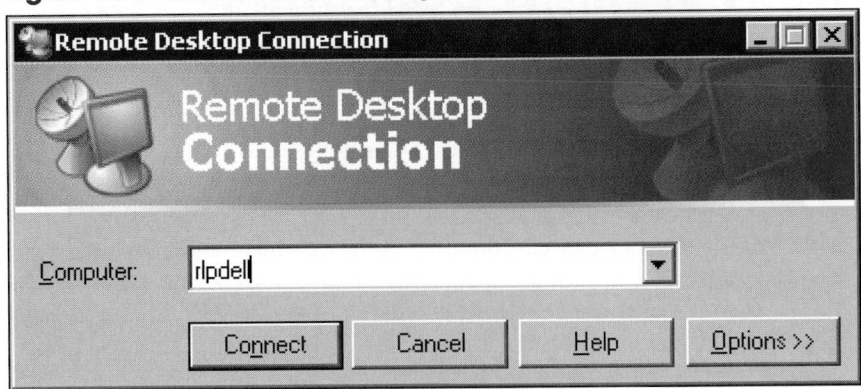

Figure 15-7 The Disconnect Windows session dialog box

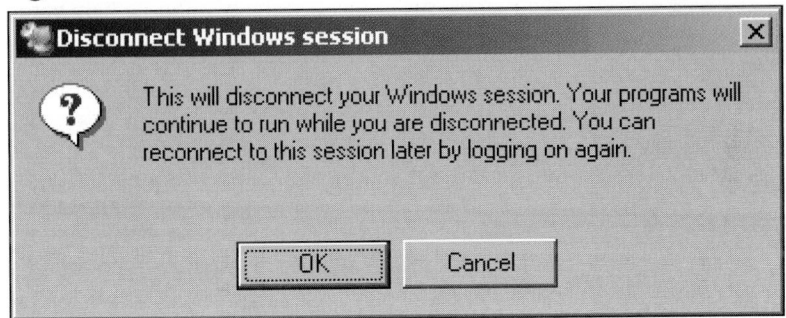

Figure 15-8 The expanded Remote Desktop Connection dialog box

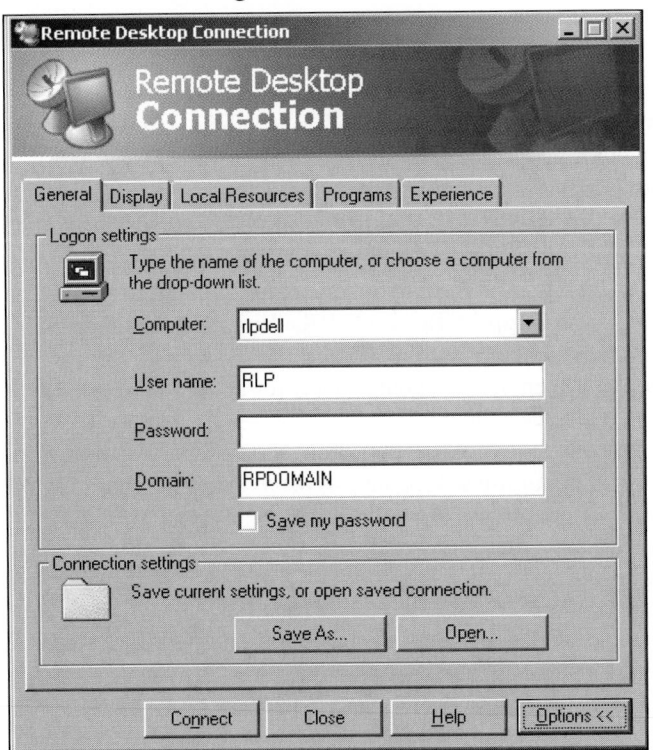

skill 3   *Using Remote Assistance*

exam objective

Manage servers remotely. Manage a server by using Remote Assistance. Manage a server by using available support tools.

overview

Remote Assistance is another capability based on Terminal Services. It is used to allow a trusted party such as a help desk support person or network technician to remotely access your system. This expert can be allowed to either just view your system or to both view and interact with your system. The Remote Assistance expert can take control of the computer and perform tasks to try to fix a problem, as long as they have received permission from the user.

Usually, a Remote Assistance session will begin with a user sending a Remote Assistance invitation through the Help and Support Center either using Windows Messenger, or an e-mail message. If the person to whom the request is directed agrees to help, he or she will open a Remote Desktop connection and connect to the other computer. The expert can also initiate the Remote Assistance session by offering help before it is requested.

You can connect to a Remote Assistance session over a LAN or over the Internet. Connections from the Internet in which the user is behind a firewall are also possible, as long as the default Terminal Services port (the default RDP port), TCP port 3389, is open. You can control whether or not users on your LAN will be able to request help over the Internet by either blocking or permitting inbound and outbound traffic through port 3389 at the firewall.

You can also set Group Policy to either allow or deny users from using Remote Assistance and you can designate whether the expert will be able to control the computer or just view it. You enable Remote Assistance on the **Remote** tab in the **System Properties** dialog box **(Figure 15-9)**. The local Administrator can choose to not enable or to disable Remote Assistance so that Remote Assistance invitations cannot be sent. The local Administrator can also clear the **Allow this computer to be controlled remotely** check box in the **Remote Assistance Settings** dialog box to prevent the Remote Assistance helper from controlling the computer **(Figure 15-10)**. However, keep in mind that Group Policy settings override settings in the System Properties dialog box.

tip
In order to use Remote Assistance, both computers must be running Windows XP or Windows Server 2003.

tip
If you want to request assistance using Windows Messenger, your helper must also be signed on to Windows Messenger.

tip
Guests cannot send Remote Assistance invitations.

how to

Request help using Remote Assistance

1. Click **Start**, right-click **My Computer**, and select **Properties** to open the **System Properties** dialog box.
2. Open the **Remote** tab. In the **Remote Assistance** section, select the **Turn on Remote Assistance and allow invitations to be sent from this computer** check box **(Figure 15-9)**.
3. Click **OK** to close the System Properties dialog box.
4. Click **Start** and click **Help and Support** to open the **Help and Support Center**.
5. In the right column, under **Support Tasks**, click the **Remote Assistance** link.
6. Click the **Invite someone to help you** link **(Figure 15-11)**.
7. Type the name of the person you are going to ask for help in the **Type the assistant's first name** text box. Click **Continue**.
8. In the **Set the invitation to expire** section, limit the time in which the recipient can accept the invitation to **30 minutes**. Type the password the helper must use to connect to your computer in the **Type password** text box and reenter it in the **Confirm password** text box. You must share this password with the recipient **(Figure 15-12)**. Click **Create E-mail Invitation**.
9. Outlook Express or Outlook (if it is your default mail client) will open with a default message entered in a message window. Enter the e-mail address in the **To** box, connect to the Internet, if necessary, and click the **Send** button.
10. The message will be sent and the window shown in **Figure 15-13** opens.

tip
Users cannot see Remote Assistance tickets created by the other users of the computer. Even the Administrator can see only his or her own tickets.

Figure 15-9 Enabling Remote Assistance

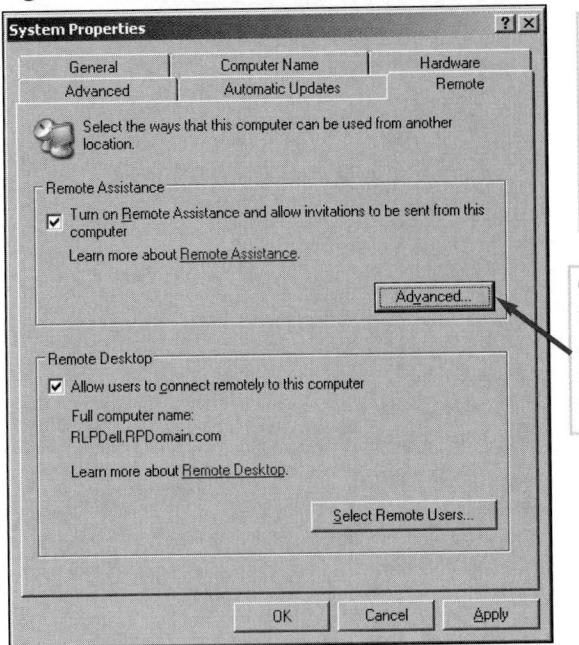

Figure 15-10 The Remote Assistance Settings dialog box

Clear to prevent the Remote Assistance expert from controlling the computer

Click to open the Remote Assistance Settings dialog box

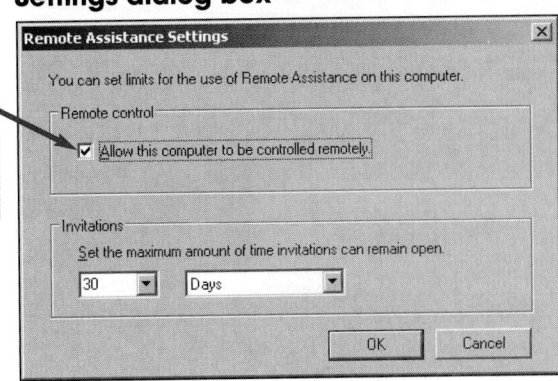

Figure 15-11 Sending a Remote Assistance invitation

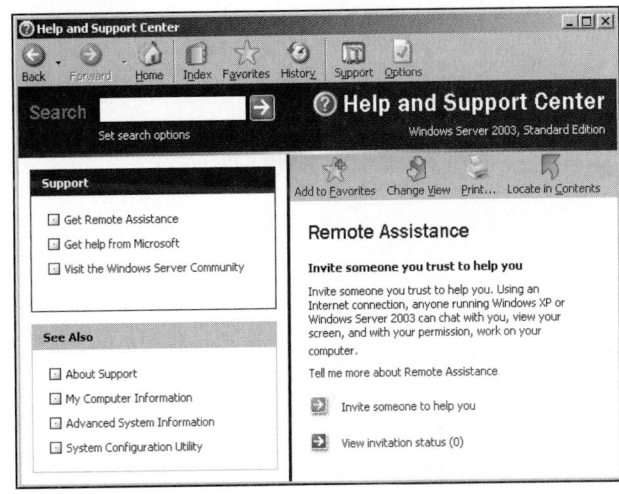

Figure 15-12 Creating an e-mail invitation

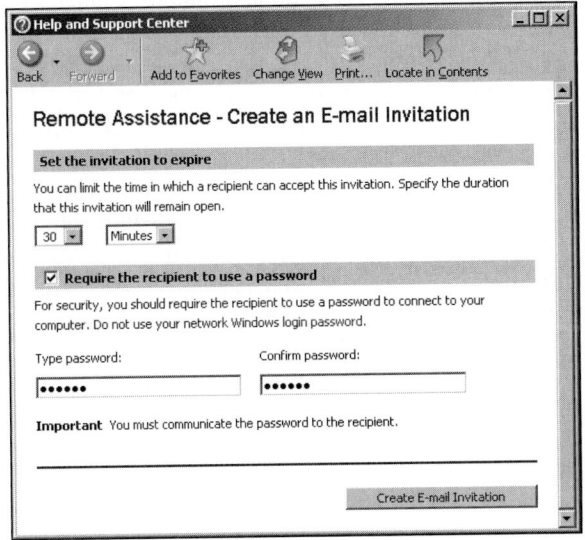

Figure 15-13 Sending the e-mail invitation

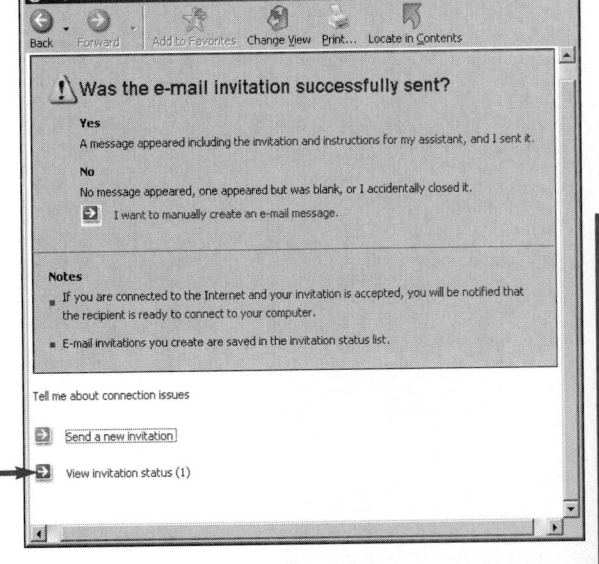

Click to view or modify the invitation

skill 3

Using Remote Assistance (cont'd)

exam objective

Manage servers remotely. Manage a server by using Remote Assistance. Manage a server by using available support tools.

how to

11. Click **View invitation status** to view or change your invitation (**Figure 15-14**).
12. On the remote computer, receive the e-mail and click the link in the message. If this is the first time Remote Assistance is being used on this computer you will be prompted to download and install the **Remote Assistance Server Control**.
13. The **Remote Assistance** Web page opens (**Figure 15-15**).
14. Click ⟨ Start Remote Assistance ⟩ .
15. The **Remote Assistance Invitation** opens. Enter the password you entered in step 8 and click ⟨ Yes ⟩ .
16. On the sending computer, a **Remote Assistance** message box will open to inform you that your invitation has been accepted (**Figure 15-16**). Click ⟨ Yes ⟩ . After the connection has been established, the user and the helper can chat and exchange files. The entire process is user-driven. If the user sends a file, the helper must accept it and specify where to store it.
17. The helper can click the **Take Control** button to ask the user if he/she can take control of the user's desktop. The user will have to click ⟨ Yes ⟩ to permit the helper to take control (**Figure 15-17**).
18. The user can either click the **Stop Control** button or press the **[Esc]** key at any time to stop control by the helper (**Figure 15-18**).
19. Click the **Disconnect** button to end the Remote Assistance session and close the Remote Assistance windows on both computers.

tip

Always use a strong password to avoid the possibility of a hacker discovering the password using a password cracking program. Never send the password in an e-mail. Use the telephone or another secure method to transmit the password.

more

To offer Remote Assistance without an invitation, open the Help and Support Center, and under **Support Tasks**, click **Tools**. Then, under **Tools** on the left side of the window, click **Help and Support Center Tools**. In the right pane, click **Offer Remote Assistance**. Enter the computer name or IP address for the computer to which you want to connect and click the **Connect** button. The **Offer Remote Assistance** policy in Group Policy (Computer Configuration\Administrative Templates\System\Remote Assistance) must be enabled and your user account must be listed as a helper, or you must be a member of the Administrators group on the computer to which you are offering Remote Assistance. The **Solicited Remote Assistance** policy must also be enabled. When you enable the **Offer Remote Assistance** policy, in the **Permit remote control of this computer** list box you can either choose **Allow helpers to remotely control the computer** or **Allow helpers to only view the computer**. The user must always give permission before the helper will be permitted to view the user's computer and the helper will only be able to take control of the user's computer if you select this option when you enable the policy. When you enable the Solicited Remote Assistance policy, you can also designate a maximum ticket time and the method for sending e-mail invitations. The Maximum ticket time can be configured in minutes, hours, or days. The method for sending e-mail invitations can be set to either Mailto or SMAPI. Computers running Windows XP can use only Simple Messaging Application Programming Interface e-mail programs.

tip

Remote Assistance is not available on either the 64-bit edition of Windows XP or the 64-bit versions of Windows Server 2003.

Figure 15-14 Viewing the status of the e-mail invitation

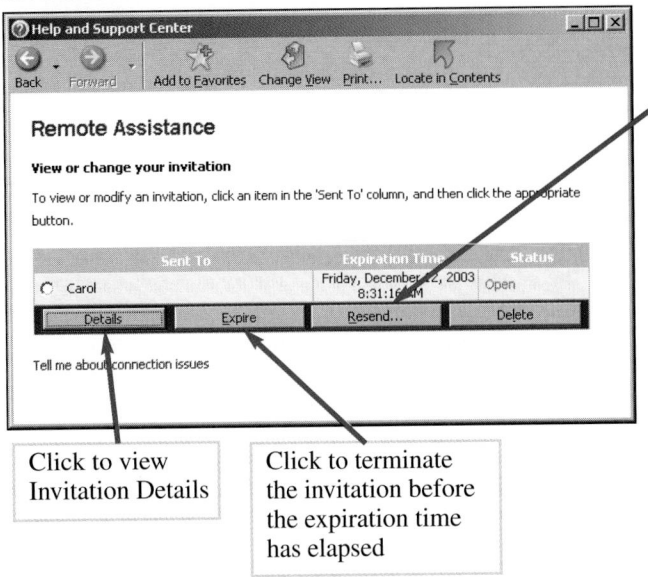

Click to resend an expired invitation

Click to view Invitation Details

Click to terminate the invitation before the expiration time has elapsed

Figure 15-16 Invitation accepted

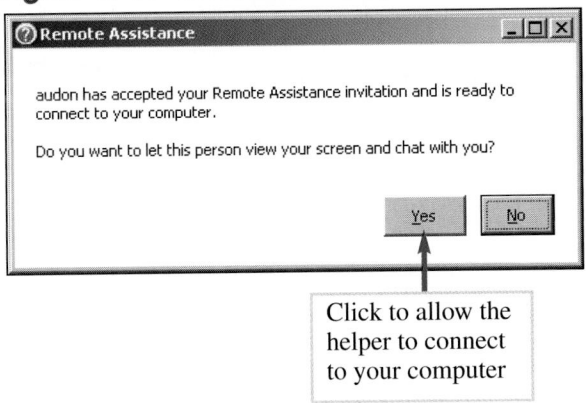

Click to allow the helper to connect to your computer

Figure 15-15 Starting a Remote Assistance session

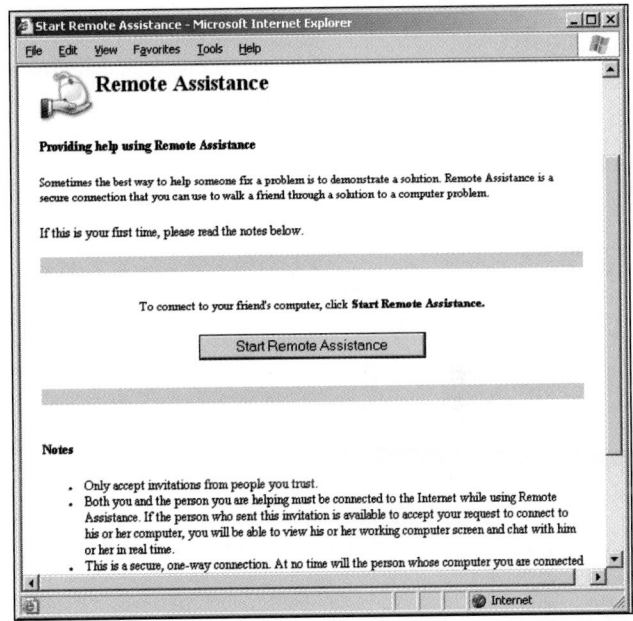

Figure 15-17 Sharing control of your computer

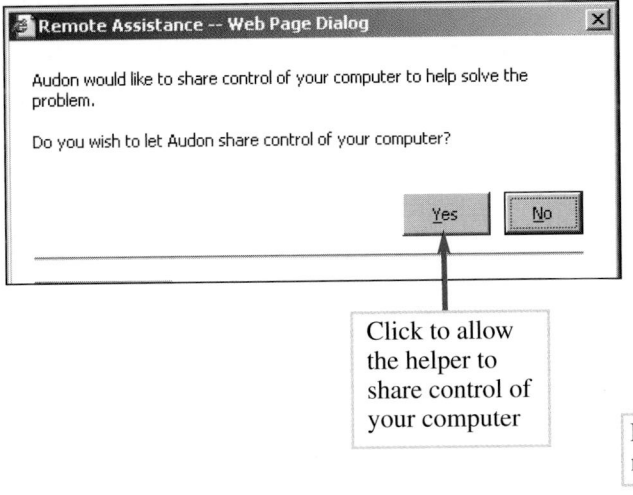

Click to allow the helper to share control of your computer

Figure 15-18 The Remote Assistance window

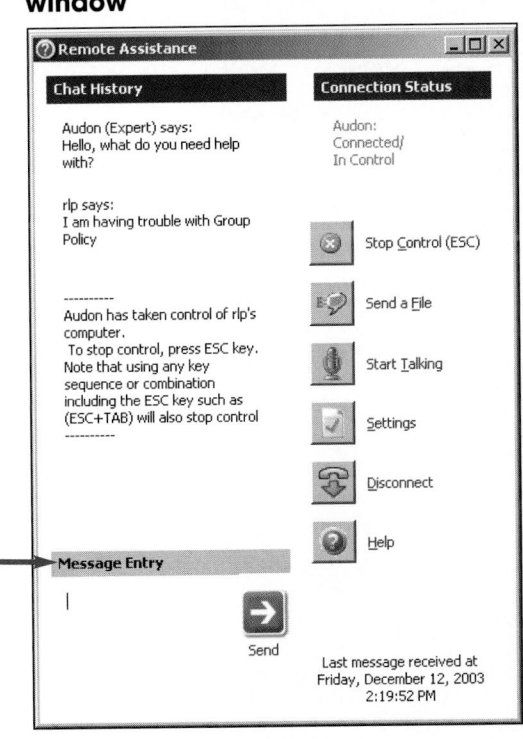

Enter chat messages

skill 4

Configuring Terminal Services

exam objective

Manage a server by using available support tools.

overview

Terminal Services is used to distribute and manage Windows-based applications. The Windows Server 2003 desktop and Windows-based programs can be delivered even to computers that might not normally have the capability to run them. Terminal Services supports multi-session access to applications, meaning that multiple clients can access multiple applications concurrently. You should install Terminal Services on a member server rather than on a domain controller because processing user logons to the domain will take CPU cycles away from terminal sessions.

In addition to installing Terminal Services, you must install Terminal Services Licensing. When applications are installed on a Terminal Server, Terminal Services registers them for multi-session access. Each client who will be accessing the Terminal Server must either be a Windows 2000 Professional or Windows XP Professional client, or must have a **TSCAL (Terminal Server Client Access License)** if it is running any other operating system. You need to have only one license server per domain or one license server per site, even if you are creating multiple Terminal Servers on the domain or site. Each of the Terminal Servers on the site or domain must be connected to the license server so that licenses can be issued for client connections. Temporary licenses will be issued to unlicensed clients for 120 days. Terminal Services Licensing does not have to reside on the Terminal Server. In fact, it is considered a best practice to install Terminal Server Licensing on a computer that is not a Terminal Server (although for simplicity's sake you will install both on the same computer in the exercise below). However, you do not need to make the license server a dedicated license issuer, since only one TSCAL will have to be issued per client and it is thus not a resource intensive process. The components of Terminal Services Licensing are described in **Table 15-1**.

You must have administrative rights to install and configure Terminal Services. After you have installed Terminal Services and configured licensing for the Terminal Server, you can use Add or Remove Programs to install applications. Applications that are already installed must be reinstalled so that they are configured for use by multiple simultaneous users. You must use Add or Remove Programs Wizard to uninstall and reinstall previously installed applications.

tip

Always install Terminal Services on an NTFS partition in order to provide the proper security environment for multi-user sessions.

how to

Install Terminal Services and Terminal Services Licensing on a member server.

1. Log on to your member server as an **Administrator**.
2. Click [⚐ Start], point to **Control Panel**, and click **Add or Remove Programs** to open the **Add or Remove Programs** window.
3. Click **Add/Remove Windows Components** to initiate the **Windows Components Wizard**.
4. Scroll down the **Components** list and select the **Terminal Server** and **Terminal Server Licensing** check boxes.
5. Click [Next >] to open the **Terminal Services setup** screen. This screen informs you that by default only members of the local Administrators group will be able to connect to the Terminal Server. You must add members to the Remote Desktop Users group in order to allow other users to connect (**Figure 15-19**).
6. Click [Next >] to open the Terminal Server Setup screen. Here, you must choose whether to use **Full Security** or **Relaxed Security**. You will have to choose Relaxed Security if some of the applications on your Terminal Server were designed for earlier operating systems (**Figure 15-20**).

Table 15-1 Components of Terminal Services Licensing

Component	Description
Microsoft Clearinghouse	A database maintained by Microsoft that stores information about all activated license servers and client license key packs that have been issued. The Microsoft Clearinghouse, which is accessed by running the Licensing Wizard in the Terminal Services Licensing snap-in activates license servers and distributes client license key packs.
Terminal server configured. client	A Windows Server 2003 computer on which Terminal Services is installed and When a user logs on to the Terminal Server, the client license must be validated. If no license is presented, the Terminal Server contacts the license server to have one issued.
License server	All Terminal Services client licenses that have been installed for a Terminal Server are stored on a license server. The license server also monitors licenses that have been issued to client computers and terminals. The license server, which must be activated through the Microsoft Clearinghouse, must be connected to all Terminal Servers on the network.
Client licenses	Each terminal or client computer that connects to a Terminal Server must have a license. The license is stored on the local computer so that it can be presented to the Terminal Server for validation each time a connection is established.

Figure 15-19 The Terminal Server setup screen

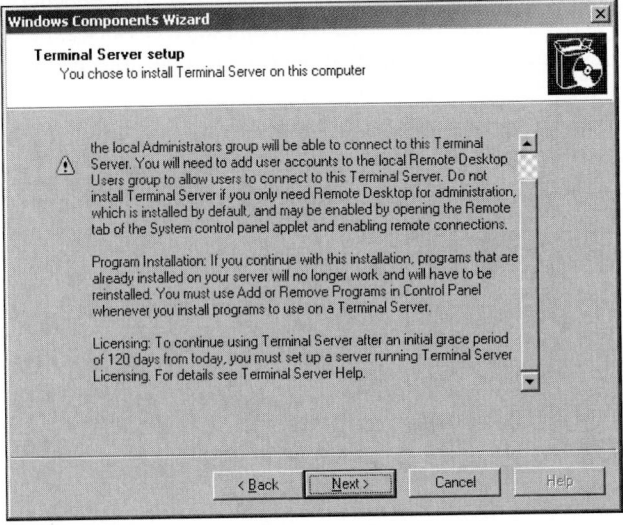

Figure 15-20 Selecting default permissions for application compatibility

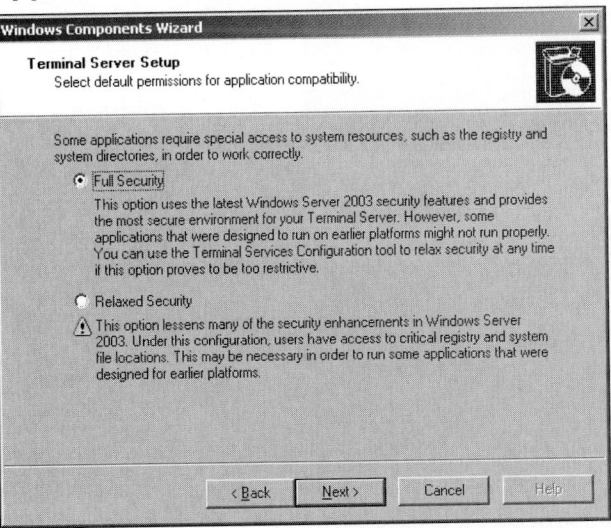

skill 4

Configuring Terminal Services *(cont'd)*

exam objective

Manage a server by using available support tools.

how to

7. Click [Next >] to accept the default Full Security setting and open the **Terminal Server Licensing Setup** screen.

8. Here, you designate whether your Terminal Server will be an enterprise license server or a domain license server (**Figure 15-21**). If you have Windows NT 4.0 domains or workgroups on your network, you must select **Your domain or workgroup**. Otherwise, click [Next >] to accept the default and open the **Configuring Components** screen.

9. You will be prompted to insert the Windows Server 2003 installation disk. The operating system builds a list of the components to be installed and copies the required files to the hard disk.

10. When the installation is complete, the **Completing the Windows Components Wizard** screen opens. Click [Finish] to close the Windows Components Wizard.

11. The **System Settings Change** message box prompts you to restart the computer so that the new settings will take effect. Click [Yes] to reboot.

12. When the computer reboots, do not log on. Instead you will log on to your domain from a client computer using the administrative account for your member server.

13. On the client computer on which you have installed the Remote Desktop Connection client, click [Start], point to **Programs** (or **All Programs**), point to **Accessories**, point to **Communications** and click **Remote Desktop Connection** to open the **Remote Desktop Connection** dialog box.

14. In the **Computer** text box, enter the name or IP address of the Terminal Server and click [Connect].

15. The **Log On to Windows** dialog box opens. Type your administrative user name, password, and domain in the appropriate text boxes and click [OK].

16. You are logged on to the Terminal Server and a **Terminal Services Help** window opens.

17. Click [Start], point to **Administrative Tools**, and click **Terminal Services Configuration** (**Figure 15-22**).

18. Select **Connections** in the console tree. Right-click the connection and click **Properties** to open the Properties dialog box for the connection.

19. Open the **Permissions** tab. Note that the **Remote Desktop Users** group has been automatically added and given the **User Access** and **Guest Access** permissions (**Figure 15-23**). You can click [Add] to add users or groups to the permissions list or you can add users to the Remote Desktop Users group in Active Directory Users and Computers.

20. Close the Properties dialog box.

21. Click [Start] and then click **Log Off** to open the **Log Off Windows** dialog box (**Figure 15-24**).

22. Click [Log Off] to log off of the Terminal Services session

tip

When you install Terminal Services, the **User** and **Sessions** objects and their counters are added to the System Monitor. You can use these counters to monitor the resources used by a user or session.

tip

When you install Terminal Services, a check box is added to the **Processes** tab in **Task Manager** to **Show processes from all users.**

more

◆ There are two types of license servers (**Figure 15-21**):

  • **Enterprise:** An enterprise license server serves all servers in a site, regardless of domain, as long as they are members of Windows Server 2003 or Windows 2000 domains. Servers outside of the site are not serviced, even if other servers that are members of the same domain are in the site. You install an enterprise license server when you have a multi-domain site, or wish to control licensing based on the site.

  • **Domain:** You install a domain license server when you want to have a separate license server for each domain. If you have Windows NT 4.0 domains or workgroups on your network, you should use a domain license server to support those clients. Only Terminal Servers in the same domain will be able to contact a domain license server.

Figure 15-21 Terminal Server Licensing Setup

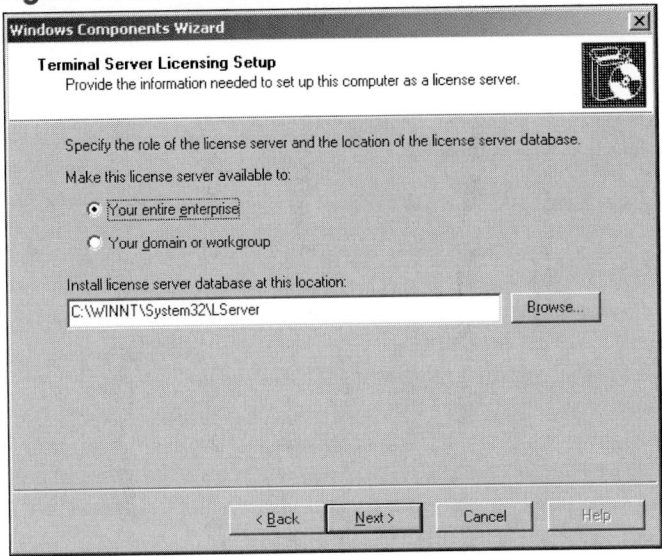

Figure 15-22 The Terminal Services Configuration console

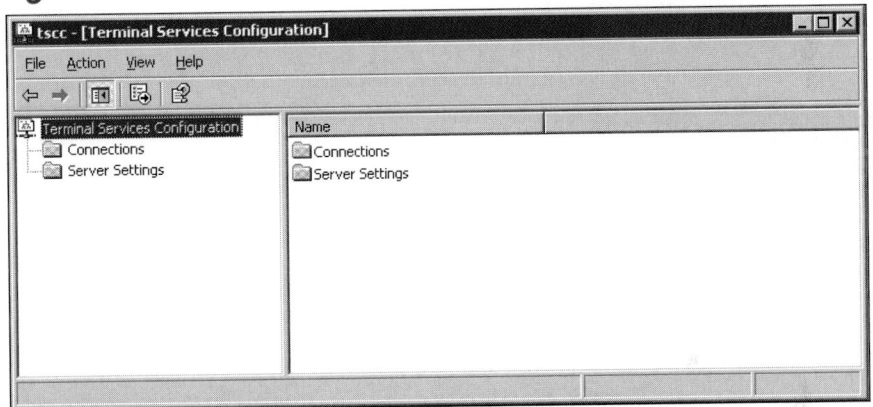

Figure 15-23 The Properties dialog box for the default RDP-Tcp connection

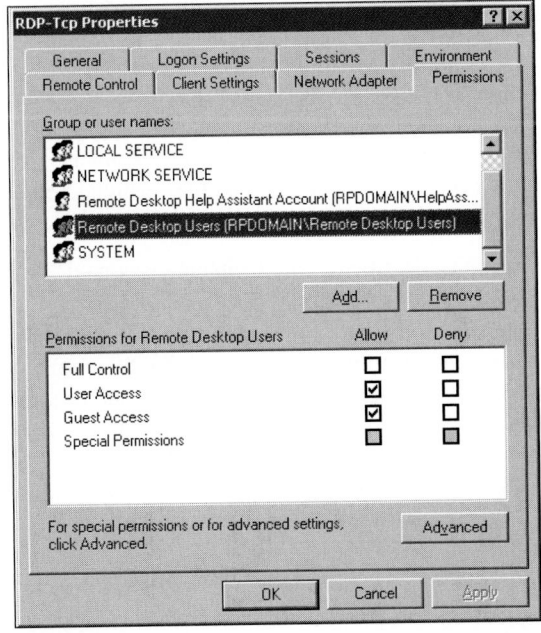

Figure 15-24 The Log Off Windows dialog box

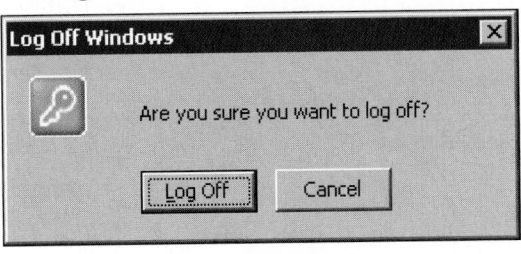

skill 4

Configuring Terminal Services (cont'd)

exam objective

Manage a server by using available support tools.

more

After you install Terminal Services Licensing, you must run the Terminal Server License Server Activation Wizard to activate the licensing server (**Figure 15-25**). If the TS Licensing server is connected to the Internet you can automatically connect to the Microsoft Clearinghouse to activate the license server (**Figure 15-26**). Microsoft then issues a digital certificate that validates the ownership and identity of the TS Licensing Server. This digital certificate will be used to make subsequent purchases of client access licenses. If the license server is not connected to the Internet but you have Internet access through another computer, you can use the Web Browser activation method. You can access the Internet from another computer and go to a secure Microsoft Web site to get a certificate for the license server. You can also activate the license server by calling Microsoft. The Licensing Wizard will help you to locate a telephone number for a customer service center and your request will be completed over the telephone. Once the license server is activated, you must install TSCALs on the server. When a client without a TSCAL logs on to the Terminal Server, the Terminal Server locates a license server and requests a new TSCAL for the client. Each client then stores its own TSCAL locally. The license server can issue temporary licenses for 120 days after installation. After this evaluation period, you must have TSCALs installed on the license server, or unlicensed clients will no longer be able to log on.

The Remote Desktop Protocol (RDP-Tcp) connection in the Terminal Services Configuration console is configured automatically when the operating system is installed. This connection is used to log on to both Remote Desktop for Administration and Terminal Services. If you have another NIC for which you want to create another connection, right-click the **Connections** node and select **Create New Connection** to initiate the Terminal Services Connection Wizard.

tip

If you reset a listener session, it will reset all sessions that are using that connection and you could cause users to lose data when they are disconnected.

tip

You must have the Full Control permission in order to reset another user's session. Resetting a user's session can cause the user to lose data on their client.

One other Terminal Services administration tool is the **Terminal Services Manager** (**Start>Administrative Tools>Terminal Services Manager**). It is used to monitor connections to a Terminal Server. You can view the configuration of the client and the processes that the client is running on the Terminal Server in the Terminal Services Manager (**Figure 15-27**). You can terminate processes, connect to and disconnect from sessions, monitor sessions, reset sessions (this boots the client off the server), send messages to users, and log off users. If multiple sessions are in progress, you can view them all in the same window. The lists you can view in the Terminal Services Manager console are described below:

◆ **Sessions:** Displays a list of active sessions between the Terminal Server client and the Terminal Server.
◆ **Users:** Displays the credentials of the users who are logged on to the Terminal Server.
◆ **Processes:** Displays a list of applications or processes running on the Terminal Server for a particular Terminal Server client.

In the Terminal Service Manager, one session is identified as the **Console** session (ID 0). This is the session on the physical console on the remote Terminal Server. If you log on to the console session, you are logging on to the session in progress at the remote Terminal Server just as if you were logging on locally. You cannot perform any administrative functions on the console session other than sending a message. **Listener** sessions monitor for and accept new RDP connections. If more than one connection is configured in Terminal Services Configuration, there will be several listener sessions.

Figure 15-25 The Terminal Server License Server Activation Wizard

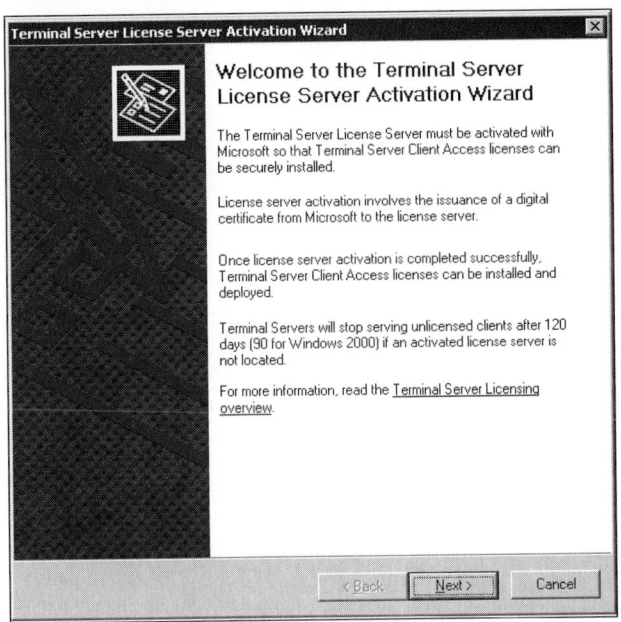

Figure 15-26 Selecting the license server activation method

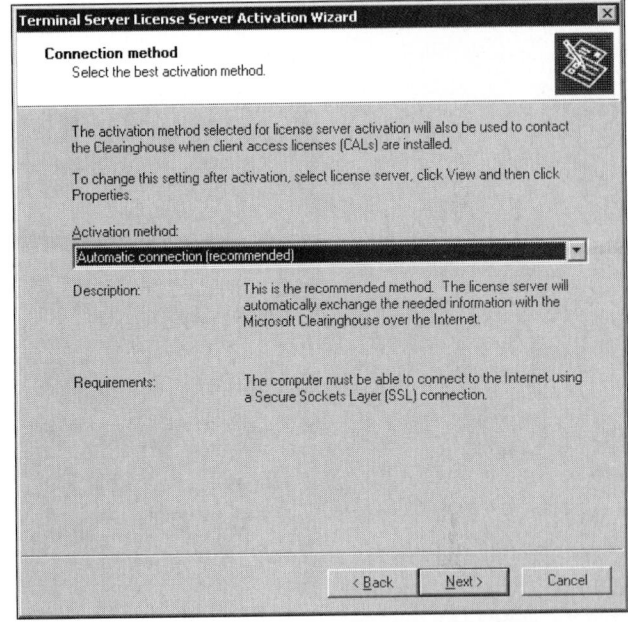

Figure 15-27 The Terminal Service Manager console

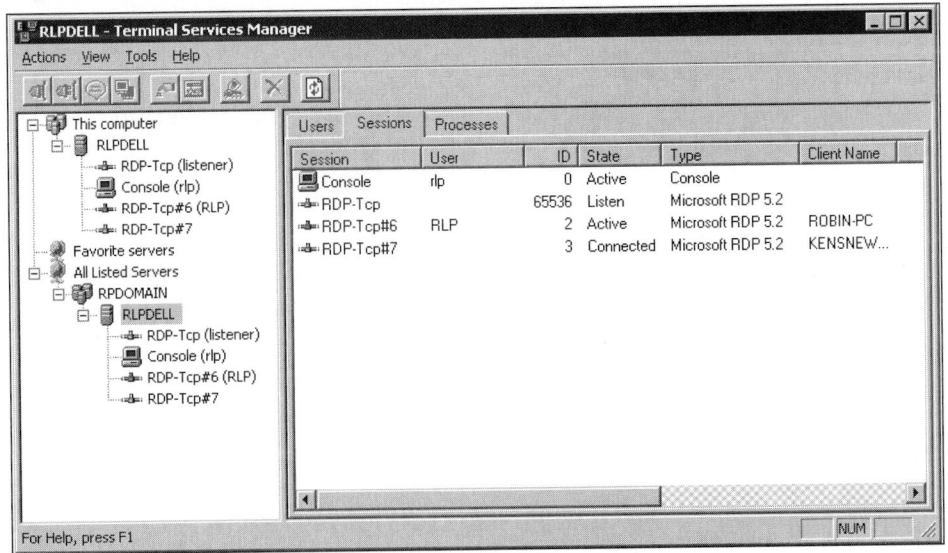

skill 5

Troubleshooting Terminal Services

exam objective

Troubleshoot Terminal Services. Diagnose and resolve issues related to Terminal Services security. Diagnose and resolve issues related to client Terminal Services.

overview

After you install Terminal Services, you should use Add or Remove Programs to install applications on the Terminal Server so that they will be configured for use by multiple simultaneous users. In general, if Add or Remove Programs is not used to install the application, it may not be available to all Terminal Services users. Once the application is properly installed and configured for multiple users, users should be able to execute and process applications remotely on the Terminal Server from their Terminal Server clients. However, problems can sometimes occur. Some difficulties you may encounter and their possible solutions are described below:

◆ **A client cannot logon:** Check the encryption and authentication settings in the Properties dialog box for the RDP-Tcp connection (or other connections you have configured for other installed network adapters) to make sure that the client can handle the settings on the Terminal Server (**Figure 15-28**). The four encryption levels are outlined in **Table 15-2**. Next, make sure that the client and the server are both using the same protocol suite, usually TCP/IP. If the Terminal Server client is using a dial-up connection, it must use PPP (Point-to-Point Protocol) and the same protocol suite, usually TCP/IP, as the server.

◆ **User is unable to run a program:** Usually this indicates that the program was installed before Terminal Services and has not been reinstalled so that it is configured for use by multiple users simultaneously. The program must be uninstalled and reinstalled. This could also be permissions related so you will have to make sure that the user in question has permission to run the program.

◆ **No connections to the Terminal Server can be established:** This may mean that the server is disconnected or inactive. Open the Terminal Services Manager on the server, right-click the server name, and click **Connect (Figure 15-29)**. This can also be due to Remote Desktop protocol connection issues.

◆ **Unable to log on to the Terminal Server automatically:** In Windows 2000 Server and Windows Server 2003, improved encryption functionality may cause the Windows NT 4.0 version of the Terminal Services client to be unable to identify the user name and password in the automatic logon section of the connection file. To log on automatically, open the **Client Connection Manager** window in Windows NT 4.0. Then, right-click the connection icon and click the **Properties** command to open the Properties dialog box. Select the **Automatic logon** check box and enter your username and password and the domain name to which you will be logging on. The best solution is probably to upgrade the old Terminal Services client software to the new Remote Desktop Connection client software. To log on automatically using the Remote Desktop Connection client software, select the **Save my password** check box on the **General** tab. The next time you log on to the Terminal Server in the specified domain, you will not have to enter a username or domain name, you will just have to enter the password. The final reason users may not be able to log on automatically is that the administrator has configured the server (either the server you are administering with Remote Desktop for Administration or the Terminal Server) to deny automatic logons. In this case, users will simply have to enter the logon information at each log on.

◆ **A user's session is stalled or the user cannot log off:** Open Terminal Services Manager, right-click the username and click **Disconnect (Figure 15-30)**.

◆ **Unable to install an .msi package from a remote Terminal Services session:** In order to install .msi packages for Terminal Services from a terminal client, you must have administrative rights and permissions on the server.

Table 15-2 Remote Desktop Protocol Encryption Levels

Encryption Level	Description
Low	56-bit encryption is used to encrypt only data sent from the client to the server. Data sent from the server to the client is not encrypted.
Client Compatible	The maximum encryption level supported by the client is used to encrypt data going in both directions. This is the same as the Medium level of encryption on Windows 2000.
High	128-bit encryption is used to encrypt all data sent from the client to the server and from the server to the client. If a client does not support 128-bit encryption, the connection will be refused.
FIPS Compliant	The Federal Information Processing Standard is used to both encrypt and decrypt all data sent from the client to the server and from the server to the client. FIPS outlines the U.S. government requirements for hardware and software crypto-modules.

Figure 15-28 Choosing the Encryption level

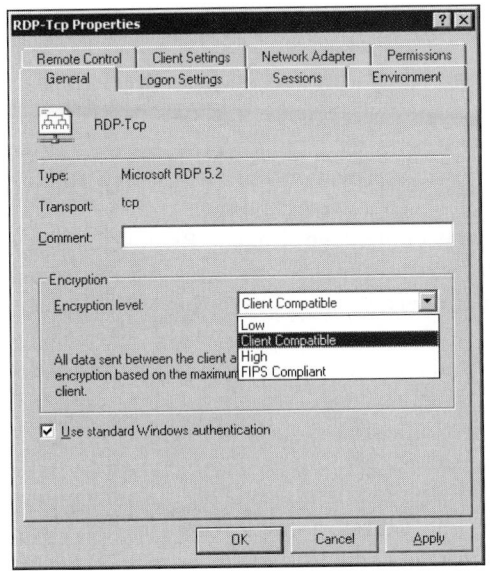

Figure 15-29 Reconnecting a Terminal Server

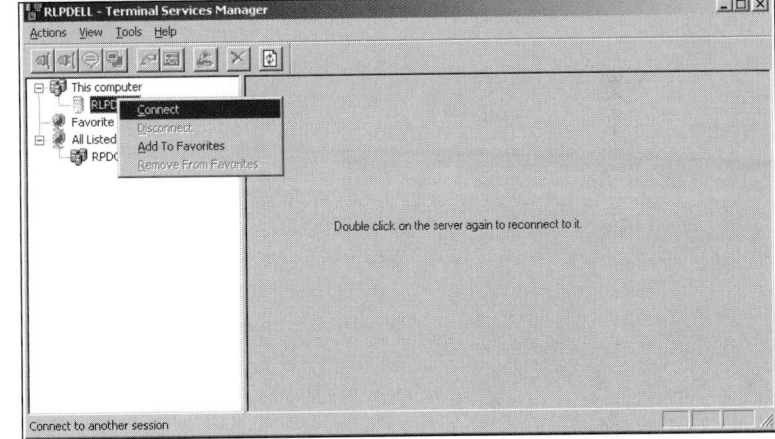

Figure 15-30 Disconnecting a user

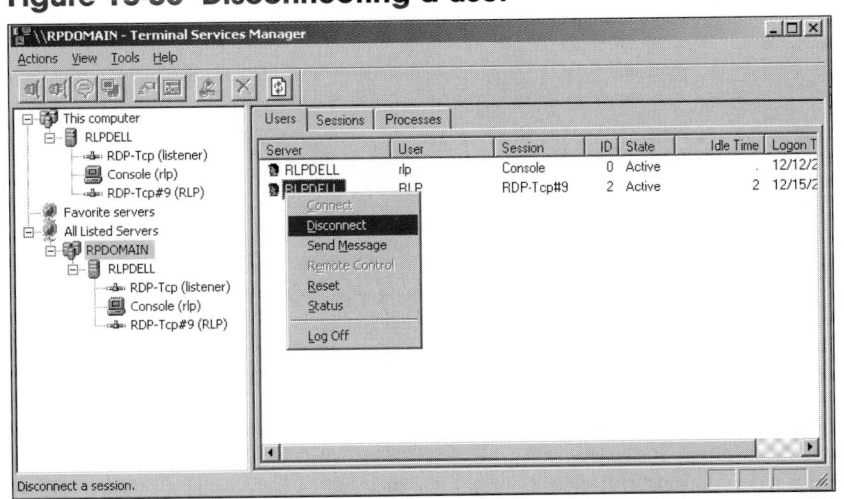

skill 5

Troubleshooting Terminal Services
(cont'd)

Troubleshoot Terminal Services. Diagnose and resolve issues related to Terminal Services security. Diagnose and resolve issues related to client Terminal Services.

overview

Remote Desktop-related issues include:

◆ **The user receives an error message that says "This initial program cannot be started":** Usually this indicates that the Remote Desktop Connection client has been configured to start a program when the connection is established and an incorrect program path and file name have been entered on the **Programs** tab in the **Remote Desktop Connection** dialog box **(Figure 15-31)**. The Terminal Server administrator may also have designated a program to start at connection in Terminal Services Configuration (on the **Environment** tab in the **Properties** dialog box for the connection) **(Figure 15-32)**. You will have to verify the program path and file name to make sure they are correct. Administrators can also use Group Policy to specify a startup program. This is done in the Group Policy Object Editor for the appropriate container object by enabling the **Start a program on connection** policy in the Computer Configuration \Administrative Templates\Windows Components\Terminal Services node **(Figure 15-33)**.

◆ **An active RAS connection cannot be disconnected with Terminal Services:** If a RAS connection is created in a Terminal Services session, the current ID for the session is added to the port. In order to disconnect the session, the current session ID must be the same as the ID that was added to the port or the disconnection will fail. You must disconnect a RAS session from inside the session in which it was established.

◆ **Slow connections:** Low bandwidth connections can impair Remote Desktop performance. One thing you can do to alleviate this problem is to set the **Background** selection on the **Desktop** tab in the **Display Properties** dialog box to **None** on the remote computer **(Figure 15-34)**. You should also avoid using programs that have high memory requirements, such as video games, over Remote Desktop Connections and consider either upgrading the modem or switching to high-bandwidth service.

◆ **The screen saver on the Remote Desktop is blank:** This is not really a problem; it is the default behavior for a Remote Desktop connection.

◆ **When the Remote Desktop Connection dialog box is minimized, the screen goes blank:** This can be caused by a password-protected screensaver on the client. You will have to disconnect the Remote Desktop connection and disable the password-protected screensaver.

more

In order to avoid Terminal Services security problems, you should follow the guidelines listed below:

◆ Add your user account to the Remote Desktop Users group on your computer so that you will not have to log on as an Administrator in order to remotely access your computer. It is never considered a good practice to log on to a computer as an Administrator when you are performing everyday tasks and functions. You should log on as an Administrator only if you must perform management functions.

◆ All members of the Remote Desktop Users group should be required to use strong passwords. If either the client or the server is connected to the Internet, this is a necessity in order to avoid dictionary attacks and other malicious password cracking assaults.

◆ Upgrade all old Terminal Services clients to the Remote Desktop Connection client.

◆ Follow all of the general security rules for a network such as restricting access to servers to only trusted personnel, logging on as an Administrator only when necessary to perform administrative tasks, and assigning users to groups and assigning permissions based on the lowest level of access necessary for those users to perform their regular duties. If you are not using any legacy programs, this can include restricted membership in the Power Users group and more extensive use of the Users group in order to avoid allowing normal users to access any administrative functions.

The Prentice Hall Certification Series Exam 70-290

Figure 15-31 The Programs tab in the Remote Desktop Connection dialog box

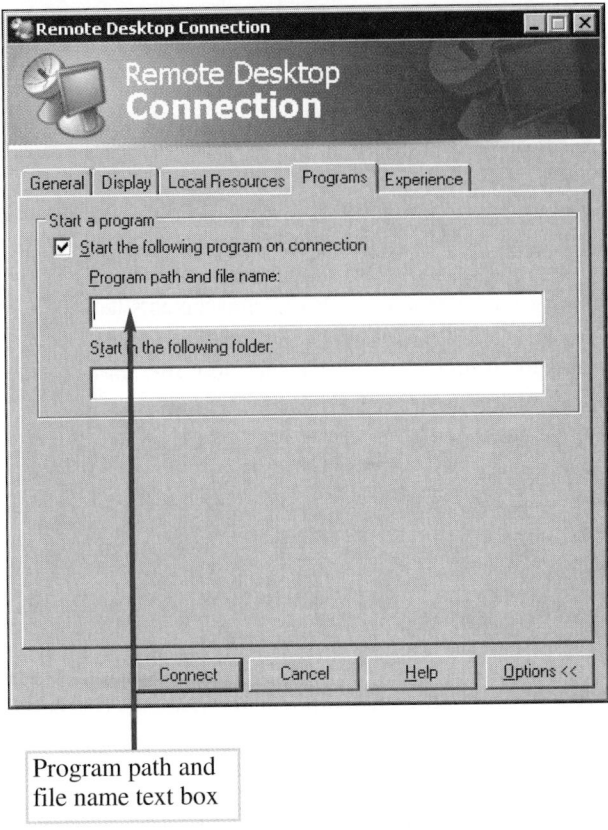

Program path and
file name text box

Figure 15-32 The Environment tab in the RDP-Tcp Properties dialog box

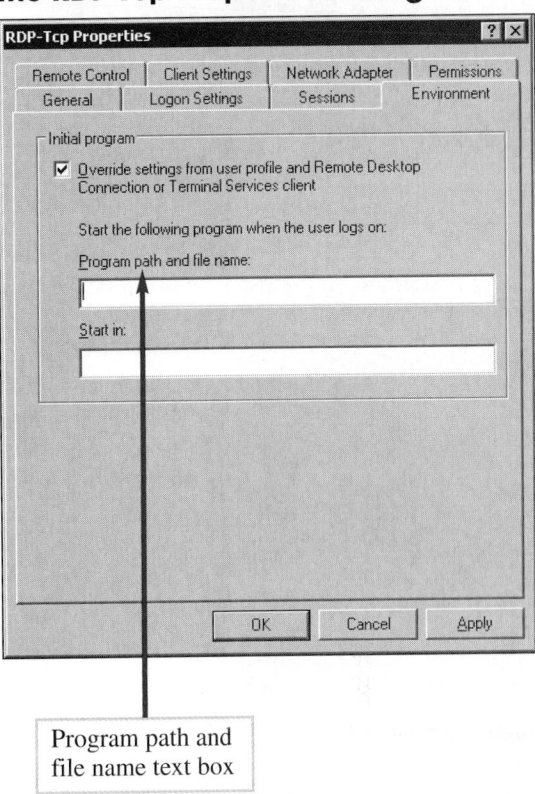

Program path and
file name text box

Figure 15-33 The Start a program on connection Properties dialog box

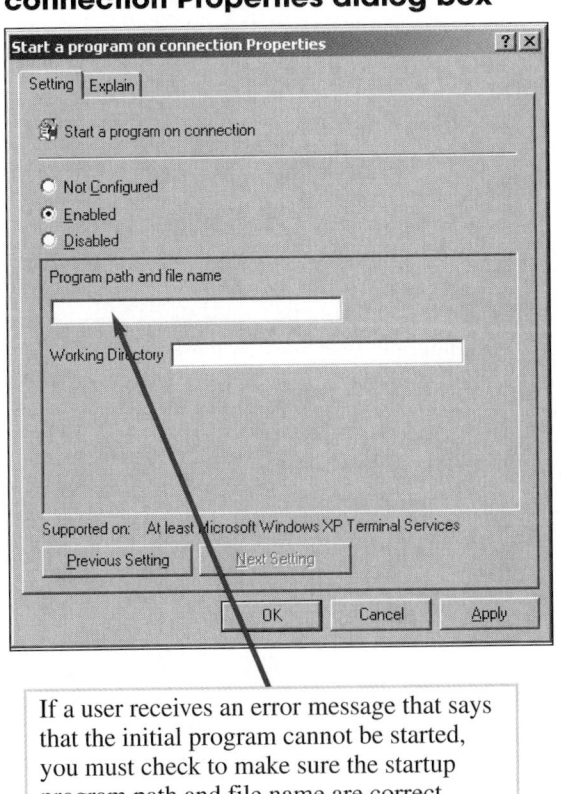

If a user receives an error message that says
that the initial program cannot be started,
you must check to make sure the startup
program path and file name are correct

Figure 15-34 The Desktop tab in the Display Properties dialog box

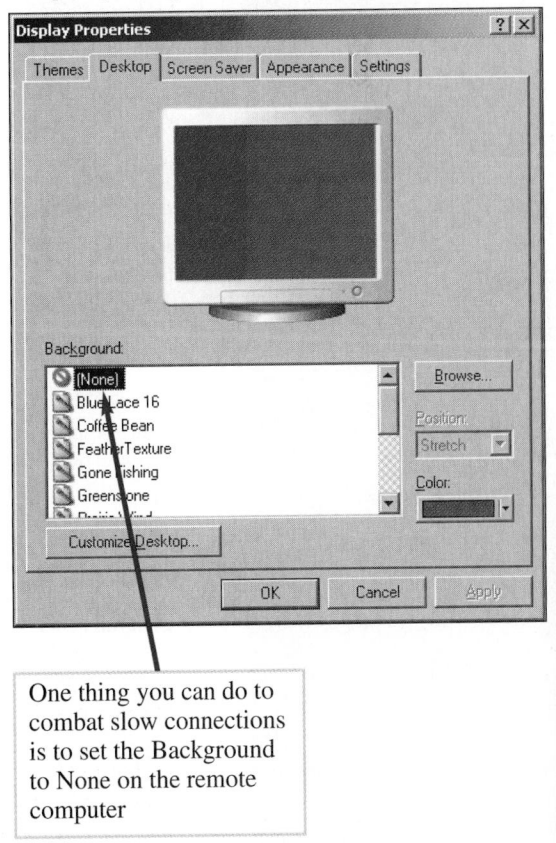

One thing you can do to
combat slow connections
is to set the Background
to None on the remote
computer

skill 6

Introducing Internet Information Services 6.0

exam objective

Manage a Web server. Manage Internet Information Services (IIS).

overview

Internet Information Services (IIS) 6.0 is the Web server for Windows Server 2003. Using IIS, you can publish Web pages and deploy scalable and reliable Web sites. For security reasons, IIS 6.0 is not installed by default when you install the operating system, as IIS 5.0 was in Windows 2000 Server. IIS 6.0 also includes new security enhancements designed to protect the content on your Web and FTP sites as well as data that users transmit to your sites. The components of IIS that can be optionally installed are outlined in **Table 15-3**. Some of the significant features of IIS are listed below:

◆ **Automatic restart:** IIS 6.0 will automatically restart in the event of a system failure or when a Web application becomes unavailable. In IIS 6.0, the FTP, NNTP, and SMTP services as well as the IIS Admin service run in **Inetinfo.exe**, while the WWW service is hosted by the service host (Svchost.exe). This separation of process spaces means that if the IIS Admin service terminates, the WWW service will not. Instead, the WWW service recognizes that the IIS Admin service (also referred to as the IIS metabase) has terminated abnormally and checks to see if **IISReset.exe** is configured for the IIS Admin service. The IIS Admin service is the parent process for all IIS services. It supplies the interface that is used to administer IIS and all of its components. IISReset.exe is the command-line utility that is used to stop and restart IIS. It is configured by default to restart the IIS Admin service. Administrators can instead choose to run a custom file, reboot the server, or take no action when IIS stops unexpectedly. Data pertaining to the malfunction is recorded in the Event log. Automatic Restart is also enabled by default for the WWW service. However, the Net start command is used to restart the WWW service. You can disable Automatic Restart for both the IIS Admin service and the WWW service. To disable Automatic Restart for the IIS Admin service, open the **Services** snap-in (**Start>Administrative Tools>Services**) and double-click **IIS Admin Service**. On the Recovery tab, select **Take No Action** in the **First Failure**, **Second Failure**, and **Subsequent Failures** list boxes (**Figure 15-35**).

◆ **Easy access to Web sites:** Each Web site has a unique socket that consists of an IP address and a port number to identify it. IIS supports **socket pooling**, which is used to optimize access to Web sites. Socket pooling allows Web sites with different IP addresses to share the same port number. Thus, you can bind multiple Web sites that share the same port to different IP addresses to optimize the utilization of the resources on the Web server.

◆ **Scalability:** Using IIS 6.0, you can assign different ports, IP addresses, or host header names to each Web site so that you can host multiple Web sites on the same Web server. This increases the scalability of your Web site. A **host header name** is the name assigned to a server on a specific network on the Internet (such as **www.prenhall.com**). The IP address, port number, or host header name identifies each Web site uniquely on the Web server. Hosting multiple Web sites on a single Web server helps reduce costs and saves time, because you will not need to create different Web servers in order to host multiple sites. You assign different ports, IP addresses, or host header names in the **Add/Edit Web Site Identification** dialog box (**Figure 15-36**).

◆ **Bandwidth management:** The network or Internet connection used by a Web server is generally also used by multiple services running on the server such as an e-mail service. Therefore, it is essential that you prioritize and then assign the available bandwidth to applications and Web resources. **Bandwidth throttling** is used to limit the bandwidth used by IIS services to a value that you, as an administrator, set. If the bandwidth used by the IIS services approaches or exceeds this limit, bandwidth throttling delays or rejects IIS

tip

You can also use the Iisreset.exe /disable command at the command prompt to disable Automatic Restart for the IIS Admin service.

tip

To disable Automatic Restart for the WWW service, in the Services snap-in, double-click World Wide Web Publishing Service, and select Take No Action in the First, Second, and Subsequent Failures list boxes.

tip

IIS 6.0 has a new kernel-mode driver that is used for HTTP parsing and caching. This is designed to increase the scalability of multiprocessor computers and throughput on the Web server so that you can host more sites on one Web server and maintain a greater number of simultaneous active worker processes.

Table 15-3 Components of Internet Information Services*

Component	Description
Background Intelligent Transfer Service (BITS) server extension	Service that transfers files using spare bandwidth and resumes data transfers if a session is disconnected or if the computer reboots. Spare bandwidth refers to bandwidth that is not currently in use. For example, if 70% of your bandwidth is currently in use, BITS will transfer files using only the remaining 30 percent. If there is a network disconnection or a reboot when the connection is reestablished, BITS will resume a data transfer from the interruption point.
Common Files	IIS program files.
File Transfer Protocol Service	Service used to install the default FTP site and to create new FTP sites. FTP sites are used to upload and download files to and from a server over the Internet.
FrontPage 2002 Server Extensions	A group of files that provide functionality for Microsoft FrontPage and Visual InterDev. FrontPage is an HTML editor, which is used to create Web sites. It provides a graphical interface that you can use to create a Web site without having to learn HTML. Using FrontPage server extensions, administrators can view and modify Web pages, create new Web pages, and manage pages from a remote location on a network. FrontPage server extensions are also used for security and site configuration.
Internet Information Services Manager	Installs the Internet Information Services (IIS) Manager snap-in, which is used to manage the IIS server.
Internet Printing	Component used to enable Web-based printer management. This allows you to administer, connect to, and view printers using a Web browser, as well as to connect to a printer using the printer's URL.
NNTP Service	Component used to configure an IIS server to act as a Network News Transport Protocol server, which can receive, distribute, and post Usenet articles. Newsreader clients can post and read messages and IIS can exchange NNTP messages with other NNTP servers.
SMTP Service	Component used to configure an IIS server to act as a Simple Mail Transfer Protocol server, which facilitates the transmission of e-mail either on your network or the Internet.
World Wide Web Publishing Service	Component used to configure an IIS server to deliver Web publishing services.

*You can add or remove these components using the Windows Components Wizard in Add or Remove Programs. If you install IIS by configuring the Application Server role using the Configure Your Server or Manage Your Server Wizards all components may not be installed.

Figure 15-35 The IIS Admin Service Properties dialog box

You can assign different ports, IP addresses, or host header names to each Web site so that you can host multiple Web sites on the same Web server

Figure 15-36 The Add/Edit Web Site Identification dialog box

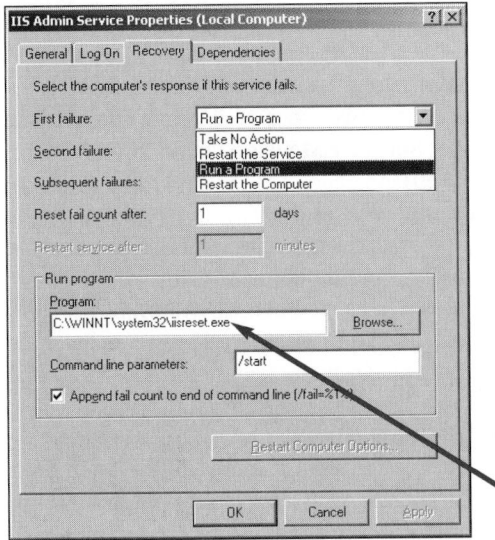

Iisrest.exe is configured to run by default

skill 6

Introducing Internet Information Services 6.0 (cont'd)

exam objective

Manage a Web server. Manage Internet Information Services (IIS).

overview

service requests until more bandwidth becomes available. This ensures that bandwidth is available to applications as well as Web services on the server (**Figure 15-37**).

◆ **Reliability:** The newly designed request-processing architecture in IIS 6.0 allows Web-based applications to run in an environment in which they are protected from the malfunctions of other applications. What this means is that one program will typically not prevent another program from running and administrators will not have to stop and start services as often in order to solve application problems. IIS 6.0 also includes application monitoring so that administrators will be able to identify applications that have not yet failed but are beginning to exhibit problems.

how to

Install IIS.

1. Click [🏁 Start] point to **Administrative Tools**, and click **Configure Your Server Wizard**.
2. Click [Next >] to open the **Preliminary Steps** screen.
3. Click [Next >] to open the **Server Role** screen. Select **Application Server (IIS, ASP.NET) (Figure 15-38)**.
4. Click [Next >] to open the **Application Server Options** screen. Select both the **Front Page Server Extensions** and **Enable ASP.NET** check boxes (**Figure 15-39**).
5. Click [Next >] to open the **Summary of Selections** screen.
6. Click [Next >] to open the **Applying Selections** screen. The operating system begins to install and configure the selected components and the **Windows Components Wizard**, **Configuring the Components** screen opens. You will be prompted to insert the Windows Server 2003 installation CD-ROM. Insert the disk and click [OK].
7. After IIS has been installed and configured, the Windows Components Wizard will close and the final page of the Configure Your Server Wizard opens to tell you that **This Server is Now an Application Server**.
8. Click [Finish] to close the Wizard.
9. If the Manage Your Server window opens, close it.
10. To configure the Web environment, click [🏁 Start], point **Administrative Tools**, and click **Internet Information Services (IIS) Manager** to open the **Internet Information Services (IIS) Manager** snap-in.

tip

IIS can also be installed through Add or Remove Programs in the Control Panel.

more

After IIS is installed, you use the **Internet Information Services (IIS) Manager** snap-in to manage the Web server and the applications running on it. A default Web site is created so that you can easily add content and create your Web environment. Because you enabled Front Page extensions and ASP.NET when you configured the IIS server in the above exercises, your Web site already has the ability to serve these two types of dynamic content. You can enable additional dynamic content in the **Web Server Extensions** node. Simply right-click the appropriate content type, for example, **WebDAV**, and click **Allow (Figure 15-40)**. **WebDAV (Web-based Distributed Authoring and Versioning)** is an extension of the HTTP protocol that is used to access files on a Web server through an HTTP connection. The HTTP connection enables users to add, modify, and delete data from Web pages to facilitate Web page authoring. While HTTP provides only read access, WebDAV provides write access. You set up a WebDAV directory on your Web server so that users can share documents over the Internet or an intranet. Resources can be locked and unlocked so that numerous people can be reading the file at the same time, but only one can be modifying it at a time. WebDAV provides a Web folder interface, similar to Windows Explorer, in which you can drag and drop folders to provide a network file system suitable for the Internet. It can be thought of as an over-the-Web document management system, a support protocol for collaborative applications, and a central tool for remote software development teams.

tip

The default setup is to configure IIS only for static content.

Figure 15-37 The Performance tab in the Default Web Site Properties dialog box

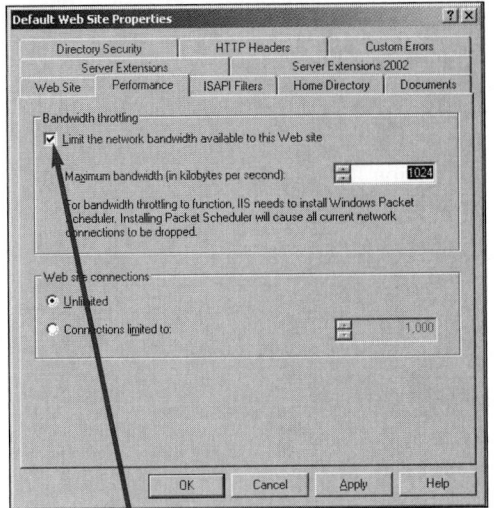

Figure 15-38 Configuring an Application Server

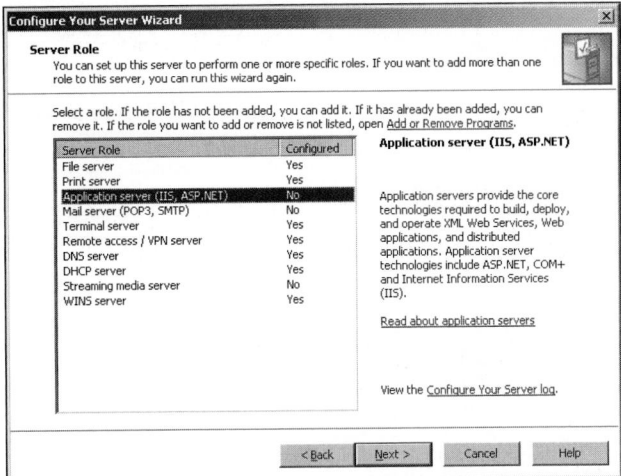

Used to limit the bandwidth used by IIS; if the bandwidth approaches or exceeds this limit, bandwidth throttling delays or ejects IIS service requests until more bandwidth becomes available

Figure 15-39 Installing dynamic content tools

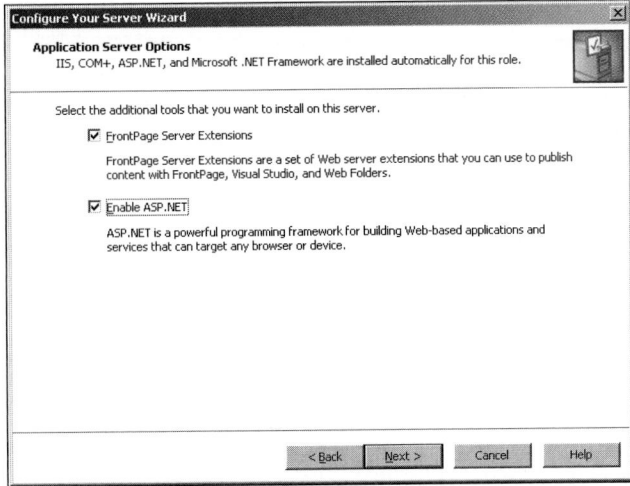

Figure 15-40 Enabling additional dynamic content tools

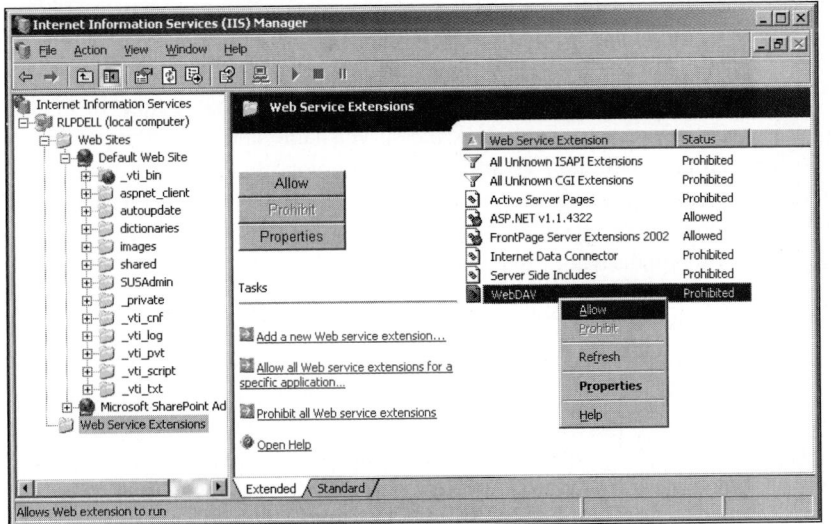

skill 7

Examining IIS Configuration Changes

exam objective

Manage a Web server. Manage Internet Information Services (IIS).

overview

In addition to the installation of the Internet Information Services (IIS) Manager snap-in, a number of other configuration changes are instituted after you install IIS. These changes include new user objects, new services added to the Services console, and additional folders on the hard drive. Understanding each of these configuration changes will help you to understand how IIS functions.

First, let's examine the two new user accounts and one new group account that are added. If you install IIS on a member server, these accounts will be added to the local accounts database and can be viewed in the Computer Management console. If you install IIS on a domain controller, these accounts are added to Active Directory and can be viewed in the Active Directory User and Computers console (**Figure 15-41**). The IUSR_<*server_name*> account is the account that will be used for Anonymous access to the IIS server. The IWAM_<*server_name*> account is the user account that will be used to start out-of-process applications and the IIS_WPG group account is the worker process group. Worker processes serve specific namespaces. For example, **www.azimuth-interactive.com** will be served by a specific worker process, which can run under an identity that is added to the IIS_WPG group, for example, AzimuthInteractiveAccount. The IIS_WPG group has no default members, and you should only add service accounts to this group.

In addition to the IIS Admin Service, to which you have already been introduced, other new services are added to the Services snap-in, depending on the components of IIS you have installed. If you have installed the File Transfer Protocol Service, the FTP Publishing service will be installed. If you have installed Network News Transfer Protocol (NNTP), that service will be installed, and if you have installed Simple Mail Transfer Protocol, that service will be installed. Finally, the World Wide Web Publishing service will be installed to provide you with a Web server that can host one or any number of Web sites (**Figure 15-42**).

The new folders installed include **Inetpub**, which is installed at the root of the system drive (*%systemdrive%*\inetpub), **Inetsrv**, which is installed in the *%systemroot%*\system32 folder, and **Iishelp**, which is installed in the *%systemroot%*\Help folder. **Inetpub** is the storage folder for all content. Sub-folders divide the content according to whether it is Web content, or FTP, NNTP, or SMTP content (**Figure 15-43**). **Inetsrv** stores all IIS programs and .dll files, and **Iishelp** contains IIS documentation.

more

When you configure IIS, you can set properties for all Web sites on the server or only for a particular site. To set properties for all Web sites on a server, referred to as **Master properties**, you use the **Web Site Properties** dialog box. In Internet Information Services (IIS) Manager, right-click the server name and click **Properties**. Likewise, to set Master properties for all FTP sites on a server, you use the **FTP Sites Properties** dialog box. Setting properties for all sites on a particular server allows you to configure properties that will be inherited by all sites of that type, rather than setting those properties for each site individually. This time-saving capability can be used to set security and performance configurations on a one-time-only basis. You can also choose not to have Master properties propagate to the individual sites if the settings do not match. For example, if the connection timeout period for the default Web site is set to timeout after 120 seconds, and you set the Master property for the connection timeout period to 180 seconds, the **Inheritance Overrides** dialog box will open. Here, you can choose which of the child sites should use the new value or you can allow the setting in the child site to override the Master setting (**Figure 15-44**).

Figure 15-41 IIS user and group accounts

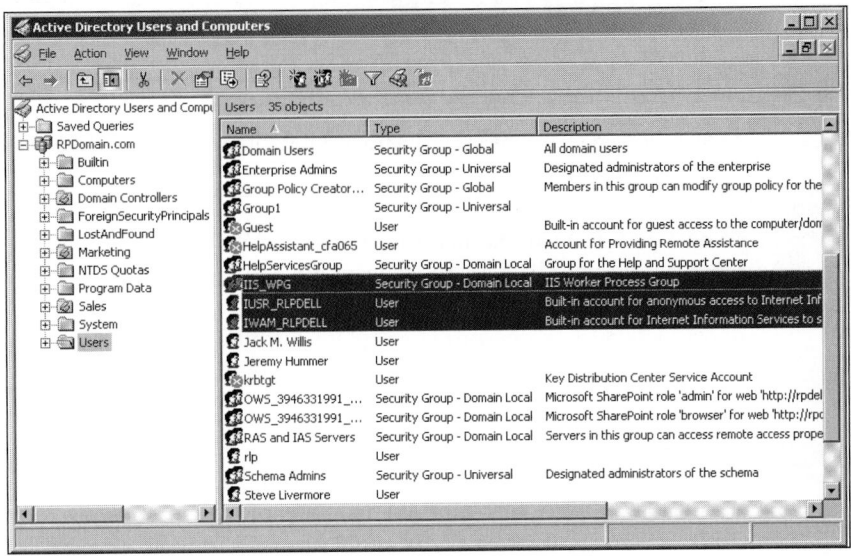

Figure 15-42 The World Wide Web Publishing Service

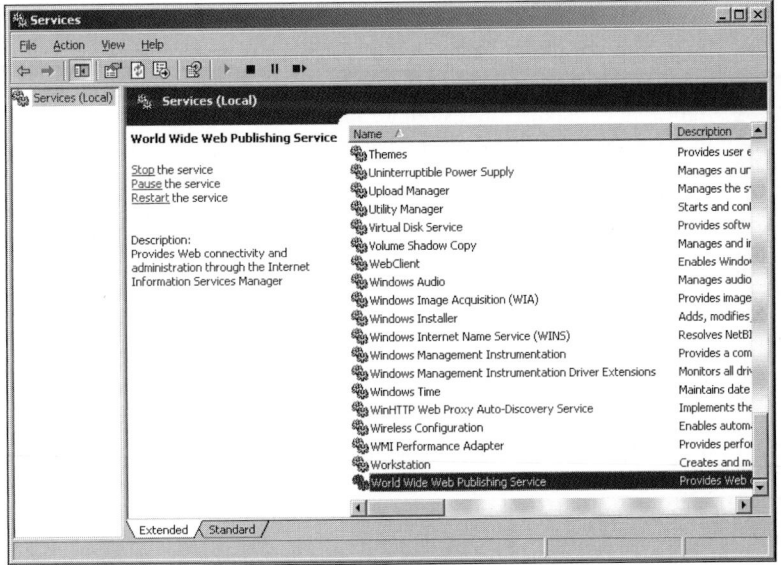

Figure 15-43 Inetpub

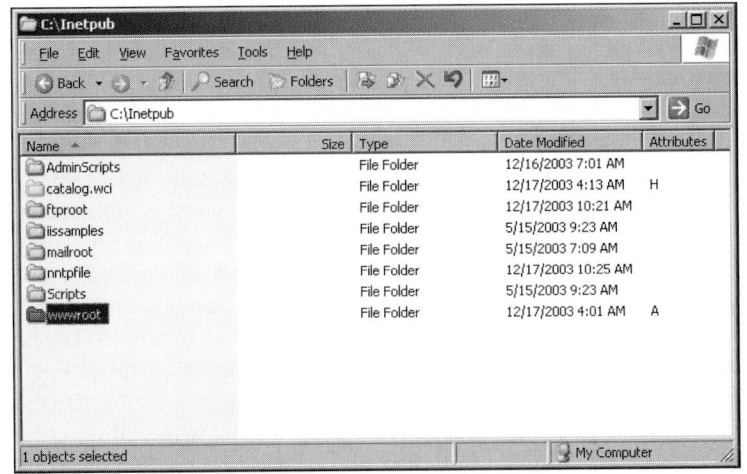

Figure 15-44 The Inheritance Overrides dialog box

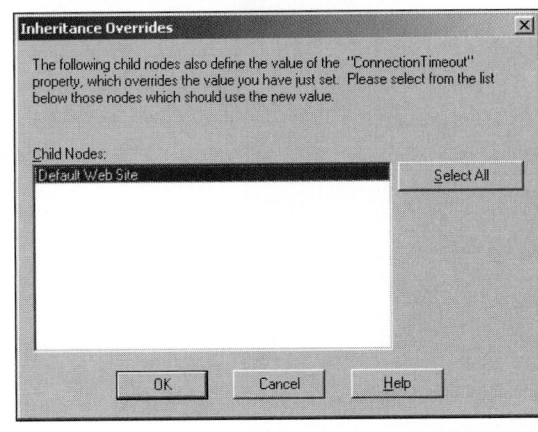

skill 8

Managing IIS

exam objective

Manage a Web server. Manage Internet Information Services (IIS). Manage a server key using available support tools.

overview

As you have learned, the Internet Information Services (IIS) Manager is the main management tool for your Web server, and you can configure properties for an individual site or for all sites on the server. Some properties cannot be set for all sites on the server and must be set on an individual site basis. Let's explore some of the configurations you can set at the site level.

First, in Internet Information Services (IIS) Manager, double-click **Internet Information Services** in the scope pane to display the name of the server. Expand the *<server_name>* local computer node, expand the **Web Sites** node, right-click **Default Web Site**, and click **Properties** to open the **Default Web Site Properties** dialog box. On the **Web Site** tab, select the IP address for the Web site in the **IP Address** list box.

To make one Web server look as if it is several Web servers, click **Advanced** to open the **Advanced Web Site Configuration** dialog box. Click **Add** to open the **Add/Edit Web Site Identification** dialog box where you can set additional IP addresses for different TCP ports. On the **Web Site** tab, you can set the connection timeout period. **Enable HTTP Keep-Alives** is enabled by default. This setting is used to ensure that the IIS server will keep a connection open while a browser is making the many requests required to download a Web page with multiple elements, for example, multiple graphics. If this is not enabled, each element will need a separate connection. The multiple requests and connections bog down the server, consume extra system resources, consume additional bandwidth, and thus, decrease server efficiency. Without HTTP Keep-Alives, the browser would also be stalled due to all of these extra requests and connections, particularly on a low bandwidth connection **(Figure 15-45)**.

On the **Performance** tab in the **Default Web Site Properties** dialog box, you can tune your Web site performance based on the number of visitors expected per day. The default setting is to accept an **Unlimited** number of connections, but if you need to conserve bandwidth you can limit the number of connections. You may need to conserve bandwidth for services such as e-mail servers, news servers, or if you have several Web sites running on the same site. Limiting the number of connections can also decrease memory usage and protect your Web server from overload attacks, which inundate the server with requests to such a degree that the server can no longer service requests from other users **(Figure 15-46)**. You can also limit the bandwidth used by your Web server. To throttle bandwidth, select the **Limit the total network bandwidth available to this Web site** check box under **Bandwidth throttling**, type the maximum number of kilobytes per second that you want to allow for the site in the **Maximum bandwidth (in kilobytes per second box)** text box, click **Apply** and then click **OK**.

On the **Directory Security** tab, you configure security options **(Figure 15-47)**. Click **Edit** if you are going to disable anonymous access or to edit the authentication method. In the **Authentication Methods** dialog box **(Figure 15-48)**, you set the type of authentication you are going to use. Select the **Basic authentication (password is sent in clear text)** check box if you are going to accept clients who are unable to send a hash. Select the **Digest authentication for Windows domain servers** check box if you want to improve security by having the user's credentials sent as an MD5 hash, also called an MD5 message digest hash. An MD5 hash transmits encrypted user credentials in an HTTP header. It can be created only by an HTTP 1.1 compliant browser such as IE 5 or above. In an MD5 hash, the user name and password are impossible to interpret from the hash. Since Digest authentication requires HTTP 1.1, older browsers will not support it and when asked by the server to provide Digest authentication credentials, the client will decline the request since it cannot comply. Digest authentication can be used with WebDAV directories. If you are going to enable Digest authentication, a Domain Administrator must make sure that all clients who will access a resource on the Web server have IE 5 or higher installed, and that the users are in the same

tip

You can use the **Web Service** object counters in the System Monitor to determine an appropriate connections limit. Monitor the **Current Connections, Maximum Connections**, and **Total Connection Attempts** counters until you determine a baseline. Then, set the connection limit accordingly.

tip

You can also limit the bandwidth used by your Web server by enabling bandwidth throttling for the entire WWW service.

tip

If anonymous access is allowed, as it is by default, the IUSR_*<server_name>* account is assigned to all users, and they will be able to visit all of the public areas of your Web site.

Figure 15-45 The Web Site tab

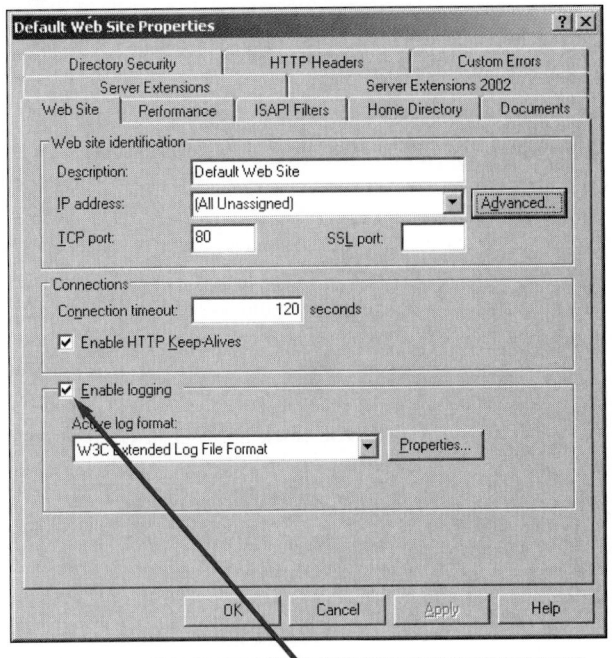

By default, the Enable Logging check box and W3C Extended Log File Format are selected; this includes logging for the Time Taken , Client IP Address, Method, URI Stem, and HTTP Status fields

Figure 15-46 The Performance tab

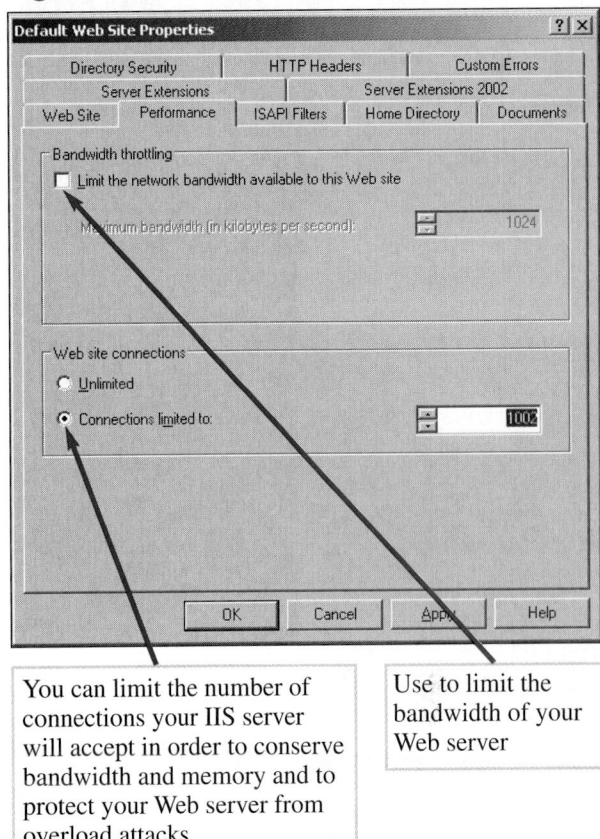

You can limit the number of connections your IIS server will accept in order to conserve bandwidth and memory and to protect your Web server from overload attacks

Use to limit the bandwidth of your Web server

Figure 15-47 The Directory Security tab

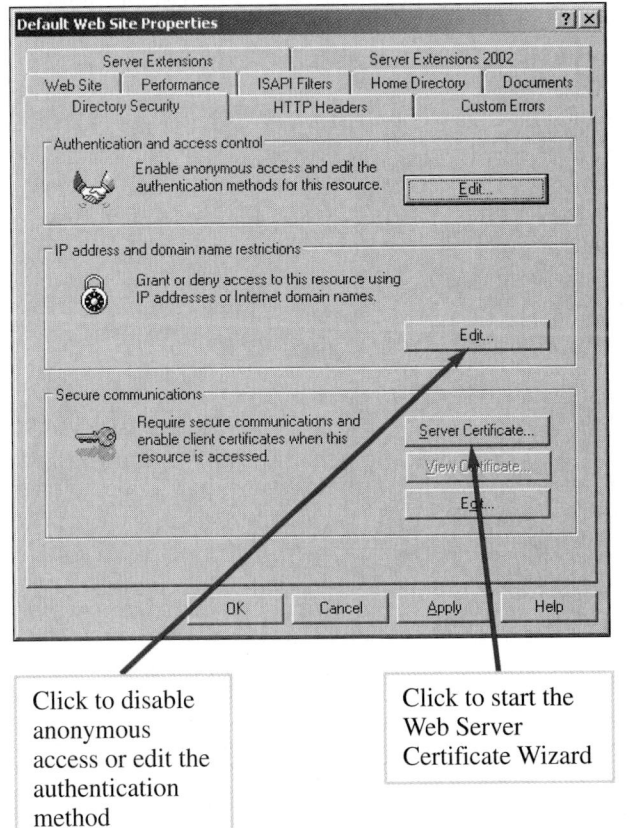

Click to disable anonymous access or edit the authentication method

Click to start the Web Server Certificate Wizard

Figure 15-48 The Authentication Methods dialog box

Clear to disable anonymous access

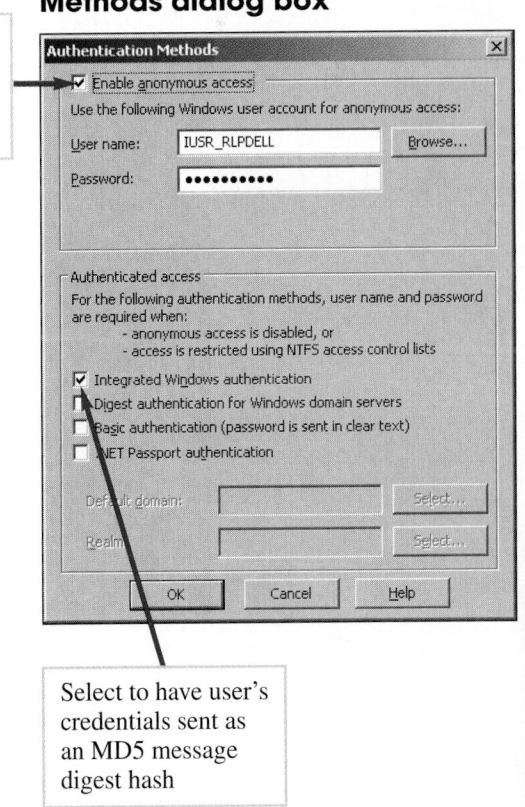

Select to have user's credentials sent as an MD5 message digest hash

skill 8

Managing IIS (cont'd)

Manage a Web server. Manage Internet Information Services (IIS). Manage a server by using available support tools.

domain or are trusted by the same domain as the Web server. Additionally, a Domain Administrator must make sure that all users have a valid user account in Active Directory, and that the domain has at least one domain controller that is running Windows 2000 or later. The IIS server must be running Windows Server 2003. Furthermore, the Store passwords using reversible encryption password policy must also be enabled. Both the Challenge Handshake Authentication Protocol (CHAP), which is used for remote access, and Digest authentication for IIS, must have this policy in effect. This policy, which you must apply to a GPO for the entire domain, creates a locally encrypted file for users' passwords. However, storing reversibly encrypted passwords is considered tantamount to saving them as plain text because the operating system, not the client's browser or IIS, decrypts them. This is why, as a general rule, you will not enable the store passwords using reversible encryption password policy, except in cases such as the use of Digest authentication, where specific requirements compel its use. The default selection, **Integrated Windows authentication**, uses either the Kerberos V5 authentication protocol or NTLM, which is also referred to as Windows NT Challenge/Response authentication. In NTLM, the user name and password are hashed before they are sent. A hashed cryptographic interchange between the user's browser and the Web server validates that the browser recognizes the password. You can also use certificates to secure communications or set IP restrictions. IP restrictions are used to limit access to a Web server to only certain, or a certain range of, IP addresses. For example, you can limit access to only a certain subnet mask or to certain domains.

.NET Passport authentication is a method in which users create a single sign-in name and passport that is used to access numerous Web sites. These sites are configured to use the Passport single sign-on service (SSI). If you configure Passport SSI for your Web site, you will not have to configure your own authentication method; however, you will still need an authorization mechanism. Passport identifies each user to the Web site, but access controls must be put in place at the site level. When a user requests one of your Web pages, the Web server redirects the authentication request back to the user. The user clicks a Sign-in button, which sends a request to a Passport server to present the user with a Sign-in page. The Sign-in page is returned to the user's browser. The user enters his or her credentials on the Sign-in page and sends them back to the Passport server. The Passport server validates the credentials, creates cookies and a query string containing the authentication details, encrypts the query string, and sends the cookies and the encrypted query string to the user's browser. The browser sends the encrypted query string to the Web server. Finally, the Web server returns the requested Web page and site cookies to the users' browser (**Figure 15-49**).

To deny access to the Web site, click the **Edit** button in the **IP Address and domain name restriction** section to open the **IP Address and Domain Name Restrictions** dialog box. Click the **Add** button to open the **Deny Access** dialog box. You can deny access to a single computer, a group of computers, or a domain name. For a single computer, you simply enter its IP address. For a group of computers, you will have to enter the network ID and subnet mask (**Figure 15-50**). If you restrict access by domain name, you must have a DNS reverse lookup for each connection, which can degrade server performance.

On the **HTTP Headers** tab, you set the expiration times for Web site content, create custom HTTP headers, and set RSACI content ratings. Setting expiration times allows you to control how long your content will be cached in clients' Web browser cache folders (**Figure 15-51**). To set content rating, click the **Edit Ratings** button. In the **Content Ratings** dialog box, select the **Enable ratings for this content** check box. You can rate content for Violence, Sex, Nudity, or Language (**Figure 15-52**). The default configuration for each is set to Level 0. You

Figure 15-49 .NET Passport Authentication

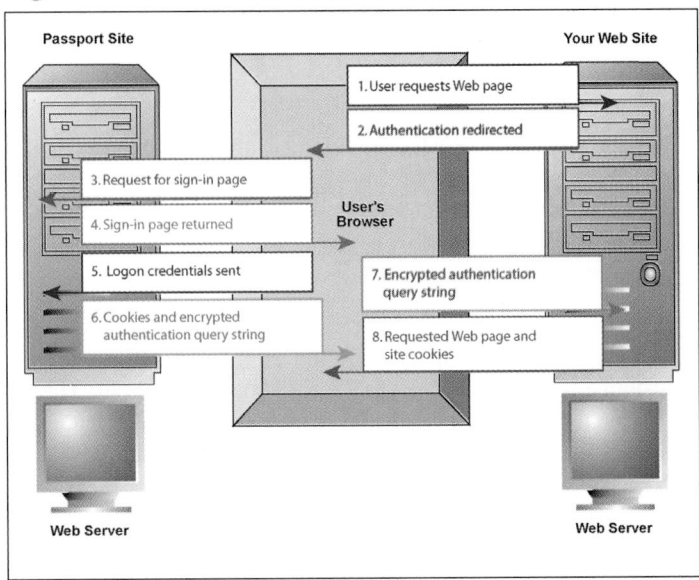

Figure 15-50 The Deny Access dialog box

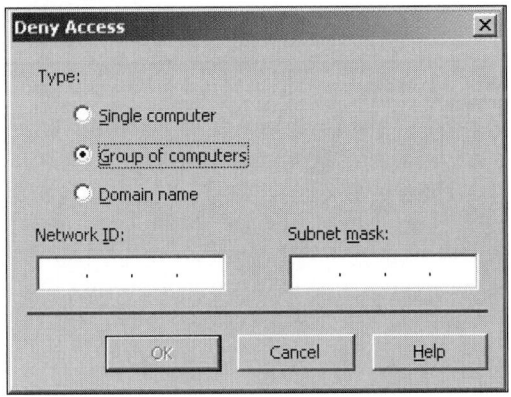

Figure 15-51 The HTTP Headers tab

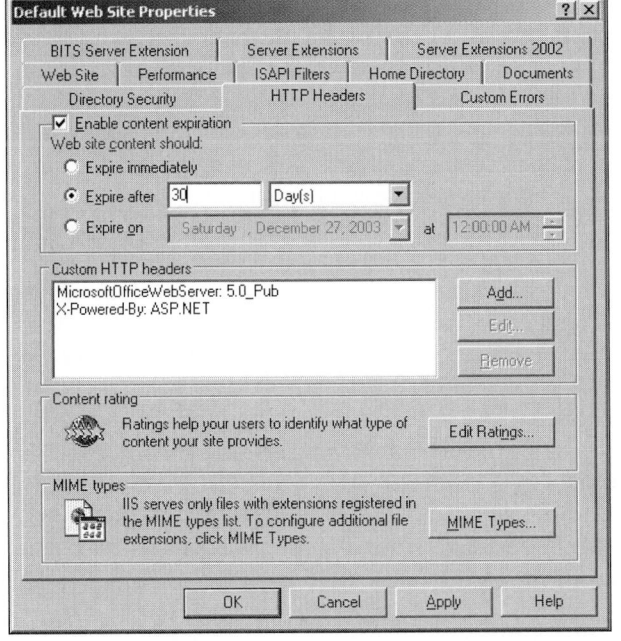

Figure 15-52 The Content Ratings dialog box

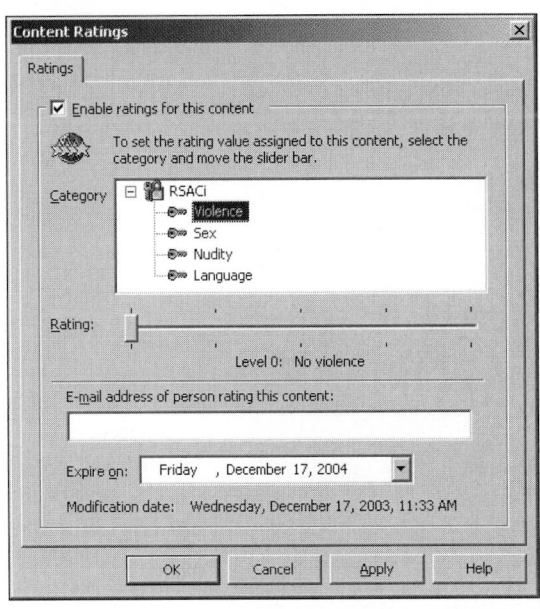

skill 8

Managing IIS (cont'd)

exam objective

Manage a Web server. Manage Internet Information Services (IIS). Manage a server by using available support tools.

overview

use the **Rating** slide bar to increase this level as appropriate. You can also enter the e-mail address for the person rating the content.

On the **Custom Errors** tab, you can customize the error message that will display in your users' Web browsers when common errors occur (**Figure 15-53**). For example, to create a custom error message for HTTP error 400, select it in the **HTTP Error** column and click the **Edit** button to open the **Edit Custom Error Properties** dialog box. The message type will generally be **File** and the **File** text box will tell you the file path (**Figure 15-54**). You can locate this file to view the default message. To edit the file, you can either open it in FrontPage (or any other HTML editor) or in Notepad. Right-click the file and click **Edit** to open it in FrontPage. Simply edit the text between the HTML tags.

On the **Documents** tab, you can designate a default Web page search order for the Web site and define a common footer to be displayed at the bottom of each Web page.

On the **Home Directory** tab, you set the path to the home directory for your Web site. You can also assign permissions for the home directory and set application settings that will execute scripts or executable files in the home directory.

On the **ISAPI Filters** tab, you set Internet Server Application Programming Interface (ISAPI) filters to regulate the functions of the Web server. ISAPI filters are .dll applications that perform a service for the Web site by processing specific HTTP requests. They are programs, driven by Web server events rather than by client requests, which respond when the Web server receives an HTTP request. You can link an ISAPI filter to a particular Web server event. When the associated event occurs, the filter is then alerted. You can install global filters that will apply to all sites on a server, or a filter can apply to only one site. If you install both global filters and site filters, the two filter lists are merged for the site (**Figure 15-55**).

more

You use the **Configuration Backup/Restore** dialog box to enable backup and restore operations for IIS. In the Internet Information Service snap-in, right-click the server name, point to **All Tasks**, and select **Backup/Restore Configuration (Figure 15-56)**. An IIS backup can be used to restore only the IIS configurations, not the content files or Registry settings. IIS backups create copies of the metabase configuration file (MetaBase.xml) and the metabase schema file (MBschema.xml). These files are stored in the *%systemroot%*\system32\inetsrv folder. There are two types of **metabase backups**: portable and non-portable. In order create a portable backup, an Administrator supplies a password that is used to encrypt the secure metabase properties in the backup files. The password cannot be changed after the backup is complete. Administrators can use the password to restore a portable backup on another computer or on a different installation of the operating system. A password does not have to be used to create a non-portable backup. Secure metabase properties are encrypted using the machine key. The machine key is unique to the computer to which it belongs. Thus, non-portable backups, as the name implies, cannot be restored on any computer other than the one on which the backup was performed. The auto-backup feature of the IIS metabase creates copies of each version of the MetaBase.xml and MBSchema.xml files in the History folder. Administrators can view these copies in the *%systemroot%*\system32\inetsrv\history folder. These are the **Automatic Backups** that you see in the Configuration Backup/Restore dialog box. The ability to restore the latest Automatic Backup can save you a lot of trouble if a critical system must be restored to a previous state. While a backup is being performed, the metabase is locked. To back up Web site content, you use the Backup utility.

tip

You can also back up the configuration settings of your IIS server by performing a System State backup using the Windows Server 2003 Backup utility.

Figure 15-53 The Custom Errors tab

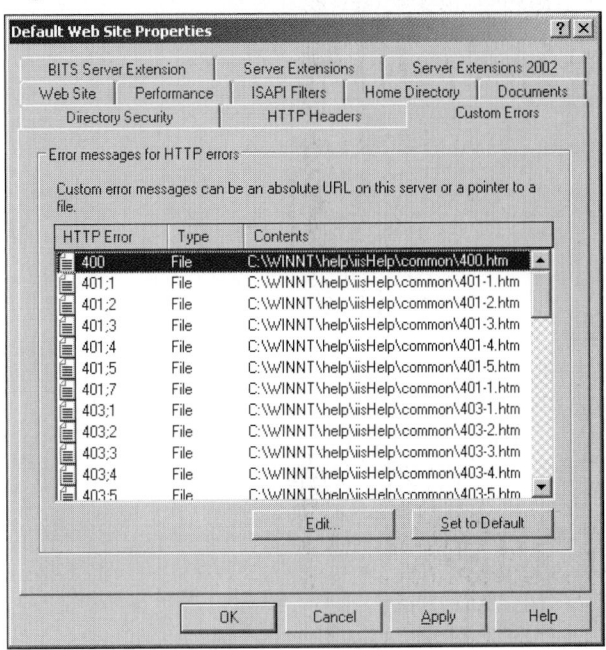

Figure 15-54 The Edit Custom Error Properties dialog box

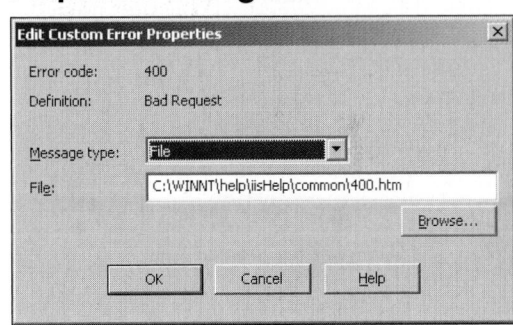

Figure 15-55 The ISAPI Filters tab

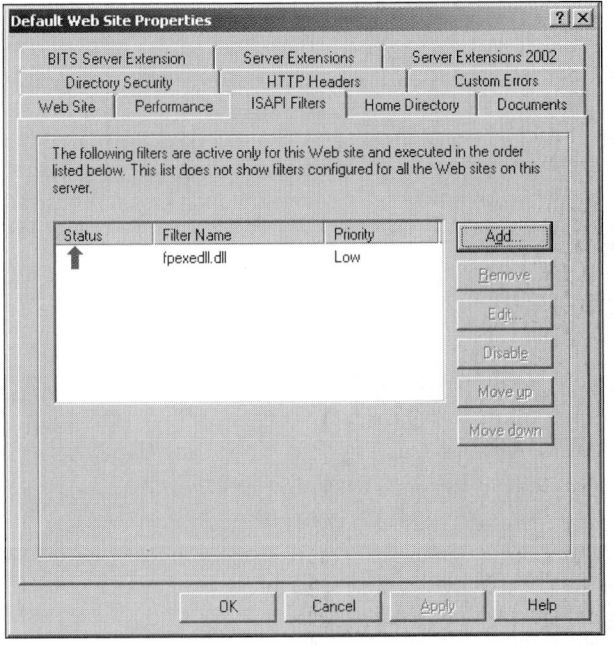

Figure 15-56 The Configuration Backup/Restore dialog box

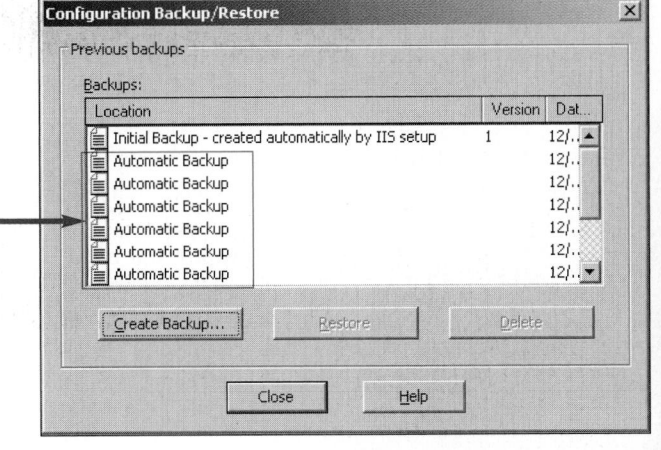

Automatic Backups

skill 9 — *Configuring IIS Security*

exam objective

Manage a Web server. Manage Internet Information Services (IIS). Manage security for IIS.

overview

You must configure security for your Web site in order to validate users, regulate user access, encrypt information, and audit Web site usage. We have already examined authentication security at the site level, as well as regulating user access by denying access to particular IP addresses and domain names. Although we examined these settings on the Directory Services tab for a site, it is important to understand that you can also configure these properties as Master properties that will apply to all sites on the server. The next level of configuration settings (down from site level) is applied at the folder level. Both authentication and access controls, as well as IP address and domain name restrictions, can be configured at the folder level. The final level of configuration settings is at the file level. Configuration settings that are changed at the site, folder, or file level override the Master properties. However, when modifying the Master properties, you can also choose to have the container objects below that level inherit the change or keep their own previously configured properties (refer back to **Figure 15-44**).

tip

Web permissions are global; they apply to all users. To apply specific permissions to users and groups, use NTFS permissions.

◆ **Access Control:** In order to control access to the resources on your Web server, you can use two types of access control permissions: **Web** and **NTFS**. Web permissions apply to all HTTP clients and determine the level of access to server resources. NTFS permissions are used to detail the level of access individual users or groups can have for files and folders on the Web server. The more restrictive permissions are applied if there is a conflict between the Web permissions and the NTFS permissions. The Web permissions are **Script source access**, **Read**, **Write**, **Directory browsing**, **Log visits**, and **Index this resource**. **Table 15-4** explains these permissions. You set Web permissions for any directory or virtual directory on a site either on the **Directory** or **Virtual Directory** tab in its Properties dialog box. **Execute permissions** are used to control application security. There are three levels of Execute permissions (**Figure 15-57**). You use the **None** permission if the directory has no executable files so that the server will not run scripts or executable files in the directory. You use **Scripts only** if only scripts such as .asp files can run on the server. The server will only be able to execute the script types you have defined on the Application Mappings list. The Applications Mappings list is found on the **App Mappings** tab in the **Application Configuration** dialog box, which can be accessed by clicking the **Configuration** button on the **Home Directory** tab in the Properties dialog box for the Web site (**Figure 15-58**). You use **Scripts and Executables** when other types of executable files can run on the server. The types of applications that can be run will not be limited to the Application Mappings list, as they are when you use the Scripts only permission.

◆ **Auditing:** It is also important to monitor Web site usage to maintain the security of the Web server. Auditing can be used to track the activities users perform on the site. Web audit policies can be configured for server events, as well as for file and directory access. You can audit user attempts to log on, both successful and unsuccessful, user attempts to access restricted accounts, and user attempts to execute restricted commands. Just as with any audit policies, you must regularly monitor the logs in order to detect unauthorized access. To enable logging at the site level, on the **Web Site** tab in the Properties dialog box for the site, select the **Enable logging** check box. This setting is enabled by default. The format selected in the Active log format list box is **W3C Extended Log File Format** by default. Click the **Properties** button to open the **Logging Properties** dialog box where you can set the log schedule

Table 15-4 Web Permissions

Read	This permission, which is selected by default, allows users to view file content and properties.
Write	Allows users to change file content and properties.
Script Source Access	Allows users to access the source code for files, for example, the scripts in an Active Server Pages (ASP) application. You can only select this permission if you have also assigned either the Read or Write permission. It also allows users to access source files. If you have assigned the Read permission, users can only read the source code. If you have assigned the Write permission, users can also write source code. Assigning the Script Source Access permission in conjunction with the Write permission presents a security risk and should rarely, if ever, be done. You do not want to allow users to both read and write source code.
Directory browsing	Allows users to view file lists and collections.
Log visits	When this permission is selected, a log entry will be created for each visit to the Web site.
Index this resource	When this permission is selected, the Indexing Service is permitted to index this resource.

Figure 15-57 Setting Execute permissions

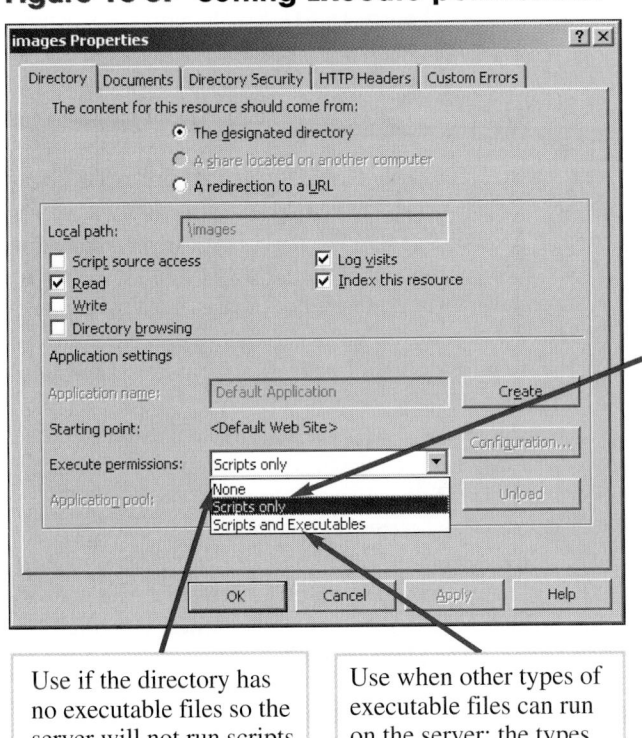

Use if only scripts such as .asp files can run on the server; the server will be able to execute only the script types you have defined

Use if the directory has no executable files so the server will not run scripts or executable files in the directory

Use when other types of executable files can run on the server; the types of applications that can be run will not be limited to the Application Mappings list as they are for the Scripts only permission

When you use the Scripts only Execute permission, the server will be able to execute only those script types you have defined on the Application Mappings list

Figure 15-58 The Application Configuration dialog box

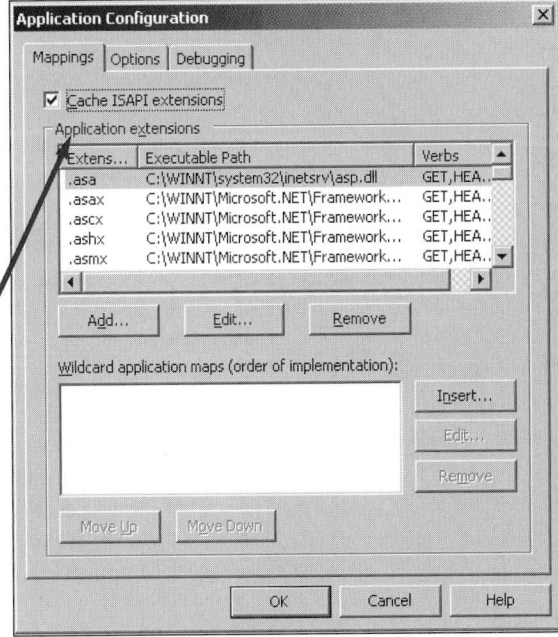

skill 9

Configuring IIS Security (cont'd)

Manage a Web server. Manage Internet Information Services (IIS). Manage security for IIS.

overview

tip

Before you can configure a working SSL Web site, you must either obtain and install a server certificate from an external CA such as VeriSign, or configure an internal CA to issue your to issue your own certificates. IIS cannot make secure connections with clients until a certificate is installed on the server.

tip

TCP port 443 is the default HTTPS port. It must be used unless users are going to be required to enter the port number when they connect to the Web site.

and change the Log file directory if desired (**Figure 15-59**). If you want, you can disable logging for a particular folder on the site. To do this, open the Properties dialog box for the directory or virtual directory and clear the check from the **Log visits** permission on the **Directory** or **Virtual Directory** tab. To set NTFS permissions for a directory or file, right-click it and select **Permissions**.

◆ **Certificates:** In IIS, digital identification files called certificates can be used to authenticate both the client and the server. You use the Web Server Certificate Wizard to request certificates, apply certificates, and to remove them from a Web site (**Figure 15-60**). You configure certificates at the Web site level. To start the Web Server Certificate Wizard, open the **Properties** dialog box for the site. On the **Directory Security** tab, click the **Server Certificate** button. The **Secure Sockets Layer (SSL)** protocol is used so that a server certificate can be accessed by users to authenticate your Web site before they send confidential data such as a credit card number (**Figure 15-61**). Server certificates include company information and the name of the issuing authority. The SSL protocol supplies data encryption and authentication between a Web client and a Web server using a variety of different cryptographic algorithms, or ciphers. These algorithms are used to authenticate the server to the client, transmit certificates, and establish session keys. Different sets of ciphers, or cipher suites, are used by clients and servers, depending on which version of SSL they support and their company policies. Data Encryption Standard (DES), an encryption algorithm used by the U.S. government; Digital Signature Algorithm (DSA), part of the digital authentication standard used by the U.S. government; RSA (Rivest-Shamir-Adleman), an extensively used public-key encryption and authentication algorithm developed by its namesakes; RSA key exchange, an SSL key-exchange algorithm based on the RSA algorithm; and Secure Hash Algorithm (SHA-1), a hash function used by the U.S. government are some examples of cipher suites. The SSL protocol actually includes two protocols: the SSL Handshake Protocol and the SSL Record Protocol (**Figure 15-62**). In the handshake phase, the SSL Record Protocol is used to send data between the SSL server and the SSL-enabled client so that they can select a cipher suite that both support. During this phase, public key encryption techniques are used to generate shared secret keys, authenticate the server to the client, and establish the encrypted SSL connection. After the SSL connection has been established, all application data flow is encrypted. The term SSL-enabled client generally refers to Web browsers that are enabled with SSL; **https://** specifies a secure SSL connection. Both Netscape (developer of SSL) and Internet Explorer browsers maintain lists of trusted CAs and the CAs' public keys. It is the browser that contacts the SSL-enabled Web server. The Web server in turn sends its certificate, which contains its public key, to the browser. The browser must verify that the certificate's validity period is applicable and that the issuing CA is on its list of trusted CAs. This is how the server is authenticated to the client before any sensitive data is transmitted (**Figure 15-63**).

• **Client certificates:** Optionally, part of the SSL Handshake Protocol can include client authentication to the server to validate users who are asking for data from your Web site. If the client is requesting a Web server resource that requires client authentication, the server requests the client's certificate. The user is authenticated by checking the data in the client's certificate, which the user has received from a third party Certification Authority.

• **Client Certificate mapping:** Another method is to map client certificates to Windows user accounts on the Web server. After you have mapped a certificate to a user account, when the user logs on using the certificate, the Web server automatically links the user to the correct Windows user account so that the user can be automatically validated

Figure 15-59 The Logging Properties dialog box

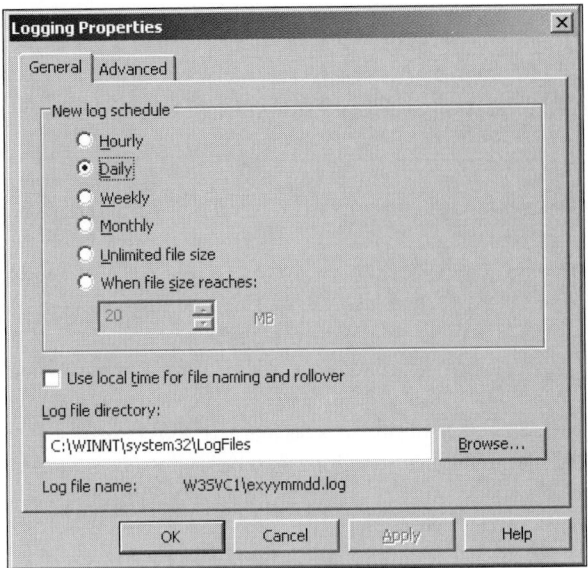

Figure 15-60 The Web Server Certificate Wizard

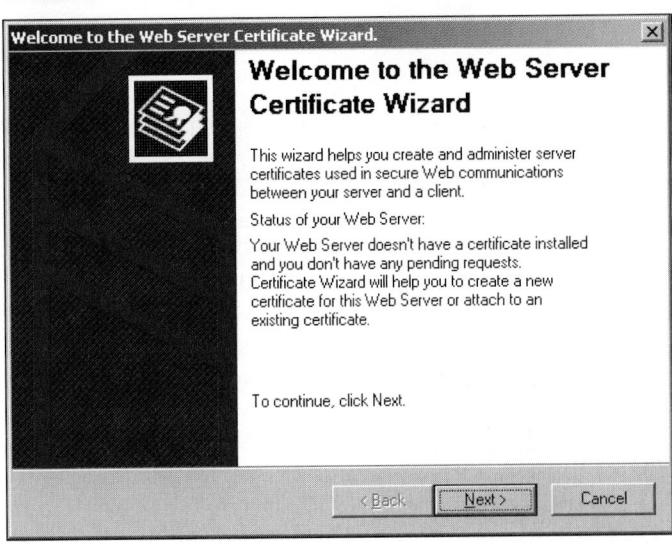

Figure 15-61 The location of SSL within the TCP/IP Protocol suite

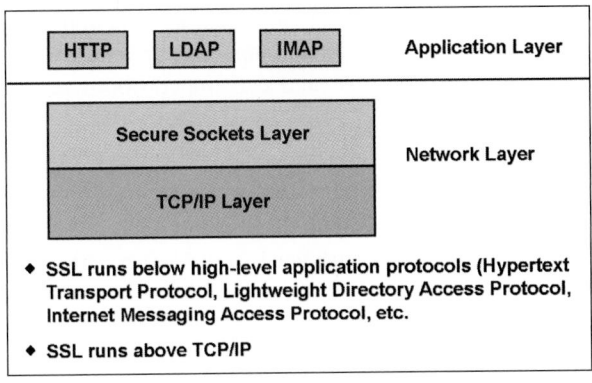

Figure 15-62 SSL Protocol layers

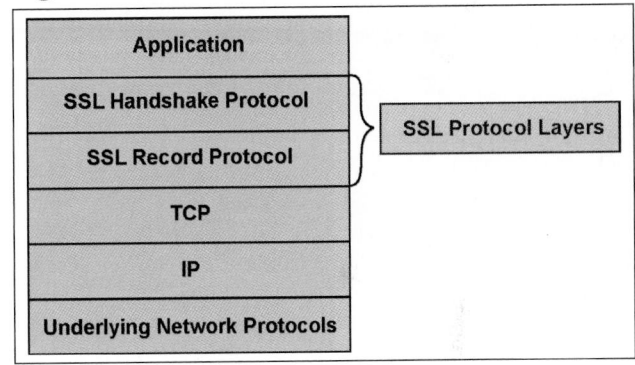

Figure 15-63 How SSL authenticates the server to the client

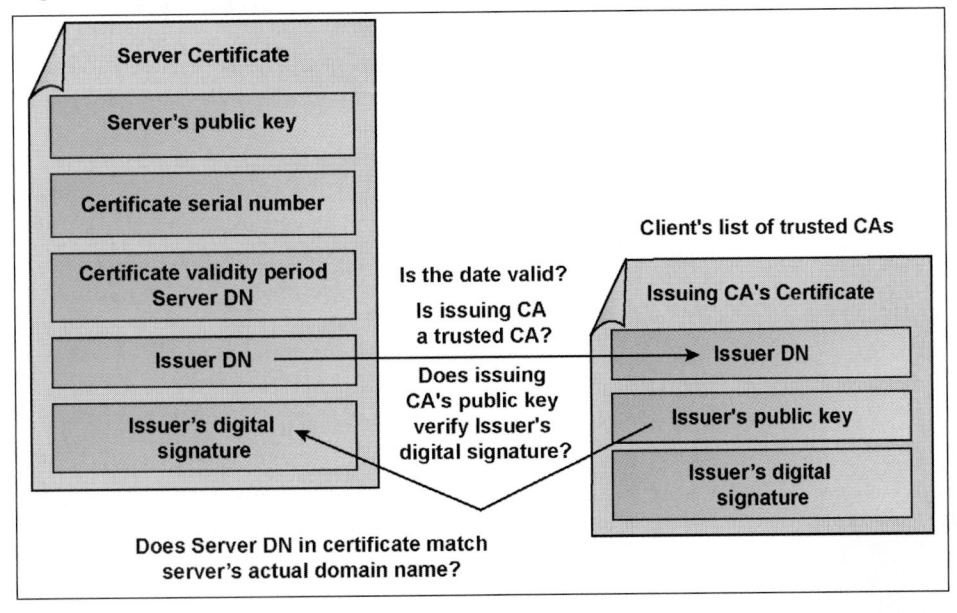

skill 9

Configuring IIS Security *(cont'd)*

Manage a Web server. Manage Internet Information Services (IIS). Manage security for IIS.

overview

without using the Basic, Message Digest, or integrated Windows authentication methods. You can also map multiple certificates to one user account. This would be done when you have several business subdivisions that each have their own Web site on your Web server so that you can map all of the client certificates for the division to its own Web site, and each Web site would be accessible only by its own members.

◆ **Encryption:** Encryption is essential if sensitive data such as credit card information and personal data, including addresses and phone numbers, is being transmitted. The SSL 3.0 protocol is the basis for IIS encryption. As you learned above, certificates include keys used to establish a SSL secure connection. You can require that an encrypted channel be used for a restricted Web site, directory, or file. However, both the user's browser and your Web server must be configured with compatible encryption and decryption capabilities. The default secure communication settings for an IIS Web server requires that the user's Web browser support a session key strength of 40 bits, or above.

As with all IIS configuration settings, when you set the security configuration for a Web site, the properties propagate to the child nodes (directories and files) for that site unless you have previously configured different settings for the child nodes. If you have, the Inheritance Overrides dialog box will open and you will have the opportunity to decide whether you want to reset these properties or keep the settings you have already configured. Keep in mind that encrypted transmissions have a significant overhead cost and can impede both server performance and transmission speed.

how to

Configure your Web server to require a 128-bit minimum session-key strength for all Secure Socket Layer (SSL) secure communication sessions. (You must have a valid server certificate installed in order to establish encrypted communications.)

tip

It is considered a best practice to configure SSL encryption and institute other IIS Manager configuration changes by logging on using a non-Administrators account and using the Run as command at the command prompt to run the IIS Manager. Type:
Runas/user:
administrativeaccountname
"mmc
%systemroot%\system32\i
netsrv\iis.msc"

1. Log on to your IIS server as an **Administrator**. You must be a member of the Administrators group on the local computer to perform this skill.
2. Click **Start**, point to **Administrative Tools**, and click **Internet Information Services (IIS) Manager**.
3. Expand the local computer node, if necessary. Expand the **Web Sites** node.
4. Right-click **Default Web site** (or whichever Web site, directory, or file for which you want to require an encrypted channel) and click **Properties**.
5. Open the **Directory Security** tab (or the **File Security** tab).
6. In the **Secure communications** section, click [Edit...] to open the **Secure Communications** dialog box.
7. Select the **Require secure channel (SSL)** check box **(Figure 15-64)**.
8. Select the **Require 128-bit Encryption** check box. This is the default for all SSL secure communication sessions for Windows Server 2003. Users must have a browser that can establish communication using a 128-bit session key in order to create an encrypted channel with your server.
9. Click [OK] to close the **Secure Communications** dialog box.
10. Click [OK] to close the Default Web Site Properties dialog box. The **Inheritance Overrides** dialog box opens to tell you that a number of child nodes define a value that overrides the value you have just set **(Figure 15-65)**. Click [OK] to allow the settings for the directories to override the Web site setting and close the dialog boxes.
11. Close Internet Information Services (IIS) Manager.

This is the Windows
Server 2003 default
for SSL secure
communication
sessions; users must
have a browser that
supports a 128-bit
session key in order
to create an
encrypted channel
with your server

Figure 15-64 The Secure Communications dialog box

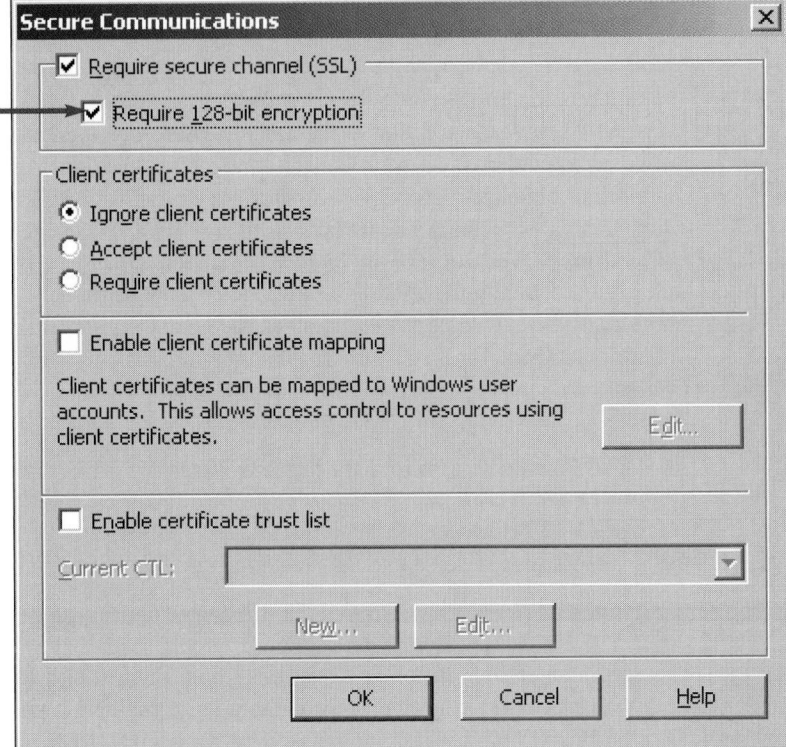

**Figure 15-65 Allowing directory settings to override
Web site settings**

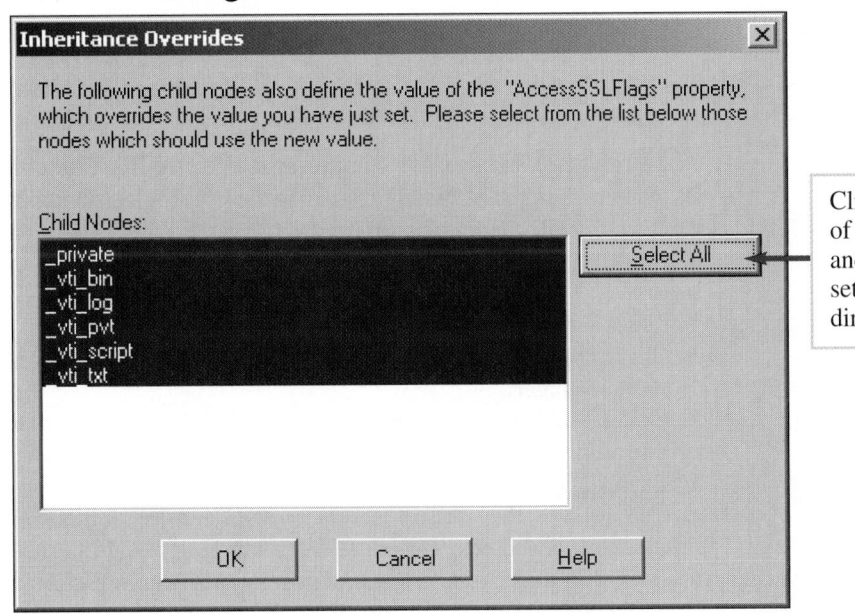

Click to select all
of the child nodes
and apply the site
setting to the
directories

Exam 70-290

skill 10

Administering the Web Environment

exam objective

Manage a Web server. Manage Internet Information Services (IIS). Manage security for IIS.

overview

IIS supports the hosting of multiple Web sites on a single Web server, so you can add new Web and FTP sites in addition to the defaults. Before you create a Web site, the content you are going to publish must be organized at a central location. You cannot publish documents that are not organized in specific directories. Every Web site must have a **home directory**, which generally contains a home page, although home pages are not necessary if browsing is enabled or if Web folders are in use. The home page is generally named index.htm, index.html, default.htm, or default.html. Home pages often also use the .asp extension. The home page will include links to the other pages on the site. You can designate more than one default home page for a site. IIS will display the first one on the list of document names, if available. When you either install IIS or create a new Web site, a default home directory is created.

By default, the home directory for the WWW service is **%*systemroot*%\Inetpub\wwwroot** (**Figure 15-66**). The default FTP service home directory is **%*systemroot*%\InetPub\Ftproot** (**Figure 15-67**). However, FTP can use the same folders as Web. In fact, many companies do this so that they can use FTP to update content on the Web server.

A **virtual directory** is used to make a directory "appear" to be within the home directory, when it really isn't. They are most often used when you have a folder structure on another disk, or on an entirely different server that you do not want to move but want to include on your Web site. When you set up a virtual directory, you give it an alias. An alias is a name that identifies the virtual directory to the Web browser. The URL for a file in the virtual directory is the full path name, server name, virtual directory alias, and filename. For example, \\WebSrv\WebPub\Webpage.html, where WebSrv is the server name, WebPub is the alias for the virtual directory, and Webpage.html is the file name. Accessing the virtual directory in this way is secure because the full path is hidden from users. An alias helps administrators change the location of directories easily by changing the mapping between the alias and the physical location of the virtual directory.

tip

You can set a different location for the home directory on the Home Directory tab in the Properties dialog box for the Web site.

how to

Create a Web site and a virtual directory on your member server.

1. Click ⊞ **Start** and then **My Computer** to open the **My Computer** window.
2. Double-click **Local Disk (C:)** to view the list of folders and files on the **C:** drive.
3. Open the **File menu**, point to **New**, and click **Folder**. Create a new folder named **Home**.
4. Copy the files for your Web site to the **Home** folder.
5. Create a folder named **Virtual** on the **C:** drive, and then copy the contents of the Home folder to the **Virtual** folder. Close the C: drive window.
6. Click ⊞ **Start**, point to **Administrative Tools**, and click **Internet Information Services (IIS) Manager**.
7. Expand the local computer node. Right-click **Web Sites**, point to **New**, and click **Web Site** to initiate the **Web Site Creation Wizard (Figure 15-68)**.
8. Click [Next >] to open the **Web Site Description** screen. You can enter a description of the new Web site so that it can be easily identified; for example, type **Research** in the **Description** text box **(Figure 15-69)**.
9. Click [Next >] to open the **IP Address and Port Settings** screen. Type the IP address for the Web site, for example, **192.168.1.45**, in the **Enter the IP address to use for this Web site** list box.
10. Type the port number for the Web site, for example, **8001**, in the **TCP Port this web site should use** text box **(Figure 15-70)**.

tip

TCP port 80 is the default HTTP port. The well-known port numbers are assigned by IANA (the Internet Assigned Numbers Authority). They run between 0 and 1023. You can use a port number above 1023 (a non-standard port number) to identify a new Web site for development and testing purposes.

Figure 15-66 Default WWW service home directory

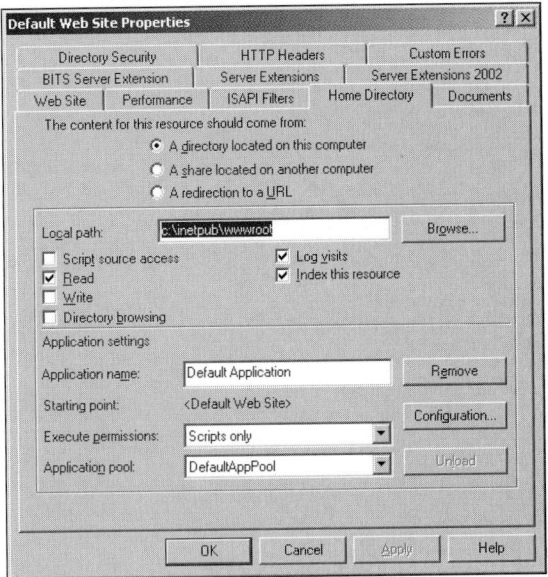

Figure 15-67 Default FTP service home directory

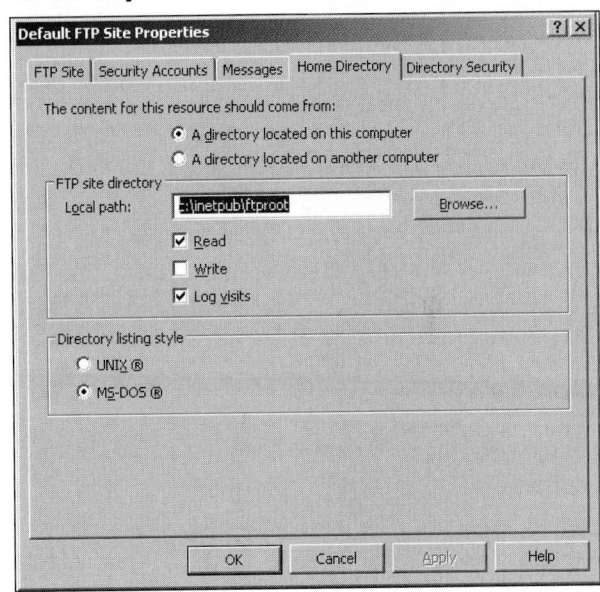

Figure 15-68 The Web Site Creation Wizard

Figure 15-69 The Web Site Description screen

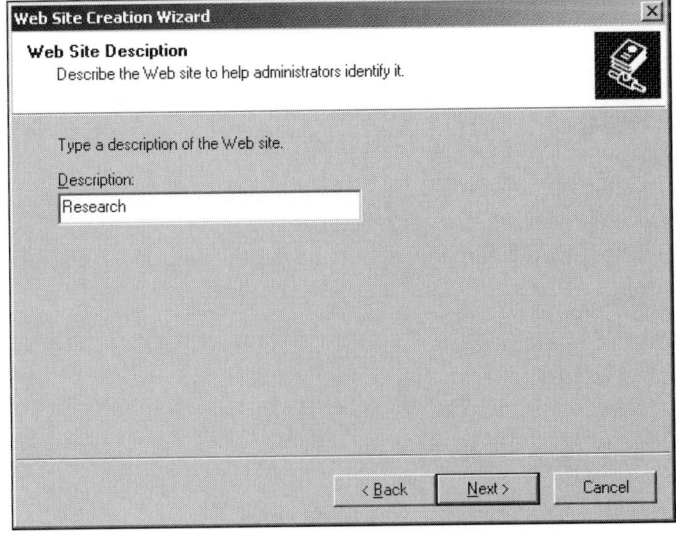

Figure 15-70 The IP Address and Port Settings screen

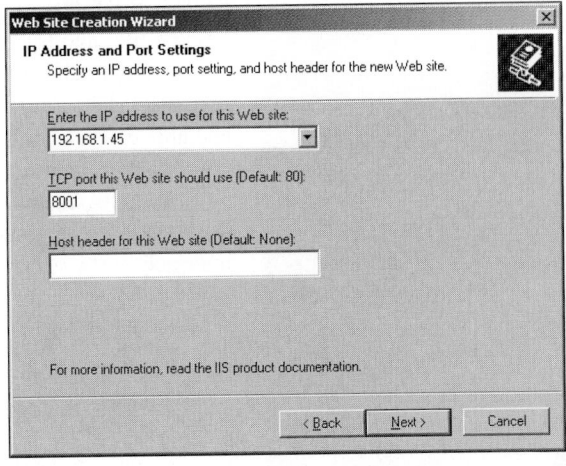

skill 10

Administering the Web Environment
(cont'd)

Manage a Web server. Manage Internet Information Services (IIS). Manage security for IIS.

how to

11. Click [Next >] to open the **Web Site Home Directory** screen. Type **C:\Home** in the **Path** text box to specify the path to the home directory (**Figure 15-71**).
12. Click [Next >] to open the **Web Site Access Permissions** screen.
13. Accept the default selections, **Read** and **Run scripts (such as ASP)**, to assign users permission to read Web pages and run scripts on the Web site.
14. Click [Next >] to open the **You have successfully completed the Web Site Creation Wizard** screen.
15. Click [Finish] to close the **Web Site Creation Wizard**. The new Web site, **Research**, is added to the console tree in the Web Sites folder.
16. With **Research** selected in the scope pane, open the **Action** menu, point to **New**, and click **Virtual Directory** to start the **Virtual Directory Creation Wizard**.
17. Click [Next >] to open the **Virtual Directory Alias** screen. Type **Sales** in the **Alias** text box.
18. Click [Next >] to open the **Web Site Content Directory** screen.
19. Type **C:\Virtual** in the **Path** text box to specify the path to the virtual directory (**Figure 15-72**).
20. Click [Next >] to open the **Access Permissions** screen. Select the **Write** and **Browse** check boxes to add these two permissions to the default permissions for accessing the virtual directory. Your users will be accessing the virtual directory rather than the Web site itself to modify existing files and upload new files (**Figure 15-73**).
21. Click [Next >] to open the **You have successfully completed the Virtual Directory Creation Wizard** screen.
22. Click [Finish] to close the Virtual Directory Creation Wizard. The **Sales** virtual directory is listed under the Research Web site in the Internet Information Services (IIS) Manager (**Figure 15-74**).

more

You can also create Web folders to access and manage the files and folders on a Web server. A **Web folder** is a shortcut to a folder on a Web server. It consists of a list of files and folders on the Web server, as well as their associated Internet addresses. If you have the Read and Write access permissions to a Web server, Web folders are created as shortcuts automatically when you access resources, such as files, on a Web server. To create Web folders, you can use the **Add Network Place Wizard**, or you can use the **Web Sharing** tab on the Properties dialog box for the folder. After a Web folder is created, you can view, manage, move, copy, and rename files and folders in the Web folders just as you do with folders in Windows Explorer. When you modify the files in a Web folder, they are saved on the Web server instead of the hard disk. Because IIS 6.0 supports Web Folders and WebDAV is integrated into IIS version 5 and above, users can navigate to a WebDAV-enabled server and the content will appear as if it is in the same namespace as the local system. Users can perform many file-system related tasks such as dragging and dropping files. They can also view and modify file properties. Using Web Folders, the local file system, network drives, and the Web site all have a uniform interface.

As you have learned, you configure the properties for a Web site at three levels: site, directory, and file. Lower levels automatically inherit properties set at the higher levels, unless you set less stringent settings at a higher level and select not to override. What we have not yet mentioned are the properties assigned to the IIS server itself (local computer). There is only one tab on the Properties dialog box for the local computer: **Internet Information Services**. On this tab, one of IIS 6.0's most significant improvements, **Direct Metabase Edit**, can be

Figure 15-71 The Web Site Home Directory screen

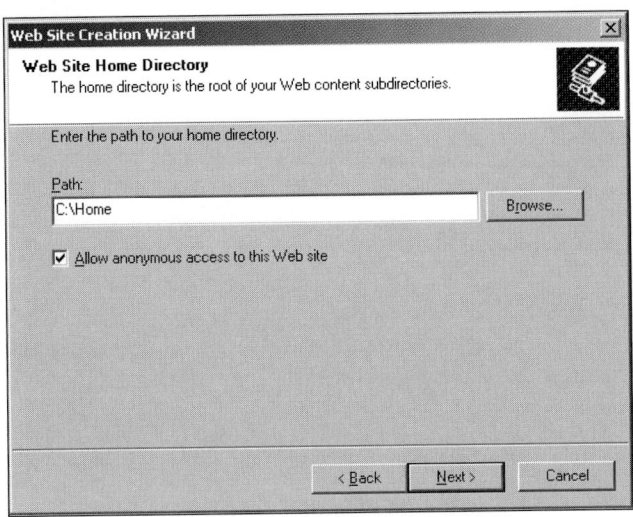

Figure 15-72 Specifying the path to the virtual directory

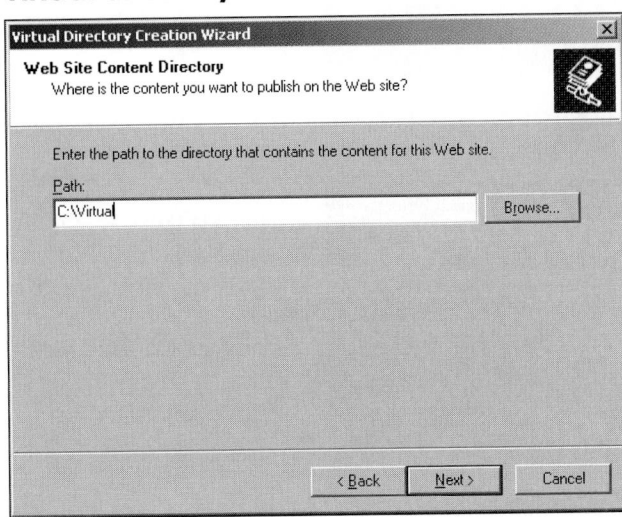

Figure 15-73 Setting Virtual Directory Access Permissions

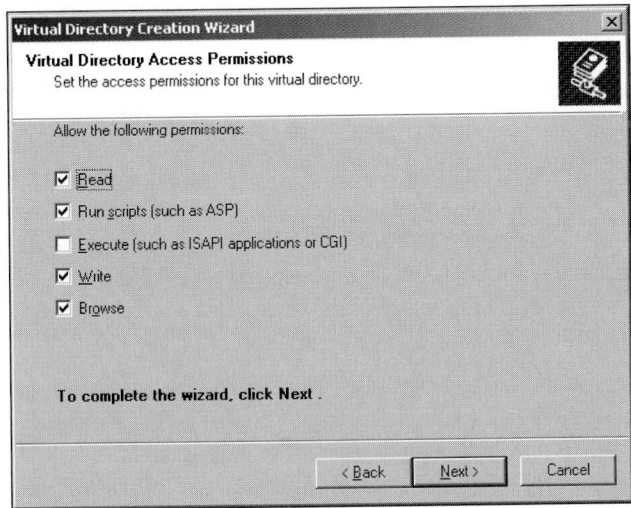

Figure 15-74 Viewing the new Web site

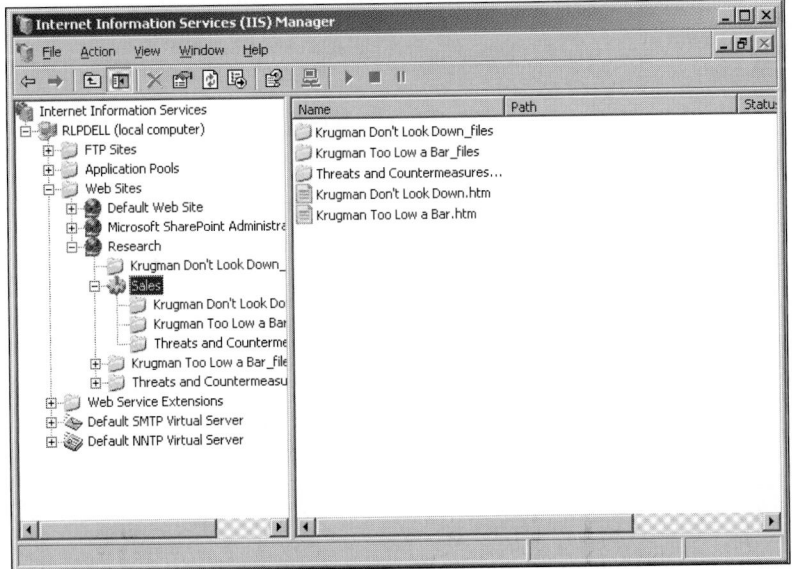

skill 10

Administering the Web Environment
(cont'd)

exam objective

Manage a Web server. Manage Internet Information Services (IIS). Manage security for IIS.

overview

enabled **(Figure 15-75)**. The ability to edit the metabase while IIS is running helps Web site administrators to avoid site downtime. When configuration changes must be made, members of the Administrators group can edit the metabase file while the service is running. The MetaBase.xml file is a text file that can be edited in any text editor such as Notepad. Microsoft recommends that Administrators log on with a non-administrative account and use the command prompt to open Internet Information Services (IIS) Manager with an Administrator's account. At the command prompt, type:

runas/user:*administrative_accountname* **"mmc %*systemroot*%\system32\inetsrv\iis.msc"**

Or to open a command prompt from which you can run other programs using secure credentials, type:

runas/user:*domain_or_machine_name/administrative_account_name* **"cmd /k"**

You will be prompted for the password and will then be able to use a secure credentials command prompt. The metabase History folder, with which you have already become familiar **(Figure 15-76)**, is the storage place for all changes that are made to MetaBase.xml. Keeping a running history is the default behavior, and this is the key to the ability to edit the metabase while IIS is running. However, Direct Metabase Edit is not enabled by default.

IIS 6.0 also includes new logging functionality, UTF-8 (Uniform Transformation Format-8-bit) logging. Logging was formerly performed by the WWW Service, but now HTTP.sys (the HTTP protocol stack) performs the logging function. You use log files to record site statistics. The additional log type can be useful because some statistics programs now use it. UTF-8 has a slight performance advantage over ASCII-based logs because it is binary rather than text.

Finally, MIME types are used to prevent attackers from sending malicious files. In IIS, only static files that have extensions on the **MIME (Multipurpose Internet Mail Extensions)** types list can be served to users. A default global list of MIME types is installed with IIS 6.0 **(Figure 15-77)**. The default Web site and all new Web sites you create automatically recognize these extensions. You can add MIME types to the global list or you can add them for a specific Web site or directory.

tip

MBSchema.xml cannot be edited while IIS is running. Changes to the metabase schema must be made programmatically.

tip

You can also use the Adsutil.vbs command line script to query the metabase to view the global MIME types list. Type **Adsutil.vbs enum/MimeMap** at the command prompt.

Figure 15-75 Enabling Direct Metabase Edit

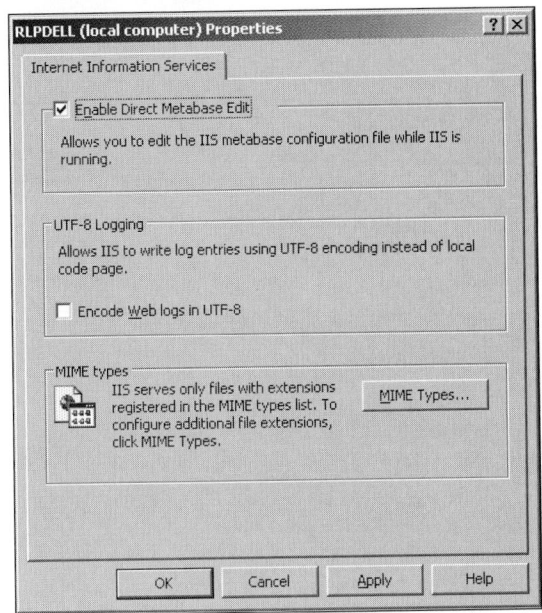

Figure 15-76 The metabase History folder

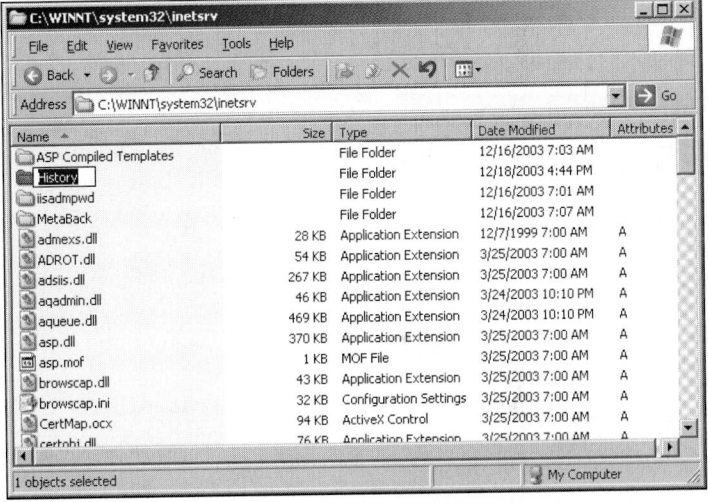

Figure 15-77 The MIME Types dialog box

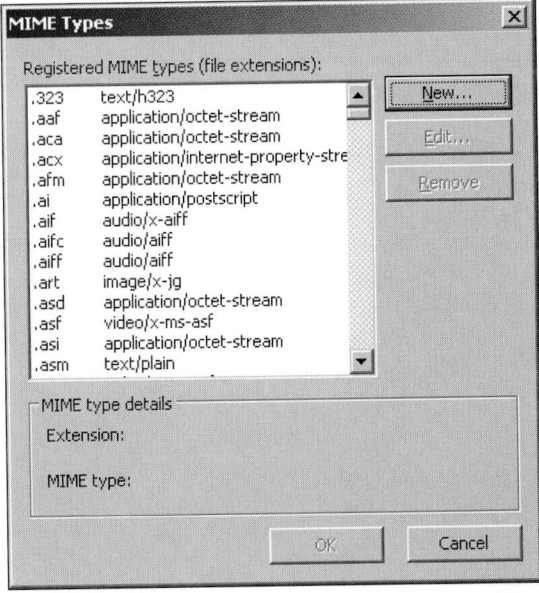

skill 11

Creating Application Pools

exam objective

Manage a Web server. Manage Internet Information Services (IIS).

overview

When you are running IIS 6.0 in worker process isolation mode, you can group Web applications into application pools. When you create application pools, you can apply configuration settings to groups of applications, as well as the worker processes servicing those applications. You can assign any Web directory or virtual directory to an **application pool**. This improves the efficiency of your IIS server and ensures that your other Web applications will not have their service interrupted when the applications in the new application pool stop.

tip

You can only create application pools when IIS 6.0 is running in worker process isolation mode.

how to

Create an application pool and assign an application to it.

1. Click ![Start], point to **Administrative Tools**, and click **Internet Information Services (IIS) Manager**.
2. Expand the *<server_name>* local computer node, right-click **Application Pools**, point to **New**, and click **Application Pool** to open the **Add New Application Pool** dialog box (**Figure 15-78**).
3. In the **Application pool ID** text box, type the name for the new application pool.
4. In the **Application pool settings** section, keep the default setting, **Use default settings for new application pool.** You can also use the settings in an existing application pool as a template for the new application pool. If you do this, you will select the existing application pool in the Application poll name list box.
5. Click ![OK] to close the Add New Application Pool dialog box.
6. Right-click the application you want to assign to the application pool and select **Properties**.
7. Open the **Virtual Directory**, **Directory**, or **Home Directory** tab, as applicable. If you are assigning a directory or virtual directory, make sure that the **Application name** text box is filled in. If it is not, click ![Create] and enter a name.
8. In the **Application pool** list box, select the name of the application pool to which you want to assign the Web site (**Figure 15-79**).
9. Click ![OK] to close the Properties dialog box.

tip

Again, it is considered a best practice to log on to your computer using an account that is not in the Administrators group, and then to use the Run as command in order to run IIS Manager as an administrator. At the command prompt type: runas/user: *administrative_accountname* "mmc %systemroot%\system32\inetsrv\iis.msc".

more

When you create an application pool, there are certain guidelines that must be followed:

1. Create an application pool for each Web site so that you can isolate Web applications on one Web site from the other sites on the same IIS server.
2. Configure a user account (process identity) for each application pool. Generally, administrators will use the Network Service account, or an account in the IIS_WPG group for security reasons, so that the least user rights necessary are used to run the application. By default, application pools operate under the Network Service account. The LocalService account also has few access rights. It can be used when you do not need access to any resource on remote computers. A final option is the LocalSystem account, but it has more user rights assigned to it than do the Network Service and LocalService accounts. This is considered to be a less secure option. LocalSystem is the account used in IIS 5.0 isolation mode (**Figure 15-80**).
3. Create a unique application pool for applications that you want to run with their own unique set of properties.

Figure 15-78 The Add New Application Pool dialog box

Figure 15-79 Assigning an application to an application pool

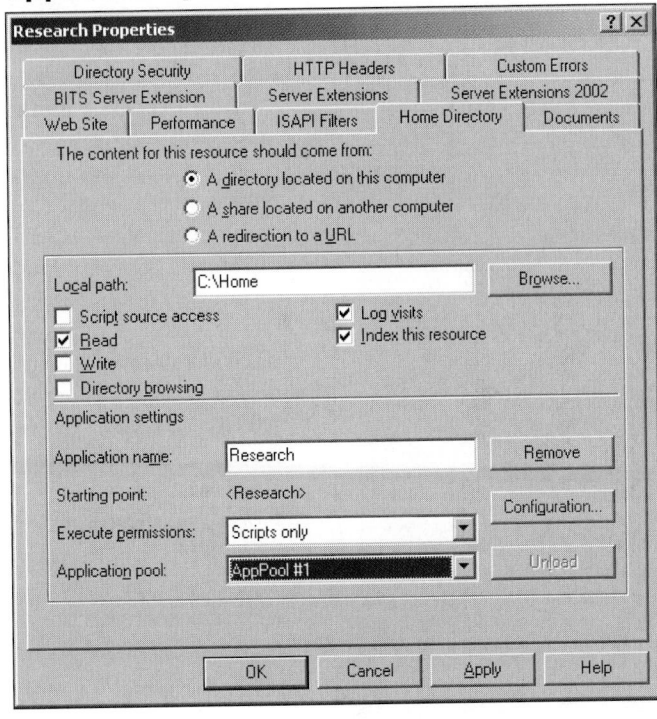

Figure 15-80 The Identity tab on the Properties dialog box for an application pool

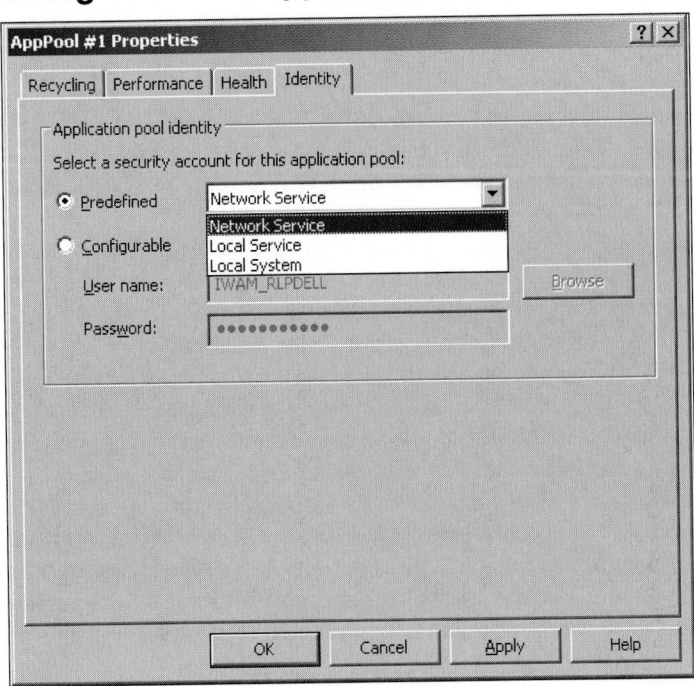

skill 12 *Troubleshooting the Web Environment*

exam objective

Manage a Web server. Manage Internet Information Services (IIS). Manage security for IIS.

overview

tip

Always check your Web site in a browser to make sure that it is functioning properly. To do this, type **http://Web_site_name/home_page_name.htm** in the address bar of the Web browser.

Some IIS problems you may encounter and their solutions are described below:

♦ **Applications are denied access to resources:** In order to understand troubleshooting this problem, first you will need some background information. There are two modes that IIS 6.0 can run in: Worker process isolation mode and IIS 5.0 isolation mode. **Worker process isolation mode** is the default (and preferred) mode for IIS 6.0. As you learned in Skill 11, when IIS 6.0 is running in worker process isolation mode, it has the capability to separate applications into isolated pools, as well as to identify unhealthy processes, resources that are being overtaxed, and memory leaks. To handle problems such as these, IIS can shut down the process or program, redirect resources, or connect the defective process to a diagnostic tool. However, whether or not IIS will install in worker process isolation mode depends on whether you perform a clean installation or an upgrade from an earlier version of IIS. If you perform a clean install, IIS will run in worker process isolation mode. If you upgrade, IIS will run the isolation mode that was previously configured. Upgrades from IIS 4.0 or 5.0 will run in IIS 5.0 isolation mode to avoid compatibility issues. If your Web site includes only static content and simple ASP applications, it is recommended that you promote to worker process isolation mode. This mode protects some of the most important parts of the World Wide Web service from malfunctioning applications. It also protects functioning applications from malfunctioning applications. IIS 5.0 isolation mode should be used if you are running legacy Web applications that may not be compatible with worker process isolation mode. Keep in mind, however, that most programs that ran correctly in IIS 5.0 should have no problem in IIS 6.0. Worker process isolation mode is more secure than IIS 5.0 isolation mode because the Network Service account is used to run worker processes, and it is granted a lower level of access than the account used in IIS 5.0 isolation mode, LocalSystem. In IIS 5.0 there are three application protection options: Low (IIS Process), Medium (Pooled), and High (Isolated). If you move programs that previously ran in Low (IIS Process) mode under LocalSystem to IIS 6.0 in worker process isolation mode, they may be denied access to resources because the Network Service Account is so much more restrictive than the LocalHost account. If you must run an application using the less secure LocalSystem account, you must create a new application pool and run the application in the application pool in its own virtual directory. This will isolate the application and reduce that possibility of attack. To configure IIS for IIS 5.0 isolation mode, right-click **Web Sites** and click **Properties**. On the **Service** tab, select the **Run WWW service in IIS 5.0 isolation mode** check box (**Figure 15-81**). After you click **OK**, you will be prompted to restart IIS (**Figure 15-82**).

♦ **Users request dynamic content and receive error 404:** The default installation of IIS is a secure locked mode with only static content enabled. In order for users to receive dynamic content, you must enable the type of content you are trying to serve, for example, ASP, ASP.NET, WebDAV, FrontPage Server Extensions, or Common Gateway Interfaces. Users will receive the 404 error if dynamic content has not been enabled and the error will be recorded in the W3C Extended log files. To enable or disable a Web service extension in IIS Manager, expand the local computer node and select **Web Service Extensions**. Select the Web service extension you want to enable or disable and click either the **Allow** or the **Prohibit** button (**Figure 15-83**). Extensions that are enabled will display with a check mark in a green circle, and when you select the extension, only the **Prohibit** and **Properties** buttons will be enabled. Likewise, if an extension has not been enabled, only the **Allow** button will be enabled.

Figure 15-81 Running the WWW service in IIS 5.0 isolation mode

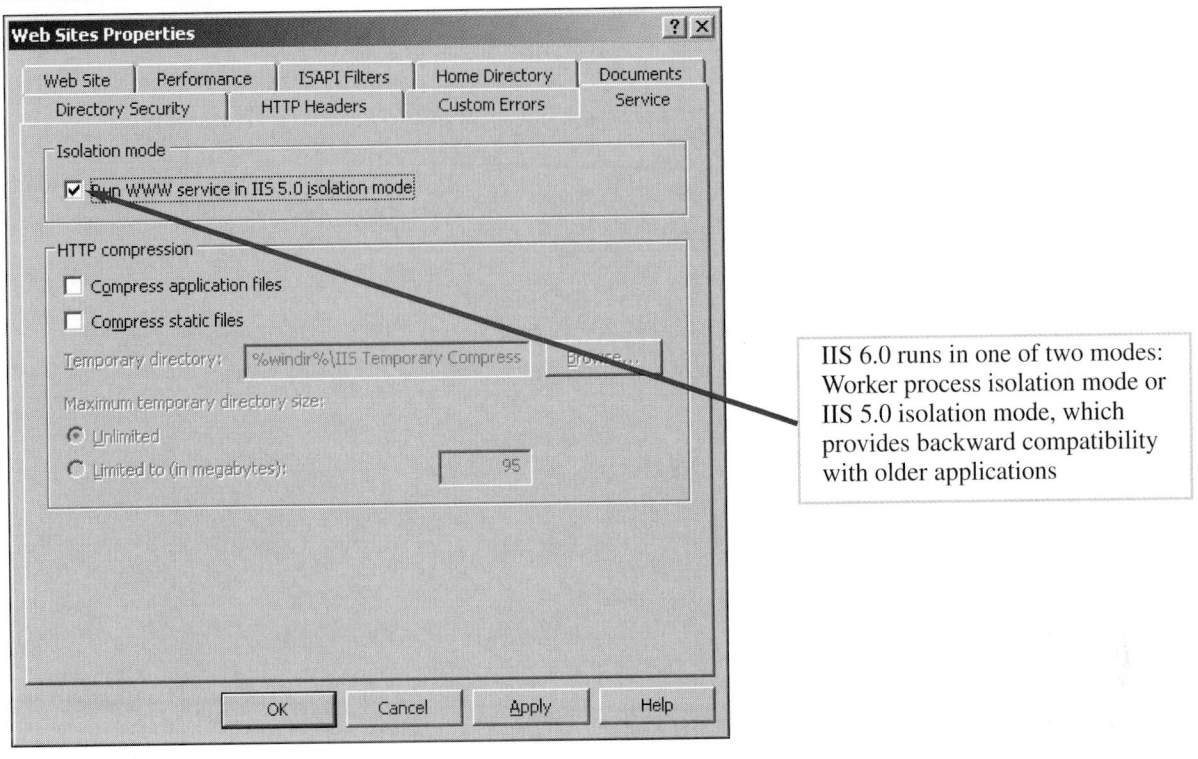

IIS 6.0 runs in one of two modes: Worker process isolation mode or IIS 5.0 isolation mode, which provides backward compatibility with older applications

Figure 15-82 Changing IIS modes

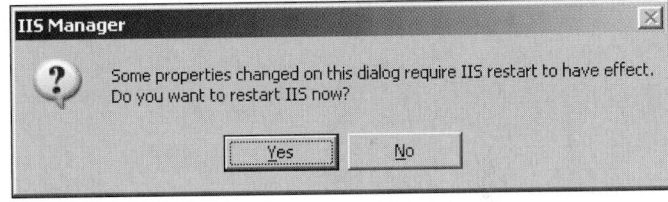

Figure 15-83 Enabling Web service extensions

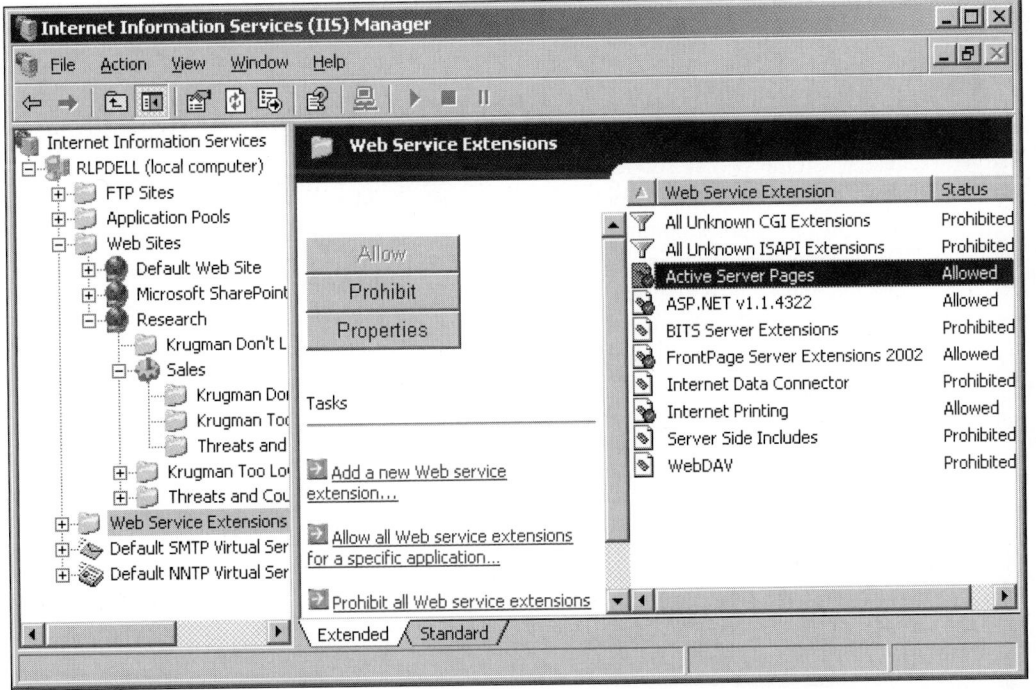

skill 12

Troubleshooting the Web Environment *(cont'd)*

exam objective

Manage a Web server. Manage Internet Information Services (IIS). Manage security for IIS.

overview

♦ **Users request static content and receive error 404:** As you have learned, if a request is made for a static file that does not have its file extension listed on the MIME types list, it will not be served to the user. IIS will deny the request and a 404 error will be logged in the W3C Extended log files. The generic 404 file is displayed to the user by default in both of these cases in order to block configuration information. You can add the file extension to the MIME list so that users will be able to access the content. You can also configure IIS to serve files with any extension by adding *application/octet-stream to the MIME list. After you update the global list, you must either restart the World Wide Web Publishing Service in the Services snap-in or wait for the worker process to recycle (120 minutes) in order for the list to update. Changes to the MIME list at the site level are instituted immediately

♦ **The application session state is dropped by worker process recycling:** A session is simply the period of time a user is interacting with a Web application. Active Server Pages (ASP) use a programmatic feature called a session state to maintain data for each user session. A unique key, stored in an HTTP cookie, is given to each user when a session begins. The Web server reads the key from the cookie to recreate the session state. Worker processes recycle after 120 minutes by default. A problem can occur if you have ASP applications that cannot store the session state while the worker process recycles. The session state can be lost and thus all data for the user session. You have two choices to solve this problem. You can either store the session state in a database, or you can disable worker process recycling. To disable worker process recycling, in IIS Manager, expand the local computer node, expand **Application Pools**, right-click the application pool, and click **Properties**. On the **Recycling** tab, clear the **Recycle worker processes (in minutes)** check box **(Figure 15-84)**.

♦ **Clients receive error 503:** Error 503 (a Service Unavailable message) is generated because the application pool is removed from service. This error can either originate from HTTP.sys (the HTTP protocol stack) or the WWW Service. First, check the error event log to find out which source detected the error. If HTTP.sys logged the error, it may be because the application pool queue length limit has been surpassed. To increase the application pool queue length limit, expand the local computer node, expand **Application Pools**, right-click the application, and click **Properties**. On the **Performance** tab, in the **Request queue limit** section, select the **Limit the kernel request queue to** check box, and enter the maximum number of queued requests **(Figure 15-85)**. Another reason for error 503 is that IIS has generated a **rapid fail protection**. This is the most common cause when the WWW service logs the error. What happens is that within a certain time period, a number of unhealthy worker processes are identified in a particular application pool and this causes communication with the WWW service to be terminated. The WWW service, recognizing that communication has ended, generates a warning or error message and restarts the worker process. You can configure worker process isolation mode for an application pool so that if this happens a particular number of times, the application pool will be disabled and rapid fail protection will be initiated. If you do not want the application pool to be removed from service so quickly, you can increase the number of unhealthy worker processes or the time period. The real solution to this problem, however, is to check the application as it is the most likely cause of the unhealthy worker processes. Memory leaks or other programmatic malfunctions may be the cause.

Figure 15-84 Disabling worker process recycling

Clear to disable worker process recycling

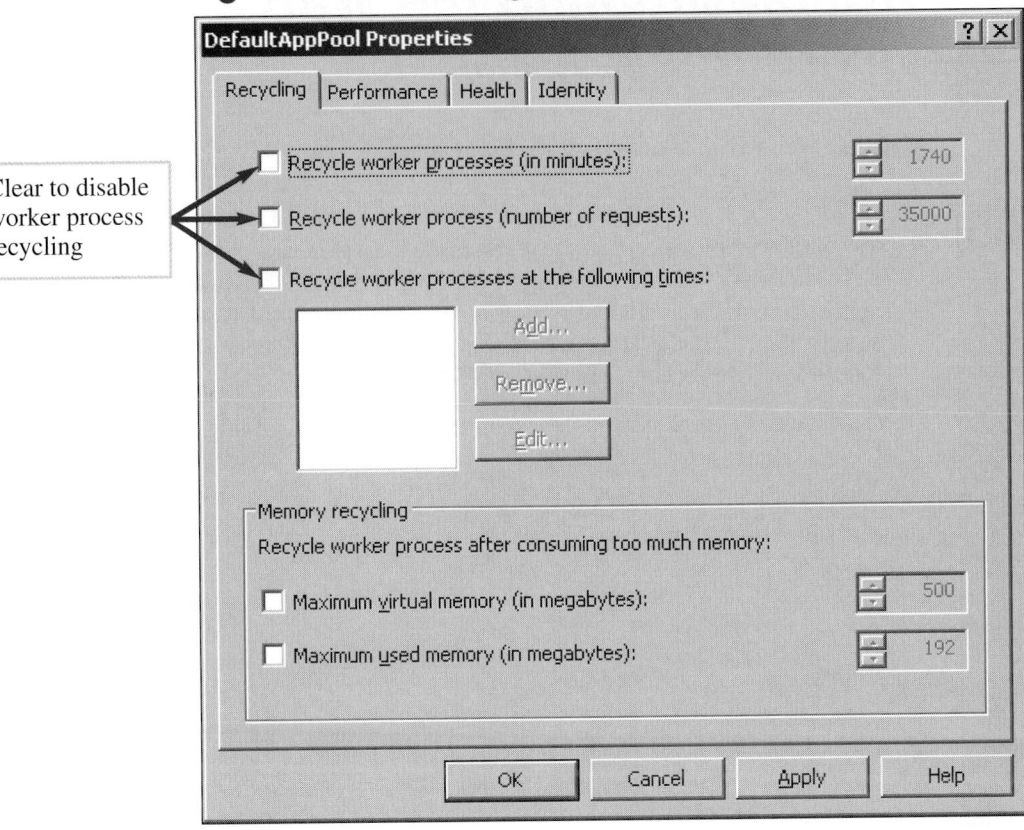

Figure 15-85 Increasing the application pool queue length limit

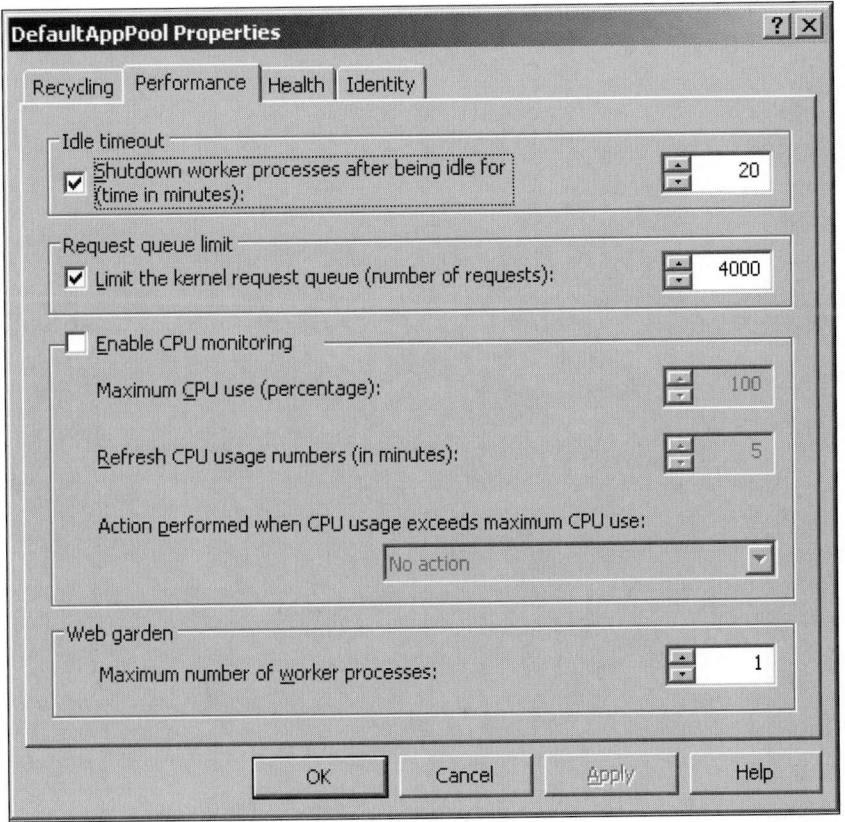

skill 12

Troubleshooting the Web Environment (cont'd)

Manage a Web server. Manage Internet Information Services (IIS). Manage security for IIS.

overview

◆   To configure rapid-fail protection, expand the local computer, expand **Application Pools**, right-click the application pool, and click **Properties**. On the **Health** tab, in the **Failures** spin box, enter the number of worker process failures to be detected before disabling the worker process. In the **Time period** spin box, enter the number of minutes during which failure totals are accumulated (**Figure 15-86**).

Client connectivity problems and their solutions are outlined in **Table 15-5**.

Figure 15-86 Configuring rapid-fail protection

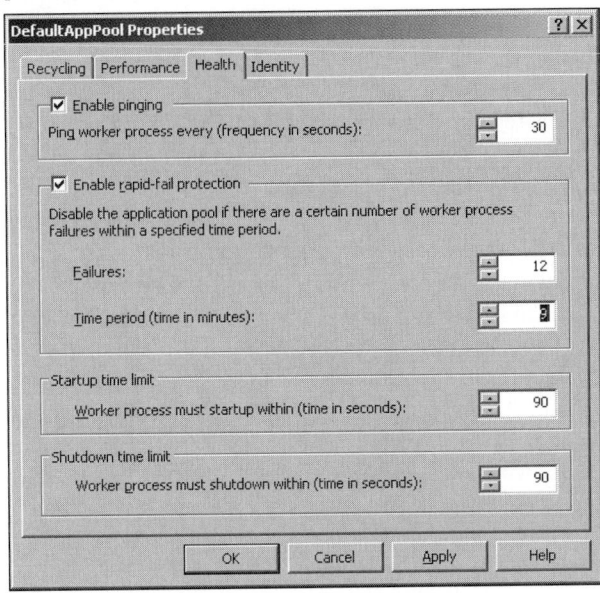

Table 15-5 IIS Connectivity Problems

Problem	Solution Set
Users cannot access the IIS Server	1. Run Ipconfig to check the TCP/IP settings on the client in order to make sure they are properly configured. 2. Use Ping to make sure the client can connect to remote computers and that it is connected to your network. 3. If you are using a proxy server, make sure that it is online and correctly configured. 4. Check the browser settings. If you are using a proxy server on your network and the client is trying to access intranet Web sites, in Internet Explorer, open the **Internet Options** dialog box on the **Connections** tab and click the **LAN** settings button. In the **Proxy server** section in the **LAN Settings** dialog box, make sure the **Bypass proxy server for local addresses** check box is selected. 5. In Internet Explorer, open the **Internet Options** dialog box on the **Advanced** tab. In the **Browsing** section, select **Show friendly HTTP error messages** to display the full details of connection errors. 6. Try running a protocol analyzer to track packets between the client and the server and locate the point where the communication breakdown is occurring.
Users cannot access a Web site	1. Make sure all users have valid user accounts if you have not enabled Anonymous access. 2. Check the connection limit for the site on the **Performance** tab to make sure it has not been exceeded. 3. On the **Directory Security** tab, check the authentication method for the site to make sure that it is compatible with the clients. Also, make sure that the clients and server are configured with compatible encryption and decryption capabilities. 4. Check the IP address and domain name restrictions. 5. Check the Web and NTFS permissions. The Users group must have the Read permission for the site and the Read Web permission must be configured for the home directory. 6. Try running ipconfig /flushdns on the client computer to flush the DNS cache and remove any invalid DNS data.

Summary

- Terminal Services is an application service that enables clients to access a server remotely to execute, process, and store data on the server. When Terminal Services is configured, each workstation runs Windows sessions on the server, all programs are executed on the server, and all processing and data storage takes place on the server. The PC merely displays the work done by the server. Since the server is handling the bulk of the work, PCs that might otherwise be obsolete can be given a second life as a terminal. An Application layer protocol called Remote Desktop Protocol (RDP) handles communication between the Terminal Server client and Terminal Server.

- Terminal Services allows clients with all down-level Windows operating systems to connect to a Windows Server 2003 computer. With the help of additional third-party software, you can also use Terminal Services to connect Macintosh-based clients or Unix clients to a Windows Server 2003 server.

- Remote Desktop for Administration allows you to access and manage a server remotely from anywhere on the network. You can perform almost any task remotely that you could while physically logged on to the server, including shutting down and restarting the computer. A server configured for Remote Desktop administration supports two simultaneous remote administration sessions. No additional licensing is required.

- Non-domain controllers are configured by default to allow Terminal Services connections by the Remote Desktop Users group. If the Terminal Server is a domain controller, you must also configure the Default Domain Policy GPO to allow the Remote Desktop Users group to connect through Terminal Services. Only the Administrators group is granted the Allow logon through Terminal Services user right by default on a domain controller.

- Remote Desktop Connection is the client software that is used to connect to a server both for Remote Desktop for Administration purposes, and if Terminal Services has been installed for application sharing by multiple simultaneous users. The Remote Desktop client is included in the default installations of both Windows Server 2003 and Windows XP Professional. For all other operating systems, you must install the client.

- Remote Assistance is used to allow a trusted party such as a help desk support person or network technician to remotely access your system. This expert can be allowed to either just view your system or to both view and interact with your system. You can connect to a Remote Assistance session over a LAN or over the Internet. Connections from the Internet in which the user is behind a firewall are also possible as long as the default Terminal Services port, TCP port 3389, is open. You can control whether or not users on your LAN will be able to request help over the Internet by either blocking or permitting inbound and outbound traffic through port 3389 at the firewall. You can also set Group Policy to either allow or deny users from using Remote Assistance, and you can designate whether the expert will be able to control the computer or just view it.

- Terminal Services is used to distribute and manage Windows-based applications. The Windows Server 2003 desktop and Windows-based programs can be delivered even to computers that might not normally have the capability to run them. Terminal Services supports multi-session access to applications; multiple clients can access multiple applications concurrently.

- You should install Terminal Services on a member server rather than on a domain controller because processing user logons to the domain will take CPU cycles away from terminal sessions. You must also install Terminal Services Licensing. Each client who will be accessing the Terminal Server must either be a Windows 2000 Professional or Windows XP Professional client, or must have a TSCAL. You only need to have one license server per domain or one license server per site, even if you are creating multiple Terminal Servers on the domain or site. Each of the Terminal Servers on the site or domain must be connected to the license server so that licenses can be issued for client connections.

- It is considered a best practice to install Terminal Server Licensing on a computer that is not a Terminal Server. After you install Terminal Services Licensing, you must run the Terminal Server License Server Activation Wizard to activate the server. After the license server is activated, you must install TSCALs on the server. When a client without a TSCAL logs on to the Terminal Server, the Terminal Server locates a license server and requests a new TSCAL for the client. Each client then stores its own TSCAL locally. The license server can issue temporary licenses for 120 days after installation. After this evaluation period, you must have TSCALs installed on the license server or unlicensed clients will no longer be able to log on.

- The Remote Desktop Protocol (RDP-Tcp) connection in the Terminal Services Configuration console is configured automatically when the operating system is installed. This connection is used to log on to both Remote Desktop for Administration and Terminal Services.

- After you install Terminal Services, you must use Add or Remove Programs to install applications on the Terminal Server so that they will be configured for use by multiple simultaneous users.

- Internet Information Services (IIS) 6.0 is the Web server for Windows Server 2003. Using IIS, you can publish Web pages and deploy Web sites. You can assign different ports, IP addresses, or host header names to each Web site so that you can host multiple Web sites on the same Web server. The new IIS 6.0 request-processing architecture allows Web-based applications to run in an environment in which they are protected from the malfunctions of other applications.

◆ Web-based Distributed Authoring and Versioning (WebDAV) is an extension of the HTTP protocol that is used to access files on a Web server through an HTTP connection. The HTTP connection enables users to add, modify, and delete data from Web pages to facilitate Web page authoring.

◆ Two new user accounts and one new group account are added when you install IIS. On a member server, these accounts will be added to the local accounts database and can be viewed in the Computer Management console. On a domain controller, these accounts are added to Active Directory and can be viewed in the Active Directory Users and Computers console. IUSR_<*servername*> is the account that will be used for Anonymous access to the IIS server. IWAM_<*server-name*> is the user account that will be used to start out-of-process applications. The IIS _WPG group account is the worker process group.

◆ The IIS Admin Service is the parent process for all IIS services. When you stop the IIS Admin Service, all other services are also stopped. IIS Admin also supplies the interface that is used to administer IIS and all of its components.

◆ When you install IIS, other new services are added to the Services snap-in, depending on the components of IIS you have installed. If you have installed the File Transfer Protocol, the FTP Publishing service will be installed. If you have installed Network News Transfer Protocol (NNTP), that service will be installed, and if you have installed Simple Mail Transfer Protocol, that service will be installed

◆ The World Wide Web Publishing (WWW) service provides you with a Web server that can host one or any number of Web sites.

◆ The Inetpub folder is installed at the root of the system drive. It is the storage folder for all content. Sub-folders divide the content according to whether it is Web, FTP, NNTP, or SMTP content. Inetsrv (*%systemroot%\system*32) is where all IIS program and .dll files are stored. Iishelp (*%systemroot%\Help*) contains IIS documentation.

◆ The Internet Information Services (IIS) Manager is the main management tool for your Web server.

◆ Master properties are configuration settings that apply to all Web sites on a server. Configuration settings can also be set at the Web site, folder, and file levels. Configuration settings that are changed at the site, folder, or file level override the Master properties. However, when modifying the Master properties, you can also choose to have the container objects below that level inherit the change.

◆ Enable HTTP Keep-Alives is used to ensure that the IIS server will keep a connection open while a browser is making the many requests required to download a Web page with multiple elements. This conserves system resources, increases server efficiency, and improves browser efficiency.

◆ IIS authentication methods are Basic authentication (password is sent in clear text), Digest authentication, Integrated Windows authentication, and .NET Password authentication. Integrated Windows authentication, by default, uses either the Kerberos V5 authentication protocol or NTLM (Windows NT Challenge/Response authentication). .NET Passport authentication is a method in which users create a single sign-in name and passport that is used to access numerous Web sites. Web sites that use .NET Passport authentication use the Passport single sign-on service (SSI) served by a partner Passport server. If you configure Passport SSI for your Web site, you will not have to configure your own authentication method; however, you will still need an authorization mechanism. Passport identifies each user to the Web site, but access controls must be put in place at the site level.

◆ The auto-backup feature of the IIS metabase creates copies of each version of the MetaBase.xml and MBSchema.xml files in the History folder. Administrators can view these copies in the *%systemroot%*\system32\inetsrv\history folder. There are two types of metabase backups: portable and non-portable. Portable backups are created with a password that is used to encrypt the secure metabase properties in the backup files. A portable backup can be restored on another computer or on a different installation of the operating system. Non-portable backups do not require a password. Secure metabase properties are encrypted using the unique machine key, so non-portable backups cannot be restored on any computer other than the one on which the backup was performed.

◆ There are two types of access control permissions for Web resources: Web and NTFS. Web permissions apply to all HTTP clients and determine the level of access to server resources. NTFS permissions are used to detail the level of access individual users and groups can have for files and folders on the Web server.

◆ The Web permissions are Script source access, Read, Write, Directory browsing, Log visits, and Index this resource. Execute permissions are used to control application security. There are three levels of Execute permissions: None, Scripts only, and Scripts and executables.

◆ In IIS, digital identification files called certificates can be used to authenticate both the client and the server. You use the Web Server Certificate Wizard to request certificates,

- apply certificates, and to remove them from a Web site. You configure certificates at the Web site level.
- The Secure Sockets Layer (SSL) protocol is used so that a server certificate can be accessed by users to authenticate your Web site before they send confidential data such as a credit card number.
- Both Netscape and Internet Explorer browsers maintain lists of trusted CAs and the CAs' public keys. It is the browser that contacts the SSL-enabled Web server. The Web server in turn sends its certificate, which contains its public key, to the browser. The browser must verify that the certificate's validity period is applicable and that the issuing CA is on its list of trusted CAs.
- The SSL 3.0 protocol is the basis for IIS encryption. Both the user's browser and your Web server must be configured with compatible encryption and decryption capabilities.
- The default secure communication settings for an IIS Web server require that the user's Web browser support a session key strength of 40 bits, or above.
- Every Web site must have a home directory, which generally contains a home page, although home pages are not necessary if browsing is enabled or if Web folders are in use. By default, the home directory for the WWW service is C:\Inetpub\wwwroot and the default FTP service home directory is C:\InetPub\Ftproot. However, FTP can use the same folders as Web. Many companies do this so that they can use FTP to update content on the Web server.
- A virtual directory is used to make a directory "appear" to be within the home directory, when it really isn't. They are most often used when you have a folder structure on another disk, or on an entirely different server that you do not want to move but want to include on your Web site. When you set up a virtual directory, you give it an alias. An alias is a name that identifies the virtual directory to the Web browser. The URL for a file in the virtual directory is the full path name, server name, virtual directory alias, and filename.

- You can also assign properties to the IIS server itself (local computer).
- One of the server settings you can implement is Direct Metabase Edit. The ability to edit the metabase while IIS is running helps Web site administrators to avoid site downtime. When configuration changes must be made, members of the Administrators group can edit the MetaBase.xml text file in Notepad while the IIS service is running. The metabase History folder is the storage place for all changes that are made to MetaBase.xml. Keeping a running history is the default behavior, and this is the key to the ability to edit the metabase while IIS is running. Direct Metabase Edit is not enabled by default.
- MIME types are used to prevent attackers from sending malicious files. In IIS, only static files that have extensions on the MIME (Multipurpose Internet Mail Extensions) types list can be served to users. A default global list of MIME types is installed with IIS 6.0. You can add MIME types to the global list or you can add them for a specific Web site or directory.
- There are two modes that IIS 6.0 can run in: Worker process isolation mode and IIS 5.0 isolation mode. If you perform a clean install, IIS will run in worker process isolation mode. Upgrades from IIS 4.0 or 5.0 will run in IIS 5.0 isolation mode to avoid compatibility issues. Worker process isolation mode protects some of the most important parts of the World Wide Web service from malfunctioning applications. IIS 5.0 isolation mode should be used if you are running legacy Web applications that may not be compatible with worker process isolation mode. Most programs that ran correctly in IIS 5.0 should have no problem in IIS 6.0. Worker process isolation mode is more secure than IIS 5.0 isolation mode because the Network Service account is used to run worker processes, and it is granted a lower level of access than the account used in IIS 5.0 isolation mode, LocalSystem.

Key Terms

Alias
Application pools
Bandwidth throttling
Direct Metabase Edit
Domain license server
Execute permissions
Enterprise license server
Home directory
Host header name
HTTP Keep-Alives
Hypertext Transfer Protocol (HTTP)
Iishelp
Inetpub
Inetsrv
Internet Server Application Programming Interface (ISAPI) filters

License server
Master properties
Metabase backup
Microsoft Clearinghouse
Multipurpose Internet Mail Extensions (MIME)
Network News Transfer Protocol (NNTP)
Remote Assistance
Remote Desktop for Administration
Remote Desktop Connection
Secure Sockets Layer (SSL)
Simple Mail Transfer Protocol (SMTP)
Socket
Socket pooling

Terminal Server
Terminal Server Client Access License (TSCAL)
Terminal Services Licensing
Terminal Services Manager
Thin client
Virtual directory
Web-based Distributed Authoring and Versioning (WebDAV)
Web folder
Web permissions
Web server
Web site

Test Yourself

1. You are the Web site administrator for your firm. You want to configure an authentication method that will require users to enter a user name and password before they can log on to the Web site, and you do not want the user name and password to be sent in clear text. Which authentication method will you choose? (Choose all that apply.)
   a. Integrated Windows authentication
   b. Anonymous authentication
   c. Digest authentication
   d. Basic authentication

2. What is the default TCP port number for HTTP?
   a. 389
   b. 3389
   c. 80
   d. 119

3. You are going to configure your Web server so that users in your company will be able to send e-mail messages. What IIS service will you use?
   a. FTP
   b. NNTP
   c. SMTP
   d. WWW

4. What user account is created when you install IIS to provide Anonymous access to the IIS server?
   a. IUSR_<server_name>
   b. IIS_WPG
   c. IWAM_<server_name>
   d. The Network Service Account

5. Which of the following administrative tools is used to modify the properties of TCP/IP connections between a Terminal Server client and a Terminal Server?
   a. Terminal Server Licensing
   b. Remote Desktop client
   c. Terminal Services Configuration
   d. Terminal Services Manager

6. What level will you use to set the connection timeout period for Web site users if you want the setting to apply to all Web sites on your IIS server?

   a. File
   b. Site
   c. Folder
   d. Master

7. On which operating systems do you have to install the Remote Desktop Connection client so that client computers can connect to a Windows Server 2003 Terminal Server? (Choose all that apply.)
   a. Windows XP Professional
   b. Windows 2000 Professional
   c. Windows 98
   d. Windows NT 4.0

8. You are the network administrator for NetLink.net. Your services are often required after working hours to troubleshoot problems. How can you fulfill these responsibilities without having to drive back and forth to your job site?
   a. Install the Remote Desktop Connection client on one of the network servers.
   b. Install Terminal Services on a server.
   c. Enable Remote Desktop for Administration on a server.
   d. Buy a remote access utility and install it on a server.

9. You have just finished making some configuration changes to your Web site and you want to back up the changes to a file that you can restore on another server. What kind of IIS backup will you perform?
   a. Portable metabase backup
   b. Non-portable metabase backup
   c. System State backup using the NT Backup utility

10. Help support personnel on your network can be contacted to provide technical support for network users through the:
    a. Terminal Services Manager
    b. Remote Desktop Connection dialog box
    c. Help and Support Center
    d. IIS Manager

Projects: On Your Own

1. Configure Master properties for the WWW service.
   a. Open the IIS Manager. Expand the server_name node, if necessary.
   b. Right-click the **Web Sites** folder and select **Properties**.
   c. Click the **Properties** button in the **Enable logging** section.
   d. In the **Logging Properties** dialog box, click the **Weekly** option button in the **New log schedule** section. Click **OK**.
   e. Open the **Performance** tab. In the **Web site connections** section, select the **Connections limited to** option button and enter **750** in the spin box.
   f. Click **OK** to close the Web Sites Properties dialog box.
   g. Expand the **Web Sites** node.
   h. Right-click **Default Web Site** and select **Properties**.
   i. Click the **Properties** button in the **Enable logging** section.
   j. Note that the Weekly setting in the New log schedule section has been inherited from its parent node.
   k. Open the **Performance** tab. Verify that connections to the Default Web site will be limited to 750 because the master property has been inherited.
   l. Click **OK** to close the Default Web Site Properties dialog box.

2. Create a Web site.
   a. In the **IIS Manager**, right-click **Default Web Site** and select **Properties**.
   b. On the **Web Site** tab, type **8080** in the **TCP port** text box. Click **OK**.
   c. Right-click **Default Web Site** and click **Stop**.
   d. When the site is listed as **Stopped**, right-click Default Web Site again and click **Start**.
   e. Open **Internet Explorer**; type **http://localhost** in the **Address** bar, and press **[Enter]**. A **The page cannot be displayed** message will open because the Default Web site is now listening for requests on port 8080.
   f. Now type **http://localhost:8080** in the Address bar, and press **[Enter]**. The **Under Construction** message will open because this is the IIS startup page.
   g. Open **My Computer** and create a new folder named **My Website** on the **C:** drive. Close My Computer.
   h. In the IIS Manager, right-click the **Web Sites** folder, point to **New**, and click **Web Site** to start the **Web Site Creation Wizard**.
   i. Click **Next**. Type **MyWebsite.net** in the **Description** text box and click **Next**.
   j. Accept the default values on the **IP Address and Port Settings** screen, and click **Next**.
   k. In the **Path** text box, type **C:\My Website**. Click **Next.**
   l. Select the **Browse** check box and click **Next**.

   m. Click **Finish**. MyWebsite.net is added to the Web Sites folder.
   n. Open **My Computer** and navigate to the My Website folder.
   o. Open the My Website folder and create a new text file named **index.txt**.
   p. Open index.txt. Type some simple HTML code: **<html><head><title>My Website.net Home</title></head><h1>My Website.net Home</h1></body></html>**
   q. Save and close **index.txt** and rename it **index.htm**. Click **Yes** in the **Rename Warning** message box. Close My Computer.
   r. Open **Internet Explorer**, type **http://localhost** in the Address bar, and press **[Enter]**.
   s. The Web page you created above opens. My Website.net Home appears in the **Title** bar and on the Web page in header style.
   t. Close Internet Explorer.

3. Configure Web site properties.
   a. In the **IIS Manager**, right-click **MyWebsite.net** and click **Properties**.
   b. Open the **Performance** tab. Enter **600** in the **Connections limited to** spin box.
   c. Open the **Documents** tab. Click the **Add** button. In the **Default content page** text box in the **Add Content Page** dialog box, type **index.html**. Click **OK**.
   d. Click the **Move Up** button until index.html is at the top of the list.
   e. Click **OK** to close the **MyWebsite.net Properties** dialog box.
   f. Open **My Computer** and navigate to and open the My Website folder. Create a new text file named **MyWebsitefooter.txt**. Open it and type **<html><body><p>My Website.net footer</p></body></html>**.
   g. Close the file and rename it **MyWebsitefooter.html**. Click **Yes** in the **Rename Warning** message box. Close My Computer.
   h. In the IIS Manager, right-click **MyWebsite.net** and click **Properties**.
   i. Open the **Documents** tab. Select the **Enable document footer** check box.
   j. Click **Browse**. Locate **MyWebsitefooter.html** and click **Open**.
   k. Open the **Directory Security** tab. Click the **Edit** button in the **Authenticated and access control** section. By default, the Web site is configured to allow anonymous access using the **IUSR_server_name** account. Integrated Windows authentication is the default authentication method. Click **OK**.

l. Open the **HTTP Headers** tab. Select the **Enable content expiration** check box. The default settings are for the content to expire in one day.

m. In the **Content rating** section, click the **Edit Ratings** button. Select the **Enable ratings for this content** check box. Examine the content ratings you can set, and click **OK**.

n. Open the **Custom Errors** tab. Scroll down and select **HTTP Error 404**. Click the **Edit** button, and write down the path to the file. Click **OK**.

o. Click **OK** to close the My Website.net Properties dialog box.

p. Open **My Computer** and navigate to the **404b.htm** file (*%systemroot%\Help\iisHelp\common*).

q. Open **404b.htm** and read the default **The page cannot be found** text. Close the file, right-click it, point to **Open With**, and select **Notepad**.

r. Locate the **<h1>** line. Edit the text so that it says **The My Website.net page cannot be found**. Save and close the file. Close My Computer.

s. Open **Internet Explorer**, type **http://localhost** in the **Address** bar and press **[Enter]**. The **MyWebsite.net** Web page opens with the footer added.

t. Type: **http://localhost/unknown** in the **Address** bar, and press **[Enter]** to view the custom error message you created.

u. Close all open windows and the IIS Manager.

Problem Solving Scenarios

1. You are the network administrator for UpClass a Manhattan fashion boutique. You are planning to install a Web server on your corporate network. The CEO would like you to create a document that outlines the steps you will follow to install and configure the IIS service. Include in this report the steps that must be followed to set up a virtual directory. Furthermore, some of the departmental managers have expressed concern about security. Some of them have also requested that they have their own Web site and that they be able to control who can access their departmental site. Add to your report a section explaining the various authentication methods that can be used and the advantages and disadvantages of each. Also include in the report the methods that can be used for controlling access to a Web site and the methods that can be used to uniquely identify each of the departmental sites on the Web server

2. The CEO is also interested in decreasing the burgeoning technical support costs at UpClass. Prepare a document explaining how Remote Assistance can be used to provide one-on-one technical support. Explain how Remote Assistance requests are sent on the network, what protections are in place to insure that only authorized users can take control of a machine, the safeguards for remote assistance invitations, and how Remote Assistance can be offered by a technical support person without an invitation. Include in your report the Group Policies that can be used to control Remote Assistance and how Remote Assistance can be used from locations not on the local area network.

16

Examining Software Update Services and License Management

Anew feature in Windows Server 2003 is the ability to download, control, and deploy updates, service packs, and patches to the operating system and its components automatically, using an internal server. This feature is called Software Update Services (SUS), and is designed to give the administrator unparalleled control over the bandwidth used by Windows Update and the service packs and updates applied by client computers using the Automatic Updates service.

By storing the content locally, your clients can now download their updates locally, rather than each client tying up WAN bandwidth retrieving each update from Microsoft. By allowing the administrator to approve each package before it is made available to the clients, Software Update Services gives the administrator the ability to approve only those updates that will not affect system stability or the stability of custom applications.

Additionally, new Group Policy features included with Software Update Services allow the administrator to define the configuration of the Automatic Updates feature on client computers on as large or as small a scale as necessary.

Goals

In this lesson, you will learn about the powerful new Software Update Services and Automatic Updates features in Windows Server 2003 and for Windows 2000 and XP clients. You will learn how to manually configure the Automatic Updates service using the GUI, as well as using the Registry Editor and Group Policy. You will also learn how to configure a Software Update Services (SUS) server, synchronize the server with the Microsoft Windows Update servers, and schedule synchronization. Additionally, you will learn how to approve updates for your organization. Finally, you will learn how to use the Licensing tool to ensure that you are in legal compliance with your licensing requirements.

Lesson 16 Examining Software Update Services and License Management

Skill	Exam 70-290 Objective
1. Installing and Configuring Software Update Services on a Client	Manage software update infrastructure.
2. Installing, Configuring, and Managing a Software Update Services (SUS) Server	Manage software update infrastructure.
3. Using a Group Policy Object to Configure Updates	Manage software update infrastructure.
4. Administrating Software Site Licensing	Manage software site licensing.

Requirements

To complete this lesson, you will need administrative rights on a Windows Server 2003 domain controller with an NTFS volume or partition and IIS installed.

skill 1

Installing and Configuring Software Update Services on a Client

exam objective

Manage software update infrastructure.

overview

Software Updates consist of two components. The first component is a client-side service, which retrieves your updates from your **Software Update Services (SUS)** server or the Internet and installs them. The second component is a server-side service that can be the central point for distributing updates to clients. As this implies, Software Updates do not require a SUS server; however, dedicating a server for this purpose can significantly reduce your update bandwidth requirements.

In order for Software Updates to work at all, the client-side service must be properly installed and configured. The client-side service is known as the **Automatic Updates** service. The Automatic Updates service is not included with any operating system except Windows Server 2003, but it is available as a free download for the following operating systems.

- Windows 2000 Professional (SP2)
- Windows 2000 Server (SP2)
- Windows 2000 Advanced Server (SP2)
- Windows XP Home
- Windows XP Professional

If your environment contains legacy operating systems such as Windows 98 or Windows NT, these computers will not be able to take advantage of Automatic Updates. A third-party product (such as MS Systems Management Server) is required to gain this functionality.

To install Automatic Updates on a Windows 2000 client or server, you simply have to install Service Pack 3. For Windows XP, installing Service Pack 1 will also install Automatic Updates. Alternatively, you can use the Windows Update Web site at: **http://windowsupdate.microsoft.com/**, or download the service as an MSI package at: **http://www.microsoft.com/windows2000/downloads/recommended/susclient/default.asp**.

After you have installed Automatic Updates, the service will attempt to contact the default SUS server, which will normally be the Microsoft Windows Update server on the Internet. The Automatic Updates service will display a Wizard to the Local Administrator 24 hours after establishing contact with the server, in order to configure the service. If this period is unacceptable, a Local Administrator can configure the computer by manually accessing the Automatic Updates service. In Windows XP or Windows Server 2003 , Automatic Updates are accessed in the **System Properties** dialog box **(Figure 16-1)**, while in Windows 2000, they are accessed through the Automatic Updates applet in the Control Panel **(Figure 16-2)**.

From the client side, there are only a few manual configuration options, each of which is detailed below:

- **Keep my computer up to date:** This setting determines whether or not Automatic Updates are enabled.
- **Notify me before downloading any updates:** This setting allows you to be notified before Automatic Updates attempts to download any updates, and also before they are installed. This method allows you to have precise control over not only which updates are installed, but also which updates are downloaded.
- **Download the updates automatically and notify me when they are ready to be installed:** This setting automatically downloads all needed updates, but refrains from installing any updates until you approve them. This is the default setting.
- **Automatically download the updates and install them on the schedule that I specify:** This setting automatically downloads any needed updates, and then installs them on the day of the week and at the specific time you specify. If necessary, this option will even restart the computer automatically.

caution

If you choose either notification option, you must be logged on to the computer as a Local Administrator to receive the update notification.

Figure 16-1 Automatic Updates Settings in System Properties (Windows Server 2003)

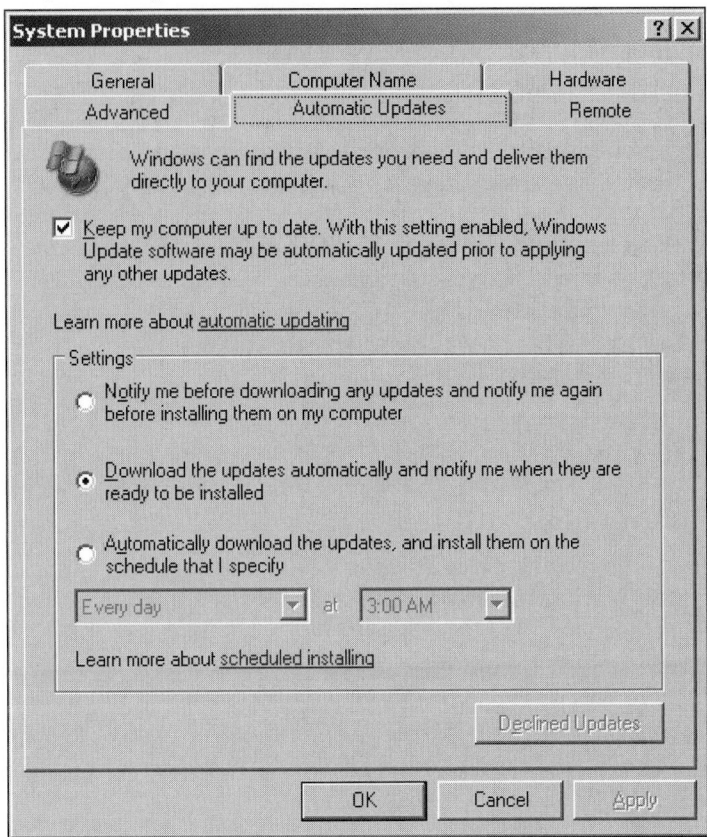

Figure 16-2 The Automatic Updates applet in Control Panel (Windows 2000 Professional)

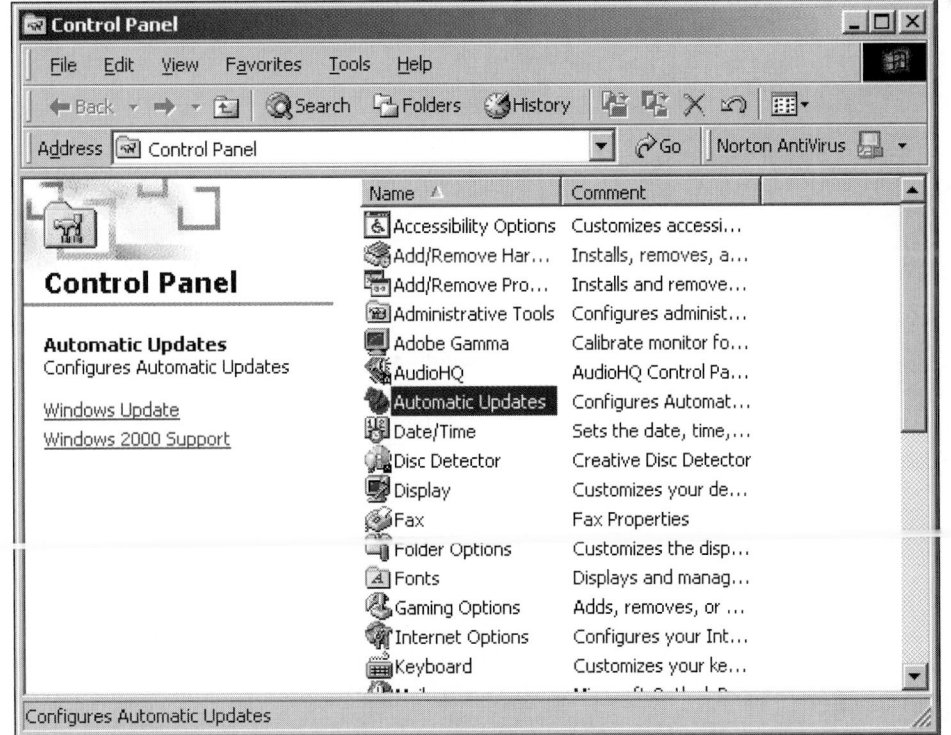

skill 1

Installing and Configuring Software Update Services on a Client (cont'd)

exam objective

Manage software update infrastructure.

overview

If you choose to notify before downloading option, a small reminder balloon will appear on the task bar when updates are ready to be downloaded. If you choose to download them automatically, a small reminder balloon will appear on the task bar when updates are ready to be installed. After you install the updates, your system may require a restart. Automatic Updates will prompt you to restart your system, but you can defer this for up to three days by choosing the **Remind me later** button. If you schedule the installation of updates, the system will automatically restart after applying the updates, if necessary.

how to

Configure Automatic Updates on a Windows XP or Windows Server 2003 computer. (To perform this exercise, you will need Automatic Updates installed.)

1. Click [Start], right-click **My Computer**, and choose **Properties** to open the **System Properties** dialog box.
2. Click the **Automatic Updates** tab to display the Automatic Updates configuration options.
3. Make sure that the check box labeled **Keep my computer up to date** is checked.
4. Choose the option **Automatically download the updates and install them on the schedule that I specify** to enable the scheduling of update installations.
5. Set the schedule using the list boxes to install your updates every Sunday at 1 AM **(Figure 16-3)**.
6. Click [OK] to accept the changes and close the **System Properties** dialog box.

more

Some of the options included with Automatic Updates are not configurable using the Control Panel applet or through System Properties. To configure these options, you must either use Group Policy or manually edit the Registry on each computer. These options are:

◆ **Reschedule Wait Time:** This setting controls how long the system waits before beginning an installation that was scheduled, but was missed. This setting is an interval of time (between 1 and 60 minutes) after the next system boot. For example, if a scheduled installation was missed, and this setting was configured at 10 minutes, the installation would begin 10 minutes after the next system boot.

◆ **No Automatic Restart with logged-on users:** This setting determines the computer's actions when a user is logged on to the system after an installation that requires a reboot is completed. In reality, this setting simply defines the presence of the restart countdown timer in the Restart dialog box. By default, this setting is enabled, which means that 5 minutes after the restart dialog box appears, the system will automatically log off any non-administrative user accounts and reboot. Local Administrators can always postpone a restart, regardless of this setting. Other user accounts can only choose to restart now or wait for the timer to expire, regardless of the setting.

◆ **Specify intranet Microsoft update service location:** This setting determines the location from which the Automatic Updates service retrieves the updates. By default, the service retrieves all updates from the Microsoft Web site. However, if you are using an internal SUS server, this setting allows you to redirect your clients to that server.

Configuring these settings in Group Policy will be covered in Skill 3. Configuring these settings by editing the Registry requires you to modify the keys listed in **Table 16-1** in the **HKEY_LOCAL_MACHINE\Software\Policies\Microsoft\Windows\WindowsUpdate\AU** section of the Registry.

Figure 16-3 Configuring Automatic Updates

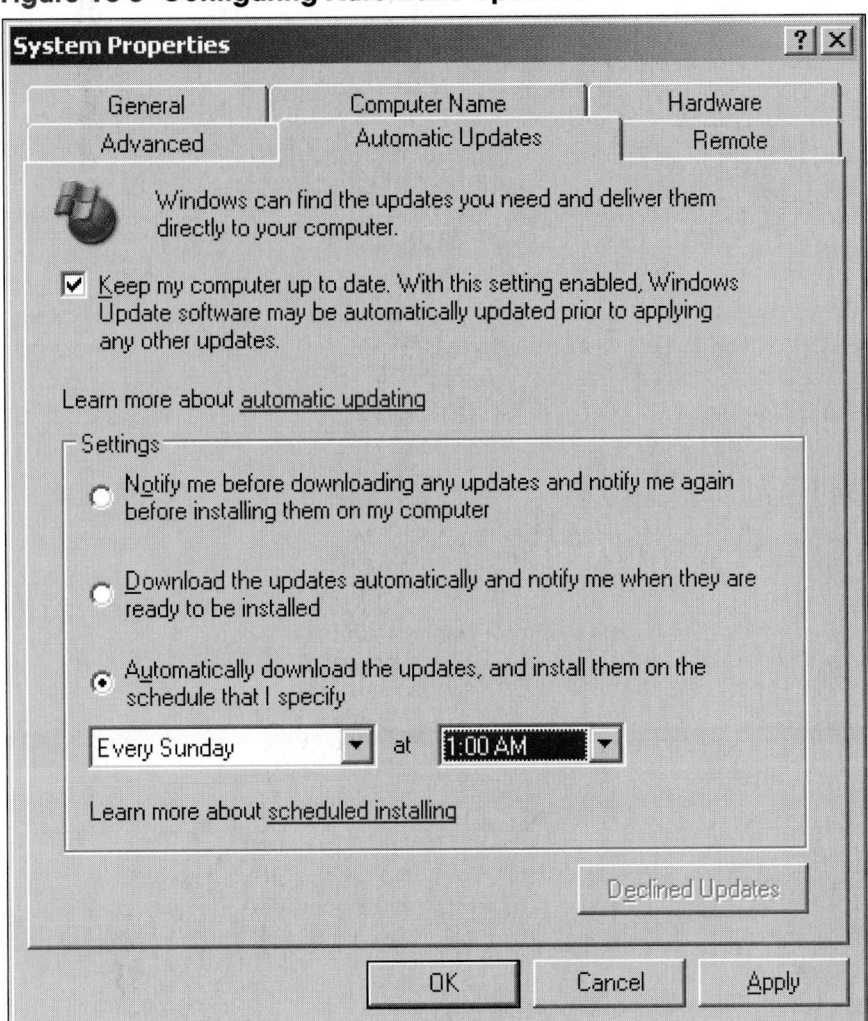

Table 16-1 SUS settings

Setting and Explanation	Registry Value	Legal Values
Reschedule Wait Time: The value for this setting is in minutes. A setting not in the listed range will schedule the update for the next day.	**RescheduleWaitTime**	1–60
No Automatic Reboot: A setting of 1 enables No Automatic Reboot (which disables the reboot timer), and a setting of 0 disables the No Automatic Reboot (which enables the timer).	**NoAutoRebootWithLoggedOnUsers**	0 or 1
Use an Alternate SUS Server: Configuring this setting to 1 enables the next two keys, allowing you to select an alternate SUS server.	**UseWUServer**	0 or 1
SUS Server Address: Listed in URL format (http://susserver).	**WUServer**	URL
SUS Statistics Server Address: Listed in URL format (http://susstats).	**WUStatusServer**	URL

skill 2

Installing, Configuring, and Managing a Software Update Services (SUS) Server

exam objective

Manage software update infrastructure.

overview

As mentioned previously, SUS is the server-side service responsible for providing updates to client computers in order to reduce the bandwidth requirements for your network and increase manageability. Using this service, in addition to significantly reducing bandwidth needs (since only a single copy of a given update needs to be downloaded for all client computers), you can also increase manageability by ensuring that updates are accepted or rejected for all computers at a central location.

To install SUS on a server, Microsoft recommends that the server meets the following requirements:

◆ Windows 2000 (SP3) or Windows Server 2003
◆ Pentium III at 700 Mhz, or equivalent
◆ 512 MB of RAM
◆ 6 or more GB of free disk space on an NTFS partition
◆ The system partition should be an NTFS partition
◆ IIS 4.0 or higher installed

These are really more recommendations than requirements, however, as SUS will install on much lower hardware than the listed minimums. The listed hardware should be capable of supporting around 15,000 computers on a dedicated SUS server.

To install SUS, you must download SUS 1.1 from Microsoft at: **http://go.microsoft .com/fwlink/?LinkId=6930**

After you download SUS, simply double-click the executable (currently SUS10SP1.exe) to install SUS. If any software requirements are not met by your server (such as IIS not being present), the install will abort. Be aware, however, that the hardware "requirements" are simply recommendations.

After the installation is complete, you will be presented with the Software Update Services Web page (**Figure 16-4**). This is where you will configure and manage most aspects of the service.

The first thing you should do after installing your SUS server is to ensure that the configuration options are correct. To do this, click the **Set options** link on the SUS Web page to open the **Set Options** page (**Figure 16-5**). Typically, the default settings shown on this page will be adequate, but let's examine each section in detail:

◆ **Select a Proxy Server configuration:** This section allows you to configure how the SUS server connects to the Microsoft Windows Update servers on the Internet. Your initial option is whether or not to use a proxy server. If you choose to use a proxy server, you can either manually specify the settings for your proxy server or let the server automatically detect your settings. The default choices: **Use a proxy server to access the Internet** and **Automatically detect proxy server settings** are typically easiest to configure, as this choice will automatically detect most NAT devices.

◆ **Specify the name your clients will use to locate this update server:** This setting is set, by default, to the NetBIOS name of your server. This should be adequate in most environments. If you use DNS naming exclusively, however, you will need to change the name to follow DNS naming conventions.

◆ **Select which server to synchronize content from:** This section allows you to choose between direct synchronization of updates from the Microsoft Windows Update servers on the Internet, or other local SUS servers on your intranet. When you synchronize from local servers, you can choose to chain updates by having only a single SUS server

Figure 16-4 The Software Update Services Web page

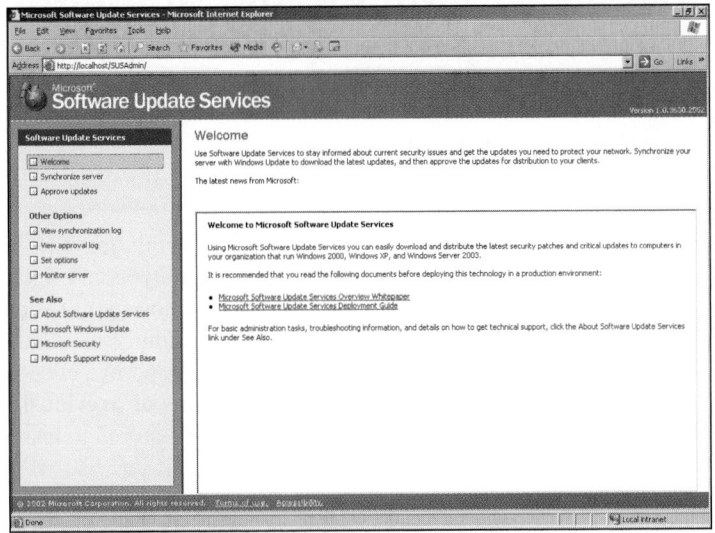

Allows you to configure how the SUS server connects to the Microsoft Windows Update servers on the Internet

This setting is set, by default, to the NetBIOS name of your server; if you use DNS naming exclusively, you will need to change the name to follow DNS naming conventions

This section allows you to choose between direct synchronization of updates from the Microsoft Windows Update servers on the Internet, or local SUS servers on your intranet

Figure 16-5 The Set options page

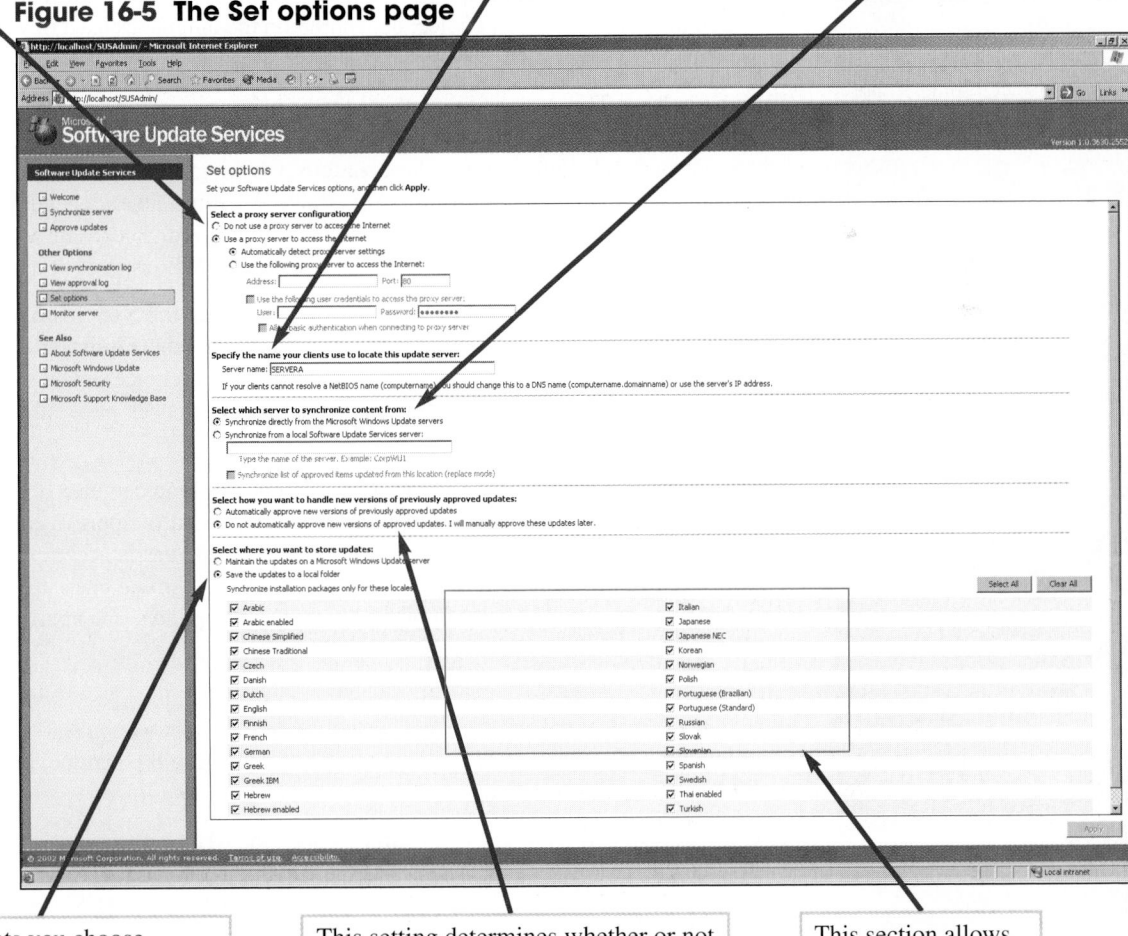

This option lets you choose whether or not to store all updates locally or leave the updates on the Microsoft Servers

This setting determines whether or not you will be required to manually approve new releases of previously approved updates

This section allows you to specify the locales supported by the SUS server

skill 2

Installing, Configuring, and Managing a Software Update Services (SUS) Server (cont'd)

exam objective

Manage software update infrastructure.

overview

download content from the Internet and allowing the other servers to pull the updates from that server. When you choose this option, you can also choose to synchronize the list of approved items from this server. This allows you to approve items at the primary server and allow all other SUS servers to simply use that server's list of approved updates. Otherwise, you will have to manually approve updates on all SUS servers.

◆ **Select how you want to handle new versions of previously approved updates:** This setting determines whether or not you will be required to manually approve new releases of previously approved updates. For example, if you had previously approved a specific IE security patch, and a new version of that patch was released, using the default settings would require you to approve the new patch as well before it would be installed.

◆ **Select where you want to store updates:** This option lets you choose whether or not to store all updates locally (conserving disk space and reducing client Internet bandwidth use) or leave the updates on the Microsoft servers. If you choose to leave the updates on the Microsoft servers, your clients will contact the SUS server for a list of available updates, but will then connect to the Microsoft servers on the Internet to retrieve them.

◆ **Synchronize installation packages only for these locales:** This section allows you to specify the locales supported by the SUS server. By default, all locales are selected, which may not be the best choice, depending on the languages used in your environment.

After you configure the server options, you should configure synchronization and download your first updates. This is done by clicking the **Synchronize server** link (**Figure 16-6**). This will open the **Synchronize server** page, where you can either choose to immediately synchronize or to schedule your synchronizations. Clicking the **Synchronize Now** button will immediately initiate a synchronization. This may take some time, depending on the locales you have selected and the speed of your Internet connection. According to Microsoft, if all locales are selected, the first synchronization can use 600 MB or more of disk space.

If you prefer to schedule synchronization, you can select the **Synchronization Schedule** button. This will open the Schedule synchronization dialog box (**Figure 16-7**), where you can choose your schedule. Regardless of your synchronization choice, when synchronization is occurring, you will see a status bar on the **Synchronize server** page informing you of its progress (**Figure 16-8**).

After you have synchronized and downloaded the updates, you can then begin the process of approving updates. Using the default settings, you will need to approve each update before clients can download and begin using them. Approving updates is accomplished by clicking the **Approve updates** link (**Figure 16-9**). You can then examine each update individually, select the ones to approve, and approve them. After updates are approved, clients will download and install the update or service pack automatically.

how to

Install the current version of SUS on your server, configure the service, perform a manual synchronization, and approve updates.

1. Click **Start** and click **My Computer** to open the **My Computer** window.
2. Double-click the (**x:**) icon, where x is the drive letter for the disk where you saved the downloaded executable file. Navigate to the folder where the SUS executable (currently **SUS10SP1.EXE**) is stored and double-click the file to start the installation.
3. Select **Next >** through all of the installation dialog boxes to install the service with the default settings.

Figure 16-6 The Synchronize server page

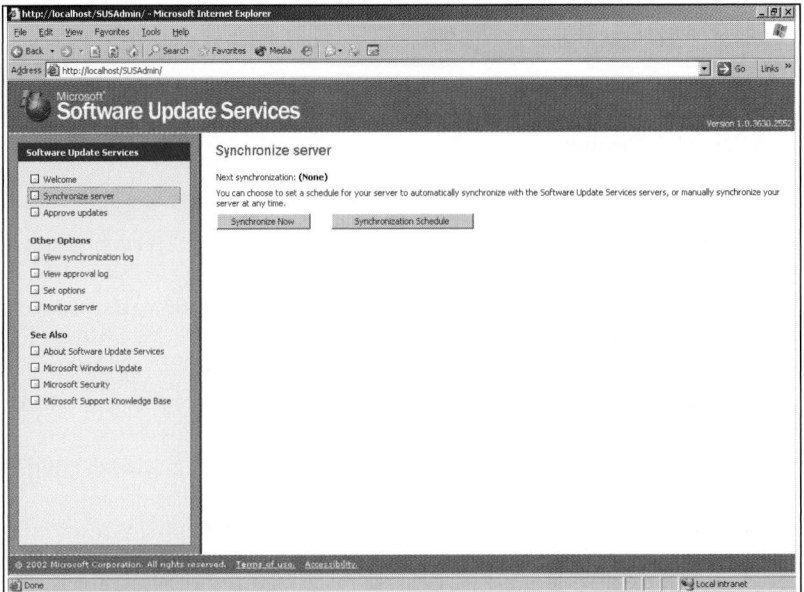

Figure 16-7 The Schedule Synchronization dialog box

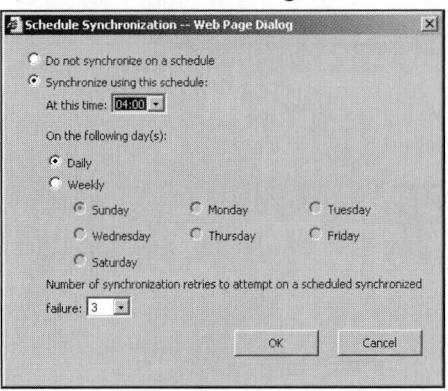

Figure 16-8 The synchronization status is shown during the synchronization process

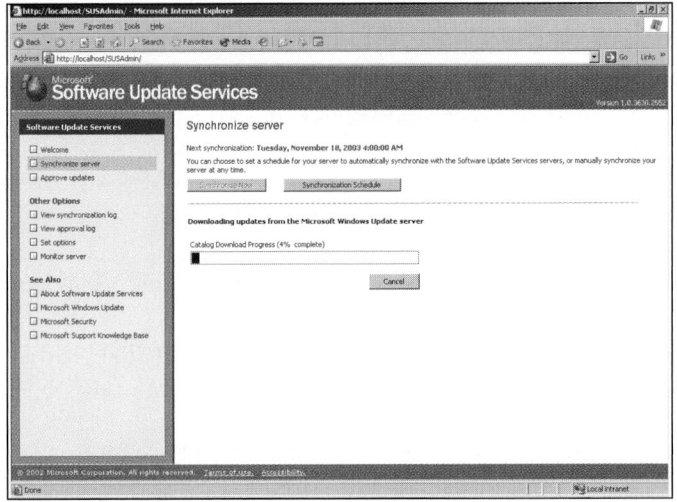

Figure 16-9 The Approve updates page

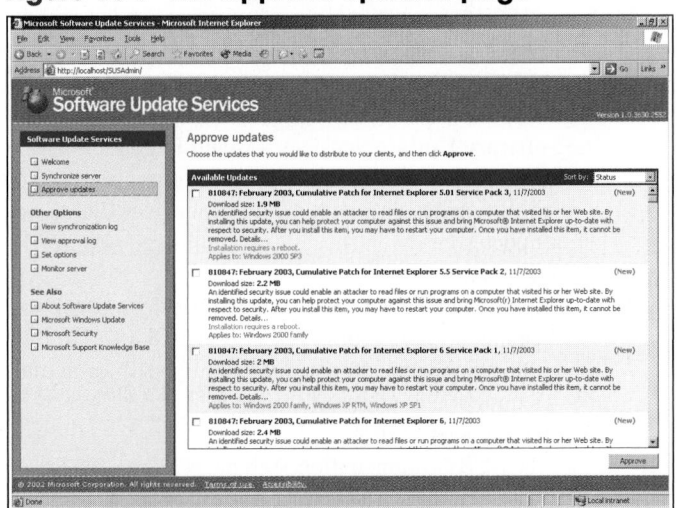

skill 2

Installing, Configuring, and Managing a Software Update Services (SUS) Server (cont'd)

exam objective

Manage software update infrastructure.

how to

tip

You can navigate to the Software Update Services configuration page at any time by typing **http://localhost /SUSAdmin/**.

4. When the installation is complete, you will be presented with the SUS welcome screen. Click the **Set options** link to open the **Set options** page.
5. In the **Select a proxy server configuration** section, ensure that the options **Use a proxy server to access the Internet** and **Automatically detect proxy server settings** are selected.
6. In the **Specify the name your clients use to locate this update server** section, the NetBIOS name for your server should be automatically entered. If it is not shown, enter it.
7. In the **Select which server to synchronize content from** section, ensure that the option **Synchronize directly from the Microsoft Windows Update servers** is selected.
8. In the **Select how you want to handle new versions of previously approved updates** section, ensure that the option **Do not automatically approve new versions of approved updates** is selected.
9. In the **Select where you want to store updates** section, ensure that **Save the updates to a local folder** is selected. Then, click [Clear All] to clear all locales, and manually select the **English** check box. This will significantly reduce the number of updates retrieved from the Internet, and reduce download time.
10. Click [Apply] to apply these options. A **VBScript** information dialog box will open to inform you that the settings have been successfully saved. Click [OK].
11. Click the **Synchronize server link** to view the **Synchronize Server** page.
12. Click [Synchronization Schedule] to open the **Schedule Synchronization** dialog box. Configure synchronization to occur daily at 4 AM. When finished, click [OK] to return to the **Synchronize Server** page.
13. Click [Synchronize Now] to initiate a manual synchronization. Note that this will begin a download of all available security updates for Windows 2000, Windows XP, and Windows Server 2003 to your server, which will typically consume no less than 500 MB. If you are using a modem to connect to the Internet, the synchronization process may take several days to complete as there is no way to load just a few updates.
14. A status bar will show you the status of the download. When the synchronization is complete, a **VBScript** information dialog box will open to inform you that your server has successfully synchronized with the Microsoft Windows Update server. Click [OK] to select and approve new updates.
15. The **Approve updates** page opens. Examine each update in turn, and select the ones you wish to be installed on your SUS clients by selecting the check box beside each update (**Figure 16-10**), and clicking [Approve].
16. A **VBScript: Software Update Services** dialog box opens to explain that your new list of approved updates is going to be applied and will replace any previous lists (**Figure 16-11**). Click [Yes] to continue.
17. The **Software Update Services — Web Page Dialog** opens to prompt you to accept the license agreement for several updates (**Figure 16-12**). Click [Accept] to continue.
18. A final **VBScript: Software Update Services** dialog box opens to inform you that the list of updates has been successfully approved (**Figure 16-13**). Click [OK] to close the dialog box.
19. Your Approve updates page will now refresh, and you should see your approved updates status change to read **Approved (Figure 16-14)**. Note that while this process approves the updates for your clients, the clients will not actually download and install these updates until you configure them to use your SUS server. This will be done using Group Policy in the next Skill.
20. Close the SUS Administration Web page.

Figure 16-10 Selecting updates to approve

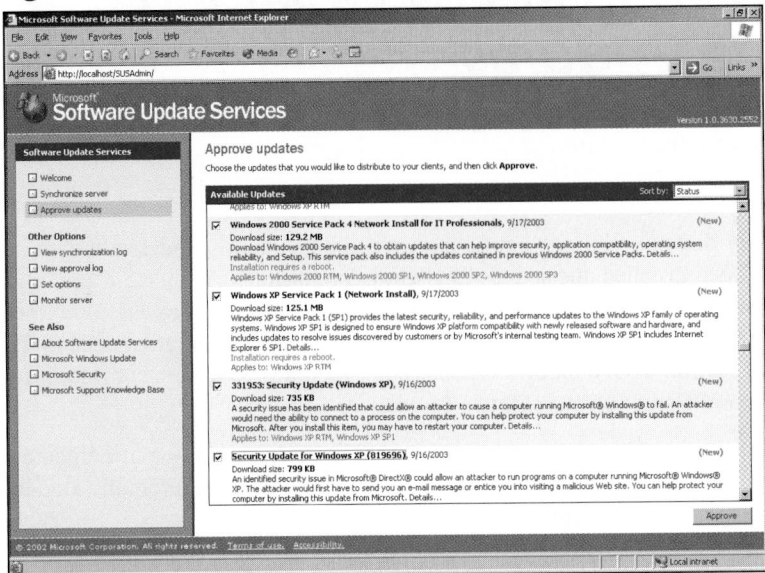

Figure 16-11 The approve updates warning dialog box

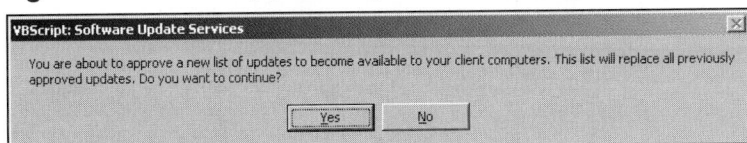

Figure 16-13 The approval confirmation dialog box

Figure 16-12 The license agreement dialog box for the approved updates

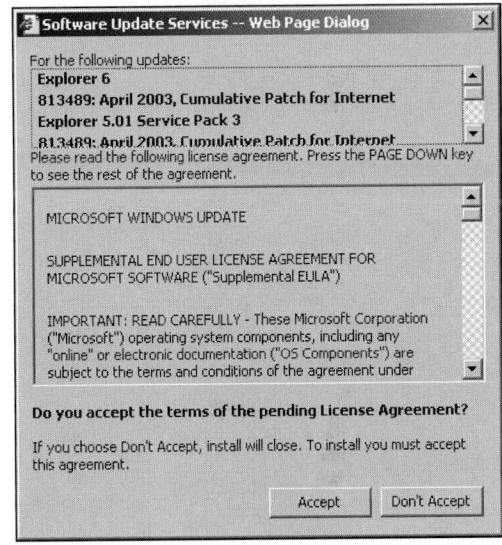

Figure 16-14 The Approve updates page, showing the status of the approved updates as "Approved"

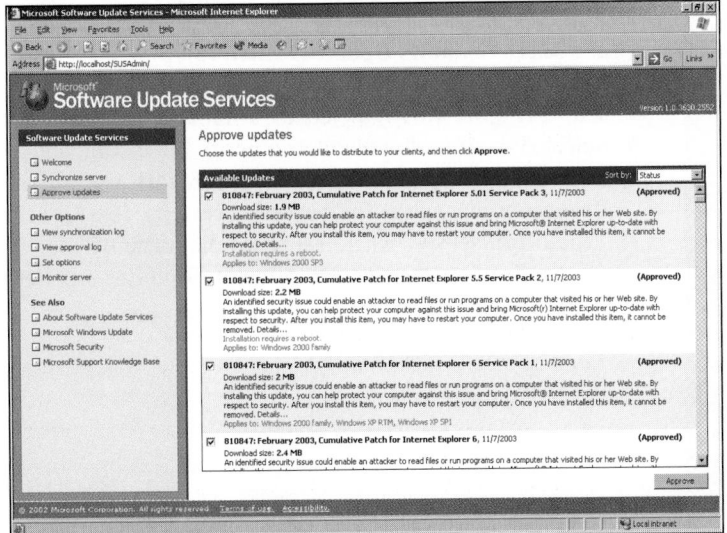

skill 3

Using a Group Policy Object to Configure Updates

exam objective

Manage software update infrastructure.

overview

In an Active Directory domain, you can configure your clients quickly and easily using a Group Policy. After SUS is installed, the new Group Policy administrative template **wuau.adm** is installed by default. This template adds the Windows Update node to the Windows Components node under Administrative Templates in the Computer Configuration node in the Group Policy Object Editor. The Windows Update node includes four new configuration options for your Windows Update clients (**Figure 16-15**):

◆ **Configure Automatic Updates:** Allows you to enable or disable automatic updates, configure the update and installation settings, and configure the automatic update scheduled install day and time (**Figure 16-16**).

◆ **Specify intranet Microsoft update service location:** Allows you to specify the internal SUS and statistics server that automatic update clients will use (**Figure 16-17**).

◆ **Reschedule Automatic Updates scheduled installations:** Allows you to specify whether Automatic Updates will immediately install missed installations after reboot and the time period to wait before beginning the installation (**Figure 16-18**).

◆ **No auto-restart for scheduled Automatic Updates installations:** This setting disables the countdown restart timer for system restarts after an update requiring a reboot has been applied. This setting has no configuration options; it can only be enabled or disabled.

Using these settings in a Group Policy, you can modify the Automatic Updates functionality for large groups of client computers quickly and easily. Be aware, however, that these Group Policies only apply to client computers running Windows Server 2003, Windows XP SP1, or Windows 2000 SP3 or later. Other clients will need the correct operating system and service pack installed, or will need to be manually configured using the Registry Editor (for pre-SP3 Windows 2000 and pre-SP1 Windows XP computers). Windows NT and Windows 9x can never make use of these new features.

how to

Edit the default domain policy to configure Automatic Updates for all of your client computers.

1. Click **Start**, point to **Administrative Tools**, and click **Group Policy Management** to open the **Group Policy Management** console.
2. Right-click **Default Domain Policy** and select **Edit** to open the **Group Policy Object Editor** for the default domain policy (**Figure 16-19**).
3. Expand **Computer Configuration**, **Administrative Templates**, **Windows Components**, and select **Windows Update** (**Figure 16-15**).
4. Double-click **Configure Automatic Updates** to open the **Properties** dialog box for the setting (**Figure 16-16**). Select the **Enabled** option button.
5. Select **3 — Auto download and notify for install**, and click [OK].
6. Double-click **Specify intranet Microsoft update service location** to open the **Properties** dialog box for the setting (**Figure 16-17**). Select the **Enabled** option button.
7. Type **http://server**, where **server** is the name of your SUS server, in both the **Set the intranet update service for detecting updates** and **Set the intranet statistics server** text boxes, and click [OK].
8. Close all open windows.

Figure 16-15 The Windows Update section in the Default Domain Policy

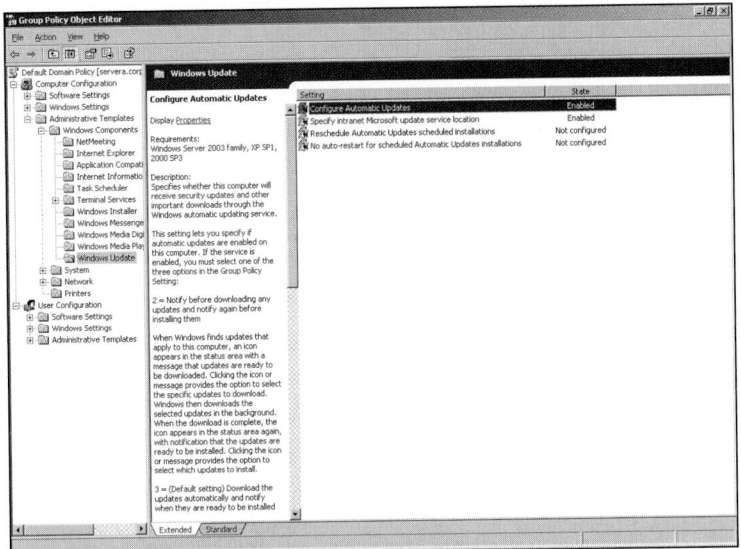

Figure 16-16 The Configure Automatic Updates Properties dialog box

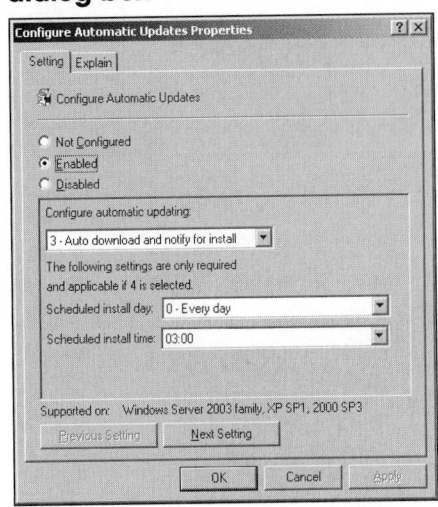

Figure 16-17 The Specify intranet Microsoft update service location Properties dialog box

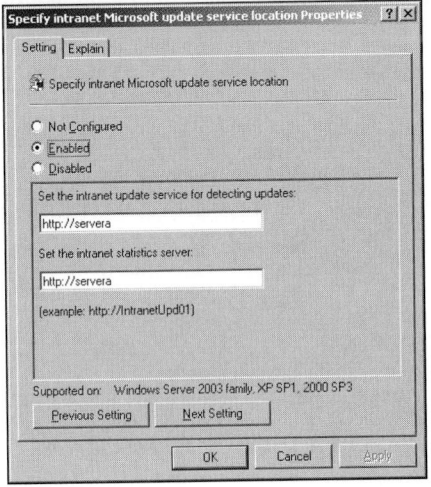

Figure 16-18 The Reschedule Automatic Updates scheduled installations Properties dialog box

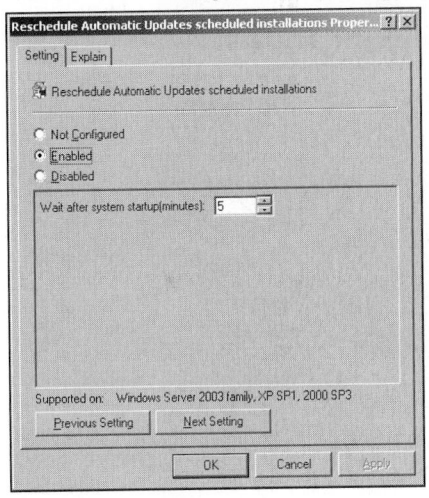

Figure 16-19 Opening the Group Policy Object Editor for the default domain policy from the GPMC

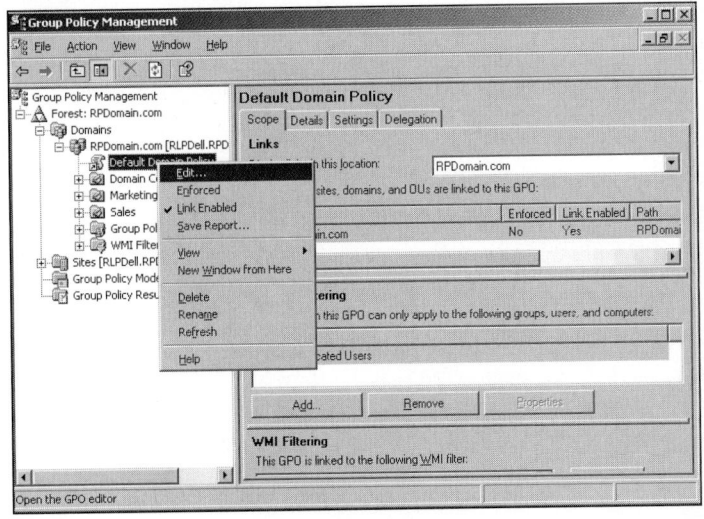

skill 4

Administrating Software Site Licensing

exam objective

Manage software site licensing.

overview

tip

Unauthenticated (anonymous) access does not require a CAL.

As mentioned in Lesson 2, Windows Server 2003 requires Client Access Licenses (CALs). CALs are licenses to access the server. CALs can be utilized in one of two modes: Per Server, or Per Device or User. With the Per Server licensing mode, a single CAL is necessary for each concurrent connection to the specific server. In this mode, you apply CALs to the servers themselves, and when the maximum number of concurrent connections to that server has been reached, no additional users can access the server. With the Per Device or User mode, a CAL is required for each client connection, but it doesn't matter which server the clients connect to. If you buy 500 CALs in this mode, you can have up to 500 concurrent users or devices connected to any of your servers and remain within licensing compliance.

Note that in Windows Server 2003, Microsoft has changed their licensing requirements somewhat. Multiple users logged on to a single machine now require multiple licenses, and a single user using more than one machine also requires multiple licenses.

To help keep track of your licensing, Windows Server 2003 provides the **Licensing tool**. The Licensing tool (Start>Administrative Tools>Licensing) is an application designed to help keep track of your CALs. Using the Licensing tool, you can view the maximum number of concurrent licenses being used, the servers that are or are not in compliance, and your license purchase history **(Figure 16-20)**.

tip

Most larger organizations have an Enterprise Licensing agreement with Microsoft, making licensing much less of a headache.

In order for the Licensing tool to function, the License Logging service must be enabled on one server on the site. The server on which the License Logging service is running is known as the site licensing server. This server is responsible for keeping track of all licenses on the site (typically, the single physical location). If you have multiple sites, you should configure a site licensing server for each site. However, be aware that cross-site accesses may utilize more than one license. In this case, you must examine the license usage to determine if multiple licenses are actually required. For example, a user accessing data on two separate sites will be using two licenses. If you are using Per Device or User mode, this access will be using an extra, unnecessary license, because one user is allowed to access data on two separate sites using only a single license. To resolve this problem, you should revoke one of the licenses.

You can enable the License Logging service in the Services console **(Figure 16-21)**. After this service is enabled, you can access the Licensing service to add licenses and monitor license usage.

Figure 16-20 The Licensing Tool

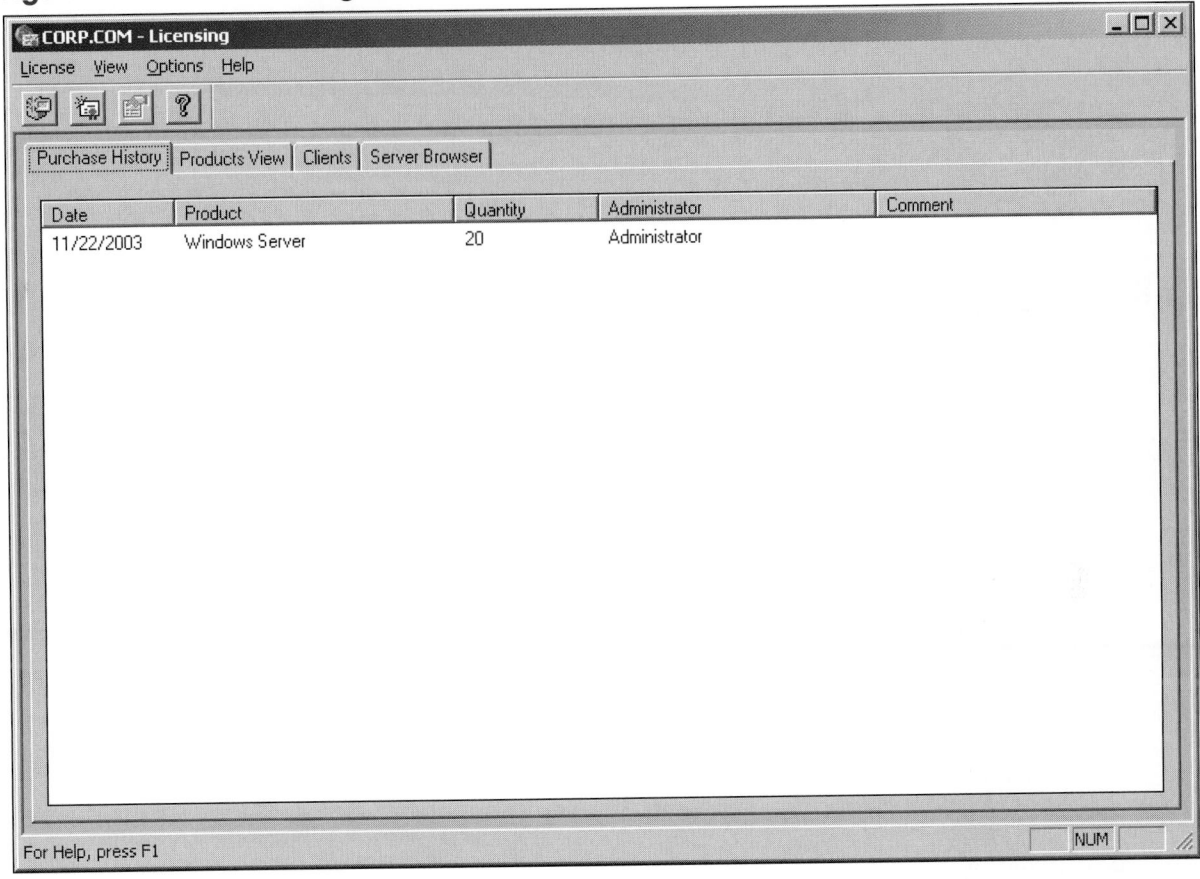

Figure 16-21 The License Logging service in the Services console

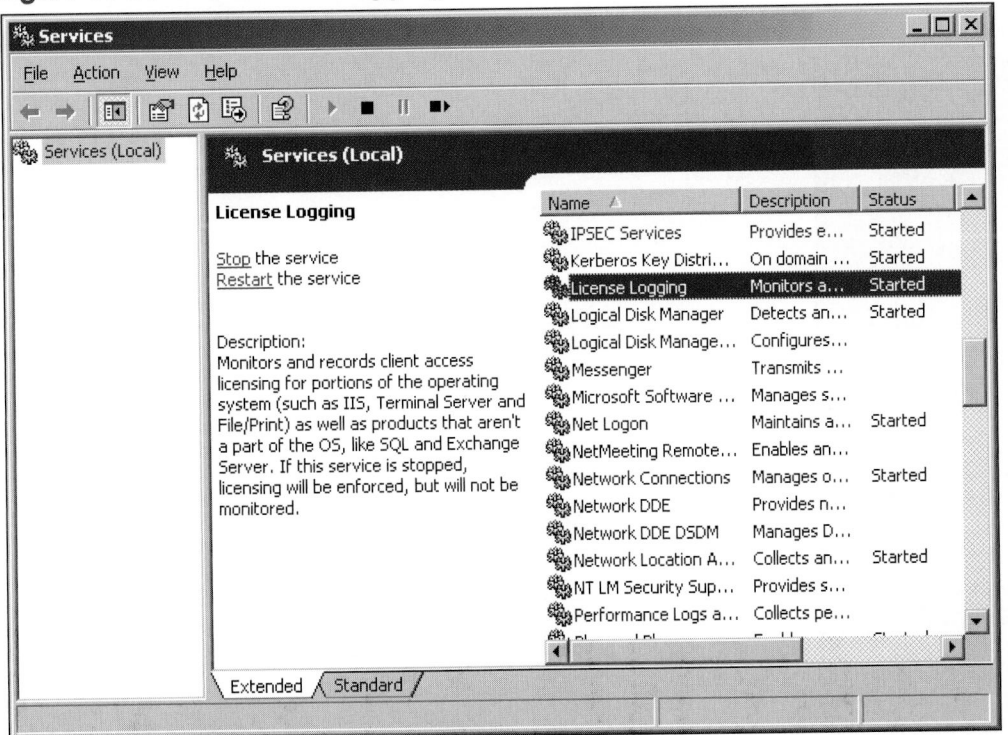

skill 4

Administrating Software Site Licensing (cont'd)

exam objective

Manage software site licensing.

overview

The Licensing tool includes four tabbed sections:

◆ **Purchase History:** Here, you can view your license purchases (**Figure 16-20**).
◆ **Products View:** Here, you can view your CALs by specific product (**Figure 16-22**). In addition, double-clicking a product allows you to see the number of accesses and the purchase history, add licenses, and show which servers are using the licenses (**Figure 16-23**).
◆ **Clients:** Displays licensed and unlicensed usage by user account (**Figure 16-24**). You can double-click an account to see the number of accesses the user has had, and, if necessary, revoke the user's license (**Figure 16-25**).
◆ **Server Browser:** Here, you can see all servers that are using this site licensing server in the Enterprise (**Figure 16-26**). You can double-click **Windows Server** after you expand a server name to change its current Licensing mode from Per Server to Per Device or User (**Figure 16-27**).

Figure 16-22 The Products View tab in the Licensing tool

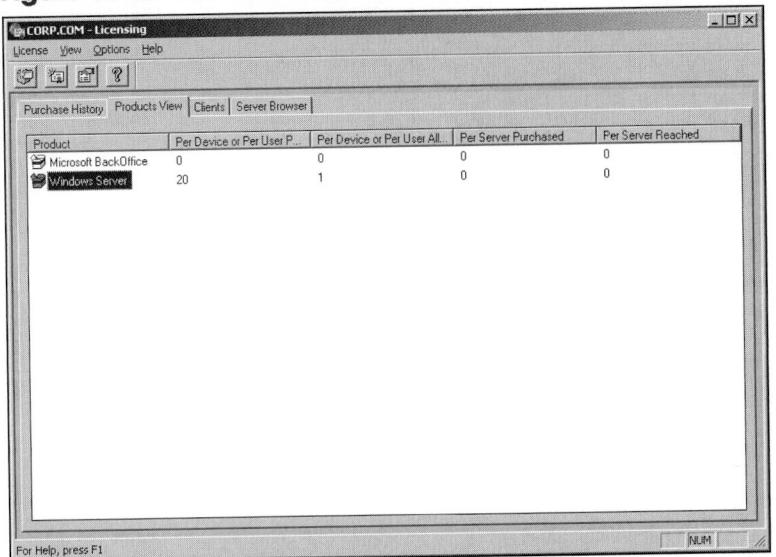

Figure 16-23 The Properties of Windows Server dialog box

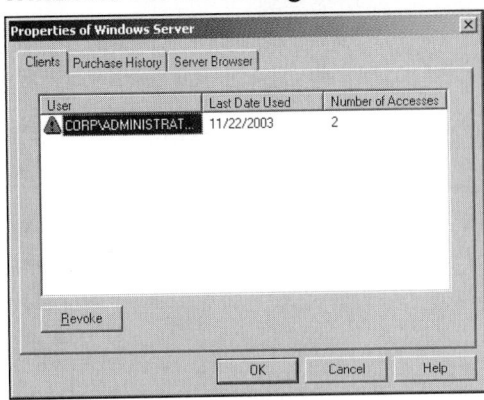

Figure 16-24 The Clients tab

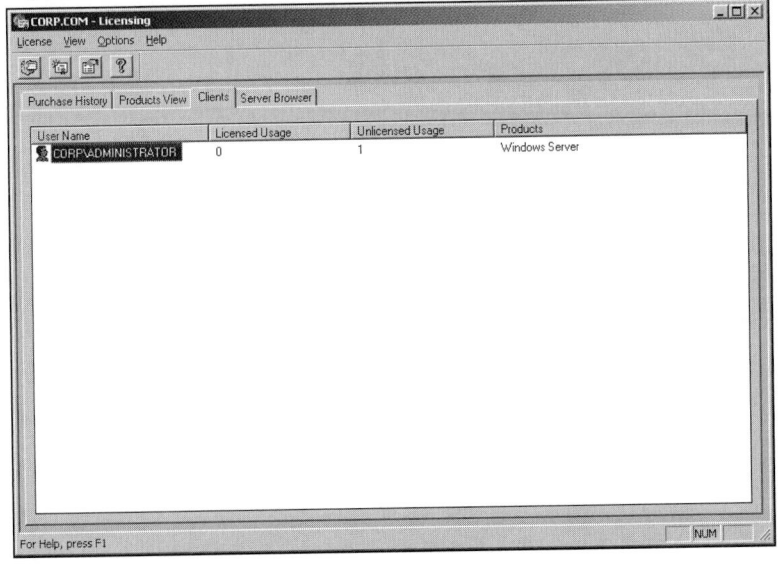

Figure 16-25 The Properties dialog box for a user account

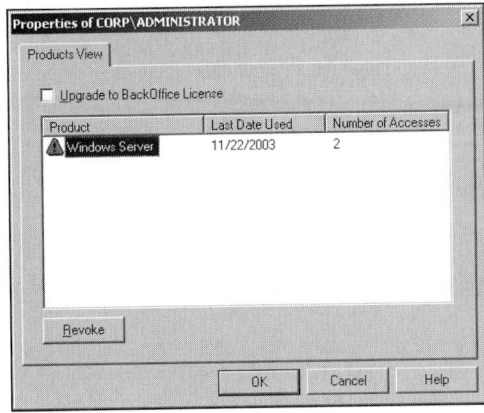

Figure 16-26 The Server Browser tab

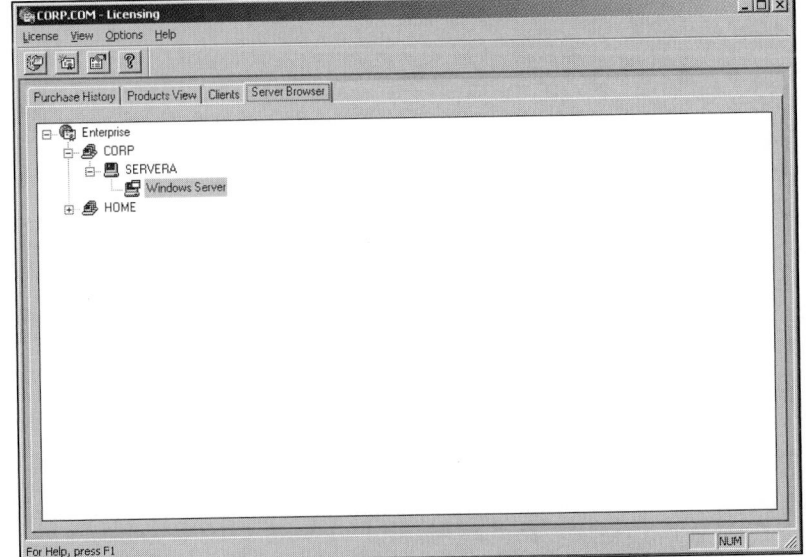

Figure 16-27 The Choose Licensing Mode dialog box

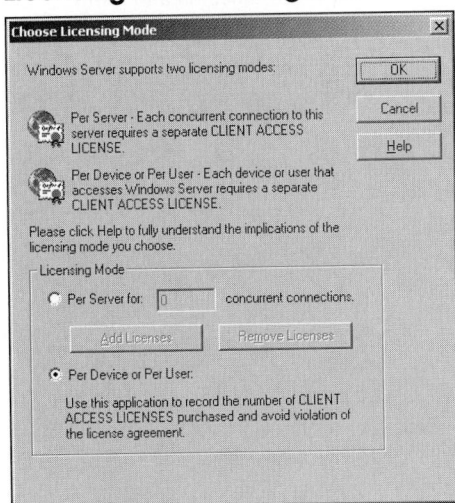

Summary

- Software Updates consists of two components, a client-side service, which retrieves your updates from your Software Update Services (SUS) server or the Internet and installs them, and a server-side service, which can be the central point for distributing updates to clients.
- In order for Software Updates to work at all, however, the client-side service must be properly installed and configured. The client-side service is known as the Automatic Updates service.
- If your environment contains legacy operating systems such as Windows 98 or Windows NT, these computers will not be able to take advantage of Automatic Updates.
- Automatic Updates can be configured on Windows 2000 using the Control Panel applet, by editing the Registry, and through Group Policy (only on SP3 or higher).
- Automatic Updates can be configured on Windows XP and Windows Server 2003 in the System Properties dialog box, by editing the Registry, and through Group Policy (only on SP1 or higher).
- The first thing you should do after installing your SUS server is to make sure that the configuration options are correct.

- Using the default settings, you will need to approve each update before clients can download and begin using them.
- When SUS is installed, the new Group Policy administrative template wuau.adm is installed by default. This template adds the Windows Update node to the Windows Components node under Administrative Templates in the Computer Configuration node in the Group Policy Object Editor.
- With the Per Server licensing mode, a single CAL is necessary for each concurrent connection to the specific server.
- With the Per Device or User mode, a CAL is required for each client connection, but it doesn't matter which server the clients connect to.
- The Licensing tool is an application designed to help keep track of your CALs.
- In order for the Licensing tool to function, the License Logging service must be enabled on one server in the site. The server on which the License Logging service is running is known as the site licensing server.

Key Terms

Automatic Updates Service
Software Update Services

Test Yourself

1. The Licensing tool is used to: (Choose all that apply.)
   a. Log performance data in a file.
   b. Track the usage of CALs.
   c. Connect to a remote terminal server.
   d. Change from Per Server to Per Device or User.

2. You have properly configured your SUS server, performed your initial synchronization, and approved the required updates. However, your clients are not receiving the updates. What could be the cause of the problem? (Choose all that apply.)
   a. Automatic Updates are not enabled.
   b. The clients are running Windows 2000 SP4.
   c. The SUS server cannot contact the Microsoft Update servers.
   d. The clients are not configured to contact the local SUS server and do not have Internet access.

3. You are the network administrator for Tropical Breeze. Tropical Breeze has 14 locations worldwide, 2,000 users, and a single domain, tropicalbreeze.com. You have configured a site license server for each site. All servers are using the Per Device or User mode of licensing. You notice that you are using 2,500 licenses during average periods and over 10,000 licenses during peak usage. What is most likely to be the cause of the problem?
   a. Too many licensing servers are configured.
   b. The License Logging service is not enabled.
   c. Users are accessing resources on multiple sites.
   d. Access to your Web site is driving up the number of required licenses.

4. You are running Windows NT 4.0 client computers and Windows Server 2003 server computers on your network.

You want to automatically deploy and install service packs and updates from a central intranet server to all of your clients Which of the following steps are necessary to do this? (Choose all that apply.)
a. Upgrade to Windows 2000 on all clients.
b. Install the Automatic Update client for Windows NT on all clients.
c. Install SUS 1.1 on the Windows Server 2003 server and synchronize.
d. Install SP3 or later on all Windows 2000 clients.

5. You have installed SUS on your Windows Server 2003 server, installed the Automatic Update client on all of your Windows 2000 clients, and configured a Group Policy to configure the clients to use your internal SUS server. You perform your synchronization on the SUS server and approve updates. However, the clients are still retrieving updates from the Internet and consuming massive amounts of bandwidth. What could be the problem?
a. You need to install SP3 on the Windows 2000 clients.
b. The No auto-restart feature is enabled in the group policy.
c. The server is not configured to store updates locally.
d. The server's proxy configuration is incorrect.

6. When you attempt to open the Licensing tool on your server, you receive an error message. What is the possible cause of the problem?
a. The server has run out of licenses.
b. You didn't modify the Registry under the HKEY_LOCAL_MACHINE/SOFTWARE/LICENSING section.
c. Your server is in Per device or User mode.
d. The License Logging service is disabled.

7. You can use the Licensing tool to: (Choose all that apply.)
a. Purchase licenses directly from Microsoft.
b. Add additional licenses to your server.
c. Change licensing mode on a server.
d. Purchase an Enterprise licensing agreement.

8. Where do you configure Automatic Updates on a Windows XP client with SP1 installed?
a. In the Automatic Updates applet in Control Panel.
b. Under Administrative Tools > Automatic Updates.
c. In system properties.
d. By typing cfgwuau.exe at the run prompt.

Projects: On Your Own

1. Configure a second SUS server and configure it to use the updates from your original SUS server.
a. Install SUS 1.1 on a Windows Server 2003 with IIS already installed.
b. On the SUS Web page, click **Set Options**.
c. In the **Select which server to synchronize content from** section, select **Synchronize from a local Software Update Services server** and type the name of your original server in the prompt.
d. Click the **Synchronize Server** link.
e. Click the **Synchronize Now** button.

Problem Solving Scenarios

1. You are the Network Administrator for Signature Consultants. Signature Consultants has 15 locations across the country connected by private WAN links. Their only connection to the Internet comes from the headquarters, which is located in Miami. You have been informed that Internet access has been extremely slow recently. After examining bandwidth usage, you notice that this is due to Windows Update services running on each computer and downloading updates automatically. You wish to improve your network performance, but you want to ensure that all computers are automatically updated. You also wish to conserve as much WAN bandwidth as possible. What solution would you advise?

Glossary

Access Control Entries (ACE) Entries in the DACL, which contain the SID of the user or group allowed or denied and the permissions associated with that user or group.

Access server A network device that can accommodate multiple modems, ISDN connections, T-carrier lines, E-carrier lines (in Europe) or other types of connections.

Account lockout threshold policy Number of invalid logon attempts that will be tolerated before a user account is locked out.

Account Logon events Event type used on a computer in a domain to audit when a request to log on to the domain is sent to the domain controller.

Account Management events Event type used to audit when an account or group is created, deleted, or modified, or a user account is renamed, has a new password set, or is activated or disabled.

Account policies Used to set the user account properties that control the logon process.

ACE See Access Control Entries.

Active Directory Provides directory database and associated services for Windows Server 2003 and Windows 2000 Server. Stores all the information about how the logical network is structured and organized and enables users to identify and locate resources on the network, such as other users and groups, shares, printers, applications, databases, and computers. Serves as the central repository for network objects and as a central administrative site so that network administrators do not have to individually manage multiple servers.

Active Directory Installation Wizard Used to install Active Directory on a Windows Server 2003 computer.

Active Directory Services Interfaces Edit See ADSIEdit.

Active Directory-integrated zone A primary DNS zone that is stored in Active Directory, inherits all security features of Active Directory, and appears as an object in the Active Directory. When you create Active Directory-integrated zones, the information is updated and replicated automatically across domains as part of the Active Directory replication cycle. You can create an Active Directory-integrated zone only if the DNS server is a domain controller.

Active partition Partition where the boot files that are required for starting the computer are stored. Also referred to as the system partition.

Add Hardware Wizard Enables you to add new hardware, remove or unplug hardware, or troubleshoot any hardware-related problems.

Add Printer Wizard Used to install a local printer. The wizard detects the print device and automatically configures the printer.

Address Resolution Protocol (ARP) Protocol that is responsible for resolving the IP address of a computer to its MAC address.

Administrative Templates Configuration setting node in the Group Policy snap-in that is used to configure Registry settings that control the behavior and appearance of the desktop and other Windows Server 2003 components and applications.

Administrator account Account used to manage the overall domain configuration.

ADSIEdit (Active Directory Services Interfaces Edit) The most commonly used scripting tool: It functions like a Registry Editor for Active Directory. ADSIEdit is an MMC snap-in that provides a means for adding, deleting, and moving Active Directory objects. Using this tool, you can view and change the attributes for an object.

A-G-DL-P strategy Microsoft-recommended strategy for using domain local and global groups.

AH See Authentication Header.

Alert Utility used to send a message, run a program, or start a log, when the value of a specific counter passes the threshold value.

Algorithm A set of instructions or formula used to solve a problem or perform a function such as encrypting and decrypting data. Algorithms must have clear-cut rules and an unmistakable end point. They can be written in any language, including English or any programming language.

Alias In IIS, a name that identifies the virtual directory to the Web browser. The URL for a file in the virtual directory is the full path name, server name, virtual directory alias, and filename.

Allocation unit Smallest unit used to allocate file storage space on a FAT partition. Also called a cluster.

Answer file Customized script that automatically answers the Setup questions for an installation. Used in an unattended installation of Window Server 2003.

Anti-replay Refers to safety measures implemented so that data packets are not retransmitted.

API See Application Programming Interface.

AppleTalk Apple Computer's protocol designed to allow communication between Apple Macintosh computers. You can enable communication between computers running the Macintosh operating system and Windows Server 2003 by installing AppleTalk and File Services for Macintosh on Windows 2000 Server.

Application directory partition New partition in Windows Server 2003 that is used to store data in Active Directory that will only be replicated to a specific group of domain controllers. Using an application directory partition, you can store DNS zones on all DNS servers in the AD forest, on all DNS servers in the AD domain, or on all servers designated in a scope that you create for the partition.

Application layer (DOD model) In the DOD model, the Application layer, at the top of the model, enables applications to access the services of the other layers and defines the protocols that applications must use in order to exchange data. Application layer protocols include HTTP, FTP, SMTP, Telnet, RIP, OSPF, DNS, and SNMP.

Application layer (OSI model) In the OSI model, the Application layer at the top of the conceptual model provides various services to applications that are specifically written to run over the network. It enables access to network services that support applications and is responsible for network access, data flow control, and error recovery.

Application pools Grouping of Web applications and the worker processes servicing those applications to which you can apply configuration settings. You can assign any Web directory or virtual directory to an application pool in order to improve the efficiency of your IIS server, and ensure that your other Web applications will not have their service interrupted when the applications in the one application pool stop.

Application Programming Interface (API) Set of definitions of the ways in which one piece of computer software communicates with another. One of the primary purposes of an API is to provide a set of commonly-used functions, for example, to draw windows or icons on the screen.

Archive attribute A property for files and folders that is used to identify them when they have changed. It is on the General tab in the Properties dialog box for a file or folder on a FAT32 partition and in the Advanced Attributes dialog box on an NTFS partition. Also known as a backup marker or archive bit.

Archive bit See Archive attribute.

ARP See Address Resolution Protocol.

Arp utility Utility used to display and modify the IP address to physical address (MAC address) translation tables that are used by Address Resolution Protocol.

AS See Authentication Service.

ASR See Automated System Recovery.

Authentication Header (AH) Security mechanism used with IPSec for authentication and data integrity purposes. AH does not provide encryption. It ensures that the correct, unmodified data is sent to the correct recipient.

Authentication Method of verifying the validity of a host or client on the network.

Authentication Service (AS) The service on the Key Distribution Center (KDC) server that validates the identity of a user and issues a Ticket Granting Ticket (TGT) that will be used for future authentication.

Authoritative restore Replicates restored data to all domain controllers on the network. You use Ntdsutil to authoritatively restore Active Directory data after you have restored the System State data but before you restart the server. Using Ntdsutil you mark Active Directory objects for authoritative restore, which modifies the update sequence number making it higher than any other update sequence number in the Active Directory replication system. Thus, data that you restore is properly replicated or distributed to the other servers on the network

Authoritative server The server where the primary zone database file is housed.

Automated System Recovery (ASR) A backup of system configuration information including key system files and the Registry that is designed to enable you to repair your system partition. You can use ASR to recover a failed server in the event of a complete breakdown.

Automatic Private Addressing (APIPA) Feature of Windows Server 2003 that can be used to automatically assign addresses to hosts on a network.

Automatic Updates service The client-side component of the Software Update Service.

Backup marker See Archive attribute.

Backup The process of creating a duplicate of a disk, program, or data so that if it is lost, it can be recovered.

BACP See Bandwidth Allocation Control Protocol.

Bandwidth Allocation Control Protocol (BACP) Multilinking protocol, usually used with ISDN (Integrated Services Digital Network) connections: BACP can be used to select a preferred client when two clients are competing to use the same bandwidth.

Bandwidth Allocation Protocol (BAP) Network protocol used with remote networks that use dial-in connections. It is often referred to as Multilink PPP because it is used with PPP to augment the use of multilinked devices. Multilinking means that multiple physical links are combined to create one logical link. All of the links are pooled and the load is balanced among the physical connection components. BAP is used to dynamically add or drop links on demand so that only as much bandwidth as is required for the current network traffic is used.

Bandwidth throttling Capability used to limit the bandwidth used by IIS services to a value that an administrator sets. If the bandwidth used by the IIS services approaches or exceeds this limit, bandwidth throttling delays or rejects IIS service requests until more bandwidth becomes available. This ensures that bandwidth is available to applications, as well as to Web services on the server

BAP See Bandwidth Allocation Protocol.

Basic storage Type of storage that divides a hard disk into primary and extended partitions. A basic disk that can have up to four partitions. Basic disks are compatible with MS-DOS, Windows 3.x, Windows 9.x, Windows NT, Windows 2000, and Windows Server 2003.

Batch files Text files that contain a series of commands for the operating system that are executed sequentially when the batch file name is typed at the command prompt or double-clicked in Windows Explorer. It batches together a number of commands into a single file so that the commands do not each have to be executed individually.

BGP See Border Gateway Protocol.

Binding A process that configures a protocol to a specific NIC and provides information about available network services, which client computers can use to make connections over a network.

Binding order The binding order establishes which protocol should be used first when a network connection is established. It is the client computer in an exchange that determines which protocol will be used to establish the connection.

Block Inheritance Setting used for GPO links for an entire domain, for all domain controllers, or for a particular OU to prevent GPOs that are linked to higher sites, domains, or organizational units from being automatically inherited by the child container.

B-node (Broadcast) NetBIOS node type that uses broadcasts to resolve names. On Microsoft machines B-nodes are referred to as enhanced B-nodes, because if the broadcast is not successful, the client will attempt to use the LMHOSTS file.

Boot partition Partition where the Windows Server 2003 operating system files (%systemroot% folder) are stored.

Boot volume The volume where the Windows Server 2003 operating system files and support files are stored (typically *Windows and* *Windows\System 32*).

Border Gateway Protocol (BGP) Routing protocol used to exchange routing information for the Internet: It is the protocol used between ISPs. Universities and corporations generally use an Interior Gateway Protocol (IGP) such as RIP or OSPF, while ISPs use BGP4 which supports CIDR.

Bottleneck Any resource, such as memory or disk space, which causes other resources to delay while it completes its assigned function.

Broadcast address The IP address in which all bits are 1 (255.255.255.255). You cannot use this address to broadcast a message to external networks because routers block it, but datagrams with this address will broadcast to all hosts on the LAN.

Broadcast Method for sending data simultaneously to all network hosts. Broadcasts can be used as a method of NetBIOS name resolution, but is inefficient because it generates a substantial amount of network traffic. It will not work on large networks that contain subnets connected by routers, because routers generally block broadcasts.

Built-in domain local groups Groups automatically created only on domain controllers. They are stored in the Users container in the Active Directory Users and Computers console. Examples include Cert Publishers, DHCP Administrators, DHCP Users, and RAS and IAS Servers.

Built-in global groups Groups automatically created on domain controllers that are stored in the Users container in the Active Directory Users and Computers console. Examples include DnsUpdateProxy, Domain Admins, Domain Controllers, and Domain Users.

Built-in groups Groups automatically created on Windows Server 2003 that have predefined rights and permissions.

Built-in local groups Groups created on all Windows Server 2003 computers. They can be viewed in the Groups folder in the Computer Management console on all non-domain controllers and in the Builtin container in Active Directory Users and Computers on domain controllers.

Built-in system groups Groups populated with users based upon how they access a computer or a resource. Network administrators cannot add, modify, or delete user accounts because the operating system does so automatically.

Built-in user accounts Accounts that are created automatically by Windows 2000 that are used to perform administrative tasks and access network resources

Burst handling Refers to a method for handling a high or burst period of WINS registration and renewal traffic.

CA See Certification Authority.

Caching-only DNS name server DNS name servers that are not authoritative for any zone which use caching to store information collected during name resolution. They are used when you need to provide DNS services locally, but do not want to create a separate zone and when you do not want to increase zone transfer traffic. Caching-only name servers do not participate in zone transfers.

CAL See Client Access License.

Certificate Digitally signed document that functions as a component of PKI: It contains the name of the subject, which can be a directory name, an e-mail name, and/or a DNS name, and a public key. Used to authenticate and secure the exchange of information on non-secure networks.

Certificate Revocation List (CRL) Record of the certificates that have been revoked, have expired, or have been removed.

Certificate Services Responsible for the issuing, renewal, and reissuing of digital certificates.

Certification Authority (CA) Entities entrusted to issue certificates to validate that the recipient, which can be a person, a computer, or an organization, which requested the certificate fulfills the conditions of an established policy.

Challenge Handshake Authentication Protocol (CHAP) Protocol used in RAS that provides authentication on the basis of a value that is calculated using an algorithm. CHAP sends a challenge message to the client as soon as the client dials in. The client applies an algorithm to the message to calculate a hash value (a fixed-length number), and sends the value to the server. The server also calculates a value and compares this value to the value sent by the client. If the value matches, the connection is established.

CHAP See Challenge Handshake Authentication Protocol.

Check Disk Tool used to check the hard disk for file system errors and bad sectors.

Child domain Domains under a parent domain.

CIDR See Classless Inter-Domain Routing.

Cipher Command line utility used to encrypt and decrypt files.

Classful IP addressing The first major addressing scheme for the Internet. There are three main address classes: A, B, and C, which have fixed 8-bit, 16-bit, and 24-bit network IDs.

Classless Inter-Domain Routing (CIDR) Internet routing method that uses classless IP addressing to allow for the more efficient allocation of IP addresses. By using a configurable, rather than static, subnet mask, the problems of wasted addresses and the diminishing capacity of Internet global routing tables are alleviated. Using CIDR, a single routing table entry can replace hundreds or thousands of entries in a global routing table.

Classless IP addressing Newer IP addressing scheme in which any number of bits can be assigned to the network ID.

Client (Respond Only) IPSec policy. Sends data packets without applying security measures such as encryption; however, if specifically requested by a server, the policy ensures that data will be encrypted before it is sent. The client does not request a secure session, but it will provide one if asked.

Client Access License (CAL) License to access or use server software. Two types: a User that allows a particular user to access licensed server software from any number of devices, and a Device CAL, which allows any number of users to access licensed server software from a particular device.

Cluster See Allocation unit.

Code signing See driver signing.

Computer Account The security principal associated with each Windows Server 2003, 2000, XP, and NT computer in a domain.

Computer Configuration node Group Policy Node used to set group policies for computers that are members of the domain, OU, or site, depending on where the GPO is configured.

Computer Management console Desktop tool that combines various administration utilities in a single console tree.

Confidentiality One of the four fundamental functions of any security system. It refers to putting protections in place to make sure that data is revealed only to the designated recipients.

Connectionless protocol A protocol in which no connection is established between communicating devices. With connectionless protocols, such as UDP, there is no guarantee that messages will reach their destination. There is no acknowledgement that data packets have been received, so data is not retransmitted.

Connection-oriented protocol A protocol that establishes a confirmed connection with the destination computer. The transfer of data occurs in three steps: connection establishment, data transfer, and connection release.

Console Consists of management applications called snap-ins that integrate applications, information, and views of a network and enables you to perform administrative tasks.

Contiguous namespace An Active Directory tree-sometimes called domain trees-form a contiguous namespace. A domain tree is formed as soon as a child domain is created and associated with a given root domain. For a technical definition, a tree is a contiguous DNS naming hierarchy.

Copy backup Backup type that creates a representation of your data at a particular point in time: It is used between Normal and Incremental or Normal and Differential backups so that when they take place, the process will not be affected by the removal of the archive bit.

Counter log Log used to record the state of object counters at specific intervals of time that you set.

CRL See Certification Revocation List.

Cryptography The process of protecting data by changing it into an indecipherable format using keys and algorithms. Only users who have a specific key can decipher it. It is used to protect e-mail messages, credit card information, and corporate data.

Csvde.exe (Comma separated values data export) Tool used to import and export group objects into and out of Active Directory using CSV files. CSV files can be used in Excel and most other spreadsheet programs.

Customized console Combination of snap-ins within a common MMC interface saved together as a file. Can be distributed for administrative purposes.

DACL See Discretionary Access Control List.

Daily backup Backup type in which files that have changed during the day are backed up. The archive attribute is not removed.

Data compression A feature that enables a user to compress files and folders to create free space on an NTFS formatted volume.

Data encryption Security technique that attempts to ensure the confidentiality of a document by scrambling it with an encryption key.

Data Link layer (OSI model) The Data Link layer supplies error control between adjoining nodes and handles the data frames between the Network and Physical layers. It ensures that frames are transferred with no errors to other computers from the Physical layer. The Data Link layer converts data packets into frames for the physical layer. At the receiving computer, it takes the raw data received from the Physical layer and packages it into data frames to send on the Network layer.

Data Store (Ntds.dit file) File where the records that make up Active Directory's database are stored. The Ntds.dit file contains the schema information, global catalog, and all of the objects stored on the domain controller. It is stored in the *%systemroot%\Ntds* folder, by default.

Database Layer Active Directory service layer that provides an object view of database information thereby isolating the upper layers of the directory service from the underlying database system. All database access is routed through the Database layer.

Datagram The message unit that IP handles and the Internet transports: The terms datagram and packet are often used interchangeably. A packet is a piece of a message transmitted over a packet-switching network that contains the destination address in addition to the data. At the IP layer in IP networks, packets are referred to as IP datagrams.

Dcdiag Command line utility that can be used to troubleshoot problems with domain controllers.

Debugging Mode Safe boot mode in which debugging information concerning the boot process is sent to another computer through a serial cable so that errors can be tracked and repaired.

Decryption Using a key and an algorithm to transform data that has been encrypted back to its original form.

Default gateway A router that links networks and manages this information so that individual TCP/IP hosts do not have to maintain complete local routing tables. It acts as an intermediate device between hosts on different network segments and functions as a gateway to remote networks.

Defragmentation Process that rearranges files, programs, and unused space to ensure that all related components of the files and programs are placed in contiguous locations on the disk, enabling files to be located and opened more quickly.

Details pane Right pane of console, which displays information and functions associated with different snap-ins.

Device driver Software that enables a hardware device to communicate with the operating system installed on a computer.

Device Manager System tool in Windows Server 2003 to manage the hardware devices installed on the computer.

Dfs link Points to shared folders on the network. A Distributed file system (Dfs) topology consists of a hierarchical structure that includes a Dfs root, one or more Dfs links, and one or more Dfs shared folders, or replicas, to which each Dfs link points.

Dfs root Stored on a server running the Dfs service. It is a local share that acts as the starting point and host to other shared resources. A Dfs root can consist of one or more Dfs links and is used to coordinate all of the shared folders that are part of the Dfs hierarchy on multiple computers on the network.

Dfs See Distributed file system.

DHCP See Dynamic Host Configuration Protocol.

DHCP lease Amount of time that the DHCP server allows the DHCP client to use a particular IP address.

Dial-up connection Establishes a non-permanent connection between a remote access server and a remote access client using telecommunications services such as an analog phone line or ISDN.

Differential backup Backs up only selected files and folders with the archive attribute, which is not removed. Therefore, even if a file has not changed since the previous Differential backup, it will be backed up again because it still has the archive attribute.

Digital message signing A method of authenticating a sender on a network in which a message digest is used to create a kind of "digital fingerprint" for a message.

Digital signature A way of validating that the message actually came from the user who claims to have sent it, and also ensures that the message has not been tampered with in any way.

Digital signature Certifies the integrity and origin of data related to device drivers, and ensures that they have not been altered after signing.

Direct Metabase Edit Functionality that allows admini-strators to edit the metabase while IIS is running. It helps Web site administrators to avoid site downtime because when configuration changes must be made, they can edit the metabase file while the IIS service is running.

Directory service Database that stores information about network objects, such as files, applications, users, or printers, in the network.

Directory Service Access events Event type used to audit a computer in a domain when an Active Directory object, such as a computer or domain, is accessed.

Directory Services Restore Mode Safe boot mode only used on domain controllers in which a directory service repair is performed.

Directory System Agent (DSA) Active Directory service layer that represents the process that provides access to the Data store, which contains the physical store of directory information located on a hard disk. The DSA is the server-side process that creates an instance of a directory service. Clients use one of the supported interfaces to connect (bind) to the DSA and then search for, read, and write Active Directory objects and their attributes. Applications need to connect to the DSA layer to access objects in Active Directory through one of the supported interfaces such as LDAP or ADSI.

Discretionary Access Control List (DACL) Set of security descriptors for each object: Each file or folder on an NTFS drive has a DACL. The DACL defines how that object can be accessed. It contains the ACEs, which include the SID of the user or group allowed or denied and the permissions associated with that user or group. By housing the list of ACEs, the DACL essentially controls access to the share.

Disjointed namespace A DNS infrastructure that includes two or more top-level domain names. The domains in the Active Directory tree are interrelated but do not always share a common root domain name. A forest is a disjointed namespace.

Disk Cleanup Utility used to locate files you are likely to want to delete such as Temporary Internet files. It also selects files that you have not accessed for some time to target them for compression.

Disk controller The circuit which allows the CPU to communicate with a hard disk, floppy disk, or other kind of disk drive: The hard disk controller controls the functions of the hard disk such as writing data to the disk.

Disk Defragmenter Utility that rearranges files and unused space on a hard disk, so that files occupy a single, contiguous space on the hard disk.

Disk duplexing Using one disk controller for each disk in a mirrored volume to ensure that if one disk controller fails, data will still be accessible.

Disk Management snap-in Utility used to view disk properties and perform disk management functions such as creating new partitions or volumes, setting an active partition, formatting drives, changing drive letters, and upgrading a disk from a conventional basic disk to a dynamic disk.

Disk quota Allocating a specific amount of disk space to each user. You can either monitor disk quotas or enforce a limit so that users cannot use more disk space than has been allotted.

Distinguished Name (DN) Distinct name that provides a unique identity to an object. All objects can be referenced using a Distinguished Name. Example: CN=Gregory Johnson, OU=Accounting, DC=ABC Corp, DC=com

Distributed file system (Dfs) An advanced file service that allows users to locate files and folders spread across the network at a single location.

Distribution folder Used for an unattended installation of Windows Server 2003. Holds the files required to install Windows Server 2003 over a network.

Distribution group Group used only for the distribution of messages by applications such as Microsoft Exchange Server. Cannot be used to assign permissions to users.

DMA (Direct Memory Access) channel Moves data directly from the memory of the computer to a device, bypassing the CPU.

DNS namespace A name for the hierarchical structure of DNS

DNS resilience Refers to the hardiness of the DNS infrastructure, specifically its ability to continue operating when individual components have been damaged.

DNS See Domain Name System.

DNS server Perform the task of name resolution to convert host names to IP addresses and to resolve service names.

DOD (Department of Defense) model Four-layered conceptual model of network architecture that includes Network Interface, Internet, Transport and Application layers.

Domain Logical group of network computers that share a central directory database that contains user accounts and security information for the domain. When used with reference to DNS, refers to nodes in the DNS hierarchical structure.

Domain controller A computer that stores a replica of the directory database. A domain controller also stores the security policies and security accounts for a domain and authenticates users to log on to the domain and access the shared resources.

Domain Dfs root Distributed file system root that is integrated with Active Directory.

Domain directory partition Partition where data pertaining to a particular AD domain, including data about objects such as users and computers, is stored. Data stored in a domain directory partition is replicated to all domain controllers in an AD domain, but it cannot be replicated to domain controllers in other AD domains. All domain controllers in the domain will receive copies of the zone even if they are not DNS servers.

Domain license server Terminal Services license server used when you want to have a separate license server for each domain. If you have Windows NT 4.0 domains or workgroups on your network, you can only use a domain license server. Only Terminal Servers in the same domain will be able to contact a domain license server.

Domain local group Group created and stored in Active Directory on a domain controller that is used to manage and access resources in a domain.

Domain Name System (DNS) The main name resolution service for Windows Server 2003 and Windows 2000.

Domain user account Account used to access resources on a computer in a domain.

Dr. Watson Utility that stops a program and records some diagnostic statistics when a program error occurs. You can view this data in the log file, *drwtsn32.log*, (in the *%systemroot%* folder) and use it to diagnose and solve system problems.

Driver signing Notifies users whether the driver being installed has passed the Microsoft certification process or not. Also known as code signing.

DSA See Directory System Agent.

Dual boot system Enables you to select between operating systems when you boot the computer.

Dynamic Host Configuration Protocol (DHCP) Standard used to automate, centralize, and simplify the process of allocating IP Addresses and other related configuration information to DHCP-enabled clients on a network.

Dynamic storage Storage method that uses volumes rather than partitions: On a dynamic disk, you can create an unlimited number of volumes and you can extend volumes onto additional physical disks.

Dynamic Update Downloads and uses critical content to enhance the Setup program.

EAP See Extensible Authentication Protocol.

EFS See Encrypting File System.

Enable Boot Logging Safe boot mode in which logging is enabled when the computer is started. Boot logging is enabled in all of the Safe modes except Last Known Good Configuration. The Boot Logging text is recorded in the *Ntbtlog.txt* file in the *%SystemRoot%* folder.

Enable VGA Mode Safe boot mode which starts the operating system in 640 x 480 pixels using the current video driver (not Vga.sys): It is used when the display has been configured for a setting that the monitor cannot display.

Encapsulating Security Payload (ESP) Security mechanism used with IPSec to transmit encrypted data. It uses encryption algorithms to guarantee the confidentiality of data packets.

Encrypting File System (EFS) A file system that is used to encrypt files and folders on an NTFS volume or partition to protect them from unauthorized users.

Encryption The process of changing or "scrambling" data so that it is unreadable to unauthorized users. It is chiefly used during data transmission, although it can also be used to protect data on an internal network. Keys and algorithms are used to make the data indecipherable.

Enforced Setting for a GPO link that is used to specify that the policy settings in the GPO link will take precedence over the settings for any child object. When the parent GPO link has precedence, the default behavior (the child container settings override the parent container settings if there is a conflict) does not apply. This was formerly referred to as the No override option.

Enrollment The process of issuing a certificate.

Enterprise license server Terminal Services license server that supplies licenses to all servers in a site, regardless of domain, as long as they are members of Windows Server 2003 or Windows 2000 domains. Servers outside of the site are not serviced, even if other servers that are members of the same domain are in the site.

Enterprise Root CA A certification authority at the top of the CA hierarchy. Enterprise root CAs sign their own CA certificates.

Enterprise Subordinate CA CA located beneath either an Enterprise root, stand-alone root, or another Enterprise subordinate CA in the hierarchy. They issue certificates within an organization either to lower level issuing CAs or directly to users and computers. Requires Active Directory.

Environmental subsystems Used by Windows Server 2003 to run a variety of applications written for different operating systems.

ESE See Extensible Storage Engine.

ESP See Encapsulating Security Payload.

Event log Used to record an entry when certain events occur such as successful execution of a program or users logging on to the system.

Event Viewer Snap-in used to monitor information about server events. Events are documented in event logs as errors, warnings, or simply information. The default event logs on a Windows Server 2003 machine are the Application log, Security log, and System log. A domain controller will also include the Directory Service log and the File Replication Service log. A DNS server will have the DNS Server log.

Execute permissions Permissions used to control application security. There are three levels of Execute permissions: None, Scripts, and Scripts and Executables.

Executive Services Responsible for performing I/O and object management, which also includes security.

Extended partition Partition that is created by combining un-partitioned free space on a hard disk. Linked to a primary partition to increase the available disk space.

Extensible Authentication Protocol (EAP) Protocol used to customize your method of remote access authentication. It supports authentication using either TLS (Transport Layer Security) or MD5-CHAP. TLS supports smart cards and certificates. MD5-CHAP uses a Message Digest 5 (MD5) algorithm to encrypt user names and passwords.

Extensible Storage Engine (ESE) layer This Active Directory service layer has direct contact with the records in the Data Store. It is based on an object's relative distinguished name attribute. This layer can support a database up to a maximum of 16 terabytes (TB) in size.

Extension snap-in Type of snap-in that extends the functionality of a stand-alone snap-in.

FAT (File Allocation Table) A 16-bit file system used to format a hard disk that supports partitions up to 4 GB in size. Also known as FAT16.

FAT16 See FAT (File Allocation Table).

FAT32 File system that supports large-sized partitions of up to 2047 GB size.

Fault tolerance Using redundancy technologies to ensure that data is protected.

FEK See File Encryption Key.

File Encryption Key (FEK) A symmetric bulk encryption key. EFS uses public key encryption in conjunction with symmetric key encryption to encrypt files and folders. The FEK is used to encrypt the file and the FEK is then encrypted using the user's public key, which is in the user's certificate. Certificates are stored in the user's profile.

File Signature Verification utility Utility used to identify unsigned files on your computer and display the related information such as the file's name, location, last modification date, file type, and the file's version number.

Folder Redirection Configuration setting node in the Group Policy snap-in under User Configuration\Windows Settings that is used to redirect Windows Server 2003 special folders to an alternate location on a network share.

Forest Discrete administrative Active Directory unit that consists of one or more trees joined together through a common forest root domain. This set of domain trees share a common schema and configuration, common global catalog, are secured by Kerberos trust, and share a disjointed namespace.

Forward lookup query Request by a DNS client to a DNS server to resolve a host name to an IP address.

Forward lookup zone Used to resolve host names to IP addresses.

FQDN See Fully qualified domain name.

Frame relay Frame relay was developed for WANs. It uses packet-switching technology and depends on virtual connection methods. Transmission speeds range between 56 Kbps and 45 Mbps.

Fully qualified domain name (FQDN) A host name that includes a domain name. It follows Internet naming conventions that use dots to separate parts of a name in addition to the simple host name. For example, server1 may be the alias for a computer on a TCP/IP network, whereas server1.finance.redhen.com. is the FQDN for the computer.

GDI See Graphical Device Interface.

Global catalog Stores a full replica of all object attributes in the directory for its host domain and a partial replica of all object attributes contained in the directory for every domain in the forest. Also stores commonly used logon and authentication data.

Global catalog server Domain controller that maintains a copy of the global catalog. Is automatically created on the initial domain controller in the first domain in the forest.

Global group Group in which members can only be drawn from the domain where the group was created, but permissions can be assigned to members for resources in any domain.

Globally Unique Identifier (GUID) A 128-bit number that defines the identity of an object in Active Directory. When you create an object in Active Directory, the Directory Service Agent (DSA) automatically assigns a GUID to the object. Even if you move an object from one domain to another, the GUID remains the same.

GPC See Group Policy Container.

GPMC See Group Policy Management Console.

GPO See Group Policy Object.

GPT See Group Policy Template.

Graphical Device Interface (GDI) Windows standard for representing graphical objects and transmitting them to output devices such as monitors and printers. It combines data, such as the word-processing codes for the file, the embedded objects in the file, and the colors and fonts for the file, with data processed by the printer driver on the client.

Group A collection of user accounts: You can also add contacts, computers, and other groups to a group.

Group nesting The process of adding groups to other groups so that you do not have to assign the same permissions for two groups separately.

Group Policy A set of configuration settings applied by administrators to objects in Active Directory. Administrators use group policies to centrally manage users' desktop environment.

Group Policy Container (GPC) An Active Directory object that stores GPO properties. It includes sub-containers for computer and user Group Policy information.

Group Policy Management Console (GPMC) A comprehensive tool for Group Policy administration for Windows 2000 and Windows Server 2003 domains. It provides administrators with the ability to backup, restore, import, and copy/paste GPOs, as well as to create, delete, and rename them. You can use it to link GPOs, search for GPOs, and to delegate Group Policy-related features such as setting permissions on GPOs and for policy-related permission for sites, domains, and OUs.

Group Policy Object (GPO) A container for Group Policy settings for sites, domains, and OUs. They contain properties that are written to the Active Directory store in an object called a GPC.

Group Policy Template (GPT) A folder structure in the *%systemroot%\SYSVOL\sysvol\<domain_name>\Policies* folder on domain controllers where Group Policy settings associated with administrative templates, security settings, scripts, and software settings are stored.

Group scope Designates the reach for a group on the network, such as to access resources in a specific domain or across domains in the network. Group scopes include Domain local, Global, and Universal.

Guest account Account used for infrequent users who must log on to access shared resources for a short duration.

GUI mode phase Consists of three stages: Gathering Information About Your Computer, Installing Windows Server 2003 Networking and Completing Setup.

GUID See Globally Unique Identifier.

HAL See Hardware Abstraction Layer.

Handle Any resource, such as a file, that is used by an application that has its own identification so that the program can access it.

Hardware Abstraction Layer (HAL) Hides the hardware interface details from the end user by acting as an interface between the user and the hardware devices.

Hardware device Any equipment connected to the computer and controlled by the microprocessor, or HAL.

Hardware profile Describes the configuration and characteristics of a device. Used to configure computers for using peripheral devices.

Hardware RAID implementation Fault tolerance is independent of the operating system and is implemented through the server's hardware. The disk controller or SCSI adapter includes a chip on which the RAID logic is stored.

H-node (Hybrid) NetBIOS node type in which the client attempts to query a WINS server first in order to resolve names. If this is unsuccessful, the B-node methods are used, i.e. broadcasts and then the LMHOSTS file. WINS clients are by default H-nodes.

Home directory Required Web page for every Web site that includes links to the other pages on the site. It generally contains a home page, although home pages are not necessary if browsing is enabled or if Web folders are in use. The home page is generally named index.htm, index.html, default.htm, or default.html, or uses the .asp extension.

Home folder Private network location in addition to the My Documents folder where users can store personal files.

Host address See Host ID.

Host header name Name assigned to a server on a specific network to uniquely identify it on the Web server. Host header names allow you to host multiple Web sites on one server. You can also assign different ports or IP addresses to each Web site in order to host multiple Web sites on the same server.

Host ID Part of an IP address, also known as the host address, which is used to identify a server, workstation, or a router on a network.

Host name Designates a particular computer either on the Internet or on a private network. At the bottom of the DNS hierarchy. Can be up to 256 characters long and can contain letters, numbers, and special characters such as "_" and ".".

Hostname Utility used to validate the host name for the local computer. The Remote Copy Protocol (RCP), remote shell (RSH), and Remote Execution (REXEC) utilities will authenticate the host name after it is received from the Hostname utility.

Hot-pluggable Used to refer to devices that can be connected and disconnected while the computer is on and that will be automatically installed and configured with no reboot necessary.

HTTP Keep-Alives Setting used to ensure that an IIS server will keep a connection open while a browser is making the many requests required to download a Web page with multiple elements. If this is not enabled, each element will need a separate connection.

HTTP See Hypertext Transfer Protocol.

Hypertext Transfer Protocol (HTTP) Standard protocol used for the transmission of data across the Internet.

I/O address A unique hexadecimal number that designates where a memory buffer for a hardware device is located.

I/O Manager Offers core services for device drivers, and translates user mode read and write commands into read or write Input/Output Request Packets (IRPs).

ICANN See Internet Corporation for Assigned Names and Numbers.

ICMP See Internet Control Message Protocol.

IEEE 802.1X New protocol in Windows XP and Windows Server 2003 that supports wireless connections.

IGMP See Internet Group Management Protocol.

IIS See Internet Information Services.

IIS Help A folder that is installed with IIS in the *%systemroot%/Help* folder that contains IIS documentation.

In-addr.arpa A second-level domain, which contains name-to-IP address mappings indexed by IP addresses. It was created to simplify the process of reverse lookup queries, which are requests to resolve a known IP address to a host name.

Incremental backup Backup type in which only selected files and folders that have the archive attribute, which is then removed. Thus, if a file has not changed since the previous backup, it will be skipped during the next Incremental backup.

Inetpub Folder installed with IIS at the root of the system drive (*%systemdrive%*) that is the storage folder for all content. Sub-folders divide the content according to whether it is Web content, or FTP, NNTP, or SMTP content.

Inetsrv Folder installed with IIS in the *%systemroot% \system32* folder that stores all IIS program and dll files.

Input/output ports (I/O ports) Channels used for data transfer between hardware devices and the microprocessor

Integral subsystems Performs various important operating system functions such as creating security tokens and tracking user rights and permissions.

Integrity One of the four fundamental functions of any security system. It refers to the accuracy of received data.

Internet Connection Sharing (ICS) Method used to share a single point of access to the Internet with other computers on a small network. The ICS enabled machine has both a public IP address and a private IP address. The clients sharing the connection request Internet access from the ICS-enabled machine, which accesses the Internet for them and passes the information to them. Unregistered non-routable private IP addresses are assigned to the client computers on the network in the Class C subnet range (192.168.0.2-192.168.0.254). The address for the ICS computer is always the Windows internal address 192.168.0.1 with a subnet mask of 255.255.255.0.

Internet Control Message Protocol (ICMP) Protocol that supports packets containing error, control, and informational messages. ICMP packets are used by higher-level protocols to solve transmission problems and by network administrators to discover where network problems are located. ICMP packets are also used by the ping utility to find out if an IP device on the network is working.

Internet Corporation for Assigned Names and Numbers (ICANN) Organization responsible for defining new top-level domains. The ICANN DNS Root Server System Advisory Committee coordinates and regulates the thirteen DNS root name servers that control the DNS name resolution process for the entire world.

Internet Group Management Protocol (IGMP) Protocol responsible for the management of IP multicasting. IP multicasting is the transmission of an IP datagram to a set of hosts called the IP multicast group, which is identified by a single IP multicast address.

Internet Information Services (IIS) 6.0 Windows Server 2003's built-in Web server.

Internet layer (DOD model) Layer in the DOD model that is responsible for addressing and routing IP datagrams. Each packet that is being sent or received is called an IP datagram. An IP datagram contains information about the source and destination addresses that are used to transfer data between computers on a network and across networks. Protocols that operate at the Internet layer include IP, ARP, ICMP, and IGMP.

Internet Protocol (IP) A connectionless protocol that is responsible for the delivery of packets, which includes the process of disassembling and reassembling them during the transmission process.

Internet Server Application Programming Interface (ISAPI) filters Filters used to regulate the functions of a Web server. They are dll scripts that manage the security of the Web site by processing HTTP requests. They are driven by Web server events rather than by client requests.

Interprocess Communication (IPC) Manager Manages IPC processes that communicate with other processes. The processes can be running on the same computer or on different computers connected through a network.

Interrupt Request (IRQ) Hardware devices use IRQ lines to send signals to the microprocessor to start receiving and sending data.

Interrupt Request for attention from the processor.

IP address A 32-bit number divided into 4 octets separated by periods. These octets have values that are 8-bit binary numbers, each of which represents a decimal number in the range 0-255. There are two parts to an IP address: the network ID and the host ID. The network ID identifies all hosts on the network and the host ID identifies a specific host.

IP See Internet Protocol.

IP version 6 IP protocol of the future. Will enable use of 128-bit IP addresses.

Ipconfig Utility used to obtain information about host computer configuration, IP address, subnet mask and default gateway.

IPSec A set of security protocols used to protect data in transit over a network.

IPX/SPX A connectionless protocol used on Novell NetWare networks.

IRQ See Interrupt Request.

ISDN (Integrated Services Digital Network) The international data transfer format for sending voice, video, and data over digital telephone lines or normal telephone wires. There are several styles of ISDN (EURO, US). ISDN uses 64 Kbps channels in conjunction with different types of services. The ISDN basic rate interface has three channels: two 64 Kbps channels used to send data, voice, and graphics, and one 16 Kbps channel used to transmit communications signaling.

Iterative query A query performed on behalf of a DNS client to assist in answering a recursive query. Iterative queries allow DNS servers to send back pointers or referrals. A DNS server that receives an iterative query can return a referral to the client if it does not have the answer.

KDC See Key Distribution Center.

KDCSVC See Kerberos Key Distribution Center Service.

Kerberos A protocol that defines how clients interact with a network authentication service. Clients obtain tickets from the Key Distribution Center (KDC). These tickets allow them to gain access to servers. Kerberos tickets represent the client's network credentials.

Kerberos Key Distribution Center Service (KDCSVC) Looks up the user account name in Active Directory as part of the Kerberos authentication process.

Kernel mode drivers Use objects by calling kernel mode support routines exported by the I/O Manager and other system components.

Kernel mode Layer of the Windows Server 2003 architecture that has access to the system data and hardware.

Key Distribution Center (KDC) The service that implements Kerberos authentication through the Authentication Service (AS) and the Ticket Granting Service (TGS).

L2TP See Layer Two Tunneling Protocol.

Last Known Good Configuration (LKGC) Safe boot mode that enables you to start the operating system using the information saved in the Registry after the last successful logon.

Layer Two Tunneling Protocol (L2TP) One of the protocols used to create secure connections in VPNs. It works over dialup lines, public TCP/IP networks (the Internet), local network links, and WAN links. If you use L2PT, a tunnel will be created, but data will not be encrypted. L2TP must be used in conjunction with IPSec which will provide data encryption. When you use L2TP, the message header is compressed.

LDAP See Lightweight Directory Access Protocol.

Ldifde (LDAP data interchange format data export).exe Utility used to import and export group objects to and from LDIF files, which are supported by many third-party LDAP applications.

License server Server configured with Terminal Services Licensing on which you install TSCALs. When a client without a TSCAL logs on to the Terminal Server, the Terminal Server locates a license server and requests a new TSCAL for the client. Each client then stores its own TSCAL locally. The license server can issue temporary licenses for 120 days after installation.

Lightweight Directory Access Protocol (LDAP) Both a protocol and an API. The LDAP protocol is the Active Directory core protocol and is the preferred method of interacting with Active Directory; the LDAP API provides access to the LDAP protocol. LDAP is used by clients to query, create, update, and delete information stored in Active Directory and domain controllers to communicate with each other.

LKGC See Last Known Good Configuration.

LMHOSTS file A text file, stored on the local computer, which contains the static mappings of NetBIOS names to IP addresses for computers on remote networks only.

Local group Group populated with user accounts that are stored in the local security database of a single computer.

Local print devices Print devices that are spooled on the local machine.

Local user account A user account that is stored in a local security database on a particular computer. It can be used to access resources on the computer on which it was created.

Local user profile User profile created the first time a user logs on to a computer. It is stored on a system's local hard disk. Any changes made to local user profile remain specific to the computer on which the changes were made.

Logical AND operation Mathematical operation that compares 2 bits: If they are both 1, the result is 1; otherwise, the result is 0. It is used to determine the network ID.

Logical partition Disk space set aside for storage within an extended partition.

Logon events Event type used to audit when users log on or off a computer or make or cancel a network connection.

Logon rights Assigned to designate who can log on to a computer and how they can log on.

Logon script Set of operations that are performed when a user logs on to a system.

Management information base (MIB) A database of network performance data that is stored on a network agent. Data stored in a MIB is accessed by an NMS. The parameters stored in the MIB can be remotely configured.

Mandatory user profile A read-only roaming profile that can be used to specify particular settings for specific users or groups of users. Changes made to the desktop settings by a user are not permanently saved.

Master properties Properties for all Web sites on a server. They allow you to configure properties that will be inherited by all sites of that type rather than setting those properties for each site individually. You can also choose not to have Master properties propagate to the individual sites if the settings do not match.

Media access control (MAC) address Unique address assigned by a manufacturer to a network interface card (NIC).

Member server A Windows NT4.0, 2000 or Server 2003 computer that is part of a domain but does not store a replica of the directory database. A member server can perform all Windows Server 2003 services except Active Directory services.

Members Users and computers that are part of a group.

Memory addresses Parts of memory assigned to the hardware device.

Message digest A shortened version of a text message created by applying a hashing algorithm to reduce it to a fixed length, generally 128, 160, 192, or 224 bits long.

Metabase backup IIS backup that creates copies of the metabase configuration file (MetaBase.xml) and the metabase schema file (MBschema.xml). There are two kinds of metabase backups: portable and non-portable. The auto-backup feature of the IIS metabase creates copies of each version of the MetaBase.xml and MBSchema.xml files in the History folder.

MIB See Management information base.

Microkernel Manages the computer's processors and handles scheduling, interrupts, exception dispatching, and CPU synchronization.

Microsoft Certificate Services Windows Server 2003 component that enables an organization to use digital certificates and certificate authorities (CAs).

Microsoft CHAP (MS-CHAP) Microsoft's version of CHAP. The challenge message is specifically designed for Windows operating systems and one-way encryption is used. MS-CHAP is used with Windows 9.x and NT and only the client is authenticated. In the extended version, MS-CHAP v1 CPW and MS-CHAP v2 CPW are updated versions of these protocols in which the user can change an expired password.

Microsoft Clearinghouse Database used to store information related to the activated license servers and client license packed issued for a Terminal Server.

Microsoft Management Console (MMC) A console framework that provides a common host environment for snap-ins used to perform administrative tasks such as managing computers, services and networks.

MIME See Multipurpose Internet Mail Extensions.

Mirrored volume Provides fault tolerance by duplicating data on two hard disks. Also known as RAID-1.

MMC See Microsoft Management Console.

M-node (Mixed) NetBIOS node type that uses broadcasts first to attempt to resolve names. If this is unsuccessful, the client attempts to query a WINS server. This node type is usually used when the WINS server is located across a WAN link.

MS-CHAP See Microsoft CHAP.

MS-CHAP2 Second version of Microsoft CHAP authentication protocol: Both the client and the server are authenticated. One encryption key is used for transmitting data, and a different key is used for receiving data. Windows 9.x clients can now be modernized so that they are compatible with MS-CHAP2.

Multi-master replication Method of creating multiple copies, known as replicas, of the directory database and making them available throughout the network.

Multipurpose Internet Mail Extensions (MIME) Internet standard used to specify the format for sending e-mail messages so that they can be exchanged between different mail systems. In IIS, only static files that have extensions on the MIME types list can be served to users. A default global list of MIME types is installed with IIS 6.0. MIME types are used to prevent attackers from sending malicious files.

.NET Framework A programming infrastructure that enhances companies' ability to integrate a variety of software applications by using XML Web services.

Name query request The process of resolving NetBIOS names using WINS starts with a client sending a to a WINS server. The WINS client asks the WINS server for the IP address for a NetBIOS name.

Name refresh request A request sent by a WINS client, before the TTL for a name registration ends, to the WINS server, asking to refresh the TTL.

Name registration request Request sent by a WINS client during the initial stages of the boot process. The WINS server checks its database for an existing entry that matches the request. If no matching records exist, the WINS server registers the NetBIOS name. After registering the NetBIOS name, the WINS server sends a positive name registration response that includes the time to live (TTL) value for the registered name.

Name release message When a WINS client no longer requires a registered name (i.e. during client shutdowns), it sends a name release message to the WINS server to release the name.

Name resolution Process by which the names that people use to identify objects can be converted into the numbers that computers use to identify objects.

Name response message Message returned to a WINS client by a WINS server if it locates an IP address corresponding to the NetBIOS name of the computer requested by the client. The name response message contains the IP address.

Namespace Bounded area in which the names that people use to identify objects are "resolved" or translated in accordance with a naming convention or system. All directory services provide a namespace; for example, a telephone directory is a namespace where the names of the subscribers are resolved or translated into telephone numbers.

NAT See Network Address Translation.

NBNS See NetBIOS Name Server.

NDIS See Network Driver Interface Specifications.

Negative name registration response Message to a client if it attempts to register a NetBIOS name that is already owned by a currently registered host.

NetBEUI See NetBIOS Enhanced User Interface.

NetBIOS Enhanced User Interface (NetBEUI) Non-routable broadcast-based protocol, which was appropriate only for small LANs consisting of 20 to 200 computers. It is no longer supported by either Windows Server 2003 or Windows XP Professional.

NetBIOS name cache Stores information about the most recently resolved NetBIOS names. Is maintained in client memory.

NetBIOS name Name used on older Windows networks for network devices. They are limited to 15 characters for the name and a single character for the service type and are registered dynamically when computers or services start, or when users log on. The WINS service is used to resolve NetBIOS names to IP addresses.

NetBIOS Name Server (NBNS) Application responsible for mapping NetBIOS names to IP addresses.

Netdiag The Network Connectivity Tester utility, included in the Windows Server 2003 Support Tools, that is used to evaluate the registration of DNS, DHCP, routing, and, generally, to help network administrators to isolate connectivity problems. It performs a series of tests to determine if your network client is functional and displays significant network status information.

Network adapter See Network interface card (NIC).

Network address See Network ID.

Network Address Translation (NAT) Protocol used so that computers on a network can share a single Internet connection. It is a service that can translate private IP addresses to public IP addresses and vice versa as they are being forwarded from client computers to a server or from the server to client computers. NAT is extendable and can be used for a larger network that has multiple routed subnets unlike ICS.

Network broadcast address The broadcast address for a specific network: It is the IP address in which all of the host ID bits are set to 1. For example, for the network 192.168, the network broadcast address is 192.168.255.255.

Network Driver Interface Specifications (NDIS) A set of Windows device driver specifications: The main purpose of NDIS is to define a standard API for NICs so that a single NIC can support multiple network protocols. NDIS also provides a library of functions, which are commonly referred to as a "wrapper." The NDIS wrapper is used by MAC drivers and by higher level protocol drivers such as TCP/IP.

Network ID Also known as the network address, the network ID identifies computers as being part of a particular network. All computers on a single network use the same value.

Network interface card (NIC) Device that transfers data from one computer or other network device to another in the form of signals through a network medium. Also known as a network adapter.

Network Interface layer (DOD model) The physical layer in the DOD model, which is responsible for sending and receiving TCP/IP packets over network media. It sends TCP/IP packets onto the network medium and receives them off of the network medium.

Network layer (OSI model) The Network layer in the OSI model is responsible for logical addressing and routing. If the router cannot send data frames as large as those it has received from the transmitting computer, the frames will be broken down into smaller units. In the receiving computer, data packets will be reassembled at this layer.

Network management station (NMS) A centrally located server that is set up to obtain and compile network performance data from SNMP agents. Administrators use it to manage remote network devices.

Network media Physical wiring that is connected to a network interface card (NIC).

Network Monitor A network monitoring tool used to capture and display statistics that can be used to optimize and troubleshoot network performance.

Network Monitor Driver A networking component (quasi-protocol) that can be installed so that the NIC on a Windows 2000 Professional or XP Professional workstation or a Windows 2000 or Windows Server 2003 server can gather network performance data that can be evaluated in the Network Monitor and System Monitor. Used to observe and troubleshoot network events.

Network News Transfer Protocol (NNTP) Member of the TCP/IP protocol suite used to configure an IIS server to act as a NNTP server, which can receive, distribute, and post Usenet articles. Newsreader clients can post and read messages, and IIS can exchange NNTP messages with other NNTP servers.

Network prefix The number following the slash notation in CIDR notation.

Network print devices Print devices that are spooled from a remote print server.

NIC See Network interface card.

NMS See Network management station.

NNTP See Network News Transfer Protocol.

Node Device which is capable of communication on a network.

Non-authoritative (normal) restore Restore operation used to restore the most recent backup of a domain controller: Restored data, including Active Directory objects, will have their original update sequence number. The update sequence number is used to detect and propagate Active Directory changes among the servers on the network. The Active Directory replication system will view data that is restored non-authoritatively as old data, and it will thus not be replicated to the other servers.

Non-routable protocol Protocol that works only on a local subnet. Examples include NetBEUI and Data Link Control (DLC).

Normal backup Backup type in which all selected files and folders are backed up whether or not they have the archive attribute: The archive attribute is removed to denote that a file has been backed up.

NT LAN Manager (NTLM) The NTLM protocol was the default network authentication for Windows NT 4.0. It has been retained in Windows 2000 and Windows Server 2003 for backward compatibility and is used for logon authentication on stand-alone Windows Server 2003 machines and workgroups.

Ntds.dit file See Data Store.

Ntdsutil A command-line utility, stored in *%systemroot%\system32*, that supplies directory-management features not found in any of the graphical tools. It is used to perform an authoritative restore on a domain controller after you have restored the System State data and before you restart the server.

NTFS File system that provides advanced features such as security, performance, and efficiency.

NTFS permissions Set of permissions that restricts access to files and folders.

NTLM See NT LAN Manager.

NWLink A protocol that emulates IPX/SPX within the Microsoft network architecture. NWLink enables computers running Microsoft operating systems to communicate with older NetWare servers and vice versa.

Object Any "thing," either tangible or intangible (abstract), about which data is stored such as files, applications, users, or printers.

Object Access Event type used to audit access to a file, folder, Registry key, or printer.

Object instances Used by the System Monitor to distinguish between multiple occurrences of the same object counter. For example, if a computer has two processors, there can be three instances for the %Processor Time counter: one for each processor and one for the total processing time.

Object Manager Responsible for creating, managing, and deleting any objects that represent operating system resources, such as process, threads, and data structures.

Organizational Unit (OU) A container object that is an Active Directory administrative partition. OUs can contain users, groups, resources, and other OUs. Organizational Units enable the delegation of administration to distinct sub-trees of the directory.

Orphan A member of a mirrored or RAID-5 volume that has failed due to a power outage or a complete hard-disk head failure: The fault-tolerant driver figures out that the orphaned member is no longer useable and it directs all new reads and writes to other volumes in the fault-tolerant volume.

OSI (Open System Interconnection) Reference Model Uses a seven-layer networking framework that consists of Application, Presentation, Session, Transport, Network, Data Link and Physical layers.

OU See Organizational Unit.

Packet Data that has been formatted into discrete units. A packet has three sections: the header, the data, and the footer or trailer.

Pagefile.sys The page file. It is used to hold temporary data which is swapped in and out of physical memory in order to provide a larger virtual memory set.

PAP See Password Authentication Protocol.

Parent domain Any domain immediately above another domain.

Parity bit The exact sequence in which data is stored on a RAID 5 volume: it includes error correction and checksum verification information so that data can be reconstructed in a RAID 5 volume.

Partition Acts as a logical division for storing data in an organized manner. Part of a hard disk drive that has been configured to act as a logically separate unit of storage.

Password Authentication Protocol (PAP) The least secure authentication protocol. It uses plain text passwords for authentication. It is used when a more secure authentication method cannot be used and this protocol may be necessary for creating dial-up connections with non-Windows networks that do not encrypt passwords.

Pathping Utility that is a combination of ping and tracert. It provides a statistical analysis of results over a period of time, which can vary depending upon how many jumps must be analyzed. It displays the computer name and IP address for each jump and also calculates the percentage of lost/sent packets to each router or link.

Per Device or Per User licensing mode Provides a separate CAL for each named user or specified device, which can then access any computer running Windows Server 2003 on the network.

Per Server licensing mode Provides a specified number of client access licenses (CALs) for the server, thereby limiting the number of client computers that can be logged on to the server at one time.

Performance counter Performance measure for an object that can be quantified, such as the percentage of time the processor is busy (%Processor Time).

Performance data Information about the use of hardware resources and the activity of system services.

Performance object A system resource such as a processor, disk, network interface card (NIC), or memory whose performance can be monitored.

PGM See Pragmatic General Multicast.

Physical layer (OSI model) Layer at the bottom of the OSI model which connects the networking components to the media that will be used to transmit data. The raw bit stream is transmitted over the physical cables at his level. And the physical structure is defined, including the cables, network cards, how the NICs attach to the hardware, how cable is attached to the NICs, and the techniques that will be used to transfer the bit stream to the cables. The Network Interface layer in the DOD model corresponds to the Data Link and Physical layers of the OSI model.

Ping The Packet Internet Groper utility is used to verify whether the host computer can connect to the TCP/IP network and it provides information about network problems such as incompatible TCP/IP configurations.

Plug and Play (PnP) Enables the computer to automatically detect and adapt to hardware configuration changes.

Plug and Play (PnP) Manager Supports boot-time Plug and Play activities and interfaces with the HAL, the Executive, and the device drivers.

P-node (Peer-to-Peer) NetBIOS node type that queries a WINS server in order to resolve names. Broadcasts are never used.

PnP See Plug and Play.

Point-to-Point Protocol (PPP) Protocol used to establish a dial-up connection: The PPP protocol allows remote clients to access network resources and provides error-checking to detect possible problems prior to data transfer. It can support many networking protocols besides TCP/IP (IPX, NetBEUI, etc.) and uses a variety of authentication protocols.

Point-to-Point Tunneling Protocol (PPTP) One of the protocols used to create secure connections in VPNs: It works over dialup lines, public TCP/IP networks (the Internet), local network links, and WAN links. PPTP uses Microsoft Point-to-Point Encryption (MPPE) to furnish encryption and does not use header compression.

Policy Change Event type used to audit when user rights, audit policies, or user security options are changed.

Positive name registration response If no matching records exist, the WINS server registers the NetBIOS name and sends this message to the client.

Power Manager Responsible for controlling all of the power management APIs, coordinating any type of power events, and generating power management IRPs.

PPP See Point-to-Point Protocol.

PPTP See Point-to-Point Tunneling Protocol.

Pragmatic General Multicast (PGM) The reliable multicast protocol supported by Windows Server 2003 to transmit messages in a multicast data stream. It operates at the Transport layer in the DOD model directly above IP but does not use either UDP or TCP. To use PGM, you must add the Reliable Multicast Protocol and create PGM-enabled applications.

Pre-copy phase Setup program executes, temporary directory is created, and all files necessary for installing Windows Server 2003 are copied by Setup to the temporary directory.

Presentation layer (OSI model) The Presentation layer converts data. It is responsible for the syntax of data transmission and for converting data structures from the method used by the computer to a network standard. It translates from the application to the network in data transmission and from the network back to the application as data is received. The Presentation layer is responsible for protocol conversion, character conversion, expanding graphics commands, data compression, and cryptography.

Primary DNS server Also known as a primary name server. The DNS name server in a zone that stores the primary zone database file. Modifications and updates can only be made to the primary zone database file. Zone transfers occur to replicate any changes to the primary zone database file to the secondary zone database files. The server where the primary zone database file is housed is called the authoritative server because it has authority over the other DNS servers in the zone.

Primary name server See Primary DNS server.

Primary partition Physical unit of storage created on a basic disk. You can create up to four partitions, or three primary and one extended partition on a basic disk, using the MBR partition style.

Primary restore Restore performed on a domain controller when you must rebuild the domain from a backup when all domain controllers have been lost. You perform a primary restore on the first domain controller and non-authoritative restores on all of the other domain controllers.

Primary zone database file Zone database file (consisting of all records about the resources in a zone) that is stored by the primary DNS server.

Print device The physical hardware device that prints data on paper.

Print queue A list of print jobs from different workstations stored on the spooler of the print server.

Print Queue object The main System Monitor performance object used to monitor the performance of both local and network printers.

Print server Most often refers to a computer that runs a server application, such as Windows Server 2003 and is connected to one or more print devices.

Printer A software program that enables users to print and manage documents on the device that prints the documents.

Printer driver A collection of one or more files containing information that Windows Server 2003 requires in order to convert print commands received from a workstation into a specific printer language that can be understood by the print device.

Printer permissions Permissions that you can assign to different types of users for controlling the access and usage of printers.

Printer pool A single printer that can queue print jobs to multiple ports and their associated print devices.

Printers and Faxes window A window that displays the printers installed on your computer: It includes the Add Printer icon, which is used to initiate the Add Printer Wizard.

Private key The confidential half of a private/public cryptographic key pair, which is generally used to decrypt a session key, digitally sign data, or to decrypt data that has been encrypted using the corresponding public key.

Privilege Use Event type used to audit when user rights are successfully exercised or when a user unsuccessfully tries to use a right that has not been assigned to him or her.

Privileges Permit users to interact with the operating system and with system-wide resources.

Process In Task Manager A process referring to an executable program that is run from within the main application, such as a Help utility in an Office program.

Process Manager Helps to create and end processes and threads.

Process Tracking Event type used to audit what each process is doing in the foreground and the background, and how long a program ran.

Product activation Technology that requires that Windows Server 2003 be activated before it can be used.

Protocol Standard that provides a set of rules and criterion for transferring data over a network.

Public key cryptography Data encryption method that uses a key pair called a public key and a private key. The key pair is mathematically related so that messages encrypted with the public key can only be decrypted by the corresponding private key. The public key is widely disseminated, while the private key is only issued to an authorized user and must be kept secure.

Public key infrastructure Defines the rules, policies, standards, and software that regulate certificates, and public and private keys. The system of digital certificates, CAs, and other registration authorities (RAs) that validate the authenticity of parties in a digital transaction.

Public key The widely disseminated half of a private/public cryptographic key pair, which is generally used to encrypt a session key, verify a digital signature, or to encrypt data that will be decrypted using the corresponding private key.

Pull Replication The process used by WINS replication partners in which a schedule is set for the partners to pull changed/updated data from the server. By default, pull replication is set to occur every 30 minutes.

Push Replication The process used by WINS replication partners in which, when the service starts or when an address in the database changes, the server can push replication by notifying its partners that changes have occurred. When the partners receive the notification, they can pull the replication data from the WINS server.

RADIUS See Remote Authentication Dial-in User Service.

RAID Level 0 See Striped volume.

RAID-1 See Mirrored volume.

RAID-5 volume Fault-tolerant striped volume on which data is written across 3 to 32 hard disks, and parity information is stored across all of the disks so that data can be reconstructed in the event of a disk failure. RAID-5 is the best fault-tolerant solution for most companies, but it is more expensive to implement than mirroring.

RDN See Relative Distinguished Name.

Realm Database holding the credentials for the security principals.

Recovery agent A user who has a recovery certificate that can be used to decrypt files that were encrypted with EFS by other users.

Recovery Console A command-line interface that you can use to troubleshoot and recover tasks, copy, rename, or replace operating system files and folders, format hard disks, repair the file system boot sector or the Master Boot Record (MBR), or to read and write data on a local drive.

Recursive query A type of forward lookup query that is used to request that a DNS name server provides the full and complete answer to the query. It is a request for the answer, not for a referral to another DNS server. When a DNS server receives a recursive query, it must follow the query to its completion.

Registry A database that stores information about the computer configuration such as user profiles, settings for files and folders, and hardware settings.

Relative Distinguished Name (RDN) Naming convention for an object that consists of one of the attributes for an object that is a part of the DN name. It is the portion of the Distinguished Name that uniquely identifies an object within the object's parent container. For example, the RDN for the user object Gregory Johnson is: CN = Gregory Johnson.

Reliable Multicast Protocol A protocol developed to support the dependable transmission of multicast data streams rather than using User Datagram Protocol (UDP), which provides no guarantee that data packets will reach their destination. PGM is the reliable multicast protocol supported by Windows Server 2003.

Remote access policy A set of rules and conditions that must be met by a remote connection before a user can gain access. The criteria, which can include parameters such as the time, groups, and connection type, are evaluated one by one when a user connects to an RRAS server. There are three components of a remote access policy: conditions, permissions, and a profile.

Remote access profile Each remote access policy you create is associated with a remote access profile that specifies the types of connections that will be available if the conditions and the permissions have been satisfied. For example, if a remote client logs on to the RRAS server on a permitted day and time, you can specify an authentication protocol, such as PAP, CHAP, or EAP, to be used to verify the credentials of the remote client.

Remote access server A computer running Windows Server 2003 and the RRAS service that is configured specifically to function using a modem, or a modem pool, to allow users to dial-in from laptops or any other remote computers that are also configured with a modem.

Remote Assistance Utility based on Terminal Services that is used to allow a trusted party such as a help desk support person or network technician to remotely access your system. This expert can be allowed to either just view your system or to both view and interact with your system.

Remote Authentication Dial-in User Service (RADIUS) Client server protocol that is used to provide centralized authentication. RADIUS clients submit authentication requests to a RADIUS server. Networks that have multiple RAS servers will often use a RADIUS server.

Remote Desktop Connection Client software used to connect to a server both using Remote Desktop for Administration and Terminal Services. The Remote Desktop client is included in the default installations of both Windows Server 2003 and Windows XP Professional.

Remote Desktop for Administration Utility based on Terminal Services technology that allows you to manage a computer from nearly any computer on your network. This technology, previously installed as Terminal Services in Remote Administration mode, can be used to perform almost any task remotely that you could while physically logged on to the server, including shutting down and restarting the machine.

Remote Installation Service (RIS) Service that allows clients to boot from a network server and use special pre-boot diagnostic tools installed on the server or to automatically install client software. Also a configuration setting node in the Group Policy snap-in under User Configuration, Windows Settings that is used to control RIS installation options available to users when the Client Installation Wizard is run.

Rendering The procedure in which the GDI formats the print file with control codes so that the correct graphics, color, and font attributes are configured for the print file.

Replica A second instance of a Dfs link.

Resolver A host or library that can perform a recursive search and can issue iterative queries. A resolver queries other DNS name servers, including the root servers, to look up DNS records on behalf of the client. If the local DNS server cannot resolve the host name to its IP address, it sends an iterative query on behalf of the client to assist in answering the recursive query.

Resource record An entry in the DNS database that identifies a host within the database. A resource record starts with a FQDN (or with a domain name followed by the name of the zone). After the FQDN are the TTL, the Record class (Internet, Hesiod, or Chaos), the record type (CNAME, PTR, A, etc), and finally the record data, which depends on the record type.

Reverse lookup query Request to resolve a known IP address to a host name. A second-level domain called in-addr.arpa, which contains name-to-IP address mappings indexed by IP addresses, was created to simplify this task.

Reverse lookup zone Used to resolve IP addresses to host names.

RIS See Remote Installation Service.

Roaming user profile User profile used primarily when users are required to work on multiple computers. The network administrator sets up a roaming user profile on a network server so that the profile is available to the user on all of the computers in the domain.

Root CA Certification authority at the top of the CA organizational hierarchy.

Root domain The top node in the DNS namespace under which all of the other domains are configured. It is represented by the trailing full stop or period (".").

Root name server DNS server that has authority for the top-most domain in the DNS namespace hierarchy, the root domain.

Root zone A zone authoritative for the root domain. A root zone is either an Internet root or an internal root (also known as a "fake root" or "empty root").

Routable protocol Protocols used on LANs and WANs that have the capability to transmit data across a router, which is a special device used to transfer data between networks. Examples of routable protocols include TCP/IP and NWLink

Route Command used to display and modify the local routing table. You can use it to set the route you want packets to take to a particular network, including the default gateway.

Router A special network device used to transfer data between networks: You can use a router to connect LANs and to connect a LAN to a WAN or the Internet.

Routing and Remote Access Service (RRAS) Service that can be configured on a Windows Server 2003 machine to create a Remote Access Services (RAS) server that can manage hundreds of concurrent connections or to receive Virtual Private Network (VPN) connections on the internal network. It can also be configured to provide shared Internet access using Network Address Translation (NAT), or to create a secure connection between two servers on the Internet to connect two LANs.

RRAS See Routing and Remote Access Service.

Safe Mode Boots your system with a minimum set of drivers so that you can fix problems that result from faulty device drivers, faulty programs, system service failures, or services that start automatically.

Schema Active Directory database design: It provides a set of definitions to describe the type of objects that can be created in Active Directory, formal definitions of every object class that can be created in an Active Directory forest, and formal definitions of every attribute that can exist in an Active Directory object. The schema can be extended by adding new object classes or new attributes.

Scope A range of IP addresses that will be assigned to DHCP clients.

Scope pane Left pane of console, where you add items to the console tree.

Scripts Configuration setting node in the Group Policy snap-in that is used to specify scripts and batch files to run at startup and shutdown for computers and at logon and logoff for users.

Secondary DNS server Also known as secondary name server. A DNS name server that stores a secondary zone database file. Its functions are to reduce the traffic and query load on the primary database zone server and to provide redundancy so that if the authoritative server is down, it can service requests.

Secondary name server See Secondary DNS server.

Secondary zone database file A copy of the primary zone database file that is stored by the secondary DNS server.

Second-level domain The child domain of a top-level domain. Second-level domains have two parts: a top-level name and a second-level name, for example, ebay.com, yale.edu, usmint.gov, and amazon.ca.

Secret key Also known as a symmetric key The same key is used to both encrypt and decrypt data.

Secret key encryption See Symmetric key encryption.

Sector The organizational unit on a FAT partition. It is the smallest unit used to transfer data to and from the disk. It can contain 512 bytes of data.

Secure Server (Require Security) IPSec policy that ensures that all communication is encrypted, which may minimize the number of client computers with which you can communicate over a network, because all communications must be secured. When you set this policy, unsecured communications with un-trusted computers are blocked. Whether or not a computer is trusted is determined by the authentication mechanism used by the client.

Secure Sockets Layer (SSL) Protocol used so that a server certificate can be accessed by users to authenticate your Web site before they send confidential data such as a credit card number. The SSL protocol supplies data encryption and authentication between a Web client and a Web server using a variety of different cryptographic algorithms.

Security Configuration Policies and security settings applied to a site, domain, OU, or local computer that can include password and account lockout policies, local security policies, user rights assignments, Registry key security, group memberships, permissions for the local file system, and more.

Security group Group used to define rights for system access and permissions for resources and objects on a computer or in a domain. Used to control access security.

Security log An event log where access and security data is recorded. Audited events are stored here. Also referred to as a Security event log.

Security principal Party (user or computer) that needs to be authenticated.

Security Reference Monitor Responsible for implementing security policies on the local computer.

Security settings Configuration setting node in the Group Policy snap-in that is used to configure machines on your network to use IP security and to specify settings for everything from user rights to system services. Account lockout policy, password policy, user rights, audit policy, public key access, Registry and Event Log access, and service operation are all controlled using security settings.

Serial Line Internet Protocol (SLIP) An older remote communications protocol that is used by UNIX computers. It does not provide security and transfers data without checking for errors. It does not support dynamically assigned IP addresses and can only be used on TCP/IP networks. The updated CSLIP (Compressed SLIP) uses header compression to reduce transmission overhead; however, the header must be decompressed when the data packets are received.

Server (Request Security) IPSec policy that always attempts to provide secure communication by requesting security using Kerberos trust from other computers. This means that, for all IP traffic, clients will be requested to provide security using authentication mechanisms, but communication with unsecured clients will not be denied. Data packets will still be exchanged, even if the other side is not IPSec capable.

Service Principal Name (SPN) Naming convention used for service principals. It often includes the name of the computer that is running the service. You can use SPNs to request Kerberos tickets, and they are required for mutual authentication.

Session layer (OSI model) The Session layer is designed to handle problems that do not involve communication issues. It enables data transport by allowing users to establish sessions and by supplying services that are needed by certain applications. Protocols in this layer are responsible for identifying the parties, managing who can send data and how long they will be allowed to send it for, and for synchronization services.

Shared folder permissions Set of permissions that prevent any unauthorized access to shared folders by users.

Shiva Password Authentication Protocol (SPAP) Authentication protocol used if you are connecting to a Shiva server. This protocol is more secure than PAP, but less secure than CHAP or MS-CHAP. Data is not encrypted.

Simple Mail Transfer Protocol (SMTP) Protocol in the TCP/IP protocol suite that is used to configure an IIS server to act as a Simple Mail Transfer Protocol server, which facilitates the transmission of e-mail either on your network or the Internet.

Simple Network Management Protocol (SNMP) A protocol in the TCP/IP protocol suite that enables servers, workstations, and network devices to compile network performance data for monitoring and troubleshooting purposes. Originally designed strictly for use with TCP/IP, it is now compatible with IPX/SPX and AppleTalk.

Simple volume Volume on a dynamic disk that consists of disk space from only a single hard drive.

Single key encryption See Symmetric key encryption.

Site Set of subnets connected by high-speed, cost effective links.

SLIP See Serial Line Internet Protocol.

SMTP See Simple Mail Transfer Protocol.

Snap-in Management application that, together with other snap-ins, forms a console.

SNMP agent The computer running the SNMP agent software. SNMP agents provide information about network performance to a network management station (NMS).

SNMP community A collection of computers that are grouped for SNMP administrative and security purposes. All network management stations and agents belong to SNMP communities.

SNMP See Simple Network Management Protocol.

SNMP service Enables you to capture network data. When you install the SNMP service on a computer, your computer becomes an SNMP agent that can communicate with an SNMP network management station (NMS). The NMS can monitor SNMP-enabled TCP/IP network devices to examine network performance, detect network malfunctions, and audit network usage.

Socket IP address and port number combination that identifies a Web site.

Socket pooling Configuration used to optimize access to Web sites by allowing Web sites with different IP addresses to share the same port number. You can bind multiple Web sites that share the same port to different IP addresses in order to optimize the utilization of the resources on the Web server.

Software RAID implementation Fault tolerance is handled by the server's operating system. Any of the RAID levels supported by Windows Server 2003 (levels 0, 1, and 5) are set up in the Disk Management snap-in. The server hardware identifies and configures the drives independently and the operating system examines them and connects them in a single logical array.

Software settings Configuration setting node in the Group Policy snap-in that is used to determine the applications that will be distributed to users via a GPO.

Software Update Services (SUS) A service designed to keep operating system files up to date.

Spanned volume Type of volume that consists of disk space from 2 to 32 disks that are combined to appear as one disk. Spanned volumes do not provide fault tolerance. When writing data to a spanned volume, Windows 2003 uses the disk space on the first available disk, and then continues to write data on other disks.

SPAP See Shiva Password Authentication Protocol.

SPN See Service Principal Name.

Spool The folder where converted print jobs are stored before they can be printed.

Spooler A file that stores the converted print commands before they can be printed.

SSL See Secure Sockets Layer.

Stand-alone Dfs root Consists of only a single level of Dfs links. Is configured locally on a computer and stores all of the information in the local Registry.

Stand-alone Root CA A top-level CA just like an enterprise root CA; however, it does not necessarily have to be a member of a domain and, therefore, does not require Active Directory access. You generally create stand-alone root CAs when you are going to issue certificates to users and computers outside your network.

Stand-alone snap-in Type of snap-in that can be used to perform administrative tasks even if no other snap-in is present.

Stand-alone Subordinate CA Can function all by itself, or it can be part of a CA hierarchy. It does not necessarily need a parent stand-alone root CA on the network, although it can have one. It can also have an external commercial CA as its parent.

Standard primary zone DNS zone that maintains information about the part of the DNS namespace for which it is responsible in a text file and stores it locally on the hard disk of the DNS server. It is the first zone to be created, is authoritative for one or more domains, and is the only copy of the zone file which can be edited.

Standard secondary zone DNS zone that maintains a read-only copy of another zone on the network. Secondary zones are created after the primary zone to provide redundancy. You cannot edit the records in the secondary zone because they are only copies.

Striped volume Two or more dynamic disks (up to 32) on which data is written in stripes across the disks, and increases disk performance. However, if one disk in a striped volume fails, you will generally lose all of your data. Also known as RAID level 0.

Stub zone An enhancement to delegated sub-domains that were added as a new feature in Windows Server 2003's DNS Server service. These zones replicate SOA, NS, and core A records from the delegated child domain to the parent domain.

Subnet ID Bits that identify the subnet for a host. In classless IP addressing, a subnet mask that is not one of the defaults is used. Bits are "borrowed" from the host ID and the host ID is divided into a subnet ID and host ID.

Subnet mask 32-bit value that is used to distinguish the network ID and the host ID in an IP address: The subnet mask blocks or "masks" a part of the IP address in order to differentiate between the two.

Supernetting The process of modifying the subnet mask to include multiple, contiguous address spaces.

SUS See Software Update Services.

Symmetric key See Secret key.

Symmetric key encryption Both the sender and the recipient must share the same session. Also known as single key encryption or secret key encryption.

System Events Event type used to audit when a computer is shut down or restarted or some event that concerns the Security log has taken place, such as clearing an event log.

System File Checker utility Utility used to scan and verify the versions of all protected system files. If a protected file has been overwritten, the correct version of the file is retrieved from the *%systemroot%\system32\dllcache* folder.

System log Contains the events that are logged by various Windows Server 2003 components.

System Monitor A tool used to view and record data about the usage of hardware resources and to monitor the activity of system services.

System partition See Active partition.

System State data On a member server, it contains the Registry, the COM + Class Registration database, the system boot files and all system files (all files under Windows File Protection), the Certificate Services database if the member server is a certificate server and the DNS zones if DNS is installed. A System State backup will also include the IIS Metadirectory if is IIS installed, and the Cluster service if the server is part of a cluster.

System volume Volume where the startup files (the files needed to boot the operating system, such as Ntldr, Boot.ini and Ntdetect) are stored.

Task Manager A tool used to monitor and manage programs and processes running on a computer.

TCP/IP See Transmission Control Protocol/Internet Protocol.

TCP/IP Subnet A grouping of devices on a network that share a common IP address range.

Terminal Server Client Access License (TSCAL) Client access license required by clients running any other operating system besides Windows 2000 or XP Professional in order to access a Terminal Server.

Terminal Server Computer on which Terminal Services has been installed for application sharing by multiple simultaneous users.

Terminal Services Licensing Tool used to configure a Terminal Services license server. The license server registers and tracks licenses issued to Terminal Services clients.

Terminal Services Manager Tool used to monitor connections to a Terminal Server. You can view the configuration of the client and the processes that the client is running in the Terminal Services Manager. You can also terminate processes, connect to and disconnect from sessions, monitor sessions, reset sessions, send messages to users, and log off users.

Terminator Device placed at the ends of the transmission line in a bus network topology to provide electrical resistance so that signals will be absorbed and cannot be bounced back to the network.

Text mode phase During this phase, Setup prompts the user for information that is required to complete installation.

TGS See Ticket Granting Service.

TGT See Ticket Granting Ticket.

Thin client Computers with minimum system resources and only a minimal operating system that are used to access a Terminal Server. A thin client is usually a small computer that runs embedded Linux or Windows CE.

Threads Blocks of program code.

Ticket Issued to users from the Ticket Granting Service. The ticket allows users to access resources on a specific server.

Ticket Granting Service (TGS) Service that issues the logon session ticket that will be used in all communications between a party and the KDC and the tickets that will arrange communication sessions between a security principal and a Validation Server.

Ticket Granting Ticket (TGT) The ticket issued by the Key Distribution Center (KDC) that is used to verify the identity of the user and grant admission to the Ticket Granting Service. The TGS will issue the logon session ticket.

Time to live (TTL) The time during which the DNS server keeps a history of query results received from other name servers in its cache memory.

Tombstoning Marks records as extinct.

Top-level domain Domains located right below the root domain in the domain namespace. They are categorized by organization type or geographic location.

Trace log Log used to monitor a particular value continuously. Events are logged by a system provider or by a non-system provider that you specify.

Tracert Utility used to search the route taken when data is transferred between communicating devices and to discover the links where communication has failed. It displays the fully qualified domain name and IP address of each gateway along the route to a remote host.

Transmission Control Protocol/Internet Protocol (TCP/IP) The core protocol for the Internet, TCP/IP is a scalable and routable suite of protocols that can be used on both large and small networks to transfer data between computers using different operating systems and widely varying structural designs.

Transport layer (DOD model) The Transport layer in the DOD model is responsible for providing the Application Layer with session and datagram communication services. The connection is established between the communicating computers using TCP, UDP and Pragmatic General Multicast (PGM).

Transport layer (OSI model) The Transport layer in the OSI model supplies control for all communications from end point to end point. Data is broken down into packets at this level on the sending computer and reassembled from the data packets at this level on the receiving computer. Protocols in this layer also supply error-checking, acknowledgement of successful data transmission, and requests for retransmission if data packets do not arrive or if they arrive with errors.

Transport mode IPSec's default mode. Only the data itself is encrypted. Because the message header and the routing information are not encrypted, it is not as secure as tunnel mode.

Tree Discrete administrative Active Directory unit that consists of a set of one or more domains in a hierarchical structure. Domains under the root domain possess contiguous names in which the child domain always contains the name of the parent domain.

TTL See Time to live.

Tunnel A secure, logical link established between a remote user and a private network. Data is encapsulated by including an additional header on the data packets or frames. The encapsulated packets are transferred through the tunnel endpoints and de-encapsulated upon reaching the destination.

Tunnel mode Used to create a secure IPSec tunnel through which data can travel from one end to the other.

Uninterruptible Power Supply (UPS) A hardware device that supplies power from capacitance cells to a computer so that when there is a loss of power, the UPS device takes over. UPS devices enable you to save your data and shut down in a systematic way when a power failure occurs.

Universal group Group used when there are multiple domains in a forest. Members can be drawn from many different domains and permissions can be assigned for resources in any domain. Universal groups are available only when Active Directory is running in Windows 2000 native mode or Windows Server 2003 mode.

Update Sequence Number (USN) Similar to the version number for the object. A domain controller with a later USN is considered to have the most up-to-date version of the object.

UPN See User Principal Name.

UPS See Uninterruptible Power Supply.

User account A user account is a form of identification for a system or a user. It includes identifying information, such as the user logon name, first name, and last name.

User Configuration node Group Policy snap-in node used to set group policies for users, which are applied when the user logs on to the domain.

User Datagram Protocol (UDP) Protocol that provides a one-to-one or one-to-many connectionless communications service. It is unreliable as it does not guarantee the delivery of data and is used when only a small amount of data needs to be transferred, such as data that can be sent in a single packet, and when the reliability of the transmission is not of primary importance.

User mode Layer in the Windows Server 2003 architecture made up of a set of components known as subsystems.

User Principal Name (UPN) The name of a system user in an e-mail address format. The user name is followed by the "at sign" followed by the name of the DNS domain with which the user is associated. An example might look like: GJohnson@ABCCorp.com. The UPN is used to identify an Active Directory object and is an acceptable format for user authentication.

User rights assignments Configured to designate the tasks a user or group is allowed to perform on either an individual system or a domain. User rights are divided into two categories: logon rights and privileges.

USN See Update Sequence Number.

Virtual directory Directory that is used to make a directory "appear" to be within the home directory, when it really isn't. They are most often used when you have a folder structure on another disk or on an entirely different server that you do not want to move but want to include on your Web site.

Virtual Memory Another term for the page file. You can set the initial and maximum sizes for the page file in the Virtual Memory dialog box. The page file is used to hold temporary data, which is swapped in and out of physical memory in order to provide a larger virtual memory set.

Virtual Memory Manager (VMM) Controls the allocation of virtual memory, which represents private, protected memory address space provided to a system or application process.

Virtual private network (VPN) Method used to securely access resources on a private network remotely through the Internet or through a private network. Tunneling and encryption protocols are used to establish a secure channel through the established infrastructure of the Internet to the LAN. The protocols keep the data flow private even though it is traveling through the public Internet.

Volume Logical division of a dynamic disk. Can consist of portions of a single hard disk or several hard disks.

Volume Shadow Copy Service (VSS) Service that can be used by applications to access locked files or files that are in use by other services or applications: The Backup utility in Windows Server 2003 makes use of this functionality so that open or locked files are not excluded from the backup process. It is also used to recover previous versions (shadow copies) of saved files that are stored on a share on a volume on which VSS has been enabled.

VPN See Virtual private network.

VSS See Volume Shadow Copy Service.

Web-based Distributed Authoring and Versioning (WebDAV) An extension of the HTTP protocol that is used to access files on a Web server through an HTTP connection, used to facilitate Web page authoring. WebDAV provides a Web folder interface, similar to Windows Explorer, in which you can drag and drop folders to provide a network file system suitable for the Internet. It is a Web document management system, a support protocol for collaborative applications, and a central tool for remote software development teams.

Web folder A shortcut to a folder on a Web server. It consists of a list of files and folders on the Web server and their associated Internet addresses.

Web permissions Permissions that apply to all HTTP clients and determine the level of access to server resources. The Web permissions are Script source access, Read, Write. Directory browsing, Log visits, and Index this resource.

Web server Server on which you configure the Web environment using IIS.

Web site Collection of interconnected text and graphic files and applications located on a Web server.

WebDAV See Web Distributed Authoring and Versioning.

Window Manager Organizes window displays and controls the screen coordinates defined for a window display.

Windows 2000 mixed mode Domain mode that allows the coexistence of Windows NT domains, Windows 2000, and Windows Server 2003 domains.

Windows 2000 native mode If your domain consists of only Windows 2000 domain controllers, you can switch to Windows 2000 native mode. This mode supports Windows 2000 and Windows Server 2003 domains

Windows File Protection utility Utility that prevents the replacement of system files in protected folders, some of which end in .sys, .dll, .ocx, .ttf, .fon, and .exe. It detects any attempt by other programs to replace or move a protected system file and looks up the file signature in a catalog file (.cat) to determine if the correct Microsoft version is being installed.

Windows Internet Naming Service (WINS) Microsoft's implementation of an NBNS.

Windows Server 2003 interim mode Domain mode used when there are no Windows 2000 Server computers and you upgrade a Windows NT PDC (primary domain controller) to Windows Server 2003.

Windows Server 2003 mode Supports the full Windows Server 2003 Active Directory implementation.

Windows Server 2003, Datacenter Edition Microsoft's most powerful server operating system. The Datacenter Edition has all of the features of Windows Server 2003, Enterprise Edition, plus support for 64-way symmetric multiprocessing (SMP) in 64-bit versions and 32-way SMP in 32-bit versions; eight-node clustering, 64 gigabytes (GB) of RAM in 32-bit versions and 512 GB of RAM in 64-bit versions.

Windows Server 2003, Enterprise Edition Designed for medium to large organizations. Contains all of the features of Windows Server 2003, Standard Edition, plus support for high-performance servers and the ability to cluster servers for greater load handling.

Windows Server 2003, Standard Edition Built on Windows 2000 Server technology. Has advanced networking features, such as Internet Authentication Service (IAS), the Network Bridge feature, Internet Connection Sharing (ICS), four-way symmetric multiprocessing (SMP), and support for up to 4 gigabytes (GB) of RAM. Designed for small to medium organizations and includes .NET technology.

Windows Server 2003, Web Edition Designed for dedicated Web serving and hosting. Takes advantage of improvements in Internet Information Services (IIS) 6.0, Microsoft ASP.NET, and .NET Framework to make it easier to build and host Web applications, Web pages, and XML Web service.

Windows Server Catalog A list of computers and peripheral devices that Microsoft has confirmed to be compatible with Windows Server 2003.

Winnt.exe The file used to initiate a manual installation. The 16-bit version of Setup used for older operating systems.

Winnt32.exe The files used to initiate a manual installation. The 32-bit version of Setup used for Windows NT 4.0 or higher compatible computers.

WINS See Windows Internet Naming Service.

WINS client Client on a network that has been configured to use WINS.

WINS database Database that holds NetBIOS name-to-IP address mappings.

WINS server The computer running WINS.

Workgroup (peer-to-peer network) Group of network computers that can share network resources, such as, files, folders, and printers, but which do not share a central directory database.

XML Web services Enable developers to easily create reusable, building-block software applications that can connect to other applications, via the Internet.

Zone database file Records about the resources in a zone.

Zone Distinct, contiguous segments of the DNS namespace that make a large domain manageable by enabling different administrators to manage different zones.

Zone transfer The process by which DNS database information is copied between primary and secondary zones.

Index

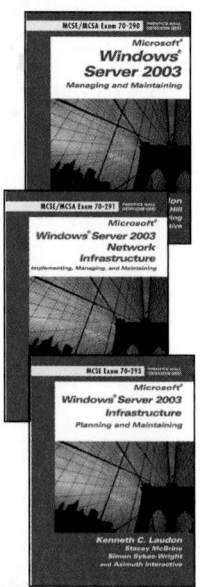

The Prentice Hall Certification Series features a building-block approach that organizes the material into a series of skills that students master one at a time. We adopted a two-page spread featuring a highly graphical approach with hundreds of screenshots that shows students how and why Windows Server 2003/Windows 2000/Windows XP works, rather than forcing them to memorize rote software procedures.

Windows Server 2003 Core Exam Texts

Exam 70-290: Microsoft Windows Server 2003: Managing and Maintaining Text: 0-13-144743-2 Project Lab Manual: 0-13-144974-5 Interactive Solution CD-ROM: 0-13-144974-5	**Exam 70-291:** Microsoft Windows Server 2003: Network Infrastructure: Implementing, Managing and Maintaining Text: 0-13-145600-8 Project Lab Manual: 0-13-145603-2 Interactive Solution CD-ROM: 0-13-145604-0
Exam 70-293: Microsoft Windows Server 2003: Network Infrastructure: Planning and Maintaining Text: 0-13-189306-8 Project Lab Manual: 0-13-189307-6 Interactive Solution CD-ROM: 0-13-189308-4	**Exam 70-294:** Microsoft Windows Server 2003: Active Directory Infrastructure: Planning, Implementing, and Maintaining Text: 0-13-189312-2 Project Lab Manual: 0-13-189314-9 Interactive Solution CD-ROM: ISBN TBD
Exam 70-297: Designing a Microsoft Windows Server 2003 Active Directory and Network Infrastructure Text: 0-13-189316-5 Project Lab Manual: 0-13-189320-3 Interactive Solution CD-ROM: ISBN TBD	**Exam 70-298:** Designing Security for a Microsoft Windows Server 2003 Network Text: 0-13-117670-6 Project Lab Manual: 0-13-146684-4 Interactive Solution CD-ROM: ISBN TBD

Value Pack Options Available

Series Features

The ONLY academic series developed by instructors for instructors that correlates to the MCSE and MCSA exam objectives.

4-color, 2-page layout
- Improves student retention through clear, easy-to-follow, step-by-step instructions.

Skills-Based Systematic Approach
- Uses integrated components: Main text, Project Lab Manual, Interactive Solution CD-ROM, and Web site with online quizzes.

Hands-on projects and problem-solving projects at the end of each lesson
- Help students better understand the material being taught.

Learning Aids
- Include Test Your Skills, On Your Own Projects, and Problem-Solving Cases at the end of each lesson.

Instructor's Resource CD
- PowerPoint slides containing all text graphics and lecture bullet points.
- Instructor's Manual that includes sample syllabus, teaching objectives, answers to exercises, and review questions.
- Test Bank with 40+ questions per lesson based on the text. Not generic MCSE questions.

Windows Server 2003 Enterprise 180 day evaluation software included in every text.